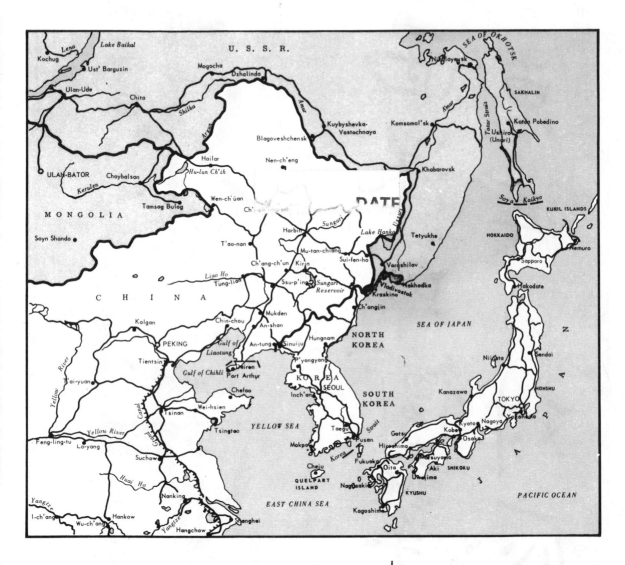

NORTHEAST CHINA,
KOREA AND JAPAN,
1945

0   200   400   600 Miles
0   200   400   600 Kilometers

ᴧᴧᴧᴧᴧ   Selected canal

━━━━   International boundary

────   Selected railroad

東亜

西洋の衝撃と東洋の対応史

SIXTH EDITION

The Far East

A History of
Western Impacts and
Eastern Responses,
1830 – 1975

PAUL H. CLYDE
Sometime Professor of History, Duke University

BURTON F. BEERS
Professor of History, North Carolina State University

WAVELAND

PRESS, INC.

Prospect Heights, Illinois

2615187l   4-8-96

Photographs used courtesy of:

Chinese Information Service, New York. Page 378

Consulate General of Japan, New York. Pages 50 (bottom right), 419, 467, 523 (right)

Duke University Archives, William MacDougall Papers. Page 181

Duke University Library, Manuscript Department:
  From the collection "Japan Today." Page 50 (top left and right, bottom left)
  Robert Eichelberger Papers. Pages 305, 414, 422, 423
  Edward James Parrish Papers. Pages 140, 144, 201, 207 (bottom)
  Van R. White Papers. Pages 26, 40

Hong Kong Tourist Association. Page 78

Library of Congress. Pages 126, 234, 283, 334, 353, 366, 400, 436

Museum of the American China Trade, Milton, Mass. Pages 70, 95, 206, 207 (top)

U.S. Department of State. Pages 448, 455, 523 (left)

For information about this book, write or call:

Waveland Press, Inc.
P.O. Box 400
Prospect Heights, Illinois 60070
(708) 634-0081

DS511.C67 1971

To Mary Kestler Clyde and Pauline Cone Beers

Contents

List of Maps and Charts

Preface

This sixth and greatly revised edition of *The Far East,* like its predecessors, has been designed to be an aid to serious study and teaching. It is addressed primarily to students, young or old, in or out of college, seeking their first systematic introduction to the history of East Asia and its meeting with the West during the last 150 years.

There was a time not very long ago when Americans regarded East Asia as a distant, rather exotic region about which there was little need to be concerned or informed. In the 1970s, following three wars fought partly or wholly in the Pacific and on the Asian continent, and having experienced recurrent controversies over the nation's far eastern policy, Americans are exhibiting a marked concern about East Asia, but as yet very few are informed. Thus, the assumption which has underpinned the planning and writing of this book is that those who would pass judgment on East Asia today must first learn how it came to be as it is. This process of learning requires a confrontation with history.

The meeting of East Asia with the West in the past century and a half, however, has been a vast, complex, and often confusing encounter.

Generations of students and teachers not infrequently have been frustrated in their efforts to reach an understanding of the story. Our aim, therefore, has been to compose a survey offering a relatively simple introduction to the most fundamental aspects of the historical record. To remain within a limited compass, it has been necessary for us to be highly selective in what to include and what to exclude. It has been our endeavor to do this without distortion of the essential historical record. From this beginning the reader will more readily pursue in-depth study and will develop his own interpretations. On those occasions when our own interpretations have intruded in this survey, we have held that these interpretations conform to the historical evidence presently available, but we have made no claims to infallibility.

A NOTE ON READING LISTS AND FOOTNOTES

Every student who aspires to the study of history will learn sooner or later that there is no substitute for planned, extensive, and intensive reading. Accordingly, we have provided guides for further reading in the footnotes and in lists at the end of every chapter. These listings are selective, for within the last quarter-century the scholarly literature on East Asia has multiplied many times. Even a very selective bibliography would fill many volumes larger than this one. In consequence, the titles noted herein are those that seem most likely to meet the needs of students and teachers using this narrative. Most of the works listed are in English, and those that are available in paperback editions are marked with an asterisk. For a guide to the vastly greater volume of literature—including studies in other European languages and in Chinese and Japanese—the reader should consult the annual bibliographies published by the Association for Asian Studies.

In some cases, scholarly works are cited in the footnotes as a means of recognizing our special indebtedness. More often, however, the footnoted materials are suggestive of issues on which scholars disagree. Students and instructors may find these references helpful as points of departure for class discussions and for research papers. The footnotes and reading lists, it should be further noted, contain not only the more recent scholarship but also works that were published twenty or even fifty or more years ago. Many of these older works have been superceded by the prodigious research of the last few years. Yet they retain importance as research tools. For example, S. Wells Williams *The Middle Kingdom,* which first appeared more than a century ago, continues to fascinate students of history who know how to use it as a source.

ACKNOWLEDGMENTS

Our debt to a host of scholars who have created a rich and specialized literature is great. It is through their patient labors that our knowledge is expanded and refined, thereby requiring periodic updating of this survey.

A number of colleagues and associates have given special help with this sixth edition. The photographic illustrations were assembled with the aid of Mr. Jerry L. Kearns, Head of the Reference Section, Prints and Photographs Division, Library of Congress; Miss Fahey Black, Acting Chief of the General Publication Division, Bureau of Public Affairs, U. S. Department of State; Mr. Francis R. Carpenter, Associate Director of the Museum of the American China Trade; Dr. Mattie Russell and Mr. David Brown, Manuscript Department, Perkins Library, Duke University; Mr. C. Y. Chang, Chinese Information Service; and the staffs of the Hong Kong Tourist Agency and Japanese Consulate General. Dr. Robert Hodgson, Geographer, and his staff, U. S. Department of State, were more than generous in providing sources for revision of the maps. Mrs. Atsuko Czupryna graciously consented to present our English title in calligraphy. Professors Fred Czupryna and Michael Metzgar, members of the history faculty at North Carolina State University, shared with us their special knowledge of Japan and China. Our planning for this edition was aided by suggestions provided by Dr. T. C. Rhee, Associate Professor of History, University of Dayton. We are especially indebted to Professor Raymond Esthus of Tulane University, who offered invaluable criticisms based on careful reading of our revised manuscript. Finally, we were fortunate once again to have the assistance of Mrs. Elizabeth B. Bond, who helped with the research, typed the manuscript, and gave our copy an initial editing.

P. H. C.
B.F.B.

The Romanization of Chinese and Japanese

Chinese personal and place names are written by the Chinese in Chinese characters that are intelligible only to students of the Chinese language. These names are reproduced in the phonetic languages of the West by attempting to write the sound, a process known as transliteration or romanization. This process is not as simple as it may seem because within China itself, Chinese characters are pronounced in various ways. The Mandarin or Peking dialect is, however, generally regarded as standard. This would seem to resolve the matter, but unfortunately the sounds of the Mandarin dialect do not always have exact equivalents in English. Thus the Mandarin sounds are indicated by some conventionalized system of English letters and accents in which the English letters do not necessarily have the normal English sound but instead represent certain Mandarin sounds.

The problem is one with which Western sinologists have long experimented with results somewhat less than adequate. The most commonly used system is the Wade-Giles spelling, which in simplified form is generally followed in this book. However as news from Eastern Asia has commanded more space in the Western press, there has come into common use a postal or journalistic spelling, which is often used in these pages to avoid confusing the student unfamiliar with the Wade-Giles spelling. For example, we spell the name of the old capital of the Manchu Empire in journalistic style as Peking; the Wade-Giles spelling would be Pei-ching. A closer approach in the conventional sounds of the English letters would be Bei-jing. The commonly used transcriptions for Chinese words are defective, chiefly in three respects: (1) they fail to use the letters *b, d, g,* and they use *j,* not with its hard sound, but for a sound closer to the English *r*; (2) they use English vowels to represent the Chinese semi-vowels in such syllables as *tzu* and *shih*; and (3) the un-English apostrophe in the Wade-Giles romanization is frequently forgotten and dropped, with the result that different Chinese pronunciations are represented by the same English letters. Since speakers of English inevitably tend to pronounce words as they are spelled, such words as "Peking" are pronounced in a way that would be unintelligible to a Chinese.

The following is a simplified guide to pronunciation in the Peking dialect according to the Wade system.

VOWELS
(as in Italian)

a as in "father"
e as in "Edward"
i as the *e* in "me"
o like "aw" (but often like
      the *u* in "cut")
u as in "lunar"
e like the *u* in "under"
ih like the *e* in "her" (no real
      equivalent in English) ..
ü like French *u* or German *u*
u is practically unpronounced

CONSONANTS

The apostrophe following a consonant indicates aspiration; the lack of the apostrophe indicates the lack of aspiration, which sounds to our ears very much like voicing. Therefore:

Unaspirated

ch sounds like the *j* in "jam"
k like the *g* in "gun"
p like the *b* in "bat"
t like the *d* in "doll"
ts and *tz* sound like *dz*
j between French *j* and English *r*

Aspirated

ch' as in "chin"
k' as in "kin"
p' as in "pun"
t' as in "tap"
ts' and *tz'* like the *ts* of "Patsy"

Most of the other consonants are similar to those in English. In the following pages the diacritical ^˘¨ marks other than the apostrophe are omitted.

Other systems of romanization are used in other Western languages. A more recent system of romanization which is not commonly used, is the Homer H. Dubs revision of C. S. Gardner's romanization. It is an attempt to modify the Wade-Giles spelling to avoid the difficulties noted above. It also represents the distinction between *ts* and *ch,* and *hs* and *s* before the vowels *i* and *ü*. This distinction is retained in most of China. Actually, only a specailly devised alphabet can be entirely phonetic. The Dubs-

Gardner romanized spelling has the advantage of suggesting approximate pronunciation in letters pronounced as they are more frequently in English.

Some examples of the three systems follow:

Postal or journalistic spelling

Chekiang	Tali	Tsinan
Kwangtung	Lanchow	Sun Yat-sen
Paoting	Kweiyang	Canton
Peking	Chang Po-ling	Wuchang
Peiping	Hsinking	Yenan
Tientsin	Chihtang	Kaifeng
Hupeh	Szechuan	Kunming
Kuling	Jehol	
Kweilin	Tsingtao	

Wade-Giles spelling

Che-chiang	Ta-li	Chi-nan
Kuang-tung	Lan-chou	Sun I-hsien
Pao-ting	Kuei-yang	Kuang-chou
Pei-ching	Chang Po-ling	Wu-ch'ang
Pei-p'ing	Hsin-ching	Yen-an
T'ien-chin	Chih-t'ang	K'ai-feng
Hu-pe	Ssu-ch'uan	K'un-ming
Ku-ling	Je-ho	
Kuei-lin	Ch'ing-tao	

Dubs spelling (and approximate pronunciation)

Je-jiang	Da-li	Dzi-nan
Guang-dung	Lan-jou	Sun Yi-sien
Bao-ding	Guei-yang	Guang-jou
Bei-jing	Jang Bo-ling	Wu-chang
Bei-ping	Sin-jing	Yen-an
Tien-dzin	Jzh-tang	Kai-feng
Hu-be	Sz-chuan	Kun-ming
Gu-ling	Re-ho	
Guei-lin	Tsing-dao	

In both Chinese and Japanese personal names, the surname comes first, followed by the given name. However, in the following pages it has seemed best to use the form with which American readers are most likely to be familiar. Thus, for example, Li Hung-chang, Feng Yu-hsiang, Chiang K'ai-shek, but T. V. Soong. The same procedure has been followed with Japanese names. However fewer Japanese given names are known to the American public, and in general the rule of surname followed by given name has been adopted. There are, however, some cases in which even this simple rule cannot be followed. There is a growing tendency among some authors and publishers to use the English word order for Japanese and Chinese personal names in title pages and book citations. In such cases there is no choice but to follow the same practice. For the romanization of Japanese words, the Hepburn system is used in which each syllable ends in a vowel, with the exception of the few syllables ending with the consonant *n*. There are as many syllables in a word as there are vowels. No syllable is accented, though there are long vowels which really constitute two syllables, as in Ōsaka. The long mark has been omitted in the following pages. Consonants in Japanese are sounded much as they are in English. Vowels are sounded as follows: *a* as in father; *i* as "ee" in feet; *u* as "oo" in food; *e* as in met; *o* as in home.

There is much variation in the spelling of Korean words in English and other western languages. During the long period of Japanese rule in Korea, 1910-1945, most maps used in the West employed the romanization of place names used by the Japanese. After 1945 there was a return to the romanized forms of the Korean terms. Perhaps the most satisfactory method of transliteration of Korean words and names is the McCune-Reischauer system (see *Transactions of the Royal Asiatic Society*, Korea Branch, XXIX, 1939) which resembles the Wade-Giles and Hepburn systems for Chinese and Japanese respectively. Consonants are sounded as in English, vowels as in Italian. The wider variation of vowel sounds in Korean than that represented in the English alphabet is usually indicated by certain diacritical notations. Some vowel sounds by way of example are: *o* pronounced as *a* in above, *o* as in moss, *u* as in full, *ae* as in bag, *oe* as the German *o*. Aspirated sounds are indicated by '. See George M. McCune, *Korea Today* (1950), xii-xiii.

The English meaning of a few common Chinese words in their romanized form will aid the beginning student.

chuan, stream

chung, middle or central (Chung Kuo, The Middle Kingdom)

fu, obsolete ending in the name of a city

hai, sea

ho, river (in north China)

hsien, county

hu, lake

huang, yellow

hung, red

kiang, river (in central and south China)

ling, range, pass

nan, south

pai, white

peh, *pei*, north

shan, mountain

si, *hsi*, west

tai, large, great

t'ien, heaven

tung, east

wan, bay

NOTE ON THIS BOOK'S TITLE

The cover design for this sixth edition is the title of the book, translated into Japanese and written with a brush. In translation, the ordering of the words is not identical with the English, and the characters convey subtle meanings that are not explicit in English usage. A literal reading of the calligraphy would be: "East Asia: Impacts (Shocks) of the West and Responses (Countermeasures) of the East, A History." In romanization the Japanese reads: "Tōa, Seiyō no Shōgeki To Tōyō no Taiōshi." A Chinese calligrapher almost certainly would employ different characters in translating the title and the form would not be the same. However, since the characters were borrowed from the Chinese writing system, a Chinese could read the Japanese. A romanized Chinese reading would be: "Tung-ya: hsī-yang chung-chī tung-yang tui-yī̄ng shǐh."

The Antiquity of China and Japan

Christian Calendar	Dynasties of China	The World of Japan	Beyond East Asia
B.C. 1300	Shang or Yin 1523–1027 B.C. (*Anyang*)		Tutankhamen, Egypt Moses
1200			Iron Age Fall of Troy to the Greeks
1100		PRE-HISTORY: Migrations from the Asiatic continent; tribal warfare.	
1000			Rigveda David and Solomon, Judah
900	Chou 1027–256 B.C.		
800			
700			Legendary Founding of Rome Zoroaster
600		Jomon Culture	Gautama, founder of Buddhism
500	(Confucius)		Darius Thermopylae Parthenon completed
400			Alexander, Socrates
300			Chandraggupta, Aristotle Asoka
200	Ch'in, 221–207 B.C.	Yayoi	Hannibal

Culture

World / Western Culture	Japan	China
		Former Han 202 B.C.–A.D. 8 (*Sian*)
Julius Caesar		
Jesus		
Kanishka		Hsin, A.D. 8–23 (*Loyana*)
Marcus Aurelius		Later Han 25–220
Mani	Founding of the Japanese State: Yamato	
		3 Kingdoms
		Western Chin
Rome sacked by Alaric		Tsin
Attila		Wei 386–534
		Sung / Ch'i / Liang
		Ch'en
		Ch'i / Chou
Mohammed	(Shotoku Taishi)	Sui, 590–618
		Tang 618–906
Harum Al Rashid	Nara, 710–784	
Charlemagne	Heian 794–1185	10 Kingdoms 907–979
		5 Dynasties

Importation of Chinese Culture

Time scale (A.D.): 100 — 0 — 100 — 200 — 300 — 400 — 500 — 600 — 700 — 800 — 900

Christian Calendar	Dynasties of China	The World of Japan	Beyond East Asia	
1000	Sung 960–1126 / Liao 947–1127	Fujiwara (late Heian)	Lief Ericsson	1000
1100			William the Conqueror	1100
1200	Southern Sung 1127–1279 / Chin 1127–1234	Kamakura 1185–1333	Magna Carta	1200
1300	Yuan (Mongols) 1260–1368		The Polos	1300
1400	Ming 1368–1644 (Nanking, Peking)	Ashikaga 1336–1573	John Wycliffe	1400
1500			Columbus / Magellan; Henry VIII	1500
1600		Tokugawa 1603–1867	Shakespeare	1600
1700	Ch'ing (Manchus) 1644–1912 (Peking)		Glorious Revolution	1700
1800			U.S. Independence / The French Revolution / War of 1812	1800
1900		Meiji, 1868–1912 / Taisho, 1912–1926 / Showa, 1926–		1900
1911	Republic (Nanking)		World War I	1911
1941			World War II	1941
1949	Communist China (Peking)			1949
1970			Korean War / Vietnam War / India's Nuclear Explosion	1970
1974				1974

The Far East

On History
in General
and
This History
in Particular

1

History, of all intellectual disciplines, is the most used and the most abused. Mr. Everyman, as Carl Becker once said, is an historian of sorts, although he may be quite unaware that he is. He can perform the simplest daily chores only because his own historical experience tells him how to perform them and to what purpose. But he uses history wisely only when he becomes a critic of his own experience and attempts to be a better historian. If he assumes that unexamined experience is all that he needs, he is abusing history.

WHAT IS HISTORY?

Any effort to define history in a few words can at best be only partially successful. In its simplest form history is the *record* of things thought, said, and done. Such a definition is a useful starting point but it leaves a host of questions unanswered. How complete is a given record? What is its quality? Is it accurate? Is it designed to mirror *what actually was,* or rather to hide or distort what was and to perpetuate a myth or a mistaken memory?

For both the professional historian and the beginning student of history the principal method for answering these questions is to master the tested principles of sound historical thinking. This process is both distinctive and difficult. The historian's task is to analyze particular situations and movements critically and to form judgments on their nature and meaning. The best history is a product of both inquiry and criticism. It involves the effort to know and to understand, and the capacity to change accepted views when the evidence so dictates. The historian's greatest problem in this regard stems from the large role played by myth, parochialism, and prejudice in the affairs of men.[1]

Furthermore, the writing and the teaching of history are beset at present with intense pressures. The modern printing press and other media pour out historical sources more rapidly than the historian can use them. Their very bulk is a problem. The increasing complexity of modern society also has made the search for historical fact and meaning increasingly difficult. In the fields of domestic and world politics, governments and pressure groups are adept in the art of sophisticated

[1] On the principles of historical thinking see Paul L. Ward, *Elements of Historical Thinking* (1971).

1

propaganda. Rivaling nations with their fierce-ly contending ideologies—such as democracy, national socialism, and communism—often seek to subvert the purposes of history. Fur-thermore, the experimental and skeptical approach of modern science has undermined many of man's inherited values and has thereby enlarged the task of the historian. Yet, man's growing respect for his critical faculties—his willingness to use them when he is permitted to do so—and his increasing sense of relativity have reduced his reliance on ideologies, old and new, and have enlarged his need for history.[2]

THE TWO HISTORIES

History of one kind or another has a universal appeal. Men and women the world over cher-ish what they consider to be their national or ethnic history for a great variety of reasons. Quite often it has merely taught them to be thankful they are not as other men. To those who regard history as a systematic, rational, scientific pursuit, it is a stern intellectual discipline, a means toward understanding the past and the present. To the receptive mind, good history can bring unsurpassed satisfac-tion and enjoyment. For those who are prac-tically inclined, it is a principal means through which man may anticipate the future.

From what has been said to this point it must be clear that there are two histories. First, there is history in theory, in the abso-lute—the actual series of thoughts and events that once occurred. This is the ideal history, never wholly recoverable. Second, there is history in all its raw distortions—the series of facts and ideas each individual affirms and holds in memory. This latter has been called the history of the specious present. People everywhere tend to believe in it as the epit-ome of their traditions and prejudices, their wishful thinking and folklore, their misinfor-mation and emotions. Its troublesome power is very great since it derives not from reality or truth, but from what men wish to think and believe.

There is naturally some correspondence be-tween the two histories; it is the business of the historian to reduce our reliance on the history of the specious present by providing a record that is as close as possible to history in the ideal—to the actual series of thoughts and events that once occurred. The historian in pursuit of this goal is sometimes thought to be subversive because the evidence he finds and the meanings which follow often run counter to the deep-seated prejudices em-bodied in the history of the specious present.[3]

THE NATURE OF THE PAST

History is concerned with the past, whether the idea or the event in question occurred one minute or a thousand years ago. Moreover, though history may appear to be a simple subject to the uninitiated, the past is not simple but rather very complex and elusive. To the question, "What has happened in the world in the twentieth century?" there is not one, but a variety of different answers. The physical scientist will not give the same an-swer as the biologist. The anthropologist, the political scientist, the sociologist, the humanist will each have his own answer and his own emphasis. Answers to more specific questions may tend to coincide, but, since each answer is drawn from a specialized background, its point of emphasis may reveal an aspect of reality or history overlooked or belittled by other intellectual disciplines.

History may thus have many points of emphasis depending on whether the historian is primarily interested in political, social, eco-nomic, artistic, scientific, or philosophical matters. All of these various approaches to history will have at least one thing in com-mon; they will all be concerned with change—with when, how, and why change takes place. In some eras of history man's ideas and

[2] Useful references are Martin Ballard, ed., *New Movements in the Study and Teaching of History* (1970), and M. I. Finley, "Myth, Memory, and History," in *History and Theory*, 4 (1965), 281-302.

[3] Carl Becker, "Everyman His Own Historian," *American Historical Review,* 37 (1932), 221-36.

institutions change with great speed and produce major alterations in the values of society. Such periods are described as revolutionary, and it is one of these revolutionary eras in a particular part of the world which forms the principal subject of this book.

EAST ASIA

This history is primarily concerned with a region which Western peoples have traditionally called the Far East but which more recently has become known as East Asia.[4] The boundaries of this area are not precise but for the purposes of this survey they include eastern Siberia, China and the border territories (Manchuria, Mongolia, Tibet), Korea, Vietnam, Japan, and other insular lands such as Taiwan (Formosa), and the Philippines.[5] It is an immense area marked by striking physical and climatic diversity and by an even greater diversity in the races, languages, and cultural development of its inhabitants. It supports an enormous population. China's alone has been estimated recently at about 800 million, while Japan, whose area is less than that of California, is inhabited by more than 100 million persons. In all, about one-third of the world's people live in East Asia.[6]

Significantly, the overwhelming proportion of this vast population are tillers of the soil. As late as World War II, Japan was the only Asian country with a highly developed industry, and even in Japan some 50 percent of the population still lived by the soil.

The climates of East Asia are varied, yet there are certain broad features that may be said to affect the continent as a whole. Of

---

[4] In the seventeenth, eighteenth, and early nineteenth centuries, Europeans and Americans who went to the East Indies, China, and Japan sailed through the Atlantic and the Indian oceans to the east. These lands thus became to them the Far East, a term which has historic rather than contemporary significance.

[5] Vietnam and the Philippines, together with Thailand (Siam), Burma, Malaya, and Indonesia, are often classified geographically as belonging to Southeast Asia.

[6] The continent of Asia and its subdivision East Asia are simply geographical terms since neither of these areas is a cultural unity. Note John M. Steadman, "The Myth of Asia," *American Scholar,* 25 (1956), 163-75.

these the best known and, to the early European navigators the most useful, is the monsoon—seasonal wind blowing south and westerly from the heart of the continent in the winter or dry season, and north and easterly from the Indian Ocean in the summer or wet season. From the sixteenth to the mid-nineteenth century, European navigators sailed to Canton on the spring or summer monsoon, and turned their course homeward on the winter monsoon. But of greater importance to the native population is the fact that the wet monsoon brings the seasonal rains that make it possible for so many to live on the land. Farther inland, where the moisture does not reach, are the arid and semiarid regions of the Mongolian plateau.

Land configuration and climate in Asia are reflected not only in the distribution of population but also in its racial and cultural traits. Its immense size, virtually impassable barriers of mountain and desert, and extreme variations of climate generally precluded communication over the continent as a whole. Furthermore, geography not only separated the great civilizations of Asia one from another, but also isolated these people from other centers of civilization such as Western Europe. Indeed it may be said that this isolation remained for practical purposes unbroken until the late nineteenth century. When the barriers of separation were finally broken by an expanding Western world, East Asia was overwhelmed. There had been no preparation to meet the West, which had been enriched and empowered by all that Europe had achieved since the Renaissance in government, trade, invention, science, industry, and literature.

Diversity in Language

The most compelling aspect of the long span of East Asian history, reaching back some three thousand years, has been the emergence and the development of Chinese civilization, primarily at the hands of the racial stock known as Mongoloid man. Language, however, not race, has been the important determinant of East Asia's cultural evolution. The predominant family of languages is the Sinitic or Sino-Tibetan, found in China, Tibet, Vietnam,

Thailand, and Burma. Chinese, the largest member of the family, subdivides into a number of languages and dialects, of which Mandarin (so-called Chinese proper) is the most common and has produced an extraordinary literature.

A second family of languages, the Altaic, includes three major groups: Mongolian, Turkish, and Tungusic. Japanese and Korean appear to be Altaic in structure. The Manchus, who conquered China in 1644, spoke Tungusic, a language which arose among nomadic peoples to the north and west of China.

Still another language family in East Asia is the Austronesian, which includes the original speech of the Philippines, Indonesia and Malaya, and of the Taiwan aborigines.[7]

THE THEME OF THIS HISTORY

Throughout the past 150 years East Asia has been the stage for a revolution perhaps unequalled in all history in the breadth and depth of its penetration. This revolution has been advanced primarily by two great movements. The first was the expansion of Western civilization in all its aspects and power into the old and traditional societies of Middle and East Asia. This movement, called the "impacts of the West," had all but conquered Asia militarily and politically by the beginning of the twentieth century. By that time, however, East Asia's responses were developing. At first faltering, uneven, and uncharted, these responses had gathered irresistible momentum by the end of World War II. The result in the mid-twentieth century was a new East Asia—chaotic, often irresponsible, jealous of its "rights" and its new-found political freedom, and torn between fiercely opposed ideologies. This new Asia, when judged by the economic standards of the West, remained abysmally poor. Yet, so determined were Asia's leaders to avoid replacing an old political "enslavement" with a newer economic "enslavement"

that they displayed a deep suspicion of deals promising a bounty from the West.

Of the many avenues of approach to a study of modern East Asia, the one that will be found here is that of history. Asia's revolution is a product of historical growth. The successes and the failures in the meeting of East and West can be understood only in the light of the disciplined background knowledge that history should provide. Within broad topics, therefore, this is a chronological survey, since time and history are inseparable. The study begins with a descriptive survey of some principal ideas and institutions of Old China and Old Japan. These, the major countries of East Asia, had developed rich and enduring civilizations very unlike the cultural background of the modern Western world. A study of the Western impacts and Asian responses must, therefore, begin with some foundations in historic Asian values.

For example, a concept that has one meaning in Europe or in the United States may have quite another meaning in China. In the West, the concepts of individual freedom and of law as preservers of individual rights have been regarded as foundations of just government. In China, individualism (a foreign notion for which a term had to be coined) suggests unordered selfishness rather than any high ideal. Likewise, law in China, compared to its role in Western society, had little to do with the rights of individuals but was of great importance as an administrative tool to be used in the interest of the state. Thus the assumption, often entertained by Americans and Europeans, that the Chinese would react as Westerners to a given proposal, is, at best, rather farfetched.[8]

The most conspicuous aspects of the meeting of West and East have been in the areas of war and diplomacy, often termed the field of international relations. Yet formal international relations alone have not been the sole means of contact, nor have they been necessarily the most significant. Accordingly, this study will emphasize the West-East traffic in

[7] An introductory reference on the cultural geography of East Asia in George B. Cressey, *Asia's Lands and Peoples* (3rd ed., 1963).

[8] See John K. Fairbank, *China: the People's Middle Kingdom and the U.S.A.* (1967).

ideas and values and the institutions through which man gives expression to them. Asia's contemporary revolutions were born in the migration of ideas from West to East that spanned the past century. Here, too, attention will be given to the ways in which the Asians received Western ideas. It is remarkable that the West has given surprisingly little attention to these subjects. The result has been a shocking failure to understand Asia's aspirations, the sources from which they arose, or the means she might use to achieve them.

It should be noted then that the scope of this survey is limited. It is not a general history of East Asia. While providing an introductory background on historic Asian institutions and values, it concentrates on the past century and a half, emphasizes the influence of the West upon East Asia, and East Asia's responses to the Western impacts. At a number of points it will also touch upon aspects of East Asia's modern revolution not related directly, if at all, to the Western impact. Both in China and in Japan, modernization has been a response to Eastern values as well as to Western influence. The impact-response theme, although of major importance, does not account for all that has happened in East Asia during the past 150 years.

A NEW INTELLECTUAL TRADITION

Moreover, this survey is concerned with a subject that is new to the Western intellectual tradition. For Europeans and especially for Americans, East Asia has remained a world apart until very recently. When, for example, in 1898 President William McKinley said he was somewhat uncertain just where the Philippine Islands might be, he was in fact speaking for the vast majority of his countrymen. The politics and geography of Asia, when they were thought of at all, were considered subjects that might well be left to academicians with a fancy for strange and outlandish regions of the world. To be sure, there were Americans—traders, businessmen, sea captains, missionaries, and historians—who were not strangers to Asia's lands and peoples; but apart from these special groups, very few Americans had any knowledge of China,

Japan, India, or the lesser countries of the East. A popular school history, published in 1863 in New York, advised its readers that "China, a vast country of eastern Asia, may be almost said to have no history of any interest to the general reader, it has so few revolutions or political changes to record."[9]

There are of course many historical factors that explain the Americans' neglect of the larger world. As men built a new society in the United States they found satisfaction in certain geographical barriers. The Atlantic Ocean enabled them to achieve that political separation from Europe which they so ardently desired. Later, when this new nation had acquired a coastline on the Pacific, men saw, to be sure, visions of a great commerce with Asia; they even pictured the Pacific as an American lake. Yet they were more than ever dominated by a philosophy of political isolation, and it was very satisfying that the Pacific Ocean was wide and the "teeming millions" of Asia were far away. If, as many early Americans saw it, there was little reason to be concerned about the political affairs of Europe (since they were largely a matter of the sinister rivalries of kings), there was even less to recommend the civilizations of Asia, inhabited as that continent was by Oriental despots and a heathen, "uncivilized" society.

"The march of events," however, often has scant respect for man's deep-rooted habits and traditions. American participation in Asia's recent military and political crises has given thousands of Americans an undreamed of familiarity with those same distant lands which their fathers and grandfathers had called strange and outlandish. Furthermore, this growing contact has been accompanied by a measure of educational reform at home. In some of America's universities, centers devoted to research on Asian societies have been established; graduate and undergraduate courses, few of which were available before 1941, have multiplied; and in a few American localities the study of Asia has even been incorporated into the public schools' curricula.

[9] Marcius Willson, *Outlines of History* (1863), 286-87. At the very moment when Willson was writing, China was in the grip of the T'ai-p'ing rebellion, one of the most devastating upheavals any society has known.

Yet, in spite of these changes, American education at all levels remains predominantly European-centered. Asian studies "still remain on the fringe of things...."[10] In consequence, the "liberally" educated student, even in the 1970's, may complete his schooling with little knowledge beyond the Western tradition. This is not to suggest that for Americans an emphasis on European institutions and their American derivatives is less than imperative. It does not follow, however, that Asian studies, as newcomers to American education, are "exotic," or that students should be encouraged to regard them as an esoteric field of study. In reality the civilizations of the Occident and Orient are now so interwoven that education built on the exclusion of one or the other can hardly be called education at all for it ignores half of human experience.[11]

Furthermore, some of the devastating reverses that have overtaken Americans, their policies, and their actions in East Asia during the twentieth century might well have been prevented if Americans and their government had been more zealous to learn about Asia and to understand its aspirations.

THE STUDY OF HISTORY

The question of how a student may best study history, or how a teacher may best teach it, has no one simple answer. There was a time when the student who, under a good deal of prodding, had memorized the names and dates of the kings of England and the presidents of the United States was regarded as one who was on the right track. In reality, what this victim had done was to develop his memory and thus prepare himself to grapple with the kings of France and, if he were so disposed, with the emperors of China. In the

[10] Holden Furber, "Asia and the West as Partners Before 'Empire' and After," *Journal of Asian Studies,* 28 (1969), 720.
[11] See Ward Morehouse, "Asia and Africa in Today's World," *Teachers College Record,* 63 (1962), 551-56; and John K. Fairbank, "Assignment for the '70's," *American Historical Review,* 74 (1969), 861-79.

study of history, one should remember that mastering the names and dates may be commendable, but it should not be regarded as an historical accomplishment.

More recently, the teaching of history, at least to beginning college students, has taken the form of broad-structured survey courses in which large classes of students listen to lectures. Save in exceptional cases, this system has only limited justification since much that is dispensed in lectures can be found in far better form in reputable books. The lecture system is most useful where it amplifies and integrates evidence the student has already acquired.

Efforts are now being made to find more meaningful ways for the beginning student to approach history. The rationale of these newer approaches is that history which has been completely prestructured for the student denies him the stimulus of discovery. This theory postulates that students learn best what they discover for themselves. Thus, in history, the most important thing for a student to learn first is how to learn, what to learn, and to what purpose. In this approach, the student is confronted with documents, the raw materials of history—original manuscripts, letters, eyewitness accounts, treaties, diplomatic and other official or unofficial correspondence. He is assigned the task of learning how to use these sources, how to draw conclusions from them, and how to test these conclusions. He thereby takes the first step toward creating his own structure of the subject. He is on the way to becoming a better historian.

As a matter of fact, none of these approaches to the study of history is either new or exclusive. Each of them has its proper place. History is as broad and all-inclusive as man's comprehension. No two students will enter the maze of history in precisely the same way or with identical objectives. What teachers and students need to bear in mind is that somewhere there is what Carl Becker called history in the absolute—the actual thoughts and deeds that once occurred. It is the search for this absolute which gives purpose to the study of history.

In the contemporary world of America and elsewhere, an encouraging sign is the increasing desire of students for intellectual pursuits that are "relevant." In some cases the relevance of a particular line of inquiry may be self-evident; relevance is often subtle and elusive. The student's ultimate discovery of relevance should be a primary goal and an unending search, but its attainment, even in some limited measure, requires first the labor and the patience necessary to master the fundamentals and the content of the subject. There can be no historical relevance for those who are unwilling to struggle with the learning process. The student of history is called upon constantly to distinguish between what is historically relevant and what is less so. The historical evidence must provide the answer, not the whim of an individual or a pressure group. Contemporaneity alone is not the badge of relevance.

Asking the Right Questions

Again, the student of history, like the professional historian, needs to develop the capacity to seek historical meaning by asking those questions that can direct the quest for answers. Sometimes the appropriate questions and the answers to them are relatively simple. It may be important, for example, to determine the exact date of a given event in order to relate it to other events on which it is presumed to have had an effect. Some historical questions are far more profound and far more frustrating. It will be noted in succeeding pages of this book that governments, even entire societies, have made specific plans for the future and have adopted careful programs of action to implement these plans. Yet the programs, even when applied with vigor, have produced conditions and results which were the antithesis of what the government or the society was attempting to achieve. How is this kind of phenomenon to be explained?

Language and Meaning

There is an additional pitfall into which the scholar and student of history can easily fall. Precise thought and precise language to give it

expression are not easily achieved. For example, there will be frequent reference in the pages which follow to "modernization" and "Westernization" in the past century or so of East Asian history. The trouble is that these terms are not precise in meaning. They may easily convey very different concepts to different people. At best they are convenient labels which continue in use for want of something better.[12]

TWO CONTRASTING MEMORIES

These introductory remarks on history in general and this history in particular may best be concluded by citing two widely accepted versions of American-Chinese relations.

Until 1949 Americans tended to regard their country's role in and toward China as one of friendship and benevolent concern. They focused on the preservation of China's territorial and administrative integrity, and on the support of her struggles to modernize. To be sure, some Americans, and a few Chinese, realized commercial profits in the process, but on the other hand, American philanthropy poured into China. In short, Americans took great pride in the historical picture they had created from their memories of American relations with China.

During those same years, the Chinese, like the Americans, were forming their own evaluations of Sino-American contacts but, strange as it may seem, their memories were very unlike those cherished by Americans. The Chinese tended to see Americans not as benevolent protectors but as creators of an unequal treaty system which reduced China to a semi-colony. Christian philanthropy and education were regarded as subverting China's traditions and culture. Americans, like Euro-

[12] On this perplexing subject of ideas and language, the student should consult: Knight Biggerstaff, "Modernization and Early Modern China," *Journal of Asian Studies,* 25 (1966), 607-20; Ardath Burks, "Modernization in Korea," *ibid.,* 27 (1968), 609-12; Marius B. Jansen, ed., *Changing Japanese Attitudes Toward Modernization* (1965),*especially ch. 1 by John Whitney Hall [Note: The asterisk indicates a paperback edition.], and John Higham *et al., History* (1965).*

peans, were the creators of China's humiliation.

In brief then, memory has left two pictures of the same scene, and they are not alike. Perhaps this is because these memories on both sides are histories of the specious present.

FOR FURTHER READING

Bibliographies. American Historical Association, comp. and ed., *A Guide to Historical Literature* (1961). American Universities Field Staff, *A Select Bibliography: Asia, Africa, Eastern Europe, Latin America* (1960), with *Supplements* (1962 and 1963). *Bibliography of Asian Studies,* published annually by The Association for Asian Studies, formerly The Far Eastern Association. Charles O. Hucker, *China, A Critical Bibliography;* and Bernard S. Silberman, *Japan and Korea, A Critical Bibliography* (1962). R. J. Kerner, *Northeastern Asia: A Selected Bibliography* (2 vols., 1939). Hyman Kublin, comp., *An Introductory Reading Guide to Asia* (3rd rev. ed., 1962). W. L. Langer and H. F. Armstrong, *Foreign Affairs Bibliography: A Selected and Annotated List of Books on International Relations, 1919-1932* (1933). Clifford H. MacFadden, *A Bibliography of Pacific Area Maps* (1941). P. K. Yu, *Chinese History: Index to Learned Articles: Volume 2, 1905-1964, Based on Collections in American and European Libraries,* No. 1 in *Harvard-Yenching Library Bibliographical Series* (1970).* Leonard H.D. Gordon and Frank J. Shulman, *Doctoral Dissertations on China: A Bibliography of Studies in Western Languages, 1945-1970* (1970).* Tienyi Li, *Chinese Fiction: A Bibliography of Books and Articles in Chinese and English* (1968). Donald Clay Johnson et al., compilers, *Southeast Asia: A Bibliography for Undergraduate Libraries* (1970).

Popular Literature. Lin Yutang, *My Country and My People* (1935), a fascinating portrayal, generally reliable, but idealized. Pearl S. Buck, *The Good Earth* (1931),* reissued repeatedly, is a novel on Chinese peasant life. Lady

Sugimoto, *A Daughter of the Samurai* (1925) a delicate and artistic account of old Japan presented through the medium of autobiography. Ishimoto Shidzue, *Facing Two Ways: The Story of My Life* (1935) depicts conflicts between traditional and modern Japan. Dennis Bloodworth, *The Chinese Looking Glass* (1967),* a popular, useful introduction to Chinese manners.

Geography and People. Daniel R. Bergsmark, *Economic Geography of Asia* (1935) is still a useful introductory survey. George B. Cressey, *Asia's Lands and People* (3rd ed., 1963), perhaps the most useful and comprehensive survey of the physical environment and cultural features. E. H. G. Dobby, *Monsoon Asia* (1961), useful reference, of uneven quality. Norton S. Ginsburg, ed., *The Pattern of Asia* (1958), general geography of Asia. Pierre Gourou, Joseph E. Spencer, and Glenn T. Trewartha, *The Development of Upland Areas in the Far East* (1949). Albert Herrman, *Historical and Commercial Atlas of China* (1935 and 1963); new edition edited by Norton Ginsburg (1966). Lionel W. Lyde, *The Continent of Asia* (1933), a detailed, technical study. Rhoads Murphey, *An Introduction to Geography* (1961), an excellent geography with maps, charts, and illustrations. Louis Richard, *Comprehensive Geography of the Chinese Empire and Dependencies* (1908), historically still very useful. L. Dudley Stamp, *Asia* (3rd ed., 1935). Guy Wint, ed., *Asia: A Handbook* (1966), handles the problems of Asia systematically and concisely. L. D. H. Buxton, *The Peoples of Asia* (1925). Inez Adams, "Rice Cultivation in Asia," *American Anthropologist* 50 (April-June, 1948), 256-82.

Government and Politics. Three important general studies are: George McTurnan Kahin, ed., *Major Governments of Asia* (1958; second ed., 1963), a symposium on political systems and processes in China, Japan, India, Pakistan, and Indonesia in modern times; Robert E. Ward and Roy C. Macridis, eds., *Modern Political Systems: Asia* (1963); and Paul M. A.

Linebarger, Chu Djang, and Ardath Burks, *Far East Governments and Politics* (1954).

Treaty Collections. Carnegie Endowment for International Peace, *Treaties and Agreements with and concerning China, 1919-1929* (1929). China, the Maritime Customs, *Treaties, Conventions, etc., Between China and Foreign States* (2 vols., 2nd ed., 1917). Henry Chung, *Korean Treaties* (1919). Hertslet's *China Treaties* (2 vols., 3rd ed., 1908). League of Nations, *Treaty Series* (1920-). J. V. A. MacMurray, ed., *Treaties and Agreements with and Concerning China, 1894-1919* (2 vols., 1921). W. M. Malloy, ed., *Treaties, Conventions, International Acts, Protocols and Agreements Between the United States and Other Powers* (3 vols., 1909-1923). W. F. Mayers, *Treaties Between the Empire of China and Foreign Powers* (3rd ed., 1901). David Hunter Miller, ed., *Treaties and Other International Acts of the United States of America* (8 vols., 1931-1948) scholarly and meticulous. W. W. Rockhill, *Treaties and Conventions with or concerning China and Korea, 1894-1904* (1904). United States, *Treaties and Other International Agreements* (1950 and subsequent years).

United States Documents. *The Annals of Congress* (1789-1824); *Register of Debates* (1825-1937); *The Congressional Globe* (1833-1873); and *The Congressional Record* (1873 to date), illuminating material from the debates in Congress on foreign relations.

Papers Relating to the Foreign Relations of the United States (1861 and subsequent years), annual volumes contain selections from American diplomatic correspondence with liberal sections devoted to East Asia. See also various periodic publications issued by the U.S. Department of State.

Periodicals. Many of the more definitive studies on aspects of modern East Asian history are scattered throughout an extensive periodical literature, in the journals of learned and professional societies, and in popular and semi-popular periodicals. The following is a selected list of some of these journals: *The American Historical Review; American Journal of International Law; American Political Science Review; Annals of the American Academy of Political and Social Science; Asian Survey; The China Quarterly; Contemporary Japan;* The Foreign Policy Association, *Bulletins and Reports; The Harvard Journal of Asiatic Studies; The Journal of Asian Studies (*before 1957 *The Far Eastern Quarterly); Journal of Asian History; Pacific Affairs; The Journal of Modern History; The Pacific Historical Review; Philippine Social Science Review; Political Science Quarterly; Transactions of the Asiatic Society of Japan; Transactions and Proceedings of the Japan Society of London;* United Nations Department of Economic Affairs, *Economic Survey of Asia and the Far East; United States Naval Institute Proceedings.*

Ways of Life
in Old China

2

The civilization of China is one of the oldest and richest known to man. It is remarkable that only recently has it become a subject of serious study in the United States. This neglect is the more curious because at various times during the past century many Americans have appeared to consider themselves as rather special friends of China, and because the government of the United States, in principle at least, often appeared as a champion of China, its independence and its political integrity. These popular and official American attitudes toward China did not lead, however, to any deep American interest in or admiration for Chinese culture, or any intellectual interest in her philosophies, her religions, or her theories of government. Thoughtful students of this history will need to consider why this was so, and to ask whether the explanation may lie in the fact that American sympathies and concern were not for an actual China that existed but rather for an imaginary China that might some day come into being through American and other benign Western influence.

Europe has on occasion been more conscious than America of the intellectual and cultural gifts China could offer, but even in Europe enthusiasm for things Chinese has

been spotty at best. The result is that although there is a long history of intercourse between China and the Western world, the two civilizations have never ceased being strangers. Thus, before entering upon the story of the Western impact upon China, there is good reason to review at least briefly some aspects of China's institutional and cultural history.[1]

THE VENERABLE AGE OF CHINA

Students are often irritated by what they regard as the curious and outmoded ideas of their elders. Similar tensions are apt to be present when a young nation is thrown into intimate contact with a very old civilization. The American people, for example, have been an independent sociopolitical group for almost 200 years; this appears as quite a respectable age until it is recalled that the Chinese people have been a cohesive social group developing a remarkable culture for more than 3,000 years.

[1] Convenient introductory references are: Frederick W. Mote, *Intellectual Foundations of China* (1971)*; L. Carrington Goodrich, *A Short History of the Chinese People* (rev., 1963)*; and H. G. Creel, *The Birth of China* (1954).*

CHINA: GREAT PERIODS IN HISTORY

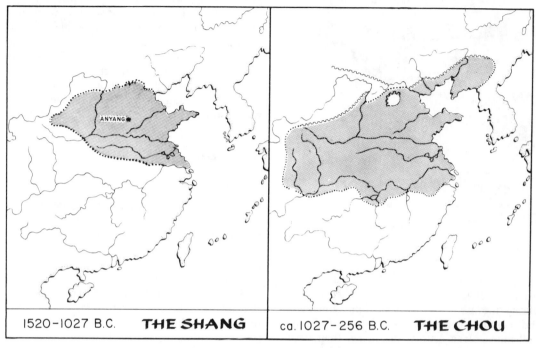

1520–1027 B.C. **THE SHANG**

ca. 1027–256 B.C. **THE CHOU**

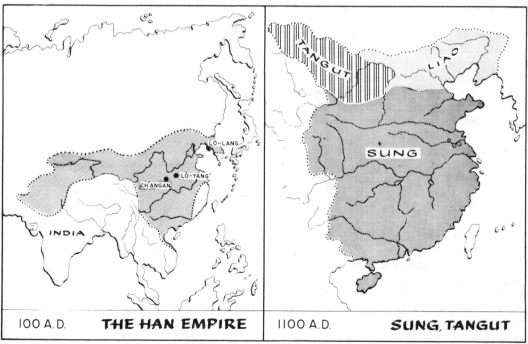

100 A.D. **THE HAN EMPIRE**

1100 A.D. **SUNG, TANGUT**

Adapted with permission from L. Carrington Goodrich, A Short History of the Chinese People *(1943).*

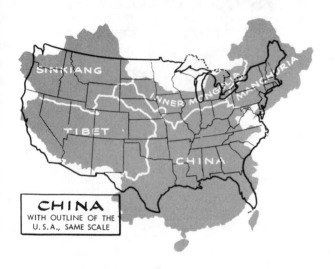

CHINA
WITH OUTLINE OF THE
U.S.A., SAME SCALE

ployed most of the important principles of the intricate modern Chinese written characters. At some very early time a calendar was invented and adjusted frequently to keep it in step with the seasons of the year. Adjustability was important in an agricultural country and among a credulous people. A ruler might lose his job, and his head too, if the seasons went astray.

DYNASTIC DIVISIONS

The earliest days of Chinese culture, prior to the eleventh century B. C., belong to what is called the Shang dynasty. It was followed by the Chou dynasty (1027-256 B. C.), during which the greatest names in Chinese history made their appearances: Confucius, Lao Tzu, and Mo Tzu. As the Chou era neared its end during years of protracted civil war (known as the period of the Warring States), China underwent political consolidation at the hands of the Ch'in, who, by military force and organizational technique, imposed their will on the Chinese world. It was a harsh and cruel experience. In the brief period 221-207 B. C., the Ch'ins made their king into China's first emperor, Shih Huang-ti, and completed the Great Wall along the northern frontier, thus emphasizing the distinction between what was Chinese and what was foreign.

The Ch'in conquest was one of the great revolutions of Chinese history, comparable only with the T'ai-p'ing of the nineteenth century or the Nationalist-Communist revolution of the twentieth century. The Ch'in revolution sought to destroy the ancient system of feudal states, thereby laying the foundations for a centralized bureaucratic state. The extent of this ruthless sociopolitical upheaval is suggested by the fact that the kings of the earlier China were aristocrats of supposed divine ancestry who, together with the nobility, were the sole possessors of political power, whereas Liu Pang, the founder of the great Han dynasty in 202 B. C., was born a peasant. But if the Ch'in revolution was con-

Stated another way, the United States has been the leader of the so-called "Free World" during the past few decades, but China was the cultural center of East Asia for two milleniums. It is hardly surprising, then, that the American and Chinese senses of value do not always coincide.

Furthermore, the Chinese are naturally very proud of their culture. They called their land *Chung-kuo,* the central country (or as the name appeared in Western literature, the Middle Kingdom), to suggest its pivotal role throughout East Asia. Indeed, an educated Chinese, whether of Confucian, communist or any other persuasion, is heir to a rich and ancient cultural tradition revealing itself in an immense and varied society, unrivaled in age by any political or social community the world has ever known.

PERIODS OF CHINESE HISTORY

The chronological chart, page xxii, gives some perspective on the matter of time and age. At the beginning of the Christian era China was already an old society. Between the sixteenth and the eleventh centuries B. C., her learned men created a system of writing that em-

structive in some respects, it was also harsh and destructive. Shih Huang-ti is remembered for his burning of books, by which he hoped vainly to narrow and discipline the course of Chinese intellectual development.[2]

The Han Dynasty, 202 B.C.-A.D. 8 and 25-220 A.D.

The Chinese like to call themselves the Sons of Han because the Han was one of the richest and most inspiring periods in China's long history. It was an era of discovery, expansion, and conquest, which made China a great power dominating much of the eastern half of Asia. Han culture enriched China's life in many ways: in literature and the arts, and in government, science, and industry. Here began the painstaking search to rediscover the proscribed classics which the Ch'ins, after the manner of dictators, had sought to destroy. The foundations were also laid for the Confucian conquest of the Chinese mind.

The creative qualities of Han culture were amazingly varied. A lunar calendar of great mathematical accuracy and a delicately sensitive seismograph were developed. By the close of the Han period glazed pottery of fine quality and elaborately embroidered silks were being produced for both domestic and foreign trade. Han ladies sought to improve on nature with face powder and rouge. Literature became richer in content and expression; scholarship was pursued actively while manuscripts were collected in an imperial library. Standard histories were written on paper which may have been made from rags.[3]

The T'ang Dynasty, 618-906

Some four centuries after the fall of the Han dynasty, China again entered upon a period of great vitality. The T'ang period is sometimes called the most brilliant in the country's history. Education was encouraged.

[2] Note C. P. Fitzgerald, *China: A Short Cultural History* (rev. ed., 1950).*
[3] Consult Richard Wilhelm, *A Short History of Chinese Civilization* (1929), and John K. Shryock, *The Origin and Development of the State Cult of Confucius* (1932).

Civil service examinations to insure bureaucratic merit, an idea adapted from the previous Sui dynasty, were stressed. Though the state cult of Confucius was favored, there was a notable measure of religious tolerance. Commerce was encouraged by extending the canal system. Stability was sought through a codification of the law.

In the middle of the eighth century, the T'ang empire covered not only the greater part of what in the nineteenth century was known as China Proper, but also south and central Manchuria and the vast area of Turkestan far to the west. Some T'ang rulers, endowed with great political perception, challenged the growing political power of Buddhism and other religions, subjecting them to the state or suppressing them. On the cultural side, architecture and sculpture reached new peaks of excellence. Ch'ang-an, the capital of T'ang China with a population of almost two million in 742, was in point of design and architecture one of the world's finest cities. In literature, the T'ang was the great age of Chinese poets: Li Po, Tu Fu, Wang Wei, Po Chu-i, and Wei Ying-wu. The breadth of T'ang interests is suggested by the encyclopedias that were compiled. The short story, which formerly dealt mainly with the world of spirits, entered the more human and mundane field of life and love. And finally, block printing was invented.

The Sung Dynasty, 960-1279

With the fall of the T'ang empire, China was again plunged into a period of political confusion. Between 907 and 960, a succession of the so-called "Five Dynasties" maintained a precarious hold on what remained of the T'ang empire. In general this was a period of rule by licentious tyrants, of such sensual refinements as the binding of women's feet (which seems to have been imposed first upon dancing girls), and of a general breakdown in the entire economic and political structure of society. It was from this chaos that the Sung empire finally arose. With the exception of the years 1127-1135, the Sung dynasty ruled China from 960 to 1279. In the main, it was

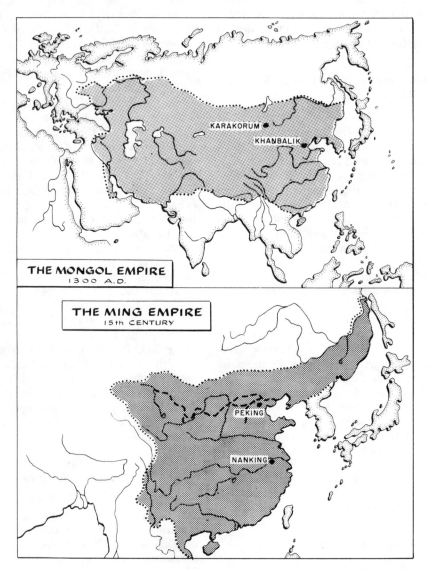

Adapted with permission from L. Carrington Goodrich, A Short History of the Chinese People *(1943).*

a period of widespread improvement in the living conditions of the people, even the common folk began to sit on chairs instead of the floor. There was a renaissance in the arts and in education. Unlike under the T'angs, when the poets excelled, under the Sungs the writers of prose took the lead. Porcelain, landscape painting, block printing, and neo-Confucianism were particularly notable in the Sung period. There was also progress in the science of algebra, perhaps introduced through the Arab trade. All in all, the civilization of Sung China may well have surpassed all others of that time, so that it was quite natural for Shao Yung to say: "I am happy because I am a human and not an animal; a male and not a female; a Chinese and not a barbarian; and because I live in Loyang, the most beautiful city in all the world."[4]

The Mongols, 1260-1368

At the close of three centuries of Sung rule, China was conquered by a foreign power, the Mongols. With this conquest, the greater Mongol empire extended in a continuous broad belt from the eastern seaboard of China as far north as the Amur, and across the heart of Asia to the borders of Arabia and far into European Russia. In their advance upon China, the Mongols took control of Mongolia by 1206, overran Korea in 1231, and made Cambaluc (Peking) their eastern winter capital in 1264. Under the leadership of Kublai Khan, Yunnan was conquered, Vietnam was reduced to vassalage, and two unsuccessful expeditions were dispatched against Japan. China had become a part of the Mongol empire. It was a period when the world was shrinking; ideas as well as merchandise traveled the caravan routes between Peking and the Danube.

The Ming Dynasty, 1368-1644;
The Ch'ing (Manchu) Dynasty, 1644-1912

As the Mongol power receded, China passed under the control of the last of its native Chinese dynasties, the Ming, which in the mid-seventeenth century was overcome by another alien conqueror, the Manchus, who ruled until the establishment of China's first so-called Republic in 1912. More will be said on these recent dynastic periods in subsequent chapters. At this point, it should be useful to summarize some of the principal ideas, philosophies, and religious concepts which dominated the everyday life of ancient China.

IDEAS BY WHICH OLD CHINA LIVED

China from its ancient beginnings to the end of the Manchu dynasty in 1912 may be called Old China, to distinguish it from Republican China, 1912-1949, or Communist China after 1949. The latter periods, as indicated by the

[4] Quoted from Goodrich, *Short History,* 163.

chart, p.xxii, are not very impressive in point of time when compared with the great sweep of Chinese history. To say, therefore, in a historical sense, that an idea, a philosophy, or an institution is "Chinese" means that it was born and nurtured as a part of Old China.

While Old China was, in the main, a remarkably stable and enduring society, it was not the unchanging society Western observers often thought it to be. In fact, Old China, at one time or another, produced an almost infinite variety of ideas, philosophies, and institutions, some of which survived into modern times. Sung China in particular was remarkable for its diversity of thought and for a relative absence of official orthodoxy.

The Ch'ing or Manchu period (1644-1912) is of particular importance to the historical narrative of these pages because it was in this period that China was subjected to the increasing pressures of European and American expansion. In the perspective of Chinese history, Manchu China saw the beginnings of an extraordinary transition from what was traditional to what is modern. The Manchu period, like earlier periods, left its own notable legacies to the China of today. Many of these legacies trace their origins to ancient China, but the Ch'ing period placed its peculiar stamp upon them. By way of illustration, one may note the following five ways in which the Manchu period contributed to the form of early modern China.

1. It was a period of empire building. During most of the age of Old China (allowing for some exceptional periods), the area of effective Chinese jurisdiction was some 1,500,000 square miles, about half the area of the United States. In the late Ch'ing period the empire covered some 4,275,000 square miles.

2. The Ch'ing period imposed on China a major population problem. In previous periods China's peak population was about 100 million. By 1850, even with an unfavorable population-land ratio and worsening economic conditions, population had reached some 430 million. By the early 1970's it was estimated at 800 million.

3. The Manchu capacity for systematic sinicization was successful. The supreme test of this policy came in the mid-nineteenth

century when, in the T'ai-p'ing rebellion (see Chapters 7 and 12), most of the scholar-official class sought to sustain their foreign Manchu masters.

4. Political, economic, and social institutions achieved greater maturity, and there was a strengthening of interregional integration.

5. Especially in the eighteenth century, there was a considerable enrichment of Chinese life. The supply of articles for mass and elite consumption increased notably. Some sectors of the populace enjoyed a rising standard of living, and the rich could afford to be extravagant.[5]

Even when allowance is made, however, for the distinctive features that set one period of Chinese history apart from another, the fact remains that the Chinese way of life exhibited an amazingly constant character. There were a number of ideas, ideals, and goals which acted as a kind of common denominator of China's political and social philosophy. At least a few of these need to be kept in mind. They had something to do with creating the very special character of Chinese culture, unrivaled as a continuous, living civilization.

The Meaning of Life

Educated Chinese have always been more concerned with the world of nature and of man than with the elusive world of the supernatural. Churches and priests played a lesser role in China than in most great civilizations. This is not to say that there were no religious motivations in China. They were present, but they expressed themselves principally through the veneration of ancestors. The point to note is that reverence for ancestors belonged to the single family group. It could not become an institutionalized national or international church.

The Chinese recognized the concept of divinity. Mountains and many other forms of nature were often given a sacred character as related to the supreme Chinese deity, *T'ien*

(Nature or Heaven); but these forces usually remained rather abstract and were personified only rarely. An important result was that the Chinese were remarkably free from religious intolerance and bigotry. When persecution occurred, it was likely to be occasioned not by religious ideas as such but by religious movements that sought to control the state. Another consequence was that for the most part the Chinese were not enticed by promised rewards in heaven or tormented by threats of everlasting punishment in hell. Such notions did not appear in China until introduced by Buddhism and other alien faiths. These attitudes on matters of the supernatural have suggested the conclusion that, in a comparative sense, the Chinese were not a religious people.[6]

The Social Philosophy

If Chinese were not greatly concerned with the other world, they were very much preoccupied with this one—namely, with nature and with man, which they considered to be one great unity. As a part of this unity man was important, but he had nothing approaching the central role in the cosmic scheme which Christian religious thought has given him. The idea was that if man was to be in harmony with the universal unity, *T'ien,* he would adjust himself to the universe, that is, to nature. The modern West, in contrast, has sought what it calls "happiness" in bending nature to the will of man. Traditional Chinese ideas would never have countenanced such practices as strip mining. Furthermore, within the universal unity of man with nature, man's problem was to find and practice the means of getting along with his fellow men. Long before the Christian era, Chinese thinkers were aware that progress in material things and power merely increases the tribulations of men unless they have first solved the riddle of human relations. This concern with the here and now, with the immediate pain and pleasure of human life, is what is usually behind

---

[5] Ping-ti Ho, "The Significance of the Ch'ing Period in Chinese History," *Journal of Asian Studies,* 26 (1967), 189-95.

[6] See the discussion by Derk Bodde, "Dominant Ideas," in *China,* H. F. MacNair, ed. (1946), 18-28.

the description of the Chinese as a pragmatic people.

Harmony and Stability

The Chinese emphasis on the temporal created a marked respect for the lessons of human experience and thus encouraged the writing of history, from which, it was hoped, man could learn how to behave. What happened for the most part was that these official historical writings often perpetuated the ideas thought to be most valid. In Chinese intellectual life, history was no idle pastime. It performed the service left to revelation in other societies, and it shaped some very strong Chinese notions on what the nature of society should be. Five examples should be sufficient to illustrate the point.

1. A Society of Status. The society of Old China was one of status. Man was born into a particular social level and, in general, was supposed to remain there. Since, however, it was sometimes possible and even desirable for individuals to rise to higher stations, the system readily accommodated a limited degree or social mobility.

2. Duties and Obligations. Great stress was laid on man's duties in his particular station, rather than on his rights. Only if one's duties were performed properly would the larger group of which he was a part (his family or clan) prosper.

3. The Unit of Society. Rugged individualism, as exalted in modern Western society, was not counted a virtue in Old China. On the contrary, it was not the individual but the family or clan that formed the basic unit of Chinese society. The primary obligations of an individual were not to himself, to his nation, or to his government, but to his family. He expressed these obligations by the formal veneration of his ancestors, by obeying and caring for the family elders, and by rearing sons to perpetuate the family and its name. The family in turn was the individual's social security, protecting him from a world that was harsh and often cruel. It was this closely knit family, perhaps more than any other institution, which preserved Chinese civiliza-

tion through periods of great political chaos. The primacy of the family in Chinese thought meant that ideas such as nationalism and patriotism, which permeated modern Western thought, exercised little influence in Old China save in a nonpolitical, cultural sense.

4. The Nature of Government. Old China had rather pronounced ideas on the subject of government. The state was considered to be one large family. The Chinese expression *kuo-chia* may be translated as nation-family. The emperor was the parent of the people; government was therefore paternalistic. If the emperor as parent was to exert the proper influence, it was recognized that he himself must live by the highest moral standards and select ministers of like character. If the common people were expected to obey, then rulers must act with high moral regard for the rights of lesser men. In contrast with the Anglo-American idea of government by law, Old China held that the best government was achieved through moral persuasion and example. Laws there were, to be sure, but they were not the most important factor in government. Old China believed that government should be by men—educated men who understood and exemplified correct conduct—rather than by inflexible rules of law (see Chapter 3).

5. Moral Foundations. In Western society Christianity has emphasized man's depravity: one must be born again. Old China, for the most part, proceeded from the more cheerful premise that man was by nature fundamentally good. Therefore, in Chinese thought, sin never achieved the exalted status it has often enjoyed in some other civilizations. The Chinese idea was that man's inherent goodness was a positive force which could be cultivated by learning. Thus great stress was laid upon education. The good man through learning achieved wisdom and thereby became a superior being.

THE IDEAL MAN IN OLD CHINA

The ideas and ideals noted in the foregoing sketch operated in a society in which the institutional framework was remarkably stable. Government, while centralized politically, was decentralized economically. Most large-scale activity, whether political, economic, military, or religious, was controlled by a great and numerous bureaucracy. This bureaucratic state was predominantly agrarian, deriving its income from the agricultural production of an illiterate but intelligent peasantry which, in addition to growing the food, provided the conscript labor for public works, such as the Great Wall or the Grand Canal, and the conscript armies for defense or conquest. The large bureaucracy of government officials who presided over the construction of public works, administered the revenue, or decided on war or peace came from the small literate element of the population who could conduct public affairs in the beautiful but difficult system of ideographic writing of the Chinese language. Since many years of education were required to master this written language and the Classical literature that went with it, it followed that only the sons of the wealthy could afford to attain literacy. It came about, therefore, that only men of wealth, the landed gentry, reared educated sons (scholars); only scholars became government officials; and government officials, in turn, invested their wealth in land. As a result, the ideal man of leadership in Old China was not a merchant, a trader, a general, or a priest, but rather a landlord-scholar official.

THE GOLDEN AGE

Most of these particular ideas, ideals, and attitudes, which gave Chinese civilization its distinctive character for more than 2,000 years, arose during a so-called Golden Age of Chinese intellectual history. The period spanned the final centuries of the Chou dynasty, from the time of Confucius (born 551 B. C.) to the establishment of the first Chinese empire, the Ch'in in 221 B. C. In these years China sired many of the great names in her political, social, institutional, and religious history. In addition to Confucius, there was Meng K'o or Mencius (ca. 372-289 B. C.), and

Hsun Tzu (ca. 298-238 B. C.). Together these three were the most notable framers of that extraordinary philosophy and way of life called Confucianism. There was that mysterious figure Lao Tzu, probably a contemporary of Confucius and the central figure along with Chuang Tzu (ca. 369-286 B. C.), in the emergence of Taoism, sometimes considered the great rival of Confucianism. Finally, there was Mo Tzu (ca. 479-438 B. C.), whose doctrines sound rather modern and un-Chinese.

THE LITERARY HERITAGE

The Golden Age bequeathed to succeeding generations a body of literature that was to have enormous influence on China's cultural history. It provided the foundations for the systems of thought that were to dominate the Chinese mind for more than 2,000 years: Confucianism and Taoism.

The inspiration for this literature goes back even to early Chou times. It consists of brief and simple oracular texts inscribed on bone, of inscriptions found on bronze vessels, and of books that were elaborated greatly in later times. One of the most notable of these is the *I Ching* or *Book of Changes,* which has had a continuing fascination for Chinese intellectuals.[7]

CONFUCIANISM

Although China has not always been dominated by professed Confucians, nevertheless Confucianism has affected China more profoundly and continuously than any other philosophy. It gave to China, among other things, a remarkable humanistic philosophy and a recognition that the true bases of society are social and mundane as well as divine in the Chinese sense of that word.

Confucius (K'ung Fu-tzu, 551-479 B. C.) was more than an academic theorist. He was also a practical statesman who spent most of his life, however, moving about the country as a teacher. His students were primarily young

[7] *I Ching, or Book of Changes,* English translation by Cary F. Baynes from the German translation of Richard Wilhelm (1967).

men of the upper classes, for whom politics was the only honorable profession. Confucius presented to them a code of high moral ideas of such force that it became the dominant philosophy of official China and, until 1911, remained as authoritative as the Christian Bible was in Western thought until about a century ago. In fact, Confucianism became so much a part of the Chinese character that it was almost taken for granted. Most Chinese said very little about it, just as some Western writers who were deeply influenced by the Bible rarely quoted it directly. Yet the Confucian tradition was in the background of every educated person's mind, since every candidate for official position concentrated on it for years. These candidates memorized longer passages from the Confucian classics than early Americans memorized from the Bible and, what is more important, became expert in applying them.

CONFUCIUS

The personality and character of Confucius cannot be disposed of in a phrase or sentence. He was doubtless a person of noble and rare virtues and of some modesty, since he does not appear to have referred to himself as an educated man (ju). He left little if anything in writing, perhaps because he did not regard his thoughts as worth recording. His followers after his death recorded what they regarded as his most memorable sayings in *The Analects (Lun Yu),* but it was not until the time of Mencius and Hsun Tzu that Confucian philosophy began to appear as an ordered and written philosophical discourse, giving strong primacy to ethical values. Actually there was very little in the lifetime of Confucius to suggest that his career was a success, and he may well have regarded himself as a failure. The Chou society in which he lived was in disorder and rapid decline. He had no patience with the ideas of the irresponsible ruling despots of that time, who, in turn, had no ear for the high ethical principles expounded by the most learned man of that day. But in reality Confucius was an almost unqualified success, since he posthumously influenced the character of Chinese civilization to a greater degree than any other single person.

The original authoritative writings on Confucianism consist of the Five Classics and the Four Books. The Five Classics, comprising the most ancient works, include: (1) *The Book of Changes,* already noted, an elaborate guide to divination through philosophical interpretation of sixty-four hexagrams and eight trigrams; (2) *The Book of History,* a fragmentary history covering the period 2400-619 B. C.; (3) *The Book of Poetry,* a collection of some three hundred poems of the Chou period; (4) *The Book of Rites,* dealing with ceremonial procedure; and (5) *The Spring and Autumn Annals,* a history of the state of Lu. While tradition often held that Confucius wrote or edited these classics, it seems clear that they are the work of many authors. It may be that Confucius as a teacher used *The Book of Poetry, The Book of History,* and *The Spring and Autumn Annals.*

In addition, perhaps a thousand years after the close of the Chou period, four texts known as the Four Books were selected from the greater mass of classical literature. These were: (1) *The Analects* or dialogues of Confucius with his disciples; (2) *The Book of Mencius,* containing the sayings of the sages; (3) *The Great Learning,* an outline of Confucian ethics; and (4) *The Doctrine of the Mean,* a similar treatise. To these basic works should also be added the voluminous commentaries, comprising thousands of volumes, produced by the tireless industry of Confucian scholars both ancient and modern.[8]

A Plan for Human Conduct

The classics and the commentaries provided a minutely detailed plan for human conduct which, if followed, would create ideal human relationships and a harmonious society. All life was to be measured by this all-inclusive

[8] Some indispensable references on early Confucianism include *The Chinese Classics,* James Legge, trans. (reprint, 5 vols., 1960)*; H. G. Creel, *Confucius and the Chinese Way* (1960)* [first published as *Confucius, the Man and the Myth* (1949)]; Arthur Waley, *Three Ways of Thought in Ancient China* (reprint, 1956)*; I. A. Richards, *Mencius on the Mind* (1932); and Hsun Tzu, *Basic Writings,* Burton Watson, trans. (1963).*

code, mastery of which would make a wise man master of himself at all times.

Since Confucius was a humanist, his philosophy, broadly considered, was a code of conduct by which man might govern himself in relations with his fellow men. Five relations were considered of first importance: the relation of prince and minister, of parent and child, of husband and wife, of elder and younger brother, and of friend and friend. Five constant virtues were stressed: benevolence, righteousness, propriety, wisdom, and fidelity. The application of these virtues to human relations would, in the Confucian view of things, achieve the true ends of life. Life would be simple, the family happy, and social relations harmonious.

Confucianism expressed the practical, the matter-of-fact, the mundane tendencies in the Chinese character. It was not a supernatural religion. To the Confucian, the idea that men live in order to die, as taught by Christianity, is incomprehensible. When his disciples asked about the gods, Confucius, with becoming modesty, replied that he knew little about them. He seems to have been mildly skeptical of the supernatural, on the theory that if man could not fully understand life, it was unreasonable to suppose he could understand death. Yet Confucianism, with commendable tolerance, encouraged such state religion as there was and tolerated sacrifices to the gods. Confucius attended these sacrifices, but left the common accompaniments of supernatural religion to others; while at times in early China there was a state priestcraft, there was no Confucian priestcraft. The concept of a future life in Confucian thought was vague, but not nonexistent. Matters such as apostolic succession, miracles, sacraments, and the future life were left for other cults to manage. Confucianism directed man in his duty to his family and to society as a whole without promising rewards or punishment in an unknown spiritual world.

What has been said to this point should not be taken to mean that the Chinese lacked a metaphysical tradition. In various ways and at various times some Chinese thinkers were much concerned with such problems.[9]

MO TZU: CHINA'S UNIQUE RELIGIOUS TEACHER

As will be noted further in Chapter 3, a great many schools of thought contending with Confucianism also had their birth in the Golden Age of Chinese philosophy. One, an offshoot of Confucianism, must be mentioned briefly. Mo Tzu, its founder, enunciated some rather remarkable ideas, but within some two hundred years his doctrines no longer sustained an active philosophical movement. Sounding in some degree like a modern, middle-class philosopher, Mo Tzu regarded utility and profit as the supreme virtues. He had no patience with ceremony, ritual, or the cultural refinements of the arts, especially music. He was China's only native religious teacher to expound a doctrine of universal love, to condemn war as the greatest of evils, and to insist on belief in the gods as supernatural beings who rewarded good and punished evil. Clearly there could be no accommodation between the Moist doctrine of loving all men equally and the Confucian insistence on first loyalty to the family. In this doctrinal battle it was the Confucians who won. Yet, as sometimes happens in history, old and forgotten ideas can prove useful to modern men. In the nineteenth century, Western Christian missionaries cited Mo Tzu's doctrine of universal love in an effort to show that ancient China had something akin to Christianity. In the twentieth century this same doctrine was a justification for Chinese revolutionaries in their efforts to break the family system and thus promote social change.

RELIGIOUS ATTITUDES

The statement was made earlier that in a comparative sense the Chinese were not a

[9] Mote, *Intellectual Foundations,* especially Chapters 2 and 6.

religious people. While this statement is quite accurate, it can easily be misleading. To assume that the Chinese lacked moral and ethical motivations of the highest order or that they lacked a sense of reverence would be a grave error. The fact that their religious motivations were different from those entertained by most Western peoples does not of itself lead to the conclusion that these motivations were necessarily absent or inferior.

Chinese religious philosophy begins with a view of the cosmos quite different from that held in the Judeo-Christian tradition. Certainly until the very recent era of modern science, Western man assumed that the universe including man was the work of a distant divine creator external to His creation. In contrast, the Chinese appear to be unique in having no such myth of genesis. Indeed, from their earliest known history the Chinese have considered the world and man not as products of an external creation, but as central elements in a spontaneously self-generating cosmos without cause or creator or will external to itself. This concept lies behind the Chinese view of the world and man as one great unity.

The philosophical view of man and the cosmos entertained by educated Chinese did not mean that lesser men were denied the delights and fears of a world of spirits and gods. Actually there were very well-developed ideas on these matters. The inhabitants of the Chinese spirit world were believed to exist somehow apart from ordinary human existence, yet they also had a material being, though one which belonged to a different state of nature from man's. In popular or vulgarized belief a spirit might assume the appearance of a god, but not of a supreme god.

To be sure, in early times popular cults existed in great variety. They were followed by the common people and occasionally by the aristocracy. Confucian intellectuals and bureaucrats paid little attention to these cults except when they took on a dangerous political tone.

The educated and the uneducated classes tended by and large to go their own separate ways in matters of religion. Neither leaned

toward monotheistic theories. The educated class revered Heaven (*Hao-t'ien*), their ancestors, and sometimes such notable names as **Confucius, Lao Tzu, or Buddha**; the common folk, on the other hand, were free to put their trust in a great variety of heavens and to fear, if they were so inclined, a vast number of hells. They often placed great reliance on charms and magic, through which they hoped to appease the spirits who controlled their fortunes. Again, the educated looked upon Confucianism, Taoism, and even Buddhism primarily as systems of philosophy, but the masses generally regarded them as religions founded by supernatural beings. Neither the educated nor the uneducated accepted any one of these systems exclusively. They usually thought of all three as different roads to a common destination—another instance of the Chinese inclination to be tolerant in matters of religion.

TAOISM: PHILOSOPHY AND RELIGION

Although Confucianism reigned supreme through most of Chinese history as the official, orthodox arena of intellectual life, it never achieved exclusive control over the Chinese mind—a fact which again points to the special character of Chinese civilization. While the Chinese were most at home with the rational and the practical, they were not quite content with these alone. In the early centuries, even as the Confucians were developing well-ordered rules of ethics and conduct for everyday life, other more imaginative minds were concerned with the whimsy of poetry, expressionistic effects in painting, and introspection and intuition in philosophy. They were creating one of the world's greatest presystematic bodies of thought, Taoism.

Taoism was to develop in two contrasting forms. It began as a magnificent mystical philosophy, which has continued to influence the Chinese mind; in time, it also assumed a secondary form as a popular religion garbed in all the trappings of superstition. As a philosophy, Taoism has appealed strongly to China's intellectuals; as a religion, it has played an immense role in the lives of the credulous masses, though it rapidly lost its appeal in the twentieth century.

Lao Tzu: the Reputed Founder

There is a good deal of uncertainty surrounding the identity of Lao Tzu, the reputed founder of Taoism and the supposed author of its Bible, the *Tao Te Ching*. It may be that Lao Tzu was the keeper of the Chou archives whom Confucius visited. It is also possible that the main ideas in the *Tao Te Ching* were brought together at that time. In any case, it is probable that Taoism had no single founder and that the *Tao Te Ching* had a composite authorship.[10]

Whatever the uncertainties about Lao Tzu's identity, the teachings attributed to him have affected China profoundly. His philosophy rejected the idea of a personal god and sought to replace any such notion by the idea of *Tao* (the way, road, or process). The *Tao* is a natural, spontaneous process—something which is so of itself. Accordingly there was no need to construct any supernatural divine plan, since the *Tao*, which does nothing, achieves everything. Taoism was a quietistic philosophy, which, if applied, would affect every phase of society. In politics, for example, the best government would be the least government. Knowledge might well be a questionable blessing because only when beauty is recognized as beauty is ugliness created; only when goodness is known to be good does evil exist.

[10] Over the centuries, Chinese have been amused and delighted by the many myths about Lao Tzu. One of these had him born of a virgin; another relates that he was carried in his mother's womb for many decades so that when he finally emerged he had a long white beard and walked with a cane.

The *Tao Te Ching* is one of the most remarkable documents in the history of philosophy and religion. Arthur Waley's effective translation renders the title as *The Way and Its Power* (reprint, 1958).* The nature and purpose of the *Tao Te Ching* are elusive. The book is a collection of brief passages of verse and prose designed to provoke meditation. For example: "The way that can be followed (or the road that can be charted) is not the true way. The word that can be spoken is not the true word." It is a book no student should miss.

Taoism was therefore opposed to moral idealism and to political realism. It did not regard the so-called great gods of Old China (Heaven, Nature) as humane. The universe was neither kindly nor righteous. It simply went its own way, ignoring human desires or the human standards of conduct in which the Confucians put so much trust. Efforts to reform morals or to right wrongs were a waste of time, since such efforts were an attempt to control the universe. The way to cope with evil was not to stress good but to reach beyond both good and evil to the pure essence of the universe, *Tao*. The principles of effortlessness, and nonaction were revered. The sage, according to Lao Tzu, relied on actionless activity and on wordless teaching.

Posterity has dealt with Lao Tzu much as it has dealt with other great teachers. Although he probably did not consider himself a religious leader, later generations of priests credited him with founding a religion. Since many of the virtues extolled by Taoism—such as patience, humility, calmness, and deliberation—were beyond the appreciation of the masses, though they might appeal to thoughtful men, the priests built a religion of Taoism by compounding a host of beliefs in the miraculous and the supernatural. Out of Lao Tzu's natural way they constructed a fascinating system of magic, myths, spells, charms, incantations, and demonology. It took control of the world of spirits and achieved an important place in the area of ancestor worship. Man's every act was affected by spirits either friendly or hostile. It was the Taoist priest who knew best when to build a house, when to celebrate a wedding, when and where to bury a corpse.[11] Thus, Taoism, diverted from its original purpose, came to provide a road on which the practical, matter-of-fact Chinese

[11] Traditional Chinese geomancy (*feng shui*) held that the prosperity of descendants depended on a properly located grave. While Westerners in China scoffed at such ideas, there were Chinese who sometimes noted that the foreigner took steps to accommodate his own dead in ways suggesting that he, too, was not immune to the influence of *feng shui*. See Andrew L. March, "An Appreciation of Chinese Geomancy," *Journal of Asian Studies,* 27 (1968), 253-67.

mind could find relief—but it was a road of unreality and mysteries, if also of fancy and poetry.

RIVAL OR COMPLEMENT?

Taoism has often been described as the great rival of Confucianism. In their contrasting views of life there is much to suggest that this was so, yet the statement is not entirely satisfactory. To use the language of British politics, it would be closer to the truth to say that Taoism was the loyal opposition: a complement to rather than a rival of Confucianism. When it is remembered that the Chinese mind was not obsessed by the demands of an exclusive and jealous god, and that Confucians often had a keen sense for the arts and literature despite their down-to-earth leanings, the complementary functions of the two philosophies seem quite clear. Confucianism satisfied the practical needs of the Chinese mind; Taoism satisfied its speculative needs.[12]

BUDDHISM

It is often quite difficult for persons of one culture and faith to achieve a full understanding of an alien religion. Those reared in the Christian tradition may have trouble understanding Buddhism. The problem is to see the alien faith as it is seen by those who accept it, and to gain some understanding of how one generation attempts to transmit its religious beliefs to succeeding generations.[13]

Buddhism was introduced into China according to official tradition about the beginning of the Christian era, but it is not known with certainty when the Chinese gained their first knowledge of this faith.[14] Gautama, the traditional founder of Buddhism, is said to have been born in northern India on the border of Nepal about 563 B. C. Of noble birth, he became dissatisfied with the transient character of worldly things, renounced the

world, and began his wanderings in search of truth. His aim was to release himself from the constant burdens that beset human life, and to achieve the spiritual training necessary to that end.

Whether Gautama regarded himself as the founder of a religion or simply as a student and teacher of ethics need not be argued here. The important fact is that from his central theme—the moral life, with its virtues of love, wisdom, and suppression of desire—his followers constructed a religion that has enjoyed widespread influence. Centuries after Gautama's death his followers divided, and it was the northern as distinct from the southern Buddhist movement that spread to Nepal, Tibet, Mongolia, Cochin China, China, Korea, and Japan. This northern school of Buddhism developed the idea of the Western Paradise (Heaven), a concept that apparently was lacking in Gautama's original teaching. Buddhism, then, in contrast with Confucianism, was much concerned with man's afterlife.

Old China must have appeared as an unpromising field for Buddhism. Its emphasis on introspection and the inner life would not seem to harmonize with the practical philosophy of the Confucian mind; and its exhortations to celibacy hardly seemed fitted for a land devoted to ancestor worship. Yet Buddhism was widely accepted in China and became one of the strongest elements in Chinese thought. The explanation for this apparent paradox lies in the fact that, during the years of Buddhism's introduction, many intellectuals were already deeply immersed in the closely related speculations of Lao Tzu, while popular Taoism was practiced widely among the common people. Buddhism, therefore, appealed to both the learned and the illiterate. As a religion it was more comprehensive than Taoism, and as a philosophy it laid great stress on the spiritual element so lacking in the Confucian ethical code.

But the primary reason for the success of Buddhism, like that of Taoism, was that Confucianism had so little to offer the unsophisticated minds of the commoners. The elaborate ritual of Buddhism had a natural appeal for the masses. And in times of chaos when life was in constant danger, Buddhism satisfied the very human need to turn in desperation to

---

[12] A very useful statement on Taoism is to be found in Mote, *Intellectual Foundations,* 67-84.

[13] Kenneth W. Morgan, *Asian Religions* (1964).*

[14] The term "Buddha" is a title meaning "The Enlightened One."

some spiritual or supernatural power. This was a refuge which Confucianism did not offer.[15]

Buddhism, however, brought much more to China than the spiritual satisfactions of a religion. Indian science and art, which accompanied it, introduced new knowledge and aesthetic values. Chinese sculpture and painting achieved more diverse forms. These were permanent contributions to China's culture. In later centuries, when Buddhism as a religion tended to give place to the rising influence of Neo-Confucianism, much of the nobility of Buddhist thought had already become a permanent part of China's intellectual and religious life.

PAINTING AND CALLIGRAPHY

At this point it would be desirable to describe in some detail the large area of Chinese art closely linked with Chinese philosophy. But space does not permit adequate discussion of those marvelous creations in bronze, jade, textiles, lacquer, enamel, and wood produced in Old China from the earliest times. There is, however, a very special interest which surrounds Chinese painting and calligraphy. In some ways these have represented the summit of China's artistic expression. Since Chinese thought tended to center on keeping man in tune with the universe or nature, landscape painting sought generalized conceptions of nature and man's place in it. Thus the painter was not apt to be concerned with particular events or objects, but rather with the ultimate meanings which nature might reveal. In calligraphy, one of the highest forms of Chinese art, the gentleman-scholar sought to perfect his mastery of form, balance, and movement. But, unlike the modern Western abstract expressionist, who at times appears to be in search of form only, the Chinese artist-calligrapher was in search of meaning beyond form.[16]

[15] Buddhism adjusted itself to ancestor worship. Who could tell better than the Buddhist priest what became of the spirits of deceased ancestors?

[16] Chiang Yee, *Chinese Calligraphy* (1954), and Michael Sullivan, "The Heritage of Chinese Art," in *The Legacy of China,* Raymond Dawson, ed. (1964),* 198-99.

CHINESE LITERATURE

Chinese literature, like Chinese art, had much to do with the special flavor of Chinese culture. In both prose and poetry the Chinese created a remarkable literary heritage. Only one characteristic can be noted here: Chinese literature tended to be utilitarian rather than aesthetic.[17] In general Chinese writers were exponents of Confucian doctrine. They sought to influence man to be moral in the Confucian sense. They viewed literature as a pragmatic vehicle, an attitude they shared with some present-day governments.

CLASS STRUCTURE

Chinese society was divided roughly into two major social classes: the gentry, an educated elite, and the common people. The distinctions between these two groups were of great importance.

The Gentry

The gentry was, in a sense, the ruling class of Old China. They tended to live by customs inherited from their fathers. Members of this group derived their income from land which they themselves did not cultivate, from government office, from academic and intellectual pursuits, and, in more recent times, from banking, industry, and commerce. Scholars, intellectuals, and government officials came almost entirely from this class since, in the main, only the sons of gentry could afford an education and thus pass the civil service examinations which provided the principal and proper avenue to government office. Through their control of the land, the gentry controlled the economy, and through their monopoly on learning they shaped the patterns of social, economic, and political life. The gentry had the power, the prestige, and most of the privileges.

[17] A good introduction to the subject is Liu Wu-chi, *An Introduction to Chinese Literature* (1966).* Note also C. T. Hsia, *The Classic Chinese Novel* (1968).*

The People

Among the nongentry the largest and most significant group, forming indeed the great mass of the people, was the peasantry. In an overwhelmingly agricultural society they were the cultivators of the land—some as farmers who owned the land they cultivated, others as tenants, and still others as simple laborers. Even as late as the mid-twentieth century something like 75 to 80 percent of China's population belonged to the peasantry. The remainder of the nongentry elements of the population included handicraftsmen, small merchants, servants, soldiers, priests, actors and, in more recent times, factory workers.

In modern times the picture of traditional China which Westerners first came to know—the China of the great sages, such as Confucius, of the great dynasties, such as the Han, the China of the literary classics and the arts—was in a major degree the China of the gentry. Historical writing has sometimes given the impression that this China was the only important China, an implication open to serious question. This misrepresentation is to some extent understandable, however, since the institutionalized patterns of thought and behavior of the gentry were accepted as ideal patterns by almost all Chinese, even if they were attainable only by the favored few. Dynasties might rise and fall, conquerors might come and go, yet from the third century B. C. until the nineteenth century A. D. these patterns of genteel life persisted. In this sense, the history of China's gentry was the key to the character and development of Chinese culture as a whole.[18]

THE PLACE OF SCIENCE

Finally, it is natural to ask what role science played in a culture that reached from ancient

[18] Interpretations of Chinese history have changed dramatically since the Communist revolution. Mao Tse-tung and his followers, not a Confucian gentry, are now the keepers of the historical record. One result of this change has been a new emphasis on the role of the common man, the peasant, in China's development. The gentry no longer are presented as idealized leaders. See two essays by Albert Feuerwerker: "China's History in Marxian Dress," *American Historical Review,* 66 (1961), 323-53; and, with Harold Kahn, "The Ideology of Scholarship: China's New Historiography," *China Quarterly* (V, 1965), 1-13.

times into the early twentieth century. One of the striking contrasts between the history of science in the West and in China is that scientific inquiry reached its heyday early in China and then fell into a long period of stagnation, whereas in the West science has continued to progress steadily, at least since the Dark Ages. One result of this difference in history is that Westerners, looking only at the China of recent times, have often come to the mistaken conclusion that the Chinese are wholly lacking in scientific aptitudes. In reality Chinese discoveries in empirical science are very extensive. They include findings in astronomy, biology, geology, archaeology, mathematics, and geography, to mention some major areas. The Chinese first discovered how to compute celestial distances. They had classified more than one hundred plant species before A. D. 500. Cast iron was produced in Western Chou 1500 years in advance of the West. The Chinese knew of the magnetic north in Shang times and had a magnetized needle to indicate direction as early as the Chou era. A Chinese map of the third century A. D. was almost as accurate as Ptolemy's. The Chinese probably invented glass (Chou period); they invented gunpowder (in T'ang), made their first bomb (about 1161), and probably the first cannon a century later. They appear to have been the first to produce paper (A. D. 105), porcelain, and printing (A. D. 600). They were using moveable type in the twelfth century.

China is also credited with the first successful immunization technique. A seismograph was in use as early as the second century. The study of anatomy dates back to medieval times. While some of these achievements were technological rather than scientific, there was a considerable body of naturalistic theory even in ancient and medieval times. There was systematic experimentation and a great deal of surprisingly accurate measurement. The theories, however, remained medieval, since the mathematization of hypotheses, developed in Europe during the Renaissance, was never advanced in China. In any case, it should now be clear that there is no foundation for the belief commonly held in the West that there was never any science or technology in China. Indeed, part of this misunderstanding may result from a lack of definition of terms. What may be called *modern* science originated only in Western Europe in the six-

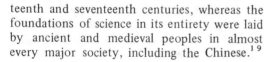

CHINESE AGRICULTURE

As a labor-intensive industry using a simple technology, Chinese agriculture has supported a large and growing population. A low level of productivity, however, has generally bound the vast majority of Chinese to the land, a factor inhibiting efforts in the twentieth century to industrialize the nation.

teenth and seventeenth centuries, whereas the foundations of science in its entirety were laid by ancient and medieval peoples in almost every major society, including the Chinese.[19]

[19] The contrasting forms of development in the Chinese and European scientific traditions point to two questions of interest: 1) Why did modern science and the mathematization of hypotheses about nature come to life only in the West at the time of Galileo? 2) How did it come about that between the second century B.C. and the sixteenth century A.D., East Asia was more effective than Europe in applying what was known of nature to useful purposes? See Joseph Needham, *The Grand Titration* (1970); and his "Science and China's Influence on the World," in *Legacy*, Dawson, ed., 234-308. Note also Sung Ying-hsing, *T'ien-kung k'ai-wu: Chinese Technology in the Seventeenth Century,* translated and annotated by E-tu Zen Sun and Shiou-chuan Sun (1966).

FOR FURTHER READING

Bibliographies. Henri Cordier, *Bibliotheca Sinica* (5 vols., 2nd ed. 1904-24). Yuan Tung-li, *China in Western Literature* (1958), continues Henri Cordier. L. C. Goodrich and H. C. Fenn, *A Syllabus of the History of Chinese Civilization and Culture* (6th rev. ed., 1958). Charles O. Hucker, *China, A Critical Bibliography* (1962); *Chinese History: A Bibliographic Review* (1958), issued by the Serivce Center for Teachers of History, American Historical Association. Charles S. Gardner, comp., *A Union List of Selected Western Books on China in American Libraries* (1938), a carefully selected list of 350 books and 21 periodicals of great importance. Kwang-ching Liu, *Americans and*

Chinese: A Historical Essay and a Bibliography (1963). See also annual bibliographies published by the Association for Asian Studies.

Geography, The Economy, and The People. George B. Cressey, *Land of the 500 Million: A Geography of China* (1955), indispensable. Rhoads Murphey, *Shanghai: Key to Modern China* (1953), an historio-geographic monograph of rare interest and value. Theodore Shabad, *China's Changing Map: A Political and Economic Geography of the Chinese People's Republic* (1956), a competent reference work. On China's population, note Ho Ping-ti, *Studies on the Population of China, 1368-1953* (1959, reprint, 1967), a major study in socio-economic history, and John S. Aird, *The Size, Composition, and Growth of the Population of Mainland China* (1961).

For information on China's economy, note E. Stuart Kirby, *Introduction to the Economic History of China* (1954), and Solomon Adler, *The Chinese Economy* (1957). Chi Ch'ao-t'ing, *Key Economic Areas in Chinese History* (1936), describes water-control measures and the shifts in China's economic center. Shen Tsung-han, *Agricultural Resources of China* (1951), an excellent study. Yang Lien-sheng, *Money and Credit in China, A Short History* (1952).

Gerald F. Winfield, *China: The Land and the People* (rev. ed., 1950), presents the interrelations among deeply rooted mores, economic conditions, and problems of political change. Also see: Mark Elvin, *The Last Thousand Years of Chinese History: Changing Patterns in Land Tenure* (1970); Keith Buchanan, *The Transformation of the Chinese Earth* (1970); and Yi-fu Tuan, *China* (1970), an historically oriented cultured geography. F. H. King, *Farmers of Forty Centuries, or Permanent Agriculture in China, Korea and Japan* (1926; reissued 1948), a standard description of the agrarian foundations of Chinese life. Fei Hsiao-t'ung, *Peasant Life in China* (1939) is based on a detailed study of a Chinese village. Morton H. Fried, *Fabric of Chinese Society: A Study of the Social Life of a Chinese County Seat* (1953). Feng Han-chi, *The Chinese Kinship System* (1948, reprint, 1967).* Olga Lang, *Chinese Family and Society* (1946).

History. Rene Grousset, *The Rise and Splendour of the Chinese Empire,* trans. A. Watson-Gandy and T. Gordon (1953), episodic but successful in conveying the flavor of China's cultural glories. Marcel Granet, *Chinese Civilization,* trans. Kathleen E. Innes and Mabel R. Brailsford (1951), a sociological interpretation of early literary remains. W. T. deBary, ed. *Sources of Chinese Tradition* (1960), the most convenient and comprehensive collection of readings on Chinese civilization from early times. Etienne Balazs, *Chinese Civilization and Bureaucracy: Variations on a Theme* (1964), a splendid sampling of the brilliant studies by the late Hungarian-French authority on Old China. Wolfram Eberhard, *History of China* (1950), translated by E. W. Dickes, a sociological interpretation emphasizing the continuity of gentry domination. Lin Yutang, *Imperial Peking: Seven Centuries of China* (1961), a picture of China's traditional humanism. Hu Chang-tu, et al., *China: Its People, Its Society, Its Culture* (1960), a survey covering all major aspects of Chinese history, culture, and life. John A. Harrison, *The Chinese Empire: A Short History of China from Neolithic Times to the End of the 18th Century* (1972);* and *China Since 1800* (1969),* succinct and readable introductions.

Joseph Needham, *Science and Civilization in China* (Vols. 1-4, 1954-1965). Thomas F. Carter and L. C. Goodrich, *The Invention of Printing in China and its Spread Westward* (rev. ed., 1955), a monumental study in Chinese cultural history.

Chang Kwang-chih, *The Archaeology of Ancient China* (1963), cultural growth of early China and its surrounding regions during a period extending from approximately 1500 B.C. to the founding of the Ch'in Dynasty in 221 B.C. Cheng Te-kun, *Archaeology in China* (1959), one of the best studies. Li Chi, *The Beginnings of Chinese Civilization: Three Lectures Illustrated with Finds at Anyang* (1957), an authoritative brief survey. Among recent studies drawing upon extensive new archaelogical work are: Edward Schafer, *Ancient China* (1967); William Watson, *Early Civilization in China* (1966); and Judith M. Treistman, *The Prehistory of China: An Archaelogical Exploration* (1972).

E-tu Zen Sun and John DeFrancis, eds., trans., *Chinese Social History* (1956), essays covering the period from the Chou to the Ch'ing dynasty. Richard L. Walker, *The Multi-State System of Ancient China* (1953) describes the relations between the various Chou states. Hsu Cho-yun, *Ancient China in Transition: An Analysis of Social Mobility, 722-222 B.C.* (1965). Woodbridge Bingham, *The Founding of the T'ang Dynasty: The Fall of the Sui and the Rise of the T'ang* (1941). Rene Grousset, *Conqueror of the World. The Life of Chingis-Khan,* Marian McKellar and Denis Sinor, trans. (1966). B. Y. Vladimirtsov, *The Life of Chinghis Khan* (1930).

Arthur W. Hummel, ed., *Eminent Chinese of the Ch'ing Period (1644-1912)* (2 vols., 1943-1944), an indispensable study. Ho Ping-ti, *The Ladder of Success in Imperial China* (1962), a statistical study of elite mobility in Ming and Ch'ing times. Franz Michael, *The Origin of Manchu Rule in China* (1942), the basic work on the Manchu conquest.

Philosophy and Religion. Chan Wing-tsit, *An Outline and an Annotated Bibliography of Chinese Philosophy* (1959). H. G. Creel, *Confucius and the Chinese Way* (1960), first published in 1949 as *Confucius the Man and the Myth,.* Fung Yu-lan, *A Short History of Chinese Philosophy,* trans. and ed. by Derk Bodde (1948) provides the best coverage of the shorter works. Fung Yu-lan, *History of Chinese Philosophy,* trans. and ed. by Derk Bodde, (2 vols., 1952-53), a comprehensive and detailed work including political theory. Lewis Hodous, *Folkways in China* (1929), a good introduction to popular religion. E. R. Hughes and K. Hughes, *Religion in China* (1950) surveys early religious practices. Arthur Waley, *Three Ways of Thought in Ancient China* (1956),* a study of the early philosophies. Arthur Waley, *The Analects of Confucius* (1938), an able translation of the sayings of Confucius. Arthur Waley, trans., *The Way and Its Power: A Study of the Tao Te Ching and Its Place in Chinese Thought* (1958), an introduction to early Taoism. C. K. Yang, *Religion in Chinese Society* (1962). Holmes Welch, *The Parting of the Way: Lao Tzu and the Taoist Movement* (1957). Arthur F. Wright, ed., *Studies in Chinese Thought*

(1953).* David S. Nivison and Arthur Wright, eds., *Confucianism in Action* (1959), essays on Confucianism in China and Japan. Arthur F. Wright, ed., *The Confucian Persuasion* (1960). Carsun Chang, *The Development of Neo-Confucian Thought* (2 vols., 1957, 1962).* Charles Eliot, *Hinduism and Buddhism, An Historical Sketch* (3 vols., 1954) traces the origins of Buddhism in India and its spread to China. Kenneth Ch'en, *Buddhism in China: A Historical Survey* (1964). Richard H. Robinson, *The Buddhist Religion: A Historical Introduction* (1970), one of the best introductions for nonspecialists. E. Zürcher, *The Buddhist Conquest of China* (1972), the formative phase of Chinese Buddhism. Peter A. Pardue, *Buddhism* (1971). Burton Watson, trans. *Hsun Tzu: Basic Writings* (1963). W.A.C.H. Dobson, trans. *Mencius, A New Translation* (1963).

Literature. Ch'en Shou-yi, *Chinese Literature: A Historical Introduction* (1961), a comprehensive survey of Chinese literature. James Legge, *The Chinese Classics* (5 vols., 1960), a reprint with minor corrections and an added concordance. C. T. Hsia, *The Classic Chinese Novel: A Critical Introduction* (1968), an eloquent and critical appreciation. Lin Yutang, trans., *Famous Chinese Short Stories* (1952).* Cyril Birch, ed., *Anthology of Chinese Literature: From Early Times to the Fourteenth Century* (1965).* Robert Payne, *The White Pony* (1967),* an introduction to Chinese poetry. Arthur Waley, *Translations from the Chinese* (1941), an introduction to Chinese poetry. Arthur Waley, *The Book of Songs* (1937),* a fine translation of the classical anthology of poetry (*Shih Ching*). Arthur Waley, *The Poetry and Career of Li Po, 701-762* (1950) gives a valuable approach to the T'ang and Sung dynasties. James. J. Y. Liu, *The Art of Chinese Poetry* (1962).* Burton Watson, *Early Chinese Literature* (1962) provides an account of Chinese writing from the time of the Chou dynasty to the middle of the Later Han dynasty. Some masterpieces of Chinese literature include: Wang Chi-chen, trans., *Dream of the Red Chamber* (rev. ed., 1958);* Clement Edgerton, trans., *The Golden*

Lotus (4 vols., 1939); Wu Cheng-en, *Monkey,* trans. from the Chinese by Arthur Waley (1958);* Chow Chung-cheng, *The Lotus Pool,* trans. by Joyce Emerson (1961). Richard Gregg Irwin, *The Evolution of a Chinese Novel: Shui-hu-chuan* (1953, reprint 1966).* John Lyman Bishop, ed., *Studies in Chinese Literature* (1965).* Henry W. Wells, *Traditional Chinese Humor: A Study in Art and Literature* (1971). Liu Wu-chi, *An Introduction to Chinese Literature* (1973).* A.R. Davis, *Tu Fu* (1971). David Marshall Lang, ed., *Guide to Eastern Literatures* (1971). Ivan Morris, ed., *Madly Singing in the Mountains: An Appreciation and Anthology of Arthur Waley* (1970).*

Art. Laurence Sickman and Alexander Soper, *The Art and Architecture of China* (1956). Dagny Carter, *Four Thousand Years of Chinese Art* (1948), one of the best of the shorter surveys. William Willets, *Chinese Art* (2 vols., 1958).* Sherman E. Lee, *A History of Far Eastern Art* (1965). Ernest F. Fenollosa, *Epochs of Chinese and Japanese Art: An Outline History of East Asiatic Design* (2 vols., 1963),* reprint of a classic study. Oswald Siren, *The Imperial Palaces of Peking* (3 vols., 1926). John D. La Plante, *Asian Art* (1968).

Ideas on Government in Old China

3

Throughout their long history the Chinese have given a great deal of thought to the subject of government. They have had much to say about what government should be, what it should do, what ideas and ideals should guide it, and so forth. The Chinese were not always in agreement on these matters; nevertheless they developed a pattern of political principles and conduct which may be described in broad general terms. It is important that this be done at the outset, since it is difficult to understand the impacts of the West upon China in the nineteenth and twentieth centuries without some basic knowledge of what kind of political society the West met in China.

The principal body of political thought that guided both the rulers and the ruled in China for some two thousand years prior to the beginning of the twentieth century was Confucianism. Two thousand years is a long time for any system to survive. What gave the Confucian political habit and tradition this power of survival? How shall its collapse in the twentieth century be explained?

As a point of departure, it is well to note that from the earliest times Chinese philosophy was concerned with politics and ethics. Confucius, the most famous of all Chinese political scientists, was a statesman as well as a teacher. In addition, politics in Old China was regarded as the most desirable profession for a young man of "good" family. Moreover, the ruling class—that is, the politicians—was the educated class. Education meant mastery of the Confucian classics and the voluminous commentaries on them made by later scholars. Political problems were discussed, debated, and solved in terms of these classics and commentaries. An apt quotation from the classics could clinch a political argument. Scholarship was also the key to passing the civil service examinations, which were the principal avenue to government office; and government office meant honor and perhaps wealth.

EARLY SCHOOLS OF POLITICAL THOUGHT

Although Confucianism as a body of political thought has had far greater influence in China than any other political philosophy or system, it has not been without rivals. Its beginnings, far back in the pre-Christian era, also saw the rise of other schools of thought.[1] The relationship among these early schools is not clear, save that no one of them was able to dominate the others. There were, for example, the *Yin-Yang* (Negative-Positive) School and the School of Names (the Logicians), of which little evidence remains concerning their theories of political action. Other schools have been more generous in apprising posterity of their political views. The Taoists (*Tao* School), followers of Lao Tzu, have left one of the great living monuments of Chinese thought. Lao Tzu denied the necessity or the wisdom of building society on elaborate laws and institutions. He would neither approve of nor be happy in either the democratic or totalitarian societies of the twentieth century. He would doubtless attribute the world's troubles to its departure from his *Tao* (way), which, in the philosophical sense, is the effortless union of man and nature.

Chuang Tzu, a follower of Lao Tzu, went even further on the path of negativism and simplicity. The best government was the least government. Men should avoid making distinctions between good and bad, high and low, the beautiful and the ugly, since such distinctions lead to moralizing and thereby put an end to simplicity.[2]

A contrasting body of thought was adumbrated by the School of Law or the Legalists, represented by men of action such as Li Li (fifth century B.C.), Shang Yang (fourth century B.C.), and especially Han Fei (third century B.C.). These men were codemakers, insistent upon a uniform body of laws and upon the theory of reward and punishment as the controllers of human action.[3]

[1] See Ch'ien Tuan-sheng, *The Government and Politics of China* (1950), H. G. Creel, *Confucius and the Chinese Way* (1960).*

[2] See Homer H. Dubs, "Taoism," in *China*, H. F. McNair, ed. (1946), 266-89. For translations from the work of Chuang Tzu see H. A. Giles, *Chuang Tzu, Mystic, Moralist, and Social Reformer* (2nd ed., 1926), and *Chuang Tzu*, Fung Yu-lan, trans. (1932).

[3] See *The Book of Lord Shang: A Classic of the Chinese School of Law*, J. J. L. Duyvendak, trans. (1928), a translation of Shang Yang's work.

Again, there was in early China the Mo School, followers of Mo Tzu (fifth century B.C.), who sought the interest of the people, opposed war as injurious to all, and wished the sovereign, aided by the ablest men, to reflect the will of the people and in turn to be obeyed by them. Mo Tzu advanced a doctrine of mutual love, mutual benefit, and something approaching the democractic spirit, though without the democratic theory or the political machinery of the democratic state.[4]

THE PHILOSOPHERS, OR CONFUCIANS

Existing alongside these various schools that prescribed what government ought or ought not to be was the *Ju* School (the Confucians). Fortunately for them, their philosophical works fared better in the burning of books by Ch'in Shih Huang Ti (259-210 B.C.) than did those of other schools. Confucianism was not formed in a political vacuum but rather in close relationship with other competing ideas. It is not wholly surprising, then, to discover that Confucian teachings are exceedingly rich in material drawn from practically all other schools of early times. Confucius himself was a person who traveled widely and had almost unlimited contacts with men in all conditions. In consequence, what emerged on his death was not one but some eight schools of Confucianism, among which could be found doctrines almost as unlike as those of the Taoists on the one hand and the Legalists on the other. Yet through all the divergent Confucian schools there ran the common factor of humanism—"Man lives with and for other men."

All the principles and values of Confucianism may be attributed to this theory of the position of man among men. Confucian ideas are concerned with what the Confucians called Rites, Virtue, Names, and the Five Relationships. Rites were the standards of sane, social living. To live by them was to practice *jen*, the

[4] See *The Ethical and Political Works of Motse* Mei Yi-pao, trans. (1929); and Mei Yi-pao, *Motse, the Neglected Rival of Confucius* (1934).

greatest Virtue. Moreover, life was a matter of status (political, social, economic, or intellectual), which was indicated by a Name, since things must be distinguished by a recognizable term if there is not to be confusion. Only when persons are designated properly may responsibility be located and honors and punishments bestowed with confidence. Nevertheless, important as status was, it is to be noted that there was very little permanent stratification of social groups in Chinese society. A man could rise from humble birth to the Confucian "aristocracy of virtue" and find an illustrious place among scholars. On the other hand, he might lose virtue and fall.

Just as the foregoing humanistic concepts provided rules of conduct for private individuals, they also served as a guide for statesmen, on the assumption that "orderly political life must come from orderly private lives." The Confucian philosophy stressed the reciprocal nature of duties and obligations between the ruler and the ruled, and the primary duty of the ruler to give good government to the people. To do this, the ruler himself had to set a high moral standard and select with care the officials who served under him. The Confucian scholar was important because only he, by his knowledge of the rules of right conduct, could properly advise the "Son of Heaven"—as the ruler was called—in his traditional duty of maintaining universal harmony between man and nature. In *The Analects,* Confucius said, "When a prince's personal conduct is correct, his government is effective without the issuing of orders. If his personal conduct is not correct, he may issue orders but they will not be followed." Right conduct gave the ruler his power.

On this basis Confucian scholars established themselves as an essential part of the government. Since the Rites tended to reflect "what was" rather than "what ought to be" (Confucius himself being a realist), the whole body of Confucian political thought leaned toward conservatism stressing legitimacy, avoiding anything revolutionary, and finding in monarchy a convenient instrument to promote a stable society.

The business of making over, so to speak, the early and fluid Confucian philosphy into an effective, applicable body of political dogma was largely the work of Former Han times (202 B.C. to A.D.8), when the first great Chinese empire was consolidated. It was also at this time that a civil service examination system began to take shape, whereby political office was virtually closed to all but Confucian scholars or at least to those who professed to be Confucians.[5]

During the first ten centuries of the Christian era, Confucianism, somewhat discredited by the fall of the eminently Confucian Han dynasty, encountered political rivals in Buddhism and Taoism. Nevertheless, by Sung times the challenge was met in the rise of Neo-Confucianism (the *Li* School of Sung and Ming times). Finally, under the Manchu dynasty, the leading Confucian school was known as the Classicists. These later schools endowed Confucianism with a spirit of inertia and traditionalism in political thought, and thus the doctrine of absolute monarchy tempered by mildness persisted—the stereotyped ideal of the literate men who ruled China.[6]

CONFUCIAN POLITICAL PRECEPTS

Since the government of Old China was affected more by Confucianism than by any other philosophy, it is worthwhile to inquire into the nature of its more important political precepts. In the course of time, these precepts came to be so deeply rooted as to be taken for granted by the ruling bureaucracy. Among the first precepts was that of unity, both social and political. To students familiar with the chaotic and amorphous China of the early twentieth century, it may be surprising that Confucius taught: "As Heaven has not two suns, so the people should not have two kings." This was a doctrine frequently invoked when the state was threatened with political division.

[5] See Ssu-yu Teng, "China's Examination System and the West," in *China,* MacNair, ed., 441-51. See also H. G. Creel, "The Beginning of Bureaucracy in China: The Origin of the Hsien," *Journal of Asian Studies,* 23 (1964), 155-83.

[6] See Ch'ien, *Government and Politics,* 27-28.

Closely allied with this concept of political unity was the doctrine of Heaven's Mandate, which appears to have been taught by Confucius, but more particularly by his disciple Mencius. This doctrine held that the supreme earthly ruler, the emperor, was elevated to his position through the favor of Heaven. The emperor was therefore the Son of Heaven, and maintained his rule by Heaven's Mandate. When an incapable or wicked ruler ascended the throne, Heaven withdrew the mandate and bestowed it on some righteous noble. It then became the duty of this noble to rebel, to overthrow the emperor, and to ascend the throne himself. In expounding this doctrine, Confucius and Mencius were really idealizing the method by which dynasties in China had been overthrown.

A number of important implications followed very naturally from this convenient doctrine of the Mandate of Heaven. It could be a justification for rebellion—a very significant point to the practical Chinese mind. It could also be used to justify conquest, once it had been achieved successfully. It could sanction submission on the part of a conquered people to the conqueror, since the latter undoubtedly also believed in the Mandate of Heaven. A conqueror, however, might sometimes be resisted, for Mencius taught that Heaven sees as the people see and hears as the people hear; the people, therefore, might well resist a conqueror who did not improve their lot. These political principles have been applied on two notable occasions in recent centuries. The Chinese accepted the rule of the Mongols (1260-1368) and of the Manchus (1644-1912) as long as these foreigners conferred substantial benefits, but overthrew them once they had lost the Mandate of Heaven.

The principle of political loyalty was also affected by the doctrine of Heaven's Mandate. Although loyalty in the Confucian code was honored frequently to an extreme degree, it was not an absolute virtue. When the ruler had lost the Mandate of Heaven, it was the duty of the. subject to be disloyal. The Western concept of the divine right of kings, demanding absolute loyalty to the throne, did not exist in the Confucian scheme of things. On the contrary, Confucianism called upon the people to pass judgment on their sovereign. As Mencius said:

"The people are the water and the prince is the boat; the water can support the boat, but it can also sink it."

The doctrine of Heaven's Mandate justified only a very limited use of force by a conqueror, for conquest ultimately was not achieved by fighting but by securing the favor of Heaven. Hence, force was proper only to subdue recalcitrants against the Will of Heaven. As a result, the Chinese, generally speaking, have been pacifists. Mencius taught that there were no righteous wars, although defensive wars were better than offensive wars. Lao Tzu and Mo Tzu likewise condemned offensive war. Virtue was more likely to impress Heaven than brute force. Consequently, Confucianism justified military expeditions only when they could be interpreted as designed to restore order and to preserve peace in a neighboring state. The record of Chinese history may appear to contradict all this theorizing about peace, for actually the Chinese have warred as generously as other peoples; but their wars of conquest were conducted mostly by rulers who were not Confucians.[7] The Confucian theory alone does not entirely explain why the Chinese have in general avoided wars of conquest. Economic considerations have also played an important part. But it does appear that, had there been no Confucian pacifism, China would have warred upon its neighbors to a much greater extent than it has. In general, Old China preferred to let her neighbors alone, provided the neighbors did not meddle in Chinese affairs.

CONFUCIAN POLITICAL INSTITUTIONS

The Monarchy

The political institution of supreme importance in Old China was the monarchy, which operated on the theory of the emperor's unlimited power. In the case of most sovereigns the actual exercise of power could be and often

[7] The whole question of Chinese pacifism, however, is a touchy one and cannot be disposed of easily. Most of China's dynasties came to power by brute force, as, for a recent example, did the Communists in 1949. This conquest was a simple matter of power, but the determination of the factors which create power is a very complex problem.

was limited in various ways. In practice, imperial power was exercised usually not by the emperor himself but by various ambitious groups: kinsmen, eunuchs, generals, or powerful families, as the case might be. Furthermore, the idea eventually developed that good government is government by men, since under unlimited power there could be no rule of law. Absolutism was made more palatable by the process of making it humane.

Under the Manchu dynasty (1644-1912) the emperor was held accountable for famine, flood, and pestilence, because such things were believed to be a consequence of his misrule. As the father of the nation, he was clothed in theory with autocratic, absolute powers; yet these powers were not to be exercised in any arbitrary manner, but in conformity with customary practices established through the ages. The succession passed in the male line to whichever son an emperor might choose; the offspring of concubines were not excluded. When there was no direct heir, the succession passed to a lateral branch of the family of a younger generation. The new emperor was thus adopted as the son of his predecessor and performed the ancestral rites to the spirits of the departed sovereigns.

The authority of the Manchu emperor was not confined within definitive politico-geographic boundaries as was the case with European sovereigns, because the philosophical base of the Confucian monarchy was cultural rather than territorial or national. The territory over which he exercised direct rule included eighteen provinces, known as China Proper, and four great dependencies: Mongolia, Manchuria (which enjoyed a privileged status because it was the homeland of the dynasty), Tibet (after 1700), and Sinkiang (after 1872). Beyond these dependencies lay the tributary states, varying in number from time to time, which recognized the overlordship of the Middle Kingdom according to Confucian political ideas. Payment of tribute was one tangible evidence of their inferior status, although the tribute was usually repaid by imperial gifts. In the course of Chinese history, bearers of tribute have come from such distant lands as Arabia, Malabar, Ceylon, and eastern India, as well as from the adjacent kingdoms of Annam, Ryukyu, Sulu,

and Korea. The theory and practice in these "foreign" relations will be treated in more detail in Chapter 14.

As legislator and administrator, the nominally autocratic Manchu emperor was bound by powerful controls: custom, the unwritten constitution of the Empire; and precedent, as defined in the edicts of his predecessors. He was influenced and not infrequently controlled by the opinions of his ministers and by his personal attendants within the palace. Under the guidance of the latter, he selected his empress from a group of daughters of Manchu nobles. Secondary consorts might be chosen from the same group. Finally, he might favor himself with an unlimited number of concubines from the families of Manchu nobles and freemen.[8]

The nobility consisted of the imperial clansmen who traced their descent directly to the founder of the dynasty; the hereditary nobility who were direct descendants of the eight princes who cooperated in the conquest of China; and finally, a number of Chinese families such as the household of the Duke of Yen, a descendant of Confucius.

Usually the function of the central administration at Peking was negative rather than positive: to check rather than to direct the actions of the provincial officials. In the middle of the nineteenth century, however, increasing contacts with Western states forced the central government, though reluctantly, to assume a more positive responsibility.

Ministers and Departments

In general, the imperial political structure at Peking consisted of six ministries or boards, namely: civil office (appointment of officials), revenue, ceremonies, war, punishments, and public works (canals, flood control). In addition to these six boards there were two other independent branches of government, the military establishment and the censorate. There were also a number of minor offices such as the

---

[8] For the methods and content of education by which in modern times a Manchu prince was prepared for the duties of an emperor see Harold L. Kahn, "The Education of a Prince: the Emperor Learns his Roles," in *Approaches to Modern Chinese History*, Albert Feuerwerker *et al.*, eds. (1967), 15-44.

imperial academy of literature, a court of review in criminal cases, and the office of history. Finally, in Ming times a grand secretariat of high officials assisted the emperor in administration, while the later Manchus created a grand council to advise on military and other important matters.

The ministers of state, the official servants of the emperor, varied in title, number, and power. Their theoretical function was to preserve the sovereign's power. Actually, they usurped for themselves whatever powers they could. Since the ministers were invariably Confucian scholars who had passed the civil service examinations, the net product of this system was the binding of public life to Confucianism. In normal times Confucianism alone opened the door to political power.

The Censors

Among the more interesting political institutions of Old China was the Court of Censors. Originally there were two classifications of censors: (1) those whose function was to impeach erring officials, and (2) those who might protest against acts of the court and propose remedies. In general, the censors provided a healthy and useful instrument of government. By Ming times (1368-1644), however, with the full development of monarchical rule, the censors tended to lose their function of remonstrating with the court. How could a monarch who had become infallible submit to criticism and still maintain his prestige?[9]

[9] See Charles O. Hucker, "Confucianism and the Chinese Censorial System," in *Confucianism in Action*, D. S. Nivison and A. F. Wright, eds. (1959),* 182-208; also Hucker, "The Traditional Chinese Censorate and the New Peking Regime," *American Political Science Review*, 14 (1951), 1041-57; and Richard L. Walker, "The Control System of the Chinese Government," *Far Eastern Quarterly*, 7 (1947), 2-21. The Court of Censors was a time-honored and useful agency of government even if, at times, it was subject to great abuse. Its beginnings probably date back to the second century B.C.; it had become a major bureaucratic organ by Sung times, about 1100 A.D.; and it reached maturity and began its decline during the Ming dynasty. As with most governmental institutions, the effectiveness of the Censorate depended on the integrity and responsibility of the emperor and his high officials and on the character and backbone of the censors. Weak censors could be afraid of the court eunuchs, while a weak emperor could admonish his censors: "Don't harass me." See Hucker, *The Censorial System of Ming China* (1966).

The Law

In Old China, ideas on the nature and function of law were quite different from those that have developed in the West. Chinese legal theory found its origins in the Chinese view of an order of nature. It was necessary for man by his actions to keep in harmony with this order, and the ultimate function of the emperor was to see to it that this was done. In theory, the emperor accomplished his mission by the moral example of his own virtuous conduct. Thus laws and regulations were thought to be unnecessary save in the case of uncivilized persons. Even here laws were regarded as only a secondary recourse in stimulating right conduct. From early times, however, the Chinese made certain compromises with this Confucian concept of law. In the third century B.C. the Legalists employed law as a bulwark of absolutism, while the eminently Confucian Han dynasty also resorted to legalisms in advancing its authority. Moreover, major codes were subsequently to appear in T'ang, Sung, Yuan, Ming, and Ch'ing times.

Chinese (Confucian) law was derived from the moral character of the natural universe. It enjoyed no divine attributes. Confucius did not claim that his insights came from divine revelation. Laws, therefore, were not inflexible rules but were to be considered as suggestive examples of proper procedures. As a consequence morality stood above law. The sanction of law was to be found in reason and experience, which may suggest why a Chinese was apt to be a Confucian when in office and a Taoist when out. Since harmony rather than abstract justice was the ideal, law was concerned with mutual respect, the principle of live and let live. In practice this meant that law was involved with the art of diplomacy and compromise, which would take into account changing conditions. The traditional skill of the Chinese in compromise and conciliation reflects their preference for accommodation over merely legalistic solutions.

Moreover, Chinese law was made by the ruler, not by a legislature or by the decisions of the courts. Little was done to establish a body of legal doctrine. Most of the law was either penal or administrative. Since business, large or small, was an affair of the family and was controlled by kinship and personal relations, private law was considered unnecessary. There was no occasion to regard a big commercial firm as a legal individual. The rights of a contract were of less consequence than the preservation of the moral order. Thus the function of law in Old China, was not to protect the political freedom or the private property of the individual. Yet it should be remembered that the Chinese were constantly concerned with achieving justice. The significant point is that they defined justice according to a set of values quite different from that which formed the legal tradition in the West.

It follows that the study of Chinese law, especially as contrasted with Western law, presents problems which no student of East Asia can afford to neglect. It is notable, for instance, that while the great dynasties from T'ang to Ch'ing times compiled their legal codes, and while popular Chinese literature delighted in stories of court trials, the Chinese did not develop a science of jurisprudence or a legal profession as it is understood in the West. In seeking answers to the legal aspects of the Chinese mind, the student will find it helpful to pursue the following questions: What were the components of the traditional Chinese legal system? Who controlled and operated the system and to what purpose? Was it a single system or a plurality and, if the latter, how were the parts related? Was Chinese society, in theory or in practice, ruled by law?

For the introductory purposes of this survey, it is sufficient to note that from a Western point of view, the weakness of the Chinese system was that the application of the law rested with the administrative bureaucracy of the empire. Thus the courts provided no check and were not intended to be a check on executive power. To a democratic society, dominated by the supremacy of law, the Chinese system was repugnant, but it was not so regarded in China. There was no popular concept of the law and the courts as the protectors of the individual. Indeed, the Chinese had a saying to the effect: "Avoid litigation; going to law is going to trouble."[10]

[10] A useful introduction is Sybille van der Sprenkel, *Legal Institutions in Manchu China* (1962).* See also Derk Bodde and Clarence Morris, *Law in Imperial China* (1967), which presents the judicial process as it actually operated and not as it was supposed to operate.

The Provinces

Under the impressive but rather passive administration at Peking, the provinces of China Proper enjoyed a large measure of autonomy. Each province was divided for purposes of administration into *tao* or circuits, prefectures, and *hsien*, which might be described as districts or counties. Over these various divisions presided a bureaucracy of officials whose status was determined by rank. In all there were nine ranks, each divided into upper and lower grades.

As long as the actions of these provincial officials did not run counter to Peking's general instructions, and as long as the appropriate revenues were forwarded promptly to the capital, a province was free to administer local affairs largely as it saw fit. This did not mean, however, that Peking had no control in the province. All provincial officials from the highest to the lowest were appointed, promoted, transferred, and dismissed by the central government. Appointment was made usually for a three-year term, and high officials were not assigned to office in the province of their birth. It followed that the personnel were constantly changing and that every official ruled among strangers. Moreover, the officials sent to a given capital were likely to be chosen from various factions or cliques in order that each might act as a check on his fellows.

The principal official of the provincial administration was the governor. With him might be associated a Tartar general in command of the local Manchu garrison. There were also a treasurer, who transmitted the revenues to Peking; a judge, who passed on appeals from prefectural and district courts, a salt commissioner, who controlled both the manufacture and sale of this article; a grain commissioner (in some provinces); and a literary chancellor, who supervised the civil service examinations.

Local Government

As mentioned above, the province was divided for purposes of administration into a number of units, the most important being the county or district (*hsien*). The county was composed of a walled city and the adjacent country with its towns and villages. In the case of larger cities, only half or a third of the city was included. The magistrate, supposedly a master of all the arts and problems of government, was the chief official. His functions were as many and varied as the problems of mankind. He collected all local revenues, with the exception of special taxes such as the salt tax and *likin,* an internal transit levy. He was judge in first instance in cases both civil and criminal. He was registrar of land, commissioner of famine and pestilence, and custodian of official buildings. In general it was his business to preserve law and order and to have a care for both the physical and the moral welfare of the people. Thus the functions of the magistrate called for rare ability. It may be added that as local administrators the magistrates were free in general to pursue whatever course seemed best as long as they could raise the necessary finances without arousing public protest and without offending higher officials or the court.

Some public functions which the government was unable or unqualified to perform, could be and sometimes were carried out by the gentry, who were an indispensable part of local government. From this circumstance, however, it should not be concluded that Old China enjoyed local self-government. The gentry were not elected or formally appointed to these duties, nor did they constitute self-governing councils free from the interference of higher authorities. Put another way, the gentry were a local elite sharing with the government the control of local affairs. Theirs was an informal power contrasting with the official government's formal power. Indeed, they were the only group empowered to represent the local community in discussions with officials or to take part in the governing process. Thus the gentry class to some extent overlapped the official class, but did not coincide with it; a member of the gentry in private life might also have an official, public capacity, but certainly not all officials were drawn from the local gentry.

The term "gentry" (there is no better designation) with its English connotations can be misleading when applied to the Chinese scene. Unlike the English gentry, whose status was hereditary, the composition of the Chinese gentry changed from time to time. Membership in the gentry depended on holding a degree or on receiving an official appointment and not on

owning landed property, the principal source of wealth. Many persons who owned land were not members of the gentry. On the other hand, the possession of wealth could ease one's course into gentry status. Wealth meant leisure, the opportunity to get an education and to take the civil service examinations, and thus to get a degree. Of course, when the government was hard-pressed for money one could sometimes buy a degree.

There were two principal ways in which the influence of the gentry played a part in local government. The first was the gentry's relationship with the commoners. The commoners looked to the gentry, as the social elite of the community, for protection against injustice and for relief in times of distress. The gentry, for example, might be expected to settle disputes among commoners. Second, the gentry could make decisions. In a sense, therefore, the gentry were the eyes and the ears of local government and of public opinion.[11]

Within a county, the towns and villages were governed by their own officials, who were nominated by the village elders and confirmed in office by the magistrate. Within the village lay the real government of China, where the spirit and the unity of the family expressed itself in a larger loyalty to the land that had supported them. The government of the village was communal and largely informal for there were no mayor and councilors; it was a moral government of the elders based on "custom and usage, the unwritten law." This was the only government that most Chinese knew. As for Peking, the villagers considered that "heaven was high and the emperor far away."[12]

[11] For extended treatment of local government and the role of the gentry see T'ung-tsu Ch'u, *Local Government in China under the Ch'ing* (1962),* and Chang Chung-li, *The Chinese Gentry* (1966).*

[12] Ch'u, *Local Government* contains an excellent account of how officials, who were "gentlemen" humanists without training in practical day-to-day problems of administration, could function in charge of the courts, of security, of welfare, and, indeed, of things in general. In the early years of the Manchu dynasty the imperial rulers, by cultivating good relations with local elites, sought to protect various groups and sections of the rural population from undue encroachment. The result was that most of the inhabitants of rural areas tended to accept alien Manchu rule as the best way to preserve local interests. In the long run, however, the Manchu system of local and rural control failed, partly because the system itself was imperfect, and also because the cumulative effects of

Economic Theory and Taxation

Economic administration in Old China considered in its narrowest sense was concerned with the problem of extracting enough revenue to maintain the Court and the necessary public services. As in all agricultural societies, most revenue was derived directly from the land, which, though belonging in theory to the emperor, was in reality owned by individuals. At times the entire system of taxation rested on the land tax. Land and taxation, therefore, were major administrative problems. Sometimes, as in the cases of salt and iron, the principle of government monopoly was applied. In general, some degree of economic regulation was regarded as a proper state function, and in times of great natural calamities this principle might be applied rather widely in public works and even in more direct measures of relief.

Education and Government

Although schools did exist in Old China, some of which were subsidized, formal public education was not regarded as the function or duty of government. The wealthy employed private tutors for their children and in some cases established a free school as an act of benevolence, but the average Chinese boy (girls rarely were educated) enjoyed no formal schooling. At the close of the nineteenth century, only a very small percentage of the people was literate in the usual sense of the word. But the word "literate" is apt to be misleading when applied to a people so compact socially and so deeply rooted in their culture as were the Chinese. A Chinese, for instance, might not be able to read, and yet he could possess extraordinary traditional skills which

would make him almost a cultured man.

The small literate group, however, provided the scholars, and scholarship in turn was of high importance, since only through learning could men rise to official position and honor. The basis of education was the Confucian classics and their commentaries, knowledge of which required much more extensive scholarship than, for example, a thorough knowledge of English literature. In addition, one also had to gain command of the voluminous Chinese histories. There was much emphasis on memory. The goal of the scholar was to be able to apply a classical phrase to the solution of a philosophical problem, and in the appropriate style. Science, mathematics, and the development of independent and critical thought were regarded as of lesser consequence in fitting a man for the responsibilities of government.

Civil Service Examinations

Scholarship achieved its rewards when the candidate had passed one or all of the civil service examinations prescribed and conducted by the government. This was the only proper avenue to public office and official distinction. There were four series of examinations, the first being held in the counties and prefectural cities twice every three years. In the counties only some 2 percent of the candidates were permitted to pass. These were admitted a few weeks later to the prefectural examinations, where somewhat more than 50 percent were likely to be successful. These men were now eligible for minor posts and could qualify to enter the provincial examinations held every three years in the provincial capitals. In great examination halls as many as 14,000 candidates ate the food they brought along, wrote their essays, and slept in their "cells" for three separate sessions of three days each. During these sessions the candidates were permitted no recesses. Once a session had commenced and the walls between the rows of cells had been bricked up, the gates of the hall were locked and none, not even the chief examiner, might enter or leave. Successful candidates in the provincial tests were eligible for the examinations in Peking. In these about 6 percent

---

physical want, economic and social inequities, and decaying administration drove the peasants to desperation. In a broader sense, developments of this kind are a reminder of a persistent conflict throughout Chinese history between bureaucracy and emperor. For an exhaustive treatment of this vital subject see Kung-chuan Hsiao, *Rural China: Imperial Control in the Nineteenth Century* (1960),* especially 501-18. Note also Lawrence D. Kessler, "Ethnic Composition of Provincial Leadership during the Ch'ing Dynasty," *Journal of Asian Studies,* 28 (1969), 489-511.

passed and they, in turn, might enter the palace examinations held in the presence of the emperor.

The significance of the Chinese examination system can hardly be overestimated. It was the great carrier of tradition. It helped, under the Ming and Manchu dynasties, to freeze the old and rich Chinese culture into a fixed pattern. It encouraged exclusive reliance upon the wisdom of the past; it discouraged freedom and independence of thought and thus prepared the way for a cultural decline that was hastened by the impact of an expanding Europe on China. It was the principal agent by which Confucianism monopolized scholarship, and by which scholarship, in turn, monopolized politics. But it went even further. The examinations became a principal road to wealth as well as to official position. This wealth was usually invested in land, and the landed gentry, the silk-gowned, frequently controlled public opinion. Thus the official did well to defer to this class, for he was a member of it either in his person or in his interests, or in both.[13]

In summary, it may be said that Confucianism as a political vehicle was concerned primarily with securing and maintaining the power of the ruling dynasty, thus ensuring the stability of the state. For a very long time it succeeded in doing this. It should also be remembered that this system's emphasis on high moral principles served to dress the despotic sovereign in a garb of respectability, thus preserving the myth that China was ruled by virtue.[14]

[13] Too frequently there was a wide gulf between theory and practice in the administration of the examination system. In addition to entering the civil service through examinations, many officials were admitted through the recommendation of relatives who had attained high position. While this practice was looked down upon, a considerable fraction of the lesser officials entered office through this *yin* system. But the question of the extent of social mobility in Old China and the relationship of mobility to the examination system can hardly be said to have been resolved. Note Ho Ping-ti, *The Ladder of Success in Imperial China* (1962).*

[14] "In traditional China, for reasons which may go back to Confucius or even earlier, external form must be impressive. The family must seem harmonious, the official must appear to govern and with pomp. Yet the realities may be very different." C. Martin Wilbur, "China and the Skeptical Eye," *Journal of Asian Studies,* 31 (1972), 765.

The foregoing sketch has suggested briefly the extraordinary influence Confucianism in its broadest aspects has exerted on the government of Old China. In the twentieth century a new China, no longer merely rebellious but openly revolutionary, has challenged not only the future but also the hallowed Confucian past. Perhaps one might find this upheaval far more comprehensible if China's revolutionists had patterned their course on models provided by eighteenth- and nineteenth-century Europe or America. On the contrary, China's revolutionists, whether of *Kuomintang* or Communist persuasion, have striven toward their own peculiar goals. No student of history expects China's dead past to determine the shape of things to come; but it would be equally naive to suppose that the political principles by which China has lived for more than two thousand years, and by which she was still living in the early years of the twentieth century, could be discarded and destroyed quickly and completely. In what ways then will political tradition be likely to reassert itself even in the midst of revolutionary change?

Authoritarianism. It is clear that the Confucian tradition is one of authority exercised (sometimes humanely) by those above upon those below. Very little evidence has emerged from twentieth-century China to suggest that this tradition has been weakened seriously. Both the *Kuomintang* and the Communists have used it, the latter with seemingly more effect than the former.[15]

Ideological Control. Confucian China is one of the best examples history provides of a society that operated by ideological control rather than by organized governmental direction. In many respects Confucianism was to China what religion has sometimes been to the West—namely, an agency for control. Chinese Communists have attempted to capitalize on this ideological tradition.

Bureaucracy. Again, it is to be noted that Confucian China was governed by bureaucracy.

[15] The authoritarian tradition is discussed ably by John K. Fairbank, *The United States and China* (3rd. rev. ed., 1971),* 96-121.

To master the difficult Chinese writing system it was necessary to begin early and to continue to study throughout life.

For Americans steeped in the democratic tradition and only recently subjected to problems of bureaucracy, it might be difficult to sense the hold which this tradition has had upon China. It was not a tradition of responsible government as the West understands that term, but rather of the responsibility of one official to another. It followed that the people, given the foundation on which bureaucratic rule stood, were not concerned with and did not regard it as their business to be concerned with affairs of state. The point is illustrated by an incident in 1851 at the time of the death of the Tao Kuang emperor. The intrepid traveler E. R. Huc, who with his fellow travelers was taking tea at an inn with some Chinese, attempted unsuccessfully to induce the latter into a political discussion. Finally, a worthy Chinese laid his hands paternally on Huc's shoulders and said, smiling ironically:

> *Listen to me, my friend! Why should you trouble your heart and fatigue your head by all these vain surmises? The Mandarins have to attend to affairs of state; they are paid for it. Let them earn their money then. But don't let us torment ourselves about what does not concern us. We should be great fools to want to do political business for nothing.*[16]

[16] E. R. Huc, *A Journey Through the Chinese Empire* (2 vols., 1859), I, 117.

Moreover, bureaucracy in a society based on personal relationships lived on standardized forms of corruption practiced so generally and openly as to become accepted institutions. Yet, whatever the shortcomings of the Chinese bureaucratic system may have been, the fact remains that as early as the beginning of the Christian era, the Chinese empire in matters of political management had many bureaucratic features not unlike those of the superstate of the twentieth century. Indeed, ancient Chinese bureaucracy when examined closely looks remarkably modern. For good or ill, it was one of China's great contributions to political theory and practice.[17]

Humanism. Although the Confucian tradition was authoritarian, it was also humanistic in that it concerned itself with human relationships and practical patterns of conduct. Although the sovereign was absolute, arbitrary, and without fear of any higher law, he was expected to have a constant regard for stability in human relationships. From this one may conclude that the Confucian tradition did not place the state completely above mankind. There was some regard for the individual, though the worth of the individual was measured in social, not in personal, terms. Success was not derived from personal initiative and individual accomplishment but from conformity with right conduct. Confucianism thus left a tradition and a principle not of individual but of social action.

Doubtless, China's past will not be the only force laboring to shape China's present and future; yet it is worth noting that the more the Chinese Communists try to create a new China, the more they seem to rely on Old Chinese ways of doing it.

[17] See Creel, "The Beginnings of Bureaucracy." The terms "feudalism" and "bureaucracy" have come to be used so loosely as to lose practically all meaning. It will be helpful to think of feudalism as a system of government in which a ruler personally delegates limited sovereignty over portions of his domain to vassals. Bureaucracy, in contrast, is a system of administration by means of professional functionaries whose functions are prescribed more or less definitely. A feudal vassal could do anything he was not expressly forbidden to do. A bureaucratic official could not properly do anything that was not part of his prescribed function.

FOR FURTHER READING

James T.C. Liu and Tu Wei-ming, eds., *Traditional China* (1970).* Sebastian De Grazia, ed., *Masters of Chinese Political Thought* (1973).* Donald J. Munro, *The Concept of Man in Early China* (1969) traces the growth of the concept of man's innate moral equality. Ch'u T'ung-tsu, *Law and Society in Traditional China* (1961), a detailed analysis of the historical relationship between Chinese law and society. Ch'u T'ung-tsu, *Local Government in China under the Ch'ing* (1962) gives details on the administration of justice, taxation, public works, and social services. On the role of the gentry see: Chang Chung-li, *The Chinese Gentry* (1955); Fei Hsiao-tung, *China's Gentry* (1953); Robert M. Marsh, *The Mandarins, The Circulation of Elites in China, 1600-1900* (1961); and Ho Ping-ti, *The Ladder of Success in Imperial China* (1962). Hsiao Kung-chuan, *Rural China: Imperial Control in the Nineteenth Century* (1960),* a monumental work covering the whole range of government activities in town and village. Hsieh Pao-chao, *The Government of China, 1644-1911* (1925), a useful introduction to the Manchu period. Derk Bodde and Clarence Morris, *Law in Imperial China: Exemplified by 190 Ch'ing Dynasty Cases* (1967).

Sybille van der Sprenkel, *Legal Institutions in Manchu China* (1962).

Examples of the vast literature on Chinese government for the years before the Manchu conquest: Brian E. McKnight, *Village and Bureaucracy in Southern Sung China* (1970); Lien-Sheng Yang, *Studies in Chinese Institutional History* (1961, reprint, 1969),* and *Money and Credit in China: A Short History* (1952, reprint, 1971);* and John Lyman Bishop, ed., *Studies of Governmental Institutions in Chinese History* (1968).* Charles O. Hucker, *The Traditional Chinese State in Ming Times, 1368-1644* (1961); E. A. Kracke, *Civil Service in Early Sung China, 960-1067* (1953)* deals with the techniques for maintaining administrative integrity among government personnel; Lin Mousheng, *Men and Ideas, An Informal History of Chinese Political Thought* (1942); Karl A. Wittfogel, *Oriental Despotism: A Comparative Study of Total Power* (1957),* a detailed analysis of the author's theory of "hydraulic society" and bureaucratic despotism.

Two brief case studies of traditional government in action are Johanna M. Menzel, ed., *The Chinese Civil Service; Career Open to Talent?* (1963),* and John Meskill, ed., *Wang An-shih: Practical Reformer?* (1963).*

Ways of Life
in Old Japan

4

Unlike China, long recognized as the creator of an East Asian civilization (Confucianism), or India, which produced a world religion in Buddhism, Japan has seemed quite unimpressive in its historic role in the making of Asian society. Moreover, it has often appeared, quite mistakenly, that an uncreative Japan could do no more than borrow from her neighbors. She absorbed much of the culture of China from the sixth to the mid-nineteenth centuries. During the past century she has drawn heavily on Western society. Yet the notable fact is that the Japanese, both ancient and modern, did much more than borrow; they adapted what they took from abroad, shaping it to their own native and sometimes prehistoric traditions. Thus they created a society which, though partaking of Chinese or Western ideas and institutions, was unmistakably Japanese.[1]

THE GEOGRAPHIC FACTOR

The capacity of the Japanese to preserve the special character of their culture notwithstanding very extensive borrowing from abroad was

[1] Two competent brief introductions to Japan's history are: John Whitney Hall, *Japan from Prehistory to Modern Times* (1970),* and Edwin O. Reischauer, *Japan: The Story of a Nation* (1970).*

reinforced by their insular position. Geography meant that Japan could open her doors to Chinese influence, or she could close them while she adjusted to what she had learned. The result was a distinctive Japanese culture and character which, while belonging to East Asia, was unlike that of any other Asian people.

Japan's early cultural borrowings from China were voluntary; they were not forced by foreign military conquest, as happened during the occupation of Japan following World War II. Japan was therefore free to accept this or reject that, and to digest what she learned from China in a comparative seclusion. Thus Chinese influence shaped and colored her own ideas and institutions but did not destroy them.[2]

[2] There is a striking geographical contrast between the immense continental position of China (some 4 million square miles) and the insular position of the four main Japanese islands (Hokkaido or Yezo, Honshu, Shikoku, and Kyushu, plus a thousand smaller islands). The total area of Japan is about 142,700 square miles, smaller than California. Due to the mountainous character of the country only some 16 percent of the land is arable. In comparison with European countries, Japan is smaller than France but slightly larger than the British Isles. In latitude the four main Japanese islands reach from approximately 31° to 46°—the same span as is occupied by most of the eastern United States, from the northern border of Florida to the Canadian border just south of Montreal.

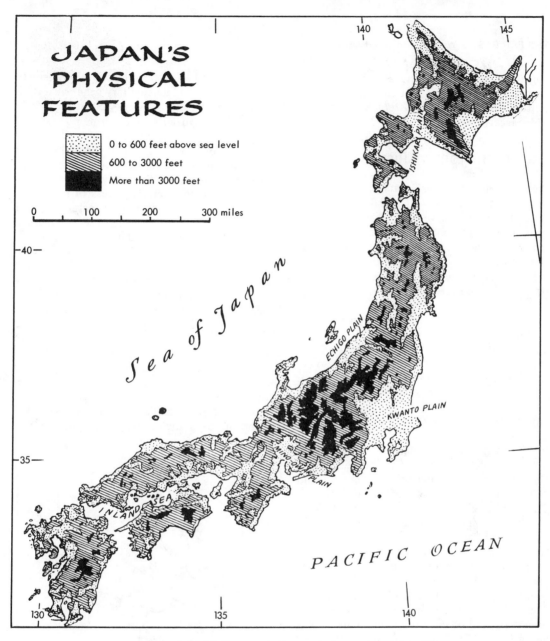

JAPAN'S PHYSICAL FEATURES

0 to 600 feet above sea level
600 to 3000 feet
More than 3000 feet

0   100   200   300 miles

Sea of Japan

ECHIGO PLAIN

KWANTO PLAIN

ISHIKARI

INLAND SEA

PACIFIC OCEAN

From Daniel R. Bergsmark, Economic Geography of Asia *(1935).*

ORIGINS OF THE JAPANESE

The peoples who were to become the Japanese of historic times were emigrants from the Asian continent of a predominantly Mongoloid racial mixture. Most of them reached Japan through Korea in successive waves of migration extending over a great period of time. Some of them may have come from the south by way of Formosa and the Ryukyu Islands. These Mongoloid folk were preceded in the islands by the Ainu, an aboriginal group whose racial identity continues to be a mystery. In historic times, roughly since the third century A.D., the Ainu inhabited northern Honshu and Hokkaido but later they were pushed steadily northward and finally were absorbed in major degree by the Japanese. In the late twentieth century only some 15,000 remain of this vanishing race.[3]

FROM PREHISTORY TO HISTORY

Precisely when the inhabitants of the Japanese islands became a coherent racial group is still uncertain. It may have been at an exceedingly early date, or not until about the third century A.D. with the establishment of the Yamato state. Evidence on the earliest known Japanese culture, called *Jomon* because of the cord pattern of its pottery, tells of a nonagricultural people who ate game, fish, and nuts. This *Jomon* culture gave way perhaps in the third century B. C. under the onslaught of new immigrants known as the Yayoi, who practiced agriculture and used irrigation in the cultivation of rice. The Yayoi were Mongoloids who had some knowledge of the more advanced civilization of China. By the first centuries A. D. there is specific evidence of a mounted warrior aristocracy controlling an agricultural population. Eventually a tribal group which had occupied the Yamato Plain in central Honshu (where the City of Nara would later be built) extended its control over neighboring tribal communities. These tribal chiefs or rulers of Yamato were also high priests claiming descent from the Sun Goddess, whose worship in time would become the cult of the land. The cult of the Sun Goddess helps to account for the matriarchal aspects of early Japan. The symbols of authority in Yamato, the so-called "Three Sacred Treasures," were a bronze mirror of Chinese origin, a sword of uncertain continental origin, and a jewel. They were to persist as important symbols throughout Japan's history.

The society over which the Yamato rulers were presiding by the fourth or fifth centuries A.D. was composed of hereditary groups of

families called *uji,* a term loosely equivalent to clan. Each *uji* had a hereditary head and a common deity. Within each *uji* were subgroups or *be*, whose members carried out special functions in agriculture, weaving, and pottery making. Some *uji* were under the authority of the Yamato rulers, some served them rather directly, while still others might be in a semiautonomous position. The ideas of hereditary rights and of the soldier as aristocrat and ruler were strong. These ideas were to show a marked capacity to survive in the Japanese mind.

It should be noted that there was a considerable contrast between the way in which the early Japanese state took form and the way in which the great dynasties of China came into being. The latter resulted from military conquest and the imposition of types of centralized control. In Japan the process tended to be more gradual. One group of *uji* eventually gained a superior position over others, resulting in a kind of hierarchy of ruling groups. Force was sometimes used but so also was the gentler art of diplomacy or conciliation, and the repeated assertion of a divine mandate from the Sun Goddess. By these various means, successive

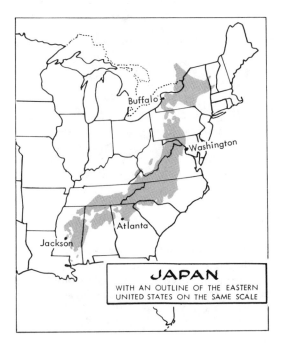

JAPAN
WITH AN OUTLINE OF THE EASTERN
UNITED STATES ON THE SAME SCALE

---

[3]Takahura Shinichiro, "The Ainu of Northern Japan, A Study in Conquest and Acculturation," translated and annotated by John A. Harrison, *Transactions of the American Philosophical Society,* New Series, 50, part 4 (1960).

priest-chiefs of Yamato established and maintained the primacy of what came to be called the Sun Line. It may be said that the system was a species of balance of power, in which the Sun Line chiefs of Yamato functioned as peacemakers between *uji* closely related to them at the center and a larger array of conquered *uji* at a distance, who had nonetheless become their "allies." In the exercise of authority there was a strong emphasis on family position and relations.

RELIGION IN PRIMITIVE JAPAN

In general the religious faith of prehistoric Japan was a simple nature worship. By the sixth century A.D. it had come to be known as Shinto, "the way of the gods," to distinguish it from Buddhism, which by that time had reached Japan from China. Shinto was an unquestioning belief in the supernatural powers, good or bad, of the spirit world, and in the intimate association of this spirit world with the family and the community. Men therefore worshipped *kami* or local spiritual forces.[4]

Kami were close at hand in many forms of nature, such as a mountain, a tree, or a rock; or they were present in symbolic form in a mirror or jewel. Sometimes these deified objects were housed in a family or a community shrine. The entrance to a major shrine might be marked by a *torii,* the symbolic gateway that is so familiar a feature of the Japanese landscape. There were *kami* for the humble family and also for the family of high estate.

Religion in Japan, as so often elsewhere, was a principal prop for political authority. Since the Sun Goddess according to mythology was the ancestress of the founder of the Yamato clan, it was natural that she should become the principal deity of Japan's indigenous religion and that this religion should become a principal support of Yamato's authority. The shrine of Amaterasu, the Sun Goddess, and the three sacred treasures were tangible evidence of the

spiritual legitimacy of the Yamato chiefs' political control throughout Japan, just as the *kami* of lesser chieftains gave sanction to their rule in the local area.

Japan's early Shinto religion, however, did much more than give support to political authority. It helped to create a social life of a comparatively high order, because Shinto placed greater emphasis on appreciation than on fear. It therefore came about that

... much that is kindly and gracious in the life of the Japanese today can be traced to those sentiments which caused their remote ancestors to ascribe divinity not only to the powerful and the awe-inspiring, such as the sun and the moon and the tempest, or to the useful, such as the well and the cooking pot, but also to the lovely and pleasant, such as the rocks and streams, the trees and flowers.[5]

Purity, the chief among the virtues of this early religion, was expressed through physical cleanliness. To be ready for religious observance one took a bath and put on clean garments. Here, deeply rooted in time, is the origin of a modern trait of the Japanese: the desire to be scrupulously clean. Here too was a tradition holding political potential. In modern times ultranationalists, sometimes successfully, identified "purity" with concepts of national loyalty and employed them as weapons in pursuit of authoritarian government and national expansion. More will be said on this aspect of the subject in later pages.

THE GROWTH OF CHINESE INFLUENCE

The birth and consolidation of the early state of Yamato was a process which lasted from the third to the sixth century. By the end of that period a fairly advanced concept of government was beginning to appear. Yamato chiefs came to think of themselves as sovereigns, and of other *uji* chiefs as their officials.

For a time the Yamato state extended its suzerain power to areas in southern Korea. Its influence there seemingly reached its peak in the fourth century, then declined and gradually came to an end. As a result in part of these

[4]While the term *kami* is usually translated as "deity" or "spirit" or "god", the basic meaning is "above" and therefore "superior." Here the problem for the student of history is to discover and to understand Japan's past in the meaning of Japanese terms.

[5]G. B. Sansom, *Japan: A Short Cultural History* (rev. ed., 1962), 47.

continental **adventures,** emigrants from mainland Asia entered Japan in increasing numbers during the fourth, fifth, and sixth centuries. They brought with them new ideas and practices of Chinese origin, which were to effect radical changes and advances within Japan— including better techniques of paddy field construction and irrigation. Of even greater import, at the beginning of the fifth century a Korean scholar named Wani introduced the Yamato aristocracy to Chinese learning through Confucian books. In time, written Chinese gradually became the official language of the Yamato court. These events paved the way for a general Chinese cultural **impact.** Buddhism was introduced about the middle of the sixth century, and soon won a body of converts. Some of these later journeyed to China as students and returned as effective missionaries of China's civilization. Eventually the Yamato court came under the control of pro-Chinese, pro-Buddhist factions. This circumstance prepared the way for the radical reform programs of the regent Shotoku Taishi, sometimes called the father of Japanese civilization.

CREATING A NEW SOCIETY

The seventh century in Japan was a time of notable transition. In 604 Shotoku Taishi, supported by the pro-Chinese-Buddhist factions, issued a code of moral injunctions superior to any political philosophy hitherto known in Japan. It expressed the Chinese theory that political power resides in the ruler. Shotoku Taishi and his supporters were seeking in Chinese political theory for a unifying principle that could break the heritage of clan barriers. It was a first attempt, under the influence of Chinese thought, to create a new political and economic structure by a frontal assault on the old clan or *uji* order. This purpose was advanced further beginning in 607, when Shotoku **Taishi** started sending embassies to China accompanied by able Japanese students who had already proven their capacity in Chinese literature and philosophy, in Buddhist studies, or as poets and artists. This educational effort

has been called one of the first well-organized and supported programs of foreign study. The students returned to Japan with the hard knowledge and the will to carry forward the transition to the Chinese pattern. In 645 they joined with others who seized control of the Yamato court and proclaimed the Taika Reform or "Great Change." These reforms meant that Yamato was intent on remaking Japan in the image of her magnificent neighbor, T'ang China. Other reform edicts followed during the entire second half of the century.

The Taika reforms, of course, did not create an immediate transformation. Change was effected slowly and under conditions of great political stress. Nevertheless, new ideas were taking hold. The Taika Reform had ordered abolition of private rice lands, proclaimed the sovereign's rights over all land resources, called for the building of a permanent capital, organized a central administration, devised a new system of land distribution to cultivators, and systematized a new means of taxation. The overall purpose was a greater centralization of power, which, with some limitations, was achieved.

The limitations on success, however, were notable. Powerful families that could not be deprived expediently of their lands were confirmed in their titles on the questionable assumption that they now held their lands in the name of the throne. In addition they were often given official posts and court rank in order to attach them closely to the court. The central government also undertook to appoint governors over provinces; but here too the practice was to confirm the existing authority of the most powerful local chief. In theory all of this was a political reorganization, yet in reality the emphasis in the Great Reform was directed to economic rather than political matters. The immediate concern of the reformers was to find more effective means of collecting wealth from the provinces.[6]

The Taika reforms were opposed at first by powerful and independent *uji*, but in the long

---

[6] K. Asakawa, *The Early Institutional Life of Japan* (1903; reissued 1963),* 295-96, 322ff.

run these changes worked to the advantage of the whole ruling class. Ultimately they converted it into a civil aristocracy (*kuge*) residing at the imperial court and enjoying the prestige of a privileged class in the new atmosphere of Chinese learning.

The reforming Japanese of the seventh and eighth centuries, steeped in Chinese influence, thought of their country as an empire and of their ruler as an all-powerful monarch in the Chinese tradition. The ruler, however, retained his original, indigenous Japanese character as chief priest while attaining this new stature. In this way Japanese sovereigns came to play a dual role: they were the Shinto high priests of Japan's divine origins as well as the absolute secular rulers, such as ruled in China. Japan's skill in adaptation was already at work. In some instances the Japanese accepted the form of a Chinese idea or institution but rejected its spirit—as when the reformers, amid all this Chinese flavor, acted to preserve the interests of a court aristocracy of birth at the expense of other groups. In China, on the other hand, there had long been an effort to create and maintain an aristocracy of learning rather than of birth.[7]

JAPAN BUILDS A CHINESE CITY: THE NARA PERIOD, 710-784

The ancient city of Nara near the modern town of that name in the Yamato Plain stood in eighth century Japan as the most striking tangible evidence of Chinese influence. Prior to this time the Japanese had not been city builders, nor had they a permanent capital. Nara was their first great city and the first permanent capital. Ch'ang-an, capital of T'ang China and perhaps the greatest city in the world at that time, was the model—a rectangle with the imperial palace at the northern end and broad straight thoroughfares intersecting at right angles. Here was the actual design and structure of Chinese architecture transplanted into Japan. The city was not so large as the Chinese model. Nevertheless, some of its Buddhist temples,

such as Horyuji and Todaiji, still stand in the twentieth century, the oldest wooden buildings in the world, and the only existing examples of the graceful Chinese architecture of T'ang.

It was at Nara that the imported Buddhism acquired tremendous influence as the new state religion. It gave to the Japanese a more sophisticated system of religious beliefs and philosophy than they had previously had. From its first introduction it was a principal vehicle for the spread of Chinese culture in Japan. As it developed into a strong institutionalized church holding great economic power, it acquired social influence and a large stake in the young nation's political affairs. Buddhism was one of the chief instruments through which the new bureaucratic government sought to strengthen its control, appointing the "right" men as chief abbots of the growing and powerful monasteries. Buddhist temples with their brilliant decorations dotted the near and the distant landscapes. Moreover, the cultured men of the Japanese court were steeped not only in Chinese religion, government, city-planning, and art, but also in the vehicle through which much of this learning came to Japan—the classical written Chinese language.

When they discovered that the writing of history had always been an important concern of Chinese governments, these aristocrats of Nara felt that they too must have histories. Their first great chronicles, the *Kojiki* or *Records of Ancient Matters,* and the *Nihon Shoki (Nihongi)* or *Chronicles of Japan* were completed in the early years of Nara, probably in 712 and 720 respectively.[8] Both of these chronicles, though official histories, are of importance in the study of early Japan. They have proven to be rather accurate accounts of the years after 400 A.D. For the earlier years they present a wealth of mythology and tradition, from which it has been possible to reconstruct much of that early and simpler Japan which existed before the coming of Chinese learning. Historians, however, are not always free to be

[7]For greater detail on Japan's cultural growth to 700 A.D. see Hall, *Japan,* 13-47, and Reischauer, *Japan,* 3-30.

[8]*Kojiki or Records of Ancient Matters,* B. H. Chamberlain, trans. (2nd ed., 1932) has been the standard translation. For the beginning student a new edition is recommended: *Kojiki,* Donald L. Philippi, trans. (1968); see also W. G. Aston, *Nihongi: Chronicles of Japan* (2 vols., 1896), a standard translation.

good historians. Sometimes they are under pressure from politicians or from advocates of this or that theory to color what they have to say. It seems that the rulers of Nara were not content that history record the simple myths and traditions handed down orally by professional chroniclers. On the contrary, they thought that matters would be much improved if history taught that the chiefs of Yamato were the unique and divine rulers of an old Japan no less glorious than its mighty neighbor China. Accordingly the historians created an impressive pseudo-history in which the Sun Goddess, a principal object of nature worship by the men of early Yamato, became the progenitress of the royal family and the grandmother of Japan's first emperor, who supposedly ascended the throne on February 11, 660 B.C. This date, which had not the slightest foundation in fact, may have been arrived at by projecting the founding of Japan a full Chinese time cycle of some 1,260 years into the past. In the twentieth century, as we shall see, these early Japanese chronicles were revived by supernationalists and superpatriots to serve the ends of a philosophy of 100 percent Japanism.

In poetry as well as history, the Nara period was one of splendid accomplishment. The great anthology of verse, the *Manyoshu* (*Collection of One Thousand Leaves*), has never been surpassed in Japanese poetry.[9]

Politically, the Nara era witnessed the beginnings of a movement in which the national government practically withered away due to the growth of tax-free estates, both secular and religious. Unlike the Chinese, the Japanese, with their strong leanings toward clan loyalty and hereditary rights, failed to develop a bureaucracy of education and learning to maintain the national domain and protect the central authority. As a consequence, the peasantry and their lands fell under the control of powerful local families with enough influence at the capital to escape the government

[9] Nippon Gakujutsu Shinkokai, *The Manyoshu. One Thousand Poems Selected and Translated from the Japanese* (1940; reissued ed. with the texts in Romaji and a new Foreword by Donald Keene, 1965).* Also Earl Roy Miner, *An Introduction to Japanese Court Poetry* (1968).*

tax collector. This meant the decline and impoverishment of royal authority and, ultimately, control of the weakened court by some powerful local family such as the Fujiwara clan, which came to the fore in the Nara period. All in all the close of the Nara era did not present a pretty picture. To be sure, artistic triumphs in temples and images were created, but they were the work of a government that lived far beyond its means and, purchasing the favor of the powerful Buddhist priesthood with generous gifts from the public domain, reduced the central authority to impotence and the peasants to the level of slaves.[10]

THE HEIAN PERIOD, 894-1185

The four centuries following the Nara period are in many respects the most fascinating and revealing period in Japanese history. Although the men who ruled at Nara were absorbed in the new learning from China, their successors in the age of Heian (meaning "peace and tranquility") had a deeper understanding of the processes of cultural borrowing, and therefore a more critical attitude toward Chinese learning in its new Japanese environment. By the ninth century the undiscriminating zeal for Chinese learning had given place to critical analysis which sought to adapt the new ideas to the peculiar background and needs of Japan. In part this more critical point of view was due to the decay of T'ang China and the resulting end, in 838, of Japanese embassies to the continent, but it should also be attributed to the growing intellectual maturity of the Japanese. It was in this period that the Japanese showed their capacity not only to borrow and imitate but also to adapt and develop the ideas and institutions of other lands to their own purposes and in their own particular ways. It was in this period, for example, that Buddhism in Japan became a Japanese rather than an Indian or a Chinese religion.

At the beginning of the Heian period the Buddhist church still retained the power to

[10] R. K. Reischauer, *Early Japanese History* (2 vols., 1937).

intimidate the government. To escape the political control of a powerful church the Emperor Kammu moved the capital to Heiankyo (City of Peace), known today as **Kyoto**, where it was to remain until the Restoration of 1868. When he had thus astutely curbed the political power of the Buddhists, he set about to fuse the church's religious power with the native cult of Shinto to create a national religion supporting the throne. The task of doing this was entrusted to two learned priest-patriots, **Kobo-Daishi** and **Dengyo-Daishi**, who became the founders respectively of the Shingon and the Tendai sects of Japanese Buddhism. Kobo-Daishi reconciled Buddhism with Shinto by a very neat doctrine which stated that the Buddhas had in part revealed themselves in Japan as Shinto deities. In this way foreign Buddhism became patriotic Japanese Buddhism and thus a bulwark of the central government.

KYOTO AND THE NEW JAPAN

The new capital, Kyoto, was the most spacious city Japan had yet known. Also modeled after the T'ang capital of Ch'ang-an, it became one of the world's most beautiful cities. Surrounded by and built into natural scenic beauty, it demonstrated the early maturing of Japanese artistic expression. Here the Japanese imperial court, the court nobility (*kuge*), the men of letters, and, to an even greater degree, the women of letters, created the masterpieces of classical Japanese literature. The second great anthology, the *Kokinshiu* (*Poems Ancient and Modern*), was completed in 922.[11] The age also brought forth Japan's ablest women of letters: Lady Murasaki no Shikibu, author of the *Genji Monogatari*[12] (ca. 1004), and Lady Sei Shonagon, author of the *Makura-no-soshi* (*Pillow Sketches*).[13] Kyoto was a cultured, refined,

[11] *Early Japanese Poets. Complete Translation of Kokinshiu*, T. Wakameda, trans. (1929) a complete translation but in inferior English.

[12] *Monogatari* means narrative. It is applied chiefly to fiction and sometimes to histories. Murasaki, like Fielding, created the prose epic of real life. The *Genji Monogatari* or *Tale of Genji* pictures the court life of the *kuge* and the ideal of the Japanese aristocratic style of the eleventh century.

[13] *The Pillow Book of Lady Sei Shonagon*, Arthur

and effeminate city. Belles lettres dominated its literature; it was the great age of the novel and poetry, of diaries and essays in the sophisticated manner, written in the native language. The duller pursuits of theology and the law were left to scholars, who wrote sometimes in rather bad Chinese.

The flowering of this early native literature in prose and poetry meant among other things that the Japanese had now acquired an adequate system for writing their native tongue. The creation of this system had taken place gradually through the ninth and tenth centuries. The method involved using simpler Chinese characters or parts of them as phonetic symbols usually representing a syllable, such as *ka, mi, ku, se,* or *to.* This syllabary or *kana* was and still is written in two forms, the one cursive, the other angular, known respectively as *hiragana* and *katakana.* Although some poetry had been written in Japanese during earlier centuries by using unabbreviated Chinese characters, it was the new syllabary that made a real and rich Japanese literature possible. It was in the new phonetic medium that the court ladies, Sei and Murasaki and others, wrote their thirty-one syllable poems, their diaries, and their novels. This was a Japanese literature expressive of a distinct Japanese culture in which Chinese influence was all but completely adapted to Japanese forms.

CHINESE INSTITUTIONS BECOME JAPANESE

In the Heian period the political and social institutions built in Japan during the previous centuries of Chinese influence also were so

Waley, trans. (1929 and 1953). The first complete English translation is Ivan Morris, *The Pillow Book of Sei Shonagon* (2 vols., 1967).* *The Pillow Book* is the earliest example of a rather unique form of Japanese writing. It is a collection of impressions, thoughts, descriptions, diary entries, lists of things liked or loathed, conversations, and poetry. It is one of the great works of Japanese literature. See also *The Gossamer Years: A Diary by a Noblewoman of Heian Japan* Edward Seidensticker, trans. (1964).* and Ivan Morris, *The World of the Shining Prince: Court Life in Ancient Japan* (1964)*—fascinating books of interest to the general reader and of instruction for the specialist.

Some of the complexities of traditional Japanese culture are revealed here: (top left) the beauty of an environment that had been changed only by the requirements of agriculture; (top right) a wayside Shinto Shrine; (bottom left) the exquisitely carved figure of Hachiman, the god of war; and (bottom right) the Golden Pavilion (Kinkakuji).

altered as to leave in some cases little evidence of their original Chinese models. For example, in China the civilian-scholar-bureaucrat chosen through civil service examinations operated in a system in which the educated class, drawn in theory at least from all walks of life, was accepted as the proper ruling class. In Japan, too, as a result of Chinese learning, the classics were studied and examinations held; but clan loyalties and hereditary rights determined who was appointed to high office. In such a situation there was no group of public servants whose

duty was to preserve the national domain. The result was that the central government, instead of developing into the stature of its Chinese model, became an empty pretense.

The imperial family continued to enjoy great prestige because of its political background and its relation to Shinto, but in actual power it was reduced to a succession of puppet emperors in the control of a powerful family—the Fujiwaras. This family, which had been a leader of the pro-Chinese factions in the seventh century, had acquired great wealth in lands and finally gained complete control of the capital and the court by marrying its daughters to the young emperors. Thus the Fujiwaras created a situation in which their clan monopolized the high if empty offices of state. Child emperors, the offspring of Fujiwara consorts, were placed on the throne, while heads of the Fujiwara house administered what was left of the state as regents (*sessho*) or as civil dictators (*kampaku*).

Ambitious and capable men who were not members of the Fujiwara clan had no choice but to seek their fortunes in distant provinces. There, by various means and as a result of varying conditions, many of them acquired great manors and built the foundations of a vigorous, militaristic, frontier society in striking contrast to the effete Kyoto aristocracy. These new landed barons had very little concern for the stability of the central government. On the contrary, their ambition was to strengthen their own local independence.

During the last century of the Heian era, these feudal barons (*buke*) and their hardy soldiers (*bushi* or *samurai*) were beyond the control of Kyoto. The once powerful Fujiwaras were forced to seek the aid of some of these new military upstarts to maintain order in the imperial capital. In the conflicts which ensued between the frontier warrior factions of Taira and Minamoto, the old civil government of Kyoto collapsed. Control of the next chapter in Japan's history was settled at the naval battle of Dan-no-ura, 1185, when the Taira were routed by their Minamoto rivals.

KAMAKURA: MILITARY DICTATORSHIP 1185-1338

By the time of the battle of Dan-no-ura, the once rude and untutored provincial aristocracy had gained considerable mastery of the new knowledge and superior skills deriving from the Chinese cultural impact. Unlike the civilian aristocracy of Kyoto, which had allowed its political authority to wither away while it wrote poetry, the provincials had developed vigorous ideas for a new society and a new political edifice. The leading actors in this coming order were mounted soldier-aristocrats, the knights (to use a European term) of what was to be Japan's era of feudal military dictator-

ship, dating from the coming to power of Minamoto Yoritomo.

The victorious Yoritomo, avoiding the mistake of his vanquished rival Taira Kiyomori, set up his seat of government not at Kyoto but at the seaside village of Kamakura near the principal estates of his relatives and allies in eastern-central Japan, not far from present-day Tokyo. At Kyoto he permitted the emperor, the Fujiwaras, and the civilian court nobility to carry on the forms of their make-believe civil government and to perpetuate the fiction that the emperor's government actually ruled. The fiction was strengthened further when Yoritomo accepted from the emperor the title shogun (generalissimo), which invested him with supreme command of all military forces. The implication was that Yoritomo commanded the emperor's army. Actually there was no emperor's army. What Yoritomo commanded was a powerful association of knights held together by family ties or by bonds of friendship arising from relations of mutual assistance. This military association under Yoritomo's leadership made up the real power and thus the real government. Moreover, with Yoritomo, the title of shogun became hereditary and therefore of greatly increased significance.

The military administration that came into being at Kamakura was known significantly as the *Bakufu* (meaning literally "tent government"), a term used originally to designate the headquarters of an army in the field, and later the administrative headquarters of a military dictator. In addition, this Kamakura administration was not a national government in the modern sense of that term but a simple machinery to control and regulate the affairs of the knights making up the Minamoto faction. Since these knights were scattered throughout the land, many of them as estate managers, Kamakura was in a position to control all areas and classes. During the time of the Minamoto shoguns and their successors, the Hojo regents, the lands of the Minamotos and their vassals were scattered thickly throughout eastern Japan, and more thinly in other areas. Sometimes the lands of a vassal lay within the domain of some independent lord. The direct authority of the shogun was thus likely to vary from complete military control in some areas to a rather shadowy suzerainty in others. But as long as the *Bakufu* retained able administrators its power was for all practical purposes supreme. The shogun was a military dictator deriving his military power from the Minamoto faction. Within this sphere, the administration of Kamakura was direct and exclusive.

These bold statements, however, require some important shading. Yoritomo, although acting the part of a military dictator, recognized the sovereignty of the throne and considered himself as exercising authority delegated by the throne. The throne therefore did not disappear with the creation of the shogunate, even though it did lose all save *de jure* authority. Emperors continued to reign in Kyoto, where they retained at times a certain social prestige and a certain negative authority. In this way the throne expressed rather vaguely a continuing concept of unity. It was significant that it should have carried this tradition, since Yoritomo probably did not think of himself as the ruler of all Japan or of Japan as a national unit. The twelfth century had already created a feudal society in which landed barons were virtually independent within their own estates and did not recognize the military power of the throne—for the throne possessed no military power. The barons did recognize the military power of the shogun, for he had the power and it was expedient for them to do so. Insofar as they were likely to bow to the shogun's legal as distinct from military authority, they did so because the former was derived from the throne and carried with it whatever prestige the throne possessed.

The Kamakura system was important itself as a system by which Japanese society of that day was ordered and controlled; but it was perhaps even more important for the influence it was to exert on the Japanese character during the succeeding six centuries of feudalism (until 1871). Kamakura planted firmly in Japan the tradition of military rule, of dictatorship of the peculiar Japanese variety, and of the principle of dual government in which an emperor reigned but a shogun ruled. It preserved the theory of the political and religious role of the imperial family. In the nineteenth and the twentieth centuries this imperial tradition was to be reasserted as a vigorous force when Japan emerged as a modern nation state.[14]

THE HOJO REGENCY, 1203-1333

On Yoritomo's death in 1199, his wife's family, the Hojo, having disposed of his heirs by various means including assassination, seized control of the shogunate and, after 1203, were its masters. Their power was exercised in a peculiarly Japanese manner. The head of the Hojo family assumed the title of regent and, in this capacity, ruled for puppet shoguns chosen from either the imperial family or the Fujiwaras. Japan of the thirteenth century thus presented the curious spectacle of a land headed by a sovereign who was emperor in name only, whose vestigial functions were sometimes assumed by an abdicated emperor, and whose real power was delegated to a hereditary military dictator (the shogun) but wielded by a hereditary regent acting for the dictator. One would suppose that this absurd-looking system, where theoretical sources of power were so remote from the offices exercising real power, would be meaningless and unworkable. Actually the Hojo regents, men of great capacity, gave Japan a government more stable, honest, and efficient than it had previously known.

THE MILITARY-FEUDAL CULTURE

With the victory of Yoritomo and the resulting era of the Hojo successors, Japan entered upon eight centuries of unbroken rule by military aristocrats. The feudal aspects of this military society bore some resemblance to feudalism in Europe, but there were also differences. For example, European feudalism under the influence of Roman law emphasized legal rights and obligations. Japanese feudalism in contrast reflected the Chinese (Confucian) principle

[14] See Minoru Shinoda, *The Founding of the Kamakura Shogunate* (1960). The Kamakura shogunate was in fact a private clan government based on vassalage but also empowered with certain public functions.

that good government is a matter of ethics (a moral problem) rather than of the inflexible, technical rule of law. The emphasis on this principle for centuries in a military society resulted in a rather general predisposition to feel that military men had greater self-effacing integrity than civilians, and thus a greater right to political authority.

The creation of the military-feudal dictatorship—a new political system—meant also the beginnings of a new cultural life involving in different ways both the fighting men and the common people. The effeminate, literary, civilian culture of the court at Kyoto did not disappear but it was faced by cultural rivals. Perhaps the most striking of the rising new philosophies was what may be called the warrior's code of behavior. This code, unlike the one prevailing in the dilettante atmosphere of the Kyoto court, laid great stress on personal loyalties, family ties, and on forms of rugged individualism which could be indifferent to suffering and even death.

In literature, prose writing such as the *Heike Monogatari (The Tale of the Taira Family)* gloried in accounts of warfare, a striking contrast to the earlier diaries of the court ladies. In religion, Buddhism developed new and popular sects—the Pure Land (Paradise) sects—which appealed to the common folk by expounding a simple belief in the redeeming power of a savior as the road to salvation.[15] The warrior aristocrats found their religious satisfactions in Zen (meditation) Buddhism, introduced from China in the latter part of the twelfth century. Zen Buddhism cast aside formalized religion and faith in the saving power of a redeemer in favor of individual effort to discover the meaning of the universe. Zen made a special appeal to the fighting men of the *Bakufu;* it was self-reliant, did not depend on scriptures, and was unencumbered by any intricate philosophy. Its stern injunction to self-examination, its freedom from the emotional, and its stress on individualism were also particularly attractive to the rugged warriors. Thus Zen, the religion of the

soldier, became in succeeding centuries a vital influence not only on the lives of military men but also on those whom they ruled.[16]

THE MONGOL THREAT

The Hojo regency was less than a century old when it was called upon to repel the attempted Mongol invasions of Kublai Khan, who, in 1263, had become emperor of China. His first unsuccessful attempt came in 1274. Then in 1281 a great Korean-Chinese fleet carrying an invading army of 150,000 men sought a landing in northern Kyushu near the modern city of Fukuoka. At this critical moment a typhoon (the *kamikaze* or divine wind) destroyed the invading fleet and thus ended the invasion. Providence, it seemed to many Japanese, had saved the land of the gods. The Hojos, with the help of their vassals, their feudal allies, and the divine wind, had met the military problem, but, as so often happens in man's experience, they were unequal to the domestic problems to which the military victory had contributed. While the Kamakura shogunate was strong enough to survive for another fifty years, increased taxes needed to meet imminent bankruptcy triggered local rebellions. Vassals and allies who had fought against the Mongol invaders, and priests whose prayers had been answered by the *kamikaze* wanted to be rewarded. But there were no available lands the Hojos could bestow as rewards.

The final destruction of the Hojos and with them the Kamakura shogunate came from an unexpected quarter. In 1331 Emperor Go-Daigo led a futile uprising to reestablish Kyoto's right to rule as well as to reign. In the tumult which followed the Hojos were destroyed along with the centralized rule of Kamakura. Then, while contending factions claimed the throne, a thoroughly unscrupulous general, Ashikaga Takauji, seized control of Kyoto and had himself appointed shogun in 1338. The Ashikaga shogunate was to survive until 1573.

[15] Readers who pursue further the subject of popular Japanese Buddhism will note its close resemblance to medieval and early modern Christianity. See Reischauer, *Japan*, 58-60.

[16] For Japan's great religious leaders, see Anesaki Masaharu, *History of Japanese Religion* (1930).

THE CULTURE OF ASHIKAGA

In matters of politics and government there is little, if anything, to be said in favor of the Ashikaga shogunate. The Ashikaga shoguns set up their capital not at Kamakura but at Muromachi, a district in Kyoto. Their years in office thus are known as the Muromachi period. The Ashikaga shoguns never exercised effective control over the military aristocracy, as the Hojos had done. The disappearance of any real central authority by shogun or emperor, and the incessant civil warfare which resulted, meant that the military class had become so large that government based on feudal ties of personal loyalty was no longer possible. A new type of political system began to appear. By the sixteenth century numerous local lords had succeeded in establishing themselves as territorial barons (daimyo), who at this time of political confusion owed allegiance to no one but themselves. These daimyo were to play a very vital role in nineteenth-century Japan.

In the nonpolitical areas of culture the Ashikaga period was notable. It was a period of great artistic and economic growth. It brought about a mingling of the provincial military-feudal society with the old civilian society of Kyoto. In Kyoto the military caste was influenced by the older civilian culture. Military men soon learned to covet the cultural trappings which wealth could buy in the capital.

The Ashikaga period was also one of Zen culture. The leading artists were Zen priests who, because of their close contacts with China, brought to Japan new aspects of Chinese art and learning, which soon blended with the native arts. For example, the No drama was developed as a major contribution to dramatic art. Japanese painting reached new heights of perfection in Chinese and native schools. Likewise, from Chinese inspiration the Japanese of the Ashikaga era developed as their own art their unsurpassed landscape gardening and their aesthetic masterpieces of flower arrangement (ikebana). The disciplinary diversion of the tea ceremeony (cha-no-yu) was developed to foster the sophisticated virtues of urbanity and courtesy.[17]

DICTATORS REUNITE JAPAN

In summary then, the Ashikaga period, which had brought great economic growth and a brilliant development of the arts, had also fostered the collapse of the central authority, whether of emperor or shogun. In the domains of the great feudal lords, the daimyo, it had created the spirit and the reality of complete local independence. Each of these domains had become a political unit unto itself, a miniature state, in which the daimyo, assisted by a bureaucracy of chosen military officers, maintained his court and government at a central castle fortress from which he ruled his peasants, merchants, and soldiers as an independent sovereign. The tendency was for each daimyo to build up his military strength at the expense of his neighbors and rivals. By this process there emerged finally a few daimyo of unrivaled strength who fought for control of the entire nation.

The first of these powerful figures moving toward the reunification of the land was Oda Nobunaga. By seizing Kyoto in 1568, and by destroying the military power of the central Buddhist monasteries, Nobunaga made himself master of central Japan. When he was assassinated in 1582, his ablest general, Hideyoshi Toyotomi, later known as the Japanese Napoleon, carried on the conquest. Wisely recognizing the force of tradition, he instilled new life into the hapless imperial court by having the throne bestow upon him the title of kampaku, regent or civil dictator. He won military control of all Japan by defeating the powerful daimyo of Satsuma in Kyushu and his remaining rivals in the east and north. With these victories behind him he embarked on the conquest of China by way of Korea in 1592.

[17] See Arthur L. Sadler, The Japanese Tea Ceremony (1934), and Harado Jiro, Japanese Gardens (1956).

His armies, however, numbering at times as many as 200,000 men, did not get beyond Korea. The resistance of the Koreans and the Chinese was too powerful, and on Hideyoshi's death in 1598 his armies were withdrawn.

Hideyoshi's successor as master of Japan was one of his own vassals and generals, Tokugawa Iyeyasu, whose home was at Edo in east-central Japan. Iyeyasu first defeated Hideyoshi's rivals, then turned upon and destroyed Hideyoshi's family. Since neither Nobunaga nor Hideyoshi had been able to make his rule hereditary, Iyeyasu was consumed with a single ambition— to fashion a political structure that would preserve the newly-acquired power in the Tokugawa family. In this ambition Iyeyasu and his successors met with astonishing success. The edifice they erected was the final and greatest of the shogunates, lasting from 1603 to 1868.[18]

FOR FURTHER READING

Reference Works. *Japan, The Official Guide* (1964), accurate, informative with many fine maps. Basil Hall Chamberlain, *Things Japanese: Being Notes on Various Subjects Connected with Japan for the Use of Travellers and Others* (1939), an informative presentation which first appeared in 1890.

Bibliographies. Hyman Kublin, comp., *What Shall I Read on Japan: An Introductory Guide* (6th rev. ed., 1961), very selective. Bernard S. Silberman, *Japan and Korea. A Critical Bibliography* (1962), more extensive. Paul H. Clyde, "Japan's March to Empire: Some Bibliographical Evaluations," *The Journal of Modern History* 21 (1949), 333-43. Hugh Borton, et al., *A Selected List of Books and Articles on Japan in English, French and German* (rev. ed.,

1954)* gives a broad coverage of many disciplines. A monumental series is Fr. von Wenckstern. *A Bibliography of the Japanese Empire* (2 vols., 1895-1907); which is continued by Oskar Nachod, *Bibliography of the Japanese Empire 1906-1926* (2 vols., 1928); *Bibliographie von Japan, 1927-1929* (1931); and *Bibliographie von Japan 1930-1932* (1935); continued by Hans Praesent and Wolf Hainisch, *Bibliographie von Japan, 1933-1935* (Leipzig, 1937). See also annual bibliographies issued by the Association for Asian Studies.

Historiography. Hugh Borton, "A Survey of Japanese Historiography," *The American Historical Review* 43 (1938), 489-99. John W. Hall, "Historiography in Japan," in H. Stuart Hughes, *Teachers of History* (1954), 284-304. John W. Hall's *Japanese History: A Guide to Japanese Reference and Research Materials* (1954). Note the essay by James W. Morley, "Historical Writing in Modern Japan," *The Development of Historiography*, ed. by M. A. Fitzsimons et al. (1954), 381-89. W. G. Beasley and E. G. Pulleybank, eds., *Historians of China and Japan* (1961).

Geography. Guy Harold Smith and Dorothy Good, with collaboration of Shannon McCune, *Japan: a Geographical View* (1943), Japan at the start of World War II. Glen T. Trewartha, *Japan: A Physical, Cultural and Regional Geography* (1945), a standard, technical study. Nasu Shiroshi, *Aspects of Japanese Agriculture* (1941). E. B. Schumpeter, ed., *The Industrialization of Japan and Manchukuo, 1930-1940* (1940). See also Carl W. Bishop, "The Historical Geography of Early Japan," *Geographical Review* 13 (1923), 40-63.

Population. Irene B. Taeuber, *The Population of Japan* (1958). E. F. Penrose, *Population Theories and Their Application with Special Reference to Japan* (1934), the ablest study prior to World War II.

General History. Herschel Webb, *An Introduction to Japan* (2nd ed., 1960), brief and well written. Hugh Borton, ed., *Japan* (1951), a col-

[18] For the period in biography, see Walter Dening, *The Life of Toyotomi Hideyoshi, 1536-1598* (3rd ed., 1930); and A. L. Sadler, *The Maker of Modern Japan: the Life of Tokugawa Iyeyasu* (1937). John W. Hall and Richard K. Beardsley, *Twelve Doors to Japan* (1965) suggests briefly what different disciplines can reveal about Japan.

lection of 23 articles on various subjects prepared by specialists. G. B. Sansom, *A History of Japan to 1334* (1958); *A History of Japan, 1334-1615* (1961); and *A History of Japan, 1615-1867* (1963) covering from antiquity to the end of the Tokugawa period. These volumes are unrivalled in quality. Tsunoda Ryusaku, William T. deBary, Donald Keene, comps., *Sources of Japanese Tradition* (1960), a source covering all Japanese history, ancient and modern. Honjo Eijiro, *The Social and Economic History of Japan* (1935). Takekoshi Yosaburo, *The Economic Aspects of the History of the Civilization of Japan* (3 vols., 1930) covering the pre-Restoration periods. James Murdock and Yamagata Isoh, *A History of Japan* (3 vols., 3rd impression, 1949), still useful though heavy in political matters and weak in interpreting the aesthetic side of Japan. Mikiso Hane, *Japan, A Historical Survey* (1972).* Yanaga Chitoshi, *Japan Since Perry* (1949), factual and, for the period after 1853, takes on the proportions of a reference history. Richard Storry, *A History of Modern Japan* (1963). Arthur Tiedemann, *Modern Japan* (1962)* is a pocket edition containing several important documents. W. G. Beasley, *The Modern History of Japan* (1963).*

Special Studies. Gerald J. Groot, *The Prehistory of Japan* (1951) depicts the Stone Age culture. Anesaki Masaharu, *Prince Shotoku, the Sage Statesman* (1948). K. Asakawa, *The Documents of Iriki, Illustrative of the Development of the Feudal Institutions of Japan* (1929). John H. Hall, *Government and Local Power in Japan: A Study of Bizen Province, 500-1700* (1966). Shinoda Minoru, *The Founding of the Kamakura Shogunate, 1180-1185* (1960) covers the formative stage in Japan's feudal system. Helen Craig McCullough, trans. (with introduction) *Yoshitsune: A Fifteenth-Century Japanese Chronicle* (1966). H. Paul Varley, *Imperial Restoration in Medieval Japan* (1971). Peter Duus, *Feudalism in Japan* (1969), an excellent introduction. Delmer M. Brown, *Money Economy in Medieval Japan: A Study in the Use of Coins* (1951) covers the period 1200 to 1600. Ruth Benedict, *The Chrysanthemum and the Sword: Patterns of Japanese Culture* (1946),* a study on the behavior of the Japanese people.

Philosophy and Religion. Alfred Bloom, *The Life of Shinran Shonin* (1968). E. Dale Saunders, *Buddhism in Japan: With An Outline of Its Origins in India* (1964), a convenient manual for beginners. Charles A. Moore, ed., *The Japanese Mind: Essentials of Japanese Philosophy and Culture* (1967). Joseph R. Kitagawa, *Religion in Japanese History* (1966), a thoughtful survey. Charles N. E. Eliot, *Japanese Buddhism* (1935), a comprehensive study emphasizing early historical trends and developments. Anesaki Masaharu, *Nichiren, the Buddhist Prophet* (1949), a study of the life and teachings of the founder of a popular and militant Buddhist sect. William Barret, ed., *Zen Buddhism; Selected Writings of D. T. Suzuki* (1956)* contains selections from the prolific writings of the principal interpreter of Zen Buddhism to the West. Ono Motonori, *Shinto, the Kami Way* (1962), a popular introduction to the indigenous religion of Japan.

Literature. Helen Craig McCullogh, *Tales of Ise: Lyrical Episodes from Tenth Century Japan* (1968). Ivan Morris, *The World of the Shining Prince: Court Life in Ancient Japan* (1964). Lady Sarashina, *As I Crossed a Bridge of Dreams. Recollections of a Woman in Eleventh Century Japan,* trans. by Ivan Morris (1971). *The Izumi Shikibu Diary: A Romance of the Heian Court,* trans. by Edwin A. Cranston. Armando Martins Janeira, *Japanese and Western Literature: A Comparative Study* (1971). E. O. Reischauer and Joseph K. Yamagiwa, *Translations from Early Japanese Literature* (1951, reprint, 1964). Donald Keene, *Japanese Literature: An Introduction for Western Readers* (1955),* is an excellent, brief treatment. The same author's *Anthology of Japanese Literature: From the Earliest Era to the Mid-Nineteenth Century* (1955)* contains superb translations from the prose, poetry, and drama of old Japan. Note also the same author's *Modern Japanese Literature: An Anthology* (1957).* Richard M. Dorson, *Folk Legends of Japan* (1962), an enjoyable collection of folk legends depicting traditional beliefs, fantasies and customs. Lord Redesdale (A. B. Mitford), *Tales of Old Japan* (1905), a free translation of early Japanese stories. Arthur Waley, *Japanese*

Poetry: The "Uta" (1946);* and *The No Plays of Japan* (1954),* reprints of standard collections. Murasaki Shikibu, *The Tale of Genji,* trans. by Arthur Waley (1960),* Japan's most famous novel written about the year 1000 by a lady-in-waiting at the Japanese court. Harold G. Henderson, *An Introduction to Haiku: an Anthology of Poems and Poets from Basho to Shiki* (1957),* a survey of Japan's most popular poetic medium.

Art and Music. Ernest F. Fenollosa, *Epics of Chinese and Japanese Art* (2 vols., 1963).

Robert T. Paine and Alexander Soper, *The Art and Architecture of Japan* (1955). H. Minamoto, *An Illustrated History of Japanese Art,* trans. by Harold G. Henderson (1935) contains reproductions with historical explanation. Charles S. Terry, *Masterworks of Japanese Art* (1956) provides illustrated commentaries on the broader history of Japanese artistic achievement. Langdon Warner, *The Enduring Art of Japan* (1952),* a classic of perceptive evaluation. William P. Malm, *Japanese Music* (1959), an extensive study of the traditional music.

The West
Discovers
East Asia

5

The discovery of East Asia by the West is a subject that presents some very real historical problems. During the centuries since the first contacts were made, China has been described in Western writings in contradictory terms: as being good and bad, weak and strong, rich and poor, wise and foolish. These Western views of China have changed from time to time. In the sixteenth century, the Jesuits thought they had found in China something akin to the ideal state. In the nineteenth century, Protestant missionaries found there a supreme example of depravity. How can such contradictory conclusions be explained? Part of the answer is that the China of the sixteenth century was not the same as the China of the nineteenth century. But a much greater part of the answer is to be found in what the foreign observers wanted to see, and in what their own cultural backgrounds permitted them to see.

EARLY WESTERN CONTACTS WITH EAST ASIA

The history of Western contacts with East Asia is a long and fascinating story; it reaches back into the pre-Christian era. In reality, the time at which Europe gained its first knowledge of

China is not known with certainty. Perhaps it was as early as the sixth or even the seventh century B.C.[1] In any event, a remarkable overland traffic in silk from China to the Roman world had developed by the early years of the Christian era, primarily due to the Roman demand for silk, not to any Chinese demand for the products of Rome. The demand for Chinese silk continued during the first six centuries of the Christian era until Europe produced its own silk.

The sixth century in Central Asia witnessed the rise of the Turks and their westward advance until they had effected diplomatic contacts with the Roman world at Constantinople. This development did not lead to direct Roman contacts with China; however, it created in Byzantine Greek literature, derived from Turkish sources, the most revealing picture of China to appear in Europe prior to the accounts of Marco Polo.

When Christianity in one of its various forms

[1] For a detailed account of early relations between Europe and China, consult G. F. Hudson, *Europe and China* (1931; reissued, 1961),* which covers the period to 1800. The student interested in how Asia has affected the West should consult Donald F. Lach, *Asia in the Making of Europe,* I, Books 1 and 2 (1965).

first reached China is uncertain. It is known that Nestorian missionaries of the Persian Church did reach China. The record of this Nestorian effort has been preserved on a monument erected at Sian in 781, though not discovered until the seventeenth century.[2] From this and other sources it now appears that the Nestorians reached T'ang China about 635, where they were honorably received by the emperor. Churches were built in several cities and, though the faith was persecuted at times, it appears to have been generally tolerated for two centuries. Then in 845 the emperor commanded the missionaries to renounce their priestly calling and to cease to pervert the institutions of the country.

During the Five Dynasties (907-960) and the Sung dynasty (960-1279) a very considerable foreign trade was conducted at Ch'uan-chou (Zayton) in Fukien and at Canton in Kwangtung. Most of the foreign merchants in this trade were Moslem Arabs, who in general seem to have been well treated; they were permitted to settle in the country, to take Chinese wives, to adjust disputes among themselves according to their own laws, and, in some cases, to hold high office in the state. It was the Arab trade which eventually was to carry into Europe a knowledge of Chinese tea.

THE RENEWAL OF EUROPEAN INTEREST IN CHINA

Christian Europe was beset by unprecedented dangers in the thirteenth century. In the south and southeast lay the fanatical power of Islam. Directly to the east was the rising threat of the Mongol Empire, whose armies in 1222 invaded Europe and defeated the Russians on the Dnieper. Simultaneously, other Mongol armies were advancing eastward upon North China. Before the close of the century, the empire built by Ghenghis Khan and his successors extended across the map of Eurasia from the western borders of Russia to the Pacific Ocean. Trade routes from Europe to China, closed for

more than four centuries, were again opened. Europe was soon to expand upon the meager knowledge of China which it had gained in the days of the silk trade. Various motives inspired this new European interest in China and the empire of the Tartars. Christian Europe was not adverse to the possibility of an alliance with the Mongols and the Chinese against the Moslems. The Crusades had created a new demand for the wares of the East. Finally, the Roman Catholic Church recognized the opportunity to carry Christianity to the pagan world. Thus faith, fear, and desire for material gain combined to inspire the embassies which Europe was soon to dispatch into Central and East Asia.

During the thirteenth and fourteenth centuries, then, Europeans representing religious, political, or commercial interests reached the capital of the Mongol Empire. John de Plano Carpini, a Franciscan, was received at the Great Khan's court in 1246. Two embassies from Louis IX of France followed in 1249 and 1252. In 1264 the two Venetian merchants, Nicolo and Maffeo Polo, were received in the court of Kublai Khan. Later, in 1275, the two brothers and Nicolo's son Marco entered the service of the Khan. From these visits came *The Book of Marco Polo,* written at the close of the century when the Polos had returned to Europe.[3] During the early years of the fourteenth century a small Christian community, the work of a Roman missionary, John of Monte Corvino, existed briefly at Cambaluc.

Although Europe had played with the idea of a sea route to the East as far back as 1300, it was not until two centuries later that this dream was brought to fulfillment. In 1488, Portuguese navigators rounded the Cape of Good Hope. Ten years later (1498-1499) Vasco da Gama reached Calicut in India. Successors of da Gama reached Malacca in 1511. From these advanced trading posts, which now for the first time could be reached by an unbroken sea voyage, the Portuguese advanced to Java, Siam, Indochina, and the southern coasts of China. Meanwhile, their naval warfare against the Arabs had made them the commercial masters of the Arabian Sea.

The China which Portuguese traders were

[2] *Sian* is the generally used modern spelling for Hsian (Wade-Giles romanization). In the spelling *Hsianfu,* the *fu* ending is a Manchu dynasty form that was not used in Nationalist China. Again, the T'ang dynasty name was *Ch'ang-an* instead of *Hsian.*

[3] A fascinating account of the Polos and their adventures in East Asia is Henry H. Hart, *Marco Polo: Venetian Adventurer* (1967).

soon to visit was ruled by the last of the great native Chinese dynasties, the Ming (1368-1644). The first century of Ming rule had been a period of commericial and maritime vigor, dominated by forceful naval diplomacy. Chinese fleets penetrated the South China Sea and the Indian Ocean, and tribute-bearing embassies from these areas visited China. After 1421, however, when the Ming capital was moved from Nanking to Peking, maritime interests were subject to increasing neglect.[4]

A Portuguese commercial expedition reached China from Malacca in 1514; though the mariners were not permitted to land, they disposed of their goods at a considerable profit.

[4] In the story of early modern contacts between Europe and East Asia (about 1500 to 1800), it should be noted that it was the Asian states that fixed the terms in which these contacts took place. At the same time a handful of Western adventurers made Europe and Asia aware of each other in some limited degree. There was some recognition in Europe that major Asian civilizations were superior to the European ones, and that Europe had much to learn from China's gifted craftsmen. The German philosopher Liebnitz suggested half seriously that the emperor of China ought to send missionaries to Europe to teach human relations. Voltaire said the sovereigns of Europe ought to follow the example of the Ch'ien-lung emperor in supporting philosphy and the arts. See Lach, *Making of Europe*, I, Book 1, xii-xiii, Book 2, Chapter VIII, "Japan,"; and Chapter IX, "China."

Carlo M. Cipolla, *Guns, Sails, and Empires; Technological Innovations and the Early Phases of European Expansion, 1400-1700* (1966),* stresses the importance of technological innovation in sailing and warfare in enabling Europeans by the end of the fifteenth century to force their way to the Spice Islands, control sea routes, and establish empires. By replacing oarsmen in the galley with sails and putting guns in the hands of the boarding party, Europeans transcended the limitations of human energy and obtained decisive advantage over non-Europeans.

Raymond Dawson, *The Chinese Chameleon: an Analysis of European Conceptions of Chinese Civilization* (1967), finds that Europe has envisaged China in a series of stereotypes: "the mighty and wealthy kingdom" reported by Polo and other early travelers; the "model [state] even for Christians" visited by Jesuits; the static China of nineteenth-century philosophers and historians; the isolated and insulated China of Kiplingesque imperialists; the "heathen Chinese" of evangelical Christians; and the "sinister" China of 1950. These stereotypes seem to owe as much in their making to the condition and need of the observer as to the actual state of the observed.

This auspicious beginning led to an official Portuguese mission headed by Thomas Pires in 1517. His embassy was well received at Canton. In 1522, however, the Chinese attacked and destroyed the Portuguese trading post at Canton, though another was soon established nearby. Later, Portuguese traders were driven from Ningpo and Amoy. These misfortunes are not difficult to explain. Reports had already reached the Ming court that the Portuguese, far from being solely interested in peaceful commerce, were intent on conquest. Then in 1557 the Portuguese established themselves at Macao, a small peninsula joined by a narrow neck of land to Hsiang-shan (Chung-shan), which lies in the delta to the south of Canton. Here the Portuguese traders were under the jurisdiction of the Chinese authorities. They themselves, however, were usually allowed to handle cases involving only their own subjects. Beyond this, Chinese control—territorial, judicial, and fiscal—was absolute.[5] It remained so until 1849, at which time the Portuguese began to persist in a claim to exclusive jurisdiction. Macao, nevertheless, was not recognized as Portuguese territory until the Protocol of Lisbon of 1887. Macao, from the time when the Portuguese first settled there until the cession of Hong Kong to Great Britain in 1842, remained the summer residence of Westerners engaged in the Canton trade.

The question arises why China, after her expulsion of the Pires mission and her subsequent experience with Portuguese lawlessness, tolerated these foreign merchants at all. In part it may be explained by the tendency of the Chinese imperial court to assert an authority which it was either unwilling or unable to enforce. Certainly the emperor could not bestow his imperial favor on surly Western barbarians who had respect neither for the dignity of the empire nor for its control over neighboring tributary states. Yet if there was profit to be derived from a limited commerce with the barbarian, he might be permitted to trade informally at a few ports. This was practical and therefore good Chinese doctrine. Actually the Chinese merchants at Canton desired the trade;

[5] H. B. Morse, *The Chronicles of the East India Company Trading to China* (5 vols., 1926-29), I, 8-9.

there were provincial officials who for a consideration would permit the trade; and at Peking, government officials, for a consideration, might pretend ignorance that there was any trade with the barbarian at all. The consequence was that trade prospered while the question of diplomatic recognition was ignored.[6]

THE DEVELOPMENT OF CATHOLIC MISSIONS

The rediscovery of China by Portuguese traders renewed the missionary interest of the Roman Catholic Church. Francis Xavier, who in 1549 introduced Catholicism to Japan, was the first zealot in the new campaign to convert the Chinese. Xavier, however, died off the coast of Kwangtung (1552), thwarted in his ambition to carry Roman Catholicism to China. He was followed by Matteo Ricci, an Italian Jesuit who

reached Macao in 1582.[7] The religious propaganda of Ricci, his associates, and successors, based on their appeal to the scientific and scholarly interests of Chinese officialdom, met with notable success. Among the converts were some princes of the blood, mandarins, and other courtiers. Ricci prepared for the Chinese a map of the world, on which he tactfully placed China in the middle; his followers corrected the Chinese calendar; others were appointed by the emperor to the post of state astronomer. A century after Ricci's arrival at Canton, the K'ang-hsi emperor granted freedom of worship to the Roman churches throughout the empire.

These official favors, however, did not exempt the missionaries from persecution. In 1616 and again in 1664 some of the Jesuits were expelled from Peking and forced to return to Canton or Macao. In fact it is surprising that in the seventeenth century there was not more persecution. Neo-Confucianism under the Ming emperors was inclined to be fixed and intolerant; Buddhism and Taoism were permitted but were regulated closely. The imperial court under the late Mings and under the first Manchu rulers did not look with favor on an exclusive authoritarian, and dogmatic religion such as Catholicism. Actually, seventeenth-century China, whatever its limitations may have been, was far more tolerant than Catholic Europe. At the very moment when the Papacy was seeking tolerance for its monks in China, Alva, as agent of the Counter Reformation, was seeking to crush heresy by the sword in the Netherlands.[8]

EARLY TRADE WITH CHINA

The Spaniards Reach the Philippines

Less than a decade after the first Portuguese navigators reached Canton, Spanish explorers

---

[6]The system of foreign trade that prevailed under the Mings is the key to politico-commercial difficulties that were to plague China's relations with the Western powers during the later eighteenth and nineteenth centuries. Under the Mings, foreign trade was considered primarily as an instrument for controlling the vassal states, not as a source of government revenue. Local officials, however, found in this trade a door to great wealth. The system worked very well in early Ming times, but with the arrival of the European barbarians (the Portuguese and those who followed them), who did not consider themselves as tributaries, it was subjected to new and powerful pressures. See Chang Tch-ch'ang, "Maritime Trade at Canton during the Ming Dynasty," *Chinese Social and Political Science Review,* 17 (1933), 264-82. Note also J. K. Fairbank, "Tributary Trade and China's Relations with the West," *Far Eastern Quarterly,* 1 (1942), 129-49; and J. K. Fairbank and Teng Ssu-yu, "On the Ch'ing Tributary System," *Harvard Journal of Asiatic Studies,* 6 (1941), 135-246. The last article is also included in John K. Fairbank and Teng Ssu-yu, *The Ch'ing Administration, Three Studies* (1960),* 107-246.

The notable Chinese voyages of discovery conducted under the early Mings suggest a striking contrast with those of the Portuguese. Culturally, the Chinese had a far more "enlightened conception" of intercultural contact; in their discoveries they set up no factories, and made no slave raids or conquests, whereas the Portuguese from the beginning considered themselves at war and were dominated by a crusader mentality. Joseph Needham, *Science and Civilization in China,* IV, Part 3, *Civil Engineering and Nautics,* (1971), 484-533.

[7]See K. S. Latourette, *A History of Christian Missions in China* (1929; Taiwan ed., 1966), 91-98.

Also, Jonathan Spence, *To Change China: Western Advisers in China 1620-1960* (1969),* 3-33, on Adam Schall and Ferdinand Verbiest, later Jesuits at the Peking court.

[8]Christianity was finally proscribed by Peking in 1724. A full and excellent discussion of the origin and development of anti-missionary feeling and anti-foreignism in China during the seventeenth and eighteenth centuries is given in Earl H. Pritchard, *Anglo-Chinese Relations during the Seventeenth and Eighteenth Centuries* (1931), Chapter 6.

were crossing the Pacific after rounding Cape Horn. In 1521, Ferdinand Magellan, a Portuguese by birth but sailing under the flag of Spain, discovered the Mariana or Ladrone (Robber) Islands, and later reached Samar in the Philippines. The Spaniards, however, were not seeking the Philippines or China, but the Spice Islands, which lay to the south. These islands, by the line of demarcation of 1494, lay, as did also the Philippines, in the Portuguese half of the world. It was not until some years later that Spain undertook conquest and exploration of the Philippines. Manila was founded in 1571, by which time the Chinese trade with the islands was considerable.

The Dutch in East Asia

Fresh from their successful struggle for national independence, the Dutch reached East Asia at the beginning of the seventeenth century. Organization of the United Dutch East India Company signaled the emerging commercial supremacy of the Netherlands and its determination, with England, to destroy the colonial and mercantile monopoly of Spain and Portugal. The Dutch attempted to open trade at Canton in 1604, and again in 1607, but on both occasions permission was denied, probably at the instigation of the Portuguese at Macao. Eventually the Dutch established themselves, first on the Pescadores Islands and later (1624) on Taiwan (Formosa). During the seventeenth and eighteenth centuries the Dutch sent four embassies to Peking (1656, 1667, 1685-1686, and 1795) seeking formal contacts with the Manchu court and commercial concessions. The ambassadors were required to perform the humiliating kowtow (nine prostrations), in return for which they received only meager commercial privileges. After 1729, however, the Dutch traded regularly at Canton.

The English Reach China

The first English vessel to reach Canton was dispatched in 1635 by the English East India Company. This was followed by a squadron of English vessels, commanded by Captain John Weddell, sent by the Courteen Association. Weddell arrived at Macao in 1637, proceeded to Canton, and at first met with opposition from the Chinese but was finally permitted to engage in trade. The English sent ships regularly to Canton after 1699, which is the probable date of the beginning of their permanent factory (trading post) there.

Other European nations played an inconspicuous role in this early China trade. The first French ship to reach Canton arrived in 1698; the first Danish ship in 1731; the first Swedish ship in 1732; and the first Russian ship in 1753. The first American ship, *Empress of China*, sailed for China in 1784.

First Russian Contacts with China

While western Europeans in the sixteenth and seventeenth centuries were making their first contacts with China by the all-sea route, Russians were moving to the East by way of Siberia. These first adventurers were a motley aggregation of explorers, fur traders, and fugitives from the law. Some of them reached the Pacific slope, while others established permanent settlements at Tobolsk, Tomsk, Yakutsk, Nertchinsk, and other points across Siberia. In eastern Siberia there was a natural geographic urge for the Russians to move south into the valley of the Amur river, where the tribal inhabitants recognized, in theory at least, the overlordship of China. The result was prolonged conflict between the Russians and the Chinese at Albazin, a Muscovite outpost on the upper Amur. In 1689 a boundary settlement was effected in the Sino-Russian Treaty of Nertchinsk, China's first treaty with a Western power. This settlement, in which Chinese negotiators were assisted by Jesuit advisers, enabled Peking to maintain and extend its claims to the Amur valley. Thirty-eight years later, in 1727, Russia and China concluded a boundary settlement to the west between Outer Mongolia and Siberia in the Treaty of Kiakhta. China was thereby assured control of the Mongols while Russia gained commercial privileges at Kiakhta as well as Nertchinsk, and the right to have an educational and religious mission at Peking.

The boundary settlements of Nertchinsk and Kiakhta, together with the commercial, diplomatic, educational, and religious concessions in these treaties, were a new departure in China's relations with the outside world. This new relationship was in marked contrast with China's attitude toward the Western Europeans who, at this time, were arriving by sea at Canton. In the eighteenth century, Russia was the only foreign power with which China had treaty relations and, more notable still, these treaties had been concluded as between equals; Russia was not listed in Ch'ing records as a tributary state. Russia was the only Western power to which China sent diplomatic missions. Russia was likewise the only foreign power having diplomatic, commercial, educational, and religious privileges at Peking. This extraordinary position of Russia was due to China's pressing need to define and consolidate her northern frontier. To gain this point the Ch'ing rulers made concessions to Russia which they would deny to all other foreign powers until well into the nineteenth century.

Like the Western Europeans in the seventeenth and eighteenth centuries, who were attempting to establish themselves at Canton, the Russians on the Sino-Russian frontier were interested primarily in trade, and the Kiakhta commerce was profitable. The principal items in this trade were cotton, silk, and tea from China; furs from Russia. On their part, the Russians adapted themselves to the "strange" ways of the Chinese much better than did the Western Europeans at Canton, and much better than they would themselves do later, in the mid-nineteenth century.[9]

THE WEST DISCOVERS JAPAN

It was more than two centuries after the travels of the Polos in China that Europeans set foot on the shores of Japan. The account generally accepted relates that in 1542 Portuguese sailors voyaging from Macao to Siam were blown from their course to the shores of Tanegashima, a small island off the southern coast of Kyushu, where they instructed the natives in the use of firearms. These visitors were followed closely by Fernando Mendez Pinto, to whom the discovery of Japan is usually credited. More Portuguese ships soon appeared, for the feudal lords of southern Japan readily accepted the idea of trade with the foreigners.

These commercial contacts with southern Japan aroused the interest of the Portuguese monks. Francis Xavier, a Jesuit who had been preaching in Goa, Travancore, and Malacca, landed at Kagoshima in 1549. For more than two years he pursued in this new field the most successful mission of his life. The Japanese, far from repelling the foreigner, welcomed both his commerce and his religion. Other Jesuits followed Xavier to Japan, where their work soon testified to their aggressive spirit and to the tolerance of the Japanese. The missionaries were heard respectfully by all classes of the people, including Buddhist priests. This may be accounted for by certain similarities between the rites and ceremonials of Buddhism and Catholicism. Also, since Catholicism was introduced directly from India, many Japanese assumed that it was a reformed Buddhism. It may be questioned whether many of the Japanese converts possessed any profound understanding of the new Western religion, for it has been noted that Japanese is a difficult language and Christianity is hard to explain.

Other causes contributed to the early success of Christianity in Japan. The feudal barons desired the profits of the foreign trade, and those in southern Japan, where most of the trade was conducted, were eager to increase their own power at the expense of the shogun's government. These barons observed the deference paid by the Portuguese traders to the missionaries. They concluded that where the missionary was, there also would be the trader.

The Spaniards in Japan

Until 1592 the Portuguese were the only Europeans to reach Japan. When Philip II of Spain ascended the throne of Portugal in 1581, he confirmed his Portuguese subjects in the exclusive right to the Japan trade. Four years later the Papacy conferred upon the Jesuits the sole right to enter Japan as missionaries.

Hideyoshi had at first been favorably disposed toward foreign priests, but he eventually became suspicious of the political implications

[9] See Clifford M. Foust, *Muscovite and Mandarin: Russia's Trade with China and Its Setting, 1727-1805* (1969); Vincent Chen, *Sino-Russian Relations in the Seventeenth Century* (1966); and James R. Gibson, *Feeding the Russian Fur Trade* (1969).

of Jesuit policy and conduct. In 1587, after subduing the *daimyo* of Satsuma, where most of the Christians lived, Hideyoshi issued an edict ordering foreign missionaries to leave Japan within twenty days. This edict was directed against the priests particularly, not against all Christians, for the Japanese desired to continue the Portuguese trade. The edict was consequently modified to permit priests to accompany Portuguese ships but not to remain in Japan. Nevertheless, for a number of reasons, even this law was not enforced effectively.

Then, in 1591, as Hideyoshi was planning the conquest of China, he sent an embassy to Manila demanding that the Spaniards there recognize Japan as their suzerain. In response the Spanish governor sent two missions to Japan, carrying among their number four Franciscan friars, who entered Japan in the guise of ambassadors and, incidentally, in violation of the papal order giving the Jesuits the sole right to proselytize in Japan. But Hideyoshi permitted these priests, and others who soon followed, to remain, on the understanding that they not preach Christianity. The Franciscans, having accepted this prohibition, immediately proceeded to violate it by conducting services in Nagasaki, Kyoto, and Osaka. Furthermore, as in China, they promoted sectarian feuds with their Jesuit colleagues. Such behavior, in open defiance of Hideyoshi's authority, served to confirm his fears regarding the intentions of the Catholic Church in Japan. Finally, the idle boasts of a Spanish pilot to the effect that the missionaries were preparing the way for political conquest led Hideyoshi to act. In 1597 a number of Franciscans, Japanese Jesuits, and Japanese laymen were crucified at Nagasaki.

JAPANESE FOREIGN POLICY

With the passing of Hideyoshi in 1598, political control of Japan passed into the hands of Tokugawa Iyeyasu, the able founder of the last great shogunate. Iyeyasu's views on foreign policy and trade were probably more enlightened than any that prevailed at the time. During his rule, the Portuguese, the Spaniards, the Dutch and the English were all welcomed in Japanese ports. The exclusion edict against foreign priests was not revoked; neither was it enforced. Spanish monks from Manila again entered Japan, and in 1608 the Papacy rescinded the restriction which had granted the field solely to the Jesuits.

In 1600 the first Dutch ship reached Japan. The pilot of the vessel was an English sailor, Will Adams, who, because of his natural wit and ability, was promptly employed by Iyeyasu as an adviser in matters of commerce and navigation. Other Dutch ships arrived in 1609, and a Dutch factory was built at Hirado near Nagasaki. News of these successes brought the first English ship to Hirado in 1613. Iyeyasu, influenced by Adams, offered the English a charter for free trade and urged them to construct a factory at his capital, Edo, the modern Tokyo. The short-sighted Captain Saris preferred to remain with his factory and trade at Hirado. There the business was handled incompetently and was abandoned in 1623, at a time when the Dutch trade was prospering.

Iyeyasu was likewise interested in developing closer commercial relations with Spain. He communicated with the Spanish authorities in the Philippines, offered to open the ports of eastern Japan to Spanish ships, and allowed it to be understood that the edicts against the missionaries would not be enforced. But it soon appeared that Spain was more likely to send missionaries than traders. As a result, Iyeyasu became suspicious of Spanish motives. The Dutch and English asserted that priests were not essential to trade. Accordingly, in 1612 Iyeyasu proscribed the Christian faith. All the Franciscan churches and many of the Jesuit establishments were destroyed. Some Japanese converts were executed in Edo (1613), and in the following year suppression of the faith was ordered throughout the land. Most of the foreign missionaries, however, were not harmed at this time, and many of the local barons refused to act against the native Christians in their domains. Hidetada, who succeeded Iyeyasu in 1616, executed some Spanish priests; but the laws were still not fully enforced. The government sought rather to have the priests leave the country voluntarily, whereas native Christians were induced by peaceful means to abandon the faith. Actually this policy failed, for the priests were defiant, and most of the converts clung to their new-found religion.

The Policy of Exclusion and Seclusion

The Catholic priesthood and its converts were, it seemed to the shogun, creating a rival authority in Japan which the shogunate was no longer willing to tolerate. Accordingly, in 1624 the Spaniards were ordered to leave the country. Direct relations between Japan and the Philippines were severed. Then in 1636 Iyemitsu, son and successor of Hidetada, proscribed Japanese trade on the high seas. No Japanese vessel might proceed abroad; no Japanese subject could lawfully leave his country; those doing so and attempting to return would suffer death. The Dutch were still permitted to trade at Hirado, but at Nagasaki the Portuguese were forced to conduct their commerce virtually as prisoners on a small artificial island known as Deshima.

These forceful measures did not end the trouble. The Shimabara revolt of 1637, a movement occasioned by feudal oppression and Christian persecutions, involved a large number of Japanese converts and was believed to have been incited by the missionaries. The government acted promptly. Spanish and Portuguese subjects were forbidden to visit Japan. Furthermore, it was decreed that if any Portuguese ship came to Japan, the vessel and cargo would be burned and the crew put to death.[10]

In this manner Japan entered upon a long period of exclusion and seclusion. It had become *sakoku,* or the closed country. The Dutch, to be sure, were permitted to carry on a limited trade confined to the island of Deshima in Nagasaki harbor, and the Chinese could send a few junks annually to the same port. Except for these contacts Japan was isolated from the outside world, and was to remain so for more than two centuries—the centuries (1638-1854) in which the Western powers built and consolidated their colonial empires.[11]

Why did Japan adopt so drastic a policy as seclusion, a policy that was to prevail for more than two centuries? The persecution of Christians in Japan was not basically of religious origin. The Buddhist church and clergy were not prime instigators, and the antagonism of the ruling class to Christianity was, in the main, political since it was the faith of Japan's potential enemies. The seclusion policy should be regarded rather as the means by which Japan's rulers sought to avoid any foreign entanglements which might endanger their fundamental aim of maintaining peace and fostering prosperity.[12]

A PERIOD OF SHIFTING INTERESTS

In summary, then, it may be said that the sixteenth and seventeenth centuries were not wholly without promise in the new intercourse between Europe and East Asia. In China there was an intelligent and tolerant audience ready to listen while Jesuits lectured on Europe's science. In Japan, the commercial and economic ideas of Tokugawa Iyeyasu far surpassed in liberality the economic policies of contemporary leaders in Europe. Yet by 1638 Japan had closed her doors to all foreign intercourse save for the annual Dutch ship and a few Chinese junks at Nagasaki. China likewise adopted a policy of cultural if not commercial exclusion. Repelled by the exclusive philosophy of the Catholic Church and by the quarrelsome character and aggressive behavior of its rival religions orders, the Chinese government expelled the missionaries in 1724. Thus the trade between Europe and Japan virtually was ended, while such trade as remained with China was confined to the single port of Canton, where it faced an uncertain future.

Yet in the eighteenth century it seemed that Europe might develop some appreciation of China as a source of things cultural and intellectual. Indeed, at the beginning of the century polite society in Europe spoke of Chinese art with ease and familiarity. The brilliant mas-

---

[10] The nature of militant Christianity is treated ably by C. R. Boxer, *The Christian Century in Japan 1549-1650* (1951), Chapters VII and VIII.

[11] On the Dutch position at Deshima see Grant Kohn Goodman, *The Dutch Impact on Japan, 1640-1853* (1967).

[12] George B. Sansom, *A History of Japan, 1615-1867* (1963),* 44. The adoption of seclusion resulted from three major concerns of the shogunate: (1) the Tokugawa drive for internal political stability; (2) the Tokugawa decision to monopolize all foreign trade; and (3) the fear of Catholic Christianity as it was revealed in the behavior of the foreign missionaries. Note the treatment by John Whitney Hall, *Japan from Prehistory to Modern Times* (1970),* 184-190.

querades of the French court were dominated by the art of China. The work of many of Europe's rococo artists was enriched if not inspired by the elaborate arts of southern China. To Europeans, the word porcelain connoted China; in England it actually was called "china," and still is. Side by side with these Chinese influences upon life in the *salon* were others playing upon the intellectual life of so-called "enlightened" Europe. Philosophers such as Leibnitz, La Mettrie, and Quesnay found support in Confucian philosophy for the rational basis of their systems of "pure thought." The physiocrats derived in part their notions on the economic nature of the state from their conception of conditions in ancient China. Lastly, in the late eighteenth century Europe's "Back to Nature" movement and the development of a sentimental nature-worship found some of their inspiration in the form and symbolism of the Chinese garden. But as the eighteenth century drew to a close, China ceased to be a source of vital inspiration to either the art or the philosophy of Europe. This was due in part to the altered views and changed status of the Jesuits. To a great degree the intellectual bridge between China and Europe had been built by the Jesuits. They had found in China something akin to what they considered the ideal state, and they had so reported to Europe. But the expulsion of these missionaries by China and the later dissolution of the Jesuits in Europe destroyed the main carrier of Chinese thought and influence.[13]

[13] See Adolph Reichwein, *China and Europe* (1925) for a full discussion of intellectual and artistic contacts in the eighteenth century. Also W. W. Appleton, *A Cycle of Cathay: The Chinese Vogue in England during the Seventeenth and Eighteenth Centuries* (1951). In fact, the discovery of China was thoroughly disturbing to the traditional thought of Europe, both religious and political. At the end of the seventeenth century Lecomte's *Nouveaux Memoires sur la Chine* raised a storm of debate because it suggested that the Chinese had known and honored the True God for more than 2000 years. The age of discovery was revealing that the Church and Europe had no monopoly on virtue and civilization. The natural religion of the deists, who denied Christian superiority, was strengthened. See Dawson, *Chinese Chameleon*, 54-55.

With the passing of the Jesuit contact, Chinese cultural influence not only ceased to reach Europe, but such influence as persisted there was subjected to attack. Save for a few remnants here and there, the China of art, letters, and philosophy had by 1800 all but disappeared from the European mind. Yet quite another China was making its appeal to Europe: a material, economic China rather than an aesthetic, intellectual one. Unlike the China that had appealed to the intellectuals of the European enlightenment, this was a China that appealed to the moneyed barons of the English East India Company. It was a China of statistics and markets, and, so the barons hoped, of larger and larger profits.

The emergence of this new attitude toward and interest in China was a product of a momentous transformation taking place in Europe itself during the late eighteenth and the early nineteenth centuries. In these years the European nation-state reached a degree of maturity. It was a product of what might be called political technology, and with it came equally marked changes in military technology. In a relatively brief span of time, leading European powers increased vastly their efficiency in the conduct of war and in the political management of their conquests.[14] Political centralization and hierarchy in political organization combined with the new military and industrial technology to become the foundations of European power after 1750.

The birth of the nation-state also created a new international system based on the idea of the equality of states. Admission to this society of "equal" states required that a state (1) define clearly the nature and source of authority and thus the locus of responsibility; (2) subscribe to the concept of the sanctity of contract to guarantee systematic and predictable conduct in trade; and (3) accept the Western concept of the universality of law and its application to the individual. These were the components of a new and powerful European sys-

[14] See Theodore Ropp, *War in the Modern World* (rev. ed., 1962).*

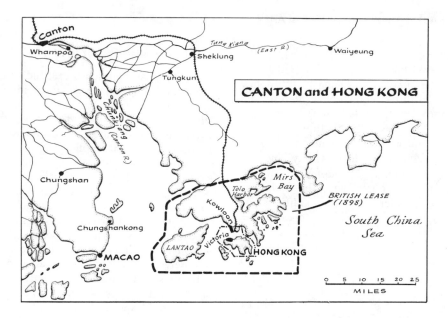

CANTON and HONG KONG

tem which was to work its will in East Asia as the nineteenth century advanced.

THE CANTON TRADE

Thus it was that in the later eighteenth century, Europe's cultural interest in China was replaced by a growing commercial interest—an interest that tended more and more to be monopolized by the British, which is to say, by the English East India Company. This did not mean that other nations were excluded from the trade of the China coast; but their share in it was circumscribed by political events. The Portuguese, who had dominated the early trade (1517-*ca.* 1600), maintained themselves continuously at Macao during the seventeenth, eighteenth, and nineteenth centuries, enjoying the profits of a small but lucrative trade. The Dutch, who dominated the eastern trade in the seventeenth century, failed to maintain this lead against the British in China. France, defeated by Britain in the colonial struggle, was unable to bid seriously for the China trade. Thus the China trade increasingly became the property of the English East India Company. Britain's victories in the colonial wars, her established position in India, and her primacy in the industrial revolution all

served to stimulate her trade with East Asia. In fact, from 1750 until 1834 it may be said that China's relations with Western Europe were essentially her relations with the English East India Company.

For most of this period China's foreign trade, as noted, was confined to the single South China port of Canton. Thus this commerce came to be known as the Canton trade. The peculiar circumstances surrounding this trade, the attitude of the Chinese toward the foreign barbarians, and the attitude of foreign barbarians in turn toward the "heathen" Chinese—all these had created by 1839 a crisis of dire proportions in the relations between Great Britain and China. It was this crisis and the wars which followed that were to determine the relations of China and the West for the succeeding century (1840-1940).

The primacy enjoyed by British trade was not a reflection of British satisfaction with the commercial system that prevailed at Canton. On the contrary, the British, like all other foreign traders in China, regarded the system as exceedingly irksome. Accordingly, between 1787 and 1816 the British sent three embassies to Peking to establish a more reasonable system of trade. These successive embassies, headed by Charles Cathcart (1787), George Macartney (1792-94), and Lord Amherst (1816), all failed.

These failures and the insults to which the British believed they had been subjected served to clarify the alternatives facing British policy at Canton. To British commercial interests and to the government it was becoming increasingly clear that there were three alternatives: (1) complete submission to a commercial system prescribed and controlled wholly by the Chinese; (2) complete abandonment of the trade (an unlikely course, since the trade was profitable even under the worst conditions); or (3) the application of force to compel the Chinese to do business on terms more pleasing to the West. Certainly a situation had arisen in which, if Britishers and Chinese were to do business at Canton, some accommodation would have to be found between their conflicting systems of foreign relations. The areas of disagreement were many and fundamental.[15]

[15] On the trade of various countries at Canton, see the tables compiled by Earl H. Pritchard, "The Struggle for Control of the China Trade," *Pacific Historical Review*, 3 (1934), 280-95. An essential study for the period is Michael Greenberg, *British Trade and the Opening of China 1800-42* (1951). Also Pritchard *Anglo-Chinese Relations*, 189-90. Note also *An Embassy to China: Being the Journal Kept by Lord Macartney during his Embassy to the Emperor Ch'ien-Lung, 1793-1794*, J. L. Crammer-Bying, ed., (1963). Although the embassy did not achieve its purposes, Lord Maccartney had the perception and the grace to write at the end of his journey: "Nothing could be more fallacious than to judge of China by any European standard." In attempting to get historical perspective on the conflicts which arose in and about the Canton trade, the reader will find it helpful to remember that the positions taken toward the Canton trade by the Manchu rulers of China seemed just as sensible to them as the views of Western traders appeared to Westerners. In attempting to understand the Manchu policy, the reader should recall that the Manchus were immersed in the very old social order of an agrarian-bureaucratic Chinese state mainly concerned with the power relations of an Inner Asian empire. There was no preparation for dealing creatively with the growth of the new maritime trade with Europe. Thus they attempted to apply at Canton/ the old administrative procedures of earlier dynasties. See John K. Fairbank, *Trade and Diplomacy on the China Coast* (2 vols., 1953),* I, 45-53. There was no disposition to consider the earlier treaties with Russia as establishing either a precedent or a practical approach to a new barbarian problem.

The "Irregularities" of the Chinese Tariff

At the time the English East India Company was assuming leadership in the Canton trade, China had developed and was applying a tariff policy that was notable in that it was designed to encourage the import and to discourage the export trade. Such a policy was not likely to win British or other foreign approval. One feature of the Chinese tariffs, though, appealed to the foreigners—the system was authorized by Peking. A system in which fiscal policy originated in the central government was quite understandable to Western Europeans. But these same tariffs, though fixed by Peking, were interpreted and applied by local or provincial authorities who functioned only nominally under the Peking government. For the most part it would appear that the rates sanctioned by Peking were reasonable. But when these rates were interpreted and applied by the local customs authorities, the tariff became far from reasonable—such, at least, was the constant complaint of the foreign traders.

This complaint was not without some foundation. The chief Chinese customs officials and their staffs had every reason to seek rapid and ready fortunes. Each chief together with his staff enjoyed only a short term in office. He had paid heavily for the office; he continued to pay for the favor of the higher authorities; he was required to see that fixed contributions reached the imperial government. Thus he would indeed be short-sighted not to make provision for his own later days of retirement. All these ends he accomplished by a constant though irregular pressure on the foreign trade. These unpredictable exactions meant fortunes to the customs bureaucracy but were an abomination to the foreign traders. In general, these merchants held that, although the imperial rates appeared to be moderate, they were so little regarded in practice that it was scarcely possible to name any fixed charge, save on a few articles.[16] In fact, the policy of the local officials at Canton was to keep the foreigner in ignorance of the actual tariff schedule.

[16] See Stanley F. Wright, *China's Struggle for Tariff Autonomy, 1843-1938* (1938), 1-5.

In the early nineteenth century, British traders, so it was said, found China as difficult to enter as Heaven and as difficult to get out of as Chancery. This was merely a way of saying that the Canton trade was a monopoly, and that the Chinese, at least a favored few of them, were the monopolists. There was nothing shocking to the English East India Company in the fact of monopoly. The Company itself was a monopoly. But when Chinese traders exacted monopoly profits at the expense of Western traders, monopoly as a principle lost some of its virtue.

The monopoly system that prevailed at Canton from 1757 to 1842 bore resemblance in some respects to commercial institutions and practices of Europe in the Middle Ages— namely, to the staple and the guild merchant or hanse. In Europe the guild merchant was a society whose primary purpose was to secure and hold a monopolistic privilege of carrying on trade. In China, the Co-hong, which corresponded to the guild merchant, was an instrumentality of imperial politics as well as of trade.

At the close of the eighteenth century the Co-hong, after a long and rather intricate history, had emerged as a group of twelve, later thirteen, so-called security merchants closely controlled by the government, directly subject to the Hoppo (the Chinese commissioner of customs at Canton), and enjoying a monopoly in the foreign trade. Every foreign vessel on arrival at Canton was "secured," that is, assigned to one of the Co-hong merchants who became responsible not only for the sale of the inbound cargo and provision for an outbound cargo, but also for every operation of whatever kind connected with the arrival, stay, and departure of the ship. The Co-hong thus became the instrument for exacting a great revenue from the foreign trade for the benefit of the Hoppo and, indirectly, through him, of the Canton officials and the court of Peking.[17] Finally, the Co-hong was to act as the sole medium of communication between the government and the foreign traders.[18]

In 1833 an event of great significance occurred. The English East India Company's monopolistic charter giving it exclusive control of English trade at Canton expired and Parliament did not renew it. So far as England was concerned, the trade was now open to any British merchant who had a mind to engage in it. This change foreshadowed grave complications in the commercial relations of Chinese and foreigners. Prior to 1833 the English traders at Canton had been under the control of a mere commercial agent, the chief factor of the Company there; but after 1833, with the abolition of the Company's monopoly, His Britannic Majesty was to be represented in the Canton trade by a "commissioned officer not only as a protector of his subjects and an overseer of their commercial activities, *but as a political and diplomatic representative*" of the British crown.[19] The crown was not likely to bow without protest to those real or supposed indignities and to the "exactions" under which, at China's will, the *Fan-Kwei* (foreign devils) had previously traded. This change in the status of British traders and of the agent who was to represent British interests at Canton set the stage for the ensuing Anglo-Chinese troubles that finally (1839-1842) resulted in the first Anglo-Chinese war, more frequently called the Opium War.

In 1833, Lord William John Napier, a Scottish peer of distinction, received a royal commission as first superintendent of (British) trade at Canton.[20] On his arrival at Macao (July, 1834) he proceeded to carry out his instruc-

[17]Pritchard, *Anglo-Chinese Relations*, 141-42. The Hong merchants were among the world's greatest

businessmen and traders of this period. Most popular with the American traders at Canton was the Hong merchant Houqua (Wu Ping-ch'ien). He is described by Thomas W. Ward of Salem as "very rich," "just in his dealings," "a man of honour and veracity," who "loves flattery and can be coaxed." Joseph Downs, "The American Trade with the Far East," in his *The China Trade and Its Influences* (1941), 15.

[18]H. B. Morse, *The Gilds of China* (2nd ed., 1932), 78. See also John Barrow, *Travels in China* (1805), 414. Barrow was private secretary to the Earl of Macartney during the latter's mission to China.

[19]See W. C. Costin, *Great Britain and China, 1833-1860* (1937).

[20]He was assisted by Sir John Francis Davis and Sir George Best Robinson as second and third superin-

Wu Ping-ch'ien (1769-1843), known to Western traders as "Houqua," was the leading Hong merchant and probably one of the nineteenth century's richest men.

tions, which, although they appeared proper enough from the Western point of view, were, if pressed, bound to result in conflict. Napier was instructed not to arouse Chinese prejudice or to endanger the trade, and not to call for armed assistance save in "extreme cases"; he was also advised by Lord Palmerston that "the establishment of direct communications with the imperial court at Peking would be desirable." At the same time he was required to announce his arrival "by letter to the Viceroy." He interpreted this to mean that he could not communicate through the Hong merchants. Neither

tendents respectively, both of whom succeeded to the post of first superintendent in the years following Napier's death. The fact that these officials were superintendents of trade precluded any possibility of their being treated as diplomatic equals by the Chinese officials. A merchant as such did not enjoy a station of honor in the official social scale of either Chinese or Japanese society.

Palmerston nor Napier appears to have realized that all these diplomatic eggs could not be carried in one basket with safety. A foreign naval officer and a representative of the British king simply could not be recognized by the Chinese unless he came as a bearer of tribute, as Napier did not.

At any rate, Napier announced his arrival at Canton by a letter to the viceroy, which, of course, the latter refused to receive. This refusal was natural enough, for Napier had violated three important rules by which the Chinese controlled foreigners. In addition to attempting direct communication with the viceroy instead of using the medium of the Hong merchants, he had proceeded from Macao to the Canton factories, located on the bank of the river outside the walled city, without asking and receiving China's official permission; and finally, he had termed his communication a *letter* instead of a *petition,* the form required by China of inferior tributary or vassal states. During the ensuing impasse Napier sickened and died, and for the ensuing five years (1834-1839) both the British and the Chinese governments followed a policy of indecision and drift.

The Legal Problem of Jurisdiction

The abolition of the English East India Company's monopoly at Canton precipitated in aggravated form another problem of long standing: the question of legal control over foreigners engaged in the trade at Canton. Most serious in Western eyes were those cases in which the Chinese demanded the surrender to Chinese justice of a foreigner accused of homicide in which a Chinese was the victim. There was already a long history of cases in which the Chinese and the foreigners had clashed on this point. One of the most notorious cases illustrative of this jurisdictional conflict was the Terranova affair. Terranova was an Italian seaman serving on the American ship *Emily* of Baltimore. In 1821, he was accused by the Chinese of having caused the death of a Chinese woman. Although convinced of his innocence and thoroughly aware that the Chinese would not give him a fair trial according to Western standards, the American merchant consul at Canton and the officers of the ship surrendered Terranova after the Chinese had stopped all American trade. Terranova was strangled, and the credit of the American merchants was saved.

For foreigners, the problem here was not simply a lack of even-handedness on the part of the Chinese. Indeed, it would appear that the Chinese authorities had no fixed desire to shield their own nationals from punishment. They insisted that justice should take its course according to well-established Chinese ideas and methods. But the foreigners regarded these as barbarous.

The Chinese attitude, however, was quite understandable. Prior to the coming of the Westerners, China's foreign relations were confined substantially to bordering vassal states which acknowledged their inferiority. If Chinese law had been accepted by these vassals, there seemed to be no good reason why special legal concessions should be made to the Western barbarians. But the foreigners argued that no matter what China's legal theories might be, her courts were utterly corrupt. In cases involving foreigners, money, it was said, was more effective than evidence. Moreover, Chinese judges were in fact disposed to give more credence to the testimony of a "civilized" Chinese than to that of an "uncivilized" barbarian, and torture was usually applied to any victim who refused to confess. This method of extracting a confession, by no means unknown in the Western world at the time, appeared more sinister when applied by "yellow" men against "white."

Finally, it should be observed that the Chinese legal theory of responsibility was thoroughly obnoxious to the English and other foreigners at Canton.

The Yellow River bursts its banks; the governor of Honan begs the emperor to deprive him of his titles, since he is responsible. A son commits an offence; the father is held responsible. A bankrupt absconds; his family are held responsible in body and estate. A shopman strikes a blow and goes into hiding; his employer is held responsible for his appearance. A province is overrun by rebels; its governor is held responsible . . . The result is that nothing which occurs goes unpunished; if the guilty

person cannot be found, convicted, and punished, then the responsible person must accept the consequences—father, family, employer, village, magistrate, or viceroy. [21]

Social Restraints on the Foreigner at Canton

If the foreigner was aggrieved when China dictated the terms on which he might conduct his trade, he was exasperated when his personal life was treated in the like manner. At Canton, the foreign factories were situated on the river bank just outside the walled city, to which the foreigner was denied access. His movements were confined to the narrow limits of the factory grounds. He was denied the use of sedan chairs—the most honorable conveyance for travel. He could not row on the river and only on rare occasions was he permitted to visit the flower gardens on the opposite bank. The markets of the walled city, with their variety of wares, were as far removed from his view as though they had been on the opposite side of the globe. He could hire Chinese servants only by connivance, not by right. Neither wives nor other foreign women could accompany the traders to Canton. They were required to remain at Macao, where all the traders were forced to return at the close of the trading season.[22] Official China, which made these rules, looked upon the foreigner as a lower order of being and treated him accordingly. In contrast with these imposed social restraints, there were frequently the most friendly and intimate relations among the trader, his Chinese agents, and the Hong merchants. Such amenities notwithstanding it was no wonder that the foreigner at times became restive; yet he was also timid. Despite all its impositions the Canton trade was profitable. On the whole, the foreign trader was inclined to bear exasperating regulations rather than risk stoppage of the trade.

The Canton trade was, in brief, much more than a mere rivalry of merchants. It was a clash

[21] H. B. Morse, *The International Relations of the Chinese Empire* (3 vols., 1910-18; Taiwan ed., 1963), I, 115.

[22] See Charles T. Downing, *The Fan-Qui or Foreigner in China* (2nd ed., 1840), III, 199-200.

between essentially different commercial, legal, and political systems. To the foreigner, as Arthur Smith, the missionary and writer, observed, it was "one long illustration of the Chinese talent for misunderstanding." Yet to the complaints of the foreigner the Chinese had a ready and plausible answer.

Why do you come here? We take in exchange your articles of produce and manufacture, which we really have no occasion for, and give you in return our precious tea, which nature has denied to your country; and yet you are not satisfied. Why do you so often visit c country whose customs you dislike?[2 3]

The Chinese System of Foreign Relations

Moreover, the Canton trade, as it had developed by the 1830's, was both an example of and a challenge to China's theory and practice of foreign relations. The traditional Chinese system of foreign relations conceived of China—the Middle Kingdom, the universal empire—as the superior party, and everyone else as lesser peoples—outer barbarians and therefore inferior. Historically, China had rarely been confronted by equals; but she had never been lacking in enemies on her borders, particularly in her great land frontier on the northeast. Even in those periods when the barbarian was able to invade and conquer China, foreign relations presented the problem of controlling the barbarians culturally.[2 4] The Chinese concept of their own superiority depended on cultural rather than physical or material power, and it derived conviction from the Confucian emphasis on the power of example. Thus the idealized relationship between China and the outer barbarians required that the barbarian recognize the unique position of the Son of Heaven as the

[2 3] Barrow, *Travels*, 413.

[2 4] Attitudes of superiority, of course, were not a one-way street. If the term "barbarian" applied to non-Chinese carried implications of inferiority, so also did European and American references to the Chinese as pagans and heathens. These terms suggested that the Chinese were to be pitied, and to pity is often to despise. See Nigel Cameron, *Barbarians and Mandarins* (1970).

ruler of mankind and be submissive to him; the emperor in turn was to be generous and benevolent to lesser peoples who showed him proper respect. This respect for and acceptance of Chinese suzerainty was given ritualistic expression and a measure of reality through the institution of tribute (usually native produce). The presentation of tribute at Peking by both the barbarians and also by the provinces of China itself signified membership in the Chinese Confucian society of peoples. In this ritual the tributary envoy might receive a patent of appointment, appointment to noble rank, and an imperial seal, in addition to the hospitality of the Chinese court. In return the tributary performed the kowtow, a symbol of submission. As elaborated at the Chinese court the kowtow consisted of three kneelings, each involving three prostrations before the emperor. It was a ceremony that left no doubt as to who was above and who was below. To Westerners recently imbued with ideas of equality it was a repugnant performance, but to men of the Confucian order it was no more than good behavior. The emperor himself performed the kowtow at the altar of Heaven and to his parents.

The tribute system and its missions had survived because it served the interests of both the superior and the inferior, of China and the outer barbarian. It served the Chinese rulers as evidence that they held the Mandate of Heaven. This prestige was important to the dynasty not only in controlling the barbarians but also in maintaining its rule over its own people. The tribute system was also China's medium of diplomacy, the process by which she kept in touch with the outside world. On the other hand, the barbarians conformed to the tribute system and were prepared to accept inferior status partly because there was no alternative, but to an even greater degree because the tribute missions became an instrumentality for conducting commerce. Indeed, by the nineteenth century tribute and trade were two inseparable factors in China's system of foreign relations.

The background of the Chinese theory of foreign relations is an important key to understanding the explosive conditions created as Western traders congregated at Canton. What mattered to the rulers of China were the ethics of tribute; what mattered to the Western barbarians were the profits of trade and, after 1834, the concept of equality. Herein lay a fundamental conflict between Confucian and Western society.[25]

The Economics of the Canton Trade

In spite of all the irritations that surrounded it, the Canton system of trade had been a profitable venture both for the English East India Company on the outside and for Chinese merchants and officials on the inside. Indeed so picturesque was this meeting of East and West in search of profits from teas and silks that the story of the old Canton trade before 1834 has often taken on the glamour of a fabulous and ideal age where merchants met as gentlemen. Within some limits, there is evidence to justify this glorification. At the same time, the Canton system failed, and the economic reasons for this collapse should be noted.

For the foreigners engaged in the Canton trade the most significant development of the early nineteenth century was the gradual decline of the East India Company's fortunes. This was partly due to the practices of the Company itself. Between 1760 and 1800, as the Company had faced a pressing need to find cargoes to pay for China's exports of silk and tea, private individuals operating under East India Company licenses were encouraged to encroach on the old Chinese junk trade with Southeast Asia. This so-called country trade began as merchants shipped to Canton products the Chinese would buy—cotton piece goods and opium from India; tin, camphor, and spices from the East Indies and Malaya. The trade deficits that plagued the Company were redressed in this way. But it was less well served when the coun-

try trade expanded and embraced all manner of services (private merchants acted as agents of London banks and insurance firms or became selling agents). As private traders with their agency houses became deeply involved in the Canton trade, the Company's monopoly became nominal. Compounding its problems, the Company faced pressures generated by England's industrial revolution. London responded to demands at home for wider export markets by looking beyond the East India Company. The Macartney (1792-1794) and the Amherst (1816) missions symbolized the erosion of the Company's role as the principal agent controlling the foreign side of the Canton trade.

The Opium Traffic

To the foregoing picture of the Company's declining monopoly in the face of the resourceful pressures of the private traders must be added the disrupting influence of opium. It was to the importation of this drug that the traders had turned much of their skill.

The first cause of this traffic lay in the unexplained development of a Chinese demand for opium. Since extensive cultivation of the poppy within China did not occur until after 1850, the demand could be met only by importation. Thus the demand within China plus the constant need at Canton for imports to balance the tea trade provided the economic bases for the growth of the traffic. As the Chinese demand grew, Indian opium came to surpass Indian raw cotton in balancing the trade. In time, too, opium production in India became an important source of government revenue there, thus tending to insure opium's place in the China trade. Indeed, this illegal traffic soon extended the opium business along the entire southeastern China coast, to the mutual financial benefit of both foreign and Chinese merchants and officials. As it happened, the phenomenal growth in the opium trade came just at the time the Company lost its monopoly at Canton. The two circumstances' coinciding brought on what may be called the Canton crisis of 1834-1840.

The rise of the opium trade presented the Peking government not only with a grave social problem but also with perplexing questions

---

[25] Fairbank, *Trade and Diplomacy*, I, 23-53. The problem was intensified because China herself was ruled by the alien Ch'ing dynasty. For example, in the Canton conflict the imperial authorities discovered that attempting to stir local Cantonese antiforeignism against the British was a dangerous weapon which, if put to extensive use, might react against the local authority of the Manchu government itself.

regarding the regulation of foreign trade. Peking had long recognized the dangers of opium and had prohibited importation and sale as early as 1729. But edicts were of no avail in light of the fact that Chinese officials from the highest to the lowest "all connived at the continuous breach of the law provided only that they found therein their personal profit."[26] Thus the opium traffic demonstrated that foreign trade, which was supposed to remain confined at Canton between the Co-hong and the foreign merchants, had grown beyond all control; and even at Canton, where the mechanism of control was nominally in place, the smuggling of opium was as prevalent as elsewhere.

Although Indian opium bulked largest in the trade, and although the British occupied a conspicuous place as the carriers, all the foreign nationals represented at Canton were involved. Portuguese, French, American, and other ships carried Persian and Turkish rather than Indian opium. Indeed, prior to 1820 American cargoes of the Persian and Turkish drug were regarded as a threat to the East India Company's interest in the trade.[27] In a word, the Canton system, contrived to meet the limited contacts of the eighteenth century, could not control the expanding contacts of the nineteenth. The system was no longer a vehicle for legitimate Western commerce or a shield for China's theory and practice of foreign relations.[28]

FOR FURTHER READING

Early Contacts with China. Edwin Van Kley, "Europe's 'Discovery' of China and the Writing of World History," *American Historical Review* 76 (1971), 358-85. Donald F. Lach and Carol Flaumenhaft, eds., *Asia on the Eve of Europe's Expansion* (1965),* a collection of contemporary accounts. Mark A. Stein. *On Ancient Central-Asian Tracks* (1933). Leonardo Olschki, *Marco Polo's Asia: An Introduction to His*

[26] Morse, *International Relations,* I, 183.

[27] Charles C. Stelle, "American Trade in Opium to China Prior to 1820," *Pacific Historical Review,* 9 (1940), 425-44.

[28] See Fairbank, *Trade and Diplomacy,* I, 56-73.

"Description of the World Called Il Milione," John A. Scott, trans. (1960), a treasury of information on medieval Asia. Henry Yule, *The Book of Ser Marco Polo* (2 vols., 1921). A. C. Moule, *Christians in China Before the Year 1550* (1930). J. de Rachewiltz, *Papal Envoys to the Great Khans* (1971). A. H. Rowbotham, *Missionary and Mandarin: The Jesuits at the Court of China* (1942). George Harold Dunne, *Generation of Giants* (1962), the story of the Jesuits in China during the last decades of the Ming dynasty. Matteo Ricci, *China in the Sixteenth Century: The Journals of Matteo Ricci: 1583-1610,* Louis J. Gallagher, trans. (1953). Henri Bernard, *Matteo Ricci's Scientific Contribution to China* (1935).

The Portuguese. Two studies by C. R. Boxer: *Fidalgos in the Far East, 1550-1770: Fact and Fancy in the History of Macao* (1948), a history of early Macao and Portuguese contacts with China; and *Four Centuries of Portuguese Expansion, 1415-1825* (1961).* See also C. R. Boxer, ed., *South China in the Sixteenth Century* (1953) contains accounts of Western travelers in China written between 1553 and 1576. Chang T'ien-tse, *Sino-Portuguese Trade from 1514 to 1644: A Synthesis of Portuguese and Chinese Sources* (1934). Lo-shu Fu, *A Documentary Chronicle of Sino-Western Relations, 1644-1820* (2 vols., 1967), a richly annotated selection of important official records from Chinese sources.

The Russians. Frank A. Golder, *Russian Expansion on the Pacific, 1641-1850* (1914). Joseph Sebes, *The Jesuits and the Sino-Russian Treaty of Nerchinsk* (1689). *The Diary of Thomas Pereira, S. J.* (1961). V. S. Frank, "The Territorial Terms of the Sino-Russian Treaty of Nertchinsk, 1689,)) *Pacific Historical Review* 16 (1947), 265-70.

Dutch, British, and American Interests. Kristof Glamann, *Dutch-Asiatic Trade, 1620-1740* (1958), a detailed examination of the Dutch East India Company in the early years. C. R. Boxer, *Jan Campagnie in Japan, 1600-1850* (1950). Philip G. Rogers, *The First Englishman* *in Japan: The Story of Will Adams* (1956). J. L. Cranmer-Byng, "Lord Macartney's Embassy to Peking in 1793," *Journal of Oriental Studies* 4 (1957-58). H. B. Morse, *The Trade and Administration of the Chinese Empire* (3rd rev. ed., 1920) treats Chinese institutions having a bearing on the foreign trade. Helen Augur, *Tall Ships to Cathay* (1951), an account of a New England firm's efforts to establish an Oriental trading company. James Kirker, *Adventurers to China: Americans in the Southern Oceans, 1792-1812* (1970). R. Coupland, *Raffles 1781-1826* (1926), an excellent study of the founder of Singapore. A popular novel recreating the color of early Hong Kong, James Clavell, *Tai-pan* (1966).*

China Submits: The Treaty System

6

The clash of interests in the foreign trade at Canton and on the southeast China coast had become monumental by 1835. The issues were not simple.[1] Beyond the matter of profits in trade, whether legitimate or contraband, they included, to mention only the more striking areas, such points as: (*1*) the British desire for diplomatic representation and equality, against China's assumptions of superiority; (*2*) the free-trading aspirations of the foreigners, against the controlled economy of the Co-hong; and (*3*) the rights of the individual in Western law, against Chinese concepts of collective responsibility. When to these basic conflicts were added the abolition of the East India Company's monopoly (1834) and the rapid expansion of the legal and the contraband trade, a degree of confusion was created in Canton which neither the British nor the Manchu government could long ignore. The policy of drift following Napier's death (1834) could not be prolonged indefinitely.

China's immediate contribution to the growing crisis came from its anti-opium move-ment, which was, first, a moral protest against the drug evil, as expressed in imperial edicts prohibiting the traffic; and, second, an economic protest resting on the mistaken belief that opium was the cause of the government's fiscal troubles. In general, the Chinese believed that as opium moved into China, silver, which was often used to pay for it, moved out. Although in some degree this was so, many other factors also contributed to the silver shortage. To the government, this shortage was a matter of grave concern. The Chinese people used copper coins in everyday transactions, but were required to convert these to silver for purposes of tax payments. When silver became more valuable in relation to copper, the tax-payer suffered. Thus the government had to choose between facing popular resentment or accepting reduced tax revenue.[2] At any rate, the government resolved to end the opium trade; for this purpose they sent the famous Lin Tse-hsu (1785-1850) to Canton in 1839. Commissioner Lin, as he was known to the foreigners, was that rare character in the Chinese bureaucracy of the time—a determined official.

---

[1] For the commercial complexities of the situation, see Michael Greenberg, *British Trade and the Opening of China, 1800-1842* (1951).

[2] J. K. Fairbank, *Trade and Diplomacy on the China Coast* (2 vols., 1953),* I, 75-76.

LIN ACTS; THE BRITISH REACT

Commissioner Lin was a man of thought as well as action, but his sources of information on the foreigners were at best imperfect. A product of China's ignorance of barbarian power, he intended to reform the Canton system on China's own terms, by attacking the problem unilaterally through the single target of opium. Accordingly, within a week of his arrival Lin had imprisoned the foreign traders in the factories and demanded delivery of the opium in their possession. The traders, through Captain Charles Elliott, superintendent of British trade, eventually surrendered some twenty thousand chests. To the astonishment of the foreign community this comfortable fortune, later valued at $6,000,000 was mixed with salt and lime and sluiced into the river. War was now certain; whereas Lin seems to have felt that his mission was accomplished, the British government could not do less than seek reparations.[3]

The First Anglo-Chinese War (1840-1842) involved two campaigns. In the first (1840), the British took Canton only to withdraw in favor of an expedition up the China coast, where they attacked Chinese garrisons and blockaded the mouth of the Yangtze. This advance brought the removal of Lin and the appointment of a Manchu, Ch'i-shan, to negotiate. He induced the British to return to the south, where, in January, 1841, an abortive convention was signed which included the transfer of Hong Kong to the British, the concession of diplomatic equality, an indemnity to the British, and provision for resumption of trade. For their trouble Ch'i-shan was promptly disgraced and Elliott recalled. In the views of their respective governments, Ch'i-shan had gone too far; Elliott, not far enough. Accordingly, the war was renewed in a second campaign (August, 1841-August, 1842). In March, 1842, the Manchu court began to consider negotiation.[4]

Meanwhile, Sir Henty Pottinger had arrived off the coast as Britain's chief representative. A British fleet moved northward, meeting no effective resistance. Early in August, 1842, Nanking, the southern capital, was at the mercy of British guns. The war was ended. The military defeat of China was decisive. A small British force, never more than 10,000 effectives, had broken what remained of Manchu military prestige. It was the beginning of a century of military defeats for China. Helpless, she sought peace on the deck of a British battleship, the *Cornwallis,* as it lay in the river off Nanking. In doing so China was choosing between danger and safety, not between what she considered right and wrong.

THE NANKING AND BOGUE TREATIES

The formal settlement of the First Anglo-Chinese War was embodied in two treaties: the Treaty of Nanking, August 29, 1842, and the supplementary Treaty of Hoomun Chai, signed at the Bogue, October 8, 1843.[5] The two treaties contained the basic principles that were to govern China's international status for a century. Later treaties between China and foreign states modified or amplified details, but the basic structure of principles contained in the first treaties remained until the end of the unequal treaty system in 1943.

Five ports, Canton, Amoy, Foochow, Ningpo, and Shanghai, were opened to the residence and trade of British merchants. Britain was to

---

[3] Lin's fascinating diary is found in Arthur Waley, *The Opium War Through Chinese Eyes* (1958).* There is no single answer to the question of whether the warfare of 1839-1842 should be called the Opium War or the First Anglo-Chinese War. It is a matter of the historian's individual judgment based on his reading of the evidence. Certainly the opium trade was the immediate occasion of the hostilities, but there were many other factors of long standing and of explosive potential. To the Chinese, the conflict has always been "The Opium War"; yet the underlying conflict was not opium but rather the clash between China's tribute system and the Western theory of the equality of states. The problem thus presents the student with an excellent demonstration of the inadequacy of labels when applied to complex historical situations. See Hsin-pao Chang, *Commissioner Lin and the Opium War* (1964). This treatment is more critical of British policy at Canton than some previous studies.

[4] P. C. Kuo, *A Critical Study of the First Anglo-Chinese War* (1935), 194-99. See also D. E. Owen, *British Opium Policy in China and India* (1934), 167-75.

[5] For texts of all important nineteenth-century treaties with China, see China, the Maritime Customs, *Treaties, Conventions, etc., Between China and Foreign States* (2 vols., 2nd ed., 1917).

appoint consular officers to these ports. The island of Hong Kong was ceded to Great Britain "in perpetuity."[6] The Co-hong was abolished, and British merchants were "to carry on their

[6] G. B. Endacott, *A History of Hong Kong* (1958) is a competent treatment of this British crown colony from the beginning to the end of World War II. Also see the same author's *Government and People in Hong Kong, 1841-1962* (1964) for the problems involved in providing a colonial government for a predominantly Chinese populace. Even at the end of the nineteenth century when Britain acquired by lease the New Territories on the mainland, adjacent to Kowloon (acquired 1860), a British colonial official was noting that the Chinese villager "does not set great store by cleanliness or better housing," does not understand British aims or ideas, or "our dismal condition of unrest" (p. 133).

mercantile transactions with whatever persons they please." China was to pay a total indemnity of $21,000,000—$6,000,000 for the surrendered opium; $3,000,000 to cover debts owed by Hong merchants to British subjects; and $12,000,000 for expenses occasioned by the war. Correspondence between the chief British representative and high Chinese officials was to be under the term "a communication," not "a petition."

China agreed to a uniform and moderate tariff on exports and imports, which came to be known as the 5 percent *ad valorem* treaty tariff. The duties fixed at this time were not to be increased save by mutual agreement. Thus, for the ensuing 88 years—that is, until

Hong Kong's Causeway Bay in 1846 and 1973.

1930—China was unable to fix her tariffs of her own free will. In 1842, however, China did not realize the importance of this act, nor was there anything in the nature of a plot on the part of British negotiators to violate China's sovereign rights, beyond meeting and correcting the circumstances in which the trade had been conducted. The British purpose was not to control China's fiscal policies but to provide a *modus operandi* for the foreign trade. Since this trade was still relatively small, and since isolation was still China's prevailing philosophy, the principle of tariff autonomy had at the time little of the significance it acquired in later years.[7] Another motive behind the tariff clause of the treaty was the aggressive free trade philosophy that then existed in Britain. In general the free traders felt that they had a divine mission to impose their creed on the world.

The first treaty settlement likewise included provision for extraterritorial jurisdiction in criminal cases (Treaty of the Bogue, Article IX)—a second major infringement on China's exercise of sovereignty. It will be recalled that for many years the foreign traders and their governments had condemned Chinese notions concerning the theory and practice of justice. At Macao the Portuguese had sought to retain exclusive jurisdiction over their nationals, and in 1833 the British, by order-in-council, provided their own court at Canton with criminal and admiralty jurisdiction. Again, it was only in later years that China realized the full implications of harboring in her seaports a foreign population over which her courts had no power.

Although China regarded opium as the primary cause of the war, the first treaty settlement, aside from stipulating the payment of $6,000,000 for the opium seized, did not mention the traffic at all. In the British view, China was free to legalize, to control, or to prohibit imports, but to enforce the latter course would be China's responsibility. The

Chinese would not agree to legalization, and thus the treaty was silent on this important question.

Finally, Britain secured the principle of most-favored-nation treatment. Article VII (Treaty of the Bogue) stated that should the emperor hereafter grant additional privileges or immunities to the subjects or citizens of other foreign countries, the same privileges and immunities would be extended to British subjects.

The new status thus acquired by Great Britain and her traders in China prompted other powers to seek treaty relations. Between 1844 and 1847 three treaties were concluded by China: with the United States (July 3, 1844); with France (October 24, 1844); and with Norway and Sweden (March 20, 1847). Of these, by far the most important was the American. Its significance may best be seen by reviewing briefly the growth of American interests in China.

EARLY AMERICAN INTERESTS IN CHINA

Even before the days of independence some notable Americans had expressed themselves on China. Benjamin Franklin (1771) hoped America would increase in likeness to her. Thomas Jefferson (1785) held that China's policy of nonintercourse was ideally adapted to American use. John Quincy Adams (1822) praised the Chinese for recognizing the virtues of the decimal system. But to most Americans China was merely a vast and remote empire—as much a curiosity as if it had been another planet.

John Ledyard, an American who accompanied Captain Cook to the Pacific (1776-1781), was among the first to tell his countrymen that furs from the northwest coast of America sold in Canton at enormous profit. The result was a voyage by the *Empress of China,* the first American ship to sail direct for Canton (1784).[8] The trade, thus begun, soon

---

[7] S. F. Wright, *China's Struggle for Tariff Autonomy, 1843-1938* (1938), 45-48. Frederick Wakeman, Jr., *Strangers at the Gate: Social Disorder in South China, 1839-1861* (1966), suggests that Cantonese hostility toward foreigners in the wake of the war was not solely a matter of anti-foreignism. It was also an expression of regional antagonism toward the Peking government and its policies.

[8] *The Empress of China,* 300 tons, carried as cargo "furs, foodstuffs, and ginseng—a wild root worth its weight in gold in the Orient as the 'dose of immortality.'" Joseph Downs, "The American Trade with the Far East," in *The China Trade and Its Influences* (1941), 13.

prospered. The Americans, like the European traders, sought Chinese silk and tea, and they encountered the same difficulties as the Europeans in finding an outbound cargo. Furs, ginseng, sandalwood, opium, and silver constituted main items in the China-bound cargoes, and various routes were followed by the ships in the early American trade. Between 1784 and 1811 Americans were the most serious rivals of the British in the tea trade at Canton. Their ships were neither so large nor so numerous as those of the English East India Company, yet in the season 1805-1806 they carried from Canton 11 million pounds of tea in 37 ships, as against British exports of 22 million pounds in 49 ships.[9]

The position of the Americans at Canton contrasted in some respects with that of the British. The Americans traded with greater individual freedom, but they possessed neither the financial backing nor the prestige of the English company, nor did they enjoy any naval protection from their home government. The first official representative of the United States in China was Major Samuel Shaw, who, after a number of voyages to East Asia, was named consul, without salary, at Canton by the Continental Congress acting on the recommendation of John Jay. It would seem that the early American trader felt little need for official support as long as he was permitted to trade on equal terms with his British rivals. But as the tension grew between the British and the Chinese after 1834, the indifference of American merchants to official backing disappeared. In May, 1839, after Lin had forced the surrender of foreign-owned opium, a group of Americans at Canton memorialized Congress to send a commercial agent to negotiate a treaty, and a naval force to protect persons and property.[10] Although expressing no sympathy with the opium traffic, they found no excuse for the "robbery" of the British. They foresaw that

England would use armed force, and they believed "that this is necessary." They recommended that the United States take *joint* action with England, France, and Holland to secure: (1) resident ministers at Peking; (2) a fixed tariff on exports and imports; (3) the liberty of trading at ports other than Canton; and (4) Chinese assent to the principle that, until their laws are made known and recognized, punishment for offenses committed by foreigners against Chinese or others shall not be greater than is applicable to a like offense by the laws of the United States or England. Thus, while many Americans in this period and later clothed their attitudes toward China in rather pious and moral phraseology, there was very little, if any, difference between what the British traders and American merchants wanted at Canton.

When the opium crisis broke at Canton, the Americans turned over their opium to the British superintendent for surrender to the Chinese; but when the English withdrew to Macao, and later to Hong Kong, the Americans remained at Canton, and conducted a lucrative business carrying cargoes of British goods to Canton when British ships were no longer permitted to enter the river.

In the broad sense, America appeared ill-prepared to formulate a political policy toward China. A fair proportion of Americans who thought about China at all harbored all manner of distorted notions concerning her. The most prevalent opinion was that the Anglo-Chinese war was "another item in the sad catalogue of [British] outrages on humanity." When in 1841 John Quincy Adams suggested in an address that the principle of equality among states was the real cause of the war in China, the idea was so shocking to the editor of the *North American Review* that he refused to print Adams' manuscript. After the first American Protestant missionaries, Elijah C. Bridgman and David Abeel, were sent to Canton in 1829, the missionary press dwelt heavily on the vices of the "heathen Chinese." The Chinese were frequently pictured as masters of deceit, cruelty, gambling, rioting, indolence, and superstition. Worst of all was their preference for rice rather than salvation. To many religious Ameri-

[9] See K. S. Latourette, *History of Early Relations Between the United States and China, 1784-1844* (1917).

[10] For a selected group of representative documents on American policy, see Paul H. Clyde, ed., *United States Policy Toward China: Diplomatic and Public Documents, 1839-1939* (1940: reissued 1964).

cans there was a shocking satisfaction in the thought that China's "depravity" offered an unlimited field for American missions. Nor were these opinions merely the fulminations of fanatics. After seventeen years in China, S. Wells Williams, one of the ablest of missionaries, succumbed at times to the prevalent conclusion:

It is much easier [he wrote] loving the souls of the heathen in the abstract than in the concrete encompassed as they are in such dirty bodies, speaking forth their foul language and vile natures exhibiting every evidence of depravity.[11]

Any thoughtful American must have been at a loss to know what to believe about China when he read that the Chinese had "some very esteemable qualities" but were "false, dishonest, and distrustful."

THE FIRST ENUNCIATION OF AMERICAN POLICY

Out of the background of these inadequate ideas on China emerged an official policy which, surprising as it may seem, so exactly expressed the reality of American interests that it survived for a century. President Tyler, on December 30, 1842—four months after the Treaty of Nanking had been signed—asked Congress to authorize appointment of a resident commissioner in China to protect the commercial and diplomatic affairs of the United States. This post was conferred upon Caleb **Cushing of Massachusetts, brilliant lawyer,** member of the Committee on Foreign Affairs, and intimate friend of the president. To Secretary of State Daniel Webster fell the task of preparing Cushing's instructions.[12] The American envoy was to secure entry of American ships and cargoes into the open ports on terms as favorable as those enjoyed by the British. He was to employ the utmost tact; to impress the Chinese with the peaceful character of his mission; and to visit Peking if possible. But in no

case was he to perform the kowtow. The instructions concluded with these significant words—the essence of American policy:

Finally, you will signify, in decided terms and a positive manner, that the Government of the United States would find it impossible to remain on terms of friendship and regard with the Emperor, if greater privileges or commercial facilities should be allowed to the subjects of any other Government than should be granted to the citizens of the United States.

Cushing reached Macao in February, 1844, welcomed neither by the Chinese, the British, nor the American communities. The treaties of Nanking and the Bogue were already in operation. Also, the Manchu negotiators had already applied, in 1842-1843, the old and well-established idea of equal treatment for all barbarians, so that the Americans in fact enjoyed most-favored-nation treatment without the asking. Thus the question arose as to what Cushing could do that had not already been done.[13]

In the face of Chinese procrastination on the subject of a treaty, Cushing intimated that he would proceed to Peking. This threat brought an imperial commissioner to Macao, and soon thereafter the first American treaty was signed (Treaty of Wang-hsia, July 3, 1844).[14] Although this treaty followed in general the principles contained in the British treaties, it was superior in point of clarity and in extending the principle of extraterritoriality to include civil as well as criminal cases. Thus the American treaty rather than the British became the basic document in China's foreign relations until the treaties of Tientsin were signed in 1858. Whereas the commercial policy set forth by Webster was in the main approved by

---

[11]F. W. Williams, *The Life and Letters of Samuel Wells Williams* (1899), 174.

[12]Webster was the special advocate of the new industrial interests appearing in the American national economy.

[13]Cushing's instructions are printed in Clyde, *Policy Toward China*, 9-12. The Manchu emperor's formal approval of the equal extension of trading privileges had been given November 15, 1843, before the arrival of Cushing in China. Kenneth Ch'en, "The Cushing Mission: Was It Necessary?" *Chinese Social and Political Science Review*, 23 (1939), 3-14.

[14]For a scholarly editing of this treaty, see Hunter Miller, ed., *Treaties and Other International Acts of the United States of America* (7 vols., 1931-42), IV. The prompt conclusion of the American treaty, once negotiations were begun, was due to Chinese "abhorrence of Cushing's intention to go to Peking," according to Ping Chia Kuo, "Caleb Cushing and the Treaty of Wanghia, 1844," *Journal of Modern History*, 5 (1933), 51. China was represented by Ch'i-ying.

American opinion, criticism of the Cushing mission was not lacking, although for the most part it was directed at the gold braid and plumes worn by the "pompous" Cushing rather than at the purposes of the mission. Journals such as *Hunt's Merchants' Magazine,* which a few months previously had bitterly denounced England's motives in China, reversed themselves, found excuses for England's behavior, and supported her policy of treaty relations. In Congress there was spirited support for Cushing, since no one knew "just how much of our tobacco might be chewed [in China] in place of opium."[15]

These more favorable reactions were not unanimous. There was a strong current of opinion that the China trade did not merit the publicity given it. Americans, it was said, might better direct their attention to the internal development of their own country. This was doubtless a very natural reaction in an America in the full tide of expansion on the frontier. Perhaps, too, the very positive character of this pioneer society reinforced the general American tendency to judge things Chinese solely in terms of American values, a tendency that contributed to tragic results in the twentieth century.

The Franco-Chinese treaty (October, 1844) followed the model of the British and American treaties. The French diplomats, however, appeared also in the role of "protectors" of Catholic missions. Their request for permission to build Roman Catholic missions at the five treaty ports, and for toleration of Chinese and foreign Catholics was granted by the emperor, though not as a part of the treaty. These concessions were extended later to Protestants.

THE RECEPTION OF THE FIRST TREATIES

The first treaty settlement viewed in retrospect reveals graphically its deep significance, but it must not be assumed that all this was clear to the contemporaries of Lin, Ch'i-ying, Pottinger,

[15] *Congressional Globe,* 27th Cong., 3rd sess., 325.

and Cushing. The fact that a handful of British troops and a small fleet had forced the Manchu court to terms did not necessarily signify that all was now well. The treaties themselves were an experiment. Would they in practice satisfy either the foreign traders and their governments or the reluctant Manchu court? Behind this question was a broad and vital problem. Did China's signature on the first treaties mean that she had broken positively with the past? Would her doors now be opened widely to Western influence, or, by evasion of the treaties, would she await the day when these doors might be closed again to a presumptuous, barbarian world?

The period from the First Anglo-Chinese War until the settlement of the second war (1861) illustrates nicely the persistence of the Chinese view that all Westerners were "irritating intruders." Confident of the greatness and self-sufficiency of her own rich culture, China in 1844 was still confident that she could control the intruders and preserve her own integrity. The defeat in the Opium War and the imposition of the treaties were considered temporary reverses, unfortunate but not fatal. Within this overall official Chinese attitude were the more particular reactions of the ruling Manchu dynasty. This dynasty, already weakened in the nineteenth century by the declining capacity of its emperors, was confronted by recurring rebellion at home as well as at the ports. Faced by these trials, the Manchus attempted at times to use the lesser trading powers, France and the United States, in an effort to thwart the main antagonist, Great Britain. The mass of memorials that flowed to Peking from high officials at Canton and, later, Shanghai insisted that the barbarian problem could best be handled by adroit "management." Accordingly, the emperor created a Barbarian Affairs Bureau to collect all records and information concerning foreign affairs, thus indicating that the government knew it was faced with a problem. In this picture, the United States by 1842 occupied a somewhat distinct position as the most important "neutral" state involved in the Anglo-Chinese struggle. Since the Americans had not joined Britain in the war, a number of Chinese officials played with the idea of "utilizing the American barbarians" in a general scheme of "using barbarians to curb barbarians." Indeed, throughout the remainder of the nineteenth century, China relied heavily on the technique of playing one power against another in her effort to resist the Western impact and to preserve her political system.[16]

CHINA AND FOREIGN AFFAIRS

China's Method in Foreign Affairs

The Treaty of Nanking (1842) had ended the old Chinese system of dealing with the foreigners through the Co-hong and the factories at Canton. This development did not mean that China's foreign relations were patterned immediately on the Western model. In the strict sense of the term there really were no official Chinese foreign relations before 1841; nor were there to be any, even in a semi-orthodox sense of the term, until the establishment of the Tsungli Yamen in 1861 and the opening of Peking to residence of ministers of the treaty powers. Thus China's foreign affairs from 1841 to 1861 were in a formative stage.[17]

The embryonic organization China used to deal with the barbarians in these years was briefly as follows: The most important official dealing directly with the foreigners at the five recently opened treaty ports was the *tao-t'ai*, or intendant of circuit. He had jurisdiction over two or more prefectures, served as an intermediary in diplomatic intercourse with the foreigners, and usually also served as superintendent of customs. A second official concerned with foreign affairs was the provincial governor (*hsun-fu*). Although the governor occasionally received the representative of a foreign state, he more frequently merely memorialized the throne on negotiations between the

tao-t'ai and the foreigner, or shifted the problem down to the *tao-t'ai* or up to the governor-general. More important, therefore, in handling foreign affairs in the new treaty period was the governor-general (*tsung-tu*), whom Westerners usually called the "viceroy." His prominence in foreign affairs was due partly to the American treaty of 1844, which stated that communications to the court were to be transmitted through this official.

The highest official outside of Peking who dealt with foreign affairs was the imperial commissioner (*ch'in-ch'ai*). Ranking above the governor-general and with a direct commission from the emperor, he might be instructed to cope with any new or alarming crisis, such as when Lin Tse-hsu was sent to Canton in 1839 to deal with the opium affair. When the Treaty of Nanking abolished the Co-hong as the agency for dealing with foreigners, the "diplomatic" function was taken over by the governor-general at Canton under the new title of "Imperial Commissioner charged with the superintendence of the concerns of foreign nations with China." All of the above officials were served by a host of underlings supposedly well versed in foreign affairs, but whose knowledge, in this period at least, was anything but impressive or accurate.[18]

Central Machinery of Foreign Affairs

Throughout the nineteenth century Western diplomats in China felt, more often than not, that China's handling of foreign affairs was a colossus of purposeful evasion, capped with downright administrative incompetence. There was certainly evasion, but the charge of administrative incompetence has been greatly overdrawn. Actually Peking's handling of foreign affairs was centralized and orderly. All such matters were dealt with directly by the emperor and the highest organ of state, the grand council (*chun chi ch'u*). Originally set up in 1729 to handle secret military affairs, the council, as a kind of inner, intimate staff of the emperor, acquired the power to interfere in any political matter. This small group, some five officials personally responsible to the emperor,

[16]Earl Swisher, *China's Management of the American Barbarians: A Study of Sino-American Relations, 1841-1861, with Documents* (1953), 1-54.

[17]The handling of foreign affairs was merely an aspect of the far larger problem of Chinese government administration as a whole. See John K. Fairbank and Teng Ssu-yu, *The Ch'ing Administration, Three Studies* (1960),* especially 107-73.

[18]Swisher, *China's Management,* 1-7.

was obviously not a foreign office, for it dealt with matters of all kinds. It had become an agency of dynastic power, negating traditional Chinese restrictions on imperial authority, although it was declining in character and initiative in the period 1841-1861. In this picture it is clear that the emperor's authority was final; however, the degree of judgment exercised by the councilors could vary greatly.

The working of this machinery for foreign affairs was regular and efficient according to the Chinese standards of that day. The foreign diplomat presented his credentials to the governor-general and imperial commissioner at Canton, or, if this had been done, he might, in specific cases of diplomatic business, deal with a governor-general, governor, or *tao-t'ai* at one of the treaty ports. The next step was a memorial from the high Chinese official to the emperor setting forth and reporting upon the business at hand. The important point is that the Western diplomat was dependent upon the case presented by the memorialist.

Chinese "Diplomatic" Officials

The Chinese official at the ports who dealt with representatives of the Western treaty powers was separated from them culturally by barriers of language, tradition, philosophy, and custom. He was therefore apt to be an inscrutable enigma or a thoroughly perverse and unreasonable being in the opinion of the foreigner. There was, however, a Chinese side to this picture that was not always comprehended by Western envoy, merchant, or missionary. What manner of men, after all, were these Chinese officials, and what ideas concerning the foreigners did they entertain in the twenty years following the first treaty settlement?

Since these Chinese officials were numerous and held posts of varying importance, from the exalted station of the imperial high commissioner down the scale of rank to semi-official and even unofficial underlings, it is only possible to give here by a few selected examples some impression of their quality as men. Among the more prominent names known to the foreigners were those of Lin Tse-hsu, who

seized the opium, and Ch'i-ying (or Kiying), who negotiated the first treaty settlement. The study of Lin's career is rewarding because in stature and influence he appears as among the greatest of Chinese statesmen of the nineteenth century. Tseng Kuo-fan and Li Hung-chang, who will be met with later in these pages, "excelled in the art of doing what was possible, [but] Lin surpassed them in the science of foreseeing what was inevitable."[19]

Lin, a native of Fukien, had first acquired fame as judicial commissioner in Kiangsu, where his judgments were regarded as so able he came to be known as "Lin, Clear as the Heavens." When, as his reputation grew, he memorialized the throne in 1838 on the opium question, he was called to Peking and, following nineteen audiences, was appointed imperial commissioner with full powers to examine and stamp out the evil of opium at Canton. The reader already knows what Lin did at Canton. When China was defeated in the war that followed and a British fleet lay off Tientsin, however, Lin was dismissed and ordered to Peking. Following a period of banishment to Chinese Turkestan, he was recalled in 1845 and thereafter served in a number of provincial posts. His fame rests not solely on his general administrative career or on his virtuosity in the opium drama at Canton. Beyond these accomplishments he was a pioneer in recognizing the power of the West. He advocated the study of Western geography and the introduction to China of Western methods and weapons of warfare as means of restoring Chinese power.

Ch'i-ying, known to contemporary Westerners as Kiying, was a Manchu imperial clansman. It was he who concluded the Treaty of Nanking with Great Britain in 1842, the Treaty of the Bogue in 1843, and the American Treaty of Wang-hsia in 1844. He also signed the later treaties with France and Sweden-Norway in 1844 and 1847 respectively. His power in China's relations with the West was unrivaled until 1850, when, under a new emperor, he was denounced as having "oppressed the people to please the foreigners." Degraded in rank, he

[19] Chang, *Commissioner Lin*, 216-17.

committed suicide in 1858. He was the victim of an uncompromising court party, and of the unpopularity of the first treaties.

Actually, the Manchu failure of 1842 was due in some measure to ignorance of the West. Even some of China's most distinguished dignitaries thought "it was because England had only a queen" that many of her subjects dared to be so unruly in China. Chinese scholars found the barbarian character "unfathomable," since it would do anything for profits. But there were reasons other than ignorance and misunderstanding for China's capitulation. The Manchu military structure had been designed to control the Chinese people, not to resist invasion from the sea.

The New Treaty Ports

The laboratory in which the new treaties were to be tried consisted of the five treaty ports: Canton, Amoy, Foochow, Ningpo, and Shanghai. In all these ports save Canton the foreigner was a stranger, and to the vast population in the interior he was all but unknown. China and the powers were entering upon a very unpredictable experiment. In the first years, 1843-1845, the way was paved for initial application of the Treaties by Ch'i-ying's policy of appeasement toward Pottinger. Thereafter, 1845-1853, there was to follow a progressive breakdown of the treaty system. This was to lead in 1854 to the creation of the Foreign Inspectorate of Customs at Shanghai, one of the most significant developments in the evolving Sino-Western system of the nineteenth century.

Only two of the first treaty ports were destined to develop as great centers of the foreign trade—Shanghai and Canton. For a few years commerce, particularly in black tea and in contract coolie labor to Cuba, flourished at Amoy. Trade at Foochow was negligible. Until the middle of 1844 not a foreign ship had entered its harbor. As a port Foochow suffered because its harbor was poor, its population, under official encouragement, was antiforeign, and its location was too close to Amoy. In the same way Ningpo was too close to Shanghai. Ningpo's later fame was due to missionary rather than commercial enterprise.

Shanghai was opened to foreign trade in November, 1843. Situated on the Whangpoo river about twelve miles from where it joins the Yangtze at Woosung, and having a native population of some 270,000, it was already an important center of China's inland and coastal trade. Here traders were no longer hampered by such monopolistic agencies as the Co-hong. There was business and opportunity for all. In 1844, forty-four foreign ships of a total tonnage of more than 8,000 entered Shanghai. Eight years later the number of ships was 182, with a total tonnage of 78,000. Shanghai exports were valued in 1846 at $7,000,000; in 1853 at $23,000,000. By 1852 Shanghai accounted for more than half of China's export trade. Many factors contributed to this rapid growth. The city bordered the great silk-producing areas; its situation at the mouth of the Yangtze was ideal for both the import and the export trade; and its inhabitants were free from the unhappy memories and the violent antiforeignism so pronounced at Canton.

The Shanghai International Settlement

The treaty status under which foreign merchants lived at the new ports was part of a peculiar, if not unique, system. At Canton and at many of the ports opened subsequently, the treaty signatories obtained from China—that is, from the emperor—grants of land known as "concessions," where the traders could erect commercial structures and residences. The concession was leased by China to the foreign power concerned, which subdivided the land into lots, granting these on long-term leases to its subjects and in some cases to other foreigners. Sometimes, as later at Tientsin, there were at one time in one open port as many as eight separate foreign "concessions." The foreign community of each concession provided, under authority of its home government, its own municipal government for the concession. Over this municipal government the consul of the given power presided. Thus at a treaty port there came to exist, in contiguous concession areas, a number of separate municipal governments, each exercising independent authority.

Shanghai met the problem in its own way. Since the local Chinese authorities there objected to the concession system, the first British consul accepted a plan whereby the Chinese

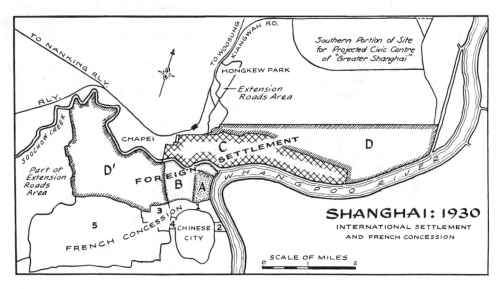

A. *Original boundaries of the foreign settlement.*
B. *Extension of the settlement boundaries, 1848.*
C. *The "American Settlement," 1863; incorporated with the foreign settlement the same year.*
D. *Further extension of the settlement, 1899.*
D' *Extension of 1899. (1) Original French concession, 1849; (2) Extended, 1861; (3) Extended, 1900; (4) Extended 1900; (5) Extended, 1914; The projected civic center of Shanghi was a project of the municipal government of the Chinese city.*

authorities set apart an area of land on the river bank in which British subjects might acquire lots from Chinese owners. A British purchaser, having reached an agreement with a Chinese owner, reported it to the British consul, who in turn reported it to the Chinese local authority, the *tao-t'ai.* This latter functionary then issued to the British subject, through his consul, a title in the form of a perpetual lease, under which the foreign buyer paid a nominal annual rent to the Chinese government, the theory being that all land belonged to the emperor and could not be alienated by outright sale.[20]

The Shanghai "settlement," as this area and its peculiar system came to be known, was at first restricted to British control. Foreigners of non-British nationality secured land therein through the consent of the British consul. This proved particularly objectionable to Americans, and so in time the right of all foreigners to lease

land within the settlement and to register such land at their own consulates was recognized. In this manner a system developed whereby each consul exercised jurisdiction over his own nationals in the common settlement area, and at the same time participated with his fellow consuls in supervision of settlement affairs.[21]

When the Shanghai settlement was first established, it was supposed that the area would be inhabited exclusively by foreigners, and for some eight years this was so. In 1853 there were only 500 Chinese residents, most of whom were servants or shopkeepers supplying the needs of the foreign residents. In the same year, however, Chinese authority in areas adjacent to the settlement broke down completely as a

[20] *Report of the Hon. Mr. Justice Feetham to the Shanghai Municipal Council* (4 vols., 1931-32), I, 27.

[21] For a brief period, separate American and French settlements existed at Shanghai, but in 1863 the American was merged with the British, forming the basis of what was to be known as the International Settlement. The French area continued to remain separate and came to be known as the "French concession," though the term is not entirely accurate.

result of rebellions and civil war, and the foreign area was soon swarming with homeless and often destitute Chinese refugees. By 1854 the Chinese population of the settlement exceeded 20,000. In this manner the whole character of the settlement was changed, and it became imperative that this unorganized community, consisting of groups of foreigners belonging to different nations, each group living under its own national laws and subject to the jurisdiction of its own consul, should provide itself with effective municipal authority for both internal administration and protection against the rebellions on its borders. To accomplish this the foreign settlement community had to acquire some degree of unity under a municipal constitution having the approval of the consular authorities. Such a constitution was adopted by the foreign merchants (known as the "renters" of settlement land) in 1854. Under this instrument adequate governing powers over the Shanghai Settlement were placed in the hands of an elected and exclusively foreign municipal council. Here then was a situation unforeseen at the time the first treaty settlement was made (1842-1844).

Foreign Relations at Canton

While the new foreign trade at Shanghai grew rapidly under generally amicable conditions, its corresponding growth at Canton was marked by friction, mob violence, and open armed conflict. To understand this contrast, one should recall that at Canton the foreign traders and some Chinese had long been in contact, and in many cases had made fortunes; but also at Canton grievances had arisen, real and imaginary, and hatreds that had finally produced war. At Canton the foreigner had been subjected to "insults" from the populace and high-handed Chinese officials. At Canton these same officials had bowed, outwardly at least, before the power of British guns. Now that the war had been won, the British proposed to assert their newly won privileges of equality. But the Chinese populace and many of the officials were by no means prepared to concede all this. The issue was soon drawn. No sooner had the city been officially opened in its new status as a treaty port (1843) than the intensity of its antiforeignism became apparent. The mere presence of Caleb Cushing in South China and his threat to proceed to Peking called forth a popular manifesto from Canton: "Ye men of America may truly dread local extermination." Foreigners were not permitted access to the walled city, and Governor Davis of Hong Kong regarded this "degrading" exclusion as a factor "provoking the insolence of the people." The treaties did not explicitly provide for entrance into the city, but the British claimed that denial of the privilege violated the spirit of the treaties and indicated the resolve of both officials and populace to preserve the old exclusive superiority. Because of this intensity of feeling, it was agreed in 1846 to postpone the "opening" of the city. The temper of the populace, however, did not improve. Foreigners, including Englishmen and an American, were stoned in a nearby village in 1847; a British fleet attacked the Bogue Forts and blockaded the river. Thereupon the viceroy agreed to open the city in April, 1849, but this settlement was not approved by the emperor. Peking in fact was torn between the demands of the foreigners and those of its own people. Until 1848, Ch'i-ying at Canton at least attempted to keep the people within the strict limits of the treaties; but his successors, Hsu Kwang-chin and Yeh Ming-ch'en, as will be seen, encouraged antiforeignism and thus contributed to a second war, which was already in the making.[22]

In summary, it may be said that the first treaty settlement was merely the beginning, not the consummation, of a new order between China and the West. By 1852 it had become merely a matter of time until Britain (this time aided by France) would demand the enforcement of the treaties and the addition of new and greater commercial privileges. This result was the more certain because Chinese leadership had neither the power nor the will to concede fully what had already been granted. At this time three factors in the Chinese intellectual milieu helped shape her attitude toward the Western impact: (1) the beginnings of a nationalistic ideology created by Chinese scholars who had long resented the alien Manchu dynasty; (2) the existence of a well-established anti-Western political tradition, in part a

[22] T. F. Tsiang, "New Light on Chinese Diplomacy, 1836-49," *Journal of Modern History,* 3 (1931), 590-91.

reaction to Jesuit efforts in the seventeenth and eighteenth centuries to plant Western technology and religious philosophy in Chinese soil; and (3) the determination of the Manchu court to apply to the Western barbarians the theory of the Middle Kingdom as the universal empire to which all outsiders were to come as inferiors and bearers of tribute. Thus China's initial response to the modern West was one of complete intellectual resistance.[23]

These intellectual limitations, which conditioned China's response to the West in the mid-nineteenth century, revealed themselves in the opinions commonly held by the scholar-officials. In the Chinese documents of the time the conventional phrases applied to Britishers, Frenchmen, and Americans were vigorous and colorful. The barbarians were inherently cunning and malicious, impatient and with no understanding of values, insatiable and avaricious, self-seekers with the feelings of dogs and sheep, fickle and inconstant, and perverse in words. If there was any fine distinction to be drawn concerning the Americans, it was that they were weak and might therefore be used in turning one barbarian against another. As for America itself, the best that was known by the scholar-officials was that it was "maritime, uncultivated, and primitive."[24]

An Unresponsive Society

The concessions China was forced to make in the first treaty settlement were a foretaste of even greater disasters that were to come at the hands of an expanding, outward-looking Europe and America; but in 1840 or 1850 there were few, if any, Chinese or Manchus who foresaw the possible scope of these imminent dangers. Herein lay the overall explanation for China's response, which, in the main, was no response at all other than a brief and futile military resistance. There were a number of major components in this failure of China to appraise the threat arising from the Western impact.

[23]Ssu-yu Teng and John K. Fairbank, *China's Response to the West* (1954),* 6-21.

[24]Swisher, *China's Management,* 44-48.

Ignorance of the West.   The first was China's almost total ignorance of Western society and, more importantly, her lack of interest in learning about it. The historic forces which had shaped the Chinese civilization had produced a long-lived, inward-looking society notable for its sense of superiority and self-sufficiency. Armed with these deeply rooted attitudes, China responded simply with a blind resistance to change, a response that was consonant with her intellectual assumptions.

Passive Government.   A second component in the Chinese response was the generally passive character of her government (see Chapters 2 and 3). The central government was to a great extent supervisory. The grass roots of administration were local, centered in the person of the district magistrate. The ideal sought by this dignitary was to so administer his area as to avoid any suggestion of trouble. Generally speaking, he was likely to follow the wishes of the local gentry, the unofficial ruling elite of the community. If trouble did arise, such as the depredations of bandits, it was wiser to buy them off than attempt to suppress them, since this would be an admission of responsibility for their existence. It was best to cover up disturbing matters—not to deal with them or report them to higher authority. The whole tendency was to deal with disputes by compromise. Society was to be harmonized, not changed. This passive philosophy of government had been a convenient and sometimes effective means of maintaining local domestic peace, but it institutionalized official corruption on a grand scale. In this context and from the Chinese point of view, the first treaty settlement was a compromise which brought peace and a measure of time. Perhaps the problem would go away.

The Role of the Gentry.   A third component in the Chinese response stemmed from the traditional role in society played by the unofficial ruling class. This class was distinguished from the common folk principally by its education and wealth, the latter most often in the form of land. Members of this elite included the literati, officials temporarily out of office, wealthy merchants and, most of all, landlords who lived on rents paid by peasants. Perpetuation of this powerful elite was insured by family ties and by the extended-family or clan system. Marriages were arranged, education was provided, and some upward mobility within the elite helped strengthen the system. Advancement and prestige awaited those who, through scholarship, passed one or more of the civil service examinations and thus became holders of a degree and perhaps an appointment in government. In addition, a certain flexibility permitted one whose family had enough money to purchase a degree. This solid, traditional system maintained the influence of the ruling elite and served the interests of its members. It was not to be disturbed by a few unruly barbarians on the coast and in the ports.

The Economic Pattern. Finally, China's unresponsiveness was a rather natural result of a very old economic system. It was a system very unsuited to the new commercial, industrial, and technological movements which at the time were propelling the expansion of Europe and leading it into such ventures as the Canton trade and the first treaty settlement. China's wealth was concentrated in a massive farm economy, worked by an almost unlimited supply of labor skilled in ancient methods of tilling the soil. Marketing, trade, and household industry were important but entirely subsidiary factors. Furthermore, Chinese economic doctrine was concerned largely with the proper use of revenue in public works, such as canals for transport and irrigation projects, rather than with the encouragement of economic growth. Capital accumulation and investment were on a very limited scale. In general, production simply equalled consumption, thereby creating the assumption of economic self-sufficiency. Modern science, technology, and entrepreneurship, which at this time were opening new economic and political vistas in the West, had not touched the Chinese economy.

FOR FURTHER READING

China Trade. Michael Greenberg, *British Trade and the Opening of China, 1800-1842*

(1951). Yen-p'ing Hao, *The Comprador in Nineteenth Century China: Bridge between East and West* (1970). Nathan A. Pelcovits, *Old China Hands and the Foreign Office* (1948) presents the thesis that the British government resisted efforts of its merchants to make the Middle Kingdom another India. Wu Wen-tsao, *The Chinese Opium Question in British Opinion and Action* (1928). George C. Allen and Audrey G. Donnithorne, *Western Enterprise in Far Eastern Economic Development: China and Japan* (1954) describes methods and policies pursued by Western firms. George Lanning and Samuel Couling, *The History of Shanghai* (2 vols., 1921-1923). E. J. Eitel, *Europe in China: The History of Hong Kong from the Beginning to the Year 1882* (1895).

American Interests Foster Rhea Dulles, *The Old China Trade* (1930). George H. Danton, *The Culture Contacts of the United States and China, 1784-1844* (1931). Two articles by Jacques M. Downs, "American Merchants and the China Opium Trade, 1800-1840," *Business History Review,* 42 (1968), 418-42; and "Fair Game: Explorative Role—Myths and the American Opium Trade," *Pacific Historical Review,* 41 (1972), 133-50. James Kirker, *Adventures to China: Americans in the Southern Oceans, 1792-1812* (1970). John K. Fairbank, "'American China Policy' to 1899: A Misconception," *Pacific Historical Review* 39 (1970), 409-20. Arthur H. Clark, *The Clipper Ship Era: An Epitome of Famous American and British Clipper Ships, Their Owners, Builders, Commanders, and Crews, 1843-1869* (1910).

Anglo-Chinese War. P.C. Kuo, *A Critical History of the First Anglo-Chinese War* (1935). Peter Fay, "The French Catholic Mission in China During the Opium War," *Modern Asian Studies* 4 (1970), 145-61; and "The Protestant Mission and the Opium War," *Pacific Historical Review,* 40 (1971), 145-61. Maurice Collis, *Foreign Mud* (1947),* a popular account of the opium dispute at Canton and of the Anglo-Chinese war that followed. Teng Ssu-yu, *Chang Hsi and the Treaty of Nanking, 1842* (1944) presents an annotated translation of a Chinese diary kept during the First Anglo-Chinese War.

Chinese Politics. Gideon Ch'en, *Lin Tse-hsu, Pioneer Promoter of the Adoption of Western*

Means of Maritime Defense in China (1934).*
Li Chien-nung, *The Political History of China,
1840-1928,* ed. and trans. by Teng Ssu-yu and
Jeremy Ingals (1956; reprint 1963)* contains
valuable chapters on the mid-nineteenth century. Alfred K. L. Ho, "The Grand Council in
The Ch'ing Dynasty," *Far Eastern Quarterly* [11]
(1952), 167-82.

The New Sino-Western Order in East Asia: 1848–1860

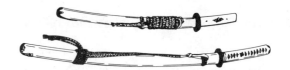

7

The first Sino-Western treaties formed the beginnings of a new order for East Asia. These agreements called for treaty relations based on a theory of the equality of states to replace the Confucian theory of relations between people that were unequal. By equality, of course, the Westerner often meant his own superiority. A victory of British arms had ordained a new order to regulate the meeting and mingling of Western states with China's Confucian society. The creation of treaty ports, the arrival of consuls, the appearance of concessions and settlements, the application of the new treaty tariff and of extraterritoriality gave tangible evidence that an old order was passing and that a new one was appearing. These obvious changes from the procedures of pre-treaty days are easily stated, but the statement itself cannot present an adequate picture of the conflict in manners and values between Confucian China and an equality-minded West. Britain had won a war, but the settlement she had imposed was to operate in an alien environment, where the Western barbarian, assuming the role of reformer in asserting his equality, was not welcome. He was feared because of his military power, but he was not respected. Thus the preliminary steps in the application of the new

order posed many questions about the future. Would this order, even if China observed the treaties, satisfy the commercial ambitions of the Westerners? How far and how rapidly could the Manchu government go toward enforcing a treaty system so repugnant to traditional Confucian concepts of foreign relations and trade? Answers to these and related questions form the basic history of the turbulent years in Sino-Western relations from 1848 to 1860. The outcome was a compromise, acceptable but not satisfactory to either side.

The crisis confronting the Manchu empire in the decade 1850 to 1860 was perhaps no less acute than that faced by Commissioner Lin at Canton in 1839. Great Britain had won the first war but was clearly dissatisfied with the ensuing peace. By 1850 most of the foreigners in the five ports regarded the first treaty settlements as inadequate if not a complete failure. Their major question was whether this settlement could be revised by diplomacy or would require resort to arms. To compound this threatening situation, conditions of political disintegration within China in some measure deprived the Manchu government of both the will and the power either to enforce or repudiate the treaties and their broad implications. The days of the great K'ang-hsi emperor (1662-1722) and the Ch'ien-lung emperor (1736-1796) were long since past. China was now almost devoid of leadership.

Thus continuing conflict between China and the West was nurtured from three principal sources: (1) the decline of Manchu power, hastened by the T'ai-p'ing and other rebellions; (2) the incapacity of the official hierarchy to adjust itself to the new order of foreign intercourse with its broad social and economic implications; and (3) the growing cooperation and strength of the treaty powers in their quest for wider and more stable commercial relations with the Middle Kingdom.

THE T'AI-P'ING REBELLION

Rebellion is an old institution in China, sanctioned by Confucian philosophy and essential in the theory of the Mandate of Heaven. When a dynasty, for whatever reason, lost its ability to rule, it was obvious that Heaven had withdrawn its mandate. The duty of the subject to rebel was then clear. This ancient theory was to enjoy wide application in nineteenth-century China. In the two decades preceding the first British war, revolts had occurred with alarming frequency in Kwangsi, Shansi, Kweichow, Kiangsi, Hainan, Hupeh, and Formosa. By mid-century there were four rebellions of major proportions: Moslem rebellions in Yunnan (1855-1873) and the Northwest (1862-1873), the Nien rebellion (1853-68), and the T'ai-p'ing rebellion (1851-1864). In these upheavals the most serious threat to the dynasty was the T'ai-p'ing rebellion.

No single condition created all this disorder. China suffered from dynastic decline, official corruption, overtaxation, excessive land rents, and official discrimination against minority groups. Compounding these troubles was a population that had increased out of proportion to land under cultivation; in 1850 China's population had reached 430 million, a 200 percent increase during Ch'ing rule, while arable land during the same period had expanded only 35 percent. As a result of these circumstances and of economic dislocations created by grow-

ing foreign trade, the peasant was degraded to virtual serfdom. Thus a permanent, floating "population of paupers" provided the raw materials for rebellion.[1]

In these circumstances there appeared one Hung Hsiu-ch'üan, a native of Hua-hsien near Canton, the youngest and brightest son of a farm family. Young Hung passed the local examinations, but failed repeatedly in the provincial tests. To this background of disappointment and failure were added mystical visions and some contacts with the Reverend Issachar Roberts, an American Baptist missionary at Canton. With the mental and spiritual equip-

[1] The nature, the meaning, and the ultimate influence of the T'ai-p'ing movement on China's twentieth-century revolutionaries (Sun Yat-sen and later the Communists) continues to be a subject of intensive research and debate. A few studies from the rich literature on the subject may be noted. On background, Frederic Wakeman, Jr., *Strangers at the Gate: Social Disorder in South China, 1839-1861* (1966); Jean Chesneaux, ed., *Popular Movements and Secret Societies in China, 1840-1850* (1972). On the literature itself, Ssu-yu Teng, *Historiography of the Taiping Rebellion* (1962).* On the sources, Franz Michael, *The Taiping Rebellion: History and Documents* (3 vols., 1966-1971)* notes the uniqueness of the T'ai-p'ings in their attack on the whole traditional social order. See also Ssu-yu Teng, *New Light on the History of the Taiping Rebellion* (1950); Vincent Y. C. Shih, *The Taiping Ideology: Its Sources, Interpretations and Influences* (1967);* Eugene P. Boardman, *Christian Influence upon the Ideology of the Taiping Rebellion, 1851-1864* (1952); G. E. Taylor, "The Taiping Rebellion: Its Economic Background and Social Theory," *Chinese Social and Political Science Review,* 16 (1933), 545-49.

On other major uprisings of the mid-century note the following: Chiang Siang-tsch, *The Nien Rebellion* (1954); Ssu-yu Teng, *The Nien Army and Their Guerrilla Warfare* (1961).* Wen-Djang Chu, *The Moslem Rebellion in Northwest China 1862-1878* (1966).* The Moslem rising spread from Shensi to Sinkiang covering almost one-fourth of China's territory. Like the T'ai-p'ing, it took unknown millions of lives.

A spirited debate continues as to whether the T'ai-p'ing movement was a rebellion or an attempted revolution, and on whether or not it was primarily an agrarian peasant movement.

An indispensable reference on the leadership of China's three modern revolutions (the T'ai-p'ing, the Republican, and the Communist) is Chun-tu Hsueh, ed., *Revolutionary Leaders of Modern China* (1971).* Note especially the introduction by Howard L. Boorman.

ment thus provided, Hung came to believe that he was commissioned to restore the worship of the true god. His original organization, the *Pai Shang-ti Hui* (Association of God Worshippers), soon recruited an enormous following from disaffected elements in Kwangsi. What first appeared to be an iconoclastic religious movement superficially bearing some resemblance to Protestantism, soon changed its course dramatically. As it grew, its devastating armies moved north to the Yangtze and captured Nanking, where its capital was established in 1853. Meanwhile Hung bestowed upon himself the title *Tien-wang* (Heavenly King), professed to rule over the *T'ai-p'ing T'ien-kuo* (The Heavenly Kingdom of Great Peace), and set for his purpose the overthrow of the Manchu dynasty. In this new theocracy God was the Heavenly Father, Christ the Divine Elder Brother, and the *T'ai-p'ing Wang* (Hung himself) the Divine Younger Brother. The Christian component in the movement was virtually restricted to the first five books of the Old Testament. Such was the notable achievement of this soured and disappointed member of the learned proletariat.

THE REBELLION AND THE FOREIGN POWERS

During the winter of 1853-1854, Hung and his rebels advanced to the north and reached the outskirts of Tientsin, but did not continue on to Peking. For the next decade they dominated the Yangtze valley in defiance of Manchu authority. A rebellion so widespread, promoting a government that threatened to rival if not overthrow the Manchus, could not but attract the attention of the foreign powers. If the T'ai-p'ing were Christians, would they not be more amenable than the Manchus to foreign treaty relations, to the commercial, social, and political concepts of the Westerners?[2] The powers realized the importance of defining their rela-

tion to the rebels when, in 1853, the Chinese walled city of Shanghai, on the very border of the foreign settlements, was captured by a rebel band known as the "Small Swords." Civil war had thus reached the edge of the settlements and retreating imperial authorities deserted the Shanghai customs house. This raised the question of whether Shanghai had become a free port, since the Chinese government was no longer capable of collecting the duties. But British and American consular authorities notified their nationals that the consuls themselves would collect the duties during the absence of imperial authorities. The British consul required his merchants to deposit promissory notes, which in fact were never paid, while the Americans were at the disadvantage of having to pay in specie. Merchants who had no consular representative took advantage of the circumstances and paid nothing. British policy also stipulated that the Shanghai settlement was to remain neutral in the civil strife that surrounded it, but in reality foreign merchants constantly gave aid to the rebels in the sale of supplies. Many ships entered and cleared the port without the payment of duties. It was during this period of confusion, inequality, and uncertainty that the rate-payers of the settlement established their own municipal council.

THE FOREIGN INSPECTORATE OF CUSTOMS

From this crisis, which in Shanghai had temporarily destroyed the power of the Peking government and threatened likewise the whole treaty structure built by the foreigners, there emerged a remarkable institution—the Foreign

---

[2] Since the foreign powers gave some support to the Manchu campaign of suppressing the rebels in the later years of the T'ai-p'ing rebellion, it should be remarked that in the early stages of the revolt the T'ai-p'ings do not appear to have been antiforeign. British, French, and American contacts with the T'ai-p'ings in 1853-54 were generally cordial. Because of

their 18 principles of human brotherhood and their realistic appraisal of Western power, the rebels tended to invite Western support. Hung Jen-k'an, a cousin of the rebel leader and T'ai-p'ing foreign minister, was an advocate of the adoption of Western institutions. The Western powers, however, were half-hearted in responding to the T'ai-p'ings' overtures. Note Teng Yuan Chung, "The Failure of Hung Jen-k'an's Foreign Policy," *Journal of Asian Studies,* 28 (1968), 125-38; and Stephen Uhalley, Jr., "A New Look at the Diplomatic Missions of 1853-54 to T'ai-p'ing-Held Nanking," *Chung Chi Journal,* 6 (1967), 171-90. The ultimate collapse of the rebellion is discussed in Chapter 12 in its chronological context.

SHANGHAI AND THE YANGTZE

Inspectorate of Customs. By agreement between the *tao-t'ai* and the consuls of the three treaty powers, Britain, the United States, and France (June 29, 1854), provision was made for the appointment of a board of foreign customs inspectors, for the creation of an adequate customs machinery, and for regulations that should define the relation of the inspectorate to the *tao-t'ai*, the consuls, and the commercial public. At first the appointing power was given to the consuls, and it was the purpose of the British consul that the British should control the new inspectorate; but within a year the British Foreign Office had ruled that the foreign inspectors were officials of China and not of the foreign countries. Thus was formed the nucleus of a new Chinese customs administration, directed by foreign inspectors, which, in 1858, was extended to all the treaty ports, where it became a model of efficient government.[3]

Throughout these early years of the T'ai-p'ing revolt, the efforts of the major treaty powers to determine what policy they should follow relative to the T'ai-p'ings were hampered by public opinion in Europe and in America. In the United States, where "Manifest Destiny"

had become the slogan of the decade, many saw evidence of a divine plan in the opening of China to Western trade. The subsequent rebellion of the T'ai-p'ings was God's instrument, destined to overthrow the Manchu dynasty and to hasten the advent of a Chinese Christian republic. Once the T'ai-p'ings had prepared the way, it was said, China would progress to republicanism and Christianity, aided by the educational forces of commercial intercourse and Christian missions. The sources on which these comforting predictions were based were rarely questioned. It was enough that the predictions were in accord with what many Americans wanted to believe.

THE OBLIGATIONS OF EXTRATERRITORIALITY

It should be noted that the growing crisis in the treaty system was not due solely to Chinese

---

[3] For detailed studies of the customs problem at Shanghai in this period, see J. K. Fairbank, "The Provisional System at Shanghai," *Chinese Social and Political Science Review,* 18 (1934-35), 455-504, and 19 (1935-36), 65-124; "The Creation of the Foreign Inspectorate of Customs at Shanghai," *ibid.,* 19 (1935-36), 469-514, and 20 (1936-37), 42-100; "The Definition of the Foreign Inspector's Status (1854-55): A Chapter in the Early History of the Inspectorate of Customs at Shanghai," *Nankai Social*

and Economic Quarterly, 9 (1936), 125-63; and *Trade and Diplomacy on the China Coast,* (2 vols., V 1953),* 371-461.

The new Chinese customs service, the so-called Foreign Inspectorate, created by joint Chinese and foreign action in 1854, became truly unique among civil services of the world, testifying to the fact that in domestic and international relations it is possible to operate on those rare qualities of efficiency and integrity where there is the purpose and the will to do so. The service was unique in its origins, in the political context in which it operated for a century, and in its devotion to honest administration. It was unique in the composition of its staff, which at times included twenty-three nationalities. It was unique in that successive heads of the service, though appointed by the Chinese government, were foreigners enjoying extraterritorial status. Moreover, the service was unique in the variety of duties it was called upon at various times to perform. While its chief function was the collecting and reporting of the customs revenue, the service also became China's most reliable fiscal agent. It was an invaluable auxiliary in liquidating the war indemnities exacted by Britain and France in 1860. In the early twentieth century it stood between China and bankruptcy in the case of the Boxer indemnity and during the financial troubles of the revolution of 1911. It functioned repeatedly as the Peking government's most trusted counselor. It helped to train China's first modern diplomats and consuls. It organized and for many years administered China's modern, infant post office and, in addition, performed many other functions not related immediately to the customs. Stanley F. Wright, *Hart and the Chinese Customs* (1950).

obstructionism and political decline. The Western governments were at times negligent in their obligations toward China. The application of extraterritoriality was a case in point. In acquiring extraterritorial jurisdiction over their nationals in China, the treaty powers had won a legal right of the greatest consequence. But the practice of extraterritoriality carried with it grave responsibilities, which, for many years, most of the powers treated with shameful disregard. At first only the British recognized and sought to meet their extraterritorial obligations.

Since under the extraterritorial grants China had surrendered the power of her own courts over foreigners, it became the duty of the treaty powers to provide competent consular courts in the treaty ports, and jails where criminals might be incarcerated. Prior to 1857, Great Britain alone took adequate steps to meet this need. A British criminal court, provided for in 1833, functioned at Canton after 1839. In 1843 an act of Parliament authorized British legal jurisdiction on foreign soil and provided the machinery for the administration of extraterritoriality, and of jails, in China. In contrast, American criminals in Chinese ports could be confined only on a national ship or, as frequently happened, by courtesy in a British jail. In 1858 American criminals were released from the British jail in Shanghai because the American consul had no funds for jail expenses. Two

years later the United States provided its first appropriation for consular jails in China.[4]

THE GROWTH OF THE OPIUM TRADE

Since 1842 the opium trade had continued to grow and to prosper. Although opium had provided the occasion for the First Sino-British war, the subsequent treaties had evaded the problem of control. Thus, although the importation of opium was still prohibited by the laws of China, foreigners and Chinese conspired to flood the market with this contraband and demoralizing drug.[5] It has been estimated that between 1840 and 1858 the annual imports increased almost 300 percent. The effects upon the Chinese were devastating, but so long as the Chinese government would not or could not enforce its law, there was little hope that the foreigners would forego a trade so profitable.

DEMANDS FOR TREATY REVISION

By 1854, despite the growth of profitable trade at Shanghai and Canton, it was evident that the

[4]For an extended treatment, see G. W. Keeton, *The Development of Extraterritoriality in China* (2 vols., 1928).

[5]*The Times* correspondent reported, 1857: "At present the [opium] trade is as open and as unrestrained in all the cities of China as the sale of hot-

Foreign factories at Canton, 1855
Tea chests are being loaded in the
foreground.

relations of China and the treaty powers were far from healthy. The abuses of extra-territoriality, a flagrant traffic in coolies for servitude in Cuba, the opium trade, and the gunboat policy of shooting first and talking afterwards, all served to reinforce the official Chinese view that the foreign barbarians were an uncouth and troublesome lot with whom China should have as few dealings as possible. On his part, the foreigner, both merchant and consul, was convinced that China had no respect for treaties and no understanding of the benefits of free commerce and free access to markets. The foreigners now regarded the treaties of 1842-1844 as inadequate, not only because China had frequently evaded them but also because these treaties confined foreign trade to the five ports. The foreign trader was still a stranger to China's vast interior; the foreign diplomat was still a stranger to Peking. Both the American and the French treaties of 1844 provided for revision after twelve years, and the British claimed this same privilege on the basis of most-favored-nation treatment. Under this claim the British held that the Treaty of Nanking would be subject to revision in 1854.

The scope of Britain's policy of treaty revision had been determined by February, 1854. The British government would insist on China's recognition of the *right* of immediate revision, but the actual revision might be delayed in view of China's domestic strife due to the T'ai-p'ing rebellion. Meanwhile, the British would seek cooperation with the Americans and the French. Britain wanted access generally to the whole interior of the Chinese Empire as well as to the cities on the coast; or failing this, free navigation of the Yangtze River and access to the cities on its banks up to Nanking. Britain also wanted legalization of the opium trade, in order that it might be limited and controlled, and abolition of internal transit duties on goods imported or purchased for export. Finally, the British government desired

"the permanent and honourable residence at the Court of Peking of a Representative of the British Crown" or provision for direct and unobstructed correspondence with that government. These official British objectives also represented approximately those general principles beginning to appear in French and American policy.

The British desire to be represented diplomatically at Peking indicated, among other things, that they were no longer willing to tolerate the Chinese system whereby the Canton viceroy was entrusted by Peking with the actual conduct of foreign affairs. With this official alone the foreigners were expected to deal, and their experience had not recommended the system. In 1848 John W. Davis, the American commissioner, after great difficulty secured an interview with the viceroy for the purpose of presenting his credentials. He was treated "with extreme rudeness" by both viceroy and governor. In fact, after 1852 "the practice of ignoring the foreign representatives became a part of the settled policy of the Chinese government."[6] A French diplomat remained at Macao fifteen months vainly awaiting a personal interview with a qualified Chinese official. Of the various successors of Davis in the period to 1855, none succeeded in securing an interview. The high commissioner was always "too busy," and in any event would have to await the dawn of "an auspicious day." Two American commissioners, Humphrey Marshall and Robert McLane, went to Nanking hoping to make direct contact with responsible officials, only to be referred back to Canton.

[6] H. B. Morse, *The International Relations of the Chinese Empire* (3 vols., 1910-1918; Taiwan ed., 1963), I, 411.

Since the Western trader was dealing with a society in China he did not understand and with a language he could rarely write or speak, business was conducted through the medium of a unique group of Chinese known as compradors. The comprador was indispensable to the foreign firm. He operated both as a Chinese and as a Western business man. Inevitably he became an agent of economic growth and change, and he was suspect in the eyes of his own countrymen as the agent of foreign traders. Yen-p'ing Hao, *The Comprador in Nineteenth Century China* (1970).

cross buns on Good Friday in the streets of London." George Wingrove Cooke, *China: Being The Times Special Correspondence from China in the Years 1857-58* (1858), 179.

Thus in 1854 the foreign traders and most of their consular and diplomatic associates were of a mind not only to extend their commercial rights but also to convert China, forcibly if necessary, to Western concepts of international law and diplomacy.

England's plan for treaty revision did not anticipate an immediate resort to war. There was to be no precipitate action. Actually the British government hoped for a cooperative policy with France and the United States. Among American merchants in the treaty ports there was general support for Britain's policy of treaty revision. This was natural because the interests of British and American traders were in many respects identical. Some support for British policy was contained, too, in the dispatches of various American commissioners in China.

In view then of the general harmony between British and American expressions of policy, England's proposals to the United States (March, 1857) for a three-power alliance (the United States, France, and Great Britain) to effect revision of the treaties were not surprising. These proposals, however, were declined; yet the dangers threatening American interests in China did prompt the appointment of William B. Reed as envoy extraordinary and minister plenipotentiary to the court of Peking.

Finally, by the early autumn of 1856, with the crisis of the Crimean War already past, Great Britain determined on a diplomatic and naval move toward Peking to hasten revision of the treaties, to expand commercial intercourse, and to destroy the exclusiveness of Chinese policy at Canton.

A JUDICIAL MURDER

In forwarding this policy Britain could count on the support of France, for in February, 1856, a French Catholic missionary, Auguste Chapdelaine, had been put to death by Chinese authorities at Sinlin in Kwangsi. Chapdelaine and some of his converts had been arrested on a charge that they were rebels—a natural enough charge, for Kwangsi had witnessed the beginnings of the T'ai-p'ing rebellion with its Christian trappings. The arrest, torture, and execution of the foreign priest and his followers are thus understandable, according to Chinese ideas at the time. The Chinese magistrate could also rest his case on the fact that under the treaties no foreigners were allowed beyond the treaty ports. Furthermore, the testimony of Catholic missionaries themselves reveals that they indoctrinated their Chinese converts with the idea of looking to "France as their support and liberator" against persecution.[7] China's fault lay in the fact that the execution of the priest violated the extraterritorial rights of France.

News of this so-called "judicial murder" reached Canton in July, 1856. It was not unwelcome to Napoleon III. France was now in a position not only to assist Great Britain in forcing, if need be, a revision of the treaties, but also to aid the Catholic Church by political means in the spiritual conquest of China. By October, 1856, France and England were able to agree upon a common policy of force.

THE AFFAIR OF THE LORCHA ARROW

The incident that was to precipitate hostilities between Great Britain and China found its origin in a system by which Chinese coasting vessels acquired temporary register under foreign flags. During the years 1853-1854, southern Chinese rebels held positions so strong in the regions of Canton and Kowloon that communications between Whampoa (the Canton anchorage) and Hong Kong were frequently broken so far as the passage of Chinese vessels was concerned. Even Commissioner Yeh asked help from the despised foreigners. In 1855 English and American authorities, in order to maintain trade between Hong Kong and Canton, believed it was necessary to grant English and United States flags with a passport to Chinese lighters for a single trip to and from Canton and Whampoa to be immediately returned and filed at the consulates by which they were issued. Out of this situation arose various ordinances of the colonial government of Hong Kong permitting residents of the colony, including Chinese, under prescribed conditions, to use the British flag on their vessels for this limited purpose. In time this right by ordinance was abused. Some

[7] W. C. Constin, *Great Britain and China 1833-1860* (1937), 202.

vessels used the protection of the British flag to engage in the smuggling trade; others carried the flags of various foreign powers with no authority whatsoever for doing so; sometimes merchant consuls, without authority from their governments, issued foreign registry to native craft. As a result it was soon difficult for Chinese authorities to distinguish between the legitimate and the illegitimate use of foreign flags by native craft.

Then, on October 8, 1856, the lorcha *Arrow,* owned by a Chinese who had resided in Hong Kong for ten years and commanded by a British subject, was boarded by Chinese police while it was lying at anchor in the river at Canton. Twelve of her Chinese crew of fourteen were arrested on charges of piracy and removed to a Chinese war-junk. Harry Parkes, British consul at Canton, promptly demanded release of the captives on the ground that the *Arrow* was a British ship carrying colonial registry from Hong Kong, that she had been boarded without communication first having been made to the British consul, and that the British flag had been hauled down by the Chinese police. British authorities at Hong Kong supported Parkes by demanding an apology and guarantees for the future.[8] The prisoners were eventually handed over by Yeh, but Consul Parkes refused to accept their release since the captives were accompanied neither by a Chinese officer of rank nor by an apology.

British naval forces thereupon attacked the forts guarding the approach to Canton. On October 29, the walls of the city were breached; but though the British could attack the city, they had insufficient forces to occupy it. In the heat of these proceedings the American flag too was fired upon by Chinese forts—a fire that was returned by American ships of war. Trade was now at an end, yet Commissioner Yeh refused all concessions.

In England, the British action was approved despite vigorous criticism from the opposition; and now that France was prepared for full

---

[8] The British registry on the *Arrow* had expired before the seizure. Chinese authorities disputed Parkes' allegation that the British flag had been lowered.

cooperation in treaty revision, the British government appointed Lord Elgin to head a special embassy. Elgin's mission was not merely to solve local grievances at Canton or elsewhere; he was to extend the opportunities for foreign trade and to establish diplomatic representation at Peking. In other words, he was to revise the treaties thoroughly.

War was now certain. The "murder" of the French priest and the affair of the *Arrow* were the convenient pretexts for armed action, the real causes of which were far more fundamental than these incidents. Britain regarded China's obstructive policy as a menace both to her actual and to her potential commercial interests, while the conduct of Chinese officials— that of Yeh in particular—was looked upon as an insult to the crown. Napoleon III was happy to be associated with the British policy. A victorious war in China would appeal to French business and the avenging of a priest's death and the providing for future religious guarantees would appeal to French Catholics and the Papacy.

After much delay, due to the diversion of British contingents to suppress the Indian Mutiny, British and French forces bombarded and captured Canton in December, 1857. British marines seized the venerable but proud and obstinate High Commissioner Yeh as this portly gentleman sought to escape over the back wall of his yamen. Fifteen months later he died, a prisoner of war, in India. Until 1860, Canton was ruled by Chinese officials acting at the command of a British and French commission.

On February 11, 1858, Britain and France were joined by the United States and Russia— through their representatives, William B. Reed and Admiral Count Putiatin—in simultaneous notes to Peking making clear the united demand of the powers for treaty revision and religious toleration, and suggesting negotiations at Shanghai. To the Chinese demand that negotiations be conducted at Canton, the representatives of the powers replied by sailing north to the mouth of the Pei-ho, at the very gateway to Peking. Alarmed by this maneuver, the Chinese court appointed the viceroy of Chihli to negotiate, but his powers were regarded by

Lord Elgin and Baron Gros of France as inadequate. They believed that only an advance to Tientsin would bring the Chinese to terms. To this end they demanded the surrender of the Taku forts guarding the mouth of the river; when this was refused, the forts were stormed and taken (May 20). Peking thereupon promptly appointed officials whose powers were regarded as adequate. Negotiations leading to new treaties were conducted with all four powers, concurrently but separately. Before the end of June, 1858, the four treaties of Tientsin had been signed.[9]

THE TREATIES OF TIENTSIN, 1858

The treaties of Tientsin were a revision and an enlargement of principles and practices set forth in the first treaties of 1842-1844. Since England and France had employed force, it was their treaties that embodied the new and valuable concessions, which, however, by reason of the most-favored-nation clause, would be enjoyed likewise by Russia and the United States. In this sense the four treaties constituted a single settlement and had a profound influence upon China's relations with the West.[10]

The new and significant privileges won by the treaty powers in the Tientsin treaties included:

1. The right to maintain a resident minister at Peking, or the right of the minister, at the

discretion of his government, to visit the capital. The minister should "not be called upon to perform any ceremony derogatory to him as representing the sovereign of an independent nation on a footing of equality with that of China."
2. The right to travel in all parts of the interior under passports issued by the foreign consuls and countersigned by the local Chinese authorities.
3. The right of foreign ships to trade on the Yangtze river, and the opening of additional treaty ports.[11]
4. The right of missionaries to protection by the Chinese authorities, since "the Christian religion, as professed by Protestants or Roman Catholics, inculcates the practice of virtue, and teaches man to do as he would be done by."[12]

The Tientsin treaties represented a common policy on the part of the four powers, for although England and France alone had used force, the United States and Russia insisted on most-favored-nation treatment. The most striking concession was the right of residence of foreign ministers at Peking, or at least the right of these ministers to visit the capital. The delay and evasion that China had constantly practiced in dealing with foreign governments would now be more difficult.

The grant of toleration to Christians, missionaries, and their Chinese converts was to become a subject of much controversy. To toleration in principle there could be no objection, but in 1858 toleration was won as a result of war and was granted in the clause of a treaty exacted as a result of war. The missionaries were already well aware that many elements in Christian doctrine had proved disruptive of China's cultural heritage; yet, since the object of the missionaries was to make this heritage subservient to Christianity, they welcomed the

[9] A study of contemporary British records is Douglas Hurd, *The Arrow War: An Anglo-Chinese Confusion* (1967). When seen in historical perspective, the affair of the lorcha *Arrow* was a weak excuse for a war. Sir John Bowring, the Governor of Hong Kong, was flexible in his treatment of the Chinese but inflexible toward their government. In the *Arrow* case "he provoked hostilities by magnifying a comparatively trivial incident. . . ." G. B. Endacott, *Government and People in Hong Kong, 1841-1962 (1964), 56.* On China's relations with her neighbors and the Western powers (1858-1880) see Immanuel C. Y. Hsu, *China's Entrance into the Family of Nations, The Diplomatic Phase, 1858-1880* (1960).

[10] It has been stated with some justification that "it became ingloriously, yet very profitably, the role of the United States pacifically to follow England to China in the wake of war, and to profit greatly by the victories of British arms." Tyler Dennett, *Americans in Eastern Asia* (1922), 159.

[11] To the five ports opened by the treaty of 1842 were added Chefoo in Shantung, Chinkiang and Nanking in Kiangsu, Hankow in Hupeh, Kiukiang in Kiangsi, Kiungchow in Hainan, Newchwang in Manchuria, Swatow in Kwangtung, Wenchow in Chekiang.

[12] All quotations are from the British treaty. The extraterritorial rights of foreigners were further defined in criminal cases. For a full account of the Tientsin negotiations see Hsu, *China's Entrance,* 21-118.

new treaty status for themselves and for their religion. As a consequence after 1858 many Chinese felt quite justified in regarding Christianity as a political as well as a religious weapon of the West.

The right of foreigners to travel in the interior was another concession on which interpretation differed widely. The traders of 1858 had complained bitterly of the restrictions that confined them to the treaty ports. They were businessmen intent on profits, and these same profits, they felt, would depend in turn on freedom of access to the entire country. Against this point of view the Chinese could argue that the people were not yet ready to receive foreigners beyond the port towns, and that, because the foreigner enjoyed extraterritoriality and would be far removed from his nearest consul when in the interior, China could exercise over him only an ineffective control if he were allowed to travel freely.

Since the powers were now bent on expanding their commerce with China, the opening of additional treaty ports (nine in China and one in Taiwan) could not long be delayed. Nevertheless, the opening of the additional ports did occasion trouble, and in the case of Nanking the port was not opened until 1899. In addition, the admission of foreign vessels to the trade of the Yangtze was a concession which could hardly be justified from the Chinese point of view. It was the great artery to the richest areas of China. The fact that the foreigners could demand and be granted access to China's coasting and inland trade is the most eloquent testimony to the decay of the Manchu dynasty.

LEGALIZATION OF THE OPIUM TRADE

Following the Tientsin settlement, negotiations were adjourned to Shanghai, where a revised schedule of rates in the conventional tariff was adopted, providing a general 5 per cent duty on exports and imports. But more significant than this revision was the legalization of the opium trade at a duty of 30 taels per 100 catties.[13]

[13] One catty equals 1-1/3 lbs.; a tael was about 1-1/3 ounces of silver.

This new legal status of opium was a triumph for British policy, which, since 1842, had been consistent, and probably sound, despite the fact that it appeared to support a nefarious traffic. The British argument ran as follows: since the Nanking settlement, the importation of opium, a contraband trade, had increased rapidly. Although most of the opium was produced in India, other sources of supply were available, and therefore prohibition by the British authorities was not likely to prove effective in stopping the trade, though it would materially reduce Indian revenue. It was the business of China to enforce her laws against an illicit traffic. England would not give protection to subjects violating China's laws, but neither would she undertake to enforce the laws for China. Since China had failed to enforce the law against opium, the trade should be legalized at a fixed duty and strictly supervised.[14]

The attitude of the United States at this time to the opium question is also of interest. Minister Reed had been instructed that his government would not seek legalization of the opium traffic, and thus the treaty that Reed signed at Tientsin made no mention of opium. But later, in discussions with Lord Elgin, Reed came to the view that "any course is better than that which is now pursued." He therefore supported the principle of legalization, and his action in this respect was accepted by his government. American business in general approved of the Tientsin treaties since it believed that, as trade with China continued to increase, cotton alone would probably more than repay the annual deficits on the imports of tea and silk.

[14] J. K. Fairbank, "The Legalization of the Opium Trade Before the Treaties of 1858," *Chinese Social and Political Science Review,* 17 (1933), 215, points out that although the imperial government in Peking took no steps to levy an official impost on opium trade before 1858, nevertheless "the unofficial or private taxation of the traffic by local [Chinese] authorities . . . appears to have been put gradually on a more regular basis." Thus the taxing of opium was applied by the Chinese authorities at some of the ports before the legalization clause was written into the treaties of 1858. Legalization served two purposes: it provided China with needed revenue, and it stabilized an important item of the foreign trade by placing it on a treaty basis.

The treaties of Tientsin were approved by the Chinese government in 1858 before the British and French forces left Tientsin. They were not to become effective, however, until ratified copies had been exchanged *at Peking*. This was done without difficulty in the case of the Russian treaty. The new Russian minister, General Nikolai Ignatiev, proceeded to Peking by the old overland route and was promptly received. The British, the French, and the American envoys, accompanied by ships of war, arrived at the mouth of the Pei-ho in June, 1859. Here it was discovered that the Chinese had strengthened the forts at Taku and had blocked the river's mouth. The envoys were informed, but only when it was too late, that they would be received at P'ei-t'ang, ten miles farther north on the coast. China intended to repel any attempt to enter the river at Taku. The British and French therefore attempted to storm the forts and break the barrier—an attempt in which they failed utterly. Accordingly, they were forced to return to Shanghai.[15]

Hostilities had thus been precipitated and a second chapter in the *Arrow* War was now inevitable. Again, the question of responsibility is difficult to assess. The British envoy, Frederick Bruce, had been instructed that it would be desirable for him to reach Tientsin in a British ship of war, but that, since definite rules of procedure could not be laid down in London, the envoy was to use discretion when to give way and when to stand firm. Bruce, faced with dilatory Chinese correspondence and evasion, followed by the blocking of the river at Taku, came to the conclusion that this was the time to stand firm. When he insisted on the approach through Taku and Tientsin he was not violating his instructions, but he *was* demanding something not granted by the British treaty. Actually neither British nor French policy in this instance could be justified in law. Both the policy and Bruce's decision were political. They rested on the conviction, for which there was considerable ground, that the Peking government had no intention to honor the extensive new concessions it had been forced to grant at Tientsin the previous year.

Meanwhile, John E. Ward, the American envoy, not restricted to any route or place for the exchange of his country's treaty, proceeded to P'ei-t'ang. At Tungchow the Chinese provided carts that carried him and his mission to Peking.[16] This was unfortunate for the dignity of the United States. Ward, a native of Georgia, was a Southern gentleman of some distinction, but being sadly ignorant of the finer points of Oriental procedure he permitted the Chinese to take full advantage of his inexperience. He should have demanded sedan chairs, the mode of conveyance used by high Chinese officials. The cart in which he rode was the kind of vehicle used to carry Korean and other tribute-bearers to the Chinese capital. Over this cart floated banners describing Ward as a tribute-bearer from the United States. Upon his arrival in Peking, Ward was requested to perform the kowtow, which of course he refused to do, and with what must have been splendid dignity informed the Chinese officials that "although he was willing to 'bend the body and slightly crook the right knee,' he was accustomed to kneel only to God and woman."[17] Having delivered himself of this impressive statement, Ward returned to P'ei-t'ang, where copies of the ratified American treaty were exchanged.

Meanwhile, British and French reinforcements reached the Pei-ho. In August, 1860, the allies stormed the Taku forts and advanced on Tientsin and Peking. The Chinese retired in confusion, and when the foreigners entered the capital, the degenerate Manchu emperor had already fled with his court to Jehol, ostensibly on a hunting trip. During the allied march on Peking, thirty-nine foreigners (twenty-six English and thirteen French, including the private secretary of Lord Elgin, who had replaced Bruce as Britain's plenipotentiary) were captured by the Chinese. At the time the victims were presumably protected by a flag of truce; the Chinese appear to have believed that by holding these hostages they would bring the allies to adopt a more moderate policy. Twenty of the prisoners were already dead when the

---

[15] During the engagement, the commander of the American naval forces, whose country was neutral, had nonetheless come to the assistance of his British cousins, explaining his action with the statement that "blood is thicker than water."

[16] The Ward correspondence is in U. S. Senate Executive Document 36-1, (30), 569 ff.

[17] Dennett, *Americans in Eastern Asia,* 342.

survivors were released. As a result, Lord Elgin ordered the burning of the emperor's Summer Palace (Yuan Ming Yuan) situated outside the city, an architectural monument which the French troops had already occupied and looted.[18]

THE PEKING CONVENTIONS, 1860

With the Chinese capital now at their mercy, the allied envoys proceeded to exchange the ratified treaties of 1858 and to exact new concessions, which were embodied in the Conventions of Peking (1860). The emperor of China expressed "his deep regret" that a "misunderstanding" had occurred at Taku the previous year; agreed that the British minister might "reside permanently" at Peking; consented to additional indemnities and to the opening of Tientsin as a treaty port; legalized the coolie trade under regulation; and consented to the cession of Kowloon on the mainland opposite Hong Kong. The French convention secured the restoration to the Roman Catholic Church of all property confiscated since 1724, a provision that was to work great hardship on the Chinese who had acquired the property. This fact does not appear to have troubled the French government or the Church. Both found a convenient justification for taking the property in an imperial edict of 1846, which had promised restoration of religious establishments to Roman Catholics. The Chinese text of the French convention (which was not authoritative) also contained a troublesome provision allowing French missionaries to rent and purchase land and to erect buildings in all provinces.[19]

[18]The Summer Palace extended over an area more than six miles in length, situated at the foot of the first range of hills some five miles to the northwest of Peking. The grounds, which might be described as a great private park, included residences, temples, pagodas, gardens, and artificial hills, some of them 300 feet in height, surrounding a lake.

[19]For a full discussion of the social and political complications arising from this alleged right of Catholic missionaries, see Paul H. Clyde, *United States Policy Toward China; Diplomatic and Public Documents, 1839-1939* (1940: reissued 1964), 107-112.

The most curious phase of events in China during 1860 remains to be told. It was in this year that rebel bands associated with the T'ai-p'ing were threatening to advance upon the wealthy and populous city of Shanghai with its growing foreign settlement. In this extremity the Chinese authorities appealed to the English and French for protection, and these latter agreed to defend the Chinese city and the foreign settlement against any attack. On August 21, 1860, British troops, assisted by some French, repelled the rebels from the walls of Shanghai. It was on this very day that British and French troops in the north were storming the Taku forts and beginning their march on Peking.

The new order in Sino-Western relations formalized by the Tientsin treaties of 1858 and the Peking treaties of 1860, has often been explained exclusively in terms of *imperialism,* a Western movement imposing itself upon an uncooperative China. This interpretation is sound, but it is not the entire explanation. Between 1840 and 1860 imperialism did work its way with China. There was also, however, a concurrent and complementary movement by means of which the Chinese state, long skilled in handling the barbarians of Inner Asia, adjusted itself to the new nineteenth-century Western intruders by drawing upon institutional devices fashioned from long experience. From the Chinese point of view there is evidence to suggest that the treaty system was added to the traditional tribute system with the idea of bringing the foreigner under the influence of the universal Confucian state. The new order was therefore not an exclusively Western creation. Seen in the perspective of Chinese historical experience with the outer barbarians, the treaty ports were modern reflections of the stations assigned for ancient tributary trade. Consular jurisdiction could be compared to the method by which the chief of Arab traders was responsible for the actions of his countrymen in China (see page 59). The most-favored-nation principle could be interpreted as contemporary evidence of the benevolence the Confucian sovereign employed toward all barbarians for the purpose of playing one against another. The treaty tariff, so antagonistic to potential Chinese industry, had its forerunner in the older and onerous Manchu policy of taxation on production and trade. Finally, even the employment of foreigners in Chinese government service had many precedents in China's history. Thus the joint Chinese-Western administration in the treaty ports can be seen as a compromise settlement. The Foreign Inspectorate of Customs at Shanghai was a preeminent example of this dual administration. Imperialism alone, therefore, does not explain what was happening in Chinese-barbarian relations in the nineteenth century.[20]

RUSSIA AND CHINA

While the *Arrow* War had been running its course in China Proper, a new chapter was being enacted in Russo-Chinese relations in northeast Asia. The treaty of Nertchinsk (1689) had been a Manchu victory over Russia, providing stabilization of China's northeastern frontier. The Ch'ing dynasty also sought to protect Manchuria from the south by sealing it off from Chinese influence; Chinese migration to the area was prohibited or limited severely. Manchuria was to be preserved culturally as a land of Manchu customs and values. Such was the official policy; but policy and reality are not always one and the same. Actually, the sinicization of Manchuria went on at an increasing pace during the entire period of Ch'ing rule at Peking. In fact, the very effort to implement the Manchu values of severe frontier militarism made the native inhabitants more susceptible to the lure of Chinese material and ideological culture as Chinese immigration both legal and illegal penetrated the area. Even Manchu governors sent to the northern areas carried with them from Peking a Chinese life style. It thereby came about that by the middle of the nineteenth century the northeast was no longer simply a Manchu cultural preserve. Materially and culturally it was becoming Chinese, no matter what the official policy might be. Both policy and practice failed to provide adequate strength against internal pressures from China

on the south or against external pressures soon to be applied by Russia on the north.[21]

During the second quarter of the nineteenth century, Siberia became increasingly important in Russian domestic and foreign policy. The growth of settlements reaching as far as Kamchatka, the expanding activities of the Russian-American Company in Alaska, and the development of the whaling industry in the Bering Sea all testified to an increasing Russian concern for her Pacific and Chinese frontiers. Furthermore, by the treaty of Nanking (1842) Britain had opened a new era in the maritime trade with China, eclipsing the Russian caravans at Kiakhta. The increasing presence of British naval units in the Pacific stimulated the Russian desire to have ports on the Pacific. In a word, after 1830 both western and eastern Siberia played prominent roles in the thoughts of the Russian government. Then, in 1847, the tsar appointed Count Nikolai Muraviev as governor-general of eastern Siberia with instructions to pursue special investigations of the Amur question. This appointment was soon to result in a new Russian advance both to the east and to the south.[22]

The Policy of Muraviev

The new governor-general applied his policy with promptness and decision. His first agents sailed down the Amur in 1848. This river, it will be recalled, was wholly within the territory of the Manchu empire according to the terms of the treaty of Nertchinsk. The following year Russian officers explored the coasts of the sea of Okhotsk as far south as the mouth of the Amur. This was a preliminary survey in Russia's general plan to prevent occupation of the area by potential enemies: Great Britain and France. Nikolaievsk was founded at the mouth of the Amur in August, 1850. These were the first major violations of the Nertchinsk treaty, to be followed by a vigorous pursuit of the new policy. Russian posts were founded at De Castries, Mariinsk,

[20] Fairbank, *Trade and Diplomacy*, I, 462-468.

[21] Robert H. G. Lee, *The Manchurian Frontier in Ch'ing History* (1970).

[22] T. C. Lin, "The Amur Frontier Question Between China and Russia, 1850-1860," *Pacific Historical Review*, 3 (1934), 1-27.

and Imperatorski bay in 1852. Sakhalin island was annexed in 1853.[23]

Up to this point China had paid little attention to the Russian advance, apparently ignoring the deep significance of the new aggressive policy. Manchu border authorities were negligent, and most of the Manchurian troops had been withdrawn by 1853 to meet the threatening northward march of the T'ai-p'ing rebels in China Proper. Even had this not been the case, China's position in 1853 did not appear on the surface to be seriously threatened on the northern frontier. Officially the policy of the Russian government was still one of respect for the terms of the Nertchinsk treaty. Nevertheless, by 1854 Muraviev had received the tsar's mandate to settle directly with Peking all questions concerning the eastern boundary. He was free to pursue his own grandiose scheme of making Russia a power on the Pacific and, if need be, "the protector of China."[24]

The Crimean War had broken out in Europe. In the Pacific the two great commercial pioneers, the Hudson Bay Company and the Russian-American Company, had agreed to remain neutral, but this did not deter Great Britain and France from attacking Russia's Pacific base at Petropavlovsk. The real value of the Amur as a road for the transport of Russian supplies to the Pacific could no longer be denied even by the "Westerners." As a result, in April, 1854, Muraviev, on the pretext of military necessity—the defense of Kamchatka—sent his first major expedition down the entire length of the Amur. No attempt was made by the Manchu frontier forces to question or stop the Russians. More troops and munitions of war descended the river the following year, and the tsar informed Muraviev that the left bank of the Amur was indispensable to Russia.

Now that Russia had occupied the river with her transports, contacts with the border Manchu authorities were inevitable. The first direct Russo-Chinese negotiations at Mariinsk in 1855 proved abortive. In 1856 Muraviev ordered his third major expedition down the river. China protested, but the Russians replied with the stationing of garrisons at strategic points on the left bank of the river.

The Mission of Count Putiatin

Meanwhile Russia was preparing a double diplomatic assault on Peking. While Muraviev was yet on the Amur, Putiatin was sent to Peking to secure for Russia whatever commercial concessions should fall to England and France as a result of the *Arrow* War. He was also to seek a settlement of the Amur question. Putiatin was refused entry at Kiakhta but reached the mouth of the Pei-ho in August, 1857, by way of the Amur and the ocean route. To his overtures the Chinese replied tersely that Russia should observe her treaty obligations. Blocked in his mission, Putiatin joined the British, French, and American envoys at Canton and proceeded north again with them to Tientsin, where in June, 1858, the four commercial treaties were signed. His influence on the Amur question was negligible. Not so with that of Muraviev.

During the progress of the *Arrow* War, Muraviev had not been idle in the north. Early in May, 1858, he succeeded in bringing China into conference at Aigun, where he demanded the river boundary which was to divide Manchuria from Siberia. China's protests received but scant consideration. On May 28, 1858, the Aigun treaty was signed. In it Russia acquired all the territory on the left or northern bank of the Amur, while the land lying between the Ussuri river and the sea (the Maritime Province) was to be held in joint control by both powers.[25] The Aigun agreement was thus signed two weeks before

---

[23]John J. Stephan, *Sakhalin: A History* (1971). Meanwhile, on the far western Sino-Russian frontier, the treaty of Ili (1851) conceded to Russia commercial privileges and the right to establish a consulate in Ili (Kuldja) in northern Sinkiang.

[24]Anatole G. Mazour, "Dimitry Zavalishin: Dreamer of a Russian-American Empire," *Pacific Historical Review,* 5 (1936), 26-37.

[25]The Chinese text of the treaty refers, in the case of territory to be held in common, only to the right bank of the Amur from the Ussuri to the sea, and not to the entire Maritime Province as is implied in the Russian text. Lin, "Amur Question," 21.

Putiatin signed the Russian treaty of Tientsin, and without his knowledge.

Although China was in no position to dispute Muraviev's advance successfully, she refused to accept the Aigun treaty in its entirety. China was prepared to cede those territories north of the Amur not already occupied by Chinese subjects, but she was not prepared to dispose of the Ussuri country. The local Kirin provincial authorities were accordingly commanded to prevent Russian encroachments. But this gesture was of no effect. When these officials failed, Peking might, and in fact did, order punishment of her helpless underlings. She also declared null and void the joint-control clause of the Aigun

NORTHEAST CHINA BORDER AREA, 1858–60

Russo-Chinese boundary according to the Treaty of Nerchinsk, 1689.

Territory taken by Russia under the Treaty of Aigun, 1858.

Territory taken by Russia under the Treaty of Peking, 1860.

0   50   100   150   200 miles
0   100   200 kilometers

treaty. But China's impotence and Russia's strength remained unchanged.

Having thus pushed her boundary to the river, and having commenced penetration of the Trans-Ussuri region, Russia now directed her final attack through diplomacy in Peking. Early in the summer of 1859, General Ignatiev had reached the Chinese capital to exchange the ratified copies of the Russian treaty of Tientsin. In addition, it was his purpose to cultivate Russian interests in other ways. In his first diplomatic overtures he sought additional commercial privileges and the outright cession to Russia of the Trans-Ussuri lands. These requests were promptly refused, and the envoy was informed that China did not regard the Aigun settlement as binding. Here matters might have rested until such time as Muraviev was again prepared to use force. But, happily for Russia, other powers came unwittingly to her aid. By October, 1860, the British and French allies, having broken Chinese resistance between Peking and Taku, occupied the capital. The Manchu dynasty appeared to be on the verge of total collapse. The T'ai-p'ing rebels were laying waste the central coast; the capital lay at the mercy of British and French arms; the Summer Palace had already been looted and burned, while a cowardly emperor and his renegade court had fled to the mountains of Jehol. Baffled and perplexed by the misfortunes that pursued the dynasty, Prince Kung, brother of the emperor, remained in Peking to seek a settlement with the victorious "barbarians."

Here was Russia's opportunity. Ignatiev played on the fears of the frightened prince. He would intervene, so he said, with the allies and thus save Peking itself from the destruction that had already consumed the Summer Palace. For these services to China he would ask only an insignificant return: the rectification of a frontier, the cession of the Trans-Ussuri country. Prince Kung was not deceived, but assuredly he was defeated. On November 14, 1860, he signed with Ignatiev the convention that, among other points, ceded the Manchurian coastline to Russia.

In large part Muraviev's dream had been realized. By the close of 1860 Russian policy in China had enjoyed a success unparalleled by that of any other state. Like the United States, she had not participated as a belligerent in the *Arrow* War, yet she was to reap all the advantages, commercial and diplomatic, won by England and France in the treaties of Tientsin. In the north, through a policy of force but without declaration of war, she had opened the Mongolian frontier to her traders and had advanced her boundary along the course of the Amur and far south along the Pacific coast to the northern tip of Korea. By conquest and colonization, yet without war in the legal sense, she had deprived the Manchu empire of some 350,000 square miles of territory. Manchuria was cut off from the sea on the east, whereas Russia possessed a new and broad road to the ocean. Before Ignatiev signed the convention that transferred the Maritime Province, Russia proceeded to consolidate her new lands; at the southern extremity of the new coastal territory Muraviev selected the harbor and site of Russia's future fortress on the Pacific. The founding of Vladivostok, "dominion of the East," was a fitting culmination to the work—aggressive, unscrupulous, but successful—of one of Russia's great empire builders.[26]

SOME UNDERLYING FACTORS

In reviewing these years of the mid-century, it will be noted that China's successive defeats in 1842-1844 and again in 1858-1860, with their resulting treaty settlements, involved much more than is suggested by new rules of intercourse and a new order between China and the West. Behind the gunboats and the treaties they produced were Western aspirations and drives of immense potential. The Europeans and later the Americans who went to China from the seventeenth to the mid-nineteenth century were propelled by a sense of mission.

[26] R.K.I. Quested, *The Expansion of Russia in East Asia, 1857-1860* (1968) is an able account of Sino-Russian negotiations. See also the same author's bibliographic review, "Further Light on the Expansion of Russia in East Asia, 1792-1860," *Journal of Asian Studies,* 29 (1970), 327-45.

As merchants they were in pursuit of the profits of commerce; as missionaries they were in pursuit of souls for the Christian God; as diplomats they were the conscious agents of Western culture—political, economic, and social. Because the purposes of the trader, the missionary, and the diplomat could not be achieved fully in the China that existed in and about 1830, China, therefore, would have to be remade in a mold more receptive to trader, missionary, and diplomat—indeed, more receptive to the entire Western culture these agents personified. This is precisely what the West set about to do in the wars of 1840 and 1856 and in the non-war on the Siberian frontier. Consequently, the Europeans and the Americans in China after 1860 were not simply foreigners who, because they enjoyed special privileges under the treaties, had really become a segment of China's ruling elite, important as this might be. Over and above this privileged status, the Westerner was an active promoter of change and, in addition, potentially an advocate of revolution in Chinese society. This fact should be recalled when seeking insights into much later Sino-Western relations, particularly in the Republican revolution of 1911, the *Kuomintang* victories of 1927-1928, and the Communist triumph of 1949.[27]

FOR FURTHER READING

The Chinese Scene and Personalities. Yen-p'ing Hao, *The Comprador in Nineteenth Century China: Bridge between East and West* (1970). Huang Yen-yü, "Viceroy Yeh Ming-ch'en and the Canton Episode (1856-1861)," *Harvard Journal of Asiatic Studies* 6 (1941), 37-127. A. W. Hummel, ed., *Eminent Chinese of the Ch'ing Period, 1644-1912,* (2 vols. 1943-1944)), a reference work of great value Ch'en Ch'i-t'ien, *Tseng Kuo-fan,* trans. by Gideon Chen (1935; reissued, 1961).* W. L. Bales, *Tso Tsung-t'ang, Soldier and Statesman of Old China* (1937) treats the campaigns of the T'ai-p'ing rebellion.

The T'ai-p'ing Rebellion. Thomas Taylor

Meadows, *The Chinese and Their Rebellions* (1856, reprint 1953), a classic on the T'ai-p'ing upheaval. Vincent Y. C. Shih, *The Taiping Ideology: Its Sources, Interpretations, and Influences* (1967). Philip A. Kuhn, *Rebellion and Its Enemies in Late Imperial China: Militarization and Social Structures, 1796-1864* (1970). S. Y. Teng, *The Taiping Rebellion and the Western Powers* (1970);* and *New Light on the History of the T'ai-p'ing Rebellion* (1950). Franz Michael, "The Military Organization and Power Structure of China During the T'ai-p'ing Rebellion," *Pacific Historical Review* 18 (1949), 469-83. Vincent Y. C. Shih, "The Ideology of the T'ai-p'ing T'ien-kuo," *Sinologica* 3 (1951), 1-15. W. J. Hail, *Tseng Kuo-fan and the T'ai-p'ing Rebellion* (1927). E. P. Boardman, *Christian Influence Upon the Ideology of the T'ai-p'ing Rebellion* (1952). John S. Gregory, *Great Britain and the Taipings* (1969). Laai Yi-faai, Franz Michael, and John C. Sherman, "The Use of Maps in Social Research: A Case Study in South China," *Geographical Review* 52 (1962), 92-111. Chester A. Bain, "Commodore Matthew Perry, Humphrey Marshall, and the Taiping Rebellion," *Far Eastern Quarterly* 10 (1951), 258-270. Teng Yuan-chung, "Reverend Issachar Jacox Roberts and the Taiping Rebellion," *Journal of Asian Studies* 23 (1963), 55-67.

China and the Powers. D. Bonner-Smith and E.W.R. Lumby, eds., *The Second China War, 1856-1860* (1954). Grace Fox, *British Admirals and Chinese Pirates, 1832-1869* (1940) treats the influence of the Admiralty on British policy. Alexander Michie, *The Englishman in China* (2 vols. 1900), the life in the East of Sir Rutherford Alcock. Laurence Oliphant, *Narrative of the Earl of Elgin's Mission to China and Japan in the Years 1857, '58, '59 (1860).* Charles Collins, *Public Administration in Hong Kong* (1952), an account of administrative machinery.

Robert J. Kerner, *The Urge to the Sea: the Course of Russian History* (1942). L. Pasvolsky, *Russia in the Far East* (1922). D. J. Dallin, *The Rise of Russia in Asia* (1949) covers the nineteenth and early twentieth centuries. A. Lobanov-Rotovsky, *Russia and Asia* (1933), popular and general. William Mandel,

---

[27] See James C. Thomson, Jr., *While China Faced West: American Reformers in Nationalist China* (1969), 3-5.

The Soviet Far East and Central Asia (1944). Perry McDonough Collins, *Siberian Journey: Down the Amur to the Pacific, 1856-1857,* Charles Vevier, ed. (1962).

Stephen C. Lockwood, *Augustine Heard* *and Company, 1858-1862: American Merchants in China on the Eve of the Opening of the Yangtze* (1971).* Tong Te-kong, *United States Diplomacy in China, 1844-1860* (1964).

Japan, 1603–ca. 1840: The Making and Breaking of the Tokugawa Regime

8

It was noted earlier in this narrative that the Heian period, 794-1185, is one of the most revealing and fascinating for the student of history in the picturesque story it presents of Japan's development. The Heian period, however, is rivaled in these and other respects by the Japan of the Tokugawas, covering the seventeenth to the mid-nineteenth century. A first key to the historical complexities of Tokugawa Japan is the somewhat abrupt change of direction taken in the early years of this period by the first Tokugawa shoguns. This change in direction set the stage for a society whose outward appearance became in time increasingly unlike its underlying realities. Something of the nature of this complex Tokugawa Japan must now be described, because it was in this period that the character of modern Japan was being shaped.

A NEW DIRECTION

As Tokugawa Iyeyasu consolidated his military victories in the first years of the seventeenth century, it appeared, as the reader will recall, that Japan would follow a policy of expanding commercial contacts with the Portuguese, the Spanish, the Dutch, and the English traders, resulting in a new Western cultural impact comparable to the Chinese cultural invasion of the seventh and the eighth centuries. Instead, Japan moved in precisely the opposite direction, adopting and implementing a policy of exclusion and seclusion. In making this vital decision, the shogunate was responding to its desire to secure a monopoly on foreign trade; to a concern with maintaining unquestioned control over its potential enemies, the *tozama daimyo* of Western Japan; and to a conviction that Roman Catholicism as taught by Portuguese and Spanish monks was a political threat to the state. Thus at the very moment when Europe had already set its course toward geographical discovery and territorial expansion, toward far-flung trade and settlement, and toward a liberal philosophy of man's rights, Japan was setting her course against these infatuations of a modern age, was turning inward upon herself, and was closing her doors to either entry or egress. Her purpose was to consolidate a political and social structure whose supreme virtues would be stability and rigid conformity to orthodox values and habits of body and mind.

The Tokugawa period, 1603-1867, has been

interpreted frequently as "an unhappy interlude" between Japan's first and second encounters with the West in the sixteenth and the nineteenth centuries. There are some grounds for this interpretation. The period was one of isolationism, of 100 percent Japanism, of extreme conservatism in social policy, and of the political tyranny of a garrison state. Such was the pattern the Tokugawas attempted to impose and, for a considerable time, did impose in the interest of political stability, a virtual synonym for unchallenged Tokugawa power. At the same time, the Tokugawa years were a far richer period than this interpretation would suggest. While the primary goal of the Tokugawa rulers was to crystallize society and, in this sense, to look backward, there were forces within Japanese society which could not be controlled so neatly and which, indeed, produced basic changes in the manner of life, preparing Japan for modern nationhood. The student who is interested in the ways in which history works will find in Tokugawa Japan a remarkable laboratory.[1]

The period was a notable and a perplexing age in which stability and change were in constant conflict, creating a kind of tension not always evident on the surface of life. Two and one-half centuries of peace—the great peace or *Taihei*, as it is called—was a new and, for most people, a welcome experience, enabling the Japanese to grapple with the pursuits and problems of peace instead of wasting their energies in civil wars. One result was a gradual vitalizing of national and cultural foundations, even though the nation was isolated from the scientific, political, and economic ideas fashioning the modern European world at that time. Government continued to be authoritarian, a monopoly of the military aristocracy, the samurai. The samurai, however, did not remain unchanged in their manner of life or in their modes of thought. In some considerable degree the samurai became a bureaucratic rather than a military elite. The shogunate's efforts to crystallize society to the end of preserving its own power in the name of peace and law and order meant that eventually it had no alternative but to be concerned with that vague ideal, the welfare of the people.

THE STRUCTURE OF TOKUGAWA

The structure of government set up by the Tokugawas was a logical result of events and of historical precedent. The military campaigns of Nobunaga, Hideyoshi, and finally of Iyeyasu and his allied *daimyo* forced the submission of all the great *daimyo* houses. After the battles of Sekigahara (1600) and of Osaka Castle (1615), the Tokugawas were the military masters of Japan. At this point their problem was one of finding a political policy and structure through which they could govern, maintain peace, and thereby preserve their own power. Most of the answers to their problem came from Japanese history itself. The emperor would continue to be the *de jure* sovereign at Kyoto. In 1603 he bestowed the title of shogun on Iyeyasu (just as it had been bestowed upon Minamoto Yoritomo at the end of the twelfth century). Thus Iyeyasu became the *de facto* ruler of Japan, with his headquarters at Edo. But this did not mean the imposition of direct rule by Edo throughout all Japan. Again turning to historical precedent, the Tokugawas decided to rule through the *daimyo* system. This meant that while the ultimate national authority resided with the shogun, the *daimyo* remained as regional rulers. This formula had all the strength that historical tradition could give.[2]

Based as it was on effective military power and a high respect for historical experience, the Tokugawa political edifice was a notable

---

[1] For a more detailed analysis than can be given here see John Whitney Hall, *Japan from Prehistory to Modern Times* (1970),* Chapter 10.

[2] The system is often designated by two different labels: (1) "centralized feudalism" stressed the feudal aspects in which the *daimyo* pledged their loyalty to the shogun; (2) the "*baku-han* system" referred to its dual character in which the shogunate (*bakufu*) ruled through the autonomous *daimyo* domains (*han*).

achievement in statecraft. It survived for more than two and one-half centuries. Its central framework, the *daimyo* system, proved to be far more effective than its appearance would suggest. In addition to having superior military power, the Tokugawas maintained control by a body of bureaucratic agents who exercised thorough supervision throughout the land. Although the *daimyo* governments did not pay taxes to the shogunate, they supported it by "presents" that were virtually compulsory. The shogunate was thus free from most of the obligations of local government and defense.

The domains of the some 270 *daimyo* varied greatly in size and in wealth, which, in Japan's agricultural society, was measured in annual rice yield. The rice yield of a *daimyo* domain was calculated in *koku* (5.11 bushels) to indicate the wealth and status of the great lord— the Tokugawas being by far the wealthiest of all. Their lands, those of their related families, and those of their most trusted *daimyo* allies were concentrated in central Japan and scattered more thinly elsewhere. The Tokugawas also controlled the growing urban commercial centers, where in time great wealth would be concentrated. The result was a central power block that could not be challenged easily. The more distant powerful *daimyo* who were potential enemies of the shogun, such as Satsuma in Kyushu, were treated, in the main, with considerable generosity.

In a political sense *daimyo* were classified in three groups: (1) *shimpan* were descendants of Tokugawa shoguns who did not succeed to this high office; (2) *fudai* were descendants of men who had accepted Iyeyasu as their overlord prior to 1600; and (3) *tozama* were descendants of lords who in 1600 had been equals, in theory at least, of Iyeyasu. The Tokugawa and the *fudai* lands, as indicated, occupied the central part of the country. The strongest *tozama*, potential enemies of the shogunate, were for the most part in the south and west. In time, smaller *fudai* holdings came to be located on the borders of these potential enemies.

The Machinery of Control

It is quite apparent that the Tokugawa political system, which sanctioned local autonomy and independent military power among the *daimyo,* could be an invitation to revolt through alliances among discontented lords. The Tokugawas created barriers against any such development through a complex system of controls. One example will illustrate their political skill in this matter.

The Tokugawa shogunate refined and made mandatory the system of *sankin kotai,* whereby the *daimyo* alternated in attendance on the shogun in Edo. *Fudai* in central Japan alternated semi-annually, while other *fudai* and all *tozama* usually alternated annually. Their wives and children remained in Edo as hostages when the *daimyo* returned to their fiefs. The great *daimyo* trains moving to and from Edo along the Tokaido (road) between Edo and Kyoto created the most picturesque scenes of Tokugawa Japan.[3]

This *sankin kotai* system was remarkably effective. It meant that half of the *daimyo* was always under the eye of the shogun at Edo. The tendency was for them to become courtiers rather than effective rebels. Moreover, the expense of maintaining an elaborate establishment at the shogun's capital drained the resources of the *daimyo* and thus contributed to their subservience to the shogun.[4]

The Central Administration

Far back in the days of Nara and Heian, the central government had failed to develop an adequate body of administrative officials loyal to and appreciative of its stabilizing role in protecting the throne and controlling the frontier clans. In contrast, the Tokugawas encouraged the growth of an educated bureau-

---

[3] Oliver Statler, *Japanese Inn* (1961),* a delightful recapturing of Japanese life at a historic inn on the Tokaido. See the delightful, ribald classic Ikku Jippensha, *Shank's Mare: Being a Translation of the Tokaido Volumes of Hizakurige,* Thomas Satchell, trans. (1960).* Note also George B. Sansom, *A History of Japan, 1615-1867* (1963).* On the position of the emperor in Tokugawa Japan, see H. D. Harootunian, "Between Principle and Personality," *Journal of Asian Studies,* 24 (1964), 115-21, and Herschel Webb, *The Japanese Imperial Institution in the Tokugawa Period* (1968).

[4] For the detailed working of *sankin kotai* and its effects on the Tokugawa system see Toshio Tsukahira, *Feudal Control in Tokugawa Japan* (1966).*

cracy loyal to the established order. In time this bureaucracy took on most of the virtues and vices of this form of government, but meanwhile it gave great strength to the Tokugawa system.

At the high level of policy making, the Tokugawas relied heavily on their council of elders (*Toshiyori*). A member of this council acted as regent when the shogun was a minor. This council was all important in fixing the relationships of the shogunate with the emperor's court and the feudal lords. The lesser vassals of the Tokugawa were regulated by a lower council of junior elders (*Wakadoshiyori*). Under these high-ranking bodies was the bureaucracy proper, comprising executive, administrative, and judicial officials together with their still more numerous underlings, who handled all the various aspects of government. The necessary personnel, as might be expected, were drawn, usually on an hereditary basis, from the Tokugawa and the *fudai* families. Among these officials there was in general a lack of any precise definition of responsibility—a circumstance which, although it can be explained in part on grounds of custom, was also a matter of intentional policy whereby the individual was prevented from building his own little empire of power. In reality it added up to a system of government by council, not by individuals. This feature was common in government in all the various feudal domains and even in the local government of the peasant village, as well as on the high plane of the shogunate. Indeed, government in the fiefs of the great lords varied little in organization from that of the shogunate. Each fief made its own laws and collected its own taxes very much on the pattern set by the Tokugawas. At the extreme local level, the village, government was directed and administered by village headmen and councilors under the watchful eye of district officers of the *daimyo*.[5]

[5] An able account of the Tokugawa central government or *Bakufu* is Conrad D. Totman, *Politics in the Tokugawa Bakufu, 1600-1843* (1967). A significant aspect of Tokugawa government was the ever-present group of officials at various levels of government held together by personal ties of loyalty

Social Classes

The foregoing details will have suggested that the machinery of government in Tokugawa Japan was comparatively simple. It was possible and logical for this to be so because in Old Japan, as in Old China, the ordering and the controlling of society was sought through social rather than through political principles and agencies. This being so, it is essential to take note of the social orders or classes as they existed in Tokugawa times. The influence of this social class structure often exerted itself after Japan had become a modern and partially Westernized state. The class system, moreover, was deeply rooted long before the Tokugawas came to power at the beginning of the seventeenth century. What the Tokugawas did was to distinguish the classes in elaborate detail and to encourage a rigid crystallization of them through more than two centuries of peace.

First in rank and in social prestige was the imperial family and the emperor's immediate vassals, the court nobles or *kuge*. The emperor, to whom land and income were granted by the shogunate, retained a real if somewhat uncertain traditional influence; but his political power had become a matter of theory only, and his court nobility subsisted on less income than that enjoyed by the poorest feudal lords. Theirs were the vaporous satisfactions of honor, not the tangible rewards of wealth.

Second in the social scale but first in power and privilege were the military men, the knights, or to use the Japanese term, the samurai. These made up the ruling class in

and common purposes. These cliques or factions were in a sense the political parties. Note the later discussion of Japan's first modern political parties in Chapter 11. The political society created in Tokugawa Japan was, in fact, derived from three social systems: the "family" or *uji* (pre-Nara); the aristocratic (Nara and Heian); and finally, the samurai (Kamakura, Ashikaga, and Tokugawa). In some notable measure, Tokugawa Japan derived its traditional loyalties from the family system, and its bureaucratic and legal techniques from the aristocratic system. See John Whitney Hall, *Government and Local Power in Japan, 500 to 1700* (1966).

Japan's military-feudal dictatorship. Within this class was a vast array of gradations from the shogun at the top of the foot soldier at the bottom. The principal ranks within this powerful caste, in descending order of grade, were (1) the *daimyo* or great lords, some two hundred and seventy in number, and who were classified according to wealth, and all of whom enjoyed an annual rice income exceeding ten thousand *koku;* (2) direct retainers of the shogun, known as *hatamoto* and *gokenin,* some of whom lived in Edo performing civil or military duties; (3) baishin, who were retainers of *daimyo* or *hatamoto,* and who according to grade within their own class served as government advisers, administrative officials, or as foot soldiers—the most numerous category within the samurai class; (4) *ronin,* or soldiers unattached to any lord; and (5) *goshi,* or samurai-peasants who acquired the status of active soldiers only in time of war. In the eighteenth century Japan's entire population was about thirty million, and of these the *daimyo* and their vassals numbered about two million; the *ronin* about four hundred thousand until about 1650.

The court nobility and the samurai belonged, in a society of status, to what may best be called the privileged classes. They were not permitted to engage in common manual labor. All others, and this included the vast majority, can hardly be said to have been bereft of privileges, but it is certain that their privileges were few and quite unimpressive.

Heading, in the Confucian sense, this multitude of common men was the farmer or peasant, who, like his betters in privileged society, was ranked and graded by various standards within his own class. The first rank among these plebians were the village headmen and councilors. In second rank came those farmers who owned their land. Finally there was the landless peasantry, the most numerous and poorest of all. It was from this group that the laboring force of the growing cities was recruited.

Differentiated from the farmer but of about the same social rank among common men were the artisans or craftsmen. They fashioned the simplest articles of daily use or created the marvelously tempered two-handed sword known as the soul of the samurai.

Neither the farmer nor the craftsman was a person of power, but since they fed and armed the samurai they were accorded a measure of honor as useful members of society.

Ranking as the commonest of common men was the merchant or *chonin* class. In the feudal-military society of early Tokugawa days, the merchant class was looked upon by both shogunate and *daimyo* as a useful tool which, so long as it had no political influence, was not likely to endanger the system. Long before the close of the Tokugawa era, however, this despised but tolerated merchant was to acquire an influence wholly out of proportion to his lowly social status.

Finally, if one scraped the bottom of the social barrel, one discovered the substratum of mankind, the *eta* or the untouchables, who were professional players, tanners, and executioners. Below the *eta* was the lowest class of society, the *hinin,* composed of beggars. One could be born into this class or be consigned to it as punishment for some crime. Districts were set apart where the untouchables were required to live unto themselves, since they could not even act as servants to commoners. They were classified as animals rather than humans, and were not even included in the census. The two names, *eta* and *hinin* were suppressed in 1871, and today descendents of these former classes are legally citizens.

The Philosophy

In seeking political stability the Tokugawa government did not confine itself to defining social classes and to spying upon its enemies. It went beyond these matters to prescribe in minute detail the morals and the behavior of the entire populace. In the Western world morals have usually been left to the management of some church, but in Japan, as in China, ethics were the concern of government, and thus moral and political philosophy became one. As a consequence the fundamental laws of the shogunate were really codes of moral injunction, such as, "Avoid what you like, and attend to unpleasant duties." Life was not considered to be the pursuit of happiness, but rather the performance of obligation. There was no place for freedom of thought because duty called for unqualified loyalty and obedience. The idea of progress was also excluded because this was a society of status in which each man occupied his proper place and was expected to stay in it.

The Confucian Foundation

The intellectual cornerstone fashioned to uphold this Tokugawa scheme of government was a cluster of Confucian ethical principles. These principles, which stressed the "proper" relations between the ruler and the ruled, appealed to the Tokugawas as exceedingly relevant to their problem of consolidating the *baku-han* (see note 2 page 110) and thus bringing order out of chaos. Since their society was moving from a purely feudal stage to one of large, well-defined social classes—from military to civil administration—fundamental priciples of government, law, and administration were needed. They were available in abundance in the more conservative interpretations of Confucianism. Confucian thought could support the concept of social classes and hierarchy in a society of status and, more importantly, it could provide a moral order prescribing the conduct of both the ruler and the ruled. The implication was that the samurai as a ruling elite would become scholars in order to be good administrators in the Confucian sense. The result would be benovolent administration and a deep concern for the welfare of the people.[6]

This Japanese effort to adopt a Confucian and therefore a Chinese moral order was reminiscent of the earlier Chinese cultural impact of the seventh and eighth centuries. Its usefulness now as a political tool was the greater because the Buddhist church had already been reduced to obedience to the state by Nobunaga and Hideyoshi, while the first Tokugawa shoguns had suppressed Christianity. The way, therefore, had been cleared for the secular morality of the Confucians. The trend to Confucianism actually was not entirely new. The samurai had long prided themselves on their regard for courage, self-sacrifice, disregard of material wealth, and loyalty to one's lord. In theory, at least, all of these qualities had been the moral stock-in-trade of the soldier since long before the Tokugawas came to power. They were qualities that the shogunate wished to strengthen. But the problem was not as simple as this would suggest. The shogunate recognized that the samurai's warlike spirit could, in times of peace, be inconvenient and even dangerous. Therefore the shogunate attempted to turn the minds of military men toward peaceful undertakings.[7]

---

[6] John Whitney Hall, "Tokugawa Japan: 1800-1853," in *Modern East Asia: Essays in Interpretation*, James B. Crowley, ed. (1970),* 62-94. Confucian thought thus formed a principal basis of the Tokugawa educational system, which ultimately included special schools for commoners. It was a system dominated by formalism, by the regimentation of students, by severe limitations on the education of commoners, and by rigid social distinctions at all levels of schooling. Nevertheless, since Tokugawa education indoctrinated all levels of society with the ideal of service to family, to community, and to country, it provided an invaluable foundation for Japan's later modernization in the nineteenth century. At the beginning of the Tokugawa period a majority of the ruling samurai class was largely illiterate. By the end of the period, most of the samurai could be described as literate, while some 40 percent of the total male population

and perhaps 10 percent of the female population had some capacity to read and write. The outstanding study is R. P. Dore, *Education in Tokugawa Japan* (1965).

[7] The prescribed philosophy of Tokugawa times especially as it applied to the samurai or ruling caste is sometimes referred to as *Bushido*, the Way of the Warrior, a term of comparatively recent origin, although the set of ideas for which it is the label is quite old. These ideas are not unlike those in the code of early European chivalry. Historically the code was the expression of early ideas on the duty of the soldier. Since Japan had been controlled by soldiers since the time of Yoritomo, there had been both the need and the opportunity to develop a set of principles on the duty of the soldier. These principles varied in degree from time to time and had not been highly conventionalized until well into the Tokugawa period, and then, in part at least, under the Confucian influence. In general, *Bushido* extolled "rectitude, courage, benevolence, politeness, sincerity, honor, disdain of money, and self-control" as ideals to be followed by the samurai. Since virtue is only as strong as those who profess it, this code was the measure of what a samurai was supposed to do, not of what he sometimes actually did.

Such then was the pattern of permanence the Tokugawas tried to impose. At first their success seemed complete. For a long time the basic character of Tokugawa institutions remained substantially without change. Yet, almost from the beginning, processes of change were at work. Indeed, the advent of unbroken peace and the closing of the country to foreign intercourse created conditions that forced the Tokugawas to tolerate and even to encourage changes in a policy that was designed to resist change.

The Tokugawa government, class structure, and politico-moral philosophy suggest that Japan had fashioned for herself a way of life that must have been very bleak indeed. Nevertheless, could a Westerner have visited Edo, Kyoto, or Osaka in, let us say, 1700, he would doubtless have been impressed not so much by the coldness of life as by its warmth, its vitality, its apparent prosperity, and its color. However gloomy the moral injunctions of shogun or *daimyo* might be, it was very evident that the city dwellers of this Japan were much concerned with the idea of progress and the pursuit of happiness. The processes of change so repugnant to Tokugawa philosophy were in operation.

The Economy

It was in the field of economics and commerce that the processes of change first became apparent. When military Japan settled down to a life of peace in the early 1600's, it was possible for trade to grow to proportions previously unknown. In peace, too, there was also less reason for local commercial restrictions, so that even though the country was still divided into the many domains of individual lords, the tendency was for the whole to become one economic unit. This tendency acquired strength from the nature of the shogun's government at Edo, to which city under the system of *sankin kotai* came all the *daimyo* with their families and a host of retainers. This official and aristocratic populace of government officials created a demand for goods and services which only artisans and tradesmen could furnish. In these circumstances the relatively simple rice economy of the individual feudal domain gradually gave

way to a money and credit economy managed by merchants, brokers, and bankers, who controlled the rice markets and storehouses of such cities as Osaka and Edo. The *daimyo* when in residence at Edo converted rice revenue into cash, spending the proceeds on elaborate furnishings, dress, and lavish entertainment. Since his income in rice did not vary greatly and maintaining social prestige was an expensive business, it was not difficult for a *daimyo* to find himself in debt to his social inferior, the merchant—not a healthy or comfortable condition for members of a ruling class.

Two points need to be emphasized in explaining how the mercantile class, which had relatively limited legal rights and no military power, could reach a point where it was able to exploit the military classes and the farmers. The first of these was the further development of Edo as a large city which had to be supplied in part by imported food and which demanded a large supply of manufactured luxuries. These factors encouraged further use of money and made the merchant indispensable. Edo's growth, as indicated, resulted from the growth of government and the enforced residence there of the *daimyo* and their families. Had the *daimyo* remained in their castle towns, their consumptive habits and those of their retainers would have developed and changed much more slowly; likewise the use of money and the growth of a merchant class to cater to these expensive habits would have been retarded. In the second place, the military class, by reason of its new consumptive habits, became more and more dependent on the merchant. Once a taste for luxury had been acquired, the nobility was prepared to mortgage its future to the merchant rather than be eclipsed in the rivalry of social living. The merchant was not liquidated because without him the necessary food and luxuries would not have been forthcoming.[8]

Years of peace and the growth of the market also affected the farmers, who, in an overwhelmingly agricultural society, comprised about 80 percent of the population. While in

[8] The complex situation which created and gave power to the merchants is portrayed in Charles D. Sheldon, *The Rise of the Merchant Class in Tokugawa Japan, 1600-1868* (1958).

many ways Japanese farming changed very little over the centuries, production during the Tokugawa era shifted from a cooperative to an individual basis. Whereas, in 1600, farming was conducted by the cooperation of families organized into kinship groups sharing land, labor, tools, and sometimes food and housing, by the end of the Tokugawa period the individual family had become the main agent of agricultural production and the focus of economic interest. The implications of this shift extended well beyond the realm of economics. Economic change, previously an aspect of kinship and social relations, became a more independent force creating its own values. Thereby the exchange of goods became less a matter of social or ritual obligation and more a question of whether the price was right.[9]

By 1700, therefore, roughly a hundred years after the Tokugawas had first risen to power, Japan had not only modified her economy but had also acquired in her larger cities a prosperous middle class. Side by side then with the extravagance of the *daimyo* and their followers in maintaining their social elegance, there appeared a new world of well-to-do merchants and their hirelings, who had their own particular ideas on how to enjoy their money. These merchants and their associates, whom the samurai regarded as uncultivated persons of low and vulgar taste, soon created through their demands for entertainment a whole new world of popular arts in literature, the theater, painting, and color prints.

The Arts

The new art was distinguished from older forms by its subject matter. It was an art that dealt with the doings and the aspirations of the newly-rich commoners, their own colorful everyday life. Here were street scenes, theaters, teahouses, and taverns of that time, the actors who had risen to stardom, and, as Sir George Sansom has said, "the easy-going ladies of the world of entertainment." The patrons of this new art were the tradespeople. In time they developed their own standards and critics, so that eventually the old aristocratic monopoly over art was broken. The processes of change were in motion.[10]

In literature and in the theater, as in art, the city folk were not wholly satisfied with the classical romances and stage plays that were the traditional fare of the military class. The tastes of the city commoners, robust and sensuous, called forth a new group of authors whose stories and plays had a wide contemporary appeal. All of this brought books and plays and an appreciation of literature and acting to a growing populace of city dwellers. Edo literature is important historically because it was another indication of change in the changeless Tokugawa pattern, and because the vacuous character of Edo writing explains in some measure the easy inroads made by European literary influence and thought in the later Meiji period, when Japan had opened her doors to Western intercourse.

THE ROOTS OF A NEW JAPAN

These bright and attractive colors in Edo's life of business and of the new arts need to be appraised against a background of contention —both social and economic. It has been suggested that the long period of peace the *Bakufu* was able to impose opened the way for a new society, which in turn eventually

---

[9] For the development of this fascinating and intricate subject, see Thomas C. Smith, *The Agrarian Origins of Modern Japan* (1965).* Note in particular the changes that occurred in land holding, labor services—a subsistence to a marketing economy—the growth of rural industries, the use of agricultural technology, and especially the development of new agricultural class relations.

[10] Hishigawa Motonobu was one of the great painters of this popular new art. The work of such men was the forerunner of the famous Japanese color print, which testified to the widely developing artistic sense of the urban classes. The great print artists (Hiroshige, for example) became popular idols. They were the creators of *Ukiyo-e*, or Floating World. *Ukiyo-e* was a picture of the passing world of pleasure. It was not unusual for proud members of the ruling aristocratic elite, the samurai, to leave the badge of their status at home in order to frequent the pleasure haunts of the commoners, who seemed to have most of the money and most of the fun.

destroyed the social and political order Iyeyasu had founded, and laid the foundations for a new state and nation. This new society, far from being confined to the markets and pleasure haunts of Edo, made itself felt in every aspect of the nation's life. Although the Tokugawas did not set out to build a modern national state, Japan during most of the Edo period was taking the first steps in the direction of modern nationalism and industrialism. The Tokugawa period saw the beginnings of prolonged struggles between a rice agriculture and industry, between a local barter economy and a national money economy, between a feudal and military aristocracy and the power of commercial and then industrial capital, between the food supply and the population that had to be fed, between what was traditional and what was not. There was much dislocation and much suffering before the birth pains of this new society with its creeping capitalism had passed.

Since every society must provide a means of feeding and clothing itself, it follows that economic conditions are often a barometer of a society's contentment and therefore of its stability. Stability was a primary goal of the *Bakufu*, but the history of the period is a story of growing dissatisfaction with economic conditions. These dissatisfactions played their part in the gradual undermining of that "massive stability" which describes the early years of the Tokugawa system. The most obvious signs of unrest occurred in the countryside among the peasantry. Peasant uprisings were not peculiar to Tokugawa times, but they increased in number and violence under the *Bakufu*. Their causes were very complex and it is possible here to suggest only a few of the conditioning factors.

First of all was the important fact that the peasant was the only regular taxpayer. A large part of his rice crop he owed to his feudal lord for the support of the whole military aristocracy. Whatever new burdens the *Bakufu* might lay on the military or business classes were passed on by them to the peasant in the form of additional taxation or through currency or market manipulations. Since a peasant paid more to his lord in a good crop year than in a bad one, a bumper crop was a questionable blessing. Although the peasant did not "own" the land he cultivated, his tenure was secure through laws that prohibited transfer of land under cultivation. Nevertheless, with the appearance of a merchant class with funds for investment, ways were found to get around these laws and thus to create a new landlord class of city merchants, who shared in the revenue derived from land on which the whole state rested. The student, however, should not jump to the simple conclusion that all the woes of the Tokugawa period can be laid at the door of a land tax on the peasantry. Actually in some areas the land tax remained static or declined slightly while the productivity of land was rising. Agrarian distress there certainly was, but it resulted not only from taxation but also from usury, flood, drought, extravagant spending, and adverse price movements. In fact, by the end of the Tokugawa period there was a large class of relatively wealthy, ambitious, and educated peasant families.[11]

Closely allied to the burden of peasant taxation was the distressing problem of population. For the first half of the Tokugawa period population increased rapidly. Through the second half it remained practically stationary at about thirty million. The initial increase bore heavily on the food supply. The growth of cities contributed to shortages of farm labor. The problem was aggravated by Japan's major dependence on a single food crop, rice, and her isolation from the outside world. In periods of crop failure there was no foreign trade, no imports and exports to relieve the crisis, and no effective means by which the price of rice could be controlled. In a fluctuating market it was the merchant who understood such matters who profited. Those who paid were the military caste and, most of all, the peasants.

The stability of the *Bakufu* was also undermined by its failure to pursue sound policies in public finance. It should be recognized that the Edo government faced extraordinary difficulties. Its military triumph at the beginning of the seventeenth century imposed upon it responsibilities that were really national in

[11] Thomas C. Smith, "The Land Tax in the Tokugawa Period," *Journal of Asian Studies,* 18 (1958), 3-19.

scope, while the state was organized in a feudal pattern: the *Bakufu* derived regular revenue from its own domains only. The consequence was a state of chronic deficit relieved but little by the drastic economic policies effected from time to time. Because of the country's political organization there could be no recourse to national loans. Instead, the *Bakufu* resorted to emergency measures. Since the peasant was already taxed to the limit that agriculture could bear, and since forced "gifts" from the *daimyo* could not be demanded too frequently, most of the special emergency levies fell upon the merchant class in the large cities under Tokugawa control. Although these levies were called loans, frequently they were not repaid; and when these levies, as was often the case, failed to meet the government's financial plight, it could and did resort to debasement of the coinage. These expedients, which at best only postponed the day of judgment, aggravated economic conditions that were already bad by encouraging wild fluctuation of prices.[12]

By the 1830's the once secure Tokugawa shogunate was infected by a deepening sense of crisis. The failure of officialdom to ease the peasant's lot was dramatized in 1837 by rebellion in Tokugawa's own ranks. Oshio Heihachiro, a minor official in the *Bakufu's* Osaka city administration, called upon an oppressed urban and rural populace to rise and kill "the heartless officials and the luxury-loving merchants who profited while the poor starved." This proved to be a minor flare-up, quickly suppressed, but it was symptomatic of a popu-

---

[12] The eventual downfall which overtook the Tokugawa shogunate has been ascribed frequently to economic stagnation. Such an interpretation now appears to be unwarranted because, in spite of all the economic troubles of this period, there was constant and gradual development reaching into remote areas and resulting in a modest rise in the standard of living of most of the population. It seems likely, therefore, that the disaster which finally overtook the Tokugawa system is to be explained rather in the inflexible character of its political and social institutions. See Susan B. Hanley and Kozo Yamamura, "A Quiet Transformation in Tokugawa Economic History," *Journal of Asian Studies,* 30 (1971), 373-84.

lar inclination to attack authority. In territory least susceptible to *Bakufu* censorship, scholars were producing literature which questioned the shogun's position. Reinterpretation of the Confucian classics and of Japan's political history produced a picture of the shogunate as a usurper of the emperor's legitimate function, a government scarcely deserving loyal obedience. Finally, the Tokugawa regime was challenged in its policy of seclusion by both the Russians and British, who, becoming numerous in Japanese waters, pressed for the opening of trade.

SUMMARY

All these various conditions, trends, changes, and schools of thought gradually destroyed the Tokugawa pattern of permanence and created in its place a society whose formal structure was no longer an adequate vehicle by which this new nation could live, move, and have its being. The Tokugawa political system had become a facade behind which grew the strivings and struggles of a disgruntled people. No class was exempt from the disturbing effects of these varied dislocations. In summary they added up to a complex anatomy of maladjustments:

1. At the top of the politico-social scale, many of the *daimyo* were plagued by the same financial ailments that beset the shogunate.
2. The samurai posed the perplexing problem of what to do with an idle standing army in a prolonged period of unbroken peace. As the finances of shogun and *daimyo* went from bad to worse, there was the irresistible tendency to cut the allowances of their samurai retainers. As a net result, the samurai had too little money and too much time on their hands.
3. The farmers, as the Tokugawa era moved into the nineteenth century, continued through peasant uprisings to protest against economic grievances magnified by periodic natural calamities of flood and famine.
4. The merchants, even with their wealth, were vulnerable and insecure. They were never free from the vexatious interference by gov-

ernment which often amounted to confiscation. Nevertheless, most of the merchants were not opposed to the regime even though many were angered by its restrictions. They resented the lowly social status from which their wealth had not freed them.

At the beginning of the seventeenth century, the Tokugawas had fashioned a society of seemingly "massive stability." For a time their plan was eminently successful. In the end, their regime of peace was their own undoing. By the end of the eighteenth century, stability was a memory. The political framework of the past still stood, but Japanese society had moved beyond this framework to create a new mode of life unforeseen by the founding fathers of the early 1600's.

In Tokugawa times, theory and practice did not always coincide. The original exclusion laws had appeared gradually. They were occasioned less by ideology than by the empirical demands of a particular situation. Even when exclusion became a national policy, its enforcement was uneven. For example, in 1720 the ban against Western books was modified to permit the study of geography, military science, and medicine. At best, exclusion, adopted without philosophical conviction, ran counter to Japan's natural economic needs. These problems were recognized early by some Japanese statesmen—Tanuma Okitsugu, for example, the most important minister in the shogunate in the late eighteenth century. The work of such statesmen indicates that Japan might have abandoned her seclusion policy voluntarily a half century before she was actually compelled to do so.[13]

The fact that the Tokugawa regime lasted for two and one-half centuries is testimony to its political and economic craftsmanship. Regulation, extended to every phase of life, would ensure stable, unchanging institutions. The policy of seclusion would be a barrier against contagion from without. Intellectually and spiritually the country would find contentment in neo-Confucianism and Buddhism.

[13] The basic study is John W. Hall, *Tanuma Okitsugu, 1719-1788: Forerunner of Modern Japan* (1955).* The fascinating story of what the Japanese learned about the West in the crucial years 1720-1830 is told by Donald Keene, *The Japanese Discovery of Europe, 1720-1830* (rev. ed., 1969).*

For a time, this planned society seemed to work quite well, but, in the longer view, institutions did change. An inflexible Confucianism failed to curb a new spirit of intellectual curiosity. Even in exclusion, Japan acquired a view of Western natural science, military science, and philosophy. Thus was the way prepared for the downfall of the last great shogunate.[14]

FOR FURTHER READING

Political History. Hugh Borton, *Peasant Uprisings in Japan in the Tokugawa Period* (2nd ed., 1968).* Susan B. Hanley, "Toward an Analysis of Demographic and Economic Change in Tokugawa Japan: A Village Study," *Journal of Asian Studies,* 31 (1972), 515-37. Kee-Ie Choi, "Technological Diffusion in Agriculture under the Bakuhan System," *Journal of Asian Studies,* 30 (1971), 749-60. Susan B. Hanley and Kozo Yamamura, *A Quiet Transformation in Tokugawa Economic History* (1971). Dan F. Henderson, "Chinese Legal Studies in Early 18th Century Japan: Scholars and Sources," *Journal of Asian Studies* 30 (1970), 21-56. Conrad D. Totman, *Politics in the Tokugawa Bakufu, 1600-1843* (1967). Peter Frost, *The Bakumatsu Currency Crisis* (1970).* Kozo Yamamura, "The Increasing Poverty of the Samurai in Tokugawa Japan, 1600-1868," *Journal of Economic History* (1971). David M. Earl, *Emperor and Nation in Japan: Political Thinkers of the Tokugawa Period* (1964) deals with Confucian influence. Nitobe, Inazo, *Bushido* (1905). Dan F. Henderson, "Japanese Legal History of the Tokugawa Period, Scholars and Sources," *Five Studies in Japanese Politics,* Robert E. Ward, ed. (1957) includes analysis of the legal system itself. Herschel Webb, *The Japanese Imperial Institution in the Tokugawa Period* (1968). John W. Hall and Marius B. Jansen, eds., *Studies in the Institutional History of Early Modern Japan* (1968). Peter Duus, *Feudalism in Japan* (1969)* G. B. Sansom, *A History of Japan: 1615-1867* (1963).* H. D. Harootunian, *Toward Restoration: The*

[14] Grant K. Goodman, *The Dutch Impact on Japan, 1640-1853* (1967), especially 212-26.

Growth of Political Consciousness in Tokugawa Japan (1970).

Economic Development. Daniel Spencer, "Japan's Pre-Perry Preparation for Economic Growth," *American Journal of Economics and Sociology* 17 (1958), 195-216. Robert Sakai, "The Satsuma-Ryukyu Trade and the Tokugawa Seclusion Policy," *Journal of Asian Studies* 23 (1964), 391-403, an important research paper from original sources. Robert G. Flershem's "Some Aspects of Japan Sea Trade in the Tokugawa Period," *Journal of Asian Studies* 23 (1964), 405-16.

Biographical Studies. Albert M. Craig and Donald H. Shively, eds., *Personality in Japanese History* (1971). Shigeru Matsumoto, *Motoori Norinaga, 1730-1801* (1970). Walter Dening, *The Life of Toyotomi Hideyoshi* (1955), a fast moving but not always accurate sketch. Arthur Lindsay Sadler, *The Maker of Modern Japan: The Life of Tokugawa Iyeyasu, 1542-1616* (1937). Philip G. Rogers, *The First Englishman in Japan: The Story of Will Adams* (1956).

Ideas and the Arts. Robert N. Bellah, *Tokugawa Religion: The Values of Preindustrial Japan* (1957).* Arthur Lindsay Sadler, *Cha-no-yu: the Japanese Tea Ceremony* (1934); and *The Art of Flower Arrangement in Japan: A Sketch of its History and Development* (1933). Faubion Bowers, *Japanese Theater* (1952),* and A. C. Scott, *The Kabuki Theatre of Japan* (1955),* a study of the traditional theatre.

The *ukiyo-zoshi,* or "tales of the floating world," offer a glittering picture of the city life which flourished during the brilliant Genroku era (1680-1740). See Howard Hibbett, *The Floating World in Japanese Fiction; Tales of the Ukiyo and Their Background* (1959). Ihara Saikaku, *Five Women Who Loved Love,* trans. by Wm. Theodore deBary (1956),* a collection of risque tales of the eighteenth century by one of Japan's literary masters, is unsurpassed for its glimpses of contemporary urban life and manners. Donald Keene, trans., *Chushingura: the Treasury of Loyal Retainers* (1971).*

Japan, ca. 1840–1864: The End of Exclusion and Seclusion

9

As Japan and the Tokugawa *baku-han* neared the mid-century mark, the prevailing temper of the country was clearly one of approaching crisis. The sources of the trouble were two-fold, internal and external.

To meet the internal crisis, described in the preceding chapter, both the shogun and the *daimyo* attempted to become reformers, seeking to evade bankruptcy in the shogunate and in the *han*. Some economic and financial measures appeared to ease the tensions for a time but did not end them. As is usual in such circumstances, those in authority, who were ultimately responsible for the general malaise, now preached to samurai and peasant a gospel of spiritual and moral rebirth as the road to the country's salvation. Doubtless a rebirth was needed, but at this point it was too little and too late. In any case, this pious effort did not cure the maladjustments that permeated the whole society. The sense and the reality of internal crisis continued and deepened.

THE EXTERNAL THREAT

The crisis arising from external sources was even more alarming to the Japanese. Since the middle of the eighteenth century they had been increasingly sensitive to the presence of Russian settlements on the coast of Siberia and to Russian explorations in the Kurile Islands. As early as 1792, the Russians sought to open trade but were rebuffed.[1] Shortly thereafter, in the 1820's, British whaling craft appeared in Japanese waters. Their continuing efforts to secure supplies led to repeated incidents and to renewed orders from Edo that foreign vessels were to be driven away. Then came the unwelcome tidings that in 1840-1842 Britain had humiliated China in war, had exacted a large indemnity, and had forced the opening of ports to foreign trade. These developments, plus the intelligence on the outside world which the *Bakufu* received annually through the Dutch trading post at Deshima, strengthened the belief that Japan might soon face the kind of crisis which had already befallen China. It was not long in coming.

THE AMERICAN THREAT

While the British continued to be preoccupied with the business of opening China, the way

[1] The definitive study is George A. Lensen, *The Russian Push Toward Japan: Russo-Japanese Relations, 1697-1875* (1959).

was cleared for Americans to pursue their designs upon Japan. A somewhat uncertain American interest in Japan dated back to earlier days of the Canton trade. At the beginning of the century, John Jacob Astor had entertained visions of an American trade between Astoria (America's Pacific northwest territory) and East Asia. Later, Senator Thomas Hart Benton advocated western expansion and settlement of Oregon and California as keys to the riches of trans-Pacific commerce. In 1837 an American firm doing business at Canton sent the ship *Morrison* to Edo bay. The unarmed ship was fired upon and forced to retire. In 1846 the American government sent Commodore James Biddle, commander of the East Indian squadron, to Edo bay with two ships of war. Hampered by his restrictive instructions, Biddle soon sailed away having gained nothing, but leaving the Japanese with the impression that the United States did not intend to force any issue. But events in America now moved rapidly. The Oregon territory was acquired in 1846; California, two years later. The United States had a border on the Pacific. This westward expansion clarified and strengthened the ideas of those Americans who believed the United States should be a trans-Pacific power. By 1851 the notion that the United States should play a larger role in the Pacific had been approved by Secretary of State Daniel Webster. The result was the appointment of Commodore Matthew C. Perry to head a naval mission, the purpose of which was to end Japan's seclusion.

THE PERRY MISSION

This decision was one of the significant turning points in American history and in American far eastern policy. In China in 1844, Caleb Cushing's prime concern was simply to secure for Americans those privileges and rights which the British had wrested from China through war; but Perry, in confronting Japan, was commissioned to destroy a national policy which the Japanese had followed for more than two centuries.

There were multiple reasons leading to this American decision. The reasons commonly cited were by-products of the American-Canton trade and the north Pacific whaling industry: to guarantee proper treatment by Japan for shipwrecked American seamen, to gain the right to secure provisions, and to satisfy the need for coaling depots. But these were not the most compelling reasons. A more powerful motive explaining Perry's appointment was the hope of increasing profits in the China trade and in the new trade that would develop with Japan. Increasing trans-Pacific commerce (protected by most-favored-nation treatment) and its resulting wealth would serve the national interest. The opening of East Asia initiated by Britain in China would be carried forward by the United States in Japan. There would be a difference, however, because a beneficent American influence—so it was said—would be the tempering agent lacking in the less scrupulous methods of the Europeans. Thus an American manifest destiny would spread American culture as well as American commerce.

AMERICAN REACTIONS

These comforting thoughts on what, it was hoped, would be America's commercial, cultural, and moral role in East Asia were embodied in the coming Perry mission. These thoughts, however, were not shared or indeed understood by all Americans. Public reaction to the whole undertaking was confused and conflicting. While optimists hoped for its success, pessimists referred to it as a "romantic notion" and "a matter of ridicule abroad and at home." A contributor to *Putnam's Magazine* thought Perry the instrument of a divine plan; trade would follow Perry's mission and thus the merchants would open "a highway for the chariot of the Lord Jesus Christ. . . ." There were also voices that cautioned care lest the United States become involved in a war with Japan. The fact the Japanese were "rude, intractable, selfish, and unsocial" was not sufficient reason for going to war with them.

These reactions are not surprising, since both in the United States and Europe pseudo knowledge had produced strange and varied opinions of Japan and the Japanese. Estimates of Japan's area ranged from 9,000 to 266,000 square miles; of population density, from 184 to 4,000 per square mile; and of total population, from 15 million to 50 million. Edo alone was sometimes said to have a population of at least 10 million. The Japanese of the "lowest orders" were said to have a yellow complexion, "like the color of cheese." As so often is the case, fancy rather than fact determined what people had to say about Japan.

With a fleet of four ships, Perry entered Edo bay and anchored off Uraga, July 8, 1853. His arrival did not take the Japanese by surprise, for they had been warned of his coming by the Dutch; yet the appearance of the American squadron precipitated one of the great crises of Japanese history. While unaware of the real nature of this crisis, Perry proceeded to the task before him with firmness, dignity, and tact. He impressed the officials of the shogun's government with the power of his fleet—it contained the first steamers seen in Japanese waters—and with his own good will. He refused to retire to Nagasaki or to deal through the Dutch there. He demanded treatment suitable to the representative of a great power. He was justified in this behavior when, in opposition to Japanese law, President Fillmore's letter was received by two high officials of the shogun's court. Then Perry sailed away, but not without informing the Japanese that he would return the next year with a more powerful fleet to receive their answer.[2]

[2] Payson J. Treat, *Diplomatic Relations Between the United States and Japan, 1853-1895* (2 vols., 1932; reprint, 1963), I, ll.

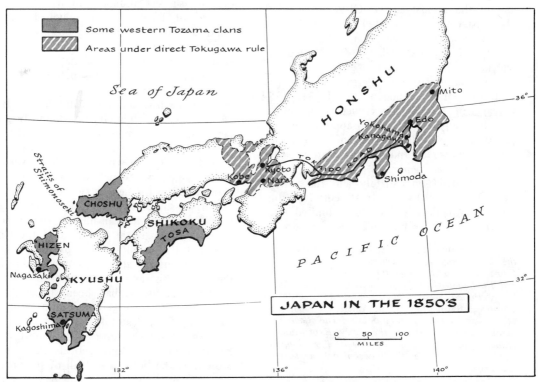

From Japan: The Story of a Nation, *by Edwin O. Reischauer. Copyright © 1970 by Edwin O. Reischauer. Reprinted by permission of Alfred A. Knopf, Inc. and Gerald Duckworth & Co. Ltd.*

PERRY'S TREATY

Perry's visit confronted the shogun with the most serious decision ever faced by the Tokugawas. An Iyeyasu would have decided the matter on his own responsibility. Now, however, the shogunate had come on sorry days, and, faced with an issue of unparalleled importance, it took the unprecedented step of seeking the advice not only of the leading *daimyo,* but also of the emperor. The preponderant opinion favored repelling the foreigner, but some few recognized the futility of armed opposition.

Perry was already hastening his return, spurred by rumors that French and Russian squadrons planned to visit Japan. This time, with an augmented fleet of seven vessels, he entered Edo bay on February 13, 1854. Fortunately, the minority at the shogun's court had prevailed, and so at Kanagawa the negotiation of a treaty proceeded amid social activities of the utmost gaiety. Gifts presented to the Japanese by the United States included a miniature railway, telegraph, books, and a variety of liquors. All these delighted the Japanese.[3]

The treaty signed by Perry and the representatives of the shogun, March 31, 1854 (Treaty of Kanagawa), viewed superficially, was in many respects a disappointment. In reality it was little more than a convention covering shipwreck and supply. It provided for peace, for the opening of two ports for supplies (Shimoda immediately and Hakodate a year later), for good treatment for shipwrecked American sailors, for a limited trade under Japanese regulations, and for supplies

[3] See Francis L. Hawks, compiler, *Narrative of the Expedition of an American Squadron to the China Seas and Japan, Performed in the Years 1852, and 1854 under the Command of Commodore M. C. Perry, United States Navy* (published by order of Congress, 1856), 375. For the Americans as Japanese artists saw them, see Oliver Statler, *The Black Ship Scroll: An Account of the Perry Expedition at Shimoda in 1854 and the Lively Beginnings of People-to-People Relations Between Japan and America* (1964).

for American ships—really a treaty of friendship. Yet viewed realistically, the treaty was a remarkable achievement against more than two centuries of Japanese exclusion. Perry's success was due to many factors: his own firmness, sagacity, tact, dignity, patience, and determination; the strength of his great naval squadron, the like of which the Japanese had never before seen; and his declaration that more ships would be sent if the just demands of the United States were not met. Reinforcing these attributes of Perry the diplomat were others over which he had no control, but without which he might well have failed: the recent frequent appearance of Russian vessels in Japanese waters, Japanese knowledge of China's defeat in 1842, and above all, those internal developments, described in Chapter 8, which had made Japan ripe for revolution.

Any estimate of Perry as naval officer, diplomat, or statesman should consider not only his success in Japan but also the broader pattern of Pacific policy which he had in mind. To Perry the opening of Japan was not an end in itself but rather one in a series of steps toward creating American maritime power in the Pacific. This pattern would include coaling stations and naval bases throughout the Pacific and especially in the Bonin Islands, the Liu-ch'iu (Ryukyu), and Formosa. Perry has sometimes been called the first American imperialist. He foresaw and supported a policy to which little heed was given at the time, but which was implemented in great detail in the next fifty years.

Perry's success was one of the most significant events in American history, though it was not so recognized at that time in the United States. Little attention was paid to it in the press, and it was almost ignored by President Pierce in his annual message to Congress, perhaps because it had been the work of a Whig government. Almost the only interest shown by Congress took the form of a protest that the cost of printing the report of the Perry mission was "outrageously extravagant." Moreover, the book was "full of pictures and most costly engravings of shells, and birds, and snakes, and bugs in Japan, with God knows how many maps that are appended to its surveys." Yet Japan's exclusion policy had been ended. The decision that effected this momentous change was made by the shogun's government, but the United States had provided the occasion that forced that decision.

EUROPE'S TREATIES

Representatives of other powers soon followed Perry to Japan and secured treaties similar though not identical with that of the United States. A British admiral, Sir James Stirling, negotiated a treaty at Nagasaki in October, 1854. The Russian Admiral, Count Putiatin, secured his treaty at Shimoda in February, 1855.[4] Finally the Dutch were released from their commercial confinement at Nagasaki and given a new treaty in January, 1856. The most-favored-nation clause made the provisions of each treaty the common property of the four powers, and expanded somewhat the rights Americans had won in the Perry treaty. These total and enlarged rights held by the four powers in 1856 included: (1) permission to secure supplies at Shimoda, Hakodate, and Nagasaki; (2) permission to trade through Japanese officials and under their regulations at these ports; (3) the right of male residence at Nagasaki; (4) permission to appoint consuls at Shimoda and Hakodate; and (5) a limited extraterritorial jurisdiction.

Three of these treaties (American, British, and Russian) were approved by the emperor in February, 1855. The importance of this was not realized at the time by the foreign powers. The treaties had been negotiated with the shogun's government and they were signed

[4] See several works on this subject by George A. Lensen: "Russians in Japan, 1858-1859," *Journal of Modern History,* 26 (1954), 162-73; "The Russo-Japanese Frontier," *History and Literature,* Florida State University Studies, No. 14, (1954), 23-40; *Russia's Japan Expedition of 1852 to 1855* (1964),* 111-26; and *Russia's Eastward Expansion* (1964).* See also W. G. Beasley, *Great Britain and the Opening of Japan* (1951), 113-44.

under the title of "taikun" (great lord). The foreigners assumed that the shogun was the proper authority to control diplomatic affairs. This was so, but what the foreigner did not know was the extent to which the authority of the shogun had already been weakened by internal dissension. This explains why the shogunate, when Perry arrived, was unwilling to accept full responsibility for signing a treaty. It had therefore referred the matter for approval to the emperor. Since the shogun's influence with the imperial court was still strong, imperial approval was given. With this approval the shogun could for a time silence the powerful opposition to the new policy.

Imperial approval insured general acceptance of the treaties, but the fact that the shogunate almost failed to secure the throne's favor revealed how the might of the *Bakufu* had declined. It had not been the habit of the Tokugawas or their predecessors to consider the will of the throne. They did so now because their old supremacy was little better than a political fiction; because they recognized the power of their feudal enemies, the *tozama* or outside lords of the western clans (Satsuma, Choshu, Hizen and Tosa), who were enemies of the Tokugawas before 1600; and because there was bitter dissension within the Tokugawa clan itself. Indeed, even among those elements that favored signing the treaties, the feeling was strong that no further concessions should be made to the foreigner—no general trade would be permitted and foreign contacts would be held to the bare treaty minimum.

TOWNSEND HARRIS IN JAPAN

Shortly after the Perry treaty was concluded, the American government sent its first consul general to reside at Shimoda. He was Townsend Harris of New York, a merchant familiar with East Asia and a man of excellent mind and character. Harris traveled by way of Siam, where he had negotiated a treaty granting extraterritoriality and a conventional tariff. He reached Shimoda in August, 1856.

This steel engraving of American sailors preparing presents for the Japanese first appeared in the officially published United States narrative of the Perry expedition.

The village of Shimoda, some 60 miles from Edo on the southern extremity of the Izu Peninsula southwest of Edo bay, was possessed of an exceptionally poor harbor that had been all but ruined by a tidal wave the previous year. The town, shut off from the hinterland by ranges of hills, was remote from the high roads and markets, and, in a word, was peculiarly ill-adapted to the needs of Harris. The Japanese had hoped to isolate the consul, if one came, and the selection of Shimoda was admirable for this purpose. Here Harris was in virtual quarantine not only from the United States but also from Japan. Fourteen months elapsed before he was visited by an American naval vessel, and eighteen months before he received additional instructions from the Department of State. On one occasion he wrote in his journal that for ten months he had not received a letter from the United States, that his supply of Western food was exhausted, and that he had lost so much weight it appeared that a vice-consul had been cut out of him. Furthermore, his position was described as that of "one honest man against a host of liars."

The principal objective of the Harris mission was to secure a full commercial treaty. The prospects of success were small. From the moment Harris landed, the Japanese used every device of obstruction and deceit to discourage and defeat him. They asserted that he had no right to land, since Japan had not approved his coming. With reluctance they assigned him an old temple as a residence. It was infested with mosquitoes, cockroaches, and large rats. The market sold him roosters that were too tough to eat. Police constantly guarded the temple on the pretext of protecting him. Wherever Harris or his Chinese servants went they were spied upon with the utmost suspicion. Japanese officials lied to him in the most flagrant manner. All this and much more Harris bore with patience, until after some months he was able to write in his journal: "The Japanese officials are daily becoming more and more friendly and more open in their communications with me. I hope this will grow and lead to good results by and by." This turn for the better in the relations between Harris and the shogun's officials must be attributed in large part to the patience, firmness, and unfailing honesty of this lonely bachelor American diplomat. He had set a high goal for himself. He proposed to serve the interests of his own country by leading Japan to a policy of full commercial intercourse, yet in so doing he was resolved not to take advantage of Japanese ignorance and lack of experience in international affairs. Harris, indeed, had become Japan's first instructor in world politics.

In June 1857, Harris witnessed the first official fruits of his labors when the Japanese signed a convention that, among other things, granted formally to the United States all that was contained in the British, Russian, and Dutch treaties. This was merely a preliminary, the great work still remained. Harris had asked for an audience with the shogun at Edo at which he would present a letter from the president. After much delay the request was granted. Harris himself described the astonishment of the officials as he stood in the presence of the shogun and looked "the awful 'Tycoon' in the face," spoke "plainly to him," and heard his reply—all this without any trepidation, or any "quivering of the muscles of the side."[5] Without the support of gunboats or marines Harris had won a great diplomatic victory.

It now remained for Harris to approach his main task—negotiating a full commercial treaty. He sought to convince the shogunate that the limited intercourse established by the first treaties was no longer adequate or practical. By January, 1858, the shogunate had agreed to the principal terms of a treaty. As the details of the treaty were perfected, Harris continued to act as instructor to the Japanese in diplomacy and international law. He continued to be that rare type of patriot who believed that the honor of his own country depended on its consideration for the rights of others.

When the treaty was completed, Harris waited impatiently month after month for the Japanese to sign. In July an American warship reached Shimoda bringing news of the Tientsin treaties with China. Harris saw in these reports both a danger and an opportunity. If the Europeans now turned their guns on Japan, his own policy would be in jeopardy. Could this potential threat from English and French warships be used to frighten the shogunate into signing the new treaty with America? Harris believed it could, and in this he was right. Despite bitter division of opinion in the shogunate, the treaty was signed July 29, 1858. It was a great personal victory for Harris, and a great diplomatic victory for his country. The treaty provided for diplomatic representation at the capitals of both powers, for the opening of new treaty ports where consuls might be stationed, for extraterritoriality, civil and criminal, for prohibition of the opium trade, for the freedom of foreigners to practice their religion, for a conventional tariff, and for the principle of most-favored-nation treatment.

The Harris treaty became the fundamental document in Japan's foreign relations until 1894. European powers accepted it as a model for their new treaties concluded in the months immediately following: the Dutch, August 18; the Russian, August 19; the British, August 26; and the French, October 7.[6] Ratifications

---

[5] See *The Complete Journal of Townsend Harris,* M. E. Cosenza, ed., (1930; rev. ed., 1959); and Carl Crow, *He Opened the Door of Japan* (1939). Also Henry Heusken, *Japan Journal, 1855-1861,* translated and edited by Jeannette C. van der Corput and Robert A. Wilson, (1964), the fascinating journal of the young Dutchman who was secretary and translator to Townsend Harris.

[6] For the Harris treaty and conventions, see Hunter Miller, ed., *Treaties and Other International Acts of the United States of America,** (8 vols., 1931-1948), VII, 598-648, 947-1170. The Harris treaty was also a triumph for those Japanese who believed Japan must move into the modern world, not away from it. Pre-eminent among these was Ii Naosuke, richest of Japan's hereditary vassals (*fudai daimyo*). See Yoshida Tsunekichi, *Ii Naosuke* (1963).

of the Harris treaty were exchanged in Washington in 1860 by the first modern Japanese embassy to the Western world. Members of this embassy, the first Japanese to see the wonders of America, were influential promoters of Japan's subsequent modernization.

DOMESTIC POLITICS AND FOREIGN AFFAIRS

The shogunate had signed the Harris treaty. Could it enforce acceptance of the new policy by its enemies at home? These latter included not only the *tozama* lords but also powerful leaders within the Tokugawa family itself. During 1857 powerful opposition against the pro-foreign policy of the shogunate had again reasserted itself. Thus, when the shogunate sought the emperor's consent to signature of the Harris treaty, the request was denied. This explains why Harris was kept waiting. Furthermore, his treaty represented a new policy adopted by the *Bakufu* without the consent of the emperor. The enemies of the Tokugawas were quick to see that by opposing this liberal foreign policy of the shogunate they could appear as loyal supporters of the "divine" emperor against a "usurping" shogun. It was clear too that the balance of power in Japan had so shifted as to enable the imperial court to issue orders to the *Bakufu*. Therefore the court told the shogun that the new treaties could be accepted only until such time as the foreign barbarians could be expelled and the old policy of exclusion resumed. In this way the imperial court at Kyoto became the center of an anti-foreign, anti-*Bakufu* party, deriving its support from the *tozama* lords, from disgruntled allies of the Tokugawa clan, and from branch families of the Tokugawa house itself, such as the Mito group.

July, 1859, was a critical month both for the shogunate and for the new treaty powers. So great was the danger of murderous attacks upon foreigners that the shogunate, refusing to open Kanagawa, which lay on the Tokaido highway between Edo and Kyoto, encouraged the foreigners to settle at Yokohama, farther down the bay and destined soon to become one of Japan's great seaports. The immediate danger was twofold. So-called ultra-patriots, samurai and *ronin*, who had detached themselves from their clans, were anxious to embarrass the shogunate by attacking foreigners. Many of the foreigners in turn had come directly from residence in China, where too frequently they had acquired the habit of regarding the Oriental as an inferior to be treated with little respect. This being so, it is surprising that in the years 1859 to 1865, when foreigners were denounced by every fanatical supporter of the throne, only twelve Westerners were killed. Two cases that had important repercussions on foreign relations may be mentioned. When in January, 1861, Henry Heusken the interpreter at the American legation, was murdered, the foreign representatives, with the exception of Harris, retired from Edo to Yokohama in protest against the shogun's failure to give the legations adequate protection. Harris took the broader view that the administration was doing everything in its power to protect them. He therefore remained in Edo, where for a time he was the only foreign diplomatic representative.

The second case had more serious consequences. In September, 1862, C. L. Richardson, a Britisher visiting from Hong Kong, was killed on the highway near Yokohama while riding with three compatriots, two men and a woman. The assassins were samurai in the feudal procession of the father of the Lord of Satsuma, a leader of the anti-shogun and anti-foreign party supporting the throne. This influential personage had just served upon the shogun a summons ordering him to appear in Kyoto to explain his conduct before the throne. There are various accounts as to what happened. There is no proof that Richardson intended to be offensive. Nevertheless, he and his companions failed to dismount while the feudal procession passed by. For this he sacrificed his life, and his companions were wounded. Although foreigners in Yokohama demanded immediate military action, saner counsel prevailed. Early in the following year

(1863), the British government made the following demands: (1) payment of an indemnity of 100,000 pounds; (2) an indemnity of 25,000 pounds to be paid by the Satsuma clan; and (3) trial and execution of the assassins in the presence of a British naval officer.

These demands came at a most unhappy moment in the shogun's career. He had already been summoned to Kyoto to explain his conduct, which could mean only that those opposed to his government and his policy were now in control of the throne. This proved to be true, for the emperor ordered that all ports be closed to foreign commerce. Meanwhile, the negotiations on the British demands continued at Yokohama, where the British and the French now offered to use their naval forces on behalf of the shogun against the anti-foreign lords. This offer the shogun declined. In June the British indemnity was paid and the powers were notified of the emperor's exclusion decree. Their reply declared that the treaties must be enforced, which, of course, the shogun fully realized. For the moment his policy would be one of delay, while he entertained the hope that some change could be effected in the attitude of his domestic enemies.

According to the imperial decree, the expelling of the foreigners and the discarding of the treaties were to be carried out by the shogun's government. However, the Lord of Choshu, a *tozama daimyo* whose lands controlled the western entrance to the inland sea, fired on an American ship lying off Shimonoseki. Later, French and Dutch vessels were also fired upon. Consequently, one American and several French war vessels hastened to attack the Choshu forts. It was evident that the shogun was unable to control the western barons. The British had already determined to take action against Satsuma to enforce compliance with the demands arising out of the Richardson affair. Accordingly, a British squadron appeared at Kagoshima in August, 1863. Here negotiations broke down, and the resulting bombardment, assisted by a typhoon and fire, destroyed more than half the town. Without securing acceptance of their demands, the British sailed away. Three months later envoys from Satsuma called upon the British

representative agreeing to pay the indemnity and to continue the search for the guilty. They also requested assistance in securing in England a naval vessel for their clan. The significance of the incident is obvious. Anti-foreignism in Satsuma was in part an artifice hiding a determination to destroy the shogunate.

CHOSHU PUNISHED

Events now took an unusual turn at Kyoto, where the anti-foreign and anti-shogunate forces were in control. Dissension appeared in these councils, where Choshu leaders were accused of attempting to seize the person of the emperor. Choshu troops were ordered to leave the capital, and when they attempted a *coup d'état,* the shogun was ordered by the emperor to deal with the rebellious clan. At this juncture, Sir Rutherford Alcock, the British minister, returned to Japan determined to unite the foreign powers in a joint expedition against Choshu. His purpose was to give needed support to the shogunate and to demonstrate to the hot-headed clans that it was no longer safe to tamper with the treaty rights of foreigners. Alcock's plan was supported by his diplomatic colleagues, and so, contrary to his instructions from London, he set about to organize a joint naval expedition, consisting of British, Dutch, and French ships, and one small American vessel, which sailed from Yokohama in August, 1864. No negotiations preceded the engagement off the Choshu coast. The fleet went straight to the task of silencing the batteries. On Choshu this lesson was as effective as the previous affair at Kagoshima. Clan leaders agreed to open the straits, not to repair the forts or to build new ones, and to pay an indemnity covering the cost of the expedition. This clan, too, now turned to the West for armaments and advice that would create an effective military machine. Since the shogun could not permit the foreign powers to negotiate with a single clan, a convention was soon concluded whereby the indemnities were assumed by the shogunate. Payment of large sums, however, proved most embarrassing to the government, and since the powers were more interested in new treaty ports and new concessions, the opportunity was favorable for a second naval demonstration.

Under the leadership of the new British minister, Sir Harry Parkes, it was planned to assemble the naval forces of the powers at Osaka, close to Kyoto, where pressure could be most effectively brought to bear upon the anti-foreign forces surrounding the throne. This time no American vessel participated, for none was available. The demands stated that two-thirds of the Shimonoseki indemnity would be remitted if Hyogo (Kobe) and Osaka were opened immediately, if the emperor gave his approval to the treaties, and if the tariff were reduced to a general 5 percent. The reply was delivered on the final day permitted by the allies' demands. The emperor—and this was most important of all—had agreed to ratify the treaties, the tariff would be reduced, and the full indemnity would be paid, for Japan was not prepared to open Hyogo and Osaka. Thus the most serious problem, the opposition of the Japanese imperial faction to the treaties, was disposed of. The western *daimyo* were no longer aligned against the foreigners, but their determination to overthrow the shogunate and restore the emperor still remained.

The first phase of Japan's nineteenth-century revolution was now complete. The two-centuries-old policy of exclusion and seclusion had been abandoned not only by the weakened shogunate but also by the throne, which derived its power from the vital western clans. Japan had now accepted full treaty relations with the major Western powers. These treaties, as in the case of those with China, imposed certain serious limitations upon Japan's sovereignty—extraterritoriality and the conventional tariff.

It should be observed that Japan's anti-foreignism in these early years of contacts with the West should not be considered merely as the emotional outburst of military patriots. Anti-foreignism had deep cultural and political roots. But its appearance after Perry's arrival must be understood in light of the economic results of opening Japan to foreign commerce. The cost of living was increased by large exports of consumer goods. The price of tea soon doubled; that of raw silk tripled. Before 1867 the price of rice, Japan's main food, had increased twelvefold. This disastrous revolution in prices was induced in part by the outflowing of Japan's gold supply due to the high and fixed price of silver in Japan. Hardships resulting from this price revolution supported the case of those factions which, for whatever reasons, regarded anti-foreignism as a patriotic duty.

SOME CONCLUSIONS

By repudiating the policy of exclusion and seclusion Japan took the first major and revolutionary step toward modernization. Later years would tell whether this dramatic change of course would lead to a slavish imitation of the West or whether, as in the earlier impact of Chinese civilization in the seventh and eighth centuries, the Japanese would again adapt what the West had to offer, shaping it to their own peculiar needs and thus preserving and enriching their own cultural identity. Certainly what had happened in Japan by 1865 was a result of the threat from the West, but it was also a result of those incoherent strivings in the later Tokugawa years toward a new order of society. The arrival of Perry meant to a few discerning leaders in the shogunate that Japan had no choice but to move rapidly toward that new order or to be forced by the Western powers to do so. In 1865 there was no one who could say with certainty what the final shape of the new order would be. Japan, to be sure, had entered the outside world, but she had not as yet found a viable structure for her own society.

FOR FURTHER READING

Foreign Relations with The West. W. G. Beasley, "Japan and the West in the Mid-Nineteenth Century: Nationalism and the Origins of the Modern State," *Proceedings of* the *British Academy* 55 (1969); and *Select Documents on Japanese Foreign Policy, 1853-1868* (1955). Manfred C. Vernon, "The Dutch and the Opening of Japan by the United States," *Pacific Historical Review* 28 (1959), 39-48. John Z. Bowers, *Western Medical Pioneers in Feudal Japan* (1969). George A. Lensen, *Report from Hokkaido: The Remains of Russian Culture in Northern Japan* (1954).

The Role of the United States. Samuel Eliot Morison, *"Old Bruin," Commodore Matthew C. Perry, 1794-1848* (1967). Roger Pineau, ed., *The Japan Expedition, 1852-1854: The Personal Journal of Commodore Matthew C. Perry* (1968). Arthur C. Walworth, *Black Ships off Japan: The Story of Commodore Perry's Expedition* (1946; reprint, 1966), a popular, readable account. Allan B. Cole, ed., A Scientist with Perry in Japan, the Journal of *Dr. James Morrow* (1947); and *Yankee Surveyors in the Shogun's Seas: Records of the U.S. Surveying Expedition to the North Pacific Ocean, 1853-56* (1947). George Henry Preble, *The Opening of Japan: A Diary of Discovery in the Far East, 1853-1856*, Boleslaw Szczesniak, ed. (1962). Alfred Tamarin, *Japan and the United States: Early Encounters, 1791-1860* (1970). Foster Rhea Dulles, *Yankees and Samurai: America's Role in the Emergence of Modern Japan* (1965). Samaki Shunzo, *Japan and the United States, 1790-1853. Transactions of the Asiatic Society of Japan,* 18 (2nd series, 1939). Edwin O. Reischauer, *The United States and Japan* (1950),* an excellent survey of U.S.-Japanese relations. Payson Jackson Treat, *Japan and the United States, 1853-1921, Revised and Continued to 1928* (1928), a standard survey. F. C. Jones, *Extra-territoriality in Japan and the Diplomatic Relations Resulting in Its Abolition, 1853-1899* (1931).

Japan Lays the Foundations of a Modern State

10

It would be difficult to exaggerate the ultimate effect of the year 1865 in Japan's modern history. By that date, and however reluctantly, the emperor and the western clans, following the course set by the shogun in 1854 and 1858, had accepted the new concept of political and commercial intercourse with the outside world, and thereby ended the long era of exclusion and seclusion. Acceptance of this new departure was a major, in fact, revolutionary, step, and the only point of consensus at the moment in Japan's internal politics. Acceptance of the new foreign policy, therefore, did not mean that Japan's crisis had passed. On the contrary, the country was now faced by an unfamiliar and aggressive Western world, which the Japanese could only regard as hostile to Japan's way of life and traditional values. In these circumstances, how would Japan proceed to revitalize her internal structure, preserve her identity, and insure her security?

Answers to these questions were not immediately apparent to Japan's ruling elites. The foreign threat signaled by the arrival of Perry, Harris, and the envoys of Britain, France, and Russia had unleashed within Japan a bitter and as yet unresolved struggle

for power. The motives of the contending leaders were mixed. There was undoubtedly a pervading passion to defend the country, but there were also dissident elements anxious to gain control of it and thus to serve personal ambitions. Between 1853 and 1865 neither the efforts of the shogunate nor those of the western clans (Satsuma, Choshu, Tosa, and Hizen) had created adequate defenses against foreign encroachment and this failure implied that the *baku-han* system was not proving equal to the task. As a result, from as early as 1858 when the shogun signed the Harris treaty without the emperor's approval, Kyoto became increasingly the center of internal politics and intrigue—a clear suggestion that the emperor, not the shogun, was emerging as the symbol of unity and perhaps as the locus of political power as well. Indeed, by 1863 the prestige of the *Bakufu* had so declined that the shogun was attempting, though unsuccessfully, to form a council of *daimyo* which, with the shogun's and the emperor's blessings, would determine matters of national policy. This failure meant that the western clans, though divided among themselves, had become strong enough to resist the shogun. Within these western *han* a vigorous younger leadership was appearing, able to control their *daimyo,* willing to oppose the shogun by force if necessary, and to rally around an emperor restored to power. This new activist leadership also included some able young members of the *kuge,* the court nobility at Kyoto. At this point interclan rivalry for control of the throne was intense. In 1866 troops of the shogun attempting to chastise Choshu for plotting at Kyoto were defeated, a turn of events which opened the way for an interclan alliance against the *Bakufu.* During 1867 the struggle for power continued. The Tokugawas vainly attempted to bolster their position by internal reforms in the clan and *Bakufu* administration. A number of the more timid *daimyo* continued to seek some form of compromise solution, but these efforts were overshadowed by the intrigues of the younger clan leaders seeking to destroy the Tokugawa power and to restore the emperor.

RESTORATION AND CIVIL WAR

Late in 1867 it seemed that a compromise solution was at hand. The *daimyo* of Tosa, disturbed by the increasing power of Satsuma and Choshu, proposed that the emperor assume political power assisted by a council of *daimyo.* Under this plan the shogun would resign but continue to serve as a kind of first councilor in the new government. This plan was promptly rejected by the more extreme *kuge* and by the younger leaders in the western clans. At the beginning of 1868 troops of these and other *han* took possession of the young emperor and proclaimed the restoration of imperial rule. In the short civil war which followed, the Tokugawa forces were defeated completely. The shogunate, which had ruled Japan for more than two and one-half centuries, had been destroyed. What kind of restored imperial government in the name of the emperor would replace it?[1]

---

[1] The Meiji restoration marked the end of what might be called Old Japan and the beginning of new Japan. It was a very complicated affair which may not have been understood by many of the participants and which has been a subject of historical controversy throughout succeeding years. It continues to raise a great many historical questions. Was it

In 1868 the restoration of imperial rule in itself could hardly be considered a revolution. Rather it was a return to a long-neglected yet revered institution, the divinely-descended monarchy and throne of ancient Japan. Since the time of Yoritomo in the twelfth century, the emperors had been relegated to a very humble and, at times, abject position, in which they carried on ceremonial functions and did the bidding of the shogun; yet the institution was not destroyed and, indeed, it had continued to evoke deep sentiments of loyalty among segments of the samurai class. Thus the emperor was the logical rallying point for those who were determined to end the Tokugawa dictatorship. At the same time the restoration leaders (slightly more than 100 might be numbered in the total group) were newcomers to the business of creating or

---

primarily a matter of throwing off the Tokugawa dictatorship and reuniting Japan under the emperor? Was it the political clothing in which Japan moved away from an economic system which was no longer useful in the face of modern industry? Was it a means by which a feudal elite and a growing class of wealthy commoners conspired at the expense of the Japanese people? Was it a case of a traditional ideology promoting a revolutionary cause? Those who were in opposition to the Tokugawas often appeared not to be proposing a new society, but rather to be reasserting old values suggested by the restoration of the emperor. Some titles in a very rich literature on the restoration include the following: Albert M. Craig, *Choshu in the Meiji Restoration* (1961) develops the idea that the restoration, far from being a revolution, was a change carried out in the name of inherited values to fulfill inherited traditions by men who had no notion of the eventual social or political results; H. D. Harootunian, *Toward Restoration: the Growth of Political Consciousness in Tokugawa Japan* (1970) finds that the restoration leaders, while having no clear view of the future, were perfectly willing to repudiate history. The values they extolled were traditional in name because that was the only vocabulary they had, but the content was new; W. G. Beasley, *The Meiji Restoration* (1973) sees the restoration's origins not in economic distress or class struggle, but in a growing sense of national danger and pride stimulated by the country's first knowledge of and contacts with the West; finally, Paul Akamatsu, *Meiji 1868: Revolution and Counter-Revolution in Japan,* translated from the French by Miriam Kochan (1972), concentrates on the political revolution of 1866-1873.

operating a national government, and they apparently had no blueprint on the shape this government should take.[2]

Judged by what these new leaders accomplished in the latter half of the nineteenth century, it is clear that they formed an extraordinary group of individuals, some of whom, later as *genro* (elder statesmen), were to have great influence on Japanese policies well into the twentieth century. As indicated, a few of them were of the court nobility, such as Iwakura Tomomi, one of the most powerful members of the group until his death in 1883. Most of them were samurai of the western clans. The majority had been raised, educated, and trained in lower- and middle-class samurai households for military and government service in the *han*. Their Confucian schooling and indoctrination in the warrior code of *bushido* instilled a loyalty to higher authority together with a sense of service to society in the Confucian sense. They were also products of Japanese political tradition which emphasized the emperor's symbolic role. Thus, they might restore an emperor, but they had no intention that he should rule. They looked toward a government based on the tradition of collective leadership, which they planned to provide. The emperor's role would be to proclaim their decisions. Furthermore, they were extremely sensitive to the threat posed by the foreign Western powers, and they were determined to so strengthen the country industrially and militarily that the powers would be forced to forgo the unequal provisions (the conventional tariff and extraterritoriality) in their commercial treaties. As individuals the new leaders were able and ambitious. In the

[2] At the time of the restoration, a young boy 15 years of age, Mutsuhito, had succeeded to the throne. The name adopted for his reign came from two Chinese characters meaning "bright" and "rule." Together they read *Meiji* or "enlightened rule," the name which would be applied to the long reign of Mutsuhito, 1867-1912. For more extended treatments of the restoration and the revolutionary changes which were to follow, see Marius B. Jansen, "The Meiji State: 1868-1912," in *Modern East Asia: Essays in Interpretation*, James B. Crowley, ed. (1970),* 95-121; and Hugh Borton, *Japan's Modern Century* (2nd ed., 1970), 79-217.

decade of the 1850's most of them had been bitterly anti-foreign, but they were also intelligent. Prior to 1868 a number of them had traveled to Britain or had had continuing close contacts with foreigners in Japan. The net result by 1868 was that a majority of the new leadership had been deeply impressed by the power, the technology, and the intellectual vigor of the Western world. It was this discovery of Western progress and leadership which converted them to the role of reformers as well as restorers. Japan's history in the decades of the 1870's and the 1880's is essentially the story of how these leaders (key figures are identified in the note below) sought, through particular methods in politics, economics, and philosophy, to make Japan modern and strong while preserving traditional values and motivations that were peculiarly Japanese.[3]

[3] See John Whitney Hall, *Japan from Prehistory to Modern Times* (1970),* 265-73. Some of the men in addition to Iwakura who were to play leading roles during the Meiji era would include: (1) Kido Koin (1835-1877) of Choshu, a builder of the western clan alliance against the Tokugawas and one of the ablest politicians in the early Meiji government; (2) Saigo Takamori (1828-1877) of Satsuma, like Kido, a maker of the western clan alliance, and later a leader of the opposition to certain policies of the early Meiji government; (3) Okubo Toshimichi (1830-1878) of Satsuma, who in the years immediately following the restoration played an indispensable role in holding the infant imperial government together; (4) Itagaki Taisuke (1837-1919) of Tosa, one of the more progressive thinkers, a believer in the separation of powers—a strange idea in the Japan of that time—and organizer of a political club, the *Risshisha,* which in 1880 was expanded into the first national political party, the *Jiyuto* or Liberal party; (5) Goto Shojiro (1838-1897) of Tosa, close associate of Itagaki, student of English affairs, and influential in matters of foreign policy; (6) Ito Hirobumi (1841-1909) of Choshu, who rose from a very humble samurai family to occupy almost every high office of state; (7) Inouye Kaoru (1836-1915) of Choshu, studied in England with Ito in 1863, saw the futility of the anti-foreign policy of the clans, and served ably in areas of foreign affairs and finance; (8) Okuma Shigenobu (1838-1922) of Hizen, trained in Dutch and English studies, at times a vigorous member of the opposition, and long associated with foreign affairs in the imperial government; (9) Yamagata Aritomo (1838-1922) of Choshu, a strong believer in authoritarian rule, and the most influential force in building Japan's modern

THE CHARTER OATH, 1868

In the early months of 1868, the restored imperial government was a very frail edifice. It lacked most of the attributes of an effective government. To be sure, the emperor now had an army (the troops of the western *han*) but its use was dependent on the will and agreement of the *daimyo*. Moreover, although Kyoto had a treasury, it was empty, and the administration had no powers of taxation. Title to the lands in the *han* was still held by more than 250 *daimyo*. There was no standard national currency, no generally approved agreement on what the framework of the new government was to be or on its future relationship to *daimyo*, samurai, peasant, artisan, or merchant. Indeed, some twenty years were to elapse before a permanent plan of government would be adopted. Meanwhile there would be almost constant alterations and shiftings in top personnel as this infant administration sought to meet immediate practical problems through the traditional method of forming councils of state directing such ministries as finance and foreign affairs. In these circumstances, with public morale threatened, some declaration of purpose and direction from on high seemed imperative. Accordingly in April, 1868, the emperor proclaimed the so-called Charter Oath. It had been composed by a few members of the young leadership, principally Iwakura and Kido Koin.

The Charter Oath set forth a number of general principles in language which was sometimes quite ambiguous. Nevertheless, these principles were to be of immense importance in the years ahead, especially to those among the young leaders who did not approve of what the government was doing at a given time. In this sense the oath was a sanction for an opposition, although this was probably not the intent of its framers.

Its overall tone was decidedly modern. It stated that government policy would rest on wide consultation, which presumably meant consultation only among *daimyo*, and samurai, and court nobility. All persons were to be free to pursue their legitimate interests. Absurd customs of the past were, it was said, to be abandoned. Finally, new knowledge would be sought wherever it could be found. If the restoration was a return to the past, the Charter Oath was a declaration that some new roads were to be opened to the future.[4]

ABOLITION OF THE FEUDAL STRUCTURE

Although the ending of exclusion, the restoring of the emperor, and the proclaiming of the Charter Oath were unmistakable evidences of the birth of a new Japan, these events in themselves had not created a state which could be governed effectively or which could meet the pressures of the foreign powers, so long as the old feudal structure preserved the political and economic autonomy of 250 *diamyo*. To men such as Kido and Okubo Toshimichi it was evident that the feudal structure must be destroyed to enable the restored emperor and his government to acquire the power to direct and rule the nation. In 1869 they persuaded the *daimyo* of the four western clans to surrender to the emperor title to their domains. Other lesser clans hastened to follow the same course. This capitulation of the *daimyo* came about because they could see no alternative and because the young leaders had convinced them they were surrendering lesser local power for greater power in the new central government. This done, the *daimyo* took up their residence at Tokyo and placed their soldiers under the command of the emperor. In 1871 the *han* were abolished formally by imperial decree and replaced by prefectures under direct administration of the restoration government. To the end of building national strength, other aspects of the feudal order suffered a like fate. The abolition of the *han* meant, of

---

army. For further detail on these and many other Meiji leaders, see Borton, *Modern Century,* Chapters 4-10.

[4] Following closely on the Charter Oath, the name of the Tokugawa shogun's capital, Edo, was changed to Tokyo (Eastern Capital). Then, amid great pomp and ceremony, the Meiji emperor, his court, and the new imperial government moved to Tokyo in 1869, where the Tokugawa's Edo castle became the imperial residence. Thereby the symbol of dual government (two capitals, Kyoto and Edo) was brought to an end.

course, the passing of the *daimyo* as autonomous feudal lords. They were compensated financially with government bonds, which helped insure their loyalty to the new regime even though they no longer played a significant role in it.

THE FATE OF THE SAMURAI CLASS

Depriving the samurai (some 6 percent of the population) of their special position in society was a vastly more complex task. The samurai, in their various gradations, were not only a military caste of great power, they were also accustomed to being supported by hereditary incomes and, in general, they had shaped the political and intellectual life of feudal Japan. They were proud, sometimes arrogant, and jealous of their privileged status. Nevertheless, the new government was now strong enough to abolish the legal base of the four feudal social classes, making all subjects of the emperor equal before the law, including even the *eta* or outcasts. This act by which the samurai were deprived of their special status was an essential prelude to the enactment of a national military service law in 1873, under which a new army of commoners was recruited and trained. A leading role in this venture was taken by Yamagata Aritomo (Choshu) who at first followed French and later German military theory and practice. The creation of this new military system was among the most revolutionary acts of the new government. It was carried through by the young samurai leaders, who, again in the interest of national strength, were destroying their own privileged and powerful caste which had ruled Japan for centuries. It should be noted that the purpose of the reformers was not to promote egalitarian principles but rather to give power to government, to free the samurai from the wasteful and frustrating restrictions of feudal society, to provide freedom of choice in occupation (a very revolutionary concept in the Japan of that time), and to promote economic activity, to create wealth, and thereby to serve the new national state. It may also be doubted whether the Meiji government had in mind a social revolution, yet almost everything it did in these early years promoted social revolution. In the emerging freer society, the two swords of the samurai, their badge of distinction and honor, would give place to education, wealth, and political position as the insignia of prestige.

Their new status as commoners was by no means welcome to many samurai. Their former income, measured in rice, had been small but it was now cut by more than 50 percent.[5] The freedom to select a vocation of one's own choosing was bewildering to men who had been schooled to believe that the bearing of arms was the only profession of honor, who regarded their former fiefs as owing them a living, and whose mental horizons were often limited to the parochial and military aspects of *bushido*. They now faced a society that deprived them of much of their income and their monopoly in bearing arms (the new national conscript army was made up largely of peasants), and, worst of all, directed them toward the despised world of business. Although there were samurai who adjusted to the new order, with some even destined to emerge as leaders in business, politics, and the professions, many found the adjustment impossible and thoroughly repugnant. These malcontents and their intellectual descendants were to play an adventuresome and at times troublesome role in Japan's later push toward empire.[6]

[5] In 1876, the samurai were compelled to convert their pensions into government bonds. Those with the largest incomes were paid off at five times the annual value of the pensions; those with the smallest, at fourteen times annual value. This gave the samurai an income on an average of one-half of their former pension income. But pension income had been about one-half of their former income. Thus, by 1877, their income was much less than one-half of what it had been.

[6] Additional useful references on these early years of Meiji include: W. W. McLaren, "Japanese Government Documents," *Transactions of the Asiatic Society of Japan*, 42 (1914) 8 ff. which contains the Charter Oath; Masakaza Iwata, *Okubo Toshimichi, the Bismarck of Japan* (1964); Hyman Kublin, "The Modern Army of Early Meiji Japan," *Far Eastern Quarterly*, 9 (1949), 20-42; Ernest L. Presseisen,

THE PEASANTS AS FREE MEN

Another victim of the abolition of feudalism was the old system of feudal land tenure, together with the traditional method of collecting taxes. Under the urging of Okubo and Inouye Kaoru, the government enacted laws providing for the private ownership of land and adopted formulae for assessing its value, fixing the tax rate on this value, and providing that the tax be paid in money as opposed to rice. In the early 1870's when this nation-wide reform was enacted, about 80 percent of Japan's population were peasants (farmers), and a majority of these were independent cultivators. Under the new order these peasants were now freed from all feudal obligations and became, nominally at least, freeholders, paying not a tax in kind on the value of their crop but a tax in money on the assessed value of their land. On the surface it appeared that the peasant had moved from serfdom to freedom. In some measure, this was so; however, the surreptitious acquisition of land by a new capitalistic landlord class, a practice which had been going on before the restoration, was now legalized and, as a result, within a few years tenant land had risen to 30 percent of the area cultivated. This process was accelerated in later years, with obvious effects upon the peasants' new-found freedom. Back in feudal days, the principle followed in matters of taxation was, generally, to leave the peasant just enough of his crop to live on and no more. Thus under the "paternal" care of his *daimyo,* the peasant neither lived nor died. Now, in the new, free society after 1871, it was sometimes said that the peasant had freedom of choice—to live or to die, to remain on the land or to leave it and go to the city. In any event, the way had been opened for the dispossession of the peasantry and for the creation of modern Japanese agriculture with its peculiar landlord-tenant relationships.[7]

These momentous changes in the structure of Japanese society revealed both strength and weakness in the Meiji administration. The more rapidly the country moved into these reforms as a prelude to the building of a strong economy, the more evident became the need for the technological knowledge and skills of modern industry, which only the West could offer. Accordingly, in 1871-1872, a special educational mission, headed by Iwakura Tomomi, vice-president of the council of state and minister for foreign affairs, visited the United States, Britain, France, and Germany, where it learned how far Japan must yet travel before she could be considered an equal of the great Western powers in political organization, industrial wealth, and military potential.

STRIFE WITHIN THE MEIJI GOVERNMENT

By 1873 the major changes in the status of samurai and peasant precipitated violent protests by both of these classes. Peasant uprisings were numerous and violent, but they were local and for the most part nonpolitical. Reactions among the samurai were more serious. Many of this class were simply not prepared to accept the new order. But they were ready followers of any leadership which would give them a renewed pride in the bearing of arms. They found this leadership within the Meiji government itself, where some of the young samurai leaders were disgruntled because they had been excluded from choice offices or had not been consulted on important policy decisions. These dissenters, led by Saigo Takamori (Satsuma), who had led the fighting against the Tokugawas, resented the "humbling" of the samurai class and saw their own role in government as declining. They now sought to embarrass the government by demanding a military expedition to punish Korea for rebuffs and insults to Japanese envoys sent to secure a treaty in 1872. Such a mission would employ large numbers of former samurai in their traditional calling as fighting men. These designs for foreign war, however, came to naught; with the return of the Iwakura mission in 1873,

---

Before Aggression; Europeans Prepare the Japanese Army (1965); and Bernard S. Silberman, *Ministers of Modernization: Elite Mobility in the Meiji Restoration, 1868-1873* (1964).

[7] For the historic position of the peasantry see Hugh Borton, *Peasant Uprisings in Japan of the Tokugawa Period* (2nd ed., 1968).*

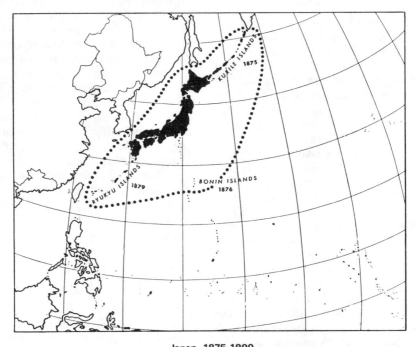

Japan, 1875-1890

Reproduced from A War Atlas for Americans *(New York: Simon & Schuster, 1944), with permission from the publisher and from the U.S. Department of State, Division of Map Intelligence and Cartography.*

the emperor directed the government to give all priority to domestic development and to forego any Korean expedition. A year later it did sanction a diversionary expedition to Formosa to punish the natives for the killing of Ryukyu islanders. But this side show did not weaken the government's resolve to build Japan internally before embarking on any major ventures in the foreign field. The adoption of Iwakura's policy also signified that opposition members of government were on the way out, and that the government was to be controlled by an even smaller group of very powerful men, principally Iwakura, Ito, Kido, Okubo, Okuma, Matsukata, and Yamagata. Saigo had already left the government and had returned to Satsuma, where in 1877 he presided over the most serious and the last of the samurai uprisings, known as the Satsuma Rebellion. The rebels numbered in excess of 40,000 but they were beaten into submission by the new national army of peasant conscripts. It was striking evidence that the day of the samurai, as samurai, was no more.

THE ECONOMIC BASE OF EARLY MEIJI

Central in the thinking of the early Meiji leaders was the need to create a financial, commercial, and industrial society competitive with the outside world and assuring Japan's security. In seeking these ends the Meiji leadership enjoyed some advantages at the beginning. It had time to plan and to experiment because it was not faced by any broadly-based revolution from the masses. Moreover, the early defeat of the Tokugawa resistance placed the large Tokugawa lands, the economic center of the country, at the disposal of the new government. At the same time the task of rapidly building a modern economic society was a gigantic one. Most of the government's meager revenues in 1868-1869 came from such limited sources as customs duties, domestic borrowing, and newly-printed paper currency. The existing currency from feudal days was a motley array of gold, silver and copper coins, and rice certificates. This monetary chaos had cost Japan dearly because it enabled the foreign merchants at the treaty ports to make huge profits by exchanging foreign silver for Japanese gold. After 1858 foreign imports, such as cotton textiles, entered the Japanese market at the low duty of 5 percent fixed by the treaties. These imports, so disruptive of native industry, were a product of Western technology, which the Japanese had yet to acquire. Foreign loans did not provide an answer to the government's overall problem because of excessively high interest rates and because the Japanese were fearful of Western exploitation.

In a word, the Meiji government decided to build economic strength through its own resources and its own initiative. The Iwakura mission, for example, implemented the statement in the Charter Oath that new knowledge would be sought wherever it could be found. For a time, foreign advisers—British, French, German, and American—were employed, but this was a temporary expedient since the Japanese learned rapidly and foreign advisers were very expensive.[8]

GOVERNMENT BUILDS INDUSTRY

Back in the later Tokugawa days, the shogunate and the western clans independently had made some limited beginnings in heavy industry (shipbuilding and munitions), and in such light industries as cotton textiles. These enterprises were taken over, expanded, and subsidized by the Meiji government. These and other ventures were financed by the government's modern banking system, at first secured largely by government bonds. The government was also the active promoter in the whole field of communications. In 1872 Japan's first railroad, from Tokyo to Yokohama, was opened. Port facilities were improved. A modern postal system was established, while telegraph lines began to penetrate all important cities. Despite these heroic efforts, Japan's financial position by 1880 was one of deep crisis. Everything the government did to promote the economy and to strengthen the state cost money, which in considerable measure the government simply did not have. Furthermore, most of the government's infant industrial enterprises were not yet making a profit. These troubles were met by the policies of Matsukata Masayoshi (Satsuma), who became minister of finance in 1881. He sold most of the government's plants in the nonstrategic industries to private interests, and applied measures of rigid retrenchment. These measures were successful; within less than ten years the financial crisis had been met and passed.[9]

THE NEW JAPANESE ENTREPRENEUR

The Matsukata policies were a turning point in Japan's industrial development. While the government would still operate many industries and foster others in direct and indirect ways, private entrepreneurship would be relied upon for basic and rapid economic growth. The industries which at this time were sold by the government went to a very small number of rich merchants able to buy them at bargain prices. Most of these industries were soon profitable, not only because of the energies and abilities of private management but also because the Japanese were mastering the necessary technological skills. Before the end of the century the success of Japan's industrialization was assured. The less favorable side of the picture was that much of this growing industry was concentrated in the hands of an

---

[8] Japan's first major success in foreign trade was in the silk industry. She developed superior methods of reeling silk and soon became a principal supplier of the Western silk market. Silk continued as her chief export into the twentieth century.

[9] For further economic background on this period see James I. Nakamura, *Agricultural Production and the Economic Development of Japan, 1873-1922* (1966).

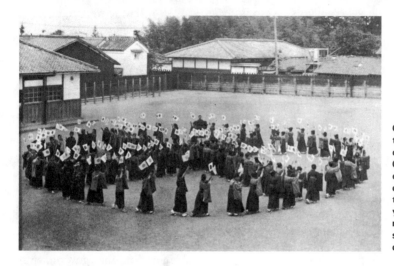

Christian missions in late nine-teenth-century Japan were less conspicuous than they were in China. Nevertheless, missionaries contributed significantly to social change, through such activities as the operation of schools for young women. The students en-rolled at the convent school shown here are performing a flag drill.

exceedingly small group of entrepreneurs. From this group would emerge later the great financial and industrial family combines known as the *zaibatsu,* which would dominate Japanese business in the twentieth century.[10]

CREATING A LITERATE PEOPLE

In these early years of Meiji one of the most striking things about the young restoration leaders was their conviction that only an

[10] The financier-industrialists of Meiji Japan were for the most part a new breed. A very few—such as the Mitsui family, successful bankers since the seventeenth century—were descendants of great merchants of Tokugawa times. Most of the modern business men, however, were of samurai origin—Iwasaki Yataro, for example, founder of the Mitsubishi interests, and second only in strength to Mitsui. Shibusawa Eiichi, another industrial genius, came from a well-to-do peasant family. He acquired samurai status in the last days of the shogunate but became one of the leading industrialists of early Meiji, especially in banking and the cotton textile industry. On the origins of Japan's business pioneers and the role of government in Meiji industry, see Thomas C. Smith, *Political Change and Industrial Development in Japan: Government Enterprise, 1868-1880* (1955), and Johannes Hirschmeier, *The Origins of Entrepreneurship in Meiji Japan* (1964).

educated Japan could become a strong Japan. This conviction was given expression in both the Charter Oath (1868) and the education laws of 1871-1872. The law which created a department of education proclaimed that "all people, high and low, and of both sexes, should receive education, so that there should not be found one family in the whole land, or one member of a family ignorant and illiterate." Although education in the later Tokugawa years had been reaching even some sectors of the common people, the law of 1871 announcing universal public education marked the beginning of a new era.

Prior to the restoration foreign travel was still forbidden. Japan's knowledge of the Western world was confined to what she had learned from the Dutch at Nagasaki, from the foreigners who had come in the wake of Perry, and from the limited company of Japanese who had ventured abroad with or without official approval. It was a new and strange world that greeted these first travelers. The reports prepared by the shogun's mission to the United States in 1860 covered every sphere of life from the constitutional position and behavior of the American president to bathroom plumbing and etiquette.

The new educational policy was a two-fold

plan. It involved, in the first place, sending selected able students to study in Europe and America. (This phase recalls how Japanese students had been sent to China for the same purpose in the seventh and eighth centuries.) They were selected and assigned to particular countries with great care. Students of business and education went for the most part to the United States. Those who would study naval and maritime affairs did so in Britain. Germany received those in science, medicine, and military affairs, while those specializing in political science, law, and government were assigned to France.

The second aspect of the new education policy, more difficult and more expensive, was to build schools and universities in Japan and to staff them with trained teachers. This was a task involving many years of effort. Yet by the end of the century almost all Japanese children were enrolled. The curriculum provided six years of compulsory elementary schooling, after which selection became more rigid for the five-year middle schools and very selective for the three-year high schools. The entire system culminated in the prestigious imperial universities, the first of which, Tokyo University, was chartered in 1877. A number of private universities would also make their appearance, together with government normal, commercial, and technical schools. Elementary education for girls was similar to that for boys, although secondary education for girls stressed woman's domestic role. By 1902 provision was made for higher education for women. In the universities there was a strong French influence, and throughout the educational system the German emphasis on vocational training was evident.

Evaluations of the educational system built by Japan in the first decades of the Meiji period need to take account of the purposes it was designed to serve. The design was to create a secular, state-controlled system to serve as an effective agent in promoting the whole spectrum of government policy. It would do this by training loyal and obedient subjects, literate and skilled in the vocations of an agricultural and industrial society. This competent populace of technicians in agricul-

ture, industry, and commerce would be directed by an elite leadership educated in the imperial universities. Judged in these terms, the new educational structure was a notable success.[11]

FOR FURTHER READING

Government and Politics. For the foundations of the Meiji see: Sakata Yoshio and John W. Hall, "The Motivation of Political Leadership in the Meiji Restoration," *Journal of Asian Studies* 16 (1956), 31-50; and Robert A. Wilson, *Genesis of the Meiji Government in Japan, 1868-1871* (1957). Harold S. Quigley, *Japanese Government and Politics: An Introductory Study* (1932), a long-time standard reference that is still useful for details. George M. Beckman, *The Making of the Meiji Constitution: The Oligarchs and the Constitutional Development of Japan, 1868-1891* (1957), important for key constitutional documents. Robert K. Sakai, "Feudal Society and Modern Leadership in Satsuma-Han," *Journal of Asian Studies* 16 (1957), 356-76. The interplay of ideas and politics is revealed in D. C. Holtom, *The National Faith of Japan: A Study in Modern Shinto* (1943); Warren Smith, *Confucianism in Modern Japan: A Study of Conservatism in Japanese Intellectual History* (1959); Masao Maruyama, *Thought and Behavior in Modern Japanese Politics,* Ivan Morris, ed. (1963);* and Kichisaburo Nakamura, *The Formation of Modern Japan as Legal History* (1965.)

Insights into the personalities of the Meiji era are offered in Roger F. Hackett, *Yamagata Aritomo in the Rise of Modern Japan* (1971); Junesay Iddittie, *The Life of Marquis Shigenobu Okuma* (1956); Hamada Kenji, *Prince Ito* (1936); Roger F. Hackett, "Nishi Amane—A Tokugawa-Meiji Bureaucrat," *Journal of Asian Studies* 18 (1959), 213-25, illustrates the interplay of change and

[11] Herbert Passin, *Society and Education in Japan* (1965)* deals among other things with the introduction of a modern educational system in the Meiji period.

continuity in nineteenth-century Japan. Marius B. Jansen, "Takechi Zuizan and the Tosa Loyalist Party," *Journal of Asian Studies* 18 (1959), 199-212, a study of the Loyalist movement in Tosa. Richard Minear, *Japanese Tradition and Western Law: Emperor, State, and Law in the Thought of Hozumi Yatsuka* (1970); and Johannes Siemes, *Hermann Roesler and the Making of the Meiji Constitution* (1966).

Economics. Henry Rosovsky, *Capital Formation in Japan, 1868-1940* (1961), a major work on the Japanese economy. Essays on early Meiji may be found in two volumes edited by W.W. Lockwood, *The State and Economic Enterprise in Japan* (1965); and *The Economic Development of Japan* (rev. ed. 1968).* See also James Morley, ed., *Dilemmas of Growth in Prewar Japan* (1965). Ohara Keichi and Okata Tamotsu, eds. and trans., *Japanese Trade and Industry in the Meiji-Taisho Era* (1957). G. C. Allen, *A Short Economic History of Modern Japan* (rev. ed. 1962) emphasizes industry, finance, and governmental economic policy. Takekoshi Yosaburo, *Economic Aspects of the History of the Civilization of Japan* (3 vols., 1930). Thomas R. H. Havens, "Kato Kanji and the Spirit of Agriculture in Modern Japan," *Monumenta Nipponica*, no. 3-4 (1970); and James I. Nakamura, *Agricultural Production and the Economic Development of Japan, 1873-1922* (1966), revisions of earlier theories on agricultural production. R. P. Dore, "The Meiji Landlord: Good or Bad?" *Journal of Asian Studies* 18 (1959), 343-56.

Japan
in the 1880s:
The Victory of
"Constitutional
Absolutism"

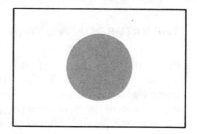

11

In the short span of two decades following the arrival of Perry in 1853, Japan had undergone some extraordinary changes, and even more were to come. With the exception of the brief Tokugawa resistance, these changes had come to pass with relatively little violence. The age-old policy of exclusion and seclusion had been abandoned. The Tokugawa shogunate had been destroyed. A divinely-descended emperor and the institution of the throne had been restored to *de facto* as well as *de jure* authority. The institutions and the social classes of feudalism had been done away with, and were replaced by a new makeshift national administration modeled on traditional Japanese ideas of collective responsibility in a council of state. These developments were Japan's first pragmatic response to the unwelcome arrival at her ports of a modern Western world too powerful to be ignored.

The second aspect of Japan's response was perhaps even more notable and certainly more difficult to appraise. Following closely on the arrival of the Western diplomats and traders, the Japanese displayed an unlimited interest in and enthusiasm for understanding and mastering every facet of this new and strange Western world. Those Japanese who traveled and studied abroad returned with graphic accounts of the power, industry, wealth, and intellectual vitality of European and American civilization. Selections from Western literature and later complete works began to appear in Japanese translations: Locke, Mill, Rousseau, Montesquieu, and many others. British capitalistic liberalism and French doctrines on the rights of man entered Japanese ports as easily as cotton textiles at the precise moment when the Charter Oath was proclaiming that "an assembly widely convoked shall be established, and thus great stress shall be laid on public discussion." Whatever these words of the divine emperor were intended to mean, it is clear that Japanese who were so disposed could interpret them as a pledge guaranteeing the rights of the "people" in some form of representative government. The decade of the 1880's was destined to clarify just what the Charter Oath meant, and what part, if any, Locke, Mill, Rousseau, and Montesquieu were to have in shaping the ultimate form and spirit of the Meiji government.

THE NATURE OF THE TASK

From the first years of the restoration at Kyoto and then at Tokyo, the men who controlled the emperor's new government were involved in two domestic political tasks of great complexity. They were determined to maintain and to strengthen their own power, and somehow to create broad national support for it. At the same time, they were attempting to determine what the nature of a more permanent government philosophy and structure was to be. The first task was on the road to solution by 1877 when the government's conscript army crushed the Satsuma rebellion. Ready solutions to the second task were by no means so easy to find. Japan was adopting Western ways in education, commerce, science, medicine, industry, and a host of other fields. There was no reason, therefore, in the view of some Japanese, why she should not also follow the West in political philosophy and structure of government. A difficulty here was that the West presented not one but a variety of philosophical and political models, such as British or French liberalism and German authoritarianism. Moreover, although the Meiji leaders had been willing to destroy many of Japan's institutions, such as the feudal dictatorship, they were still traditionalists in many ways. They had restored to power an emperor and a throne which were as traditionally Japanese as any institutions could be. Among all these conflicting currents of thought and action, Japan was pursuing a quest for a new grand design in government.[1]

[1] Fukuzawa Yukichi (1835-1901) was one of the great exponents of the West to his countrymen. He had visited Europe and the United States prior to the restoration. A prolific author, he wrote about practically everything Western life had to offer both materially and intellectually. He came of lower-strata samurai stock and accepted no posts in government, but he founded one of Japan's best private universities, Keio. Note Carmen Blacker, *The Japanese Enlightenment, A Study of the Writings of Fukuzawa Yukichi* (1964); G. B. Sansom, *The Western World and Japan* (1950); and *The Autobiography of Fukuzawa Yukichi,* Eiichi Kiyooka, ed., (1966). Fukuzawa's career exemplifies the doubts that beset the intellectuals of the emerging Japan. In his early writings, Fukuzawa found his moral precepts in natural laws, as expounded in Western society. He considered these to be applicable universally, thus minimizing cultural diversity and the unique qualities of a people. Later, he was to become critical of some aspects of Western civilization, and to be concerned about the spiritual emptiness of Japan's cultural revolution. There were limits, he thought, beyond which cultural borrowing should not be pushed; traditional values and institutions should also be components of the new Japan. See Fukuzawa Yukichi, *An Encouragement of Learning,* David A. Dilworth and Umeyo Hirano, trans. (1969).

While Japanese of nearly all classes shared in the nineteenth-century enthusiasm for Western culture, the wealthy, especially those having class contacts with the West, were best able to indulge themselves fully. Kichibei Murai, for example, an industrialist with ties to American tobacco interests, built one home (he had six altogether, including some that were built in traditional Japanese style) according to Western architectural fashion and entertained there in the manner of the American rich. These photos were taken about 1900.

THE APPEAL OF REPRESENTATIVE INSTITUTIONS

The fascinations which the Japanese found in their introduction to things Western were at first undiscriminating, but in a relatively short time first reactions gave place to more reasoned views on what Japan should adopt or reject from the West and on why this should be done. For example, it has been noted that the Meiji leaders wanted to create strong and stable political institutions. They observed that in the West constitutionalism, defining the government's powers and its relations with the people, appeared to promote strength and stability in the most enlightened states. Constitutionalism, therefore, might also serve Japan. Furthermore, Japan desired relief from the stigma of the conventional tariff and extraterritoriality in the commercial treaties. Constitutionalism and representative institutions, it was believed, would contribute to this end by convincing the powers of Japan's progress.

In 1874 Itagaki Taisuke of Tosa and some councilors from Hizen, irked by the near monopoly of power and office held by councilors from Satsuma and Choshu, resigned from the government. As a means of protest, Itagaki formed a popular political society at first expressive of samurai discontent. The movement was soon joined by well-to-do peasants and merchants and, before the end of the decade, it was calling for the establishment of "people's rights." Frightened by this development, the government, through the emperor, instructed all councilors to make proposals on constitutional government. What followed were a number of dramatic moves by Okuma Shigenobu of Hizen, who was still in the government. Okuma charged high officials with corruption in the sale of Hokkaido government properties to private interests, and he advocated immediate adoption of the British system of parliamentary government. To protect itself, the government effected an immediate reorganization and ousted Okuma from office.[2]

[2] The Hokkaido scandal which Okuma exposed was a huge and notorious scheme by members of the government and by others close to government

A CONSTITUTION IS PROMISED

The ouster of Okuma meant that the most traditionalistic members of the government, such as Iwakura Tomomi and Ito Hirobumi, were in control.[3] At this point an imperial edict announced that a parliament would be convoked in 1890. The constitution establishing the parliament would be drafted, however, in secret. It was already evident that Japan's new constitution would reserve great powers to the sovereign and his ministers, and that the role of the people would be restricted severely.

THE BIRTH OF POLITICAL PARTIES

During 1881 and 1882 three political parties made their appearance: the *Jiyuto* (Liberal Party) led by Itagaki, the *Kaishinto* (Progressive Party) headed by Okuma, and the *Rikken Teiseito* (Imperialist Party) supported by the government. For the moment these parties seemed to be concerned primarily with advocating one or another form of Western constitutional government. This interest in politi-

to profit at the expense of the taxpayer by selling the properties (real estate, factories, mines, etc.) of the government-sponsored Hokkaido Colonial Office to two private companies organized to receive them. The price was to be less than 400,000 yen; the value of the properties was in excess of 20 million yen. It should not be assumed, however, that Okuma, Itagaki, Goto and others of the growing opposition were interested primarily in the purification of Japanese politics. Their primary purpose was to regain power by embarrassing the government. A goodly number of Japan's Meiji leaders entered politics as poor samurai. Many of them died immensely wealthy. On the politics of the years 1875-1882, see Andrew Fraser, "The Osaka Conference of 1875," *Journal of Asian Studies,* 26 (1967), 589-610; Joyce C. Lebra, "Okuma Shigenobu and the 1881 Political Crisis," *ibid.,* 18 (1959), 475-87; and Andrew Fraser, "The Expulsion of Okuma from the Government in 1881," *ibid.,* 26 (1967), 213-36.

[3] In July, 1881, before Okuma was forced out, Iwakura had submitted a memorial to the throne setting forth the steps Japan should follow in moving toward constitutional government. He proposed announcing the creation of an investigation commission and drafting the constitution in secret within the palace. This memorial foreshadowed almost exactly the precise course followed.

cal theory and political forms was not entirely spurious, but it was of secondary importance. The stated principles and platforms were usually exceedingly vague and broad. In any case, Japanese political thought tended to emphasize the political leader rather than any body of principles. It followed then that political parties tended to be aggregations of individuals bound by personal loyalty to a particular man, as was the case in feudal times, rather than a group held together by ideological concerns. To some extent, of course, economic and social considerations also played a part in the formation of parties.[4] From what had been said it should not be assumed that Western political theory, constitutionalism, and liberalism, played no part in the thinking of Japanese politicians and intellectuals, for indeed they did. Yet, at the same time, it would be a mistake to assume that Japanese political parties were inspired primarily by Western concepts of constitutionalism, or that the early "liberal" in Japanese politics was a replica of the nineteenth-century English liberal.

From 1881, when the first party appeared, until about 1900, there seems to have been some genuine enthusiasm among the politicians for the principles of responsible government. But between 1900 and 1918 the power of the elder statesmen, the *genro* (see p. 150) and the special groups that supported them—aristocrats, bureaucrats, and militarists—was so entrenched that generally the party politicians gave up the struggle for liberal principles (for which there was no long background of tradition as there was in England); they then sought the spoils of office by selling their parliamentary support to the oligarchy. In turn, oligarchs such as Ito Hirobumi and militarists such as Katsura Taro accepted the presidency of major political parties. Considering the character of these leaders, the parties obviously could no longer stand effectively for responsible government.

[4] R. K. Reischauer, *Japan: Government-Politics* (1939), 29-30, 95-97.

THE ECONOMIC BASE OF THE MEIJI PARTIES

The *Jiyuto,* or Liberal Party, of 1881 presented the seemingly incongruous spectacle of liberalism promoted by a class of rural landowners. This was due to the peculiar character of Japan's rural economy in the restoration era. Landed proprietors occupied a dual position; they combined the functions of semifeudal landlord with those of commercial capitalist. They collected the profits of agriculture in the form of land rent paid by tenants in rice; these profits, converted into money at the best possible rate, were usually invested either in land or in rural industries, such as the manufacture of *sake* (rice wine) or *miso* (bean paste). Thus the landowner became a local rural industrialist, rice broker, or merchant. It was in these latter capacities that the manufacturing-landlord entered politics in 1881, combining his efforts with those of other groups in the formation of the *Jiyuto.* He did so because he was opposed to the government's policy of financing its military and naval program by increasing taxation on the products he manufactured, and because he objected to paying the bulk of the nation's income in the form of the land tax while the government bestowed its favors and protection on the financial oligarchy of the cities. Other rural groups also had their special complaints. The tenant cultivator wanted reduction in his rent. Those who owned their land were already threatened with dispossession. Thus from these various groups, particularly from the landed, rural manufacturers, came the crusade for "Liberty and the People's Rights." In this sense Japanese liberalism sprang from the countryside and not from the cities. In contrast, the ideological leadership of the movement came from quite a different group. Its nucleus was made up of samurai from Hizen and Tosa who had been pushed out of the new government bureaucracy by the samurai politicians of Satsuma and Choshu.

The second and rival political party, the *Kaishinto,* led by Okuma, included in its membership other disgruntled bureaucrats who were out of office, a scattering of liberal intellectuals who favored the British parliamentary system, and, significantly from the economic point of view, some of the wealthier urban merchants and industrialists, including representatives of the Mitsubishi interests. In ideology, the *Kaishinto* was a mild reflection of the current English liberalism and utilitarianism.

From 1880 until 1918 the oligarchy, led by the *genro,* was able to channel within narrow limits all movements of political liberalism, and thus to uphold its authoritarian concepts on the economic and social structure of society. It accomplished this in a number of ways. It neutralized the parties by playing one against another. It won some of the party leaders over to its own fold by various means, not excluding bribing them with offices. Freedom of speech and of the press were seriously hampered. The Press Law of 1875 and the Peace Preservation Ordinance of 1887 were the nineteenth-century manifestations of what came to be known in the twentieth century as the control of "dangerous thoughts." Thus the first liberal political parties were for a time suppressed entirely, depriving the economically and socially depressed masses of any political leadership. What is more, when the resurrected *Jiyuto* (Liberal Party) took its place in the first Diet of 1890, it had been shorn of its liberalism. By 1900, when it became the *Seiyukai,* it was the party of the great landlords and rural capitalists.[5]

CONSTITUTIONAL PREPARATIONS

Meanwhile, as the *Jiyuto* and the *Kaishinto* clamored for a popular and liberal constitution, the government set about the task of drafting a document that would preserve the power of oligarchy. It created a commission

[5] See G. E. Uyehara, *The Political Development of Japan, 1867-1909* (1910), 89-106; Yusuke Tsurumi, "The Liberal Movement in Japan," in his *The Reawakening of the Orient* (1925), 68 ff.; and W. W. McLaren, *A Political History of Japan During the Meiji Era, 1867-1912* (1916), 153-77.

on constitutional investigation headed by Ito Hirobumi. In 1884 a new nobility was created to draw together and unify the conservative and aristocratic elements that were to dominate the new government. It was also decided to create the executive branch prior to the adoption of the constitution. This would enable the executive to become a functioning organ familiar with its duties before it would be required to adjust itself to a parliament. Accordingly, a cabinet (*nai kaku*) was set up in 1885, modeled on the German cabinet. Then in 1888 a privy council was established with Ito, head of the constitutional commission, as president. As further preparation for the constitutional regime, a merit system was introduced into the civil service and new codes were prepared in both public and private law. A penal code and a code of criminal procedure, begun in 1873 and completed in 1880, were adopted in 1882; they were strongly influenced by French law. The larger task of constructing a civil code, begun in 1870, was completed and put into effect in 1899, in which year extraterritoriality was terminated. The civil law also showed strong French influence. A code of civil procedure was operative as early as 1891, and adopted with the commercial code, German in origin, in 1899.

DRAFTING THE CONSTITUTION

Some of the more important instruments of a new government had been created and were in operation before the constitution itself was created. Although this procedure lent stability to political affairs in a period of transition, it also enabled the ruling faction, headed by Ito, to maintain its monopoly of power.

The foundations of a constitutional regime had been laid as early as 1868, when the Charter Oath was proclaimed. Two years later, in 1870, Ito visited the United States, where he studied the American constitutional system, delving deeply into the pages of the *Federalist*. More important in shaping Ito's ideas, however, was the advice of General Grant, given in 1879, that Japan in designing a constitution should give full regard to her own peculiar traditions. Then, in 1882, a year after the emperor had promised a constitution, Ito studied in Germany, where the successes of Bismarck had brought new prestige to the political philosophy and institutions of Prussia. Back in Japan, Ito was commissioned in 1884 to draft a constitution. He called on the services of three able assistants, all of whom had traveled abroad: Inouye Tsuyoshi, Ito Myoji, and Kaneko Kentaro. With Ito, these men constituted a bureau attached to the imperial household, thus precluding any popular political pressure. When their draft of the constitution was completed, it was ratified by the privy council, which had been created by Ito for this specific purpose and which was to be maintained under the constitution as the highest advisory body to the sovereign. Finally, on February 11, 1889, the anniversary of the traditional founding of the state of Yamato in 660 B.C., Emperor Mutsuhito bestowed the constitution as a royal gift upon his people. Every precaution had already been taken to ensure an obedient and peaceful acceptance by the people at large. Tokyo was subject to quasi-martial law under a special Peace Preservation Ordinance. Most of the more outspoken newspapers had already been suppressed, while the press in general was under strict instructions to refrain temporarily from all critical comment. As a consequence the public reception was peaceful.[6]

The constitution which emerged in 1889 has been described in various formulae, none of which is very precise. For example, it has been seen as a document embodying Japanese political principles under the guise of representative institutions. In this view it is a kind of hybrid, a unique blend of authoritarianism and constitutionalism, or, to put it another way, an absolute constitutional monarchy. While there is little about the constitution that could be described as liberal, it would appear that its authors opposed extreme conservative views almost as vigorously as they rejected parliamentary authority. The result was a distinctly Japanese product. Certainly the Meiji leaders were reluctant to share political power. Yet in the constitutional struggle they did so, even if grudgingly. As Ito saw his task in drafting the constitution, it was to seek a means of controlling and rendering as harmless as possible any encroachment by political parties in the area of political authority.[7]

THE ESSENTIALS OF THE CONSTITUTION

The Law and the Constitution of 1889

The fundamental law of the empire consisted of the constitution, the imperial house law, imperial ordinances, statutes, and international treaties.[8]

The nature of the constitution was best revealed by the position of the emperor. Since the constitution was a gift of the throne, only the emperor could initiate amendments. These required the consent of the House of Peers (*Kizoku-in*) and the House of Representatives (*Shugi-in*). Interpretation of the constitution rested with the courts, and, in a case of dispute, with the privy council.

---

[6] McLaren, *Political History*, 186; Uyehara, *Political Development*, 109-23. The official interpretation of the constitution is by Ito Hirobumi, *Commentaries on the Constitution of the Empire of Japan,* Ito Myoji, trans. (2nd ed., 1906). Note particularly the concept of *kokumin*—the relation of nationalism and liberalism, the state and the individual—as discussed by Barbara J. Teters, "Kuga's Commentaries on the Constitution of the Empire of Japan," *Journal of Asian Studies,* 28 (1969), 321-37.

[7] George Akita, *Foundations of Constitutional Government in Japan, 1868-1900* (1967), and Joseph Pittau, S.J., *Political Thought in Early Meiji Japan, 1868-1889* (1967). Very dissimilar theories have developed with regard to the intent of the makers of the Meiji Constitution. Students of Japanese politics in the earlier part of this century stressed the authoritarian aspects of the constitution. More recent scholarship has tended to challenge this emphasis. A helpful presentation of major interpretations is Joseph Pittau, S. J., "The Meiji Political System: Different Interpretations," in *Studies in Japanese Culture,* Joseph Roggendorf, ed. (1963).

[8] For a concise summary of the organization of Japan's government see Reischauer, *Government—Politics,* Chapter 4.

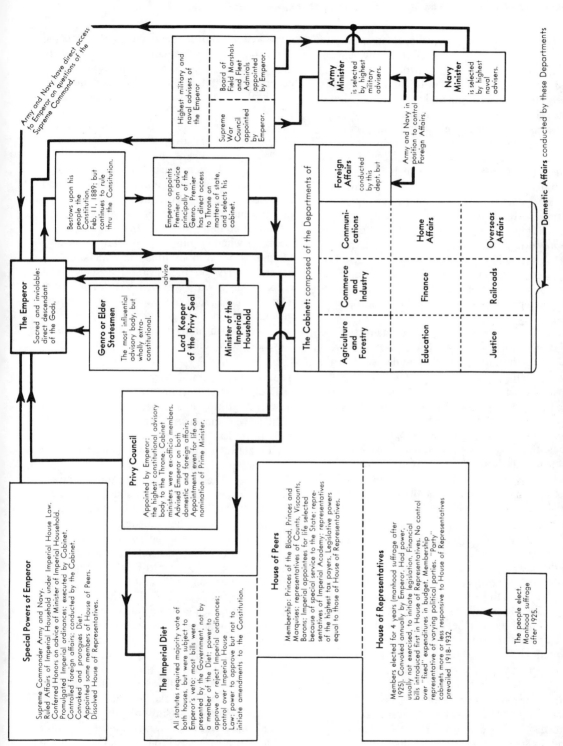

Principal Features of the Government of Japan under the Constitution of 1889

The Emperor

Sacred and inviolable; direct descendant of the Gods.

Army and Navy have direct access to Emperor on questions of Supreme Command.

Highest military and naval advisers of the Emperor

Board of Field Marshals and Fleet Admirals appointed by Emperor.

Supreme War Council appointed by Emperor.

Army Minister is selected by highest military advisers.

Navy Minister is selected by highest naval advisers.

Army and Navy in position to control Foreign Affairs.

Bestows upon his people the Constitution, Feb. 11, 1889; but continues to rule thru the Constitution.

Emperor appoints Premier on advice principally of the Genro. Premier has direct access to Throne on matters of state, and selects his cabinet.

The Cabinet: composed of the Departments of

Foreign Affairs conducted by this dept. but

Agriculture and Forestry	Commerce and Industry	Communications	Foreign Affairs
Education	Finance	Home Affairs	
Justice	Railroads	Overseas Affairs	

Domestic Affairs conducted by these Departments

Genro or Elder Statesmen

The most influential advisory body, but wholly extra-constitutional.

advise

Lord Keeper of the Privy Seal

Minister of the Imperial Household

Special Powers of Emperor

Supreme Commander Army and Navy. Ruled Affairs of Imperial Household under Imperial House Law. Conferred Honors on advice of Minister of Imperial Household. Promulgated Imperial ordinances; executed by Cabinet. Controlled foreign affairs; conducted by the Cabinet. Convoked and prorogues Diet. Appointed some members of House of Peers. Dissolved House of Representatives.

Privy Council

Appointed by Emperor; the highest constitutional advisory body to the Throne. Cabinet ministers were ex-officio members. Advised Emperor on both domestic and foreign affairs. Appointments even for life on nomination of Prime Minister.

The Imperial Diet

All statutes required majority vote of both houses, but were subject to Emperor's veto; most bills were presented by the Government, not by a member of the Diet; power to approve or reject Imperial ordinances; control over Imperial House Law; power to approve but not to initiate amendments to the Constitution.

House of Peers

Membership: Princes of the Blood, Princes and Marquises; representatives of Counts, Viscounts, Barons; Imperial appointees for life selected because of special service to the State; representatives of the highest tax payers; representatives of Imperial Academy; representatives of the highest tax payers. Legislative powers equal to those of House of Representatives.

House of Representatives

Members elected for 4 years (manhood suffrage after 1925). Convoked annually by Emperor. Had power, usually not exercised, to initiate legislation. Financial bills introduced first in House of Representatives. No control over "fixed" expenditures in budget. Membership representative of varying political parties. "Party" cabinets more or less responsive to House of Representatives prevailed 1918-1932.

The people elect. Manhood suffrage after 1925.

The imperial house law occupied a unique position. It could not be affected by legislation, was beyond the control of the Diet, and could be amended only by the emperor with advice of the imperial family council and the privy council. The imperial house law, not the constitution, determined the succession.

Great powers were exercised by the emperor through imperial ordinances of three kinds: (1) prerogative—imperial house law; (2) administrative—executive acts in the interest of the general welfare, and (3) emergency— actions taken when the Diet was not in session. These last required at time of issue approval by the privy council (*sumitsu-in*), and ultimately approval by the Diet, unless repealed before a new session. It is thus clear that in a very large field the ordinance powers of the emperor were beyond legislative control.

Statutes were enacted by the majority vote of both houses of the Diet, whose powers over legislation were the same, save that money bills were to be presented first in the lower house. The emperor's veto power over all laws was absolute. In practice most legislation was initiated by the government. Treaties were to be ratified by the emperor with the consent of the privy council. Treaties were regarded as superior to ordinary law: they were not subject to change by ordinance, but could not be in conflict with the constitution or the imperial house law.

The Power Elite and the Constitution

Japanese government was dominated after 1889 by a power elite composed of the imperial family, the *genro* (elder statesmen), and the House of Peers. In this group were the former *kuge* (the civilian court nobility), the former *daimyo,* those samurai who engineered the restoration, and, finally, a select few from the professional classes.

The Emperor. The emperor's powers as defined by the constitution were extremely broad. He possessed the rights of sovereignty and exercised them within the constitution, convoked and prorogued the Diet, dissolved the House of Representatives, issued ordinances, determined the organization of the government, and acted on appointments and dismissals of all officials, save in those cases where other provision was made by the constitution. He exercised the administrative and command powers over the army and navy, declared war, made peace and concluded treaties, proclaimed martial law, conferred all high official ranks and honors, appointed and removed judges. All these constitutional powers and prerogatives of the emperor were to be exercised *only* on the advice of his advisers, whether ministers of state, ministers of the imperial household, or chiefs of the general staffs of the army and navy. The emperor, in a word, reigned but did not rule. The problem for the student of Japanese government in the period after 1889 is to discover which individuals and groups ruled through the sovereign.

The Genro. From shortly after the promulgation of the constitution until 1931, the most powerful group in Japanese government and politics was the *genro*. This group was extraconstitutional. It was composed of trusted and tried statesmen who had assumed leadership in the making of the new Japan in the years 1880-1900. These men exercised the real power in government under the constitution. No important decisions were made without their consent; in fact they made the decisions. Although the power of the *genro* was contested as early as 1913, it was not until about 1922 that their supreme control in all important affairs of state, domestic and foreign, began to be questioned. The *genro* illustrate clearly the fact that although constitutional government in Japan often appeared to be Western in structure and performance, actually it was Japanese. The *genro* as personalities, not as constitutionalists, were the real makers of the new Japan in the later years of Meiji. They included Ito Hirobumi (Choshu), maker of the constitution; Yamagata Aritomo (Choshu), the builder of Japan's modern army; Inouye Kaoru (Choshu), influential in reforms in taxation; Oyama Iwao

(Satsuma), a great soldier; and Matsukata Masayoshi (Satsuma), of great prominence in taxation and finance. These were the original members. Later General Katsura Taro (Choshu) and Saionji Kimmochi *(kuge)* were added.[9]

Study of the appearance of the *genro,* of why this decision-making structure emerged at a particular time and took a particular form, is a rewarding pursuit. The *genro* was more than a manifestation of the general tendency in Japanese society to make decisions through group consensus. Since all the original members of the *genro* held at one time or another prior to 1900 all major posts in the civil and military bureaucracy and the government, there was practically no distinction between bureaucracy and government. Moreover, in the late nineteenth century, Meiji leaders needed above all to find a consensus on goals and to resolve the conflict between traditional Confucian moral education and so-called *jitsugaku* or education for practical affairs associated with Western learning as preparation for service in bureaucracy and government. There was no one person who could be entrusted with such decisions and such responsibility. Restraint was placed on the emergence of such a leader by the peculiar status of the emperor. Thus the small group character of the *genro* was all but inevitable.[10]

The House of Peers. This body, the upper house of the legislature, included: (1) all princes of the blood who had reached majority; (2) princes and marquises twenty-nine years of age; (3) representatives of counts, viscounts, and barons, elected by their orders for terms of seven years; (4) imperial appointees selected for life because of distinguished service to the state or in recognition of scholarship; (5) representatives of the Imperial Academy elected by their colleagues to serve seven-year terms; and (6) elected representatives of the highest taxpayers from each prefecture. The House of Peers was a body distinguished for its conservatism of blood, wealth, and title. Its power was guaranteed by the constitution.

The Bureaucracy

The bureaucrats were the civil office holders. Their position was based on ability and on appointment. Their loyalties were to the aristocrats rather than to the common people. Of first importance among the bureaucratic elements was the imperial household ministry. The lord keeper of the privy seal and the minister of the imperial household headed this group. Both, because of their close personal relationship with the emperor, had great influence as advisers to the throne. It was through them that audience with the sovereign was secured. These ministers were appointed by the emperor on the advice of the prime minister.

The Privy Council. The second group in the bureaucracy was the privy council. Created in 1888, it was designed to review and accept the constitution and to be the highest constitutional advisory body to the emperor. Its membership numbered twenty-six, appointed for life by the emperor on the advice of the prime minister and with the approval of the president of the council. Ministers of state were *ex officio* councilors. The council proved itself an effective curb against representative tendencies.

The Civil Service. The great body of civil servants—the rank and file of bureaucracy, numbering nearly half a million members—was selected by competitive examination. Usually the most rigid application of these examinations was in the foreign office (*gaimusho*), whereas in the home ministry they were less

[9] Ito was assassinated, 1909; Katsura died, 1913; Inouye, 1915; Oyama, 1916; Yamagata, 1922; Matsukata, 1924; Saionji, 1940. It is significant that no *genro* was ever assassinated in Japan or by a Japanese. But as indicative of the weakening prestige of the group, attempts were made on the life of the aged Saionji.

[10] For further development of this subject see two articles by Bernard S. Silberman: "Bureaucratic Development and the Structure of Decision-Making in the Meiji Period: the Case of the *Genro,*" and "Bureaucratic Development and the Structure of Decision-Making in Japan: 1868-1925," *Journal of Asian Studies,* 27 (1967), 81-94; and 29, (1970), 347-62.

effective in competition with the spoils system.[11]

The Military

In no modern state, save perhaps, Prussia,
has the professional soldier played so influential a role in politics as in Japan. The
unbroken dominance of the military men, the
samurai, began in the twelfth century. In
Tokugawa times the soldier acquired a preeminent social status and a monopoly of
political power. The restoration of 1868 did
not destroy the influence of the military class.
It tended rather to transfer power from the
upper to the middle and lower ranks among
the former samurai. The military conscription
law of 1873 destroyed, in theory at least, the
distinction between samurai and commoner,
but in reality the personnel of the army and
navy, especially the professional officer class,
retained the old samurai tradition and attitude
of moral and social superiority. The mentality
continued to be that of a ruling class. Yet this
superior attitude did not prevent the appearance of cliques among those who controlled
the new army. As early as 1879, the three
main military functions—operations and
strategy, military administration, and training
and inspection—were being carried out by
three separate sections of the army. In 1885
when the cabinet was set up as a preliminary
to constitutional government, only one of the
three functions—military administration—was
placed even under partial control of the civil
government. Thus the principle of the separation of the command power (*tosuiken*) from
routine military administration (*gunsei*) was
established before the constitution. Under the
constitution, the prime minister accepted the
nominees of the services as the ministers of
war and of the navy in his cabinet. The
services thus had the power to destroy a
government by forcing the resignation of a

service minister and refusing to nominate a
new one.[12]

The Politicians and the House of Representatives

The constitution provided for a bicameral
legislature or Diet, which the Japanese called
gikai. The purpose of the framers was to
prevent the legislators from indulging in hasty
legislation and to give decisive legislative
power (in the House of Peers) to the aristocracy. The House of Representatives, according
to the *Commentaries,* was to regard itself as
"representatives of the people of the whole
country," though prior to 1925 there were
high property qualifications both for candidates and for the franchise. The constitution
required annual sessions of the Diet, which
were frequently supplemented by extraordinary sessions caused by frequent dissolutions. Originally the House of Representatives
consisted of 300 members, but this number
was increased to 381 in 1900, and to 466 in
1925, when manhood suffrage was adopted.
All statutes required approval by the House of
Representatives as well as by the House of
Peers. The same applied to amendments to the
constitution and to imperial ordinances if

[11] Robert M. Spaulding, Jr., *Imperial Japan's
Higher Civil Service Examinations* (1967). Modernization, which destroyed the civil service examinations
in China, created a system of examinations in Japan.

[12] The background of the subject is discussed by
Yale C. Maxon, *Control of Japanese Foreign Policy*
(1957), especially Chapter 2. The army and the navy
liked to think of themselves as unique guardians of
the throne and of the so-called "national spirit." In
practice, however, they were the most flagrant viola-
tors of the commands of the throne. An imperial
rescript addressed to service men (1882) set forth
that: "Service men should not involve themselves or
interest themselves in politics." Under the constitution they did not vote. Nevertheless, no group in
Japanese society was more jealous of its political
fortunes than the military. See K. W. Colegrove,
Militarism in Japan (1936); also E. E. N. Causton,
Militarism and Foreign Policy in Japan (1936); O.
Tanin and E. Yohan, *Militarism and Fascism in
Japan* (1934). Ernest L. Presseisen, *Before Aggression: Europeans Prepare the Japanese Army* (1965),
demonstrates that in the modernization of the
Japanese army after 1870 far more was involved
than the selection of the German as the ideal
military model.

these latter were to remain in effect after the Diet came into session. However, the Diet, and consequently the House of Representatives, held only limited control over the nation's finances. All items of so-called "fixed expenditures" were beyond its power: salaries, and expenses of the imperial household; and fixed budgets of administrative branches of the government, such as the army and navy. Furthermore, the constitution provided, in Article LXXI, that: "When the Imperial Diet has not voted on the budget, or when the budget has not been brought into actual existence, the government shall carry out the budget of the preceding year." Thus the framers of the constitution were careful not to place control of the national purse in the hands of the representatives of the people.

The Ministry and the Cabinet

Under the constitution no formal provision was made for a cabinet. The constitution merely noted that: "The respective Ministers of State shall give their advice to the emperor, and be responsible for it." All laws, ordinances, and rescripts required the countersignature of a minister of state. But, as noted, a cabinet was created in 1885, and it continued to function as the ministry under the constitution. The prime minister was selected by the emperor on the advice of the *genro*. This is another way of saying that the cabinet's responsibility was primarily to the emperor, and only secondarily to the Diet.

Such, in brief, were some of the main structural features of Japan's national government as established by the constitution of 1889. Historians are still seeking a satisfactory explanation for the form that this Meiji political structure assumed. How and why did the Japanese bureaucracy acquire almost a complete monopoly of decision making and administration? Why did the institution of the emperor emerge as it did—that is, the emperor as the state?[13]

[13] For the application of structural-functional analysis in the area of political systems as an aid in finding answers, see Bernard S. Silberman, "E. H. Norman: Structure and Function in the Meiji State, a Reappraisal," *Pacific Affairs*, 41 (1968-69), 553-59.

The Meiji constitution of 1889, even when allowance is made for its decidedly authoritarian character, was a notable achievement in the history of Japan's modernization. It was a major example of Japan's unique response to the Western impact. The adoption of constitutionalism suggested that Japan was becoming Western, but the content of the constitution suggested that while Japan was adopting a Western form (constitutionalism), she was creating a pattern of government that was unmistakably Japanese. What had been happening in Japan especially in the years 1868 to 1889 may best be described as an intense struggle to determine what manner of value system Japan was to have in the modern world. The Meiji constitution was evidence that in the political sphere the Japanese advocates of Mill and Rousseau were no match for the traditionalists who found that ultimate value rested in the prerogatives of the emperor and of themselves. This principle of authority, applied so successfully in politics in 1889, was also to determine the value structure that would prevail in every phase of the new Japanese culture.

In a very large measure, the political, economic, and social values which the Meiji leaders had devised by 1889 were a product of deeply ingrained and traditional habits of thought. First in importance was the Confucian idea of unity, which applied to the family, the clan, and the family-state. Only through these groups had the life of the Japanese individual acquired meaning and become an expression of what has sometimes been called loosely the Japanese spirit. In the modern West, science, philosophy, literature, and religion had struggled, not always successfully, to free themselves from control by state or church. This quest for individualism resulted in a diversity of value systems, with resulting conflicts among them. This self-seeking, individual diversity, often confusion, in Western thought did not make sense to the traditional Japanese mind, in which philosophy, religion, economics, and politics were one and indivisible. Consequently, a Japanese was a Confucian, a Buddhist, and a Shintoist simultaneously. Nothing, it was believed, should be permitted to interfere with this idea of oneness. There could be no place in Japanese society for the rugged individualism of the capitalist, the parochial school of an exclusive church, the class struggle of the communists, or even the conflicting platforms of political parties.

The application of this principle of unity to practical politics was best exemplified by the Japanese attitude toward the emperor system. In Shintoism the emperor was the descendant of the gods; in Buddhism, of the supreme Buddha; and in Confucianism, he was the fountain of the great virtues from which the good society would come. He symbolized the complete unity of the family-state in its philosophical, religious, political, and economic concerns.

An American school child learns at a tender age that "all men are created equal." Japanese children, however, learned to recognize inequality as a principle that is both self-evident and natural. As in the case of unity, the doctrine of inequality was sanctioned by the dominant systems of thought. Shintoism explained inequality in terms of blood, the emperor being what he was because of his direct descent from the Sun Goddess. The respective stations of all persons in society were determined by the stations of their divine ancestors. Buddhism gave equal stress to the inequality of men as they struggled toward salvation. Confucianism rated men as having superior or inferior virtue. One man was, therefore, not as good as another. Within the circle of Japanese culture he held a particular station that was determined by nobility of blood, Buddhist enlightenment, and Confucian virtue. This theory of society would not harmonize easily with the modern world into which Japan had begun to move even before the end of the Tokugawa period. How could a society that was moving toward new institutions be controlled during a period of unprecedented change? Since Japan was an agrarian society, much would depend on main-

taining some stability in the rural life of the nation. In rural Japan, nationalism, constitutionalism and industrialization were meaningless terms, but the traditional language of loyalty and obligation (now directed to the throne) was understandable to samurai and peasant alike. Therefore it was this language of tradition that the leaders of Meiji used to support an orderly revolution. They used old values to justify a new society.

THE FUNCTION OF LAW

There were also great differences to be reconciled between traditional Japanese ideas on law and the constitutional law of the West toward which Japan appeared to be moving. In the Anglo-American tradition, constitutional law stressed regulation arrived at in democratic fashion through the legislative process. It implied that law is the essential factor in safeguarding equal opportunity and individual rights in the interest of the common good. A traditionally-minded Japanese, however, did not see society in this light. He looked to man as the answer to good government. More specifically, the will of the sovereign defined the welfare of society. Laws were simply an expression of what the sovereign believed to be best at a given time. Their purpose could not be the protection of individual freedom because such a purpose would presuppose Western notions of individualism. Furthermore, a society based on inequality meant that there were rulers and those who were ruled. Written law was considered a guide to the former rather than a protection of the latter.

THE VALUES IN SHINTOISM

The use made of the old and indigenous cult of Shinto also exemplified the way in which Meiji modernization drew upon Japanese tradition. From the beginning of the Meiji period there was a conscious, deliberate, and organized effort not only to perpetuate old cultural values but also to give them new strength. These efforts created in the late nineteenth and early twentieth centuries out of Japan's mythological past a foundation for the modern Japanese state that was essentially religious in character. Marked by a high degree of organization and formalization, these religious foundations were clothed with a sanctity that made them immune to free debate or criticism. Since they were concerned essentially with the origins of the state, their authority could be invoked at all times to stifle criticism and thereby negate the principles of democratic practices. This state religion, so intimately a part of modern Japanese nationalism, was commonly known as State or Pure Shinto, to distinguish it from popular sectarian cults of Shinto that had no official standing.

For many centuries after its early, simple flowering, Shinto had been all but submerged by Buddhism, just as was Confucianism in China. But, with the rise of military feudalism, Shinto, taking on a new intellectual vigor, not only freed itself by degrees from Buddhist control but even asserted its superiority over Buddhism. This regeneration of Shinto, strongly nationalistic, sang the praises of early Japan as it was before the coming of Confucianism and Buddhism. In Tokugawa times, although the shoguns patronized Chinese learning and although Buddhism was the established religion, Shinto scholars nevertheless were able to revive interest in the *Kojiki,* to make it a Bible of nationalism and a proof of Japan's unique superiority. During the early nineteenth century, the popular appeal of the Shinto myths was revealed in the rise of numbers of Shinto sects which eventually attracted many adherents from among the common people, thus testifying to the inadequacy of modern Japanese Buddhism as a popular religious vehicle. One of the early decisions of the Meiji leaders involved the disestablishing of Buddhism and the reestablishing and revitalizing of Shinto. An office of Shinto affairs became one of the highest organs of the new state. By this means it was possible to reinvigorate Shinto and to use it con-

sciously as the spiritual foundation of the new national state.

The nationalistic values in Shinto mythology were exploited to the full. From Japan's ancient myths re-emerged a pantheon of deities headed by the Sun Goddess, who was now ministered to by tens of thousands of priests at thousands of sacred places. The dogma of state Shinto cannot be treated here in detail, but its character may be suggested by three essential tenets of this politico-religious faith.

The first was the dogma, announced in the first and third articles of the Meiji constitution, of unbroken, divine imperial sovereignty. The emperor was the living heir and embodiment of the divine ancestors of the race. The second dogma of state Shinto, closely related to the first, was the belief in Japan as the land of the gods. Here the concept was that Japan, far from being merely the product of ordinary geographical and historical forces, was peculiarly endowed with grace by the divine ancestors. The third dogma was the belief in Japan's benevolent mission or destiny. Modern Japanese were taught that the land of the gods, uniquely formed, was possessed of a divine mission to extend its righteous sovereignty over less fortunate peoples. Thus the dogmas of divine descent, the land of the gods, and benevolent destiny, all served to reinforce traditional Japanese thought, and by so doing to create a climate inhospitable to democratic ideas.[14]

CHRISTIAN MISSIONS

Even before the restoration government removed in 1873 the two-centuries-old ban against Christianity, British and American Protestant missionaries in some numbers had been well received. In 1875 the founding of Doshisha English School (later Doshisha University) in Kyoto marked the beginnings of

[14] The subject of Shinto nationalism is treated in great detail in D. C. Holtom, *Modern Japan and Shinto Nationalism* (1943; rev. ed., 1947; reprint, 1963).

Christian education by Japanese converts. Five additional Christian schools and colleges had been founded by 1890. At first the Christian movement was welcome, perhaps for itself but also because it contributed to Westernization. In time it met opposition from: (1) advocates of English empiricism who taught evolution and agnosticism; (2) zealots of Buddhism and Shintoism; and (3) extreme disciples of the new nationalism, who held that Westernization was being carried too far. Although Christian theology made only a limited imprint in Meiji Japan, the influence of Christian principles of social responsibility and humanitarianism was, though indeterminate, by no means inconsiderable.

NEW CUSTOMS IN A BEWILDERED SOCIETY

The social and intellectual temper of Japanese life from 1870 to 1900 was not only complex, it was also subject to constant and bewildering change. In the earlier years there was, as indicated, a mad mania for Westernization, a willingness to replace everything that was native with anything that was foreign. Confusion in thought was followed by confusion and contradiction in action. The dictum of the Charter Oath of 1868 that "absurd customs" would be discarded was at first taken as an invitation to wholesale change. Buddhist priests were told to take wives, to raise families, and to eat beef. Since beef eating was common in the West, it was inferred that it must be a symbol of advanced civilization. Married women and former court nobles (*kuge*) were told to stop blackening their teeth and shaving their eyebrows. For men the western haircut, instead of long hair done in a top knot, came to symbolize that the wearer was modern and progressive.[15]

[15] On the thought of the Japanese intellectuals of the period see Thomas R. H. Havens, "Comte, Mill, and the Thought of Nishi Amane in Meiji Japan," *Journal of Asian Studies,* 27 (1968), 219-28; and George M. Wilson, "Kita Ikki's Theory of Revolution," *ibid.,* 26 (1966), 89-99.

Particularly in the early years of their new contacts with the West, the Japanese showed a deep sensitivity to Western opinion. Since they were determined to be well thought of by the "more advanced" Europeans and Americans, there was a general scramble to discard or to hide institutions and customs that might subject them to ridicule or moral scorn by the foreigners. Abortion and infanticide, both common practices in Tokugawa times, were now prohibited. Mixed bathing at public bath houses, the social clubs of feudal times, met a similar fate. By 1885, however, although the mania for things Western remained strong, it was countered by a conservative reaction—a demand for the preservation of Japanese values.

THE TEMPER OF MEIJI JAPAN

It must be clear that Meiji Japan compresses itself into no easy historical nutshell. Indeed, it has much in common with Stephen Leacock's hero who rode off in all directions. This is not to imply that there was no purpose in the Meiji revolution. In fact, the purpose—to enable Japan to overtake the West and become overnight a powerful national state—was never in doubt. If there were confusions and contradictions, these were the natural garments of a people torn between the old and the new, between what was indigenous and what was foreign, between a native heritage they understood and alien cultures they could scarcely comprehend. Historically, the point to observe is that before the end of the century the pattern of the new Japan had been made and applied. In material things and purposes it was a modern and even a Western Japan, where politics was constitutional in form, where wages replaced kinship and loyalty, and where businessmen wore coats and trousers instead of the kimono. At the same time, the leaders directing this revolution were men of the samurai tradition, and they preserved and invigorated that tradition as the moral and spiritual foundation of the new nation.

An understanding of this late nineteenth

century Japan involves the measurement of Western penetration and influence. This task is beset by many pitfalls. For example, it has often been assumed that Germany provided Ito with the model for the Meiji constitution. Certainly, Ito saw merits in the German structure, but it should not be forgotten, as Sir George Sansom notes, that Japan, it would seem, would have produced a political system almost precisely like the one adopted even without the German experience to draw upon.[16]

Finally, Westernization and modernization in Meiji Japan were not always the same thing. It would seem that the Meiji leadership had taken deeply to heart the principle that "foreign ideas and institutions must be adopted *in degree* so that they appear to supplement and enrich the society rather than challenge and defy it. . . ."[17]

FOR FURTHER READING

Government in Action. Robert A. Scalapino, *Democracy and the Party Movement in Prewar Japan: The Failure of the First Attempt* (1953), a general history emphasizing the social basis of politics. Nobutaka Ike, *Japanese Politics: An Introductory Survey* (1957); and Chitoshi Yanaga, *Japanese People and Politics* (1956), analytical studies. Robert E. Ward, ed., *Political Development in Modern Japan* (1968). E. Herbert Norman, *Soldier and Peasant in Japan: The Origins of Conscription* (1943). John A. Harrison, *Japan's Northern Frontier* (1953).* Delmer M. Brown, *Nationalism in Japan: An Introductory Historical Analysis* (1955) surveys Japanese nationalism from earliest times. Ienaga Saburo, *History of Japan* (4th ed., 1959).*

[16] Sansom, *Western World,* 358-63.
[17] Robert A. Scalapino, "Environmental and Foreign Contributions: Japan," in *Political Modernization in Japan and Turkey,* R. E. Ward and D. A. Rustow, eds. (1964),* 89. See also Donald H. Shively, ed., *Tradition and Modernization in Japanese Culture* (1971).

Japan and the West. Robert S. Schwantes, *Japanese and Americans: A Century of Cultural Relations* (1955). Grace Fox, *Britain and Japan, 1858-1883* (1969). Sir Ernest Satow, *A Diplomat in Japan* (1921). Harold S. Williams, *Tales of Foreign Settlements in Japan* (1958), bright and episodic.

On the return of Christian missions to Japan see: Joseph J. Spae, *Christianity Encounters Japan* (1968); Irwin Scheiner, *Christian Converts and Social Protest in Meiji Japan* (1970); S. N. Eisenstadt, ed., *The Protestant Ethic and Modernization: A Comparative View* (1968);* and Ikao Fujio and James R. McGovern, comps., *A Bibliography of Christianity in Japan: Protestantism in English Sources, 1859-1959* (1966).

Social and Intellectual Transformations. Marius B. Jansen, ed., *Changing Japanese Attitudes toward Modernization* (1965);* R. P. Dore, ed., *Aspects of Social Change in Modern Japan* (1967);* Donald H. Shively, ed., *Tradition and Modernization in Japanese Culture* (1971); and Centenary Culture Council, ed., *Japanese Culture in the Meiji Era* (10 vols., 1955-58). John F. Embree, *Suye Mura: A Japanese Village* (1939),* a case study focusing on a small village in Kyushu. Hani Setsuko, *The Japanese Family System* (1948).

The Arts. Donald Keene, comp. and ed., *Modern Japanese Literature: An Anthology* (1956),* a selection from prose, poetry, and drama. Kokusai Bunka Shinkokai, *Introduction to Contemporary Japanese Literature* (1939). Kunitomo Tadao, *Japanese Literature Since 1868* (1938).

Zoe Kincaid, *Kabuki, the Popular Stage of Japan* (1925), a detailed study based on secondary sources. Earle Ernst, *The Kabuki Theatre* (1956).* Faubion Bowers, *Japanese Theatre* (1952, 2nd printing, 1954),* a very good general introduction to the various forms of Japanese theatre with illustrations.

China,
1860–1870:
The Return
to Tradition

12

The new Sino-Western order in East Asia, fashioned during the 1840's and the 1850's by diplomacy and war, could hardly be described in 1860 as a promising vehicle for the future of China's relations with the great Western powers. The expanded privileges bestowed upon Westerners by the treaties of Tientsin (1858) and the conventions of Peking (1860) had been exacted from a country which seemed to have no government, and much of whose territory was either controlled or devastated by the T'ai-p'ing and other major rebellions. Peking was still occupied by British and French troops. The unhappy Hsien-feng emperor, a mental and physical degenerate, remained in hiding with his court at Jehol, where he had fled when the British and the French occupied Peking, and where he died in August, 1861. Left at Peking to salvage what he could in this humiliating scene was I-hsin (1833-1893), usually known as Prince Kung, a half-brother of the fugitive emperor. Prince Kung, emerging from a most unlikely background, was to have a brief but seemingly constructive influence on China's relations with the powers during the next few years.

Prince Kung's rise to power at this moment was due to both international and domestic politics and intrigue. When the court fled, he had been left at Peking to deal with the invading armies of Britain and France as best he could. He seemed ill-prepared for this task since he had been bitterly antiforeign. Yet, in a measure, Prince Kung did succeed, against what appeared to be overwhelming odds. To be sure, he signed humiliating conventions with Britain, France, and Russia; but the barbarian troops left Peking. To many Manchus and Chinese it seemed that Prince Kung had done the impossible. He had saved the dynasty and he had shown a capacity to manage the barbarians.

CONTROL OF THE T'UNG-CHIH EMPEROR

The death of the Hsien-feng emperor at Jehol (1861) and the succession of his only son, born of an antiforeign concubine, precipitated a violent factional struggle for control of the new infant sovereign, the court, and the administration. On his death bed the fugitive emperor had named an administration from which the former concubine, now the empress dowager Tz'u-hsi, and Prince Kung were excluded. This maneuver drove Tz'u-hsi and Prince Kung to join forces. Their opponents were crushed ruthlessly; some were permitted to hang themselves, others were beheaded. The empress dowager had achieved mastery of the dynasty. She would continue to dominate the court for nearly half a century until her own death in 1908. But, since it was considered that Prince Kung had rescued the dynasty from the barbarians, there was nothing she could do but curb her antiforeignism for a time and appoint Kung as prince regent, grand councilor, and head of the newly-formed Tsungli Yamen, a kind of embryonic foreign office. Meanwhile, the child sovereign was enthroned as the T'ung-chih emperor (1862-1874). Such was the frail political edifice at Peking on which Prince Kung would try to build a policy of peace with the treaty powers.

THE TSUNGLI YAMEN

To implement this new policy of treaty observance the Tsungli Yamen was created on the recommendation of Prince Kung and with imperial sanction. It was a special body under the grand council, designed to deal with all matters relating to the Western powers. The creation of this special board, which was often staffed with able and powerful officials, was a major step toward a ministry of foreign affairs (*wai-wu-pu*), which was not established until 1901.

Prince Kung had seen the futility of China's blind resistance. Accordingly, as head of the Tsungli Yamen, he organized the beginnings of a Westernized Manchu army, tried to revitalize the Peking administration, acted as regent for the child T'ung-chih emperor, and, until his dismissal from the Tsungli Yamen in 1884, directed his influence toward maintaining peace with the Western powers, on the theory that only through peace could China gain strength. A vital weakness in Prince Kung's policy was his inability, for reasons that will be apparent later, to reassert the influence of Peking in the provinces after the defeat of the T'ai-p'ings. Nor was he able to free himself wholly from the stifling influences of an ignorant, retrograde, and antiforeign Manchu court.[1]

[1]On the role of the Tsungli Yamen, see Masataka Banno, *China and the West, 1858-1861: the Origins of the Tsungli Yamen* (1964), and the

MINISTERS FROM THE TREATY POWERS

The first ministers of the treaty powers reached Peking during 1861. The powers had won the right to maintain resident ministers at the capital. With Prince Kung's approval they were permitted to set up permanent residence. The group included Frederick Bruce (Great Britain), M. de Bourboulon (France), and Anson Burlingame (United States). Their reception seemed to indicate that the new order was being accepted, but with some qualifications. When a representative of Prussia appeared, the Chinese granted his country the commercial privileges won by the treaty powers but denied him the right to reside at Peking. This case suggested that the antiforeignism of the court was still very much alive even under Prince Kung's new policy.

THE COLLAPSE OF THE T'AI-P'ING REBELLION

In this China of 1860-1861, internal ills were as great as, if not greater than, the malady of Western pressures. The T'ai-p'ings had continued to threaten the Manchu dynasty throughout the years 1851-1863, a period in which the pressure of the foreign powers on the coast had been at its height. The conditions, political, economic, and social, which had occasioned this and other rebellions have already been suggested (see p. 92). The basic importance of the T'ai-p'ing movement lay not only in its weakening effect upon the Manchu dynasty, already under threat from the foreign powers, but also in the fact that the T'ai-p'ing may be considered the opening phase of a profound process of reform and revolution reaching far into the twentieth century.

The nature of the T'ai-p'ing movement is still a subject of debate among historians. Some of the emerging conclusions indicate: (1) the T'ai-p'ings desired to establish a dynasty that

administrative history by S. M. Meng, *The Tsungli Yamen: Its Organization and Function* (1962).* At the time of its creation, the Tsungli Yamen was considered to be a temporary agency which would be dispensed with when the crisis was passed. It dealt with many matters other than foreign affairs.

would be new in kind and in name; and (2) the T'ai-p'ings planned full-scale reorganization of social and economic life. Under the rule of the Heavenly King, the T'ai-p'ings envisioned a state providing a system of total control of all life. Drawing upon the concepts of the father-hood of God and the brotherhood and equality of all men, the rebels held that the state should provide security and protection for the aged, the handicapped, the widowed, and the or-phaned. Women were to be the equals of men, and would be permitted to enter military serv-ice, to take government examinations, and to hold office. Such ancient customs as footbind-ing, prostitution, and polygamy were to be abolished, and movable goods were to be con-signed to a public treasury for redistribution on the basis of need. In short, the T'ai-p'ing's creed embraced the vision of a revolutionized society; but this vision was embraced mostly by the leadership. The great majority of T'ai-p'ings were peasants seeking redress of traditional grievances rather than the transformation of society.[2]

In any event, the fact remains that the de-struction and devastation of life and property in the decade of the rebellion were almost beyond description. How many lives were de-stroyed, directly or indirectly, no one knows, but the estimates run as high as thirty million. In the beginning the movement was idealistic and disciplined. Its leadership included some men of ability and responsibility. Unfortun-ately, many of these men lost their lives in the early years and were replaced by men of lesser caliber. As a result, vast areas controlled by the T'ai-p'ings were subject to maladministration, while border areas were pillaged by both T'ai-p'ing and imperial forces.

The ultimate collapse of the rebellion cannot be ascribed to a single cause. Fundamental was its failure to win the support of the literati. These influential elements were alienated in part by the presence of Christian concepts in

T'ai-p'ing ideology, but more especially by the T'ai-p'ing attack on the Confucian bureaucracy as intellectually hollow and socially corrupt.[3] Furthermore, the later T'ai-p'ing leadership evi-dently found the recesses of the harem more congenial than the edifice of reform. In any case, the movement headed toward destructive ends from what appeared as constructive begin-nings. Its leadership was eventually captured by the traditions and abuses against which it had taken up arms: provincialism, familism, and nepotism. This loss of the ardor for reform coincided with the revival of dynastic spirit at Peking under Prince Kung. Moreover, the T'ai-p'ings did not solve the problem of recruiting and training young leaders to perpetuate their new order. T'ai-p'ing military leadership suf-fered the same decline as its political leadership. The military's failure to capture Peking was fatal.

If China was slow in meeting the threat of the T'ai-p'ing rebellion, she was not wholly without resolve. It was the T'ai-p'ing revolt that brought into prominence two of China's all too few great nineteenth-century leaders, Tseng Kuo-fan of Hunan and Li Hung-chang of Anhui. These men, unlike so many of their colleagues, had fought the rebellion from its beginnings; but it was not until after 1860 that they achieved, with foreign assistance, any major success.[4]

Among the foreigners who entered the Chinese military service to fight the T'ai-p'ings were Frederick Townsend Ward, an American soldier of fortune from Salem, Massachusetts, and an organizer of a Chinese force known as the "Ever Victorious Army"; and Major Charles George Gordon of the British army, who took command of the "Ever Victorious Army" in

[2] For a brief discussion of the historiographic problems see Paul A. Cohen, "Ch'ing China: Con-frontation with the West, 1850-1900," in *Modern East Asia: Essays in Interpretation*, James B. Crowley, ed. (1970),* 29-61.

[3] Joseph R. Levenson, *Confucian China and Its Modern Fate*, Vol. II, *The Problem of Monarchical Decay*, (3 vols., 1964),* 112.

[4] Teng Ssu-yu, *New Light on the History of the T'ai-p'ing Rebellion* (1950), especially 35-73. Also by the same author, "A Political Interpretation of Chinese Rebellions and Revolutions," *Tsing Hua Journal of Chinese Studies*, 1 (1958), 91-119. Eugene P. Boardman, *Christian Influence upon the Ideology of the T'ai-p'ing Rebellion, 1851-1864* (1952), excepically 41-105. Also Helmut G. Callis, *China, Confucian and Communist* (1959).

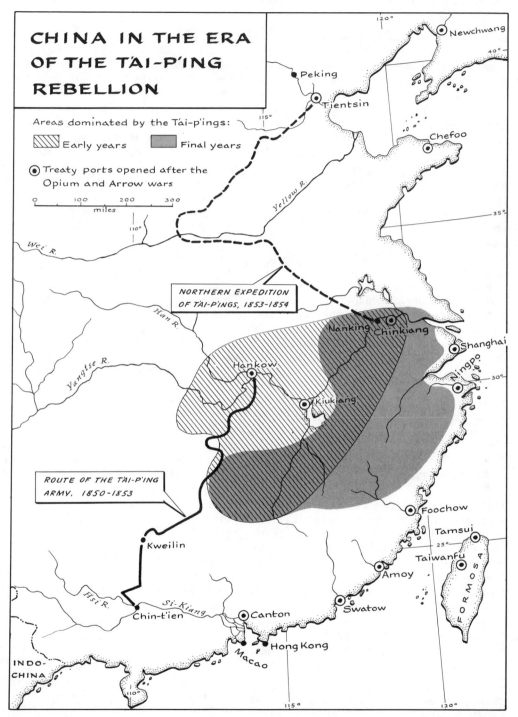

CHINA IN THE ERA OF THE T'AI-P'ING REBELLION

Areas dominated by the T'ai-p'ings:

Early years   Final years

Treaty ports opened after the Opium and Arrow wars

miles
0   100   200   300

NORTHERN EXPEDITION OF T'AI-P'INGS, 1853-1854

ROUTE OF THE T'AI-P'ING ARMY, 1850-1853

Newchwang
Peking
Tientsin
Chefoo
Yellow R.
Wei R.
Han R.
Yangtse R.
Nanking
Chinkiang
Shanghai
Ningpo
Hankow
Kiukiang
Foochow
Tamsui
Taiwanfu
Kweilin
Amoy
FORMOSA
Hsi R.
Si-Kiang
Chin-t'ien
Canton
Swatow
Hong Kong
Macao
INDO-CHINA

Adapted from J.K. Fairbank, E.O. Reischauer, and Albert M. Craig, East Asia: The Modern Transformation *(1965), pp. 160, 339.*

1863 after Ward's death. The military campaigns of Tseng, Li, and their foreign colleagues, together with the aid of the British and the French governments, resulted in the slow but sure destruction of the rebel military power on the lower Yangtze. The city of Soochow, one of the strongest rebel bastions, fell in December, 1863. In the following year the T'ai-p'ing "Heavenly King," debauched and degenerate, committed suicide shortly before his capital of Nanking fell before the armies of Tseng Kuo-fan. So ended the T'ai-p'ing rebellion. During its course through the middle decades of the century, twelve of the richest provinces were devastated, millions of people were exterminated, and poverty and despair made an unprecedented conquest.

In some respects the rebellion played a decisive part in the relations of China and the West. It helped to encourage European intervention in China. For instance, the conclusion of the treaties of 1858 and 1860 stamped the T'ai-p'ings as rebels. They could no longer be regarded as potential allies of the Western powers, nor as potential successors to the Manchus. Furthermore, the indemnities for the *Arrow* War depended on the fate of the Peking dynasty.[5]

CHINA'S MILITARY ESTABLISHMENT

The final suppression of the T'ai-p'ings was a reminder that the Confucian dynasty had narrowly escaped destruction from domestic foes. How had it come to pass that Peking had so little capacity to meet her enemies at home or from abroad?

When the crises of the mid-nineteenth century befell China, her military establishment, set up by the Manchus some two centuries earlier, was all but useless as a fighting force. Prior to the conquest of China (1644), the Manchus

[5] W. J. Hail, *Tseng Kuo-fan and the Taiping Rebellion* (1927), 290. For a graphic account of Ward and Gordon, see Jonathan Spence, *To Change China: Western Advisers in China 1620-1960* (1969),* 57-92. Also J. S. Gregory, *Great Britain and the T'ai-p'ings* (1969).

had been organized in military-administrative groups, known as "banners," which served the civil and economic as well as the military activities of the Manchu rulers. After the conquest of China, the Manchus sought to rule their new subjects in a Chinese way while, at the same time, preserving their own identity as Manchus. The banner organization was thus maintained and banner garrisons were placed throughout the empire. These garrisons were heaviest about Peking, along the northwestern frontier, and in the provincial capitals and larger cities. Although some Chinese, mainly from the northern frontier, had been admitted to the banners, these military units and their families remained a class apart from the conquered people.

With the consolidation of the Manchu conquest, the bannermen emerged as a hereditary, privileged military group or caste, excluded from trade and labor though not always from the civil service. Like the samurai in Japan under the Tokugawa dictatorship, they were perpetuated through generations of comparative peace. In time they lost their character and capacity as warriors, lapsing into the role of tragic and useless idlers.

The Manchus had also maintained in the provinces a second and Chinese military force, known as the Army of the Green Standard. This force was descended from certain Chinese armies that had assisted the Manchus during the conquest. Some of these forces had been taken into the banners, but in the south they remained distinct and formed the beginnings of a separate Chinese army under Manchu rule.

Some of the Green Standard were used to assist the banner garrisons on the northwestern frontier or to help suppress rebellious factions in various parts of the empire, but the far greater portion appeared to be devoted to detecting and preventing robbery and other crimes, protecting government property, or escorting criminals from one locale to another. The Green Standard could thus hardly be counted an army at all. Nevertheless, it was an integral part of the central bureaucratic administration through which the Manchus ruled China, and in the earlier and more vigorous years of the dynasty the Green Standard had served understandable purposes.

As the leadership and competence of the dynasty declined in the late eighteenth and the nineteenth centuries, the military services, both the bannermen and the Green Standard, no longer served effectively the original purposes for which they were designed, and were next to useless against the guns and disciplined troops of the Western powers. Worst of all, corruption had depleted these services of whatever morale they once possessed. As the dynasty no longer led the nation, so the officers of the Green Standard no longer led their troops. It had become common practice for officers to use their men as servants, to ride in sedan chairs when an infrequent march was undertaken, to withhold soldiers' pay for their own use, to charge the government for companies at full strength when actually no more than a handful of men were really in service. In times of emergency or for purposes of some official inspection, units were hastily recruited to full strength by gathering in a rabble of bandits, idlers, and criminals, who could be discharged just as promptly once the inspectors had moved on. Thus it was that Chinese diplomacy at Nanking in 1842 and at Tientsin and Peking in 1858 and 1860 operated in a vacuum: there was no effective military power behind it. This same lack of military power also had much to do with the early successes of the T'ai-p'ings and with their ability to remain in occupation of so much of central China long after their movement had lost direction and momentum.

To the abler members of China's ruling class, the scholar gentry, witnessing the spectacle of crisis, it seemed that the rebellion at home rather than the barbarian in the treaty ports was the occasion for the more intense alarm. The immediate, and presumably the ultimate, purpose of the barbarian was trade, and this, it was assumed, could eventually be confined and controlled; on the other hand, the T'ai-p'ing rebels, entrenched in the heart of China, were pseudo-Christian, anti-Confucian, and anti-Manchu—and thus a positive and immediate threat not only to the established governmental system but also to the vested interests of all who enjoyed the favor of those in power. Some members of the official scholar gentry were moved to action against this threatened calamity, in the interest of the dynasty, of the socio-political system, and of their own stake therein.

In the beginning the resultant movement to create regional armies was nothing more than an effort by some of the gentry to organize local militia for the defense of their home communities against the T'ai-p'ings. Since the regular troops—the bannermen and the Green Standard—had failed to destroy the rebels, the central government was in the unhappy position where it had to accept and even encourage this kind of local initiative. Accordingly, in 1853, the emperor ordered Tseng Kuo-fan, who had a reputation for scholarship and experience as an official at Peking, to organize forces in his native Hunan to fight the T'ai-p'ings. In a Confucian society Tseng's lack of military background was considered no drawback. He soon justified the Confucian theory that scholarship and virtue fit a man for any public service. His Hunan army, as it came to be known, was built on quality rather than numbers. His recruits were hardy, loyal peasants, not the dregs of the slums and jails. Moreover, these soldiers were well paid and were led by officers selected for character and ability. Early in its career this army gained its first battle training suppressing banditry in its home province. This strategy gave Tseng control of the area from which his financial support had to come, demonstrated to the populace the value of the army, and guaranteed the necessary replacements in troops. Moreover, what was done by Tseng in Hunan was repeated by Li Hung-chang in Anhui and by a few men of initiative in other areas.[6]

[6] Among the important studies on the military power under the Manchus is Franz Michael, *The Origin of Manchu Rule in China* (1942). On the new military leaders of the nineteenth century, see Arthur W. Hummel, ed., *Eminent Chinese of the Ch'ing Period, 1644-1912* (2 vols., 1943). On politico-military aspects during the T'ai-p'ing rebellion, see Franz Michael, "Military Organization and Power Structure of China during the Taiping Rebellion," *Pacific Historical Review,* 18 (1949), 469-83; James T. K. Wu, "The Impact of the Taiping Rebellion on the Manchu Fiscal System," *ibid.,* (1950), 265-75; Ralph L. Powell, *The Rise of Chinese Military Power, 1895-1912* (1955); and Stanley Spector, *Li Hung-chang and the Huai*

IMPLICATIONS OF REGIONAL MILITARISM

It was armies such as these which, bolstered with some foreign assistance, finally destroyed the incubus of the T'ai-p'ing rebellion. The military importance of these armies in preserving the life of the Manchu dynasty was thus immediate and apparent. It was not so apparent that, while these armies were saving the dynasty from the T'ai-p'ings, they were not saving the dynasty from itself. This was so because, unlike the traditional banners and Green Standard armies, which were closely integrated with the central political authority, the new nineteenth-century armies were not national; they were regional and private armies, recruited from and financed by local areas. The financing of these armies by the local authorities who organized them meant that new sources of revenue had to be found. One such source was a tax called *likin* (literally, "one thousandth"), a commercial tax on goods in transit imposed and collected by provincial or other local authorities.

The point to be noted in particular is that Peking had little part in conceiving, directing, or controlling these matters. China was saved from the T'ai-p'ings, but it was not the dynasty that did the saving. All that was left for Peking was to acquiesce in what local leaders of initiative were doing by appointing them, as Prince Kung did, as governors or governors-general of provinces, and by placing its seal of approval on subordinates they selected, on the local laws they passed, and on the taxes they collected. This meant that Peking was losing its power of control as local and regional administra-

tion was being taken over by the provincial leaders of the new militia armies. It meant, in addition, that after 1860 the balance which the dynasty had maintained between Manchu and Chinese officials began rapidly to favor the Chinese, many but not all of whom were of the scholar-official class. From 1861 to 1890 the number of Manchu governors-general appointed was ten, while the number of Chinese was thirty-four. Manchu governors appointed during the same period numbered thirteen, while the Chinese totaled 104.

The conclusion is inescapable: the structure of political power within China was altered radically as a result of the T'ai-p'ing upheaval. The centralized military organization, effective in the early years of the dynasty, had lost its practical power. Military power, no longer centralized, was diffused in various provincial and local areas. With this diffusion of military authority went also a comparable diffusion of fiscal authority and ultimately of Peking's administrative control. A governor or governor-general who owed his position to a local army, to local taxation, and to his control of local administration was not a mere servant of the dynasty. Thus began a continuing conflict between centralism and regionalism which was to have far reaching results in the twentieth century. These shiftings in the politico-military focus of power within China had a very direct bearing on China's relations with the foreign powers. The military impotence of Peking was a constant invitation to the treaty powers to use China's treaty violations to demand further treaty concessions.

THE COOPERATIVE POLICY

Although the growth of regional or private armies betokened declining strength in the dynasty, Peking did make a number of constructive efforts to deal rationally with the treaty powers. In these cases Prince Kung reasoned that China would have peace if she observed the treaties, and peace would open the way for self-strengthening. A few powerful officials held the same view: Tseng Kuo-fan, Li

---

Army: A Study in Nineteenth Century Chinese Regionalism (1964). Note in particular the difficulties of evaluating the policies of Chinese leaders of this period. It seems fair to say, for example, that while Li Hung-chang took ample personal profit from his industrial enterprises, his primary concern was regional development and the strengthening of the state. In the years of the T'ai-p'ing rebellion, regional militarism supported the central authority of Peking in important ways. See David Pong, "The Income and Military Expenditure of Kiangsi Province in the Last Years (1860-1864) of the Taiping Rebellion," *Journal of Asian Studies,* 26 (1966), 49-65.

Hung-chang, Tso Tsung-t'ang, and the Manchu Grand Councilor Wen-hsiang.

This new policy of cooperating with the barbarians was what the treaty powers wanted, but what they had hardly dared to hope for. For the most part they took the position that so long as China cooperated in observing the treaties it would be good policy for them to sustain the Ch'ing administration, meanwhile helping to guide it into the modern world. This form of altruism would pay off, so it was said, in more commerce and more profits. For the moment at least both Peking and the powers found common cause in this single cooperative policy. Implementation of the policy was helped along because the ministers of the powers then at Peking happened to be men disposed by personality to work together with some understanding of China's difficulties.[7]

The role of the United States in this cooperative policy was notable. Burlingame, who was under instructions to "consult and cooperate" with his diplomatic colleagues, achieved an informal status of leadership among his peers, a status that was the more remarkable because his own country was torn apart by civil war and because he was a novice in the diplomatic techniques of commercial imperialism. He described for Secretary of State William H. Seward in 1862 the principles through which the United States might apply a "cooperative" policy in China. These principles, approved by Seward, included:

1. No acquisition of Chinese territory by the United States.
2. No interference "in the political struggles of the Chinese further than to maintain our treaty rights."
3. Active assistance to Chinese authorities, in cooperation with other powers, in maintaining treaty rights against pirates, bandits, and rebels, to the end that should the other powers "menace the integrity of the Chinese territory then the very fact that we had acted with them for law and order would give us greater weight against such a policy."

[7] In 1862 these ministers included Bruce (Great Britain), Berthemy (France), de Balluseck (Russia), and Burlingame (U. S.), known together as the four B's.

Burlingame believed that the danger of continuing foreign aggression was very real. To meet this danger he reiterated a principle already expressed by U.S. Commissioner to China Humphrey Marshall nearly a decade earlier, to the effect that it would be sound policy for the treaty powers to guarantee the neutrality of China.

From 1862 until he retired as American minister in 1867, Burlingame and his three colleagues applied the cooperative policy with some success. In essence the policy achieved two things. First, China, confronted by united diplomatic action from the powers, was held to a stricter observance of the treaties, and this lessened the danger of resort to a gunboat policy. Second, as a result of this increased diplomatic stability, there was less temptation to individual powers to take advantage of China's weakness.[8]

THE T'UNG-WEN KUAN

A further indication that Peking was moving cautiously toward accommodation with the West was the creation in 1862, on Prince Kung's recommendation, of the *t'ung-wen kuan* or interpreters' college, as it came to be called. Since English and French texts were the only authoritative versions of the British and the French treaties of Tientsin, China's need for native linguists could hardly be denied even by the most conservative members of the court. The original faculty, composed of Western instructors, included an American missionary, W. A. P. Martin, appointed as instructor of English in 1864. Within a few years the school was offering not only foreign language but also a very modest liberal arts curriculum, which included such subjects as mathematics, chemistry, physics, and international law. Similar schools came into being at Shanghai (1863), Canton (1864), and Foochow (1866). The influence of these schools cannot be judged with certainty. For the most part, the better qualified students did not attend them, since

[8] It was in these years, too, that the newly-organized Chinese Customs Service became a stabilizing force in Sino-Western relations under Robert Hart, appointed inspector-general in 1863.

families of influence did not send their sons to an untried venture such as the *t'ung-wen kuan.* Nevertheless, these schools were China's first effort in Western education.[9]

WESTERN INTERNATIONAL LAW

Prior to joining the staff of the *t'ung-wen kuan,* W. A. P. Martin undertook to translate into Chinese Henry Wheaton's *Elements of International Law.* In doing this Martin was prompted, first, by China's obvious need for such a work, and, second, by his conviction that the principles of international law were one of the worthy products of Christian civilization. Through the influence of Burlingame, the translation was given in 1864 to Prince Kung and the Tsungli Yamen, where it was put to an immediate practical test. Armed with this new Western weapon, Prince Kung rebuked the newly-arrived Prussian minister for his seizure of Danish merchant ships in Chinese waters near Taku. The minister was not received until he had released the ships. The incident was convincing evidence to at least some members of the Tsungli Yamen that international law could serve China as well as the West.[10]

[9] Knight Biggerstaff, *The Earliest Modern Government Schools in China* (1961) provides a fine understanding of the Chinese approach to Western learning. Western innovations in education met opposition from high places at court, led by the Grand Secretary Wo-jen, a Mongol scholar of great reputation, a tutor to the emperor, and head of the Hanlin Academy. His objections to Western learning expressed the traditionalism that was still dominant. Wo-jen declared that if mathematics was to be taught by Westerners the damage to China would be great. The way to establish and strengthen a nation, he said, was to lay emphasis on propriety and righteousness (Confucian virtues), not on power and plotting. No nation, he asserted, had ever raised itself from decline by the use of mathematics. As for other aspects of Westernism, he pointed out that Christianity had already deceived many ignorant Chinese.

[10] At the time of this incident, Prussia and Denmark were at war. The fact that the barbarians could be confounded by their own rules was a pleasant surpise to the Tsungli Yamen.

A FIRST DIPLOMATIC MISSION

An additional sign of new behavior at Peking was China's first semi-diplomatic mission to western Europe. The decision to send such a mission was a particularly difficult one for the Ch'ing administration. China, of course, had every right to be represented abroad, but she had little disposition to move in this direction. To send ambassadors abroad would be another indication that China was no longer the Middle Kingdom but merely a nation among nations. Until 1860, when foreign envoys gained the treaty right to reside permanently at Peking, they had always been excluded from the capital, except for brief periods when they came as bearers of tribute. On the other hand, Prince Kung and the Tsungli Yamen could not remain entirely insensitive to the value of foreign intelligence direct from their own diplomatic agents. They were moved finally to a first timid step by the counsel of Anson Burlingame and Robert Hart. Hart later confided that he believed foreign representation abroad would have a double effect: it would safeguard China's independence and freedom of action, and it would bind China to the West and promote her modernization. Accordingly, in 1866, as a kind of tentative substitute for regular diplomatic intercourse, the court approved a semiofficial mission headed by an elderly Manchu functionary of low rank, Pin-ch'un. Since he was a person of little consequence, any indignities he might suffer abroad could be ignored. Pin-ch'un visited widely throughout Europe. He paid little attention to political affairs but was impressed greatly by the spotless hotels, the brightly-lighted streets that did not become muddy in the rain, and by the fact that Queen Victoria was unable to act without the sanction of a parliament.[11]

THE BURLINGAME MISSION

Of greater immediate importance was China's invitation in 1867 to Burlingame, who was

[11] Knight Biggerstaff, "The First Chinese Mission of Investigation Sent to Europe," *Pacific Historical Review,* 6 (1937), 307-20.

about to retire as American minister at Peking, to serve as one of China's first official envoys to the treaty powers. Prince Kung and his colleagues took this unprecedented action in the hope that misunderstandings might be avoided, that there might be closer contact with foreign governments, and, most importantly, that in the approaching revision of the treaties the powers might be persuaded to show forbearance on the theory that China was already "progressing" as rapidly as could be, so that demands for further concessions would be inexpedient. Burlingame had so won the confidence of Peking that he was considered the ideal envoy to achieve these ends. Associated with him on a basis of equality in the mission were Chih Kang, a Manchu, and Sun Chia-ku, a Chinese.

The Burlingame mission was also due in some measure to the fact that after 1861 Prince Kung, Wen-hsiang (his chief assistant), Tseng Kuo-fan, and Li Hung-chang, while more favorably inclined toward revolutionary changes than their predecessors, were able to see that China must make adjustments to the West if she hoped to survive. It was against this background that the Tsungli Yamen in 1867 required the provincial governors to give Peking their views on what should be done when the foreign powers pressed for further treaty revision. The replies of these officials are of importance historically, since they reveal the attitude of high Chinese officials to the problem of foreign relations in general and to specific questions in particular; thus they provide an approach to the history of China's foreign relations during the next half century. In general the views expressed in this secret correspondence with Peking in 1867-1868 are a fair indication of the rough road China was to travel in foreign affairs. For the most part the opinions from the provinces may be summarized as follows: (1) foreigners and the countries from which they came were still held in low esteem; (2) no further treaty concessions should be granted to foreign merchants; and (3) no further expansion of foreign missionary activity should be permitted. Only three high officials who engaged in this correspondence (Li Hung-chang, Tseng Kuo-fan, and Shen Pao-chen) showed any understanding of the possible values to China of

railways, telegraphs, steamships, and mining machinery. Perhaps not more than five of these officials sensed the gravity of the problems posed for China by an aggressive Western world.[12]

The Burlingame mission was received in America with an enthusiasm not unlike what small boys accord a circus. Burlingame, an idealist and above all an orator, gave free reign to his eloquence. He pictured China, the oldest nation, seeking Westernization and progress through America, the youngest of nations. He pictured a China that stood with arms extended to receive "the shining banners of Western civilization"—strange-sounding words to the ears of Prince Kung and his associates in Peking. Many an American editor assumed that Burlingame's words meant what they said. The *Farmer's Cabinet* of Amherst, New Hampshire, was moved to observe that China's exclusiveness was ended. This "must give an enormous development to our trade, and the interests of Christianity will be more effectively promoted by this action of the Chinese Emperor, than by any other political event of the last two centuries." Although Burlingame's intentions were the best, he laid the foundations for a species of colorful reporting on China that was to deceive the American public from that day far into the twentieth century.

In Washington, Burlingame and his Chinese colleagues were received by President Johnson and the Congress. On July 28, Burlingame and Secretary Seward concluded eight supplementary articles to the American treaty of Tientsin. These articles provided that China might appoint consuls at United States ports, that Americans in China and Chinese in the United States should enjoy complete freedom of religion, and that rights of residence and travel were to be available to the nationals of both countries. Moreover, the United States disavowed "any intention or right to intervene in the domestic administration of China in regard to the construction of railroads, telegraphs or other material internal improvements,"

[12] Knight Biggerstaff, "The Secret Correspondence of 1867-1868: Views of Leading Chinese Statesmen Regarding the Further Opening of China to Western Influence," *Journal of Modern History,* 22 (1950), 122-36.

China being conceded the right to determine the time for such undertakings; and, finally, China and the United States recognized "the inherent and inalienable right of man to change his home and allegiance. . . ."[13]

On September 19 the mission reached London, where it received Lord Clarendon's assurance that the British government would show forbearance in seeking further commercial concessions and would deal only with the central government in seeking redress of wrongs to British subjects. From London the mission visited Paris, Belgium, Prussia, Denmark, Sweden, Holland, and Russia. In Russia, on February 23, 1870, Burlingame died of pneumonia. Meanwhile, although the foreign press in the treaty ports had heaped abuse on the mission, declaring that it did not represent the real purposes of Peking, the Chinese government ratified the Seward-Burlingame articles, thus demonstrating its faith in an envoy who, though exceeding the stricter limits of his instructions, had presented China's case with enthusiasm, if not with complete candor. The general success of the Burlingame mission in weathering, for the moment at least, the problem of treaty revision inspired unwarranted confidence at the Manchu court, for it now seemed evident that the foreigners could be managed for a price—the modest cost of the Burlingame mission.

It required another ten years, however, for the Manchu court to establish its first diplomatic mission in Britain (1877). This mission provided a nice example of the processes by which China was learning, slowly, to comprehend the West. When Kuo Sung-t'ao, a loyal, learned, incorruptible official, and the first Chinese minister at London, returned to Peking, he said, to the astonishment of his colleagues: "Confucius and Mencius have deceived us." By this he meant not that he was converted to Western ideas, but that he had learned there were ways other than the Chinese of governing civilized countries. For a distinguished Chinese official to acknowledge that there were barbarian governments untouched by Confucian culture that were both "civilized and rational" was unprecedented if not subversive.

In the United States the first Chinese legation was opened in 1878 by Ch'en Lanpin and Yung Wing, who had been in charge of an educational mission. By 1880 China had legations in most of the leading Western states and Japan. But it was only through dire necessity, rather than free, positive choice, that China thus entered the world community.

THE T'UNG-CHIH RESTORATION

To that small number of contemporary Westerners who had some knowledge of China, the decade of the 1860's held considerable promise for the future of Sino-Western relations. The seemingly enlightened attitude of Prince Kung, the final defeat of the T'ai-p'ings, the cooperative policy, the good sense and restraint of the Western ministers at Peking, the beginnings of Western education at such schools as the *t'ung-wen kuan,* the appearance of an interest in Western international law, the Pin-ch'un and Burlingame missions, together with some reforms in the Confucian bureaucracy and some government relief to areas devastated by the T'ai-p'ings[14]—all pointed to new and constructive beginnings in China's approach to her internal affairs and to the Western world. The powers could therefore surmise that the Ch'ing

---

[13] For the Burlingame mission, see Knight Biggerstaff, "The Official Chinese Attitude Toward the Burlingame Mission," *American Historical Review,* 41 (1936), 682-702; and Knight Biggerstaff, "A Translation of Anson Burlingame's Instructions from the Chinese Foreign Office," *Far Eastern Quarterly,* 1 (1942), 277-79.

[14] The task of reconstruction following the devastation of the T'ai-p'ing twenty-year civil war was, however, enormous, and far beyond the vision or the capacities of the Ch'ing government. Rebuilding and public relief to the homeless and destitute was, therefore, done largely through the leadership of the local gentry encouraged by the government, and through the stamina and work of the peasants and other common folk. The government did at times remit the land tax or reduce tax rates, but these acts assisted landlords rather than tenants. The landlord might pay less in taxes while the tenant rarely paid less in rent.

dynasty was entering a new era with fresh vitality.

Some Chinese and Manchus also looked upon the period as one of great promise, but for very different reasons. To the Peking government the new beginnings were simply the application of a little new knowledge, along with conventional wisdom, to specific problems. The purpose was not to change China but to restore its Confucian order through a revival of traditional ethics and virtues. In economics, for example, the government wanted to revitalize the traditional system rather than to break new ground. For such reasons, this period has come to be known as the T'ung-chih restoration.

It should not have been surprising that the Chinese response of the 1860's took this particular direction—a return to tradition. Although the previous two decades, marked by Western barbarian invasion and unprecedented internal rebellion, had laid bare the pitiable state of China's government and of her society at large, this did not mean that the gentry, the ruling bureaucracy, or the Manchu dynasty saw these ills as signifying the failure of the Confucianism system by which the Chinese had lived for two thousand years. That system had given China a self-sufficiency and a cultural durability unique in the world's political and social history. The immediate crisis, therefore, could only be considered as temporary. It would pass; meanwhile it would be met in two ways, both of which were traditional.

The first way would call for flexibility in accommodating the barbarian in his appetite for treaties and trade. This process would give China the time to master the secrets of barbarian power, particularly barbarian military power, which would then be used to quell rebellion at home and eventually to expel the barbarian. All this could be justified under the old principle of conciliation, which China had used many times. It was this kind of strategy in the 1860's that made it appear to the Westerners that China's modernization was at hand. Prince Kung's policy of observing the treaties, the appearance of the more modern armies that defeated the T'ai-p'ings, the establishment of modern academies (the *t'ung-wen kuan,* for example), and the first Chinese missions to the West all implied that China was adopting what the West liked to call progress.

The second and simultaneous way in which the crisis would be met was neither known to nor comprehended by the treaty port foreigners or their governments. It was to be a revival of the traditional order, a process of self-strengthening which would cleanse the system of abuses so that its virtues might prevail. Through old and tried Confucian ideals and methods, through scholar government and the practice of virtue, China, its leaders believed, would again become strong. China would not become Western; she would become more Confucian. This happy outcome would provide the solution to both foreign invasion and domestic rebellion. A conservatism which would not see what it did not wish to see would restore China to greatness.[15]

FOR FURTHER READING

Confucian Tradition and Reform. Various aspects of China's traditional intellectual framework are presented in: Arthur F. Wright, ed., *Studies in Chinese Thought* (1953),* David Nivison and Arthur F. Wright, eds., *Confucianism in Action* (1959);* Arthur Wright, ed.,

[15] The pioneer collection of documents on this subject is Ssu-yu Teng and John K. Fairbank, *China's Response to the West* (1954).*

It is vital for the Western student not to confuse modern Chinese conservatism of this period with Western conservatism. To be sure, they both wished to conserve but, beyond this, they had little in common. Western political conservatism was concerned to preserve "the Christian, antirationalist, aristocratic, and feudal strains of pre-Enlightenment European Society." Chinese conservatism of the later nineteenth century was bent on preserving Confucian, rationalist, gentry and non-feudal strains of earlier Chinese society. The Chinese conservative had no interest in Western political and philosophic ideas. He believed in a rational, cosmopolitan order and in a rational national order that might even subordinate private property to group interests. He believed in man's innate goodness, and in the ideal of the universal state. These beliefs bear no resemblance to the preoccupations of the modern Western conservative with a divine plan in history, a sense of sin, a distrust of reason, and a conviction that private property is sacred. On these points, see Mary C. Wright, *The Last Stand of Chinese Conservatism* (1957),* 1-3.

Confucian Persuasion (1960);* Arthur Wright and Denis Twitchett, eds., *Confucian Personalities* (1962);* and Joseph R. Levenson, *Confucian China and Its Modern Fate: The Problem of Intellectual Continuity* (1958); and *Modern China and Its Confucian Past* (1964), studies on the most influential tradition.

Among the specialized studies focusing on problems of reform in the Confucian tradition are: Chang Chung-li, *The Chinese Gentry: Studies on Their Role in Nineteenth Century Chinese Society* (1955)* which emphasizes the scholarly bureaucratic foundation of the dominant social class; Fei Hsiao-t'ung, *China's Gentry,* rev. and ed. by Margaret Park Redfield (1953),* a study of political and social classes stressing the disruptive influences of Western commerce; Robert M. Marsh, *The Mandarins: the Circulation of the Elites in China, 1600-1900* (1961), a study of eminent Chinese to determine whether advancement in government service was due to bureaucratic factors or to family background. For biographies of key personalities see Kwang-ching Liu, "Li Hung-chang's Formative Years, 1823-1866," *Harvard Journal of Asiatic Studies* (1970); and Princess Der Ling, *Old Buddha* (1932).

Establishing Diplomatic Contacts. S. M. Meng, *The Tsungli Yamen: Its Organization and Functions* (1962).* Banno Masataka, *China and the West, 1858-1861: The Origin of the Tsungli Yamen* (1964), a detailed case study of the clash between Chinese and Western political traditions. S. S. Kim, "Burlingame and the Inauguration of the Cooperative Policy," *Modern Asian Studies* (October, 1971). Wang Tseng-tsai, "The Audience Question: Foreign Representatives and the Emperor of China, 1858-1873" *Historical Journal 14* (September, 1971), 617-626.

China, 1870–1890: Signs of Trouble

13

For some two decades following the T'ung-chih period China was relatively free from serious internal rebellion. The resulting peace, along with a consequent revival of some dynastic prestige, suggested that there might also be increasingly stable relations between China and the treaty powers. This expectation was not fulfilled for, in fact, China had already entered upon a period of tense relations with her Western residents and of increasing pressures from their governments. The T'ung-chih restoration, with its feeble efforts at self-strengthening, was on the road to failure.

THE ROLE OF THE EMPRESS DOWAGER

China's unhappy position in these decades following 1860 was guaranteed, as it were, by the character and the personality of the Empress Dowager Tz'u-hsi. She had won an increasing dominance over the dynasty and the administration. Although a shrewd manipulator of men, she had little that could be called education and no comprehension of the modern

Western world that was imposing itself on China. Her overweening ambition was to achieve for herself a monopoly of power, to which end she even set aside dynastic laws and traditions in effecting the succession of the Kuang-hsu emperor (1875-1908). As Prince Kung lost her favor she began to listen to her most traditionally-minded advisers. To a very great degree she was responsible for the ultimate failure "to regenerate the dynasty and modernize the country."[1]

[1] Immanuel C. Y. Hsu, *The Rise of Modern China* (1970), 368. The different outlooks of the Empress Dowager and Prince Kung should not be overdrawn. Both were traditionalists, bent on preserving the old order. Even Prince Kung had supposed, naively, that when he created the post of superintendent of trade at Tientsin, the barbarian chieftains (the ministers of the powers then resident at Peking) would find they had nothing to do and so would go home. From 1870 on, when Li Hung-chang accepted the Tientsin post, his office took over most of the foreign affairs functions of the Tsungli Yamen, while Li himself became to all intents and purposes China's foreign minister for the remainder of the century. The Manchu court was still striving to keep foreign affairs as far from Peking as possible.

THE PROBLEM OF TREATY REVISION

The British Treaty of Tientsin was subject to revision in 1868, but, at London, Lord Clarendon had assured Burlingame that the British government would exercise forbearance. This was significant. Chinese officialdom was convinced that the treaties offered too much; the British, and most of the foreign merchants in the ports, that they conceded too little. There was always the danger, too, that attacks upon foreigners by lawless or antiforeign elements of the Chinese populace would lead to a resumption of the gunboat policy. Americans, like all Westerners, were subject to these armed attacks.

Skillful diplomacy was needed if the legal rights of the powers were to be honored, if the uncompromising demands of the merchants were to be curbed, and if Chinese officialdom was to be convinced that its best interests would be served by educating its people to a fuller observance of the treaties. A few Chinese officials did have some understanding of all this. Li Hung-chang, for example, advocated a more unbiased approach. Discarding the view that foreigners were a plague on Chinese soil, he observed with brutal frankness that "The outrageous craft and malignity of the Chinese exceeds even that of the foreigners."

The foreign merchants in the treaty ports and Hong Kong also had their ideas on what should be done. They were appealing already to their home governments on the subject of treaty revision to redress their real or imagined grievances. However, Sir Rutherford Alcock, British minister at Peking, believed that China could better be induced to adopt a progressive policy if coercion were not applied. He recognized that a moderate policy would never satisfy the merchants, but he added that they had no claim to consideration since they refused to appreciate the difficulties of reform and progress in a land as old as China, and since they themselves were guilty of "fraudulent practices and want of good faith." Accordingly, Lord Clarendon decided to delay pressing for treaty revision until 1872-1873, when the young T'ung-chih emperor would attain his majority.

In this decision the other treaty powers concurred.

THE DEVELOPMENT OF CHRISTIAN MISSIONS

The question of treaty revision and, in fact, the larger problem of China's relations with the West were connected intimately with the Christian missionary problem. The reader is already familiar with some aspects of Roman Catholic missions in China during the sixteenth, seventeenth, and eighteenth centuries. In the nineteenth century, coincident with the opening of China and Japan, Protestant Christendom also became active in the field of foreign missions. In 1805 the London Missionary Society sent Robert Morrison to China, traveling on an American ship because the English East India Company, fearful of offending the Chinese, refused him passage on a Company ship.[2] In the early 1820's the American Bible Society also entered the field. During the first year of its work in China the Society distributed 500 copies of the New Testament. Eighty years later it was giving away more than half a million copies, including an elegantly bound edition to the empress dowager on her sixtieth birthday. After 1830, American Protestantism was represented in China by an expanding group of churches and missionary societies.

THE TREATY STATUS OF MISSIONARIES

Christianity and those who preached it had acquired an internal legal status in China as a result of the toleration clauses of the Tientsin treaties of 1858; the Russian and the French treaties permitted the missionaries *to travel* with passports in the interior. The Chinese text of the Franco-Chinese convention of 1860 conceded the right of missionaries *to reside* in the interior, to acquire land, to build churches and schools, and to propagate Christian doc-

[2] See K. S. Latourette, *A History of Christian Missions in China* (1929, Taiwan ed., 1966) 212.

trine without hindrance. The French text, which was authoritative, contained no such concessions, and was kept secret from the other legations at Peking for ten years. Whatever the explanation of this discrepancy in the texts, its effects were explained clearly by Frederick F. Low, American minister at Peking in 1870:

The missionaries of this Roman Catholic Religious Faith have, in addition to the right of residence as Bishops and Priests, assumed to occupy a semi-official position which places them on an equality with the native officers where they reside. They also claimed the right to protect the native Christians from persecution, which practically constituted the missionaries the arbiters of their disputes and the judges of their wrongful acts, and removed this class from the control of their native rulers. The absolute right of the Roman Catholic Clergy to exercise, in the name and by the authority of the French Government, a protectorate over native Christians was claimed .. and insisted upon by some of the earlier representatives of France in China.[3]

Chinese officialdom feared and resented these pretensions of the missionaries. Not only did the officials see immediate political implications involving their own power, they were also suspicious of Christianity because it was an alien and exclusive faith that was frequently in conflict with fundamental concepts of Chinese social and religious life. It will not be difficult, then, to understand how easily the masses might be aroused to attack the missionaries and their property. All classes of Chinese found ample evidence to support their distrust of the foreign missionary. His intolerant dogmas could scarcely be reconciled with Chinese philosophy, which was essentially tolerant, practical, and mundane; Christian love and Christian intolerance were difficult for many Chinese to reconcile; and Christian theory did not seem to be practiced with much vigor by the foreign merchants in the ports. From these critical conclusions grew others born of ignorance and fanaticism. It was a common rumor, for instance, that Christian hospitals and orphanages purchased hapless infants from indigent mothers

and extracted their eyes to compound direful drugs which, when taken, converted the victim to Christianity.[4]

From a background of such suspicion, hatred, and fear came the so-called Tientsin Massacre of 1870. A Chinese mob destroyed a Roman Catholic orphanage and the adjoining church, and killed the French consul, two priests, ten nuns, three Russians, and some thirty Chinese servants. Alarm soon spread to many of the treaty ports, and French, British, and American warships appeared off Tientsin. The demands of France led to the death penalty or banishment of some of the perpetrators. China paid an indemnity of 250,000 taels and sent a mission of apology to France. Peking proposed a number of rules to govern and safeguard the work of missionaries, but only the American minister was willing even to discuss them.

Thus less than ten years after Burlingame had reached China, and two years after negotiation of the Burlingame-Seward treaty, the policy of patience and forbearance was headed for rough weather. The responsibility for the Tientsin massacre cannot be laid at the door of one country or one group of individuals. It was an ugly creation of Chinese officials and agitators, and of foreign missionaries, their churches and their governments.

During the remainder of the nineteenth and on into the twentieth century China's relations with the West continued to be complicated by the political and other implications of the Christian missionary movement. A balanced picture of the missionary at work must give full weight to the sincerity and humanity with which many missionaries labored; the educational and the medical work of the missions

[3] To Secretary of State Hamilton Fish. Printed in Paul H. Clyde, ed., *United States Policy Toward China: Diplomatic and Public Documents, 1839-1939* (1940, reissued 1964), 108, 112.

[4] Paul A. Cohen, *China and Christianity: The Missionary Movement and the Growth of Chinese Antiforeignism, 1860-1870* (1963). Also James E. Kirby, Jr., "The Foochow Anti-Missionary Riot, August 30, 1878," *Journal of Asian Studies,* 25 (1966), 665-79. In the view of Chinese officials, the missionary was unwelcome not only because of his religious ideology but also because he was a disturber of the peace. The missionary's appeal for protection (to which he was entitled under the treaties) imposed special burdens on Chinese officialdom. What the Western diplomat demanded on behalf of the missionary, the Peking government often granted—even if it were in no position to enforce the grant.

brought forth the highest praise. Nevertheless, George F. Seward, while American minister at Peking (1876-1880), found that the majority of the grievances with which the legation was called upon to deal concerned missionaries. He regretted a situation that made the diplomatic agent of the American government the right arm of the propagandists of the Christian faith.

THE AUDIENCE QUESTION

The thirteen-year period from 1860 to 1873 had shown that the Ch'ing dynasty, as directed by Prince Kung, was capable of at least faltering steps toward adjustment to the new world of the West. At the same time, this Manchu-Chinese capacity to take one step forward was countered more often than not by a genius for taking two steps backward. The granting by the emperor in 1873 of the first official audience at Peking to the ministers of the treaty powers resident there suggests how this genius worked. When a minister from a treaty power reached China, he would, if Western practice prevailed, be received in audience by the emperor to present his credentials. Such an audience, however, would imply that the Son of Heaven was a mere equal of the Western sovereigns, an admission Peking could not bring itself to make. As late as 1867 the court had been most careful in its instructions to the Burlingame mission to guard against committing the emperor on this point. Consequently, all requests for audience made by the envoys in Peking had been denied. From 1861 to 1873 the Tsungli Yamen was able to evade and delay a decision on the ground that the emperor was a minor. But this excuse could not be used indefinitely. The powers were in general agreement that eventually the audience must be insisted upon. It seemed that 1873, the year of the emperor's coming of age, would be the appropriate time.[5]

[5] The Chinese attitude toward the audience question may be stated in this way: Apparently the court was not unwilling to grant imperial audiences during the 1860's. It merely demanded that foreign envoys conform to certain ceremonial usages to which the foreign envoys objected. Hence came the desire of the Chinese to postpone grappling with the question. Note W. W. Rockhill, *Diplomatic Audiences at the Court of China* (1905).

The date for the first audience was finally set for June 29, 1873. During the previous months the ministers of the Tsungli Yamen and the foreign envoys had engaged in an unprofitable wrangle, the former demanding that the foreigners kneel before the throne. Three bows were finally accepted as a substitute. Then came the appointed day when the T'ung-chih emperor entered the *Tzu Kuang Ko* (Throne Hall of Purple Effulgence) located in an imperial park adjacent to but not in the imperial palace. The Japanese ambassador, Soyejima, outranking his European colleagues, was received first and alone. Then the representatives of the Western powers were led in together by Prince Kung: General Vlangaly of Russia, Frederick F. Low of the United States, Thomas F. Wade of Great Britain, M. de Geofroy of France, and M. Ferguson of the Netherlands. All bowed three times as they advanced to the center of the hall and placed their letters of credence on the Dragon Table. After the reading of a congratulatory address in French, the emperor acknowledged receipt of the letters by a slight inclination of the head and a few words in Manchu addressed to Prince Kung. The envoys now stepped backwards bowing repeatedly until they had reached the entrance to the hall. The entire ceremony had taken less than half an hour.

So ended the first audience granted the foreign powers since the establishment of treaty relations. It was an event of primary importance to the powers, for, as Minister Low had said, friendly relations could not be cultivated unless the "arrogance and conceit" of high Chinese officials was curbed by a ceremonial recognition that China was not superior to the foreign nations. On the surface, therefore, the powers could pride themselves on a ceremonial diplomatic victory. Their triumph, however, was not so complete as they supposed. The Manchu-Chinese court had succeeded in snubbing the foreigners at the very moment their equality was seemingly recognized. The *Tzu Kuang Ko*, where the audience was held, was a pavilion used for receiving tribute missions from the rulers of lesser kingdoms, such as Korea, Burma, and the Ryukyu Islands. Furthermore, the envoys were not permitted to enter the grounds by the main gate but through a side entrance, just as lesser officials were required to enter at the side gate of a yamen. Finally, the Chinese account of the audience notes particularly that the foreign ministers were admitted "after an interval of some duration"; that is, after they had been kept waiting, a favorite method of making a caller feel his inferiority.

In reality, therefore, the audience had accomplished very little, for the Peking authorities were convinced that they had succeeded in maintaining their superior position. Moreover, a year and a half later (January 12, 1875) the T'ung-chih emperor died. Under the influence of the Empress Dowager Tz'u-hsi, and against all precedent, the court named as successor Tsai-tien, a child of the same generation as the deceased monarch. The new sovereign, the Kuang-hsu emperor (1875-1908), was a son of Tz'u-hsi's sister and of Prince Chun, her most ardent supporter in the imperial family. For the next fourteen years Tz'u-hsi, as regent, was again the ruler of China. This development did not improve China's relations with the treaty powers.

TREATY REVISION AND THE MARGARY AFFAIR

British traders had long speculated on the possibilities of reaching China's western provinces of Kweichow, Yunnan, and Szechuan by way of the Burma border. One expedition from British India had proceeded to Bhamo on the upper Irrawaddy in 1868; a second expedition, under Colonel Horace A. Browne, was organized in 1874 to enter Yunnan. The British legation in Peking was asked to secure passports and an interpreter from the consular service. For this post Minister Thomas Wade selected Augustus Raymond Margary, who, traveling overland with six Chinese, reached Bhamo in January, 1875.

In February the Browne expedition left Bhamo. It was preceded by Margary and his Chinese, whose purpose was to discover whether the route might be traveled in safety. The answer to this question was given when Margary and five of his Chinese associates were killed. Responsibility for this outrage is not easily placed. The Burmese sovereign was opposed to the opening of trade routes, as were

also the local Chinese authorities in Yunnan. The border tribes were irresponsible and frequently beyond Chinese control. Yet the British government took the position that local Chinese authorities could not be absolved of negligence, if not connivance. What is really significant is that the murder of Margary was seized upon by British Minister Wade as an appropriate incident to be used in forcing a settlement with Peking of all outstanding Anglo-Chinese questions.

Wade formulated his demands promptly: (1) China was to send a mission of investigation accompanied by British officers; (2) permission was to be granted for a second expedition from India; (3) 150,000 taels were to be placed at the British minister's disposal; (4) the emperor was to grant a fitting and satisfactory audience to Her Majesty's minister; (5) British goods were to be freed from all *likin* taxation; and (6) all British claims were to be satisfied at once. On reflection, Wade reduced his demands to the first three, the government in London approved one and two but reserved judgment on point three.

The Chinese government accepted the demands in principle but objected to the blunt manner of Wade's diplomacy. It was not until August, 1876, that Wade met with Li Hung-chang at Cheefoo, where in September an agreement known as the Cheefoo Convention was signed. It was ratified by China four days later, but not by Great Britain until July, 1885.[6]

The Chefoo convention was an impressive document embodying three sections. The first, which dealt with the Yunnan-Margary case, provided for the issuance of proclamations in the provinces, drew up regulations for the Burma-Yunnan frontier trade, approved a second mission from India, stationed British officers for five years at some city in Yunnan, established an indemnity of 200,000 taels for the families of those murdered, and for expenses incident to the whole case, and recognized the claims of British merchants. Finally, China was to send a mission of apology to London.

[6] For text of the Chefoo convention, see China, The Maritime Customs, *Treaties, Conventions, etc., Between China and Foreign States* (2 vols., 2nd ed., 1917), I, 491-505. Note S. T. Wang, *The Margary Affair and the Chefoo Agreement* (1940), and Immanuel C. Y. Hsu, *China's Entrance into the Family of Nations, The Diplomatic Phase, 1858-1880* (1960), 176-79.

Section two of the convention dealt with "Official Intercourse." China was to invite the foreign powers to consider with her a code of procedure and official etiquette designed to insure proper treatment of the foreign ministers at Peking and of the consuls at the treaty ports. China was also to invite the powers to joint consideration of means of insuring more effective administration of justice at the treaty ports.

Section three, dealing with trade, provided for stationing a consul at Chungking, and for the opening of additional treaty ports (Ichang, Wuhu, Wenchow, and Pakhoi) as well as several ports of call on the Yangtze. Other clauses defined more clearly the foreign settlement areas in the ports.

In general the Chefoo convention was a substantial supplement to Britain's treaties of 1842, 1858, and 1860, in that it secured practically all the concessions the British minister had been demanding over a period of nearly two years. However, the convention was not well received by representatives of the other treaty powers. There were objections from the Russians, the Germans, and the French, a point of importance since by the nature of its content, most of the convention required the ratification of these powers also. Some British merchants were also opposed to it, on the ground that it would be better to hold China to a strict observance of the 1858 settlement than to require new concessions of her. The Chefoo convention illustrated not only how pressure was exerted on China to revise treaties, but also how difficult it was to attain agreement among the treaty powers themselves.

IMMIGRATION: PRINCIPLE AND PRACTICE

While these problems of treaty revision and interpretation were still being debated, China's relations with the United States were disturbed by the emigration of Chinese laborers to California. During the nineteenth century Chinese emigration had been of two kinds: free emigration of coolie laborers, for the most part to California and Australia, and contract-labor emigration to Cuba and Peru, known as the coolie trade. After 1862 the coolie trade was prohibited in American ships, and was brought under rigid regulation in British vessels sailing from Hong Kong. Nevertheless, until 1874 this nefarious trade continued to flourish from the Portuguese settlement at Macao. S. Wells Williams wrote in 1866 from Peking that "the most flagitious acts have been committed by the Chinese natives upon each other, under the stimulus of rewards offered by foreigners to bring them coolies." Burlingame reported that in the season 1865-1866, 13,500 coolies were sent to Cuba alone, mostly from Macao.[7] Until this vicious traffic was brought to an end in 1874 there was no logic in Western moralizing on the shortcomings of China in international affairs.

In contrast with the pitiable Chinese coolie laborer in Cuba and Peru, the free laborer who went to California enjoyed a personal and economic freedom he had not known in China. So relatively prosperous, indeed, was the lot of these immigrants that by 1880 there were 75,000 Chinese in California—9 percent of the population. They had been attracted by news of the rich opportunities offered in the gold fields, by the demands for labor in the building of the first transcontinental railroad, and by the retail trade in San Francisco and other towns. At first the Chinese were welcomed. They provided cheap, convenient labor and were able to live on "the smell of a greasy rag." In the beginning, too, their qualities of industry and docility were seen as virtues. This attitude prevailed until the great depression of the seventies, at which time the cry was raised that the "Chinaman" was robbing the white man's dinner pail and destroying his standard of living. The "Chinaman's" virtues became vices. The New York *Nation* noted derisively in 1883 that the Chinese on the Pacific Coast were perpetuating "those disgusting habits of thrift, industry, and self-denial. . . ." It became clear,

[7] United States, Department of State, *China Despatches*, Vol. 23. No. 27, and Vol. 24, No. 130, cited in Clyde, ed., *Policy Toward China*, 76-79.

to those who wished so to think, that the Chinese also had many other vices. They lived to themselves, frequently in hovels; they were impervious to the beneficent influence of Americanization; they gambled, they smoked and smuggled opium; and, since they had no wives with them, they consorted with prostitutes. There was some truth in all these charges, but no evidence has yet been unearthed to indicate that in these respects the Chinese were any worse, or better, than virile "Americans" of Irish and other descent who at this time made up the vociferous element on the Pacific Coast.

Violence against the Chinese in word and deed reached a shameful intensity in 1877. San Francisco harbored the backwash of the depression of 1873: the scum of the labor market, rowdies, and political adventurers. In this group were many Irish, naturalized and unnaturalized, who readily accepted the leadership of one Denis Kearney, an Irish-born, recently-naturalized agitator, famous for his charismatic power. It was Kearney who shouted as he held a noosed rope in his hand, "The Chinese must go!" "Christian" followers of Kearney held that the Chinese didn't have souls, and even if they did, they weren't worth saving. So the Chinese were attacked, their store windows broken, their freshly laundered clothing trampled in the gutter, their queues snipped with scissors, their bodies kicked and stoned. Finally, there were boycotts of Oriental labor and cold-blooded murdering of some of the Chinese.[8]

THE CHINESE BECOME A POLITICAL QUESTION

What was basically an economic and sociological problem soon became political. Western politicians and members of Congress were determined to be rid of the Chinese. The attitude of the eastern states was different only in degree. As early as 1855 a governor of California was denouncing the Chinese to satisfy his constituents, anti-Chinese memorials were in circulation, and anti-Chinese bills were being offered in the legislature. Charges were made that the Chinese in California, like those in Cuba and Peru, were under servile contracts.

The Civil War quieted the agitation for a time, and the transcontinental railroad construction that followed absorbed all available Chinese labor. But the Central Pacific was finished in 1869, at which time the roads were employing nearly 10,000 men, of whom some 9,000 were Chinese—who were noted to be "peaceable, industrious and economical, apt to learn and quite as efficient as white laborers." In defiance of all forecasts, however, the completion of the railways did not usher in prosperity. On the contrary, land values failed to rise and thousands of white and Chinese laborers were thrown out of employment. The California State Democratic platform of 1869 was rabidly anti-Negro, anti-railway, and anti-Chinese. The Republicans, too, found it politically expedient to be nominally anti-Chinese. In 1876 the California Senate sent to Congress, in the guise of an impartial investigation of the Chinese, a viciously partisan document designed to inflame race prejudice and win an election. Against this testimony were the words of a former American Minister at Peking, J. Ross Browne, usually regarded as severe in his judgments of the Chinese:

The Chinese do not seek to interfere in our political struggles; they are peaceful and law-abiding; they are always willing to bear their equal burden of taxes; and all they ask is to be treated with common humanity.[9]

The unhappy fate of the Chinese on the Pacific Coast made it abundantly clear that Seward and Burlingame had misjudged the nature of American attitudes when in 1868 they had written into their Sino-American treaty a proclamation of "the inherent and inalienable right of man to change his home and allegiance." It now appeared either that this principle itself was not valid or that many Americans were not so closely wedded to it as had been supposed. At any rate, the American government was faced with the embarrassing task of informing China that her people were not wanted here.

[8] See M. R. Coolidge, *Chinese Immigration* (1909), Chapters 1-7; R. W. Paul, "The Origins of the Chinese Issue in California," *The Mississippi Valley Historical Review,* 25 (1938), 181-96; and the study by H. F. MacNair, *The Chinese Abroad* (1924).

[9] Department of State, *China Despatches,* Vol. 25, No. 1.

Prompt action by the federal government could not be delayed, for in 1879 Congress passed a law prohibiting any ship from bringing to the United States more than fifteen Chinese on any one trip. President Hayes vetoed the bill on the ground that it was virtual exclusion and, therefore, in violation of the Burlingame treaty. In the West, Hayes was burned in effigy, while the East greeted his act as "wise and manly." Thereupon the president sent to China a commission composed of James B. Angell, William H. Trescot, and John F. Swift. One who is unfamiliar with the background traced here, and who reads only the instructions of Secretary Evarts to the commission (June, 1880) might well suppose that in that year it was the United States rather than China that had suffered injury. The commissioners were to concern themselves with: (1) "making our commercial privileges more clear, more secure and more extensive"; (2) impressing upon the Chinese that if they could collect *likin* and other "discriminatory" taxes, they could also prevent their collection; (3) entertaining any ideas the Chinese might have for reconciling the systems of jurisprudence, American and Chinese, in applying extraterritoriality in China; and (4) explaining to the Chinese why "this Government finds great public interests to require in our relations to China and the movement of its population to our Pacific coast, what may appear to be a modification of our universal hospitality to foreign immigration." In November, 1880, the commission signed two treaties with China, the one commercial, the other giving the United States the right to "regulate, limit or suspend" but not to "absolutely prohibit" the immigration of Chinese laborers. When Congress responded to this new treaty provision by suspending Chinese immigration for twenty years, President Arthur vetoed the measure (April, 1882) as "unreasonable"—that is, not within the meaning of "suspension." A compromise was found in a second bill, also in 1882, suspending Chinese immigration for ten years. The President accepted this measure. The law of 1882 was amended and strengthened in 1884. In 1892 immigration was suspended for another ten years, and in 1894 China agreed by treaty to

extend it to 1904. When exclusion by treaty ended in 1904, Congress renewed the exclusion without time limit.[10]

Even this diplomatic settlement and the legislative program against the Chinese did not for a time put an end to anti-Chinese riots in the United States. Twenty-eight Chinese were murdered in Wyoming in 1885; the federal government was powerless to intervene in what

---

[10] United States, Department of State, *China Instructions,* Vol. 3, No. 1. For more than half a century following the coming of Chinese exclusion in 1882, this subject was interpreted largely as an aspect of sectionalism. In essence the sectional or California thesis, as it has been called, was that the clamor raised by immigrant Irish in that state, and supported by politicians and demagogues near and far for their own purposes, changed the entire policy of a nation, committing the United States to race discrimination in immigration—a position wholly at variance with American principles of government and with the theory of the melting pot. In this interpretation there was the comforting implication that the Eastern States were quite virtuous, that iniquity was confined to the West Coast, that the excessive prejudice of Californians alone was responsible for Chinese exclusion. The evidence now indicates that, while California led the movement, that state was aided and abetted by forces and popular attitudes which were national, not sectional, and which long antedated the arrival of the Chinese in California. Since the beginning of American commercial contacts at Canton in the late eighteenth century, American traders, followed by American diplomats and Protestant missionaries, had created an American image of the Chinese as a people steeped in a wide spectrum of depravity. While there were many exceptions, the overall attitude of Americans was that the Chinese were a race incapable of progress, yet peculiarly adept in the arts of cruelty, deceit, cunning, despotism, idolatry, and sexual deviation; they were a people unfit for permanent residence and citizenship in America. Thus more recent interpretations tend to the view that, because of the widespread acceptance of this ugly image of the Chinese, Californians had no difficulty in leading the nation to adopt Chinese exclusion, the first departure from open immigration in favor of discrimination on ethnocultural grounds. The California thesis is presented in Coolidge, *Immigration.* Other more recent, and important, studies include Gunther P. Barth, *Bitter Strength: A History of the Chinese in the United States, 1850-1870* (1964); Stuart C. Miller, *The Unwelcome Immigrant: the American Image of the Chinese, 1785-1882* (1969); Alexander Saxton, *The Indispensable Enemy: Labor and the Anti-Chinese Movement in California* (1971); and James W. Loewen, *The Mississippi Chinese: Between Black and White* (1971).

was purely a state matter. The best that Congress could do was to vote an indemnity.[11]

The facts of the Chinese immigration question in the late nineteenth century lead to conclusions that are not pleasant. On a number of points the evidence is perfectly clear. Most of the Chinese in the United States were here legally; as a group they were industrious and peaceable; their vices may have been different but it would be a wise man who could affirm that they were worse than those of other immigrants, or for that matter of native-born Americans. Indeed, the Chinese had been encouraged to come to the United States not only by economic opportunity but also by the diplomacy of two Americans, Seward and Burlingame. Burlingame was undoubtedly influenced by idealism, Seward by the more mundane considerations of cheap labor. Their combined motives resulted in the writing of a treaty in 1868 which embodied the ideal and the principle of free immigration. Within twelve years this ideal had become unworkable. Thereupon the problem was permitted to fall into the hands of demagogues, agitators, and political hoodlums, who thought of themselves as "100 percent American." Their policy of total exclusion was even more barren in statesmanship than was the naive "free immigration" of Burlingame and Seward.

CHINESE STUDENTS ABROAD

In the years when agitation against the Chinese was particularly strong in California, China was sending her first young students abroad to receive a Western education in the United States, Great Britain, and France. The training of Chinese in science and mathematics had already been undertaken at the *t'ung-wen kuan* in Peking and elsewhere, but ultimately the need for young Chinese to study abroad gained some recognition. Two principal student

---

[11] Coolidge, *Immigration*, Chapters 9-17. On the status of historical studies on the immigration question and on other aspects of U. S.-China relations 1850-1895 see the excellent survey by Kwang-ching Liu, "America and China: the Late Nineteenth Century," in *American-East Asian Relations: A Survey*, Ernest R. May and James C. Thomson, Jr., eds. (1972), 34-96.

missions followed. The first sent 120 Chinese students to the United States between 1872 and 1881; the second sent thirty students to England and France for technical training. As in other matters, it was Tseng Kuo-fan and Li Hung-chang who implemented these missions. Their memorial of 1871 to the Tsungli Yamen declared that there was no way to master Western ideas, techniques, and machines "unless we have actually seen them and practised with them for a long time." Or, in the words of the Chinese proverb, "To hear a hundred times is not as good as to see once."

In the United States the education of these Chinese students gave promise of significant results. The way for them had been paved by the enthusiasms of Yung Wing (1828-1912), the first Chinese to graduate from an American university (Yale, 1854). But the venture ended as suddenly as it had begun. In 1881 the students were recalled for reasons that bear directly on China's intellectual attitudes in this period. In part the premature death of China's efforts in foreign education was hastened by jealousies among those Chinese who administered the program in America; but more important, it would appear, was the discovery that the students were mastering American studies to the exclusion, or at least the neglect of, Chinese studies. This revelation was too much for the traditionalists in Peking, and even Li Hung-chang felt that China had gone too far, though there was a touch of understanding in his remark that it was hard for young Chinese abroad "to avoid indulging in foreign customs."[12]

HISTORICAL REFLECTIONS ON SELF-STRENGTHENING

China's record in the new world of Western diplomacy, 1860 to 1890, does not lend itself to easy analysis. The general failure to understand what was happening in China at the time was shared by both Chinese and foreigners. The contemporary official reaction to China in both

---

[12] Y. C. Wang, *Chinese Intellectuals and the West, 1872-1949* (1966). This exhaustive study of Chinese students abroad reaches the pessimistic conclusion that Chinese education abroad was a failure, a conclusion to which some exception has been taken.

America and Europe vacillated between hope and despair: hope that China would soon accept the virtues of Western modernization and despair that she would ever free herself from the dead hand of her past. Even so astute an observer as John Russell Young, American minister at Peking, 1882 to 1885, saw only the surface manifestations of China's troubles. His dictum that China had largely herself to blame for her woes, that she had no government worthy of the name, and that her efforts in foreign affairs amounted to simple "trifling" was substantially true, but it did not touch the core of China's real problem. The essence of that problem was the reaction of the intellectual scholar-official class, the ruling bureaucracy, to the Western assault not simply upon China's seacoast but, more importantly, upon her institutions and the ideas and values from which they were created. Of this reaction the West knew almost nothing. The ways through which China's educated men sought to fathom the alien and powerful West and to protect their own culture from its contagion is therefore a subject of prime import.

QUESTIONABLE ASSUMPTIONS

The historical puzzle posed by China's response in the nineteenth century to the Western impact was complicated by two decisive factors. The first was the Chinese attitude of superiority to, if not disdain of, the Western barbarian. The second was the capacity of Europeans and Americans to approach the Chinese question armed, for the most part, with very questionable assumptions on what China was and what it wanted to be. This capacity to see in China what one wanted to see rather than what was actually there was not new in the nineteenth century. It went back to far earlier European and later American contacts with China.

For example, Marco Polo, with an amazing flair for exaggeration, described China as a land of great material prosperity. Later, in the sixteenth and seventeenth centuries, the Jesuit missionaries depicted China (save for its religions) as an ideal society. Then came the assumption, widely cultivated by some notable historians (Leopold von Ranke, for example), that China was timeless and unchanging. From this idea grew the notion that there was a peculiarly "Asiatic" type of society. Thus "Asiatic" became far more than a geographical term. It began to connote an assortment of meanings, political, social, and philosophical, most of which were general, vague, and at best misleading. Lastly, whereas the Jesuits reported that China approached the ideal society, nineteenth century Protestantism found China to be anything but ideal. It was heathen and in a state of moral degradation. In this view even the greatest minds of China were necessarily inferior.[13]

These misconceptions were expanded in the late nineteenth century. Evidence suggests that what many Americans at that time chose to believe concerning China was fanciful, though often well-intentioned. Burlingame had told his American audience of a China bent on mastering the fundamentals of Western civilization. These were sweet words to Americans in the era of Manifest Destiny. They carried the implication that, given the chance, China would gladly foresake her outmoded ways for the modern manners of America. This slender thesis was to intrude itself repeatedly into American thought on China. In sharp contrast, however, the testimony of J. Ross Browne, who succeeded Burlingame as American minister at Peking in 1868, was a direct and explicit denial of much that Burlingame had said. But Browne's words did not reach the American public. They were for the confidential ears of Secretary William H. Seward:

An impression [said Browne] *seems to have obtained in the United States that the Government of China is peculiarly friendly to our country, and that great advantages to our commerce are about to accrue from this preference. . . .*

I need scarcely say these anticipations are without foundation. The Government of China

[13]Raymond Dawson, "Western Conceptions of Chinese Civilization," in *The Legacy of China,* Raymond Dawson, ed. (1964),* 1-27.

Candidates for the Imperial civil service were sequestered for many days in cells such as these while they wrote their examination papers. These examination cells, which had been built by the thousands in provincial capitals, symbolized the Confucian monopoly of learning and political power in Old China.

may have preferences; but it has no special regard for any foreign power.[14]

CHINA'S FIRST RESPONSE

The Canton crisis of 1834-1840 had revealed China's original intellectual response to the West. It was pre-eminently Chinese. It did not assume that China might profit through learning from the West; this was natural since the Chinese tradition was one of self-sufficiency. At Canton, therefore, in 1839, Lin did what any able and traditional Chinese could be expected to do. He applied force against the British while, at the same time, by letter, he delivered himself of a sermon to Queen Victoria, exhorting that lady to control her subjects within the bounds of Confucian virtue. This formula of force plus persuasion was the traditional method by which China had controlled the barbarians on her borders. Lin, however, although traditional, was also observant. The subsequent debacle at Canton convinced him that China should purchase and manufacture Western armaments, translate Western books, hire foreign technical advisers, and train Chinese technical personnel; but these ideas were so revolutionary that he confided them only to

his most intimate friends. China was to wait another twenty years before embarking timidly on such ventures. Meanwhile, the Chinese response, particularly at Canton, took the form of bitter and violent antiforeignism, which meant anti-Westernism.[15]

THE POLICY OF CONCILIATION

Although Lin's policy failed and Chinese arms met defeat, China's traditional diplomatic arsenal was not thereby exhausted. If an enemy could not be forced and persuaded, it was good traditional policy to conciliate him through negotiation; this was what the Ch'ing dynasty did when it accepted the first treaties of 1842-1844 and 1858-1860. Under this strategy the treaties were regarded officially as temporary devices for pacifying the barbarians and thereby bringing them under control. A forceful exponent of this policy was the imperial Manchu clansman Ch'i-ying, who negotiated with Sir Henry Pottinger of Great Britain

[14] Department of State, *China Despatches,* Vol. 25, No. 7, November 25, 1868; quoted by Clyde, *Policy Toward China,* 93-94. Note also Harold R. Isaacs, *Scratches on our Minds* (1958),* 63ff.

[15] Lin's letter to Queen Victoria and his comments on Western arms, etc., in Ssu-Yu Teng and John K. Fairbank, *China's Response to the West* (1954),* 23-30. The perceptive student will wish to seek answers to the question: "Why have certain Western ideas been warmly received in China while others have been met with cold indifference?" See Benjamin Schwartz, "The Intellectual History of China," in *Chinese Thought and Institutions,* John K. Fairbank, ed. (1957),* 15-30.

(1842), Caleb Cushing of the United States (1844), and Th. de Lagrene of France (1844).

ᐧAlthough the policy of conciliation was not regarded as a concession to Western ways or as a reform of Chinese ways—it was, after all, traditional procedure—even so distinguished an official as Ch'i-ying, the agent of conciliation, was in constant danger of being denounced to the court as subversive on the theory of guilt by association. The barbarians being untouchables, there was a fine line of distinction between conciliation that was appeasement and conciliation that was not. Proper conciliation was a delaying tactic designed to hold and then to divide the enemy, to "manage" him adroitly by playing one barbarian against another.[16]

On the positive side, however, the period of conciliation, 1842-1860, produced, in time, a new type of Chinese official, a man familiar with the barbarians and one who, presumably, knew how to deal with them. Some of these new officials were on friendly terms with foreigners, but it is important to note that their memorials to Peking continued to denounce the barbarian, his opium, his ignorance of Confucian virtue, and his Christian religion.

The foregoing background on Chinese reactions to foreign influence illustrates why China and the West appeared to make little headway toward mutual accommodation and understanding. What has been called the "restoration mentality" in China was not a very useful instrument in moving toward what the West called "progress." One of the notable creators of restoration thought provides a further example. Feng Kuei-fen was a Soochow scholar, versed in the classics and experienced in government, who developed an interest in modern scientific knowledge. As an associate of Tseng Kuo-fan and Li Hung-chang, he knew many foreigners. It was he who opened the school of Western language and science at Shanghai in 1863. He came to believe that pressures from the West presented a complex of ideas and forces unlike any invasion China had ever known. Therefore, Western science and language must be mastered and used to supplement Chinese knowledge. He did not question the superiority of Confucian ethics; they would remain as the foundation of Chinese society. But Western technology, if not Western learning in general, could be useful and, therefore, should be learned.

THE APPEAL OF WESTERN TECHNOLOGY

Although the theory of Feng Kuei-fen that Western "know-how" should become the servant of a Confucian society was stoutly opposed in some quarters, it was also widely held and sometimes applied. Tseng Kuo-fan, Li Hung-chang, and Tso Tsung-t'ang (1812-1885), the great administrators of the period, were all advocates of Western weapons.

At the time of the downfall of the T'ai-p'ings, Tseng Kuo-fan was probably the most influential man in China. He had employed foreigners and their weapons in his fight against the rebels. Long before the *Arrow* War (1857-1858) he had urged the building of a Chinese navy. He built arsenals in the provinces of Hunan and Kiangsi and, together with Li Hung-chang, the Kiangnan arsenal at Shanghai (1865). In these matters of armament Tseng was a Western convert. Yet he never deserted the Confucian ideal of the good statesman. His formula for dealing with the foreigners was to treat them with Confucian virtue. In treaty revision, for example, what could be conceded should be conceded; that which could not be conceded should be resisted with resolution. As he said, "We should never hem and haw [literally, half spit and half swallow]."

EFFORTS TOWARD INDUSTRIALIZATION

The emphasis that Chinese leadership placed in the late nineteenth century on the problem of defense against the West led inevitably to concern with industrialization. Here there was a natural train of thought, beginning with the

[16] Earl Swisher, *China's Management of the American Barbarians: A Study of Sino-American Relations, 1841-1861, with Documents* (1953), 1-54.

idea that China must use Western arms and armament and ending with the conclusion that China herself must manufacture these arms. In 1872, organization of the China Merchants Steam Navigation Company led to the opening of the Kaiping coal mines near Tientsin. Transportation of the coal from mine to port called for railroad construction.

As a result of the great energy and foresight of Li and Tso a great variety of industrial enterprises were planned, and some were actually established between 1863 and 1890. These included technical schools, arsenals, shipyards, machine factories, Western-style fortifications, coal and iron mines, a steamship company, railroads and a dockyard, a telegraph from Taku to Tientsin in 1879, and plans for a navy and a naval school.[17]

Yet, for all its variety, the movement toward industrialization was slow and ineffective. The scholar-official of China had yet to be converted to wholehearted support of industrial development. When it was discovered, for example, that the first steamships built in China cost more than was anticipated and proved to be inferior to foreign ships, some officials advised abandoning the whole business. Li Hung-chang protested against this proposed retreat from industrialization in a memorial of 1872: "Our scholars and officials have confined themselves to the study of stanzas and sentences and are ignorant of the greatest change of the last several thousand years." But in the China of Tseng and Li, one must recall, such protests were necessarily framed in a context in which the idea of industrialization, already a century old in Europe, was still new.

GOVERNMENT SUPERVISION: MERCHANT OPERATION

The failure of the early industrialization effort to meet China's goal of self-strengthening and defense was not due primarily to the advantages enjoyed by the foreigners or even to competition from them. In the same period Japan faced similar competition but succeeded in creating a strong industrial foundation, based on initial government capital, operation, and control. But in China quite a different system of control and management was followed, one derived from traditional methods of economic administration. Under this system merchants provided a part of the capital, but management was half business and half politics. The manager was apt to be of official status and to have enough influence with local authorities to be able to secure special privileges, such as exemption from taxation. There might even be two managers, one to run the business, the other to manage the government. Initially, the purpose of the system was to enlist private capital from merchant sources. What happened more often than not was that officials, using the names of merchants, invested in these semi-governmental enterprises and placed their own relatives in charge as managers. The whole system went under the name of "official supervision and merchant operation."

The evils that resulted from this mingling of Confucian bureaucracy and Western business were described vividly in 1892 by a contemporary Chinese comprador-scholar, Cheng Kuan-ying, who knew many foreigners and much Western literature.

In recent days [he wrote], *although the court has ordered the governors-general and governors to develop commerce and open all kinds of manufacturing bureaus, and has authorized the inviting of merchants to manage them, yet the officials and merchants have habitually been unable to get along together. . . . Businessmen who have undertaken many affairs, although they understand clearly that there are profits to be made, nevertheless hesitate to accept the invitation to manage government enterprises. . . If a surplus or profit is made by the company, all the local officials request some contribution and overstep their proper duty to meddle in the company's affairs.*[18]

Moreover, the modern type of enterprise started in China in this period failed to bring about a real industrial revolution. China continued to be preoccupied with dividing the

---

[17] Kwang-ching Liu, Anglo-American Steamship *Rivalry in China, 1862-1874* (1962), a case study revealing the complex interplay between Chinese and foreign enterprise.

[18] Quoted in Teng and Fairbank, *China's Response,* 113-14.

static economic product among landlords, merchants, and officials. Thus there was no recognition of the need to increase the product and, therefore, no real undermining of traditional institutional barriers.[19]

THE NATURE OF CHINESE LEADERSHIP, 1860-1890

By the year 1890, China had passed through three decades of effort in "self-strengthening." What had the movement achieved? During the 1860's there were signs that a new order was in the making, but during the next two decades such signs were not easy to discern. The move-

[19] See Albert Feuerwerker, *China's Early Industrialization* (1958),* 242-51. The tendency of the Ch'ing administration to resist reform and to preserve institutions that should have been abolished is illustrated in the study by Harold C. Hinton, *The Grain Tribute System of China, 1845-1911* (1957).*

For indispensable insights into political institutional developments in China from 1870 to the close of the century, the student should consult Albert Feuerwerker, *et al.,* eds., *Approaches to Modern Chinese History* (1967), especially the essays by Kwang-ching Liu on Li Hung-chang, by John L. Rawlinson on the nineteenth century Chinese navy, by Paul A. Cohen on the ideas of Wang T'ao, and by Akira Iriye on Chinese public opinion. In these materials will be found at least a partial answer to the proposition that the Manchu dynasty survived as long as it did precisely because it was weak.

In the case of the mineral industries, the Ch'ing government in its early years had permitted small-scale local development as a supplementary factor in the general economy. Later the government engaged in substantial participation itself through direct sponsorship, supervision, or financial subsidy and purchasing in the production and distribution of minerals and metals. In the late eighteenth century, the government took the additional step of recruiting wealthy investors who were expected to carry the undertaking to a successful conclusion. This concept of *chao-shang* (recruiting investors) meant that private fortunes were called upon by government to meet the latter's needs. In such cases political motives were likely to be more influential than economic ones. The Hong merchants at Canton were a manifestation of *chao-shang.* See E-tu Zen Sun, "Ch'ing Government and the Mineral Industries Before 1800," *Journal of Asian Studies,* 27 (1968), 835-45.

On China's monetary system see Frank H. King, *Money and Monetary Policy in China, 1845-1895* (1965).

ment appeared to lose rather than to gain in strength. In explanation it may be noted that the entire period was, with some exceptions, one of peace, in which the Western powers used the pressures of negotiation rather than of war; it would appear that this softer policy was interpreted by the great majority of the scholar-bureaucrats to mean that the crisis was passed. If the crises of 1840 and 1860 were not forgotten, at least their forebodings seemed less ominous.

How shall this lack of sustained purpose be explained? Some of the factors involved are reasonably clear. Basic among these was the nature of the Confucian leadership which the mid- and later nineteenth century had produced. It was not that China had no men of political stature. Prince Kung, Tseng Kuo-fan, Li Hung-chang, Tso Tsung-t'ang, and others were administrators of ability who perceived the danger of foreign control and sought a defense against it through Western scientific techniques. Beyond this point, however, they were unprepared to go. Their answer to the West was to use Western science to make China more Confucian. When it appeared, as in the case of Chinese students abroad, that Confucian values would suffer from sustained contact with the West, even China's most progressive leaders drew back. The students were recalled.

THE QUALITY OF LEADERSHIP AT PEKING

There were two areas in which Chinese leadership, and the lack of it, were of the greatest import: (1) at Peking, in the Manchu court and the central administration, and (2) in the provinces, where vigorous administrators such as Tseng and Li held office.

At Peking the hopeful course set by Prince Kung in 1860 was soon abandoned. For five years as a member of the regency and as head of the grand council and of the Tsungli Yamen, he had shown an awareness of China's plight and had wielded sufficient influence to direct policy accordingly. By 1865, however, when the immediate threat of dynastic collapse had passed and the T'ai-p'ings had been suppressed, the incubus of court conservatism reasserted its power in the person of Tz'u-hsi, the empress dowager (1835-1908). This able and ambitious Manchu woman was a concubine of the Hsien-feng emperor (ruled 1851-1861) and mother of the T'ung-chih emperor (1856-1875). She had become co-regent with the Hsien-feng emperor's first wife when her own son ascended the throne in 1862. Some reference has already been made to the uneasy alliance between Prince Kung and this remarkable woman. On the death of her childless son in 1875, she adopted and placed on the throne the son of Prince Kung's brother, Prince Chun, and her own sister; she thus maintained her power as regent for the new child emperor, Kuang-hsu (ruled 1875-1908). From then until her death in 1908, except for a brief period, 1889-1898, she was the power in the Peking government.

Two principal traits highlighted the character of this woman as a ruler. By the power of her inflexible will and her knowledge of human frailty she dominated the court and thereby the central administration, and she won or controlled officials of court and government by an amazing assortment of methods. According to the need of the moment, she exhorted, flattered, bribed, commanded, or pleaded to get what she wanted. By placing an increasing number of Chinese in high provincial office she somewhat strengthened the loyalty of the scholar-bureaucrats to the Manchu monarchy. At the same time the high price she placed on her official favors raised the fine art of bribery (gifts to the empress dowager) to new and fantastic levels.

Against her limited success in reviving the loyalty of Chinese officialdom must be placed her incapacity to face repeated crises in foreign affairs. She hated the foreigners and their works. Though she usually followed the advice of her ministers, there were few who could advise her with intelligence. As Li Hung-chang wrote in 1881, "The stupidity and confusion of our scholar-officials, and the lack of men of ability in the court are really ridiculous."

From these circumstances came the confusion of the empress dowager's rule. Under her authority vast sums had been collected to give China a modern navy. The money was spent in rebuilding the Summer Palace. The warnings of Wen-hsiang, one of the able assistants of Prince Kung, were like a small voice calling in the wilderness: "When Your Majesty is concerned to work diligently, then your ministers . . . dare not follow their traditional dawdling habits. Otherwise . . . the disaster will be unspeakable." These were prophetic words, but the empress dowager did not understand them.

In the provinces the prospect for leadership had more substance. The efforts of Tseng,[20] Li, and others meant that there was some awakening among the scholar-bureaucrats. At the same time this awakening was so hedged about by mental obstructions and the carrion weight of traditionalism that not even Li saw the alternatives from which China might choose. The time had not yet come for Chinese-Manchu leadership to question the dead hand of the past. Moreover, and this is historically quite understandable, history had not bequeathed China a sense of political patriotism. The urge to adopt Western technology and science was often seen as a means whereby officials and merchants might make profits for themselves rather than as a method of saving the country from foreign aggression. Although the progressive governors were for the most part steadfast in their loyalty to Peking, their local successes in provincial finance and military affairs were at the expense of the central authority and, therefore, at the expense of a unified and coherent effort to save the empire through self-strengthening.[21]

A NINETEENTH-CENTURY CONTRAST

The ways in which China and Japan responded in the nineteenth century to the Western impact form an arresting study in contrasts. How did it come about that the Japanese alone met the Western intrusion with vigor, seeking survival in strong, independent nationhood and

---

[20] Note Chen Shen Han-yin, "Tseng Kuo-fan in Peking, 1840-1852: His Ideas on Statecraft and Reform," *Journal of Asian Studies*, 27 (1967), 61-80.

[21] Undoubtedly a significant factor in the general failure of the reform movement may best be described as bureaucratic inertia. Certainly Chinese leadership in this period was inept. At the same time, individuals within the leadership were sometimes thwarted in efforts at reform by the very ideas and institutions that had given Chinese society its stability. In some

readily employing modern science and technology to refashion traditional Japanese society on industrial foundations, while the Chinese in the same years failed to make a positive, constructive response? Satisfying answers are the more elusive because what actually happened was just the reverse of what informed contemporaries might well have predicted. They might have noted that Japan was at a grave physical disadvantage in the struggle for power and wealth. Her farmlands were crowded, her minerals scanty. She was not well located either as to materials or markets. In mid-nineteenth century she was still bound by feudalism and by the self-conscious power of a warrior caste antagonistic to modernization. In contrast China might have seemed ready for the modern world. In location and wealth she was superior. She had traditions of freedom and social mobility, of private property, of pragmatism and materialism, of humane political ideals, and of knowledge as the key to office. All in all China appeared uniquely equipped to adopt the secular, rational, utilitarian democratic culture of the West. Yet it was Japan, not China, that embraced the modern world in the nineteenth century. No simple explanation can explain why and how this occurred but the following factors are suggestive of the processes at work.

1. Traditional philosophical attitudes, especially those attributable to Confucianism and Taoism, with their emphasis on indirection, may well have conditioned the Chinese response. In Japan the code of the samurai taught that an enemy was met by direct action, and most of Japan's Meiji leaders were samurai.

2. Most important in Japan's response was her capacity to combine the two essential conditions of successful adaptation and growth: (a) leadership in technological and social change, and (b) teamwork and discipline in organization, giving order and momentum to the process of change. The fitness of the leaders to rule and the willingness of the majority to follow characterized Japanese organization.

3. Japan's response was aided by the fact that her society, above the family, was more pluralistic in structure than was China's. Initiative in Japan thus tended to be dispersed among a number of centers. Groups such as the business elite, barred from the hereditary aristocracy, had built their own money power, thereby undermining the ruling caste; particular families, such as the Western clans, became the pioneers in Western technology and later the leaders of political revolution.

4. Japan's response was more vigorous because her internal crisis, unlike that of China, was potentially revolutionary. Within Japan the mid-century tensions were such that powerful elements of the ruling class were ready to adopt modernization even if it meant the downfall of feudalism and the liquidation of their own class.

5. Historically Japan was a frontier society, a cultural borrower, and, as it happened, the Western impact reached her shores at the precise moment when internal frictions had already prepared the way for great changes in her society.[22]

---

measure these institutions were so hallowed by time and so infected by bureaucratic confusion and indecision and by widespread corruption and nepotism that, as one example, the maintenance of a respectable navy would have been impossible regardless of the number or quality of warships China might build or buy. Note John L. Rawlinson, *China's Struggle for Naval Development, 1839-1895* (1967). Another case in point was the use by Li Hung-chang of a traditional institution, the *mu-fu* (tent friends) system—a coterie of tried associates—where the emphasis was on personal loyalty rather than on competence. Although the system had often worked in the past, it simply opened the door to abuse in the nineteenth century. Note Kenneth Folsom, *Friends, Guests, and Colleagues: the Mu-Fu System in the Late Ch'ing Period* (1968). For an able portrayal of China's patterns of behavior in this period, see Paul A. Cohen, in *Modern East Asia: Essays in Interpretation,* James B. Crowley, ed., (1970),* 29-61.

FOR FURTHER READING

For materials dealing with political tradition and reform see the citations in Chapter 12.

[22] See W. W. Lockwood, "Japan's Response to the West: the Contrast with China," *World Politics,* 9 (1956), 37-54.

Economics and Industrial Development.
Stephen C. Lockwood, *Augustine Heard and Company, 1858-1862: American Merchants in China on the Eve of the Opening of the Yangtze* (1971).* Yeh-chin Wang, "The Fiscal Importance of the Land Tax during the Ch'ing Period," *Journal of Asian Studies* 30 (1971), 829-42. Albert Feuerwerker, *China's Early Industrialization: Sheng Hsuan-huai (1844-1916) and Mandarin Enterprise* (1959).* C. F. Remer, *The Foreign Trade of China* (1926). Harold Hinton, *The Grain Tribute System of China, 1845-1911* (1956).* Edwin G. Beal, *The Origin of Likin* (1958) treats economic developments in the late nineteenth century. Kwang-ching Liu, *Anglo-American Steamship Rivalry in China, 1862-1874* (1962), a good specialized study. Stanley F. Wright, *Hart and the Chinese Customs* (1950). Marion J. Levy, *The Rise of the Modern Chinese Business Class* (1949). Norman Jacobs, *The Origin of Modern Capitalism and Eastern Asia* (rev. ed., 1959) seeks an answer to the question: why did modern industrial capitalism arise in Japan and not in China? Ellsworth C. Carlson, *The Kaiping Mines, 1877-1912* (1957),* a study of China's first modern coal-mining enterprise. Frank H. H. King, *Money and Monetary Policy in China, 1845-1895* (1965). Two works by Chen Ch'i-t'ien: *Tseng Kuo-fan, Pioneer Promoter of the Steamship in China(1961);* and *Tso Tsung-t'ang: Pioneer Promoter of the Modern Dockyard and the Woolen Mill in China* (1961),* brief biographies of China's first industrialists. C. John Stanley, *Late Ch'ing Finance: Hu Kuang-yung as an Innovator* (1961).*

Education and the Press. Adrian A. Bennett, *John Fryer: the Introduction of Western Science and Technology into Nineteenth-Century China* (1967).* William Ayers, *Chang Chih-tung and Educational Reform in China* (1971). Knight Biggerstaff, "Shanghai Polytechnic Institution and Reading Room: An Attempt to Introduce Western Science and Technology to the Chinese," *Pacific Historical Review* 25 (1956), 127-49. Lin Yu-t'ang, *A History of the Press and Public Opinion in China* (1936).

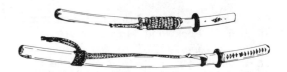

China, 1870–1895: The Fate of the Border Territories

14

The annexation of Hong Kong by Great Britain in 1842, and the southern advance of Russia to the Amur and her annexation of the Maritime Province in 1858-1860 were early indications that the Western impact upon China involved a vital territorial dimension. In the years 1870 to 1895 this issue, gaining new momentum, collided with China's theory and practice of empire and concept of world order. China's position on these matters had been given tangible expression through her dealings with the outer zone territories, the so-called border dependencies (Manchuria, Mongolia, Sinkiang, and Tibet), on the north and west and the tributary states of Korea, Liu-ch'iu, Vietnam, Siam, Burma, Nepal, and Bhutan on the east, the south and the southwest. It was these complex relationships between China, the superior Middle Kingdom, and the inferior border states that the great Western powers, together with the new Japan, began to challenge.

CHINA'S WORLD ORDER: THE THEORETICAL BASIS

Old China did not have a theory or practice of what the modern West has regarded as foreign relations. Nevertheless, Old China did have a very logical and impressive concept and practice of what may be called the Chinese world order. This concept, which matured over the centuries, was a product of geographic and historical circumstances.

The various societies of East Asia had, as it were, a common cultural ancestor in ancient China. For example, Japan, Korea, Liu-ch'iu (Ryukyu), and Vietnam came to be, in some major though varying degree, influenced by Chinese culture. The extent of China, her age, wealth, cultural richness, and power gave her an unrivaled pre-eminence over her neighbors. Thus there developed an Eastern world of which China was the center. She was in fact the Central Country or Middle Kingdom. Quite naturally, therefore, the Chinese came to regard their relations with neighboring peoples as a means by which the Chinese social order (Confucianism) would be bestowed upon less fortunate communities. *T'ien-tzu,* the Son of Heaven, would realize the desirable Confucian ideal of unity, of *T'ien-hsai,* "all under Heaven." In this concept of China as the center, there was a pronounced assumption of Chinese superiority. China's neighbors were not considered her equals, an attitude which reflected the inequalities of status within Chinese society itself.[1]

The formal relationship that came to prevail between China and her tributary states suggests the Confucian relationship of the elder and the younger brother. It was a relationship not always definite or uniform, but it was apt to include the following: (1) China, the superior, taught and admonished the lesser state; (2) the lesser state might be under close supervision or the contacts might be largely ceremonial; (3) the lesser sovereign received investiture from the Chinese emperor; (4) the lesser state could be required to furnish men and supplies when China engaged in missions of "correction"; and (5) tribute-bearing missions from the lesser state were sent to China, thereby recognizing the primacy of China in the Confucian family of nations.[2]

In theory, and generally in practice, China did not seek through these means to control directly the internal affairs of the border states. In fact, the border states were largely autonomous so long as their rulers kept the peace, lived with their peoples on the Confucian model, and performed the ceremonial and other duties of their inferior status. In practice, however, many of the men who have controlled China have been politicians rather than pure Confucian theorists. It was possible for such men to use the theory of the superior and the inferior state to serve the ends of power politics and thus to make the border states mere satellites of the Middle Kingdom.

With all influence flowing outward, with no competing cultures or authority against which the barriers of definite boundaries need to be raised, China had no need for the legal concept of the state. Its control was through ideas which

[1] See Chapter 5, p. 72, on China's system of foreign relations.

[2] The nature of the Chinese world order is treated in John K. Fairbank, "China's World Order: The Tradition of Chinese Foreign Relations," *Encounter* (December, 1966), 1-7; Immanuel C. Y. Hsu, *China's Entrance into the Family of Nations, The Diplomatic Phase, 1858-1880* (1960), 3-18; and M. Frederick Nelson, *Korea and the Old Orders in Eastern Asia* (1945), 3-20. See also, John K. Fairbank, ed., *The Chinese World Order* (1968) for an extended treatment.

could be confined within no physical boundaries. The marking off of a certain territory within which its word was the highest law and beyond which its precepts were unrecognized was not contemplated in Chinese theory. Furthermore, the field of governmental influence embraced the entire social life of man, not merely certain fields that were deemed public, such as foreign relations.

China's controls were applied through propaganda, appeal to reason, and example rather than through the enactment of laws enforced by the authority of the state. None of this was understood by the Western powers when, in the nineteenth century, they sought to open relations with or to control China's border states. To the West it appeared simply that China was the "suzerain" over various "vassal" or "tributary" states. This was so; but these terms did not connote in China what they meant in the West. In Korea, for example, Westerners found a people who were neither sovereign enough to conduct independent relations nor subject enough to throw responsibility for their actions on China. As a consequence, when Western states in the nineteenth century sought relations not only with China but also with the border states, they precipitated a conflict between Confucian theory and Western concepts of international law, centering around the question of the legal equality of states.

CHINA'S WORLD ORDER IN PRACTICE

China's theory of her central position in a world order was no mere product of Confucian philosophizing. It reflected the fact that Chinese administration in the Han period had generally been confined to the eighteen provinces known as China Proper. In the north and northwest, from very early times, the Great Wall delimited China Proper from a second region, the outer territories, inhabited originally by non-Han peoples though controlled in greater or lesser degree by China. The territorial limits of these outer regions were vague, unmarked, and tended to shift with the ebb and flow of power. Administration of these outer territories was quite distinct from that in the provinces of China Proper. There were periods when China's control might vanish in one area or another but reappear in time as a result of diplomacy, military force, or commercial arrangement. Thus the degree of Chinese influence or control varied greatly from time to time in Tibet, Sinkiang, and Mongolia. There were periods, too, when Korea and Vietnam were under some degree of direct Chinese administration. After 1644, Manchuria was a special area among the outer territories, since it was the homeland of the conquering Ch'ing dynasty.

The tributary states were distinguished from the outer territories in that they generally were absolved from Chinese administrative control. These tributary states, however, by engaging in the ceremony of the tribute missions, acknowledged the fact of China's overlordship and their own inferiority. It was in both the outer territories and the tributary states that China's historic forms of control were about to be called into question.

Case I: The Ryukyu Islands

The island kingdom of Ryukyu (Liu-ch'iu), the chain of small islands reaching from Kyushu in southern Japan southward to Taiwan (Formosa), had sent tribute to China since late in the fourteenth century, a fact that placed it in the Confucian community of states over which China presided. Feudal Japan, however, also exercised certain political claims over Ryukyu. The royal family of Ryukyu was said to be related to the Minamoto clan; this may explain why it was that the Ryukyuans sent tribute to Japan in the fifteenth century. Early in the seventeenth century the Japanese *daimyo* of Satsuma attacked the islands and brought the northern group under his immediate control, leaving the southern group semi-independent in a species of tributary status. Thus in the middle of the nineteenth century the unfortunate little state found itself tributary to both China and Japan. In 1871, some Ryukyu islanders, wrecked on the shores of Taiwan, were murdered by the aborigines. When China in response to Japanese overtures disclaimed re-

sponsibility for acts of the Taiwanese, Japan sent a military expedition to Taiwan (1874). In addition, the Japanese continued to occupy a portion of the island, pending a settlement of the dispute with China. This was finally secured through British mediation; China agreed to indemnify the families of the murdered men and to pay for the roads Japan had built in Taiwan. The significant implication of this settlement was that Japan assumed the role of protector of the Ryukyu islanders. For a time China refused to accept this view, and Ryukyu continued to send tribute missions to Peking. Attempts at mediation by ex-President Grant in 1879 failed; but in that year the Ryukyuan king was removed to Tokyo, where he was granted a title of nobility, and the islands were incorporated into Japan as a prefecture under the name of Okinawa. In 1881 China finally accepted a situation which she was powerless to alter.[3] The Ryukyu incident was important because in this case Japan succeeded in breaking the Confucian concept of international relations and in substituting for it the Western code of state responsibility.

Case II: The Ili Crisis

Sinkiang or Chinese Turkestan, one of the outer zone territories lying northwest of China Proper, is an immense area almost three times the size of Texas. In the northwestern sector of Sinkiang, bordering on Russian Turkestan, was the prefecture (*fu*) of Ili, rich in natural resources and strategically located for the control of all of Sinkiang. Following conclusion of the Russo-Chinese treaty of Ili (1851), permitting Russia to establish consulates, a growing and prosperous transborder trade developed.

---

[3] Payson J. Treat, *Diplomatic Relations between the United States and Japan, 1853-1895* (2 vols., 1932; reprint, 1963), I, 473-75, 568-69; II, 71-78, 98-104, 126-27, 141-44; Hyman Kublin, "The Attitude of China During the Liu-ch'iu Controversy, 1871-1881," *Pacific Historical Review*, 18 (1949), 213-31. Also Robert K. Sakai, "The Ryukyu (Liu-ch'iu) Islands as Fief of Satsuma," and Ta-tuan Ch'en, "Investure of the Liu-ch'iu Kings in the Ch'ing Period," in Fairbank, ed.

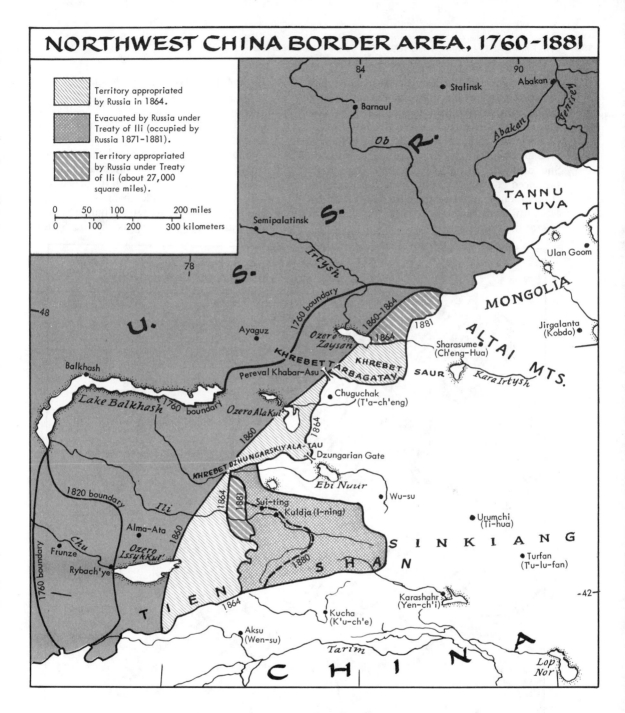

NORTHWEST CHINA BORDER AREA, 1760–1881

Territory appropriated by Russia in 1864.

Evacuated by Russia under Treaty of Ili (occupied by Russia 1871–1881).

Territory appropriated by Russia under Treaty of Ili (about 27,000 square miles).

0   50   100   200 miles
0   100   200   300 kilometers

Stalinsk
Abakan
Barnaul
Ob R.
Abakan
Yenisei
TANNU TUVA
Semipalatinsk
S.
Irtysh
Ulan Goom
MONGOLIA
U.
Ayaguz
1760 boundary
Ozero Zaysan
1860–1864
1881
1864
ALTAI MTS.
Jirgalanta (Kobdo)
Sharasume (Ch'eng-Hua)
Balkhash
KHREBET TARBAGATAY
SAUR
Kara Irtysh
Pereval Khabar-Asu
Chuguchak (T'a-ch'eng)
Lake Balkhash
1760 boundary
Ozero Alakul
1864
1860
KHREBET DZHUNGARSKIY ALA-TAU
Dzungarian Gate
Ebi Nuur
Wu-su
1820 boundary
Ili
1864
1881
Sui-ting
Kuldja (I-ning)
Urumchi (Ti-hua)
S I N K I A N G
Alma-Ata
1860
1880
Turfan (T'u-lu-fan)
1760 boundary
Chu
Frunze
Ozero Issykkul'
Rybach'ye
T I E N
1864
S H A N
Karashahr (Yen-ch'i)
Kucha (K'u-ch'e)
Aksu (Wen-su)
Tarim
C H I N A
Lop Nor

Political conditions in Sinkiang were far from stable. The Manchus had conquered this territory in the mid-eighteenth century; they ruled it with an oppressive military administration centered at Ili, and subjected the Uighur Moslem populace to heavy and arbitrary taxation which served no purpose other than pandering to the extravagance of the ruling Manchu military bureaucracy. The result was a long series of revolts culminating in a major uprising in the mid-1860's. Yakub Beg, the adventurer who led the uprising was encouraged by the British in India, who hoped to restrain the southward expansion of Russia. Since China seemed unable to reassert her authority in Sinkiang, the way was opened for Russia. She occupied Ili in 1871, giving as pretexts the need to protect her own border from Moslem raids and to safeguard Chinese interests until such time as the Manchus could reinstate their authority.

Since China was beset at the time by other Moslem rebellions in the provinces of Kansu and Shensi, it was not until 1877 that her armies under Tso Tsung-T'ang reconquered Sinkiang, except for Ili, which was still occupied by Russia. Two years later an incompetent Chinese mission to Russia concluded the treaty of Livadia, which returned only part of Ili to China while giving Russia a large indemnity, the right to set up numerous consulates, and navigation rights on the Sungari

THE ADVANCE OF COLONIALISM IN SOUTHEAST ASIA

Major colonial areas ca. 1840

Additions by 1900

Adapted from J. K. Fairbank, E. O. Reischauer, and A. M. Craig, East Asia: The Modern Transformation *(1965), p. 411; H. J. Benda and J. A. Larkin,* The World of Southeast Asia *(1967), p. ix.*

river in Manchuria. Thoroughly outraged by what its ambassador had done, the Tsungli Yamen refused to accept this treaty. Finally, in 1881, a second Chinese mission, headed by Tseng Chi-tse, the son of Tseng Kuo-fan, concluded the treaty of St. Petersburg, which returned most of Ili to China and reduced the number of Russian consular posts, but increased the indemnity China was to pay. In Peking this treaty was interpreted as a Chinese diplomatic triumph, a view which encouraged the complacency of the traditionalists. At best it was a very limited victory but it did prompt Peking in 1884 to make Sinkiang a regular province of China Proper.[4]

Case III: Eastern Indochina

In the mid-nineteenth century the large peninsula of Southeast Asia extending southward from China toward the East Indies was a complex mix of races, native dynasties, and cultural modes—a meeting ground of native, Indian, and Chinese cultures. In political terminology the area included: Burma, Siam, Laos, Cambodia, Malaya, and to the east a group of dynastic states whose geographical boundaries were very imprecise. It was not until the coming of French colonial rule in the second half of the century that this eastern area assumed its modern politico-geographical form comprising three defined areas: Tonkin in the north, Annam on the central coastal region, and Cochin China in the south—making up what is now called Vietnam, a name deriving from ancient times. Parts of this area had been under varying Chinese influence since the third century B. C. In modern times tribute missions went to Peking during the Ming (1368-1644) and the Manchu (1644-1911) periods. Life in the north centered in the rich valley of the Red River and the cities of Hanoi and Haiphong. Far to the south the city of Saigon drew its wealth from the fertile lands of the Mekong delta.[5]

[4] See Immanuel C. Y. Hsu, *The Ili Crisis: A Study of Sino-Russian Diplomacy, 1878-1881* (1965), and *The Rise of Modern China* (1970), *381-88.*

[5] For historical background, John F. Cady, *Southeast Asia: Its Historical Development* (1964), and D. G. E. Hall, *A History of Southeast Asia* (1964).

The Coming of the Europeans

European interest in Southeast Asia generally and French interest in the Indochina area more particularly dates back well beyond the nineteenth century. In the early days of the Canton trade, adventuresome Europeans, seeking new and profitable ways to acquire spices, set up their first trading posts on the shores and islands of this rich area. The Portuguese, Dutch, French, and British entered this part of the world not as colonizers but as merchants. They began with no conscious or deliberate purpose of building empires, though in the long run that was precisely what they did: the Portuguese at Macao and Timor, the Dutch in the East Indies, the British in Burma and Malaya, and the French in Indochina.[6]

The French in Indochina

French traders and Catholic missionaries had reached Indochina by the seventeenth century, but the foundations of French political power there date from the years 1747 to 1858. In the earlier years of this period France made contacts with native mandarins hoping to open trade and to use the region as a base for attacks on Dutch and British commerce. A first treaty was concluded in 1787. The hope was that it would further French commerce and Catholic missions but in fact it led to violent anti-Christian movements and a general refusal by native rulers to receive French diplomatic and naval missions. As a result it was not until the mid-nineteenth century that France was ready to force a settlement to serve her purposes. When in 1855 a mission sent by Napoleon III failed to secure a new treaty, the ostensible purpose of which was to put an end to the killing of French and Spanish ecclesiastics, the two powers sent a naval expedition in 1858, at the time of the *Arrow* War in China. Successful campaigns were conducted against Tourane (Da Nang) and Saigon, the latter being oc-

[6] These empires were usually referred to as colonies though they were only such in the fact that they were not self-governing while they were subject to alien authority and economic control, by foreign merchants who were not colonists.

cupied by French troops in 1859. In 1862 the city and some surrounding territory was ceded to France. The French gained the right to propagate Catholicism; three ports were opened to French and Spanish trade and, of course, the victors won an indemnity. The following year Cambodia was made a French protectorate and additional territory was annexed to what the French now called Cochin China.

Within the following decade, French agents discovered the commercial advantages of access to China's Yunnan province by way of the Red River through Tonkin. Accordingly, in 1874, a new treaty confirmed France in control of Vietnam's (Annam and Tonkin) foreign relations and conferred on France navigation rights on the Red River. Technically, Vietnam retained her independence. In fact, by the treaties of 1862 and 1874 she had become a French protectorate. China took note of what was going on by refusing to recognize the treaties on the ground that Vietnam was a tributary state of China. By 1880 French troops were stationed at Hanoi and Haiphong, yet Vietnam continued to send tribute missions to Peking. By 1883 the French were in occupation of the Red River Valley and had secured a further treaty giving them a protectorate over Tonkin. This treaty virtually excluded the Vietnamese administration from that province. French Residents with suitable garrisons were to reside in the towns of Tonkin with authority over the Vietnamese. This development led to hostilities between the French and the Chinese on the Tonkin-China border in 1883.

China's Response

Among China's ruling elite there were two principal schools of thought on what should be done in the Vietnam crisis. Prince Kung and Li Hung-chang cautioned that China was in no position to resist French incursions in her dependencies or to provoke France, and should fight only if invaded. Opposing this view as appeasement, the so-called *Ch'ing-i*

(literati) party, made up of younger scholars and leaders, such as Chang Chih-tung, advocated a policy of vigorous military resistance. Thus faltering between war and peace, China made a further effort at negotiation. An agreement between Li Hung-chang and French naval authorities was acceptable neither to Paris nor Peking. Then in 1884 a French fleet attacked and crippled the south China port of Foochow. China responded by declaring war on France, though she had neither the will nor the means to prosecute it. In 1885, neither power having a mind to pursue hostilities, a formal settlement was reached. Its essential point was that China recognized the treaties that had been forced upon Vietnam by France. Thus, Vietnam ceased to be a tributary state of China and became a part of the French empire.[7]

Case IV: Burma

Burma, lying between India and China's Yunnan province, is a large and picturesque country approximately the size of Texas. Geographically it has two rather distinct areas. Lower Burma in the south includes the delta and plains of the Irrawaddy, the Sittang, and the Salween, the Province of Arakan, and the Tenasserim peninsula. This area produces rice, tin, and lumber. Upper Burma with its towering mountains and narrow valleys is rich in minerals. Burma's early history reflects her

---

[7] See Lloyd E. Eastman; "Ch'ing-i and Chinese Policy Formation during the Nineteenth Century," *Journal of Asian Studies,* 24 (1965), 595-612; and *Throne and Mandarins: China's Search for a Policy during the Sino-French Controversy, 1880-1885* (1967). On China's naval strength at the time, John L. Rawlinson, *China's Struggle for Naval Development, 1839-1895.* (1967), 190-198. Among the economic reasons for French interest in Tonkin were the coal resources in China's Kwangtung province and gold in Yunnan. Later in 1885 the French secured a new treaty at Hue, the Vietnamese capital, providing for the stationing of French officials in the provinces of Annam. (Annam became the French term for what remained of Vietnam after the cutting off of Cochin China in the south and the gaining of a protectorate—virtual colonial control—over Tonkin).

buffer location between the two great civilizations of Asia, the Indian and the Chinese. Her early peoples came principally from Tibet and western China. A strong cultural bond with India dates from the eleventh century, when the country was converted to Hinayana Buddhism. Mongol invasions of Burma in the thirteenth century left a legacy of conquest and military rule over diverse ethnic and language groups: Burmese, Karen, Tai and Shan.[8]

The Europeans in Burma

Europe's interest in Burma dates from the seventeenth century when English, French, and Dutch merchants engaged in the export of teakwood. Later, as the British and French contended for supremacy in India, each country gave aid to rival Burmese political factions, a process that soon led to entanglements in Burma's internal affairs. Britain's ultimate triumph in India, together with exaggerated estimates of Burma's natural wealth, led to three Anglo-Burmese wars, 1824-1826, 1852, and 1885-1886. The net result of these conflicts was that Burma became a British possession. Since Burma was a tributary state of China, and since China was in no position to stop the British, an Anglo-Chinese agreement in 1886 softened the blow to Chinese pride by permitting Burma to send a tribute mission to Peking once every decade. It was a face-saving device which did not alter reality.[9]

Case V: Korea

Korea (Chosen) was among the more important tributary states of China. In area it is almost precisely the size of the state of Minnesota. Its location is strategic in the defense of north China both by land and by sea. Regular tribute missions to Peking had been sent from the early years of the Yi dynasty in the fourteenth century. More than 200,000

[8] Excellent background is in John L. Christian, *Modern Burma* (1942).

[9] See John F. Cady, *A History of Modern Burma* (1958), especially useful on the nineteenth century. Also G. E. Harvey, *British Rule in Burma,, 1824-1942* (1946).

Chinese troops in Korea turned back the armies of Hideyoshi at the end of the sixteenth century. This kind of history created a close cultural and political relationship between China and this lesser state. China's Confucian influence predominated in Korean institutions and culture.[10]

The West Discovers Korea

The earliest European contact with Korea occurred in 1593 when the Spanish Jesuit, Gregario de Cespedes, administered spiritual consolation to Japanese Christian soldiers during Hideyoshi's abortive invasion. A number of Dutch sailors were shipwrecked on Korean shores in the seventeenth century and later escaped to Japan. Some attempts were made to open trade toward the end of the eighteenth and the beginning of the nineteenth centuries. During these developments Roman Catholic Christianity reached Korea by the way of the Jesuit mission in Peking; later, French priests entered the country surreptitiously. The conflict between Christianity and Confucianism, and the increase in the number of converts (there were some 9,000 in 1839) led in that year to the persecution and death of many converts and three priests. When, in 1846, France sought explanations, she was informed that Korea was subordinate to China, to whom all questions of foreign relations must be referred. By this statement Korea was attempting to avoid relations with the West rather than to describe her own status, for actually she had negotiated directly with foreign states, such as Japan, though not with states that were outside the Confucian system.

After 1860 a number of powers attempted to trade with Korea: the British and the Russians in 1861, the French the following year. To a second Russian mission in 1866 the Koreans declared that they were a dependent state of China. This policy of denying autonomy was implemented from 1863 until 1898

[10] On the geographic setting, see George B. Cressey, *Asia's Lands and Peoples* (3rd ed., 1963), and Shannon McCune, *Korea's Heritage: A Regional and Social Geography* (1956).

by the regent, father of an infant king, who was vigorously anti-Western and anti-Christian.

France in Korea, 1866

In 1866 a great wave of anti-Christian persecution virtually wiped out the Christian community of some 18,000 converts; only three of a score of French priests escaped with their lives. A French force from China prepared to attack Korea, and the Peking government, which disclaimed any authority over Korea, was informed that France herself would seek satisfaction. The military-naval expedition that followed suffered a decisive defeat, and for a time France abandoned any further action. The fact that China apparently did not assume any responsibility for the acts of Korea confirmed France in the belief that China had voluntarily surrendered any claim to suzerainty over this former tributary state.

The United States and Korea

The United States showed an official interest in Korea in 1866, when Secretary of State William H. Seward, thinking that Korea was about to be partitioned, proposed a joint France-American expedition. The French had brought back word from Korea that an American merchant ship, the *General Sherman,* had been wrecked on the Korean coast and that the natives had burned her and killed the crew. To Burlingame's inquiries at Peking, China replied that her connections with Korea were only "ceremonial." Seward's joint expedition was not undertaken, but American naval vessels did some charting on the Korean coast, and it was decided to seek a treaty with Korea for the protection of Americans shipwrecked there. When the American naval expedition reached Korea in May, 1871, it was fired upon. In retaliation, it destroyed a number of Korean forts, but got no treaty.[11] Indeed, the Koreans made it clear to China that they wished to continue the old Confucian relationship, and they hoped China would make this clear to the barbarians. This, China

made little effort to do. Thus American diplomats in Peking, like their French colleagues, continued to hold the view that China had recently renounced control over Korea's foreign affairs in order to avoid responsibility for Korea's involvements with Western powers.

Japan and the Opening of Korea

Japan sent a mission to Korea in 1868 to announce the restoration of the emperor and to seek the reopening of relations. This mission and subsequent ones in 1869 and 1871 were treated with scant respect by the Korean government, since Japan was regarded as a traitor to Confucian society because of her adoption of Western ways. Then, in 1875, a Japanese gunboat engaged in marine surveys on the Korean coast was fired upon. Here was an incident that could serve to bring Korea into treaty relations with Japan and at the same time detach Korea from its posture of Confucian dependency on China. Recognizing, however, that her success in Korea might well depend on the attitude of China, Japan first dispatched to Peking a mission under Mori Arinori to seek a more definite Chinese avowal of Korea's independence. But China refused to grant more than that the relationship was one of "dependence yet no control." Nevertheless, Li Hung-chang agreed to aid Japan in securing a friendly reception at Seoul.

The mission that Japan sent to Korea soon secured a treaty (February 26, 1876) which opened three Korean ports to trade and provided for diplomatic intercourse. In English translation, Article I read: "Chosen, being an independent State (*tzu chu*), enjoys the same sovereign rights as does Japan." Some Chinese, however, translated this article more favorably to China. For instance: "Chaohsien [Chosen], being an autonomous (*tzu chu*) state, shall enjoy the rights of equality with Japan."[12]

---

[12] Hsu Shuhsi, *China and Her Political Entity* (1926), 109. *Tzu chu* is usually translated "self-governing" or "autonomous," rather than "sovereign" or "independent." On aspects of Japanese policy, see Marlene J. Mayo, "The Korean Crisis of 1873 and Early Meiji Foreign Policy," *Journal of Asian Studies,* 31 (1972), 793-819.

[11] C. O. Paullin, *Diplomatic Negotiations of American Naval Officers, 1788-1883* (1912), 282-328.

Nevertheless, despite arguments over the precise meaning of Article I, certain points were quite clear. The Japanese intended by their treaty to make Korea "independent" as the West understood that term, whereas China was intent on at least preserving the ancient relationship. As for the Korean government, it signed a "Western treaty" with Japan, making at the same time a mental reservation to continue the old Confucian relation with China.

China and Korea

China recognized the danger of losing her ancient Confucian dominance over Korea. Following the loss of Ryukyu, Li Hung-chang noted that: "We can no longer refrain from devising ways and means for the security of Korea." Accordingly, China adopted a threefold course of action: she urged Korea to strengthen her military forces; she increased her diplomatic contacts with Korea in the hope of exercising greater influence at Seoul; and she urged Korea to conclude treaties with those powers which, unlike Japan and Russia, would be less likely to have territorial ambitions. Of these powers the United States was the first to show a renewed interest in treaty relations with Korea. Commodore Robert W. Shufeldt was sent to seek, with Japanese aid, a commercial treaty. The mission failed, but Shufeldt was encouraged by Li Hung-chang to try again through China's good offices. In 1882 the first American-Korean treaty was concluded. It provided among other things for the exchange of diplomatic and consular officers, and for trade with Korea on the most-favored-nation principle. It also stated:

If other Powers deal unjustly or oppressively with either Government, the other will exert their good offices, on being informed of the case, to bring about an amicable arrangement, thus showing their friendly feelings.

Li had asked, and Shufeldt had refused, to include a clause acknowledging the dependence of Korea upon China. The matter was disposed of by a letter from the Korean king to the American president acknowledging the subservient status. The United States, however, took the position, stated by Secretary of State Frederick T. Frelinghuysen,

. . . that we regarded Corea as de facto independent, and that our acceptance of the friendly aid found in China was in no sense a recognition of China's suzerain power.[13]

The principal European powers soon followed the example of the United States by securing treaties through China's good offices: Great Britain and Germany in 1883; Italy and Russia in 1884; and France in 1886. In each case Korea, while negotiating as a sovereign power, set forth in accompanying letters her dependent position upon China.

Korean Politics and Chinese Relations, 1882

Prior to the conclusion of these treaties, the international status of Korea had been affected by other developments. The first of these was China's intervention in a palace revolution at Seoul; the other was the conclusion of certain Sino-Korean trade regulations.

There were two major factions at the Korean court: one favored relations with foreign powers; the other was intensely antiforeign. The rivalry of these two factions, together with bad economic conditions, led to a conspiracy in 1882 to do away with the queen. The plot failed, but in the course of the fighting Korean mobs attacked the Japanese legation and drove its occupants to the coast, where they were rescued by a British ship. Both Japan and China stepped into the picture by sending troops to restore order. China, claiming to act in her traditional Confucian capacity, seized the king's father and sent him to Tientsin for punishment. Japan on her part exacted from Korea an agreement providing for an apology, an indemnity, the right to station a legation guard at Seoul, and permission to travel in the interior. To the Western powers all this was thoroughly confusing. China was intervening in the internal affairs of Korea, for which she professed to have no responsibility, using troops to restore order, issuing proclamations in the name of the king, and carrying off a great lord of the court to answer for his deeds. On the

---

[13]United States, Department of State, *China Instructions*, Vol. 3, No. 30.

other hand, Japan was ignoring the Chinese and dealing directly with Korea.

The second development of 1882 was the conclusion by China and Korea of new regulations on trade. This agreement, asserting that there was no change in Korea's status "as a boundary state of China," gave to the Chinese advantages over other foreigners in matters of residence, travel, trade, and import duties. It was evident that Chinese control over and intervention in Korea was becoming more pronounced. High Chinese military officers even proposed the annexation of Korea and war with Japan. Li Hung-chang, however, adopted measures short of this, sending an official of the Peking government to Korea as inspector-general of Korean customs. He also sent a number of Chinese "commercial agents" who would "actually assist the King to decide political issues." Indeed, Korea had ceased to be merely a Confucian appendage of China, for Li Hung-chang was now asserting, "I am King of Korea whenever I think the interests of China require me to assert that prerogative."[14]

The Tientsin Convention, 1885

Japan also had become more active in Korea. By 1884 the Japanese minister at Seoul was openly criticizing the policies of China, adding that Japan would welcome complete Korean independence. In December, 1884, the Korean "progressives" seized the king and called upon the Japanese for military protection. Yuan Shih-k'ai, commanding Chinese troops, promptly drove the Japanese to the coast and restored the king to his conservative counselors. For this affair, the Japanese exacted an indemnity from Korea; but they also sent a mission headed by Ito Hirobumi to Tientsin to discuss the Korean question with Li Hung-chang. The convention

[14] United States, Department of State, *China Despatches,* Vol. 65, No. 230, Young to Freling-huysen, August 8, 1883. Also, Dong Jae Yim, "The Abduction of the Taewongun, 1882," *Papers on China,* 21, published by the East Asian Research Center, Harvard University (1968), 99-130.

of Tientsin (April 18, 1885) was a partial victory for Japan. The two powers agreed to withdraw their troops from Korea and, in case of future disturbances, neither was to send troops *without notifying the other.* Thus, Japan gained a position of equality with China in the matter of military intervention.

Between 1885 and 1894 Li Hung-chang so strengthened his control over Korea that the country became a Chinese protectorate rather than a dependent state in the old Confucian sense. Li accomplished this end by various means. To the control which he already exercised through foreigners in the employ of the Korean government and through Chinese commercial agents, he added the appointment of Yuan Shih-k'ai as Chinese Resident in Korea, a post superior to that of a regular diplomatic representative. By the control which he exercised through these agents, Li attempted to destroy any idea in the minds of the powers that Korea was fully sovereign. Li also sought economic as well as political influence at Seoul. In 1885 China obtained a monopoly in the Korean telegraph, and attempted to get control over future loans sought by the Korean government. So successful was Li's policy that in 1892 even Japan approached Korea through China when seeking satisfaction for losses occasioned by certain Korean embargoes on the exportation of cargoes to Japan.

Immediate Background for War

By the early months of 1894, the context for an impending struggle between China and Japan concerning the international status of Korea was clearly discernible and can be summarized as follows: (*1*) the impact of the West had already deprived China of her principal dependent states such as Burma and Annam; (*2*) Korea appeared to be headed toward what the West called "sovereign independence" (this was indicated by the Japanese treaty of 1876, the American treaty of 1882, and the European treaties of 1883 and after); (*3*) Li Hung-chang, however, was determined to preserve China's influence in this strategic peninsula against the designs of either Japan or Russia, and to do so by Western as well as Confucian techniques if necessary; and, (4) since no one of the Western powers was prepared to act upon the fact as well as the principle of Korean independence, it remained for Japan to do so. When Japan did act it was relatively easy for her to give the impression that her motives were benevolent—to rescue Korea from China and Russia, and to bestow upon the Hermit Kingdom the independence, sovereignty, and progressive outlook which Japan herself enjoyed.[15]

Korea: The Approaching Crisis

Thus, in 1894 the Korean situation was critical; it had already become "a sort of focal point for great European rivalries, as well as for Asiatic antagonisms."[16] The Russians, for example, wanted an ice-free port in Korea and the British were determined they should not have one. It was against such European rivalries that the Japanese policy of 1894 was launched.

By 1894, Japan's political position in Korea was woefully weak, but her economic position was showing steady growth. Ninety percent of Korea's foreign trade was with Japan. Li had made strenuous efforts to counter Japan's economic advance. He was acquiring an army and navy, and was creating a naval base at Port Arthur. He was also planning a railway from Shanhaikwan to the Manchurian border near Vladivostok. News of this project created considerable excitement in Russia, where in 1891 the decision had been made to build the Trans-Siberian Railway. This railway was looked upon in Europe as of the utmost importance, and it was viewed with misgivings by both China and Japan. The Japanese believed that if Russia completed her system of communications, her advance into East Asia could not be stopped; at the same time, they also believed that Korea must be independent or controlled by Japan if the empire were to be secure. Japanese domestic worries also figured in their thinking. The constitutional government inaugurated in 1890 was not going well; cabinets that considered themselves responsible only to the emperor were faced with a succession of recalcitrant diets that refused to accept naval estimates presented by the government until appealed to directly by the emperor.[17] With young and inexperienced parliamentarians in such a mood, some of the bureaucrats and militarists in the government were ready to welcome a foreign war that would unite the home front.

Immediate Preliminaries To War

From 1871 until 1894 the peace party in Japan, headed in the later years by Ito Hirobumi, maintained its ascendancy over the militarists, and consequently there was no war over Korea. But after 1890 the "obstructive" tactics of the diet gave the war party its opportunity. The *Tong Hak* ("Eastern Learning Society"), originally a Korean religious sect, had acquired a political complexion, drawing the politically oppressed into its membership and assuming a program that was antiforeign, anti-Christian, and anti-Japanese. When rebellion finally occurred in the southern provinces, Korean government troops sent to quell the disturbance were themselves defeated. Acting on the advice of Yuan, Li Hung-chang promptly decided to send Chinese troops (June 6, 1894) and, in accord with the Tientsin convention, notified Japan that he was doing so. Untactfully, China's notice referred to "our tributary state." Japan replied the same day that she too would send troops owing to the "grave nature" of affairs in the peninsula, and added that she had "never recognized Korea as a tributary state of China." By the time the Japanese troops arrived, the Chinese had already suppressed the revolt. Japan proposed joint Sino-Japanese action to

[15] The most detailed account of Japanese-Korean relations is Hilary Conroy, *The Japanese Seizure of Korea: 1868-1910* (1960).

[16] William L. Langer, *The Diplomacy of Imperialism, 1890-1902* (2 vols., 1935; 2nd ed. in one vol., 1951), I, 168. Note Chapter 6 for a discussion of European aspects of the crisis.

[17] Takeuchi Tatsuji, *War and Diplomacy in the Japanese Empire* (1935), 109-110.

effect financial, administrative, and military reforms in Korea. China replied that she could not interfere in the internal administration of Korea and added that Japan had no right to do so either. Japan then turned to the Korean government, demanding a declaration indicating whether Korea was tributary to China. When Korea's reply proved ambiguous to the Japanese, their troops seized the king, and a reorganized Korean government "ordered" Japan to expel Chinese troops. The Sino-Japanese War had begun. The declarations were issued on August 1, 1894.

The War

The diplomatic front was by no means favorable to Japan when she embarked on a policy of war. Britain indicated that she would not agree to Japanese annexation of Korean territory. Russia, too, gave her diplomatic support to China, seemingly on the theory that it was better to have Korea controlled by a weak China than by a young and vigorous Japan. As a result, Japan gave assurances to the powers that she was interested only in Korean reform, had no designs on Korean territory, and, in the interests of European commerce, would refrain from attacking Shanghai. These assurances were accepted, probably because it was generally believed in the West that Japan would be defeated anyway. But these early forecasts were shattered by the September victories of Japanese arms at Pingyang and the Yalu river. It soon became evident that Chinese forces were no match for the small but relatively efficient Japanese military machine.

A diplomatic revolution was soon under way. British opinion, reacting to the Japanese victories, invited France, Germany, Russia, and the United States to intervene to seek a settlement that would include Korean independence, a European guarantee to Korea, and indemnity for Japan. The proposal was dropped when Germany and the United States refused to join. Li Hung-chang also sought the support of Europe and America to end the disastrous war before China was completely humbled.

During the winter months of January and February, 1895, the Japanese had taken Wei-hai-wei; their armies were crossing southern Manchuria; and in early March they had occupied Newchwang and Yingkow, from which they might soon advance on a frightened and humiliated government in Peking, where the empress dowager, instead of building a navy, had employed government funds to rebuild the Summer Palace. When the United States offered its good offices to both belligerents, Japan replied significantly that her objectives would not be reached "until China finds herself in a position to approach Japan directly on the subject of peace."

Indeed Li Hung-chang did send a succession of peace missions to Japan. Finally, when all these failed and when hope of European aid or of a victory for Chinese arms had vanished, Li himself accepted the humiliating task of asking for peace. As he left for Japan he still hoped for a diplomatic victory through European intervention, although he was warned by Charles Denby, American minister at Peking, that what China needed was a sincere, friendly rapprochement with Japan.

China's failure to prevent Korea's detachment from the tributary system has often been explained simply by saying that her foreign policy was weak, inept, and uninformed. In a limited degree this interpretation is sound, but it should also take into account the fact that the Tsungli Yamen, though constantly blocked by the tradition-bound board of rites, did advance new ideas and try new methods. In the Korean case the Tsungli Yamen showed remarkable flexibility; its efforts were nullified, however, by obstruction at home and the complexities of dealing with the Koreans and Japanese.[18]

JAPAN IN EAST ASIA

Japan's military and naval victory marked the beginning of a new era in East Asia, the effects of which were to be felt almost as

[18] Mary C. Wright, "The Adaptability of Ch'ing Diplomacy," *Journal of Asian Studies*, 17 (1958), 363-81.

Kichibei Murai and his staff inspecting a petroleum site in northern Honshu

Murai Brothers Company Ltd. coal mine

Mine workers' housing

Coporate farming operations in Korea

JAPAN'S NEW ECONOMY

Japan's new international power was based partly on a rapidly developing industrial and financial base. For example, the Murai Brothers Company Ltd. had applied modern business practices in several areas by 1900. In addition to the activities depicted above, the firm controlled a large bank and manufactured cigarettes in association with the American Tobacco Corporation.

much in Europe as in Asia. The immediate question was: "What would be Japan's demands?" At Tientsin in 1885 Ito had been forced to accept what China was willing to give. At Shimonoseki in 1895 China would be forced to give whatever Ito demanded. The specific nature of Japan's demands was not known until they were presented to the Chinese on April 1. They included: (*1*) China to recognize the full and complete independence of Korea; (*2*) to cede Taiwan,[19] the Pescadores, and the Liaotung Peninsula in South Manchuria to Japan; (*3*) China to pay Japan an indemnity of 300 million taels[20]; and (*4*) China to conclude with Japan a new treaty of commerce, granting, among other things, most-favored-nation treatment to Japan, and opening seven new treaty ports. Since neither Europe nor the United States was prepared at this time to come actively to China's aid, Li was forced to accept Japan's

[19] Japan's interest in Taiwan dated back to 1872. For a few brief weeks in the spring of 1895 the terms of the Shimonoseki settlement were challenged by the appearance of the Republic of Taiwan, "A republican state, autonomous but not sovereign, presided over by a ruler who sought to function as both a Taiwanese president and Chinese governor." See Harry J. Lamley, "The 1895 Taiwan Republic," *Journal of Asian Studies,* 27 (1968), 739-62.

[20] The tael (Chinese, *liang*) was a unit of weight and when applied to silver was often used as a currency unit. There were in practice a number of taels of varying weights but about 1-1/3 ounces was most common. As a standard money of account, the tael was seldom minted in coin. Transactions were carried on with silver ingots, checks or bank notes in taels, or Spanish-Mexican dollars.

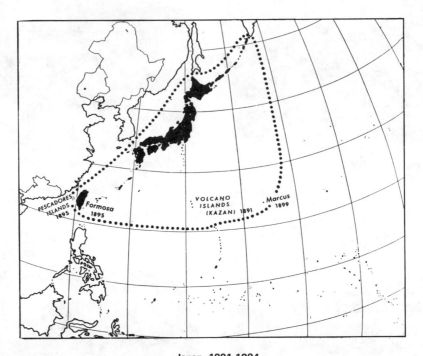

Japan, 1891-1904
Reproduced from A War Atlas for Americans *(New York: Simon & Schuster, 1944)
with permission from the publisher and from the U.S. Department of State, Division
of Map Intelligence and Cartography.*

terms, though with some modifications. The treaty of Shimonoseki was signed on April 17, 1895.

The efficacy of war as a stabilizer of Japanese politics was immediately evident. By the declaration of war, Ito and the *genro* achieved notable results. The nation was unified; peace prevailed between the government and the diet; huge war budgets (one of 150 million yen) were passed without a dissenting vote; and a resolution was adopted unanimously to appropriate any amount of funds needed for the prosecution of the war.

Japan had taken the first step in what was to be a vigorous policy of expanding her role on the Asian continent. With Port Arthur and the Liaotung Peninsula in her possession she could look forward to a controlling influence at Peking. In short, she had made it clear that both territorially and diplomatically she pro-

posed to be a part of whatever pressures were exerted upon China.

For China the results of the war were no less momentous. The proud Middle Kingdom had been defeated by a people looked upon not only as inferior but also, by reason of their Westernization, as traitors to the Confucian ideal. In naval, military, and political affairs the Manchu government had met humiliating defeat. To a few thoughtful Chinese it appeared that the dynasty had lost the Mandate of Heaven. Now, with Japan's victory, the old Confucian theory of international relations, which China had maintained for centuries, was destroyed. There was no longer in theory or in fact an East Asian Confucian world order. China was no longer the Middle Kingdom, for there were no longer any dependent states that recognized her superior status. Her efforts to protect herself from the inroads of the powers had been frustrated by the same institutional obstacles, by the same bureaucratic incubus that had blocked internal reform.[21]

FOR FURTHER READING

General. Franz Michael, *The Origin of Manchu Rule in China, Frontier and Bureaucracy as Interacting Forces in the Chinese Empire* (1942) develops Chinese-nomad relations. Owen Lattimore, *Inner Asian Frontiers of China* (2nd ed., 1951).*

Ryukyu Islands and Ili. Clarence Glacken, *The Great Loochoo: A Study in Okinawan Village Life* (1955). George H. Kerr, *Okinawa: the History of an Island People* (1958). Martin Norins, *Gateway to Asia: Sinkiang Frontier of the Chinese Far West* (1944). Rene Grousset, *The Empire of the Steppes: A History of Central Asia* (1960).

Southeast Asia. Harold C. Hinton, *China's Relations with Burma and Vietnam* (1958).

---

[21] The impact of a war can not always be gauged by reading accounts of the battles or the terms of the peace settlement. Hostilities in the Sino-Japanese war lasted only a few months and were confined mainly to coastal areas. For a nation that suffered repeated defeats at the hands of Western powers, the treaty of Shimonoseki was not the first humiliation. Yet it may be suggested that China's defeat in 1884-1895 was in many respects the most significant event of the nineteenth century in East Asia. It was a humiliation that affected the Chinese world more deeply than the whole history of the treaty system which had been imposed by the West in 1842-1844 and in 1858-1860. The treaty system with its special privileges—treaty ports, extraterritoriality, conventional tariffs, and the right of proselytism—however distasteful, had become a part of an established, if not entirely acceptable, order. Chinese officialdom could construe this modified order as one that was still essentially Confucian, and, therefore, one that was susceptible to salvation by Confucian-scholar-bureaucrats. These hopes vanished in the defeat of 1895 and in the tragic events that were to follow, 1896-1900 (see chapter 15). As a consequence, younger Chinese intellectuals for the first time despaired that China could be revitalized in the Confucian way. See Harold Z. Schiffrin, *Sun Yatsen and the Origins of the Chinese Revolution* (1970).*

Among the general studies of historical Southeast Asia see: John F. Cady, *Southeast Asia: Its Historical Development* (1964), a fluent survey written especially for the college level. D. G. E. Hall, *A History of South-East Asia* (2nd rev. ed., 1964) is a standard reference work. Among the shorter and stimulating general treatments are: Brian Harrison, *Southeast Asia: A Short History* (3rd ed., 1966); Nicholas Tarling, *A Concise History of Southeast Asia* (1966); and John Bastin and Harry J. Benda, *A History of Modern Southeast Asia: Colonialism, Nationalism, and Decolonization* (1968).*

For European penetration of Burma and the Indochina area see: John F. Cady, *A History of Modern Burma* (1958), especially recommended for the years 1800-1885. Maung Htin Aung, *A History of Burma* (1968) presents a Burmese statesman's view. See also the latter author's *The Stricken Peacock: Anglo-Burmese Relations, 1752-1948* (1965)* which reveals some of the inadequacies of Western writings without contributing any new research. G. E. Harvey, *British Rule in Burma, 1824-1942* (1946), standard reference. Particularly useful for the pre-modern period of Vietnamese history are: Joseph Buttinger, *Vietnam: A Dragon Embattled* (1967)* and Lethanh Khoi, *Le Viet-Nam: Histoire et Civilisation* (1955). Details on people, agriculture, industry, and foreign trade are found in Charles Robequain, *The Economic Development of French Indo-China* (1944), and Olov R. T. Janse, *The Peoples of French Indo-China* (1944). Selected aspects of French rule are treated in Roger Levy, Guy Lacam, and Andrew Roth, *French Interests and Policies in the Far East* (1941).

Tibet. Li Tieh-tseng, *Tibet: Today and Yesterday* (1960). Shen Tsung-lien and Liu Shen-chi, *Tibet and the Tibetans* (1953). Charles Bell, *The People of Tibet* (1928), and *The Religion of Tibet* (1931). Helmut Hoffman, *The Religions of Tibet* (1961). Li Tieh-tseng, *The Historical Status of Tibet* (1956) covers Tibet's dealings with T'ang China. Schuyler Cammann, *Trade through the Himalayas: The Early British Attempts to Open Tibet* (1951) also covers early Ch'ing relations with Tibet. Alastair Lamb, *Britain and Chinese*

Central Asia (1960). Robert Brainerd Ekvall. *Cultural Relations on the Kansu-Tibetan Border* (1939).

Korea. William E. Henthorn, *A History of Korea* (1971). Sohn Pow-key et al., *The History of Korea* (1970). Woo-keun Han, *The History of Korea,* trans. by Lee Kyong-shik and ed. by Grafton K. Mintz (1972). Takashi Hatada, *A History of Korea,* trans. by Benjamin H. Hazard and Warren W. Smith, Jr. (1969). C. I. Eugene Kim and Han-kyo Kim, *Korea and the Politics of Imperialism, 1876-1910* (1967). Mary C. Wright, "The Adaptability of Ch'ing Diplomacy: The Case of Korea," *Journal of Asian Studies* 17 (1958), 363-81. Marlene J. Mayo, "The Korean Crisis of 1873 and Early Meiji Foreign Policy," *Journal of Asian Studies,* 31 (1972), 793-819.

W. W. Rockhill, *China's Intercourse with Korea from the XVth Century to 1895* (1905). *Korean-American Relations: Documents Pertaining to the Far Eastern Diplomacy of the United States,* Vol. 1, George M. McCune and John A. Harrison, eds. (1951), and Volume 2, Spencer J. Palmer, ed. (1963). Fred H. Harrington, *God, Mammon, and the Japanese* (1962), a biography of Horace Allen, missionary, businessman, and first American Minister to Korea. Tyler Dennett, *Americans in Eastern Asia* (1922; reprint, 1963) contains chapters on Korea's nineteenth century foreign relations.

Imperialism
in Full Flower:
1895–1899

15

Japan's quick, complete, and unexpected victory in the Sino-Japanese war, and the territorial settlement she exacted in the treaty of Shimonoseki were striking testimony that this diminutive Oriental state, emerging so recently from its feudal isolation, had not only joined the modern Western world but had also mastered its vehicles for power—the political philosophies commonly referred to as modern nationalism and imperialism.

In her adoption of the practices of competitive nationalism, Japan had followed the great European powers, which had sought to increase their security by imposing their sovereignty on less developed peoples and by controlling the resources and skills of those peoples, while at the same time bringing them the blessings of a "superior" civilization. These European practices had come to be known as imperialism, and, by the late nineteenth century, they had produced intense rivalries, a contest which the United States was beginning to join. Thus, the sudden emergence of Japan as a power was not welcomed in the West. Japan, in her victory over China, was seen as far too apt a student of modern-

ization. The time was at hand, therefore, for the West to respond.[1]

[1] Imperialism in its varied aspects has defied precise definition, and the word has been used so loosely as to become almost meaningless. For example, there is disagreement as to the conditions, forces, and states of mind in the late nineteenth century which gave rise to imperialism. Certainly the period brought the conviction to those who espoused imperialism that rapid change was the order of the day in technology, methods of warfare, and international relations. Many of these changes were reaching the underdeveloped areas of the world, and what would happen in these areas, so ran the argument, must be controlled by the more advanced nations; the imperialists must control lesser peoples in order to "civilize" them. Thus, insofar as fear of what the developing nations might do as they gained power was a motive here, it seems that imperialism, often described as a philosophy of self-confidence, could also be described as a philosophy of uncertainty and insecurity. Moreover, East Asia affected the late nineteenth century development of Western imperialism in two ways. First, many imperialists had become convinced that their future power and security would be determined by their influence in or control over East Asia. Secondly, since no single imperialistic power could control all of East Asia, there was a tendency for the rivals to curb their rivalry by a strategy that would divide the spoils. See the analysis

An American warship in the Wangpu River anchorage, Shanghai.

Offices of the American firm, Russell & Company, Shanghai, 1866. The firm traded in tea and silk and, for a few years, operated a steamboat line on the Yangtze River.

THE TRIPLE INTERVENTION

Six days after the conclusion of the treaty of Shimonoseki (April 23, 1895), the representatives in Tokyo of Russia, Germany, and France presented notes to Count Hayashi, deputy foreign minister, which said:

by Akira Iriye, "Imperialism in East Asia," in *Modern East Asia: Essays in Interpretation,* James B. Crowley, ed. (1970),* 122-50. For some differing interpretations of American imperialism note Ernest R. May, *American Imperialism* (1968); Marilyn B. Young, *The Rhetoric of Empire* (1968); W. A. Williams, *The Roots of the Modern American Empire* (1969).*

. . . the possession of the Peninsula of Liaotung, claimed by Japan, would be a constant menace to the Capital of China, would at the same time render illusory the independence of Korea, and would henceforth be a perpetual obstacle to the peace of the Far East.

The three powers, protesting that in this manner they were giving new proof of their friendship, advised Japan to renounce possession of Liaotung. For a week the diplomatic scales hung in uneasy equilibrium until, on May 5, Japan accepted the advice. She asked, however, that the treaty of Shimonoseki be ratified in its original form prior to the re-

Tea-tasting room of George H. Macy & Company, about 1885.

Peddling American-made cigarettes in northern China, about 1900.

trocession, and that she be given additional indemnity; this the powers granted. Ratification took place at Chefoo, where, significantly, a Russian squadron in the gray paint of war and with its decks cleared for action lay at anchor. The Liaotung Peninsula was returned to China by a convention signed November 8, 1895, in which China agreed to pay an additional indemnity of 30 million Kuping taels.[2]

Thus Japan, who had won the war, lost the

[2]See note 20, Chapter 14.

peace. For the brief duration of the war she had bid for and held diplomatic leadership in East Asia. But the triple intervention of Russia, Germany, and France demonstrated that the European powers would not stand idly by while Japan gained a strategic foothold on the Asian continent.

During the Shimonoseki negotiations Prime Minister Ito and Foreign Minister Mutsu had realized that an unfriendly European intervention was in the making. Accordingly, Mutsu attempted to forestall action by the powers by insisting that Japan's negotiating position not include territorial demands on

Adapted from J. K. Fairbank, E. O. Reischauer, and A. M. Craig, East Asia: The Modern Transformation *(1965), p. 399; and Dun J. Lee,* The Ageless Chinese *(1965), p. 423.*

the mainland. In this he was opposed by pressure from the military and naval staffs, who saw Japanese possession of the Liaotung Peninsula as a territorial gain which would enable Japan to dominate Peking. The debate over this policy question within Japan ended the temporary truce in her domestic politics. Eventually, the militarists had their way; they forced the government to demand concessions from China which, as Mutsu and Ito knew, the

powers would soon force it to renounce. When the inevitable European intervention came and the government bowed to it, the Japanese public, which had been elated with the news of their country's military and naval triumphs, became indignant; they were not quieted until the emperor snactioned an imperial rescript stating that the retrocession in no way compromised the dignity or honor of the nation. Actually, the government was aware that such was not the case, and that the excessive demands of the militarists had turned military victory into diplomatic defeat.

Seen in historical perspective, the triple intervention had lasting effects on Japanese policy and on the temper of the Japanese people. The powers intervened just at the moment when Japan appeared to have mastered the techniques of success as the world measured such matters. In 1894, on the eve of the Sino-Japanese War, Japan had finally won release from the unequal treaties that had been imposed after the Perry mission. Great Britain had led the way, signing a treaty relinquishing extraterritorial rights. Then had come the intoxicating victory over China. It thus was against a background of an surging national pride that Japanese viewed the forced return of Liaotung, the symbol of Japan's entry into the company of the imperial powers. In seeking Liaotung, Japan's expansionists could say that they were merely following in the footsteps of Portugal, Spain the Netherlands, France, Russia, and Great Britain—all of whom had seized territory in East Asia. When some of these same powers forced Japan to adhere to a different standard of conduct, the triple intervention became grounds for the cultivation of an intensified ultranationalism. As time would reveal, Japanese patriotism could feed on adversity and self-denial.

EUROPEAN BACKGROUND OF THE INTERVENTION

The reasons that led to this dramatic three-power intervention are clear, as are also the reasons why Britain did not participate. Up to the time of the war, British policy, though favoring independence for Korea, had been decidedly pro-Chinese, opposing any thought of Japanese annexations on the continent. Japan's demands were, therefore, disturbing to the British, for they threatened to upset whatever balance of power there was in East Asia. At the same time the British admired Japan's aggressive efficiency. Furthermore—and this was the determining point—they were not insensitive to the fact that the commercial

clauses of the peace settlement could be very profitable to British business in China.

For her part, Russia had attempted to remain on friendly terms with Japan until 1895. She had ample opportunity to intervene in the war but was more interested in preserving the status quo. All this, however, was changed by Japan's amazing victory. The tsar vacillated several times and then, having the assurance of German and French support, decided to thwart Japan's imperial ambitions.[3] Russia, endeavoring to acquire an ice-free port on the Pacific, saw numerous advantages in this policy. It would exclude Japan from any share in the partition of China (a partition which the Japanese were already considering), and it would make Russia appear as the savior of China, which would dispose Peking favorably to subsequent Russian territorial demands.

Germany's participation in the intervention is explained largely by her fear that a partition of China was possible; in that case it would be well to be active in events leading to that end. The Germans had their eyes on several bases in East Asia; here the views of the German foreign office were influenced by Max von Brandt, who for a quarter of a century had been the leading German diplomat in the Orient. Furthermore, anything that encouraged the Russians to become involved in East Asia would presumably react to German advantage in Europe.

The participation of France is explained by considerations of general policy. France feared that the Japanese would resist intervention, and that they might be joined by the British, thus precipitating a general conflict. Therefore, France initially favored letting the Japanese have their gains while the powers would seek their own territorial compensation elsewhere in China. When, however, Russia decided to act, France joined her in the interest of their dual alliance.

FINANCING WAR AND PEACE

While Japan paid for her diplomatic defeat with loss of her territorial gains in Manchuria, China

[3] George A. Lensen, "Japan and Tsarist Russia—the Changing Relationships, 1875-1917," *Jahrbucher fur Geschichte Osteuropas* (1962), 337-48.

paid for her unpreparedness with cold cash. Her efforts to float domestic loans during the war had failed. Consequently, the Peking government financed the war with two loans totaling some £4,635,000 from the British Hong Kong and Shanghai Bank. After the war, China was confronted with the Japanese indemnity totalling 230 million Kuping taels (about $172 million gold). The Russians were particularly anxious that this bill be paid to hasten the Japanese evacuation of Liaotung; but they were equally concerned that the indemnity be met in such fashion as to leave China in a kind of politico-financial dependence upon Russia, thus preventing the extension of British financial influence at Peking. The Germans and the French shared in this desire. The result was a Franco-Russian loan to China, July 6, 1895, of 400 million francs. The political motive behind the loan was indicated by China's pledge not to grant any foreign power the right of supervision or administration over its revenues unless the same rights were extended to the Russian government. Count Witte, Russia's minister of finance, had won the first round in the financial battle for dominance at Peking. The Germans, who had not been admitted to the Franco-Russian loan, joined the British bankers in a loan of £16 million on March 23, 1896. Two years later the Anglo-German banking group extended another loan in the sum of £16 million. The era of international rivalry to finance and thus to control China was well under way.

RUSSO-CHINESE AGREEMENTS, 1896

The indemnity loans, virtually forced upon China by Russia and France in 1895, were not considered adequate compensation for "the diplomatic aid" these powers had given Peking. The shape of future Russian policy was made clear during 1896. Since 1891 the Russians had been engaged in construction of the Trans-Siberian Railway. It was obvious that such a huge undertaking, involving a line some 5,000 miles in length, was not designed primarily to connect European Russia with Vladivostok or any other port which was ice-bound four or five

months each year. Since as early as 1857, Russian statesmen had played with the idea of a Peking terminus for a Siberian railway; what Russia now wanted was a port in southern Korea or Manchuria. But in the months immediately following the peace this was out of the question unless she was prepared to fight Japan. By 1896, however, Russian fortunes in Korea took an unexpected turn for the better. The Koreans had not taken kindly to Japan's energetic suggestions on reform and, when the Japanese minister was implicated in the murder of the Korean queen, the king fled to the Russian legation in Seoul. Still, even this development did not result in immediate Russian seizures in Korea.

Meanwhile, in December, 1895, Witte had chartered the Russo-Chinese Bank, ostensibly a private corporation but officially approved and inspired. In fact, it was a slightly disguised branch of the Russian treasury with the capital coming from French banks. This new concern was to be the financial arm of the Trans-Siberian Railway. Its powers were notable in that it could collect taxes, finance the business of local government, coin money, and secure commercial and industrial concessions.

Another phase of the Russian far eastern plan concerned the route of the Trans-Siberian Railway from Lake Baikal to Vladivostok. To run the line wholly in Russian territory north of Manchuria and the Amur would entail 350 miles of additional construction through difficult terrain. If, however, it were run directly across central Manchuria, it would not only shorten the distance but it would also be the first step to Russian control of all Manchurian commerce and of railroad development in North China. For a time, however, the Russians made little headway at Peking. The Chinese were aware that Russian railway demands could not be pushed aside, but they hoped to strike a better bargain by sending Li Hung-chang to the coronation of the new tsar. Actually this arrangement was exactly what Witte wanted. Li was met at Port Said by Witte's agent, Prince Esper Ukhtomskii, whose colorful writings on the cultural and philosophical unity of Russians and Asians were well known. The prince's role was to prepare Li for Witte's more practical proposals on Russo-Chinese industrial unity in Manchuria. The argument as presented to Li was that Russia had plenty of territory and therefore had no designs on that of China; that culturally the tie between the two nations was great; that by building the railroad across Manchuria, Russia would be in a position to aid China against attack; and, finally, that China herself was not in a position to finance or build the road. There seems little doubt that Li was also bribed handsomely by Russian agents, but his decision was probably based on his realization that British aid was not forthcoming, as well as on his intense hatred of the Japanese. An alliance with and concessions to Russia seemed only natural.[4]

Li was not alone among Chinese politicians in wishing to play Russia against Japan and the other powers. Japan's victory in 1895 had awakened and alarmed the Chinese scholar-official mind as had no crisis in the previous half century. The Sino-Japanese war illumined the empty pretense of the program of self-strengthening and hustled the high command of the Confucian bureaucracy back again to the older weapon of using barbarian to fight barbarian. Even among Li's rivals there were supporters of his Russian policy, such as Chang Chih-tung (1837-1909). In 1895 Chang wrote that Russia was China's natural ally, "because England uses commerce to absorb the profits of China, France uses religion to entice the Chinese people, Germany has no territorial boundary with us, and the United States does not like to interfere in others' military affairs." So China got the Russian alliance she wanted, but she got it by granting concessions which within two years threatened the break-up of the empire.

The Russo-Chinese secret alliance, known as the Li-Lobanov treaty, was signed June 3, 1896, and remained in force for fifteen years. Among other things it provided: (1) for mutual assistance against Japanese aggression; (2) for the use of Chinese ports by Russia in the event of war; and (3) for China's consent to the construction of the Trans-Siberian Railway

across Manchuria—construction and operation of the road to be accorded to the Russo-Chinese Bank. Although rumors of this agreement soon became public, it was not until many years later that the exact nature of the alliance was revealed.

THE CHINESE EASTERN RAILWAY

What the public did learn was that on September 8, 1896, the Russo-Chinese Bank and the Chinese government had agreed to the construction and operation by the Chinese Eastern Railway Company of a railway line from Manchouli on the western border of Manchuria to Pogranichnaya on the southeast border near Vladivostok. The statutes of the new Chinese Eastern Railway Company were to conform to Russian law; the president was to be named by China; but the Russian general manager would exercise greater power. The political nature of the line was indicated by the fact that over the "lands actually necessary for the construction, operation, and protection of the line" the Company was to have "the absolute and exclusive right of administration." China was to grant reduced tariff rates to goods entering or leaving by the line; there was to be no interference with the movement of Russian troops or munitions on the line; and the Company was to have "the complete and exclusive right to operate the line."

These terms were confirmed in December, 1896, when the Russian government sanctioned the statutes of the Chinese Eastern Railway Company. These statutes obligated the Company to construct telegraph lines and to carry Russian mails free. Although the Chinese government was to adopt measures for the protection of the line, "the preservation of law and order on the lands assigned to the railway and its appurtenances shall be confided to police agents appointed by the Company." After eighty years the railroad was to become Chinese property without payment. Thirty-six years after its completion China could purchase it by paying to the Company the full outlay with interest.

Construction of the Chinese Eastern Railway was completed in 1904. From this great trunk

[4] *The Memoirs of Count Witte*, A. Yarmolinsky, ed. (1921) is of great value but incomplete and unreliable in Witte's estimates of his own role.

line, nearly 1,000 miles in length, Russia hoped to build a political and commercial empire, providing easy access to the Pacific and insuring Russian economic dominance in North China. This was the Russian policy: peaceful penetration.

THE YAMAGATA-LOBANOV AGREEMENT

Li Hung-chang was not the only distinguished Oriental guest at the Russian coronation in 1896. Japan was represented by Yamagata Aritomo, the most powerful of the Choshu clansmen, father of the modern Japanese army, and the leading exponent of the military tradition. The Japanese wanted a compromise settlement of Russo-Japanese rivalry in Korea, a compromise that would maintain the balance until the army and navy expansion program could be effected. Accordingly, Yamagata proposed to the Russians that the two powers divide Korea at the 38th parallel into a northern, Russian sphere and a southern, Japanese sphere—an arrangement that would give the Japanese control of Seoul, the capital. The Russians turned down the offer. For the present they regarded it as good policy to play along with England and the United States in respecting the integrity of Korea. In the long run, they hoped to get control of the entire peninsula. As a result, two general and unsatisfactory compromise agreements were reached. At Seoul the Russian and Japanese representatives advised the Korean king to return as soon as possible to his palace from his refuge in the Russian legation. The Japanese were to withdraw most of their troops. This understanding, reached at Seoul on May 26, was supplemented by the Yamagata-Lobanov agreement made at Moscow (June 9). It stipulated that both powers would support the Korean king's efforts to restore and maintain order and both would guarantee foreign loans so that adequate police could be maintained and foreign intervention avoided. Korea was thus recognized as a Russo-Japanese joint problem. A secret article provided that in case it became necessary to send troops to Korea, the two powers would consult with a view to fixing a neutral zone between their spheres of action. Korea had become a kind of joint protectorate.[5]

GERMANY AND EAST ASIA

The German intervention against Japan in 1895 had been prompted not only by the desire to involve Russia in East Asia and thus weaken the Franco-Russian alliance in Europe, but also by the German ambition to secure a naval and commercial base in China. For a time Germany appeared to be interested in various islands on the Korean coast, and in Wei-hai-wei, Chusan, Woosung, Amoy, Samsah Bay, and Mirs Bay.[6] But in the summer of 1897 she decided to take Kiaochou on the south Shantung coast. This decision rested on the enthusiasm of the kaiser; on the reports of Admiral von Tirpitz, commander of the German far eastern fleet in 1896; and German harbor-construction engineers; and, less directly, on the earlier advice of Ferdinand von Richthofen, perhaps the outstanding European authority on China of his time. Von Richthofen, who had brought back much valuable scientific, geographic, and socioeconomic data from his various travels through China—and, incidentally, dramatized for Europe the dire consequences that would follow if Asian labor were loosed on the world's economy—had first pointed out the strategic and economic advantages of Kiaochou.

To avoid any collision with Russia, whose fleet had already wintered at Kiaochou, thus establishing a sort of priority in the place, the kaiser appealed to the tsar and was evidently given a green light. Accordingly, Germany notified China of her need for the harbor. Apparently the plan was for the German fleet, uninvited, to winter at Kiaochou—a friendly

[5] William L. Langer, *The Diplomacy of Imperialism, 1890-1902* (2 vols., 1935; 2nd ed. in one vol., 1951), I, 405-07.

[6] German commercial and colonial activity in the Pacific area dated back to the activities of Hamburg merchants in Samoa (1857); by 1885 Germany had possession of a large section of New Guinea, and of the Bismarck and the Marshall islands.

but unmistakable gesture calculated to bring the Chinese to terms. The way was made even easier when, in November, 1897, two German Catholic missionaries were killed by Chinese robbers in southern Shantung. Admiral von Diederich landed German troops at Kiaochou Bay. For a time the Chinese government refused to come to terms but, on March 6, Germany secured her agreement. This convention was prefaced with the remark that "The Imperial Chinese Government considers it advisable to give a special proof of their grateful appreciation of the friendship shown to them by Germany." How deep this "friendship" was, and how significant its results, may be judged from the terms of the convention. Among other points it provided for: (1) a "neutral" zone 50 kilometers wide surrounding Kiaochou Bay, in which zone China would permit the free movement of German troops, and in which China would take no measures without the consent of Germany; (2) a ninety-nine year lease to Germany for both sides of the entrance to Kiaochou Bay, including use of the port of Tsingtao as a naval base; (3) the exercise by Germany during the term of the lease of sovereign powers over the leased area; (4) a Chinese pledge to "cede to Germany a more suitable place" in the event that the Germans returned the territory prior to the expiration of the lease; (5) a German pledge not to "sublet" the territory to another power; (6) permission for the construction of two railways by a Sino-German company in which the nationals of both powers might invest; (7) the right of Germans to mine coal within 30 *li* (10 miles) of the railways; and (8) a commitment from China to the effect that

. . . the Chinese Government binds itself in all cases where foreign assistance, in persons, capital or material, may be needed for any purpose whatever within the Province of Shantung, to offer the said work or supplying of materials in the first instance to German manufacturers and merchants engaged in undertakings of the kind in question.[7]

[7] John V. A. MacMurray, ed., *Treaties and Agreements with and concerning China, 1894-1919* (2 vols., 1921), I, 112-16. John E. Schrecker, *Imperialism and Chinese Nationalism: Germany in Shantung* (1971), throws light on Chinese attitudes toward the West, and on many aspects of German policy.

Germany's descent upon Kiaochou necessitated changes in Russia's plans. She had considered taking Kiaochou herself in the winter of 1895-1896. Now, although the Germans had taken the one good naval harbor in North China, there were still plenty of harbors in Korea. Back in Moscow in 1896 Li Hung-chang had even advised the Russians to take a Korean port. But when Russia turned to Korea in late 1897 and attempted to make a Russian the financial adviser of the king and to oust a Britisher, M'Leavy Brown, from control of the Korean customs, she was met with the appearance of a strong Anglo-Japanese squadron in the harbor of Chemulpo. Accordingly, in November, 1897, the Russian government began to consider occupation of the harbor of Talienwan on the Liaotung Peninsula in South Manchuria, a few miles northeast of Port Arthur. In Peking, the Chinese government, though petitioned by some of the most powerful viceroys, such as Chang Chih-tung, to resist Russian overtures and to seek an alliance with Japan and England, had determined on a policy of surrender. And so in March, 1898, less than three weeks after Germany had leased Kiaochou, China leased to Russia for twenty-five years the southern tip of the Liaotung Peninsula, containing Port Arthur and Talienwan. This was the exact spot from which Russia, France, and Germany had ousted Japan three years earlier. North of the leased area a neutral zone would stretch to the base of the peninsula. Finally, the convention accompanying the lease granted to the Chinese Eastern Railway Company the right to connect Talienwan by rail with the main line in central Manchuria. Thus, to quote the terms of the agreement, Russia's naval forces had acquired "an entirely secure base on the littoral of northern China."

FRANCE LEASES KWANGCHOU-BAY

During the winter of 1897-1898, when Germany and Russia were maturing their plans at Kiaochou and Port Arthur, France was still paying lip service to the principle of China's integrity. Yet it was obvious that France was not unaffected by the German and Russian moves. Since 1885 France had possessed a great empire of colonies and "protectorates" in Indochina. In that year China had renounced control over Annam, had agreed to respect Franco-Annamite agreements, and had promised to open two cities in Yunnan to French commerce. In 1895, French influence, now more strongly entrenched in northern Indochina (Annam and Tonkin), was looking to industrial concessions across the frontier in China's southern provinces. Within a month of the famous triple intervention of that year, France reaped her first reward. In June, 1895, it was agreed that

... *for the exploitation of its mines in the provinces of Yunnan, Kwangsi, and Kwangtung, [China] may call upon, in the first instance, French manufacturers and engineers....*

The principle that the railways of Annam might be extended into China was also established. Following close on the heels of this agreement, France secured a concession from China in June, 1896, to construct a railroad in Kwangsi from the border of Tonkin to Lung-chow. In the same year a French expedition explored the interior of the island of Hainan, and, in January, China promised France never to alienate it to any other power. It is not surprising, then, that France was ready with new demands once Germany and Russia had taken action at Kiaochou and Port Arthur. These demands led to extensive new gains. In April, 1898, China agreed not to alienate any of her territories on the border of Tonkin. At the same time she agreed: (1) to grant France a concession for a railroad from Tonkin to Yunnan-fu (Kumming), completed in 1910; (2) to lease to France for ninety-nine years the bay of Kwangchou as a naval station and coaling depot; and (3) to appoint Frenchmen as advisers to the newly-proposed Chinese postal service. These measures were designed not only to give France a strategic foothold and industrial concessions in South China, but also to draw Chinese commerce away from British influence at Hong Kong and Canton and to center it under French control in the Gulf of

Tonkin. The net result was a French sphere covering Kwangtung, Kwangsi, and Yunnan.

GREAT BRITAIN: KOWLOON, WEI-HAI-WEI

The British government during 1897-1898 had failed to place any effective restraints on the development of German, Russian, or French policy in China. British policy had been basically commercial rather than political, but it could not remain unaffected by the new position occupied in China by the other great European powers. In other words, if leaseholds, preferential concessions, and special spheres were to be the order of the day, it behooved Britain to have her share. From February through July, 1898, Britain and China concluded a series of agreements of the utmost importance. China agreed: (1) never to alienate any territory in the Yangtze valley; (2) to insure that the inspector-general of the Chinese maritime customs should be a British subject so long as British trade predominated; (3) to lease Wei-hai-wei to Britain as a naval harbor "for so long a period as Port Arthur shall remain in the occupation of Russia"; and (4) to extend the British territory of Kowloon in a ninety-nine year lease over the entire peninsula lying between Deep Bay and Mirs Bay. With this British advance went an Anglo-German loan to China in the amount of £16 million and various preliminary agreements between the Hong Kong and Shanghai Banking Corporation and Chinese authorities concerning the financing of the Shanghai-Nanking and the Peking-Newchwang Railways. Thus, by November, 1898, the British had secured nine railroad concessions totaling 2,800 miles; the Russians, three concessions, 1,500 miles; the Belgians, one concession, 650 miles; and the French, three concessions, 400 miles.[8]

These developments, culminating in the spring and summer of 1898, made it quite evi-

[8] Details on railroad concessions in E-tu Zen Sun, *Chinese Railways and British Interests, 1898-1911* (1954).

dent that the integrity of China was worth very little. Germany, Russia, and France had all expressed great respect for this principle, but their leaseholds and their railroad and non-alienation agreements indicated that these protestations were not to be taken seriously. It was obvious that an era of special and exclusive privilege prevailed in China. Britain disliked the tendency, for she had more to gain in an open market where all traded on terms of equality. But no power, not even the United States, would align itself with the British. Consequently, Downing Street, having protested, decided to join the robbers.[9] In London, opponents of this policy of imitation spoke in sarcastic terms of "Port Arthur Balfour" and "a triumph of diplomatic incompetency." The opposition called Wei-hai-wei, "Woe! Woe! Woe!" The fact was that the four great powers of Europe had begun the business of tampering with Chinese sovereignty. To be sure, each of the leasehold agreements carefully reserved to China her full sovereignty in the leased areas. But, as Langer has said, "This was mere camouflage and the statesmen knew it." The most serious phase of the business was that there was no unity of purpose within China herself, no constructive program of reform and resistance, and no able leadership.

HUMILIATION COMPOUNDED

By the end of 1898 it appeared that the break-up of China was at hand. Since 1840 her great Confucian society had suffered successive military defeats; she had been subjected to the unequal treaty system; her influence and control over the tributary states had been destroyed; and as the century drew to a close her strategic harbors had become foreign naval bases. For half a century her foreign trade had been dominated by Western merchants and now Western industry, beginning with the railroads

and mines, would be built, administered, and controlled by aliens. The naval leaseholds and the railroad zones in the various spheres of influence were quasi-colonial areas governed and policed by the West. To informed and thoughtful Chinese as well as to many in the outside world there seemed little reason to believe that either the Manchus or their empire could long survive these major assaults by the forces of imperialism.[10]

THE PHILIPPINES

While the great scramble for leaseholds and spheres of influence was engulfing China, the United States was projecting Manifest Destiny into East Asia. It has been said with some truth that in the months preceding May, 1898, no idea was so remote from the mind of the American people as the conquest and annexation of the Philippine Islands. Yet within the following year the United States had taken a great Asiatic territory 6,000 miles across the Pacific from San Francisco, and in the process had projected itself into the main currents of world politics. These stirring events came just at the moment when Europe seemed bent on the dismemberment of China.

[9] Russian action in Manchuria could only be halted by war and British foreign policy showed no inclination to pursue such a course with geography favoring the Russian position. Japan's gain in all this concession-hunting was a pledge by China that she would not alienate to any other power any part of Fukien province opposite Formosa.

[10] The role of foreign investment in China's economic development was to become increasingly important and controversial in the twentieth century. Certainly during the past 100 years economic contact with the West had been important but was hardly the only factor affecting the Chinese economy. The most common interpretation, especially by Chinese, has been that the foreign economic intrusion was detrimental to the Chinese economy—economic imperialism designed to subjugate China to the West. The most commonly used arguments in support of this view are: (1) foreign trade and investment ruined Chinese handicraft industries and disturbed agriculture; (2) foreign trade and investment drained wealth from China; and (3) foreign enterprises in China enjoyed special advantages which placed Chinese-owned modern enterprises at a hopeless disadvantage. These arguments against the foreign economic impact were believed strongly by the Manchu government in the last decades of the nineteenth century, as well as by more recent governments. Actually, the evidence now available tends to challenge the validity of all these arguments. Chiming Hou, *Foreign Investment and Economic Development in China, 1840-1937* (1965).

Americans were long familiar with the acquisition of contiguous territory. The nineteenth century was filled with the territorial advance of Americans through Louisiana and Florida, through Texas to the Rio Grande and California, and across the plains of Kansas to Oregon. The movement was completed by mid-century; now the business of Americans, so it was said, was to remain at home to develop what they possessed. Yet, a new overseas expansion had been foreshadowed. In Seward's purchase of Alaska, 1867,[11] there was the suggestion of the earlier ideas of Commodore Perry in Japan and Peter Parker in China that the United States needed coaling and naval stations on the Pacific. As early as 1854 President Pierce and Secretary of State Marcy tried but failed to annex the Hawaiian islands by treaty. The Midway islands were easier marks; a thousand miles northwest of Hawaii, they were occupied by an American naval force in August, 1867. In 1878 the American Navy acquired the use of a harbor in the Samoan islands of the South Pacific, and a decade later the state department resisted German encroachment there with vigor.[12] This official American interest in Samoa and the harbor of Pago Pago, 5,600 miles from Panama, was significant because it was an

... assertion by the United States, not merely of a willingness, but even of a right to take part in determining the fate of a remote and semi-barbarous people whose possessions lay far outside the traditional sphere of American political interests.[13]

And, if Americans previously had not been

seriously interested in annexing Hawaii, the Senate in 1887 secured an equivalent—the exclusive right for the United States to use Pearl Harbor as a naval station; by 1893, Americans were debating the proposals of the Harrison administration to bring the islands under the American flag. Against the pro-expansionist arguments of Captain Alfred T. Mahan—that the islands controlled the commerce of the North Pacific and were strategically essential—were those of the anti-expansionists and anti-annexationists: men such as Carl Schurz, E. L. Godkin, editor of *The Nation,* and James Gordon Bennett, Jr., publisher of the Democratic *New York Herald.* This opposition to expansion expressed views running the gamut from the constitutional and ideological objections of Schurz to the polemics of Godkin who asserted that if Hawaii were admitted to the Union,

... men would come into our Senate worse than those from Nevada, Wyoming and Idaho and which will be sent from Utah, Arizona, New Mexico and Oklahoma after they are admitted into the Union.[14]

THE NEW MANIFEST DESTINY

In the decades immediately preceding the threatened partition of China the popular American mind had not kept pace with "the march of events in the Pacific." The official arm of the United States had carried the Stars and Stripes far afield, to Alaska and the Aleutians, to Midway and to Samoa, and to Pearl Harbor. Yet the vast majority of Americans had no interest in these places, no understanding of why their government was projecting itself into those distant fields, and certainly no thought of setting up a colony in Asia. Disciples of a New Manifest Destiny there were, but they were few compared with those Americans who followed the more timid philosophy of Grover Cleveland, called by the expansionists "the Buffalo lilliputian!"[15] Even American "big business,"

---

[11] On the Alaska purchase, see V. J. Farrar, *The Annexation of Russian America to the United States* (1937); F. A. Golder, "The Purchase of Alaska," *American Historical Review,* 25 (1920), 411-25; T. A. Bailey, "Why the United States Purchased Alaska," *Pacific Historical Review,* 3 (1934), 39-49; and the popular account in F. R. Dulles, *America in the Pacific* (1932), Chapter 6.

[12] George H. Ryden, *The Foreign Policy of the United States in Relation to Samoa* (1933), Chapters 7-9.

[13] John Bassett Moore, in *The Cambridge Modern History,* VII, 663.

[14] E. L. Godkin, "Hawaii," *The Nation,* 56 (1883), 96.

[15] For further readings on the beginnings of American imperialism in the Pacific, see Julius W. Pratt, *Expansionists of 1898* (1936),* Chapter 1,

usually considered the spearhead of imperialism, was not of one mind. In 1893 no less a person than the vice-president of the Great Northern Railroad was saying publicly that the Chinese

. . . is as poor as a rat, and has nothing with which to pay for our high-priced products except silk handkerchiefs and bamboo pipes. . . . The Great Northern is coming . . . to do business with the Pacific slope, not with Asia.

"The New Manifest Destiny"; H. W. Bradley, "The American Frontier in Hawaii," *Proceedings, Pacific Coast Branch, American Historical Association* (1930) 135-50; Allan Nevins, *Grover Cleveland* (1934), Chapter 30; C. C. Tansill, *The Foreign Policy of Thomas F. Bayard, 1885-1897* (1940), Chapter 12; A. T. Volwiler, "Harrison, Blaine, and American Foreign Policy, 1889-1893," *American Philosophical Society Proceedings,* 79 (1938), 637-48; and studies cited in note 1.

[16] See A. Whitney Griswold, *The Far Eastern Policy of the United States* (1938),* 8. Thomas J.

Nevertheless, a new far eastern policy for the United States was taking shape in the minds of some Americans. It voiced a point of view that added new political ideas to old commercial ones.[16] The patron saint of expansion, John Louis O'Sullivan, close associate of Polk, Pierce,

---

McCormick, *The China Market: America's Quest for Informal Empire, 1893-1901* (1967)* explores the background of the decisions to annex Hawaii, Guam, and the Philippines, and to dispatch the Open Door Notes. He concludes that American action was influenced less by the accidents of war, pressures of public opinion, or force of personalities than by an evolving purpose on the part of the Cleveland and McKinley administrations to discover ways to assist in the development of American foreign trade. David Healy, *US Expansionism: the Imperialist Urge in the 1890's* (1970) holds that seeking an island empire in the Pacific was a new departure, not just an extension of the earlier commercialism.

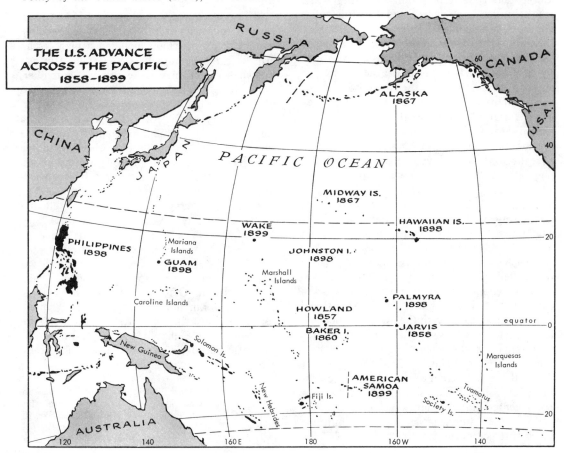

THE U.S. ADVANCE ACROSS THE PACIFIC 1858-1899

and Buchanan and coiner of the phrase "Manifest Destiny," died in 1895; but his philosophy was kept alive by John W. Burgess of Columbia University, under whom Theodore Roosevelt sat as a student, by Senator Albert J. Beveridge, and by Captain Alfred Thayer Mahan, whose lectures at the Naval War College were later published under the title, *The Influence of Sea Power upon History*. The composite doctrine, the larger policy, that emerged from the writings and speeches of these and other men was that the United States had come of age; that it could no longer be held within the old continental borders; that the commerce of the world was beckoning to American enterprise; and that benighted areas and backward people were calling to the beneficent forces in American civilization. The United States could no longer ignore the responsibilities of the "white man's burden" to civilize and to Christianize less fortunate peoples. There was also the additional thought that if, in the course of doing all this, some Americans made an honest profit in the new business fields, so much the better.

To a notable degree the stage was set for new adventures in American foreign policy when, on April 19, 1898, the Congress of the United States passed a joint resolution that precipitated the Spanish-American war. Actually, the roots of this war were connected only remotely, if at all, with the white man's burden and the larger policy it entailed. There were few Americans in the spring of 1898 who entertained any notion that the war with Spain would place the United States among the great colonial powers, much less that her new colonies would lie on the fringe of Asia. There was in fact no official suggestion that, if war came, it would lead to colonies at all. On the contrary, the war resolution voiced traditional principles associated with the Monroe Doctrine. It stated that Cuba was and ought to be free "of right"; it demanded the withdrawal of Spain from Cuba; it instructed the president to secure these ends by use of the armed forces; and it expressly denied any intent on the part of the United States to annex Cuba.

Thus the American policy and purpose which emerged during and immediately following the Spanish-American war were not a direct result of the vague shibboleths of the "larger policy" implied in the call to a new Manifest Destiny. In reality, they had a much clearer identity. The condition of the American economy after 1870, culminating in the panic of 1893, had suggested to some industrialists and politicians that industrial overproduction could only be cured through overseas markets. Therefore foreign markets had to be kept open to insure equal commercial opportunity for Americans. In the vast Pacific, so it was said, there would be a need for island stepping-stones to major markets, such as China, which, defeated by Japan in 1895, would surely awaken and throw open her doors to American commerce. It made no difference that China had not given the slightest evidence that she intended to do this.

These ideas also found support in the planning of American naval strategists for a possible war with Spain, which included a plan for an attack on the Spanish fleet at Manila. This was known to McKinley as early as September, 1897. Thus a Pacific offensive was an accepted plan when Theodore Roosevelt became assistant secretary of the Navy. Roosevelt wanted a war to annex the Philippines, and the evidence suggests that not only he but others, including perhaps the president himself, were not unaware that the conflict could result in annexation. If the opportunity came it would not be unwelcome to many industrialists, who felt that nothing, at least, should be done to impede it. Nevertheless, these speculative factors appear to have been a secondary consideration in the shaping of war plans. The main objective was quick and effective damage to Spain. When Roosevelt in October, 1897, sent George Dewey to command the American Asian squadron, and later cabled him to destroy the Spanish fleet in the Philippines in the event of war, the basic purpose was to win a war, not necessarily to open a market in China.[17]

[17] The last word has not been written on American thinking and resulting policy in this period. On the role of naval interests, see W. R. Braisted, *The United States Navy in the Pacific, 1897-1909* (1958). Walter LaFeber, *The New Em-*

When war did come, Dewey moved his fleet thirty miles up the China coast into the waters of Mirs Bay, "an isolated locality" where, "independent of international complications," supplies could be received secretly and temporary repairs effected. "We appreciated that so loosely organized a national entity as the Chinese Empire could not enforce the neutrality laws," wrote Dewey.[18]

Dewey's fleet sailed for the Philippines on April 27. On the morning of May 1, while it was yet dark, his ships passed the guns of Corregidor and sent the Spanish fleet to the bottom as it clung to its base at Cavite. Dewey promptly established a blockade of the bay and city of Manila and informed Washington that the city could be taken, but that 5,000 men would be needed to hold it. In Washington, the decision to send troops to the support of Dewey involved many questions. No clear political policy as to the future of the Philippines had yet emerged, and even the military policy for the immediate future was in a formative and tentative stage. For what specific purposes were the troops to be sent? Were they to engage in the conquest of the entire archipelago? How many troops should be sent? Illogically, the last question was answered first. The fact was that Dewey's dramatic victory had taken the country by surprise. Neither the government nor the people were prepared for the vital decisions that his victory demanded. Thus McKinley's cabinet, groping for an immediate and long-range policy, dispatched troops to Manila; by the end of July some 8,000 had arrived. This was to make possible the eventual capture of Manila, but it did not clarify the political atmosphere in the islands, where Filipino nationalists, with American encouragement and assistance, had taken the field against Spain and, with Dewey's approval, harassed the outskirts of Manila while the American commodore awaited the arrival of an American army. On August 12, 1898, a few hours after a protocol of peace had been signed in Washington, Manila surrendered to American forces.

THE EMBARRASSMENTS OF VICTORY

From May 1, the date of Dewey's naval victory, until February 6, 1899, when the Senate ratified the treaty of Paris by a margin of only two votes, the government and the people of the United States were embarrassed by a naval victory which had given them a tropical archipelago and some six to seven million "little brown wards." At first the experience was intoxicating. When the news came of Dewey's triumph,

. . . the country went wild with excitement. "Dewey Days" were celebrated in the principal cities. Streets were renamed for Dewey. Young women wore "Dewey" sailor hats, sipped "Dewey" cocktails, chewed "Dewey Chewies"—a new brand of gum—and wrote letters on "Dewey blue" stationery. Men smoked cigars made of Sampson Havana filler and Dewey Manila wrappers, while those who were so inclined resorted to the corner saloon and called for Dewey brand whiskey. Meanwhile the President notified Congress that: "At this unsurpassed achievement the great heart of our nation throbs, not with boasting or with greed

pire: An Interpretation of American Expansion (1963)* sets forth the economic underpinnings of American decisions. Thomas McCormick, "Insular Imperialism and the Open Door," *Pacific Historical Review,* 32 (1963), 155-69 applies LaFeber's insights to the annexation of Pacific islands. A lively argument persists between the economic determinists and their critics. The latter admit that the economic transformation of the United States provided stimulus to the new policy, but that too much stress has been given to economic arguments. Some of the economic arguments were simply absurd save as corollaries of "duty and destiny." In assessing the force of economic factors, it has been pointed out that the determinists often neglect the differences in means advocated by those who were agreed on the need for increased government aid to business. Some were annexationists, mild or extreme. Others advocated expanding foreign markets through an assertive diplomatic service, or reform of the consular service, or construction of an isthmian canal. These distinctions are important since they suggest that the emerging American drive to the Western Pacific was based less on rational calculation than it has sometimes been said to be. Note the comments of Marilyn Blatt Young, "American Expansion, 1870-1900: The Far East," in *Towards a New Past: Dissenting Essays in American History,* Barton J. Bernstein, ed. (1968),* 176-201.

[18]*Autobiography of George Dewey* (1916), 175-90.

of conquest, but with deep gratitude that this triumph has come in a just cause. . . .[19]

But the problem of what to do with these Oriental fruits of victory still remained.

THE EMERGENCE OF A POLICY

The expansionists wanted annexation of all the Philippines. Senator Henry Cabot Lodge urged this policy on McKinley and his secretary of state, Judge William R. Day. Then, early in July, the Congress, by joint resolution, annexed the Hawaiian islands; by the time Manila fell, public opinion and pressure groups were swinging definitely toward expansionism. There were petitions to Congress and to the state department picturing the Philippines as the key to far eastern commerce. Publications of the Protestant churches favored annexation almost unanimously, for church editors saw God's hand and new missionary fields in Dewey's victory.

McKinley was attaching more and more importance to public opinion. The earlier public clamor for war with Spain was very fresh in his mind. It was easy for him to be persuaded that the people wanted the Philippines. Indeed, some historians go so far as to say that McKinley thought only of his own and his party's leadership, and was concerned only incidentally with real or imagined interests abroad.[20]

Powerful forces in international politics also exerted pressure on McKinley and his cabinet. Great Britain and Germany, in their bitter colonial rivalry, were each determined that the Philippines should not fall into the hands of the other if by chance the United States turned them loose. Great Britain, whose attitude when the war began was in doubt, later urged Washington to retain the islands. She did not wish to be placed in a position where she would have to oppose German claims directly. Japan's attitude at the time, though not very significant, was an added voice urging American annexation.

Unquestionably, the Germans were interested in the Philippines. They had hoped to prevent the war and were alarmed by signs of Anglo-American friendship and the prospects of American commercial rivalry in Asia. During the war German public opinion, favorable to Spain, had aroused the suspicions of Americans, who were still sensitive over Germany's threatened encroachments in Samoa. Then, too, there was a story, widely believed, that at Manila the German admiral, von Diederich, had interfered with Dewey's blockade, and had withdrawn only when threatened by a British squadron. This was a far cry from what actually happened, but the story served nonetheless to arouse American resentment, and so to support the advocates of American annexation.[21]

The protocol of peace, drawn up by McKinley's cabinet and signed with Spain on August 12, was diplomatically vague concerning the future status of the islands, though it foreshadowed occupation of at least part of them. The annexationist implications of the protocol were soon reflected in the appointment by McKinley of a peace commission that was dominated by expansionists. While the commissioners sailed toward Paris, John Hay was crossing from the London embassy to become secretary of state and to be one of the decisive influences on McKinley's final decision (October 26): "The cession must be of the whole archipelago or none."

The treaty of Paris was not signed until December 10, 1898, for Spain's opposition to relinquishment of the Philippines was persistent and bitter. The Spanish commissioners had not been slow to point out that in their view the United States could not claim the Philippines by right of conquest, since Manila had been captured several hours after the signing of the protocol of peace. As a compromise, the treaty, which set up American sovereignty in the Philippines, Puerto Rico, and Guam and provided for Spain's withdrawal from Cuba, also stipulated that the United States pay Spain $20 million.

[19] H. R. Lynn, *The Genesis of America's Philippine Policy*, unpublished manuscript, University of Kentucky (1935), 8.

[20] See Ernest R. May, *Imperial Democracy: the Emergence of America as a Great Power* (1961).*

[21] T. A. Bailey, "Dewey and the Germans at Manila Bay," *American Historical Review*, 45 (1939), 59-81; L. B. Shippee, "Germany and the Spanish-American War," *ibid.*, 30 (1925), 754-77.

One more hurdle remained: ratification of the treaty by the Senate. This was secured February 6, 1899, by the narrow margin of two votes. It was preceded by some of the most dramatic debates in the Senate, in the press, and on the public platform. The arguments centered primarily on the Philippines. In Congress the opposition to expansion and imperialism was led by Senator George F. Hoar of Massachusetts. Although his eloquence in opposing imperialism failed to curb the popular enthusiasm for empire either within or outside Congress, the result was in doubt until news of the outbreak of the Filipino insurrection against American control (February 4) raised the issue of what was called "national honor." This questionable slogan strengthened the position of the annexationists. For better or worse, the decision to keep the islands was one of the most momentous of American history, though, as time was to show, it was not necessarily one of the wisest. The United States had acquired a dependency that was in revolt against its new master. The country had fought a war to free Cuba from Spain, and this it had done; but it had also gained a colony in the far western Pacific where young nationalism was as opposed to America as it had been to Spain. Moreover, this colony was acquired at a rather inconvenient moment. If the United States had any design to protest the inroads of the powers on China, she could now do so with little grace or effect. She had herself captured an empire in East Asia.[22]

FOR FURTHER READING

Diplomacy of Imperialism. Paul H. Clyde, *International Rivalries in Manchuria* (rev. ed., 1928), a general survey of international relations. For more specialized studies of the European powers and Japan see: Philip Joseph, *Foreign Diplomacy in China, 1894-1900* (1928); R. Stanley McCordock, *British Far Eastern Policy 1894-1900* (1931); L. K. Young, *British Policy in China, 1895-1902* (1970), based on recently opened archives; John F. Cady, *The Roots of French Imperialism in Eastern Asia* (1954), a thorough and able study. D. J. Dallin, *The Rise of Russia in Asia* (1949); Andrew Malozemoff, *Russian Far Eastern Policy, 1881-1904, with Special Emphasis on the Causes of the Russo-Japanese War* (1958); Akira Iriye, *Pacific Estrangement: Japanese and American Expansion, 1897-1911* (1972); G. A. Ballard, *Influence of the Sea on the Political History of Japan* (1921); Francis Hilary Conroy, *The Japanese Frontier in Hawaii, 1868-1898* (1953); T. A. Bailey, "Japan's Protest against the Annexation of Hawaii," *Journal of Modern History* 3 (1931), 46-61.

Role of the United States. Kwang-ching Liu, "America and China: The Late Nineteenth Century," in *American-East Asian Relations,* James Thomson and Ernest May, eds. (1972), an extended introduction to historical literature. Varying interpretations of the origins and course of American expansion may be sampled in the works cited in various footnotes in this chapter and in Walter LaFeber, *The New American Empire: An Interpretation of American Expansion, 1860-1898* (1963).

Trade, Investment, Treaties. See two basic studies by C. F. Remer, *The Foreign Trade of China* (1926), and *Foreign Investments in China* (1933). Cheng Yu-kwei, *Foreign Trade and Industrial Development of China: An Historical and Integrated Analysis through 1948* (1956), a convenient factual summary covering the century of the Western impact, but the interpretations are open to serious qualifications. John V. A. MacMurray, ed., *Treaties and Agreements With and Concerning China, 1894-1919* (2 vols., 1921); and W.W. Willoughby, *Foreign Rights and Interests in China* (2 vols., rev. ed., 1927), basic reference works.

[22] Rubin F. Weston, *Racism in U. S. Imperialism: the Influence of Racial Assumptions on American Foreign Policy, 1893-1946* (1972) concludes that the inhabitants of the new insular possessions (Hawaii, the Philippines, Guam) were regarded as colored, hence inferior—a view shared by both imperialists and anti-imperialists in 1898.

A Reformation That Failed: China, 1890-1901

16

The final decade of the nineteenth century was one of the great turning points in the history of modern China. It was in that decade that China took her first faltering and, for the moment, ineffective steps toward creating a new society. In this effort she was responding to the Western impact and to the ills and the needs of her own ailing society, just as half a century earlier the Japanese were also reacting to the internal demands of their own society in responding to the West.

There were many reasons why China attempted to move in a new direction at this particular time. Since 1860 Peking had made continuing efforts to deal with major crises both domestic (the T'ai-p'ing and other rebellions) and foreign (pressure by the Western powers). The ideology behind these first efforts had been entirely traditional. The Chinese called the T'ung-chih period (1862-1874) a restoration (*chung-hsing*), since it was essentially an appeal to the past. Its only innovations were some feeble efforts to modernize the fighting forces and to create the beginnings of a foreign office (the Tsungli Yamen), both of which, designed to be temporary measures, did not contemplate fundamental institutional change. They were tactics in the movement

called self-strengthening. Since China's problems were still considered traditional problems, they sought to solve them by the traditional methods of revitalizing and applying the virtues of the Confucian system. Gradually, as the ineffectiveness of the restoration became more obvious (as demonstrated by the defeat of China by France in 1885), the need for more meaningful reform gained some acceptance. But the idea of change was so unorthodox that it was usually disguised in various ways to make it more palatable to the traditional mind. The process was exemplified by the career of Chang Chih-tung.

CHANG CHIH-TUNG AND REFORM

By the 1880's Chang Chih-tung was fast becoming one of the outstanding regional administrators of China. He had a brilliant scholastic background and was an eloquent exponent of traditional Chinese culture. His influence in the scholar-bureaucracy is suggested by a career in which he served as governor-general at Canton (1885-1889), at Nanking (1894-1896), and at Wuhan (the cities of Wuchang, Hanyang, and Hankow) (1889-1894 and 1896-1907). China's defeat by France turned Chang into an advocate of modernization. His program in the last years of the century called for industrializing, opening mines, building foundries, constructing railroads, and modernizing education to include Western technology as well as the Confucian classics. His overall purpose was to save Chinese society and the Manchu dynasty by using Western technology, but especially by reviving all that was best in the Confucian system. In this program there would be no place for Western political, economic, or social institutions—such as democracy, with its constitutional monarchies, parliaments, doctrines of the rights of the people, individual freedom, and free enterprise. It was a plan, to use Chang's phrase, of "Chinese learning for the essential principles, Western learning for the practical applications." The phrase was at best a dubious formula, but it was an effective shield against traditional critics. Thus Chang Chih-tung represented a step toward reform but reform that would somehow preserve the traditional culture.[1]

BIRTH OF RADICAL IDEAS

While a few Chinese statesmen, such as Li Hung-chang and Chang Chih-tung, were proposing to use Western technological methods to achieve Chinese ends (a strong Confucianism), others were beginning to suggest that this limited formula was impractical and inadequate, and that China must grapple with the fearful idea of institutional reform, questioning even the Confucian foundations. For example, Kuo Sung-tao, China's minister to Britain and France (1876-1878), reported when he returned to Peking that these countries had a distinct and illustrious history of their own, together with political and economic institutions which had made them prosperous. Such institutions were worthy, he noted, of careful study. But Kuo's ideas were regarded by his colleagues at Peking as preposterous and disgraceful.

Another Chinese whose views were remarkable for his time was Wang T'ao (1828-1897). Because of his early favorable views on the T'ai-p'ings he was regarded as a subversive. As an independent scholar and journalist closely associated with the foreigners at Shanghai and Hong Kong, Wang assisted James Legge in the translation of *The Confucian Classics.* He spent two years in Europe, wrote a book on the Franco-Prussian war, delivered a lecture at Oxford in 1868, visited Japan, and founded his own newspaper in Hong Kong, in which he launched editorial attacks on the Manchu-Chinese administration of the time. While never losing his love of Confucian civilization, he became an ardent admirer of Western law and constitutional government on the British model. Though his comments on Western politics were often acute, his observations on social matters may have been overdrawn, as when he wrote that "most women in the state of Massachusetts have preferred to get concubines for their husbands."[2]

Another advocate of reform in methods was Hsueh Fu-ch'eng, successively secretary to Tseng Kuo-fan and Li Hung-chang, and later a member of China's diplomatic service at London and Paris. Hsueh remained a staunch opponent of those Western social customs, such as freedom of choice in marriage, which he thought honored woman but degraded man;

[1] Another advocate of conservative reform was Weng T'ung-ho (1830-1904). Weng, who had all the prestige of a Confucian scholar-official, was tutor to both the T'ung-chih and the Kuang-hsu emperors. He was deeply loyal to the dynasty and to the Confucian tradition, but came to believe that neither would survive without reform. His career illustrated the intense personal rivalries within the ranks of officialdom: one of Weng's purposes was to seize leadership in the reform movement from Li Hung-chang and Chang Chih-tung. Note Ho Ping-ti, "Weng T'ung-ho and the 'One Hundred Days of Reform,'" *Far Eastern Quarterly,* 10 (1951), 125-35.

[2] See excerpts from Wang's writings in Ssu-yu Teng and John K. Fairbank, *China's Response to the West* (1954),* 137-40; and Henry McAleavy, *Wang T'ao: The Life and Writings of a Displaced Person* (1953). See also Paul A. Cohen, "Wang T'ao and Incipient Chinese Nationalism," *Journal of Asian Studies,* 26 (1967), 559-74. A central problem in the mind of a nineteenth-century Chinese intellectual was that by tradition he tended to view China as a world rather than as a nation. Thus China was not a part of something bigger. Consequently, the Western invitation to China to join the world was incomprehensible, if not impudent. As Chinese reformers moved toward a concept of nationalism, their attitudes toward the West often combined an acute resentment and a grudging respect.

but, like Wang, he saw in constitutional government the answer to China's ills. In these views Wang and Hsueh went far beyond technological reforms. Hsueh, like many of the reformers who followed him, was also concerned with the philosophical problem of finding precedent in Chinese history for institutional reform. If such precedent were there, then China could safely learn from the West without surrendering her own foundations. To those who clung to the traditional methods Hsueh remarked, "We cannot expect to excel others [the Westerners] merely by sitting upright in a dignified attitude."

These men and other reformers, such as Ho Kai (or Ho Ch'i, 1859-1917), disillusioned by the self-strengthening philosophy of most officials, stressed not only the need to develop Chinese commerce, industry, and agriculture, but also to find political solutions to China's ills. Thus Chinese reformism acquired a new orientation, demanding political change and parliamentary institutions, as early as the decade that preceded the Sino-Japanese war.[3]

CHRISTIAN MISSIONS AND REFORM

One of the important sources from which the Chinese acquired their ideas on reform was the Christian missionary movement, especially as carried on by British and American Protestants. What the missionaries said and did shaped in major degree the ideas that Chinese intellectuals held concerning the West. Moreover, the Protestant missions came to have a broad social as well as a religious purpose. They were concerned to improve through education the lot of the convert in this world as well as in the world to come. From the earliest days, schools were

[3] Lloyd E. Eastman, "Political Reformism in China Before the Sino-Japanese War," *Journal of Asian Studies,* 27 (1968), 695-710. It was the humiliation suffered by China in the Sino-French war of 1884-1885 that suggested the barrenness of the self-strengthening philosophy and the need for institutional change.

regarded as an essential part of the missionary establishment. Shortly after 1830 two of the first American Protestant missionaries at Canton, David Abeel (1804-1846) and E. C. Bridgman (1801-1861), opened a school and began publication of the famous *Chinese Repository* (1832-1851). The first American missionary hospital and medical school at Canton was the work of Peter Parker (1804-1888). After the second treaty settlement (1858-1860), which legalized inland missions, there was a marked expansion in both Catholic and Protestant establishments. English and American Protestant missionary scholars took the lead with the assistance of Chinese associates in publishing Chinese translations and digests of Western books on history, literature, and science. Among the British contributing to this cultural invasion were William Muirhead (1822-1900), Joseph Edkins (1823-1905), Alexander Wylie (1815-1887), James Legge (1815-1897), translator of the Confucian classics, and Timothy Richard (1845-1919), who at the invitation of Li Hung-chang edited a Chinese daily at Tientsin. The Americans included W. A. P. Martin (1827-1916), S. Wells Williams (1812-1884), John Fryer (1839-1923), and Young J. Allen (1836-1907). Fryer and Allen compiled and translated into Chinese the first textbook in science for Chinese students.[4]

The cultural and intellectual influence of the missionary in support of reform, however, was limited in many ways. His direct contacts were confined to the treaty ports and a few inland posts. He reached only a handful of the scholar-official and gentry classes, by whom he was regarded as a subversive influence, especially when he sought to protect his converts from the course of Chinese justice—a practice especially notable among Catholic missionaries. Furthermore, the religious role of the missionary became in the Chinese mind inseparable from Westernization in general. The consequence was that the growing anti-missionary

[4] See Teng and Fairbank, *China's Response,* 133-93.

movement from 1860 onward retarded the entire process of learning from the West and thereby hindered any genuine reform movement.[5]

K'ANG YU-WEI

The man who was to dramatize the cause of institutional and thus radical reform was K'ang Yu-wei (1858-1927), a native of Canton and member of a scholarly family. His education was thoroughly grounded in Neo-Confucianism. His interest in Western studies dated from the early 1880's when he first saw Hong Kong and the International Settlement at Shanghai. If the British could administer these areas efficiently on the borders of China, he reasoned that their home country must be a model of government. From this point on, K'ang immersed himself in the study of Western books in Chinese translation. He came to the conclusion that what the West called progress was not only desirable but also imperative. From this position he moved to a reinterpretation of classical tradition, challenging the Neo-Confucian orthodoxy as a philosophy based on spurious texts. The result was his portrayal of Confucius as a reformer, thus creating the philosophical foundation for a reform movement—a Chinese (Confucian) justification for institutional change. Confucianism in K'ang's thought was to be revised, not abandoned.

[5] The missionary was both a source of ideas on reform and a target of Chinese attack. He was valued by some Chinese reformers for the ideas he might contribute to a new China, but he was resented by the gentry-official class as an agent of foreign and subversive doctrines, religious and political. It is hardly surprising that the Ch'ing dynasty was never able to deal effectively with the problem; internally it was faced by anti-missionary riots and externally it was faced by demands from the powers for concessions and for the dismissal of officials who failed to protect the missionary from popular Chinese ire. See Edmund S. Wehrle, *Britain, China and the Antimissionary Riots, 1891-1900* (1966). How American pressures were exerted is treated in George E. Paulsen, "The Szechwan Riots of 1895 and American 'Missionary Diplomacy,'" *Journal of Asian Studies,* 28 (1969), 285-98.

K'ang Yu-wei's attacks in his teaching and in his first books on the officially-accepted interpretation of the Classics were thoroughly upsetting to the whole Chinese world of scholar-officials. In 1894 the government seized and burned the printing blocks of his books. Nevertheless, the following year K'ang passed the metropolitan examination over strenuous efforts to fail him. He had reached the top of the ladder of learning. These events in his career coincided with China's defeat in the Sino-Japanese war. In 1897, the year in which Germany seized Kiaochou, K'ang was recommended to the young and troubled emperor by moderate reformers at the court.

THE HUNDRED DAYS OF REFORM

It was this march of events—China's defeat in 1895 and the subsequent scramble for leaseholds and spheres of interest between 1896 and 1898—rather than the strength of the reform movement itself that unexpectedly plunged K'ang Yu-wei and his associates into power, and as rapidly into defeat, exile, or death. In the spring of 1898 the question of reform as presented in the memorials of K'ang and others touched the imagination of a few progressive officials at the Peking court and, more importantly, of the Kuang-hsu emperor. Since 1889 this weak, ineffectual, and inexperienced but well-intentioned young sovereign had been ruling in his own right. Frightened by the tidings of disaster and emboldened by the urgings of the reformers, the emperor announced the need for reform in a decree promulgated on June 11, 1898. K'ang Yu-wei, Liang Ch'i-ch'ao, one of K'ang's students, and others were appointed to advise the sovereign on proposed reforms and K'ang was allowed to submit memorials directly to the throne. The result was an unparalleled flood of ill-devised decrees known as the "Hundred Days of Reform." The problems tackled were as varied as the ills of this sick civilization. China was to have able diplomatic representation abroad, and officials were ordered to recommend men "who are not enveloped in the narrow circle of bigoted conservatism." China was to have a new order in which all the nation would unite in a march to progress. High conservative officials were advised to seek education in Europe. The old education was to be replaced by "practical" subjects; temples and monasteries were to be made into modern schools and colleges in every province; a transportation and mining bureau was to be set up in Peking; the army was to be reorganized; useless government posts were to be abolished; foreign works on politics and science were to be translated. From June until September some forty decrees attempted to remake the old society. It is small wonder that the effort failed; the reformers lacked experience, and the young emperor was not a magician. Undoubtedly he meant well, but he was emotionally unstable and intellectually diffuse. He possessed no adequate appreciation of the practical difficulties of constructive reform or of the conservative forces, personified by the empress dowager, that would oppose him.[6]

THE CONSERVATIVE REACTION

The program of the One Hundred Days proposed extreme departures from hallowed Confucian heritage, but far more important in its immediate impact was the fact that this program struck at the vested interests of every conservative officeholder in the Manchu-Chinese administration. Manchus feared an ouster in favor of Chinese. The plan to turn monasteries into schools infuriated the clergy. Military reforms threatened incompetent officers of the Manchu banners and the Chinese Green Standard. Abolition of the old civil serv-

[6] See Meribeth E. Cameron, *The Reform Movement in China* (1931), Chapter 2. K'ang Yu-wei hoped to transform China within the framework of the Confucian tradition. He wanted reform and transformation as opposed to revolution, and he wished the people of China to be active framers of their political future. See Jung-pang Lo, ed. and trans., *K'ang Yu-wei: A Biography and a Symposium* (1967). Recent research on Chinese reform is presented in papers by Richard C. Howard, Yen-P'ing Hao, Hao Chang, Charlton M. Lewis, and John Schrecker in "The Chinese Movement of the 1890's: A Symposium," *Journal of Asian Studies*, 29 (1969), 7-54.

ice examinations as the only proper road to government appointment jeopardized holders of degrees who were seeking office. The abolition of useless offices affected a host of political favorites. If corruption (bribery) were done away with, most high officials would lose an important source of income. It all added up to the fact that conservatives were opposed to radical reform not only because it was unorthodox but also because it could destroy their positions and wealth. The net effect of the One Hundred Days was to unite the conservatives behind the empress dowager and the policy of self-strengthening, which had failed partly because it was no more than a form of creeping modernization.[7]

THE DOWAGER IN COMMAND

Since 1889 the empress dowager had lived in retirement at the Summer Palace, but her influence over the court, the weak emperor, and the administration was undiminished. As China's troubles increased after 1885 she had shown some disposition toward the moderate reforms of the self-strengthening movement, but she remained inflexibly opposed to any change she considered radical or subversive of her own power. Such power was based primarily on the philosophy of classical education with all it implied, and on institutionalized corruption. These bulwarks of her power were the chief targets of K'ang Yu-wei's program.

Accordingly, when she judged that the conservative opposition to the One Hundred Days had become sufficiently strong, she acted swiftly, with the aid of her Manchu military commander, Jung-lu. The Kuang-hsu emperor was forced into seclusion on the pretext of illness and the empress dowager assumed the regency. The One Hundred Days of Reform thus passed into history.

Many of the reformers suffered summary execution, but the leaders, K'ang Yu-wei and Liang Ch'i-ch'ao, escaped to British Hong Kong

[7] It was no coincidence that Chang Chih-tung's *Exhortation to Study* was printed and circulated by imperial order in 1898 in justification of self-strengthening as the approved road to China's salvation.

and Japan, where in safety they could read the decrees condemning them to death by "slicing." For ten years the Kuang-hsu emperor lived on, a prisoner of the regent empress dowager. That he was permitted even this existence was due, among other things, to the intervention of the powers, to the regent's fear of provoking the southern progressives, and to the desire to hide the fact that China was again being ruled by a woman.

REACTION AGAIN IN POWER

The collapse of the reform movement gave renewed evidence of the stubborn power and "the elegant perfumed ignorance" of the court reactionaries. Furthermore, the conflict at Peking for and against reform was merely one aspect of a complex struggle for power between Manchus and Chinese, between northern and southern factions at court, and between the personal ambitions of rival officials. In this context the empress dowager symbolized the craving for personal and dynastic power and the aroused inertia of the system-bound eunuchs and officials through whom her influence was maintained. In the closing months of 1898 it was the fashion among the foreigners in Peking to dismiss Kuang-hsu's reforms as a case of misguided zeal; in this light it was easier to understand the determination of the Chinese conservatives to have their way. At the same time the empress dowager never ceased to protest her own enthusiasm for reform.

The return of the empress dowager to power was coincident with a stiffening of the government's opposition to further foreign demands. In March, 1899, when Italy demanded the lease of San Men Bay and the setting aside of the greater part of Chekiang province as her sphere of influence, she received a polite but firm refusal. In fact, no further major concessions were secured by the powers during 1899 or the early months of 1900. Nevertheless, as the last days of 1899 approached, the Chinese scene was filled with dire forebodings. In addition to the naval leaseholds secured by Germany, Russia, France, and Great Britain, hardly a square foot of Chinese territory remained which was not claimed or about to be claimed as a sphere of influence. The Russians were ex-

tending their influence into Mongolia. From Shantung the Germans were looking westward into the northwest provinces. Great Britain was firmly entrenched in the great Yangtze valley. And France was expanding her concessionary rights in Yunnan, Kwangsi, and Kwangtung.

THE THREATENED PARTITION OF CHINA

The Sino-Japanese war of 1894-1895, precipitated a train of events which resulted in a movement threatening the partition of China. This development, against which the Manchu government seemed helpless, had, by 1899, reduced strategic areas in China to semi-colonial status. For example, Tsingtao, under lease, had become a German city protected by a German squadron; the Chinese derived such consolation as they might from the fact that sovereignty in the abstract was reserved to Peking. Beyond Tsingtao throughout populous Shantung province, the birthplace of Confucius and thus China's Holy Land, German capital had acquired a practical monopoly in railroad and mining development. Indeed, the stage was set in China for an era of special monopolistic privilege for German capital in Shantung, for Russian capital in Manchuria, for British capital in the Yangtze valley, and for French capital in the areas bordering Indochina.

This state of affairs would not have come about but for the inability of Peking to protect its territory and to enjoy the respect that power invites. In fact Peking was not only weak, it was growing weaker. There was no effective leadership in China's capital. Popular discontent among the masses suggested that the dynasty had lost the Mandate of Heaven, and that the foreigner, with his leaseholds, railways, and Christianity, was not looked upon by the Chinese people as an adequate substitute for Heaven's favor.[8] After 1898, the political and military impotence of Peking served as a constant invitation to the great powers in their competitive quests for Chinese markets that

[8] For background manifestations of political weakness and of anti-dynastic and anti-foreign reactions, see Paul H. Clyde, ed., *United States Policy Toward China: Diplomatic and Public Documents, 1839-1939* (1940; reissued 1964), Chapter 29.

could be controlled politically. Thus, once the first steps had been taken in 1897-1898 to cut the Chinese melon, once the leaseholds and spheres of influence had been acquired, the powers were under the temptation to cut deeper—to make "spheres" into protectorates, and protectorates into annexations. This threat to China's sovereign existence was an important by-product not only of China's weakness but also of that intense European rivalry which was to result finally in World War I.

THE OPEN DOOR POLICY

Against the background of this rivalry among the great powers, and of incompetency at Peking, the United States sought to protect its interests by proposing a doctrine designed to create a commercial market in China that was free and open to all.

The major interest of the powers in China during the nineteenth century had been commercial. After the first treaty settlement of 1842-1844, these commercial interests were pursued within the limitations imposed by the most-favored-nation clause contained in all the treaties. Commercial privileges or concessions extended by China to one power were thus automatically enjoyed by all. As a result, the principle of equal commercial opportunity was maintained with a fair measure of support from all the powers, and in particular from the United States and Great Britain.[9] When, in the winter of 1897-1898, Germany and Russia launched the scramble for naval leaseholds and spheres of influence, the British opposed the idea. They were confident that a free and open market for British commerce and capital was the best guarantee of their continued economic supremacy in China. Realizing, however, that it could not hope for success by playing a lone hand, the British government appealed to the

United States in March, 1898, and again in January, 1899, for some form of joint action to maintain what the British called an open door.[10] Neither President William McKinley nor Secretary of State John Sherman was disposed to act on the British suggestion for neither possessed any deep understanding of previous American policy in China. Accordingly, Britain went into the business of leaseholds (Kowloon extension and Wei-hai-wei) and spheres of influence (Yangtze valley) on a magnificent scale.

In the case of the British overtures, the United States was completely unresponsive to the call of a historic American policy. The principle of equality implied in most-favored-nation treatment was as old as American independence itself and had been applied in European as well as in far eastern treaties. The state department had been advised repeatedly by Ambassador John Hay in London and Minister Charles Denby in Peking that the leaseholds and the spheres threatened not only equal opportunity in commerce but the territorial and political integrity of China as well.

Only on the basis of a number of factors can this blindness of 1898 in failing to defend the principle of equal opportunity be explained. Principal among these were (1) Secretary Sherman's incompetence in diplomacy and his fear of being "used" by the British; (2) the preoccupation of government and people with Cuba and the Spanish-American war; and (3) the fact that America's material and commercial stake in China was small—hardly 2 percent of the total United States foreign trade. Consequently, it was with very hesitant steps that the American government moved to reassert its interests in its historic policy in China.[11] In the winter of 1898-1899, Lord Charles Beresford, returning to England from China, aroused his Ameri-

---

[9] The background of the British attitude is given in Lord Charles Beresford, *The Breakup of China* (1899). On the all-pervading comprador system by which Europeans and Americans conducted their business both economic and sometimes political in China, see Y. C. Wang, "Tu Yueh-Sheng (1888-1951): A Tentative Political Biography," *Journal of Asian Studies,* 26 (1967), 433-55.

[10] The relevant correspondence is treated in A. L. P. Dennis, *Adventures in American Diplomacy, 1896-1906* (1928), Chapter 8, with documents.

[11] The direction of American policy at this point was unclear. Edwin Conger, American minister at Peking, recommended in 1898 that the United States join the European powers, take possession of a port in China, and claim Chihli province as an American sphere.

can friends with a picture of China preserved by an Anglo-American open door policy. This idea appealed to American businessmen, especially after Dewey's victory at Manila Bay in May, 1898, as the concept of China as a free market accorded well with their interest in expanding American commerce in Asia.[12] The American government began to react to the pressure of these ideas in the fall and winter of 1898. The Anglophile John Hay was now secretary of state. McKinley told the Paris peace commission and the Congress that exclusive treatment could not be allowed to prejudice the sale of American products in China. But the President was still uncertain of his course; the second British overture for joint action on the open door policy was rebuffed in January, 1899, despite the fact that more than 1,000 American missionaries in China were at one with American business in wanting a "strong" policy from Washington.

Principal among the factors prompting the reassertion of America's traditional China policy was the threat to British commercial supremacy in China brought about by the success of the Russian, German, and French drives to create special positions for themselves through their respective spheres of influence. The British government had reacted to this threat by approaching Washington to seek a joint open door declaration; but at the same time it considered seriously, if reluctantly, the creation of its own sphere in the Yangtze valley. It was argued that, in the new era of railroad and mining enterprise in China, there was logic in a system of spheres of concentration as against an open door policy whereby the powers would be milling around jostling each other in the scramble for concessions. In other words, so the official British argument ran, it would be useful to keep an open door in matters of trade in consumer goods while at the same time protecting future capital investment through the principle of spheres. As a result, the British were not particularly disturbed when Sherman turned them down in March, 1898; but John Hay, then the American ambassador to London, was. Hay knew nothing about China, but he thought it poor business to rebuff the British needlessly. The net result was

that when Hay became secretary of state in the summer of 1898 his thoughts were moving toward an open door policy at the very moment when, unbeknown to him, the British government, while giving the idea lip service, was actually moving away from it by appropriating a Yangtze valley sphere and by leasing the Kowloon extension across from Hong Kong.

At this point an Englishman, Alfred Hippisley, second ranking official of the Chinese Imperial Maritime Customs Service, returned to England on leave and urged upon his friend W. W. Rockhill, Hay's new adviser on far eastern affairs, that the United States do something to preserve an open door for commerce in China. The spheres, he said, might as well be accepted as realities and, if they applied only to railroads and mines, might do little harm. What he feared was that other sphere-holding powers would tamper with the Chinese customs administration as the British had already done at Kowloon. These ideas made a strong impression on Rockhill and Hay. At Hay's suggestion, Rockhill prepared recommendations for a policy based on Hippisley's ideas, and these recommendations were approved by the president.[13]

THE HAY OPEN DOOR NOTES

These were the antecedents of the Hay Open Door Notes sent to Britain, Germany, and Russia, September 6, 1899.[14] These prosaic notes, which were to plague American diplomats for half a century, began with some background of Hippisley and Rockhill's ideas and with a denial of any American recognition of the spheres, though both Hippisley and Rockhill accepted as axiomatic that the spheres were facts whose existence could be challenged only by force. The real substance of the notes was a three-point technical formula by which each power within its sphere was requested (1) not

[12] See Julius W. Pratt, *Expansionists of 1898* (1936),* 278.

[13] For the background of the Hay open door policy, see George F. Kennan, *American Diplomacy, 1900-1950* (1951),* 21-37.

[14] Similar though not identical notes went to Japan (Nov. 13), to Italy (Nov. 17), and to France (Nov. 21). See A. Whitney Griswold, *The Far Eastern Policy of the United States* (1938),* Chapter 2; for texts of the Hippisley memorandum, Rockhill memorandum, and drafts of the final notes see pp. 475-500.

to interfere with the administration of treaty ports; (2) not to impede the equitable administration of Chinese customs; and (3) not to charge discriminatory railroad rates or harbor dues. It appears that there was no attempt by the government in Washington to appraise the formula in terms of what its practical application in China was likely to be. Actually, the formula seems to have been an expression of what the Chinese Imperial Maritime Customs Service wanted at that particular time. Hippisley had secured the support of the United States without Rockhill or Hay's realizing the degree to which their formula might be contrary to the real purposes of the British government.

The powers to which they were addressed received the Hay Open Door Notes with no enthusiasm, and their replies were plainly evasive. The British response, the most favorable of any, was clearly conditional, accepting the formula in so far as others might accept it. The Russians did not wish to reply at all, and when they did they were completely evasive. Although the replies were all but worthless, Hay, on March 20, 1900, announced he had received "satisfactory assurances" from all the powers and that he looked upon these responses as "final and definitive." This piece of sheer diplomatic bluff did not deceive the powers, but it did deceive the American people. It created the impression that the American government by a stroke of diplomatic genius had saved China from the evil purposes of predatory powers.[15]

It is not belittling the Hay policy of 1899 to say that it was inadequate to protect either immediate American commercial interests or the historic American principle of equal opportunity. One need only recall that "in the Far East the powers were dealing with the fate of an empire of upward of three hundred million souls and no less than five major states were

disputing the spoils."[16] This was not the sort of thing to be arrested by polite diplomatic notes. The spheres were still there, and they still represented a state of intense international rivalry for preferential treatment in railroad, mining, and investment concessions.[17]

THE BOXER CATASTROPHE

The victory of the empress dowager in the *coup d'etat* of 1898 meant that there was to be no meaningful reform, that the court was in the hands of those opposed to meeting China's crises by inquiry and enlightenment. It was a victory for the Manchus over those Chinese officials who could be accused of radical or even moderate leanings toward change. Nevertheless, the empress dowager and her intellectually barren cohorts sorely needed domestic allies in the midst of China's humiliations. Since she had just suppressed reform by scholar-officials at the top, the alternative to which she would soon turn was to seek allies and popular support from violent elements at the bottom. In little more than a decade the alternative would destroy the dynasty and heap additional humiliation on the country in the form of the Boxer catastrophe of 1900. Its causes were many and exceedingly complex. Only a few of them can be suggested here.

Antiforeignism. A widespread state of mind paving the way for the Boxer tragedy had been in the making since 1860, when, by treaty, Christian missionaries were permitted to reside and preach in the interior. From that date until 1900 outbreaks against both missionaries and

[15] Paul H. Clyde, "Historical Reflections on Continuity in United States Far Eastern Policy," in *Southeast Asia in the Coming World,* Philip W. Thayer, ed. (1953), 17-24; and "The Open Door Policy of John Hay," *Historical Outlook* (May 1931).

[16] William L. Langer *The Diplomacy of Imperialism, 1890-1902* (2 vols., 1935; 2nd ed. in one vol., 1951), II, 677.

[17] It is Langer's conclusion that to this point "the efforts of Hay, then, had no practical bearing on the situation as it was at the turn of the century." *Diplomacy,* II, 688. Tyler Dennett, *John Hay* (1933), 295, gives the following comment on the whole negotiation: "It would have taken more than a lawyer to define what new rights had been recognized, or acquired, or even what had actually been said."

their converts were a common occurrence. Popular hostility to the missionary was shared by all classes, and was often stimulated and directed by the gentry. This increasing antiforeignism derived its strength from powerful tradition reinforced by the acceleration of imperialism at the close of the century. Beyond the long-standing resentment against the intrusion of the West in general—it was easy to blame the Westerner for all China's ills—there was the age-old assumption of China's cultural superiority. As the missionary moved into the interior he became more conspicuous and was a visible symbol of a foreign cultural assault on everything Chinese. His very presence was an offense. Moreover, his behavior was a challenge to the leadership of the gentry since, by the very nature of his mission, he appeared in the role of a teacher whose instruction, more often than not, ran counter to the most hallowed Chinese values.[18]

Economic Depression. Years of economic depression and dislocation, aggravated by natural calamities, also helped bring on the Boxer troubles. The T'ai-p'ing and other rebellions had left a legacy of famine and starvation; destitute peasants sought survival through banditry or in the conspiracies of secret societies. Increased taxation and disastrous floods in 1898 in Shantung, Anhwei, Kiangsi, and Kiangsu gave rise to additional discontent. It was always possible for agitators to inflame the populace by attributing all these calamities to the evil influence of the foreigners, their concessions and leaseholds, and especially their religion: to kill the missionary and his converts was to strike at the disease which had infected and weakened China.

The Boxers. The leadership of the popular movement designed to save China from the foreign menace came from a traditional type of secret society, this one by the name of *I-ho*

ch'uan, translated loosely as Righteous and Harmonious Fists. Members engaged in Chinese physical exercises, involving posturing, which were said to coordinate brain and brawn for combat; hence the name Boxers. These ritual exercises, Taoist in origin, were supposed to make the Boxer immune to foreign bullets—a comforting gospel which strengthened the old idea of popular rebellion. The specific goal of the Boxers at first was expressed in their battle-cry, "Overthrow the Ch'ing; destroy the foreigner." Later, in 1899, as conservative officials both Manchu and Chinese began to patronize Boxer leaders, the slogan became, "Support the Ch'ing; destroy the foreigner." In the winter and spring of 1900 thousands of Boxers ravaged the countryside of Chihli, burning Christian missions and butchering Chinese converts. The freedom with which they moved suggested that the empress dowager had made the fateful decision to allow a violent popular movement to attack and, hopefully, destroy the foreigner. In any case, she left little reason to doubt her antiforeign sentiments; in June, 1900, while the Boxers were besieging the foreign areas at Peking and Tientsin and the powers were preparing a military relief expedition, the dowager declared war on the foreigners.

Southern Neutrality. Fortunately for the foreigners and for China, the central and southern provinces ignored the lunacy at court and the dynasty's declaration of war. Li Hung-chang at Canton, Liu K'un-i at Nanking, Chang Chihtung at Wuhan, and Yuan Shih-k'ai in Shantung sought to avert complete catastrophe through diplomacy with the powers. They neutralized all China save the northern provinces, and they enticed the powers to accept the theory that what had occurred was a rebellion not actually supported by the dynasty. It was an obvious fiction designed to save China, which, within limits, it did. From this point until the later relief of the besieged legations (August 14, 1900), the empress dowager played a fantastic dual role. She supported both her advisers at Peking who sought extermination of the foreigners and, in words at least, her governors-general in the south who were striving to restore peace.

[18] See Paul A. Cohen, *China and Christianity: The Missionary Movement and the Growth of Chinese Antiforeignism, 1860-1870* (1963), and the same author's "Ch'ing China: Confrontation with the West, 1850-1900," in *Modern East Asia: Essays in Interpretation,* James B. Crowley, ed. (1970),* 29-61.

International Complications. From June through the summer of 1900, the violence in North China continued. Thousands of super-stitious and fanatical Boxers, prompted by conservative officialdom, joined in a debauch of slaughter and destruction in Shantung, Chihli, Shansi, and Manchuria. They tore up railroads and telegraphs, burned churches, and murdered Christian missionaries and their converts. A British relief expedition from Tientsin was forced to retire and the siege of the legations dragged on until August 14, when an allied army of Americans, British, French, Germans, and Japanese entered Peking. Again, as in 1858, China's inability to adjust to the West, and the blind reaction of court officialdom, had opened the gates of Peking to foreign armies. This time, however, the threat to China's integrity was far greater. In 1858 it was a question of a few commercial concessions; but in 1900 the question was whether China as a state would continue to exist.

The Boxer outbreak, following closely on the "final and definitive" assurances Hay said he had received from the powers, meant that if there was little structure on which to hang the open door in 1899, there was even less in 1900. The powers were engaged in armed intervention at Peking. As a result of the Boxers' attack on the Chinese Eastern Railroad, which forced the Russians out of Mukden and Tsitsihar and put Harbin under seige, the Russians were soon to occupy strategic areas in Manchuria. Kuro-patkin, the Russian minister of war, had ex-claimed when he heard of the Boxer outbreak: "This will give us an excuse for seizing Manchuria." By October, 1900, Russia was in complete military control of the three eastern provinces. As a response to Hay's Open Door Notes the actions of the powers may have been "final and definitive," but not in the way Hay intended.

During the first half of 1900, Edwin H. Conger, American minister at Peking, reported to his government on the chaos in North China and cooperated with his diplomatic colleagues in joint protests to the Chinese government. This procedure was in line with the Hay notes of 1899 and had precedent in Burlingame's

cooperative policy of the 1860's. But opera-tional procedures were reversed between March and June and Conger was told to act "singly and without the cooperation of other powers." Then, on the eve of the attacks on the Peking legations, Rockhill told Hay that the Boxer movement was not likely to "cause any serious complications," and the state department, again partially reversing itself, told Conger that he might act "concurrently" with other powers "if necessity arises."

CHINA'S POLITICAL INTEGRITY

To Hay the time seemed ripe for a clarification of American policy. On July 3, 1900, in a circular to the powers he said, in words de-signed to be quieting, that the United States had no thought other than

... to seek a solution which may bring about permanent safety and peace to China, preserve Chinese territorial and administrative entity, protect all rights guaranteed to friendly Powers by treaty and international law, and safeguard for the world the principle of equal and im-partial trade with all parts of the Chinese Empire.

This principle of China's territorial integrity was not new in the language of American policy. It had been expressed by Humphrey Marshall in 1853 and by Anson Burlingame in 1862. Although it had been absent from, if not repudiated by, the Hay policy of 1899, which tacitly acknowledged the reality of leaseholds and spheres, it was now revived in July, 1900, in a new and stronger form. Hay not only invited "respect" for China's integrity but also suggested "a collective guarantee" by the powers—a guarantee, however, that was not forthcoming since, with the exception of Great Britain, none of the powers even replied to the July circular.

Yet the important point is that in late 1900 the threatened partition of China was again arrested. Why was this? The note-writing of Hay probably had some psychological effect, but it does not appear to have been the determining factor. What counted was the rivalry and the mutual jealousy of the powers, and their retreat from cooperative policy to bilateral negotiations. Great Britain and Japan were slowly drawing together to stop Russia in Manchuria and in the Middle East. Germany's equivocal position in Shantung, between Russia and Great Britain, had resulted on October 16, 1900, in an Anglo-German agreement favoring the open door and the integrity of China; but this was an innocuous affair. John Hay referred to it as "a horrible practical German joke on England." He failed, it would seem, to realize that if this were so, it was an equally horrible joke upon himself and everything he had been attempting to do in China. There was no conversion of the powers to the idea of China's integrity. Rather, the business of melon-cutting was stopped because each of the potential aggressors, fearful of the debacle that would follow, hesitated to make the first move.

Then, ironically, in the midst of this lull, Hay himself joined the concession hunters. In December, 1900, under pressure from the American navy, he sought a naval coaling station at Samsah Inlet, north of Foochow on the coast of Fukien province. Japan, when consulted, blocked the move, reminding Hay, presumably with some delight, of his own recent efforts to preserve the territorial integrity of China.[19] In subsequent years this incident did not strengthen the moral influence of the United States in East Asia.

THE BOXER SETTLEMENT

With the defeat of the Boxers and the occupation of Peking by an international army, the powers set about the long, drawn-out business of deciding how to punish China and how to provide security for the future. The final settlement embodied in the peace protocol of September, 1901, was thus achieved only after prolonged and involved negotiations.

During the advance of the international relief expedition on Peking there had been relative harmony among the powers, for the plight of the besieged foreigners in the capital was desperate. The international relief army was one of the most remarkable ever assembled: 8,000 Japanese, 4,500 Russians, 3,000 British, 2,500 Americans, and 800 French. Available German troops were held back to protect Kiaochou and the coast. To please the kaiser the honor of commanding the allied forces had been given to Field Marshal Count von Waldersee, who, perhaps fortunately, did not arrive until after Peking was in allied hands. This was a severe blow to German imperialistic pride; the kaiser was forced to see the glory of leadership go to General Linievitch, the Russian commander.

The general tension increased during the autumn and winter of 1900-1901, when the powers became convinced that Russia was preparing to control not only Manchuria but also the province of Chihli. This led to all manner of attempts by the powers for additional concessions for themselves from China. In these unhappy circumstances, suggesting renewed danger of partition of the empire, the Boxer protocol was concluded, September 7, 1901.

The terms were severe and humiliating for China and the wisdom of the settlement has often been questioned. From the standpoint of the powers it could be argued that Peking's responsibility was great. The Manchu government had regarded itself as at war and, therefore, had now to pay the price of its defeat and treachery. The terms were dictated against a background of punitive expeditions against many localities where foreigners had been attacked and of occupation by allied troops of the Imperial City within Peking itself.[20]

---

[19] Hay consulted Japan because the latter regarded the province of Fukien, opposite Formosa, as a Japanese sphere of influence. Hay's effort to secure Samsah was not made public until 24 years after the event. The navy again urged the project on Hay in December, 1901, and in May, 1902. See Griswold, *Far Eastern Policy,* 83-84. Hay's "integrity of China" notes of 1900 were an effort to preserve the old treaty system at a time of crisis. John K. Fairbank, "Dilemmas of American Far Eastern Policy," *Pacific Affairs,* 36 (1963-64), 430-37.

[20] The terms of the protocol may be summarized as follows: (1) apology to Germany and Japan for the murder of the German minister and the Japanese chancellor of legation, and erection of a memorial to von Ketteler on the spot where he was assassinated; (2) punishment of responsible Chinese officials; (3) erection of monuments in desecrated foreign cemeteries; (4) suspension of official examinations in all cities

Japan's role in suppressing the Boxers who were beseiging the Peking quarter was illustrated in a series of widely distributed drawings. This one was circulated under the title "The Occupation of Peking Castle by Allied Armies."

In the long view the Boxer uprising was to exert a profound influence upon China's political future. It hastened the end of the Manchu dynasty and the creation of the Republic. In this respect it was a dynamic step in the progress of China's revolution. The

Boxers had no constructive program of reform; they attributed China's ills to the "foreign devils" who must be destroyed along with their machines and inventions, "their strange and

where attacks had occurred; (5) China's payment of an indemnity of $333 million, creation of an effective 5 percent tariff, and prohibition for at least two years of importation of arms, ammunition, and materials for their manufacture; (6) destruction of the Taku forts and creation of a legation quarter in Peking under exclusive control of the powers, which they might make defensible; (7) occupation rights by the powers

to thirteen places as a guarantee of free communication with Peking; (8) China's agreement to the amendment of commercial treaties and to the creation of a ministry of foreign affairs; (9) Chinese publication of preventive edicts against further outbreaks; and (10) provision for the right of the allies to maintain legation guards at Peking. The American share of the indemnity, $25 million, was, as in the case of all the powers, far in excess of justifiable claims. Substantial portions of it were returned to China in 1907 and 1924.

intolerant religion, their insufferable airs of superiority."[21] Yet, with all its weakness, its lack of constructive program, its blind fanaticism and reaction, the Boxer movement was an unmistakable symptom of China's growing unrest, of her resentment against foreign intrusion and exploitation, and of her will to resist.

FOR FURTHER READING

Chinese Intellectual and Institutional Change. Herrlee G. Creel, *Chinese Thought from Confucius to Mao Tse-Tung* (1953).* Joseph R. Levenson, *Liang Ch'i-ch'ao and the Mind of Modern China* (1953),* an intellectual history of modern China. Liang Ch'i-ch'ao, *Intellectual Trends in the Ch'ing Period,* trans. with introduction and notes by Immanuel C. Y. Hsu (1959) contains the memoirs of one of the leading revolutionaries of the late nineteenth century. Hao Chang, *Liang Ch'i-ch'ao and the Intellectual Transition in China, 1890-1907* (1971). Benjamin I. Schwartz, *In Search of Wealth and Power, Yen Fu and the West* (1964).* Laurence A. Schneider, *Ku Chieh-kang and China's New History: Nationaliam and the Quest for Alternative Traditions* (1971). S. A. M. Adshead, *The Modernization of the Chinese Salt Administration, 1900-1920* (1970). Ying-wan Cheng, *Postal Communication in China and its Modernization, 1860-1896* (1970). Ralph L. Powell, *The Rise of Chinese Military Power, 1895-1912* (1955). Stanley Spector, *Li Hung-chang and the Huai Army* (1964) I. Losing Buck, *Land Utilization in China* (1937), a principal source on the agrarian economy. Yang Lien Shang, *Money and Credit in China: A Short History* (1952).*

Christian Missions. Kenneth Scott Latourette, *A History of Christian Missions in China* (1929). Robert McClellan, *The Heathen Chinese: A Study of American Attitudes toward China, 1890-1895* (1971). Paul R. Bohr, *Famine in China and the Missionary: Timothy Richard as Relief Administrator and Advocate of Reform, 1876-1884* (1972).* Kwang-ching Liu, ed., *American Missionaries in China:*

---

[21] R. F. Johnston, *Twilight in the Forbidden City* (1934), 44.

Papers from Harvard Seminars (1966).* Jessie Gregory Lutz, *China and the Christian Colleges, 1850-1950* (1971). Paul A. Varg, *Missionaries, Chinese and Diplomats. The American Protestant Missionary Movement in China, 1890-1952* (1958). Kwang-ching Liu, "Early Christian Colleges in China," *Journal of Asian Studies* 20 (1960), 71-78. Chen Chi-yun, "Liang Ch'i-ch'ao's Missionary Education: A Case Study of Missionary Influence on the Reformers," *Papers on China* 16 (1962), 66-125. Chan Wing-tsit, *Religious Trends in Modern China* (1953).

The Open Door and China's Integrity. Marilyn B. Young, "The Quest for Empire" in *American-East Asian Relations: A Survey.* James Thomson and Ernest May, eds. (1972), 131-42, a basic bibliographic introduction. Among titles not listed already in Chapter 15 are: Thomas McCormick, *The China Market: America's Quest for an Informal Empire, 1893-1901* (1967),* W. A. Williams, *The Roots of the Modern American Empire: A Study of the Growth and Shaping of Social Consciousness in a Market-Place Society* (1969).* Paul A. Varg, *Open Door Diplomat: The Life of W. W Rockhill* (1952); Julius W. Pratt, *America's Colonial Experiment* (1950). Also see Warren I. Cohen, *America's Response to China* (1971).*

The Boxer Uprising. Chester C. Tan, *The Boxer Catastrophe* (1955),* the basic study. Victor Purcell, *The Boxer Uprising: A Background Study* (1963). Peter Fleming, *The Siege of Peking* (1959). L.R. Marchant, ed., *The Siege of the Peking Legations: A Diary by Lancelot Giles* (1970). G. N. Steiger, *China and the Occident, the Origin and Development of the Boxer Movement* (1927). Richard H. Wilde, "The Boxer Affair and Australian Responsibility for Imperial Defense," *Pacific Historical Review* 26 (1957), 51-65. Michael E. Hunt, "The American Remission of the Boxer Indemnity: A Reappraisal," *Journal of Asian Studies* 31 (1972), 539-59.

An End
and A New
Beginning:
China,
1901–1910

17

For the Manchu dynasty the first decade of the new century was a triumph in consummate irony. In these years the Manchus, who, with Chinese allies, had destroyed the program of the One Hundred Days in 1898, turned about and attempted to implement most of K'ang Yu-wei's reforms. The purpose was a desperate effort to save the dynasty and, incidentally, the China over which it ruled. What the dynasty actually did was to assist at the birth of a new force in Chinese life—nationalism. This ironically implied that the end of the dynasty was at hand and, moreover, that Confucianism as a political system had lost its power. The outcome of events was far from what the dynasty had in mind, and far from the expectations of the traditionalists among the literati. A dynasty which had ruled China since 1644 and a political system which had prevailed for more than two thousand years were coming to an end; a new force in nation-building would appear.

THE DOWAGER TRIES REFORM

Until that mid-summer madness called the Boxer rebellion, the empress dowager Tz'u-hsi,

giving some support to the old self-strengthening movement, had been steadfastly opposed to significant—that is, institutional—reform. The scuttling of the One Hundred Days (1898) was due directly to her. Her return to power in the capacity of regent signaled an intensification of reaction. This tendency was given its fullest expression in the policies and actions of the court as the Boxer movement got under way. The empress dowager was in full sympathy with the antiforeign, anti-Christian philosophy of the Boxer patriots. It was not by accident that government troops were allowed by the court to join forces with the Boxers.[1] The dowager had set her course not only against reform at home but also against the treaty powers that personified the impact of all things Western.

When foreign armies again entered Peking in the midst of the Boxer troubles the dowager fled from the capital for a second time, as in 1860. Before her return to Peking in January, 1902, after the Boxer protocol had been signed, Tz'u-hsi professed to be a converted woman. She had hardly become a progressive, for she had no understanding of such things, but she

[1] R. F. Johnston, *Twilight in the Forbidden City* (1934), 46.

was converted to "reform," at least as she defined the term. From 1901 until three years after her death in 1908, the dynasty supported a program that bore striking resemblance to the reforms she had so ruthlessly suppressed. The new reform program was to involve the educational system, the army and navy, the form of government, and a great array of miscellaneous matters, including a crusade against the opium traffic. In 1902 reform edicts removed the ban on intermarriage between Chinese and Manchus, advised the Chinese to abandon the practice of binding the feet of their women, ordered the sending of intelligent Manchus abroad for study, and abolished a number of sinecures. All this seemed to indicate that the empress dowager was intent on a housecleaning. There were still, however, questions as to the depth and sincerity of her conversion, and as to the capacity for leadership of this masterful but unscrupulous woman.

THE NEW OUTLOOK

This striking about-face by the dynasty was not a result of its capacity to provide either intellectual or political leadership. On the contrary, it was due to a growing consciousness among all politically-minded Chinese that imperialism must be stopped—that China must be saved. This was not a completely new idea in 1901. It was central to the abortive reforms of 1898; but it was the events of 1895-1898, culminating in the colossal Boxer tragedy of 1900, that gave the idea wide acceptance and a previously unknown intensity. Against this rising national feeling even the most blind among the traditionalists, Manchus or Chinese, could not but acknowledge their own failure. They tended to lapse into silence and, in general, were ignored. This mood gave the dynasty no choice but to seek safety in reform.

The new embryonic nationalism in 1901 was fragmented; in no sense was it one united and organized movement. No accepted political leaders had emerged, but some major components of the movement's intellectual content and purpose could be identified. The first point in this consensus has already been suggested: China must have a government that could restore and protect the nation against the inroads

and the power of the Western imperialists and Japan. Second, the classical tradition had come to be regarded as a political guide which had failed to provide the needed strength. Third, China must have a political structure derived from Western and Japanese experience. Fourth, China's social structure, hallowed by time, would still be adequate for the future if rid of some obvious abuses. There was, to be sure, very little agreement on how all these changes were to be brought about, but the way was open for Peking to demonstrate its eleventh hour conversion to reform.[2]

EDUCATIONAL REFORM

The decision to reconstruct China's educational system involved a revolutionary departure from the past. Some rather futile efforts in this direction, important in spite of their failure, had already been made in the late nineteenth century. The traditional Confucian education leading to the civil service examinations had been sanctified by a thousand years of history and guarded jealously by the ruling scholar-bureaucrats as the fortress of their position and power. A few progressive scholars had dared to say that the classical education alone was no longer adequate for a China harassed by the modern world, but it was not until 1887 that mathematics became a subject for examination. Even then the weight of tradition was so strong that few candidates prepared for it. In 1897 a special examination on political economy was suggested in order that some candidates might be encouraged to learn about current affairs. At the time of the fateful One Hundred Days of Reform, Liang Ch'i-ch'ao and more than a hundred other progressives asked for abolition of the traditional civil service examination system. Nothing came of these preliminary requests until 1903, however, when Chang Chih-tung, governor-general at Nanking, and Yuan Shih-k'ai, governor-general at Tientsin, suggested gradual abolition. The weight of their prestige encouraged other memorialists, with

[2] Ernest P. Young, "Nationalism, Reform, and Republican Revolution: China in the Early Twentieth Century," in *Modern East Asia: Essays in Interpretation*, James B. Crowley, ed. (1970),* 151-65.

the result that on September 2, 1905, an imperial decree announced the immediate, permanent end of the examinations.

The Boxer protocol (1901) had already suspended the civil service examinations for five years in cities where foreigners had been attacked. An imperial edict, also in 1901, had called for the building of a national school system. Instruction was still to be in the Confucian classics, but it would also include Chinese and Western history, government, and science. In 1904 this educational plan was revised and extended on the model of the educational system prevailing in Japan. It would provide for kindergartens, primary schools, middle schools, high schools or provincial colleges, and an imperial university at Peking. Unlike in Japan, however, there was a notable lack of provision for the education of women.

Substantial evidence indicates that many Chinese accepted the new educational reforms with enthusiasm if not always with understanding, but there was also persistent opposition. Fitful waves of reaction followed the first waves of reform. While temples were being turned into schools and the empress dowager was curtailing her theatricals to equip an academy for girls, some of the erstwhile reformers turned conservative, reemphasized Confucian studies, and belittled the Western learning. Still greater opposition came from some local mandarins. Peking might decree reform in education, but it would remain a dead letter until the local officials were prepared to implement it. Even where the attitude of local officials was favorable, the educational effort frequently dissipated itself in the construction of colleges rather than primary schools.

Of equal difficulty were the problems of financing the new schools and staffing them. Finance was left to the ingenuity of the local community, with results that were "precarious and unsatisfactory." In the teacher problem, the missionaries and the native graduates of the mission schools offered the greatest hope. The missionaries, however, were deterred from accepting appointment by a rule forbidding the teaching of religion in government schools. As a result, a large proportion of the new teachers came from Japan. They worked for lower salaries than Westerners, and culturally they fitted more easily into the Chinese environment.

Meanwhile, in 1905, the empress dowager, intent on building, through education, a new body of public servants capable of strengthening the dynasty and resisting the pressure of the foreign powers, urged more students to study abroad. At this time there were probably 8,000 Chinese students in Japan. A lesser number went to Europe and to the United States. Some undoubtedly profited by the experience, while others were mere adventurers, seeking the prestige that a few months of foreign residence would give. Those who came to America were assisted through Boxer indemnity funds which the American government returned to China after 1907.[3] By 1911 there were some 800 Chinese students in the United States and about 400 in Europe.

These were encouraging signs. In the years 1909-1910, China could point to 57,267 schools, 89,362 teachers, and 1,626,529 enrolled students. In the light of only ten years of educational reform the figures are impressive until one recalls that China's population was in excess of 400 million, of whom some 65 million were children of school age. On this point, however, it should be recognized that the reforms were not intended to provide either mass or liberal education. The basic aim was to prepare an elite of government officials, trained specialists in modern knowledge, who would use their newly-found skills to create and administer a new, strong China. In time, however, the net effect was far broader than the official intent implied. Once the old examination system was gone, a new type of student appeared whose horizons were broadened by reading, in translation, the works of important and provocative Western writers—for example, Dickens, Scott, Balzac, and Dumas in fiction,

---

[3] In 1908 the American Congress by joint resolution authorized President Roosevelt to reduce the United States share of the Boxer indemnity from $24,440,000 to $13,655,492. The original figure had far exceeded American claims. United States, *Foreign Relations, 1907* Pt. I, 174-75; *ibid., 1908,* 64-65, 71-72.

and Adam Smith, John Stuart Mill, and Montesquieu in political economy and philosophy. The new education could certainly produce government officials but it could also produce revolutionaries.

MILITARY REFORM

By 1901 the need for military reform, for the creation of a national Chinese army, was obvious even to the Manchus. China's military humiliation had reached a new height in the Sino-Japanese war and in the Boxer uprising, and during the Russo-Japanese war (1904-1905) the hapless dynasty had no alternative but to open Manchuria to the battling armies of two great foreign powers.

China had acquired a number of regional armies in the days of the T'ai-p'ing rebellion. They suppressed the rebellion but, in so doing, weakened the central government at the very moment they were saving it. The effectiveness of these armies against the T'ai-p'ings suggested a means by which China in time might defend herself against the Western powers. Accordingly, Li Hung-chang and others among the new Chinese scholar-militarists had set about to buy arms and munitions from the West, to seek Western military advisers, and to establish arsenals. All this was done without pattern or plan, so that a small body of troops might find itself carrying thirteen kinds of rifles and even more brands of ammunition. The picture was not wholly negative but, as so often in nineteenth-century China, what the right hand acquired the left hand took away. What was learned in the classroom, for instance, was rarely applied in maneuvers, either because young officers scorned the drill field or because their old-fashioned commanders blocked reform. Since the reform spirit rarely penetrated Peking, progress was confined to the local level. In the end, the militia armies tended to degenerate once the T'ai-p'ings had been suppressed, until they were not much better than the defunct Banners and the Green Standard. Apparently, military reform was fashionable only when disaster was imminent.

But China's humiliating defeat in 1895 and the subsequent scramble of the powers for leaseholds opened a new chapter in the nation's stumbling search for military power. In the first place, there was now evidence of some popular demand among the Chinese for reform. In the second, even the Manchu court was no longer wholly blind to the dangers from within or from abroad invited by its military weakness. The central figure in the new military reforms was Yuan Shih-k'ai, who had been Li Hung-chang's agent in Korea in the years before the Sino-Japanese war. Yuan, a Chinese, was born in Honan, 1859, in a family of the smaller landed gentry; he had failed the literary examinations and had purchased his first post and rank in government. He appears to have decided quite early that in the China of his day a primarily military career was the surest path to power. In any event, he became a staff officer in 1880, and between 1882 and 1894, established, through service in Korea, a reputation as a military man and a diplomat. By 1895 he had formed high connections at Peking with such Manchu officials as Prince Ch'ing and Jung-lu, the Manchu president of the board of war, and was promptly placed in command of an army corps in which many of the young officers were graduates of Li Hung-chang's military school at Tientsin. Yuan set about to make his corps the best-trained, -equipped, and -disciplined army in China.

The One Hundred Days made possible Yuan's complete ingratiation with the Manchu dynasty. By this time Yuan had formed connections with Chinese reformers as well as with the conservatives of the court. In the events of 1898 he betrayed the reformers and thus opened the way for the suppression of the reforms and for the return to power of the empress dowager. From then until 1908 Yuan had the confidence of the Manchu court.

Indeed, Yuan's position at the turn of the century was compounded by the play of multiple forces in delicate balance. He was described by Lord Charles Beresford in 1898 as intelligent, well-informed, patriotic, and deeply concerned for the fate of his country. At the same time Yuan was ambitious to achieve military and political power for himself. His advancement up to 1900 had been due to his liaison with an ailing dynasty as well as to ability and energy. Yet he had also had close association with those Chinese who wanted reform, and, when the Boxer troubles occurred, Yuan displayed notable independence of judgment. Far from aiding the dynasty in its ill-advised support of the Boxers, Yuan, who had recently been named governor of Shantung, gave no quarter to the Boxers, maintained order in the province, protected the foreigners, and thus, enjoying the favor of the powers, aided in the return of the fugitive court to Peking after the Boxer settlement. This, then, was the background of the empress dowager's new-found ardor after 1901 for military reform, and for the role of Yuan Shih-k'ai in implementing the program.

The Manchu military reform program, 1902-1911, like the other efforts of the dynasty to rebuild its prestige and power, was notable in purpose rather than in performance. Under decrees inspired by the empress dowager, provincial governors were ordered to modernize their troops. Military schools were to be reformed and the entire program was to be directed by a commission for army reorganization headed by Prince Ch'ing. Meanwhile, Yuan Shih-k'ai, on the death of Li Hung-chang (1901), was named governor-general of the province of Chilhli and was entrusted with the direction of military and foreign affairs in North China. His own Peiyang army, now expanded to something between 50,000 and 80,000 men, was commanded by officers who were Yuan's men. Many of these politico-military subordinates were later to hold high office during the early years of the Republic.[4]

[4] Feng Kuo-chang was president, 1917-1919; Tuan Ch'i-jui, several times premier and chief executive of the provisional government, 1924-1926; Wang Shih-chen, premier, 1917-1918; Hsu Shih-chang, president 1919-1922; and Ts'ao K'un, president 1923-1924. Yuan's military schools graduated other men who figured in the subsequent struggle for power: Wu Pei-fu, Sun Chuan-fang, and Feng Yu-hsiang, the "Christian general."

It is important to note a distinction between the earlier nineteenth century armies which suppressed the T'ai-p'ings, and which in some degree were regional armies, and the Peiyang Army in the decade of reform. The earlier armies appeared at a time when reform was an almost inconceivable idea at Peking. By the turn of the century, however, a sense of nationalism was

At this point the plan of the Manchu court to enforce the general principle of governmental centralization of authority in Peking affected the military reform program. In his rise to power Yuan had made enemies at court, particularly among high Manchu officials. These officials found in the idea of centralization a means of wresting from Yuan the command of his army. In 1907, control of two-thirds of the Peiyang army was assumed by the ministry of war. A few months later Yuan was further isolated from military power when he was appointed minister of foreign affairs and elevated to the grand council. When in 1908 the empress dowager died, Yuan was dismissed from office and sent into retirement. With Yuan out of the way, the ministry of war attempted to organize a national army under its immediate control. All manner of elaborate plans were drafted setting forth the control, equipment, and training of this force, including the necessary military industries of munitions and supply. Some progress in fact was made. In 1909 about 700 young Chinese were being trained as officers in Japan.

The army itself, however, grew very slowly. What held it back was both the costliness of the expansion program and the uncertainties involved in financing it. In the absence of a centralized fiscal system, any major army expansion was bound to be a charge on the provinces, which were unlikely to pay for an army they did not control. In the long run, it turned out that the principal achievement of military reform was social; the army came to be regarded as an instrument of the new nationalism, thus giving a military career a respectability it had

appearing in China. Belatedly, the dynasty itself had turned to national reform. It was in these circumstances that Yuan Shih-k'ai rose to power. He did not operate in the same circumstances as the mid-nineteenth century commanders. Nor was he a military separatist in the pattern of the later warlords (1916-1927). His control of the Peiyang army, which was not a highly personalized army, came from his influence with the empress dowager and the central administration. Stephen R. MacKinnon, "The Peiyang Army, Yuan Shih-k'ai, and the Origins of Modern Chinese Warlordism," *Journal of Asian Studies*, 32 (1973), 405-23.

never previously enjoyed in the scale of Chinese values. It opened a new avenue to careers of leadership to the sons of gentry. An officer in the new army became a symbol of patriotism, a decidedly new virtue in the Chinese scheme of things.

CENTRAL ADMINISTRATIVE REFORM

Reforms of the educational system and of the army in the China of 1901-1910 were made the more difficult because the country did not have a modern, national administrative structure with which to operate modern institutions or to enforce its mandate in the provinces. Historically, Peking had exercised a limited local control through the appointment and removal of provincial officials, but beyond this its role in the provinces was supervisory. Provincial regionalism was strong and it had grown even stronger in the later nineteenth century (see Chapter 12), just at the time when central control was needed if there were to be any source of authority to speak and act for the country as a whole.

The first administrative reform of this period was due to the terms of the Boxer protocol, which required that the Tsungli Yamen be remodeled into a modern ministry of foreign affairs. Later (1905), a ministry of police was created, foreshadowing a ministry of internal affairs; other ministries, such as education and war, followed. A ministry of commerce, established in 1903, was eventually expanded to include agriculture and industry. As these new agencies took shape, the old historic boards gradually lost their functions and tended to disappear.

One of the most difficult reforms attempted was in the area of national finance. Any change here would affect directly a host of vested interests. These interests were imbedded in old practices which could hardly be called a system at all, but which were designed to finance an elite rather than to operate a modern state. There was little budgeting or accounting and no single central treasury at Peking. Moreover, the newer revenues from foreign trade, collected by the Imperial Maritime Customs Service, were pledged to meet war indemnities and foreign loans. Nevertheless, between 1908 and 1910, some efforts were made to estimate national revenue as a basis for a national budget. There was, however, no coordination between Peking and the provinces even in these belated efforts. Peking might propose but the provinces were still in a position to dispose.

Legal reform presented another example of the weight of tradition. The need for legal reform was widely recognized because such reform would determine when China could throw off the stigma of extraterritoriality. But a new draft criminal code, prepared in 1907 and based on German and Japanese models, was promptly rejected as far too radical. It would have dismantled the Confucian social order with its emphasis on family and filial piety and its distinctions based on age, sex, and status. In 1910 a mild revision of the Ch'ing code was adopted. It reduced the crueler forms of corporal punishment and provided for individual instead of collective responsibility. The timidity of this beginning was again a reflection of the long Confucian background which did not accord law a primary place in Chinese society.

CONSTITUTIONAL REFORM

It has been noted that the empress dowager, her frightened dynastic household, and her chief advisers undertook political reform not as a means toward enlightened government but rather as a desperate effort to save the dynasty. As early as January, 1901, the dowager, while still an exile at Sian, had decreed that the best political methods of foreign countries should be studied. The idea was that there must be some germ of strength in Occidental governments which, if known, would give China strength and reestablish her position of superiority.[5] Accordingly, in 1905 she sent official missions to Japan, Europe and the United States to study constitutional government. The reports of these commissions, given to the throne in 1906-1907, revealed the limited steps the dynasty was prepared to take. Constitutionalism, in so far as it might be adopted, was to be justified on prac-

[5] Harold M. Vinacke, *Modern Constitutional Development in China* (1920), 54.

tical rather than theoretical grounds. The commissioners argued that a constitution would make the emperor's powers more effective and would make the people more responsive and industrious subjects, thus increasing production and revenue.

The commissioners were particularly impressed by what they saw in Japan. To them it seemed clear that (1) Japan's strength was due to her adoption of Western institutions, and (2) Japan had provided herself with a constitution without sacrificing the power of the imperial house. Why then could not the empress dowager by similar reforms satisfy her subjects, strengthen the empire, and preserve her own power? She proceeded on the assumption that real power was to be reserved to the throne, with the people tendering advice when requested to do so through their representatives. Furthermore, she proposed to act slowly in order to placate the conservative opposition. By the close of 1907 three cautious steps had been taken on the road to constitutional government: (1) the principle itself had been accepted; (2) a commission had been created to advise on procedure; and (3) an edict had been issued authorizing a national assembly and provincial assemblies.

During 1908 these cautious preliminaries assumed more tangible shape. The throne approved specific regulations for provincial assemblies that were to meet within a year. Underlying principles of the future constitution were decided upon and promulgated. A national parliament was to meet after nine years, and a preliminary constitutional program to that end was adopted. The new provincial assemblies were to be an integral part of the national machinery, their powers in no case infringing on the imperial prerogatives—an indication that the official reformers were under the influence of Japanese and German models. The assemblies were conceived as sounding boards of provincial opinion; in large part, their discussions were to be limited to matters submitted to them by the viceroy or governor. The right to vote for electors, who in turn would choose members of the assembly, was strictly limited by property or scholastic qualifications.

As time would show, these assemblies were to make their presence felt in two ways: they reflected public opinion to a considerable degree, and they checked the efforts of the central government to increase its own power.

On the subject of constitutional principles, the court reformers were perfectly clear in their position. "The government of China," said one memorial, "is to be constitutional by imperial decree. ... The principles of the constitution are the great laws which may not be lightly altered. ... The constitution is designed to conserve the power of the sovereign and protect the officials and the people." All legislative, executive, and judicial authority was reserved to the Manchu sovereign.

Parliament was given power to propose legislation ...; it might adopt measures of government; and it might impeach ministers for illegal acts, but no action it took had any weight or validity save that derived from the Imperial sanction.[6]

As W. W. Rockhill, American minister at Peking, commented, the purpose of the imperial reformers was "a perpetuation of the existing system under a thin veil of constitutional guarantees."[7]

Application of this program of political reform was to take place gradually over a period of nine years. In 1909 the provincial assemblies met for the first time, conducted themselves with considerable dignity, and led in the public agitation for early calling of a parliament. The following year the National Assembly held its first meeting (October 3, 1910). Of the 200 members, 100 were chosen by the throne, the remainder by the provincial assemblies from their own members. Contrary to expectation, this Assembly, far from proving a mere rubber stamp, forced the government's decision to convoke a parliament in 1913 instead of 1917. It also forced the throne to consider concessions toward the establishment of a responsible ministry. In general it showed a remarkably independent attitude.

---

[6] Vinacke, *Constitutional Development,* 77.

[7] Quoted in Vinacke, *Constitutional Development,* 79.

The independence shown by this hand-picked National Assembly of 1910 confirmed a more general political awakening than the Manchu government with all its reforms had been willing to acknowledge. Moreover, this national awakening had found two potential leaders, who differed widely in intellectual background and in the means by which they proposed to achieve China's salvation. These men were Liang Ch'i-ch'ao and Sun Yat-sen.

LIANG CH'I-CH'AO (1873-1929)

After his escape to Japan in 1898 from the wrath of the empress dowager, Liang moved rapidly forward as a philosopher, writer, and editor from the reform philosophy of his teacher K'ang Yu-wei. A reinterpretation of Confucianism was no longer enough for Liang. The Chinese must become a "new people," reborn by a new patriotic and cultural movement. By the force of his reputation as a scholar, and by the vigor of his pen, Liang became the first great teacher of modern Chinese citizenship. He was among the first of the scholar-elite to free himself from the Confucian tradition. Probably no Chinese of the time was so influential in popularizing modern knowledge, especially among the student class at home and in Japan. There was little place in Liang's doctrine for the feeble reformism of the empress dowager.[8]

As an exile in Japan, Liang became a vigorous and eloquent exponent of Western ideas, established a school for Chinese students at Tokyo, and eventually became the mentor of a whole generation of young Chinese intellectuals who studied in Japan in the decade following the Boxer affair. Liang was thoroughly grounded in Chinese classical learning, had exceedingly broad intellectual interests, wrote forcefully on a great variety of subjects, and so became the most admired author of the period. By going far outside Chinese learning he launched a great reappraisal of Chinese history, which has continued since his time.

Liang's vision of the future China pictured a constitutional monarchy with a parliament operating on the principle of responsible government. Since he did not believe the Chinese people were ready for full representative democracy, he advocated gradual constitutional change. Consequently he aroused the ire of both the Ch'ing government and of those who would destroy it. In his role as an intellectual aristocrat, Liang's political philosophy stressed moral virtues derived from both the Confucian and the Western world, but rarely practiced by either. Among these were self-respect, moral renovation, enterprise, the rule of law, and loyalty to the nation. This set of virtues showed how far Liang had moved from his Confucian background, yet the Confucian base was not absent. Moreover, with a rare intellectual honesty, he did not look upon the Ch'ing dynasty as the author of all China's troubles.[9]

SUN YAT-SEN (1866-1925)

Contrasting sharply with Liang's intellectual drive to shape the mind of modern China was the career of Sun Wen or, as he was generally known, Sun Yat-sen—the activist, the professional revolutionary. Unlike Liang, born an aristocrat and raised in classical scholarship, Sun Yat-sen came of peasant stock in the Canton-Macao region, an area far from Peking and the birthplace of many of China's rebels. Some of Sun's relatives had supported the T'ai-p'ings. At age thirteen he was sent to Honolulu, where an older brother enrolled him for three years in a Church of England school. Returning to his native village as a Christian convert, he outraged the community with his idol smashing and was again sent away. At Hong Kong he

[8] For an interpretation of Liang, 1898-1911, see Joseph R. Levenson, *Liang Ch'i-ch'ao and the Mind of Modern China* (1953),* 55-169. See also Robert A. Scalapino, "Prelude to Marxism: the Chinese Student Movement in Japan, 1900-1910," in *Approaches to Modern Chinese History*, Albert Feuerwerker, et al. eds. (1967), 190-215.

[9] Philip C. Huang, *Liang Ch'i-ch'ao and Modern Chinese Liberalism* (1973). Liang's ideas about the nature of man and the needs of modern China were a fusion of particular Confucian, Meiji Japanese, and Western concepts. At the heart of his program was the picture of the "new citizen" who would combine the Confucian stress on morality, Liang's own high regard for freedom of thought, and the Meiji belief that an awakened citizenry could create a state notable for its liberal democracy and its national power.

studied medicine at a British mission hospital, practiced briefly at Macao, but soon thereafter turned to his first interest, the remaking of China through the traditional method of revolt instigated by secret societies. On the eve of the Sino-Japanese war he had formed his own secret society, the *Hsing-chung Hui* (Revive China). Its attempt in 1895 to take over the Canton government failed and Sun went into exile in Japan, where he took the Japanese name of Nakayama, meaning "central mountain". The following year, Sun was seized in London and imprisoned in the Chinese legation, where the plan was to get him back to Peking for execution. But the plot was discovered and the efforts of Sir James Cantlie, his former teacher at Hong Kong, along with an aroused public opinion, prompted the British government to secure his release.

THE SAN MIN CHU-I

During the next turbulent decade (1896-1905), the years in which China's humiliations reached new heights, revolutionary movements and groups were increasing among Chinese at home and abroad, but they were in competition one with another and were without coordination, a common ideology, or united programs of action. This vacuum propelled Sun into devising his own particular doctrine and program. It was to be known as his Three Principles of the People, the *San min chu-i*. The first of the three principles, *min-tsu chu-i*, rendered as "nationalism," was a term suggesting people and race. To Sun it was a call to end the alien Manchu rule and China's semi-colonial status under the unequal treaties and the foreign naval leaseholds. The second principle, *min-ch'uan chu-i* —"people's rights" or "democracy"—included a great cluster of political notions, such as election, initiative, referendum, and recall, plus the classification of government branches and powers under such headings as executive, legislative, judicial, control, and examination. The control (supervision) and examination functions were derived from Confucian institutions, the censorate and the civil service examinations. The third principle, *min-sheng chu-i*—"people's

livelihood"—was Sun's particular form of socialism. It was not based on the Marxian concept of class struggle, but rather on the single tax theory of Henry George, which held that the state should take all unearned future increment in land values in order to defeat speculation and monopoly. Sun's socialism, however, did not contemplate redistribution of land; such an idea would have had little appeal to landlords and merchants whose support Sun needed. They were interested in a political but not an economic or social revolution.

THE T'UNG-MENG HUI

The Three Principles provided Sun with effective political doctrine and, thus armed, he moved to the creation of a party designed to unite all revolutionary factions. With support coming from Chinese communities in Honolulu, the United States, Europe, and Japan, the Chinese United League (*Chung-kuo T'ung-meng hui*) was formed at Tokyo in 1905 with Sun, now 39, as its leader. Branches of the League were to be formed secretly in the provinces of China and it was to have overseas offices at San Francisco, Honolulu, Brussels, and Singapore. For a time following these developments the fortunes of revolution seemed to be prospering.

Sun Yat-sen had become the most widely known of China's revolutionaries but he had not achieved a preeminent leadership among those favoring a new China. As a Chinese trained abroad, he had little standing as yet with the scholar-elite; he was still regarded in many quarters not as the sage to lead China into a new era but merely as an able conspirator. Nevertheless, the League, with its new ideology of republicanism, made a strong appeal, especially to Chinese students. In *Minpao (The People),* the journal of the League, able associates of Sun, such as Wang Ching-wei and Hu Han-min, advanced the idea that Liang Ch'i-ch'ao's gradual constitutional reform was not enough and that China was capable of a quick and thorough republican revolution.

This optimism of the revolutionaries was premature since, even within the League, unity in the revolutionary movement had not been achieved. In 1906 a revolt in Hunan province was suppressed easily. In 1907, as a result of protests from the Ch'ing government, Sun was expelled from Japan. In 1908, agents of the League were ousted by France from her Vietnam colonies. Meanwhile, the further success of Peking in arresting and executing conspirators discouraged funding of Sun's movement by overseas Chinese. By 1910, the prospects for Sun and the League were at best uncertain.[10]

ECONOMIC REFORM

Side by side with the Manchu reform program and the revolutionary agitations of Liang and Sun, China witnessed in the first decade of the twentieth century the beginnings of an industrial revolution. After 1896 nationals of the treaty powers enjoyed the right not only to trade but also to engage in industry and manufacturing in the treaty ports. The appearance of this new foreign-owned factory industry, employing cheap Chinese labor, coincided with the appearance of the foreign naval leaseholds and the spheres of influence. This industrial activity, seeming to pose a threat to China's rural handicraft industries, stirred the Manchu-Chinese government to encourage the development of modern Chinese industry. Invention was invited by the offer of patents and monopolies; by 1906 a ministry of agriculture, industry, and commerce had been created at Peking; codes of commercial and company law were issued. As a result, there was some growth of Chinese factory industry, including cotton textile mills, electric plants, flour mills, match and tobacco factories, steel mills, and silk filatures, along with the construction of railroads.

Financing of these enterprises was aided, though ineffectively, by the founding of the first modern Chinese banks to compete with the great foreign banking houses of the treaty ports. These developments, the beginnings of modern Chinese industrialization, were obviously of great significance but, in general, the Manchu industrial reforms, as part of the "self-strengthening" movement, were designed less to encourage industry than to save the dynasty. China's meager capital accumulation went into the purchase of land or into usurious loans to the peasantry rather than into needed industrial development. Furthermore, what efforts were made toward industrialization were joint official-merchant undertakings, and thus a prelude to the bureaucratic capitalism which was to develop in republican China.[11]

REFLECTIONS ON REFORM

By the end of 1910 China had had a decade of reform, but the country remained bewildered and baffled. A dynasty which had ruled for more than two and one-half centuries and which had finally sought refuge in reform was now reduced to impotence. In turning to reform it had turned away from tradition, and in deserting tradition it lost its claim to rule. Philosophically, the strongest claim of the alien Manchus to rule in China rested on their historic support of Confucianism. But Confucianism's hallowed tradition was no longer a convincing political vehicle.

On the positive side, the answer to China's ills seemed to lie in some form of modernization and Westernization. Yet neither the liberal followers of Liang Ch'i-ch'ao nor the revolutionaries led by Sun Yat-sen had shown the power to take command and to lead the nation into a new life.

The central problem for China in 1910, as it had been for Japan a half-century earlier, was how to survive. Japan had met her crisis di-

[10] The fame of Sun Yat-sen as the father of China's first modern revolution was due to his skill as improviser, not to the quality of his ideas or his capacity as a political philosopher. At first considered to be no more than an uncouth conspirator, Sun improved his political stature with China's growing and disaffected intellectual elite between 1896 and 1910. But it was political style, not ideas, that made him unique. See Harold Z. Schiffrin, *Sun Yat-sen and the Origins of the Chinese Revolution* (1970),* 1-9; Harold Z. Schiffrin, "Sun Yat-sen's Early Land Policy," *Journal of Asian Studies,* 16 (1957), 549-64; and Robert A. Scalapino and Harold Z. Schiffrin, "Early Socialist Currents in the Chinese Revolutionary Movement," *Ibid.,* 18 (1959), 321-42.

[11] Peking's efforts toward industrialization in the first decade of the century were aided by the stirrings of nationalism and by anti-dynastic movements. For background see En-han Lee, "China's Response to Foreign Investment in Her Mining Industry (1902-1911)," *Journal of Asian Studies,* 28 (1968), 55-76.

rectly and with vast self-confidence; China's slower response was due to an absence of self-confidence. But why? The answer would seem to be that China's catastrophes of the nineteenth century were not simple political and military defeats; they were cultural and psychological defeats. They had called into question the great tradition by which the Chinese had always lived and which had become so much a part of their being that it was largely taken for granted. In her long history China had suffered military defeat many times. She had always recovered and survived and, indeed, had absorbed the conqueror into her cultural system. But in the nineteenth and the early twentieth centuries it seemed to increasing numbers of Chinese that they were powerless both politically and culturally. They felt, and with reason, that the barbarian world was determined not only to defeat China on the battlefield but also to destroy her civilization, to humiliate her spirit, and to deny her any sense of self-worth.[12]

[12] The way in which the Chinese saw the fate that was befalling them is particularly difficult for Americans to appreciate, for the simple reason that Americans, at least to this point, have experienced nothing remotely comparable to what had been happening in China. See Lyman P. Van Slyke, "China and the United States," *Stanford Observer* (April, 1972), 7.

There have been many points in this study where the reader has been faced with the perplexing historical question: Why did the Confucian system fail? One answer, frequently encountered, tends to idealize the Confucian tradition and to explain China's recent and contemporary problems as a product of departures from the Confucian tradition, departures brought about either by weak monarchs and scholar-bureaucrats within or by the arrival of the Westerners from without. The weakness of this interpretation lies in the fact that the Confucian tradition itself was not lacking in defects. For example, Confucianism of the nineteenth century illustrates almost perfectly a historic Chinese capacity to create and more especially to preserve unworkable systems. The rather inflexible Confucian order based on an agricultural economy was viable only while new arable land was available. When such land was no longer available, a system and a tradition which could not adjust to new realities failed. See Harold C. Hinton, "China: An Overview," *Problems of Communism* 18 (1969), 45.

FOR FURTHER READING

General. Jung-pang Lo, ed., and trans., *K'ang Yu-wei: A Biography and A Symposium* (1967). Sun E-tu Zen, "The Chinese Constitutional Missions of 1905-1906," *Journal of Modern History* 24 (1952), 251-68. Wolfgang Franke, *The Reform and Abolition of the Traditional Chinese Examination System* (1960).* Samuel C. Chu, *Reform in Modern China: Chang Chien, 1853-1926* (1965). Mary C. Wright, ed., *China in Revolution: The First Phase, 1900-1913* (1968).* E. Backhouse and J. O. P. Bland, *Annals and Memoirs of the Court of Peking* (1914). Hu Shih, *The Chinese Renaissance* (1934; reissued 1963). Robert A. Scalapino and George T. Yu, *The Chinese Anarchist Movement* (1961). K'ang Yu-wei, *Ta t'ung shu: The One World Philosophy,* trans. by Lawrence G. Thompson (1958). John Gilbert Reid, *The Manchu Abdication and the Powers, 1908-1912* (1935), a basic and detailed study. Marion J. Levy, *The Family Revolution in Modern China* (1949).* Florence Ayscough, *Chinese Women, Yesterday and Today* (1937).

Sun-Yat-sen and other Revolutionaries. Sir James Cantlie, *Sun Yat-sen and the Awakening of China* (1912). Hsueh Chun-tu, *Huang Hsing and the Chinese Revolution* (1961), an uneven study of one of Sun Yat-sen's close associates of early revolutionary days. Marius B. Jansen, *The Japanese and Sun Yat-sen* (1954),* a very able study, S. Y. Teng, "Dr. Sun Yat-sen and Chinese Secret Societies," *Studies on Asia* (1963), 81-99. Harold Z. Schiffrin, *Sun Yat-sen and the Origins of the Chinese Revolution* (1968).* Michael Gasster, *Chinese Intellectuals and the Revolution of 1911: The Birth of Modern Chinese Radicalism* (1969); and Mary B. Rankin, *Early Chinese Revolutionaries: Radical Intellectuals in Shanghai and Chekiang, 1902-1911* (1971).

Manchuria and Korea: 1900–1910

18

The closing years of the nineteenth century had witnessed a tremendous unleashing of imperialism in East Asia (see Chapter 15). In returning at this point to the further development of that story there is reason to review briefly some of the major steps taken in the early years of that extraordinary movement, since they bear directly on what was about to happen in Manchuria and Korea during the first decade of the new century.

By the year 1900, East Asia had become a primary focal point in the rivalry of the great imperialistic powers, who had reached the conclusion that their future strength and security would be determined in some major degree by their influence in or their control over areas in East Asia. The industrial revolution had come of age in the West; the Japanese, while far behind in the industrial race, had shown a remarkable capacity to learn from the industrial strong men of Europe and America; and China, once the center of a great Confucian civilization, had sunk to the level of a semi-colonial area, seemingly an easy prey in the next advance of foreign imperialism.

A major transformation had been imposed upon China since 1842-1844 and 1858-1860

when Western commercial ambitions had devised the unequal treaty system. That system was still the foundation of the powers' position in China, but the superstructure of the system had been greatly enlarged. On China's borders and off her coasts, Burma, Indochina, the Philippines, Taiwan and the Pescadores had become colonies of Britain, France, the United States, and Japan. Within China, naval leaseholds and spheres of influence marked the imperial advance of Russia in Manchuria, Germany in Shantung, Britain in the Yangtze valley, and France in the southern provinces. Japan was seeking a sphere in Fukien, and the United States was toying with the idea of a coaling station somewhere on the China coast. The older commercial interest of the treaty system was still strong and growing stronger, but it had been overtaken and surpassed by new impulses toward capital investment, industrial exploitation, and the political influence to protect these assets. Because it was assumed that China could not or would not provide this protection, the task was undertaken by the powers themselves, singly or collectively.

The theory that China could not be counted upon to act responsibly was confirmed in the minds of the powers by the ghastly spectacle of the Boxer rebellion, aided and abetted by the dynasty's declaration of war. Incredible as it may seem, the Boxer upheaval took the powers by surprise. It was this surprise, coupled with anger and fright, which produced cooperation: the international relief army and the policy of seeking a common settlement in which China would be confronted by a united front. It was a plausible and, on ethical grounds, even a defensible policy; in a measure it succeeded. It produced the Boxer protocol of 1901. Yet the policy also failed, in that Russia, while negotiating in common with the others, was also attempting secretly to make a separate agreement that would give her exclusive control in Manchuria.[1]

THE RUSSIANS IN MANCHURIA

During 1900 the antiforeignism and violence of the Boxer movement spread to Manchuria, where the Russians were building the Chinese Eastern Railway across central Manchuria and the southern branch line from Harbin to Port Arthur and Dalny (later named Dairen) in the Liaotung (Kwantung) leased territory. This violence was the pretext which put a Russian army of 175,000 men into Manchuria. By November, Russia was in complete military control of the Three Eastern Provinces (Manchuria), and Admiral E. I. Alexeiev, governor-general of Russia's leasehold, had exacted a provisional agreement from the Manchu military governor at Mukden, giving Russia a free hand in Manchuria in all but name. The Manchu court, though frightened and in exile at Sian, refused to ratify this agreement. By February, 1901, Russia was demanding of China a treaty (separate from the joint negotiations at Peking) which in phraseology appeared to restore Manchuria to China but which in reality preserved the Russian occupation: Russian troops would be known as railway guards.

The powers promptly warned China not to accept any separate agreement with Russia prior to conclusion of the joint negotiations on

the Boxer affair. Similar warnings came from China's diplomats abroad. Finally, the harassed Ch'ing government refused the Russian demands. Russia's military occupation continued.[2]

THE ANGLO-JAPANESE ALLIANCE

Russia's determination to have her way in Manchuria produced a vigorous response in Japan and Great Britain. As early as the crisis of 1898, when Russia leased Port Arthur, there had been preliminary feelers between London and Tokyo on an Anglo-Japanese alliance. Japan was particularly sensitive because, since 1895, Russian rather than Japanese influence had prevailed not only in Manchuria but also in Korea. Moreover, Russia's lease of Port Arthur was by no means welcome to the British. Nevertheless, these preliminary soundings were premature; Britain still hoped for a compromise settlement with Russia; and Ito Hirobumi believed that Japan's interests in Korea could be restored by an arrangement with Russia rather than with Britain. Consequently, it was not until August, 1901, with Russia in full occupation of Manchuria, that serious Anglo-Japanese negotiations were undertaken. By that time Ito had resigned as prime minister and had been replaced by General Katsura Taro, a protege of General Yamagata Aritomo. Yamagata, unlike Ito, believed that war with Russia was inevitable. Thus the decision was made at Tokyo and London to conclude the Anglo-Japanese alliance.

This alliance, signed January 30, 1902, pledged the signatories to support "the status quo and general peace in the Extreme East," the "independence and territorial integrity" of China and Korea, and the open door policy. These points were diplomatic window dressing. The real importance of the alliance was its recognition of the special interests of both powers in China, and the special interests of Japan "politically as well as commercially and industrially" in Korea. These terms were clearly

[1] Chester C. Tan, *The Boxer Catastrophe* (1955).*

[2] Texts of the agreements can be found in John V. A. MacMurray, ed., *Treaties and Agreements with and concerning China, 1894-1919* (2 vols., 1921). See also George A. Lensen, *The Russo-Chinese War* (1967).

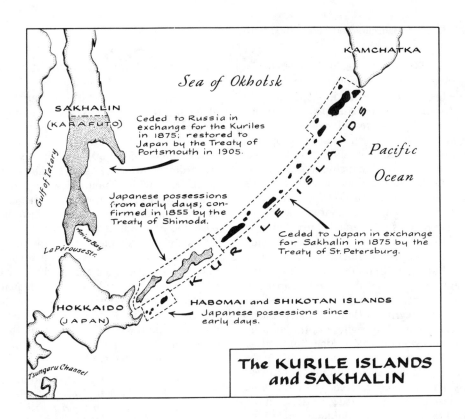

KAMCHATKA

Sea of Okhotsk

SAKHALIN
(KARAFUTO)

Ceded to Russia in
exchange for the Kuriles
in 1875; restored to
Japan by the Treaty of
Portsmouth in 1905.

*Pacific
Ocean*

Gulf of Tatary

Aniva Bay

La Pérouse Str.

Japanese possessions
from early days; con-
firmed in 1855 by the
Treaty of Shimoda.

KURILE ISLANDS

Ceded to Japan in exchange
for Sakhalin in 1875 by the
Treaty of St. Petersburg.

HOKKAIDO
(JAPAN)

HABOMAI and SHIKOTAN ISLANDS
Japanese possessions since
early days.

Tsungaru Channel

**The KURILE ISLANDS
and SAKHALIN**

a victory for the principle of spheres of influence; they were an equally obvious defeat for the policy of the open door. The alliance went on to pledge each signatory to neutrality if the other were at war with another power, and to come to the other's assistance if attacked by more than one state. Since it was evident that the alliance was aimed at St. Petersburg, Russia and France replied with a declaration (March, 1902) taking cognizance of it and reaffirming their adherence to the status quo and the integrity of China.

This unprecedented alliance between an Eastern and a Western power ended Britain's splendid isolation, elevated Japan to unquestioned great power status, and gave her a new freedom to deal with what she regarded as the Russian menace in Manchuria and Korea.[3]

[3] Ian Nish, *The Anglo-Japanese Alliance* (1966) includes the full text of the alliance and the secret diplomatic notes covering naval cooperation. For Ito's views and his attempts to reach a settlement with Russia see Takeuchi Tatsuji, *War and Diplomacy in the Japanese Empire* (1935), 124-28. The work of the alliance propagandists is portrayed by C. N. Spinks, "The Background of the Anglo-Japanese Alliance," *Pacific Historical Review*, 8 (1939), 317-39.

THE RUSSO-JAPANESE NEGOTIATIONS

The most immediate and specific effect of the Anglo-Japanese alliance was a Russo-Chinese agreement (April, 1902) by which Russia said she would evacuate her troops from Manchuria in three stages over an eighteen-month period. This agreement provided some easing of the tension but it did not answer the question, uppermost at Tokyo, whether Russia would recognize and respect Japan's special interests in Korea noted in the Anglo-Japanese alliance. Japan was acquiring strategic property in Korea; she was aware of Russian plans to exploit the timber resources of the Yalu River valley in northwestern Korea; and, as time went on, she was alarmed by Russia's failure to proceed with scheduled troop evacuation, and by new demands presented by the Russians to China (April, 1903). If accepted, these demands would have transformed the Russian sphere into a protectorate.[4]

[4] Among these demands, Russia stipulated that China agree: (1) to open no new treaty ports or to admit no additional consuls in Manchuria, and (2) to employ no foreigners save Russians in Manchuria. *United States Foreign Relations, 1903*, 53-54.

In June, 1903, Japan decided to open discussions with Russia. Her position would be to acknowledge Russian rights in Manchuria in return for Russian recognition of Japan's special interests in Korea. Japan's first proposals in August brought counterproposals from Russia in October. In sum, these counterproposals insisted that Manchuria was an exclusive Russian concern, that there should be a neutral zone in Korea, and that Japan was not to use her position in Korea for strategic purposes. Negotiations continued into January, 1904. By this time the tsar's advisers had made the decision to concede much to the Japanese in Korea, but the full implications of this decision were not conveyed to the Japanese. Japan's final terms said that if Russia respected the territorial integrity of China and Manchuria, and respected the treaty rights of other powers there, Japan would regard Manchuria as a Russian sphere, but Russia must agree not to interfere with Japan's special interests in Korea. No reply having been received by February 4, the Japanese government made the decision for war. As Japan broke off diplomatic relations and as Russian troops crossed the Yalu into Korea, Admiral Togo Heihachiro attacked and crippled the Russian squadron at Port Arthur, February 8. Two days later Japan declared war. To neither power did war come as a surprise; history presents few better examples of a war fought by both powers for imperialistic ends. In assessing the relative responsibility of Tokyo and St. Petersburg, if indeed this be possible, "... it can at least be said for Japan that her policy was based upon a real need. The argument for self-preservation is in her favor."[5]

[5] W. L. Langer, "The Origins of the Russo-Japanese War," *Europaische Gesprache* 4, 279-335. See Shumpei Okamoto, *The Japanese Oligarchy and the Russo-Japanese War* (1970) on how the Japanese decisions were made; on Russian policy, see Andrew Malozenoff, *Russian Far Eastern Policy 1881-1904* (1958). From the beginning, the negotiations were complicated by irresponsible factionalism among the advisers and friends of the tsar. For example, toward the end of the negotiations the Russians decided to no longer insist on a neutral zone in north Korea. This was a significant change in Russian policy, but Rear Admiral A. M. Abaza deliberately misrepresented the

THE U. S. AND MANCHURIA, 1901-1905

The Russian occupation of Manchuria, a serious challenge to Japan, was also a rebuff to the United States since it was designed to destroy John Hay's open door of 1899 and his pronouncement of 1900 on China's integrity. Accordingly when Russia sought a separate agreement with China, Hay warned Peking (February, 1901) of the danger of making any separate arrangement without the full knowledge and approval of all the powers. While this was simply a statement of an all too obvious truth, there was the hope that it might bolster Peking's morale. When the Anglo-Japanese alliance was announced, Hay, inadequately informed by his diplomatic service, was taken by surprise. As the Russians announced the intended withdrawal of their troops from Manchuria, he wrote to President Theodore Roosevelt with unadorned realism:

We are not in any attitude of hostility towards Russia in Manchuria. On the contrary we recognize her exceptional position in northern China. What we have been working for two years to accomplish, and what we have at last accomplished, if assurances are to count for anything, is that, no matter what happens eventually in northern China and Manchuria, the United States shall not be placed in any worse position than while the country was under the unquestioned domination of China.[6]

In Hay's comments there was the rather clear intimation that China's integrity was, after all, not very important in American policy at that time. What was important were American treaty rights.

The outbreak of the Russo-Japanese war increased the danger to any open door policy and

Russian decision to Kurino Shinichiro, Japan's representative at St. Petersburg. The tsar was responsible for these cross purposes within his administration, yet it appears that he hoped to avoid war with Japan even at the price of giving Japan a relatively free hand in Korea. See Raymond A. Esthus, *Theodore Roosevelt and Japan* (1966), 21-22.

[6] Roosevelt Papers, quoted by Tyler Dennett, *Roosevelt and the Russo-Japanese War* (1925), 135-36.

to China's integrity. Accordingly, President Roosevelt reasserted the Hay policy of 1900, asking the powers to respect "the neutrality of China and in all practical ways her administrative entity." Thus the conception of *de jure* Chinese sovereignty over Manchuria was restored to American diplomacy. In this sense a traditional American policy in China was reinforced at least formally, but at the same time it was weakened by the evident American willingness "to follow Great Britain's example and abandon . . . [Korea] to its Japanese fate." Russia was quick to ask why the United States opposed her in Manchuria while giving Japan a green light in Korea.[7] At the same time, in far western China the claim of integrity was rebuffed by the British. In the course of Anglo-American discussions on Tibet, the British referred to Chinese sovereignty there as a "constitutional fiction" and a "political affectation."

While the Russo-Japanese war was in progress, the United States made two more efforts to keep alive the principle of China's integrity. The first of these was a diplomatic circular, January 13, 1905. The Russian response gave no satisfaction. The second was President Roosevelt's demand upon Japan for assurance that she "adhere to the position of maintaining

[7] A. Whitney Griswold, *The Far Eastern Policy of the United States* (1938),* 96-97. American diplomats in East Asia—Griscom at Tokyo, Allen at Seoul, as well as Hay and Rockhill—looked to Japan as the only, if not the most desirable, solution of the Korean problem.

the open door in Manchuria and restoring that province to China." Without this assurance the president was not prepared to act as mediator. It would be foolish, however, to ignore the fact that the open door and the integrity of China meant little to the powers and that they were hardly given more than diplomatic lip-service. Until such time as the United States was prepared to attack the spheres directly, its policies of the open door and China's integrity were destined to savor of the doctrinaire. Moreover, there was nothing to indicate that American public opinion would have sanctioned stronger measures even had the department of state wished to apply them. Finally, there was the embarrassing fact that American policy had not always remained true to its own announced principles. Hay himself, at the behest of the U.S. Navy, had indulged in concession hunting and, what is more, had told Roosevelt that China's integrity in Manchuria was of little concern so long as American treaty rights there were not adversely affected.

WAR ON LAND AND SEA

A peculiarity of the Russo-Japanese war was that it was fought primarily in Manchuria, which was Chinese and hence neutral territory. Since Russia, however, was in military occupation of Manchuria after 1900, and since Peking lacked the power to oust her from the three eastern provinces, there was nothing for China to do but recognize an area of hostilities and

An artist's version of Japanese army operations in the war with Russia. Note the appeal to patriotism in this picture and the one portraying Japanese operations against the Boxers (Chapter 16).

thereby imply her consent to military operations there by the belligerents.[8]

As hostilities got under way there was a vast difference in the morale of the two combatants. In Japan the war was a popular cause and there was a notable unity of purpose; in Russia there was no unity. The more extreme elements were turning to revolutionary activity, while many in business and intellectual circles hoped for a Russian defeat in Manchuria. Only defeat, it was felt, would free the tsar from the adventurers among his advisers and open the way for the political modernization of an autocratic, irresponsible regime.

In her military advance, Japan landed armies in Korea, drove the Russians from north Korea, and began the invasion of Manchuria. After a five-month siege Port Arthur was captured, January 2, 1905. In March, the Japanese took Mukden after a battle in which close to 400,000 troops were engaged on each side. Each major engagement forced the Russians to retire further to the north though their armies were not destroyed or routed. Then in May came Russia's defeat at sea. The Baltic fleet, having made the long voyage from Europe, was destroyed in the Korean Straits by the Japanese under Admiral Togo.

PROBLEM OF PEACE

Efforts to find a basis for peace had been undertaken early in the war. Although Japan had won military victories on land and had destroyed Russian sea power, she had failed to destroy the Russian armies. Each victory removed Japanese armies further from their base, and the nation's economy had been strained to the point of danger. On the other hand, although Russia's position showed some improvement in a military sense as the war dragged on, her funds were exhausted and French bankers were not disposed to extend further credits. In addition, revolutionary movements within Russia threatened the entire war effort.

[8] Takahashi Sakuye, *International Law Applied to the Russo-Japanese War* (1908), 250; and Amos S. Hershey, *The International Law and Diplomacy of the Russo-Japanese War* (1906).

It was Japan that made the first formal proposal for peace in May, 1905, when she requested President Theodore Roosevelt on his own "initiative to invite the two belligerents to come together for the purpose of direct negotiation." Roosevelt's subsequent approach to the tsar was accepted June 6, and two days later the United States sent formal invitations to the belligerents, offering good offices. Both powers accepted. Roosevelt had acted because, as he said:

> *I believe that our future history will be more determined by our position on the Pacific facing China than our position on the Atlantic facing Europe.*[9]

It is unnecessary here to treat in any detail the preliminaries of the peace settlement made at Portsmouth, New Hampshire: the appointment of delegates, Witte and Rosen for Russia, Komura and Takahira for Japan; the death of Secretary Hay, July 1, 1905; the renewal of the Anglo-Japanese alliance, August 12, 1905, recognizing Japan's "paramount political, military, and economic" interests in Korea; the signing of the secret treaty of Bjorko between the kaiser and the tsar, the alleged success of Witte in capturing American sympathy for Russia's case; the capacity of the Japanese "by their stiffness and taciturnity" to lose in the negotiations the advantage won by their military and naval victories; and the other repeated crises into which the negotiations fell.[10]

[9] A. L. P. Dennis, *Adventures in American Diplomacy, 1896-1906* (1928), 406.

[10] It is now clear that Japan's senior oligarchs were both cautious and realistic in their control of the negotiations which led to war and in the decision to make peace on the basis of minimal war aims. In contrast, the most outspoken advocates of a quick declaration of war and a harsh peace were party politicians, leaders of patriotic societies, journalists, and some academics. The weakness of the oligarchy was that it did not lead this activist public opinion into more moderate and realistic channels. See the excellent study cited earlier, Okamoto, *The Japanese Oligarchy*. In regard to American public opinion, see W.B. Thorson, "American Public Opinion and the Portsmouth Peace Conference," *American Historical Review*, 53 (1947-48), 439-64.

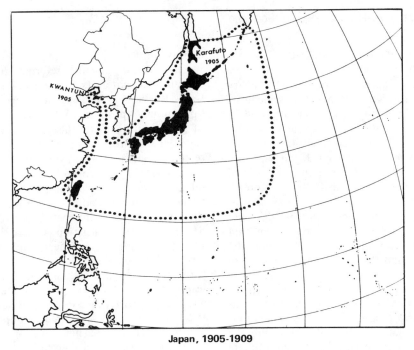

Japan, 1905-1909

Reproduced from A War Atlas for Americans *(New York: Simon & Schuster) 1944, with permission from the publisher and from the U.S. Department of State, Division of Map Intelligence and Cartography.*

THE TREATY OF PORTSMOUTH

The treaty of Portsmouth, September 5, 1905, was destined to become one of the most consequential agreements in the modern history of East Asia. By it Japan acquired from Russia, subject to the consent of China, the Liaotung leased territory and the southern section of the Chinese Eastern Railroad from Kuan-ch'eng-tzu (near Changchun) to Port Arthur, along with certain coal mines which belonged to or were worked by the Russians. Both powers agreed "to evacuate completely and simultaneously Manchuria," except the Liaotung leasehold, within eighteen months after the treaty became effective. Both powers, however, reserved the right "to maintain guards" to protect their respective railway lines in Manchuria. Russia declared that she did not have in Manchuria "any territorial advantages or preferential or exclusive concessions in impairment of Chinese sovereignty or inconsistent with the principle of equal opportunity." Both Japan and Russia engaged "not to obstruct any general measures common to all countries, which China may take for the development of the commerce and industry of Manchuria." The two powers also agreed to "exploit their respective railways in Manchuria exclusively for commercial and industrial purposes and in no wise for strategic purposes with the exception of the railways in the Liaotung leased territory." With regard to Korea, Russia acknowledged that Japan possessed in Korea paramount political, military, and economic interests, and engaged not to obstruct such measures as Japan might deem necessary to take. The southern half of the island of Sakhalin was ceded to Japan in lieu of a war indemnity, and Japan was granted fishing rights in certain territorial waters of Siberia on the Pacific. Above all, the war had convinced both powers of the futility of working at cross-purposes. Indeed, the treaty of Portsmouth was soon to open the door to a period of Russo-Japanese collaboration in Manchuria.

JAPAN'S NEW POSITION IN KOREA

Prior to 1905, Japan considered her primary interests to be in Korea rather than Manchuria. The decade 1894-1904 had been a period of intense but intermittent Russo-Japanese economic rivalry in Korea. The Anglo-Japanese alliance, (1902) recognized that Japan was "interested in a peculiar degree politically as well as commercially and industrially in Korea." With the outbreak of the Russo-Japanese war, Korea proclaimed her neutrality but took no steps to defend it, believing, it would seem, that benevolent protection would come from the United States and the great powers of western Europe. Japan, however, was no longer concerned with Korean neutrality or Korean independence. In the military sphere, Korea was looked upon as a necessary base of operations against Russia, and in the political sphere the peninsula was soon to be subjected to intimate Japanese control. Japanese forces occupied Seoul (February 8, 1904) the day Admiral Togo attacked Port Arthur, and a protocol signed February 23 laid the groundwork for the subsequent Japanese protectorate. Korea was to place "full confidence" in Japan and to "adopt the advice of the latter with regard to improvements in administration." Japan would definitely guarantee the independence and territorial "integrity" of Korea and to this end might interfere in Korean affairs. Korea was pledged not to conclude with third powers any agreement "contrary to the principles" of the protocol. In additional agreements (August 19-22, 1904), Japan was empowered to appoint advisers to the Korean departments of finance and foreign affairs. By the beginning of 1905, Japan had assumed responsibility for policing the Korean capital and had placed a Japanese police inspector in each province. Moreover, international sanction was promptly given to Japan's new position in Korea. William Howard Taft, Roosevelt's secretary of war, in conversations with the Japanese prime minister, General Count Katsura, gave his approval, later confirmed by the president, to a Japanese suz-erainty in Korea.[11] In August, the renewed Anglo-Japanese alliance referred to Japan's "paramount" interests at Seoul and, in September, Russia likewise acknowledged Japan's "paramount" position (Article II of the treaty of Portsmouth). With this international sanction, Japan, through pressure exerted at Seoul, secured from the Korean government an agreement giving Japan control of Korea's foreign relations and the right to appoint a Japanese resident-general at Seoul. On the following day the United States instructed its Minister at Seoul to close the legation. Willard Straight, a young virtuoso in American diplomacy, described this diplomatic retreat as "like the stampede of rats from a sinking ship." The establishment of the Japanese protectorate in Korea was complete. Having consolidated her position at Seoul, Japan was prepared to implement in South Manchuria the new position which the treaty of Portsmouth had given her.[12]

STEEL RAILS AND POLITICS

In general, the treaty of Portsmouth divided Manchuria into "North Manchuria," where Russia still claimed a sphere of influence, and "South Manchuria," where Japan was about to create a sphere.[13] Since Japan had professed to

[11] H. F. Pringle, *Theodore Roosevelt* (1932),* 384. Japan in turn satisfied Roosevelt by a disavowal of any aggressive purpose in the Philippines. For the nature and meaning of the so-called Taft-Katsura understanding see Raymond A. Esthus, "The Taft-Katsura Agreement—Reality or Myth?" *Journal of Modern History,* 31 (1959), 46-51, and Jongsuk Chay, "The Taft-Katsura Memorandum Reconsidered," *Pacific Historical Review,* 37 (1968), 321-26.

[12] For a Japanese account of the Korean negotiations, see Takeuchi, *War and Diplomacy,* 160-62.

[13] The line of demarcation between these spheres (North and South Manchuria) was defined in the secret Russo-Japanese treaties of 1907, 1910, and 1912. See E. B. Price, *The Russo-Japanese Treaties of 1907-1916 Concerning Manchuria and Mongolia* (1933); also, Kungtu C. Sun assisted by Ralph W. Huenemann, *The Economic Development of Manchuria in the First Half of the Twentieth Century* (1969).*

be fighting for the open door and the integrity of China in Manchuria, the conclusion of peace was greeted with general popular enthusiasm in Europe and America; but American investors and merchants in East Asia disapproved of the treaty because they feared that Japan would now curb their activity in the Orient, particularly in the promising frontier area of South Manchuria. In its simplest form, the question was whether Manchuria was to be open on terms of equality to the commerce, industry, and capital of all nations, or whether it was to be an exclusive economic preserve of Russia and Japan, buttressed by Russian and Japanese political control in derogation of Chinese sovereignty and administration.

Although ratifications of the treaty of Portsmouth were exchanged at Washington (November 25, 1905), the former belligerents had agreed to an eighteen-month period in which to complete evacuation of their armies. This meant that for more than a year Manchuria remained partly under military occupation. Although agreements of this type were common at the termination of hostilities, they were often the subject of abuse or misunderstanding. In the case of South Manchuria, as early as March, 1906, the United States called to Japan's attention charges from American interests in China that Japanese actions could result only in the exclusion of all but Japanese trade by the time the territory was evacuated. Thus within six months of the conclusion of peace the United States was calling upon Japan, as it had previously called upon Russia, to respect the principle of equal opportunity.

SINO-JAPANESE TREATY, 1905

The treaty of Portsmouth, which had provided that the transfer to Japan of Russian territorial, railway, and other rights in South Manchuria, was to be conditional on the consent of China. This consent was secured by Japan's foreign minister, Baron Komura Jutaro, in negotiations with Yuan Shih-k'ai at Peking in a treaty dated December 22, 1905. An additional Sino-Japanese agreement of the same date contained

important provisions: (1) China agreed to open sixteen cities in Manchuria to international residence and trade; (2) Japan agreed to withdraw her troops and railway guards (if Russia would withdraw her railway guards) when "China shall have become herself capable of affording full protection to the lives and property of foreigners"; (3) Japan secured the right to maintain the military railway she had built from Antung on the Korean border to Mukden; and (4) China consented to formation of a Sino-Japanese corporation to exploit the Yalu forests.

Moreover, this formal Sino-Japanese treaty and the additional agreement were said by the Japanese government to be supplemented by secret "protocols." the most important of which pledged the Chinese government not to construct any mainline railway "in the neighborhood of and parallel to" the Japanese South Manchuria Railway (running from Changchun to Port Arthur and Dalny), or any branch line "which might be prejudicial" to the Japanese line.

To manage the railroad and the other properties acquired from Russia in South Manchuria, the Japanese government created the South Manchuria Railway Company—a joint stock company in which the Japanese government owned one-half of the capital stock and controlled appointment of the principal officers. Shareholders were limited to the Chinese and Japanese governments and to subjects of these two countries. The president and vice-president were responsible to the Japanese prime minister. The company was empowered to engage in subsidiary enterprises such as mining, water transportation, electric power, real estate, and warehousing within the railway zone. In addition, the company possessed broad civil administrative powers and authority to collect taxes within the same zone. This company became an amazingly effective agent of Japanese penetration in Manchuria. Protection of the railroad was provided by the government of Japan's leased territory of Kwantung (Liaotung), which was under a governor-general of high military rank who also exercised civil administrative power in the leased territory. Indeed, the development of South Manchurian resources resulting from the capital, energy, and efficiency of the South Manchurian Railway Company not only excited the jealousy of other foreign nationals, principally British and American, but also inspired the fear that Japanese railroads, using the S.M.R. as the trunk, would branch out east and west, to the exclusion of all non-Japanese enterprise.

JURISDICTION IN MANCHURIA

Among the more significant features of Japan's emerging special position in South Manchuria after 1905 were certain jurisdictional powers. Within the Kwantung leased territory she possessed all rights of administration pertaining to sovereignty except the power to transfer the territory. In addition, Japan and Russia exercised special jurisdictional and administrative powers in their respective railway zones. Powers exercised by Japan included: ordinary rights of administration pertaining to sovereignty, taxation, police, and transfer of real property; employment of a limited number of railroad guards to protect the railway; and ordinary police power and the customary functions of municipal and local administration. Over and above the foregoing powers, Japan enjoyed, as did also other treaty powers, extraterritoriality and consular jurisdiction—privileges long established in the China treaties. In North Manchuria, Russia continued to hold a comparable position, save that she no longer possessed a leasehold.

INTENSIFICATION OF RIVALRY

Although after 1905 China's sovereign rights in Manchuria were specifically reserved in the Kwantung territory and the various railway zones, *de facto* administration was exercised by Russia (the Chinese Eastern Railway) in North Manchuria, and by Japan (the Government General of Kwantung and the S.M.R.) in South Manchuria. Far from decreasing foreign (Russian) control in Manchuria, the Russo-

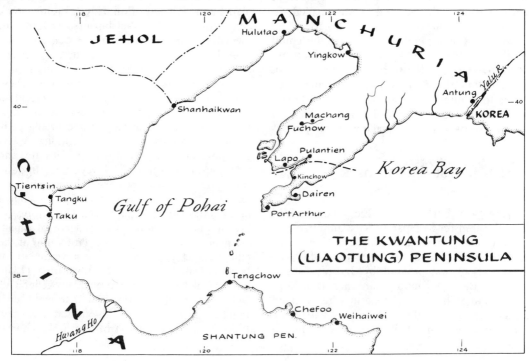

THE KWANTUNG (LIAOTUNG) PENINSULA

Japanese war had paved the way for Sino-Russian and Sino-Japanese agreements by which two powers instead of one claimed spheres of influence there. In these circumstances there were few grounds for optimism on the future of the open door doctrine and the integrity of China. Foreign business interests in China, British and American in particular, had rather naively anticipated great opportunities for their goods and capital in South Manchuria once peace was restored. These opportunities had not appeared, and the powers were concerned to discover how far Japan and Russia were bent on a policy of preference, if not monopoly, for their own commerce, industry, and capital. A test case was soon forthcoming.

BRITAIN AND MANCHURIA

In November, 1907, the Chinese government contracted with a British firm to build a short railroad from Hsinmintun to Fakumen. In its origins this contract was an outgrowth of agreements made as early as 1898 between the Chinese government and the (British) Hong Kong and Shanghai Banking Corporation for the construction of certain railways in Manchuria. Its revival in 1907 was due to private British and American interests seeking to challenge Japan's strategic position. The Japanese government promptly protested that the proposed line violated the secret "protocols" of 1905, the new road being in the Japanese view "parallel" and "prejudicial" to the S.M.R. The success of the Japanese protest was assured when the British government refused to support the British concessionaires or to call in question the validity of the "protocol" on which Japan's protest was based.

FRANCE AND MANCHURIA

Japan's post-war position in Manchuria was reinforced by diplomatic measures far more fundamental than the blocking of a small proposed railway. High on the list of Japanese aims was the difficult one of coming to workable terms with her recent enemy, Russia. This objective was rendered easier by the fact that statesmen friendly to an entente were in power

at Tokyo (Saionji, Hayashi, and Motono) and at St. Petersburg (Iswolsky). The road to a general Russo-Japanese rapprochement was paved by France. France had opposed Japan in 1895 (the triple intervention); she was allied with Russia during 1904-1905; therefore, in view of Japan's victory, it was now good policy for France to clarify her relations with Tokyo and to aid in creating a Russo-Japanese entente. The Franco-Japanese treaty, which materialized on June 10, 1907, and which provided the formula for subsequent Russo-Japanese agreements, is notable "... for its complete *sang-froid*, its subtle implications, and its bold assumptions."[14] The two powers, after agreeing "to respect the independence and integrity of China, as well as the principle of equal treatment in that country for the commerce and subjects or citizens of all nations," went on to assert that they possessed "a special interest" in preserving peace and order "especially in the regions of the Chinese Empire adjoining the territories where they possess rights of sovereignty, protection or occupation." These two powers then proceeded to constitute themselves as the guardians of peace in vast area of China which they defined as including, in the case of France, the Chinese provinces of Kwangtung, Kwangsi, and Yunnan; and, in the case of Japan, Fukien and the regions of Manchuria and Mongolia.

Following promptly this remarkable Franco-Japanese treaty came important Russo-Japanese agreements. These included a treaty of commerce and navigation and a fisheries convention,[15] and two political conventions, one public, the other secret. The public convention subscribed, as always, to the "independence and territorial integrity of the Empire of China," and pledged the signatories "to sustain and defend the maintenance of the status quo and respect for this principle by all pacific means within their reach." The secret convention (not revealed until published by the Soviet government in 1918) established precedents of the greatest importance:

1. It drew a line of demarcation between North and South Manchuria (the Russian and the Japanese spheres).

[14] Price, *Treaties,* 26-31.

[15] MacMurray, *Treaties,* I, 643-48.

2. North of this line Japan undertook not to seek for herself or her subjects, not to obstruct Russian efforts there to secure concessions for railroads or telegraphs.

3. Russia undertook neither "to interfere with nor to place any obstacle in the way of the *further development*" of the "relations of political solidarity between Japan and Korea."

4. Japan, "recognizing the special interests of Russia [in Outer Mongolia] undertook . . . to refrain from any inference with might prejudice those interests." [16]

THE UNITED STATES AND MANCHURIA

The Franco-Japanese and the Russo-Japanese agreements of 1907 reinforced the doctrine of spheres of influence, and by implication weakened further China's territorial integrity and the principle of equal opportunity. Indeed, what had become of the open door in Manchuria has never been described more realistically than by ex-President Roosevelt to his successor, President Taft:

. . . *As regards Manchuria, if the Japanese choose to follow a course of conduct to which we are adverse, we cannot stop it unless we are prepared to go to war. . . . The "Open Door" policy in China was an excellent thing . . . , but as has been proved by the whole history of Manchuria, the "Open Door" policy completely disappears as soon as a powerful nation determines to disregard it, and is willing to run the risk of war rather than forego its intention.* [17]

The foregoing explains why the American government under the presidency of Theodore Roosevelt was not prepared to lead any offensive against Japan's claim to special interests in South Manchuria. There were Americans, however, both in and outside government who did attempt to challenge the Japanese position. In 1905, E. H. Harriman, hoping to build a round-the-world transportation system, had

reached an understanding with Ito and Katsura to finance the reconstruction of the railway (S.M.R.) which Japan hoped to acquire from Russia at the end of the war. After peace came, Japan dropped the scheme. In Tokyo it seemed better policy to secure funds in London, where the Anglo-Japanese alliance had recently been renewed. Moreover, the scheme probably would have foundered in any event due to rivalry among American bankers.

Far more active than Harriman in furthering American commerce and capital in Manchuria was Willard Straight, consul-general of the United States at Mukden, 1906-1908. Straight was convinced that the weakness of the United States in East Asia was due to the relatively small American capital investment in China. A Sino-American publicity bureau which he inspired was so active that the Japanese protested and the bureau was liquidated. Straight made little progress with his official superiors as long as Roosevelt remained in the White House. Indeed, the president was less concerned with Japan's response to American capital in Manchuria than he was with the possibility of hostile Japanese action against the Philippines. Roosevelt's ideas had been shaped in part by the crisis of 1906 in American-Japanese relations when the San Francisco school board segregated Oriental students in the city schools. The "Gentleman's Agreement" of 1907-1908 restored in part a sense of diplomatic calm, but war talk was such in the summer of 1907 that the president sent to General Leonard Wood, commanding the troops in the Philippines, special instructions for meeting a Japanese attack. In October, he sent Taft to Tokyo, from where he reported that Japan was anxious to avoid war. Still, to meet the crisis in more fundamental ways Roosevelt had decided on two lines of action: (1) he sent the American fleet on a world cruise including Japanese ports (March, 1907 to February, 1909); and (2) he refused to take the offensive against Japan's position in Manchuria. [18]

While the American fleet pursued its course in foreign waters the president employed the

---

[16] Text in Price, *Treaties,* 107-11. (Emphasis added.)

[17] Roosevelt to Taft, December 22, 1910, quoted in Griswold, *Far Eastern Policy,* 132.

[18] T. A. Bailey, *Theodore Roosevelt and the Japanese-American Crises* (1934), Chapters 9 and 12.

less provocative arts of diplomacy with the Japanese in Washington. A five-year arbitration treaty with Japan was concluded May, 1908. It was an innocuous affair excluding all questions of "vital interests," but nonetheless a peaceful gesture. This treaty was followed by an exchange of notes between Secretary of State Elihu Root and the Japanese Ambassador Takahira (November 30, 1908), which "was as important for what it left unsaid as for what it definitely stipulated." Since the phraseology of the notes was delightfully general there was ground for the belief that the exchange meant more than appeared. Certainly it would seem that the Root-Takahira exchange gave some sort of moral sanction to the special position of Japan in Korea and Manchuria. At the same time there is nothing to indicate that Root intended to give Japan a free hand in Manchuria. To the American government the notes meant guarantees on the Philippines, Hawaii, and Alaska, a reiteration of the open door and integrity of China, and a quieting of war talk. To the Japanese the notes gave assurance of peace, a guarantee of Taiwan, and acceptance by the United States of the treaties giving Japan a special position in East Asia.[19]

THE SHIFT TO DOLLAR DIPLOMACY

The Roosevelt-Root policy toward Japan and Manchuria was soon to give way to a new American strategy. William Howard Taft and Philander C. Knox became president and secretary of state respectively at a time when American capital was to look increasingly to foreign fields for investment. Government was sympathetic and, as Taft said later, its policy substituted "dollars for bullets" and combined "idealistic humanitarian sentiments" with "legitimate commercial aims." The commercial machinery of the department of state was enlarged and, from November, 1908, until June, 1909, its far eastern division was headed by Willard Straight, who worked incessantly to maintain Harriman's interest in Manchurian railway finance and to enlist the interest of New York bankers. Early in 1909 these efforts bore fruit. At the instance of the state depart-

ment an American banking group was designated "as the official agent of American railway financing in China," with Straight as its Peking representative. The department then demanded of China that the American bankers be admitted to the Hukuang railway loan (see p. 270) then under negotiation between China and three banking groups representing British, French, and German interests. The new American policy was striking at European financial monopoly in China Proper as well as at the Japanese in Manchuria. This was in line with the objective of Taft and Knox "to force American capital by diplomatic pressure" into a region of the world where it would not go of its own accord. Also it meant that Secretary Knox was attempting what was diplomatically impossible, to "smoke Japan out" of her position in Manchuria despite the fact that Japan by 1907 "had given general notice of her determination to dominate as much of Manchuria as she could."[20]

Implementation of the smoking-out experiment was begun by Straight and Harriman, who in 1909 were also attempting to buy the Chinese Eastern Railway from Russia. What Harriman really wanted was the Japanese S.M.R., but the Japanese had refused to sell. Harriman, therefore, would force the sale by buying the Russian road and connecting it with the Gulf of Pechihli by a new line parallel to the S.M.R. from Chinchow (near Shanhaikwan where the Great Wall meets the sea) to Aigun on the Amur. If the threat of construction did not bring the Japanese to terms, then actual construction of the Chinchow-Aigun line would be undertaken. "He [Harriman] would smash competitors in Manchuria exactly as he had smashed them at home."[21] But Harriman died on September 10, 1909, and although Straight secured from the Manchurian government a preliminary agreement to finance (by the American group) and to construct (by a British firm) the Chinchow-Aigun line, the bankers in New York became timid without Harriman's leadership. Harriman's railroad politics had failed.

[19] T. A. Bailey, "The Root-Takahira Agreement of 1908," *Pacific Historical Review,* 9 (1940), 19-35.

[20] J. G. Reid, *The Manchu Abdication and the Powers* (1935), 75.

[21] Griswold, *Far Eastern Policy,* 152-53; Reid, *Manchu Abdication,* 42.

THE KNOX NEUTRALIZATION PROPOSAL

Still not discouraged, on November 6, 1909, Secretary Knox made two striking (some would say fantastic) proposals to Great Britain: (1) that the foreign-owned Manchurian railways (C.E.R. and S.M.R. systems) be "neutralized" by providing China with funds to purchase them through a great multipower loan, during the life of which the railroads would be under multinational foreign control; and (2) in case "neutralization" proved impracticable, that Great Britain join with the United States in supporting the Chinchow-Aigun project and in inviting powers "friendly to complete commercial neutralization of Manchuria to participate." These propositions were as Gargantuan as they were romantic.

Sir Edward Grey approved "the general principle" of the neutralization proposal but thought it "wiser to postpone" any consideration of its application. As to the Chinchow-Aigun proposal, Sir Edward thought nothing should be done until China had agreed to Japanese participation. With this British approval in principle but refusal in fact, Knox approached the Chinese, French, German, Japanese, and Russian governments. Russia and Japan, after consulting with each other, rejected the neutralization scheme in notes that showed a marked similarity. In addition, they warned China that they must be consulted before foreign capital was employed in Manchurian railway enterprise. As a result, France and Great Britain gave notice that they would not support the United States in the Chinchow-Aigun line. The plans of Harriman, Straight, and Knox had miscarried. But this was not all, Secretary Knox had hastened, and assured, a tightening of the Russian and Japanese spheres in Manchuria. On July 4, 1910, Russia and Japan signed two conventions, again, as in 1907, one public and the other secret. They announced to the world "the perfecting" of their connecting railway service in Manchuria. They refrained from any mention of China's integrity and the open door, but engaged publicly, in case the status quo should be menaced, to decide "the measures that they

may judge necessary to take for the maintenance of the said status quo." Secretly the two powers reaffirmed the line of demarcation drawn between their spheres in 1907, and strengthened their "special position" by recognizing "the right of each, within its own sphere, freely to take all measures necessary for the safeguarding and the defense of those interests." Finally, the secret convention provided for "common action" in defense of their special interests. The significance of dollar diplomacy as practiced by Knox in this instance is that it had not opened—on the contrary, it tended to close—the door to American capital in Manchuria.

Summarized in broad perspective, the years between the end of the Russo-Japanese war and the close of the Taft administration formed a chapter in American far eastern diplomacy distinguished for virility, if not for judicious purpose and method. Japan and Russia were creating a new balance of power in East Asia. In China the collapsing Confucian order was giving place to impotency and revolution. Into the tumult of these changes stepped American finance and its government, seeking to play a decisive role. Leadership was provided by the brilliance of young Willard Straight, hero or evil genius according to interpretation. Although possessed of personal charm and intellectual acuity, Straight was a pathetic failure as a diplomat, financial agent, and judge of men and nations. He set the American pattern in anti-Japanese thought which was to be of consequence in later years. All the efforts of Harriman, Straight, Knox, the bankers, and the so-called Manchurian wing of the department of state failed to reverse the pattern set by the Root-Takahira exchange. On the contrary, dollar diplomacy in East Asia stimulated the very things it was designed to destroy—Japan's and Russia's spheres of influence.[22]

[22]For an extended study, see Charles Vevier, *The United States and China, 1906-1913* (1955), especially 35-170. The Taft-Knox offensive with dollar diplomacy in Manchuria was simply one aspect of a much wider, emerging American far eastern policy. A basic influence on American naval policy in the Pacific throughout the period 1909-1922 was "the develop-

THE ANNEXATION OF KOREA

By 1905 Korea had become a Japanese protectorate, and was so recognized internationally. Roosevelt had written to Hay (January 29, 1905): "We cannot possibly interfere for the Koreans against Japan. They could not strike a blow in their own defense." Nevertheless, the emperor of Korea persisted in the belief that the United States would come to his country's rescue because of the "good offices" clause in the Korean-American treaty of 1882. The department of state, however, had taken the view that Korea, by not protesting Japanese-Korean agreements of 1904, which had created a Japanese protectorate, had deprived herself of any further grounds for appeal under the good offices clause.

Despite the fact that by 1907 the Korean royal palace was guarded by Japanese police, an official Korean delegation, bearing credentials from the emperor and advised by H. B. Hulbert, an American teacher long resident in Korea, arrived at the Hague peace conference. The mission's purpose was to make known "the violation of our [Korean] rights by the Japanese" and to re-establish "direct diplomatic relations" with the powers; but neither the conference nor the Dutch government would receive the mission. Japan, too, acted promptly in response to this challenge to her authority. The elder statesmen felt that "the hour had not yet come to push to extreme limits [*i.e.,* annexation] the chastisement for the felony committed." Instead "the [Korean] emperor king was forced to abdicate the throne in favor of his son" and a new agreement was concluded "whereby the Japanese resident-general became a virtual regent." Under this agreement all matters of internal administration as well as foreign relations were to be controlled by the resident-general.

With Japanese control tightening its grip on the entire Korean administration, the Korean problem as seen by the Japanese government became an integral part of the larger Manchurian scene, where Japan and Russia had come to an understanding (in the 1907 secret treaty). As early as the spring of 1909, Foreign Minister Komura had secured the approval of Premier Katsura and Prince Ito to a memorandum "strongly recommending" Korean annexation, a proposal which soon had the approval of the cabinet and the emperor. Meanwhile, Ito, having resigned as resident-general (June, 1909) to become president of the privy council, went to Harbin (October, 1909) to meet Russian Minister of Finance Kokovtseff and to prepare the way for a closer understanding with Russia. In July, 1909, Viscount Sone, who had replaced Ito in Korea, had secured an agreement placing the administration of Korean courts and prisons under direct Japanese control. Indeed, every preparation had been made for executing the predetermined policy of annexation. The assassination of Ito by a Korean in Harbin (October 26, 1909) served only to increase the popular and public demand in Japan for immediate action. On June 24, the day on which the draft Russo-Japanese treaties of July 4, 1910, were shown to the British and French governments, the Korean police were placed under the command of the Japanese resident-general. General Terauchi, minister of war, "under heavy guard," reached Seoul on July 23. All organs of public opinion had been "suspended or ruthlessly suppressed." In the audience that followed, Terauchi presented the young Korean sovereign with a face-saving means of escape: a request for annexation from the emperor of Korea to the emperor of Japan. The treaty of annexation was signed August 22, 1910, and proclaimed seven days later.

With the annexation of Korea by Japan in 1910, a particular phase of modern East Asian history was brought to a close. During the previous thirty years, the traditional Chinese world order had been destroyed, step by step, by Great Britain in Burma, by France in Indochina, and by Japan in Taiwan, the Liu-ch'iu islands, and Korea. Moreover, the powers (France, Great Britain, Germany, Japan, and Russia) had acquired a new stake within China through their spheres of influence. Even the United States had taken a colony in the Philippines. The old China-centered order had been

---

ment of bases and other forms of support that would enable the United States to dispatch and maintain a fleet in the western Pacific sufficiently powerful to win naval dominance in those waters from Japan." William R. Braisted, *The United States Navy in the Pacific, 1909-1922* (1971), 35.

replaced by the disorder of intense rivalry among the great Western powers and Japan.

China had sunk to semi-colonialism, while her former tributary states had become the colonies of other powers. In general these states lacked both the power and the motivation to achieve or maintain independence. The case of Korea was notable: there the Yi dynasty, authoritarian, paternalistic, yet lacking any effective machinery for centralization, had been the prey of its own degenerate court politics for three centuries. Thus, given the temper of the times, Korea's fate in 1910 was the natural result, however undesirable, of the general march of events.[23]

AMERICAN ATTITUDES

The critical posture of popular American reactions to Japan's annexation of Korea was hardly surprising. The honeymoon period in American-Japanese relations had come to an end with Japan's emergence as a great power. Korea now shared in the "paternalism and . . . benign sentimentality" which had long marked some popular American attitudes toward the Middle Kingdom. Rather mystical feelings of friendship for China had long been nourished by the belief that she was seeking moderniza-

tion, that she was plagued by dreadful natural calamities, that she was a victim of European and Japanese aggression, that American—particularly church—philanthropy in China had achieved far more than it actually had, and that these American efforts were in line with the aspirations of the Chinese people. It was quite easy for Americans to assume that the same philanthropic spirit was at the heart of official American policy in China. But paradoxically, this same American public which "believed" so devoutly in China was uninformed about and indifferent to her save in moments of crisis. Actually, American public sentiment and official policy were not one and the same, though they usually appeared to be because the official language used to describe American policy (for example, the phrases "the Open Door" and "China's independence and territorial and administrative integrity") implied a concern for China rather than a concern for American interests. Thus, both in America and abroad, the impression was created that the United States had become the guardian of China, protecting her from the ravages of European and Japanese exploitation. This fanciful myth was to persist in the popular American mind until the communist conquest of China in 1949.[24]

FOR FURTHER READING

General. Lung Chang, *La Chine a L'aube Du XX Siecle: Les Relations Diplomatiques De La Chine Avec Les Puissances Depuis La Guerre Sino-Japanaise Jusqu'a La Guerre Russo-Japanaise* (1962). Stephen Uhalley, Jr., "The Wai-wu Pu: The Chinese Foreign Office from 1901-1911," *Journal of the China Society* 5 (1967), 9-27.

The Russo-Japanese Conflict. Asakawa Kanichi, *The Russo-Japanese Conflict: Its Causes and Issues* (1904), an important contemporary

[23] In a number of phases of modern East Asian history, the student will come upon what may be described as the *conspiratorial theory of history.* A case in point is the Japanese seizure of Korea. In this instance the conspiratorial theory postulates that beginning with the early years of Meiji, Japan developed and adhered to a master plan for the conquest of Korea. In reality, this type of interpretation, while having the virtue of simplicity, tends to minimize the play of other complex forces. Japan's actions in Korea, like the actions of other powers elsewhere, were often treacherous and cruel, but it does not appear that the thesis of "conspiracy" has been proved. An able summary of what happened to Korea is C. I. Eugene Kim and Han-kyo Kim, *Korea and the Politics of Imperialism, 1876-1910* (1967), 219-23. Note also the fundamental studies by Hilary Conroy, *The Japanese Seizure of Korea: 1868-1910* (1960); and "Lessons from Japanese Imperialism," *Monumenta Nipponica: Studies in Japanese Culture,* 21 (1965), 335-46. For a summary of conflicting interpretations see George Totten, *et al.,* "Review Article," *Journal of Asian Studies,* 22 (1963), 469-72.

[24] For the full development of the subject see Paul A. Varg, *The Making of a Myth: the United States and China, 1897-1912* (1968), especially 1-13. Thomas J. McCormick, "American Expansion in China," *American Historical Review,* 75 (1970), 1393-96, comments critically on Varg's thesis.

Japanese view of the causes of the war. Edwin A. Falk, *Togo and the Rise of Japanese Sea Power* (1936), the best account of the life of one of the outstanding naval figures of modern times. John A. White, *The Diplomacy of the Russo-Japanese War* (1964). Jonathan Steinberg, "Germany and the Russo-Japanese War," *American Historical Review* 75 (1970), 1965-86. Shumpei Okamoto, *The Japanese Oligarchy and the Russo-Japanese War* (1971), a pioneering study revealing the interplay of domestic politics and foreign policy. John J. Stephan, *Sakhalin: A History* (1971), a brief synthesis drawn from Russian and Japanese sources.

Among the older studies of the American role Tyler Dennett, *Roosevelt and the Russo-Japanese War* (1925), and A. L. P. Dennis, *Adventures in American Diplomacy, 1896-1906* (1928) have been superseded in some measure by Raymond A. Esthus, *Theodore Roosevelt and Japan* (1966), and Charles Neu, *An Uncertain Friendship: Theodore Roosevelt and Japan, 1906-1909* (1967). Eugene P. Trani, *The Treaty of Portsmouth: An Adventure in American Diplomacy* (1969), a brief, competent study of the president's role.

Manchuria.   Shun-hsin Chou, "Railway Development and Economic Growth in Manchuria," *China Quarterly* (January-March 1971). E.W. Edwards, "Great Britain and the Manchurian Railway Question, 1909-1910," *English Historical Review* 81 (October 1966). Three legalistic studies: C. Walter Young, *The International Legal Status of the Kwantung Leased Territory* (1931); *Japan's Special Position in Manchuria: Its Assertion, Legal Interpretation and Present Meaning* (1931); and *Japanese Jurisdiction in the South Manchuria Railway Areas* (1931). Owen Lattimore, *Manchuria: Cradle of Conflict* (rev. ed., 1935) presents Manchuria's regional relationship to China. Sun E-Tu Zen, *Chinese Railways and British Interests, 1898-1911* (1954). Chang Chiao, *China's Struggle for Railroad Development* (1943).

The American Role.   Ralph E. Minger, "Taft's Missions to Japan: A Study in Personal Diplomacy," *The Pacific Historical Review* 30 (1961), 279-94. Edward H. Zabriskie, *American-Russian Rivalry in the Far East: A Study in Diplomacy and Power Politics, 1895-1914* (1946). W. A. Williams, *American-Russian Relations, 1781-1947* (1952). Richard T. Chang, "The Failure of the Katsura-Harriman Agreement," *Journal of Asian Studies,* 21 (1961), 65-76. Richard D. Challener, *Admirals, Generals, and American Foreign Policy, 1898-1914* (1973). Paul A. Varg, *The Making of a Myth: The United States and China, 1897-1912* (1968). Charles Vevier, *The United States and China, 1906-1913: A Study of Finance and Diplomacy* (1955). James Lorence, "Business and Reform: The American Asiatic Association and the Exclusion Laws, 1905-1907," *Pacific Historical Review,* 39 (1970), 421-38.

Akira Iriye, *Pacific Estrangement: Japanese and American Expansion, 1897-1911* (1972). Floyd J. Fithian, "Dollars Without the Flag: The Case of Sinclair and Sakhalin Oil," *Pacific Historical Review* (May 1970). Thomas J. McCormick, "American Expansion in China," *American Historical Review* 75 (1970), 1393-96.

China,
1911–1916:
The Gray Dawn
of a Republic

19

In 1911 the Manchu dynasty had ruled China for 267 years. Like other successful conquerors of the Middle Kingdom, it had recognized the superior cultural attainments of the conquered people, and it had associated Chinese with Manchus in government. Thus the dynasty not only held the Mandate of Heaven but also ruled at times with distinction. By 1900, however, the Manchus faced economic dislocation, bureaucratic ineptitude, and the impact of the Western world of ideas and power on their seaboard. These conditions called for radical adjustments in China's political, economic, and social structure—adjustments which the Sino-Manchu political hierarchy could neither visualize nor implement. To be sure, in the face of impending disaster, the aging and opportunistic empress dowager had sought refuge in reform, but her conversion had failed to halt the decline in Manchu prestige and authority.

A series of events that may be described as the immediate causes of the impending Revolution of 1911 began in 1908. There was the death of the unfortunate young Kuang-hsu emperor on November 14, and on the following day the old empress dowager died. She had provided for the succession by placing an infant

on the throne with the Manchu Prince Ch'un as regent. Thus, when death removed the hold of the empress dowager, the helm of state was in the keeping of a child directed by a regent who was to prove devoid of political wisdom. The seriousness of these events should be considered in relation to the larger picture in China during the first decade of the century: the abortive reforms of 1898, the disasters of the Boxer revolt, the inroads of the Western powers and Japan, the use of Chinese soil as battlegrounds in the Russo-Japanese war, and the reduction of Manchuria to the status of Russian and Japanese spheres of influence. All of these events called for the appearance of able leadership at Peking. It was not forthcoming. Moreover, adding to the political void was the forced retirement of Yuan Shih-k'ai. With Yuan there also went into retirement many of the abler lesser officials whom he had trained and who were responsive to his leadership. In October, 1909, Chang Chih-tung, the great Yangtze viceroy, died. The result was that, while officially the reform program was continued, it became little more than a succession of edicts and blueprints.

The National Assembly, created by the Manchu reforms and designed to be a willing tool of the dynasty, met for the first time in October, 1910, but, to the chagrin of the court and in spite of all its hand-picked conservatism, it showed a remarkable spirit of independence. It forced the government to promise a parliament in 1913 instead of after the longer nine-year period of preparation provided in the reform program. It threatened to impeach members of the government and attacked its fiscal and administrative policies with vigor. Early in 1911, it demanded a responsible cabinet, winning the demand, in principle at least, before adjournment.

FLOOD, FAMINE, AND TAXES

Evidence of revolutionary stirrings was not confined to Peking. Recurring crises of famine occasioned by increasing population and by flood and drought were not new to China but in the twenty-five years preceding the Revolution of 1911, population had increased by perhaps as much as 50 million. Some of these people found new homes in Manchuria and others in sparsely populated areas of the empire or in immigration abroad to Indochina and the Malay States, but these movements provided slight relief for the basic problem of livelihood. The years 1910 and 1911 marked the culmination of a series of bad seasons. Hundreds of thousands died, and several millions were on the verge of starvation. Those who survived were psychologically prepared for any movement that promised relief.

Throughout China discontent had also been fanned by rising taxes. Every measure in the reform program of 1901 and in subsequent programs had called for more revenue: new army, new railroads, new educational system. In addition, there were the charges on the Japanese war indemnity of 1895, and the more onerous charges of the Boxer indemnity of 1901.[1]

[1] Taxation as a cause of revolt, however, was a political argument rather than an economic pressure, for it would seem that in its final years the Manchu government was taking a smaller share of the national produce than it had in, say, 1750. Yeh-chien Wang, "The Fiscal Importance of the Land Tax during the Ch'ing Period," *Journal of Asian Studies*, 30 (1971), 829-42.

Closely linked with popular criticism of tax policies was the hard fact that the reform program encroached on the traditional autonomy of the provinces. Insofar as the reform program possessed a real purpose other than that of saving the dynasty, it was to give China a national government capable of exercising the sovereignty of the state and of protecting it from foreign encroachment. This objective required the sacrifice of the autonomy of the provinces, where vested local interests were loath to part with the prerogatives which time and custom had afforded.

The issue came to focus on the question of financing and thus controlling proposed trunk line railroads, designed to be the first step in solving China's problem of communications. There had been a strong local demand for constructing railroads on a provincial rather than a national basis, and for financing these lines with Chinese rather than foreign funds. It was a natural reaction to foreign concession-grabbing and foreign financial control, while at the same time it was an equally natural expression of traditional Chinese political habits. But it was an impractical policy. The huge sums necessary could not be raised in the provinces and even such sums as were collected were dissipated in wild speculation or unadulterated graft. Accordingly, early in 1911, Peking began to pursue with vigor its policy of railroad centralization. Foreign loans were contracted for the Hankow-Canton and Hankow-Szechuan trunk lines. At the same time the government sought to reach a settlement with the provincial interests involved. This proved to be difficult. Official protests were lodged at Peking, and in Szechuan there were public demonstrations on a wide scale.[2]

[2] The railroad controversy involved such matters as government centralization as opposed to the traditional and relative autonomy of the provinces, and the new and as yet ill-defined spirit of nationalism as opposed to local vested interests. Most of China's railroads were owned and operated by foreign powers—the Russians and the Japanese in Manchuria, the Germans in Shantung, the French in Yunnan. Other lines owned nominally by Peking were mortgaged in fact to foreign banks and bond-holders. This practice

THE WUHAN REVOLT, 1911

Peking had been emboldened to pursue its national railway policy because it underestimated provincial opposition and because, among other things, revolution did not appear to be imminent. Sun Yat-sen's *T'ung-meng Hui,* while united in theory, had not established practical bases of operation within China. To be sure, a number of isolated and scattered revolts had occurred since 1906, but all had been suppressed. What Peking did not understand was the degree to which these outbreaks, together with peasant rice riots and the growing fears of the gentry, jealous of its local autonomy, had destroyed the authority of the dynasty and its capacity to rule. It was at this point that one of the great accidents of history occurred.

In the province of Hupeh on the central Yangtze, groups of students and soldiers had been holding secret meetings to study ways and means of planning revolt. When this activity was discovered some three thousand troops at Wuchang revolted at once; that was on October 10, a day since celebrated as Double Ten—the tenth day of the tenth month. The Manchu governor-general promptly fled; the city was in rebel hands. While there was some local resistance, the Wuchang revolt was popular, primarily because it was a rebellion against the

---

of foreign finance had produced by 1910 the first four-power consortium of foreign bankers (British, French, German, and American), which financed the national railway policy decreed by Peking in 1911. The first undertaking was to be trunk lines from Canton to Hankow and from Hankow westward into Szechuan—known together as the Hukuang railways. A Hankow-Peking line had been opened in 1905. To the new Chinese nationalists and also to the holders of vested interests in the provinces, it was clear that Peking, in pursuit of a national policy, had sold out to unscrupulous Chinese promoters at home and to imperialistic bankers abroad. One example of these Chinese politico-industrial promoters was Sheng Hsuan-huai, who had become powerful in the service of Li Hung-chang and Chang Chih-tung. He controlled a steamship line, an arsenal, and iron and coal mines, which he had financed through Japanese loans. As a government superviser of telegraphs and textile mills he had amassed a fortune and he saw great opportunities to enrich himself further in the government's national railway plan.

Manchus. Since the rising had not been planned for this particular time it had no senior military or political leadership. In consequence the young soldier-rebels dragged their commander, Colonel Li Yuan-hung from under his bed and presented him with the choice of immediate death or leadership of rebellion. Being a practical man, though at the time far from a revolutionist, Colonel Li chose the latter. Within a brief period the three Wuhan cities—Hankow, Hanyang, and Wuchang—were in rebel hands.

From this center the revolt spread rapidly, particularly in the provinces south of the Yangtze; generally speaking the north remained loyal to the imperial government. The pattern was one of a series of local and largely bloodless rebellions seemingly uncoordinated and without unified leadership or a predetermined national plan.[3] While the Wuchang group was attempting to coordinate the movement by inviting provinces which had declared their independence to send delegates to a Wuchang revolutionary council, the revolution spread to Shanghai, where a new rebel government under the leadership of Ch'en Ch'i-mei was organized. Wu T'ing-fang, a Cantonese and former minister to the United States, was made chief of diplomatic affairs. He attempted to speak for the revolution as a whole. Interrevolutionary politics was thus making its appearance. The Shanghai group was dominated by Cantonese who were determined that leadership in the rebellion should not remain with the Yangtze provinces centered at Wuchang. Fortunately, all the revolutionary groups were at one in their determination that the Manchus must go. This and Li Yuan-hung's willingness to give way to Shanghai's so-called "military government" prevented an open break and permitted the Canton elements to lead.[4]

REACTIONS AT PEKING

The Manchu government, frightened by the turmoil caused by its national railway policy,

[3] P. M. A. Linebarger, *Government in Republican China* (1938), 145.

[4] Harold M. Vinacke, *Modern Constitutional Development in China* (1920), 102.

was to be even less resolute in dealing with the anti-dynastic revolt at Wuhan. The government was embarrassed also by the reconvening on October 22, less than two weeks after the Wuchang rising, of the National Assembly. Heartened by the general spirit of rebellion, the Assembly demanded responsible cabinet government, insisted that a constitution be adopted only with the consent of the Assembly, and urged that political offenders be pardoned. On November 3, the dynasty gave its approval in edicts establishing a constitutional monarchy. Meanwhile the regent, Prince Ch'un, had induced Yuan Shih-k'ai to return to Peking by promising him unlimited powers. Yuan promptly resumed his command of the military forces and, on November 8, the National Assembly elected him premier.

THE POLICY OF YUAN SHIH-K'AI

Yuan Shih-k'ai's critics have dealt harshly with his record. A soldier and diplomat from the north, he has been characterized as narrow in outlook, altogether a tradition-bound official despite his up-to-date ideas—an opportunist and a realist in politics. Actually, Yuan was far more than these. While he had his limitations, and they were exceedingly large, he had shown progressive tendencies. He was indeed an opportunist and a realist, but he was not altogether tradition-bound. He was a progressive capable of carrying out needed reforms, as the previous decade had shown, and a tried administrator in civil and military affairs. He was not a republican and did not believe in 1911 that republicanism was the answer to China's ills, in which view he was by no means alone. Like many other Chinese of sober thought, Yuan seems to have held the view that it would be fatal for China to attempt a complete break with the spirit or the political machinery of the past, and that the stability of reform would depend in some major degree on Confucian mores and not exclusively on the adoption of Western ideologies.[5] Now that he was invested by the dynasty with supreme powers, and endowed by the National Assembly with the post of prime

[5] A. M. Kotenev, *The Chinese Soldier* (1937), 82-83.

minister, Yuan's task was to put a stop to rebellion and to carry on the constitutional reforms of the Assembly. Yuan, however, entertained purposes more subtle than these. Although he was not seeking the destruction of the dynasty, Yuan was willing to permit the spread of the southern rebellions in order to force the Manchus to accept and play the role of a passive, constitutional monarchy. Yuan's imperial forces were superior in every respect to the revolutionary armies of Li, yet the northern armies were never permitted to push their advantages to ultimate and decisive victory. So long as these conditions prevailed Yuan was able to impose his will in Peking.

Opposed to Yuan, to the dynasty, and to the National Assembly stood the rebel armies of Li Yuan-hung, the so-called "military government" (Cantonese) at Shanghai, and the southern provinces that had declared their independence. In October when the Hankow incident occurred, Sun Yat-sen, ideological leader of the southern rebels, was in the United States. Not until two months later (December 24, 1911) did he reach Shanghai.

THE PEACE NEGOTIATIONS

The return of Sun Yat-sen, although inspiring to the revolutionists, did not alter the fact that they were incapable of carrying the revolution to a successful conclusion or of holding its leadership. The balance between the hoary traditions of dynastic rule and the mysteries of republicanism was held not by Sun Yat-sen but by Yuan Shih-k'ai. With a subtle appreciation of his political and military advantage, Yuan attempted to negotiate a settlement with Li Yuan-hung, finally agreeing with Li's consent to deal with the republican group at Shanghai. Meanwhile, at Li's suggestion, delegates from the "independent" southern provinces assembled at a national convention in Nanking and elected Sun Yat-sen provisional president. It was this more unified republican regime that finally concluded the peace settlement with Yuan's representative, T'ang Shao-yi, an American-educated Cantonese. In these negotiations the monarchy was brought to an end by abdication and a republic, in name at least, was created. Sun Yat-sen stepped down from the presidency, and at his suggestion the Nanking convention elected Yuan Shih-k'ai first provisional president of the Republic of China. Sun's relinquishment of the presidency could be rationalized by his desire to remain solely the ideological leader of the new China, and by the more decisive factor, the political and military power of Yuan.

The new Republic was to be inaugurated with the arrival of Yuan at Nanking. Nanking, however, represented the south and was controlled by the southern republicans, while Yuan's armies were around Peking. This explains why a military mutiny, perhaps engineered by Yuan near Peking, made it inconvenient for the new president to leave the old capital. By this means Yuan was able to force the republicans to come to Peking, the home of tradition and conservatism. Furthermore, the Manchu abdication edicts, dictated by Yuan himself and promulgated on February 12, 1912, implied clearly that the new president derived his power by transfer from the throne rather than by mandate of the Republic.

The end of dynastic rule and the emergence of Yuan Shih-k'ai as president of the Republic were not due solely to the political and military advantages enjoyed by Yuan within China. Both the Republic and Yuan's leadership therein were in part the creation of the foreign powers. From 1908, and even earlier, the fate of the Manchu dynasty rested on its capacity to prevent further disintegration, to arrest foreign concession-hunting, and to forestall the partition of the empire by the powers. Between 1908 and 1912, however, the powers failed both singly and collectively to support the imperial government to these ends. Indeed, the rivalries of the powers in their efforts to control China politically and economically weakened what little prestige was left to the dynasty and thereby invited provincial opposition to Peking's national railway policies. Moreover, the reforms which Peking planned for the border territories of Tibet, Mongolia, and Manchuria—reforms designed eventually to bring these areas into a national China—were frowned upon by Britain, Russia, and Japan. From the Wuhan rebellion in October, 1911, until the

Manchu abdication edicts of February, 1912, the powers did nothing to prevent the collapse of the imperial regime. On the contrary, they assisted Yuan Shih-k'ai in his ambitions to head the new Republic. As a result of conflicting power-interests and of commitments from some of the powers, Yuan was able to count on foreign diplomatic and financial support before the conclusion of his negotiations with the southern republicans and before his elevation to the presidency.

EARLY PHASES OF YUAN'S GOVERNMENT

With the establishment of the Republic, China did not enter an era of republicanism but rather one of militarism. The "national" army organized by Li Hung-chang and Yuan Shih-k'ai was a northern army, not a national army; its officers thought of themselves as lieutenants of Yuan, not of the state. Authority in the southern provinces during the revolution had shifted to provincial leaders who could command the personal allegiance of troops in their respective areas. Thus, both during and succeeding the revolution, military authority was also political authority. Since the number of men under arms increased rapidly as a result of revolutionary conditions, there were few checks upon the power of these personal armies.

Not being in a position to destroy or disband these independent provincial armies, Yuan's only recourse was to make allies of them. This he did by appointing their commanders as provincial military governors. Eventually he hoped to replace them by civil administrations responsive to his Peking government. This would be done by coaxing the provincial militarists into various government posts in the capital, thus separating them from their armies, the source of their strength.

Meanwhile, the new government was attempting to get under way at Peking under the terms of a provisional constitution adopted at Nanking in March, 1912. Being the product of southern republicanism, this constitution was shaped with the idea of making the president subject to parliamentary will. In August, Sun Yat-sen announced the organization of his new political party, the *Kuomintang,* to which Yuan replied by organizing his own Progressive Party, the *Chinputang.* When the National Assembly under the provisional constitution met early in 1913, the *Kuomintang* held the strongest position, but the hope for republican government received a fatal blow with the assassination in March, 1913, of Sung Chiao-jen, the parliamentary leader of the *Kuomintang.* After it became known that Yuan's men were responsible for this deed, a rebellion broke out against Yuan which was supported by part of the *Kuomintang* and a few southern warlords. When Yuan successfully suppressed the outbreak, Sun Yat-sen and some of his followers fled to Japan. In October the remaining members of the Assembly removed Yuan's provisional status by electing him president of the Republic. Less than a month later, Yuan ousted from the Assembly those *Kuomintang* members who had not already fled, and banned the *Kuomintang.* Then by presidential decree, January, 1915, he "suspended" the Assembly and replaced it with his own constitutional council. This body brought forth on May 1 its own constitution, known as the Constitutional Compact, It created a "presidential government," and "legitimatized" Yuan's dictatorship.[6]

In this manner Yuan was attempting to pave the way for a restoration of monarchy, with

himself as the monarch. There was much to support the idea that constitutional monarchy as proposed in 1898 by K'ang Yu-wei was more likely to succeed than republicanism. This view was presented to Yuan in a memorandum, August, 1915, by his American constitutional adviser, Professor Frank Goodnow. Goodnow pointed out the desirability, viewing China's problem of government in the abstract, "of establishing a constitutional monarchy *if* there was general demand for it rather than of maintaining the trappings of a republicanism without operative democracy.[7] As a result of "a circus of plebiscites and constitutional councils," constitutional monarchy was proclaimed in December, 1915. It was short-lived. No considerable body of the Chinese people had any understanding of the relative merits of constitutional monarchy or republicanism, but there were provincial and republican leaders with following enough to oppose Yuan as a monarch of any kind. Revolt promptly flared in Yunnan and spread rapidly through the south. Yuan renounced the throne in March, and died three months later, June 6, 1916.

DOLLAR DIPLOMACY AND THE REVOLUTION

It has been noted that the collapse of the Manchu dynasty was due in part to the acquiescence of the powers. In like manner, the hope of a stable regime under Yuan depended on the financial policies of the same powers. The republican government of 1912 was without funds and with increasing unpaid obligations. China's quest for foreign financial aid, however, could not be divorced from implications of foreign political control. It should be recalled that the Revolution of 1911 was, among other things, a reaction and protest against the foreign scramble for concessions which followed the Sino-Japanese war of 1894-1895, and which continued with increasing intensity in subsequent years. Indeed, the politico-financial rivalry of the powers was so great that they themselves had begun to favor pooling certain

---

[6] While Sun Yat-sen had remained titular head of the revolutionary forces, actual party leadership had devolved in considerable measure on Sung Chiao-jen, a Hunanese who had coordinated the uprising in Wuhan, 1911, against the Manchus. It was Sung, not Sun, who advocated parliamentary government, and it was Sung who actually transformed the *T'ung-meng Hui,* a secret society, into an open political organization, the *Kuomintang.* Sung believed that the KMT would become an instrument for strengthening parliamentary government. Sun, on the other hand, advocated strong presidential powers. See Tamada Noriko, "Sung Chiao-jen and the 1911 Revolution," *Papers on China,* 21, published by the East Asia Research Center, Harvard University (1968), 184-229. The assassination of Sung Chiao-jen set a political style which was to stifle any democratic tendencies in China from that day to the present. This political style was supported by two principles: (1) that those in power are above the law, and (2) that the best way to deal with political opponents is to "dispose" of them.

[7] Noel Pugach, "Embarrassed Monarchist: Frank J. Goodnow and Constitutional Development in China, 1913-1915," *Pacific Historical Review,* 42 (1973), 499-517.

types of loans to China through an international banking agency called the consortium. This agency was to be composed of groups of bankers designated by their respective governments. Thus loans made through the consortium would be subject to a double test: their acceptability to the bankers on economic grounds, and to the powers on political grounds. In its embryonic stage in 1909, the consortium included only the British, French, and German banking groups that were proposing to finance and construct the Hukuang railways in Central and South China for the Manchu-Chinese government.[8] An American group was admitted in 1911 after President Taft appealed to the Chinese regent.

After the Revolution and the establishment of the Republic, the interest of the consortium, on the surface at least, was directed toward providing the impecunious government at Peking with funds to maintain itself. In the view of the Chinese government and of many foreign bankers not included in the various groups, however, the consortium was an attempt to create a monopoly controlling the Chinese loan market. Not surprisingly, Russia and Japan, though borrowing countries themselves, soon demanded admission to the consortium, and their banking groups were admitted in June, 1912. Clearly, in such a climate of intense rivalry, it was not going to be easy to carry out the principle of assisting the Republic through international financial cooperation.

In the midst of this complicated politico-financial wirepulling at Peking, the Wilson administration came into power in Washington. The American banking group asked whether it would continue to enjoy the active support of the department of state in its China investments. President Wilson replied on March 18, 1913, by withdrawing official support from the American group, because he found the control measures of a proposed reorganization loan "to touch very nearly the administrative independence of China itself." Taft had pushed

American bankers into China to preserve the open door; Wilson now refused to support them there because their activities threatened China's independence. Nevertheless, the reorganization loan agreement was concluded without American participation on April 26, 1913.

As for the open door as an instrument of American policy, the best that can be said is that to this point the going had been very rough. Between 1899 and 1910 the policy of the open door and the integrity of China had passed through three phases. The labels used by American politicians remained the same, "the open door" and "the integrity of China," but the policies they represented did not. In the first phase, under Hay, the open door meant the preservation of equal commercial opportunity in an area where there was no equal investment opportunity; for the most part Hay abandoned the integrity of China in the face of Russian power in Manchuria. In the second phase, under Elihu Root, it was assumed that the spheres were facts and that more harm than good would come from any direct attack upon them, but, nevertheless, Root struggled to keep alive the concept of China's integrity. In the third phase, under Taft and Knox, the open door was supposed to encompass equal investment as well as commercial opportunity, thus abolishing the spheres and insuring China's integrity. New policies were simply attached to old words. If Americans did not understand all this, it is hardly surprising that Japan and the powers, not to mention China herself, were puzzled.[9]

SEPARATIST MOVEMENTS IN BORDER TERRITORIES

The transition from Manchu empire to Chinese republic was the occasion for rebellions and independence movements in the dependencies of Mongolia and Tibet. During the decade preceding the Revolution of 1911, the Mongol nobility had grown restive as Chinese settlers

[8] C. F. Remer, *Foreign Investments in China* (1933), 126. Charles Vevier, *The United States and China, 1906-1913* (1955), 88-110.

[9] Raymond A. Esthus, "The Changing Concept of the Open Door, 1899-1910," *Mississippi Valley Historical Review*, 46 (1959), 452-53.

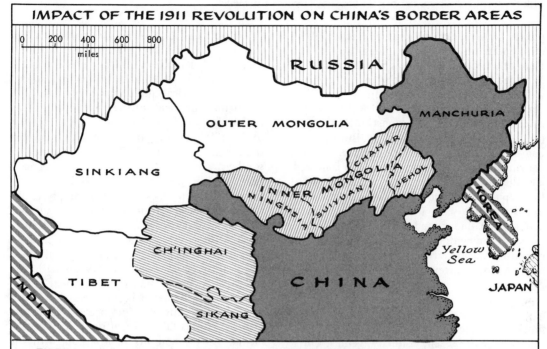

IMPACT OF THE 1911 REVOLUTION ON CHINA'S BORDER AREAS

TIBET   Manchu nominal control to 1912; Chinese Republic in 1912 created provinces of Ch'inghai and Sikang.

SINKIANG   Chinese dependency to 1878; then made 19th province of China. Russian influence dominant by 1941.

OUTER MONGOLIA   Until 1912 controlled by Manchus; 1915, autonomous under Chinese suzerainty but in reality a Russian protectorate; 1924, Mongolian People's Republic, independent but increasingly under Russian control.

INNER MONGOLIA   Manchu control to 1911; divided into four provinces by Chinese Republic, 1912.

encroached on Inner Mongolia and as Peking attempted to extend the government of China Proper to this area. Mongol disaffection was encouraged by Russia, whose agents fostered Mongol nationalism. In December, 1911, an independent Mongol government came into being at Urga. The Chinese combatted the movement by attempting to re-establish their authority in Inner Mongolia, only to be countered by Russian recognition of the Urga government in November, 1912. A year later (November, 1913) Russia and the Republic of China agreed that Outer Mongolia was "autonomous" but not "independent." Nearly two years later (June, 1915), Mongolia accepted this status in an agreement involving herself, Russia, and China.

The Revolution of 1911 was also the signal for trouble in Tibet. The Tibetans drove the Chinese garrison from the country and con-cluded an agreement (January, 1913) with the new Mongolian government. When Yuan Shih-k'ai sought to re-establish China's authority at Lhasa by force; he encountered British diplomatic opposition. It was not until 1914 that an agreement was worked out among Tibet, China, and Britain whereby western Tibet (Tibet proper) would be autonomous, with the Chinese maintaining a resident and small guard at Lhasa; in eastern Tibet the authority of China would be retained.

ANALYSIS OF THE OLD FIRST REPUBLIC

The years 1911 to 1916 were but a prelude to even more dismal things to come before the final collapse of the first republic in 1928. Indeed, it had fallen to Yuan Shih-k'ai to preside over one of the most fantastic failures in modern history. The Chinese Republican Revolution, 1911-1912, was an attempt to set aside the Confucian monarchy and to replace it with a parliamentary constitutional republic. On paper this republic appeared to have everything needed for success: constitutions, parliamentary procedures, codes of law. But since the constitutions were just so much paper, the parliamentary procedures were not followed, and the law codes were never enforced. What the republic did not have was much more important than what it had. It did not have a people who understood parliamentary institutions, government by law, or the rudiments of responsible democratic citizenship. When at the beginning of the Revolution of 1911, a council of representatives was convoked by the southern republicans, these representatives were not elected: there was no election machinery in the provinces; indeed, no one knew what an election was. Sun Yat-sen, visionary, genius, Christian, and for the moment provisional president, not only prayed to his Christian God for guidance in directing the young Republic, but also supplicated the spirits of the Ming emperors, the last Chinese rulers of China. Yuan Shih-k'ai rose to the presidency over Sun Yat-sen not by any Mandate of Heaven or even a mandate of the people, but by double-crossing both the dynasty and the republicans through his military power, supported later by foreign loans. He dispersed the *Kuomintang*-dominated Assembly and acquired one that would do his bidding. Then, not content with the reality of this presidential dictatorship in a nominal republic, Yuan became a romantic. His scheme to restore the monarchy with himself as monarch failed not because it was a move away from democracy, as so many Americans then and later imagined, but because Peking did not have enough power to suppress the southern insurrection. By 1916, when Yuan Shih-k'ai joined the spirits of his ancestors, the first Republic of China had been perverted into an immense failure.[10] Moreover, his effort to find

an acceptable relationship between a dying Confucianism and the new Western world of science and democracy had not found success.

The beginnings of the first Republic are still beset by historical questions. How did it come about that the ideals of the early revolutionary leadership could produce only the presidency of Yuan Shih-k'ai, who was neither a revolutionary nor a republican? Was it due to the southern rebels' lack of ideology and organization, to their military and financial inferiority, to foreign support of Peking, or simply to the skill of Yuan in turning events to his own advantage? Yuan, it has often been said, maneuvered the court and the revolutionaries into a situation in which they neutralized each other. Then, through superior military strength and foreign support, he emerged as president—a first step in his scheme to become emperor. To a degree, all of this was true because Yuan did profit from his talent for intrigue, his position in the North, and his relationship with the powers. At the same time, the importance of his wiliness has been overemphasized. Many other factors entered into his rise to the presidency. He was supported not only by the court

[10]P. M. A. Linebarger, Djang Chu, and Ardath W. Burks, *Far Eastern Governments and Politics* (1954), 120-32.

In the West the distinctive role of the individual in history has made biography a special field in literary and historical writing. In traditional China, on the contrary, where there was no similar cult of the individual, the ultimate purpose of biography was not to portray the individual realistically, as a fallible person, but to instruct officials in orthodoxy. This explains why a Chinese has been able to write an effective study of Yuan Shih-k'ai as a politician but not as a person. As will be seen later, "in the People's Republic of China, biographical writing is largely shaped by a mechanistic view of history which stresses the role of impersonal economic factors in determining the development of social organization and the course of human relations and institutions. Virtue and vice are polarized, the worthy 'model worker' standing in sharp contrast to the socially irresponsible 'bourgeois intellectual,' doomed by his gentry background, his liberalism, and his Harvard Ph.D. Yet the current situation [in Communist China] still contains incongruities. At the same time that both party and academic historians are constrained by the general demands of orthodox Communist doctrine, they also dwell in a specific political environment dominated, in apparent contradiction to that doctrine, by a single individual: Mao Tse-tung. Mao himself is not only the exception to all the rules but also, like Confucius, the imposer of new precepts." Howard L. Boorman, "The Biographical Approach to Chinese History," *Journal of Asian Studies*, 21 (1962), 454.

but also by some of the southern rebel leaders, who, in reality, were not outmaneuvered in giving Yuan the presidency. The suppression of radical revolutionary forces was effected by other revolutionaries and not primarily by Yuan. Moreover, Yuan's military superiority, if it existed, was not as great as supposed, and he had only limited support from the powers until after he became president. In a word, Yuan alone did not determine the outcome of the Revolution of 1911.[11]

As a government, the first Republic of China was a failure, but as a symbol of what could happen it was filled with meaning. The fact that the Republic had come into being following two thousand years of Confucian monarchy meant that a revolutionary process was well under way.

To anticipate and to emphasize the story that will be told later (in Chapter 24), it should be noted that the ascendancy of Yuan Shih-k'ai marked the beginning of warlord rule, which was to dominate China for nearly forty years, far into the *Kuomintang* era. What the warlords did held significance far beyond their own struggles for power. Their seemingly meaningless warfare destroyed the always tenuous internal cohesion of the country, ravaged its economy, and reduced a large part of its people to desperation. In these circumstances, China became very susceptible to a host of new influences, because under warlord leadership power passed to men whose semi-Western military training gave them an awareness of the value of innovation, and whose comparative lack of training in neo-Confucian orthodoxy made them rather prone to abandon tradition and to adopt new and foreign ideas.[12]

MADE IN JAPAN

China's republican revolution of 1911, surprising as it may seem, was "made in Japan," a fact of some historical import. During the late nineteenth century, Japan's success in modernization made a striking appeal to thoughtful Chinese, whether moderate reformers or radical revolutionaries. Most Chinese who studied abroad went to Japan, not only because it was close at hand but also because the Japanese experience seemed most relevant. K'ang Yu-wei and Liang Ch'i-ch'ao sought refuge in Japan from the wrath of the empress dowager; Sun Yat-sen was a refugee there in 1895. When the Manchus turned to reform in 1901, it was the Japanese model in education, constitutionalism, and military affairs which made the greatest impression upon the Peking government. It was in Japan that the Chinese reformers and revolutionaries developed and debated their ideas and their plans of action to create the new China. In this sense the revolution of 1911 was a product of Japanese influence.

The cooperative attitude of the Japanese, until 1907, toward Chinese political exiles was associated with Japan's own experience in the Meiji period. Japan's intense nationalism in the years 1890-1919 sometimes took a form later called ultranationalism. It had shown itself in the early samurai revolts of the 1870's as well as in the liberal movement for the people's rights. One nationalistic doctrine (sometimes called the Okuma doctrine of 1898) was that Japan, having modernized rapidly and successfully, should assist China, her historical cultural benefactor. Such aid could lead to a pan-Asiatic movement designed to free the peoples of the East from Western domination. This hope helps to explain the association in Japan at the turn of the century of political leaders such as Okuma Shigenobu and others with K'ang Yu-wie, Liang Ch'i-ch'ao, Sun Yat-sen, and other Chinese political exiles.

At the same time, it must be said that pan-Asianism was a far less significant force in Japanese thought than her emerging philosophy of imperialism, stimulated by victory in the Sino-Japanese war and defeat in the triple intervention. Vague ideas of kinship between the Japanese and their continental neighbors did not mean that the goal of Japanese imperialism was Asia for the Asians.[13]

[11] See Ernest P. Young, "Yuan Shih-k'ai's Rise to the Presidency," in *China in Revolution: The First Phase, 1900-1913,* Mary Clabaugh Wright, ed. (1968),* 419-42. The limitations of the revolution are studied in Edward Friedman, "Revolution or Just Another Bloody Cycle? Swatow and the 1911 Revolution," *Journal of Asian Studies,* 29 (1970), 289-307.

[12] Donald G. Gillin, "China and the Foreigner, 1911-1950," *South Atlantic Quarterly,* 68 (1969), 208-19.

[13] For background on this complex and elusive subject see, Marius B. Jansen, *The Japanese and Sun Yat-sen* (1954),* and Akira Iriye, "Imperialism in East Asia," in *Modern East Asia: Essays in Interpretation,* James B. Crowley, ed. (1970),* 143-49.

FOR FURTHER READING

General. H. F. MacNair, *China in Revolution* (1931); and *Modern Chinese History: Selected Readings* (1923).* Li Chien-nung, *The Political History of China, 1840-1928,* Teng Ssu-vu and Jeremy Ingals trans. and eds. (1956).* Pan Wei-tung, *The Chinese Constitution, A Study of Forty Years of Constitution Making in China* (1945). Franklin W. Houn, *Central Government of China, 1912-1928: An Institutional Study* (1957), a rather formal presentation of what was supposed to be rather than what was. Tsao Wen-yen, *The Constitutional Structure of Modern China* (1948). A. H. Holcombe, *The Spirit of the Chinese Revolution* (1930).

Sun Yat-sen. Lyon Sharman, *Sun Yat-sen, His Life and Its Meaning, A Critical Biography* (1934).* Henry B. Restarick, *Sun Yat-sen: Liberator of China* (1931). Bernard Martin, *Strange Vigour* (1944). P. M. A. Linebarger, *The Political Doctrines of Sun Yat-sen* (1937). Francis Price, trans., *San Min Chu I, The Three Principles of the People* (1928). Leonard Hsu, *Sun Yat-sen, His Political and Social Ideals* (1933). Stephen Chen and Robert Payne, *Sun Yat-sen: A Portrait* (1946).

Other Leaders. Jerome Ch'en, *Yuan Shih-k'ai, 1859-1916* (1961) Stephen R. Makinnon, "Liang Shih-i and the Communications Clique," *Journal of Asian Studies* 29 (1970), 559-80. K.S. Liew, *Struggle for Democracy: Sung Chiao-jen and the 1911 Revolution* (1971).

Foreign Interests. Marianne Bastid, "La diplomatie francaise et la revolution chinoise de 1911," *Revue d'histoire moderne et contemporarie* 16 (1969), 221–45. Key Ray Chong, "The Abortive American-Chinese Project for Chinese Revolution," *Pacific Historical Review* 41 (1972), 54-70. Walter V. and Marie V. Scholes, *The Foreign Policies of the Taft Administration* (1970). Roy Watson Curry, *Woodrow Wilson and Far Eastern Policy, 1913-1921* (1957). Tien-yi Li, *Woodrow Wilson's China Policy* (1952).

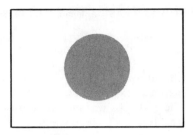

Japan, 1889–1918: Government and Society under the Oligarchy

20

As this narrative resumes the story of Japan's internal political, economic, and social growth, it will be recalled that on February 11, 1889, the Meiji emperor had bestowed a "gift" upon his people, the nation's first constitution. That constitution has been described (see Chapter 11) as a document designed to perpetuate what may be called "constitutional absolutism," because it provided for representative institutions reflecting concessions to modern Western ideas even as it perpetuated and strengthened the myth of the emperor's absolutism. Its purpose was to insure the continuing control of government by the Meiji oligarchs, from whom was emerging that inner select group, the *genro*. For some thirty years, that is until 1918, the Meiji Constitution functioned very much as the oligarchs had planned. The methods they employed and the nature of the groups which opposed them form the principal subjects of this chapter. As a part of this story there will also be some discussion of the economic and social life of this period. Japan's extraordinary growth at the time not only placed her in the company of the great industrial powers but also subjected her society at home to unprecedented strain and conflict.

It was also during these years of rule by the oligarchy that Japan achieved great power status and acquired an empire. In foreign affairs the nation was completely united; when differences occurred they centered usually on questions of method rather than policy. On the domestic front, in contrast, the struggle between the oligarchy and the political parties for control of government was unrelenting and, at times, vicious.

EXPANSION OF OLIGARCHICAL LEADERSHIP

On July 1, 1890, Japan held her first elections under the constitution. It was, in most respects, a model performance. Of the some 450,000 eligible voters (one out of every hundred persons had the right to vote), all but 27,000 resorted in orderly fashion to the polls and cast their ballots. The result was a decided victory for the *Jiyuto* (Liberal Party) and the *Kaishinto* (Reform or Progressive Party), both of which had appeared initially in the 1880's as an opposition to Choshu-Satsuma leadership. As aspirants for parliamentary seats, party candidates in 1890 continued their opposition, attacking the government for failing to abolish the unequal treaties and for grossly inflating national expenditures. Moreover, the force of these attacks was magnified by the election to the House of Representatives of independent opposition candidates, whose numbers swelled the total anti-government membership to more than two hundred of the three hundred contested seats. The government counted only ninety supporters in the House of Representatives, but it controlled the House of Peers through appointment, thus remaining in a position to block unwelcome legislation.

The appearance of a noisy opposition in a political tradition previously marked by authoritarianism was certainly a notable development. In time this trend would become a foundation for democratic institutions, but this was not its immediate significance. Rather, the elections admitted to government members of a small but politically conscious and articulate element that hitherto had been excluded from political leadership. Among this excluded element were men of substantial economic means. As a group drawn from the ranks of ex-samurai, they were also the social equals of the ruling authorities. In effect, by holding elections under the constitution, Japan substantially enlarged the political oligarchy.[1]

Among the older oligarchs were some who believed that the enlarged leadership would strengthen an already thriving state. The opposition, it was said, would be converted to support of the government as power was shared. Furthermore, the parliamentary experiment was to be carefully controlled. The parties' access to power was to be "partial, gradual, and carefully hedged."[2] Actual experience, however, produced results quite different from these expectations. Once elected, the party members were not easily tamed. Within two years, by 1892, a cabinet resigned after suffering defeat in the Diet, and this upset was by no means the end of the trouble. Thus the fashioning of a working relationship between the older oligarchs and the parties became one of the first tasks of the new constitutional era.

Other adjustments, too, were required by the growth of Japan's civil, military, and economic institutions. In contrast with the early Meiji period, when trained personnel were scarce, Japan after 1890 had a growing and able civil bureaucracy, centered around several thousand university graduates. Both as masters of a rigorous academic training and as "officials of the emperor," these bureaucrats enjoyed high social prestige. They drafted legislation for the Diet, had access to cabinet ministers, and generally controlled the administration of the law. Well before 1918 an increasing number of this group was finding itself appointed to policy-making positions. A similar growth in authority was enjoyed by the army and navy, which, in an imperialistic age, experienced little difficulty in demonstrating their importance. By the outbreak of the Sino-Japanese war (1894) the army had an authorized wartime strength of more than a quarter of a million men, while the navy had twenty-eight modern vessels aggregating 57,000 tons. Substantial headway had also been made in creating military industries. The training of officers had been brought abreast of the latest Western practices, and roughly a third of the national budget was allocated to military purposes. These were the realities that gave substance to the privileged powers of the military under the constitution.

Japan's governing elite was further enlarged in the years 1889-1918 by the involvement of the great commercial and industrial combines, the *zaibatsu*, in decision-making processes. While business groups claimed no constitutional role, cooperation between economic and political leaders was fostered by their joint agreement on mutually compatible goals. Thus the growth of political and economic power tended

[1] Edwin O. Reischauer, *Japan: The Story of a Nation* (1970),* 138-44. Among the original instigators of the imperial restoration, Ito Hirobumi, Okuma Shigenobu, Yamagata Aritomo, and Inouye Kaoru were the most important still living at this time. For details on relations between the oligarchs and parties see Hugh Borton, *Japan's Modern Century* (2nd ed., 1970), Chapter 11.

[2] George Akita, *Foundations of Constitutional Government in Japan, 1868-1900* (1967).

to become increasingly intertwined. Moreover, as the costs of political campaigning increased, politicians turned to businessmen for help in defraying campaign expenses. Channels were thereby opened enabling business executives to make their views known to the oligarchs and to the party leaders.

Political processes also were altered by changes in the personnel of Japan's older leadership. Prior to 1918 the Choshu-Satsuma oligarchs had lost none of their luster as founding fathers, but their vigor was sapped by advancing age. Those who survived into the new era turned administrative chores over to their proteges and, as *genro* (elder statesmen), gave directives from behind the scenes. Leadership patterns were further changed by the death in 1912 of the Meiji emperor, a vigorous man who occasionally had contributed to major decisions. His successor, Taisho Tenno' (1912-1926), who had been sickly as a child and was mentally ill in later years, was not involved in the daily activities of government. His role was even more exclusively symbolic than his father's.

Thus it may be said that between 1890 and 1918 the ranks of government leadership and of its supporting bureaucracy were enlarged greatly as the tasks of government at home and abroad grew in complexity. Japan was becoming a highly-organized bureaucratic state in which the functions of government multiplied and became increasingly specialized. This enlarged leadership with its expanding bureaucracy was fertile ground for the cultivation of rival elites (factions within the governing elite), each competing for position and power. Government was outgrowing the more informal habits and procedures of former times. Controversies could move from the closed committee rooms to the open floor of the Diet. Yet, with all of these changes, the old oligarchs remained in control. Japan's government was modernizing, but it was still a paternalistic, authoritarian state.

THE OLIGARCHY VERSUS THE PARTIES

The political history of Japan from 1890 until 1918 holds a special interest because it was in these years that the Japanese fashioned the particular structure of political compromise that enabled the constitution to function with some success. There were three stages in the development of this formula in constitutional compromise. The first, from 1890 to 1895, was marked by antagonism and separation between the ruling oligarchy and the opposition parties. The second, from 1895 to 1900, involved a series of unstable ententes between the parties and the oligarchy. The third, from 1900 to 1918, was distinguished by leadership in which the oligarchy, enlarged by the incorporation of the parties, employed devices of parliamentary government as part of the political process.

The period of complete estrangement between the government oligarchy and the popular parties was of great importance because it taught the Japanese that compromise was indispensable if there was to be any constitutional government at all. In this particular instance, however, compromise was not easy. The oligarchy had been entrenching itself in power during all the years that had elapsed since the restoration of 1868. It was confident of its power. Furthermore, prior to the meeting of the first Diet, Premier Kuroda Kiyotaka and Ito Hirobumi had proclaimed the government's policy of "transcendent" cabinets, by which they meant that the government under the constitution derived all its power from the throne and was concerned with all the emperor's subjects rather than with the desires of political parties. This policy, while complying with the explicit terms of the constitution, was at variance with the platforms of the *Jiyuto* and the *Kaishinto,* both of which made it clear in 1890 that they would use the constitution to subordinate the oligarchy to the rule of party cabinets responsible to the House of Representatives.

So matters stood when in November, 1890, a hostile government, headed by the Choshu militarist, Premier and General Yamagata Aritomo, faced equally hostile parties in the first Diet. The spirit of "arrogance and contempt" with which the premier addressed the House of Representatives was equalled only by the verbal violence with which the parties used the only constitutional weapon they possessed—a limited power to strike at the government's budget.

Yamagata was speaking for the oligarchy and its servant the bureaucracy—the vast body of office holders, great and small—when he called on the House for unity with and unqualified trust in the government and its officialdom. In response, the parties attacked and clipped the budget. In doing this they were not engaging merely in a general assault designed to reduce taxes or to assert their supremacy. The assault was aimed directly at a more specific target. The principal cuts in the budget proposed by the House involved the personal income of officials: salaries, pensions, and residence and travel allowances. Aiming the attack directly at the lesser civil and military bureaucracy was in the realm of everyday practical politics, since it struck at the real and indispensable foundation supporting the oligarchy. In meeting this attack, the government, as expected, was prepared to use all its resources, fair or foul. As a beginning it employed two devices often resorted to in future years: (1) it stood firmly on the constitutional provision prohibiting reduction of expenditures already fixed; and (2) it resorted to intimidation of members of the parties by hired gangsters. When these methods failed to move the parliamentarians, the government resorted to bribery of the weaker party members. A budget more acceptable to the government was then passed.[3]

In the light of Yamagata's rather trying experience, no member of the oligarchy welcomed the prospect of becoming the next premier. Yet under the policy of the oligarchy it was desirable that the post be held by a member of this group. Thus when Yamagata resigned, his minister of finance, Matsukata Masayoshi of Satsuma, an able financier but certainly undistinguished as a political leader, accepted the premiership, May 6, 1891. When the second Diet met, it followed precedent by

[3] For details of these early party battles with the oligarchs see Robert A. Scalapino, *Democracy and the Party Movement in Prewar Japan* (1953). For a statistical analysis of Japanese national elections, 1892-1937, and their bearing on Japan's political modernization, see Robert A. Scalapino, "Elections and Political Modernization in Prewar Japan," in *Political Development in Modern Japan*, Robert E. Ward, ed. (1968), 249-91.

attacking the government's budget, but in this case the reductions were leveled at new expenditures such as the naval program. To meet this crisis the government dissolved the Diet and ordered a special election for February, 1892, which turned out to be "the most brutal election in Japanese history." The government had decided to show the parties no quarter and, if possible, to break their hold on the electorate. Voters were intimidated by hired thugs, some party candidates were arrested arbitrarily, and the property of others was burned. Before the election was over at least twenty-five persons had been killed and nearly 400 wounded. Yet, the government did not achieve its purpose. In the new Diet, the parties, with 163 seats, maintained a clear majority.

Thus the battle was soon renewed. When Matsukata resigned, August, 1892, Ito accepted the premiership and formed a cabinet that included most of the *genro*. This time the House used its ultimate weapon. It memorialized the throne to impeach the ministry. The emperor's reply, written undoubtedly by the oligarchy, was a major blow to popular government: the House was told that its function was "to aid" the government. Matters were thus deadlocked when the outbreak of the Sino-Japanese war in 1894 brought peace to internal Japanese politics. The constitutional question was forgotten as all factions united in prosecution of the war.

OLIGARCHY-PARTY ENTENTES, 1895-1900

During the brief period from the close of the war until the turn of the century, the oligarchy and parties experimented with political ententes. The first of these was between the Ito cabinet and the *Jiyuto*. The general pattern set by this and succeeding ententes required party support for the government's program in return for which the party received a post in the cabinet, appointment of party members to office, and, to phrase the matter delicately, contributions to the party's treasury. These shaky alliances enabled a party to get one foot in the door of administrative authority. On the debit side they contributed little to the advancement of the principle of party government, since neither oligarchy nor party had surrendered their extreme and opposing views as to what government should be. Nor did the alliances bring political stability. From 1895 to 1900 there were no less than six different cabinets and four dissolutions of the Diet, leaving chaos and corruption in their wake. Finally, the ententes, by providing power and spoils to only selected members of the parties, increased factionalism among the parties and destroyed what little chance there was for a united front among the parliamentarians.[4] It was at this time, too, that Yamagata, the unrelenting opponent of popular government, gave the military services an even greater advantage in successive administrations when in May, 1900, he secured an imperial ordinance requiring that only generals or lieutenant generals on the active list might hold the post of minister of war and only admirals or vice admirals on the active list the post of minister of the navy.[5] The requirement meant that no popular party would be able to form a cabinet unless it complied with the wishes of the military oligarchs.

THE OLIGARCH AS PARTY LEADER

As the new century opened, Japan's constitutional government, now a decade old, had failed to produce a working pattern for the stress and strain of everyday politics. In this respect the record was one of dismal failure. Yet Japan, through the genius of Ito, was about to find a solution that would give some stability to her constitutional structure. In essence the solution rejected both the strong-arm methods of Yamagata and the ententes of recent years. Ito's purpose was to find a means through which a political party might be created as an administration party, thus providing support for the oligarchy. This was not a

[4] During this period there was a brief interlude of the so-called party cabinet of Okuma and Itagaki in 1898. The two leaders had recently formed a new constitutional party, the *Kenseito*.

[5] The ordinance was modified in 1913, enabling reserve officers of these ranks to qualify but reverted to its original form in 1936.

new idea with Ito; he had been considering it since the elections of 1892.

In 1900 a group of politicians in the recently formed *Kenseito* party provided Ito with the opportunity to try his idea in practice. The group asked Ito to become its leader, and Ito agreed on condition that the new party accept his terms: (1) the party must be dissolved and a new and more representative party must take its place; and (2) party members must accept orders from the leader. The *Kenseito* accepted the terms. On September 16, 1900, a new party was born, the *Rikken Seiyukai* (Association of Friends of Constitutional Government), with Ito as its president. This development meant that the party men (or at least most of them) were willing to renounce the principles of party government if by so doing they might gain access to administrative authority. From the beginning Ito had left no doubt as to his purposes. His *Seiyukai* would stand for the "true"—that is, the imperial—interpretation of the constitution.[6] Party members might be invited to join a cabinet, but this action was not to imply that the cabinet had thereby become responsible to the party or to the Diet. Since the *Seiyukai* was the only strong political party, Ito's formula effectively ended the wholesale attacks on the cabinet by the House of Representatives. The formula, however, did not bring an end to factionalism in the parties or the oligarchy. Indeed, the oligarchy had already regrouped into rival factions behind Yamagata and Ito, respectively. From 1901 to 1918, contests between these factions and their successors were a principal feature of Japanese politics.

Ito's plan for oligarchic leadership of the parties was soon to mean that the daily conduct

[6] For conflicting interpretations of the theory of imperial powers, see H. S. Quigley, *Japanese Government and Politics* (1932), 67-68; R. K. Reischauer, *Japan: Government-Politics* (1939), 167-69; G. E. Uyehara, *The Political Development of Japan, 1867-1909* (1910), 19; Nakano Tomio, *The Ordinance Power of the Japanese Emperor* (1923), 5; H. Sato, *Democracy and the Japanese Government* (1920), 1; E. W. Clement, "Constitutional Imperialism in Japan," *Proceedings of the Academy of Political Science*, 6 (1916), 325; and U. Iwasaki, *Working Forces in Japanese Politics* (1921), Chapter 2. The Japanese doctrine postulating the identity of the emperor and the state is known as *kokutai*.

of government was placed on the shoulders of younger men while the old leadership continued its control from behind the scenes. In 1901, following the collapse of Ito's first cabinet, Yamagata, who was of no mind to face Ito and a hostile *Seiyukai,* chose a military protege, General Katsura Taro of Choshu, to serve as premier. Within two years Ito was appointed to the privy council and retired from administrative duties. His place as titular head of the *Seiyukai* was given to his protege, Saionji Kimmochi. For twelve years, 1901-1913, Katsura and Saionji were to alternate in leadership of successive cabinets. The list of prime ministers, 1898 to 1918, suggests the preeminent role of the oligarchy:

Yamagata	*November,*	*1898-October, 1900*
Ito	*October,*	*1900–June, 1901*
Katsura	*June,*	*1901–January, 1906*
Saionji	*January,*	*1906–July, 1908*
Katsura	*July,*	*1908–August,1911*
Saionji	*August,*	*1911–December, 1911*
Katsura	*December,*	*1911–February, 1913*
Yamamoto	*February,*	*1913–April, 1914*
Okuma	*April,*	*1914–October, 1916*
Terauchi	*October,*	*1916–September, 1918*

GOVERNMENT BY ACCOMMODATION

It should be noted, too, that political rivalry within the Japanese oligarchy during the early years of this century was controlled by an extraordinarily even balance of forces and by a resulting self-imposed discipline. What has been called the "Katsura-Saionji truce" meant that opposition could be carried only so far. Among rivals there was conflict but there was even more cooperation in many areas. The consequent smoothness with which, in the main, government operated in these years was due partly to Ito's scheme of "sharing" power with the party politicians, but in an even greater degree it appears to have been due to the nation's general sense of well-being. This sense of achievement came from Japan's rapid industrial modernization, from her victory over Russia (1905), and from the annexation of

Korea (1910). These stirring events had a great deal to do with lowering political tempers at home. The rule of the oligarchs was a great success story, resulting in a political climate in which there was a disposition to find accommodation among rivals within the oligarchy and between the oligarchy and the party politicians.

The foregoing is not to suggest that the system always worked without problems. For example, The Taisho political crisis of 1911-1912 (named after the emperor who had just ascended the throne) occurred when Premier Saionji's (and the *Seiyukai's*) program of financial retrenchment challenged the army's determination to have two new divisions for Korea. After consulting with Yamagata but not with the premier, the army minister resigned, and Saionji's cabinet collapsed. The problem then was to find a replacement. Yamagata favored General Terauchi Masatake—one of his own proteges—as the new prime minister, but other oligarchs believed that a militarist would be unacceptable to party leaders. Other names were considered without result until General Katsura agreed to form his third cabinet. While Katsura was an army man, he had been cooperative in his dealings with the *Seiyukai* and he was known to lean toward Saionji's ideas on retrenchment. Moreover, he had broken with his old mentor, Yamagata. Nevertheless, Katsura's role was difficult, first, because party leaders suspected that he had instigated Saionji's dismissal and, second, because the navy was demanding new battleships. Indeed, the navy threatened to follow the army's lead by withholding its nomination for the cabinet if its demands were not met. When Katsura countered with an imperial rescript forcing the navy to furnish a minister, political agitation spilled into the streets. The opposition interpreted Katsura's action not as an effort to curb the military but as an undemocratic, high-handed use of imperial authority. Lacking a majority in the Diet, Katsura resigned. Some degree of political peace was restored only when the oligarchs agreed upon Admiral Count Yamamoto Gombei of Satsuma as premier. He commanded support from the military and from the *Seiyukai.*

In the following two years the old oligarchs were to name additional premiers. In 1914, after the navy was implicated in scandals touching battleship construction, the Diet refused to pass the budget and Yamamoto resigned. His successor was Marquis Okuma Shigenobu, who in turn was succeeded by General Terauchi in 1916. By 1918, however, age had weakened seriously the oligarchs' system of governing through their proteges. Furthermore, the once-docile political parties were showing a marked trend toward independence. Back in 1913, Katsura had attempted to rule by forming his own political party, the *Doshikai,* following Ito's strategy. The *Doshikai* was designed as a counterweight to the growing power of the *Seiyukai.* Okuma as prime minister in 1914 relied on this new party for support in the Diet, and he named the party's president Kato Komei (Takaaki) as foreign minister in his cabinet. Despite this gesture, the oligarchs were soon to find the *Doshikai* no more manageable than the older *Seiyukai.* Both parties wanted increased power in government. It was an indication that the younger oligarchs did not have the prestige or the power of an Ito or a Yamagata and that the capacity of the oligarchy to maintain its unchallenged rule was weakening.

Hara Kei (Takashi), named president of the *Seiyukai* in 1913 and one of the most prominent party leaders, symbolized the new popular forces in Japanese politics. Born a generation later than the early Meiji leadership and hailing from northeastern Honshu (far from Satsuma and Choshu), Hara was an "outsider" who had gained Ito's patronage. After a period in journalism he entered the foreign ministry, where he rose rapidly. At various times he was editor of a great daily newspaper, a bank official, president of a business firm and a member of the Diet. He had helped to found the *Seiyukai* in 1900 and, as expressed in a later program, his political goals were not very different from those of the oligarchs: "the perfection of national defense, the expansion of education, the encouragement of industry, and the expansion of communications." His methods, however, were those of a party organizer. During three terms as home minister, he resorted to the pork barrel to build party support. Districts which voted for the *Seiyukai* got roads, schools, and rail lines. In like manner, bureaucrats offering support were favored with special appointments and promotions. The political machine that Ito and Saionji had used against Yamagata was, in fact, largely Hara's creation.

In fact, the *Seiyukai* and its managing genius, Hara, were achieving new and increased power as the rule of the *genro* declined. Hara's methods brought a new stimulus to the party movement. For example, after analyzing the *Doshikai* victory in the election of 1915, Hara took advantage of specific areas of tension between the oligarchs and the *Doshikai.* He thereupon sought and reached an understanding with the arch-militarist and oligarch, Yamagata. Accordingly, when General Terauchi, Yamagata's man, became prime minister in 1916 he received a notable measure of support from the *Seiyukai.* This strategy was justified when in 1917 the *Seiyukai* won a majority in the Diet. Hara, it was obvious, was providing a type of political planning and creating a base of political power which the oligarchy could no longer ignore. This development was the more striking because Hara was a "commoner" among titled aristocrats.[7] The result was that in the troubled months of 1918 as World War I was ending, the *genro* took the unprecedented step of recommending Hara, the "commoner", as Terauchi's successor. The fact was that in the economic disorders of that time—resulting from war-time industrial expansion and a postwar recession—Hara had no rival. The significance of his appointment as prime minister (September, 1918) was very great indeed. It marked the end of rule by the *genro* and the clansmen of Satsuma and Choshu. It marked the beginnings of what appeared to be a new era of rule by party politicians, in which the commercial, industrial, and financial sectors of a bourgeois society would attempt to displace the feudal-authoritarian traditions of an earlier day.

ECONOMIC AND SOCIAL CONCERNS

Japan's adoption of constitutional government

[7] Although Hara made much of his lack of title, he actually came from a noble family (a *kaoru*), higher in status than Saionji. This background contributed to the rapid growth of his career in his early years. For the early years see Tetsuo Najita, *Hara Kei and the Politics of Compromise, 1905-1915* (1967).

(1890) and the ensuing struggle, which brought a political party, the *Seiyukai,* and its leader, Hara Kei, to power in 1918, was naturally of supreme importance; but it was only one aspect of Japan's march to modernization in these decades at the turn of the century. It was an extraordinary period in Japanese history. As recently as 1868-1871, Japan had been a feudal-military dictatorship just emerging from two centuries of isolation. Yet in the years covered by this chapter she had defeated China and Russia in war, had become the ally of the world's greatest industrial and naval power, and had acquired an empire as well as her own peculiar form of constitutional and representative government. These achievements could not have occurred had there not been, in addition, sweeping movements of modernization in the country's economic and social structure. There was the problem, for instance, of finding the resources to pay for war and for empire, and the even more vexing problem of adjusting the people's social values in a society now living in a new world.

THE NATIONAL TEMPER

The most pervasive social as well as political force in these years was nationalism of a peculiarly Japanese variety. Japan's early modern nationalism had been born in the nation's response to Perry. It had been a motivation in the restoration, and it had much to do with creating the constitutional movement and the structure of the modern economy. Japan, it was said, must master and apply the secrets of Western power in order to be strong herself. Yet Western values were not to replace fundamental Japanese values. Here there was the historical precedent of the eighth and ninth centuries, when Japan adopted the superior learning of China but promptly reshaped it in a distinctly Japanese mold. So it was that in the Meiji period Japan imported the technology and techniques of the West along with Western political, economic, and social ideas, but she attempted to integrate them into her own in-

digenous institutions and values. The role played by the *genro* in the early years of the Meiji constitution is a striking example.

THE EDUCATIONAL AGENT

One indispensable agency shaping Japan's modernization was the system of universal education created by the early Meiji leadership (see Chapter 10). By the first decades of the twentieth century it had become a minutely-designed and highly-organized state system serving a people among whom illiteracy had become all but unknown. By the turn of the century some 5 million children were attending 27,000 elementary schools. Secondary education heavily emphasized vocational and technical training, while the imperial universities provided higher education for the elite, the sons of the well-to-do. This development of technical (there were 240 technical schools by 1903) and university education was a major stimulus to the nation's industrial advance, and the entire educational system provided the ideological base of Japanese nationalism. The constant stress on such themes as familism, emperor-loyalty, and selfless, patriotic devotion served both the cause of modernization and the interests of the oligarchy and its ideal of government.

Textbooks were written under the supervision of the educational bureaucracy. They emphasized three particular themes: (1) the emperor was not merely the repository of sacred authority, he *was* that authority; (2) the nation was a super-family, united by filial piety and emperor-loyalty; and (3) the ethic of patriotism was the backbone of the country. By this system of indoctrination, diverse values and concepts, Eastern and Western, were drawn together to build a national morale deriving much of its rationale from various doctrines of Shintoism and Confucianism, and from the German theory of state sovereignty. The goal of education was not how to think, but what to think. It rested on the techniques of totali-

This poster, which was distributed to Japanese elementary schools by the Ministry of Education, 1909, illustrates the emphasis placed on "moral instruction." From the pictures and accompanying text, a youngster learned the proper way to greet an elder.

tarianism, and drew support from traditional patterns of subservience to authority.[8]

THE ECONOMIC COMPLEX

It will be recalled that the beginnings of Japan's economic and social reform antedated the constitutional movement by some years. The abolition of class and occupational restrictions in the 1870's had been a severe shock to the samurai

[8] Wilbur M. Fridell, "Government Ethics: Textbooks in Late *Meiji* Japan," *Journal of Asian Studies,* 29 (1970), 823-33. The philosophy of the educational system permeated every sector of society. For example, the position taken by the great entrepreneurs of the *zaibatsu* is of interest. It was not uncommon for them to say that the great personal fortunes they amassed were gained, so to speak, by accident. Their real purpose, so they affirmed, was to perform a selfless, patriotic function—serving the national interest by increasing the nation's wealth and insuring its security. All this at a time when scandalous relations of discrimination and favoritism existed between government and particular personalities in business. Nevertheless, the patriotic interpretation was a beautiful rationalization, acceptable to most Japanese. Note Marius B. Jansen, "The Meiji State: 1868-1912," in *Modern East Asia: Essays in Interpretation,* James B. Crowley, ed. (1970),* 117.

class, but it opened the way for a great release of human energy and ability in modern professions, in business, and in the creation of skilled and specialized labor. It was not, however, until after 1885 that Japan's modern economic growth became substantial. By that time the fiscal reforms of Matsukata Masayoshi had created a sound banking system, headed by the Bank of Japan, and had imposed on the government a budgetary system and a sound currency designed to prevent the recurrence of the financial crises of previous years.

SILK AND COTTON

The first major indicators of Japan's economic growth were in the so-called light industries of silk and cotton. Silk had long been a part of Japan's village economy. Modernization of the industry and the establishment of controls in quality for the European market created an enormous demand for Japanese silk. By the turn of the century, the country had become the largest single source of raw silk. This success story in the export of silk was repeated in the new cotton-spinning industry. Its new factories used economical, surplus rural labor (mostly female). By 1910 Japan had between 1½ and 2 million spindles, and was producing nearly 500 million pounds of cotton yarn each year. Together, these two industries gave Japan her first strength in the balance of foreign trade. By 1900 the textile industries provided more than 50 percent of the jobs in factory employment. The heavy industries, such as steel, machinery, and ship building, were also growing, but at a slower rate. Designed at first to serve only strategic needs, they did not become an important factor in world competition until the close of World War I.

POPULATION AND LABOR

Japan's rapid economic growth in the late years of the Meiji era and during World War I was fostered by an abundant supply of well-trained, docile, and cheap labor. In the fifty years following the Meiji restoration, the population increased nearly 100 percent to about 60 millions, partially as a result of modern medical services and improved hygiene. Much of this increased labor supply had been trained in native traditional industries, and thereby possessed skills of value for the modern factory. Since unused agricultural land was almost non-existent, the increasing surplus rural population moved to the cities and to the new industries; but even in this period of industrial growth the supply of labor increased faster than the demand for it. Wages, therefore, remained low. The consequence was that there was no rapid rise in the standard of living of the laboring classes and, as will be seen, of the farming classes. While an impoverished peasantry and the surplus labor it produced for the factories enjoyed some benefits from better and less expensive manufactured goods (such as cotton cloth) and from modern public services (schools and electric power), there was very little upgrading in the fundamentals of housing and diet.

POSITION OF THE RICE FARMER

Until well into the twentieth century, as mod-

ernization and industrialization continued, half or more of Japan's population remained rural. These were the rice farmers who produced the principal staple of the Japanese diet. The income of farm families was restricted in the first instance by the small size of their land holdings (about 2.6 acres). At the time of the restoration about 30 percent of all agricultral land was cultivated by tenants. By 1910 about 45 percent of the paddy fields were cultivated by tenants, and about 39 percent of the farmers owned no land. The brave gesture of the restoration in making the peasant the owner of the land had not worked very well. Its failure had been hastened by the land tax, to be paid in money, imposed by the early Meiji government as its main source of income. In poor crop years, peasants who could not meet the tax were dispossessed, although the land confiscated by the government and auctioned for sale usually was many times the value of the taxes in arrears. Tenant farmers paid land rents in kind, amounting to 45 to 60 percent of the crop on rice land. Moreover, the farming populace was paying a far larger percentage of its income in taxes than the city merchant or the industrialist.

INDUSTRIAL GROWTH

Although Japan's industrial growth was remarkable it did not at first keep pace with her obligations. Her wars against China and Russia imposed unprecedented burdens on the national budget. War indemnities reduced but did not meet rising expenditures. In 1897 Japan adopted the gold standard, established her credit abroad, and became a heavy borrower of foreign capital. It was World War I that presented Japan with the opportunity to become a great industrial power. The war brought orders to Japan for munitions, various war supplies, and civilian goods. Countries of East and South Asia, no longer able to buy from Europe, turned to the Japanese market. As indicative of the result, exports of Japanese cotton cloth increased 185 percent between 1913 and 1918 (from 412 million to 1,174 billion linear yards). The Japanese merchant fleet increased from

1,577,000 gross tons in 1914 to 2,840,000 tons in 1919. By the latter year, Japan's foreign assets exceeded her outstanding debts by Yen 1,300 billion. Five years earlier Japan had been a debtor by approximately the same figure. This fantastic transformation was accompanied by expanded bank credit, price inflation, exhorbitant profits, and wild speculation. All Japanese, of course, did not share in this massive prosperity; indeed, these were the conditions which led to the rice riots of 1918, the fall of the Terauchi government, and the appointment of Hara as prime minister.

CONTROLLING PROTEST

Finally, it should be noted that Meiji constitutionalism, subservient as it was to the idea and goal of a centralized, industrial state, was biased in favor of power rather than of the welfare of the common man. This is not to say that the Meiji oligarchy took no steps to curb abuses, yet the first factory labor law drafted by the government in 1898 was not submitted to the Diet because of the opposition of the industrialists. When the Japan Social Democratic Party was formed in 1901 by Katayama Sen and Kotoku Denjiro, it was ordered dissolved by Home Minister Suematsu Kencho, son-in-law of Premier Ito, within three hours of its founding. During the Russo-Japanese war the socialist movement became more radical, international, and intellectual. In 1907, rioting by miners in protest against outrageous working conditions resulted in millions in property damage and in the arrest of more than 200 miners and labor leaders.

The policy of repression directed against socialistic parties and associations was merely an extreme aspect of the oligarchy's attitude toward political freedom in general. Although the constitution made reference to civil liberties, suppression continued after 1890. Oftentimes the government, seeking a gradual transition, had a plausible case against the tendency of dissident groups to resort to violence. At first the series of peace preservation laws that were in effect when the constitution was promulgated were opposed bitterly by the parties in the first Diets, and the most obnoxious of

the statutes was repealed in 1898, only to be re-enacted two years later in a form virtually precluding the legal organization and maintenance of labor unions. This law persisted until 1926, though it was not always enforced.

FOR FURTHER READING

Social, Economic, and Intellectual Bases of Politics. For the pattern of Japanese culture, see Ruth Benedict, *The Chrysanthemum and the Sword* (1946).* G. C. Allen, *Modern Japan and Its Problems* (1928) studies the effect of Western influences. W. W. Lockwood, *The Economic Development of Japan* (1954)* provides valuable insights into the political significance of economic processes. On this topic see also Araki Mitsutaro, *Financial System in Japan* (1933); Yamasaki Kakujiro and Ogawa Gotaro, *The Effect of the War Upon the Commerce and Industry of Japan* (1939); and Ohara Keishi (comp.), *Japanese Trade and Industry in the Meiji-Taisho Era,* trans. and adapted by Okata Tomatsu (1957). On the emergence of the labor movement see Katayama Sen, *The Labor Movement in Japan* (1918), and Kohno Mitsu, *Labour Movement in Japan* (1938). See also Kawabe Kisaburo, *The Press and Politics in Japan, A Study of the Relation Between the Newspaper and the Political Development of Modern Japan* (1921). H. L. Keenleyside and A. F. Thomas, *History of Japanese Education* (1937) reveals the political philosophy behind the educational system.

History of Political Thought. Ito Hirobumi, *Commentaries on the Constitution of the Empire of Japan,* Miyoji Ito, trans. (1889). Fujisawa Rikitaro, *Recent Aims and Political Development of Japan* (1923). *The Autobiography of Fukuzawa Yukichi* (1934). Kawai Tatsuo, *The Goal of Japanese Expansion* (1938), for the so-called philosophy of *musubi.* Tokutomi Idiiro, "The Life of Yoshida Shoin," *Transactions of the Asiatic Society of Japan,* 45, (1917), Part I. Joseph J. Spae, *Ito Jinsai: A Philosopher, Educator, and Sinologist of the Tokugawa Period. (Monumenta Serica Monograph Series* 12, 1948) presents the important position of Yoshida Shoin with a bibliography on Japanese Confucianism.

Political History and Government. H. P. Mason, *Japan: First General Election* (1969), the first detailed description in English. See also Chitoshi Yanaga, *Japanese People and Politics* (1956).* Delmar Brown, *Nationalism in Japan: An Introductory Historical Analysis* (1955). C. B. Fahs, *Government in Japan* (1940). Fujii Shinichi, *The Essentials of Japanese Constitutional Law* (1940). W. W. McLaren, *A Political History of Japan during the Meiji Era, 1867-1912* (1916). Two studies by E. H. Norman, *Japan's Emergence as a Modern State* (1940), and *Soldier and Peasant in Japan: The Origins of Conscription* (1943) deal with the early years of the oligarchy.

Japan
and China
in World War I,
1914 – 1918

21

Considered in the perspective of its immediate causes and its military and naval campaigns, World War I was primarily a European conflict. No major battles were fought on Asian soil or in Asian waters. Nevertheless, at one time or another all the major lands and people of Asia were aligned with the allied and associated powers. By their participation in the war, Asians became parties to major changes in the international order wrought by the war. In 1914, all of the great peoples of Asia, the Japanese excepted, were in a colonial or semi-colonial status; five years later, native spokesmen in colonial Asia, employing the Wilsonian principle of national self-determination, were demanding an end to Western and Japanese domination.

WAR COMES TO EAST ASIA

Japan's entrance into World War I derived its sanction from a double basis: the nation's commitments under the Anglo-Japanese alliance, and the larger political and military purposes of Japan's emerging Asian policy.

On August 7, 1914, three days after her own declaration of war, Great Britain requested

Japan to destroy the German fleet in Pacific waters. The decision of the Japanese government, made on August 8, was to demand of Germany not only surrender of its armed ships in Asian waters (thus complying with the British request) but also surrender of the Kiaochou leasehold in Shantung. Later in the month, on August 23, as Germany ignored Tokyo's ultimatum, Japan entered the war. This momentous decision to join Great Britain in the war (as explained by Count Kato Komei, the foreign minister) was not based on legal obligations of the Anglo-Japanese alliance, for "the general conditions were not such as to impose upon Japan the duty to join the war under treaty obligations," but "as a voluntary expression of friendship toward Great Britain under the Alliance."[1] What Japan meant was that she welcomed an opportunity to destroy German influence in East Asia and to enhance her own international position.

The outbreak of war in Europe had aroused great alarm in Peking. China's interests, so its government reasoned, would best be served by exclusion of her territories and waters from the zone of hostilities. Peking first proclaimed her

[1] Takeuchi Tatsuji, *War and Diplomacy in the Japanese Empire* (1935), 169.

neutrality and later delimited a war zone in the areas adjacent to Kiaochou. Both of these measures were futile. Following promptly on her declaration of war, Japan proceeded to the investment of the Kiaochou leased territory and its port of Tsingtao. With this port under naval blockade, Japanese military forces landed on Chinese soil far to the north, moved to attack Tsingtao from the rear, and occupied the railway zone reaching from Tsingtao to Tsinan far in the interior of the province.[2] Kiaochou surrendered, November 10, and Japan took over not only the leased territory but also all German interests in Shantung, including the Tsingtao-Tsinan Railway.[3] Japan also took over from

[2] A small British force was also engaged for "token" purposes.

[3] The nature and scope of German rights which Japan was to claim as a result of her victory were as follows: (1) the 99-year lease of both sides of Kiaochou Bay which China had conferred upon Germany, on which Germany had erected fortifications and in which she exercised "rights of administration"; (2) German troops held the right of freedom of passage within a zone of 50 kilometers of the bay, in which Chinese administration was subject to German approval; (3) the right Germany acquired to construct certain railroads in Shantung, a provision that resulted in the building of the Tsingtao-Tsinan Railway by a Sino-German concern, the Shantung Railway Company; (4) the right Germany also acquired to mine coal within 30 *li* of the railroads; (5) Germany's right, should she desire to return Kiaochou to China before the expiration of the lease, to have China lease her "a more suitable place"; and (6) China's agreement to approach German nationals if assistance in the form of capital, services, or materials were needed for any undertaking in Shantung province. In addition, although Germany had engaged not to sublet the territory to another power, there was no provision regarding the transfer of the territory by Germany to another power as a result of conquest, such as the Japanese action of 1914.

Under these various concessions, Germany had built a modern port at Tsingtao, had extended a railroad far into the interior of the province, and had developed broad commercial undertakings, while at Kiaochou she had created a naval base for the Pacific squadron. How these German rights had worked out in practice is treated by John E. Schrecker, *Imperialism and Chinese Nationalism: Germany in Shantung* (1971). The German navy and the German foreign office failed to agree on their China policy; in addition, Chinese resistance was more effective in thwarting German purposes in Shantung than has been sup-

the Chinese, on the plea of military necessity, the policing of the railroads outside the leased territory. Japanese replaced Germans in the Chinese customs house at Tsingtao. Indeed, the ousting of the Germans was thorough and complete. As in 1904, China was unable to keep war from her shores or to control its course within her borders.

While Japanese naval and military forces were engaged in the reduction of Tsingtao and in taking over other German interests in Shantung, units of the Japanese navy were operating in the Pacific and Indian Oceans in cooperation with the British against German commerce raiders. Early in these operations, while the Australians were occupying German colonies and islands south of the equator, the Japanese occupied the German islands north of the equator. These included the Marianas (excepting Guam), the Carolines, and the Marshalls. From this point on, that is from the beginning of 1915, Japan's relationship to the war became essentially noncombatant. Still, while Japan's factories equipped the Russian armies on the eastern front, her policies in China posed a threat not only to Western commerce but also to the political principles emerging in the pattern of Allied war aims.

THE TWENTY-ONE DEMANDS

On January 18, 1915, Japanese Minister Hioki at Peking presented to President Yuan Shih-k'ai a group of twenty-one demands designed to "insure" Japan's position in China at a time when Europe was preoccupied with war. Japan was launched upon new steps in her policy of expansion. In particular she hoped to establish a solid legal basis for her special interests in Manchuria. Although European powers had recognized Japanese claims there, China had not. A second phase of Japanese policy in 1915 concerned itself with the nation's position and influence south of the Great Wall in China

posed. After 1915, the Japanese who replaced the Germans in Shantung were far more effective, because the Japanese home economy developed the Shantung trade aggressively.

Proper. In the scramble there for railway and mining concessions, Japan, as a debtor nation, was at a disadvantage against European and American competitors. As seen in Tokyo, the weakness of Japan's position could only be corrected by the assertion of specific rights and, if possible, of a general and paramount influence over all of China. To achieve these purposes, Japan presented demands divided into five groups: Group 1 would preclude Germany's return to Shantung at the close of the war; Group 2 demanded that China concede Japan's *paramount* interests in South Manchuria and eastern Inner Mongolia; Group 3 would convey to Japanese interests a monopoly over mining operations in designated regions of the Yangtze valley; Group 4 required China to pledge non-alienation of her coastal territory; and Group 5, termed "requests" rather than "demands," provided for (a) the appointment of Japanese advisors in key positions in the Chinese government; (b) the extension of Japanese rights to own hospitals, temples, and schools in China's interior; (c) the establishment of joint Sino-Japanese police forces in regions where clashes had occurred; (d) an agreement by China to purchase arms in Japan; (e) the grant of railway construction rights in South China; and (f) concession to Japanese of the "right of preaching in China." So sweeping were these latter "requests" that world opinion identified Japanese policy with Group 5 rather than with the more specific demands relating to Shantung, Manchuria, and eastern Inner Mongolia. Group 5 seemed to justify extravagant speculation as to Japan's real purpose, not excluding the possibility that her motive was the creation of a protectorate over China.

THE COURSE OF NEGOTIATIONS

The demands were presented to President Yuan Shih-k'ai with insistence upon secrecy. China's response was to defend herself by permitting the terms to become known through unofficial channels. Garbled accounts appeared in the Chinese and foreign press, touching off violent reactions in Chinese public opinion. Both the United States and Great Britain expressed reservations on a number of the demands. Thus, as

the unhappy negotiations dragged on, Japan, finding more resistance than she had anticipated, resorted to an ultimatum on May 7. Two weeks later, on May 25, China and Japan signed a number of treaties and notes embodying many, though by no means all, of the terms set forth in the original twenty-one demands.

The more important treaty commitments gained by Japan included: (1) recognition of Shantung as a Japanese sphere, in return for which the German leasehold in Shantung was to be returned to China after the close of the war; (2) extension of the Kwantung leasehold to 99 years, together with increased railroad and other privileges in South Manchuria; and (3) the right of Japan to be consulted first in case China required foreign capital for railway or harbor construction in Fukien. On paper at least, Japan had won the basis for a commanding position in China.

INTERNATIONAL REPERCUSSION

The price paid by Japan for this diplomatic victory was a mounting Western suspicion of Japanese ambitions. The Anglo-Japanese alliance in particular was weakened by Japan's resort to secrecy and her insistence on playing a lone hand in China. Some two years before delivery of the twenty-one demands, Count Kato Komei, before leaving London to become foreign minister, had informed Viscount Grey that Japan awaited only the "psychological moment" to obtain "permanent occupation of Kwantung Province," but Japan failed to provide her ally with advance notice of the concessions to be demanded of China in the twenty-one demands.[4] During the Sino-Japanese negotiations, Great Britain pressured Japan mainly with respect to demands that crossed British interests in central China. She did not press Japan more vigorously in 1915 because of their common war effort against Germany. British restraint, however, did not conceal an emerging official view that Japanese expansion was inimical to British far eastern interests.[5]

[4] Paul S. Dull, "Count Kato Komei and the Twenty-one Demands," *Pacific Historical Review,* 19 (1950), 151-61.

[5] The depth of British concern and the nature of her interventions in negotiations over the twenty-one

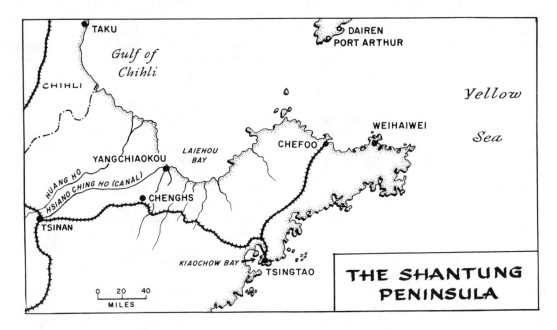

In American-Japanese relations, the twenty-one demands increased President Woodrow Wilson's determination to oppose Japanese expansion. Since Japan had sought to implement her policy in China at a time when Europe was involved in war, the United States alone was in a position to act in East Asia if she desired to do so. Wilson had already shown his concern for China. He had been the first to extend formal recognition to the Republic; he had repudiated the Taft-Knox policy regarding the consortium, which in his view infringed China's administrative independence; and he

had approved of an effort to assist in the maintenance of China's neutrality at the outbreak of war. His policy in the case of the twenty-one demands was to "protect China out of sympathy, and American rights out of interest, but to move cautiously lest Japan be antagonized against the United States and be more severe with China."[6]

In consequence, the policy of the American government, as initially formulated in a detailed memorandum from Secretary of State Bryan to the Japanese ambassador on March 13, raised specific objection to several of Japan's demands on the ground that they violated the open door and China's administrative and territorial in-

---

demands have been revealed by the recent openings of foreign office archives. The new materials, however, have led to disagreement among historians on the structure of British priorities in Asia. Robert J. Gowen, "Great Britain and the Twenty-one Demands: Cooperation *vs.* Effacement," *Journal of Modern History,* 43 (1971), 76-106; and Peter Lowe, *Great Britain and Japan, 1911-1915: A Study of British Far Eastern Policy* (1969) stress London's defense of British interests in China. On the other hand, Don Dignan, "New Perspectives on British Far Eastern Policy, 1913-19," *University of Queensland Papers: Departments of Government and History,* I, (1969), 263-302, emphasizes British fears that Japan was promoting the rise of Indian nationalism.

[6] At the outbreak of World War I, many serious and responsible Chinese assumed that American support of the open door meant that the United States would guarantee China against any territorial aggression or disregard of her sovereignty. How fantastic these Chinese hopes were was revealed by Acting Secretary of State Lansing when he informed the American legation in Peking that although the United States was prepared to promote China's welfare by peaceful methods, "it would be quixotic in the extreme to allow the question of China's territorial integrity to entangle the United States in international difficulties." United States, *Foreign Relations, 1914 (Supplement),* 186-87, 190.

tegrity. To these objections, however, Bryan added an important observation concerning the areas in which Japan claimed spheres of influence:

While on principle and under the treaties of 1844, 1858, 1868 and 1903 with China the United States has ground upon which to base objections to the Japanese "demands" relative to Shantung, South Manchuria and Eastern Mongolia, nevertheless, the United States frankly recognizes that territorial contiguity creates special relations between Japan and these districts.[7]

Stated briefly, the United States was offering to strike a bargain with Japan. Insofar as China was concerned, the bargain called for American recognition of Japan's claims to spheres of influence in return for concrete Japanese pledges of support for the open door in the remainder of China. While this offer was undoubtedly more modest than Japan might have wished, it did seem to foretell a significant shift in the policy of the nation which had presented the greatest opposition to the spheres.[8]

But Japan did not respond to the American offer. Thus, later in the negotiations, as a result of Japan's ultimatum to China, the United States appeared less conciliatory. In identical notes to China and Japan on May 11, Secretary Bryan informed these powers that the United States would not recognize

. . . any agreement or undertaking which has been entered into or which may be entered into between the governments of Japan and China, impairing the treaty rights of the United States and its citizens in China, the political or territorial integrity of the Republic of China, or the international policy relative to China commonly known as the open door policy.[9]

---

[7] *Foreign Relations, 1914, Supp.,* 189-190.

[8] For the origins of the proffered bargain see Burton F. Beers, "Robert Lansing's Proposed Bargain with Japan," *Pacific Historical Review,* 26 (1957), 391-400. Sir Edward Grey, the British prime minister, toyed with the idea of an Anglo-Japanese bargain which was similar in substance to the one suggested by the United States. Grey's idea was to make concessions to Japanese economic interests in areas of China where Britain claimed exclusive investment privileges in return for Japanese pledges forswearing attacks on British imperial holdings. See Dignan, "New Perspectives."

[9] *Foreign Relations, 1915,* 146.

This note was sent after China's acceptance of the ultimatum, but two weeks before the signing of the Sino-Japanese treaties and notes of May 25. The procedure was unusual, and the doctrine that was set forth (that of nonrecognition), though it was later to play a most conspicuous part in American policy, had no immediate effect upon the Sino-Japanese settlement. The United States in 1915, although sympathetic to China and concerned for American interests therein, was not prepared to challenge Japan openly. Tokyo did not fail to note, however, that, by reserving the right to reopen all issues raised in the twenty-one demands, the United States had established a basis for future opposition to Japanese expansion.

CHINA'S DISINTEGRATING POLITICAL ORDER

The extreme caution of Britain and the United States in defense of China's integrity suggested that effective opposition to Japan must come primarily from China herself. Yet in 1915, and during the remainder of World War I, Chinese politics generated less, rather than more, resistance to foreign encroachment. Although the twenty-one demands stirred unprecedented resentment in segments of the Chinese populace, bringing a semblance of unity among politicians, this display of infant nationalism did not produce an effective national government. In the spring of 1915 President Yuan Shih-k'ai was already planning (see Chapter 19) to restore the monarchy with himself as the monarch. These pretensions precipitated new uprisings. Leaders in eight provinces in the south and west were in open revolt against Peking when Yuan died suddenly on June 6, 1916.

With Yuan gone, there was no political figure with sufficient prestige to assert a national authority. Power passed to provincial military governors, who, between 1916 and 1928, competed one with another as "warlords." Commanding newly-swollen forces equipped with modern weapons, and using China's new railways and river steamers, these militarists moved about establishing provincial or regional bases of power. To buttress their claims to legitimacy, the warlords adopted benign political slogans and created some of the trappings of civil government, but few succeeded in building any genuine popular support. In these circumstances, China was fragmented politically, and constantly at war with herself.

Nominally, the Republic survived. Peking continued to present some of the appearances of a parliamentary government, operating under a presidential system. It was this Peking warlord government which, prior to *Kuomintang*-Nationalist triumphs in 1927-1928, was recognized by Japan and the Western powers as the government of China. But the reality was that this "government" was simply the pawn of a succession of rival warlords. Control in Peking offered victorious militarists some of the symbols of authority and, more important, access to foreign loans. The old capital, therefore, remained a prize in China's civil wars, but it was no longer the center of a governmental system accepted throughout the country. In 1917, for example, Sun Yat-sen re-emerged from political eclipse to join forces with southern members of parliament and local warlords in establishing a rival regime at Canton.

Such political fragmentation provided rich opportunities for Japanese imperialism. Tuan Ch'i-jui, Peking's sometime warlord premier, financed his domestic wars by borrowing heavily from Japan. In return for this financial assistance, he made a military alliance with Japan, imported Japanese military instructors, and worked closely with other pro-Japanese politicians. When nationalists complained that the premier was selling China to foreigners in order to reinforce his personal powers, Li Yuan-hung, then serving as president, resigned. Tuan's response was to coerce what remained of the parliament into selecting a new presidential figure who would be more in tune with his policies.

CHINA ENTERS THE WAR

In the midst of her domestic political chaos, China was called upon in February, 1917, to resolve the question of breaking diplomatic relations with Germany. President Wilson, having announced the severance of American relations with Germany, called upon neutral powers to follow the American example. The American minister at Peking, Paul S. Reinsch, not only conveyed the appeal to the government through Premier Tuan, but also proceeded with great zeal to urge its adoption. This pressure from Reinsch touched off a flurry of international activity. Japan, fearing that Reinsch's moves marked the beginning of close Sino-American ties, first sought to block China's break with Germany. Later Japan reversed her course and led the European powers in urging the severance of relations. Thus the way for a diplomatic break between China and Germany had already been paved when, on February 24, the torpedoing by a German submarine of the French ship *Athos* in the Mediterranean resulted in the death of 543 Chinese coolies. (Thousands of coolies had been employed by the French and British to work in the Flemish and French military zones in 1916-1917.) On March 14, China formally terminated relations with Germany. Unknown to China, however, was the price that she had paid for being a party to the maneuvering just described. Before accepting the idea of a break between China and Germany, Japan secretly asked for and obtained (in February and March, 1917) pledges of support from her European allies for her claims in Shantung as well as in the German islands in the North Pacific (the Marianas, Carolines, and Marshalls).[10] Even China's formal declaration of war on August 14 had its price. During the summer of 1917, the question of the country's belligerency became an issue in the tangled maneuverings of the warlords. Tuan was briefly forced from power by rivals who proposed to maintain China's neutrality. Before he returned as premier, China's titular leader, President Li Yuan-hung, had resigned and the parliament's *Kuomintang* membership had fled. Thus China not only lost to Japan, but the

[10] These concessions were the product of diplomacy in which Japan played upon Allied fears that a deal with Germany would take her out of the war. See Frank Ikle, "Japanese-German Peace Negotiations during World War I," *American Historical Review*, 71 (1965), 62-76.

controversy over the war also served to magnify her political chaos.

As a belligerent, China was neither able nor willing to contribute much to the war effort, except by sending labor battalions to France, Mesopotamia and Africa. Not until the latter part of 1918, when the collapse of Germany seemed assured, did Tuan's government bestir itself to adopt a vigorous war policy through effective control of enemy aliens and liquidation of enemy property. These tardy steps were a last-minute bid for consideration at the forthcoming peace conference. They were also a recognition by the northern warlords that Chinese public opinion was becoming more sympathetic to the cause of the Allied and Associated Powers. China, however, was not solely responsible for the shortcomings of her war record. Against the acts of her irresponsible warload government must be weighed the tortuous diplomacy of the Allies. Japan, Britain, and France had assisted in pushing China into the war neither for high moral purpose nor in the hope that she would become an effective belligerent, but rather with the specific intent of eliminating German commercial and industrial competition from post war China. If American diplomacy was less self-serving, it was also thoroughly ineffective in saving China from the powers or from herself. And finally, it should be noted that when China issued her declaration of war, she did so without definite assurance of concessions, financial or otherwise, from the West.

PEACE

Although Japan's participation in the war was marginal, Tokyo made extensive preparations for the peace conference. Just as World War I had swept away the old balance of power in Europe, so it had gone far to destroy the balance of power in East Asia. Prior to 1914, Japan had been accorded nominal status as a so-called great power, a result of victories over China in 1895 and over Russia in 1905. Actually, however, the great powers of Europe had not considered Japan a full ranking member of their select company. It was the World War of 1914 that elevated Japan to a new status. The

war had provided Japan with an opportunity to expand her economy and armed forces, as well as to demonstrate her supremacy in China and the Pacific. Japan, therefore, approached the peace conference conscious of her new-found power. She was prepared to seek general recognition of her status as a great power and specific recognition of her hegemony in East Asia.

The opposition to Japan's objectives was to come principally, though not exclusively, from the United States. Since May, 1915, the Wilson administration, concerned with upholding China's administrative and territorial integrity as well as with the protection of specific American interests, had labored to forestall the establishment of a Japanese political and economic monopoly in China. The United States had urged American investors to underwrite major construction projects and had revived negotiations for the creation of a new consortium, an organization which would safeguard Peking from financial dependence on Japan. Diplomacy had sought to obtain pledges limiting Japanese aspirations. But these efforts had been invariably hampered by the war. American investors, for example, had been hard-pressed to find funds for China in the face of war demands elsewhere. Again, the necessity of maintaining at least the facade of unity among the Allied and Associated Powers while the war lasted had prevented the United States from exerting much diplomatic pressure on Tokyo. But, in 1917, the United States invited Viscount Ishii Kikujiro to Washington. During the subsequent conversations Secretary of State Robert Lansing urged Japan to relinquish her claims to special privilege in China, but he dared not press too hard, lest Japan withdraw from the war. When Japan refused to yield, Lansing and Ishii signed notes, carefully worded, to conceal the disagreement they embodied. But as the peace conference drew near, the United States, free at last from the responsibility of belligerency, sought new means by which to block Japan in her efforts to gain special privilege in China.

JAPAN AT VERSAILLES

At the Versailles conference, Japan presented three demands: (1) she asked for cession of the former German islands in the North Pacific (the Marianas, the Carolines, and the Marshalls); (2) she asked confirmation of her claims to the former German rights in Shantung province; and (3) she asked for a declaration of racial equality among states as a basic principle of the proposed League of Nations. Unassailable as Japan may have believed these objectives to be, they led nonetheless to widespread and bitter opposition from some of her former allies and associates in arms. Japan's claim to the German islands violated the Wilsonian principle of no annexations; her claims to Kiaochou and Shantung ran counter to a young and virile Chinese nationalism; and her demand for a declaration of racial equality raised a storm of protest from some of the British dominions, particularly Australia.

Nevertheless, Japan's representatives, Baron Makino Nobuaki and Viscount Chinda Sutemi, approached their task with confidence, for Japan's demands in the case of the German islands and Shantung were supported by powerful legal claims, and, in the case of racial equality, by high moral principles.[11] The German islands and Kiaochou had been captured by Japanese arms and were in Japanese possession. Moreover, Japan's claims were sustained by secret concessions of European allies and by the treaties and notes signed with China in May, 1915. Whatever moral or legal strength China's resentment against the 1915 treaties may have had, it was weakened seriously in 1918 when China again gave her explicit consent to the transfer of Kiaochou to Japan, on the understanding that Japan would in turn restore the leasehold to China but would retain in expanded form Germany's economic rights in the province. Thus Japan's legal case was strong; despite the desire of the Allies and the United States to block her further expansion, they were not prepared to challenge the legal basis of her claims, lest this challenge rebound upon the whole system of unequal treaties pertaining to China.

[11] Japan's ranking delegate was Prince Saionji Kimmochi, ex-premier and member of the *genro*.

CHINA ENTERS THE CONFERENCE

If the demands on which Japan was to insist were brutally clear, they were also a logical result of the policy on which she had embarked in 1914-1915 and to which her preparations had been pointed for many years. In contrast, the role that China might play at the peace table was not so predictable. It is true that by 1918 there was the beginning of a young and extremely vocal Chinese nationalism, but neither the warlord government at Peking nor the insurgent government which had been established at Canton appeared to represent anything with political substance. Indeed, the program that China presented at Paris was merely a product of opportunism and of the particular personalities in her peace delegation. Although the Peking and Canton governments had not achieved unity at home, they presented a facade of unity at Paris, for the Chinese peace delegation was composed of representatives of both governments. In terms of political strategy and showmanship, this Chinese delegation was unsurpassed at Paris, for to the able political strategy of C. T. Wang was added the eloquent English of Wellington Koo. These men fashioned the Chinese presentation as the program of a young, progressive, revolutionary, and idealistic China—a program that must have sounded strange in the ears of Peking's warlords. It should be added that no delegation supported the Wilsonian program with greater eloquence. Nevertheless, China's delegation was regarded with suspicion by the European Allies and Japan: first, because in the light of China's internal politics it was questionable whether any delegation could speak for the country; and second, because it was soon evident that Wang and Koo were less concerned with the problem of making peace with Germany than with using the conference to free China from her semicolonial status. To most of the Allied statesmen this purpose was alarming, for it implied an attack not only on Japan's "special interests" but also upon the larger system of spheres of influence and the "unequal treaties" in general, to which all the victorious great powers were parties. In addition, the mistrust of Japan, England, and France was further aroused because, both before and during the Paris conference, Wang and Koo systematically set out to cultivate the sympathies and enlist the support of the American delegation, which in turn was not loath to give the Chinese encouragement.

THE DEBATE AT PARIS

Japan's demand for the "unconditional cession" of the German rights in Shantung was made on January 28, 1919. The following day, China's counter-demand that Kiaochou and the German rights be restored directly to China was presented. To President Wilson, the obvious answer to this deadlock between China and Japan was to be found in his own program, which promised a new world of international justice under a League of Nations. But Wilson could make no progress against the Japanese on

this score while Australia, New Zealand, South Africa, France, Italy, and Belgium remained insistent on annexing the German colonies in their respective regions. The best that Wilson could eventually get was the system of mandates, which, with the exception of those in Class A, gave to the mandatory power a control which for practical purposes was indistinguishable from annexation. Under the Class C mandate, Japan acquired the former German islands in the North Pacific, and the British dominions got those in the South Pacific.

Having "compromised" by accepting a mandate instead of annexation in the Pacific islands, Japan turned to her third objective. With the approval and aid of President Wilson and Colonel House, her delegation presented as an amendment to the draft covenant of the League of Nations a resolution affirming the principle of racial equality.

This resolution, approved by Wilson, was a logical if not an essential complement to the whole spirit of the Wilsonian program as well as

Japan, 1910-1919

Reproduced from A War Atlas for Americans *(New York: Simon & Schuster) 1944, with permission from the publisher and from the U.S. Department of State, Division of Map Intelligence and Cartography.*

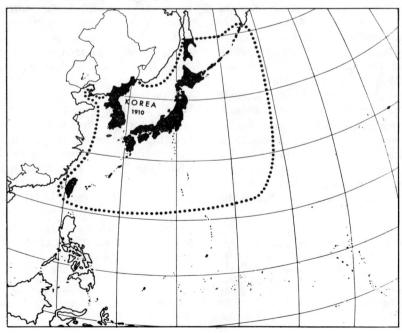

to the League itself; but, in newsroom parlance, it was a "hot potato." It aroused the unrelenting opposition of Premier William H. Hughes of Australia, who was supported by the chief British delegates, Arthur Balfour and Robert Cecil. The argument advanced against any provision on racial equality was that it implied the right of the League to interfere in questions concerning immigration and the rights of aliens, which every nation regarded as matters of purely domestic concern. Great Britain feared embarrassment in some of her middle eastern colonies. Hughes saw the resolution as endangering the "white" Australia policy, and he **threatened to arouse an outraged public** opinion in the British dominions and the United States unless the amendment were dropped. At the same time he stooped to convince the Japanese press that it was the United States and not Australia that was blocking the amendment.[12]

Wilson's dilemma was real. If the racial equality debate was brought into the open, as Hughes had threatened, what would be the reaction of the American Pacific Coast, especially California, which had already enacted the discriminatory alien land law of 1913 aimed at the Japanese? But this was not all. American policy at Paris was attempting to hold Japan in check on many fronts. There was Shantung, which Wilson wanted to restore directly to China. There was the prospective four-power consortium, into which he hoped to entice Japan in order to preserve a financial open door in China. There was eastern Siberia (see Chapter 22), which it was hoped could be rescued from Japan's military expansionists despite its occupation at the time by more than 70,000 Japanese troops. And there was the Island of Yap in the Japanese mandate, where it was hoped the

United States might be given submarine cable privileges. Would not American policy have a better chance of achieving these objectives if Japanese racial pride were satisfied by even an emasculated concession to the principle of racial equality? Thus, on grounds of high principle and practical politics, Wilson desired adoption of the amendment.

The vote on Japan's amendment[13] was favorable, eleven to six, but for reasons which seemed good to him, Wilson ruled against adoption of the amendment because the vote was not unanimous and announced defeat of the measure. The newsmen had been right; racial equality was a "hot potato." Wilson could not risk the issue in open debate, and he feared that Hughes would force it into the open if it could be defeated in no other way.

Two of Japan's objectives at Paris had now been disposed of: in the Pacific islands there had been a "compromise" which Japan had accepted but did not like; on racial equality she had accepted a defeat particularly galling to Japanese pride, since the race issue was a symbol of discrimination, a label of an inferior people. Japan's government was, therefore, in no mood to accept further reverses as it approached the debate on its next objective: transfer to Japan, in the terms of the peace treaty, of the former German rights in Shantung. Here Japan was determined to accept neither compromise nor defeat. The problem was the more difficult because Wang and Koo had by this time gone far beyond their original demand for the direct restoration of Kiaochou and the German rights. Encouraged by the support of public opinion in the West and in China, the Chinese delegates demanded abrogation of all the 1915 treaties and notes. This was a direct thrust not only at Japan's pretensions in Shantung but also at her "special position" in South Manchuria and eastern Inner Mongolia, and at her general ambitions in China as a whole. It was a challenge which the Japanese

---

[12] Hughes' vehemence on the racial issue was directed at Japanese expansion. The Australian Premier's fears of eventual conflict with Japan led to views that were frequently at cross purposes with the Anglo-Japanese alliance. See L.F. Fitzhardinge, "Australia, Japan, and Great Britain, 1914-1918: A Study in Triangular Diplomacy," *Historical Studies,* 14 (1970), 250-58.

[13] It had become merely an "endorsement of the principle of equality of nations and just treatment of their nationals."

promptly accepted. They stood firm and demanded Shantung, threatening to withdraw from the conference if it were denied them. Wilson thought that this Japanese stand permitted only one choice—acceptance. In this he differed from some of his close advisers, who felt that the Japanese were bluffing. Wilson, however, was right and his advisers were wrong.[14] With Wilson's opposition ended, Japan was permitted to insert articles into the treaty giving her free disposal of German rights in return for oral assurances that Chinese sovereignty in Shantung would be restored at some unspecified time. China's response was her refusal to sign the treaty.

CHINA'S BALANCE SHEET OF WAR

Although China refused to sign the treaty of Versailles between the Allied and Associated Powers and Germany, and although her defeat on the Shantung issue was a reverse of great magnitude, her balance sheet of war was not written wholly in red ink. The war had terminated China's old "unequal" treaties with Germany, Austria, and Hungary, thus opening the way for new treaties with those powers negotiated on a basis of equality.[15] And, more than this, the war contributed in complex ways to the growth of Chinese nationalism. A word about the intellectual foundations of the new China in the aftermath of the Revolution of 1911 will explain this contribution.

In an immediate sense, the Revolution of 1911 was profoundly disappointing to its partisans. While the Manchus had been ousted, the first Republic had not provided the setting for any rapid political transformations in Chinese life. The cold facts were that Chinese society was largely unchanged; furthermore, the new

political institutions of the Republic itself were attacked by Yuan Shih-k'ai and succeeding warlords. Yet, for all its apparent superficiality, the Revolution held a deep significance that was manifest even as early as World War I. By sweeping away a dynasty that, though foreign, was culturally orthodox in subscribing to Confucian traditions, the Revolution had encouraged new directions in nationalist thinking even as it removed the stoutest defender of old faiths. Before 1911, opposition to the Manchus had imparted to nationalism a high content of anti-foreignism; with the dynasty gone there was an increased tendency to concentrate on the ills of Chinese society. Similarly, young nationalists lost interest in attempts to synthesize Confucian and Western ideas and turned to the examination of foreign ideas which presumably would provide the footings for the new China. In this new context, patriotism no longer required the retention of Old China's cultural grandeur. Service to the nation legitimized cultural unorthodoxy.[16]

Leadership in promoting these ideas was provided primarily by an able body of intellectuals fathered at Peking National University. There in September, 1915, the magazine *New Youth,* founded by Ch'en Tu-hsiu who was both Western-educated and a fervent advocate of Western liberalism, began a campaign to direct the rebuilding of China along new lines. Ch'en advocated the destruction of Confucianism and the erection of a society on an entirely fresh base. The first number of the *New Youth* was a call to young Chinese to abandon traditional deference toward elders and to assume the initiative in shaping a new order. Subsequent numbers advocated a modern China built on science and democracy. At about this time Ch'en, in collaboration with the American-educated Hu Shih, also inaugurated literary reforms aimed at making literature a tool for the remodeling of China. Writers were to compose their works in the vernacular rather than classical Chinese; and they were to express the emotions and thoughts of contemporary China instead of those of the dead past. From these beginnings came the

---

[14] See Russell Fifield, "Japanese Policy Toward the Shantung Question at the Paris Peace Conference," *Journal of Modern History,* 23 (1951), 265-72.

[15] China did sign the treaty of St. Germain with Austria, September 10, 1919; the treaty of Neuilly with Bulgaria; and the treaty of Trianon with Hungary. China's war with Germany was ended officially September 15, 1919, by proclamation of the Chinese president.

[16] Joseph R. Levenson, "The Intellectual Revolution in China," in *Modern China,* Albert Feuerwerker, ed. (1964),* 154-68.

New Culture Movement. Lu Hsun, who joined the movement in 1918 and became one of its leaders, captured one aspect of the thinking of young literati in his popular short stories, which depicted the majority in Old China leading dull, meaningless lives amid conditions of poverty, ignorance, and misery. Such attacks on the traditional order and calls for a new one stimulated endless debates over how Western liberalism, pragmatism, utilitarianism, anarchism, or one of several varieties of socialism might be adapted to Chinese purposes. In short, young intellectuals, rejecting the conservative traditions of the past, embarked upon a search for new standards for Chinese society.

While forces within China provided most of the impetus for the New Culture Movement, the direction of the movement and its impact on the country were affected by events outside the country. During World War I, the emphasis given by the Allied and Associated Powers to democracy and self-determination of people bolstered the orientation of young intellectuals toward the West. By the end of the war, however, it was evident that this orientation was being affected by the Versailles settlement and the spectacle of revolutionary regimes being established throughout Europe. Indeed, young China reacted violently to the provisions of the treaty of Versailles concerning Shantung. On May 4, 1919, such wild demonstrations were staged against Peking's role at Paris that the entire cabinet was ultimately forced to resign. This marked the first time in the history of the Republic that public opinion had broken the power of a governing clique. But Peking was not the only loser in this episode. Beginning with the May Fourth incident, the West was included in the attacks of Chinese nationalists. From this point onward young literati increasingly found impossible the achievement of fundamental reforms without the elimination of foreign influence and intervention in Chinese affairs. Moreover, this attack on imperialism was associated with growing skepticism that the West provided useful models for the construction of a new China. For example, Liang Ch'i-ch'ao, formerly a champion of Western liberalism, published an article in 1920 which criticized the development of science and material culture in the West at the expense of human values. According to Liang, Western civilization was bankrupt. As an alternative to Western precedents, some intellectuals were attracted by the Bolshevik experiment. In August, 1920, through the so-called "Karakhan Manifesto," Moscow announced its intention of relinquishing all special privileges which had been inherited by the Soviet Union from treaties concluded between Tsarist Russia and China. Later China was to discover that reservations were attached to this gesture, but these were not immediately apparent. What seemed clear to young Chinese was that the Soviet Union was abandoning imperialism, while Japan and the West clung to it. Finally, Chinese thinking was touched by news of successful revolutions not only in Russia but also in Finland and the Dual Monarchy. Whereas the New Culture Movement had been directed initially toward the modernization of China through thought reform, it tended after 1919 toward direct action.

Nor were these shifts in the New Culture Movement the only influences on Chinese nationalism deriving from events outside China. The prominence achieved by advocates of the New Culture was itself in some measure related to World War I. Between 1914 and 1919 Western trade with China dropped sharply. As a result, Chinese light industry expanded, swelling the number of factory managers and industrial workers, stimulating migration from the countryside to cities, and causing dislocations in rural economies.[17] One consequence was the weakening of the landlords and the gentry, who

[17]Between 1913 and 1918, Chinese imports from Great Britain fell from $156,480,000 to $79,870,000; those from France declined from $8,476,000 to $2,445,000; and those from Germany from $47,240,000 to zero. The number of Chinese textile firms rose from 22 in 1911 to 54 in 1919 and 109 in 1921; flour mills from 67 in 1916 to 86 in 1918; modern banks from 7 in 1911 to 131 in 1923; steamships from 893 (tonnage, 141,024) in 1913 to 2,027 (236,622 tons) in 1918; and coal production from 12.8 million tons in 1913 to 20.1 million tons in 1919. Immanuel C. Y. Hsu, *The Rise of Modern China* (1970), 583-84.

were prime proponents of the Confucian tradition. At the same time, economic and social change presented new opportunities for the cultivation of revolutionary concepts. Thus it appears that World War I created a paradoxical situation for China. Even as the war led to fresh encroachments on Chinese sovereignty, it was indirectly helping to lay the foundations of a new nation.

FOR FURTHER READING

Japan and World War I. For general bibliographic reviews see two essays by Burton F. Beers and Roger Dingman in *American-East Asian Relations: A Survey,* Ernest May and James C. Thomson, Jr., eds. (1972). The essay by Dingman introduces Japanese language materials. Charles R. Hicks, *Japan's Entry into the War, 1914* (1944). On politics relating to the war see Shimasa Idditti, *The Life of Marquis Shigenobu Okuma* (1940), and A. Morgan Young, *Japan Under Taisho Tenno, 1912-1926* (1928), as well as the study by Takeuchi cited in footnotes. A. M. Pooley, *Japan's Foreign Policies* (1920) recounts the growth of ambitions toward China. Ernest B. Price, *The Russo-Japanese Treaties of 1907-1916 Concerning Manchuria and Mongolia* (1933) gives the text of the treaty of 1916 by which Russia and Japan sought further to define their spheres of influence. Differing interpretations on the origins of this treaty are given in Pauline Tompkins, *American-Russian Relations in the Far East* (1949), and W. A. Williams, *American-Russian Relations, 1781-1947* (1952). Discussion of Japan's secret treaties with her European allies is found in F. S. Cocks, *The Secret Treaties* (2nd ed., 1931). Barbara Tuchman, *The Zimmerman Telegram,* (1958)* sifts the evidence on the rumored alliance between Japan and Germany. Japan's troubles with the United States are surveyed in William L. Neuman, *America Encounters Japan: From Perry to MacArthur* (1963).*

China and World War I. Madeline Chi, *China Diplomacy, 1914-1918: Harvard East Asian Monographs* #31 (1970),* draws on Chinese archival material. On China's internal politics

see George T. Yu, *Party Politics in Republican China, 1912-1924* (1966). Older but still useful are: Thomas E. LaFargue, *China and the World War* (1937); H. F. MacNair, *China in Revolution* (1931); H. B. Morse and H. F. MacNair, *Far Eastern International Relations* (1931); and H. M. Vinacke, *Modern Constitutional Development in China* (1920), Jerome Ch'en, *Yuan Shih-k'ai* (2nd ed., 1972), tones down the criticism offered in the first edition. R. T. Pollard, *China's Foreign Relations, 1917-1931* (1933), superseded by more recent research but useful as a reference. George M. Dutcher, *The Political Awakening of the East* (1925), an early effort to appraise the impact of the war on Asian nationalism. Chow Tse-tsung, *The May Fourth Movement: Intellectual Revolution in Modern China* (1960)* and *Research Guide to the May Fourth Movement* (1963)* deal with China's intellectual ferment between 1917 and 1921. Judith Blick, "The Chinese Labor Corps in World War I," *Papers on China,* Vol. 9, published and distributed by the East Asian Research Center, Harvard University (1955), 111-45, a well-organized pioneer study on the subject.

American Far Eastern Policy. On Wilson's policy see R. W. Curry, *Woodrow Wilson and Far Eastern Policy, 1913-1921* (1957); Tien-yi Li, *Woodrow Wilson's China Policy, 1913-1917* (1952); and Russell H. Fifield, *Woodrow Wilson and the Far East: The Diplomacy of the Shantung Question* (1952; reprinted, 1965). Burton F. Beers, *Vain Endeavor: Robert Lansing's Attempts to End the American-Japanese Rivalry* (1962), more critical of the Wilson policy than any of the foregoing. Note also A. W. Griswold, *The Far Eastern Policy of the United States* (1938).* O. J. Clinard, *Japan's Influence on American Naval Power, 1897-1917* (1947) contains very debatable interpretations. Kamikawa Hikomatsu, ed., *Japan-American Diplomatic Relations in the Meiji-Taisho Era,* trans. by Kimura Michiko (1958) is based partly on Japanese sources. Warren I. Cohen, "America and the May Fourth Movement: The Response to Chinese Nationalism," *Pacific Historical Review,* 35 (1966), 83-100.

Versailles Conference. This topic is covered in several works already cited. Additional studies are: W. L. Godshall, *The International Aspects of the Shantung Question* (1933); Victor Birdsall, *Versailles Twenty Years After* (1941), an excellent study of the Peace Conference in general with a penetrating chapter on Japanese strategy. A basic work is David Hunter Miller, *The Drafting of the Covenant* (2 vols., 1938).

On the disposition of the Pacific islands see Werner Levi "American Attitudes toward the Pacific Islands, 1914-1919," *Pacific Historical Review* 17 (1948), 55-64; and Paul H. Clyde, *Japan's Pacific Mandate* (1935; reprinted 1967). Wunsz King, *China at the Paris Peace Conference in 1919* (1961),* is by a junior member of the Chinese delegation.

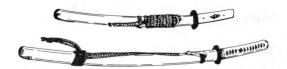

The Legacies of War in East Asia, 1919–1924

22

As World War I receded into the category of things past, new and specific international problems—some created by the war, others magnified by it—appeared to threaten the peace. These new points of friction were by no means limited to particular geographic areas; they were in the Old World and in the New World alike. But they were particularly acute in the sphere of East Asian international relations. By 1920, for example, there was a widespread popular conviction in the United States and Canada, and to a lesser degree in Great Britain and France, that Japan had shown little interest in the defeat of German militarism and that she had used the war primarily to advance Japanese hegemony in China. In Japan, on the other hand, there was a widespread conviction that the Western powers, especially the United States, were seeking to undermine legitimate Japanese aspirations.

The appearance of these recriminatory views was traceable directly and immediately to the differences that had arisen out of Japan's ambitions in the Pacific as revealed in her seizure of German-controlled islands, out of her independent dealings with Yuan Shih-k'ai and the warlords, out of her programs as presented at Paris, and, finally, out of an episode yet to be discussed—the joint American-Japanese expedition into Siberia in 1918. Underlying the diplomacy of these clashes was the determination of the Japanese military, whose influence on policy had been enhanced by the war, to forestall a resurgence of Western domination in Asia by uniting the Chinese and non-Bolshevik Russians behind Japan. The emerging Japanese military program viewed Japan's national security as resting on her leadership of a new Asian "international" order, sometimes called pan-Asianism, rather than on her cooperation with Europe and the United States. This position of the Japanese military was decidedly at variance with Great Britain's determination to protect her imperial holdings in South and Southeast Asia and her economic stake in China. France, too, had shown no disposition to withdraw from Southeast Asia. Moreover, Japanese expansionism was at cross purposes with Woodrow Wilson's vision of a modern China emerging under American tutelage.

The deterioration in Japan's relations with the West had not as yet (1919) produced an extreme crisis. The European war and settlement, seemingly far removed from East Asian affairs, were the principal American, French, and British concerns prior to 1920. Similarly, the Japanese government and public displayed little inclination to resort to further warfare as a means of advancing national interests. Beginning in the autumn of 1918 with the ministry headed by Hara Kei, Japan's government was led by men who, while no less determined than their predecessors to defend and to strengthen their country's vital interests, sought their objectives through economic expansion and international cooperation. This new emphasis was derived from the new importance of civilian bureaucrats and politicians in policy making. These men were responsive to manufacturing, mercantile, and banking interests with a stake in international trade and stability. Japanese policy also reflected the conviction that the diplomacy of imperialism had been discredited by Wilsonian internationalism, and that a policy embodying old principles could only lead to isolation and trouble.[1]

Japan, therefore, like Britain, France, and the United States, had some disposition to seek peaceful solutions to issues which had survived the war or which had been created, in part at least, by the war. Such an undertaking, however, presented a varied assortment of problems of great magnitude and complexity. First, the Russian revolutions had created a political vacuum in Siberia and on the long Sino-Russian frontier reaching into inner Asia. Second, the Chinese Revolution of 1911, despite all its hopes and aspirations, had seemingly degenerated by 1916 into a meaningless chaos of contending warlords who made a mockery of all the eloquence of Wang and Koo at Versailles. Third, there was the uninviting prospect of a new world naval race, in which the leading contenders would be the United States, Great Britain, and Japan. And fourth, there was the old, perplexing, and emotion-laden problem of oriental immigration to the United States. The approach to and disposition of these formidable matters is the subject to which this narrative must now turn.

[1] Akira Iriye, "The Failure of Economic Expansion, 1918-1931," An unpublished paper presented at the Conference on Taisho Japan, Duke University, January, 1968 (in manuscript).

THE SIBERIAN INTERVENTION

International difficulties arising from the inter-Allied intervention in Siberia were full-blown when the war ended. Late in 1917 the Russian Revolution had created a political vacuum in Siberia and in the zone of the Chinese Eastern Railway in north-central Manchuria. During the years 1918-1920 and after, Siberia, North Manchuria, and Outer Mongolia became a confused battleground for armies, political creeds, and irresponsible brigands, in which all the major powers—Great Britain, France, Japan, and the United States—became involved. In tracing these various developments in some detail a word should first be said about events in Siberia itself.

The bonds that had held together Siberia's vast territorial expanse were either weakened or destroyed by the ousting of the tsarist regime, the collapse of Kerensky's provisional government, and the resulting warfare between revolutionary and anti-revolutionary forces. The collapse of the imperial government brought first a revival of the late nineteenth-century movement for Siberian autonomy. Opposed to these "regionalists" from November, 1917, to the summer of 1918 was the rising influence of the local soviets. The defeat of these groups in the summer of 1918 paved the way for the Kolchak White government at Omsk, which claimed all power in Siberia from November, 1918, to January, 1920. Although Kolchak's government was accorded *de facto* recognition by the supreme council of the Allied and Associated Powers, it was by no means the only pretender to power. Among the nondescript array of these Siberian pretenders great and small was Cossack Captain Grigorii Semenov, who had been commissioned by Kerensky's provisional government to recruit troops in the Trans-Baikalia. There was also Baron Ungern von Sternberg, who used Mongolia as a base from which he hoped to set up a pan-mongolian empire. And there were social revolutionaries of divergent shades, some of whom operated reluctantly with Kolchak, others with the Bolsheviks. In the Russian railway zone at Harbin there were two principal factions. One was headed by the anti-Bolshevik, Lt. General Dimitrii Horvath, the other by Petr Yakolivich Derber, whose "government" was composed of center-left social revolutionaries. In addition to these there were many other groups led by Cossack adventurers and more concerned with opportunities for pillage and plunder than with the political stability of Russia. Finally, there were almost innumerable bands of peasant "partisans," who had no understanding of the mad political events in which they were enmeshed and by which they were impoverished.

Another factor complicated conditions in Siberia. Early in World War I a Czechoslovak army was formed in Russia and fought as a division of the Russian army against the Central Powers. During the period of Kerensky's provisional government, this Czech force was increased to some 50,000 men. As the Russian armies disintegrated in the first months of Bolshevik rule, the Czech legions remained intact. They were placed under the Supreme French Command by the Czech National Council in Paris, where the decision was made to transport the force around the world by way of Vladivostok and the Pacific to serve with the French armies on the western front. Permission was granted the Czechs by the Bolsheviks to cross Siberia en route to France. However, in the conditions prevailing, clashes soon occurred between the Czechs and Bolsheviks. During May and June, 1918, anti-Bolshevik governments appeared at Samara and Omsk, sheltered by Czech arms.

THE QUESTION OF ALLIED INTERVENTION IN RUSSIA

This checkered pattern of forces and events was a matter of deep concern to Great Britain, France, and Italy, all of whom were hard-pressed by the Central Powers. They feared that Germany would use the Bolsheviks to convert Russia into a granary for the Central Powers, would gain control of vast stores of war materiel at Archangel and Vladivostok, and, finally, would be free to transfer major reinforcements from the eastern to the western front. Furthermore, they tended to believe reports that the Bolsheviks were planning to spread their revolu-

tionary creed into Central Europe through indoctrination of German and Austro-Hungarian prisoners of war held in Russian and Siberian camps. In a word, the Allies thought it imperative that Russia be brought back into the war quickly under non-Bolshevik auspices. To this end they urged either that Japan send an expedition eastward to the Ural Mountains or that such an expedition be sent jointly by Japan and the United States. A military expedition, it was reasoned, could provide the dual advantage of reviving the eastern front and providing a rallying point for non-Bolshevik factions.

For seven months, December, 1917, through June, 1918, neither Japan nor the United States yielded to mounting Allied pressure.[2] Although the Japanese army favored intervention on the grounds that it would provide a means for

[2] Both countries wavered during this period. Japan indicated interest in the idea in December, 1917, and again in March, 1918. On this latter occasion the United States considered going into Siberia if Japan acted.

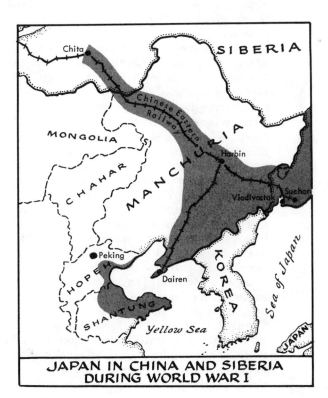

JAPAN IN CHINA AND SIBERIA DURING WORLD WAR I

combatting Bolshevism and for obtaining a voice in a Russian settlement, the Terauchi ministry hesitated because the purposes were too large and the results too uncertain for Japan to undertake·the risks alone. The American government felt that an expedition was unlikely to revive the eastern front and, in any event, would divert needed energies from the main centers of fighting in Western Europe.

Both Japan and the United States, however, began to shift their respective positions when the Czechs broke with the Bolsheviks in late May, 1918. The Czech hold on the Trans-Siberian Railway and their strategic position in the Volga region provided the first tangible possibility of reopening an eastern front. Moreover, the Wilson administration overcame some of its inhibitions against intervention when the supreme war council decided, June 1, to send a force including American troops to Murmansk in northwestern Russia, held by the British since March, and also to occupy Archangel. Thus, a month later, on July 6, the United States agreed to a Siberian expedition on the grounds that the Czechs needed help. Ostensibly, Wilson had accepted the idea that the Allied and Associated Powers could not win on the western front even in 1919 unless the Germans were forced to keep troops in the east.

In reality the President's reasoning was far more complex than this statement would imply. Wilson feared that a continuation of differences over the Siberian expedition would weaken the united front against the Central Powers. If one was an ally, one must act like an ally. Since the Allies insisted on going into Siberia, the United States would go along with them. Beneath this reasoning were concealed Wilson's apprehensions concerning Japan. While Tokyo had opposed going into Siberia alone, Wilson knew that this stand was closely contested in Japan itself. The Japanese army, riled by the eastward march of Bolshevism, had used every pressure for permission to send troops to Siberia. Indeed, even as the army argued, its agents were contacting Semenov, Horvath, and others in a search for Russian allies. Moreover, in May, 1918, Japan signed agreements with China providing for cooperation in military measures, and granting permission for Japanese troops to move in Chinese territory. The effect of these understandings would be to safeguard the rear of Japanese forces, if they became engaged in Siberia and the Sino-Russian borderlands. Moves such as these cast doubt on any assumption that Japan would long continue to oppose intervention. To Wilson this prospect suggested a final reason for agreeing to the venture. By taking the lead the United States would be able to say later: "Now let us come out" instead of "now you come out." Convinced that Japanese expansionists would use any intervention for their own purposes, Wilson felt that he could "impose greater restraint on Japan within rather than outside" the intervention. The important thing, he felt, was to maintain the open door in Siberia and North Manchuria against Japanese pretensions.[3]

On July 17, 1918, the United States informed the Allied ambassadors of its decision to intervene, and of its objectives, to which it asked their adherence.

Military action is admissible in Russia . . . only to help the Czecho-Slovaks consolidate their forces and to get into successful cooperation with their Slavic kinsmen and to steady any efforts at self-government or self-defense in which the Russians themselves may be willing to accept assistance. . . . The only legitimate object for which Americans or Allied troops can be employed . . . is to guard military stores which may subsequently be needed by Russian forces and to render such aid as may be acceptable to the Russians in the organization of their own self-defense.[4]

From August until November, 1918, troops of the Allied Powers—British, Japanese, French,

[3] Betty Miller Unterberger, "President Wilson and the Decision to Send American Troops to Siberia," *Pacific Historical Review*, 24 (1955), 63-74, is the clearest statement of this generally accepted interpretation. Also see Unterberger, "The Russian Revolution and Wilson's Far Eastern Policy," *Russian Review* (April, 1957), 35-46. For a different view of Wilson's motives see Christopher Lasch, "American Intervention in Siberia: A Reinterpretation," *Political Science Quarterly*, 77 (1962), 205-23.

[4] United States, *Foreign Relations, 1918, Russia*, II, 288.

and American—were landed at Vladivostok. It was Wilson's intention to curb the Japanese by an agreement limiting the American and Japanese contingents to some 7,000 troops each. In the end the United States sent 9,000 troops, the Japanese something in excess of 72,000.[5]

THEORY AND PRACTICE IN SIBERIA

Now that Allied contingents were in Siberia, what were they to do? There was as much

[5] It appears that Japan was careful to reserve the liberty to send additional troops if in her view circumstances demanded it. See United States, *Foreign Relations, 1918, Russia*, II, 324-26.

disagreement on this question as there had been on the original point of intervention. The policy of the American military forces, commanded by Major General William S. Graves, had been determined by Wilson. It required that the troops refrain from "any interference of any kind with the political sovereignty of Russia" and from "any intervention in her internal affairs." Since these American troops were on Russian soil, these were admittedly difficult instructions to follow. Nevertheless, General Graves attempted to carry them out. Where American troops patrolled the railroads, they did so for all Russians, whether White or Red. Graves' actions in this respect appear to have been proper, but they led to a tense situation, since of all the key personalities in

Japanese troops march by American army headquarters in Vladivostok, November 15, 1918.

General William S. Graves, U.S. Ambassador Roland S. Morris, and the Japanese Chief of Staff, General Inagaki, prepare to leave Vladivoskok on an inspection trip along the Trans-Siberian railway.

the intervening armies he alone held unswervingly to his instructions and to the announced purposes of the intervention. On the other hand, most of the Allied representatives, including many Americans, completely disregarded the principles of noninterference and neutrality in Russian affairs. The European governments, the Japanese, and some American officials thought the purpose of the intervention was to fight the Reds. The announced purposes of the intervention were no longer to be the real purposes. Thus England, France, and Japan, with the willing support of certain American consular officials and members of the department of state, became the *de facto* allies of Semenov. Moreover, the Allies, mainly the British and French, had been responsible for bringing Admiral Alexsander Vasilevich Kolchak to Siberia, where they installed him as head of a White government at Omsk. There this well-meaning but mild and ineffectual sailor was surrounded by discredited Russian Whites, and by British and French military missions, which seemed unaware that Russia could not be pressed back into the political and economic mold of the tsars. From November, 1918, until January, 1920, Kolchak, the Czechs, and their British and French allies fought the Bolsheviks, long after Germany had fallen and the need of an eastern front had disappeared. The European Allies and Japan had altered the original stated purposes of the intervention, without Wilson's consent, in favor of interference in the internal politics of Russia.

As was inevitable, the Siberian and Chinese Eastern Railways became the focus of these conflicting aims. Whoever controlled these railways controlled Siberia. Late in July, 1918, when Semenov's forces were hard pressed by the Reds, Japan invoked her military agreements with China and dispatched troops to the zone of the Chinese Eastern Railway. These troops soon controlled the line and occupied most of the railway towns. Once established, the Japanese utilized their position to direct supplies to Horvath and other friendly Cossack leaders. From these events it became clear that Japan was expanding her sphere of influence into North Manchuria and was fostering puppet regimes in Siberia.

At first the United States did no more than formally protest these Japanese moves. Presumably the American government feared that uncompromising opposition might so alter the political balance within Japan as to lead to Japanese withdrawal from the war. Later, after the armistice was signed, the American stand was firmer. On November 16, 1918, Secretary of State Robert Lansing stated flatly that Japan's monopoly of the Manchurian railways was opposed by the United States; and he demanded that Japan demonstrate her intention to cooperate by turning over control of the railroads to an inter-Allied commission.[6] In making this demand, the United States was not only taking advantage of the war's end, it was also assuming that the effect of America's demonstration of military power in Europe would not be lost on the Japanese. Furthermore, when a new Japanese cabinet was formed by Premier Hara following the resignation of Count Terauchi on September 19, the United States assumed that the new ministry, less subservient to the army, would seek in some degree to meet American desires. Subsequent events supported the wisdom of these considerations. In December, Tokyo informed the United States of her intention to withdraw more than half of her troops from Siberia and Manchuria. A month later, January, 1919, an inter-Allied railway control board was established with Japan's assent. The Hara government thus made substantial moves to eliminate Siberia as a source of American-Japanese friction.

THE END OF INTER-ALLIED INTERVENTION

Unhappily, these steps toward establishing some accord did not bring a fundamental settlement. As the months of 1919 dragged on, evil days settled upon the entire Siberian adventure. The high purposes of military strategy for which it was conceived no longer had any meaning, for Germany had long since collapsed and the war in Europe was over. The real purpose of the European powers and

6 *Foreign Relations, 1918, Russia,* II, 433-35.

Japan—to crush Bolshevism—had resulted in dismal failure. By the end of 1919 the remnants of Kolchak's armies were in complete rout before the rising Red tide and the infuriated peasant partisans. The White elements both within and outside Russia had failed to provide a program or a leadership which the Russians would accept. The United States Ambassador Roland S. Morris in Tokyo went far to explain this when he said:

The advent of Allied forces [in Siberia] has led to the hope among former [Russian] officials, civil and military, that they will regain the power and influence they had before the revolution. The attitude of these officials indicates that they will be relentless in their endeavor to suppress all liberal or moderate movements. Possibly nothing but their inevitable failure will bring them to reason.[7]

As for the European Allies and the United States, by 1920 they were tired of the whole business. The scheme for cooperative management of the railways had broken down during the long weeks of the Paris peace conference; rivalries among forces in Siberia had intensified; and the Western forces were therefore withdrawn, leaving Siberia to the Russians—and to the Japanese.

For two years the Japanese remained. The Japanese government and the army regarded the whole eastern Siberian question as being still very decidedly Japan's business. The growth of revolutionary ferment in Russia and the discrediting of the Whites appeared as the prelude to a communist society touching the shores of the Pacific, which would be a threat to Japan's position in South Manchuria and even to the social fabric and political structure of her society at home. The massacre of Japanese at Nikolaievsk, near the mouth of the Amur River, opposite northern Sakhalin, in 1920 seemed to confirm the wisdom of army expansionists, who desired to annex the Maritime Province along with Vladivostok. So Japan stayed on, temporarily in control of a great circular area reaching from Vladivostok to Chita, an area traversed by the Chinese Eastern and the Amur Railways. She entertained the hope that a buffer state, friendly to Japan and free of Bolshevik contagion, would yet arise in East Asia. But whatever justification there may have been for this hope, it had already been destroyed by the bungled inter-Allied intervention. In any case, the Russians in general appear to have been just as happy to see the Allies go as the Allied soldiers were to leave. Writing in 1931, General Graves noted that the participating governments seemed to take "very little pride in this venture. Who can blame them?"[8]

THE FOUR-POWER CONSORTIUM

Throughout the two years (1918-1920) of international wrangling in Siberia there had been a continuous succession of clashes between American and Japanese policy. One such area of conflict was in the arena of international finance in China as a whole. In 1913 President Wilson, disapproving of the control measures employed by the first or six-power consortium as infringements upon the "administrative integrity" of China, informed the American banking group that it would not enjoy official support. In the five years that followed, the basic principles of Wilson's policy toward China—territorial and administrative integrity and the open door—did not change, but his views on the means of achieving and maintaining these principles did. By November, 1917, the president, though not fully convinced that independent loans to China were impractical as political weapons, had decided to encourage the organization of a new, four-power consortium. The following year, on the initiative of the American government, a new American banking group was formed. The bankers, however, were not of a mind to enter the field of Chinese investments save in concert with British, French, and Japanese banking groups, and with the assured support of the American government. These conditions the American government accepted, insisting in turn that the prospective consortium must respect the well-established principles of American policy in China—principles which were well-known to be at variance with Japan's theory of "special interests" and with the theory of the British and the French on spheres of influence.

[7] *Foreign Relations, 1918, Russia,* II, 414.

[8] William S. Graves, *America's Siberian Adventure* (1931), 356.

The reasons for this complete reversal of method by the Wilson administration are significant. The World War had given Japan a free hand in financing China, and it had also destroyed temporarily any possibility of China's receiving British or French credits. But more was involved than the matter of investment. Wilson was forced to recognize that, China's political position being what it was, the political aspects of American policy could no longer be detached with safety from economic considerations. This was made particularly clear during 1918, when, as a result of the mysterious maneuverings of Nishihara Kamezo, personal representative in China of Japanese Premier Count Terauchi, the Peking government of Premier Tuan and his Anfu clique contracted Japanese loans in the amount of about Yen 120 million. These were not investments in the usual meaning of that word. Rather, they were payments to officials then in power in exchange for certain agreements that would promote Japanese policy, particularly in Manchuria.[9] Japan was thus buying an economic and political stake from a Chinese government in Peking that was willing to sell.

Against Sino-Japanese financial politics of this type, doctrinaire slogans of American policy on the open door and the integrity of China were useless unless implemented by more realistic factors. Wilson, therefore, sought to revive and apply international cooperative action through a new consortium, his hope being that with British and French support Japan could be held in line and her efforts to gain a financial monopoly at Peking frustrated.

Actual negotiations toward the birth of a new consortium were delayed until the closing days of the Paris peace conference; once started, they appeared at first to progress smoothly. Britain and France agreed to support the American plan for the organization and operation of the consortium. Japanese bankers also agreed, presumably because they preferred cooperation with rather than competition from

[9] For the Japanese origins of the scheme see Frank C. Langdon, "Japan's Failure to Establish Friendly Relations with China, 1917-1918," *Pacific Historical Review,* 26 (1957), 245-58.

their foreign colleagues. Within a short time, however, Japan's position hardened as it became evident the proposed agreement would infringe upon her "special interests." Indeed, it required another year before a compromise agreement for the new four-power consortium could be reached. In this compromise the United States, England, and France pledged their "good faith" to "refuse their countenance to any operation [of the consortium] inimical to the vital interests of Japan." These powers also agreed to exclusion of the zone of the South Manchuria Railway from the joint activities of the consortium. It meant that while the powers would now pool all loans, administrative and industrial, in China Proper south of the Great Wall, Japan still retained her "special position" in South Manchuria. Contrary, however, to official and popular expectations, China showed no enthusiasm for the consortium and declined to do business with it. Chinese political leaders in general took the view that the consortium was a "threat of international control of Chinese finance" and a "monopoly or attempted monopoly" designed to deprive China of a free world market where she could borrow on the best terms available. Again it was evident that "preserving" China and serving American interests at the same time was not a simple task.

THE WASHINGTON DISARMAMENT CONFERENCE

The troubles in Siberia and the arguments over the consortium only served to underscore another area of friction. As World War I came to a close, Japan and the United States found themselves involved in an appalling naval race. Under the Naval Appropriation Act of 1916 the United States fleet would soon equal and perhaps surpass the British fleet. Japan's building program would enable her to maintain her rank as the third naval power. To what end was this construction now that the war was over? Amicable relations between Great Britain and the United States gave some credence to the suspicion that America and Japan were preparing to fight each other in the Pacific.

The prospect of a naval race was cause for general concern. The United States government was seriously embarrassed; there was reason to doubt that American voters, disillusioned with war as a means of resolving world problems, would continue to support projected naval construction for a Pacific defense, especially as the Pacific was an area in which the public had shown little interest. Furthermore, the fact that the United States had repudiated the League of Nations and had elected Harding in 1920 did not mean that the Wilsonian peace program had been blotted from the American consciousness. Among Harding's advisers and in the Republican Party at large were a number of men, such as Charles Evans Hughes, the new secretary of state, who were committed to the principle of arms reduction and to American leadership to this end.[10] Nor was there much enthusiasm in

[10]The Republican Platform of 1920, although repudiating the League, had called for "an international association" designed to preserve the peace.

Japanese government circles for the continuing naval rivalry. The construction of dreadnoughts imposed burdens on an economy which was sagging as Japan encountered post war competition. Furthermore, peaceful pursuits such as trade and diplomacy, rather than militarism, were now favored as the means for advancing the national interest. Thus Japan, like the United States, was prepared at least to listen to proposals for ending the naval race.[11]

The uneasiness in Washington and Tokyo on the naval question was shared by London and the capitals of the Commonwealth nations. London was concerned by reports published in the United States that Great Britain, as an ally of Japan through her obligations under the Anglo-Japanese alliance, would be involved in

[11]Early accounts based largely on American documents suggested a reluctance on Japan's part to attend the Washington conference. Recent investigations of Japanese archives call these findings into question. See Ian H. Nish, "Japan and the Ending of the Anglo-Japanese Alliance," in *Studies in International History*, K. Bourne and D.C. Watts, eds. (1967), 369-84.

Japan, 1920-1930

Reproduced from A War Atlas for Americans *(New York: Simon & Schuster) 1944, with permission from the publisher and from the U.S. Department of State, Division of Map Intelligence and Cartography.*

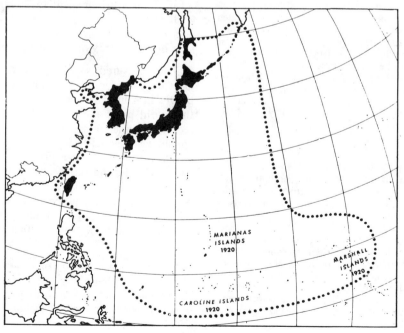

309

any American-Japanese war. These reports, though ill-founded, threatened Anglo-American relations. The Commonwealth countries were troubled by the prospect of an Anglo-American antagonism upsetting their own amicable relations with the United States. Thus it was that Commonwealth prime ministers, conferring just prior to the imperial conference at London, June, 1921, came up with a proposal calling for termination of the Anglo-Japanese alliance and its replacement by a new and broader agreement covering the Pacific.[12] As a result of this action, Great Britain prodded the United States to call a disarmament conference. Formal invitations to discuss disarmament and problems relating to East Asia and the Pacific were sent from Washington on August 11, 1921, to Great Britain, France, Italy, Japan, and to four lesser powers: Belgium, China, the Netherlands, and Portugal.[13]

---

[12] See J. Chalmers Vinson, "The Imperial Conference of 1921 and the Anglo-Japanese Alliance, *Pacific Historical Review*, 31 (1962), 257-66. Drawing on recently opened British sources, Ian H. Nish's *Alliance in Decline: A Study in Anglo-Japanese Relations, 1908-23* (1972) plays down the importance of the imperial conference of 1921 in British decision-making. Prior to the conference, London had decided that promises of continued Anglo-Japanese military cooperation were not worth concessions to Japanese imperial ambitions. The larger British interests seemed likely to be better served by cooperation with the United States than by an exclusive relationship with Japan. In effect, the pressures applied by the Commonwealth nations at the imperial conference only accelerated the drift of British policy. Ira Klein, "Whitehall, Washington, and the Anglo-Japanese Alliance, 1919-1921." *Pacific Historical Review*, 41 (1972), 460-83, generally supports Nish's contentions.

[13] These latter powers were selected on the basis of their real or supposed interest in the Pacific. It was not anticipated that they would participate in the arms discussions. Since German and Austrian interests in East Asia had been liquidated by the war, these powers were excluded. The absence of the Soviet Union could be explained only on the basis of a quarantine with which the victorious powers hoped to isolate that government. For another aspect of representation problems, see J. Chalmers Vinson, "The Problem of Australian Representation at the Washington Conference for the Limitation of Naval Armament," *Australian Journal of Politics and History*, 4 (1958), 155-64.

THE WAY TO DISARM IS TO DISARM

It was an illustrious assembly of notables that gathered in Washington's Memorial Continental Hall on November 12, 1921, to hear President Harding's exuberant remarks of welcome. He was followed immediately by Secretary Hughes, chairman of the conference, who, avoiding the platitudes of diplomacy, declared that the nations had come together "not for general resolutions . . . but for action."[14] Thereupon he presented to the startled delegates and the galleries a plan for immediate slashing of naval strength. In brief, the American plan called for:

1. A 10-year naval holiday in capital ship construction.
2. The scrapping of many ships, including some already in commission and others in the process of building.
3. Application of the program of scrapping so as to leave the navies of the United States, Great Britain, and Japan in a ratio of 5-5-3; France and Italy, without scrapping would fit into this ratio as 1.75-1.75.
4. Capital ship replacements limited by treaty to 500,000 tons each for the United States and Great Britain, and to 300,000 tons for Japan.
5. Similar ratios applied to aircraft carriers, cruisers, destroyers, and submarines.[15]

The measured words of Secretary Hughes electrified not only the audience which sat before him but also the far larger audience of the world press and public. The impact of the secretary's plan was suggested by unrestrained applause in the galleries. Yet, in the final analysis, acceptance of the proposed naval ratio would not depend on emotional response. The armament race had not developed in a vacuum. No great power was prepared to surrender any relative naval advantage it felt it could maintain. Great Britain, for obvious reasons, was

---

[14] *Conference on the Limitation of Armament, Washington, November 12, 1921-February 6, 1922*, (1922), 58.

[15] United States, Sen. doc. 126, 67th Cong., 2nd Sess., *Conference on the Limitation of Armament*, 41-63.

ready to accept naval parity with the United States, however distasteful the idea, but only if assured of the safety of her interests in the Pacific. Japan, whose armed forces opposed any relative reduction in naval power, would certainly reject any inferior ratio without corresponding compensations. Could the diplomats develop an alternative to the Anglo-Japanese alliance?[16] Would the conference discover a formula that would reconcile the traditional American policy of upholding China's integrity with Japan's determination to retain her "special interests"? It was upon the answers to questions such as these that the fate of Hughes' disarmament proposal hinged.

THE FOUR-POWER PACT

The conference first approached the troublesome Anglo-Japanese alliance. Great Britain wanted to expand the alliance to include the United States, but Hughes would have none of this proposal, for it would have amounted to American recognition of the "special interests" of Japan and Great Britain in East Asia. Rather, Hughes countered with a plan for a four-power treaty (the United States, Britain, France and Japan) which would embody the principles of the Root-Takahira notes of 1908. This idea, which won quick acceptance, became the heart of the four-power treaty signed December 13, 1921. By this ten-year pact, superseding the Anglo-Japanese alliance, the signatory powers agreed:

1. To respect one another's rights in the regions of the Pacific in respect to their "insular possessions and insular dominions."
2. To meet in joint conference "for consideration and adjustment" of any "controversy arising out of any Pacific question and involving their said rights which is not satisfactorily settled by diplomacy."
3. To "communicate with one another fully" if

[16] During the Washington Conference, as in earlier years, American East Asian policy was shaped by the nation's political leadership and the state department bureaucracy without much consultation with the navy. For detailed studies of naval planning and the navy's role see William R. Braisted, *The United States Navy in the Pacific, 1897-1909* (1958); and *The United States Navy in the Pacific, 1909-1922* (1971).

the rights of the contracting parties "are threatened by the aggressive action of any other Power."

The early signature of the four-power treaty materially advanced the fortunes of the conference. The inclusion of France was one of the moves designed to win that country's acceptance of the inferior naval ratio (1.75 as against 5-5-3 for the great powers) assigned to it by the Hughes plan. By ending the Anglo-Japanese alliance and substituting the broader pledge of "consultation," the treaty went far to remove American and Commonwealth fears of Anglo-Japanese cooperation in some future war. Furthermore, by combining principles of the Root-Takahira notes of 1908 with those of the Bryan treaties of 1914, the United States had been given a renewed pledge against aggression in the Philippines; this was a matter of consequence since Japan, now in possession of the Marshall, Mariana, and Caroline Islands, lay athwart direct American approaches to Manila.[17]

LIMITING NAVAL ARMAMENT

Japan's assent to the four-power treaty did not mean that Tokyo was prepared to accept without major qualifications the Hughes program of naval limitation. While desirous of ending an unwelcome rivalry, Japan was determined to maintain her own naval supremacy in the western Pacific. To this end she wanted definite assurances that Great Britain and the United States would not develop naval bases at Hong Kong, Manila, Guam, and other Pacific islands. Since this was clearly Japan's price for even considering the principle of the Hughes plan, the Big Three quickly reached agreement on the nonfortification principle, which later became Article XIX of the five-power naval treaty. It was agreed that "the status quo at the time of the signing of the present Treaty, with regard to fortification and naval bases, shall be maintained" in specified possessions.[18]

[17] J. Chalmers Vinson, "The Drafting of the Four-Power Treaty of the Washington Conference," *Journal of Modern History*, 25 (1953), 40-47.

[18] Specifically, the territories in which new fortifications were prohibited were: for the United

The negotiations then shifted to the Hughes naval formula. In consequence of pressure exerted by France, the original plan was whittled down to apply only to capital ships. As finally concluded, the naval treaty provided for:

1. A 10-year holiday in capital ship construction.
2. Scrapping specified vessels in commission and under construction (United States, 845,000 tons; Great Britain, 583,000 tons; Japan, 435,000 tons). Under a replacement program to begin after the 10-year construction holiday, battleship tonnage would be limited to: United States, 525,000 tons; Great Britain, 525,000 tons; Japan, 315,000 tons; France, 175,000 tons; and Italy, 175,000 tons. A similar ratio with lower tonnage limitations was specified for aircraft carriers.
3. Limiting the tonnage of individual battleships and aircraft carriers to 35,000 and 27,000 respectively, and the caliber of their guns to 16 and 8 inches respectively.

The treaty was to apply until December 31, 1936, and might be terminated thereafter through two-years' notice by any signatory.

The terms of this epochal treaty are easily stated, but its immediate effect upon the interplay of national policies in the Pacific and East Asia cannot be reduced to simple evaluation. Nonetheless, it may be conceded that Japan had won tangible and specific advantages. If her sensitive national pride was wounded by the inferior capital ship ratio, her security was greatly increased by the nonfortification agreement, by her mandate over the former German islands in the North Pacific, and by the resulting liberty she enjoyed to pursue her own specific aims in China.

Britain also profited. Although she did forego the right to add to the fortifications of

Hong Kong and islands in the Central Pacific, she retained full liberty to fortify Singapore, Australia, and New Zealand, which were thus not likely to be threatened so long as Japan observed the nonfortification clause. In a word, Britain gave up little and received much. Her advantage was the more striking because East Asia, although of great importance, was of much less significance in British policy than were the Middle East and Europe.

Did the United States win advantages comparable to those gained by Britain and Japan? Conceding that the conference had made Japan the naval master of the western Pacific and arbiter of China's future, and that the United States had agreed as regards naval fortifications to remain east of Pearl Harbor, it would appear that Secretary Hughes had given up a great deal to get a ten-year naval holiday in capital ship construction. Hughes, however, viewed these concessions in conjunction with the terms of the nine-power treaty which emerged from the concurrent conference on East Asian questions.

THE FAR EASTERN CONFERENCE

This nine-power treaty may best be understood as a culmination of nearly a century of American policy in East Asia. That policy had rested essentially on three principles. The first was the most-favored-nation principle, to which in 1899 and 1900 had been added the principles of the commercial open door and the integrity of China. The resulting composite policy was one of self-interest, not sentiment. Practically, it was vulnerable in the highest degree, because American commercial interests in China were relatively small and because the American people had shown no willingness to defend the open door or the integrity of China by force. Between 1900 and the end of World War I, the powers had violated the open door and China's integrity whenever they regarded it as advantageous to do so and whenever they were not restrained by their mutual jealousies and fears. American policy may have served to retard these encroachments; it did not prevent them.

States—the Aleutians, Guam, Pago-Pago, and the Philippines; for Great Britain—Hong Kong and British insular possessions in the Pacific, east of 110 east longitude, excepting islands adjacent to Canada, Australia, and New Zealand; for Japan—the Kurile Islands, Bonin Islands, Amami-Oshima, the Liu-ch'iu (Ryukyu) Islands, Taiwan, and the Pescadores.

In negotiating the nine-power treaty, Hughes sought to remedy this weakness by making these principles the heart of a treaty. By so doing, the historic American principles would become international law binding upon each of the signatories. For the first time, Hughes reasoned, Japan and the other powers would be definitely restrained from seeking "special interests" in China.

The conclusion of the nine-power open door treaty on February 6, 1922, was a signal triumph for Hughes. The signatory powers (the United States, Great Britain, France, Japan, Italy, Belgium, the Netherlands, Portugal, and China) consented to the following provisions:

1. The contracting parties, other than China, agree to respect and support the sovereignty, independence, and the territorial and administrative integrity of China; they further agree to provide the fullest opportunity for China's development and to maintain the principle of equal opportunity for the commerce and industry of all nations in China.
2. No treaty, agreement, arrangement, or understanding infringing the above principles shall be made.
3. The nationals of the contracting parties will not be supported by their governments in any agreement, arrangement, or understanding which infringes the above principles.
4. China's neutrality shall be respected.
5. The parties will consult fully in circumstances requiring the application of the treaty.

Imbedded in the language of these provisions, however, were some ambiguities suggesting future trouble. But in 1922 the American delegation was not aware of them or chose not to emphasize them. Clearly the treaty was a tangible advance over any previous enunciation of American policy in East Asia. What seemed important was the measure of agreement that had been achieved. During the remainder of the conference, the United States and Japan experienced little difficulty in cooperating on the disposition of additional issues.

Among the questions before the Far Eastern Conference was China's demand for immediate restoration of tariff autonomy and abolition of extraterritoriality. The United States and Japan joined other powers in opposing this demand.

The powers were willing to grant only that China be permitted a moderate increase in tariff rates (the "Washington surtax") and that commissions be established to study the termination of the extraterritorial system. Nor did China find the powers any more willing to abrogate the Manchurian clauses of the treaties and notes of May, 1915. None of the powers was prepared to concede the Chinese claims that the treaties were invalid because obtained by force. Such an admission might have opened the way for an attack on practically all the treaties negotiated over nearly a century.

Although the Far Eastern Conference itself did not attempt to deal with the Shantung question, Hughes and Balfour of Great Britain were responsible for bringing the Chinese and Japanese together in Washington and for breaking the deadlock between them. The Chinese were still demanding full and direct restoration of former German rights, as they had at Paris three years earlier. The Japanese were equally emphatic. They were prepared to restore the leasehold, but only under the terms of the 1915 and 1918 treaties and through direct negotiations with China.[19] But the good offices of Hughes and Balfour finally resulted in Sino-Japanese discussions extending through thirty-six meetings with British and American "observers." Even then the negotiations were only sustained through persistent and powerful British and American pressure at Peking and Tokyo. The Sino-Japanese treaty which resulted (February 4, 1922) returned Kiaochou to China; Japan, however, would retain control of the Tsinan-Tsingtao Railway for fifteen years, during the life of the loan through which China purchased the road. The settlement was obviously a compromise. Japan temporarily retained a measure of economic and political control, while China had won something more than the mere principle of her claim.

The conference also provided an opportunity for discussion of two other problems outstanding between the United States and Japan. Hughes won from the Japanese (January 23, 1922) a pledge that their military forces would soon be withdrawn from Siberia and

---

[19] The principle was one on which the Japanese had insisted ever since the Shimonoseki negotiations of 1895.

North Sakhalin. In obtaining the pledge Hughes scored another victory in the name of the open door. It appears, however, that pressure from within Japan rather than the diplomacy of Hughes was responsible for Japan's withdrawal. Finally, but not as a part of the conference, the United States raised again with Japan its claims concerning the island of Yap. These negotiations brought forth an American-Japanese treaty (February 11, 1922), whereby the United States recognized the Japanese mandate over the former German islands in the North Pacific, and Japan in return granted to American citizens residential, cable, and radio rights on Yap.

JAPANESE IMMIGRATION

Only one major issue in American-Japanese relations was not the subject of negotiation at the Washington conference: Japanese immigration to the United States and American treatment of the Japanese immigrant. The exclusion of the issue from the agenda was due to considerations of tactics rather than lack of concern on either side. The issue had been a serious source of friction during the decade before America's entry into World War I. In the aftermath of war there were signs that it would once again become the source of trouble as Americans, stirred by intense nationalism, agitated for an immigration law which, among other provisions, would exclude Japanese from the United States.

Washington had been embarrassed by the issue since 1906. When, in that year, the San Francisco school board segregated Japanese students on grounds of racial inferiority, President Theodore Roosevelt branded the action a "wicked absurdity" and attempted unsuccessfully to change the board's decision. Roosevelt feared that discriminatory treatment against the people of a vigorous Oriental state would destroy most-favored-nation treatment for American commerce in East Asia and render illusory the open door in China and the security of the Philippines. To avert possible danger, Roosevelt had the immigration law of 1902 amended to stop the entry of Japanese into

Hawaii and, in 1907-1908, reached an understanding with Tokyo—called the gentlemen's agreement—through which Japan herself would refuse passports to laborers seeking residence in the United States.[20] These measures, intended to give assurance to Californians that they would not be overwhelmed by Japanese, did little to calm Western fears, however ill-founded. In 1913, the California legislature prohibited aliens ineligible for citizenship from owning land and imposed a three-year limit on land leases. Since this measure was clearly aimed at the Japanese, it was Woodrow Wilson's turn to be concerned; but, like Roosevelt, he was unable to quiet the anti-Japanese uproar. His efforts were thus confined to trying to soothe Japanese feelings and to head off similar bills in other legislatures.[21]

By the time Congress began consideration of new immigration bills after World War I, Secretary Hughes, aware that the Japanese were acutely sensitive about American treatment of their nationals, was alert lest another affront be given. When, in December, 1923, bills were introduced in the Senate and House denying entry to aliens who were ineligible for citizenship, Hughes himself testified before the House

[20] The gentlemen's agreement is not contained in a single document. Its text, on the contrary, consists of correspondence exchanged between the United States and Japan during 1907 and 1908. A resume is printed in United States, *Foreign Relations, 1924,* II, 339-69. It was printed in 1939.

[21] Reaching any accommodation with Japan was complicated by the tendency of the United States to subordinate questions on the treatment of Japanese immigrants to other issues. Roger Daniel, *The Politics of Prejudice: The Anti-Japanese Movement in California and the Struggle for Exclusion* (1962),* for example, reveals Wilson in 1913 as reluctant to embarrass Democratic Party leadership in California. Later, during World War I, the common cause against the Central Powers took precedence. Finally, in the closing days of the Wilson administration, an informal understanding was developed whereby the United States and Japan would negotiate a treaty covering immigration and discrimination. But neither the outgoing Wilson nor the incoming Harding proved willing to implement the understanding. On this occasion, American interest in settling the issue was subordinated to larger considerations in East Asian policy. See Kell F. Mitchell, Jr., "Diplomacy and Prejudice: The Morris-Shidehara Negotiations, 1920-1921," *Pacific Historical Review,* 39 (1970), 85-104.

Committee on Immigration. He argued that although Japanese immigration should be controlled, the method proposed was inadvisable. In his opinion, it was bad policy to offend Japan unnecessarily when, by assigning Japan an immigrant quota such as those proposed for other nations, not more than 250 Japanese would be admitted annually. Furthermore, the proposed legislation would, the secretary felt, "largely undo the work of the Washington Conference." Nevertheless, in March, 1924, the House Committee recommended legislation excluding all aliens who were ineligible for citizenship. The bill passed the House on April 12 by the overwhelming majority of 326 to 71.

Simultaneously, the Senate was considering rather favorably Hughes' arguments when, on April 14, an attack was launched on a memorandum prepared by Japanese Ambassador Hanihara. In this memorandum, which had been sent originally as a note to the state department, Hanihara reviewed the history of the gentlemen's agreement, defined Japan's objections to legislation embodying exclusion, and, in conclusion, "truthfully but most ill-advisedly" referred to "the grave consequences which the enactment of the measure [exclusion law] retaining that particular provision would inevitably bring upon the otherwise happy and mutually advantageous relations between our two countries." Hughes disliked the phrase "grave consequences," for there were few stronger phrases in diplomatic language, but he regarded the Japanese analysis of the gentlemen's agreement as sound and, therefore, sent the note to Congress as support for his contentions. Congress, however, found the note offensive. It was described as "impertinent," as not to be "tolerated" by even a fourth-class power, and as a "veiled threat." The Hughes compromise was voted down, and on April 16 the Senate followed the House by voting 71 to 4 to exclude aliens who were ineligible for citizenship. Last-minute efforts of President Coolidge to delay application to Japan of the exclusion clause in the hope that a new treaty might be negotiated also failed, and on May 15 the immigration bill emerging from conference was passed by House and Senate, the votes being 308 to 62 and 69 to 9. It was to become effective July 1, 1924. The President, in signing the bill on May 26, announced that had the exclusion clause not been an integral part of the larger bill, he would have vetoed it on the ground that the method adopted by Congress in securing Japanese exclusion was "unnecessary and deplorable at this time."

Immediate reactions to the abrogation of the gentlemen's agreement were, naturally, more pronounced in Japan than in the United States. Japan's official protest was a mild reflection of bitter outbursts in the Japanese press and of deep resentment in the Japanese popular mind. In the United States reactions were varied because the issues involved were more complex. Public opinion throughout the country, though favoring rigid control of Japanese immigration, does not appear to have favored the method used by Congress. Naturally this view was more pronounced in the East than on the Pacific Coast. The Senate, however, was not guided by the general flavor of public opinion, but rather by known public reactions to specific domestic issues. The immigration debate was largely controlled by concurrent domestic reactions that might be expected from "the Southern vote in its relation to the Dyer anti-lynching bill, the issue of Congressional prerogative, the questions of the Senatorial investigations and of party loyalty, the need of thinking of the Pacific Coast's presidential vote, to say nothing of the Pacific Coast's racial future."[22] Undoubtedly many Americans believed, as did *The Cincinnati Enquirer,* that "the crux of this matter is that the United States, like Canada and Australia, must be kept a white man's country." A heroic step, so it was thought, had been taken, not in the implementation of race prejudice but in "producing a civilization peculiar to the American race and suited to a static society."

After 1924, influential American groups, business and professional, advocated revision which would give Japan and China a quota, but this move was halted by the Manchurian crisis, 1931. Japanese exclusion was not repealed until 1952, the year in which an American-Japanese peace treaty was signed. In the meantime, during World War II, with the intent of protecting the national security, the United States carried out the relocation to the interior from the

[22] Rodman Paul, *The Abrogation of the Gentleman's Agreement* (1936), 99.

Pacific coast of all persons of Japanese extraction. Chinese exclusion was repealed in 1943, and China was assigned an annual immigration quota of 105.

IN SUMMARY

Five years elapsed between the close of the debate on Shantung at Paris and the enactment of the Quota Immigration Act of 1924. For British, American, and Japanese statesmen they were years filled with problems caused or heightened by World War I. How is their work to be viewed? To what extent were they successful in resolving an increasingly troublesome American-Japanese rivalry?

Certainly there was much in the record which pointed to an easing of tensions. The Hara government's effort to cooperate with the United States in the operation of Siberian railways, the compromise on the consortium, the termination of the naval race, and the signing of the four- and nine-power treaties contributed to an easing of fears on both sides of the Pacific. Even in the enactment of the exclusion law, the Japanese could take some comfort in the thought that American opinion was divided, and in the hope that the measure would eventually be repealed. Moreover, advocates of conciliation were influential in both Washington and Tokyo. Secretary Hughes' determination to achieve limitation of armaments was matched in Japan by the "Friendship Policy" of Baron Shidehara Kijuro, foreign minister, 1924-1927.

Yet, notwithstanding these hopeful signs, the foundations of peace remained exceedingly fragile. Chinese nationalism, which by 1924 was gaining strength (see Chapter 24), was not content with the Washington conference settlements. Young China was continuing to demand abolition of the "unequal treaties." Moreover, while Japan's key leadership had displayed a cooperative spirit in nearly all postwar negotiations with the West, there were those who resented British and American initiatives terminating the Anglo-Japanese alliance. Among Japan's military leadership especially, there was a strong conviction that Japan had

been isolated politically and must look to her own security. It was in such an atmosphere that the Japanese navy identified the United States as Japan's probable enemy and began to shape its plans accordingly. Some Japanese leaders developed their own special interpretation of the nine-power treaty. In this interpretation, attention focused on a clause in Article I in which the signatory powers were pledged to refrain "from countenancing action inimical to the security of the [signatory] States." Since Japan could argue that her "special interests" in South Manchuria and Inner Mongolia were vital to her security, this clause was read as modifying the pledge to support the open door. According to this construction, the other parties to the nine-power treaty accepted Japan's claims and were pledged not to interfere with them.[23] In a word, tensions had been eased, but their root causes had not been removed.

FOR FURTHER READING

Two bibliographical essays by Roger Dingman and Akira Iriye in *American-East Asian Relations: A Survey,* Ernest May and James C. Thomson, Jr., eds. (1972) afford the most comprehensive review of literature on the years 1919-1924. Akira Iriye, *Across the Pacific: An Inner History of American-East Asian Relations* (1967)* studies of origins of changing American and Japanese perceptions of each other. Eleanor Tupper and George McReynolds, *Japan in American Public Opinion* (1937) draws heavily on the American press.

---

[23] The degree to which this special interpretation of the nine-power treaty was shared by Japan's leadership has not been established. See Sadao Asada, "Japan's 'Special Interests' and the Washington Conference, 1921-1922," *American Historical Review,* 67 (1961), 62-70, a pioneering article which first noted these private interpretations. For evidence suggesting limited acceptance of the view in Japan see Thomas H. Buckley, *The United States and the Washington Conference, 1921-1922* (1970), 152-54. Malcolm D. Kennedy, *The Estrangement of Great Britain and Japan, 1917-1935* (1969), which stresses Japanese disillusionment with the British for abandoning their alliance, is of special value because the author enjoyed wide contact with highly-placed Japanese officials.

Siberian Intervention. George Kennan, *Soviet-American Relations, 1917-1920: The Decision to Intervene* (1958),* based on American, Japanese, and Russian sources. John A. White, *The Siberian Intervention* (1950), especially useful for the study of inter-Allied diplomacy. Betty M. Unterberger, *America's Siberian Expedition, 1918-1920: A Study of National Policy* (1956), the most thorough study of American archival materials. James A. Morley, *Japan's Thrust into Siberia* (1957), indispensable for the development of Japanese policy. The most satisfactory documentary treatment of the period from April to December, 1918 is James Bunyan, ed., *Intervention, Civil War, and Communism in Russia* (1936). Elena Varneck and H. H. Fisher, eds., *The Testimony of Kolchak and Other Siberian Materials* (1935), valuable for the editorial annotation of the sources presented. Richard Luckett, *The White Generals* (1971), the failures in the leadership opposing the Bolsheviks. Clarence A. Manning, *The Siberian Fiasco* (1952).

The Consortium. Selected correspondence is in Carnegie Endowment for International Peace, *The Consortium* (1921), and Paul H. Clyde, *United States Policy Toward China* (1940; reissued, 1964). There is a brief exposition in C. F. Remer, *Foreign Investments in China* (1933). F. V. Field, *American Participation in the China Consortium* (1931), a sound specialized study.

Washington Conference. R. L. Buell, *The Washington Conference* (1922), the best contemporary account. On sea power and politics note E. B. Potter, ed., *The United States and World Sea Power* (1955); and E. A. Falk, *Togo and the Rise of Japanese Sea Power* (1936). J. Chalmers Vinson, *The Parchment Peace: The United States Senate and the Washington Conference* (1955), the most incisive study of American politics in the Washington Conference. Ichihashi Yamato, *The Washington Conference and After* (1928), by a long-time professor of Japanese history and government and secretary to Admiral Baron Kato, Japan's chief delegate to the Conference. Chapter 21 of Takeuchi Tatsuji, *War and Diplomacy in the Japanese Empire* (1935) covers Japanese politics and the Conference. B. E. C. Dugdale, *Arthur James Balfour* (2 vols. 1936), information on the British role. Although outdated in some respects by Vinson's article on the Imperial Conference of 1921 (cited fn. 12 this chapter), J. B. Brebner, "Canada, the Anglo-Japanese Alliance and the Washington Conference," *Political Science Quarterly* 50 (1935), 45-58, is an excellent article. H. F. MacNair and D. F. Lach, *Modern Far Eastern International Relations* (1956), and George F. Kennan, *American Diplomacy, 1900-1950* (1951)* should also be consulted.

Japanese Immigration. John Roger Stemen, *The Diplomacy of the Immigration Issue, A Study in Japanese-American Relations, 1894-1941* (Ph.D. dissertation, Indiana University, 1960), draws heavily on Western sources. The standard study of the Gentlemen's Agreement is T. A. Bailey, *Theodore Roosevelt and the Japanese-American Crises* (1934). A Japanese interpretation is Ichihashi Yamato, *Japanese in the United States* (1932). R. D. McKenzie, *Oriental Exclusion* (1928) presents an able analysis of the working of the 1924 law. E. G. Mears, *Resident Orientals on the American-Pacific Coast* (1928) surveys legal and other relationships of the races. The broad outlines of immigration in the entire Pacific area are given in J. B. Condliffe, ed., *Problems of the Pacific* (1928), 146-61. Contemporary American concerns with the role of racial minorities in American life have stimulated studies of the Japanese immigrant. The view presented emphasizes the insensitivity of American democracy to the rights of a minority. Bill Hosohawa, *Nisei: The Quiet Americans* (1969); *Audrie Girdner and Ann Loftis, *The Great Betrayal: The Evacuation of Japanese-Americans during World War II* (1969); Dillon S. Myer, *Uprooted Americans: The Japanese-Americans and the War Relocation Authority during World War II* (1971); and Roger Daniels, *Concentration Camps U.S.A.: Japanese-Americans and World War II* (1971);* James W. Loewen, *The Mississippi Chinese: Between Black and White* (1971); and Louise H. Hunter, *Buddhism in Hawaii: Its Impact on a Yankee Community* (1971).

Japan,
1918–1931:
Experiments
with
Party Government

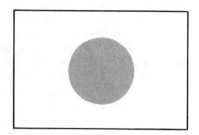

23

In the years 1918-1931, while the powers searched for a settlement of their East Asian rivalries, Japan's oligarchs were challenged by a new generation of reformers at home demanding fundamental changes in the policies and procedures of government. High on the reform agenda were demands for an end to imperialism and for the adoption of a cooperative attitude, especially in matters of disarmament. The reformers also wanted a new day in the domestic political process. Stated broadly, Japanese progressives called for government conducted by party cabinets responsible to the majority in the lower house of the Diet, election of the lower house by universal manhood suffrage, and guarantees of civil liberties for the entire population. These proposed advances in democratic and responsible constitutional government were to be joined with internationalism to usher in a new political era. Consequently, in 1918, the downfall of the militarist Terauchi ministry and the selection of Hara Kei, the untitled president of the *Seiyukai,* as prime minister were hailed by reform-minded Japanese as the dawn of the new era. The stage was seemingly set for the end of rule by oligarchy and for the beginnings of more popular inter-

pretations of government under the constitution.[1]

THE BASE OF THE NEW POLITICS

The new movement for party government recalled the early demands for "restoration" of imperial rule and for the adoption of Western ideas early in the Meiji era. Like those earlier efforts, the call for party government in 1918 and after, and for a fresh approach to foreign affairs was a product of pronounced changes in Japanese society, including the appearance of

[1] In the study of this period of Japan's modern political history when the nation was seeking modernization, especially through Western ideas, methods, and technology, there is the natural tendency for American and British students to view Japan's political development against the background of Anglo-American democratic institutions. A closer and more meaningful comparison is found between Japan and Germany prior to World War I. Politically, Japan and Germany were by no means identical, but there were some striking similarities in the values and institutions motivating their politics. The long, evolutionary struggle of representative and democratic forces in British development was alien to the Japanese experience.

an intellectual liberalism opposed to state orthodoxy. Allied victories in World War I had infused Japanese democratic currents with new vitality. During the war years, Japan's propaganda had derided German militarism's attacks on liberty and had publicized Wilsonian ideals. Thus, Yoshino Sakuzo (1878-1933) found magazine editors during the postwar years ready to publish his plans for a restructured government under party control. In addition, a theoretical basis for curbing absolutism was set forth in the writings of Minobe Tatsukichi, a distinguished scholar and jurist, who held that the emperor was an organ of the state rather than the embodiment of the state. Among literary figures the novelist Mushakoji Saneatsu captured the new spirit, saying that "only a country without authority is liveable."[2]

The extension of the wartime boom also contributed to the demands for reform. While the Japanese economy suffered temporarily from the cancellation of war contracts and the renewal of European competition, Japan, in the main, retained the commercial advantages won during the war. New highs in the export of raw silk and cotton textile goods stimulated development of a more diversified system. In the postwar years, Japan produced most of her own textile and electrical machinery, railway rolling stock, and bicycles, and maintained a thriving ship-building industry. Electric generating

[2] See Frank O. Miller, *Minobe Tatsukichi: Interpreter of Constitutionalism in Japan* (1965); and Bernard S. Silberman, "The Political Theory and Program of Yoshino Sakuzo," *Journal of Modern History,* 31 (1959), 310-24.

capacity increased fourfold (to four million kilowatts) in the decade 1919-1929. This enlarged capacity in heavy industry and large-scale commercial operations was a tribute to the leadership of the great *zaibatsu* combines—Mitsui, Mitsubishi, Yasuda, and Sumitomo. Operating as subcontractors or suppliers for these giants were a vast number of small, family-owned enterprises. By 1930 this latter type of business accounted for 30 percent of total manufacturing. This growth in the whole industrial complex multiplied the expanding elite of business executives and increased their demands that business have a greater political role. Party government in turn was the immediate beneficiary of these developments, since businessmen and party politicians already had close connections. Businessmen, moreover, sought through the parties political leverage that no longer could be exercised through the *genro.* By the end of World War I, the old oligarchs were all but gone; Itagaki died in 1919; Matsukata abandoned politics well before his death in 1924; and Yamagata and Okuma died in 1922. Saionji, the only remaining *genro,* was sympathetic toward party government.

Thus politics after 1918 rested on foundations quite different from those of 1890 or even 1914. Among the divergent elements in Japan's postwar elite—militarists, bureaucrats, businessmen, and intellectuals—no single group possessed either the prestige or the power of the old oligarchs. Moreover, this new elite, reflecting special interests, lacked the unity of purpose which characterized the *genro.* In these circumstances, the Diet and the party system

Year	Prime Minister	Party Affiliation
1918	Hara Kei (Takashi)	Seiyukai cabinet
1921	Viscount Takahashi Korekiyo	Seiyukai cabinet
1922	Admiral Kato Tomosaburo	nonparty cabinet
1923	Admiral Count Yamamoto Gombei	nonparty cabinet
1924	Viscount Kiyoura Keigo	nonparty Peers cabinet
1924	Viscount Kato Komei (Takaaki)	Kenseikai cabinet
1925	Viscount Kato Komei (Takaaki)	Kenseikai cabinet
1926	Baron Wakatsuki Reijiro	Kenseikai cabinet
1927	General Baron Tanaka Giichi	Seiyukai cabinet
1929	Hamaguchi Osachi (Yuko)	Minseito cabinet
1931	Baron Wakatsuki Reijiro	Minseito cabinet
1931	Inukai Tsuyoshi	Seiyukai cabinet

assumed importance as mechanisms for balancing contending factions. The parties also benefited from progressive lowering of property qualifications for voting. By 1918 the bulk of the urban middle class, but not the peasantry or factory laborers, had acquired the franchise. From these developments the parties acquired an image as vehicles of a more popular form of government.[3]

Between 1918 and 1932 twelve cabinets guided Japan's destiny. Their average life was a little more than one year. As the record indicates, Japan was led by a succession of party or semi-party cabinets, thus making it possible to describe the administration as being in some measure responsible to the Diet. Indeed, the process of governing through party cabinets became so established that, at the time, it was known as "the normal course of constitutional government." It should be noted, however, that this era did not bring a complete break with the past or an unqualified achievement of responsible government. The military service ministries remained beyond party control. The principles of oligarchical government remained firmly entrenched in the House of Peers, privy council, imperial household, and among the bureaucrats. Furthermore, the parties themselves were weakened by defects of character and organization.

THE HARA GOVERNMENT, 1918-1921

As prime minister, Hara Kei applied himself in the beginning to the tasks of political reconciliation; the expansion of public education and some liberalization of the franchise were offered as concessions to the new popular forces. Party leadership was honored by appointment of *Seiyukai* members to the cabinet and to posts in the bureaucracy. The prestige of the old leadership—civil bureaucrats, militarists, and oligarchs—was upheld through the device of accepting representatives of each into the *Seiyukai* and giving them key appointments.

[3] Tetsuo Najita, *Hara Kei and the Politics of Compromise, 1905-1915* (1967); and Peter Duus, *Party Rivalry and Political Change in Taisho Japan* (1968) are detailed studies of party development.

General Tanaka Giichi, for example, a protege of Yamagata, became minister of war. In economic and social matters, Hara's policies favored landowners and businessmen rather than workers. Fears of radicalism were quieted when the administration suppressed socialist groups, thereby strengthening its ideological image.

The Hara political formula was successful, at least for the time-being, in restoring peace in a riot-torn society, but it did not encourage experimentation with basic reforms. Two such areas for potential reform were the expansion of the franchise (still limited by tax qualifications) and implementation of the principles of parliamentary government. On the matter of the franchise, universal manhood suffrage had been proposed in 1902 and passed by the House of Representatives in 1911; it was rejected immediately by the House of Peers. The subject then remained dormant until 1919 when the *Kenseikai* opposition party, under the leadership of Kato Komei, favored reintroduction of a universal manhood suffrage bill. Hara and his more powerful *Seiyukai,* in contrast, took the position that while the party would favor expansion of the suffrage sometime in the future, there should be no immediate consideration. He feared that enlargement of the franchise would increase the urban vote, to the advantage of the *Kenseikai,* and weaken the position of the *Seiyukai* among the rural elites and the older traditional leadership.[4] Neither Hara nor his party was ready to be so closely identified with the so-called common man. In fact, Hara's government followed a policy of ruthless suppression of strikes and of the labor movement in general. It was a policy, however, which promoted rather than retarded the growth of Marxism among intellectuals and students, and it embittered the growing mass of urban workers. In November, 1921, Hara was assassinated by an employee of the government railways.

For the moment this was to be the end of party government. Hara had not advanced appreciably the theory or the practice of party

[4] Edward G. Griffin, "The Universal Suffrage Issue in Japanese Politics, 1918-1925," *Journal of Asian Studies,* 31 (1972), 275-90.

government. He did not curb the immense power of the bureaucracy. He did not increase the prestige of the House of Representatives, which was allowed to consume its energy in debates on trivia while many of its members indulged in profitable forms of corruption. Hara appears to have been a person of integrity, but he could be blind to misconduct among his party colleagues. Still, allowing for all these shortcomings, Hara did build the most powerful party Japan had known to that time.

NON-PARTY CABINETS

With Hara's assassination, his finance minister, Takahashi Korekiyo, an able financier but no party leader, became premier. Within months the *Seiyukai* had become a minority party through desertions. Takahashi resigned in June, 1922. Stunned by all these disturbing events, the elder statesmen reverted to tradition by giving the nation a succession of three non-party cabinets within two years, from June, 1922, to June, 1924. The first, headed by Admiral Kato Tomosaburo, naval minister in four preceding cabinets and chief of Japan's delegation to the Washington conference, survived little more than a year, to September, 1923. Kato, who had died the previous month, was succeeded by Admiral Yamamoto Gombei, who held the premiership for four months while the government struggled with the chaos of the Tokyo earthquake and fire (September, 1923). When in the midst of these tribulations an attempt was made on the life of the prince regent, Yamamoto resigned and was replaced by Viscount Kiyoura Keigo, president of the tradition-bound privy council. Kiyoura held onto office for five months until June, 1924. By that time it was obvious that the two-year reversion to non-party cabinets had been a complete failure. Kiyoura, for example, received no support at all save in some sectors of the oligarchy. The House of Representatives simply refused to work with the cabinet. Kato Komei, president of the *Kenseikai*, brought other parties into a joint declaration demanding party government, the end of special privilege for the oligarchs, and united action to achieve these ends. The result

of this unprecedented unity brought dissolution of the Diet (January, 1924). The following election gave the parties complete control of the House of Representatives with 284 seats, while the oligarchs controlled only 180; the *Kenseikai* was the strongest party with 153 seats.[5]

THE KATO GOVERNMENTS, 1924-1926

The prospect for responsible government had never been so high as it was in 1924, when Kato Komei formed the country's first coalition party cabinet from the *Kenseikai*, (of which Kato was president), the *Seiyukai*, and the *Kakushin Club*. Kato had a long and distinguished political career. From the presidency of the *Doshikai* in 1913 and later of the *Kenseikai*, he had become foreign minister in the Okuma cabinet of 1914, and had challenged, if unsuccessfully, the *genro* and the militarists on numerous occasions. By 1924, when he became premier, he had long admired British political institutions, and was unquestionably Japan's outstanding exponent of responsible government. Far from being a commoner, he was an aristocrat guided by a philosophy of enlightened conservatism, a quality which enabled him to face the oligarchs without fear.

As a reforming government, Kato's coalition made some notable headway. A major achievement was the passage of a universal manhood suffrage bill in 1925, through which the electorate (all males 25 and over) was increased from three million to more than twelve million. Four divisions were cut from the army in 1924 as part of a retrenchment program. Similar economies trimmed the bureaucracy by some twenty thousand persons. Moreover, social legislation favorable to labor was passed. The law that had been used against labor unions was abolished; a national health insurance law and a labor disputes mediation law were enacted; and improved working conditions were encouraged by new factory legislation. Altogether, these measures laid the basis for popular support from the rising nonrevolutionary socialist move-

[5] For greater detail on these political developments see Hugh Borton, *Japan's Modern Century* (2nd ed., 1970), 339-66.

ment. Yet there was also a darker side of the picture for the advocates of responsible government. Passage of the suffrage act was preceded by the "Peace Preservation Law," which, though aimed at anarchists and Communists, could be used against the press, the universities, and indeed any movement critical of things as they were. It was legislation indicative of a determination to limit the range of political alternatives open to the newly-enlarged electorate. Further limitation on responsible government appeared in Kato's failure—like Hara's—to carry through fundamental reforms of the governmental system. If military budgets were pared, the armed forces nevertheless retained tremendous influence through training programs that were introduced in middle schools, in high shcools, and through veterans' organizations.[6] There was in addition the utter failure of Kato's plan for curtailing the powers of the House of Peers. With the passing of the *genro,* the importance of the Peers as a check on the electorate and their representatives had increased.

THE TANAKA GOVERNMENT, 1927-1929

The meaning of Kato's failure to deal with reform of the Peerage was soon evident. On Kato's death, January, 1926, Wakatsuki Reijiro, one of Kato's political proteges, succeeded to the premiership and presidency of the *Kenseikai.* The troubles of government mounted as the army attacked the conciliatory policy toward China of Foreign Minister Baron Shidehara Kijuro; but it was opposition from the privy council, which, with the House of Peers, was the fortress of the Imperial point of view, that wrecked the Wakatsuki cabinet by the simple expedient of declaring unconstitutional certain emergency measures of the gov-

[6] Richard J. Smethurst, "The Creation of the Imperial Military Reserve Association in Japan," *Journal of Asian Studies,* 30 (1971), 815-28, deals with military values which opposed individualism and thus democracy.

ernment for dealing with the banking crisis of 1927.

Meanwhile, the *Seiyukai,* thirsting for a return to power and having no leader within its ranks, bestowed its presidency on General Tanaka Giichi. From the beginning Tanaka faced grave problems of political stategy. As a result of the first election under the new manhood suffrage law, the *Seiyukai* held 219 seats, the new *Minseito* (*Kenseikai* plus *Seiyuhonto*) held 217, and the remaining 30 seats were held by independents and representatives of the new labor parties. What followed were legislative scenes of wild uproar. There was the grotesque spectacle of the opposition, presumbably the advocates of responsible government, attacking the cabinet for its adherence to the treaty for the renunciation of war on the ground that the phrase "in the names of their respective peoples" was an affront to the emperor. With this opposition from the politicians, it was hardly surprising that the privy council blocked the treaty until the government gave assurances that this democratic phrase did not apply in the case of Japan.

Even more suggestive of the frail basis of party government was the incident that forced the resignation of the Tanaka cabinet. As prime minister, Tanaka spoke of a "positive foreign policy"—that is, strengthening Japan's position in Manchuria and taking a tougher attitude toward Chinese nationalism. Tanaka's purpose was to reassure his own people, but the hard line provoked anti-Japanese boycotts in China. Further trouble appeared when officers of Japan's Kwantung army sought to deal on their own with the dangers of Chinese nationalism by assassinating the Manchurian warlord, Chang Tso-lin, on the assumption that his successor would be more subservient to Japan. Premier Tanaka first told the young emperor the army was not responsible. Later, with the support of his cabinet including the service ministers, he sought to punish the conspirators and re-establish discipline in the army, but he was blocked by the general staff and the powerful military affairs bureau. The conspirators were not punished and Tanaka's government resigned. It was a victory for irresponsible military officers and for the army's independent political power.[7]

THE MINSEITO CABINET, 1929-1931

The surviving *genro*, Saionji, then recommended a *Minseito* party cabinet with Hamaguchi Yuko, party president, as prime minister. Coming into office with a strong program calling for clean politics, economy, arms reduction, and a moderate China policy, this cabinet failed more tragically than its predecessors. Its plans to reduce the lesser bureaucracy were challenged successfully, and although the government finally won ratification of the London naval treaty, October, 1930, it incurred the wrath of the army, navy, and the oligarchs of the privy council. In addition, the *Seiyukai*, led by Inukai Tsuyoshi, joined with these bureaucrats in denouncing the government.[8] The real political issue was whether a party cabinet with a majority in the lower House and with the apparent confidence of the electorate could successfully challenge the independent and irresponsible power of the militarists and the oligarchs. Hamaguchi maintained that the navy's approval of the London treaty was beside the

---

[7] See Paul S. Dull, "The Assassination of Chang Tso-lin," *Far Eastern Quarterly*, 11 (1952), 453-63. The Japanese public had no way of knowing at the time that Tanaka's resignation was due to insubordination and internal conflict within an army which had clothed itself in self-righteous patriotism. Note Borton, *Modern Century*, 356 and 365.

[8] The problem of marshaling domestic support for naval disarmament was to become increasingly complex for Japan's leadership because many Japanese came to believe that more was at stake than a naval ratio. The London agreements came ". . . to symbolize the existing order of international and national life in Japan. To oppose the Japanese-American agreement in London was not only to protest against specific disarmament arrangements but also to challenge the structure of the Washington [conference] system which, it was widely believed, provided the framework for the continuation of a cooperative foreign policy and a conservative fiscal and social policy at home." Akira Iriye, "1922-1931," in *American-East Asian Relation: A Survey*, Ernest R. May and James C. Thomson, Jr., eds. (1972), 221-42. This essay offers valuable suggestions for further reading in American-Japanese relations.

point because the constitution provided that the emperor alone, on the advice of the cabinet, exercised treaty-making powers. The premier was insisting that in foreign policy the military members of the cabinet did not have a veto.

Hamaguchi's victory was short-lived. In spite of the importance of the constitutional issue involved, the opposition *Seiyukai* did everything in its power to embarrass the government. In addition, economic depression coupled with retrenchment policies were creating alarming unemployment. The oligarchs, most of the bureaucracy, the extreme nationalists and expansionists in the military services, and the secret societies were as one in the belief that the Hamaguchi policies of conciliating China and of overriding the advice of the army and navy were subversive, designed to undercut the power of these special groups. Added support for this view came from politicians, the press, and the public, all of whom were sensitive to any implied weakening of Japan's special position in China. Six weeks after his victory on the London naval treaty, Hamaguchi was shot at the Tokyo railroad station by a nationalist "patriot." While he survived for nearly a year, he could no longer be an effective leader. Wakatsuki, who followed as premier, could lead neither the party nor the nation. There was no one to curb the Japanese militarists in Manchuria. On September 18, 1931, these militarists began the seizure of Manchuria. For a brief interlude the *Seiyukai*, under Inukai, returned to office but not to power. The day of party cabinets was ended, and with it the prospect for responsible civilian government.[9]

PARTY GOVERNMENT; A SUMMARY

By 1931, Japan for more than a decade had attempted a transition from oligarchic government to responsible government under a party system. In the early years of the period the parties had revealed a new popular influence as the potential heirs of the *genro*-sponsored oligarchs. Long before the end of the period, however, there was massive evidence that popular

---

[9] Borton, *Modern Century*, 360-62.

support of the parties was uncertain, that the parties themselves were not dedicated to the principles on which free representative government could survive, that the politicians were unwilling to seek basic constitutional reform, and that, though all of the *genro* save Saionji were gone, the principles of oligarchy had not been outlived. Political power had not passed from the bureaucracy and the oligarchs to the representatives of the people.

No simple statement can explain this failure to develop or mature a Japanese democracy. The obstacles in its path were formidable. In the first instance, problems were created by Japan's constitutional structure. The Diet was constitutionally weak. It lacked both legal and financial controls over the cabinet. Such power as was given the elected lower House was shared by the appointed upper House. Moreover, other established centers of authority, such as the bureaucracy, the privy council, the military services, the *genro*, and the imperial household, could veto attempts to curtail their power. Second, the political parties, grounded in personal loyalties, and long accustomed to subservience to the oligarchy, were ill-equipped to lead an aroused public opinion in obtaining concessions on behalf of popular government. United more by the hope of receiving the crumbs of office than by agreement on principle, the parties battled each other for advantage instead of joining in an attack on arbitrary authority.[10] In addition, the self-seeking appearance projected by the parties seriously limited their popular appeal. Third, the forces of representative government were frightened into retreat by labor and radical movements after 1918. The Japanese labor movement,

socialist in its origins, grew rapidly during World War I with the organization of the first trade unions. At the same time Marxism had become popular among professors, writers, and university students. The intimate relation between the labor movement and this vocal, proletarian radicalism was as alarming to the political parties as it was to the oligarchs. All agreed that the extension of civil rights might result in radicals overturning the established order. In consequence, both Hara and Kato countered each of their measures toward political freedom with new executive powers by which the government could control the people. Fourth, compounding all of these difficulties was a social and economic order which provided only a narrow basis for supporting an attack on authoritarian government. The development of a sense of individualism, personal responsibility, and self-confidence were essential to the proper functioning of responsible government, but were checked in the Japanese populace by the functioning of most social groups. The educational system, as it had since the beginning of the Meiji era, fostered acceptance of oligarchical government. Business mergers tending to enlarge the size and power of the *zaibatsu* also contributed to the suppression of individualism by promoting inequality of income and perpetuating concepts of status and authority in industry. These were some of the obstacles on the road to representative institutions. When they are seen in the perspective of Japan's international position during the 1920's, the fate of Japanese democracy becomes more understandable.

RESPONSIBLE GOVERNMENT AND WORLD POLITICS

The failure of responsible party government was to have a vital bearing on methods used in Japan's foreign policy. In Japan, as in other lands, efforts at liberal political reform had not precluded a vigorous policy of expansion. Proponents of party government, such as Saionji after the Russo-Japanese War and

[10] The picture of self-seeking politicians should not be overdrawn. Parties in Japan were utterly without historical precedent. Moreover, party members confronted ethical assumptions, for example, sincerity between men, unselfish dedication to serve all of society, and a spiritual consensus based on personal loyalty, which served as obstacles to the operation of parties. See Tetsuo Najita, "Inukai Tsuyoshi: Some Dilemmas in Party Development in Pre-World War II Japan," *American Historical Review,* 74 (1968), 492-510.

Okuma in 1915, had not hesitated to implement Japan's special position in China and Manchuria. After World War I, Japanese "liberals," such as Hara, Kato, Shidehara, and Hamaguchi, were no more prepared to forego the nation's privileged status in Manchuria than were the militarists, but they were sensitive to the implications of military coercion. So it was that, under their direction, foreign policy in the era of party government became identified with economic rather than military expansion, with informal rather than formal empire. Moreover, this new policy guided the approach to many fundamental problems: the situation created by the failure of the inter-Allied intervention in Siberia, the extension of naval disarmament, and the challenge to Japanese interests from Chinese nationalism. When economic diplomacy failed to produce the promised results, foreign policy and party government alike came under attack.

JAPAN AND RUSSIA, 1922-1929

A striking development in the period immediately after the Washington conference was the formal improvement in Japan's relations with Soviet Russia. At the end of 1922 the last Japanese forces left the mainland of Siberia. Their withdrawal was due to many pressures. In addition to diplomatic pressure exerted on Japan at the Washington conference, the Japanese public no longer supported a policy that had cost the taxpayer some Yen 700 million, alienated the Russians, aroused the suspicions of the Western powers, and finally, served to hasten rather than retard the union of eastern Siberia with communist Moscow. The economic as well as the political interests of both Japan and Russia demanded an end to the chaos created by revolution and intervention. As a consequence of protracted negotiations begun in June, 1923, a treaty was signed on January 20, 1925, restoring relations between the two powers.[11]

[11]George A. Lensen, *Japanese Recognition of the U.S.S.R.: Soviet-Japanese Relations, 1921-1930* (1970) provides a detailed account of Soviet-Japanese negotiations with the full text of major agreements and extensive quotations from other Japanese and Russian documents.

The rapprochement represented by this treaty was a product of significant and varied forces playing upon Japanese policy. It had become evident even to Japan's chauvinists that military and political intervention had failed utterly to isolate eastern Siberia from the advance of Bolshevism. Furthermore, since there was an increasing demand in Japan for the products of Siberia's mines, forests, and waters, the re-establishment of normal relations in which commerce and industry might develop with some freedom was the natural alternative despite Japan's fear of the infiltration of "dangerous thoughts." Moreover, the success of Russian influence with the Chinese Nationalists at Canton and the conclusion of the Russian treaties with Peking and Mukden in 1924 emphasized Japan's isolation. Indeed, this isolation was now looming much larger in Japanese eyes than it had at the time of the Washington conference. There was no longer an Anglo-Japanese alliance as a prop to Japanese policy, and "the insensate method" taken by the American Senate in the quota immigration act of May, 1924, to exclude Japanese from the United States was interpreted by the Japanese press, the government, and public opinion as again indicative of an American attitude basically unfriendly to Japan's interests and purposes.

A PERIOD OF SINO-JAPANESE AMITY

The period in which normal diplomatic relations between Japan and Soviet Russia were restored also saw the growth of happier prospects in Sino-Japanese affairs. During the greater part of the decade 1922-1931, Japan's foreign policy was colored by the personality and the philosophy of Baron Shidehara Kijuro, a career diplomat who had married into the Iwasaki family, which controlled the powerful Mitsubishi trust. Shidehara had become the spokesman of those elements that saw the future of Japan's commercial and industrial expansion in membership in the League of Nations, limitation of naval armament, and the development of a policy of conciliation and adjustment to China's new nationalism—without, of course, renouncing

Japan's "life line" in South Manchuria. From 1924 to 1927 and from 1929 to 1931, while he was foreign minister, Shidehara pursued a conciliatory policy. He summarized the principles of the policy before the Japanese Diet in January, 1927:

1. To respect the sovereignty and territorial integrity of China.
2. To promote solidarity and economic rapprochement between the two countries.
3. To entertain sympathetically and helpfully the just aspirations of the Chinese people.
4. To maintain an attitude of patience and tolerance in the present situation in China, and to protect Japan's legitimate and essential rights and interests by all reasonable means at the disposal of the government.

As applied to the situation in China, these principles produced Japanese cooperation with other powers in modifying rates under treaty tariffs and in expressing readiness to restore tariff autonomy after January, 1929 (concession of autonomy was actually delayed beyond that date). Negotiations on the refunding of the Nishihara and other loans were marked by restraint seldom evident in earlier Sino-Japanese dealings. In Manchuria, Japan's stress on economic rather than military measures was seen in the appointment of additional commercial officers.

On two occasions during Shidehara's first term at the foreign office, Japan did resort to the use of troops "for the protection of Japanese interests in China." In December, 1925, when Kuo Sung-ling, a lesser militarist in Manchuria, revolted against Chang Tso-lin, Japan dispatched some troops to the Mukden area. Again in April, 1927, Japanese marines were used to resist Chinese mobs attacking the Japanese concession at Hankow. But Japanese naval forces did not join in the Anglo-American bombardment of Nanking in March, 1927, despite the fact that the Japanese consulate had been attacked by the Chinese and several Japanese nationals had been wounded. The crux of the Shidehara policy was a serious effort to reconcile China's aspirations with Japan's interest.

TANAKA AND THE POSITIVE POLICY

Shidehara's "weak" policy, which had been pursued in the face of mounting civil war and antiforeignism in China, aroused bitter opposition among Japanese militarists and bureaucrats and in some business circles. The sentiment was particularly strong in the powerful privy council, which forced the resignation of the first Wakatsuki cabinet in April, 1927, thus opening the way for the "positive policy" of Tanaka and the *Seiyukai*. The nature of this so-called "positive policy" toward China merits some further comment.

The positive policy distinguished between the attitude Japan would adopt toward China Proper and her attitude toward Manchuria and eastern Mongolia. With respect to China Proper, Tanaka reiterated policies which had been repeatedly announced—noninterference with the Chinese civil war, respect for China's "popular will," sympathy for the demands of the more moderate elements of the *Kuomintang*, and determination to protect Japanese lives and property. In Manchuria and eastern Mongolia, on the other hand, Tanaka emphasized that Japan had "special interests," that it was her duty to maintain peace and order there, " and that her rights and interests in these areas would be protected if threatened by disturbance incident to the Nationalist movement or other civil strife." As guiding principles, these pronouncements were scarcely distinguishable from those of Shidehara. What imparted a difference in practice was Tanaka's military background, his party's commitment to a "stronger" policy, and, above all, the application of these principles just as the *Kuomintang* was moving toward military unification of China.[12]

[12] Akira Iriye, *After Imperialism: The Search for a New Order in the Far East, 1921-1931* (1965),* Chapter 4. Associated with the history of the "positive policy" is the so-called "Tanaka Memorial," a document which, purporting to contain the decisions reached at a foreign office conference, first made its appearance in 1929, and after 1931 was reprinted many times and widely circulated as evidence of Japan's predetermined policy vis-a-vis China in general

For Tanaka, as for Shidehara, the problem was to reconcile Chinese aspirations with Japanese interests. Chinese industrialization in Manchuria (particularly the building of Chinese-owned railroads) would, it was felt, threaten Japan's South Manchurian Railroad, and therefore her "special position." Moreover, the power of left-wing elements in the *Kuomintang* until 1927 was alarming to the Japanese government and particularly to the leaders of the Japanese Kwantung army in South Manchuria, which consistently urged strong measures. Chinese nationalist tendencies to move away from rather than toward an accommodation with Japan had distressed Shidehara and had prompted, with his blessings, a thorough re-evaluation of Chinese relations. Thus it was against a background suggesting that something more must be done that Tanaka approved the use of Japanese troops in Shantung to check the advance of *Kuomintang* forces and thereby to prevent the immediate union of Manchuria with the Nationalist cause. The prime minister was less conscious of intervening in China's civil war than of satisfying his own military subordinates and *Seiyukai* colleagues.[13] The

---

and Manchuria in particular. Japanese policy in Manchuria and China after 1931 bore a striking resemblance to specific points in the "Memorial." The disputed authenticity of the document is discussed by W. W. Willoughby, *Japan's Case Examined* (1940), 146-53. The "Memorial" was undoubtedly a forgery, but the program outlined represented the thinking of some Japanese expansionists. Robert A. Scalapino, *Democracy and the Party Movement in Prewar Japan* (1953), 236.

The difference between the "weak" policy of Shidehara and the "positive" policy of Tanaka involved more than an argument over principles to be applied in relations with China. In some considerable measure, Shidehara represented the commercialism of Japan's light industries and their quest for expanding export markets. Tanaka was more closely identified with Japan's heavy industries. A strong armament policy enabled the army and navy to place large contracts with Japan's heavy industries, thus in fact subsidizing them, for which reason the heavy industries tended to be willing to go along with the Tanaka policy. But in order to justify armaments and preparedness, Tanaka was forced to adopt a "positive" policy, to maintain that a warlike crisis was perpetually just around the corner on the continent of Asia.

[13] Iriye, *After Imperialism,* 146-47.

effect, nevertheless, was to revive military diplomacy and to enlarge the initiative exercised by military extremists, especially after the failure to punish Chang Tso-lin's assassins. From this time on, especially as Tanaka resigned in July, 1929, the course of Japanese foreign policy was under the constant and increasing threat of extreme militarists and of a general staff that was unable or unwilling to restore discipline in its own service or to permit the civilian wing of the government to take steps to that end.

JAPAN AND THE LEAGUE OF NATIONS

As the pendulum of Japanese politics swung uneasily between the "weak" and "strong" policies of Shidehara and Tanaka, Japan continued to play a respectable and in some cases a distinguished role as a member of the League of Nations. A number of Japan's ablest statesmen, jurists, diplomats, and public men served with the League. Until 1926, Nitobe Inazo, one of the best known of Japan's liberals abroad, served as an under-secretary general and as a director of the international bureau. He was succeeded by Sugimura Yotaro as under-secretary general and director of the political section.

Japan was also active in the field of arbitration and adjudication of international disputes. She was a signatory of the Convention for the Pacific Settlement of International Disputes, a product of the Hague peace congresses of 1899 and 1907. When, under the League of Nations, the principle of international adjudication acquired new life, Adachi Mineichiro was named a member of the League committee that drafted the statutes for the new Permanent Court of International Justice, commonly known as the World Court. A Japanese, Oda Yorozu, was one of the original eleven judges of the court. He in turn was succeeded in 1930 by Adachi Mineichiro, who served also as president of the court. However, on account of the so-called "optional clause" in the statutes of the court imposing compulsory acceptance of its jurisdiction in specified cases, Japan did not accept the court's full jurisdiction.

NAVAL RIVALRY IN THE PACIFIC

The Washington conference had made a beginning toward holding within bounds the race in naval armament among the great powers. After 1924, however, when the United States passed the quota immigration act excluding aliens who were ineligible for citizenship, there was noticeable tension in American-Japanese relations and a growing interest in the question of armaments. A naval race was still quite possible, for the Washington conference ratio-5-5-3 for the United States, Great Britain, and Japan—was applicable only to capital ships. Indeed, the naval race was already under way, for while the United States failed to maintain its naval strength either in auxiliary categories or in the capital ships to which it was entitled under the Washington agreement, the other powers, Japan and Great Britain, continued to build.[14]

Without adequate preparation, President Coolidge on February 10, 1927, invited the powers to a disarmament conference at Geneva. Although France and Italy declined to attend, Great Britain, the United States, and Japan attempted to extend and supplement the principles adopted at Washington. The United States wanted to apply the 5-5-3 ratio to all categories and to reduce total cruiser tonnage. No agreement was reached, however, and the conference ended in failure. This was the more lamentable since there was little doubt that public opinion at this time in all three countries favored further limitation. The conference was defeated both by the naval experts and by lobbyists of special groups.

Anglo-American-Japanese relations continued to deteriorate after the Geneva conference. There appeared to be no solution to the

naval problem so long as Great Britain and the United States remained as far apart as they were at Geneva. By late 1929 this doleful picture had been retouched and brightened. Shidehara was back at the Japanese foreign office, and President Herbert Hoover and Prime Minister Ramsay MacDonald had talked amicably at the president's fishing camp at Rapidan, Virginia. Evidence of the improved international temper came with a British invitation to the powers, October 7, 1929, to a disarmament conference in London. As at Geneva, this conference was soon mired in the technical details of the experts. Yet, on April 22, 1930, the London naval treaty was signed by Britain, the United States, and Japan. France, who had demanded a political agreement assuring her of military support, and Italy accepted only part of the treaty. Nevertheless, the results of the conference were positive, if limited. The three major powers had accepted a maximum upper limit in all categories of vessels. Britain acceded to an over-all principle of parity with the United States. Japan accepted a 10-10-6 ratio in heavy cruisers, was granted a 10-10-7 ratio in light cruisers and other auxiliary ships, and parity with the larger powers in submarines. An escalator clause could release any signatory from its obligations if its position was jeopardized by the naval construction of a non-signatory.

At the London naval conference Japan sought "three fundamental claims": (1) a 70 percent ratio relative to the United States in 10,000-ton, 8-inch-gun heavy cruisers; (2) a 70 percent ratio in gross tonnage relative to the United States in all auxiliary craft; and (3) parity with Britain and the United States in submarine tonnage at the then high existing strength of some 78,000 tons. This program of the Japanese naval staff, supported by the press, was designed to give the nation greater relative strength in far eastern waters than was provided by the 5-5-3 capital ship ratio of the Washington treaty. In Japan it was generally regarded as "adequate for defense in any contingency." What Japan achieved by the specific provisions of the 1930 treaty fell

---

[14] For discussions of the growing armament problem, see B. H. Williams, *The United States and Disarmament* (1931); J. W. Wheeler-Bennett, *Disarmament and Security Since Locarno, 1925-1931* (1932), Chapters 1 and 2; and Giovanni Engely, *The Politics of Naval Disarmament*, H. V. Rhodes, trans. (1932), Chapters 1, 2 and 3.

short of the 70 percent ratio in the heavy cruiser class. The United States agreed informally, however, not to complete its heavy curiser construction schedule until after 1936, thus giving Japan an actual 72 percent ratio in heavy cruisers vis-a-vis the United States during the life of the treaty (scheduled to terminate, with the Washington treaty, at the end of 1936). But this informal understanding was unacceptable to the naval experts at Tokyo, and the Hamaguchi government met violent opposition from the naval staff and all ultranationalistic groups. Admiral Kato Kanji, chief of the naval general staff, personified the resolute position of the military services and their supporters. The decision to accept the compromise was, therefore, a major victory for civilian as opposed to military dominance in the government. Furthermore, it strengthened the constitutional theories of Minobe Tatsukichi, who held that the power to determine the military and naval strength of the state did not belong to the supreme command. In his view, it was the prerogative of the cabinet and not of the military services to advise the emperor.

Japan's adherence to the London treaty marked the high point in the nation's struggle toward responsible government. But, as already noted, the victory was fictitious; there was no united public opinion to support a government that was fighting for democratic and responsible control.

FOR FURTHER READING

Tsunoda Ryusaku and others, eds., *Sources of the Japanese Tradition* (1958).* Chapter 26, "The High Tide of Prewar Liberalism" presents pertinent documents and penetrating editorial notes. H. S. Quigley, *Japanese Government and Politics* (1932), a good reference work. R. K. Reischauer, *Japan: Government-Politics* (1939) has an excellent brief chapter on "The Party Politicians in Power, 1918-1932." A useful summary is also to be found in Delmar M. Brown, *Nationalism in Japan: An Introductory*

Historical Analysis (1955). Something of the diversity of Japanese political thinking is suggested by two studies: Douglas H. Mendel, Jr., "Ozaki Yukio: Political Conscience of Modern Japan," *Far Eastern Quarterly* 15 (1956), 343-56; and Walter Scott Perry, "Yoshino Sakuzo, 1873-1933: Exponent of Democratic Ideals in Japan," (1956, University Microfilm Publication 17,734). Tatsuo Arima, *The Failure of Freedom: A Portrait of Modern Japanese Intellectuals* (1969), concludes that the failure of constitutional government in the 1930s was due at least in part to the failure of the dominant intellectuals to recognize it as a protector of their own intellectual freedom. A. Morgan Young, *Japan Under Taisho Tenno, 1912-1926* (1928), and *Imperial Japan, 1926-1938* (1938), though journalistic, are packed with valuable observations on Japanese politics and the social order. Hugh Byas, *Government by Assassination* (1942) is another valuable journalistic account. Scholarly studies of the social order underpinning politics are John F. Embree's, *Suye Mura; A Japanese Village* (1939),* and *The Japanese Nation, A Social Survey* (1945); and Andrew J. Grad, *Land and Peasant in Japan, An Introductory Survey* (1952). Individual chapters of the following touch on aspects of domestic politics and foreign relations: Chitoshi Yanaga, *Japan Since Perry* (1949); W. G. Beasley, *The Modern History of Japan* (1963);* and Nobuya Bamba, *Japanese Diplomacy in a Dilemma: New Light on Japan's China Policy, 1924-1929* (1973) contrasts the differing perceptions of Shidehara and Tanaka. On Japanese radicalism, see Henry D. Smith, II, *Japan's First Student Radicals* (1972), a history of the national student movement in the 1920s. Kawai Tatsuo, *The Goal of Japanese Expansion* (1938); Hyman Kublin, *Asian Revolutionary, The Life of Sen Katayama* (1964); George M. Beckman and Genji Okubo, *The Japanese Communist Party, 1922-1945* (1969). Peter Duus, "The Era of Party Rule: Japan, 1905-1932," *Modern East Asia: Essays in Interpretation*, James B. Crowley, ed. (1970),* 180-206.

China, 1916-1931: Warlords, the Kuomintang, and Nationalism

24

The China that emerged from the catastrophe of World War I was a paradox of indescribable chaos and of magnificent rebirth. From the death of Yuan Shih-k'ai in 1916 until 1931, China endured civil war, took the first steps toward unity under the revolutionary *Kuomintang,* and began to free herself from the semi-dependent status to which she had succumbed. A unique assortment of movements and personalities was to distinguish this perplexing story. There was the phantom warlord government at Peking, which was the only government recognized *de jure* by the foreign powers, 1916-1928. There was the insurgent Canton revolutionary government of Sun Yat-sen, which, under the *Kuomintang,* was to formalize China's new nationalism at Nanking after 1927. Between these two political forces and within each there were crusades of factionalism, duplicity, civil war, and massacre. And between all of these and the foreign powers there were intrigue and consipiracy in a battle for position, influence, and control in the China that would emerge.

AN ERA OF WARLORDISM

In an immediate sense, China's warlord era, 1916-1928, was traceable to Yuan Shih-k'ai's

ill-favored schemes. Under Yuan's leadership, local armies had been permitted to swell on the theory that China's military power was thereby enhanced. More realistic appraisals revealed that these military increments bolstered local leadership often in opposition to the central government, but this development was not immediately apparent. While Yuan lived, he presided over an uneasy coalition, balancing contending forces. Only with his death did Peking lose control and was the stage set for civil war. Thus, in stimulating militarism Yuan contributed to the chaos that followed his demise. Yet Yuan was himself the victim, not the author, of the deeper revolutionary forces attacking the central authority which until recently had been wielded by the Manchus. The Revolution of 1911 had dealt a death blow to the principle upon which central authority had been based, and for nearly two decades thereafter political authority rested, in the absence of other sanctions, primarily on local military power. Not until the *Kuomintang* devised a new program uniting the populace did government issue from something other than a gun.

While the warlords were alike as destroyers of political unity, they differed widely in ability, temperament, and ambition. Some entertained no purpose save enjoying whatever fortunes their powers accumulated, but others, though not qualifying for the title of revolutionary, were touched by nationalism and directed their efforts toward regeneration of their country. One such reforming warlord was Yen Hsi-shan, governor of Shansi, 1911-1930. Yen denounced the land-owning gentry for their "oppression" of the peasantry, reduced the authority of the gentry in the countryside, and introduced land reforms. He also established a school system with the aim of providing instruction in technology and science, as well as traditional subjects, and promoted modernization of agriculture. Moreover, he gave uncompromising support to the economic modernization of Shansi, irrespective of the cost in terms of traditional values and institutions. Significantly, these steps were not taken as part of any conscious effort to establish a new order in Shansi. Yen, who embraced many of the values of the Confucian gentry and aspired to membership in that class, regarded his actions as necessary to his retention of power. Nevertheless, Yen contributed to change. Whatever his motives, his actions in Shansi suggested that a new society might be built, one which was not Confucian.

Secure in his territorial base, Yen met political changes of the greatest magnitude. Like other warlords, he shifted allies as expediency dictated. Thus, in 1927-1928, unable to check the *Kuomintang's* northern progress, he joined party forces, assisted in the capture of Peking, and accepted a ministry in the *Kuomintang*-Nationalist government. A short time later, following the collapse of a coup directed against Chiang Kai-shek, Yen fled to Manchuria, only to return in 1932 to another alliance with *Kuomintang* leadership. When Japanese troops invaded northern China, Yen's troops joined the Communists in staging a joint defense, but these allies in turn became enemies at the end of World War II. Indeed, it was the Communists who finally ended Yen's political career in Shansi, sending him along with the rest of the *Kuomintang* into refuge on Taiwan.

What Yen's career suggests is that the warlords bequeathed no simple legacy. As independent (the *Kuomintang*-Nationalist government, except in the most nominal sense, never ruled in Yen's Shansi province) and sometimes brutal leaders, the warlords were scorned by nationalists intent upon ushering China into a new era.

It was much later before the more positive aspects of the reforming warlord regimes were recognized. In an era when Confucianism was destroyed and new values were sought, warlords such as Yen helped introduce some of China's masses to a more modern world.[1]

SOCIAL TRANSFORMATIONS

As noted earlier, World War I, by reducing the commercial and industrial role of the great Western powers in China, opened the way for an era of growth in Chinese-owned commerce and industry. The consequent increase in the Chinese industrial force (numbering between one and two million in the 1920s), and its concentration in industrial urban centers such as Shanghai, created socio-economic conditions which in turn nourished a new kind of social ferment fostering political agitation. Migration of sons and daughters to the cities as independent wage-earners eroded the self-contained, authoritarian family system. In a society where cheap labor was inexhaustible, the results were predictable: sweat shops, long hours, extreme exploitation of female and child labor, and wages low even by Chinese standards. All of these conditions produced China's first labor organizations, espousing a variety of so-called radical solutions in a China already beset by the political chaos of warlordism.

Meanwhile in rural China, a decided decline in the prestige and authority of the Confucian-oriented gentry marked a further general deterioration of the whole quality of Chinese life. Population increases, warlordism, and the growth of tenantry multiplied peasant miseries. In addition, the countryside was plagued by an ever growing number of landless peasants—illiterate, rootless, jobless, and, so, ready recruits for banditry, warlord armies, or mass coolie labor.

INTELLECTUAL FOUNDATIONS

Beneath the turmoil of warlordism and social

[1] See Donald G. Gillin, *Warlord: Yen Hsi-shan in Shansi Province, 1911-1949* (1966); James S. Sheridan, *Chinese Warlord: The Career of Feng Yu-hsiang* (1966)*; and Winston Hsieh, "The Ideas and Ideals of a Warlord: Ch'en Chiang-ming (1878-1933)," *Papers on China*, 16, published by the East Asian Research Center, Harvard University (1962), 198-252.

change there were real, if submerged, strivings toward a new order. The New Culture Movement continued the search for the intellectual underpinnings of a modern China. During the postwar years, young intellectuals no longer debated how Western civilization might be employed to save an ancient Chinese cultural heritage. The revolutionary view held that Confucianism was dead and that all its vestiges should be uprooted. It was China, not her culture, that must be saved. Thus, one-time radical leaders such as Yen Fu, an old-style scholar and pioneer translator of Western works, lost virtually all influence. Among the new leadership two trends were discernible. First, one group, in which Ch'en Tu-hsiu figured prominently, responded to disappointment over Western behavior by drawing closer to the ideas of Marx and Lenin. Ch'en and Li Ta-chao, the latter honored officially by the Chinese Communist Party as its founder, established Marxist study groups.[2] Some indication of the new leanings toward communism was the unprecedented welcome extended by Chinese intellectuals to the Soviet representative, Adolph Joffe, when he arrived in Peking in August, 1922. Second, Hu Shih, who had been one of the early leaders of the New Culture Movement, stood out among those continuing to support reform in accord with Western liberal traditions. In 1919, this group sponsored

a series of widely acclaimed lectures by the American philosopher John Dewey.[3]

In advancing their respective causes there were some points upon which Marxists and liberals agreed. Trends in Chinese thought during the 1920s underscored young China's acceptance of certain Western values, such as materialism and pragmatism. In 1923, to cite a single example, Ch'en Tu-hsiu and Hu Shih joined the defense against an attempt by Chang Chunmai (Carsun Chang) to substitute for materialism a metaphysical system derived from the intuitionism of Henri Bergson and the neo-Confucian School of the Mind. Similarly, most young literati could applaud Hu Shih's critical study of Confucianism (*Outline of the History of Chinese Philosophy*), which helped to destroy whatever prestige was retained by the classics, and could unite in denouncing the retention by foreign powers of the "unequal treaties." The really crucial differences dividing young intellectuals concerned the methods which were to be applied to the problems of Chinese life. Hu Shih was a spokesman for the view that looked toward evolutionary change and stressed individualism. Marxists, on the other hand, dismissed gradualism with the argument that only radical solutions would serve nationalist aims.

These intellectual strivings toward a New China found popular expression in a literature which built upon reforms of the World War I era. In the postwar years, Chinese writers moved beyond earlier attempts to invigorate the vernacular language as a vehicle for spreading Western ideas. Literature followed philosophy in seeking a unique synthesis of new concepts. Literary associations (more than one hundred between 1922 and 1925) sponsored journals reflecting a broad spectrum of opinion. Among young writers were a few concerned with aesthetics alone, but most, including such men as Lu Hsun, Kuo Mo-jo, and Mao Tun,

---

[2] Ch'en, not Li, was actually the first leader of the Chinese Communist Party, serving in that capacity from 1921 until his expulsion from the Party in 1927. Communist histories were later to revile him as a "traitorous revisionist." Li's importance in the party is suggested by his role in negotiating with Sun Yat-sen the coalition between the Communists and the *Kuomintang*. The subsequent reputations of the two men, however, owed less to their actual party roles than to their ideas. Ch'en regarded the total failure of Chinese traditions as a source of renewal and looked outside China for the basis of the new society. Li, on the other hand, looked to tradition as well as Marxism. Drawing upon his own rural background, Li saw in the peasantry the true spirit of China and the strength for its renaissance. In advancing these latter views, Li anticipated Mao Tse-tung, who in these early party years served as Li's assistant in the library of Peking University. For a study emphasizing Li's ideas see Maurice Meisner, *Li Ta-chao and the Origins of Chinese Marxism* (1967).*

[3] Dewey delivered thirty-two lectures at Peking National University alone. The schedule arranged by his followers kept Dewey in China for the better part of two years. John Dewey, *Lectures in China, 1919-1920,* trans. from the Chinese and ed. by Robert W. Clopton and Tsuin-chen Ou (1973).

were firmly aligned with the adage, "Art should reform life." On this assumption literature became an ever more self-conscious tool of social reform.[4]

Writers were not the only intermediaries between the intellectuals and masses. Following World War I, this role was assumed increasingly by students. The students' influence was traceable directly to the historic position of scholarship and the scholar in Old China. Many Chinese looked to the students for answers in the chaotic revolutionary years. The students, especially after the demonstrations of May 4, 1919, had shown their power and, in turn, had voiced their opinions with an air of authority. Since some considerable number of them had received a modern education in Japan, Europe, or America, and since in the turmoil of prevailing conditions many graduates could not find jobs which they considered commensurate with their training, they readily became active critics of government. So it was that a growing body of students became revolutionary agents. Among themselves, students did not agree on the details of the revolutionary blueprint, but from their continual, often clamorous, debates a consensus did emerge: China was to be unified, to be relieved of the "unequal treaties" which infringed her sovereignty, and to become the seat of a new civilization.

THE NEW *KOUMINTANG*

It was in these circumstances of warlord politics, of intellectual strivings for a new order,

and of student activism that the *Kuomintang,* China's first nationalist party, made its bid for power.[5] During World War I, it had been by no means certain that this party would emerge as an important factor in Chinese politics. After the *Kuomintang* members left the Peking government in 1917 and fled to southern ports, the party went into eclipse. South China, like the north, had its full quota of provincial warlord-governors who made alliances or fought each other for personal advantage under not the slightest control of the "government" in Peking. In this general confusion, Sun Yat-sen and his following made little immediate headway. The *Kuomintang* had no effective organization other than personal bonds of loyalty to Sun. It was filled with factionalism and diverse political creeds and, of course, had no army.

Nevertheless, these dark years created the beginning of a new era in party history. Since, in an age of warlordism, control of Peking offered no sure approach to power, Sun set about creating a military base in the south. A deal was struck with Yunnanese warlords whereby the latter would protect the *Kuomintang* in return for access to public revenues. This proved an unstable arrangement, lasting barely two years, but the alliance gave the *Kuomintang* time to look to its own defense.[6] Important, too, was the way Sun used the interval to link the *Kuomintang* with other revolutionary elements.

Just after World War I, Sun, giving heed to the nationwide student uprising protesting the Shantung settlement at Versailles, brought stu-

---

[4] Judged by standards of comparable Western literature, the quality of this Chinese writing was pitiful. Russian or Scandinavian works, through which Chinese authors sought inspiration, reached China through poor English or Japanese translations. It would be difficult to find in any of the journals of the 1920's a mature example of literary criticism. See Yi-tsi M. Feuerwerker, "Tradition and Experiment in Modern Chinese Literature," reprinted in *Modern China,* Albert Feuerwerker, ed. (1964),* 169-83; and Charlotte Furth, *Ting Wen-chiang: Science and China's New Culture* (1970). Chinese experiments with scientific ideas during these years reveal little about science but much about young China's search for an identity of its own. See D.W.Y. Kwok, *Scientism in Chinese Thought, 1900-1950* (1965); and Bonnie S. McDougall, *The Introduction of Western Literary Theories into Modern China, 1919-1925* (1971).*

[5] *Kuo* means country, *min* means people, and the combination *kuomin* means national (citizen) or, as an adjective, nationalist. *Tang* is Chinese for party. Thus *Kuomintang*—the (Chinese) Nationalist Party.

[6] Relations between the Yunnanese army and the *Kuomintang* were not severed by the collapse of the original alliance. The warlord army under several of its old officers was incorporated into the *Kuomintang's* Third National Revolutionary Army. This practice of incorporating old elements without assimilating them completely later served the *Kuomintang* in coming to terms with other warlords. It seemed that the *Kuomintang* was less successful in destroying warlordism than in modifying a system which remained decentralized and militaristic. See Donald S. Sutton, "The Kuomintang and Warlordism: The Yunnanese Army in Kwantung, 1923-1925," Paper presented at the annual convention of the Association for Asian Studies, Philadelphia, March, 1968 (in manuscript).

dent leaders into the party, thereby bringing to the movement a younger element ripe for revolution. Then, in 1922, Sun, whose appeals to the Western democracies for aid against the Peking warlords had gone unanswered, met Adolph Joffe, who had been sent by Moscow to cultivate both the Peking regime and the *Kuomintang*. By the following January, Sun and Joffe had reached an agreement. Sun declared that neither communism nor the Soviet system was suitable for China, while Joffe, concurring in this view, assured Sun of Russian sympathy and support in the achievement of China's most pressing needs—national unification and full independence. The Chinese Communist Party, which had been founded in Shanghai during the summer of 1921, pledged support to the *Kuomintang,* and Communists as individuals were permitted to join Sun's forces.

The considerations which prompted this alliance are noteworthy. Both sides saw advantages for themselves. The Comintern, based in

Chiang Kai-shek in the 1920s.

Moscow, had picked China as the chief area of activity for the years after 1922. In extending aid to Sun, the objective of the Comintern was to help the Chinese Communist Party establish itself within the *Kuomintang* and eventually to control it. Sun explained his side of the deal by saying simply that he had to seek help where he could get it. While not subscribing to communism, Sun, especially as the alliance ripened, recognized fully the usefulness of communist methods. The apparent similarity of the communist vision of society and his own principle of "people's livelihood," as well as a mutual antipathy to imperialism, permitted Sun to believe that the two parties could cooperate. Nor was he concerned that the Chinese Communists might ultimately dominate the *Kuomintang*. The Chinese Communists, Sun believed, were just "youngsters," only some 300 in number in 1922, (as compared to his own following of 150,000), whom the Soviets would disavow if necessary in order to maintain its relationship with the *Kuomintang*.

While Sun was overly optimistic about his ability to handle the Communists, he had discovered in the student movement and in proffered Russian aid the means for revitalizing his following. Within two years the *Kuomintang*, theoretically, was a totalitarian party in structure and discipline, though its doctrine had not become communist. Much of this radical reorganization was the work of communist advisers from Moscow, headed by Michael Borodin, a revolutionary of international repute. Simultaneously, the *Kuomintang* set about organzing a party army, the officer corp of which was trained at the newly-founded Whampoa military academy, under the command of a young officer just returned from observing the Red Army at Moscow. His name was Chiang Kai-shek. Moreover, Sun, in a series of lectures which he delivered to party officials in 1924, enunciated in its most developed form a basic manifesto that set the frame for future party and government relations. Called the *San min chu-i*, the Three Principles of the People, this manifesto contained ideas that had been basic with Sun since before 1905 (see Chapter 17), but it was not until these ideas were modified and expressed in the context of the postwar years that they became powerful weapons of propaganda.

Sun's first principle was *Min-tsu chu-i*, meaning "people's nationhood" or "Nationalism." In its original form this principle held simply that the Manchus, an alien dynasty, be ousted. Events since 1911, however, had demonstrated that this was not enough to make China a nation. The people remained—in Sun's words— a "sheet of loose sand," lacking solidarity. Thus in its revised form the principle of nationalism embodied the idea of a unity embracing Chinese, Manchus, Mongols, Tibetans, and various minorities. With respect to the principle's internal implications, Sun did not spell out clearly the program for unification, because here he faced problems of extreme delicacy. Unification involved not only patriotism to the state but also the problem of determining what kind of a state. Was it to be a state in which the Chinese, as the overwhelming majority, were to have a corresponding ascendancy over such people as the Mongols? Or was it to be a federated state in which the Mongols and Tibetans were to have the standing of majorities within their own territories? A number of Mongol-*Kuomintang* followers of Sun believed that the eventual outcome would be a federated state, but for Sun, by 1924, it was extraordinarily difficult to make a decision. Open advocacy of a federated system, in view of China's weakness at the time, might expose the frontier people to annexation or near annexation by foreign powers.

If, however, it was difficult for Sun to resolve the internal character of nationalism, there was no such problem externally. Stung by the way the West had spurned his party, 1919-1924, Sun viewed China's lack of national solidarity as stemming in large measure from the legacy of foreign domination. In consequence, his first principle was frankly anti-imperialistic. While Sun had once represented the vanguard of a nationalism inspired by the West, he now deprecated the West and sought in Chinese traditionalism a basis for his new nationalism.

Min-ch'uan chu-i, translated as "people's power" or "democracy," was Sun's second principle. In 1905 Sun proclaimed his support of democracy mainly by attacking advocates of

a constitutional monarchy as proponents of "absolutism." By 1924 he was more explicit about what the term meant. His ideas on democracy were derived from four principal sources: (1) Western republicanism; (2) the Swiss doctrine of initiative, referendum, election, and recall; (3) Soviet democratic centralism; and (4) Chinese ideas of examination and control. The result was a plan of government which he believed would insure popular control through electoral processes, yet give a strong executive wide powers to deal with the business of government. In operation the plan was to rest on the division of men in Confucian fashion into first-, second- and third-class citizens. These would be, respectively: (1) the leaders, who could understand the past and thus guide men into the future (a Confucian idea); (2) those who could interpret the leaders to the masses; and (3) the rank and file, bereft of understanding but able to say whether they liked what they got. Political power was to be exercised through five branches: three of these—executive, legislative, and judicial—are familiar to students of American government, while the remaining divisions—"examination" and "control"—were based on models provided by Chinese history. Training for the exercise of political power would be given to the people by the *Kuomintang* during the period of tutelage that was to follow immediately the military reunification.

The third principle was called *Min-sheng chu-i* or "people's livelihood," a phrase used to embrace a number of social and economic theories which had attracted Sun's attention. Often Sun and his followers used *Min-sheng* as an equivalent for socialism, drawing upon the popularity of this idea, but Sun rejected Marxism's basic tenets. Drawing upon a work little known in the West, *The Social Interpretation of History* by a Brooklyn dentist, Maurice Williams, Sun refuted the theories of class struggle and economic determinism. More important to Sun were the single tax ideas of Henry George. While Sun never developed a precise economic program, he appears to have envisaged a tax on the unearned increment of land as the means for equalizing land tenure, eliminating inequality in wealth, and providing capital for the expansion of production. To promote China's industrial development, Sun stressed the recovery of tariff autonomy and erection of protective tariffs. Sun's recommendations for agriculture were confined mainly to the need for technological improvement.[7]

THE PASSING OF SUN YAT-SEN

While his new *Kuomintang* was acquiring a new power, Sun still hoped for the peaceful unification of China through an acceptable agreement with Peking. Late in 1924 the prospect seemed hopeful. The warlord president at Peking, Ts'ao K'un, had been driven from office and his place as provisional chief executive taken by Tuan Ch'i-jui. Accordingly, Sun went to Peking seeking a basis for settlement. There in March, 1925, he died, calling on his followers to carry on the revolution.

The passing of Sun Yat-sen had disrupting effects, all of which were not apparent immediately, upon the nationalist movement and upon the fortunes of the *Kuomintang*. So long as Sun lived, his shortcomings had been obvious not only to many of his immediate followers but also to his enemies. Now that he was gone the failures of the man whom many had regarded as a visionary were forgotten. Sun became the embodiment of all the idealism within the nationalist movement, and the personification of all the revolutionary fervor of the reconstituted *Kuomintang*. As Confucius had become the sage of ancient China, so would Sun Yat-sen inherit the role in twentieth-century China. Confucianism would give place to Sun Yatsenism. Yet, since no single leader had emerged to take Sun's place, rivalry among his immediate associates was a natural consequence of his death—a rivalry that tended to rest its case on divergent interpretations of Sun's political and economic philosophy. Here there was ample ground for ideological warfare and party strife because of the vague, general, and uncertain

terms in which Sun had so frequently expressed his ideas.[8]

For the time being, however, unity, as the price of military victory, kept factionalism within bounds. The Canton government was declared formally to be the *Kuomintang*-Nationalist government. It was a committee administration with Wang Ching-wei, generally considered to be of the left, as chairman. This leftist orientation was unsuccessfully challenged in November, 1925, when a group of rightist leaders, professing to hold a session of the central executive committee of the party in the Western Hills at Peking, passed resolutions denouncing the leftists and expelling the Communists. At the second national congress of the *Kuomintang,* January, 1926, the sacredness of Sun's teachings, the soundness of the Russian

---

[7] Key Ray Chong, "Cheng Kuan-ying (1841–1920): A Source of Sun Yat-sen's Nationalist Ideology?" *Journal of Asian Studies,* 28 (1969), 247-67; and Stephen Uhalley, Jr. "Sun Yat-sen and Chinese History," *Journal of the Hong Kong Branch of the Royal Asiatic Society,* 8 (1968), 109–18, should be read along with the articles cited in Chapter 17.

[8] The sources of these intense factional quarrels remain a matter of dispute. Official *Kuomintang* interpretations attribute the trouble to communist plots. Communist versions maintain that Michael Borodin, whom the *Kuomintang* claims was behind the intrigue, did not have much influence in party affairs and that factionalism arose from efforts of "feudal" elements, the bourgeoisie, and imperialist representatives to bolster Chiang Kai-shek. Both of these explanations, however, in keeping with the common tendency of all Chinese to venerate Sun Yat-sen, ignore the roots of factionalism before 1925. Both the *T'ung Meng-hui* and later the early *Kuomintang* suffered from extreme factionalism throughout their histories; indeed, Sun's role in these parties was for a time that of a factional leader. When his leadership was no longer disputed, Sun did not purge the party of dissidents, but rather operated through persuasion and compromise, balancing forces to keep the party intact. While Sun lived, the *Kuomintang* elite, who were linked with their chief through personal ties and who conceded his sole authority, held their own rivalries in check. With Sun's death, restraints were removed and deeply ingrained rivalries emerged. In this perspective, intraparty battles assume the appearance less of ideological rivalries than of a search for a leader whose relationship with various elements would impart new unity. The difficulties presented by the search are suggested by Wang Ching-wei's observation that the *Tsung-li* (Sun's title as party leader) was not an office but a person. James R. Shirley, "Control of the *Kuomintang* after Sun Yat-sen's Death," *Journal of Asian Studies* 25 (1965), 69-82; and George T. Yu, *Party Politics in Republican China: The* Kuomintang, *1912-1914* (1966) suggest that Western-style parties contained no magic solution for Chinese problems.

orientation, and the purpose to carry the revolution to the people were all affirmed. The Western Hills group was expelled and more Communists joined the party. Meanwhile, *Kuomintang* forces had crushed all military opposition from the Kwangtung and Kwangsi warlords.

With this added security in its southern base, the *Kuomintang* proposed to move to the military unification of all China. For many reasons the decision was regarded as dubious. Neither the military nor the political position of the Canton regime was strong. The surface unity in the *Kuomintang* did not reflect the factional bitterness beneath. Nevertheless, the military counsel of Chiang Kai-shek, commander of the armies, prevailed. Within three months *Kuomintang*-Nationalist armies were on the Yangtze. The Canton-based government was moved, January, 1927, to the sister cities

of Hankow, Hanyang, and Wuchang, where it became known as the Wuhan Regime. Here the growing conflict between Nationalists and Communists came in view. While Wuhan demonstrators (Communists and *Kuomintang* leftists) attacked foreign concessions at central Yangtze cities and demanded a socialist revolution, Chiang Kai-shek and *Kuomintang* conservatives formed their own government at Nanking, April, 1927, from where they launched widespread attacks on Communists and leftists in the lower Yangtze.[9] Simultaneously, seized documents exposed Russian ambitions in China. Chang Tso-lin, the Manchurian warlord then heading the Peking government, raided the Soviet offices there. Other disclosures came from the Wuhan Regime, which finally expelled its Russian advisers, dissolved itself, reappeared briefly in Canton, and then was reunited with Nanking. On top of these developments the northern march of the *Kuomintang* continued. Some northern warlords, Feng Yu-hsiang, the Christian General, and Yen Hsi-shan, the Model Governor, joined the Nationalist cause. Chang Tso-lin retreated from Peking to Manchuria, where he was slain by the Kwantung (Japanese) army, but his son Chang Hsueh-liang, the Young Marshal, raised the Nationalist flag at Mukden, December, 1928. No southern *Kuomintang* soldier entered Manchuria, but the Republic of China at Peking was dead. The *Kuomintang* had won the war of unification.

CHINA'S REVOLUTION AND THE FOREIGN POWERS

The perplexing course of China's internal revo-

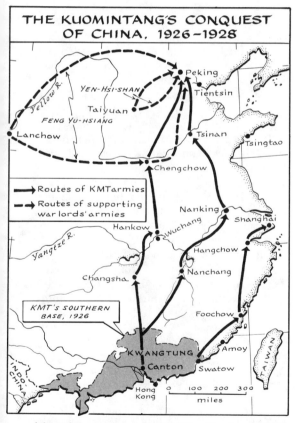

THE KUOMINTANG'S CONQUEST OF CHINA, 1926-1928

→ Routes of KMT armies
-→ Routes of supporting war lords' armies

KMT'S SOUTHERN BASE, 1926

Adapted from Immanuel C.Y. Hsü, *The Rise of Modern China* (1970), p. 660.

[9] The split with the Communists marked a decided shift in Chiang's political orientation. Chiang was initially an advocate of the left-wing, but his relations with Communists cooled notably after 1925. Both Chiang and the Communists at first were inclined to conceal their differences. When the rivalry broke into the open, an unprincipled struggle for power ensued. Seeking to deny the Communists control of Shanghai, for example, Chiang resorted to deals with the city's extensive underworld, whose forces surprised and defeated Communists forces. For aspects of this struggle see Wu Tien-wei: "Chiang Kai-shek's March Twentieth Coup d'Etat of 1926," *Journal of Asian Studies*, 27 (1968), 585-602; and "A Review of the Wuhan Debacle: The *Kuomintang*-Communist Split of 1927," *ibid.*, 29 (1969), 125-43.

lution had been watched with anticipation and fear by the West and Japan. Would this revolution produce a stable China that would take its place within the international political and legal community of the Western powers? The protestations of Chinese spokesmen at Paris (1919) and Washington (1922) implied that this would be so. Yet there were also dire forebodings of trouble. Both the May Fourth and New Culture Movements had directly challenged the unequal treaty system dating back to 1842, the foreign concessions and settlements, naval leaseholds, spheres of influence, and, in fact, the entire structure of foreign position and influence through which China had sunk to a semicolonial position. It was not Sun Yat-sen and *Kuomintang* followers alone who inveighed against imperialism. Even the warlord government in Peking could not resist the popular pressure demanding revision or abolition of "unequal treaties."

Peking's delegates at the Washington conference on the limitation of armaments had sought extensive revision of China's treaty structure. The powers, of course, united against these demands, agreeing only to certain steps toward the ultimate relinquishment of their privileges. Subsequently, the actions taken at Washington did lead to partial satisfaction of Peking's aims. Before 1922 nearly one hundred foreign post offices operating on Chinese soil were closed.[10] In the same year Japan withdrew her troops from Siberia and the Allied and Associated Powers terminated their control of the Chinese Eastern Railway. Finally, Japan executed her pledge to transfer to China the title to Germany's former "special interests" in Shantung.

These developments, however, were balanced by Peking's unsuccessful efforts in 1923 to reopen with Tokyo the question of the termination of the Sino-Japanese treaties and notes of May, 1915. Nor was Peking much

more successful in concluding other desired agreements. During the Washington conference, the British had agreed to surrender Wei-hai-wei as a means of facilitating a Sino-Japanese settlement on Shantung. Negotiations were conducted to this end by an Anglo-Chinese commission, but complete agreement was not reached until April, 1930. Difficulties between the Peking government and France over repayment of the Boxer indemnity delayed until 1925 the implementation of agreements reached at Washington to raise China's tariff to an effective 5 percent *ad valorem* level, to return to China the Kwangchow leasehold, and to establish a commission to consider abolition of extraterritoriality. Further disappointment to Chinese nationalists derived from the failure of the commission on extraterritoriality to set a date for the termination of foreign jurisdiction in China. The commission recommended only that the powers cooperate in the progressive modification of their extraterritorial rights. National frustration engendered by this report was not relieved by the recommendations of the tariff conference (convened in Peking, October, 1925) that China should not be accorded tariff autonomy until January 1, 1929. Chinese sentiment had been demanding immediate abolition of the conventional tariff along with all other "unequal treaties." As a result, Peking became increasingly aggressive in its efforts to revise China's treaty structure, but with only minor success.[11] When the *Kuomintang* came to power in 1927, the "unequal treaties" were part of its inheritance.

Although it was not evident at the time, the foregoing diplomacy profoundly affected China's revolutionary course. The treaty powers' continued recognition of the warlords in Peking, their tendency to be tied to protocol and to let treaty revision drift, and their steadfast refusal to deal with Sun Yat-sen all served to increase popular resentment against imperialism. Moreover, this Western diplomatic record played directly into the hands of the

---

[10] The exact numbers were: Great Britain, 12; Japan, 66; France, 13; and the United States, 1. The powers were permitted to maintain post offices in leased territories "or as otherwise specifically provided by treaty." Under this provision the Japanese continued to maintain post offices in the zone of the South Manchurian Railway.

[11] A treaty between Austria and China, October 19, 1925, confirmed the war-time ending of Austria's extraterritorial rights. On October 26, 1926, China and Finland negotiated a treaty as equals.

Soviet Union. In contrast with the half-hearted efforts of the West and Japan to effect treaty revision, the Soviet Union approached China simultaneously through open diplomacy and revolutionary subversion. Prior to the expulsion of Soviet advisers from Wuhan in 1927, the Soviet Union maintained contact not only with the *Kuomintang* but also with the young Communist Party, with the Republic in Peking, and with semi-independent Manchuria.

SOVIET POLICY AND THE CHINESE REVOLUTION

Soviet Russian policy toward China had begun to unfold in 1918 with the Karakhan declaration, which appeared to concede China's political rights in the Chinese Eastern Railway zone while reserving Russia's financial and economic interests. Later, in 1920, the Russians went further, declaring treaties concluded with China by former Russian governments null and void. Then, in 1922, Adolph Joffe arrived in Peking seeking to re-establish diplomatic relations, to get Peking's approval of the new "independent" People's Revolutionary Government which the Russians had set up in Outer Mongolia in 1920, and to regain a position of influence in the Chinese Eastern Railway. Unsuccessful initially in Peking, Joffe went on to Shanghai to meet Sun Yat-sen. The result of that meeting was the immediate and remarkable growth of Soviet influence in the new *Kuomintang*. Furthermore, during the course of these first contacts with China, Soviet representatives in touch with Ch'en Tu-hsiu and other Marxists were helping to establish Communist party apparatus.

These Soviet gestures to Chinese national feelings served the interests of Russia rather than China. With Japan's withdrawal from Siberia (1922), the way had been cleared for the adherence to the Soviet Union of the eastern Siberian regime known as the Far Eastern Republic. Accordingly, Peking was in no position to rebuff further Russian overtures presented by L.M. Karakhan, September, 1923. A treaty signed by Wellington Koo and Karakhan, May 31, 1924, provided for resumption of formal relations, surrender by Russia of extraterritorial rights and of concessions at Hankow and Tientsin, restoration of Russian legations

and consulates and property of the Orthodox Church, Russian recognition of China's suzerainty in Outer Mongolia, and withdrawal of Russian troops. In addition, Russia recognized Chinese sovereignty in the Chinese Eastern Railway zone and agreed that China might redeem the line "with Chinese capital" in return for Chinese pledges that the future disposition of the line would be determined by China and Russia to the exclusion of third parties, and that management of the road would be a joint Russo-Chinese concern. Since the Chinese Eastern Railway lay in the Manchurian territories actually controlled by the warlord Chang Tso-lin, a similar agreement was negotiated (September 20, 1924) with the Manchurian leader. In effect, as a result of hard bargaining, Moscow had reclaimed much of the tsarist position in Northeast Asia.

These Russian diplomatic victories in northern China coincided with outbreaks of antiforeign violence in the south at Shanghai and Canton. On May 30, 1925, a Chinese crowd in the Shanghai International Settlement, aroused by student agitators, denouncing the killing of a Chinese in a Japanese-owned cotton mill, was fired upon by Indian and Chinese constables. The order to fire, given by a police inspector of British nationality, resulted in the death of eight demonstrators. Chinese anger at this "inexcusable outrage" took the form of a general strike supported by virtually all sections of the populace. Business in Shanghai was at a standstill and remained so during most of the summer. Meanwhile, another shooting incident, June 23, 1925, involving Anglo-French troops and cadets from the *Kuomintang's* Whampoa academy, resulted in the death of fifty-two Chinese in Canton and a strike that crippled Hong Kong for fifteen months.[12] Both the Communists and the *Kuomintang* profited directly from these unhappy events. Communist party membership increased from 1,000 in 1925 to 58,000 in 1927. Moreover, both incidents intensified national feeling and imparted a new confidence to the *Kuomintang* and its armies as the northern march began.

[12] See the study by Lennox A. Mills, *British Rule in Eastern Asia* (1942). Popular antiforeign outbreaks, boycotts, etc., were not entirely spontaneous. There was often organized intimidation of the populace.

THE *KUOMINTANG* AND THE POWERS

These manifestations of an aroused Chinese nationalism forced the powers by 1926 to deal with the Canton-based *Kuomintang* regime. A general strike of industrial labor in the Wuhan cities called in November was followed by mass demonstrations in an anti-British crusade. The agitation was so effective that the British government proposed that the Washington Conference treaty powers: (1) legalize what Canton was already doing by agreeing to immediate collection of the "Washington surtaxes" (see p. 313); (2) recognize and deal with regional governments; (3) implement a grant of tariff autonomy immediately upon China's promulgation of a national tariff; and (4) seek to develop better relations with China even while no national government existed. Britain's gesture of concession, far from satisfying the Nationalists, spurred them to new outbursts of fury. The British policy was described as a design to weaken China by creating regional governments and by encouraging militarists to seize the ports and to profit by collection of the proposed surtaxes.

Before the powers could reply to the British proposal, the anti-British crusade on the upper Yangtze had been carried still further. During the first week of January, 1927, under the threat of mob violence, the British abandoned their concessions in Hankow and Kiukiang. Both concessions were immediately taken over for administrative purposes by the Chinese. Likewise, without waiting for action by the powers, whatever Chinese groups happened to be in control of the treaty ports applied the surtaxes without further ado. This developing situation brought forth hurried assurances from the Japanese and the American governments expressing sympathy with China's "just aspirations" and indicating willingness to aid their attainment in an orderly fashion. In the light of this rising tide of nationalism, Great Britain, already disposed to find a new basis for her relations with China, concluded agreements with the Nationalists during February and March, 1927, handing over the Hankow and Kiukiang concessions.

Almost immediately following these agreements, Britain's policy of conciliation faced new trials at Nanking late in March. No sooner had the old southern capital been captured by the Nationalists than it became the scene of violent and seemingly premeditated attacks by *Kuomintang* troops upon foreign persons and property. Three British, one French, one American, and one Italian national were killed, and a number of Japanese subjects were wounded or subjected to outrageous but less fatal treatment. Foreign property was looted. Nor was there an end to these doings of the *Kuomintang* soldiery until British and American gunboats laid a protective barrage about the properties of the Standard Oil Company, where surviving foreigners had taken refuge. The United States, England, France, Italy, and Japan demanded (April 11) an apology, reparations, and guarantees for the future. China's reply was evasive, but despite this the powers did not press for an immediate settlement. To have done so would have strengthened the radical wing of the *Kuomintang*-Soviet leaders at Hankow. Actually, the powers were hoping for the success of a new, conservative, and non-Soviet national regime at Nanking.

NANKING'S NEW TREATY RELATIONS

With the ousting of the old Peking regime, June, 1928, the *Kuomintang*-Nationalist Government at Nanking promptly took over the conduct of China's foreign relations. It issued a declaration calling for new treaties negotiated with full regard to the sovereignty and equality of states. Although this declaration was by no means welcome to the powers, they were nevertheless disposed to negotiate. Indeed, there was no alternative unless they proposed to use force to impose the old treaties. Moreover, China's break with Russia and the new conservative orientation of the *Kuomintang* were pleasing to foreign business groups and, in the main, to their governments.

The United States was the first power to act. By a treaty concluded at Peking on July 25, 1928, it conceded tariff autonomy to China, subject to most-favored-nation treatment. The agreement was one of the most significant in China's recent foreign relations, for it shattered the old international bloc long opposed to any concessions. The tariff agreement with the United States was followed before the end of 1928 by similar agreements with other powers. Indeed, by January, 1929, Japan was the only power that had not concluded a new tariff agreement. This situation was due to a number of questions outstanding between the two countries. Not until Japanese troops had retired from Shantung and China had agreed to revenue allotments for the security of certain Japanese loans was an agreement reached (May 6, 1930).

Meanwhile, new Chinese tariff treaties with Belgium, Denmark, Italy, Portugal, and Spain contained provisions for abolition of extraterritoriality, subject to a similar concession by all the powers. Accordingly, on April 27, 1929, Nanking adressed the United States, Great Britain, and France requesting abolition at the earliest possible date. Similar notes went to Brazil, the Netherlands, and Norway. The replies of Britain, France, and the United States (August 10) were an emphatic denial that China was as yet entitled to full jurisdictional sovereignty. While complimenting China on the progress she had made, they noted that the recommendations of the commission on extraterritoriality had not been carried out. In September, 1929, China protested this attitude both directly to the powers and in the Assembly of the League of Nations. In December, Nanking went a step further, announcing the unilateral ending of extraterritoriality as of January 1, 1930, but softening the blow with the assurance that China would negotiate with powers willing to do so.

By 1931, in addition to terminating the treaty tariff and opening negotiations looking to the end of extraterritoriality, the *Kuomintang*-Nationalist government could claim other successes in whittling away foreign privileges: the Shanghai Municipal Council and Mixed Court, long the exclusive preserve of foreigners, had been given a Chinese voice; Nanking had issued new law codes and secured new treaties placing some foreign nationals under Chinese jurisdiction; Chinese control had been established over the Maritime Customs Administration, the Salt Revenue Administration, and the Post Office; and foreign concession areas had been reduced from thirty-three to thirteen.

These achievements of the Nanking government's early years, 1927-1930, seemed to promise that China was finding a new, matured stability; that the day of the warlord was gone; that the Russian bid for control had failed; that the unequal treaty system would be ended by force plus diplomacy; and, finally, that Sun Yat-sen's program for a new China was assured.

FOR FURTHER READING

Development of Nationalism. Nathaniel Peffer, *The Far East: A Modern History* (1958),* perceptive chapters on China in the 1920s. Teng Ssu-yu and Jeremy Ingals, eds. and trans., *The Political History of China, 1840-1928* (1956),* a Chinese account of the national movement. Franklin W. Houn, *Central Government of China, 1912-1928: An Institutional Study* (1957), an excellent account of China's struggle for constitutional government, but the conclusion that the collapse of constitutionalism inclined the country toward communism is debatable. Milton J.T. Shieh, *The Kuomintang: Selected Historical Documents, 1894-1969* (1970),* a semi-official history designed to correct the "misconceptions" about the party; Jean Chesneaux, *The Chinese Labor Movement, 1919-1927* (1968); and *Popular Movements and Secret Societies in China, 1840-1950* (1972), important opening references on the social basis of revolution. Intellectual currents are assessed in Chester C. Tan, *Chinese Political Thought in the Twentieth Century* (1971),* which is best for its concise introduction to non-Communist theorists; Donald J. Munro, "Humanism in Modern China," in *'Nothing Conceded': Essays in Honor of Liu Yu-yun,* Frederic Wakeman, ed. (1970), focuses on Fung Yu-lan and Hsiung Shih-yun; Laurence A. Schneider, *Ku Chieh-kang and China's New History: Nationalism and the Quest for Alternative Traditions* (1971), a difficult but rewarding study of a Chinese intellectual's effort to base a revolutionary creed on tradition. Huang Sung-k'ang, *Lu Hsun and the New Culture Movement* (1957), an excellent highly condensed outline of the intellectual revolution as it applied to the modernization of literature, 1917-1930. Amitendranath Tagore, *Literary Debates in Modern China, 1918-1937* (1967) focuses on the controversies between the right and left. William Theodore de Bary and others, eds., *Sources of Chinese Tradition* (1960),* two chapters—"The Nationalist Revolution" and "The New Culture Movement"—in which pertinent documents and editorial comment are combined. The student movement is surveyed in Chiang Wen-han, *The Chinese Student Movement* (1948).

Rise of the *Kuomintang.* On Sun Yat-sen see: Harold Z. Schiffrin, "The Enigma of Sun Yat-sen," *China in Revolution: The First Phase, 1900-1913.* Mary C. Wright, ed. (1968).* P.M. A. Linebarger, *The Political Doctrines of Sun Yat-sen: An Exposition of the San Min Chu I* (1937). Lyon Sharman, *Sun Yat-sen: His Life and Its Meaning* (1934; reprinted, 1965),* a full length critical biography; Stephen Chen and Robert Payne, *Sun Yat-sen: A Portrait* (1946), a briefer but suggestive study. Early biographies of Chiang Kai-shek include: Chen Tsung-hsi and others, *General Chiang Kai-shek, the Builder of New China* (1929); H. K. Tong, *Chiang Kai-shek* (2 vols., 1937); T'ang Leang-li, *Wang Ching-wei* (1931) is by an associate of the subject. P. M. A. Linebarger, *Government in Republican China* (1938), an able and sympathetic account of the National Government's philosophy and structure. On the *Kuomintang's* program see also Sun Yat-sen, *The International Development of China* (1941). For data and interpretations of the period of Soviet orientation see: two studies by David J. Dallin, *The Rise of Russia in Asia* (1949), and *Soviet Russia and the Far East* (1948), which are based on Chinese as well as Russian sources, and exhibit shrewd insights into Soviet thinking. Allen S. Whiting, *Soviet Policies in China, 1917-1924* (1954),* a major work of scholarship. Conrad Brandt, *Stalin's Failure in China, 1924-1927*

(1958),* a standard reference for understanding the initial Soviet failure in the Chinese revolution. C. Martin Wilbur and Julie Lien-ying How, eds., *Documents on Communism, Nationalism, and Soviet Advisers in China, 1918-1927: Papers Seized in the 1927 Peking Raid* (1956) reveals Communist tactics and intra-party rivalries. T'ang Leang-li, *The Inner History of the Chinese Revolution* (1930) gives a favorable interpretation of the rise of the *Kuomintang* and a justification of both the Soviet orientation and its later repudiation. Leng Shao Chuan and Norman Palmer, *Sun Yat-sen and Communism* (1960) shows how the Western failure to assess correctly Chinese nationalism inclined Sun toward the Soviet. Xenia J. Eudin and Robert C. North, eds., *Soviet Russia and the East, 1920-1927* (1957) includes documents pertaining to China. Xenia J. Eudin and Robert C. North, *M. N. Roy's Mission to China, the Communist-Kuomintang Split of 1927* (1963). Howard L. Boorman and Richard C. Howard, eds., *Biographical Dictionary of Republican China,* (4 vols., 1967-1971).

China and the Powers. Wesley R. Fishel, *The End of Extraterritoriality in China* (1952), a detailed historical study. See also S. F. Wright, *China's Struggle for Tariff Autonomy, 1843-1938* (1938). For the special role of the United States see Dorothy Borg, *American Policy and the Chinese Revolution, 1925-1928* (1947); and Nemai Sadhan Bose, *American Attitude and Policy to the Nationalist Movement in China, 1911-1921* (1970). Marius B. Jansen, *The Japanese and Sun Yat-sen* (1954),* an important study. In addition to the studies of Sino-Soviet relations listed above note Peter S. H. Tang, *Russian and Soviet Policy in Manchuria and Outer Mongolia* (1959).

A Decade of Kuomintang-National Rule, 1928–1937

25

The task of nation-building which confronted the *Kuomintang*-Nationalist government in 1928 was without precedent in China's modern history. Until 1911 a predominantly agrarian China had been ruled by a Confucian monarchy and government deriving its sanctions from custom and tradition. It was a system based primarily on ideology and culture rather than on law and politics. It had enjoyed a magnificent success. It had made China into the Middle Kingdom, the center of a world order, as the Chinese liked to consider it. Now, in the early twentieth century, the system had met with disaster. The impact of the West had destroyed the Chinese world order and with it the Confucian monarchy and its edifice of Confucian government. The tragedy was that China had not yet found an adequate substitute to take its place. In 1911 the Wuhan revolt appeared to open the way to fill this vacuum with what was called a republic; but while this republic had constitutions, codes of law, and parliaments, it did not have a body of citizens who understood these things or a leadership that could make them function. The outcome, therefore, was

the brief rule of Yuan Shih-k'ai and the subsequent fiasco of the warlords.

Thus, in 1928 the tasks confronting the *Kuomintang* and its newly-established national government at Nanking were of immense proportions. In a sense the problem was twofold. First, if the Nationalist government was to be national in anything more than name, it must find the immediate means by which its rule and authority would be felt throughout China—certainly no mean undertaking. Second, and in the longer view, it must devise a program in political education whereby Sun Yat-sen's revolutionary creed—nationalism, democracy, and livelihood—could be made the living, working, political and social philosophy of 400 million people, most of whom had not the slightest understanding of these doctrines.

From the beginning of the *Kuomintang*-Nationalist era, the history of the nation-building effort was a compound of three ingredients, each amazingly complex in itself. The first was the character of the *Kuomintang* and of the national government which it created and controlled. The second was the nature of the opposition to the *Kuomintang* within China. The third was the obstruction of China's revolution from the outside, principally though not exclusively by Japan.

THE NATIONAL GOVERNMENT AND THE *KUOMINTANG*

The *Kuomintang*-Nationalist government that ruled over much of China from 1928 until 1949 was the first which attempted to administer China as though it were a Western nation-state. The government's structure was established under the First Organic Law of 1928. Under this instrument, power was concentrated at the top and was exercised through five *yuan* (departments or divisions) rather than the three—legislative, executive, and judicial—common to Western governments. Of these five, the executive *yuan* was in a sense the cabinet. The legislative *yuan,* a body of eighty-eight members, was neither a parliament nor a legislature as those terms are understood in the West. Basically its function was the researching and drafting of legislation. Justice was administered through the judicial *yuan,* while the examination *yuan* was concerned with applying the merit system to all government officials, excepting those top political positions. Finally, the control *yuan* suggested the censorate of Old China. Its function was to denounce (in the legal sense, bring suit against) irresponsible officials. Presiding over this structure until his death in 1943 was President Lin Sen, a scholar and follower of Sun Yat-sen.

The First Organic Law provided for extensive presidential powers, but in 1931 the promulgation of the provisional constitution shifted authority to the executive *yuan.* Meanwhile, the single party rule of the *Kuomintang* from 1928 onward meant that policy decisions belonged to top leaders of the party, men who at times might also hold top offices in the government. In a word, the national government was the creation and the creature of the *Kuomintang.*

This intimate relationship of the national government and *Kuomintang* did not result in

the new regime's achieving a singleness of thought and purpose. While the *Kuomintang* had no rivals within the government, the party itself became divided after achieving power. This was partly due to the loss of Sun Yat-sen, whose personality had served as a powerful unifying force. Gone, too, was the compulsion toward unity which had developed out of the requirements of the northern expedition, 1925-1927. But beyond these considerations was the fact that *Kuomintang* membership became exceedingly diverse after the party came to power. Among the members the most active were college and middle school graduates, who were employed as party workers, civil servants, teachers, and editors. In time, further important categories of membership included small shopkeepers, factory workers, and postal and railway employees. The interests of this membership, which in the 1930's may have totaled more than two million (exclusive of armed forces), were by no means identical. As a result, some members, frightened by Communist activities, pushed the party toward the right, to the delight of every opponent of Sun and his revolution. Simultaneously, the *Kuomintang* was also pulled toward the left by others inspired by the revolutionary program that had brought the party into being and by the obvious needs for agrarian and labor reforms. Finally, party harmony was taxed by sharp rivalries in its leadership. These rivalries, however, did not shatter party organization. That structure retained the form given it by Sun Yat-sen. Operating through various levels of authority, the party extended from the national congress of the *Kuomintang* and central executive committee at the top to the local party cells. Since the congress met infrequently and the central executive committee proved cumbersome, authority tended to gravitate to a smaller standing committee. Power within the party hierarchy was divided among rival leaders. Hu Han-min, a scholar and conservative, Wang Ching-wei, the brilliant and opportunistic demagogue, and Chiang Kai-shek, leader of the armies, were the more outstanding. Of these three, the first two later became leaders of the so-called right and left factions respectively. Chiang Kai-shek's position was more fluid, his eminence being derived more from his command function than from ideological factors. Lesser factions included the C. C. Clique of Ch'en Li-fu, minister of education, and Ch'en Kuo-fu, head of the central political institute, both of whom were master political manipulators; the Regenerationists or Blue Shirts, who mimicked a Fascist pattern; the secret police organization; and the milder Political Science Group, which eschewed violence and was hardly revolutionary. During the first years at Nanking, none of these men or factions achieved a position that could completely control the party or the government.[1] Because of the personal basis of Chinese politics, factionalism was to be expected. It was to prove, however, a luxury which the *Kuomintang* could ill afford. Once in power, the party tended to lapse into a mood of assurance, to lose its dynamic character. Factional strife contributed decidedly to this tendency.

CHIANG KAI-SHEK AND *KUOMINTANG* MILITARISM

Both governmental machinery and competing factions were eventually dominated or balanced by the *Kuomintang's* military chief, Chiang Kai-shek. Possessed of remarkable courage and a sense of timing, Chiang was a master in dealing with factional politics. As a leader of a fledgling party army before 1927, Chiang was considered a leftist, working closely with Soviet advisers and Communist officers; but in 1926, and again in 1927, when the Communists threatened his control, Chiang turned on his associates, "disposed" of them, or expelled them from the party. Once the *Kuomintang* was in power, Chiang cooperated with or opposed the party's right

[1] The problem of establishing leadership was complicated by the party's decision that Sun should continue to hold the title *Tsung-li* even after his death. Consequently, it was difficult when Sun was gone for anyone to seek exclusive leadership without doing violence to Sun's memory. It was not until 1938 that a new title of leadership, *Tsung-ts'ai,* was created and given to Chiang Kai-shek.

and left, as circumstances demanded. What made Chiang indispensable to *Kuomintang* leaders of every persuasion was the power of his armies. The party's tactic of absorbing or allying with warlord rivals, rather than eliminating them, and the party's failure to exterminate the communist opposition meant that in every year after 1927 the *Kuomintang*-Nationalist government was fighting or negotiating somewhere in China in the name of national unity. Moreover, Japan's conquest of Manchuria, her penetration of North China after 1931, and her eventual resort to all out war in 1937, made Chiang the one person to head the national resistance. Thus, in 1938, after a decade of growing but not unchallenged power, Chiang was designated party leader. One of his principal rivals, Hu Han-min, had died two years earlier, while another, Wang Ching-wei, was shortly to desert the *Kuomintang* and to align himself with the invading Japanese.

In circumstances of continued warfare, the *Kuomintang* army played a decisive role in Chinese politics. After 1928 Chiang, with the aid of German advisers, reorganized the army and strengthened his own position as commander-in-chief. The program of the Army Staff College was modernized. The men trained there, and a growing number educated in the finest foreign academies, formed the first competent body of middle-grade officers in China's modern era. Troops were schooled in German military methods and equipped with German-style arms. By 1937 the Central Army numbered about 300,000, while more than a half-million men were organized in subsidiary units. A beginning was also made in the organization of a navy and air force. While these units varied greatly in fighting efficiency, training, and equipment, the best of them were excellent, as was demonstrated by the Nineteenth Route Army when it met Japanese forces at Shanghai in January, 1932. Its defense of Shanghai, one of modern China's first victories over a foreign power, instilled confidence in other *Kuomintang* forces. This confidence was further reflected as an expanding military bureaucracy, operating with substantial autonomy under the executive *yuan,* intervened in the tasks of political and economic construction. Even before the Japanese invasion plunged China into total war, the military had displaced civil government in important areas of Chinese life.[2]

AUTHORITARIAN TENDENCIES

Acting on Sun Yat-sen's dictum that government and the people must be linked as one being, the *Kuomintang*-Nationalist regime devised an administrative structure to carry central authority to the local level. *Hsien* (county) magistrates were placed under orders from Nanking. Separate from the *hsien* government but also responsible to Nanking were local administrative units in charge of the military, the customs, transportation, and other matters. The *Kuomintang* also maintained party units under central control parallel to governmental administration. Below the *hsien* were further subdivisions leading down to individual households. The theory was that the government would train the people for democracy through direct administrative contact with the populace during a period of tutelage.

These forms of political practice emphasized authoritarian control. The 1930s saw the growth of local police, secret police, press censorship, directed education, and the *pao-chia*, a mutual guarantee system borrowed from Old China in which households were grouped so as to enable everyone to police everyone else. This did not mean, however, that all political opposition was proscribed. In fact a number of minor parties, consisting usually of a small nucleus of leaders and a few thousand followers having aims quite different from the *Kuomintang's*, not only operated but also were permit-

[2] Hung-mao Tien, *Government and Politics in Kuomintang China, 1927-1937* (1972), shows that by 1931 the center of power was no longer at Nanking at all but at Chiang's anti-communist field headquarters at Nanchang. By that time Chiang's chairmanship of the military council was the most powerful position in the party-state; government and party organs in Nanking fumbled ineffectually with paper plans and procedural problems.

ted, in 1941, to form a federation of democratic parties. Known as the "Democratic League," its purpose was to oppose one-party rule, party armies, secret police, and corruption. Even so, there were limits beyond which criticism was not tolerated. During the 1930s, pressures were exerted on opponents of the regime, several of whom were associated with colleges in the old capital city, now renamed Peiping. Student critics were jailed, and teachers and editors were intimidated.

Accompanying these developments was an attempted revival of Confucianism in the guise of the New Life Movement, which sought to instill in the populace a martial spirit and a social consciousness through the resurrection of ancient standards. These were: *li*, defined variously as propriety, proper behavior according to status, or a regulated attitude; *i* (or *yi*), righteousness or justice (in the Platonic sense); *lien*, integrity; and *ch'ih*, conscience. In order to render these classical concepts more understandable to the masses, some one hundred specific rules were issued as guides in their application. For example, the populace was admonished: do not eat noisily; correct your posture; keep your gown buttoned; do not spit; kill rats and flies. Through such inspiring exhortations, the Chinese people were to be led to practice orderliness and cleanliness. Between 1934 and 1937 the New Life Movement was also responsible for other activities, many of which were of doubtful value in promoting China's regeneration but which certainly reflected Nanking's tendency to justify itself through the authoritarian traditions of Old China.

For those in the New Culture Movement, who hoped for the eventual emergence of a democratic republic, the dictatorial policy and methods of the Nanking regime were profoundly disappointing. Hu Shih, who remained an eloquent and courageous spokesman for this group, continued in the decade after 1928 to espouse liberal principles in a manner that was reminiscent of a Confucian scholar admonishing his rulers to transform their hearts and minds. But the doctrines of gradual reform, progress, and democracy lacked the persuasive powers that Confucianism once had enjoyed. This was partly because Chinese liberals lacked an organizational backing; neither Hu nor his associates were political activists. They seemed to many of their concerned countrymen to be out of tune with their time. Hu was seen as failing to recognize the vast differences between China and the United States, where his political theories had been nurtured. While Hu's ideas were applauded by American liberals who knew very little about China, they often appeared to be doctrinaire in a China torn by violence and revolution and where there was as yet no well-established and accepted political system.[3]

NANKING'S EFFORTS TO EXTEND ITS TERRITORIAL BASE

In the period 1928-1937, Nanking was less concerned with the reform of government than with extending its military and police authority over regions where its control was nominal or where it faced outright defiance. The problem had three major aspects. In the first place, warlordism had not been destroyed completely. In the second, communist groups and forces which had escaped Chiang's purge at Shanghai and elsewhere were now engaged in rebuilding their political base. Third, after 1931 there was the obvious need to resist the Japanese who had occupied Manchuria.

MANAGING THE WARLORDS

Establishment of the Nanking government in 1927-1928 did not mean that all of China's warlords had been liquidated or had submitted themselves to the *Kuomintang* or its government. For example, in Shansi province General Yen Hsi-shan, the so-called Model Governor, was so entrenched that Nanking could do no more than seek his support as an ally, not his allegiance. Indeed, some of the surviving mili-

tarists were so completely independent of Nanking that the government's negotiations with them has been likened to an aspect of its "foreign policy."[4] Yet Nanking was not devoid of resources for destroying warlordism. In such provinces as Szechuan, where the government faced a coalition of contending militarists rather than a single authority, the methods of attrition could be applied. For a time after the *Kuomintang*-Nationalist government was established the supremacy of the Szechuan militarists was so complete that there were no Nanking officials in the province. By the mid-1930's, however, provincial rivalries, popular unrest, and the dangers posed by marauding communist forces cracked local resistance enough to permit Nanking to send some army officers. These were followed by civil officials. In 1937 the centralizing process was ended abruptly by the Japanese invasion. Before that event, however, Nanking had discovered in its military and administrative arms, devices that worked with some success against local authority.[5]

COMMUNIST OPPOSITION TO THE *KUOMINTANG*

The power of the *Kuomintang* was affected also by the armed challenge of rival revolutionary forces under Communist leadership. Following their ouster from the *Kuomintang* in 1927, the Communists first staged abortive uprisings and then were forced underground. Some Communist Party leaders retreated to the cities where they continued to plot for an urban-based revolution. Another group, in the mountainous border region of Kiangsi-Hunan provinces, established a territorial base commanded by Mao Tse-tung as chairman of the council of people's commissars, and by Chu Teh as commander-in-chief of the Communist army.

[3] See Jerome B. Grieder, *Hu Shih and the Chinese Renaissance: Liberalism in the Chinese Revolution, 1917-1937* (1970). Mission schools were an important source of American ideas in China; see Jessie Gregory Lutz, *China and the Christian Colleges, 1850-1950* (1971).

[4] For discussion of Nanking's efforts to deal with powerful warlords other than Yen Hsi-shan, see Donald Gillin, "Problems of Centralization in Republican China: the Case of Ch'en Ch'eng and the *Kuomintang*," *Journal of Asian Studies,* 29 (1970), 835-50.

[5] Robert A. Kapp, "Provincial Independence vs. National Rule: A Case Study of Szechuan in the 1920's and 1930's," *Journal of Asian Studies,* 30 (1971), 535-49. Note Kapp's description of the warlords as "sub-national militarists."

From these vantage points the Communist Party increasingly became a contender for leadership of China's revolution.

Foundations of Chinese Communism

The appeal of communism to Chinese intellectuals lay partly in its promised solutions to pressing problems. The doctrine's condemnation of the past justified attacks on traditional Confucian values; its justification of force offered a short cut to a modern China; and its demand for an end to colonialism supported the determination of young China to terminate the "unequal" treaty system. Moreover, acceptance of communist doctrine was encouraged by the New Culture Movement's emphasis on positivism, pragmatism, and materialism. While all of these tenets could be embraced by such an eloquent anti-Communist as Hu Shih, for others they inevitably suggested communist ideology. For them, positivism meant the Marxist science of life; pragmatism, as applied to achieving social revolution, was identified with Leninism; and materialism in general was regarded as a first step toward making the dialectical materialism of Marx the reigning philosophy. Finally, some Chinese saw an affinity between the principles of communism and those propounded by Sun Yat-sen. Sun himself had recognized that communism's emphasis on a state-controlled economy, rule by a party elite under strong leadership, and struggle against colonialism could be construed as identical with his doctrines of people's livelihood, democracy, and nationalism.[6]

[6] In considering the appeal of Marxism to Chinese revolutionaries, the world-wide impact of communist theory during the last century should be recalled. Marxism in one reading or another had become the frame of reference of most of the labor movement and intelligentsia over large areas of the globe, not to mention its privileged position as the official philosophy in communist countries. Its success in these areas was derived less from any logical coherence or scientific method than from an appeal to men's emotions and sense of morality. Marxism presented a richly secular theology in which history appeared to be working toward the ultimate Utopian society. Here, in an age of science and reason, was a new faith by which men could live and die. On these points see

While these intellectual trends favored the growth of communism, the Chinese Communist Party (CCP) had great difficulty establishing a broadly based popular following. One explanation was the party's subservience to Moscow during the first decade after its founding in 1921. It was Moscow that decided on the alliance and merger with the *Kuomintang,* and that directed the Chinese party to comply with the decision. Moscow saw greater potential in Sun and his followers than in a pitiful handful of Chinese Marxists having no influence. By theorizing that a united front was vital to the defeat of the warlords and imperialism, and that the *Kuomintang* was the one Chinese organization embracing all revolutionary classes, Moscow justified its view of the *Kuomintang* as the central revolutionary force. Whatever may be said of this theory, the stand was one which favored the expansion of Russian influence in China at the expense of Chinese nationalism and the Chinese Communist Party. Nevertheless, the Chinese Communist leadership accepted Russia's direction in this matter, as it did in virtually all others.

Under the tutelage of Soviet advisers the CCP was transformed from a loose coalition of Marxist study groups into a band of professional revolutionaries, disciplined and trained to concentrate on the organization and seizure of power. Moreover, the alliance with the *Kuomintang* during the latter's northern march provided party leaders with opportunities to instigate mass uprisings among peasants and workers. Yet the CCP suffered when Moscow, underestimating both the dangers posed by Chiang Kai-shek and the revolutionary potential of the poor peasantry, refused, first, to allow retaliation against Chiang for his purge of Communist rivals in 1926 and, second, to permit party leaders in 1927 to capitalize on the peasant revolts they had instigated. After 1927 the CCP, then outside the *Kuomintang,* was further injured when it accepted Stalin's

Robert C. Tucker, *The Marxian Revolutionary Idea* (1969).* For the story of how an important Chinese intellectual was converted to Marxism see David T. Roy, *Kuo Mo-jo: The Early Years* (1971).

view that the revolution must be continued through conspiracy and armed insurrection. In accord with this new line the party staged the Autumn Harvest Uprings (led by Mao Tse-tung) among peasants in Hunan, seized the port of Swatow for a week in September, 1927, and led a four-day uprising in Canton, When these and similar efforts collapsed, the party, following still another directive from Moscow, attempted to incite the urban proletariat to revolt. These uprisings, called the "Li Li-san line" after one their leading advocates, were doomed by labor apathy and vigorous *Kuomintang* suppression. Thus, after ten years, the CCP could claim no significant victories.[7]

Development of Rural Bases

The CCP's survival—and eventual re-emergence—during these early years must be ascribed largely to its appeal to the peasantry. In 1925, acting on Lenin's admonition that peas-

[7] A succinct synthesis of research on Soviet Russian involvement is in Lucien Bianco, *Origins of the Chinese Revolution, 1915-1949* (1971), 53-81. Much of the spadework on Sino-Soviet relationships, it should be emphasized, remains to be done. For example, a recently published study takes issue with the generally accepted contention that Li Li-san was made the scapegoat for Russian mistakes in ordering the ill-fated uprisings in China's cities. This new research points to the development of strategy jointly by Chinese and Russians in 1927-1928, calling for the creation of a Chinese Communist army, development of rural bases of Red power, and preparation for protracted struggle. Li's urban uprisings were not intended to set off a great national uprising but were intended to divert *Kuomintang* attentions from the Communists' real purposes. Li was punished not for having headed an abortive effort, but for having procrastinated in sharing leadership with emerging Communist military officers. This interpretation also holds that in creating an armed force in the Kiangsi base, Mao was acting more nearly in line with Moscow's directives than has been assumed. See Richard C. Thornton, *The Comintern and the Chinese Communists, 1928-1931* (1969). Suggestive of still other unsolved puzzles are the memoirs of two Communist pioneers: Sheng Yueh, *Sun Yat-sen University in Moscow and the Chinese Revolution: A Personal Account* (1971);* and Chang Kuo-t'ao, *The Rise of the Chinese Communist Party, 1921-1927* (1971). Both relate their experiences in dealing with the Russians, and Sheng specifically comments on his frustrations over the breakup of the Communists and *Kuomintang* in 1927.

ants could assist with, if not lead, revolutions, the party organized peasant associations in areas which were controlled by revolutionary forces. Peasants, burdened with extortionate rents and other exactions by landlords, and stirred by a tradition of rebellion, responded enthusiastically to Communist leadership in the redistribution of land, the reduction of taxes, and the confiscation of the wealth of local gentry. Within a few months, the peasant associations claimed a membership of 180,000. As the Communists (collaborating with the *Kuomintang*) started the northern expedition, so many peasants cooperated with them that the party could not provide adequate leadership to direct the peasant movement. Membership in the peasant associations soon surpassed the three million mark, thus eclipsing the urban labor movement.

The party, however, did not immediately seek to exploit the opportunities of peasant support. Chinese Communist leadership was inclined by background, temperament, and intellectual outlook to regard massive peasant support as a liability rather than an asset. The party's founders, having come mainly from families of landowning gentry or rich peasants, and being bound by the Marxist dogma that the only genuine source of revolutionary initiative was the industrial working class, were unwilling to identify themselves with the peasantry. Party policy subordinated peasant interests to those associated with carrying forward an urban-based revolution. Indeed, the "Li Li-san line" was inaugurated partly in an effort to bring the revolutionary effort in the cities abreast of that in the countryside.[8] But if the leadership was unwilling to capitalize on peasant discontent, the possibility of a peasant-based revolution did not escape Mao Tse-tung. As early as 1927, Mao launched a campaign to have the party regard the peasant rather than the industrial worker as the driving force of China's communist revolution.

While Mao had been active in the communist cause throughout the 1920s, his rise to prominence in a personal and ideological sense

[8] Urban Communists, unlike those in the countryside, were unable to offer the masses any immediate benefits as inducements for revolutionary activity.

occurred in the party's second decade. Following the collapse of the Autumn Harvest Uprising (September, 1927), Mao, joined by Chu Teh and what was left of Communist forces, retreated to the remote, mountain-girdled plateau region of the Hunan-Kiangsi border. Here a start was made in developing programs that were to give the Chinese Communist movement new life. The Hunan-Kiangsi region was converted into a territorial base.[9] Here in the provincial borderlands Mao constructed a bastion within which the Communists could organize the economic basis of power and defend themselves against attack, and from which Communist rule could be extended to the rest of China. Since Mao and Chu treated the peasants well, the peasantry furnished recruits for the Red Army, supplies, intelligence reports on enemy movements, and concealment for the Communists when they retreated in the face of superior forces. The Red Army in turn was trained to look upon itself as the defender of the peasants and the very embodiment of their aspirations. Wherever the Red Army went, land was redistributed and the powers of landlords, moneylenders, and gentry were broken. These efforts were so successful that by early 1930 the Red Army was conquering large stretches of territory, mostly in Kiangsi but also as far north as Hupeh.

These improved fortunes did not immediately elevate Mao to leadership of the party. The officially designated party leaders, those who were recognized in Moscow, remained in urban areas where (as noted) they strove frantically to rouse the proletariat. Thus it was not until the collapse of the "Li Li-san line" and Li's subsequent disgrace that Mao's fortunes improved appreciably. In 1932 Mao used his new power to force the party's central committee to move from Shanghai to the area under his control.[10]

[9] For a study of the geographic factor in Chinese Communist history see Robert W. McColl, "The Oyuwan Soviet Area, 1927-1932," *Journal of Asian Studies,* 27 (1967), 41-60.

[10] Ideological differences were by no means the only trouble between Mao and the party's central committee. Mao was a "non-Bolshevik Revolutionary," who "though an active revolutionary through-

Collapse of the Kiangsi Soviet and the "Long March"

In November, 1931, a Chinese Soviet Republic, having its capital in Juichin, Kiangsi, and claiming altogether sixteen territorial bases, was proclaimed with Mao as its president. The Kiangsi base alone had a population of 2.5 million. Even more impressive was the demonstrated capacity of the Communists to survive *Kuomintang* military pressures. Between 1930 and 1933, the Kiangsi central base alone was subjected to no less than four successive "Extermination Campaigns."

It was the fifth of these campaigns that brought the Communists to near disaster. Confronted by *Kuomintang* superiority in men and arms, an ever-tightening economic blockade, and a military situation which deprived Red forces of their best weapon—mobility—the Communist leadership decided to flee Kiangsi in search of another base. Some 90,000-100,000 forces broke through the *Kuomintang*-Nationalist encirclement to begin a 6,000 mile march through southwest and western China, a march that has become legendary in party history. During 370 days Red forces fought their way toward remote and desolate Shensi province. There in 1935, Mao, now firmly in command, with perhaps 7,000-8,000 followers, made new beginnings

out the 1920s, was much too busy to master the fundamental Marxist categories. He was a revolutionary before he became a Communist. A natural leader of men, he found it difficult to subordinate himself to the strict party discipline inherent in a Leninist democratic central regime." He proved to be shrewd and tenacious, bowing to the party leadership whenever that was expedient, but otherwise working steadily to maintain and to increase his own power base. In these latter respects he was not greatly different from such warlords as Yen Hsi-shan or Feng Yu-hsiang. What ultimately distinguished Mao from the warlords was his vision of a transformed China and his ability to marshal mass support. Before he could realize his vision, however, Mao had to fight his way to political power. John E. Rue, *Mao Tse-tung in Opposition, 1927-1935* (1966), 24. See also Hsiao Tso-liang, *Power Relations within the Chinese Communist Movement, 1930-1934* Hssiao Tso-liang, *Power Relations within the Chinese Communist Movement, 1930-1934* (2 vols., 1961-1967).

under conditions which, if anything, were less promising than those in 1927.[11]

Shensi province, economically poor and far from the concentrations of population through which the CCP aspired to build its revolution, appeared as an unlikely base of operations. Yet the party was not without resources. In a decade and a half, the Communists had become a disciplined revolutionary organization, had developed techniques for converting peasant discontent into revolutionary action, and had laid the groundwork for modern guerrilla warfare. Under Mao, moreover, the party was becoming far less subservient to directives from Moscow.

ECONOMIC FOUNDATIONS OF *KUOMINTANG*-NATIONALIST CHINA

Nanking's determined efforts to lay the political foundations of its authority were not matched by its promotion of economic and social development, though some headway was made in this direction. In the decade before the Sino-Japanese war (1937), light and staple industries, communication systems, and export-import firms continued the gradual expansion that had begun during World War I. Moreover, the *Kuomintang*-Nationalist regime fostered some essential foundations for economic growth. These were fiscal reforms, such as the centralization of industrial taxation, national control over tariff policy, and the establishment of annual national budgets. The government built some additions to the communications system. Power industries were enlarged. These achievements were publicized as evidence that the new regime was mastering its economic problems.

Under Nanking's rule, China was a developing country.[12] This trend, however, while

important to an assessment of long-term economic growth, was acutely disappointing to those nationalists who had anticipated a vigorous broadening and quickening of modernization. Of critical importance was the government's failure to effect far-reaching economic and social reforms. While economic activity was increased through expenditures to modernize and expand the *Kuomintang's* armies, resources and labor were diverted from the production of consumer goods and services. Experiments in rural reconstruction were permitted under provincial administrations, but they received little encouragement from Nanking. Nor were land laws aimed at protecting the peasantry rigorously enforced.[13]

---

[11] The actual number of survivors was larger, since some of the Red Army, including Chu Teh, followed a more westerly route to Shensi.

[12] Paul K.T. Shih, ed., *The Strenuous Decade: China's Nation-Building Efforts, 1927-1937* (1970) emphasizes the achievements of the *Kuomintang* in power. On economic development see especially the essay by Arthur N. Young. John K. Chang, "Industrial Development of Mainland China, 1912-1939," *Journal of Economic History,* 27 (1967), 56-81, places Nanking's programs in the context of long

term trends. For two critical assessments see Douglas Paauw: "Chinese National Expenditure during the Nanking Period," *Far Eastern Quarterly,* 12 (1952), 3-26; and "The *Kuomintang* and Economic Stagnation," *Journal of Asian Studies,* 16 (1957), 213-20. The root of the conflicting appraisals given in these studies is to be found in the relativism of the term "economic stagnation." In an absolute sense the term was inaccurate for China as a whole. Manchuria under Japanese rule enjoyed an industrial boom. Nor was the term literally accurate even for regions under *Kuomintang*-Nationalist control. Between 1925-1936 the industrial growth rate was 4.7 percent; for the years 1931-1937, the figure was 9.3 percent. Thus there was substance to Nanking's claims. Moreover, these statistics should be kept in mind while examining the Communists' later claims of economic achievement. Progress in China's economic transformation was not confined to the years after 1949. Yet, it also must be remembered that the economic growth disappointed the expectations that had been stirred as the *Kuomintang* assumed authority. Given the militaristic orientation of production underlying the growth figures and the government's failures in other fields, indices on economic growth lead to varying interpretations.

[13] Arthur N. Young, an American who served as a high level financial adviser to the *Kuomintang*-Nationalist government, has written of the strengths and limitations of Nanking's economic programs in *China's Nation-Building Effort, 1927-1937: The Financial and Economic Record* (1971). Ramon H. Myers and Thomas R. Ulie, "Foreign Influence and Agricultural Development in Northeast China: A Case Study of the Liaotung Peninsula,. 1906-1942," *Journal of Asian Studies,* 31 (1972), 329-50, is suggestive of the problems of transforming agriculture in support of economic modernization. See also Myers, "The Commercialization of Agriculture in Modern China," in *Economic Organization in Chinese Society,* W.E. Willmott, ed. (1972), which finds steady modernization in agriculture,

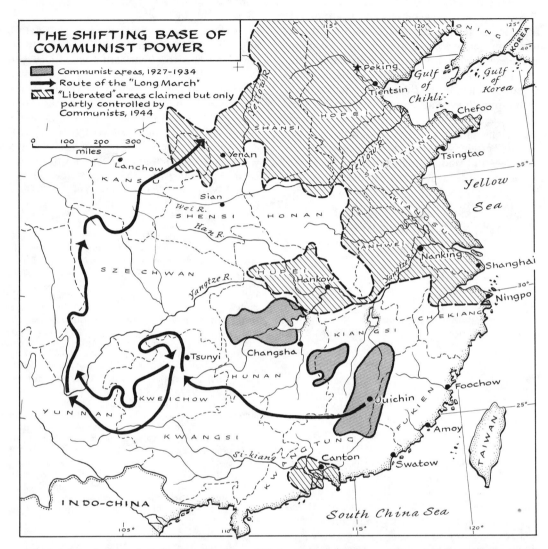

Adapted from Immanuel C. Y. Hsu, The Rise of Modern China *(1970), p. 660; and J. K. Fairbank, E. O. Reischauer, and A. M. Craig,* East Asia: The Modern Transformation *(1965), p. 853.*

1870-1937, but little indication that the peasantry benefited from the change. For evidence that the Chinese Communists were not alone in perceiving the fundamental importance of rural reform see James C. Thomson, Jr., *While China Faced West: American Reformers in Nationalist China* (1969). Here are recounted the activities of American missionaries who worked with Chinese reformers in efforts to transform rural life and livelihood. Initially, many of these Americans identified their concerns with those expressed by Mao Tse-tung and his Communist fol-lowers, but they rejected Communist methods as inhumane. With respect to the Nanking government, their views underwent a transformation. Despite an early conviction that the *Kuomintang*-Nationalist government was little interested in their work, these Americans eventually drew close to the regime, not because the government gave support, but because of the *Kuomintang's* success in national unification (sti-mulating hopes of eventual reform) and of the Generalissimo and Madame Chiang's protective atti-tude toward Christianity.

To be sure, the tasks of economic development were exceedingly difficult. The divisions within the *Kuomintang* arising from sharply contrasting personal philosophies and rivalries were not conducive to agreement on economic policy. The *Kuomintang*, moreover, was called upon to revolutionize China's economy during a period when depression was creating havoc throughout the world and when Japan posed a constant military threat. In addition, the popular demand for economic change was not always matched by a general determination to abandon traditional ways. The nature of this difficulty is suggested by the tendency of educated Chinese to insist upon white-collar jobs that most nearly approximated the prestigious vocations of Old China. Such tendencies safeguarded individual self-esteem but they deprived the country of talents badly needed in other areas. Finally, in these years the *Kuomintang*-Nationalist government had to cope with a treaty system which, by giving foreigners and foreign business special privileges, diminished Nanking's authority in the economic realm. When all of these factors are taken into account, it is easier to understand the *Kuomintang's* determination to unite China through military measures rather than to concentrate on political and economic reform.

Meanwhile, the position of the *Kuomintang* and the *Kuomintang*-Nationalist government had been challenged from the outside first by Russia in North Manchuria in 1929 and then by Japan in South Manchuria in 1931 and after (see Chapter 26). In the case of North Manchuria, Nanking could do no more than bow to the terms Russia imposed on Manchurian authorities. In the case of South Manchuria, Nanking could and did appeal to the League of Nations, but Manchuria itself passed into Japanese hands while the Young Marshal Chang Hsueh-liang reassembled his army west of Peiping. During 1934-1935, when Japan's Kwantung army attempted to set up an autonomous state around Peiping, the *Kuomintang*-Nationalist government played a delicate game of appeasement, neither obstructing the Japanese completely nor conceding all they asked. To this point the *Kuomintang's* policy was to placate Japan. Confronted with dissension within its own ranks and opposed vigorously by the Communists, the party had decided to crush internal foes before turning against foreign invaders.

Village street in Honan Province, 1934.

This policy was soon met with a rising demand throughout China for a united front against Japan. Japanese pressure since 1931 in Manchuria and North China and at Shanghai had gone far to subordinate conflicting groups and class interests of Chinese society and to produce a widespread demand for armed resistance. The popular humiliation before Japanese arms affected all classes, high and low, urban and rural, including the *Kuomintang,* the Communists, and others who might be called nonpartisans. A manifestation of this national feeling was a revolt in 1933 in Fukien by *Kuomintang* and other elements demanding resistance to the Japanese and democracy for the Chinese. Later, in 1936, Nanking faced a revolt by southern generals and their political followers in Kwangtung and Kwangsi, who professed to represent regional branches of the central executive committee itself. Again the demand was for resistance to Japan, and again Nanking met the emergency with force, patronage, and assurances that resistance was coming.[14] The culmination of these revolts against the *Kuomintang*-Nationalist government came in December, 1936, when Chiang Kai-shek was seized on a visit to Sian and held prisoner by Chang Hsueh-liang. The kidnapping was clearly a protest against Nanking's orders to fight the Chinese Communists. Chang's commanders and troops were more concerned with fighting

[14] The *Kuomintang*-Nationalist government's procrastination eroded its support among the educated middle classes and college students. The Communists were slow to exploit this opportunity, but by 1936 they were doing so. Students were in the vanguard of those supporting the Communist call for a united front against Japan. See Jessie Lutz, "December 9, 1935: Student Nationalism and the China Christian Colleges," *Journal of Asian Studies,* 26 (1967), 627-48. John Israel, *Student Nationalism in China, 1927-1937* (1966), concludes: "It is quite likely that no government faced with the succession of foreign and domestic crises that plagued the KMT from 1927 to 1949 could have acted to the satisfaction of revolutionary students." See also Jerome B. Grieder, "Communism, Nationalism, and Democracy: The Chinese Intelligentsia and the Chinese Revolution in the 1920's and 1930's," in *Modern East Asia: Essays in Interpretation,* James B. Crowley, ed. (1970),* 207-34.

the Japanese and regaining their homeland. Indeed, there had been fraternizing rather than fighting between the Manchurian troops and the Communists in the northwest. What Chang wanted was a pledge that the Nanking government would join forces with the Communist Party against Japan, an idea which then was supported by the Communist leadership. Presumably such a pledge was obtained prior to Chiang Kai-shek's release. The *Kuomintang* was clearly being forced to give top priority to the repelling of foreign aggression.

FOR FURTHER READING

Economic and Social Conditions. Cheng Yu-kwei, *Foreign Trade and Industrial Development of China: An Historical and Integrated Analysis through 1948* (1956) painstakingly collects widely scattered data. On the position of labor see: Augusta Wagner, *Labor Legislation in China* (1938); Nym Wales (pseudonym of Mrs. Edgar Snow), *The Chinese Labor Movement* (1945); and Ning Lao-T'ai-t'ai, and Ida Pruitt, *A Daughter of Han* (1945),* the autobiography of a Chinese working woman. Victor Purcell, *Problems of Chinese Education* (1936); Chang Jen-chi, *Pre-Communist China's Rural Schools and Community* (1960); and John DeFrancis, *Nationalism and Language Reform in China* (1950) are suggestive of the role of education in the Nationalist movement. Andrew James Nathan, *A History of the China International Famine Relief Commission* (1965),* based almost entirely on foreign sources. Mary E. Ferguson, *China Medical Board and Peking Union Medical College: A Chronicle of Fruitful Collaboration, 1914-1951* (1970), a fine narrative on the college but no adequate treatment of the Chinese response. Jay Leyda, *Dianying: Electric Shadows, An Account of Films and the Film Audience in China* (1972), offers original insights into films as social and political documents of the 1930s and later. Lao She, *Cat Country: A Satirical View of China in the 1930's* (1971).

The *Kuomintang*. Biographical treatment of *Kuomintang* and Communist party leaders is given in Chun-tu Hsueh, ed., *Revolutionary Leaders of Modern China* (1971),* and Howard L. Boorman and Richard C. Howard, eds., *Biographical Dictionary of Republican China* (4 vols., 1967-1971). P. M. A. Linebarger, *The China of Chiang K'ai-shek* (1941) is an able and sympathetic study. F. F. Liu, *A Military History of Modern China, 1924-1949* (1956) is the first penetrating account of the rise and fall of the Whampoa clique. On this subject see also R. L. MacFarquhar, "The Whampoa Military Academy," *Papers on China,* Vol. 9. Published and distributed by the East Asia Research Center, Harvard University, (1955); and E. F. Carlson, *The Chinese Army: Its Organization and Military Efficiency* (1940). Mary C. Wright, "From Revolution to Restoration: The Transformation of *Kuomintang* Ideology," *Far Eastern Quarterly* 14 (1955), 515-32, is an important brief study. John Carter Vincent, *The Extraterritorial System in China: Final Phase* (1970)* focuses on the years between the two world wars.

The Communist Party. "Chinese Communism," in William T. deBary and others, eds., *Sources of Chinese Tradition* (1960);* and Helene Carrere D'Encausse and Stuart R. Schram, *Marxism and Asia, An Introduction with Readings* (1969) provide an excellent introduction to the relationship of Communist ideology to evolving Chinese thought. Jacques Guillermaz, *A History of the Chinese Communist Party, 1921-1929* (1972)* is a detailed narrative. On Moscow's link with the Chinese Communists see Harold Isaacs, *The Tragedy of the Chinese Revolution* (3rd. ed., 1961); and Conrad Brandt, *Stalin's Failure in China, 1924-1927* (1956)* which reach opposing views on Stalin's responsibility for Communist

failures in China. C. P. Fitzgerald, *The Birth of Communist China* (1966);* and Franklin W. Houn, *A Short History of Chinese Communism* (rev.ed., 1973),* offer differing perspectives on the formative years. Chao Ku-chun, *Agrarian Policy of the Chinese Communist Party, 1921-1959* (1960); and Tso-liang Hsiao, *The Land Revolution in China, 1930-1934; A Study of Documents* (1969) are most useful for these early years. Hsia Tsi-an, *Enigma of the Five Martyrs: A Study of the Leftist Literary Movement in Modern China* (1962), employs tools of literary criticism to reveal Chinese Communism's intraparty struggles in the 1930s. Dick Wilson, *The Long March, 1935; The Epic of Chinese Communism's Survival* (1972), a scholarly study written with a journalist's verve. Edgar Snow, *Red Star Over China* (1944)* gives a sympathetic description of early Communist struggles. C. Martin Wilbur and Julie Lien-ying How, *Documents on Communism, Nationalism, and Soviet Advisors in China 1918-1927* (1956); and Conrad Brandt, B. I. Schwartz, and J. K. Fairbank, eds., *A Documentary History of Chinese Communism* (1952)* offers translations of Chinese documents with editorial commentary. O. Edmund Clubb, *Communism in China, As Reported from Hankow in 1932* (1968). Howard L. Boorman, "Mao Tse-tung, the Lacquered Image," *China Quarterly* 16 (1963), 1-55, is a short but carefully documented biography of Mao. As examples of the specialized research that appears frequently in *The China Quarterly* see Harold R. Isaacs, "Documents on the Coming Chinese Revolution," (January-March 1969); Jerome Ch'en, "Resolutions of the Tsunyi Conference, 1935; Translation and Commentary," (October-December 1969); and Chi-hsi Hu, "Hua Fu, the Fifth Encirclement Campaign and the Tsunyi Conference," (July-September 1970).

Resort to Militarism: The Manchurian Crisis and Ultranationalism in Japanese Politics, 1929–1937

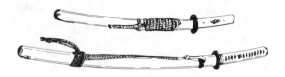

26

The years during which the *Kuomintang* established its leadership in China also produced a developing crisis in East Asian international relations. At issue was the status of Manchuria, a vast territory that both the Manchu dynasty and the later Chinese Republic had said was a part of China but which, in fact, had been subjected to substantial Russian and Japanese control. After 1928 the special position enjoyed by these powers in Manchuria became the target of an assertive Chinese nationalism. As in other parts of China, *Kuomintang* propaganda dwelt ceaselessly on the necessity of recovering lost sovereign rights, on the abolition of the unequal treaties, and on the wickedness of imperialism. Neither Russia nor Japan, however, was disposed to concede what the Chinese demanded in Manchuria. Both nations considered Manchuria (sometimes called the Three Eastern Provinces) of great strategic importance, and both valued it for its vast economic resources. By 1928, for example, Manchuria's agricultural products, including such crops as soy beans, kaoliang, wheat, millet, and barley, most of which were exported, totalled some $650 million annually.

There had also been extensive exploitation of the rich timber lands and of such minerals as coal, iron, and gold. Thus, to a greater extent than in China Proper, Chinese nationalism and its propaganda in Manchuria challenged the foreign interests of two major powers, Russia and Japan.

Moreover, in Manchuria, Russia and Japan were dealing with Chang Tso-lin, an erstwhile bandit turned statesman, and his son Chang Hsueh-liang, who assumed political control on the death of his father in 1928. Between 1905 and 1931 these two warlords, like others of their kind, played an intricate political game, alternately attacking and supporting China's central government. In December, 1928, the younger Chang announced his allegiance to the newly-established *Kuomintang* regime, accepting the Nationalist flag and becoming Nanking's commander-in-chief of the Northeast Frontier Army. So far as the internal administration of Manchuria was concerned the association with Nanking was nominal. The Nanking government merely confirmed what Manchurian authorities were pleased to do. This theoretical allegiance of Manchuria to the Nationalist government did, however, bring notable results in Manchuria's foreign outlook. To the *Kuomintang's* anti-imperialist campaigns, Manchurian officialdom added a nationalistically-oriented "forward policy" of their own.[1]

THE SINO-RUSSIAN CRISIS OF 1929

Sino-Russian relations had grown progressively worse since the *Kuomintang's* expulsion of the Communists in 1927. In Manchuria, relations with Russia were severely strained by the pronounced anti-communism of local Manchurian authorities. Chang Tso-lin bitterly resented the Soviet Union's use of the territorial base afforded by the Chinese Eastern Railway and the use of Soviet railway personnel in broadcasting propaganda undermining his rule. The conflict came into the open in 1927 when Chang, at the time still master of Peking, raided Soviet headquarters there, charging Russian violations of the no-propaganda clauses of the 1924 Sino-Soviet agreements. Two years later, in May, 1929, Chang Hsueh-liang entered Soviet consulates along the Chinese Eastern Railway, arrested Communist agents, and seized documentary evidence of Soviet subversion. In July, Chang's forces took over the railroad telegraph system and arrested Soviet employees, replacing them with Chinese and White Russians. When China did not respond to an ultimatum addressed to both Nanking and Mukden, the Soviets broke off relations and sporadic fighting erupted on the Siberian-Manchurian border.

These border hostilities were a direct challenge to principles of the recently signed treaty for the renunciation of war, August, 1928, (the Kellogg-Briand treaty). Accordingly, the American secretary of state, Henry L. Stimson, acting on the theory that the treaty should be "a practical instrument for preserving peace," reminded both Russia and China of their obligations to employ peaceful

means of settlement. This appeal, approved by other major signatories, brought assurances from Russia and China that they would resort to force only in self-defense.[2]

Meanwhile, negotiations between the Soviet Union and local Manchurian officials and between the Russian ambassador and the Chinese minister in Berlin were abortive. By November there was open though undeclared warfare on the Manchurian border. A Soviet army invaded Manchuria from the west. The forces of Chang Hsueh-liang retreated in confusion. On December 3, Chang agreed to Russia's demands, and Nanking followed suit on December 22.

This brief, undeclared war had shown that (1) in Manchuria, Soviet Russia was as jealous of her interests and as ready to defend them by force as had been tsarist Russia; (2) the Kellogg-Briand treaty was an ineffective preventive of war; and (3) the national government at Nanking, involved in suppressing opposition in central and northwest China, was incapable of exerting power in the border provinces of the northeast. These conclusions were not lost on Japan's determined expansionists.

SINO-JAPANESE ISSUES IN MANCHURIA

Manchuria had come to represent, by 1931, a fundamental clash of Sino-Japanese as well as Sino-Russian interests. Chinese nationalism regarded it as the first line of defense; Japanese governments, as a life line. Chinese called it the "granary of China," while the migration of Chinese peasants to it was a sort of safety valve easing the pressure in overcrowded areas, such as Shantung.[3] The Japanese felt that

---

[1] Akira Iriye, "Chang Hsueh-liang and the Japanese," *Journal of Asian Studies,* 20 (1960), 33-43, dissects the motivations of the Manchurian warlords.

[2] In the Kellogg-Briand pact the signatories: (1) "condemned recourse to war for the solution of international controversies"; (2) renounced war "as an instrument of national policy"; and (3) agreed that the settlement of all disputes should be by none but pacific means. All signatories reserved the right of self-defense.

[3] By 1931 Manchuria had an estimated population of 30 million persons, of whom some 28 million were Chinese (including a small percentage of native Manchus), 500,000 or more Mongols, 800,000 Koreans, 150,000 Russians, and some 230,000 Japanese.

they had won Liaotung in 1895; that they had saved Manchuria from Russia in 1905; that Japanese capital was principally responsible for the development of the country; and that by reason of patriotism, defense, and exceptional treaty rights they had acquired a "special position."

Principal among specific issues were conflicts arising out of the Sino-Japanese Manchurian treaty and notes of May, 1915. Whereas Japan insisted upon the fulfillment of the treaty, the Chinese persistently denied its validity. The issues tended to become more acute after 1928 when the *Kuomintang* was established in Manchuria. After 1927, too, there was a movement among the Chinese to divest the South Manchuria Railway of its political and administrative functions, making of it a purely commercial enterprise. This was a natural nationalistic aspiration, but it struck at the very basis of Japan's position, which in Manchuria was definitely political. Furthermore, although the Russo-Chinese Railway Agreement of 1896 conferred upon the Chinese Eastern Railway Company the "absolute and exclusive administration of its [railway] lands," the Chinese government denied that this conferred political control in the railroad zone. In additon, the activities of Japanese railway guards, both in and outside the railway zone, and of the Japanese consular police became increasingly irritating as nationalist sentiment in Manchuria grew. These police were located not only in the railroad areas but also at Japanese consulates in various towns: Harbin, Manchouli, and the Chientao district on the Korean border. A further source of conflict was the presence in Manchuria of 800,000 Koreans, who after 1910 were Japanese subjects. As in the case of the Japanese, the Chinese opposed acquisition of land in Manchuria by Koreans. Japan, on the other hand, refused to recognize the naturalization of Koreans as Chinese.

Finally, China and Japan had long quarrelled over the construction and financing of railways in Manchuria. Japan, utilizing the tactics which the Russians had employed in operating the Chinese Eastern Railway, obtained from her control of railway transportation in South Manchuria not only for profit but also political advantage. The semi-official, efficient, profitable, and wealthy S.M.R. (South Manchuria Railway) made it its policy to finance the construction of only such Chinese lines as would be "feeders to its own road terminating in the great port of Dairen. The increasing power of this transportation system under Japanese ownership and control and, in fact, its very existence were repugnant to Chinese nationalists. After 1924, the Chinese, in spite of Japanese protests that their action violated the secret protocol of the Sino-Japanese treaty of Peking, December, 1905, built lines paralleling and competing with the S.M.R. system and connecting with the Chinese-controlled ports of Yingkow and Hulutao. These lines were quite successful in diverting traffic from the Japanese roads. But this was not the only aspect of China's offensive. China would neither repay loans of Yen 150 million which had been expended in the construction of four major and a number of minor Chinese railways, nor appoint Japanese railway advisers, as required by prior agreements. China contended that the loans were primarily strategic and political, that they had been made by the S.M.R. with the idea of monopolizing railway investments, and that the lines were heavily overcapitalized and could not be put on a paying basis. The legal merits of these disputes were never resolved. Moreover, to this legal tangle there was added a miscellaneous assortment of railway and other disputes involving Sino-Japanese agreements, most of which had political and strategic overtones. One of these, the Wanpaoshan affair (1931), was of little importance in itself, but it led to anti-Chinese riots and bloodshed in Korea, and from there to an anti-Japanese boycott in China. While this furor was at its height, a Japanese intelligence officer, Captain Nakamura, was killed by Chinese troops in Inner Mongolia.[4]

[4] Daniel B. Ramsdell, "The Nakamura Incident and the Japanese Foreign Office," *Journal of Asian Studies*, 25 (1965), 51-67, examines the impact of the incident on Japanese policy making.

Thus the Sino-Japanese Manchurian question by mid-September, 1931, had produced a collision of irreconcilable policies. As the tension increased, both sides made some efforts toward peaceful solutions, but these were unproductive. The more rabid Chinese nationalists had so aroused public opinion as to render negotiations virtually impossible. Among the Japanese the disposition to conciliate Chinese nationalism through concessions was rapidly fading. Moreover, for those in China and Japan who favored and planned a policy of force to settle Manchurian issues, September, 1931, was a time well chosen. The West was going through a period of economic chaos to which its governments seemed unable to respond effectively. Great Britain deserted the gold standard: the situation in Europe called forth the Hoover moratorium on debt payments, and the United States, of course, was still in the throes of the depression. If force were applied in Manchuria, it was unlikely that Europe or America would interfere.

On the night of September 18, 1931, the Japanese Kwantung army seized Mukden. The hostilities were precipitated, according to the Japanese, by a Chinese attempt to blow up the tracks of the S.M.R. In the light of new materials brought out at the Tokyo war crimes trials (diaries, memoirs, and autobiographies), it appears that the Manchurian incident of September 18 was engineered by Japanese civilians as well as military extremists who were anxious to find a quick solution to unsolved political problems.[5] Because of advanced preparation for these initial military operations, the Japanese were able to move quickly to seize Changchun and Kirin. During the next three months, the Japanese expanded their operation southward toward the border of China Proper and northward beyond the

[5] Yoshihashi Takehiko, *Conspiracy at Mukden* (1963), offers details not available in other English language sources.

Japan, 1931-1933

Reproduced from A War Atlas for Americans *(New York: Simon & Schuster, 1944), with permission from the publisher and from the U.S. Department of State, Division of Map Intelligence and Cartography.*

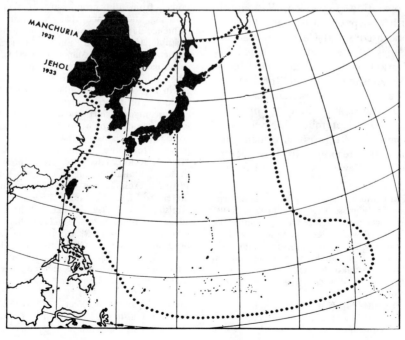

main line of the Chinese Eastern Railway. On January 2, 1932, the Kwantung army, dispersing the last southern remnants of Chang Hsueh-liang's armies, captured Chinchow, near the Chinese border. As 1932 advanced, Japan completed her military conquest of Manchuria.[6]

Throughout these months, persistent but ineffective efforts were made to halt the Japanese military advance and to resolve the issue through peaceful means. Responding to China's appeal under Article XI of the Covenant, the League of Nations tried vainly to interest the powers in imposing sanctions on Japan. On October 24, the League issued an order to the Kwantung army to withdraw to the S.M.R. zone, which Japan ignored. Finally, on December 10 a commission (the Lytton commission) was sent to investigate the issue.[7] Meanwhile, the League sought to strengthen its hand by enlisting the support of the United States. The United States, however, concerned lest isolationist sentiment be aroused, maintained that it would act independently and agreed only to consult informally with the League on possible moves. Later, as Japanese operations expanded, Washington took the further step of authorizing Prentiss Gilbert, American consul at Geneva, to participate in meetings of the League Council involving application of the Kellogg-Briand pact. Apart from its consultations with the League, the United States made representations of its own in Tokyo. The first of these was markedly conciliatory. On September 22, Secretary of State Henry L. Stimson informed the Japanese "that the responsibility for determining the course of events with regard to the

liquidating of this [Manchurian] situation rests largely upon Japan," and he hinted that both the Kellogg-Briand pact and the nine-power open door treaty were at stake. At this point Stimson thought it unwise to speak more sternly to the Japanese. The secretary held that the road to resolving the Manchurian affair lay in "giving Shidehara and the Foreign Office an opportunity, free from anything approaching a threat or even public criticism, to get control of the situation." It was the difficult problem of letting "the Japanese know that we were watching them and at the same time to do it in a way which will help Shidehara."[8] Later, as it became clear that the foreign office would not undo the work of the Kwantung army, Stimson moved toward diplomatic coercion. On January 7, 1932, after informing the British and French of his intention but without waiting for their concurrence, Stimson informed China and Japan that the United States

---

[6] The ultimate intentions of Japan in Manchuria were unclear in September, 1931. It appears, however, that the decison to seize all of Manchuria originated entirely within the Kwantung army and in opposition to the central army authorities and government, both of which sought a settlement on a more limited scale. Sadako No Ogata, *Defiance in Manchuria: The Making of Japanese Foreign Policy, 1931-1932*, (1964), 187.

[7] Detailed treatment is in W. W. Willoughby, *The Sino-Japanese Controversy and the League of Nations* (1935), Chapter 3.

[8] Henry L. Stimson, *The Far Eastern Crisis* (1936), 34-37. Recent probing of Japanese records reveals the exceedingly fragile basis of Stimson's hopes. Japan's bureaucratic in-fighting had stripped power from the proponents of conciliation, thus reducing the chance that American policy would influence Japanese conduct. In the foreign office, for example, the so-called "Europe-America" faction lost influence during the Manchurian crisis. Control gradually passed to a group headed by Arita Hachiro, who, while opposing reckless adventures, favored Japan's progressive domination of China and the exclusion of Western interests. Much the same kind of bureaucratic shift occurred within the navy ministry, a body which appeared less identified with continental expansion than the army. Here power passed from the "administrative" faction to the "fleet" faction. This latter group pressed for an end to naval limitation and preparation for a southward advance, even at the risk of war with the United States. See Usui Katsumi, "The Role of the Foreign Ministry," and Asada Sadao, "The Japanese Navy and the United States," in *Pearl Harbor as History: Japanese-American Relations, 1931-1941*, Dorothy Borg and Shumpei Okamoto, eds. (1973), 127-48 and 225-60. For critical comment on Stimson's diplomacy by one of the secretary's contemporaries, see George A. Lensen, "Japan and Manchuria: Ambassador Forbes' Appraisal of American Policy toward Japan in the Years, 1931-1932," *Monumenta Nipponica: Studies in Japanese Culture*, 23, 1967 66-89.

. . . cannot admit the legality of any situation de facto nor does it intend to recognize any treaty or agreement entered into between those governments, or agents thereof, which may impair the treaty rights of the United States or its citizens in China, including those which relate to the sovereignty, the independence, or the territorial and administrative integrity of the Republic of China, or to the international policy relative to China, commonly known as the open-door policy; and that it does not intend to recognize any situation, treaty, or agreement which may be brought about by means contrary to the covenants and obligations of the Pact of Paris, of August 27, 1928, to which treaty both China and Japan, as well as the United States, are parties.

This nonrecognition doctrine was derived from Secretary Bryan's caveat of May, 1915, while the note as a whole was a reassertion of traditional American policy. Stimson assumed that Britain and France would see their far eastern interests as identical with those of the United States and would also make representations in Tokyo, but this assumption was unfounded, for neither country associated itself with this American move.[9]

[9] American diplomacy during the Manchurian crisis was shaped by countervailing pressures. Not

In 1935, imperialistic groups in Japan favored creation of an autonomous North China, free from the political control of Nanking and under the tutelage of Manchuko.

Courtesy of the New York Times.

HOSTILITIES SPREAD INTO CHINA PROPER

Toward the end of January, 1932, Sino-Japanese hostilities spread from Manchuria to Shanghai, where a most effective boycott of Japanese goods became the occasion for a naval bombardment of Chinese sections of the city. But, unlike in Manchuria, where there had been a policy of retreat, at Shanghai a Chinese army (the Nineteenth Route Army) held its position until the arrival early in March of heavy Japanese army reinforcements. Britain, whose interests were now seriously affected, protested Japanese bombings at Shanghai, and concurrently with the United States sent naval and marine reinforcements to the International Settlement. Meanwhile, China invoked Articles X and XV of the League of Nations Covenant, under which the League was required to assess responsibility and apply sanctions. This led to appointment of a League committee at Shanghai, consisting of the local consular representatives of the League states, to report directly on conditions there. The United States, making use of an open letter from Secretary Stimson to the chairman of the Senate foreign relations committee, issued on February 24 a general appeal to the powers to associate themselves with the nonrecognition doctrine.

---

only was the Hoover administration limited by the Senate's decisive rejection of American membership in the League of Nations, but it was also caught in the growing crisis of the great depression. These problems dictated less, rather than more, foreign involvement. Yet Hoover and Stimson saw the Japanese invasion as threatening a great deal more than China's integrity. At stake was the world-wide peace-keeping structure embodied in such understandings as the Washington conference treaties and the Kellogg-Briand pact. Thus, when efforts to encourage Japanese self-restraint failed, the United States was determined to take some action. "If the fruits of aggression should be recognized," wrote Stimson, "the whole theory of the Kellogg Pact would be repudiated, and the world would be at once returned to the point of recognizing war as a legitimate instrument of national policy. Nonrecognition might not prevent aggression, but recognition gave it outright approval." Quoted in Norman A. Graebner, "Hoover, Roosevelt, and the Japanese," *Pearl Harbor*, Borg and Okamoto, eds., 29.

For a time it seemed that Japanese expansion might yet be checked by international pressure. The League Assembly, March, 1932, aligned itself with the nonrecognition doctrine and, in May, China and Japan made peace at Shanghai on terms worked out by the consular committee of the League. But these prospects were at best temporary. There was, in fact, very little basis for collective action. For example, although Great Britain saw great dangers not only to its commercial interests in China but also to its imperial domains in South and Southeast Asia, London could devise no practical formula for checking Japan. Like virtually every other power, Britain confronted an economic crisis at home which demanded the highest priority. Moreover, the British were not impressed either by Nanking's ability to defend China or by the American theory that Japan would be constrained by moral sanctions. Indeed, British officials despaired of cooperating with the United States. As a result, no united front developed, and Japan was accorded a virtual free hand.[10]

Since the beginning of 1932, the Japanese had encouraged and promoted the organization of local self-governing bodies throughout Manchuria. These had gradually combined into a new "state," which had declared its independence of China and the Nanking government, February 18, 1932. On March 9, the former and last emperor of China, known as Henry P'u-yi, became regent of this new state of Manchukuo, and on September 15 Japan

[10] At the height of the Shanghai crisis, Stanley Baldwin expressed a common view among British officials: "You will get nothing out of Washington but words, big words, but only words." Thus, Great Britain guarded itself against the appearance of too close cooperation with the United States. The British were persuaded that, if Japan were provoked, the Americans would offer no real support. For an example of the limited cooperation that London would permit, see the study of Anglo-American naval cooperation in the Pacific by Gerald E. Wheeler, "Isolated Japan: American Diplomatic Cooperation, 1927-1936," *Pacific Historical Review*, 30 (1961), 165-78. The basic study of British attitudes is Christopher Thorne, "The Shanghai Crisis of 1932: The Basis of British Policy," *American Historical Review*, 75 (1970), 1616-39.

extended formal recognition to the regime it had created. In a dramatic scene at Geneva, the Japanese delegation walked out of the Assembly (February, 1933) and gave notice of Japan's intention of withdrawing from the League altogether. In January, 1933, Japanese troops began the invasion of Jehol province while others fanned out through the Peiping area south of the Great Wall. These latest Japanese conquests were accorded a measure of Chinese recognition in a truce agreement signed at Tangku, May 31, 1933, by which China accepted the creation of a broad "demilitarized neutral" zone. Thus through the establishment of an autonomous buffer state, the invasion of North China led directly to expanded Japanese control.

MANCHURIA: INTERPRETATIONS

Japan had gained control of nearly half a million square miles of territory by the application of force in a manner which the international legal opinion of governments did not regard as war, and which the Japanese termed euphemistically an "incident." The effect was to reshape East Asia more radically than any "incident' since the British had fashioned the treaty of Nanking in 1842. Japan's creation of Manchukuo was an effort to establish a continental power in Asia as a counterbalance to the maritime power which Western nations had exercised over China through nearly a century.

In a broader sense, the Manchurian "incident" was a second and more disheartening test of collective security as a principle, and of the means of enforcement. As Russia used direct action in North Manchuria in 1929, so Japan used force in South Manchuria and North China from 1931 to 1933. Neither France nor Great Britain was prepared to apply sanctions against Japan without the active support of the United States. While the United States cooperated to a limited degree with the League of Nations she remained outside the world's only permanent machinery dedicated to the principle of collective security, and the American administration was constantly fearful of public reaction should it appear that it was using Manchuria as a back-

door entry into the League. In reality, American policy, as the Manchurian affair developed in 1931, remained true to traditional principles of the open door and the integrity of China as embodied in the Washington treaties, and it called upon Japan to observe these covenants and the Kellogg-Briand pact. It prodded the League toward similar action. Whether more could have been expected from a government representative of the same political faith which a decade earlier had repudiated the Wilsonian program of collective security is a matter on which there has been no general agreement. At all events, neither the League, the United States, nor the two together stopped Japan, and the integrity of China was not preserved by reassertion of the nonrecognition doctrine.

JAPAN, 1931: THE POLITICAL ATMOSPHERE

When the Kwantung Army defied the cabinet in Tokyo and acted on its own authority in Manchuria, it had the potential support in Japan of a people prepared to follow any leadership that offered positive solutions for the nation's economic ills. By 1931 party politicians had lost much of their earlier appeal. This growing disesteem sprang partly from a conviction that the makers of Japan's foreign policy were not delivering promised results. Japan's self-restraint and cooperative spirit under the Shidehara diplomacy had neither moderated outbursts of Chinese nationalism nor ended criticism of Japanese ambitions by the West. Moreover, these apparent failures in foreign affairs led to increasing criticism of party government and its handling of domestic affairs. Japan was deep in the world depression; population was increasing at nearly one million *per* year, overtaking the country's food supply. The national economy was not absorbing the more than 400,000 new workers annually seeking employment. The farmer, already debt-ridden, faced decreasing income. Capital was concentrated in a few, great, family-owned *zaibatsu* combines, while small business, near bankruptcy, was without a voice in economic policy. Thus the stage was set perfectly for those who had long been ready to say that responsible party government was a fraud and that Japan must return to the leadership of her "true" patriots.

Caught in this political crossfire, Japan's party leaders failed utterly to keep the military under control. Within hours after the outbreak of fighting in Manchuria, the Wakatsuki cabinet adopted a policy limiting the military theater. But this decision, like others seeking to discipline the Kwantung army, was ignored. It was a case of a united military command exercising its will upon a divided civilian leadership. While a majority in the cabinet opposed the Manchurian conquest, several ministers were outspoken in their support of expansionist policies. In consequence, the government temporized until it finally resigned in December. Wakatsuki's successor, Inukai Tsuyoshi, committed by principle and membership in the *Seiyukai* to the practice of party government, suffered an even crueler fate. Since by the time Inukai took office the conquest of Manchuria was nearly complete, the prime minister concentrated on checking further insubordination. He attempted negotiations with the Chinese and sought an imperial rescript restraining the Kwantung army. These efforts not only failed, they also brought an end to party cabinets. Inukai was assassinated by ultranationalists on May 15, 1932. The next two prime ministers (Saito Makoto, May, 1932-July, 1934; and Okada Keisuke, July, 1934-March, 1936) were admirals, selected by Saionji, the only surviving *genro,* on the theory that they would be acceptable to, and more manageable than, Japan's generals. Some party members continued to criticise the military from the floor of the Diet, but the parties themselves were split by the Manchuria crisis into impotent, quarreling factions.

The new political atmosphere encouraged the pretensions of civilian and military extremists. These right wing social critics had long been a part of the Japanese scene. Early in the Meiji era, ultranationalists had proclaimed their loyalty to the throne, their mystical belief in Japan's destiny as leader of all Asia, and their conviction that the Japanese possessed superlative inborn qualities

which set them apart from other peoples. Organizations espousing these ideas however, were not numerous until the 1920s, when some 600 or more such groups were spawned in response to the pressures of economic and social changes. Even then, most of these societies were short-lived and had little voice in national policy. It was the Manchurian incident, which resulted partly from plots hatched by members of one of the ultranationalist societies, the *Sakurakai* (The Society of the Cherry), that tipped the balance toward the extremists. After 1931 ultranationalist organizations increasingly tended to interlock with the military, especially with junior officers. The common ground between civilian extremists and the young officers was the conviction that Japan's postwar liberalism and democracy pointed toward national decline. Among the military, this conviction was strengthened by sympathy for the plight of the oppressed peasantry. Since the military drew heavily from a rural and small town populace, the officer corps shared peasant resentment of the businessman's political and economic ascendency. Indeed, after 1931 the military became a champion of agrarian interests against city groups, especially the capitalists.[11]

THE NEW JAPANISM

The tone and temper of rightist ultranationalism, the new Japanism, was best personified by General Araki Sadao, who had risen from humble birth and from labor in a soy sauce factory to become minister of war, 1931-1934. In appearance and temperament

---

[11]While these economic and social tensions were aggravated by the worldwide crisis caused by the great depression, they were even more fundamentally a product of the priorities set by Japan's own leadership. To insure national power, the Meiji oligarchy had chosen to stress industrialization at the expense of agriculture. Thus Japan in the 1930s was wrestling with a product of its own modern development. See especially the essays by James Morley and Edwin O. Reischauer in *Dilemmas of Growth in Prewar Japan,* James Morley, ed. (1972).

more like a mild and ascetic priest than a saber-rattling samurai, Araki was nontheless a soldier, simple in personal habits and single-minded in his devotion to *Kodo,* the imperial way. It was Araki who became the spiritual leader and the politico-ethical spokesman of the new Japan. As this Japan faced a world hostile toward her because of her continental expansion, Araki rationalized ultranationalism and foreign conquest as high ethical principles, clothing them in the traditional Japanese doctrines of *Kodo, Kokutai* (national polity),[12] and *Hakko ichiu* (the world under one roof). The implications of these doctrines were reinterpreted as Japan's universal and benign mission to bring peace to the world. In East Asia, this mission would spread the beneficent rule of the emperor to those benighted peoples whose rulers had failed them or who had fallen a prey to Western exploitation and the doctrines of capitalism and liberalism. At home *Kodo* would direct Japanese footsteps into the forsaken paths of her own indigenous culture. From these paths she had been enticed, so it was said, by pernicious Western cults—liberalism, capitalism, democracy, individualism, and even communism—and the result had been a Japan where political life was usurped by corrupt political parties, where capitalists grew wealthy while peasants could not eat the rice they grew—a Japan weakened at home and thus denied the right to rescue Asia from European and American exploitation.[13]

Organizations such as the *Yuzonsha* (Society to Preserve the National Essence)

[12] *Kokutai* as used by the Japanese is meant to suggest that unity of the state which results from the unqualified loyalty of the people to the imperial line "unbroken through ages eternal."

[13] D. C. Holtom, *Modern Japan and Shinto Nationalism* (rev. ed., 1947), 21-23. On the subject of Japanese nationalism during the past century, the student should consult R.P. Dore, *Education in Tokugawa Japan* (1965); Delmer M. Brown, *Nationalism in Japan* (1955); and "A Symposium on Japanese Nationalism," *Journal of Asian Studies,* 31 (1971), 5-62, with contributions by Kenneth B. Pyle, Tetsuo Najita, and Harry D. Harootunian. It should be recalled that nationalism, either in Japan or elsewhere, fits into no simple definition. Moreover, the study of nationalism, undoubtedly the most powerful political emotion in the modern world, has been impeded by the heat of ideological conflicts.

nurtured other national messiahs, such as Kita Ikki and Okuwa Shumei, whose writings called for a new authoritarianism safeguarding and promoting military power under the emperor's guidance. Other reformers proposed a return to an agrarian-centered economy.

In addition to these revolutionary groups, there were conservatives of the oligarchy, the army, the bureaucracy, and business, who, fearing revolution and upholding the imperial interpretation of the Meiji constitution, were emphatically antidemocratic. The most active personalities of this grouping were organized in the *Kokuhonsha* (National Foundation Society). The new mood as reflected in the drift of Japan's leadership was suspicious, if not fearful, of democratic trends. By 1933, the *Seiyukai* was parroting the slogans of the young officers, and was appealing to Japanese education and Shintoism to revive the Japanese spirit and the imperial way.

CURBING DANGEROUS THOUGHTS

The advocates of ultranationalism were alert to ferret out the enemies that bored from within. Those Japanese reputed to be friends of Westernism, democracy, and responsible government were especially suspect as purveyors of "dangerous thoughts." The most famous case of this sort of attack on intellectual freedom had as its victim Minobe Tatsukichi, a distinguished professor of constitutional law. His books were widely known and he was a respected member of the Peers. He was not a radical and it would be difficult to know on what grounds he could even be called a liberal. His theory of the emperor was not exactly a democratic doctrine; in its simplest form it was that the emperor was an organ of the state and not the state itself. But this proposition was all that was needed by the superpatriots in their search for subversives. The fact that the doctrine had long been taught and accepted by many respectable men was irrelevant. What did matter was that in 1935 the ultranationalists had deemed Minobe a traitor to the imperial way. Minobe's logical protest, that if the emperor's sovereignty was inherent in his being and person then the Meiji constitution was mean-

Emperor Hirohito (astride the white horse) as he was pictured in an official Japanese publication in 1935. Compare this portrayal with another official picture on page 419.

ingless, fell on deaf ears. The clamor of the nationalists, and also of the *Seiyukai* politicians, forced Minobe's resignation from the Peers and from his professorship. Hardly a voice was raised in his defense.[14]

Such irresponsible assaults on respectable men did not mean that the chauvinists were all of one mind. Within the top echelons of the army were violent factional disputes, which were carried in some cases to solution by murder. Furthermore, as the 1930s advanced, there was faltering opposition to the extremes of militarism from conservative officials of the court as well as from other sources. Moreover, while by 1940 the old political parties had dissolved themselves to make way for a single, exclusive, and official party (the Imperial Rule Assistance Association), extremists never created, in concept or

[14] Minobe's "organic theory" brought him into direct conflict with the "historical school" of constitutional lawyers, who maintained that by his doctrine he had violated the principles and essence of Japanese nationalism, known as *national polity*. The advocates of Japanese expansion could not tolerate a philosophy that claimed the emperor was a mere functionary of the state. See Frank O. Miller, *Minobe Tatsukichi: Interpreter of Constitutionalism in Japan* (1965). For a study of the opposition to Minobe see George M. Wilson, *Radical Nationalist in Japan: Kita Ikki, 1833-1937* (1969).

reality, a *Fuhrer*. Even General Premier Tojo Hideki, the man who carried Japan into total war in 1941, was never a Hitler. Japan's authoritarianism borrowed from the West but did not imitate the West.

EXTREMISTS SEEK CONTROL

The political history of Japan after 1931 is a history of extreme nationalism nurtured in a historically strong military tradition and directed by a politically-minded, authoritarian military caste. In 1932, as the success of the Manchurian invasion gave weight to demands for a "stronger foreign policy," the activities of the ultranationalists became violent. On February 9, Inouye Junnosuke, former finance minister and manager of the *Minseito,* was murdered; on March 5, Dan Takuma, managing director of the Mitsui interests was also murdered. These deaths came before that of Prime Minister Inukai who was assassinated by a small band of naval officers and farmers who believed Japan could not be purified until the old politicians and parties were destroyed. Significantly, all of the dead had been outspoken foes of those who sought expansion of Japanese foreign interests through force.

Ten days after Inukai's assassination, the *Seiyukai* cabinet resigned, thus destroying the last vestige of party government. While the fall of the cabinet ended an era begun by Hara in 1918, the event did not mean the immediate adoption of a new theory or structure of government, or that the extremists were in unchallenged control. What happened was an attempted return to tradition, a return to government by elder statesmen who could balance opposing political elites, preserve national unity, and prevent revolution or exclusive army control. When, in 1932, Saionji recommended that the emperor call on Admiral Viscount Saito to form a national government, he was appealing to the Japanese political genius of the late Meiji period. Saito, an admiral and a man of aristocratic rank, was acceptable in a society where status still prevailed.

The new Saito cabinet included five party men—three from the *Seiyukai,* and two from the *Minseito*—two bureaucrats, three militarists, and three members of the House of Peers. It survived until 1934. Thereafter until 1941 nine governments trampled on the heels of their predecessors. The high mortality in these administrations was symptomatic of the turbulent instability of Japanese politics. Saito's immediate successor, Admiral Okada Keisuke, followed the Saito pattern in cabinet personnel. Thereafter cabinets became less "national" and more representative of the growing power of the militarists and the ultra-nationalists.[15]

[15] On Saito's position, see Ippei Fukuda, *Sketches of Men and Life* (1933), 27-34. On the fall of cabinet government, see Robert A. Scalapino, *Democracy and the Party Movement in Prewar Japan* (1953), 370-71. Premiers who headed "national" cabinets, 1931-1941, included: 1932, Admiral Viscount Saito Makoto; 1934, Admiral Okada Keisuke; 1936, Hirota Koki; 1937, General Hayashi Senjuro; 1937, Prince Konoe Fumimaro; 1939, Baron Hiranuma Kiichiro; 1940, Admiral Yonai Mitsumasa; 1940, Prince Konoe Fumimaro; 1941, Prince Konoe Fumimaro; 1941, General Tojo Hideki. From 1939 on, cabinet changes hardly affected national policy. Policy was determined not by cabinets but by a small, flexible group of military and civilian oligarchs finding some compromise between factions seeking power. It was the *genro* idea, without any genuine *genro* since Saionji's power had declined with age and circumstances. He died in 1940.

Indicative of these trends were efforts to undo the work of the elections of February, 1936, in which the nationalist parties and the *Seiyukai* lost ground, and in which leftist parties and the more moderate *Minseito* made a surprisingly strong showing. Extremists reacted swiftly to this evidence of continued opposition to their cause. On February 26, four days after the announcement of the election returns, junior officers and a regiment of troops en route to Manchuria attempted to overthrow the Okada cabinet by force. The mutineers murdered Takahashi Korekiyo, the minister of finance; Admiral Viscount Saito Makoto, lord keeper of the privy seal; and General Watanabe Jotaro, inspector general of military education. They attempted to kill Premier Okada but murdered his brother-in-law by mistake. For three days the heart of Tokyo was held by the mutinous troops.[16]

Although for the moment the army's prestige was weakened by these outrages, it soon recovered when apologists painted the assassins as young men pure in heart whose sole motive was to restore the "national spirit." Fundamentally the political picture had not been changed, for although the new government formed by Hirota Koki, March 9, 1936, was composed of moderate militarists and civilian bureaucrats, the influence of the army remained high, each minister having been approved by General Count Terauchi Juichi, the minister of war. Perhaps more important was the way in which the maneuverings of the moderates versus the extreme militarists added to the confusion of thought and alignment among civilian groups. Factionalism was already present in the bureaucracy, and among the major political parties the *Seiyukai* had long since shown its willingness to support extremes of nationalism. Now there were signs that the great Mitsui house was beginning to look with quali-

[16] The seriousness of this attempted coup is underlined by the fact that, while the actual mutineers were junior officers, they received encouragement and support from their seniors. The government's initial response was confused and ineffectual. It was the emperor's outraged resistance to his palace military advisors that turned the tide. See Ben-Ami Shillony, "The February 26 Affair: Politics of a Military Insurrection," in *Crisis Politics in Prewar Japan,* George M. Wilson, ed. (1970), 25-50.

fied favor toward extremists at home who could be counted as expansionists abroad. Younger and lesser-known capitalists, such as Aikawa Yoshisuke, heading army-sponsored industry in Manchukuo, had already accepted army backing as a convenient means of breaking into the industrial monopoly of the established *zaibatsu*. As the crosscurrents of domestic conflict increased, the Hirota cabinet moved steadily toward "bureaucratic totalitarianism."

Until 1937 a number of politicians and indeed Japan's electorate showed at times a healthy skepticism toward all moves in the direction of fascism and irresponsible military expansion. The force of this resistance, however, was worn away by assassinations, terrorism, the appeal of foreign conquest, and constant reiteration of nationalistic themes. Military budgets reached all-time highs, while the influence of the Diet continued to decline. Further evidence of the army's involvement in politics came in January, 1937, when the emperor called upon General Ugaki Kazushige to succeed Hirota. Yet the military ascendency by no means guaranteed Japan a unified, resolute political leadership. The depth of divisions within the military was revealed when the army blocked Ugaki's appointment by refusing to appoint a minister of war. Still another cabinet headed by another general, Hayashi Senjuro, collapsed after the prime minister failed to win the nation's unified support. In these circumstances, Prince Konoe Fumimaro, a member of one of Japan's oldest aristocratic families and a man with close ties to the imperial household, was called to head the government. The hope was that Konoe, as a symbol of imperial authority, might end the political confusion and thus unite the nation.

CONSOLIDATION OF MANCHUKUO AFTER 1932

Meanwhile the new state of Manchukuo was the scene of striking economic developments. Prior to the Manchurian incident of 1931, Japanese investments in the South Manchurian sphere of influence amounted to 1.617 billion yen, nearly 50 percent of which represented outlays of the South Manchuria Railway. In 1938, total Japanese investments in Manchukuo were about 3.441 billion yen, and by the end of 1939 the figure had reached 4 billion. Much of this investment took the form of imports of mining, factory, and textile machinery, and of consumer goods.[17]

Politically the fiction of an independent state was maintained. On March 1, 1934, Henry P'u-yi, who had been serving as the Japanese-appointed regent, was enthroned as the Emperor Kangte. Under a constitution of the same date, Manchukuo became a monarchy with both executive and legislative authority exercised by the emperor, though the latter powers were subject to the approval of a legislative council. Real power, however, remained in the hands of the Japanese and Manchukuo troops and the governor of the Kwantung leased territory.

In line with the American nonrecognition doctrine, none of the great powers, save Japan, at first recognized Manchukuo—and of the small powers, only El Salvador, the Papacy, and the Dominican Republic had extended recognition by 1934. Germany, however, gave qualified recognition in a trade agreement of the same year, renewed for a second three years in 1937; and in November, 1937, Italy formally recognized the puppet state. Full German recognition came on May 12, 1938, and was soon followed by recognition from Poland and Hungary. On February 24, 1939, Manchukuo became a signatory of the anti-comintern pact concluded by Germany and Japan on November 25, 1936. Soviet Russia extended a *de facto* recognition; after two years of negotiations, 1933-1935, Russia sold its rights in the Chinese Eastern Railway to Manchukuo, the payment being guaranteed by Japan.

During the decade of the 1930's, the international politics and government of Manchukuo were more orderly than the outside world of nonrecognizing powers was pre-

[17] E. B. Schumpeter, ed., *The Industrialization of Japan and Manchukuo, 1930-1940* (1940), 398.

pared to admit. Under the authoritarian, regimented rule of Manchukuo there was greater stability in Manchuria than at any other time in its modern history. Chinese who resisted were hunted down and eliminated, but for those who accepted the regime there could be increased security for life and property.[18]

By 1937 Japan had made considerable progress toward integrating the economic and strategic values of Manchukuo with those of the homeland. In general, the idea had been that Manchukuo would provide the raw materials in minerals and foodstuffs lacked by Japan's growing industrial society. On the credit side, Manchukuo's population was rapidly increasing, new farm lands were being opened, and industry, particularly coal, iron, and steel, was expanding. On the debit side was the instability of the international picture, pervaded by the insatiable fever of the Kwantung army to insure the borders of the new state by pushing its boundaries into Mongolia and by forcing the establishment of a secure buffer zone in North China.

FURTHER JAPANESE ADVANCES

The first step in Japan's advance was the creation by the Kwantung army of an autonomous Mongol province in western Manchuria incorporating part of Jehol, which had been added to Manchukuo in 1933. Here, by guaranteeing the Mongols possession of their grazing lands, by insuring and respecting their autonomous government, and by fostering the privileges of the Lama priests, the Japanese hoped to appeal to the Mongols in general, including those in Outer Mongolia. The scheme was not entirely successful, since the Mongol princes also bargained with the Chinese Nationalists at Nanking.

Just as the Kwantung army felt it necessary to move westward into Inner Mongolia, so it

[18] Although in general this was true, there is also evidence that those who suffered from Japanese rule were not solely those who resisted. See in particular the picture presented by W. I. Ladejinsky, "Manchurian Agriculture under Japanese Control," *Foreign Agriculture*, 5 (1941), 309-40. Moreover, there was great economic pressure on the people of Manchuria as Japan's war program developed. These factors all served to keep alive a Manchurian resistance movement.

thought it even more essential to establish friendly governments in the northeastern sections of China Proper, especially in the provinces of Hopei, Shantung and Shansi. These provinces could be linked, so it was thought, with the Inner Mongolian provinces of Chahar and Suiyuan (yet to be conquered) to give Japan control of all bordering territory to the south and west of Manchukuo. In the two years following the Tangku truce (May, 1933), postal service and railway traffic were resumed between Manchukuo and China, though without the latter extending formal recognition. By 1935, the Kwantung army had exerted enough pressure to force the retirement of Chinese troops from Hopei and to liquidate the *Kuomintang* in that region. Yet, as in Inner Mongolia, these measures failed to establish the friendly government the Japanese military was determined to have. By sanctioning cooperation between local Chinese authorities and the Japanese, Nanking retained at least a show of authority in northern China.

Simultaneously with the Japanese infiltration into North China came renewed efforts by Japanese diplomacy to reach an understanding with China as a whole. There was always the hope among Japanese statesmen that a workable arrangement could be reached for close political and economic planning among Japan, Manchukuo, and China. Japan's success in Manchukuo and the continued factional strife within China lent some encouragement to the Japanese hope. Indeed, on the surface, Japan appeared to make some progress. There were elements within the *Kuomintang*-Nationalist government which were prepared to adopt a policy of appeasement, either from personal conviction on the principle of a pan-Asian policy or because they regarded resistance by China as hopeless. Consequently, during 1935, Nanking made some efforts to stop anti-Japanese boycotts, to prevent publication of inflammatory anti-Japanese articles, and to suppress the student movement. Yet Nanking was not entirely subservient. When in 1934 Japan warned the League powers and the United States to follow a policy of "hands off" China, the Nanking government denied the right of Japan to assert a monopoly of political interest in East Asia. It all added up to a situation in

North China in which by 1936 there was no Sino-Japanese war but neither was there a Sino-Japanese peace.

FOR FURTHER READING

George Alexander Lensen, *The Damned Inheritance: The Soviet Union and the Manchurian Crises, 1924-1935* (1974), the most recent of Lensen's exhaustive probing of Russia's far eastern diplomacy. Peter S. H. Tang, *Russian and Soviet Policy in Manchuria and Outer Mongolia* (1959) has a chapter on the undeclared Sino-Soviet war of 1929. Material on Sino-Soviet difficulties is also to be found in Max Beloff, *Foreign Policy of Soviet Russia, 1929-1941* (2 vols., 1953). For interpretations of issues between China and Japan see: H. L. Kingman, *Effects of Chinese Nationalism upon Manchurian Railway Developments, 1925-1931* (1932); K. K. Kawakami, *Manchoukuo: Child of Conflict* (1933), an able Japanese apology; and Seiji G. Hishida, *Japan Among the Great Powers: A Survey of Her International Relations* (1940). The official Chinese case as presented to the Lytton Commission is *Memoranda Presented to the Lytton Commission* (2 vols., 1932). Oka Takashi, "Saionji and the Manchurian Crisis," *Papers on China*, Vol. 8. Published and distributed by the East Asian Research Center, Harvard University (1953) emphasizes the Japanese political background.

W. A. Williams, "China and Japan: A Challenge and a Choice of the Nineteen Twenties," *Pacific Historical Review* 26 (1957), 259-79, views Stimson's diplomacy in the light of American policy over the preceding decade. Paul H. Clyde, "The Diplomacy of 'Playing No Favorites': Secretary Stimson and Manchuria, 1931," *Mississippi Valley Historical Review* 35 (1948) reveals the caution and limited purpose of the Secretary. For an American Ambassador's memoirs see Joseph C. Grew, *Ten Years in Japan* (1944). R. Basset, *Democracy and Foreign Policy: A Case History; The Sino-Japanese Dispute, 1931-33* (1952) studies British public opinion. Harriet L. Moore, *Soviet Far Eastern Diplomacy,*

1931-1945 (1945) chronicles what Russia said and did. See also Frank M. Tamagna, *Italy's Interests and Policies in the Far East* (1941). Sara R. Smith, *The Manchurian Crisis, 1931-1932* (1948) is useful chiefly for its discussion of the League of Nations. On legal aspects see Robert Langer, *Seizure of Territory: The Stimson Doctrine and Related Principles in Legal Theory and Diplomatic Practice* (1947).

On Japan in Manchuria after the crisis note: F. C. Jones, *Manchuria Since 1931* (1949); and John R. Steward, *Manchuria Since 1931* (1936). Norton S. Ginsburg, "Manchurian Railway Development," *Far Eastern Quarterly*, 8 (1948-49), 398-411, covers the period 1931-45 in the light of Japan's strategic purposes respecting Russia. Ch'ing Hsuan-t'ung, *The Last Manchu*, ed. with an introduction by Paul Kramer; Kuo Ying Tsai, trans. (1967), excerpts from the original manuscript of the last Ch'ing emperor who also served as the titular head of Manchukuo.

Politics and Government. A hardheaded scrutiny of Japan's ultranationalistic political organizations and forces during the fateful decade of the 1930s is found in Richard Storry, *The Double Patriots: A Study in Japanese Nationalism* (1957). James B. Crowley, "Japanese Army Factionalism in the Early 1930's," *Journal of Asian Studies* 21 (1962), 309-26, modifies the findings of Storry and others on the intraplay of groups within the army. Royal Jules Wald, *The Young Officers Movement in Japan, ca. 1925-1937, Ideologies and Actions* (Unpublished Ph.D. dissertation, University of California, Berkeley, 1949) supplies much information about the various secret organizations among the "young" officers. Pertinent documents and comment on the nature of militarism and the role of the military are contained in Tsunoda Ryusaku and others, eds., *Sources of the Japanese Tradition* (1958),* Chapter 27. John Maki, *Japanese Militarism, Its Cause and Cure* (1945) exemplifies the view of Japanese society as basically autocratic and militaristic. Robert K. Hall, ed., *Kokutai no hongi. Cardinal Principles of the National Entity of Japan,* trans. by John O. Gauntlett, with introduction by the editor (1949) provides a Japanese text published by the Ministry of Education to further nationalism. Charles B. Fahs, *Government in Japan* (1940); Hugh Borton, *Japan Since 1931* (1940); and R. K. Reischauer, *Japan: Government-Politics* (1939), especially Chapter 7, are three studies which supplement each other. See also Evelyn Colbert, *The Left Wing in Japanese Politics* (1952) which traces left wing developments from the 1918 proletarian movement through the 1950 purge. Maruyama Masao, *Thought and Behavior in Modern Japanese Politics,* ed. by Ivan Morris (1963)* interprets the rise of ultranationalism.

Economics. Material on the important and complex economic basis of politics include the following: E. B. Schumpeter ed., *The Industrialization of Japan and Manchukuo* (1940); E. F. Penrose, *Food Supply and Raw Materials in Japan* (1930); Asahi Isoshi, *The Economic Strength of Japan* (1939); three works by G. C. Allen, *Japan the Hungry Guest* (1938), on Japan's economic needs resulting from industrialization; *Japanese Industry: Its Recent Development and Present Condition* (1939), on the impact of the Sino-Japanese War on the industrial structure; and *Western Enterprise in Far Eastern Economic Development: China and Japan* (1954), in collaboration with A. G. Donnithorne.

From the Marco Polo Bridge to Pearl Harbor, 1937–1941

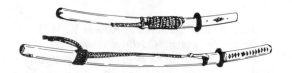

27

Following Japan's conquest of Manchuria in 1931, politics carried both China and Japan closer to a broader conflict. Although China was by no means unified under the new *Kuomintang*-Nationalist government, Chinese nationalism, often unorganized, incoherent, even leaderless, had become vehement against foreign encroachment. There were growing pressures on Nanking to abandon its policy of appeasement in favor of resistance against the Japanese. In Japan, on the other hand, the ascendency of ultranationalists portended further changes in foreign policy. From 1933 to 1937 Japan had sought to bind China to her purposes by measures short of open warfare, but the birth of Manchukuo, Japanese penetration of Inner Mongolia, and the effort to create an autonomous state in North China had all failed to create a subservient China. These failures had proved exceedingly irritating. By 1937, while the ultranationalists had not established complete control over the Tokyo government, the prominence of military leaders in politics increased the likelihood that solutions to Japan's problems would be sought through armed force. The result was the renewal of Sino-Japanese hostilities on a grand scale in the bloody, undeclared war of 1937-1941, and the final merging of this conflict with the world conflagration that began with the German invasion of Poland.

JAPAN'S SEARCH FOR SECURITY

Japanese expansion into China and, subsequently, into Southeast Asia was rooted in deep-seated feelings of insecurity. In a situation of great social and economic crisis, Tokyo's military leadership won popular support for the theory that Japan, despite a half-century of growth in her international status, was threatened by ever-growing crises. The challenge posed by Chinese nationalism to Japan's leadership in Asia was intensifying. Soviet power, a communist system inimical to Japanese government under an emperor, was firmly established in Siberia. Finally, there was growing suspicion of the United States and Great Britain, both of which identified their interests with the preservation of China's integrity.[1] Accordingly, it was said, Japan must establish hegemony in Asia. In the

[1] Northern China was not the only target of Japanese military expansionists, 1931-1933. In the aftermath of the Manchurian incident, a faction within the army, the *Koda-ha* (imperial way), which was organized around such men as General Araki

phraseology of one editor, Japan was to "advance with a policy of Asia for Asiatics—an Asiatic Monroe Doctrine." The substance of this concept was to be the ultranationalists' solution of the China problem: (1) China was to be forced to recognize Manchukuo; (2) her economic and diplomatic dependence on Western powers was to be terminated; and (3) the country was to be brought into full cooperation with Japan for the benefit of both nations. Later, from 1940 to 1941, after Europe went to war and the United States threw its support to Great Britain and a Dutch government-in-exile, Japan spoke of the necessity of eliminating "encirclement" from the south. The nation's earlier determination to found her foreign policy on international cooperation was gone. Faced with an apparently ever more serious foreign danger, the Japanese people were to submit to the discipline of a planned economy and expanded governmental authority. Meanwhile the military called for a crash expansion program for the navy and the army.[2]

MARCO POLO BRIDGE: HOSTILITIES, NOT WAR

On the night of July 7, 1937, in the vicinity of the Marco Polo Bridge about nine miles southwest of Peiping, fighting broke out between a Chinese garrison and a Japanese force. The latter was conducting maneuvers beyond the localities where foreign troops were permitted under the Boxer protocol. The area was important strategically because of the Peiping-Hankow railway. Moreover, without treaty right, the town of Fengt'ai, through which a connecting line passed, had been garrisoned for more than a year by Japanese troops. Although in 1913 the Chinese government had authorized foreign commanders to drill their troops in the region, the magnitude of the Japanese maneuvers following the long period of tension since the Tangku truce of May, 1933, was an invitation to trouble. As on previous occasions, efforts were made to settle the dispute locally. But at the end of July, Japanese reinforcements reached the Peiping area and demanded that Chinese troops withdraw south of Peiping and Tientsin. When this demand was refused, Peiping and Tientsin were occupied by the Japanese. The Japanese emperor ordered Prince Konoe to start negotiations with the Nanking government. Nanking, however, having presumably decided that it could tolerate no further erosion of its sovereignty in this region, indicated that it was prepared to use armed force in order to retain North China. Japan's response was to abandon further efforts to control the area through economic and political pressures and to resort to arms herself.[3]

After occupying the area of Peiping and Tientsin, the Japanese drove into Inner Mongolia, occupied Kalgan, and thus severed China's principal line of overland communication with Soviet Russia. Suiyuan province was

Sadao, demanded a "preventative" war with the Soviet Union. Such was the influence of this faction that tensions in 1933 foreshadowed a resort to violence. General Araki's dismissal as war minister, January, 1934, however, was symptomatic of a decline in *Koda-ha* fortunes and of a definite shift in Japanese interests toward China. See Ikuhiko Hata, *Reality and Illusion: The Hidden Crisis between Japan and the U.S.S.R., 1932-1934,* Occasional Papers of the East Asian Institute, Columbia University (1967).

[2] See James B. Crowley, *Japan's Quest for Autonomy: National Security and Foreign Policy, 1931-1938* (1966); and his suggestive essay, "A New Deal for Japan and Asia: One Road to Pearl Harbor," in *Modern East Asia: Essays in Interpretation,* James B. Crowley, ed. (1970),* 235-64. In contrast to Crowley's writings, which emphasize the fears of Japan's whole leadership and its turn toward military solutions, earlier researchers explained Japanese militarism largely in terms of "conspiracies" of army and navy officers. This view suggested that Japan was in fact maneuvered into a program of conquest. See Yale C. Maxon, *Control of Japanese Foreign Policy* (1957); Richard Storry, *The Double Patriots* (1957); and Masao Maruyama, *Thought and Behavior in Modern Japanese Politics,* Ivan Morris, ed. (1963).*

[3] While the Konoe government pledged to "wage a war of chastisement" until China capitulated and reflected on "the error of its ways," the army general staff displayed decided skepticism. The general staff did not believe that Japan had the means of conquering Chiang Kai-shek's forces, and did not relish making heavy commitments in China while the Soviet Union was building its forces in the Maritime provinces. Thus the general staff persisted until the end of 1937 in an effort to persuade the government to negotiate a settlement. This effort was overruled on January 18, 1938 by a basic cabinet decision promising to "annihilate" the Chinese Nationalist government and "to foster new regimes for a rejuvenated China." See Crowley, "New Deal."

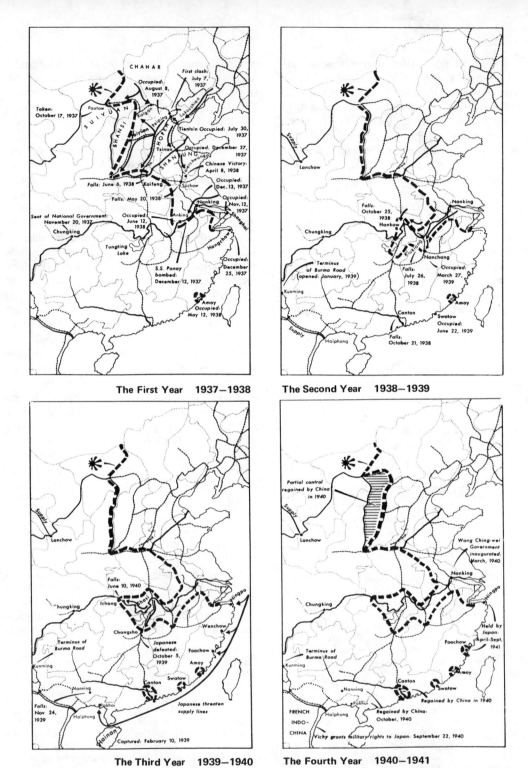

The First Year 1937–1938

The Second Year 1938–1939

The Third Year 1939–1940

The Fourth Year 1940–1941

Reproduced from A War Atlas for Americans *(New York: Simon & Schuster, 1944), with permission from the publisher and from the U.S. Department of State, Division of Map Intelligence and Cartography.*

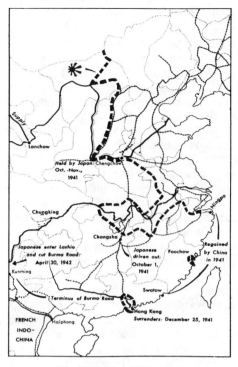

The Fifth Year 1941-1942

the International Settlement at Shanghai. This strategy failed again, as in 1932, for the Chinese at Shanghai were defeated after heroic resistance, and the Japanese moved up the river to capture Nanking in December, 1937, where local commanders permitted their troops to engage in wholesale acts of brutality against the local Chinese populace. The fall of Naking, however, did not result in the capture of the *Kuomintang*-Nationalist government. The regime had moved to Hankow and was eventually to retire further westward to Chungking. Nor did the Japanese advance signify the collapse of Chinese resistance in Central China. A humiliating defeat at Taierchwang, near the southern base of the Shantung peninsula, delayed the union of Japan's northern and central armies until May, 1938, when the Japanese won control of the two north-south railways: the Peiping-Hankow and Tientsin-Pukow lines. Five months were required for the Japanese to reach Hankow on the upper Yangtze, which was taken in October, 1938. Ichang still further up the Yangtze was not captured until June, 1940.

This pattern of initial success followed by virtual stalemate was repeated in the south. Canton, the great southern port, fell without resistance in the autumn, 1938, giving credence to reports that the city had been "sold." In November, 1939, the Japanese landed at Pakhoi in Kwangtung. From this base a drive into Kwangsi brought the capitulation of the provincial capital, Nanning. But China's over-all strategy was showing improvement. In Hunan province the Japanese were forced to stop their advance on Changsha. Thus Japan had invaded China on three major fronts, yet Chinese resistance seemed only to stiffen. To meet these difficulties Japan resorted not only to new military measures but also to diplomacy. Bomber raids were launched, especially on the new temporary capital at Chungking and key points on China's supply line from the south, the Burma road. In February, 1939, the Japanese navy seized the island of Hainan off the South China coast, occupied the Spratley Islands a month later, and continued a blockade of Chinese shipping at principal Chinese ports. Meanwhile the Japanese put forward a series

overrun and occupied, placing the Peiping-Suiyuan railway in Japanese hands. Other Japanese forces moved into Shansi to strike at strongholds of the Chinese Communists both there and in bordering Shensi. But here the Japanese met their first significant reverses at the hands of the Eighth Route (Communist) Army, so-called since its nominal incorporation with the Nationalist armies in August, 1937. Employing guerrilla tactics against forces overwhelmingly superior both in numbers and weapons, the Communists frustrated Japan's attempt to control northwest China. When the United States entered the war at the end of 1941, Japanese lines in this region were approximately where they had been in 1938.

Meanwhile, hostilities spread to the Yangtze valley. China was largely responsible for this development. Japanese interests would have been best served by confining the conflict to North China. Nanking, on the other hand, hoped for the involvement of other powers if Japan disregarded the neutrality of

of peace proposals involving Japanese control of strategic Chinese areas, recognition of Manchukuo, and the formation of an economic bloc of China, Japan, and Manchukuo. Although these feelers played upon existing dissensions within the *Kuomintang,* they were all rebuffed by Chiang Kai-shek in December, 1938.

THE PROPAGATION OF PUPPET REGIMES

Having failed to conquer China or to bring her government to acceptance of peace, Japan decided to ignore the *Kuomintang*-Nationalists as a government and to seek the establishment of a new Chinese regime which would do away with the folly of anti-Japanism. To this end Japan proposed to set up a puppet government similar to the regime that had functioned in Manchukuo since 1932. The first of these was the Provisional Government of the Republic of China, proclaimed at Peiping in December, 1937. Its authority and ability to govern the people of North China were successfully challenged from the beginning by a new Chinese administration called the Border Government of Hopei, Shansi, and Chahar, organized by Chinese Communists with initial approval of the *Kuomintang*-Nationalist government. This border government became one of the great forces of guerrilla resistance to Japanese penetration in the north.[4]

Since the Provisional Government at Peking never possessed more than a wavering local appeal, it was incumbent on Japan to find a Chinese national personality who could head a new puppet regime at Nanking with some prospect of claiming the allegiance of the Chinese people. Their choice settled upon Wang Ching-wei. Wang had a long and distinguished, if erratic, revolutionary record. An intimate of Sun Yat-sen, he had held many of the highest posts in the *Kuomintang* and the *Kuomintang*-Nationalist government. Although originally a leader of the left wing in the

Kuomintang, he had come to oppose the Communists, had developed a bitter spirit of rivalry toward Chiang Kai-shek, and had been recognized as the leader of appeasement. Moreover, prior to 1941, Wang had convinced himself that China's future lay in cooperation with Japan. At Nanking, March 30, 1940, the new National Government, under the leadership of Wang, was proclaimed. Declared to be the true guardian of the principles of Sun Yat-sen, this "returned" and "Reorganized Government" retained the *Kuomintang* ideology and the structure of the Nationalist Government as it had existed at Nanking. Its personnel was composed in considerable part, though not exclusively, of *Kuomintang* members who had deserted with Wang. Wang's government, soon recognized by Japan, concluded a treaty with Tokyo, November, 1940, providing for joint defense against communism and for cooperation in economic development. Recognition was also accorded to the Wang regime, July, 1941, by Germany, Italy, Spain, Rumania, and other totalitarian governments of Europe.[5]

[4] The techniques of resistance as they developed in North China are portrayed by George E. Taylor, *The Struggle for North China* (1940).

[5] The popular appeal of Wang's National Government was exceedingly limited. Although its "independence" was proclaimed, the government operated only in areas occupied by Japanese troops, and Wang's administration was manifestly under Japan's direction. Wang thus became in the eyes of many Chinese nothing less than a traitor. When the war ended, *Kuomintang* troops desecrated his tomb (he died in November, 1944). Yet Wang was not without his defenders. An impressive physical presence and a demeanor which recalled the Confucian ideal of a *chun-tzu* (superior man) combined to make Wang an enormously attractive individual. Moreover, it was argued that Wang's collaboration was not instigated by any desire to betray China. Chiang's Nationalist Government had been able neither to unite China nor to defend it against Japanese invaders. Collaboration with Japan, on the other hand, held possibilities of destroying the Chinese Communist movement, driving Western imperialists from East Asia, and speeding the modernization of Chinese society. Viewed in these terms, Wang was not a "traitor" but a wiser patriot than Chiang. According to his followers, Wang's tragedy was not that he failed the cause of Chinese nationalism but that Japan failed in her promise to assist Wang with China's salvation. See John Hunter Boyle, *China and Japan at War, 1937-1945: The Politics of Collaboration* (1972).

The area of China thus occupied or controlled by Japan constituted a rich block of territory comprising the Yangtze valley from Shanghai to Hankow in the south to Peiping and Chahar province in the north. Here Wang's nominal jurisdiction extended over more than a half million square miles of territory with a population of 200 million. It included much of the wealthiest and most densely populated areas of China. Japan turned to economic exploitation that would integrate this area into the co-prosperity framework with Manchukuo and Japan. The groundwork was prepared by intensive campaigns of propaganda to eliminate anti-Japanese sentiment. Against this background the whole economic and commercial structure of central and northeastern China was reorganized. All forms of communication and industry, including mining, were to be capitalized and directed by new companies in which Japan held half the stock. Ultimate authority rested with the newly-organized China affairs board, created in Tokyo, December, 1938. The general plan contemplated concentrations of high-precision industry in Japan; heavy, chemical, and electrical industry in Manchukuo; and salt production and light industry in North China.

RESISTANCE IN INDEPENDENT CHINA

Both for China and for the world at large the most significant and compelling fact of the four years of undeclared warfare, 1937-1941, was the resistance of independent China. Actually more than half of the territory and population of China Proper remained beyond the control of Japanese arms, although in economic wealth it was much the poorer half. Chinese nationalism thus had no alternative but to base its resistance on the great interior hinterland, where political and economic modernization were all but unknown. To this ancient west country, into the provinces of Szechuan, Kweichow, and Yunnan, trekked an astonishing migration of the wealthy, the educated, the politically influential, students, professors, skilled laborers, and some with no designation other than that of patriot. They

traveled by boat, by cart, and on foot, carrying what possessions they could. In the old interior, where ancient and feudal traditions were still predominant, they set up the wartime capital of Chungking and reassembled transplanted schools, universities, and factories.

In northwest China the resistance movement was led by the Communist party. As the Japanese offensive came to a standstill in Shansi, the Eighth Route Army began to push its way back into that province and thence out onto the North China plain. In 1938 this force was joined by the New Fourth Army. The Communist objective was to organize war bases in the less accessible border areas between provinces. Beginning with the Shansi-Hopeh-Chahar border region, set up in 1938, and moving later into the Shansi-Hopeh-Honan-Shantung border area, the Communists by 1941 had organized territory containing a population of about fifty million persons. Within these so-called "liberated areas" Communist troops, having been trained to regard themselves as defenders of the populace, depended upon the civilian population for food and quarters. The utilization of civilian intelligence networks enabled these armies to dispense with much of the usual centralized military organization. In consequence, the Communist armies operated as scattered, mobile forces, appearing and disappearing in the rural areas behind Japanese lines.

Ostensibly the Communist resistance effort was linked to *Kuomintang*-Nationalist leadership. Beginning in August, 1935, both the Chinese Communist party and the Comintern called for a united front against the Japanese, presumably because a nationwide resistance would serve the dual purpose of diverting the Japanese from an attack on the Soviet Union and keeping the *Kuomintang*-Nationalist regime from attacking its Communist opponents. At the end of the following year, more tangible evidence of the Communist desire for a united front was forthcoming as the party leadership helped engineer Chiang Kai-shek's release after the Sian kidnapping. As Japanese pressure increased, the Communists announced in September, 1937, their willingness to make peace with the *Kuomintang* on the understanding that the Red Army would be placed

Chunking during wartime.

under the Nationalist government's command as the Eighth Route Army, that the Chinese Soviet Republic would be disbanded and the territory under its control organized into a special-area government under the Nationalist government, that the Communists would halt the confiscation of land, and that the Communist party would subscribe to Sun Yat-sen's "Three Principles." For the *Kuomintang,* Chiang issued a statement endorsing the Communist proposal.

But these steps toward unity did not constitute a genuine political settlement. Relations between the *Kuomintang* and Communists were embittered by ten years of relentless civil war, and each side remained dedicated to the eradication of the other. In these circumstances, the truce, while it produced temporarily closer relations, led eventually to deeper conflicts. The Communists proved unwilling to submit wholly to *Kuomintang* leadership either in military or political matters. The Communist strategy of prolonged resistance through guerrilla warfare,

which was to be one of China's strongest military weapons, was not supported by the *Kuomintang* leadership. Nor could the *Kuomintang*-Nationalist government fail to be alarmed by the Communist practice of establishing local administrations, loyal to the Communists, in areas liberated by the Red armies. To the *Kuomintang* leadership, it seemed that the Communists were utilizing the war to promote their own political fortunes.[6] After 1938, while the war with Japan went forward, the *Kuomintang* and the Communists diverted some of their best troops to watch each other. From then on there were periodic clashes between *Kuomintang* and Communist armies.

THE SINO-JAPANESE CONFLICT IN WORLD POLITICS

The outcome of the Sino-Japanese conflict, however, was not to be determined solely by

[6] According to Communist claims, the Red Army increased from 80,000 in 1937 to 470,000 in 1943. An army of one million was claimed by 1945.

events in East Asia. As the two nations sank ever more deeply into the morass of undeclared war, the great Western powers sought to define their interests and positions with respect to the unpredictable contest. The diplomatic maneuverings which resulted from shifting national policies profoundly affected the power balances in East Asia. The worldwide diplomatic struggle that developed along with the undeclared war after 1937 involved the East Asian policies not only of the totalitarian powers but also of Great Britain and the United States.

The historical cleavage which had frequently existed between American and British policy in Asia was not ended with Japan's invasion of Manchuria in 1931. In January, 1932, Great Britain declined to give its formal support when the United States enunciated the so-called Stimson nonrecognition doctrine. British policy held that it was not the business of the British government to defend "the administrative integrity of China until that integrity" was "something more than an ideal."[7] By 1937, however, Japan's resort to war worked a fundamental change in British views. Japan's conquests in China posed immediate challenges to important British economic and political stakes. In addition, London foresaw a time when Japanese militarism would menace Britain's vast possessions and interests in Southeast Asia, India, and the western Pacific. This reassessment ushered in a new British policy of benevolent neutrality that favored China by giving her moral support and limited material aid, but nonetheless aimed at preventing a breakdown in Anglo-Japanese relations.[8]

[7] See I. S. Friedman, *British Relations with China, 1931-1939* (1940), 18-42.

[8] The stiffening of British resistance to Japanese expansion contrasted markedly with London's appeasement of Hitler. The disparity was explained by Great Britain's view that German ambitions were more limited than Japan's. Concessions to Germany would presumably relieve tensions, but concessions to the Japanese would only lead to more demands. Even so, British opposition was tempered by the recognition that she had little practical aid to give China and by her deep concern over Europe's problems. Nothing was to be gained by breaking with Japan at a time when there were great dangers of war nearer home. See Bradford A. Lee, *Britain and the Sino-Japanese War, 1937-1939: A Study in the*

In time, this revised British policy was to produce a basis for Anglo-American cooperation in Asia. The United States, like Great Britain, attached special significance to the outbreak of fighting in China. President Roosevelt adopted the thesis that the "China incident" was symptomatic of world-wide tendencies toward militarism. In consequence, the president and Secretary of State Cordell Hull assumed personal direction of American East Asian diplomacy as an aspect of a fresh search for ways of bolstering world peace. (Between 1932 and 1937 most of the negotiations concerned with this region had been conducted routinely by second- and third-ranking state department officials.) Roosevelt's famed "quarantine" speech, October, 1937, suggesting the isolation of aggressors, represented a possible new direction in American policy. But these broad parallels in British and American policy did not produce immediate agreeement on short-range tactics. When London suggested that the United States join an economic mission to China with the aim of rehabilitating Nationalist finances, the United States refused. Washington, preoccupied with efforts to end the great depression, leaned heavily toward a political philosophy of pacifism and isolation, fearing that the British proposal would lead to involvements Americans had no mind to assume.[9]

Dilemmas of British Decline (1973). For the thesis that joint Anglo-American efforts to check Japanese expansion by means short of war might have worked until as late as 1938, see Nicholas R. Clifford, *Retreat from China: British Policy in the Far East, 1937-1941* (1967).

[9] The definitive study of transformations in American policy is Dorothy Borg, *The United States and the Far Eastern Crisis of 1933-1938: From the Manchurian Incident through the Initial Stage of the Undeclared Sino-Japanese War* (1964). Roosevelt's efforts to infuse American policy with new vigor contrasted sharply with an earlier tendency to allow matters to drift. On taking office in 1933, Roosevelt put an end to Stimson's provocative note-writing and permitted no direct challenges to Japanese expansion. Yet he neither conceded the principle of American opposition nor encouraged his subordinates to seek a settlement with Japan. For observations on the ambiguities of American policy during Roosevelt's first administration see the essay by Waldo H. Heinrichs, Jr., in *American-East Asian Relations: A Survey*, Ernest B. May and James C. Thomson, Jr., eds. (1972), 243-59.

These continuing British-American differences over China were a natural product of the failure of the more general peace-keeping arrangements that had followed World War I. The years 1932-1937 saw the collapse of limitation on naval armaments. The world disarmament conference, meeting in Geneva while Japanese forces consolidated their position in Manchuria and fought with the Chinese at Shanghai, rejected an American proposal either to abolish all offensive weapons or to reduce existing armaments by 33 percent. In December, 1934, Japan gave the two-years' notice of her intent to denounce the Washington naval treaty of 1922 and made clear her intent to seek naval parity at the next disarmament conference. Accordingly, when her demand was denied, Japan withdrew from the London naval conference of 1935-1936. The treaty agreed upon by Britain, the United States, and France at London, March, 1936, without the adherence of Japan and Italy, thus became an empty gesture. Nor was this the only blow to international cooperation. On October 6, 1937, the League of Nations Assembly finally resolved that Japan's invasion of China was a violation of the nine-power treaty and the Kellogg-Briand pact, and suggested that the signatories find a solution to the Sino-Japanese dispute. This latter suggestion led to a meeting of nineteen powers in Brussels, from November 3 to November 24, 1937. All original and later signatories of the nine-power treaty were invited, along with Germany and the Soviet Union. Japan declined to attend, since she had been condemned, and took the position that the dispute concerned herself and China alone. Germany also stayed away. At Brussels the delegates talked, while some waited for the United States to propose sanctions. In the end the delegates reaffirmed, Italy dissenting, the applicability of the nine-power treaty, and went home. Japan was offered no inducement to make peace and there was no thought of collective force if she refused. The Brussels effort was stillborn.

The breakdown of the West's peace-keeping machinery was all the more striking because its deterioration was paralleled by the emergence of a new international force. At Berlin on November 25, 1936, Japan and Germany signed an anti-Comintern pact, providing for cooperation in "defense against the disintegrating influence of Communism." This pact, which was followed by a similar one between Japan and Italy, provided Tokyo with safeguards against Soviet Russian interference with her ambitions in China. Indeed, the existence of the pact encouraged the Japanese the following year to meet Chinese resistance with armed force. Interpreted more broadly, the agreements with Berlin and Rome were the first formal manifestation that Japan's ambitions had been accorded a measure of international acceptance.

THE NEW ORDER IN EAST ASIA

In autumn, 1938, Japan took stock of her position. She was convinced that the democracies would continue to do nothing and that the Soviet frontier would continue to be quiet. But the Japanese conquests in China, which had reached to Canton and Hankow, had not broken Chinese resistance. Japan had won the battles but she had not won China. The war was a stalemate and seemed likely to remain so indefinitely. Japan, therefore, sought a new policy to capitalize on her gains in the conquered territories of eastern China. This policy, announced by Premier Konoe, November 3, 1938, was "a new order in East Asia." Its purpose was to bring stability and coordination under Japanese leadership between Japan, Manchukuo, and occupied China.

The hard-core meaning of the new order was soon evident as Japan attempted to destroy all non-Japanese foreign business in China. The policy and purpose were two-fold: to create a near-monopoly for Japanese economic interests and, on grounds of military necessity, to stop foreign aid to the Nationalists. In June, 1939, Japan blockaded the British and French concessions at Tientsin, publicly stripping and searching foreigners as they entered or left the concessions. This was an effort to persuade Chinese spectators that Western colonialism was dead and that Japan was the liberator of Asia. Beyond this, Japan was trying to force the surrender of the silver bullion held by the British as backing for Chinese currency, in order to destroy this currency in favor of new issues by Japan's puppet governments. Even Germany, Japan's new partner, did not escape injury as the Japanese destroyed the West's economic interests in occupied China. Nevertheless, in spite of Japanese pressure the West did not completely capitulate. Britain refused to give up the bullion, and the United States, responding to the ousting of American business from areas reached by the Japanese army, gave notice that it was terminating its treaty of commerce with Japan.

JAPAN STARTS SOUTH

When World War II broke out in late summer, 1939, Japan announced that she would not be involved in the European struggle; she would bend all efforts to settle the China affair. The European war, however, quickly intruded into Asian politics. While officially neutral, the United States, as early as November 4, 1939, began to supply aid to European democracies on a cash-and-carry basis. In May and June, 1940, Holland, Belgium, and France fell before German armies, and the Battle of Britain began. These events gave Japan a freer hand. She was able to obtain British assent to a suspension of traffic in supplies flowing into Nationalist China from Hong Kong and Burma. In French Indochina, Japanese pressure closed the border into China, secured the use of certain airfields and the right to station troops, and obtained transit rights for troops attacking southwest China. A Japanese economic mission was sent to the Netherland Indies, where it bargained, initially without success, for greatly increased quotas of oil. In short, during the West's preoccupation with its own war, the Japanese army sought opportunities not only to improve its strategic position but also to augment its slender economic resources by tapping Southeast Asia's rich supplies of oil, bauxite, tin, and rubber.

As early as March, 1939, the Japanese army had been pressing for a full alliance with Germany. Germany had already indicated that she was prepared to overlook the damage done by Japan to her economic interests in China in order to obtain a pact which would give her added weight in Europe. Yet it was not until September, 1940, that the desired treaty, including Italy as a partner, was concluded. By that time the pact was aimed clearly at the United States; Germany believed that it would deter the expansion of American aid to Britain. In Japan it was viewed as a warning against American interference with Japanese moves, especially the full-fledged drive into Southeast Asia which the army was contemplating. The United States, however, was not Japan's only concern. If Japan moved south, what would the Soviet Union do? Japan had been disappointed in her earlier expectation that the Soviet Union would remain quiet. As recently as August, 1939, the prolonged Russo-Japanese rivalry had erupted in a battle along the Manchukuo-Outer Mongolian border in which the Kwantung army suffered some 18,000 casualties.[10] This renewed tension offered the prospect of a Soviet strike in the north when Japan's attentions were directed elsewhere. To eliminate this danger Japan entered protracted negotiations to settle immediate issues related to the northern frontier and, in general, to dispose of the possibility of a general war with the Soviet Union. At Moscow, April 3, 1941, Foreign Minister Matsuoka Yosuke proudly signed the Soviet-Japanese nonaggression pact. Japan's northern flank seemed secure. Only one problem remained—to keep the Americans inactive while Japan took over Southeast Asia and liquidated Chinese resistance.[11]

[10] Assessments of the origins and outcome of the Soviet-Japanese conflicts are provided in two essays by Alvin D. Coox, "Soviet Ousting of Japanese Consulates, 1937-38," *Orient/West,* 9 (1964), 49-58; and "High Command and Field Army: The Kwantung Army and the Nomohan Incident," *Military Affairs,* 33 (1969), 302-11. Also see Katsu H. Young, "The Nomohan Incident: Imperial Japan and the Soviet Union," *Monumenta Nipponica: Studies in Japanese Culture,* 22 (1967), 82-101. For insights into contemporary Soviet scholarship see Leonid N. Kutakov, *Japanese Foreign Policy on the Eve of the Pacific War: A Soviet View,* ed. with a foreword by George A. Lensen (1972).

[11] The slowness of Japan's military to recognize the possibility of war with the United States deserves

AMERICA MOVES TOWARD WAR

Meanwhile the United States was moving cautiously away from neutrality. As early as November, 1939, Congress had repealed the arms embargo, enabling Britain and France to purchase and ship war goods in and from the American market. By June, 1940, as all Western Europe save the United Kingdom lay prostrate at Hitler's feet, President Roosevelt promised aid to "the opponents of force" and the speedy rearmament of America itself. Congress followed the president's lead with unprecedented appropriations for the armed services and the first peacetime selective service act. Fifty over-age destroyers still useful for submarine patrol and convoy duty were given to the British in

September in return for the right to maintain American military bases in British possessions from Newfoundland to Guiana. Since the destroyer deal was a clear departure from neutrality, it indicated how rapidly the United States was moving toward a shooting war. After the president had been elected for a third term he called for making the United States the "arsenal of democracy." Congress implemented the proposal, March 11, 1941, with passage of the lend-lease act, which meant that the United States would lend goods instead of money to the democracies. This was a complete denial of neutrality. At the same time, British and American military and naval officers were jointly planning the coordination of military efforts for the time when the United States might enter the conflict. There had been close planning for mutual defense between the United States and Canada dating back to August, 1940. By July, 1941, the United States Navy was convoying British lend-lease material as far as Iceland. In August, Churchill and Roosevelt issued the Atlantic Charter, proclaiming the goals of the free world. Thus, in early 1941, the United States had moved far along the path to belligerency in the Atlantic. These events encouraged Japanese expansionists to believe that the United States, faced with war in Europe, would not fight in Asia if she were offered some expendable concessions.

The United States policy of aid to Britain, however, was accompanied by a growing resolve to resist Japanese aims in the Pacific. In July, 1939, Washington gave Tokyo the required six-months' notice terminating the Japanese-American commercial treaty of 1911, paving the way for a policy of progressive economic sanctions against Japan, which began in July, 1940. At first only aviation gasoline and number one grade scrap metal were embargoed; the following September all scrap metal; and by November, all types of iron and steel.

As Japanese-American relations rapidly deteriorated, unofficial talks were initiated to see if somehow an agreement might take the two governments off a collision course. Two Catholic priests who had talked with Japanese leaders, Father Drought and Bishop Walsh, arrived in the United States early in 1941 and con-

---

further emphasis. Although the crisis psychology of the 1930s had evoked images of enemies on all sides, the reality of a coming conflict was not accepted even by most senior army and navy officers until well into 1941. During the late 1930s, Japanese commanders, bogged down with their troops in China, spoke of economic cooperation with the United States. Even after decisions were shaped to move toward Southeast Asia, there was much wishful thinking about avoiding conflict with the United States. Influential army officers assumed that the United States would not act if Japan left the Philippines alone. When the realization that the United States might well go to war finally dawned on Japan's militarists, they refused to be deterred, even though the army and navy had failed to develop joint plans for such a conflict. Naval officers generally would not admit that their fleets were unlikely to win a prolonged conflict with the United States. Army officers preferred to accept the optimistic estimates which their naval colleagues prepared but did not believe. In 1941 the problem was much the same as it had been in 1937 when Tokyo had proved unable to limit the hostilities that had broken out at Marco Polo Bridge. On that earlier occasion General Ishihara Kanji had complained that "we do not have the capacity to take a large view of policy and strategy and to pass judgments on the basis of the larger picture." For important summations of Japanese research in military archives, see two review articles by Akira Iriye in the *Journal of Asian Studies,* 23 (1963), 103-13, and 26, (1967), 677-82. An extraordinarily rich series of essays focusing on the interplay of Japanese and American bureaucracies is to be found in Dorothy Borg and Shumpei Okamoto, eds., *Pearl Harbor as History: Japanese-American Relations, 1931-1941* (1973). See especially Fujiwara Akira's essay on the Japanese army, and Asada Sadao's on the navy.

ferred with Secretary of State Hull and Japanese Ambassador Nomura Kichisaburo. Nomura thereupon drafted a proposal which was presented to Hull and to Tokyo. By its terms Japan would agree to employ only peaceful measures in the Southwest Pacific and would aid Germany under terms of her alliance only if that country were the victim of aggression. The United States in return would restore normal American-Japanese trade, assist Japan in obtaining raw materials in the Southwest Pacific, and press the *Kuomintang*-Nationalist government to make peace. When the Japanese government reviewed these terms, the proposed restrictions on Japan's role under her alliance were omitted, and Tokyo demanded that the United States stop aiding Britain. Furthermore, Japan deleted the pledge prohibiting the use of force in the Southwest Pacific. The United States was to be offered only guarantees on a "neutralized" Philippines.

Secretary of State Hull pursued the American side of the talks by asking Japan's acceptance of four principles which, as he had been saying for years, must be the basis for agreement on specific issues. The first of these was respect for the sovereignty and territorial integrity of nations. The second was the principle of noninterference in the internal affairs of other states. The third was support of the principle of equality, including equality of commercial opportunity. The fourth was nondisturbance of the status quo in the Pacific except as it might be altered by peaceful means. From this confrontation two things were clear: (1) the United States was advancing ethically unimpeachable principles which could become the foundation of a program sharply limiting Japanese expansion, and (2) the Japanese were requiring an end to embargoes and to American aid to China, not a debate on principles.

The Hull-Nomura conversations, which began in April just after the conclusion of the Soviet-Japanese nonaggression pact, were to continue until the Pearl Harbor attack in December. From beginning to end they were as futile as diplomatic discussions could be. The American refusal to abandon announced principles showed that the Japanese had badly miscalculated the growing seriousness of American intentions in East Asia. At the same time Japan had no intention of getting out of China save

on its own terms, or of foregoing expansion in Southeast Asia. The only virtue of the talks was that they gave both powers more time to prepare for what was coming, and the United States needed that time desperately.

By early summer the march of events was propelling the United States and Japan toward a momentous crisis. Germany's invasion of the Soviet Union, June 22, 1941, without previous advice to Japan, spurred action in Tokyo. On July 2, an imperial Japanese conference agreed to an advance in Indochina, to observe the nonaggression pact with the Soviet Union, and to join the European war when the defeat of Russia became imminent. General mobilization was ordered. New bases in Indochina were demanded of the Vichy government. By the end of July, new Japanese armies were in the French colony. Operational plans were hastened looking to invasion of Malaya, the East Indies, and the Philippines. The navy began practice for an attack on Pearl Harbor, which had been considered as early as January.

On the American side, Roosevelt reacted swiftly to the Japanese occupation of Indochina by issuing, July 26, an executive order freezing all Japanese assets in the United States. The order, which was based on the existence of an "unlimited national emergency," meant the virtual end of trade between the United States and Japan.[12] Most important of all, it meant a

[12] Donald S. Friedman, *The Road from Isolation: The Campaign of the American Committee for Non-Participation in Japanese Aggression, 1938-1940* (1968),* is a study of a pressure group seeking the imposition of economic sanctions on Japan. The firm policy advocated by this group and ultimately adopted by the Roosevelt administration was intended to demonstrate its deep concern over the East Asian situation and the danger to Japan of violating the principles upon which American policy rested. Sanctions presumably would strengthen the hands of those Japanese who opposed war with the United States. In this presumption, the United States probably was wrong. Among the Japanese military, especially middle grade officers, American trade restrictions only "proved" the inevitability of war. Moreover, insofar as American restrictions depleted Japan's ability to wage the "inevitable" war, sanctions gave substance to arguments that Japan was being "encircled" and that she should pursue the southern strategy. See Hosoya Chihiro, "Twenty-five Years after Pearl Harbor: A New Look at Japan's Decision for War,'" in *Imperial Japan and Asia: A Reassessment,* Grant K. Goodman, comp., Occasional

full embargo on oil. At this point Japanese proponents of a peaceful settlement began what was to be a final effort to avoid war. In August, Premier Konoe Fumimaro proposed a meeting with President Roosevelt somewhere in the Pacific. The meeting was never held, for the president informed Nomura that Japan must first stop her military advances and give a clearer statement of her purposes. With the collapse of this proposal the Japanese high command, led by the Minister of War Tojo Hideki and his Kwantung officer clique, increased its pressure for a decision on war with America. An imperial conference, September 6, concluded that, if in a month there were not substantial evidence that the United States would accept Japan's position, war would be forthcoming.[13] The substantial evidence was not forthcoming; Nomura had nothing to offer that

Hull would accept. American principles and Japanese purposes were as far apart as they had been in May. The time had come when Tojo was to have a free hand; Konoe resigned and, on October 18, Tojo became prime minister.

The war plans of the Tojo cabinet were approved by another imperial conference, November 5. It was agreed that (1) a new proposal would be made to the United States, which must be accepted by November 25; and (2) failure would mean war, with simultaneous attacks on Pearl Harbor, Manila, and Singapore. Kurusu Saburo, a special Japanese envoy, reached Washington, November 17, but had no new instructions. To keep the negotiations going while a Japanese fleet moved toward Pearl Harbor, Japan presented new proposals on November 20. They provided an avenue to new troubles rather than an end to old ones. In reply, Hull gave Nomura, on November 26, a comprehensive proposal for a peaceful settlement. It was not an ultimatum, for it left Japan a choice of four alternatives, but it was a denial of everything Japan had set out to do since 1931. She could choose to reverse her policy, to continue the war in China but refrain from further southern advances, to retreat, or to march on. On December 1, an imperial conference made the final decision for war with the United States.[14] The American government had long known that some sort of zero hour was near, for Japanese codes had been broken. Yet it was not known where the Japanese would strike. The prevailing assumption in Washington was that Japan would attack British and Dutch territories in Southeast Asia, but not American territory. The question was whether Congress and American people would support the administration in war on Japan if her next attacks were confined to British and Dutch holdings.[15]

---

papers of the East Asian Institute, Columbia University (1967), 52-63. Joseph C. Grew, the American Ambassador to Japan, was the most important official personage warning that American policy would not deter the Japanese. Citing "psychological factors," Grew reminded Washington that Japan remained a land of "hard warriors," whose values would not permit them to be intimidated by American pressures. See Waldo H. Heinrichs, Jr., *American Ambassador: Joseph C. Grew and the Development of the United States Diplomatic Tradition* (1966).

[13] The timing of the decision was due in part to the fact that, until September 4, Tokyo did not believe Hull was serious about incorporating his four principles into an agreement with Japan. When the Japanese government discovered the American intention, its reaction was colored by a belief that the United States had suddenly stiffened its demands. This belief in turn encouraged acceptance of the ideas that the United States was not negotiating seriously and that war was the only recourse. These ideas, it appears, sprang from Tokyo's being misinformed about the American position. While Hull strove to make American insistence on its principles clear throughout his talks, Amabassador Nomura, committed personally to a settlement and handicapped by inexperience in diplomacy as well as deficiencies in his comprehension of English, glossed over the secretary's demands in his reports. See Robert J. C. Butow, "The Hull-Nomura Conversations: A Fundamental Misconception," *American Historical Review,* 65 (1960), 822-36. Hosoya Chihiro has written more comprehensively on this subject in "The Role of Japan's Foreign Ministry and Its Embassy in Washington, 1940-1941," in *Pearl Harbor,* Borg and Okamoto, eds., 149-64.

[14] See Nobutaka Ike, *Japan's Decision for War: Records of the 1941 Policy Conference* (1967), a translation of documents revealing the thought of Japanese leadership.

[15] While Roosevelt was concerned whether Congress would declare war in response to a Japanese attack on British or Dutch possessions in Asia, he committed his administration to assist Britain in the event of such an attack. The commitment was made informally and was gradually expanded. By December 3, the president promised help even if

Moreover, since the American army and navy were demanding more time for preparation, one final effort—if not for peace, at least for delay—was made. On December 6, President Roosevelt sent a direct appeal to the emperor. It reached Grew in Tokyo almost at the moment of the Pearl Harbor attack.

Nomura and Kurusu presented Japan's reply to Hull at 2:20 P.M., December 7. It was a summation of Japan's case against the United States and an announcement that the negotiations were ended. Delays in decoding had prevented its presentation at 1:00 P.M., just in advance of the attack on Pearl Harbor. Thus when the note was presented Hull knew, but the Japanese envoys did not, that the bombs had fallen. Hull looked at the note (he already knew what was in it), told his callers that it was "crowded with infamous falsehoods," and directed them to leave. Later in the afternoon Japan declared war. The following day Great Britain and the United States declared war on Japan; Germany and Italy declared war on the United States, December 11.

PEARL HARBOR

Japanese planes launched from carriers had crippled the United States Pacific fleet at Pearl Harbor and had destroyed most American aircraft in the Hawaiian Islands. The casualties were as staggering as the damage to the fleet: 2,343 dead, 1,272 wounded, 960 missing. That much of the crippled fleet was back in service within a year was belated compensation for the greatest naval disaster in American history. Providentially, the Japanese did not follow up their victory with an effort to invade the Hawaiian Islands. Having for the time being paralyzed American naval power in the Pacific, Japan was free to pursue her immediate objective, the conquest of southeastern Asia—Hong Kong, Malaya, the Philippines, and the Indies.

Responsibility for the Pearl Harbor disaster presents a complex problem in historical interpretation. By July, 1946, there had been eight

Britain went to war in response to a Japanese attack on Thailand. See Raymond A. Esthus, "President Roosevelt's Commitment to Britain to Intervene in a Pacific War," *Mississippi Valley Historical Review,* 50 (1963), 28-38.

official investigations, yet it still seemed that the full story had not been revealed. Although the earliest investigations, made by Secretary of the Navy Frank Knox and Associate Supreme Court Justice Owen Roberts, laid the major responsibility on the Pearl Harbor commanders, Admiral Husband S. Kimmel and General Walter C. Short, later investigations including that of a joint Congressional committee, tended to lay less blame on the commanders and more upon departments and personalities in the government at Washington. Whatever the ultimate verdict of history may be, the Pearl Harbor attack was of tremendous importance not merely as a military catastrophe but also as a political awakening. If on the morning of December 7 any lingering doubts remained in the American mind as to the role of the United States in the struggle against totalitarianism, Pearl Harbor removed them.

Americans sought what satisfaction they could by labelling the catastrophe Japan's "sneak attack." At best, this was consolation only to the thoughtless. At worst, it was a convenient diversion from the hard and cold fact that it was the business of the government and of the armed services not to be taken by surprise. There were both immediate and long-range reasons suggesting that the attack should have been anticipated. American carriers in war games in 1932 had carried out a successful Sunday morning attack on Pearl Harbor; Grew had warned the state department eleven months in advance that if war came Japan might open hostilities with an attack on Pearl Harbor; from September on, intercepted Japanese messages revealed a sharp interest in the location of ships at Pearl Harbor; as the American-Japanese conversations were drawing to a close in November, Grew and Hull had given repeated warnings that the Japanese might depend upon surprise and on simultaneous attacks at several points. Such warnings, of course, were not the only ones received. From diplomatic channels and intelligence, the Roosevelt administration obtained a flood of conflicting evidence on what Japan might do. Some of this, admittedly, supported the prevailing assumption that Japan would attack Dutch and British possessions, not American territory. Even so, by early December, Washington was sufficiently persuaded of the possibility of war that field commanders were alerted. Yet in spite of this alert both the American government and armed forces were taken by surprise.[16]

FOR FURTHER READING

The Sino-Japanese Undeclared War. Paul H. Clyde, "Japan's March to Empire: Some Bibliographic Evaluations," *Journal of Modern History* 21 (1949), 333-43. Alvin D. Coox, *Year of the Tiger* (1964), excellent essays on such topics as the "rape" of Nanking, *Panay* crisis, and the *Ladybird* affair. F. F. Liu, *A Military History of Modern China, 1924-1949* (1956), one of the fullest accounts of China's mobilization and military effort. Further insight into the Chinese war effort may be had from T. A. Bisson, *Japan in China* (1938); L. K. Rosinger, *China's Wartime Politics, 1937-1944* (1944); H. F. MacNair, ed., *Voices from Un-*

[16] The years immediately preceding Pearl Harbor have been studied intensively by historians. These years are rich in historical source and secondary materials on the events and policies which led Japan and the United States into war in 1941. This richness in the record, and in historical studies upon it, has not produced any single, definitive interpretation of the causes of war. Among the widely differing conclusions that have been reached by American, British, and Japanese historians, only a few can be suggested in broad terms. (1) the war came because of Japanese aggression in China; (2) the war was brought about by American blundering, or by her sinister intentions manifested in policies that deceived the American people and provoked Japan; (3) Japanese expansion was a response to Russian communism, and the economic sanctions applied by the United States forced Japan to move southward and to go to war; and (4) Japanese policy, according to certain recent interpretations, was not the result of a conspiracy of the Japanese military, but rather of the pursuit of legitimate national aims by both civilian and military leaders. In this latter interpretation, Japanese policy is described as an expression of what can be expected in a world ruled by ultranationalistic great powers. Japan's basic aim, in this case, was survival, an aim which could not be compromised. An excellent analysis of the historical literature on the coming of the war is Louis Morton, "1937-1941," in *American-East Asian Relations,* May and Thomson, eds., 260-90.

occupied China (1944); and E. F. Carlson, *Twin Stars over China* (1940).

The Conflict in World Politics. F.C. Jones, *Japan's New Order in East Asia, Its Rise and Its Fall, 1937-1945* (1954) studies Japanese diplomacy from a global viewpoint. Seiji G. Hishida, *Japan Among the Great Powers: A Survey of Her International Relations* (1940), heavy on Japanese official interpretations. A brief and excellent study in German of Japan's dealings with the Soviet Union is Hubertus Lupke, *Japan's Russlandpolitik Von 1939 Bis 1941* (1962). Frank W. Ikle, *German-Japanese Relations, 1936-1940: A Study of Totalitarian Diplomacy* (1956); and Ernst L. Presseisen, *Germany and Japan: A Study in Totalitarian Diplomacy, 1933-1941* (1958) are complementary studies emphasizing respectively the Japanese and German sides of diplomacy. Johanna M. Meskill, *Hitler and Japan: The Hollow Alliance* (1966), emphasizes the failure of the Axis as a military partnership. Paul W. Schroeder, *The Axis Alliance and Japanese-American Relations, 1941* (1958) concludes that the Axis alliance was a lesser factor in Japan's decision to attack the United States than was the rigidity of American Policy.

The United States and Japan. W. L. Langer and S. E. Gleason, *The World Crisis and American Foreign Policy: The Challenge to Isolation, 1937-1940,* (Vol. 1); and *The Undeclared War, 1940-1941* (Vol. 2) (1952-1953) sets the far eastern crisis in the perspective of world conflict. Herbert Feis, *The Road to Pearl Harbor: the Coming of the War between the United States and Japan* (1950),* an intensive study of American records. Robert J. C. Butow, *Tojo and the Coming of the War* (1961);* and David J. Lu, *From the Marco Polo Bridge to Pearl Harbor: Japan's Entry into World War II* (1961) are careful studies that lead to different interpretations. Roberta Wohlstetter, *Pearl Harbor: Warning and Decision* (1962)* explains why Americans were surprised.

East Asia in World War II: Colonialism versus Nationalism

28

Japan's attack on Pearl Harbor dramatically expanded the undeclared war that had been waged in China since 1937. No longer were Chinese and Japanese the sole adversaries, fighting their exclusive war on the China mainland. Swift Japanese offensives carried hostilities into vast areas of the Pacific and into Southeast Asia, where the colonial empires of the French, British, Dutch and Americans were invaded and conquered. In these early months of 1942, the great battles in Asia and the Pacific took their place with those in Europe to form the indescribable conflict, World War II. For Japan, the expanded war was fought for enormous stakes. Earlier, 1937-1941, she had sought a more limited objective—to subdue Chinese nationalism, turning it to her own purposes. After December 7, 1941, Japan aimed at nothing less than the total destruction of the Western challenge to her leadership in all of greater East Asia. In addition, Japan intended to establish a colonial empire that would supplant those controlled by the West.

MILITARY OFFENSIVES AND THE DIPLOMACY OF WAR, 1941-1945

Coordinated Japanese offensives were launched from the Caroline Islands and Taiwan, from naval bases and airfields which the Vichy French had permitted Japan to acquire in French Indochina, and from bases acquired in Thailand after December 8. Less than three weeks were required to subdue Hong Kong, the great commercial city which had been a British possession for a century. Japanese troops, trained for tropical and jungle warfare, moved southward on the Malay Peninsula to capture Singapore on February 15, 1942, and westward to occupy Burma by June, 1942. An attack on the Philippines, which came a few hours after the assault on Pearl Harbor, placed these islands, after five months of bitter fighting, under Japanese control. With speed unabated, Japan moved on to the conquest of the rich Netherland Indies and the Bismarck and Solomon Islands. She invaded New Guinea, south and east of the Philippines, with the ultimate objective of attacking Australia.[1] But here the stubborn, heroic resistance that had been maintained by slim forces since Pearl Harbor checked the Japanese. New Guinea remained partly in Allied hands.

On May 7 and 8, in a naval-air battle over the Coral Sea, American planes broke up a

[1] For the techniques of the Japanese occupation, military, political, and economic, see Robert E. Ward, *Asia for the Asiatics* (1945).

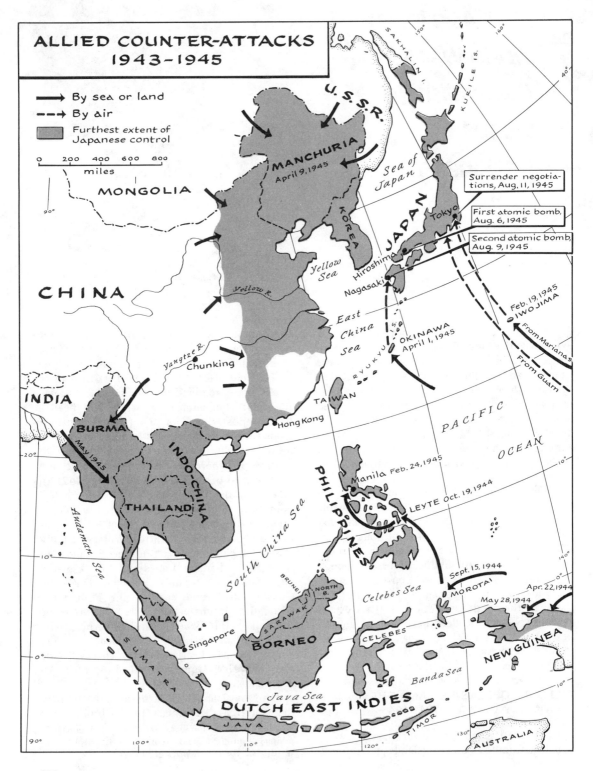

ALLIED COUNTER-ATTACKS
1943-1945

→ By sea or land
⇢ By air
▨ Furthest extent of Japanese control

0   200   400   600   800
        miles

U.S.S.R.

MONGOLIA

MANCHURIA
April 9, 1945

KOREA

Sea of Japan

SAKHALIN I.

KURILE IS.

JAPAN

Tokyo

Surrender negotia-
tions, Aug. 11, 1945

First atomic bomb,
Aug. 6, 1945

Second atomic bomb,
Aug. 9, 1945

CHINA

Yellow Sea

Yellow R.

Hiroshima

Nagasaki

East China Sea

RYUKYU IS.

OKINAWA
April 1, 1945

Feb. 19, 1945
IWO JIMA

From Marianas

From Guam

PACIFIC

OCEAN

Yangtze R.

Chunking

INDIA

BURMA

May 1945

INDO-CHINA

THAILAND

TAIWAN

Hong Kong

Andaman Sea

MALAYA

Singapore

SUMATRA

South China Sea

BRUNEI
NORTH B.
SARAWAK

BORNEO

PHILIPPINES

Manila Feb. 24, 1945

LEYTE Oct. 19, 1944

Sept. 15, 1944

MOROTAI

Apr. 22, 1944

May 28, 1944

Celebes Sea

CELEBES

NEW GUINEA

Java Sea

DUTCH EAST INDIES

JAVA

Banda Sea

TIMOR

AUSTRALIA

Japanese attempt to cut the Australian supply lines across the southwestern Pacific to Honolulu and the American Pacific coast. The first major Japanese reverse was the naval-air battle of Midway, June 4-7, 1942, which inflicted heavy losses (21 ships) on her fleet and prevented the occupation of Midway and possibly the invasion of the Hawaiian Islands. Indeed, this proved to be a pivotal encounter. After Midway, save for their invasion of the Aleutians, the Japanese were no longer a menace in the central or eastern Pacific. Elsewhere, Allied actions in the southwest Pacific (Solomons, Guadalcanal, and New Guinea) and the CBI (China-Burma-India) theater destroyed Japanese opportunities for driving further toward Australia and India.

The year 1943 marked the end of Japan's march to conquest and the beginning of her ultimate defeat. In the Pacific and Asia, as in Europe, defeat could not come, however, until the enemies of the Axis had achieved a realistic unity in over-all policy and strategy, had won the battle of production, and had brought their newly-created power to bear on far-flung battle fronts on the land, the seas, and in the air.

From the beginning of the war in Europe and Asia, it had been the ill-concealed boast of the totalitarian powers that their opponents were incapable of unity in resistance. Nevertheless, in a series of momentous conferences, the principal powers united behind a plan aimed at winning a speedy military victory. On January 1, 1942, in response to an American proposal, twenty-six governments at war with the Axis pledged their united action in prosecuting the conflict, agreeing to conclude no separate peace. Thus the principles of the Atlantic charter became a basic manifesto of these united nations and the preliminary blueprint for war and eventual victory in Asia as well as in Europe.

At Quebec, August 11-24, 1943, Roosevelt, Churchill, and T. V. Soong approved policies designed to (1) strike at Japan through greater aid to China; (2) achieve closer collaboration with Russia; and (3) speed the invasion of Italy. The Moscow conference of foreign ministers was a logical sequel. There, October 19-30, 1943, Britain, the Soviet Union, and the United States proclaimed the principles of the coming peace: fascism was to be destroyed and war criminals brought to justice. China also joined in declarations demanding "unconditional surrender" by the Axis and promising the creation of a postwar international organization based on the sovereign equality of states and designed to maintain peace and security.

Since Russia was not at war with Japan, the Moscow conference of foreign ministers had not dealt specifically with war plans in Asia. Such plans were the subject of the meeting of Roosevelt, Churchill, and Chiang Kai-shek at Cairo, November 22-26, 1943. The war was to be prosecuted until Japan accepted "unconditional surrender;" Japan was to be deprived of all the lands which she had seized since 1894; and Korea was "in due course" to be free and independent. Following immediately on Cairo came the first meeting of Stalin with Roosevelt and Churchill at Teheran, December 2-7, which gave final shape to plans for destruction of Hitler's Germany, and produced Russia's first promise to enter the war against Japan.

Meanwhile, at Dumbarton Oaks in Washington, D.C., representatives of the United States, Great Britain, Russia, and China drafted preliminary proposals for an international organization to replace the League of Nations. This organization was later to materialize as the United Nations. Subsequently, at Yalta in the Crimea, February, 1945, Roosevelt, Churchill, and Stalin again met and, among other things, announced a coming international conference at San Francisco to create a charter for the permanent organization of the United Nations.

Even before the achievement of a complete diplomatic and military coalition, the Allies were winning their first campaigns. In the Pacific these included, as already noted, the battle of Midway and the campaigns at Guadalcanal. In the Aleutian Islands, at the far eastern extremity of the Asian and Pacific battlefront, American forces took the offensive in May, 1943, and by August had reconquered the entire archipelago. Simultaneously, British and American forces broke the German and Italian armies in North Africa (May, 1943); Soviet armies stopped the German advance at Stalingrad (September-

November, 1942), and in 1943 engaged in the first great Soviet counteroffensive. In September, 1943, came the unconditional surrender of Italy. By the spring of 1944, the Germans had been driven from all of southern Russia.

Axis reverses in Europe permitted the Allies to mount offensives in three widely separated areas in Asia and the Pacific. In the summer of 1943, American forces advanced through cruel campaigns in New Georgia, Bougainville, and New Guinea toward Rabaul, Japan's principal military and naval base in the southwest Pacific. To the north, the capture of the Gilbert and Marshall Islands (November, 1943, and February, 1944) was the prelude to a great naval offensive in the summer of 1944. Striking westward toward the China coast, American forces moved to the conquest of the major islands of the Mariana group (Saipan, July 9, and Tinian, July 23) and to the reconquest of Guam (August 3), all of which were captured only after the bitterest fighting and great loss of life. Far to the west in the CBI, offensives—long delayed by impenetrable jungles, devastating heat, disease, scarcity of transportation, and paucity of supplies and troops—were begun in northern Burma and along the Manipur-Imphal front. Especially important in this theater was the work of American and Chinese forces in northern Burma (1944) covering construction of the Ledo road, the new supply route from India to China.

Other pressures, too, were reducing Japan's power to resist. By the summer of 1944, American submarines had sunk a total of nearly 700 Japanese vessels. These losses contributed to the eventual collapse of Japanese war production at home. To speed the process, the United States employed the B-29 bomber, which flew from secret airfields deep in China. The first raid by these flying superfortresses against southern Japan was made on June 15, 1944. Later raids struck at the eastern part of North China and Manchuria.

The weight of this military and naval power moved ever closer to Japan itself in the closing months of 1944 and into 1945. Fol-lowing successful campaigns in the western Carolines and the Halmahera group off northern New Guinea, the Philippines were invaded (October 19, 1944) in a series of related military and naval operations which resulted in serious Japanese losses at sea and the ultimate destruction of twenty-three Japanese divisions. Meanwhile the capture of Iwo Jima, March 16, 1945, and of Okinawa in Liu-ch'iu (the Ryukyus), June 21, prepared the way for massive air assaults on Japan's home islands. The first of these in the early months of 1945 were concentrated on industrial centers— Tokyo, Nagoya, Osaka, Kobe—and on the destruction of Japanese airfields, principally in Kyushu. Although American losses in all these attacks were heavy, they cannot be compared with the frightful destruction wrought in Japan. By June 1, 1945, more than fifty square miles of Tokyo had been reduced to rubble and ashes. In July, 1945, British carrier planes joined the attack. By the same month, more than 2,000 American planes were sometimes over Japan in a single day. The land-based air attacks were supported by carrier-plane attacks and by naval bombardment of Japan's coastal cities. In the final two and one-half months of the war the combined Anglo-American Third Fleet destroyed or damaged nearly 3,000 Japanese planes and sank or damaged some 1,600 enemy naval and merchant vessels, thus completing the destruction of Japan's power on the sea and in the air by August 1, 1945. Moreover, as these great assaults developed, Japan's defenses were struck not only in her homeland but also on the further edges of her conquered and now crumbling empire—in Bangkok, Taiwan, Saigon, Rangoon, Penang, and Kuala Lumpur.

By the summer of 1945, Japan's military position was hopeless. In Europe, Germany had already collapsed. It was now possible to warn the Japanese people that particular cities would be destroyed if they continued to fight. The resulting raids carrying out these threats made it increasingly clear to the Japanese populace that their own defenders were powerless. At least some of Japan's leaders recognized the inevitability of defeat, as indicated by the removal in April, 1945, of General Koiso Kuniaki from the premiership and the installation of Suzuki Kantaro, whose appointment departed from the army's insistence that the premier be a general in active service. The appointment, however, did not mean that control had passed to peace advocates. As late as June 9, Suzuki, replying to President Truman's warning that Japan would be destroyed unless she surrendered, declared that Japan would fight on. Then, on July 26, during the Potsdam conference, the United States, Britain, and China delivered a final ultimatum to Japan demanding immediate unconditional surrender.[2] Japan replied (July 30) that she would ignore the demands of the Potsdam declaration.

While ultranationalistic Japanese fanatics were determined to keep fighting other events conspired to end hostilities without an invasion. On August 6, the Japanese city of Hiroshima and its army base were destroyed in the space of minutes by the first atomic bomb used in warfare. Nearly a month earlier (July 13), the Japanese government had asked Russia to intervene with Britain and the United States to bring about peace. Russia's reply, not delivered until August 8, announced immediate severance of her diplomatic relations with Japan and stated that "from August 9 the Soviet Government will consider itself to be at war with Japan." Within hours of Russia's severance of relations, a second atomic bomb destroyed the city of Nagasaki and its naval base. On the same day Russian armies invaded Manchuria; three days later they seized the Korean ports of Rashin and Yuki and advanced on the southern or Japanese half of Sakhalin Island. On August 10, the Japanese government announced its willingness to accept the Potsdam terms (to which Russia had now subscribed), provided they comprised no "demand which prejudices the prerogatives of His Majesty [the emperor] as a sovereign ruler." The reply of the United States (August 11) stated that "the authority of the Emperor and the Japanese Government to rule the State shall be subject to the Supreme Commander of the Allied Powers." Japan accepted

these terms August 14, and the surrender was effected on board the U.S. battleship *Missouri* in Tokyo Bay, September 2, 1945.

The Japanese decision to surrender was hastened by the atomic bomb and the Soviet Union's declaration of war. These events intensified an existing crisis and gave the Japanese emperor an extraordinary role in a decision that had long been in the making. It was a case in which the personal opinion of the emperor became an imperial decision and, therefore, the will of the state. The crisis of July and August had given the men who had long known that Japan must surrender the chance to stop the fanatics and to allow the historic influence of the throne to end the carnage.[3]

The emperor's announcement of surrender presented the Japanese with one of the great crises of their history. A proud and sensitive people, having met military defeat, was called upon to face a future compounded of social confusion in the homeland and of uncertainty in its relations with the outside world of conquerors. Before passing to the account of the postwar era, however, some attention must be given to the fate which befell Southeast Asia as Japan's legions reached the borders of India. Wartime developments in Japan and in China will be treated in the chapter which follows.

[3] See Robert J. C. Butow, *Japan's Decision to Surrender* (1954),* 228-33. The atomic bomb killed some 75,000 persons at Hiroshima and 35,000 at Nagasaki. Larger numbers were injured. The use of the bomb had been preceded by incendiary bomb raids over Japanese cities. On March 9, the most destructive of such raids over Tokyo killed more than 80,000 people, injured 40,000, and left one million homeless. Whether the use of the atomic bomb was necessary remains an unresolved debate. It would appear that Japan had been defeated by American sea power prior to the use of the bomb. The question was, when would she surrender? Her decision came when the emperor intervened, but even then military extremists threatened revolt to continue the war. See Russell F. Weigley, *The American Way in War: A History of United States Military Strategy and Policy* (1973), 310-11, 364-65. On the use of the atomic bomb as a weapon of war and as an instrument of foreign policy, see Martin J. Sherwin, "The Atomic Bomb and the Origins of the Cold War: U.S. Atomic-Energy Policy and Diplomacy, 1941-1945," *American Historical Review,* 78 (1973), 945-68.

[2] Text in United States, Department of State, *Occupation of Japan* (1946), 53-55.

SOUTHEAST ASIA:
THE RESPONSE TO COLONIALISM

When Japanese forces invaded Southeast Asia, they seized a region that had been ruled for three-quarters of a century or more by Western colonialism: Great Britain controlled Burma and the Malay states, the Dutch governed in the East Indies, and France and the United States, respectively, were sovereign in Indochina and the Philippines. In all of Southeast Asia, only Siam (Thailand) had retained its independence, and this, on the sufferance of the great powers.

The establishment of these colonial empires was noted earlier (Chapters 14 and 15) in describing the West's challenge to Old China's world order. The Western impact, it will be recalled, destroyed the tributary system through which China had exercised a cultural, and at times a political, overlordship in the border territories such as Vietnam, which exchanged an ancient Confucian tributary status under China for a modern, Western colonial status under France. One of Japan's principal designs, through the medium of World War II, was to take over all Western colonial empires in Southeast Asia, to free these peoples from Western bondage, and to bring them within Japan's "new order for East Asia"—a pleasant phrase which, in reality, meant Japan's particular variety of colonialism. In an earlier age, Japan's colonial ambitions might well have been fulfilled. By the time of World War II, however, colonialism was in some disrepute even in the thinking of some powers who still practiced it. Furthermore, in a number of Southeast Asian states, national independence movements could no longer be ignored. The United States, for whatever reasons, had promised independence to the Philippines, and the British had edged Burma in the direction of independence in 1937.[4] The climate fostered

---

[4] The government set up in Burma in 1937 was a dyarchy. The British colonial administration still had exclusive control over the most important functions such as defense, foreign affairs, and monetary policy. Responsibility for other governmental matters was transferred to Burmese, but even legislation on "transferred subjects" was subject to the colonial governor's veto.

by World War II nourished Southeast Asian nationalism among elite native groups and suggested that the Western colonial order had outlived its usefulness.

In describing wartime Southeast Asia, the experience of Indochina will be given particular attention for a number of reasons. A part of this French colony, the ancient kingdom of Vietnam, by virtue of long historical association with China, belonged to the East Asian culture area with which this entire narrative is primarily concerned. Indochina is also emphasized because of the importance it was to assume in the postwar years.

FRENCH INDOCHINA:
ITS COLONIAL EXPERIENCE

During the late nineteenth and early twentieth centuries, France presided over a great empire in Southeast Asia. It was an empire which had been won by diplomacy, by the aggressive policy and tactics of Roman Catholic missionaries, and by military force. This empire included Cochin China (southern Vietnam), the protectorates of Annam and Tonkin (central and northern Vietnam), Laos, and Cambodia. The total area, slightly less than 300,000 square miles, approximated the combined areas of Texas and West Virginia. Its population on the eve of World War II was some 24 million, including 500,000 Chinese and 42,000 Europeans, almost all of whom were French.

THE NATIVE CULTURES

The Vietnamese, a Mongoloid people, probably entered the Red river valley from South China in prehistoric times. For more than a thousand years (111 B.C. to A.D. 939) northern Vietnam was a part of the Chinese empire. After 939, Vietnam was a tributary state of China although there were occasional, short periods of direct Chinese rule. Thus between the tenth century and the French conquests of the nineteenth century, Vietnam had a political life of its own, while at the same time its ruling elites fashioned their governmental and cultural patterns on Chinese

(Confucian) models. The life of the common folk, however, was shaped by indigenous Southeast Asian styles as well as by Chinese influence. In addition, all of Southeast Asia (including Vietnam) received cultural influences from India. These influences, especially in law and religion, were particularly strong in Cambodia. Thus the people of France's Indochinese empire—Vietnamese, Laotians, Cambodians, and montagnards, (an indigenous hill people inhabiting portions of Laos and Annam)—lived in a borderland of mixed and mingling Asiatic cultures, to which France was to add a frosting of Europeanization in politics and religion.

In building their Indochinese empire, the French discovered the advantages of preserving and capitalizing upon the distinctiveness of native life. French penetration of Cambodia, for example, was speeded by a policy of aiding King Norodom (reigned 1860-1904) against local rebels. French forces thereby were in a position to terminate Cambodia's dependence on Siam and to effect the King's acceptance of French directives. Vietnam's Nguyen dynasty, which had been established in 1802 after a period of civil war and peasant uprisings, proved more difficult to manage. Under this monarchy, long-existing Chinese patterns in government had been stressed and implemented. Confucian institutions (ministries, Hanlin academy, the censorate) administration (tax collecting methods, sale of offices) and the court (Hue, the capital, was a kind of miniature Peking) all emphasized that the Chinese model was ideal and the tributary status natural.[5] Under this dynasty, all of Vietnam (the north, the center, and the south) was united for the first time; thus, Vietnam's kings had the power to slow French

encroachment. When they were finally overcome, their dynasty was not destroyed. The French installed a compliant emperor and turned the monarchy against those who opposed alien rule.

THE FRENCH COLONIAL SYSTEM

The French colonial system was based on the assumption that the colonies and protectorates would be drawn progressively closer to France as integral parts of a closely-knit empire. French imperialists could conceive of no higher goal than making cultured, brown-skinned Frenchmen out of Vietnamese. Of all Westerners in East Asia, the French showed the least racial bias; they were willing to treat as equals those Asians who, in their opinion, had achieved equality with the French in education and refinement. Such an attitude was tolerant of cultural, but not of political, native nationalism. France would not admit the possibility of political equality with herself. Prior to 1941, she succeeded with indoctrinating many native intellectuals with her political and religious philosophy, thereby strengthening her hold on Indochina. She failed, however, to win any broad native loyalty, save among the elites whom she kept in power and through whom she ruled.[6]

Colonial administration fitted no neat pattern, but it reflected the aforementioned governing philosophy and the conditions that the French had found. Cochin China was ruled directly as a colony; Annam (central Vietnam) and Tonkin (northern Vietnam) were ruled more indirectly, on the surface at least, as protectorates with the Nguyen emperors still occupying their thrones; and Cambodia and the kingdom of Luang Prabang in Laos were ruled by their respective native kings. There was a direct French colonial administration in the remainder of Laos, the area of the ancient kingdoms of Vientiane and Champassak. The system advanced the cause of French authority, since it made foreign rule less obvious and, therefore, more acceptable.

Its effects on the native populace are more difficult to evaluate. Despite geographic prox-

---

[5] The extent to which the Chinese style was copied is suggested by the fact that Vietnamese emperors were Sons of Heaven to petty rulers within their own territory; that they regarded the Cambodians as barbarians; and that they termed their own land, Vietnam, the central country in dealing with Laos. Yet Vietnamese social conditions and Sinitic ideals sometimes did not mesh. Thus the tasks of the Nguyen emperor included the mediation of disputes between local officials and zealous Confucian bureaucrats. For a study of the adaptation of Chinese institutions in a society that was not Chinese, see Alexander B. Woodside, *Vietnam and the Chinese Model* (1971).

[6] The basic study is John F. Cady, *The Roots of French Imperialism in Eastern Asia* (1954).*

imity and long exposure to the same colonial rulers, the people of Indochina often had quite different colonial experiences. Cambodia, as a territorial state, remained largely intact under its kings, whereas the alienation of Cochin China from northern and central Vietnam weakened the unity that had been established by the Nguyen dynasty. In Vietnam, French rule seriously weakened the traditional Confucian political system, but no new system took its place. On the economic side, through the expropriation of land in Cochin China, some fifty percent of the better agricultural areas passed into the hands of the estate owners (French and native collaborators), creating a plantation system in which peasants served as landless laborers beset by the usual evils of usury and sharecropping.[7]

VIETNAMESE NATIONALISM

Among those subjected to French rule, the Vietnamese offered the most pronounced resistance, which ran the gamut from mild reform proposals to outright nationalism. By the late nineteenth century, Vietnamese intellectuals, like their Chinese counterparts, advocated strengthening their Confucian-like state by the use of Western technology. In the 1890s, scholars urged that K'ang Yu-wei's reforms be applied to Vietnam. The French, however, ignored these voices of moderate reform; their policy required punishment of those who openly challenged their authority. Thus Phan Boi Chau, who advocated Vietnam's independence under a constitutional monarchy, became a political exile in Japan. Returning to his homeland in 1909, Phan turned to republican agitation, only to be imprisoned four years later. When nationalistic scholars opened a school at Hanoi in 1907, it was closed by the French and its leaders exiled. Some years later (1918), the French

[7] Milton E. Osborne, *The French Presence in Cochinchina and Cambodia: Rule and Response, 1859-1905* (1969) documents the diversity for two regions.

did permit the opening of the more conservative University of Hanoi, but there was no encouragement of modern education for the people in general.

The failure of the early nationalists to achieve any significant reform opened the way for more extreme elements. Ho Chi Minh, born in the early 1890s, began his political career as a Vietnamese nationalist. Ho went to France, took part in the organization of the French Communist party after World War I, and studied Communist theory and tactics at Moscow. By 1925, he was at Canton as a subordinate of Borodin. When the *Kuomintang* ousted the Communists from the party in China, Ho went to Russia and finally at Hong Kong drew together a variety of dissident groups to form the Communist Party of Indochina (1930). In the same year nationalist revolts within Vietnam, including peasant uprisings, were crushed by the French with such severity that the nationalist movement—both moderate and Communist—appeared to be broken. Ho was jailed in Hong Kong (1931-1933); the Vietnamese Communist party organization was in disarray.

INDOCHINA DURING WORLD WAR II

Japan's advance during the early phases of World War II provided a favorable setting for the revival of Vietnamese nationalism. In contrast with her practice elsewhere in Southeast Asia, Japan did not at first assume direct control over Indochina. Until very late in the war, she permitted the German-dominated Vichy government of France to remain in authority; the acceptance of Japanese military forces in Indochina was one manifestation of the willingness of the Vichy colonial administration to serve Japan's interests. The arrival of the Japanese, however, meant that native nationalists had two targets: the French and the Japanese. Moreover, *Kuomintang*-Nationalist China provided the Vietnamese nationalists an opportunity to reorganize. During the spring of 1941, Ho Chi Minh was permitted to establish a base of operations in China just north of the Indochina border. There he undertook to rally nationalists of every political coloration in a united front against foreign rule in Vietnam. Leadership was to be provided by the *Vietminh* (League for the Independence of Vietnam), a coalition in which Ho served as secretary-general.

By the time Japan surrendered, August, 1945, the *Vietminh* had become a formidable body. Backed by a guerrilla army led by another Communist, Vo Nguyen Giap, the *Vietminh* had established in 1944 a "liberated" zone just inside northern Tonkin. From this territorial base, the *Vietminh* began the steady infiltration of Tonkin, eventually reaching the Red River delta area. Meanwhile the declining fortunes of the Axis powers weakened the French colonial administration. In March, 1945, the Japanese, facing defeat and seeking desperately to organize fresh support, took over administration from the French and bestowed titular leadership in Vietnam upon Emperor Bao-dai, a figure in the old Nguyen dynasty, but this new government proved no match for the *Vietminh* in appealing for popular support. On August 26, the day that American occupation forces landed in Japan, Bao-dai abdicated in favor of the *Vietminh*-backed "Democratic Republic of Vietnam." Within a few days, September 2, 1945, Ho Chi Minh proclaimed Vietnam's independence.[8]

[8] See Huynh Kim Khanh, "The Vietnamese August Revolution Reinterpreted," *Journal of Asian Studies* (1971), 761-82, a detailed analysis of the crucial role played by World War II in destroying the forces which had suppressed Vietnamese nationalism. One of the most striking aspects of Vietnam's recent history has been the persistent strength of the Communists in the independence movement. This can be partly explained by two factors: (1) the organizational and theoretical talents of the Communists; and (2) the assistance which the Communists received from Russia and China. Furthermore, their success is also partially attributable to local conditions not of their own making. Communist forces faced little effective opposition from more moderate elements. The Communists operating in the *Vietminh* were unified in their purpose, but the non-Marxist elements were plagued by factionalism and irresolution. For a case study, see William J. Duiker, "Phan Boi Chau: Asian Revolutionary in a Changing World," *ibid.,* 31 (1971), 77-88. Phan was the best known nationalist during the first quarter of the twentieth century. Yet after two decades spent in tireless

The Vietnamese independence movement which confronted the French as they returned to Indochina after the war epitomized the striking changes that had been occurring generally in Southeast Asia. Before Pearl Harbor it was evident that the entire region lying between the Indian border and the Philippines had been transformed under the Western impact. Dynastic states, or, as in the case of the Philippines, politically primitive local regimes, had been superseded by territorial states and colonial bureaucracies. Livelihood no longer rested solely on subsistence economies but rather was supplemented by international trade and the exploitation of rich natural resources. Moreover, under the influence of these new political and economic forces, population had increased and had shifted about, while traditional social foundations had been eroded. Finally, to the exceedingly rich and diverse Hindu and Confucian cultural influences had been added cultural drives coming from the West. World War II had contributed vibrant national feelings, which for the first time had become organized to challenge Western authority. Liberated France was not alone in meeting resistance when it sought to reestablish colonial rule; the Dutch found Indonesian nationalists organized and prepared to fight, and anti-colonial forces were operating against the British return to Burma and Malaya. Only in the Philippines, where plans for national independence were well-advanced before 1941, did it appear that the postwar era was not to be marked by a native-led test of colonial power.

Japan's occupation of Southeast Asia, 1941-1945, was an immediate source of this new nationalistic vitality. Within six months after Pearl Harbor, all of Southeast Asia had been brought, directly or indirectly, under a single authority. Japan's immediate purpose was to bind the region to herself in support of the war effort, and to this end her colonial administrations emphasized the production of industrial raw materials and foodstuffs. Gener-

pursuit of Vietnamese independence, he left behind neither a party organization nor a theory upon which followers might build a new Vietnam.

ally speaking, these efforts did Japan little good for as the war progressed, shipping losses denied the Japanese the advantages they sought. Moreover, Japanese policy created new problems, since the products of plantation economies were assigned low priorities. The result was widespread hardship, which, in turn, fed popular resistance movements. Thus, well before V-J Day, Southeast Asia's rejection of Western colonialism was bolstered by resentment against Japanese rule.

National sentiment was strengthened further by Japan's intense labors to extirpate the cultural influence of the old colonial powers and to insinuate herself into the favor of the native populace. Language instruction proscribed Western tongues while emphasizing native languages; Japanese administrators encouraged the formation of youth organizations, air raid associations, auxiliary police corps, and paramilitary forces in efforts to lay a popular basis for propagandizing the "New Asia" and "Asia for Asiatics." The Japanese enlisted native leaders into government service, where they enjoyed some prestige if not much power. These measures produced results precisely the reverse of those desired. Japan's new order did not win acceptance; instead, it broadened the popular basis of native nationalism and instilled a new sense of self-confidence in native leaders.[9]

In summary, it may be said that in 1941, when the war in the Pacific began, Southeast Asia was a vast array of economically rich and prestigious Western colonial empires. Their strategic import was symbolized by the great British naval base at Singapore. Although the stirrings of nationalism and independence among native elites had been present for many years, there had been no serious threat to the political authority of the colonial powers. On the surface, the area seemed blessed with a notable stability. The war and Japan's conquest of these colonies in the name of her "new order" brought an equally notable instability. Although the Japanese made "heroic"

[9] John Bastin and Harry J. Benda, *A History of Modern Southeast Asia: Colonialism, Nationalism, and Decolonization* (1968),* 123-52.

efforts to appear in the role of liberators, their efforts won few converts. In the minds of native nationalist elites, Japan's early victory had destroyed the moral authority of Britain, France, and the Netherlands as colonial powers. Then, in turn, Japan's defeat in 1945 destroyed whatever prestige she might have possessed in the minds of these same elites. This significant change in the thinking and the temper of Southeast Asia as the war came to an end was soon to be ignored, especially by France and the Netherlands, with results that will be recounted in a later chapter.

FOR FURTHER READING

Military and Naval Affairs. Louis Morton, *The War in the Pacific; Strategy and Command: The First Two Years* (1962) offers careful description and. analysis of American military policy. Samuel Eliot Morison, *History of United States Naval Operations in World War II* (14 vols., 1947-1960) is the most detailed operational history of American naval warfare. On the United States Army's role, see appropriate volumes in three officially sponsored series: *United States Army in World War II; The Army Air Forces in World War II*, and *Operational Narratives of the Marine Corps in World War II*. Among the more specialized accounts are: Forrest C. Pogue, *George C. Marshall: Organizer of Victory, 1943-1945* (1973), especially Chapters 8 and 22; Samuel B. Griffith, *The Battle for Guadalcanal* (1963); Stanley L. Falk, *Bataan: The March of Death* (1962); James A. Field, *The Japanese at Leyte Gulf* (1947); W. W. Smith, *Midway: Turning Point of the Pacific* (1966); Masanobu Tsuji, *Singapore, The Japanese Version* (1960); Hashimoto Mochitsura, *Sunk: The Story of the Japanese Submarine Fleet, 1941-1945*. E. H. M. Colegrove, trans. (1954); Joyce Lebra, *Jungle Alliance: Japan and the Indian National Army* (1971); and K.K. Ghosh, *The Indian National Army: Second Front of the Indian Independence Movement* (1969), offer contrasting insights into the war in

Burma. For literature not suggested by the foregoing see Louis Morton, "Britain and Australia in the War Against Japan: Review Article," *Pacific Affairs* 34 (1961), 184-89, and "World War II: A Survey of Recent Writings," *American Historical Review,* 75 (1970), 1987-2008.

The decision to use atomic weapons against Japan has produced historical controversy. Lansing Lamont, *Day of Trinity* (1965) is a readable account of scientific and technological development leading to the bomb. Louis Morton, "The Decision to Use the Atomic Bomb," *Command Decisions,* K. R. Greenfield, ed. (1960) is based on the memoirs of American officials; the complex military, political, and moral issues involved in the decision are treated in Herbert Feis, *The Atomic Bomb and the End of World War II* (rev. ed., 1966);* Robert J. C. Butow, *Japan's Decision to Surrender* (1954),* and T. Kase, *Journey to the Missouri* (1950). The timing of the attacks, nature of the orders issued, and other operational details are covered in appropriate volumes of the naval and air force histories cited above. The effect of the bombing is told in John Hersey, *Hiroshima* (1946);* the recollections of some survivors are in Arata Osada, ed., *Children of the A-Bomb* (1963) and Robert J. Lifton, *Death in Life: Survivors of Hiroshima* (1967).* Among volumes sharply critical of the decision to use atomic weapons are: Fletcher Knebel and Charles W. Bailey, *No High Ground* (1961); R. C. Batchelder, *The Irreversible Decision* (1962); and Gar Alperovitz, *Atomic Diplomacy* (1965).* The latter argues that the decision was prompted by a desire to pursue a tough line with the Soviet Union, and not to save lives or to hasten peace.

Wartime Diplomacy. Herbert Feis offers the fullest scholarly treatment in a series of four volumes: *The China Tangle: The American Effort in China from Pearl Harbor to the Marshall Mission* (1953);* *Churchill, Roosevelt, Stalin: The War They Waged and the Peace They Sought* (1957);* *Between War and Peace: The Potsdam Conference* (1960);* *The Atomic Bomb* (cited above); and *Contest over Japan* (1967).* On the Yalta Conference see: Walter Johnson, ed., *Roosevelt and the Russians: The Yalta Conference* (1949); John L. Snell, ed., *The Meaning of Yalta,* with a foreword by Paul H. Clyde (1956);* and Athan G. Theoharis, *The Yalta Myths: An Issue in U.S. Politics, 1945-1955* (1970). Details on the lack of cooperation in the Axis partnership are given in F.C. Jones, *Japan's New Order in East Asia: Its Rise and Fall, 1937-1945* (1954). George A. Lensen, *The Strange Neutrality: Soviet-Japanese Relations during the Second World War, 1941-1945* (1972), a pioneering work drawing upon extensive Soviet and Japanese sources.

Japan's Decision to Surrender. In addition to the volumes by Butow and Kase noted above see: *United States Strategic Bombing Survey, Japan's Struggle to End the War* (1946); Lester Brooks, *Behind Japan's Surrender: The Secret Struggle that Ended an Empire* (1968); and Pacific War Research Society, *Japan's Longest Day* (1968),* a translation of exhaustive research conducted in Japan.

Indochina. Joseph Buttinger, *A Dragon Defiant: A Short History of Vietnam* (1972),* a good introduction to the long struggle for national identity. For insights into the culture of the Indochina area see: Charles Robequain, *The Economic Development of French Indo-China* (1944); Gerald Hickey, *Village in Vietnam* (1964);* F.M. LeBar and A. Suddard, eds., *Laos: Its People, Its Society, Its Culture* (1960); David J. Steinberg, *et al., Cambodia: Its People, Its Society, Its Culture* (1959). Two studies of Vietnam's struggles against the French are in David G. Marr, *Vietnamese Anticolonialism, 1885-1925* (1971);* and Helen B. Lamb, *Vietnam's Will to Live* (1972). King C. Chen, *Vietnam and China, 1938-1954* (1969), studies the dealings of Vietnam's nationalists with both *Kuomintang* and Communist China. On Ho Chi Minh see: Bernard B. Fall, ed., *Ho Chi Minh on Revolution: Selected Writings, 1920-66* (1967);* Jean Lacouture, *Ho Chi Minh: A Political Biography* (1968);* and Jean Sainteny, *Ho Chi Minh and His Vietnam: A Personal Memoir,* trans. from the French by Herma Briffault (1972).

Southeast Asia. David J. Steinberg, *et al., In Search of Southeast Asia: A Modern History* (1971), the most recent and most successful effort to capture the unifying themes in the recent past. John F. Cady, *Southeast Asia: Its Historical Development* (1964); and D.G.E. Hall, *A History of South-East Asia* (2nd. rev. ed., 1964), are strongest in their portrayal of national histories. Useful extracts from the sources may be found in Harry J. Benda and John A. Larkin, eds., *The World of Southeast Asia: Selected Historical Readings* (1967);* and John Bastin, ed., *The Emergence of Modern Southeast Asia, 1511-1957* (1967).*

Willard Elsbree, *Japan's Role in Southeast Asian Nationalist Movements, 1940-45* (1953), a pioneering and able general account. The more specialized studies of the Japanese colonial era have focused thus far on Burma and the Philippines: Frank N. Trager, ed., *Burma: Japanese Military Administration; Selected Documents, 1941-1945* (1971); Royama Masamichi and Takeuchi Tatsuji, *The Philippine Polity: A Japanese View* (1967); Grant Goodman, *Davao: A Case Study in Japanese-Philippine Relations* (1967);* and David J. Steinberg, *Philippine Collaboration in World War II* (1967).

Leads into the immense volumes of specialized literature are provided by Donald Clay Johnson, et al., *Southeast Asia: A Bibliography for Undergraduate Libraries* (1970); Stephen N. Hay and Margaret H. Chase, *Southeast Asian History: A Bibliographic Guide* (1962); and Peter W. Stanley, "The Forgotten Philippines, 1790-1946," in *American-East Asian Relations: A Survey,* Ernest May and James C. Thomson, eds. (1972). *The Journal of Southeast Asian History,* published by the Department of History, University of Singapore (1960-present) carries recent scholarship of high standard.

China and Japan, 1941–1945: The Impact of World War II

29

In 1941-1942, both Nationalist China and Japan viewed the expanded Asian war with ill-conceived optimism. For the *Kuomintang* leadership, China's membership in a global coalition seemed to foreshadow the ultimate defeat of Japan, the triumph of a party-led revolution, and the elevation of China to the envied position of a great power. These were hopes for the future; against them the realities of early 1942 were ominous. No one could be certain when the triumph over the Axis would come or, indeed, whether it would come at all. Moreover, the promise of a bountiful victory was balanced against a meager present. Locked in China's great western interior, and faced with an isolation that became almost complete as all of Southeast Asia fell to Japan, the Nationalist government was in no position to take full advantage of the munitions, guns, and planes that the United States was producing. Compounding these difficulties were signs that Chiang Kai-shek, having settled for a stalemate on the battlefield and having avoided new initiatives in the transformation of Chinese society, was rapidly losing favor with the populace. When the end of the war finally came, the Nationalist government, while num- bered among the victors, reaped limited bless- ings from Japan's defeat. By 1945, China's *Kuomintang* party and government had lost much of its revolutionary vitality, and its popularity with the Chinese people had been seriously eroded.

When Japan precipitated the larger war in the Pacific by her attack on Pearl Harbor in 1941, she was carrying to its logical conclu- sion the philosophy and policy first applied in the seizure of Manchuria in 1931, applied again in the undeclared war upon China begun in 1937, and yet again in her subsequent moves to set up an entirely new order in greater East Asia. This grandiose policy, nur- tured by military fanatics who saw it as Japan's divine and benign mission, had, by 1941, gained wide acceptance in non-military circles as Japan's only road to national security. It was widely assumed that as the Axis powers would undoubtedly win in Europe, so Japan would win in East and Southeast Asia. Since victory would require a supreme effort, Japan moved during the first years of the war toward totalitarian controls. But as early vic- tories were succeeded by even greater defeats, and as the air war was carried to Japan's

The problems of supplying *Kuomintang* China with foreign military assistance are suggested by this photograph of the Ledo (Stilwell) Road. Altogether this route traversed 1,079 miles between Ledo, India, and Kunming, China.

homeland, optimism could no longer be sustained in the face of unbelievable destruction of life and property. As in China, where the experiences of war served only to erode further the authority of the *Kuomintang*-Nationalist government, so in Japan there was increased questioning of a military-dominated government whose conduct had brought not victory but seemingly certain defeat, if not total destruction.

CHINA: THE *KUOMINTANG'S* DECLINING AUTHORITY

Basic among Nationalist China's wartime problems was the deterioration of her economy. The retreat into the undeveloped hinterland, however heroic in terms of human endurance, cut deeply into productive capac-

ity. Government assistance had been given to effect the removal of industries to the interior, but since many coastal enterprises were foreign-owned, only about 600 private factories and 117,300 tons of machinery were actually transferred. While additional plants were built with government capital, the peak value of total production, reached in 1943, was only 12 percent of prewar levels.[1] Light arms were manufactured, but there was not one factory in *Kuomintang* China that could produce a truck, a tank, or an airplane. To meet her most pressing needs, the *Kuomintang*-Nationalist government welcomed such imports as could be obtained from the Soviet Union, the United States, and, after 1941, even from Japan.[2]

Adding to the production crisis was one of the greatest monetary inflations of all time. While this problem was undeniably rooted in prewar financial and fiscal practices, its immediate and direct causes were tied to the war.[3] Since the Japanese invaders collected the custom-duties which had previously served as a major source of income, Chungking's heavy war-induced expenditures had to be based on

[1] In 1943 Nationalist China produced 147 million kilowatts of electricity, 84,300 tons of pig iron, 10,400 tons of steel, 6 million tons of coal, less than 6,000 tons of basic chemicals, and 14 million gallons of liquid fuel. See Cheng Yu-kwei, *Foreign Trade and Industrial Development of China* (1956).

[2] Imports from Japanese sources trickled through long, thinly-manned battle lines. Between 1942 and 1945, Nationalist China's imports from the Japanese ranged from 20 to 35 percent of the total from all sources.

[3] In the period 1928-1937, *Kuomintang*-Nationalist government finance, although substantially strengthened by reform, presented a number of unsound characteristics: the allocation of one-third of annual state revenues to service the national debt; a heavy reliance (as much as one-fifth of the total spent) on loans to finance national expenditures; and dependence on customs revenues for about half of the national income. This was a situation that reflected Nanking's failures to wrest important sources of income from warlord control. It also reflected the government's tendency toward the expedient course. For example, it was relatively simple to tap the revenues collected by the maritime customs service, an inheritance from the era of the "unequal treaties." Taxation through internal reform presented a more difficult problem.

the resources of a few poor provinces; naturally, price stability was constantly imperiled. In consequence, by 1945 a businessman making a simple transaction was accompanied by coolies who carried enormous stacks of banknotes. These conditions beggared government officials and lesser bureaucrats as well as China's new middle class. To survive, officialdom resorted to wholesale graft. Still another result was to deprive the government of its most progressive supporters in business, and to give the extreme right wing increased power and authority.

The *Kuomintang*-Nationalist government faced another problem in rising peasant unrest. After 1937, the horrors of war multiplied the burdens already suffered by peasants as a result of tenancy and indebtedness. As Japanese forces invaded China, villages were looted and burned and the populace abused. Behind Nationalist lines peasants were indiscriminately conscripted into the army—some provinces were stripped of as many as one-half to two-thirds of the male population of military age—and were often treated brutally by their officers. Nationalist armies commandeered men, carts, and draft animals without regard to local need or peasant sensibilities. Even worse was the government's use of troops to collect food while peasants starved. To a peasantry thus treated, the Nationalist government assumed the appearance of a devouring tyrant; on occasion, peasant mobs attempted to disarm the troops. As the war progressed, Nationalist armies became increasingly unreliable as their ranks were filled by sullen, sometimes rebellious, peasant conscripts.

Still other problems were connected with the multiple objectives of the Nationalist government's political leadership. The *Kuomintang,* as the source of the government's authority, faced the Herculean task of providing leadership in prosecuting the war and expelling the Japanese, while at the same time maintaining its claim to be the guardian and the vehicle of Sun Yat-sen's continuing revolution. Since the government was under one-party political tutelage, a staggering responsibility rested on the *Kuomintang* hierarchy. This hierarchy professed to maintain its political power on a broad base of popular consent.

Yet obtaining this consent was peculiarly difficult in the atmosphere of wartime China, not only because Chinese politics were traditionally very personal, but also because constitutionalism did not exist in fact. Since those who were outside the party, as well as many of the party's rank and file, had no effective means of influencing policy, they became something less than ardent adherents of *Kuomintang* leadership.[4] This problem of leadership was the more serious because, in addition to the challenge from the Communists, the *Kuomintang* was confronted by a whole group of minor political parties jealous of *Kuomintang* power, all of which thought they knew what ought to be done. During the early war years beginning in 1937, the minor parties, although allowed no share in the *Kuomintang's* monopoly of political power or in responsibility for the conduct of war, sought to cooperate with the government even when their status as independent parties was not fully recognized in law. After 1941, however, when the *Kuomintang*-Communist united front failed, the Nationalist government revived a policy of repression which in turn alienated popular support at the very moment it was most needed.[5]

[4] On the structure of the Nationalist government as affected by the Japanese invasion, see Liu Naichen, "The Framework of Government in Unoccupied China," in *Voices from Unoccupied China,* H. F. MacNair, ed. (1944), 1-15.

[5] Ch'ien Tuan-sheng, *The Government and Politics of China* (1950),* 371-75. A wide array of political ideas and programs were represented by the minor parties. The Young China party (sometimes called the Chinese Youth party) had been organized in Paris, 1923. It called itself democratic and filled its platform with vague aspirations, extreme nationalism, and anti-communism. The National Socialist party, dominated at the outset by university professors, had been formed in 1931 by Carsun Chang among intellectuals who had been followers of Liang Ch'i-ch'ao. The party was largely an attempt to restore traditional values modified by Western thought. The National Salvation Association was organized by intellectuals at Shanghai, 1936, to promote armed resistance against Japan. Its thinking was leftist, for which many of its members were imprisoned, though in reality its objective was unity of the country above all party considerations. During the war the *Kuomintang* continued a policy of suppressing this movement. Two additional minor groups, the National Association for Vocational Education and the Rural Reconstruction Group, favored popularizing vocational education and implementing

Also contributing to the *Kuomintang's* difficulties in marshaling broad support was the party's failure to supply dynamic leadership either on the battlefield or in the political realm. The indispensible party leader at the time of the outbreak of war was Chiang Kai-shek, whose emergence from party ranks was due principally, though not exclusively, to his status as a soldier. Chiang had won a new degree of unity within China by defeating most of the warlords. The luster derived from this achievement, however, dimmed as Chiang grappled with the exceedingly complex problems of resisting Japan from 1937 to 1945. For one thing, Chiang's forces, while numerically impressive, were in general unequal to Japanese armies in equipment, training, and morale. Moreover, Chiang's inability to deal effectively with political problems of military control and organization meant that he exercised only limited authority over some of the troops under his command. After 1938, except where a pitched battle and frontal attack on a better equipped enemy appeared mandatory, Chinese troops were ordered to avoid decisive engagements, to yield in the face of Japanese assaults, and to attack only thinly defended points. By such means Chiang hoped to hang on, keeping his armies in the field until help arrived and Japan was overcome by Allied forces. The strategy was designed to achieve the survival of the Nationalist government and, given the handicaps under which Chiang labored, was understandable. Nevertheless, Chiang's essentially defensive effort produced no political or military heroes prepared to pay any price for victory.[6]

The conduct of hostilities was only a single aspect of the problem of leadership. In a land where nationalism was a vibrant, popular aspiration rather than a realized system of administration, Chiang was expected to implement Sun's revolution through appropriate political, economic, and social reforms. These needs for political and social leadership came at a time when nearly half of China's territory was in the hands of the invader, when factionalism within the *Kuomintang* was increasing rather than decreasing, and, finally, when Chiang's position was constantly under challenge by the Communists and by non-Communists both inside and outside the *Kuomintang*. In 1937 and 1938, Chiang appeared to be rising to the crisis that called him. In response to popular demand he made peace with the Communists and moved in the direction of constitutionalism. He showed some qualities of political as well as military leadership, and of ethical stature; but unlike Sun Yat-sen, he was not a "political philosopher and utopist" who could stir the loyalty of men by his power of expression, nor was he a saint like Gandhi who could convince a world of his selfless devotion.[7]

Chiang's political creed was revealed not only by what he did, but also by his book, *China's Destiny*, first published at Chungking in Chinese in 1943.[8] It is a textbook on Chinese nationalism in which Chiang appears as a disciple of nineteenth-century nationalism similar to the models provided by Germany, Italy, and Japan. Chiang's program, as pre-

---

rural reform. These groups were less important as political parties than as symbols of political needs. Finally, the Democratic League, founded in 1941 by progressives of the People's Political Council, had a more valid claim to the label "democratic" than any other political group. In the *Kuomintang*-Communist conflict during and after the war the League was divided between those inclined toward close cooperation with the Communists and those aspiring to be neutral mediators.

[6] See P. M. A. Linebarger, "Ideological Dynamics of the Postwar Far East," in *Foreign Governments*, F. Morstein Marx, ed. (1949), 555.

[7] See P. M. A. Linebarger, "Government in China," in *Foreign Governments*, Marx, ed., 597.

[8] Editions in English include: (1) Chiang Kai-shek, *China's Destiny*, authorized translation by Wang Chung-hui, with an introduction by Lin Yutang (1947); (2) Chiang Kai-shek, *China's Destiny and Chinese Economic Theory*, with notes and commentary by Philip Jaffe (1947). Although there has been much controversy as to the relative merits of the two English editions, as a matter of fact "as translations they are about equally faithful to the author's original," despite "the servile acceptance of Lin Yutang" and "the bitterly hostile presentation of Mr. Jaffe." See the evaluation on this point by Earl Swisher in *Far Eastern Quarterly*, 10 (1950), 89-95.

sented, was also closely parallel to the reform philosophy of Meiji Japan. Emphasis was on an emotional race and national consciousness with the Yellow Emperor presented as the common ancestor of Chinese, Manchus, Mongols, Tibetans, and Mohammedans, just as Amaterasu, the Sun Goddess, became the ancestress of the Japanese emperor and the Japanese race. Chiang reviewed the decline and the fall of the Manchus, the story of Western imperialism (the unequal treaties), the subversion of the Revolution of 1911 by Yuan Shih-k'ai and the warlords, the reorganization and triumph of the *Kuomintang,* its record of national reconstruction from 1928 to 1937, and, finally, China's achievement of new nationhood signified by termination of the unequal treaties with Great Britain and the United States in 1943. China's revolution, therefore, could be held together no longer by anti-imperialism. It required a new positive nationalism that Chiang proposed to base on Confucian morality, which he believed could still inspire the nation. The weakness of his position lay in the fact that his plea for loyalty to the state was backed by no sound political theory relevant to the wartime China of 1937-1945.[9]

Whatever may be said of *China's Destiny* as a sincere revelation of Chiang's mind and soul, as a political manifesto it was a lamentable miscarriage. It opposed the intellectual trends of the prewar years by berating those Chinese

[9] "The weakness and confusion of his [Chiang's] thesis lie in the fact that Confucian morality has been outmoded for several generations of students and political leaders who regard it as old-fashioned, and the additional fact that Confucius' political philosophy is moralistic, non-legal, and anti-state and thus ill-suited to modern nationalism, even of the conventional sort. The fact that Chiang tried to append an argument for a government of law over a government of men only serves to confuse his dominant and basically untenable thesis.... No attempt is made to reselect from China's rich tradition those elements that would support a new and modern state; no search is made for the democratic elements in China's history and philosophy." Swisher, *Far Eastern Quarterly,* 10 (1950), 93. The view that Chiang's ideological shortcomings were less serious than his failure to stay in touch with the broad spectrum of political factions is advanced in Pichon P. Y. Loh, "The Politics of Chiang Kai-shek: A Reappraisal," *Journal of Asian Studies,* 25 (1966), 431-51.

who had sought inspiration from the West. It scolded Chinese businessmen of the treaty ports for their Western free enterprise while it advocated restriction of private capital and a government-planned economy. It alienated the youth of China by offering nothing more than an exhortation to obedience and frugality. It sought political and social stability by appeals to tradition which had no meaning in the ferment of modern China and which served only to alienate political allies in the struggle against Communism.

RESURGENCE OF CHINESE COMMUNISM

Another difficulty besetting the National government's leadership after 1941 was the progressive breakdown of the *Kuomintang-*Communist united front. Proclaimed in September, 1937, the united front rested on an agreement between the *Kuomintang* and Communists to abandon their war against each other and to act jointly in the defense of China. The motivating force behind the agreement was China's growing determination to resist Japanese imperialism; it did not signify any lessening of hostility between the two contending parties. On the contrary, both Chiang and Mao Tse-tung were intent upon resuming their warfare at the earliest feasible moment. The unification movement, therefore, was soon gripped by creeping paralysis. Both the Nationalist government and the Communists continued to fight Japan, but after late 1938, the united front became merely a name, and eventually, by 1944, not even that. The total effect was to cripple China's limited powers to resist Japan and to pave the way for renewed civil war.

In contrast to the *Kuomintang,* the Communists during the war years enjoyed a dramatic revival. Prior to the Japanese invasion, Mao Tse-tung and his followers, pinned to China's desolate northwest and threatened by fresh "extermination campaigns," faced a future more perilous than in their years in Kiangsi. Yet, when Japan surrendered in 1945, these Communist forces claimed nineteen base areas in northern China with a population of 90 million, an army of 930,000 plus a militia of 2.2 million, and a party membership of 1.2 million. So greatly improved were the party's fortunes by 1944 that some informed observers were asking whether the Communists had not already won the struggle for China.

Guerrilla warfare became the vehicle for this Communist advance. From their stronghold in Shensi, guerrilla armies infiltrated the countryside to organize the populace in opposition to the Japanese. Here, in a region where many *Kuomintang* officials had resigned or fled as the Japanese approached, the Communists appeared as protectors, offering villagers the means for retaliating against the indignities and brutality of the foreign occupation. Indeed, Japanese excesses proved to be the Communists' greatest ally. Throughout the north, the Japanese army replied to opposition with "mopping-up" campaigns that involved systematic destruction and indiscriminate slaughter. In these circumstances, which capitalized upon a rural people's lack of organization, the Chinese frequently found their greatest security as members of a guerrilla band.

In this phase of party history, the Communists pictured themselves as patriots whose prime concern was the nation's salvation. The Communists' goals were portrayed not only in initiatives looking toward a united front with the *Kuomintang,* but also in the party's identification with the principles of Sun Yat-sen. In a treatise entitled "On New Democracy," Mao Tse-tung praised Sun's program as one which required only a theory of mass organization to make it entirely applicable to existing conditions. The effect was to provide party organizers with the means for stimulating national feeling and for presenting the party's "border region government" as the prime bulwark of Chinese civilization.

These efforts to play upon newly-instilled national patriotism resulted in a decided de-emphasis of the more revolutionary aspects of the party's economic and social programs. Earlier calls for the confiscation of large land holdings were replaced by the enforcement of regulations reducing and limiting land rents, reducing interest rates to a maximum of ten percent a year, and introducing a scheme of progressive taxation. These measures, which appeared as reforms of an existing system, were linked with positive demonstrations of the Communists' concern with popular needs. Guerrilla forces pressured local despots to accept their authority and to change their ways, even disciplined mothers-in-law who mistreated daughters-in-law, and admonished husbands to deal humanely with their wives. The Communist military, moreover, stood in sharp contrast to other forces, whether Japanese or *Kuomintang,* in its practice of treating the peasantry with consideration. In addition, the party drew popular support through its operation of public councils, which introduced the peasantry to what was said to be mass-style democracy.[10]

The party's growth and its revision of tactics in no way diminished Mao's authority. Party membership, old and new, was regularly subjected to rigorous ideological indoctrination aimed at making it completely responsive to the direction of higher authority. This process, known as the *cheng-feng* movement, involved party members in intensive study of authorized texts, group discussion, public con-

[10] See Lucien Bianco, *Origins of the Chinese Revolution, 1915-1949* (1971), 140-66. The ingredients of Communist success in northern China remain a source of controversy. The thesis that the party advanced by capitalizing on peasant discontent was set out in a pioneering study by Benjamin Schwartz, *Chinese Communism and the Rise of Mao* (1951).* A more recent statement, which applies this contention specifically to the war years, is Donald Gillin's "Peasant and Communist in Modern China: Reflections on the Origins of the Communist-led Peasant Movement," *South Atlantic Quarterly,* 60 (1961), 434-46. Differing interpretations are in Chalmers Johnson, *Peasant Nationalism and Communist Power* (1962),* which holds that the party's success in arousing and organizing national feeling against the Japanese invader was the key to its success; and in Shanti Swarup, *A Study of the Chinese Communist Movement, 1927-1934* (1966), which argues that the Communists succeeded only when they perceived the necessity of combining national and social revolutions with the operational tactics of warlordism. Mark Selden's *The Yenan Way in Revolutionary China* (1971)* reveals the importance of involving the populace in the processes of decision making. Whatever the reasons, the Communist strategy worked.

fession, and self-criticism. By these means dissident elements were eliminated from the party and a fresh sense of revolutionary fervor gripped the membership. When World War II terminated with Japan's surrender, therefore, there was a powerful Communist Party in China, whose expanded organization, discipline, and newly-won popularity created fresh challenges for the *Kuomintang*-Nationalist government.

KUOMINTANG COUNTER EFFORTS

The spectre of expanding Communism greatly alarmed the Nationalist government and triggered counterefforts. Initially the Nationalists broke up Communist front organizations within their reach and launched guerrilla attacks of their own behind Japanese lines; but lacking both an ideology and program of action to match the Communists' in popular appeal, neither of these activities had much success. There followed a military blockade of the Communists' northern stronghold to prevent infiltration into Nationalist territory. The expansion of Communist forces outside the regions designated in the truce agreements led to a series of "incidents," which culminated in the battle called the "New Fourth Army incident" of January, 1941, leading to the beginning of intensified civil war.

Nevertheless, in spite of frequent incidents and continual friction, the stated policy of the Nationalist government remained that of seeking a political settlement with the Communists. At meetings of the people's political council, some minor parties attempted mediation with the object of preserving *Kuomintang*-Communist cooperation. On a number of occasions there were direct negotiations between Nationalist and Communist officials in which suggestions for a "coalition government" were brought forth. Although no settlement was reached, it appeared that from May to September, 1944, the Nationalist government and the Chinese Communist party were at least going through the motions of seeking a peaceful settlement. But behind these maneuvers was the government's fear of offending elements within the *Kuomintang* if "radical measures of reform" were passed, and

the government's well-justified conviction that the Communists would extend their power at the first opportunity.

EFFORTS TO BOLSTER CHINA

Although China was isolated from the other theaters of World War II, her war effort was supported by her allies. In the early stages of the Sino-Japanese conflict, the Soviet Union, although officially at peace, provided assistance in the form of $250 million in credits, five air wings with Soviet pilots, and the stationing of Soviet troops at Hami to block Japan's access to Sinkiang. This aid, however, which had been prompted by fears that the German-Japanese anti-Comintern pact of 1936 pointed to an utlimate Japanese assault on the Soviet Union, was not sustained beyond the outbreak of World War II. Beginning in 1941, the United States became the chief source of foreign aid to China.

At first this American aid was little more than verbal assurance that the war would be fought until Japan was defeated. But financial aid followed, a $500 million loan in 1942.[11] There was also implementation of long-range planning to reopen communications with Chungking. The chief of the American military mission to China, General Joseph Stilwell, became chief-of-staff to Generalissimo Chiang Kai-shek and commander of ground forces in the CBI theater. After the retreat from Burma, it was Stilwell's task to train Chinese troops for its reconquest, to open air transport from India over the Hump of the Himalayas to Chungking, and to construct the Ledo road from Assam through northern Burma to link with the upper Burma road. One of the heroic stories of the war was written by the Americans who, beginning with scanty equipment, flew lend-lease supplies to Chungking.[12] There was also aid to China from the American Volunteer Group. Under General Claire L. Chennault, these American "Flying Tigers"

[11] Previous loans had been made in the prewar years.

[12] See Charles F. Romanus and Riley Sunderland, *Stilwell's Mission to China* (1953) for an authoritative account of American military aid.

had operated prior to Pearl Harbor under contracts with the Chinese government to protect the Burma road. Later they continued to function in China as the Fourteenth Air Force of the United States Army Air Forces.

On the political and diplomatic front, the United States moved to bolster Chinese confidence by discarding the last remnants of the unequal treaty system. Tariff autonomy had been conceded to China more than a decade earlier. On January 11, 1943, both the United States and Great Britain concluded treaties with China providing for immediate relinquishment of their extraterritorial rights and for the settlement of related questions. This act and similar relinquishment of special rights by all the remaining "treaty powers" completed the long process of restoring and recognizing the full sovereignty of China. At the same time, impelled by the pressures of war, Congress ended Chinese exclusion on December 17, 1943. Under the new law, a presidential proclamation fixed an annual quota of Chinese immigrants at 105.

The fuller significance of the ending of extraterritoriality and the exclusion laws was given at the Cairo conference, November 22-26, 1943, where Roosevelt and Churchill met with Chiang Kai-shek to consider problems of war and peace in East Asia. The implications were that China was accepted as one of the great powers, that the Nationalist government had the full support of Britain and America, and that postwar East Asia would be built around a fully sovereign, independent, and strong China. Indeed, the year 1943 revealed new heights in America's traditional and sentimental admiration for China. This newly aroused enthusiasm was associated with Madame Chiang Kai-shek, who had come to the United States early in 1943 to win American support for the Nationalist government and to criticize the strategy of merely holding the front against Japan until the defeat of Hitler had been achieved. Her eloquence and charm appeared to personify the heroism of a China that had refused to be beaten. Chinese unity and Chinese democracy were accepted uncritically under the spell of

her magnetic personality. Madame Chiang spoke of the highlights; she avoided the shadows. Neither she nor other spokesmen of the Nationalist government were in a position to say what all knew—that China's prosecution of the war had reached its lowest point since Japan struck at Lukouchiao in July, 1937.

Although there had been warning rumors in 1943, it was not until early in 1944 that an alarming picture of China's deteriorating war effort and morale broke through Chungking's censorship to reach the United States. President Roosevelt, fearing that China would not hold together until the end of the war, pressed for a renewed *Kuomintang*-Communist truce. In support of this policy, an American army observer group nicknamed the "Dixie Mission" was sent to Yenan to report on expanding Communist operations, and Vice-President Henry A. Wallace was sent to Chungking to impress upon Chiang the importance of giving the highest priority to defeating Japan.[13] The American government

---

[13] The "Dixie Mission" included state department as well as military personnel. Moreover, American newspaper reporters were permitted to enter Communist-controlled areas. In consequence, the reporting on the Chinese Communists was comprehensive and by no means confined to military operations. David D. Barrett, *Dixie Mission: The United States Army Observer Group in Yenan, 1944* (1970),* is the memoir of the commander of the "Dixie Mission." American diplomatic documents relating to the "Dixie Mission" are printed in United States, Department of State, *Foreign Relations of the United States: Diplomatic Papers, 1944: Volume VI, China* (1967). While contacts between the American observer group and the Chinese Communists proved to be temporary, the mission's records reveal American knowledge of and attitudes toward the Communists before the onset of cold war tension. Chapters dealing with these early American attitudes are found in Dorothy Borg, *The United States and the Far Eastern Crisis of 1933-1938: From the Manchurian Incident through the Initial Stage of the Undeclared Sino-Japanese War* (1964); and Tang Tsou, *America's Failure in China, 1941-50* (1963).* A study of changing American conceptions is Kenneth E. Shewmaker's *Americans and Chinese Communists, 1927-1945: A Persuading Encounter* (1971). Warren W. Tozer, "The Foreign Correspondents' Visit to Yenan in 1944: A Reassessment," *Pacific Historical Review*, 41 (1972), 207-24, contends that newspaper accounts had little effect on American opinion.

also wanted Chiang to form a war council representing all Chinese forces. This latter body was to be presided over by General Joseph Stilwell.

Great obstacles, however, soon confronted these American efforts to assist China. Acting on the theory that China should assume the full obligations of a major ally, General Stilwell proposed to Chiang a list of fundamental military reforms: *Kuomintang* forces were to be reduced; those remaining were to be thoroughly retrained; and the command structure was to be reorganized. Stilwell regarded these measures as indispensable to China's military effectiveness, but Chiang perceived in them a challenge to the foundations of his political power. The Generalissimo much preferred the advice of General Claire Chennault, who, by proposing to win the war through air assaults, planned to avoid any interference with China's political or military structure.[14] In August, 1944, General Patrick J. Hurley went to Chungking as the President's personal representative to Chiang to sweeten the bitter relations between Chiang and Stilwell, to keep China in the war, and to unify all Chinese military forces against Japan. Hurley soon come to the view that relations between Chiang and Stilwell over the question of China's war effort and the means of promoting it had deteriorated beyond repair. Accordingly, following Hurley's recommendation,

[14] A brief, interpretative portrait of Stilwell is in Jonathan Spence, *To Change China: Western Advisers in China, 1620-1900* (1969),* Chapter 9. Barbara Tuchman' full-length biography, *Stilwell and the American Experience in China, 1911-45* (1971),* sees the General's mission as "America's supreme try in China." In some respects, few other men could have been better suited for the assignment: Stilwell gave his maximum effort; ". . . he never slackened and he never gave up." Yet Stilwell and his government failed, because the goal was unachievable: "The impulse was not Chinese. Combat efficiency and the offensive spirit, like the Christianity and democracy offered by missionaries and foreign advisers, were not the indigenous demands of the society and culture to which they were brought. . . . The American effort to sustain the status quo could not supply an outworn government with strength and stability or popular support. It could not hold up a husk nor long delay the cyclical passing of the mandate of heaven. In the end China went her own way as if the Americans had never come." (531)

Stilwell was recalled and Major General Albert C. Wedemeyer was designated to replace him as Chiang's chief-of-staff, October, 1944. Coincident with these events, Clarence E. Gauss, ambassador to China and an exceedingly able diplomat, resigned November 1, 1944, and was replaced by General Hurley, who continued as ambassador until November 26, 1945. Hurley's activities included: (1) efforts to mediate between the Nationalists and Communists; and (2) efforts to clarify relations between China and the Soviet Union. By this time, however, the American offensive against Japan through the Philippines and the Mandated Islands was reducing the China theater to lesser importance in American military planning. As a result there was less effort to deal with the problem of Nationalist military and political power. General Hurley was instrumental in a resumption of negotiations between the Nationalists and the Communists, but the basic question of power between the two groups remained unresolved. Thus matters stood as, with Japan's surrender, hostilities in the Pacific came to an end.

JAPAN DURING THE WAR

When the war in the Pacific began in 1941, the Japanese public had long been indoctrinated with high expectations. By mid-1942, with far-flung victories won, Premier Tojo Hideki told the nation that Japan's first purpose had already been achieved: the defeat of the United States, Great Britain, and the Netherlands. The task that remained was consolidation of the fruits of victory. Peace and security would be established in the former Western colonial empires through military bases at Singapore, Manila, and Hong Kong. Prosperity would be fostered through a self-contained economy covering all of the "Greater East Asia Co-prosperity Sphere." The former Western colonies would be given "independent governments" friendly to Japan. To achieve these ends, the Tojo government set about to create a totalitarian government at home equipped with new and greatly enlarged administrative machinery to direct and manage its empire abroad.

BUREAUCRATIC TOTALITARIANISM

The political philosophy and structure of government which had developed in Japan by 1941, and which were to persist throughout the war, were in many respects logical developments of earlier steps taken after 1931 toward totalitarian control. Yet neither before nor after 1941 did Japan become a corporate state in the manner of Germany or Italy. She produced no all-powerful Nazi or Fascist party and no single political leader capable of emerging as a dictator. In matters of economics and production, she failed to create the full corporate state in the manner of her European allies. What happened in Japan both before and during the war was influenced by these European pace-setters, but Japanese conditions, problems, and the methods of dealing with them remained essentially Japanese.

When, by her attack on Pearl Harbor, Japan engulfed the Pacific area in World War II, she was operating under a governmental structure that had been altered vastly since the invasion of Manchuria a decade earlier. The movement toward parliamentary government, from which so much had been expected in the decade, 1920 to 1930, had been extinguished. The imperial Diet had declined in political importance, though its influence had not been entirely destroyed. The traditional political parties, the *Seiyukai* and the *Minseito,* had abolished themselves under the pressure of extremists in 1940, and the country had returned to nonparty ministries. The armed services had secured increasing control over the civil administration but had been unable to gain a monopoly of political power in the cabinet and especially in the office of the prime minister. The functions of government had been increased greatly, in part by cabinet-inspired legislation in the Diet, and by a much greater use of imperial ordinance, ministerial orders, and departmental regulations. When she attacked Pearl Harbor, Japan seemed to be close to the goal of the corporate state. Yet the corporate state that was appearing was peculiarly Japanese. The most important results of the governmental changes

from 1931 to 1941 were the increase in the number and the power of bureaucratic agencies, the enhancement of the prestige and the political influence of the bureaucracy as a whole, and thus the creation in wartime Japan of what may best be called "a dictatorship of the bureaucracy."[15]

The growth of bureaucratic agencies and of bureaucratic power in Japan after 1931 was not unique.[16] There were similar tendencies in the Western world and particularly in the United States under the New Deal. Nevertheless, throughout the history of modern Japan, bureaucracy had a greater political force, a broader and more complex mechanism, than

---

[15] Charles Nelson Spinks, "Bureaucratic Japan," *Far Eastern Survey,* 10 (1941), 219-25.

[16] The term "bureaucracy" as applied to government in Japan is used in a much broader sense than is common in Western usage. It includes not only the civil servants but also the agents of the military services and, at times, of the political parties and the *zaibatsu.* Thus the enlargement of the bureaucracy may be said to have proceeded along two major lines: (1) There was an expansion of ministerial agencies and the creation of extraministerial boards under the jurisdiction of the cabinet. Some of the more important of these created in the immediate prewar years included: the Manchurian affairs board, entrusted with the coordination of policy between Japan and Manchukuo; the cabinet planning board, a species of politico-economic general staff; the China affairs board, responsible for furthering the New Order in occupied China; and the cabinet advisory council, an effort to recognize the modern would-be *genro* and through them to find a means of reconciling rival bureaucratic factions. (2) Of great importance was the multiplication of the national policy companies, which were the instruments of Japanese expansion at first in Manchuria and then in occupied China. The idea involved in this kind of an organization was not new. It had been employed early in the Meiji era in such cases as the Hokkaido Development Company and the Yawata Iron Works. As an instrument of national expansion abroad, the system was first fully matured in the South Manchurian Railway Company, founded in 1906, in whose hands Japan's exploitation of the South Manchuria sphere remained a practical monopoly until 1932. The pattern of organization for which the S.M.R. provided the model was that of an official corporation in which the government held a controlling number of shares. In the later national policy companies, the companies were holding concerns controlling subsidiary companies which conducted the business enterprises involved.

in other countries. During the entire constitutional period the ministers of state (the cabinet) were linked more intimately with bureaucratic elements than with the Diet. In addition some factions of the bureaucracy—the army and the navy, particularly—enjoyed a position of political independence and power guaranteed by constitutional organization. Again, Japan's bureaucrats enjoyed a unique political strength because of the influence they wielded in the formulation as well as in the execution of policies. Ministers of state in Japan's bureaucratic cabinets long recognized that the government's fortunes depended less on the adoption of important national policies than on appropriate political recognition of each major bureaucratic group and the maintenance of a balance among these groups. As the bureaucratic agencies of government increased in size and number after 1931, and as the political parties lost influence and finally disappeared, it became the function of the prime minister to act as a mediating officer between these factions of permanent office-holders.

The absence of commanding political leadership in prewar and wartime Japan was as notable as the power of the bureaucracy. There were efforts, indeed, to perpetuate the *genro* system. In a limited way it lived on in a loose organization made up of the lord keeper of the privy seal, former prime ministers, and high representatives of the army and navy. Its influence, however, never equalled or even rivalled that of the Meiji *genro*. Outstanding among the so-called new *genro* was Prince Konoe Fumimaro, who headed three cabinets on the eve of the war. Konoe was chosen not because of his ability to lead but because of the aristocratic prestige of his family and his capacity, despite nebulous political thinking, to keep on reasonably good terms with all factions.

As the power of the bureaucracy increased, successive governments after 1932 sought to provide the prime minister with agencies through which he might exercise more effective leadership. A five-minister conference or inner cabinet had become fully established by 1940. In the spring of 1941, Premier Konoe turned to a second expedient, the creation of an unofficial but informally recognized "big three of the cabinet," including the premier, the vice-premier, and the minister of finance. This device, although more flexible than the five-minister conference, failed. A third device designed to increase the efficiency of Japan's top bureaucratic leadership was the *Taisei Yokusan Kai* (Imperial Rule Assistance Association, IRAA), which made its appearance on the demise of the traditional political parties in 1940. The idea of a single political party had been inspired by the European fascist model. Konoe was prevailed upon to lead the movement. The new associaton emerged as an agency of "spiritual mobilization" and was soon controlled by the army. Early in the war, the political importance of the IRAA led to the creation of a new and closely related organization, the Imperial Rule Assistance Political Society (IRAPS). This body, at first associated with the efforts of the government to pack the Diet with "approved candidates," enjoyed only a very limited success. As the war progressed, the IRAPS tended to become a species of Diet members' club, dominated by conservative, but not extremist, party leaders.

The Economic Pattern

Although political power in prewar Japan had gravitated toward a cumbersome and leaderless bureaucracy, and although there was increasing state intervention in economic life, the nation was still far from possessing a planned economy. As late as 1941, most of the nation's business was financed and operated by private enterprise with only limited government interference. From the autumn of 1940, however, the need for national control of industry became more pressing, but there was no agreement as to the degree of control desirable or as to who should exercise this control. Extremists in the army, the navy, and some factions of the bureaucracy clamored for total control in which the state would simply take over all industry. The business interests, particularly the *Zaibatsu*, were opposed to this program and remained so throughout the war. They were not hostile to greater wartime integration of industry enforced by the state—in fact, they perceived some advantages to themselves in such a system—but they were determined that their ownership and their prerogatives of management should be safeguarded and preserved.

The Search for Effective Government

The Tojo cabinet, which replaced the third Konoe ministry on October 18, 1941, was supposed to be the answer to this riddle of leadership. General Tojo Kideki was a product of the Kwantung Army School, a former commander of the gendarmerie in Manchukuo, chief of staff of the Kwantung Army, vice-minister of war in the first Konoe cabinet, and finally minister of war in the third Konoe cabinet. He had a reputation as an able administrator, and in his political and economic thinking it was assumed that he shared the attitude of the "state planners." He was thus acceptable to the militarists and the fascist extremists, but in addition he appears to have been regarded by the *zaibatsu* as a reliable leader. As Japan's wartime premier, Tojo held more offices and acquired greater power than any prime minister in Japan's history. He held concurrently the posts of premier, war minister, and home minister. After he had relinquished the last of these, he took over the new ministry of munitions and became chief of staff. Tojo's accession to power seemed to guarantee the creation in wartime Japan of a full-fledged, military, corporate state, if not a personal dictatorship.

This expectation, however, was not fulfilled. Tojo was confronted with the industrial monopolies of the *zaibatsu,* operating in general as semi-autonomous units linked neither with each other nor with the government through any effectively coercive administrative authority. Even with unprecedented authority at his command, the prime minister proved unable to overcome the problems emerging from this system. Finally, in January, 1944, after two war years of chaotic administration, the major enterprises were placed under the control of the newly created ministry of munitions. This centralized control and relatively efficient management of war production were not a political victory for the militarists

and extreme advocates of "state planning," but rather an acceptance by the government of control measures proposed by and acceptable to the industrialists, the *zaibatsu*. Indeed, the Tojo government, whose fumbling in directing home-production contributed to Japan's first military and naval reverses, fell and was replaced in July, 1944.

Although the war forced a greater concentration of administrative power than Japan had previously known, the failure of these belated measures to achieve victory, together with the rising specter of defeat, encouraged a return to traditional politics under the more conservative guidance of the so-called new *genro*. When the Tojo cabinet fell, the ministry that succeeded was essentially a military cabinet headed by a Kwantung army extremist, General Koiso Kuniaki, but was tempered by the presence of Admiral Yonai Mitsumasa as deputy prime minister and navy minister. Koiso's cabinet survived less than a year in the face of mounting military reverses. On April 7, 1945, it was succeeded by a ministry headed by Admiral Baron Suzuki Kantaro. Suzuki was a former lord chamberlain and had been attacked by the extremist assassins in 1936. His cabinet represented a careful balancing of conservative bureaucracies, the military services, and the business interests, and a conscious effort by the elder statesmen to defeat all extreme forms of political control. It was the Suzuki cabinet that tendered Japan's surrender in August and then gave place, September 16, 1945, to a new ministry under a prince of the imperial household, Higashikuni Naruhiko, a cousin of Emperor Hirohito. The selection of an imperial prince as premier was an effort to stabilize public opinion as the Japanese people witnessed the occupation of their homeland by a foreign army. Once the first phase of the occupation and demobilization was complete, Higashikuni resigned, October 5. He was succeeded the following day by one of Japan's few surviving "liberals," a man whom the nation had repudiated in 1931, Baron Shidehara Kijuro, who remained in office until April 22, 1946. It was Shidehara who faced the first problems of a defeated and broken Japan—the problems of food, housing, and inflation in a nation without leadership or purpose. These crises were beyond the grasp of the aged Shidehara, and in May the premiership passed to Yoshida Shigeru.[17]

Although Japan's unconditional surrender was brought about by the overwhelming powers of American armament, the time and the manner of the surrender were conditioned by the political, economic, and bureaucratic character of the Japanese state. Indeed, Japan's surrender could have come earlier if the political structure of the nation had permitted a more rapid and decisive determination of national policies or if the allies had been content with something short of unconditional surrender. As early as mid-1944, those Japanese leaders who possessed the basic information foresaw the economic collapse which was already underway and which assured the coming military disaster. By August, 1945, even without direct air attack, the level of Japan's production would have declined below the peak of 1944 by 40 to 50 percent, solely as a result of the interdiction of overseas imports. As it was, the damage from air attacks approximated that which was suffered by Germany. Approximately 30 percent of the urban population of Japan lost its homes and much of its possessions. With this appalling physical disaster came declining morale. Japan's civilian casualties numbered about 806,000, of which 333,000 were deaths. A declining belief in the power to win was accompanied by loss of confidence in both the military and the civilian leaders. Although a few of Japan's statesmen foresaw the ultimate defeat as early as February, 1944, it was not until May, 1945, that the supreme war direction council, a creation of the Koiso cabinet, seriously considered means to end the war.

FOR FURTHER READING

China. For graphic detail some of the older studies of wartime China remain the best

[17]Shidehara died in 1951. See Hugh Borton, *Japan's Modern Century* (2nd ed., 1970), 466-67.

sources: John K. Fairbank, *The United States and China* (1st ed., 1948), provides a wealth of information on the *Kuomintang* and its government which is omitted in later editions; Lawrence K. Rossinger, *China's Wartime Politics* (1945) also stresses *Kuomintang* China. On economic problems see Chang Kia-ngau, *The Inflationary Spiral: The Experience in China, 1939-1950* (1958); and Chou Shunhsin, *The Chinese Inflation, 1937-1949* (1963). The story of the ways in which foreign aid was utilized in China is told by a long-time Chinese financial adviser, Arthur N. Young, *China and the Helping Hand, 1937-1945* (1964). Oliver J. Caldwell, *A Secret War: Americans in China, 1944-1945* (1972). Paul A. Varg, *The Closing of the Door: Sino-American Relations, 1936-1946* (1973).

Grahan Peck, *Two Kinds of Time* (1950),* a reflective account of Chinese life, 1940-1947, based on first-hand observation. Other vivid portrayals are to be found in Theodore H. White and Annalee Jacoby, *Thunder Out of China* (1946); and Han Suyin, *Birdless Summer* (1968), part of a trilogy, autobiographic, and passionately patriotic.

On the Communists see: Franklin W. Houn *A Short History of Chinese Communism* (2nd rev. ed., 1967);* Boyd Compton, *Mao's China: Party Reform Documents, 1942-1944* (1952);* Edgar Snow, *Random Notes on Red China, 1936-1945* (1957);* and Lyman M. Van Slyke, *Enemies and Friends: The United Front in Chinese Communist History* (1967).

Japan. T. A. Bisson, *Japan's War Economy* (1945) stresses the role of the *zaibatsu*. Jerome B. Cohen, *Japan's Economy in War and Reconstruction* (1949) is the ablest general study. B. F. Johnston, *Japanese Food Management in World War II* (1953) is a voluminous reference work. Douglas G. Haring, ed., *Japan's Prospect* (1946) is by scholars who trained personnel. for military government in Japan. Yale C. Maxon, *Control of Japanese Foreign Policy: Study of Civil-Military Rivalry, 1930-1945* (1957) provides a careful study of a crucial aspect of Japanese politics. J. Morris, *Traveller from Tokyo*

(1943), an eye-witness account of Japan at the beginning of the war. William Craig, *The Fall of Japan* (1967)* emphasizes the human dimensions of surrender. Among the apologies written by Japanese leaders are Shigemitsu Mamoru, *Japan and Her Destiny: My Struggle for Peace* (1958); and Togo Shigenori, *The Cause of Japan* (1956).

The Occupation of Japan, 1945–1952

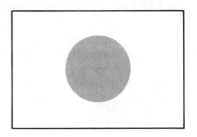

30

V-J Day, August 14, 1945, ended the hostilities of World War II in the Pacific and East Asia, but it did not bring peace. To be sure, the Allies' victory freed the Orient of the incubus of Japanese militarism and imperialistic expansion; however, it did not and could not rid Asia of all the ills from which it suffered. In many areas, men continued to fight to achieve the things they desired. Many of their goals were old and could not be traced exclusively to the recent policies and behavior of Japan. Rather, they were the recurring manifestations of an Asia stirred by a political and social revolution underway before World War II. But if the processes of modernization were not introduced into East Asia by the war, these processes were in many respects accelerated by the conflict, and they continued to operate with even greater force after the hostilities had ceased. Throughout the entire area there was not a single country unaffected by dynamic forces of change. Thus Japan's surrender was but the first step toward meeting a vast array of perplexing questions which war had not solved, and which in some cases were made more difficult by the war.

Basic to Asia's postwar turmoil was the fact that the traditional "low" standard of living was made even lower by the ravages of war—the destruction of life savings and property, the interruption of trade, the displacement of large segments of population, and the general dislocation resulting from extreme shortages and uncontrolled inflation. Some areas of East Asia were affected more adversely and radically by the war than others. Yet the words of Manuel Roxas, a Filipino leader, to the effect that war and the Japanese had brought "physical ruin" to the Philippines, could well be applied to larger areas of East Asia. This was not to say that Asia's economic problems had become insuperable. It was, rather, that the destruction wrought by war exacerbated the region's long-standing economic problems—relative poverty in resources, population pressures, subsistence income of the peasant masses, lack of industrial capital, and traditional social habits that were in conflict with a modern world. Clearly, economic independence and new standards of living remained a hope for the future.

Politics no less than economics were disrupted by the war. Traditional views of Asia's political status became untenable. Japan, the one "great power" of East Asia, was reduced to the status of a third- or fourth-class power. China, for one hundred years a quasi-dependent area, regained her full sovereignty and was dignified with nominal inclusion among the great states. The Philippines became an independent republic. Other native republics, semi-independent in fact, were born in French Indochina and the Netherland Indies, and independence "in due course" was promised to Korea. The Mongolian People's Republic acquired nationhood under Soviet patronage. Burma and India entered upon a new and independent political future. These signs of vital political consciousness were partly a result of nationalism, (a refusal to be governed longer by alien powers), but were also symptoms of a much broader social unrest. The enticements of modernization brought East Asia out of her seclusion, affected her intellectual as well as her material life, created the stirrings of a new social consciousness, and supplied her with a new intellectual and social leadership, whether in the person of a Chiang Kai-shek or a Mao Tse-tung in China, a Roxas or a Taruc in the Philippines, a Sukarno in Indonesia, a Ho Chi Minh in Indochina, a Syngman Rhee or a Kim

Il-song in Korea. The principle common to all these leaders was the concept of Asia's inherent right to political independence. What they had not resolved was the political, economic, and social structure in which independence was to function.

JAPAN AS A VICTIM OF WAR

The legacies of war in Japan were manifest everywhere. The country that had embarked on arrogant conquest was vastly different from the one that bowed before the victors in 1945—a picture of physical destruction, economic collapse, and social and spiritual emptiness; yet a Japan that had responded with habitual discipline to the emperor's bidding to surrender. The catalogue of the nation's losses included nearly two million lives and some 40 percent of the aggregate urban area including two million buildings. Nearly 700,000 buildings were destroyed in Tokyo alone, where population in the terror of bombing attacks shrank from more than 6.5 million to less than 3 million.

Frightful as the physical destruction was, its consequences were by no means so damaging as the breakdown of the economy at the war's

Hostilities ended in Asia and the Pacific when Japan surrendered formally in ceremonies aboard the *U.S.S. Missouri*. General Douglas MacArthur signed for the Allies; General Yoshijiro Umezu signed for the Japanese army.

end. The extraordinary gains of the prewar decade (1930-1940), during which industrial output doubled, were wiped out by defeat, leaving the nation in 1946 with less than a third of its 1930 production. The only immediately useful vestige of Japan's wealth was the paddy field. The peasant became an important person as desperate city dwellers sought food through the illicit channels of the black market. Prized family possessions were traded for rice; vegetables were grown where houses had stood; inflation consumed the meager savings that millions of people had gathered through long, hard years.

Possibly most damaging of all to a disciplined people was the enforced departure from discipline. Men defied authority or they perished. It was no longer possible to live within the law. The price was paid in morale and in character. Petty lawlessness and juvenile delinquency flourished, while gangsterism and protection rackets terrorized whole communities.[1]

At the same time, the picture of Japan as the victors found it was not hopeless. Millions of Japanese accepted surrender and humiliation with dignity. They met the cruel reality of defeat, surrender, and hunger, and, with little effort to shift the blame to others, accepted it as their own responsibility as well as that of their leaders. Whatever later successes the occupation enjoyed were attributable in a major degree to this attitude that enabled the Japanese people to cooperate with the inevitable. Troops of the occupation were received without visible animosity: a strange and friendly reception for Americans who had been taught, or had learned in battle, to hate the Japanese.

THE AMERICAN CONCEPT OF OCCUPATION

From the moment of Japan's defeat it was clear that the United States would assume a predominant position in the occupation of Japan. Although America gave assurance that it would consider the wishes of the principal Allied

powers, it was emphatic that "in the event of any differences of opinion among them, the policies of the United States will govern." This idea of a completely free hand for the United States in fashioning the new Japan did not meet with international favor. Since the control of Japan would have a direct bearing on larger questions concerning East Asia, it was to be expected that China, Russia, Australia, Great Britain, and France would seek a voice in policies applied in Tokyo.

The problem was eventually resolved in December, 1945, when the foreign ministers of Great Britain, Russia, and the United States, after consultation with China, agreed upon the creation of a Far Eastern commission and an Allied council for Japan. The functions of the commission, located in Washington, were to formulate policies, to review on the request of any member any directive issued to the supreme commander, and to consider other matters referred to it by agreement among the participating powers. In theory, the Far Eastern commission was a severe limitation on the freedom of the United States to formulate policies, but the reality was that the United States had not lost its predominant position. The United States retained responsibility for interpreting policy decisions and issuing directives to General Douglas MacArthur, to whom was assigned the post of Supreme Commander of the Allied Powers (SCAP). General MacArthur in turn applied the directives in accordance with his own interpretation. Nor was this free hand checked by the Allied council sitting in Tokyo, since this was a consultative and advisory body without power to act.[2]

Initial plans to establish a full scale military government in Japan were altered by Tokyo's

---

[1] A graphic account of Japan in defeat is given by Edwin O. Reischauer, *The United States and Japan* (rev. ed., 1961).*

[2] The limitations on the authority of the Far Eastern commission were revealed early in the occupation. In March, 1946, a majority of the commission's membership attempted to delay General MacArthur's program for activating a new Japanese constitution so that the commission could review all of SCAP's requirements. When the United States threatened to veto the majority decision, the commission dropped its delaying tactics and requested only an opportunity to see an advance copy of the final draft of the constitution. The American representative on the commission approved this latter action, but MacArthur refused to honor it.

sudden surrender and the subsequent peaceful reception accorded American forces.[3] Instead of administering Japan directly through American military officers, authority was to be exercised through the emperor's government. Under this concept, staff sections were created as a part of MacArthur's headquarters to plan the execution of occupation policy in respect to political, economic, and social problems involved in the remaking of Japan. Corresponding roughly to the ministries in the Japanese cabinet, these American staff sections were to transform policy directives into specific programs and to transmit the programs to the appropriate Japanese agency. In this way the private Japanese citizen acted on instructions from his own government.[4]

The ultimate objectives of the occupation were to insure that Japan would cease to be a threat to peace and security, and to encourage the development of responsible government supported by the freely expressed will of the Japanese people. These objectives were to be secured by: (1) limiting Japanese sovereignty to her main islands and a few outlying ones; (2) destroying Japan's military establishment and the economic base which supported it; (3) barring from office persons who were associated

[3] With Japan's surrender the United States faced a situation quite different from the one presented by a defeated Germany. Germany's Nazi party, for example, could not be equated with any single element in Japan. Nor did Germany have any institution similar to the Japanese imperial throne. American planning, therefore, took into account such problems as how the emperor was to be treated, the continued existence of the Japanese government as an entity, and the wisdom of direct American rule (as in Germany). For a description of the evolution of American planning by one who participated in it, see Hugh Borton, *American Presurrender Planning for Postwar Japan,* Occasional Papers of the East Asian Institute, Columbia University (1967).* Borton's "Preparation for the Occupation of Japan," *Journal of Asian Studies,* 25 (1966), 203-12, contains additional information especially on the emperor question.

[4] In practice this operation was less precise than the description suggests. While Washington regarded the occupation forces as the instruments of policy and not the determinants of policy, many of the day-to-day decisions were determined by events and by personalities commanding the occupation forces.

closely with Japan's militaristic policies and punishing war criminals; (4) encouraging the development of organizations in labor, industry, and agriculture that would facilitate expression of the popular will; (5) promoting policies which would encourage the wide distribution of income and ownership of the means of production and trade; and (6) revamping the educational system to encourage the acceptance of democratic reforms through reorientation of Japanese thought.

The implementation of the occupation was directed by MacArthur's staff of military officers in key posts and by civilians, some of whom were at relatively high levels. This small group undertook the amazing task of renovating politically, economically, and socially a nation of more than 80 million people. Many members of the occupation staff were persons with wide or specialized knowledge of Japan; others, although not conversant with Japan, had brilliant records in government, business, or the professions in the United States. To their staggering tasks in Japan they brought not only expert knowledge but also, and perhaps as important, a crusading zeal to create a new and revolutionary, though peaceful and democratic, Japan. As the occupation continued, however, it became increasingly difficult to procure and hold staff personnel of high competence. In addition, the occupation by its very nature tended to pervert its own members, who enjoyed standards of living no Japanese could afford, and whose judgements were always right while the Japanese were always wrong. Nevertheless, it should be added that the "corruption of conquest" would have been far greater had not the majority of occupation personnel retained their perspective and their honesty of purpose.

Throughout the occupation, both the staff of SCAP and the Japanese government upon which it operated felt the unique personal influence of MacArthur. To Japanese as well as to Americans, his name was synonymous with military tradition. Entering Japan as conqueror, he came, as it were, to assume, with the emperor's approval, the role of super-emperor. Autocratic, austere, decisive, always the drama-

DISPOSITION OF JAPAN'S EMPIRE, 1945

A – Southern SAKHALIN and KURIL ISLANDS occupied by U.S.S.R.

B – MANCHURIA to China; temporary Russian occupation.

C – KOREA: North occupied by Russia; south by U.S.A.

D – RYUKYU and BONIN ISLANDS occupied by U.S.A.

E – TAIWAN occupied by Nationalist China.

F – Occupied and administered by U.S.A. under U.N. trusteeship.

G – SOUTHEAST ASIA: Limited occupation by British, French, and Dutch, and by Chinese Nationalists.

tist, yet benevolent, MacArthur personified qualities which, although respected and admired by the traditional Japanese mind, were not wholly representative of the American democracy which was about to re-educate Japan. Certainly, MacArthur was a stabilizing influence on the war-shaken Japanese. They understood his insistence on personal loyalty. His personal leadership and his apparent desire to preserve the emperor reassured them at a time when their own leaders had failed. He became, in brief, a national idol, the spirit of the occupation and the promise of a new Japan, though not necessarily a democratic one.

THE OCCUPATION AT WORK

The work of remaking Japan, a task of almost inconceivable complexity, was essentially a fourfold undertaking. It involved: (1) the disassembling and demilitarizing of the former Japanese empire; (2) the building of a new peaceful political structure; (3) the insuring of sufficient economic well-being to guarantee survival of the new political edifice; and (4) the fashioning of new social and educational foundations.[5]

Disposal of Japan's territorial empire was forecast by the Cairo conference, December, 1943; by the Potsdam proclamation, July, 1945, later adhered to by Russia, limiting Japanese territory to Honshu, Hokkaido, Kyushu, Shikoku, and some minor islands; and by the Yalta conference, February, 1945, where it was agreed that Russia would receive the Kurile Islands and Southern Sakhalin. Since there was no further elaboration on Japan's territorial limits, the ultimate legal disposition

awaited a general Japanese treaty. Meanwhile, Japan's overseas territories were taken over by those victors who belived they had a right to them or who were determined to get possession of them. Korea ceased to be a part of the Japanese empire. Chinese *Kuomintang* forces occupied Taiwan, the Pescadores, and part of Manchuria. United States forces remained in the Caroline, Marshall, Mariana, Bonin, and Ryukyu Islands. Russia took *de facto* possession of Southern Sakhalin and the Kuriles.

Demilitarization in the Japanese homeland involved the effort to destroy both the physical machinery of war and the intellectual or spiritual sources of war. It was easy to cope with the former.[6] Those parts of the industrial machine that directly fed the military services were closed, naval bases were destroyed, and the army and navy were disbanded. Atomic research was proscribed. Steel, chemical, and machine tool industries were limited. There remained, however, the second objective, to destroy the authority and influence of those who had led Japan into foreign conquest.

The most spectacular phase of this effort in political fumigation was the Tokyo trial of twenty-five Japanese leaders, in which the prosecution attempted to show that these men were personally responsible for Japan's misdeeds and were guilty of crimes against humanity. The Tokyo trial was instituted pursuant to the Potsdam declaration, July 20, 1945, and the Instrument of Surrender, September 2, 1945, and was conducted under the terms of the charter of the international military tribunal for the Far East, approved by the Supreme Commander of the Allied Powers, January 19, 1946, with amendments, April 26. In the indictment, Japan's "major war criminals" were charged with crimes against peace, murder, and conventional war crimes and crimes against humanity. The specific purpose of the trials, as expressed by

---

[5] Basic documents and commentary on the occupation to the end of 1947 are in Edwin M. Martin, *The Allied Occupation of Japan* (1948). The period 1948-1950 is covered in Robert A. Fearey, *Occupation of Japan: Second Phase, 1948-1950* (1950). Two major official accounts are of interest: SCAP, Government Section, *Summation of Non-Military Activities in Japan* (35 vols., 1949); and SCAP, Government Section, *Political Reorientation of Japan, September, 1945 to September, 1948* (2 vols., 1949). Both cover the period to 1948.

[6] The demobilization of Japanese forces in the home islands and the return of forces from overseas was conducted with amazing speed. Much of the work was accomplished within six weeks. By January, 1946, the occupation had abolished Japan's army and navy ministries, and had ordered one of the two occupying American armies to return to the United States.

The Occupation: Constitutional reforms ushered in dramatic changes in official Japanese portrayals of Emperior Hirohito. No longer depicted as the remote, militaristic personage of the 1930s and war years, the Emperor became fully human, a bespectacled and bookish man who pursued avidly the study of marine biology.

The decision of the military tribunal handed down in December, 1948, condemned seven defendants to be hanged and consigned the remainder, with the exception of two, to life imprisonment. Along with the trials, there was also the dissolution of some 1,300 Japanese chauvinistic societies and organizations and the disbarment of nearly 200,000 persons from public office. These latter were disqualified on grounds of having contributed to militarism and aggression. As was anticipated, these measures contributed to the appearance of new personalities in Japanese politics, men not associated with the military regime. If the trial and punishment were designed to convince the Japanese people that the real culprits had been brought to justice, however, it must be concluded that the effort failed. The Japanese public did not appear to be convinced that the magic of the judicial process had solved the question of war guilt.[8]

THE NEW POLITICAL STRUCTURE

The political policy of the United States for postwar Japan involved some inherent contra-

Joseph B. Keenan, chief of counsel, was to confirm the already recognized rule that such individuals of a nation who, either in official positions or otherwise, plan aggressive warfare, especially in contravention of sound treaties, assurances, and agreements of their nations, are common felons and deserve and will receive the punishment of ages meted out in every land to murderers, brigands, pirates, and plunderers.[7]

[7] Documents, including the opening statement of the prosecution, the charter of the international military tribunal, and the indictment, are in *Trial of Japanese War Criminals*, Department of State Publications 2613, Far Eastern Series, 12 (1946). See also, *Judgment of the International Military Tribunal for the Far East* (10 vols., 1948).

The case for the natural law school of international law as manifested in the trials in Germany and Japan is J. B. Keenan and Brendan Brown, *Crimes Against International Law* (1950). The juridical basis of the Tokyo war crimes trial and of the corresponding earlier trial in Nuremberg was also given by Henry L. Stimson, "The Nuremberg Trial: Landmark in Law," *Foreign Affairs*, 25 (1947), 179-89.

For an able attack on the theory of the trials, see

Nathan April, "An Inquiry into the Juridical Basis for the Nuremberg War Crimes Trial," *Minnesota Law Review*, 20 (1946), 313-31.

In a pioneering study of the impact of the war crimes trials on the Japanese, Kazuko Tsurumi concludes that the effect was the opposite from the one intended. The conviction of war criminals failed to illustrate Japan's need of democratic and peaceful "values." Rather, the convicted men regarded their impending executions as a final sacrifice for traditional, authoritarian values. This perception may have stemmed from the parallel between the international military tribunal's hierarchical, authoritarian structure and the Japanese army's similar structure. If this were the case, the international tribunal was scarcely an appropriate vehicle for inculcating new social values. Kazuko Tsurumi, *Social Change and the Individual: Japan Before and After Defeat in World War II* (1970).

A less technical but equally stinging indictment is Richard H. Minear's *Victor's Justice: The Tokyo War Crimes Trial* (1971).

[8] Elsewhere in East Asia about 5,000 lesser Japanese figures were placed on trial. For example, in the Philippines, in 1946, a number of Japanese military leaders were tried for alleged war crimes, were sentenced to death, and were executed. Among these were Generals Yamashita Tomoyuki and Homma Masaharu. Other trials were held in Shanghai.

dictions. The policy was to foster "a peaceful and responsible government" and to see that this government conformed in general "to principles of democratic self-government," while at the same time it assured the Japanese that no form of government would be imposed on them that "was not supported by the freely expressed will of the people." How were these objectives to be brought about with a people who were not democratic, and by means that would not prostitute the essence of democracy itself?

The demilitarization program was the first major, though negative step toward a democratic political structure. By demilitarization it was hoped to liquidate both the leaders and many of the agencies of totalitarianism. As this ground-clearing proceeded, the occupation also undertook its positive program to remodel the old political and legal edifice which had been built since the early days of Meiji. The result was the complete revision of the Meiji constitution, amounting really to the writing of a new constitution, though this was done by procedures well established under the Meiji constitution: namely, amendments initiated by imperial ordinance and later approved by the Diet. The task of revising the old constitution was undertaken at the bidding of SCAP late in 1945, but the results were meager, and a satisfactory draft constitution emerged only after vigorous suggestion and, indeed, dictation by the occupation. The new constitution, proclaimed by the emperor with MacArthur's approval, was adopted and became effective, May 3, 1947.[9]

[9] An initial draft of the constitution was produced by a committee appointed by Prime Minister Shide-

Government of Japan under the Constitution of 1947

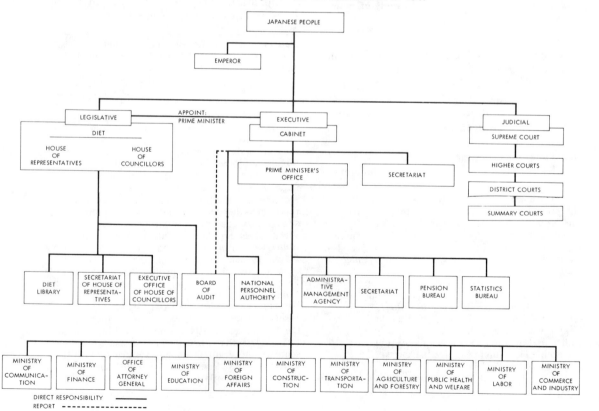

The constitution of 1947 was, for the Japanese, a revolutionary document. In it, sovereignty reposes with the people, not with the emperor. This popular sovereignty was defined in an extensive bill of rights spelling out such principles as: equality of the sexes; freedom of thought; the right to "minimum standards of wholesome and cultured living"; equality of education; and the right and obligation of the workers to work and to organize. The emperor was stripped of the vast constitutional powers he had held under the Meiji constitution, and became the symbol of the state and of the unity of the people. This change in the emperor's status was theoretical rather than actual, since even under the Meiji constitution the emperors had not exercised their constitutional powers.

The new constitution created a new constitutional balance by conferring overwhelming political power upon the Diet, elected by the people. The new Diet remained bicameral but was wholly elective, while the electorate itself no longer labored under disabilities of income, sex, or status in an aristocracy. The lower house, elected for a four-year term, remained known as the House of Representatives; the old House of Peers was replaced by the House of Councilors, elected for six years. The House of Representatives could pass measures over the objections of the House of Councilors by a

hara Kijuro. Headed by Matsumoto Joji, a distinguished professor of law, this drafting committee was an able but conservative body. Thus SCAP's objections focused on the committee's failure to incorporate the principles of responsible government into its document. According to this draft, the emperor was to retain his central authority; the privy council was to be continued as a chief advisory body; and there were no guarantees on human rights.

On February 2, 1946, General Courtney Whitney, MacArthur's chief aide, intervened in the drafting process and ordered the government section of SCAP to produce a draft that met American specifications. This task was completed in a week. SCAP and the Japanese cabinet then met for two days in almost continuous session. It appears that the sessions were devoted to negotiations and the production of acceptable English and Japanese language texts. For accounts by Hugh Borton, a specialist who was close to these events, see "The Allied Occupation of Japan, 1945-47," in *The Far East, 1942-1946*, F. C. Jones *et al.*, eds. (1955); and *Japan's Modern Century* (2nd. ed., 1970), 462-64. The official American version of the origins of the constitution is given in SCAP, *Political Reorientation* I, 82-118; the various drafts are in II, 625-55; 671-77.

two-thirds vote, and the budget over the objections of the upper house by a simple majority vote in the lower house.

As for the executive branch (the prime minister and his cabinet), the new constitution made it directly responsible to the Diet. The prime minister was to be selected by the Diet, and a majority of his cabinet were to be Diet members. Thus the Diet, through its control of the cabinet and the budget, was given the constitutional power to direct the formerly all-powerful bureaucracy. The first step taken by the Diet in this direction was enactment of a new civil service code.[10]

While the Diet and executive suggested the British model, the new Japanese judiciary was patterned after American ideas. Recognition was given to the principle of an independent judiciary, beginning with a supreme court that passed on all questions of constitutionality. This court nominated judges in the lower courts, although the actual appointment of the judges was to be done by the cabinet. Members of the supreme court were also to be appointed by the cabinet, but such appointments were subject to review by the people at the next general election.

Local government, formerly a mere agent of the central power, was strengthened in the new constitution by provision for the popular election of the chief local officials, the abolition of compulsory neighborhood associations, the elimination of the centrally controlled police, and the delegation of larger powers to local legislative bodies.

In the constitution of 1947, Japan renounced war and the right of belligerency forever. To some, this clause seemed to have little value beyond an expression of human aspirations for a more decent world. In a sense it recalled the pious hopes embalmed in the Kellogg-Briand treaty for the renunciation of war, 1928. It also appeared paradoxical that militaristic Japan should be the first to ban war. Nevertheless, the renunciation appealed to many Japanese as further evidence of Japan's unique character and mission.[11]

[10] On the broad subject of Japanese law, see Thomas L. Blakemore, "Postwar Developments in Japanese Law," *Wisconsin Law Review* (July, 1947), 632-53.

[11] The origins of the clause renouncing war have not been clearly established. While the outlines of

NEW SOCIAL AND ECONOMIC PATTERNS

Practically all activities of the occupation were undertaken with the object of bringing about in Japan a reformation in values and ideals. The more perceptive counsels of the occupation recognized that no paper reforms, such as new constitutions, could possibly outlive the occupation unless the Japanese people acquired a sense of democracy. Therefore, in the occupation's view, it was imperative that authoritarianism and paternalism be replaced by equality and individualism.

While this was admittedly an ambitious undertaking, the moment for basic reform was opportune, because the Japanese, stunned by defeat, retained little confidence in their traditional ways. Intellectually, they sought feverishly for new horizons; in consequence, during the first years of the occupation, broad social and economic reforms enjoyed wide popularity. To the vast majority of the Japanese, democracy (however vague their concept of it might be) appeared as a happy substitute for a way of life that had led to war and disaster.[12]

[12] The popularity of the occupation's social reforms may be gauged by the rapidity with which the word *demokurashi* became part of the common vocabulary. The actual implementation of reform, however, was impeded by the population's uncertainty as to how to proceed. Did democracy require a man in a crowded streetcar to offer his seat to a woman in recognition of her recently elevated status, or was it more democratic for the man to keep his seat on grounds that men and women had become equal under the law? Compounding such practical problems were the confusing acts of the occupation itself. While the occupation might proclaim democracy, it frequently did not practice it. Reminiscent of the old days was the rigid censorship imposed on imported printed matter lest "dangerous thoughts" enter the country. Criticism of the occupation and of Allied countries was banned. American occupation personnel, civilian and military, were subject in word and deed to military controls. They were the agents of a policy, and it is doubtful whether any policy can be promoted in an occupied country if that policy is not followed at all levels. In occupied Japan the censorship was aimed

Japan's new constitution were developed in Washington and were transmitted to SCAP, this clause was not part of these outlines. It is known, therefore, that the clause was first proposed in Japan. Kenzo Takayanaga, who was involved in the drafting process, attributes the authorship to Prime Minister Shidehara. See Kenzo's "Some Reminiscences of Japan's Commission on the Constitution," in *The Constitution of Japan: Its First Twenty Years, 1947-1967,* Fenno Henderson, ed. (1968), 86-87. For doubts on this theory see Borton, *Modern Century,* 487. Borton holds that the clause originated in SCAP.

In the early postwar era Japanese confronted basic problems of survival. Fuel was scarce and the sight of women gathering such combustible materials as they could find was familiar to accupying forces. The photographs on the facing page are of a school lunch program started by the Occupation to combat malnutrition and of an American-style town meeting which was organized by the Occupation for discussion of food shortages.

EDUCATIONAL REFORM

Since the prewar educational system had been consciously designed to produce willing servants of the state, it was subjected to wholesale change. Specific educational reforms effected by the occupation were aimed at creating a more intelligent and critical public mind and at training the younger generations for responsible citizenship. The period of compulsory education was extended from six to nine years. Beyond the elementary training required under the old system, there were created a three-year compulsory junior high school, a three-year senior high school, and a four-year college course. An effort was made to equalize the quality of education at all levels, and to provide the fullest opportunity for children of both sexes to pursue programs that would contribute most fully to the development of their individual talents. But these innovations, initially at least, suffered from lack of democratically trained teachers, and from the serious question of how penniless Japan was to pay for this

quite specifically at communist propaganda; nevertheless, occupation personnel, not being free to voice independent judgments, were handicapped from the start in attempting to behave as democrats. In a word, the Japanese citizens found in the occupation few examples of democracy in action.

major expansion in schools and curriculum. In the curriculum itself, the traditional emphasis on ethics (a synonym for supernationalism) gave way to concern for social studies. Efforts were made to rewrite the textbooks, to introduce modern methods of instruction, and to break the stifling centralized control of the old ministry of education.

SOCIAL REFORM

Having set out to remodel Japan's schools, the occupation, partly by desire, partly by compulsion, found it necessary to go further into the tangled areas of social reform. A first step was to strike at the traditional form and behavior of the Japanese family. Equality, a strange principle to Oriental ears, was applied to the sexes by the new constitution. Japanese women acquired equal legal rights with men in politics and education. Furthermore, this principle of equality, and the new educational program in general, tended to weaken the control formerly exercised by family heads over the youth and even over other adult members of the family. Tendencies toward individualism which had appeared in Japan long before World War II were encouraged by the occupation. This shifting from the family to the individual as the

basic unit of society was among the most vital effects of the Western impact of East Asia.[13]

RESHAPING ECONOMIC INSTITUTIONS

The occupation's reforming zeal was also directed at the concentrations of wealth which had supported authoritarianism. Old elites of businessmen and landlords were to be destroyed and a new system based on economic competition installed. Reform proceeded on the theory that democracy required a measure of equality in the distribution of income, wealth, and ownership. Eventually these reforms were augmented by efforts to stimulate economic growth. A society enjoying a rising standard of living, it was reasoned, would have a stake in a reformed economy. Among the most striking of all occupation reforms was the redistribution of agricultural land. Essentially this reform entailed: (1) enforced sale to the

[13] Kazuya Matsumiya, "Family Organization in Present Day Japan," *American Journal of Sociology*, 53 (1947), 105-10. SCAP's tendency to develop programs for every aspect of Japanese life is illustrated by MacArthur's encouragement of the Christian missionary movement. To the general, Japan seemed a spiritual vacuum, a country that might go communist if the void left by the "destruction of Shinto and Buddhism" were not filled. Thus, the occupation welcomed Christian missionaries of every persuasion, gave preferential treatment to Japanese Christians, and supported denominational efforts to raise mission funds in the United States. American Christians in turn gave unprecedented support to the mission effort: by 1950, more than 2,500 missionaries had reached Japan; some ten million Bibles were distributed; and several million dollars were expended on Christian education. Yet this boom in Christian influence scarcely survived MacArthur's dismissal in 1951. MacArthur's successor, General Matthew Ridgway, was meticulous in his own religious observances, but he ventured no pronouncements on behalf of Christianity. Among Japanese, Christianity proved far less appealing than many Americans had hoped. By 1951, there were about 200,000 Christians in Japan—approximately the same number as before the war. See Lawrence S. Wittner, "MacArthur and the Missionaries: God and Man in Occupied Japan," *Pacific Historical Review,* 40 (1970), 77-98. For two studies of SCAP's disestablishment of Shinto, see William P. Woodard, *The Allied Occupation of Japan, 1945-1952, and Japanese Religions* (1972).

government of all land held by absentee landlords; (2) resale of these lands to former tenants who had cultivated them; and (3) permission for farmer-landlords to retain the land cultivated by their families and in addition some two and one-half acres of tenant-cultivated land. The program of purchase and resale was effected at prewar values, making it a possible transaction for the tenants but virtual confiscation for the former owners. The extent of this reform was suggested by the fact that by 1952 more than five million acres of land had been purchased from landlords and sold to working farmers. This meant that about 90 percent of all cultivated land had been acquired by those who worked it, as compared with less than 50 percent in 1945. Moreover, legislation reduced land rents by about 50 percent and provided further protection by means of rent ceilings. Although this land reform implied social consequences of the utmost importance, it was in no sense a magic formula. Japan's basic agricultural problem—how to feed too many people from too little land—was still unsolved.[14]

Equally fundamental was the occupation's dissolution of the *zaibatsu,* the great industrial and commercial conglomerates which held a commanding position in Japan's economy. As a first step, family control and ownership of the firms (Mitsui, Mitsubishi, Yasuda, and Sumitomo were the largest) were to be liquidated. Family-owned holding companies, the key organizations, were dissolved; stock held by *zaibatsu* families in related, underlying companies was confiscated and sold; and *zaibatsu* family members were prohibited from working for the

[14] The problems created by tenantry had become so serious that Japanese—including some landlords—had been calling for reform long before the occupation. Plans had been formulated by governmental agencies, but these had never been implemented. Thus, SCAP became a catalyst, moving Japan's society along lines that many Japanese themselves wanted to follow. It is doubtful, however, that Japanese officials would have supported as strong a program as the one put into effect by the occupation. On these and other economic reforms see Hugh T. Patrick, "The Phoenix Risen from the Ashes: Postwar Japan," in *Modern East Asia: Essays in Interpretation*, James B. Crowley, ed. (1970),* 298-336.

companies that they had once owned. The cumulative effect of these measures was to wipe out family fortunes and to force prominent men into permanent retirement.

The breakup of the conglomerates themselves proved less easy. Interlocking directorates were dissolved; *zaibatsu* subsidiaries and affiliates were reorganized on a basis of independent ownership; and such large *zaibatsu* firms as the Mitsubishi Trading Company were broken up into a number of competing companies. As in agriculture, the reform program did much to redistribute income, wealth and ownership. Yet the occupation fell short of its determination to establish a wholly new business environment. Even under new management and ownership, ex-*zaibatsu* firms continued to deal with one another in a manner that recalled the past. Moreover, as the occupation began to emphasize economic recovery, there was a notable decline in its reforming spirit. In late 1947 SCAP considered an additional 1,200 companies for breakup into smaller units. When American businessmen protested that this would prevent permanently Japan's recovery, the list was shortened to 325. During the entire occupation, 83 holding companies were dissolved, and 5,000 companies were put through some measure of financial reorganization.

On the opposite side of the industrial picture, the occupation paved the way for Japan's first free development of a labor movement. Labor leaders, who had been jailed during the 1930s and 1940s, resumed their organizational activities with startling success. Unions were formed in industries of every size, and were generally linked in nationwide federations. By 1950 some seven million workers (an all-time high of 56 percent of the labor force) had been unionized. Union activities, however, disappointed SCAP's expectation that organized labor would focus primarily on improving the workers' economic status. National federations stressed political rather than economic objectives. There were efforts by some unions through strikes to take over policy control of industries, while sabotage under Communist instigation became the policy of the more militant organizations. This latter kind of behavior was not tolerated by the occupation; instead, in its later stages, the occupation, concerned by labor's more radical tendencies, joined forces with Japan's conservatives who had shown little sympathy with a responsible role for labor in either industry or politics.

POLITICS DURING THE OCCUPATION

The effect of the occupation upon Japanese government and politics was profound from the beginning. SCAP's reforms broke old political patterns and forced many established leaders from office. Communists, who were released from prison or returned from exile, formed their first legal party under Nozaka Sanzo, who was to become one of the ablest postwar political manipulators. The Social Democrats (*Shakaito*), refusing a united front with the Communists, formed their own party, drawing strength from intellectuals and labor. More conservative elements were grouped in the Liberal (*Jiyuto*) and the Progressive (*Shimpoto*) parties, the former led by Ashida Hitoshi and Yoshida Shigeru, the latter by Shidehara Kijuro. Most of the members of these latter parties had belonged to the old *Seiyukai* or *Minseito*.

While the formation of new political groupings and the reshuffling of old ones imparted a new character to Japanese politics, the parties were not free immediately to seek goals that were entirely of their own devising. In October, 1945, for example, when the occupation directed implementation of a "bill of rights" guaranteeing basic human freedoms, the releasing of political prisoners, and the curbing of the ministry of home affairs and its powerful centralized police, the surrender cabinet of Prime Minister Higashikuni resigned on the ground that it could not maintain order. The Liberals, whose gains in the election of April, 1946, enabled them to form a ministry headed by Yoshida, were given the responsibility of installing the "MacArthur Constitution," and of carrying the purge of undesirable persons into the area of local politics. While the Yoshida government's popularity suffered from occupation-imposed policies, the cabinet's eventual collapse was not precipitated by Japan's own political processes. Early in 1947, General MacArthur blocked a general strike called to protest the economic condition of workers. The Communists thus suffered a setback, and the government announced that a new general election was to be held. The latter step, which was in effect a declaration of no confidence in Yoshida, was preliminary to the selection of a government headed by Katayama Tetsu, president of the Social Democrats. Not until mid-1949 did MacArthur indicate that close control by the occupation of Japanese domestic affairs was no longer necessary. By this time Yoshida was back in power with a Liberal party government which he was to lead until 1954. By this time, too, the cold war was exercising a pronounced influence on Japan's politics. Confronted with the increasing influence of Communism, Japanese political thought and organization became more deeply divided into right and left wings; Communist party strength declined, and conservatism was reborn.

ECONOMIC REBUILDING, 1948-1950

From the beginning of 1948, the Japanese government and the occupation gave less attention to reform and more attention to the historical problem of increasing manufactures to support a population that had increased, 1945-1948, by nearly eight million. In part, this new emphasis was dictated by deteriorating living standards. When the war ended, the average daily diet provided only 1,530 calories. Two years later, July, 1947, starvation no longer threatened, but in order to survive the typical Tokyo family was still obliged to deal on the black market, going ever deeper into debt. Behind this bleak picture was a general economic instability: wages that failed to keep pace with inflation; a heavily unfavorable trade balance; and limited export opportunities (silk, the largest prewar export, had been replaced by nylon). Thus the occupation moved belatedly in 1948 to meet this crisis through an all-inclusive program of stabilization, balancing the budget, limiting credit, renovating the tax structure, and dealing with tax evasion. At the same time the United States encouraged expansion of industrial production and export by favoring the eventual

dropping of reparations payments, extending economic aid (through loans rather than outright grants), and, when the Korean War broke out, placing orders with Japanese firms.

In this new climate fostered by the occupation, reform no longer was favored. The *zaibatsu* dissolution, for example, was virtually halted on grounds that it was disruptive to normal economic processes. Moreover, by 1948 the United States was losing interest in policies that had a punitive flavor. With the onset of the cold war, Japan seemed much less of a military threat than the Communist nations. Indeed, American policy began to view Japan as a potential ally to be assisted and encouraged with her rebuilding, rather than as a defeated enemy to be punished for her misdeeds.[15]

By 1950, Japan's economic and financial status showed substantial improvement resulting from rapid economic growth. This is not to say, however, that prosperity had been achieved. Recovery had begun when production was at such a low level (output in 1945-1946 approximated that of 1914) that prewar per capita production was not attained until 1954-1955. Furthermore, the apparent link between Japan's rebuilding and American aid (a matter of nearly two billion dollars, 1945-1950) gave rise to the thought that the economy was not yet on a sound foundation.[16]

[15] Chalmers Johnson, *Conspiracy at Matsukawa* (1972), a book written with the verve of a detective story, epitomizes the changing climate of opinion. Johnson's subject is a train wreck at Matsukawa in the summer of 1949, the indictment of 20 Communists and union leaders on charges of conspiracy, and the legal proceedings which extended through five trials and required fourteen years. The first trial took place during the time when the American view of communism was colored by the impact of the cold war. The initial proceedings resulted in a death sentence for five defendants and life sentences for five others. By the fifth and last trial all defendants were acquited and were subsequently paid $211, 555, the largest damages in Japanese judicial history.

[16] In the post-occupation years, as Japan regained a sense of self-confidence, Japanese frequently expressed disappointment that the occupation shifted from reform to the encouragement of economic growth. The critics did not object to prosperity as such, but they believed that affluence might have come at the expense of changes that were needed in

THE JAPANESE PEACE TREATY

The outbreak of war in Korea emphasized the need, as the United States saw it, of ending the occupation by concluding a peace treaty with Japan, thereby bringing her into the company of the free world against the Communist powers.[17] Earlier efforts toward a treaty had

---

Japanese society. The purge of Japan's old political leadership and business executives, for example, was seen as having been halted because the Americans needed the cooperation of Japanese conservatives. Commenting on these half-measures, the *Asahi Shimbum*, a great daily newspaper, printed an ambitious series of essays reviewing American-Japanese relations, which noted "Like so many other Occupation policies, the 'bloodless revolution' [the purge] . . . ended inconclusively . . . [and] produced some serious repercussions." The problem was compounded by the tendency of the Japanese to acquire a taste for some of the more unsavory characteristics of American life. Among contemporary Japanese are many who recall nostalgically the edifying, American-made movies which SCAP permitted to be imported during the early days of the occupation. These are contrasted favorably with the tough movie dramas and cartoon books glorifying violence that later made their way from the United States to Japan. "The darker side of American culture is filtering its way into Japan. . . . You might say that American movies sowed the seeds both of democracy and of a passion for violence." See the Staff of the *Asahi Shimbum, The Pacific Rivals: A Japanese View of Japanese-American Relations* (1972), 166, 136. For American criticism of United States policy, see John W. Dower, "Occupied Japan and the American Lake, 1945-1950," in *America's Asia: Dissenting Essays on Asian-American Relations*, Edward Friedman and Mark Selden, eds. (1971),* 149-197.

[17]While in general it was true that the decision to terminate the occupation rested with the Americans, the Japanese influence on the final stages of the occupation must be noted. By 1949, as the Japanese electorate began to manifest a returning self-confidence, Japan's leadership demonstrated some independence of American policy. In an effort to ensure the establishment of democracy, SCAP had shown a preference for working with the less conservative elements, but Japanese voters gave a landslide victory to the Liberal-Democratic party (*Jiyu-Minshuto*), which led to the formation of the third Yoshida cabinet. The shift in occupation policies after the years 1948-1949 should not be attributed entirely to American reactions to the onset of the cold war. Conservative forces in Japan, which were beyond American control, were beginning to reassert themselves. Thus the student may well ask whether the American occupation could have been maintained much longer, even if its termination had not proved expedient. See Justin Williams, "Com-

---

broken down in 1948. On American initiative, conversations among the former allies were resumed in September, 1950, resulting a year later in the San Francisco peace conference and a treaty of peace with Japan. By July, 1951, there was sufficient agreement for the United States and the United Kingdom to issue a joint invitation to the fifty-five powers at war with Japan to a peace conference to be held at San Francisco on September 4, 1951. Suggested revisions of the draft treaty enclosed with the invitations were to be submitted promptly so that the final text might be circulated by August 13. The treaty would thus be completed before the conference assembled.

Accordingly, at San Francisco, September 8, 1951, a peace treaty was signed by Japan and forty-eight nations (Communist powers refused to sign). Japan agreed to seek membership in the United Nations, to respect the civil rights of her people guaranteed in her own new constitution, to accept the territorial clauses of the Potsdam declaration, to recognize the independence of Korea, to forego her claims to Taiwan, the Pescadores, the Kuriles and Karafuto (southern Sakhalin), and to agree to a United Nations trusteeship in the Ryukyu and Bonin Islands. The treaty recognized Japan's right of self-defense. Within three months after the treaty was in force, occupation armies would leave, though limited foreign forces might continue to be stationed there under special agreements. The occupation came to an end April 28, 1952, the day the treaty became effective. Also on September 8, 1951, Japan and the United States concluded a security agreement permitting American forces to remain in Japan for an unspecified period, which meant that the United States was assuming responsibility for Japan's defense indefinitely.

The peace treaty with Japan was a necessary step toward ending the war, but it was not a solution of Japanese problems. Rather, it was merely the formal beginning of Japan's efforts as a sovereign state to chart her course at home and abroad in the postwar world. Insofar as the reforms of the occupation, including the constitution of 1947, could be taken at face value,

---

pleting Japan's Political Reorientation, 1947-1952: Crucial Phase of the Allied Occupation," *American Historical Review*, 73 (1968), 1454-69.

Japan was a democracy, but she had had as yet no free experience in making democracy work: her peoples were not of one mind as to what democracy meant; she did not have a stable and prosperous economy that could afford policies of drift; and in world affairs she was on the explosive Asian frontier between Communism and the free world. From 1952 onward, therefore, Japan's political, economic, and social history was to be a reflection of her efforts to find a new life in the ominous turmoil of these pressures.

FOR FURTHER READING

General Accounts. For differing appraisals of the occupation, see Robert B. Textor, *Failure in Japan: With Keystones for a Positive Policy* (1951); Kazuo Kawai, *Japan's American Interlude* (1960); Herbert Passin, *The Legacy of the Occupation* (1968); and Robert E. Ward, "Reflections on the Occupation and Planned Political Change in Japan," in *Political Development in Modern Japan,* Robert E. Ward, ed. (1968). Allen S. Clifton, *Time of Fallen Blossoms* (1951) describes the simple dignity of the country people of Japan in the early postwar years. Mishima Sumie, *The Broader Way: A Woman's Life in the New Japan* (1953) portrays life during and after the hostilities. Elizabeth Gray Vining, *Windows for the Crown Prince* (1952) contains delicate and sympathetic sketches of Japan and upper-class Japanese culture by the tutor of the Crown Prince. Frank Gibney, *Five Gentlemen of Japan: The Portrait of a Nation's Character* (1953) tells of the impact of the occupation on Japanese life through sketches of the Emperor, a farmer, an admiral, a newspaperman, and a steel worker. Robert S. Schwantes, *Japanese and Americans: A Century of Cultural Relations* (1955) deserves careful reading.

Government, Politics, and Parties. Paul M. A. Linebarger, Djang Chu, and Ardath Burks, *Far Eastern Governments and Politics: China and Japan* (1954). Chitoshi Yanaga, *Japanese People and Politics* (1956)* emphasizes the

forces of politics rather than the structure of government. A briefer but enlightening study is Nobutake Ike, *Japanese Politics: An Introductory Study* (1957). H.S. Quigley and J.E. Turner, *The New Japan: Government and Politics* (1956). An excellent specialized study is Robert E. Ward's "The Origins of the Present Japanese Constitution," *American Political Science Review* 50 (1956), 980-1010. Hans H. Baerwald, *The Purge of Japanese Leaders under the Occupation* (1959) combines a factual account with discussion of the moral and administrative dilemmas implicit in the purge. For biographical details and excellent scholarship on Japanese Communists, see Roger Swearinger and Paul Langer, *Red Flag in Japan: International Communism in Action, 1919-1951* (1952); Robert A. Scalapino, *The Japanese Communist Movement, 1920-1966* (1967); and George M. Beckman and Okubo Genji, *The Japanese Communist Party, 1922-1945* (1969).

Economics. B. V. A. Röling and C. F. Rüter, eds., *The Tokyo Judgement: The International Tribunal for the Far East* (2 vols., 1972). Edward Ackerman, *Japan's Natural Resources and Their Relation to Japan's Economic Future* (1953) explains Japan's problems in supporting her expanding population on her meager resources. For a statistical analysis of Japan's postwar economic problems, see Jerome B. Cohen, *Economic Problems of Free Japan* (1952). For specialized studies see: Martin Bronfenbrenner, "Japanese Labor Economics as Economic Analysis," *Journal of Asian Studies,* 31 (1972), 605-9, useful notes contrasting the philosophies of American and Japanese labor as brought out in the occupation. T. A. Bisson, *Zaibatsu Dissolution in Japan* (1954); Ronald P. Dore, *Land Reform in Japan* (1959); Laurence I. Hewes, Jr., *Japan—Land and Men: An Account of the Japanese Land Reform Program, 1945-1951* (1955); and Sherwood M. Fine, *Japan's Postwar Industrial Recovery* (1953).

Social Ideals and Religion. Jean Stoetzel, *Without the Chrysanthemum and the Sword: A Study of the Attitudes of Youth in Postwar*

Japan (1955) surveys the impact of defeat and occupation on young Japanese. The role of religion in the postwar era is assessed in Richard T. Baker, *Darkness of the Sun: The Story of Christianity in the Japanese Empire* (1947); and Yanaihara Tadao, *Religion and Democracy in Modern Japan* (1948). Herbert Passin, *Society and Education in Japan* (1965),* essays and documents touching traditional and modern Japan to 1947. A basic treatment on educational reforms is Robert King Hall, *Education for a New Japan* (1949).

The Japanese Peace Treaty. Bernard C. Cohen, *The Political Process and Foreign Policy: The Making of the Japanese Peace Settlement* (1957) studies the means by which American pressure groups were brought to accept the peace treaty. Also note R. H. Rosecrance, *Australian Diplomacy and Japan, 1945-1951* (1962). Frederick S. Dunn, et al., *Peace-making and the Settlement with Japan* (1963).

From Kuomintang into Communist China, 1945–1949

31

The end of hostilities in World War II altered decisively the long-standing conflict between the *Kuomintang* and the Chinese Communists. With the removal of Japanese power by surrender, these contending parties abandoned all pretense of a united front and engaged in a violent scramble for Japanese-occupied China, which included Manchuria and the whole area of central and eastern-seaboard China. In this struggle the Communists had advantages they had not possessed in 1937. No longer confined to a relatively small region in the northwest, they controlled the countryside in the north and central regions, thus presenting formidable obstacles to Nationalist occupation efforts. The Communist party, reorganized and strengthened by the *cheng-feng* movement, had increased in membership from about 40,000 to more than a million. While the Red army remained inferior to the Nationalist force in men and equipment, its size was growing (the Communists claimed a force of 930,000 in 1945), and it was supported by an effective militia. The Nationalist government, on the other hand, had declined as a vital force. Its status was marked by loss of fervor in its revolutionary program, widespread corruption, spiraling inflation, and deteriorating morale, civilian and military. In consequence of

this new balance of forces, even though the Nationalist government had been accorded nominal big power status by its allies, its survival after 1945 was not assured.

Altered, too, was the international setting of the *Kuomintang*-Communist conflict. With Japan's defeat both the Soviet Union and the United States acquired new Asian bases from which pressure could be exerted on China. In 1945 the Soviet Union reassumed a position of great strength in northeastern Asia. She had entered the war against Japan by invading Manchuria, August 9, 1945, and concluded a Sino-Soviet treaty of friendship, with the *Kuomintang*-Nationalist government on August 14. The practical effect was to give Russia immediate control of Manchuria, to restore old historic rights in the Manchurian railways and the Kwantung leased territory, and to guarantee the "independence" of Outer Mongolia under a government controlled by Moscow. In return for these Manchurian and Mongolian concessions, Russia was pledged to give moral support and material aid only to the Nationalist government as *the* government of China, to respect China's sovereignty in Manchuria, and to refrain from interference in the internal affairs of Sinkiang. These conditions were acceptable to Nanking because they appeared to deny to the Chinese Communists any support from Russia. The fact, too, that Russian military operations in Manchuria and Korea continued long after the Japanese surrender contributed further to Russia's position in practical power. Within a few weeks and with the expenditure of a minimum of effort, Russia acquired a stronger position in the key area of northeast Asia than she had ever held before.

Against this focal area of revived Russian power was the even greater though more widely dispersed power of the United States in East Asia. This predominant American position was a creation of the military campaigns of the war and not of a historical development of American policy. Immediately following Japan's surrender, the United States was (1) master of the Philippines and the entire Western Pacific, (2) in a position to set the terms on which the Dutch, French, and the British might reoccupy their empires in Southeast Asia, (3) the only external power other than Russia capable of exerting strong pressure on the Chinese Nationalist government, (4) the unqualified military and political master of Japan, and (5) in occupation of Korea south of the 38th parallel. This extraordinary position of power did not mean, however, that the United States could dispose of Asian problems by simple mandate or in complete disregard of forces of opposition which it did not and in all probability could not control. In the Philippines and in Japan the United States was at greater liberty than in other areas to pursue its own purposes, but even in these areas its power was subject to various restraints imposed by local conditions or by the traditions of its own institutions and historic policies. With respect to China, the power of the United States to make decisions designed to influence or to determine the future of that state was limited by (1) the inhibitions of traditional American policy there, (2) the reoccupation of northeast China by Russia, and (3) the division of Chinese power itself between the *Kuomintang* and the Communists.

THE NATIONALIST ATTEMPT TO GAIN CONTROL

At the end of the war in Asia, Chiang Kai-shek, as Allied commander-in-chief in the China theater and as head of the *Kuomintang*-Nationalist (and recognized) government, was to receive the Japanese surrender in China and in northern Indochina. Three major tasks confronted the Nationalists: (1) to take over the occupied territory from the Japanese armies and to re-establish administrative control; (2) to reach a settlement of the Communist problem; and (3) to revive China's war-torn economic and social orders.

Accepting the Surrender

For the task of accepting the Japanese surrender, Nationalist forces could hardly have been in a less advantageous position. They had been driven by the Japanese into southwestern China. Nevertheless, in late 1945 the Americans airlifted Nationalist troops to key points in the east and north, while 50,000 American Marines occupied port areas and airfields on the Nationalist behalf at Tsingtao, Peking, and Tientsin. Within three months, except for the villages and countryside in the north where Communists continued in control, the whole of the rich coastal region from Canton to Peking was in *Kuomintang*-Nationalist hands. Only in Manchuria did the Nationalists suffer reverses in their race for territorial control. There the Russians permitted Communist guerrillas to advance through the countryside, capturing whatever Japanese arms they could find, and to establish strongholds. When *Kuomintang* forces eventually took over Manchuria from the Russians, their authority was confined largely to urban areas.[1]

The Nanking government also derived postwar advantage from its official role as the leader of the national resistance. Whereas ten years earlier Chiang Kai-shek had been condemned by articulate Chinese for his vacillation in the face of Japanese encroachment, he now was hailed in most reoccupied areas as a national hero. His government was credited with China's advance into the company of the great powers.

[1] Lacking troops to occupy Manchuria immediately after the war, the Nationalists requested the Russians to delay turning Manchuria over to Chinese authorities. An early transfer would have served the Chinese Communists. The Russians complied, but they held the territory longer than the Nationalists desired.

Moreover, as the recognized Chinese authority, the *Kuomintang*-Nationalist regime was the recipient of foreign financial assistance to meet pressing needs. Yet, in spite of these apparent advantages, three and one-half years later, in 1949—to anticipate the story—Chiang was a fallen leader, forced to resign as president of the Republic and to take refuge on Taiwan while his Communist opponents proclaimed the establishment of a new Republic in Peking.

Efforts at Political Settlement

The ultimate collapse of the *Kuomintang* as a governing party was foreshadowed in the futility which marked their immediate postwar negotiations with the Communists. On August 28, 1945, Mao Tse-tung himself arrived in Chungking to discuss the formation of a "democratic coalition government." These talks, which were conducted even as the two opposing armies competed for territory, reflected the deep longing of the Chinese populace for peace. Neither side could afford to display an unwillingness to negotiate. The *Kuomintang's* participation in these talks was further explained by American pressure. In the closing months of the war, American policy, recognizing that the *Kuomintang* had ceased to be an effective unifying force and that the Chinese Communists were serious contenders for power, looked toward the formation of a political coalition as a means for building China's internal peace, and thereby her strength.[2]

[2] For an example of the quality of information on the *Kuomintang*-Communist struggle that was available to American officials, see Lyman P. Van Slyke, ed., *The Chinese Communist Movement: A Report of the United States War Department, July, 1945* (1968). Based on more than 2,500 reports, pamphlets, and books, and completed in June, 1945, this report represented an attempt by the military intelligence division of the war department to evaluate the strength, nature, and intentions of the Chinese Communist party. Aside from the specific information it contained, the report was very significant because, although clearly anti-Communist and anti-Russian, it did not hesitate to characterize the *Kuomintang*-Nationalist government as an inefficient dictatorship which had alienated almost every sector of society.

It was this policy which Ambassador Patrick Hurley tried to implement between September, 1944 and November, 1945. There were clear distinctions, however, between solutions acceptable to the Communists on one hand and to the *Kuomintang* on the other. While the Communists professed a willingness to enter a coalition government and to place their military forces under the control of that government, they demanded guarantees that they would have a position of strength in the new regime before giving up control of their armies. The *Kuomintang*, although willing to give political promises for the future, was determined to have military integration first under its own control. In consequence, the Mao-Chiang talks ended with a statement which exuded good will but settled nothing.

The Marshall Mission

In an effort to promote a coalition, President Truman sent General George C. Marshall to China late in 1945 to seek "the unification of China by peaceful, democratic methods." This effort was based on specific premises: (1) that American assistance would not be extended indefinitely to a China that could achieve no unity within itself; and (2) that a united and democratic China was essential to world stability and the proper functioning of the United Nations. Marshall was initially successful in persuading the Nationalists and the Communists to meet, January, 1946, in a body called the Political Consultative Conference (PCC), and to accept three agreements foreshadowing a settlement: (1) a military truce, (2) a political and constitutional agreement,

The Communists were pictured as politically well-organized, highly disciplined, progressive, and popular. Nevertheless, in a summary of the report, Brigadier General Peabody emphasized the *Kuomintang*-Nationalist government's legitimacy and international status as though these had some sacred validity which made the concept of revolution unthinkable.

On the relative positions of the *Kuomintang* and of the Communists at this particular time, see the analysis by Paul A. Varg, *The Closing of the Door: Sino-American Relations, 1936-1946* (1973), 205-28. Note in particular the discussion of the problems of American policy.

and (3) an agreement on the reorganization and control of military forces.

Under the truce agreement, military advances were to be halted and local outbreaks settled by truce teams composed of a Nationalist, a Communist, and an American officer. The second or political agreement confirmed the Nationalists or the Communists in control of the territory each held and provided for a state council in the Nationalist government in which all political groups would have representation. This new body was to determine policy. Moreover, the political agreement provided for a parliamentary system when constitutional rule was achieved. The third or military agreement, to which General Marshall contributed in the discussions, provided an arrangement whereby the Communist army was to become a part of a Chinese national army. All three of these basic agreements were interdependent. A failure of one meant a failure of all.

For many complex reasons, the fragile agreement effected by the Marshall mission did not succeed in unifying China. In general, it failed because it did not answer the all-consuming and bitter internal question of what party, clique, or faction was to emerge in China as the custodian of Sun Yat-sen's revolutionary program. That program, the three principles of the people (the *San min chu-I*), meant many different things to various Chinese factions; but on one principle, nationalism (*min-tsu chu-i*), there was no disagreement. There was, indeed, a broad popular determination that foreigners whether Russian or American, should not regain a privileged position even suggestive of the old days of the unequal treaty system. In 1945-1946, when General Marshall was sent to China, American policy (like Russian policy of a later date) underestimated the strength of this Chinese nationalism, and underestimated the problem of how, given the conditions prevailing in China, the United States could possibly play in the role of impartial mediator between the *Kuomintang*-Nationalists and the Communists. While Marshall himself maintained a notable impartiality, the United States continued to furnish aid to the Nationalists. The Communists seized upon this contradiction and denounced America for interfering in Chinese affairs. The *Kuomintang* on their part held that the United

States was pursuing unattainable goals. Marshall, like Stilwell, they said, was attempting to persuade Chiang to adopt reforms which would erode his powers.[3]

America's alleged deficiencies as mediator, however, appear to have contributed less to Marshall's failure than the determination of the two Chinese camps to finish the fight they had

[3] The ambiguity in America's position had been noted by American diplomats well in advance of the Marshall mission. Ambassador Hurley, for example, had held to the theory that wartime China had to "furnish her own leadership, make her own decisions and be responsible for her own domestic and international policies." Yet with equal firmness he rejected principles or actions that "would weaken the National Government or the leadership of Chiang Kai-shek." In practice, as conflict between the *Kuomintang* and Communists intensified, the ambassador tended to honor the latter principle more than the former. This in turn led to disagreement within the embassy's own staff. Staff members maintained that it was hopeless for the United States to pose as mediator unless its purposes were impartial, and that American favoritism toward the *Kuomintang* would eventually result in further trouble. George Atcheson (acting in Hurley's absence as the embassy's chargé d'affaires), noted that, "Although our intentions have been good and our actions in refusing to deal with or assist any group but the Central Government have been diplomatically correct, if this situation continues and our analysis of it is correct, chaos in China will be inevitable and the probable outbreak of disastrous civil conflict will be accelerated." Correspondence on this topic appears in the United States, Department of State, *Foreign Relations of the United States: Diplomatic Papers, 1945: Volume VII, The Far East: China* (1969). In his later years, Hurley joined partisans of the *Kuomintang* who asserted that the United States had "sold out" China to the Communists. He claimed that his embassy's staff had sabotaged efforts to shape a coalition government. Moreover, he held that state department career officers had deceived President Roosevelt with respect to the implications for China of the Yalta accords. These later views were at variance with the ones entertained by Hurley while he held office. In 1944-1945, Hurley supported Roosevelt's efforts to bring the Soviet Union into the war against Japan and to win Russian support for the *Kuomintang*-Nationalist government. To these ends, Hurley was prepared to recommend even larger concessions to the Russians than those agreed upon at Yalta. See Russell D. Buhite, "Patrick J. Hurley and the Yalta Far Eastern Agreement," *Pacific Historical Review*, 38 (1968), 343-53. For a description of Hurley's relationship with his staff, see Robert T. Smith, "Alone in China: Patrick J. Hurley's Attempts to Unify China, 1944-1945," unpublished Ph.D. dissertation, University of Oklahoma (1966). See also Varg, *Closing the Door*, 291-92.

begun twenty years earlier. At Sian in 1937 the *Kuomintang* and the Communists had suppressed their differences in the face of the Japanese invasion; but in 1946 against whom could there be a united front, and for what purposes? Neither side now perceived foreign aggression as China's number one problem. Rather, "One intended to seize power, the other to retain it; one was determined to promote social revolution in the countryside, the other to prevent it."[4] Given these circumstances, disputes over means of control in local and provincial areas became inevitable. Communist demands for greater representation in the state council were countered by an insistence on the part of the right-wing *Kuomintang* that the PCC agreements be disavowed altogether. Armed clashes became increasingly frequent and serious in Manchuria in the spring of 1946. By the beginning of the following year, all pretense of keeping the agreements had vanished. To this failure, renewed civil war was the answer.[5]

A CASE OF CRUMBLING FOUNDATIONS

Facing the prospect of a desperate civil war and recognizing at last the need to gain popular support, the Nationalist government sought to save itself by a belated appeal to constitutionalism. A national convention open to all parties, but attended only by the *Kuomintang* and some of the minor groups, adopted a constitution generally in line with the principles of the PCC agreements. Providing for a parliamentary

[4] Lucien Bianco, *Origins of the Chinese Revolution, 1915-1949* (1971), 172.

[5] John F. Melby, a state department officer who worked with General Marshall in mediating between the *Kuomintang* and the Communists, recorded in his journal (November 16, 1946): "I suppose coalition had to be attempted, even though it was an impractical notion at best and the very nature of this kind of political struggle has precluded success except on a temporary basis and then only under great stress. I know Marshall now believes he made a mistake in ever thinking coalition was desirable or useful or possible," *The Mandate of Heaven: Record of a Civil War, China, 1945-49* (1968),* 172.

system, the constitution became effective, formally at least, in December, 1947; but during the emergency of civil war, large special powers were to be retained by Chiang as president.[6]

The efforts toward constitutionalism and parliamentary government in 1947 were doomed from the beginning. They were made at a time when the Nationalist government was not only beset by civil war but also had already lost the revived prestige it enjoyed briefly when Japan surrendered in 1945. At that time there was still hope that the government's economic and financial assets, including foreign aid, if used wisely, could provide a sound economic structure to serve as a base for the intelligent political reform demanded by business, professional, and intellectual classes alike. But neither the *Kuomintang* nor the Nationalist government found or effected the means of using these assets wisely. In a period when the productive capacity and support of the business community were needed more desperately than ever, the government did the very thing best designed to alienate private enterprise. It seized the Japanese industrial plants in occupied China and operated them as state concerns. This amounted to confiscation in some cases, since many of the firms had been privately owned. Even worse was the government's use of foreign aid in support of state owned or controlled undertakings, and its excessive exactions on firms that remained in private hands.

Equally ruinous to *Kuomintang*-Nationalist fortunes was a vicious inflationary spiral. As *Kuomintang*-Communist warfare intensified, Nanking sought to pay its way by printing more and more paper money. In mid-1947, the

[6] The new constitution and the parliamentary system came largely from the efforts of Carsun Chang, head of the Social Democratic party, who had striven to overcome party dictatorship and militarism through adoption of the parliamentary principle. His plan was so modified by the national convention as largely to subvert the representative principle. Thus when the new government under the constitution was formed, many of the minor parties, united in the Democratic League, refused to cooperate and allied themselves with the Communists. See Chang Chun-mai (Carsun Chang), *The Third Force in China* (1952).

Chinese national currency rate to the U.S. dollar was 45,000 to 1, and the deterioration was continuing. The foreign financial reserves, which the government held in 1945 had been spent. There was, in fact, no budget. Expenditures, especially by the military, were wasteful, and in any event no one could tell what proportion of the taxes collected reached the treasury, due to the flagrant dishonesty of tax collectors.

It would appear, however, that the worst effects of inflation were neither economic nor military, but moral. The unending spiral of worthless paper corrupted everyone who was forced to use it. For those dependent on salaries and wages the problem was not one of inequity but of survival. Soldiers, lesser officials, and the intellectuals suffered most. These last, who could have contributed so much to the *Kuomintang,* were at best ignored; at worst they were persecuted or liquidated. These were the men who had recognized that ideology was important in China. They were the carriers of the Chinese revolution that had begun in the nineteenth century. Most of them were not Communists. Perhaps a majority of them were opposed to civil war and favored compromise with the Communists and the establishment of a representative government. When the PCC agreements failed and the full civil war was resumed in 1947, many of these intellectuals were dismissed from their positions or arrested, and some were slain.[7] This type of repression was another example of the policies that had undermined the Nationalist government and the *Kuomintang* from within, at the very moment when this government and party were to meet

in full battle all the power which the Chinese Communists could bring against them.

THE COMMUNIST MILITARY VICTORY

The civil war that followed the failure of the Nationalists and Communists to effect a political solution was of brief duration, 1947 to 1949, and resulted in the complete collapse of the Nationalist armies. Spreading over thousands of miles and involving millions of men on both sides, this civil war was for the most part a massive series of small battles. In the initial stages, Nationalist forces, capitalizing upon their superiority in men and equipment and upon the Communist propensity for getting out of the way when the odds were against them, advanced into the North Chinese and Manchurian countryside. For a time, Nationalist forces even held Yenan. It was not long, however, before this effort to seize and hold the maximum territory reacted against the Nationalists. As Nationalist forces spread out from their bases, they became increasingly vulnerable to the Communist style of war. Government forces were subjected to ambushes, skirmishes, and attacks on isolated garrisons, which, in effect, nullified their superiority. Meanwhile, the Communists, flushed by an accumulation of minor successes, enlarged their armies, supplied them with equipment turned over by the Russians or captured from the Nationalists, and stepped up their offensive.[8]

---

[7] The student segment of the Chinese intelligentsia has been described by Jessie G. Lutz: "The acceptance of the Chinese Communist Party and the rejection of the *Kuomintang* in the course of the student movement of 1945 to 1949 came with the conviction that the Chinese Communist Party and not the *Kuomintang* could achieve the goals of Chinese nationalism. Transfer of loyalties occurred not because of the attractiveness of communist ideology, but because student activists after 1947 believed that only communist victory could bring peace and political unity; only the leadership of the Chinese Communist Party could restore the centralized and sovereign state essential for modernization." "The Chinese Student Movement of 1945-1949," *Journal of Asian Studies,* 31 (1971), 95.

[8] Nanking's American military advisers urged Chiang to avoid moves which would overextend his forces and expose his lines of communication. The disastrous consequences of going against this advice were expressed by General Wedemeyer, September, 1947, when he reported to Washington that Manchuria was close to Communist control. The General recommended to the Nationalist government and to Washington that China ask the United Nations to end Manchurian hostilities, and that Manchuria be placed under a trusteeship composed of China, Russia, the United States, Britain, and France. The effect of the proposal was to require the Nationalists to admit that Manchuria was not China, and that Nanking was unable to deal with the Communist challenge. The plan also would have required the United States to pledge military forces in a civil war. Since the United States was determined to avoid these implications, its response was again to advise concentration of Nation-

Soviet troops removing Japanese industrial equipment from a Manchurian factory for shipment to Russia.

Major Nationalist reverses came first in Manchuria. Although Chiang had sent his best troops into this region, they could not cope with a Communist plan which used saboteurs to cut rail lines and isolated *Kuomintang* garrisons in major cities. These tactics were carried into North China, accompanied by a southward thrust toward the Yangtze River. By the end of 1947, the Communists had won virtual control of Hopei and Shansi provinces, prompting Mao Tse-tung to claim that, "The revolutionary war of the Chinese people had reached the turning point; . . . a turning point in history."[9]

alist forces in North China. Chiang simply ignored the Americans and pursued the Manchurian campaign. By 1948, the Communists had cut Manchurian rail lines, thus isolating the Nationalists in the cities, where they were dependent on supplies brought in by air.

[9] "The Present Situation and Our Tasks," *Selected Works* (4 vols., 1961-1965), IV, 157. The inner history of the play of forces in Manchuria between the Russians, the *Kuomintang,* and the Chinese Communists must await further evidence. The subject is of historical importance because Manchuria was controlled by Russia at the end of the war and was also the initial base of the Chinese Communist offensives which finally ended in the conquest of all China. During the early years of the cold war, critics of American policy attributed the military success of the Chinese Communists to the concessions President Franklin Roosevelt made to Russia in Manchuria at the Yalta conference. In later years, however, it has been suggested that, as early as 1946, Russia was not entirely

The decisive battles of the *Kuomintang*-Communist civil war came in 1948. In North China the Red army enlarged its territorial base with the conquest of key cities and surrounding countryside in Honan and Shantung. By September, Communist forces launched their biggest offensive, a campaign which in two months brought the fall of Manchuria. Two months later, November, 1948, Communist and *Kuomintang*-Nationalist troops were locked in one of the great battles of modern history as they fought on the vast plain of the Hwai River near Suchow. Into this conflict Chiang Kai-shek threw his remaining military resources. In January, 1949, the Nationalist commander, General Tu Yu-ming, surrendered. His action wiped out the best part of the surviving Nationalist

in accord with emerging Chinese Communist objectives. The evidence does not point to one simple conclusion. For example, Russia permitted Chinese Communist forces to occupy the Manchurian countryside; in addition, the eventual Russian military withdrawal was timed to the advantage of the Chinese Communists and to the disadvantage of the Nationalists. Yet initially, Russia denied the Chinese Communists access to Manchurian cities and their rich industrial plants and capital, much of which the Russians took with them when they left. For analysis of Russian policy, see Charles B. McLane, *Soviet Policy and the Chinese Communists* (1958); and Adam Ulam, *Expansion and Coexistence: The History of Soviet Foreign Policy, 1917-1967* (1968).

forces. The Red army at last had gained numerical and material superiority.[10]

At this point Chiang Kai-shek could no longer ignore demands for negotiations. He resigned the presidency. General Li Tsung-jen became acting president and opened talks with the Communists. In essence, the Communists demanded unconditional surrender. When the Nationalists refused, the Communists renewed their attack, penetrating southward to Canton and westward to Chungking. With the remnants of the Nationalist armies, Chiang Kai-shek escaped to Taiwan, where, in March, 1950, he resumed the presidency of all that was left of *Kuomintang*-Nationalist China.

The Communist takeover in China fitted neither the traditional Marxist concept of an urban insurrection nor the Maoist vision of a general peasant uprising. Rather, the pattern was one of systematic military conquest by armies which moved from rural bases in the north to seize and occupy the entire mainland. As a military victory, it came as much from *Kuomintang* failures as from Communist military power. Indeed, by 1949, the collapse of the Nationalist government was so far advanced that the Communists often met little or no resistance. They moved, in the main, into a political vacuum.[11]

The rapidity of the Communist military victory was the more surprising and foreboding to the outside world because it had been supposed that Chiang and his German military advisers of former years had built a modern and effective army. Yet this army had failed to cope with a mobile enemy not given to defending a fixed position. It appeared that in the selection of

Nationalist military leadership too high a premium had been placed on personal loyalty to Chiang rather than on military competence. The resulting mismanagement and mistreatment of the common soldier destroyed morale while generating despair and desertion. From 1947 on, desertions from the Nationalists to the Red army were so great that the Communists were unable to provide the customary indoctrination and training for these volunteers.[12]

In contrast, the Communists and the Red army enjoyed increasing popular support. Japan's surrender had removed much of the pressure for a united front, thus enabling the Communists to resume openly their role of social reformers. Their timing was most effective, because the reestablishment of Nationalist rule in Japanese-occupied China had brought the peasantry no relief. The old order of landlord control continued under the returned *Kuomintang* as it had under the Japanese. In consequence, the Communists were able to appeal successfully for peasant support by reactivating the agrarian policy of their early years in Kiangsi: redistribution of land; indictment of landlords; and cultivation of direct peasant action through the Poor Peasants Association. By these means the Communists created a strong foundation for their military offensives. In Manchuria, for example, where land distribution came earliest and was most thorough, some 1.6 million recruits were added to the Red army between June, 1946 and June, 1948.[13]

A CHINESE FORMULA

The Chinese Communist victory, military and political, was ominous to the non-communist world and particularly to the American people. Since it seemed to suggest a Chinese Communist formula for world revolution, it strengthened the growing belief in the United States that there was a united, world-wide communist conspiracy. Mao Tse-tung's formula (a disciplined party and army plus an economic and social program with strong peasant appeal) would bring revolution, it was said, in the third world of Asia, Africa, and Latin America. What-

[10] O. Edmund Clubb: "Chiang Kai-shek's Waterloo: The Battle of the Hwai-hai," *Pacific Historical Review,* 25 (1956), 389-99; and "Manchuria in the Balance, 1945-1946," *ibid.,* 26 (1957), 377-89.

[11] General David G. Barr, chief of the United States Joint Military Advisory Group attached to the Nationalists, commented on the reasons for Nanking's military collapse when he wrote that since his arrival in China, the government had not lost a single battle for the lack of ammunition or equipment. "Their military debacles in my opinion can all be attributed to the world's worst leadership and many other morale destroying factors that lead to a complete loss of will to fight." "Report to the Department of the Army, November 16, 1948," in United States Department of State, *China White Paper, August, 1949* (reissued ed., 1967), 358.

[12] Bianco, *Origins,* 183.

[13] Bianco, *Origins,* 187-90

ever the validity of this frightening picture, it failed to take into account the uniqueness of the Chinese setting and experience. Mao's influence, for example, was derived less from communist theory (important as that theory might be) than from the ability to capitalize on Chinese conditions as he found them. The nationalist fervor on which he seized was not a creation of the Communists. It was a product of a century of Western imperialism, and of the even older Chinese cultural assumption that the Chinese were superior to the barbarians. In addition, Mao capitalized on every growing weakness of the *Kuomintang*-Nationalists. Those weakenesses were not due primarily to the Communists, but arose from the failure of Chiang and the *Kuomintang* to implement Sun Yat-sen's revolutionary program in the years before the Communists had become serious contenders for power. In a word, the Chinese formula, if there was one, was specifically Chinese.[14]

[14] The Communist takeover of 1949 in China will long present the student of history with an amazingly fertile field for historical analysis. Already there has been a progression of interpretations. It has been seen as simply a matter of *Kuomintang* failures: political, military, economic and social. Hu Shih, the distinguished Chinese educator and philosopher, attributed the Communist victory to Russian intrigue. A number of American politicians and critics professed to find an explanation by indiscriminately charging that incompetence and even subversion in the American diplomatic service and the department of state had brought about what they called America's "loss" of China. More recent scholarship has developed the concept that the Chinese revolution by the 1940s had developed an urgency and an energy which no *Kuomintang*-sponsored reforms could possibly satisfy. This is to say, Chiang and the *Kuomintang* had lapsed into the role, not of revolutionaries, but of protectors of an established order, and were thus unable to perform the double function of remaining in power while at the same time transforming the country. In this view, the politics of mass mobilization incorporating the peasantry called for a new kind of leadership. Variants on this more recent interpretation render more understandable Chiang's view that reform only served the cause of rebellion. They also tend to confirm General Marshall's opinion that, since the United States was unable to influence opposing Chinese forces sufficiently, the only course in the American interest was disengagement from the Chinese mainland. See the "Foreword" by John K. Fairbank in the able study by

REACTIONS IN THE UNITED STATES

The Communist conquest of China was regarded in the United States as an unprecedented catastrophe, not only for the Chinese but also, and perhaps more importantly, for Americans and for the historic East Asian policies of their government. Following the republican revolution of 1911-1912 and the later truimph of the *Kuomintang* in 1927-1928, large and influential sectors of American public opinion, responding to the reports and the pleas of American Christian missionaries, assumed an extraordinary feeling of responsibility—a kind of guardianship—for the future of China and the Chinese. In turn, this sense of guardianship fostered in the American mind very high expectations of what China was to be. The conviction grew that China, discarding her benighted past, was on the road to modernization, and that this modernization, under kindly American guidance, would bring forth a new China with marked resemblances to the United States. What could be more natural or more desirable than that America should be the model for the new China?[15] This mental and imaginative background provided a degree of comfort to Americans during the war years, 1941-1945. They had come to believe, and they were encouraged to believe, that with the defeat of Japan, China would be reborn as a great sovereign state under the *Kuomintang*, and that this party would direct China's modernization and transformation into a strong, democratic, peaceful, and friendly nation particularly well-disposed toward the United States. These pleasant beliefs were shattered completely by the Communist victory of 1949. At first the news was simply unbelievable to most Americans. It appeared to make a mockery of a half century of American expectations. There was now a vision of a new Chinese empire dedi-

Foster Rhea Dulles, *American Policy toward Communist China: The Historical Record, 1949-1969* (1972); also Bianco, *Origins;* and Pinchon P.Y. Loh, *The Kuomintang Debacle of 1949: Conquest or Collapse?* (1965).*

[15] Varg, *Closing the Door,* 3.

cated to the principles of world revolution. China, it was said, would communize its neighbors, converting them into satellites much as Old China had controlled the border states by Confucianizing them.[16]

CHINA IN AMERICAN POLITICS

Americans, sometimes led by public officials, plunged into a vast debate aimed ostensibly at fixing responsiblity for the "loss of China." This inquiry soon turned into a crusade, pursued in a manner and in an atmosphere of irresponsibility and unbelievable recrimination. American partisans of the *Kuomintang* both in and out of Congress (the so-called China bloc and China lobby) charged that the collapse of the Nationalist government was not due to its own weakness and revolutionary vacuity, but to the failure of the American government to give it adequate support. This theory, if true, meant that the administration of President Truman, indirectly if not directly, had assisted the Chinese Communists to power. From this position it was charged that either the administration had so miscalculated affairs in China as to bring disastrous defeat, or had knowingly pursued a course that was manifestly easy on communism if not sympathetic to it.[17] These unproven charges were welcomed in greater or lesser degree by a wide variety of American individuals and factions intent on exploiting China's revolution for political purposes in the United States.[18]

To an American public which had never given sustained, serious attention to East Asia in general or to the Chinese revolution in particular, the charges made by the promoters of the politics of fear seemed plausible enough in the 1950s, and to some extent thereafter. Hunting the "culprits" in the "loss of China" was popular politics. Of course, even from the beginning of these political battles there were some Americans who, though often silenced, did not fail to observe that it is difficult for one to "lose" what one had never possessed.[19]

THE BALANCE OF POWER

Beyond the China problem there was a further sense in which historic American-East Asian

[16] Since Americans prior to 1949 had generally felt that China would have no part in the Communist movement, Mao's victory was interpreted by some to mean that the Chinese must be helpless victims (perhaps the puppets) of an international conspiracy centered in Moscow. "The obsession with the threat of international Communism, the feeling of insecurity born of the pressures of the Cold War, made it all too easy [for Americans] to see in the events in China no more than a calculated move by the Soviet Union to carry its offensives against the West to another front." Dulles, *American Policy*, 41. During the 1950s, the names of America's China specialists and scholars who cautioned that there was grave error in such oversimplified explanations all but disappeared from America's popular press.

[17] The fullest statement of this thesis is in Anthony Kubeck, *How the Far East Was Lost: American Policy and the Creation of Communist China, 1941-1949* (1963).

[18] An amazing variety of personalities, public and private, and pressure groups worked separately and together in this emotional attack on America's China policy. Eventually it was Senator Joseph R. McCarthy, Republican from Wisconsin, who became the uninhibited spokesman for the view that the American government was "soft" on communism and that the state department was the key to the Communist conquest of China. For a reliable summation of the evidence bearing on the McCarthy charges, see Dulles, *American Policy*, 33-148. A specialized scholarly study of McCathyism is Robert Griffith, *The Politics of Fear: Senator Joseph R. McCarthy and the Senate* (1970).

[19] In time it was recognized that the China bloc, the China lobby, and Senator McCarthy did a major disservice to the American people and their government. Roger Hilsman, former assistant secretary of state for far eastern affairs, noted some of the unfortunate results: ". . . before the McCarthy business had run its course, the twenty-some China specialists in the Foreign Service had either resigned, retired, or run to cover in jobs dealing with other parts of the world." *To Move A Nation* (1967), 297. The repressive effect of McCarthyism on the academic community was also pronounced. In the emotionally charged atmosphere of American public opinion during the cold war, conclusions reached in scholarly research were unwelcome except when they supported the claims of the *Kuomintang*. Tang Tsou, *America's Failure in China, 1941-1950* (1963),* vii-viii, suggests that the reluctance of some American politicians and lobbyists to encourage scholarly investigation was due to their fear that the scholars could not find an "identifiable group of scapegoats" who might be blamed for the "loss of China."

policy was in trouble. During the twentieth century, the United States had sought to preserve a balance of power in East Asia by opposing Japan's ambitions in China. World War II destroyed Japanese power, but it had also destroyed the power of Britain, France, and the Netherlands in East Asia. The result was that after 1949 Russia and China replaced Japan and Western Europe as political factors in continental East Asia.[20]

In 1947 the United States went to the aid of Greece and Turkey to save Europe, it was said, from the advance of communism. Pressure groups in the United States demanded that similar, massive aid be extended to sustain China's Nationalist government and, after 1949, to support its return from Taiwan to the mainland. During the months before the outbreak of the Korean War in June, 1950, the Truman administration yielded in some degree to these pressures. It continued to recognize Chiang's government as the government of China and extended limited aid to it, but it refrained from any massive commitment. The administration had been disheartened by its failure to create a coalition between Nanking and Yenan. It no longer believed that the Nationalists could regain control of China even with unlimited American economic and military assistance. Furthermore, American military authorities, mindful of Japan's failure to conquer the Chinese mainland, opposed involvement in a great and perhaps interminable land war in China. There was also a clear danger of Soviet intervention in Europe or the Middle East if the United States were committed deeply to China.

[20] Louis Morton has written: "The Allies, though they defeated Japan and won the war, gained little and lost much. China, which the United States had hoped to make the bulwark of the free world in the Far East, was lost to communism; and the former colonies, freed from Japanese domination, showed little inclination to return to their former status. . . . The Western Powers, who had expected to be restored to their former position in the area taken from them by Japan, were ultimately driven from Southeast Asia. In a sense, the efforts of the United States today to reestablish Western influence in that region may be viewed as an effort to achieve what the Allies failed to achieve in World War II." "World War II: A Survey of Recent Writings," *American Historical Review*, 75 (1970), 1987-2008.

In any case, it was hoped that, if the Communists indeed established themselves in firm control of mainland China, the United States could somehow get along with them.[21] Consequently, by January, 1950, the Truman administration had adopted a policy of marking time and keeping American options open. The administration opposed the admission of the Chinese Communists to the United Nations and refused to follow the lead of the British government in extending diplomatic recognition to the newly-proclaimed Chinese People's Republic; but it also made public its intention "at this time" to refrain from establishing military bases on Taiwan. "The United States," a White House press statement said, "will not pursue a course which will lead to involvement in the civil conflict in China."[22]

COMMUNIST CHINA AND THE POWERS

The Communist military victory and the establishment, October 1, 1949, of a central government at Peking called the People's Republic of China was followed immediately, October 2, by Russian recognition of the new regime. By January, 1950, Mao's government had also been recognized by Russia's satellites, and by India, Burma, Britain, Finland, Sweden, Israel, and Denmark; soon thereafter recognition was extended by Ceylon, Pakistan, Afghanistan, Indonesia, the Netherlands, and Switzerland. Britain's early recognition was extended in the hope of protecting her territorial and commercial interests, and of counterbalancing the preponderant Russian influence. The Indian position as expressed by Prime Minister Jawaharlal Nehru was that power had passed to the Chinese Communists, that they rather than the *Kuomintang* had popular support, and that the people of Asia must be allowed to decide their political future without foreign interference.

These early gestures toward accepting Communist China into the family of nations savored of self-interest or were somewhat doctrinaire,

[21] Herbert Feis, *From Trust to Terror: The Onset of the Cold War, 1945-1950* (1970), 204.

[22] See Dulles, *American Policy,* 64-69.

since Chinese policy in the early months of 1950 did not place a premium on recognition by the Western powers or even on admission to the United Nations. Peking's priorities emphasized securing the new government's position against enemies from within and without, and for these tasks of consolidation the Soviet Union offered practical assistance. Moscow had repudiated its treaty of 1945 pledging support to the Chinese Nationalist government. In January, 1950, Soviet delegates initiated a boycott of United Nations proceedings in protest against the Security Council's refusal to eject the Nationalist Chinese representative. On February 14, 1950, Mao Tse-tung signed a treaty of alliance and mutual assistance with Moscow. The treaty aligned China in international affairs with the Soviet bloc of states and tightened the economic and cultural ties between Mao's government and the Soviet Union. In the context of a deepening Russo-American rivalry, China's preference was made even clearer when Peking seized United States' consular properties and continued to charge that American policy was imperialistic. At the same time Mao appeared willing to tolerate Soviet imperialism in Manchuria, Mongolia, and Sinkiang, even if he did not welcome it.

FOR FURTHER READING

A number of titles which are pertinent to the subject of this chapter are listed in Chapter 29. Among additional works on China's revolution see: Conrad Brandt, Benjamin Schwartz, and John Fairbank, *A Documentary History of Chinese Communism* (1952) * offers translations of documents relating to the Nationalist-Communist competition that ended in 1949. Frederic Wakeman, Jr., *History and Will: Philosophical Perspectives of Mao Tse-tung's Thought* (1973), studies the processes through which Mao applied Marxist ideas to Chinese circumstances. Chang Chia-ao, *The Inflationary Spiral: The Experience in China, 1939-1950* (1958) is a study of the economic disintegration of the Nationalist government by a former cabinet minister in the government. Milton J. T. Shieh, *The Kuomintang: Selected Historical Documents, 1894-1969* (1970)*, a semi-official history designed to correct "misconceptions."

Ch'ien Tuan-sheng, *The Government and Politics of China* (1950; reissued 1967)* should be noted for its explanation of Nationalist failures. C. P. Fitzgerald, *Revolution in China* (1952) * focuses skillfully on the indigenous forces underlying the revolution. See also Harold Isaacs, *The Tragedy of the Chinese Revolution* (rev. ed., 1951).* Chiang Chung-cheng (Chiang Kai-shek), *Soviet Russia in China: A Summing-up at Seventy* (1957) * is important as Chiang's explanation of his failure.

For the military climax of the *Kuomintang*-Communist struggle see Lionel Max Chassin, *The Communist Conquest of China: A History of the Civil War, 1945-1949* (1965), and Chapter 8 in O. Edmund Clubb, *20th Century China* (1964).* Robert B. Rigg, *Red China's Fighting Hordes* (1952) describes the leadership, organization and tactics of the Communist armies. William W. Whitson with Huang Chen-hsia, *The Chinese High Command: A History of Communist Military Politics, 1927-1971* (1973), a sophisticated, technical analysis.

Among significant eyewitness accounts of the Communist conquest are: Derke Bodde, *Peking Diary: A Year of Revolution* (1950);* and Jack Belden, *China Shakes the World* (1949)*. Kuo Ping-chia, *China: New Age and New Outlook* (1956) assesses the events of 1945-1949 against the background of history. Sun K'o, *China Looks Forward* (1944) is a summing-up by the son of Sun Yat-sen of the *Kuomintang's* accomplishments and failures.

Max Beloff, *Soviet Policy in the Far East, 1944-1951* (1953); Aitchen K. Wu, *China and the Soviet Union* (1950); and Henry Wei, *China and Soviet Russia* (1956) offer narratives describing the formation of the Sino-Soviet alliance of 1950. William Mandel, comp., *Soviet Source Materials on USSR Relations with East Asia, 1945-1950* (1950). An able and extensive survey of American far eastern policy is Harold Vinacke, *Far Eastern Politics in the Postwar Period* (1956). United States Department of State, *United States Relations with China, with Special Reference to the Period 1944-1949* (1949) provides selections from once-secret documents and an official explanation of American policy. The privately reissued edition is cited in footnote 11. Paul H. Clyde, "Historical Reflections on American Relations with the Far East," *The South Atlantic Quarterly* 61

(1962): 437-49, is a critical interpretation. Among important recent references: John K. Fairbank, *The United States and China* (3rd. ed., 1971),* the updating of a standard work; Athan G. Theoharis *The Yalta Myths: An Issue in U.S. Politics, 1945-1955* (1970); and John S. Service, *The Amerasia Papers: Some Problems in the History of U.S.-China Relations* (1971),* the defense of a career Foreign Service officer to charges by McCarthyites of "traitorous" conduct. Judith Coburn, "Asian Scholars and Government: The Chrysanthemum on the Sword," in *America's Asia: Dissenting Essays on Asian-American Relations.* Edward Friedman and Mark Selden, eds, (1971),* 67-107, advances the thesis that American scholarship has been distorted by government financing. For bibliographic essays offering differing perspectives on Sino-American relations in the Roosevelt-Truman eras see: Jim Peck, "America and the Chinese Revolution, 1942-1946: An Interpretation"; and Robert Dallek, "The Truman Era," in *American-East Asian Relations: A Survey,* James Thomson and Ernest May eds. (1972) 319-55, 356-76.

China
under Mao:
The Great
Transformation

32

The year 1949 was unique in the political traditions of Chinese civilization. When Communist armies in that year drove the *Kuomintang* and its government from the mainland, they seemed to repeat great and climactic events from China's long past—the destruction of a government that had failed and the substitution of another professing to have the Mandate of Heaven. To some extent, then, the Communist conquest suggested the old cyclical theory of Chinese history by which dynasties rose in virtue and fell in decay. After 1911, however, this theory was not so satisfying. The republican revolution of that year did not seek merely the installation of another dynasty; rather, it sought a new order that mingled modern, Western values with traditional, Chinese ones. It was as proponents of this revolution in its most extreme form that the Communists seized power in 1949. Indeed, their conquest rested on assumptions of total revolution, uninhibited, for the moment at least, even by the traditions and values taken from China's long history. Here lay the uniqueness of 1949.

For the tasks of reshaping China while at the same time uniting a people who in the fullest sense had not lived under a centralized government since the fall of the Manchu dynasty, the Communists possessed endowments greater than any other group that had claimed leadership in the twentieth century. Years of bitter struggle had created a leadership which, initially at least, was remarkably united and determined under Mao Tse-tung. In addition to skill in the politics of opposition and destruction, the Communists came to power with experience derived from actually governing in China's Northwest. Furthermore, from their revolutionary heritage, from the teaching of their ideology, and from study of precedents supplied by the communist state in Soviet Russia, this new leadership had obtained a clear conception of its immediate goals and of the means for achieving them. But would these qualities suffice for the larger tasks ahead? Would the new regime succeed in discarding a traditional social order which rested on the inequality of man and an economy based on subsistence farming, so as to achieve the proclaimed goal of a classless society blessed with material abundance? Would revolutionary innovations survive the regime's first years? Indeed, would communism provide answers for China's problems that were any more satisfactory than those of the regimes whose failures marked the past half century? Since the Chinese Communist era is contemporary history, these and similar questions are necessarily lacking in definitive answers. Moreover, the historical picture of Communist China has been and is incomplete, distorted by inadequate or inaccurate data. The Chinese government has completely controlled all media of communication and manipulated the flow of information for its own purposes. Foreign observers, especially those with training and background for specialized analysis, have enjoyed only limited access to China for firsthand study. Thus historical scholarship on Communist China in the 1970s is necessarily tentative.[1]

[1] The limitation imposed on research by the inaccessibility of Communist China has been suggested by Walter Galenson's "The Current State of Chinese Economic Studies," in United States Congress: Joint Economic Committee, *Studies Prepared in the Joint Economic Committee, Congress of the United States: An Economic Profile of Mainland China* (90th Congress, 1st sess.: Joint Committee Print, 2 vols., 1967), I, 3-7, which points out that in the period 1960-1967, Chinese authorities published scarcely a single significant figure relating to the country's economy. No public announcements were made of the magnitude of steel or coal production, of machinery output, or of the size of harvests. Peking simply attempted to block the publication of useful data outside the country.

The early 1970s, however, brought some improvements in opportunities for travel in China. Earlier, during the cold war decades, 1950-1970, Americans were virtually barred from China—other foreign nationals enjoyed somewhat larger opportunities—since both Washington and Peking maintained barriers to travel. Beginning in 1969, the United States relaxed some of its prohibitions, and shortly thereafter the People's Republic began to invite selected Americans—scholars, journalists, artists, athletes, but not casual tourists—to visit and even to have audiences with high officials. By mid-1973, some 6,000 Americans had been to China and 200 of them had written about their experiences. This "China witnessing" was a supplement to "China watching," an activity that had generally been conducted from a distance. Even so, the portrayal of revolutionary China remained no easy task. In so vast a country there were limits to what the most indefatigable traveler could see or was permitted to see. The reporting of foreign visitors, moreover, was colored by the individual reporter's experience with and knowledge of China, as well as by his reaction to a communist revolution. Compare the perspectives, for example, of Felix Greene, *Awakened China: The Country Americans Don't Know* (1961) and Edgar

POLITICAL AND ADMINISTRATIVE FOUNDATIONS

As the Communists moved toward military victory, 1948-1949, they prepared for the establishment of a national government. A first step, September, 1949, was the convening of the Chinese People's Consultative Conference, which met in Peking and adopted three basic documents: the common program of general principles, to serve as an interim constitution; the organic law of the central people's government, to establish a provisional government; and the organic law of the Chinese People's Consultative Conference. In Communist legal theory this conference and its documentary products imparted to the regime a legitimacy unattainable through military conquest alone. Thus, only after the conference completed its work did the Communists proclaim on October 1, 1949, the existence of the Chinese People's Republic.

Ostensibly the new government was a broad coalition in which the Communists, functioning as a party of proletarians in alliance with the peasantry, served along with a number of "democratic" parties. These "democratic" parties held seats in the Chinese People's Consultative Conference, and their representatives received appointments to governmental posts. Yet the real substance of the coalition was suggested by the requirement that the "democratic" parties operate under Communist leadership. These parties generally were not permitted to build grass-roots support or propagandize on their own behalf. They provided window dressing for the claim that the new government represented all people and not a single class. Moreover, insofar as they were compliant tools, these parties assisted in educating and guiding people in the way the Communists wanted them to go;

Snow, *The Other Side of the River: Red China Today* (1961),* both of which were based on extensive travels during the late 1950s. Examples of more recent reporting are to be found in Ross Terrill, *800,000,000: The Real China* (1971)*; Charlotte Y. Salisbury, *China Diary* (1973); Lois Wheeler, *China on Stage: An American Actress in the People's Republic* (1972); and Committee of Concerned Asian Scholars, *China: Inside the People's Republic* (1972).*

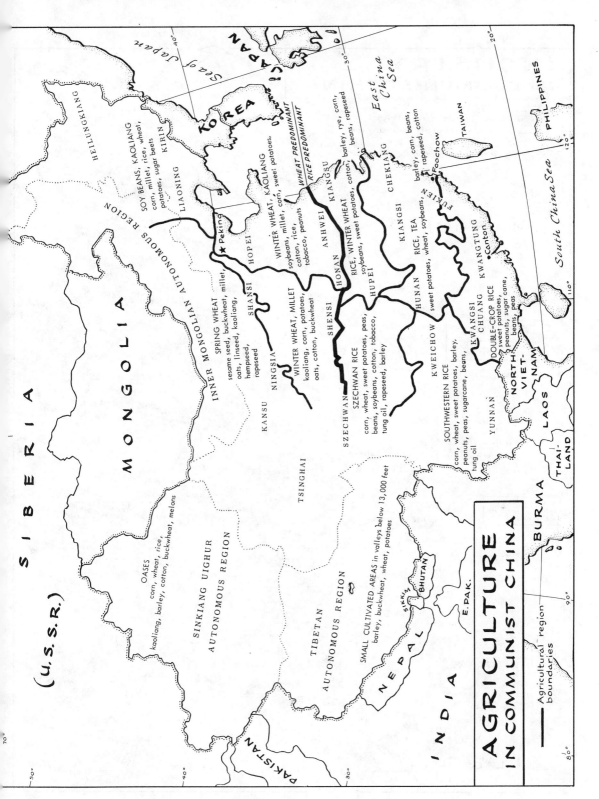

SIBERIA

(U.S.S.R.)

HEILUNGKIANG

KIRIN

LIAONING

KOREA

JAPAN

Sea of Japan

MONGOLIA

INNER MONGOLIAN AUTONOMOUS REGION

SOY BEANS, KAOLIANG, corn, millet, rice, wheat, potatoes, sugar beets

Peking ★

HOPEI

WINTER WHEAT, KAOLIANG, soybeans, millet, corn, sweet potatoes, cotton, rice, tobacco, peanuts

WHEAT PREDOMINANT
RICE PREDOMINANT

ANHWEI

KIANGSU

RICE, WINTER WHEAT, cotton, barley, rye, corn, soybeans, sweet potatoes, beans, rapeseed

East China Sea

CHEKIANG

RICE, TEA, barley, corn, beans, rapeseed, cotton

TAIWAN

120°

PHILIPPINES

SHANSI

SPRING WHEAT, millet, sesame seed, buckwheat, oats, linseed, kaoliang, hempseed, rapeseed

NINGSIA

SHENSI

WINTER WHEAT, MILLET, kaoliang, corn, potatoes, oats, cotton, buckwheat

HONAN

HUPEI

FUKIEN

Foochow

30°

South China Sea

KANSU

SZECHWAN

SZECHWAN RICE, corn, wheat, sweet potatoes, peas, beans, soybeans, cotton, tobacco, tung oil, rapeseed, barley

HUNAN

RICE, sweet potatoes, wheat, soybeans, beans

KIANGSI

KWEICHOW

SOUTHWESTERN RICE, corn, wheat, sweet potatoes, barley, peanuts, peas, sugarcane, beans, tung oil

KWANGTUNG

Canton

KWANGSI CHUANG

DOUBLE-CROP RICE, sweet potatoes, peanuts, sugar cane, beans, peas

110°

TSINGHAI

SINKIANG UIGHUR AUTONOMOUS REGION

OASES
corn, wheat, rice, kaoliang, barley, cotton, buckwheat, melons

TIBETAN AUTONOMOUS REGION

SMALL CULTIVATED AREAS in valleys below 13,000 feet
barley, buckwheat, wheat, potatoes

YUNNAN

NORTH VIET-NAM

LAOS

BURMA

THAI-LAND

SIKKIM

BHUTAN

NEPAL

E. PAK.

INDIA

PAKISTAN

70°

50°

40°

30°

90°

80°

AGRICULTURE IN COMMUNIST CHINA

——— Agricultural region boundaries

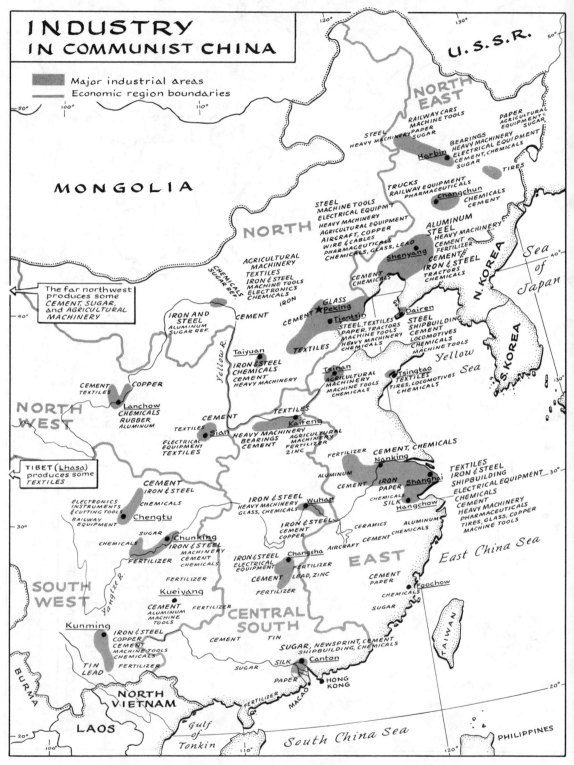

INDUSTRY IN COMMUNIST CHINA

Major industrial areas
Economic region boundaries

U.S.S.R.

NORTH EAST

MONGOLIA

NORTH

RAILWAY CARS
MACHINE TOOLS
PAPER
SUGAR

STEEL
HEAVY MACHINERY

PAPER
AGRICULTURAL
EQUIPMENT
SUGAR

BEARINGS
HEAVY MACHINERY
ELECTRICAL EQUIPMENT
CEMENT, CHEMICALS
SUGAR

Harbin

TIRES

TRUCKS
RAILWAY EQUIPMENT
PHARMACEUTICALS

Changchun

CHEMICALS
CEMENT

STEEL
MACHINE TOOLS
ELECTRICAL EQUIP'MT
HEAVY MACHINERY
AGRICULTURAL EQUIPMENT
AIRCRAFT, COPPER
WIRE & CABLES
PHARMACEUTICALS
CHEMICALS, GLASS, LEAD

ALUMINUM
STEEL
HEAVY MACHINERY
CEMENT
FERTILIZER

Shenyang

CEMENT
IRON & STEEL
TRACTORS
CHEMICALS

N. KOREA

Sea
of
Japan

AGRICULTURAL
MACHINERY
TEXTILES
IRON & STEEL
MACHINE TOOLS
ELECTRONICS
CHEMICALS

CEMENT
CHEMICALS

The far northwest
produces some
CEMENT, SUGAR,
and AGRICULTURAL
MACHINERY

IRON AND
STEEL
ALUMINUM
SUGAR REF.

CEMENT

IRON

CHEMICALS
SUGAR REF.

GLASS
CEMENT ★Peking

Tientsin

Dairen

STEEL, TEXTILES
PAPER, TRACTORS
MACHINE TOOLS
HEAVY MACHINERY
CHEMICALS

STEEL
SHIPBUILDING
CEMENT
LOCOMOTIVES
CHEMICALS
MACHINE TOOLS

S. KOREA

Yellow
Sea

Taiyuan

IRON & STEEL
CHEMICALS
CEMENT
HEAVY MACHINERY

TEXTILES

Tsinan
AGRICULTURAL
MACHINERY
MACHINE TOOLS
CHEMICALS

Tsingtao
TEXTILES
TIRES, LOCOMOTIVES
CHEMICALS

NORTH
WEST

CEMENT
TEXTILES

COPPER

Lanchow
CHEMICALS
RUBBER
ALUMINUM

CEMENT

TEXTILES

TEXTILES

Kaifeng

Sian
ELECTRICAL
EQUIPMENT
TEXTILES

HEAVY MACHINERY
BEARINGS
CEMENT

AGRICULTURAL
MACHINERY
FERTILIZER
ZINC

FERTILIZER

CEMENT, STEEL
Nanking

ALUMINUM

CEMENT

IRON
PAPER

Shanghai

TEXTILES
IRON & STEEL
SHIPBUILDING
ELECTRICAL EQUIPMENT
CHEMICALS
CEMENT
HEAVY MACHINERY
PHARMACEUTICALS
TIRES, GLASS, COPPER
MACHINE TOOLS

TIBET (Lhasa)
produces some
TEXTILES

CEMENT
IRON & STEEL

CHEMICALS

IRON & STEEL
HEAVY MACHINERY
GLASS, CHEMICALS

Wuhan

CHEMICALS
SILK

Hangchow

ELECTRONICS
INSTRUMENTS
& CUTTING TOOLS
RAILWAY
EQUIPMENT

Chengtu

IRON & STEEL
CEMENT
COPPER

CERAMICS

ALUMINUM
CEMENT CHEMICALS

SUGAR

Chunking
IRON & STEEL
MACHINERY
CEMENT
CHEMICALS

AIRCRAFT

CHEMICALS

FERTILIZER

IRON & STEEL
ELECTRICAL
EQUIPMENT

Changsha

FERTILIZER
LEAD, ZINC

EAST

CEMENT
PAPER

Foochow

SOUTH
WEST

Kueiyang

CEMENT
ALUMINUM
MACHINE
TOOLS

FERTILIZER

CEMENT

FERTILIZER

CENTRAL
SOUTH

CEMENT
PAPER

SUGAR

CHEMICALS

East China Sea

TAIWAN

Kunming

IRON & STEEL
COPPER
CEMENT
MACHINE TOOLS
CHEMICALS

FERTILIZER

CEMENT

TIN

SUGAR, NEWSPRINT, CEMENT
SHIPBUILDING, CHEMICALS

TIN
LEAD

SUGAR

SILK

Canton

BURMA

NORTH
VIETNAM

PAPER

HONG
KONG

PHILIPPINES

MACAO

FERTILIZER

LAOS

Gulf
of
Tonkin

South China Sea

Adapted from Communist China Map Portfolio *(U.S. Central Intelligence Agency, 1967).*

they helped to mobilize enthusiasm and energies for the work of "socialist construction." When they no longer served these purposes, they disappeared.

The Communists set up mass organizations to implement their rule. Among those organizations were: the All-China Federation of Democratic Youth, the All-China Federation of Cooperatives, the All-China Federation of Democratic Women, the Peasants' Association, and the National Committee of the (Christian) Churches in China for the Realization of Self-Administration. Other mass organizations, such as the Sino-Soviet Friendship Association, the Red Cross Society of China, and the Chinese People's Committee for World Peace and Against American Aggression, represented some specific purpose. Unlike the "democratic" parties, these organizations—and there was one for nearly every conceivable group or purpose—did not conceal their Communist leadership. The All-China Federation of Trade Unions, for example, had as its honorary chairman Liu Shao-ch'i, a top party official. The inclusion of practically everybody in one or another of the mass organizations helped to create the impression at home and abroad that the Communists enjoyed overwhelming popular support, and the organizations themselves provided additional mechanisms for publicizing and implementing party programs.

The provisional government established in 1949 was comprised of four main branches. The central people's government exercised legislative, executive, and judicial powers. Administrative responsibilities and control of the armies were vested respectively in the government administrative council and the people's revolutionary military council. And finally, complementary to the executive organs but subordinate to them were the procurator general's office and the supreme people's court. Directly beneath this structure was local government, comprising everything from the provinces on down. In contrast with the old imperial system, which extended only as far as the *hsien* (county), Communist government penetrated the lowest levels to the towns and to the wards and streets in towns.[2] This centralized structure was

[2] The Communists experimented with different administrative systems below the central structure. Upon coming to power, they took over nearly intact

modified only by the establishment of autonomous local governments in regions inhabited by national minorities. In 1949, however, it was unclear whether the Communists intended to permit these minorities a significant degree of autonomy.

With the convening of the National People's Congress and the adoption of the constitution, September, 1954, the government was formalized, but there were no fundamental political changes. Aside from imparting an additional claim of legitimacy to the regime, the new constitution was important chiefly as a legal basis for the forthcoming socialist transformation of the national economy, the nationalization of natural resources, and the inauguration of centralized planning. Governmental processes under the constitution also offered China's masses elections and opportunities for office holding, both of which provided them with a sense of participation. In this respect, government, like the mass organizations, became an instrument for enlisting popular support.[3]

the existing system with its regional, provincial, county, and district divisions. Later the regional divisions were eliminated and changes were made in appointing local officials so as to tighten Peking's control. During the "Great Leap Forward" of 1958, village governments were often consolidated into a single commune congress. Also, there were changes in the means of directing this structure. The Chinese initially followed the Soviet example of creating complex bureaucracies for the management of subordinate organs, but in 1956 party members functioning in provincial and local governments were given enlarged authority in making decisions. The latter move did not imply a loosening of central control; rather it reflected confidence that party members would do the bidding of their leaders. This reliance on the ideological soundness of party members had worked remarkably well in giving direction to scattered bands of revolutionaries before 1949. Moreover, the new system undoubtedly recommended itself to Peking because it contained echoes of traditional Confucian concepts concerning man in government. On this latter point see H. F. Schurmann, "The Roots of Social Policy," *Survey,* No. 38 (1961), 156-69. See also Richard H. Solomon, "On Activism and Activists: Maoist Conceptions of Motivation and Political Role Linking State to Society," *China Quarterly,* No. 39 (1969), 76-114.

[3] See Derek J. Waller, *The Government and Politics of Communist China* (1971),* a succinct description and analysis, emphasizing the interplay between the government and the party. Party theory has embraced two contradictory concepts: on the one hand, the supremacy of the collective interest, popular activism, and popular political consciousness have

THE ROLE OF THE COMMUNIST PARTY

For most of the regime's first twenty years, until the advent of the "Great Proletarian Cultural Revolution," 1966-1969, the Chinese Communist party was central to the operation of the government, the army, and every other agency by which authority was maintained. The party's organization was so designed that its reach extended from Peking to the grassroots. Between 1949 and 1961 membership expanded from 4,448,080 to some 17 million. Thus the party was equipped with the personnel necessary to control key posts in all organizations. It was through party members, acting as a cohesive, disciplined body, that public policy was implemented. It also was through control of the party that Mao Tse-tung and a handful of veteran colleagues, such as Liu Shao-ch'i, Chou En-lai, Chu Teh, Ch'en Yun, Teng Hsiao-p'ing,

and Lin Piao, irrespective of official titles, determined national policy, assigned responsibility, and prescribed the ways and means for carrying out decisions.

Leadership during the regime's early years was characterized by a remarkable unity of purpose. Mao's authority was unquestioned, and top officials seemed immune to the devisive influence of factionalism. Throughout the party, unity and a high level of political consciousness and revolutionary competence were maintained by unremitting indoctrination. Every member constantly engaged in *hseuh-hsi* (study or training) in order to sharpen his perception of Marxist-Leninist principles and the "thought of Mao Tse-tung." The party's frequent resort to *cheng-feng,* the rectification campaigns which had proven so effective in building unity, required members not only to intensify their studies but also to expose their innermost thoughts in group meetings directed toward criticism and self-criticism. This latter mechanism proved especially effective in enabling party leadership to detect undesirables and to eliminate them.

---

been stressed; on the other, the leading role of the party has been postulated. The result in practice has been popular participation more as a matter of form than of substance. Thus, Chinese have enjoyed "limited opportunities for participation in the management of minor affairs." Such opportunities, moreover, have been limited to those things which "support socialism as defined by the Party." See James R. Townsend, *Political Participation in Communist China* (1967).* Also, A. Doak Barnett, ed., *Chinese Communist Politics in Action* (1969), a collection of essays dealing with relationships between formal government structure and the populace.

RESHAPING THE MASSES

Attainment of Mao's vision required enthusiastic popular support, not mere acquiescence to his will. Thus, with their power secured after

No Chinese communist party leader other than Mao Tse-tung himself has proven more durable than Chou En-lai, who is shown here in a meeting with American officials. By 1974, however, Chou, succumbing to the ills of old age, had retired from heavy administrative responsibilities.

1949, the Communists applied themselves to the elimination of old loyalties, the encouragement of greatly enlarged expectations, and the identification of themselves with those expectations. In pursuing these goals, the party, especially during its first years in power, sometimes used harsh tactics. According to Communist theory and practice, enemies of the revolution—their identity was determined by the Communists alone—were not entitled to civil rights and were to be treated sternly. Under this rationalization the regime supported in 1951-1953 the extermination of untold numbers of "landlords" and the redistribution of their land. These measures, by destroying a local leadership noted for its conservatism and for its attachments to China's old traditional order, were of the utmost importance in clearing the way for a new era.

But, in the balance, propaganda and persuasion sometimes proved more important in Communist China than force. China's involvement in the Korean war, for example, while costly in terms of trained military manpower and resources, demonstrated, in the regime's early days, its ability to appeal successfully to nationalistic feelings. Moreover, the Communist leadership's confidence in its ideological control (a traditional Confucian method) was bolstered by successes with the *cheng-feng* movement of the 1940s and subsequent rectification efforts.

Education, also a powerful force in Old China, became a major instrument for introducing the new society. The Communists, avoiding the old tradition of education for a chosen few, began construction of a system of schools for the masses designed to meet two major needs: (1) the training of a largely illiterate populace in the technical skills necessary for a modern society; and (2) the mass inculcating of concepts that would sustain Peking's revolutionary programs. While these schools provided for a high degree of political indoctrination, the curriculum was for the most part constructive. It was designed to counteract traditional disdain for manual labor, to stress science and technology, and to integrate research and study with practical application. By 1959 there were some 86 million children attending elementary schools, 12 million in middle schools, and 660,000 in colleges and universities. In addition, part-time schools provided for combined

work and study. Measured in quantitative terms (college-level enrollment in 1963 was five times that of 1947, the highest year for the pre-Communist era), these were impressive figures. Yet, generally speaking, the quality of the nonpolitical aspects of the curricula was not high; nor was the progress of the first decade sustained into the 1960s. Economic pressures imposed by the Great Leap Forward (to be discussed later) retarded expansion of the school system. Further trouble arose when the higher levels of the educational system became a target of doctrinal dispute. It was charged that the specialized programs of the advanced schools were violating the egalitarian aspects of the revolution. This was another way of saying that the higher schools were a breeding ground for new elites who in time would capture the revolution and subvert it. During the Cultural Revolution of the late 1960s, the schools were closed as students were caught up in political agitation which stressed the importance of being "red" rather than "expert."[4]

Beyond the school system the Communists campaigned incessantly and intensively to reshape the whole character of Chinese thought. Literature, the press, the stage, films, and radio became evangelists of the new China. The populace was organized by trained party workers into groups of a dozen or so for critical discussion and appraisal of their own activities in the light of party directives.[5] The numbers en-

---

[4] Mao accused some Communist party leaders he was attempting to purge of being supporters of an elitist-oriented educational system. Yet, despite the rhetoric of this confrontation, Mao and the party's leadership recognized that they were facing a dilemma. Realizing that modern specialists were required in the new China, Mao at times had spoken approvingly of quality education, and the party had supported educational opportunities for peasants and workers. The problem was one of balancing the conflicting demands of academic excellence and political indoctrination. See Donald J. Munro, "Egalitarian Ideal and Educational Fact in Communist China," in *China: Management of a Revolutionary Society*, John M. H. Lindbeck, ed. (1971)* 256-301. Descriptive materials are to be found in Ronald F. Price, *Education in Communist China* (1970). See also Charles P. Ridley *et al.*, *The Making of a Model Citizen in Communist China* (1971).

[5] The power of the Chinese Communist party to effect wide social and intellectual control was due mainly to its trained staff workers, the *kan pu* or cadres. These were young party or sympathetic work-

listed in campaigns of this kind cutting across the entire society can hardly be estimated. In 1951-1952, for example, the "Three Antis-Movement" was designed to arouse the Chinese to expose "corruption, waste, and bureaucracy" in a campaign to eliminate unworthy Communists from the party and to expose former *Kuomintang* officials the regime had found useful but who were no longer needed. The "Five Antis-Movement" of the same period, which had for its targets "tax evasion, bribery, cheating in government contracts, theft of economic intelligence, and stealing national property," enlisted public support in driving "enemies" of the state from business. Targets of other campaigns were "feudalism," "American imperialism," and "running dogs of capitalism." During the later 1950s, the period of the Great Leap Forward, increased industrial production became a major propaganda theme. By controlling all the communications media, by piling one campaign on another, by arousing public opinion on behalf of selected objectives, the Communists proposed to keep opponents off-balance and to maintain in their own hands the initiative for transforming China.

The Communist insistence on conformity with the new ideology held special implications for Chinese intellectuals. Traditionally leaders of opinion, the intellectuals presented Peking with either a threat or a promise, depending on their attitude toward Communist leadership. The problem was that in 1949 many intellectuals, while disenchanted with the *Kuomintang,* saw little advantage in the new regime. In consequence, these people became a target of intensive persuasion. Among lesser figures conversion was attempted through the pressure of opinion. Meetings were staged at which individuals were subjected to ridicule, urged to

confess the erroneousness of their ideas, and encouraged to adopt a new course. These efforts at thought-remolding (or more popularly, brainwashing) were softened somewhat for more prominent personages, but the intent remained the same.[6] Faced with the eradication of free thought, many intellectuals sought escape, but the great majority, for whom escape was undesirable or impractical, remained to serve the Communists. Thus the Peking government achieved a substantial success in an area where the *Kuomintang* had failed. The Communists soon claimed the services of a considerable portion of the country's modern-trained scholars, although outbursts of criticism from intellectuals during the Hundred Flowers campaign of 1957 and the subsequent Cultural Revolution cast doubt on the regime's success in eliminating all independent thought.[7]

---

[6] The process of thought-remolding is described by an American scholar who underwent the experience in Harriet Mills, "Thought Reform: Ideological Remolding in China," *Atlantic Monthly,* No. 204 (1959) 71-77. A psychiatric appraisal is given in Robert J. Lifton, *Thought Reform and the Psychology of Totalism: A Study of "Brainwashing" in China* (1960).*

[7] The Hundred Flowers campaign, which drew its name from the ancient saying, "Let a hundred flowers bloom, let a hundred schools of thought contend," represented a momentary relaxation of thought control. Intellectuals, encouraged by party leaders to engage in free discussion, spoke out on every phase of the Communist transformation of China. The criticism, however, apparently became more widespread and intense than was anticipated. The critics went so far as to challenge the relevance of Marxism-Leninism to the Chinese revolution, and anti-Communist demonstrations occurred in several universities. At this point further criticism was forbidden, and those who had spoken were punished. Translations of statements made during the Hundred Flowers campaign are given in R. MacFarquhar, *The Hundred Flowers Campaign and the Chinese Intellectuals* (1960); and Dennis J. Doolin, trans., *Communist China: The Politics of Student Opposition* (1964).* The latter collection suggests a generation gap among Chinese intellectuals. Students were less opposed to communism than their elders. Their criticisms were directed toward disparities between theory and practice, and failures to measure up to the promises of "liberation." For the recollections of an intellectual who served the Communists before becoming disillusioned, see Chow Ching-wen, *Ten Years of Storm: The True Story of the Communist Regime* (1960).

---

ers educated for leadership in government and party activities. Their chief qualifications were capacity to develop loyalty, obedience, initiative, and ability in organizing the masses. The Communists had begun the formal training of cadres back in the days at Yenan. This training consisted of both classroom learning and of field work whereby the student acquired a mastery of doctrine and technique and also an intimate knowledge of how the common people lived and thought. This vast army of trained workers was kept "pure" in thought and deed by periodic rectification.

THE BALANCE SHEET ON SOCIAL REFORM

Communist rule forced the pace of fundamental social transformations. One of the most significant revolutions was in family life. Under the marriage law of 1950 women gained full equality with men in marriage, divorce, and ownership of property. Communist practice encouraged children to criticize and to inform on parents for persisting in traditional ways. Through the adoption of such measures Peking hoped to eliminate intense family loyalties which competed with allegiance to the state. Another objective was the mobilization of women for productive work outside the home.

Yet in some areas the government's assault on traditional culture was something less than total. While the regime was anti-religious and desired the ultimate eradication of what it held to be superstition, campaigns against religious bodies were determined in the light of their probable political effect. Organized cults with no foreign ties, such as Taoism, were severely treated, but outward deference was shown Buddhism and Islam, which claimed many adherents in Southeast Asia and other regions where the Communists had interests. Toleration and even encouragement were also accorded the traditional concepts of political and cultural unity, some traditional etiquette and customs and much traditional art and literature.[8]

[8] While in general tradition was permitted to survive if it served the Communist state, the process of determining what remained and what did not was by no means simple. Ralph C. Crozier's *Traditional Medicine in Modern China: Science, Nationalism, and the Tensions of Cultural Change* (1968) finds that the Communists championed such traditional medical treatments as acupuncture because, in a country desperately short of medical personnel, they were anxious to provide treatment in which the people had confidence. The past also was used to bolster national feeling. "Popular" and "progressive" factors from tradition were rescued from obscurity and refurbished to demonstrate China's equality with or even superiority to the West. Yet in resurrecting the past, the Communists were careful to distinguish between those things that were relevant to the present and those that belonged solely to the past. Thus the memory of Confucius could be honored while his ideas as applied to the modern world were condemned. Joseph Levenson has likened the procedure to a vast "museum" in which artifacts might be admired without being adopted. The Chinese revolution, Levenson observes,

Indeed, there were qualifications in the entire Communist effort to reshape Chinese society. Peasants welcomed the extermination of landlords enthusiastically, but they were unhappy about the subsequent introduction of cooperatives, collectives, and heavy taxes. Industrial workers discovered small improvement in their conditions under Communism; national minorities became restive as their so-called autonomous governments lost their autonomy.

ECONOMIC DEVELOPMENT

As Marxists, Peking's leaders identified their society of the future with the world of science and technology and with the triumph of modernization over a backward peasant society. The plentiful peoples' society was to replace the rule of special privilege and poverty. Yet between this future and a meaner present loomed a perilous struggle not only against external enemies who, it was said, were determined to destroy the revolution, but also against internal barriers to progress. Thus Peking embarked upon a program of rapid modernization, emphasizing initially the building of heavy industry rather than light industry and consumer goods. Agriculture was to be reorganized and updated in support of industrialization. Furthermore, Marxist convictions encouraged the determination to direct the whole process of modernization through centralized planning, decision making, and collectivism.

Lacking both capital and personnel for the material transformation of China, Peking looked to its Communist neighbor, the Soviet Union. Early in 1950, China and the Soviet Union signed a treaty of alliance and a number of collateral economic agreements, providing for a $300 million loan, reciprocal trade, and Soviet technical assistance. Subsequent understandings expanded the amount of Soviet aid. In 1956 alone, for example, provision was made for the exchange of some 2,000 persons. Thousands of Russian technical experts were sent to

has been "against the world to join the world, against their past to keep it theirs, but past." *Confucian China and Its Modern Fate, Volume III: The Problem of Historical Significance* (1965).* See also Ralph C. Crozier, ed., *China's Cultural Legacy and Communism* (1970).*

China, while additional thousands of Chinese went to the Soviet Union for technical education and on-the-job training. Soviet loans to China were estimated to have totaled about two billion dollars for economic development and one billion for military purposes.[9] By the later 1950s, however, Sino-Soviet aid agreements were expiring, and were not renewed as tensions between these allies increased. In retrospect, while Soviet aid never approached the dimensions desired by China, its effectiveness was enhanced by careful selection of projects and by relatively efficient use of available resources. Without this assistance China's industrial goals would have been far more limited than they eventually were.

The economic system inherited by the Communists bore little resemblance to the one they hoped to build. Industrial facilities were comparatively small and localized. A major asset was the heavy industry left by the Japanese in Manchuria. Some light industries, mainly textiles, remained from foreign investment in China's coastal cities, especially in Shanghai and Tientsin. The railway system was concentrated in Manchuria, save for the trunk lines in China Proper. Agriculture differed little from that of Old China. Altogether these were limited facilities, and all had suffered the ravages of foreign and civil war.

On their takeover, the Communists gave particular attention to repair of railways, the construction of new lines, and the administration of barge traffic on the rivers still so important to Chinese transportation. Light industry revived more rapidly than heavy industry. Agriculture responded to a succession of good crop seasons. Most important, however, in the Communist economic recovery were measures to control inflation. The improvements achieved here were due to rigid restrictions on credit and to government control of prices through the release of major commodities by state trading companies. These measures were bolstered by a firm national budget and a system of national taxation enforced relentlessly. Additional government rev-

enue accrued from fines upon businessmen or confiscation of their property. By 1952 production was nearly at prewar levels. Moreover, the Communists were in command of the machinery for generating further advances. Trade, industry, and bank loans and deposits were substantially in the hands of government agencies and enterprises. Meanwhile, under the agrarian reform act of 1950, landlords were stripped of their property and land was distributed among millions of peasants. One of the consequences of this step was the establishment in the countryside and villages of a ruling peasant class which owed its new status to the Communist regime.

Upon these foundations the new industrialization of China was built. While the five-year plan announced in 1953 did not go into specifics, Peking's intent was the establishment of a heavy industrial base in many regions, including the remote and technologically primitive areas of the interior. State control over this expansion was maintained through centralized planning and the socialization of enterprise. Financing was obtained through the imposition of austere living standards which prevented the loss of surplus income through personal consumption. The peasantry was goaded into a forced pace to produce an agricultural surplus that could be converted into foreign exchange and industrial raw materials.

In some periods and areas, the accomplishments in industry were both visible and impressive. Steel production, though small, increased from 1952 to 1957 by a total of some 325 percent, while coal production increased about 200 percent. A total of 4,084 kilometers of new rail lines was constructed.[10]

[9] Hu Chang-tu *et al., China: Its People; Its Society; Its Culture* (1960), 391.

[10] While these percentage increases were impressive, total production remained extremely small for a country of China's size and population. According to official claims, between 1952 and 1957 the output of key industries rose as follows:

Steel	1.35 to 5.35 million (metric) tons
Pig iron	1.9 to 5.94 million tons
Coal	63.53 to 130 million tons
Electric power	7.26 to 19.3 billion KWH
Cement	2.86 to 6.86 million tons
Machine tools	13.7 to 28 thousand sets

The Communists also faced problems in agriculture as they attempted to shift from individual enterprise to collectivism. Beginning in 1953, the government announced that small, individualized land holdings were unsuitable for mechanized farming. Individual holdings, which averaged two-and-a-half acres after land distribution, were pooled so that productivity might be raised through increased use of machines, irrigation, and chemical fertilizers. But by 1957 the attempt to raise production and to change simultaneously the entire land tenure system produced only a widening gap between agricultural output and demand. Complicating this picture were declining Soviet aid and the loss of momentum in the expansion of industries.

The "Great Leap Forward"

Faced with these problems, Peking, late in 1957, turned to a crash program of intensive exploitation of Chinese labor. Production goals were revised upward drastically, the populace was remobilized, and the so-called "Great Leap Forward" was launched in 1958. The Communists proclaimed their intention to surpass Britain's industrial production in fifteen years. To this end agricultural productivity was to be raised through large scale irrigation projects, deep plowing, and intensive tillage. The state extensively invested in the expansion of selected heavy industries. Individuals were to work harder than ever at their regular jobs and were to assume additional productive tasks at the same time. This latter arrangement permitted established production facilities to be augmented by thousands of small scale projects utilizing available labor but requiring little investment capital. Workers in their spare time would operate "backyard furnaces" smelting scrap iron, plant tree seedlings, or build water control projects, thereby stimulating the economy through additional labor. For the individual, however, the eight-hour day proclaimed by the party in 1931 became less than a vision as the workday stretched to fourteen or more hours.

The commune, an administrative unit which in the countryside encompassed on the average 10,000 acres and 5,000 households, became an essential framework for organizing the forced pace of the Great Leap. Although the Communists had little experience with communes before their attempt to create some 26,000 of them in 1958, they were attracted to the device by the possibilities presented for completely mobilizing all available labor. In each commune, workers from 200 to 300 households were formed into a production brigade, which was shifted from job to job as need required. This was viewed as an advance over the collectives in that the latter pooled labor only for agricultural purposes. Moreover, by placing large numbers under single direction, the commune was equipped to undertake bigger projects (for example, reforestation of an entire watershed). Still other advantages were anticipated from new patterns of communal living: community mess halls would cut household labor and tighten control over food consumption; labor expended on care of the very young and old would be reduced by the establishment of nurseries and homes for the aged; and de-emphasis of the family as the primary social unit would strengthen discipline. In short, the commune provided machinery for controlling the individual's economic activity, working conditions, place of residence, and family life.

For a time this regimentation of Chinese life resulted in a fury of human activity having few parallels in history. By the end of 1958, Peking was claiming an increase of 100 percent in agricultural production. The output of iron and steel was also said to have doubled. Similar "leaps" were claimed in other key enterprises. Yet as time passed the government's production estimates were reduced, and there were other signs of forced retrenchment. Some features of the commune system, such as community mess halls and rigid direction of work brigades, were modified or abandoned. Many of the much publicized economic experiments, most notably the "backyard furnaces," were accounted failures. It seemed that the Communists had attempted too much too fast. On the credit side, the Great Leap Forward was responsible for increased momentum resulting in temporary increases in industrial production, the establishment of new plants, expansion of transportation facilities, modernization of some aspects of agriculture, and consolidation of the regime's hold on the populace. Nevertheless, many new and staggering problems were created. Beginning in 1959, China experienced a distinct economic setback as plants whose machinery had been overtaxed to the breaking point closed for repair, and as new construction was cut drastically by general disorganization. Even more serious was a breakdown in agriculture. In 1960 a drop in grain production to the levels of eight years earlier created the necessity for importing wheat from Australia, Canada, or wherever it could be obtained.

Retrenchment

To surmount these problems, Peking retreated from the more extreme features of the Great Leap Forward. Centralized planning, which had been cast aside in the fury of expansion, was re-emphasized, agricultural production was given priority, and industrial investment was reduced. Official concern for quality and variety replaced an earlier emphasis on rapid growth in output. The party acknowledged the necessity of increasing production of consumer goods and of improving market conditions. The greatest transformations, however, occurred in rural communes, where the administrative structure was altered to bring management closer to the producer. Peasants were allowed private plots to use as they wished.[11]

These retrenchments in 1961-1962 effected a partial recovery. Thereafter the regime moved cautiously in preparing for further development. On the theory that peasant energies, properly channeled, could transform China, the party looked to the "socialist education campaign" for the psychological preparations for still another economic drive. Meanwhile, pending the establishment of the proper intellectual

[11] For the impact of the Great Leap on traditional patterns in economic behavior, and the force of tradition in breaking the Great Leap, see G. William Skinner, "Marketing and Social Structure in Rural China: Part III, Rural Marketing in Communist China," *Journal of Asian Studies*, 24 (1965), 371-73; 397-99; and Kenneth R. Walker, *Planning in Chinese Agriculture: Socialization and the Private Sector, 1956-1962* (1965).

and emotional climate for that drive, the party retained many of the adjustments of the retrenchment period—the private plots, rural markets, and local direction of production. Economic progress under these circumstances was such that by 1965 party officials spoke optimistically of an upsurge that would soon lead to the announcement of a third five-year plan.

REVOLUTION IN CRISIS

These optimistic pronouncements hid for a time deep disagreements within China's leadership. Some of Mao's closest associates, including Liu Shao-ch'i and other high Communist party officials, had become disillusioned with the chairman's incessant campaigns. These critics dwelt upon the destruction and waste of the Great Leap Forward and the seemingly pervasive weariness of the people. In their view, the revolution should advance through rational planning and the application of regularized procedures. This was a position with which Mao did not concur. While Mao, too, was frustrated by the revolution's failures, his remedy was more campaigning, not less, to arouse the people and unleash their energies. He was disturbed by apparent indications that China's new leaders were becoming soft and complacent. Communist cadres, for example, were reportedly exploiting their leadership in order to obtain special privileges. Indeed, Mao professed to fear that the vitality of the entire party was in decline.

These intraparty disagreements and tensions eroded the previously unified support of major policies. Mao and his colleagues in earlier years had unanimously endorsed Soviet models as guides to China's economic transformation. Liu Shao-ch'i and his associates continued to affirm their faith in these models, advocating centralized planning, heavy industrial development, and urbanization. Mao, on the other hand, increasingly espoused the ideal of a transformed peasantry and a self-sufficient countryside where men would combine the talents of farmers, craftsmen, and militia soldiers.

These ideological conflicts within the Chinese Communist leadership paved the way for ideological and political tension between China and her Communist ally, the Soviet Union, and for competition between these two giants of Communism for position and influence in the third world countries of Asia and Africa (see Chapter 36). Apparently these developments only served to heighten Mao's determination.

THE GREAT CULTURAL REVOLUTION

Mao had looked to the "socialist education campaign" of 1962 for the cure of these ideological ills. The campaign was to have been a rectification movement which would "counter modern revisionism" and train "revolutionary heirs" by forcing party cadres and intellectuals to perform physical labor. But in practice this effort to infuse the Communist party with fresh vitality accomplished little. While party bureaucrats, wrestling with daily problems, complied formally with Mao's commands, their actual performance lacked enthusiasm. As a result, Mao, confronted by a party that would not reform itself, turned to the Red army, then under the command of his close associate Lin

Red Guards demonstrate during the Great Cultural Revolution.

Piao, and to students outside the party for support in conducting a fresh rectification campaign—the "Great Proletarian Cultural Revolution"—which soon developed to unprecedented proportions.

Beginning as a movement to heighten revolutionary fervor among intellectuals (hence the name "Cultural Revolution"), this new drive soon swept virtually all of China into a tumult of mass meetings, parades, and propaganda displays praising Mao's leadership.[12] By the summer of 1967, there was the spectacle of millions of young revolutionaries, dubbed "Red Guards," staging "anti-rightist" demonstrations, "dragging out" and humiliating alleged "power-holders in the party taking the capitalist road," wrestling authority from incumbent officials, and shattering the party and its governmental machinery in many provinces. This pandemonium was a reflection not only of bitter conflict in the top leadership (Mao versus Liu) but also of conflict and resulting confusion in lower ranks of party officialdom, the bureaucracy, and the general populace. In the end (the movement ran roughly from May, 1966, to April, 1969), Mao, whose victory stemmed from control of the communications media and the Red Guards, and from the logistical support of the Red army, could boast of a thoroughly purged party and bureaucracy. But the party, suffering from public abuse of its leaders (Mao's friends and foes alike), from rapid turnover among its members, and from a consequent failure of normal operations, was displaced, temporarily at least, from a key leadership role. When a semblance of order was restored, Lin Piao's designation as China's second in command meant the emergence of the army as a

[12] Earlier rectification campaigns had been controlled by subjecting critics at every level to the control of senior party officials. In 1966 Mao not only insisted that youths be permitted to detect "rightists," but also that the usual restraints be abandoned.

The opening rounds of the "Cultural Revolution" are detailed in two articles by Stephen Uhalley, Jr.: "The Wu Han Discussion: Act One in a New Rectification Campaign," *China Mainland Review*, I (1966), 24-38; and "The Cultural Revolution and the Attack on the 'Three Family Village,' " *China Quarterly* No. 27 (1966), 149-61. Franklin W. Houn, *A Short History of Chinese Communism* (rev. ed., 1973),* Chapter 7, views the "Cultural Revolution" against the background of party rectification.

controlling element. Peking proclaimed that Lin was more "Red" than "expert"—which in Maoist terms was accounted an advantage.

RETURN TO MATERIALIST OBJECTIVES

Mao's Cultural Revolution took a heavy toll in production and in human resources. For nearly three years schools were closed, transportation disrupted, and factories fell far behind schedule. Disorders also reached into the countryside but, in general, agricultural output was not cut as seriously as manufacturing. Peking's official view was that these costs were not too high for a revitalized revolutionary leadership and party.

By early 1969, as the Cultural Revolution appeared to have served its political purposes, China's domestic programs began to show a fresh concern for the material bases of the revolution. Schools were reopened, though at first educational authorities stressed politics rather than academics; university admissions were determined more by political than by intellectual fitness. To enter a collegiate program, a candidate was expected to present credentials showing not only successful completion of two years in middle schools but also a nomination by a production brigade. Moreover, students were required upon completion of their schooling to find work in the countryside; few were permitted to enter white collar professions in the cities. Some of these more extreme legacies of the Cultural Revolution faded in time, but they did not disappear. In 1974 school teachers were still criticized for stressing subject matter at the expense of ideology. On the other hand, university admissions were tied to entrance examinations, graduation was determined by success in course work, and the policy of requiring graduates to move into rural communities appeared to be forgotten. Other retreats from the Cultural Revolution were evident in the revival of economic planning, the rehabilitation and reappointment of purged party and government officials, and a decided lessening of the Red army's direction of civil affairs.

Chou En-lai an indefatigable worker, a gifted administrator, and the new second-in-command, was generally credited with having guided China toward these new policies. By 1974 Lin Piao was dead, reportedly as the result of a plane crash in Mongolia. His memory was publicly vilified. According to official accounts, Lin had betrayed the revolution, using his high position to plot against Mao. His "schemes" had been discovered and his death occurred as he fled toward safety in the Soviet Union. These charges suggested that the wounds suffered by China's once-unified leadership had not healed. Nevertheless, the authority of the central government, which had been challenged during the Cultural Revolution, had been reestablished. Peking was again directing basic social and economic change. Furthermore, Chou's position as Mao's chief deputy enabled him, 1972-1974, to direct a foreign policy that broadened China's official contacts with the United States and Western Europe.

ASPECTS OF CONTEMPORARY CHINA

In the early 1970s, Communist China stood in marked contrast to both Old Confucian China and to the China of Chiang Kai-shek. The Communists had established a new, totalitarian society reaching from Peking to the remotest village, an economy mobilized for purposes of national power, and a social order motivated by Communist ideology. No longer the helpless state of the later years of the Manchus, China had become a world power.

Yet if Communist leadership was vital in this Chinese transformation, it must be remembered that the Chinese revolution was not a Communist creation. Many of the most fundamental innovations of which Peking boasted did not originate with the Communist leadership. The Communists were by no means the first to seek the development of modern industry or the establishment of modern governmental institutions. Nor did they introduce such concepts as nationalism or patriotism to China. Rather, in fostering the adoption of modern institutions and values, the Chinese Communists, while going further than any of their predecessors, capitalized on changes set in motion by a century of Western impact on China. Moreover, when viewed in the light of China's long history, even the most modern aspects of the

Communist state might be seen as containing some echoes of the past. While no government of Old China operated with the power or effectiveness of the contemporary regime, Communist China had inherited a political tradition dominated by concepts of authoritarianism, centralization of government, and control of the populace. The Communist emphasis on remolding the masses was reminiscent of the Confucian and neo-Confucian stress on ideological orthodoxy, conformity, and thought control. The individual, the creature of the state, was traditionally subordinated in China to the family and to other social groups. Contemporary China, while presenting a new face to the world, remained linked with its history. This is not to say that the Communist state was simply a Confucian state in modern dress or an Eastern copy of other Communist regimes. On the contrary, emerging China appeared to be taking shape as a distinctive nation, drawing its inspiration from many sources, old and new, Eastern and Western.[13]

[13] Scholars have employed various metaphors in efforts to picture the transformation of China and its emergence under Mao's leadership. John K. Fairbank has written of change and continuity. He notes that both the *Kuomintang* and the Communists have echoed the past in their efforts to train a new type of scholar-bureaucrat in a new ideology in order to revive the functions once performed by the Confucian literati and the classics. The Communists have sought a balanced economy basically managed by the state, and they have advanced an ideological orthodoxy which guides all forms of human activity. Yet, if the revolution has not lost touch with Old China's great traditions, these legacies have become "curiously intertwined with new motifs." Maoist doctrine "believes in progress toward a future millennium, not a cyclical repetition descending from a golden age. Dynastic absolutism has been replaced by party dictatorship .... Government used to be thinly spread out and superficial and the peasant passive, a sub-political animal. Today the government penetrates every hut, and peasants are people unless they misbehave." *The United States and China* (3rd rev. ed., 1971),* 403-06. Benjamin Schwartz has likened the revolution to the transformation of a complex chemical compound. The new compound contains many elements from the old one but is nothing at all like the one from which it was derived. See Schwartz's essays: "A Brief Defense of Political and Intellectual History ... with Particular Reference to Non-Western Culture," *Daedalus,* 100 (1971), 98-112; and "Limits of Tradition versus Moderates as Categories of Explanation: The Case of the Chinese Intellectuals," *ibid.,* 101 (1972), 71-88. For more specialized insights focusing on the debts of contemporary nationalism to Old China's cultural

In any event, China under Mao is the latest phase of a Chinese revolution that had its beginnings more than one hundred years ago. Fantastic as it may be, the fact is that for most of that period this revolution was all but ignored by the Western democratic world. When belatedly the concept of a new, revolutionary China finally became acceptable in the West, it was on the very questionable assumption that this new China would be a free and democratic society. When, therefore, China turned to extreme totalitarianism, it was often said, particularly in the United States, that Mao's China was merely a passing phase. It was tempting to impute to the Chinese a widespread desire to overthrow a regime that was very unpopular in the United States. But most Chinese, with little or no exposure to democracy, were unlikely to be concerned about—or indeed aware of—their lack of democratic freedom.[14]

traditions as well as to the activities of the *Kuomintang* as ruling party, see Joseph R. Levenson, "The Past and Future of Nationalism in China," *Survey,* No. 67 (1968), 28-40; and Chalmers Johnson, "The Changing Nature and Locus of Authority in Communist China," in *China,* Lindbeck, ed. 34-76.

[14] In recent years, particularly since the People's Republic demonstrated its survival beyond the Cultural Revolution, China-watchers have been more preoccupied with questions pertaining to the soundness of Mao's revolutionary program than with those relating to whether the regime will survive. The answers given to these more recent concerns, like those offered to earlier ones, reflect sharply conflicting assumptions. Stanley Karnow's *Mao and China: From Revolution to Revolution* (1972) views Mao as a deeply frustrated visionary in "collision" with his own country. Mao's problems stem from his opposition to the imperatives of "administrative routine" and "technical specialization." Mao, the poet of revolution, cannot adjust to the "prose of stable administration." Thus the Cultural Revolution was rooted in Mao's obsessive urge to launch still another revolution—an old man's last leap toward utopia. Other writers reject the view that the Cultural Revolution was merely unorganized enthusiasm substituting for rational planning. For example, Franz Schurman's "The Attack of the Cultural Revolution on Ideology and Organization," in *China in Crisis: China's Heritage and the Communist Political System,* Ping-ti Ho and Tang Tsou, eds. (1968),* 525-64, accepts the Maoist view that the Communist elite had become conservative and was subverting the revolution. Accordingly, temporary reverses stemming from disorder, suspension of schooling, and disruption of production were imperative if the revolution were to survive. The essays in Bruce Douglass and Ross Terrill, eds., *China and Ourselves: Explorations and Revisions by a New Generation* (1970),* suggest that the views of foreign observers

It was also evident that the Communists were the captives of China as well as its masters. The Communist regime had said and promised many things, only to see events belie its words. To be sure, some promises materialized, but China has not become the often-promised utopia. The basic facts of Chinese life could not be wished away: a Chinese populace still largely without education for a complex industrial society and an industrial base smaller in 1949 than the Russian base of 1917. The glaring miscalculations by the Communists on the Great Leap Forward certainly compounded the problem. Finally, the most important limiting factor was the pressure of population on available resources. The first five-year plan assumed a population of about 480 million, but the census of 1953 revealed a total of some 580 million. In subsequent years the Communists faced a population growing at a rate of 2 percent annually, which meant that there were some 732 million Chinese in 1970; if continued, this growth rate would place China's population at a billion in 1980. This rapid population increase created food shortages, aroused popular unrest, and slowed industrialization beyond all expectation. While the grain imports and renewed emphasis on food production mentioned earlier helped remove the sense of impending crisis, these measures failed to solve basic problems since growing production barely kept pace with minimum consumer needs. As in the past, production might prove adequate to permit further development of China's national power but inadequate to give substance to the promise of a better life for her millions.

FOR FURTHER READING

Government.   Joseph B. R. Whitney, *China: Area, Administration, and Nation Building* (1970), the problems of transforming China from a predominantly cultural entity to a

political entity in the twentieth century. Richard H. Solomon, *Mao's Revolution and the Chinese Political Culture* (1971).* Frank H. Trager and William Henderson, eds., *Communist China, 1949-1969: A Twenty Year Appraisal* (1970), an uneven collection of fourteen essays. Among translations of Communist documents are John Lewis, ed., *Major Doctrines of Communist China* (1964);* Center for International Affairs and the East Asian Research Center, Harvard University, *Communist China, 1955-1959: Policy Documents with Analysis* (1962);* Theodore H. E. Chen, *The Chinese Communist Regime: Documents and Commentary* (1967).* Peter S. H. Tang, *China Today: Domestic and Foreign Policies* (2nd. rev. ed., 1961) is an exhaustive description of the first decade. See also A. Doak Barnett, *Communist China: The Early Years, 1949-1955* (1964);* Robert A. Scalapino, *Elites in the People's Republic of China* (1972).* John W. Lewis, *Leadership in Communist China* (1963) is a brilliant study of politics before the "Cultural Revolution." John Wilson Lewis, ed., *Party Leadership and Revolutionary Power in China* (1970). Ezra Vogel, *Canton Under Communism (Programs and Politics in a Provincial Capital, 1949-1969)* (1969),* the first extended study of local government under communism. John W. Lewis, ed., *The City in Communist China* (1971). For insights into the army and its political role, see Samuel B. Griffith, *The Chinese People's Liberation Army* (1967); John Gittings, *The Role of the Chinese Army* (1967); Ying-Mao, et al., *The Political Work System of the Chinese Communist Military* (1971); and William Whitson, *Military in China in the Nineteen Seventies: Organization, Leadership, Political Strategy* (1972).

Economic Development.   Rhoads Murphey, "Man and Nature in China," *Modern Asian Studies,* 1 (1967), 313-33, emphasizes the intellectual underpinnings of the drive to industrialize China. Theodore Shabad, *China's Changing Map: A Political and Economic Geography of the Chinese People's Republic* (1956),* a reference work. On the early years

---

may be influenced by changes in their own environment as well as by change in China. These are essays by a new generation of China specialists who, unlike so many of their older colleagues, accept the reality of the People's Republic and are not surprised that it came into being.

of economic transformation, see Li Choh-ming, *Economic Development of Communist China: An Appraisal of the First Five Years of Industrialization* (1959); T. J. Hughes and D. E. T. Luard, *Economic Development of Communist China, 1949-1960* (2nd rev. ed., 1962). Katharine Huang Hsiao, *Money and Monetary Policy in Communist China* (1971), deals with the essential role of money in a planned economy. Chen Chi-yi, *La Reforme Agraire en Chine Populaire* (1964). Kang Chao, *Agricultural Production in Communist China, 1949-1965* (1971). Two sophisticated studies of food production having anti-collectivization biases are John L. Buck, Owen L. Dawson, and Yuan-li Wu, *Food and Agriculture in Communist China* (1966); and Owen L. Dawson, *Communist China's Agriculture: Its Development and Future Potential* (1970). Alexander Eckstein, *The National Income of Communist China* (1962); and Liu Tachung and Yeh Kung-chia, *The Economy of the Chinese Mainland: National Income and Economic Development, 1933-1959* (1965) develop base lines against which development may be measured. See also Alexander Eckstein, "Sino-Soviet Economic Relations: A Reappraisal," in *The Economic Development of China and Japan,* C. D. Cowan ed. (1964).

Intellectual and Social Life. Aspects of intellectual developments are presented in Mu Fusheng, *The Wilting of the Hundred Flowers: The Chinese Intelligentsia under Mao* (1963); Franklin Houn, *To Change a Nation: Propaganda and Indoctrination in Communist China* (1961); Albert Feuerwerker, ed., *History in Communist China* (1968)*; Stephen Uhalley, Jr., "The Controversy over Li Hsiu-ch'eng: An Ill-timed Centenary," *Journal of Asian Studies* 25 (1966), 305-17; Merle Goldman, *Literary Dissent in Communist China* (1967).* See also Cyril Birch, ed., *Chinese Communist Literature* (1963); and Sidney H. Gould, *Science in Communist China* (1961). A sympathetic report is William Hinton, *Fanshen: A Documentary of Revolution in a Chinese Village* (1966).* William T. Liu, *Chinese Society under Communism* (1967)* reveals patterns of control. The revolution's impact on family life is treated in Yang Ch'ing-k'un, *A Chinese Village in Early*

Communist Transition (1959). Two important studies pointing to the persistence of traditional legal practices in a revolutionary society are Stanley Lubman, "Mao and Mediation: Politics and Dispute Resolution in Communist China," *California Law Review* 55 (1967), 1284-1359; and Jerome A. Cohen, *The Criminal Process in the People's Republic of China, 1949-1963* (1968).

Holmes Welch, *The Practice of Buddhism, 1900-1950* (1967); *The Buddhist Revival in China* (1968); and *Buddhism under Mao* (1972), three important studies on Buddhism in modern China. Richard C. Bush, *Religion in Communist China* (1970). Francis P. Jones, *The Church in Communist China: A Protestant Appraisal* (1962). Wingtsit Chan, *Religious Trends in Modern China* (1953).

Ideology. Franz Schurman, *Ideology and Organization in Communist China* (1966),* the best discussion of the nature and causes of China's unique patterns. James Chieh Hsiung, *Ideology and Practice: The Evolution of Chinese Communism* (1970),* views communist ideology as a modern substitute for the Confucian *li*. Benjamin I. Schwartz, *Communism and China: Ideology in Flux* (1968),* broadly-ranging essays. Stuart Schram, *The Political Thought of Mao Tse-tung* (rev. ed., 1969)*; Arthur A. Cohen, *The Communism of Mao Tse-tung* (1964)*; and "What is Maoism: A Symposium," *Problems of Communism* 15 (1966), 1-30. Rhoads Murphey, "City and Countryside as Ideological Issues: India and China," *Comparative Studies in Society and History* 14 (1972), 250-67.

Biography. Donald W. Klein and Anne B. Clark, *Biographical Dictionary of Chinese Communism, 1921-1965* (2 vols., 1971). For differing perspectives on Mao Tse-tung, see Stuart Schram, *Mao Tse-tung* (rev. ed., 1967)*; Jerome Chen, *Mao and the Chinese Revolution* (1965)*; and Han Suyin, *Morning Deluge: Mao Tse-tung and the Chinese Revolution, 1893-1954* (1972). Edward E. Rice, *Mao's Way* (1972). Li Tien-min, *Chou En-lai* (1970); and Hsu Kai-yu, *Chou En-lai: China's Gray Eminence* (1968),* are biographies by writers who began as collaborators but broke when they reached quite different conclusions with regard to Chou. Martin Ebon, *Lin Piao* (1970).

Cultural Revolution. Robert S. Elegant, *Mao's Great Revolution* (1971), able journalism. Thomas W. Robinson, ed., *The Cultural Revolution in China* (1971), essays by researchers associated with the Rand Corporation. Wen-shun Chi, ed., *Readings in the Chinese Communist Cultural Revolution* (1971). James R. Townsend, "Intraparty Conflict in China: Disintegration in an Established One-Party System," in *Authoritarian Politics in Modern Society,* Samuel P. Huntington and Clement H. Moore, eds., (1970). Thomas W. Robinson, "The Wuhan Incident: Local Strife and Provincial Rebellion during the Cultural Revolution," *China Quarterly* (1971), 413-38.

Recent Developments. Allan B. Cole and Peter C. Oleson, comps., *Fifty Years of Chinese Communism: Selected Readings with Commentary,* Publication No. 47, Service Center for Teachers of History: The American Historical Association (1970) serves both as a guide to further reading and an interpretation of Chinese Communist history. Study of the current scene may be pursued in excellent periodicals: *Pacific Affairs; Asian Survey; China Quarterly; Far Eastern Economic Survey; Journal of Asian Studies;* and *Bulletin of Concerned Asian Scholars.* See also annual volumes of collected essays published by the Union Research Institute under the title, *Communist China.*

New Economic Giant
in Asia:
Japan,
1952 and After

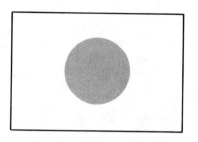

33

With the ending of the American occupation in 1952, Japan contended with problems as complex as any in her modern history. She was faced with making the transition from a defeated, humiliated, and occupied state to a sovereign nation responsible for her own destiny. Her immediate tasks included maintaining a stable and prosperous economy in islands poor in natural resources, and strengthening the infant democratic political and social order brought to the islands by the occupation. Moreover, by virtue of her location on the periphery of the Communist world and her treaty obligations to the United States, Japan was involved immediately in tense international questions. In fact, the post-occupation years were to be filled with the pressures, domestic and foreign, that had been remolding Japanese life for a century. But what was to be the impact of these pressures on the occupation's reforms? Would democratic institutions survive, or would there be a return to authoritarianism? How durable was an alliance that denied the Japanese their age-old links with the China mainland? Was Japan capable of support-

ing an expanding population without resort to another drive for empire?[1]

Economic rebuilding was a fundamental task in a land described by Joseph M. Dodge, MacArthur's financial adviser, as having "too many people, too little land, and too few natural resources." While Japanese cities were still scarred by war, the country as a whole suffered less from actual fighting than from the loss of 311,514 square kilometers (46 percent) of its prewar territory. No longer did Japan have direct control of the mineral and agricultural resources of Korea and Manchuria, the sugar and rice of Taiwan, or the pulp of Sakhalin. Nor could her fishing fleets exploit the waters of Korea and the Kuriles and other regions of the northern Pacific. Obviously, the problem of supporting an expanding population on this reduced economic base was an immediate and

[1] Two brief but basic studies of Japanese development since 1952 are in Edwin O. Reischauer *Japan: The Story of a Nation* (1970),* 242-340; and John K. Fairbank, E. O. Reischauer, and Albert M. Craig, *East Asia: Tradition and Transformation* (1973), 824-54.

pressing concern. The return of some 6 million Japanese from the colonies, and a high birth rate boosted Japan from a nation of 72 million in 1945 to one of 90 million a decade later. Furthermore, there was the problem of rebuilding foreign markets to provide exchange for the imports Japan must have to survive. Some of Japan's former customers, especially in Southeast Asia, remembering the tragedies of World War II, traded elsewhere. Even worse was the disappearance of Japan's most numerous customers, the Chinese and North Koreans, behind the Bamboo Curtain. Altogether these manifold problems imperiled the economic recovery that had begun in the later years of the occupation.

Yet the economic outlook was not hopeless. Japan retained the skills and energies which had made her a major competitor for international markets. In the context of the cold war her human resources assumed a new importance in the struggle for control of the Western Pacific and Southeast Asia. Japan became a major supplier of industrial goods and services for United States forces in this area. American expenditures, first for direct aid and later for special procurement, reached about $800 million a year in 1952-1953 and continued at better than $500 million annually through 1957. These expenditures provided a powerful stimulus to economic development, enabling Japan to balance her payments and build a surplus in foreign exchange even though imports were generally larger than exports during these years. Furthermore, through the negotiation of technical assistance contracts, Japanese industrialists imported technology and capital from the West, especially the United States, in a wide range of concerns from shipbuilding to electronics. With this help, Japanese enterprise invaded new fields of activity, thus compensating for time lost during the war.

MAKING AN ECONOMIC MIRACLE

The forecasts of gloom that described Japan's economic future during the occupation years were all but forgotten in the two decades which followed. Just prior to the end of the occupation, Japan's gross national product was pegged at $15.1 billion; it leaped to $51.9 billion in 1962 and to $290 billion in 1972. In annual per capita income, these figures translated into a phenomenal increase from $146 in 1951 to $2,000 in 1972. Japanese government projections estimated per capita income at $8,000 by 1980. What these figures reveal is that Japan, overcoming the destruction and dislocations of war, entered an era of intense development which, by the late 1960s, had boosted her to third place (behind the United States and Soviet Union) among the world's industrial powers and had made her Asia's undisputed industrial leader. By the early 1970s, Japan produced more than half of the electrical energy generated in all of Asia, excluding Soviet Siberia. Ranked against all nations, Japan was fifth in production of crude steel and fourth in production of cement. She led the world in the building of merchant shipping, and her automobiles, television sets, cameras, and other sophisticated goods were major competitors in world markets. Moreover, by 1970, the end of this development was not in sight. Japan's economy had gained such momentum that the nation's appearance as a so-called "superpower" by the late 1970s or early 1980s was widely predicted.[2]

While Japan's postwar economy was a notable example of the so-called private enterprise system, it should be observed that it enjoyed very substantial favors from government. Just as in the days of Meiji Japan, there was a remarkably close partnership between private business and government; indeed, foreign business competitors often referred to "Japan, Inc." The success of the system was due to private initiative plus government benevolence. Rapid business expansion was fostered by favorable government policies. National fiscal programs encouraged a high rate of capital investment, while private firms received further

[2] Note, for example, the statement by Herman Kahn: "It is now almost inevitable that at some point in the 70's or early 80's the Japanese economy will attain a level entitling it to such descriptions as 'giant' or 'super.' " *The Emerging Japanese Superstate: Challenge and Response* (1970),* 87.

stimulus from rapid depreciation allowances, cheap loans, subsidies, and light taxation. Government agencies assisted with economic planning that identified growth industries in need of special assistance, helped management in estimating market potentials, and enabled individual firms to set realistic production goals. Technological development leading to increased productivity was also subsidized. A virtual monopoly of lucrative home markets was guaranteed to Japanese producers by tariffs and legislation sharply limiting foreign investment in Japan.[3] Beyond these skillfully conceived programs of national assistance, economic growth was fostered by an unusual combination of favorable developments. Agricultural advances enabled Japan to achieve self-sufficiency in rice, though not in most other crops. And confidence in Japan's future was encouraged by success in limiting population expansion; projections indicated a leveling off at about 120 million by the end of the century.

Since much of Japan's industrial plant had been destroyed by war, her new factories employed the latest technology and were, therefore, the world's most efficient. At a time, too, when the United States and Soviet Union were allocating upwards of ten percent of their gross national products for national defense, Japan, prohibited by her new constitution from rebuilding military forces, could devote virtually all her resources to growth-producing industries.

For a nation poor in natural resources, the postwar liberalization of world trade policies also proved a boon of the greatest importance. In contrast to the earlier days when Japan's empire builders dreamed of national self-sufficiency, the Japanese in the 1960s became important figures in the international market. Japan's imports grew from $974 million in 1950 to over $18 billion in 1971. Three-quarters of these imports consisted of industrial raw materials—ores, coking coal, steel scrap, rubber, cotton, wool, and lumber. Trade bills were discharged by exports, which in the years 1950-1970 rose from $820 million to $25 billion.

RISING LIVING STANDARDS

For the Japanese people this economic boom produced an impressive rise in living standards. The traditional staples of diet were expanded to include dairy products and meat. There was an abundance of clothes for all seasons. The demand for housing created a backlog which the building trades, though erecting new structures at a furious pace, seemed unable to reduce. The nation's inadequate system of roads was crowded with motorized vehicles—buses, trucks, taxis, private cars, and motorized scooters.

In the late 1950s, a home equipped with a television, a refrigerator, and a washing machine signified a family's new prosperity. Within the space of five years the symbols had become an automobile, a color television, and a room air conditioner. By the early 1970s, the "foreign visit" was the popular goal, the symbol of prestige. Indeed, so many Japanese were traveling abroad on business and pleasure that the Honolulu Chamber of Commerce counted 13,000 visiting Oahu in a single week in 1972; and in Rome, guide books were being printed in Japanese as well as English. This is not to suggest that Japan had become an economic paradise; slums, malnutrition, and sweatshops remained in the picture. Nevertheless, she had become the richest country in Asia once again, and her people were sharing in this prosperity to a degree unparalleled in their history.

SOCIAL CHANGE

The American occupation had laid the foundations of a social revolution designed to uphold democractic political institutions. At the upper levels, the power of the hereditary aristocracy and military elites had been broken and traditional business leadership had been shaken seri-

[3] See Robert B. Hall, Jr., *Japan: Industrial Power of Asia* (1963),* 54-70. By the late 1960s, as the Japanese economy was soundly established, Tokyo came under heavy foreign pressure to liberalize its policies. The issue was particularly acute in American-Japanese relations, and led to negotiations in which Americans were granted some concessions. See Leon Hollerman, *Japan's Dependence on the World Economy: The Approach toward Economic Liberalization* (1967).

ously. At lower levels, the occupation by inculcating democratic values, had sought to expand individual opportunity and to build safeguards against a return of authoritarian government. These reforms stimulated the appearance of an evolving society which, while not breaking completely with its past, was new and distinctive both in structure and outlook. It was Japan's own economic boom, however, rather than the occupation, which forced the pace of social change.

The lure of new industrial jobs became a major force eroding the older social bases of society. In 1950, farm households, where authoritarian traditions had continued to prevail, numbered 6.18 million, and farm families constituted about half of the total population. Twenty years later the number of farm households had dropped to 5.34 million, while the farm-based populace comprised only twenty percent of the total. Picturesque villages which had appeared immune to change withered as young people deserted traditional occupations and manners in the search for new lives in the cities. In many places old villages simply were swallowed by advancing city limits. Some portions of the main Japanese islands, excepting Hokkaido, took on the character of a sprawling megalopolis. Even those villages that escaped such transformation lost their old isolation and were tied in various ways to nearby cities by improved highways and rapid transit systems.

Among the most important social changes was the appearance of a new and enlarged middle class. Some middle-class recruits came from the old aristocracy whose wealth and position had been destroyed by the war, inflation, and the occupation's reforms. Far more numerous, however, were additions from the humbler social orders. In the cities, enlarged opportunities in business and government awaited individuals, irrespective of social origins. In the countryside, upward social mobility was the product of land reform, technological improvement, and unprecedented prosperity. Meanwhile, as the middle class expanded, the lesser social groupings shrank to a point where they constituted a smaller proportion of the populace than before the war.

The tendency toward economic leveling also contributed to a striking transformation in popular attitudes toward authority. While the Japanese remained conscious of class distinctions, the old practices and manners associated with a traditional, elitist society were eroding. Marked displays of deference shown by inferiors to superiors before the war tended to diminish. As family controls were relaxed, the younger generations spoke with a louder voice in the choice of their schooling, their vocations, and their marriage partners. Women showed an increased self-confidence, assertiveness, and independence, not only in feminine fashions but also in politics.[4] Far less formality characterized social contacts and personal relationships. Everyday behavior in personal contacts suggested less of status and more of equality. This new spirit was not as yet dominant, but its further development, backed by new legal codes and strengthened by social fluidity, appeared likely.[5]

[4] A sampling of voter behavior in 1963 suggests the extent of the transformation wrought by the removal of the sex barrier to political participation. The sample revealed that levels of education and income were more important than sex in determining an individual's participation in political processes. In general, Japanese in the lower ranks of education and income, irrespective of sex, participated less than did those in the higher ranks. See Alice and Yasumasa Kuroda, "Aspects of Community Political Participation in Japan: Sex, Education, and Generation in the Process of Political Socialization," *Journal of Asian Studies,* 27 (1968), 229-51.

[5] The interplay of traditional and modern behavior in contemporary Japanese life is revealed in patterns among corporate executives. A college graduate typically enters a firm as a staff member immediately after graduation. He works toward appointment as a deputy section manager in seven to ten years and as section manager in an additional four to six years. This latter position represents a major achievement for, in addition to having ten to twenty subordinates, the young executive acquires social prestige. Only about two out of ten section managers will continue to rise further along the promotion ladder. Thus life is extremely competitive. Section managers work hard and socialize with superiors late into the night, sacrificing family life. Yet once a man joins a firm he rarely leaves it, since frequent job changes are regarded as evidence of undependability. Companies in turn seldom fire an employee unless he performs disgrace-

Striking too were shifts in Japanese attitudes toward the nation and nationalism. The post-occupation years were marked by a gradual revival of national pride. After 1945 and until well into the 1960s the Japanese flag was rarely flown. By degrees, however, as the more searing memories of defeat faded and were replaced by a growing awareness of Japan's new role in world affairs, there were signs of new self-confidence. The press expressed unabashed pride in the accolades the nation received for its staging of the 1964 Tokyo Olympics and the 1970 Osaka Exposition. Yet nationalism in its extreme forms was no longer a beloved emotion. Very few Japanese displayed any interest in new political overseas adventures and, when proposals were advanced to amend the constitution to provide a legal basis for rearmament, there was strong opposition.

A rejection of political authoritarianism was revealed in the treatment accorded the emperor, formerly the divine personification of the nation before whom all bowed. In his altered

fully. The ambitious young executive conforms to the seniority system, whereby a junior officer seldom gets more money than his senior regardless of capability. Senior officers not infrequently counsel subordinates in business and personal matters. In consequence, the subordinate develops an obedient, filial relationship with his boss and works hard as a member of a "family" team. The Japanese firm values group spirit more than individual capability or willingness to take responsibility. Such industrial practices reflect the persistence of traditions and attitudes, particularly those of feudal Japan when loyalty and benevolence, duty and respect for authority were social moralities; when lords assured the securities of life in return for the loyalty of vassals. For a case study see John E. Thayer, III, "Tokugawa vs. Madison Avenue: Age-old Traditions Behind East-West Conflicts in a Modern Tokyo Advertising Agency," *Papers on Japan,* published by the East Asian Research Center, Harvard University (1967), 215-27. Other aspects of changing social attitudes are treated in two articles by George DeVos and Hioshi Wagatsuma: "Value Attitudes toward Role Behavior in Two Japanese Villages," *American Anthropologist,* 63 (1961), 1204-30; and "Attitudes toward Arranged Marriage in Rural Japan," *Human Organization,* 21 (1962), 187-200; and Ezra F. Vogel's "The Democratization of Family Relations in Japanese Urban Society," *Asian Survey* 1 (1961), 18-24. See also Marius B. Jansen, ed., *Changing Japanese Attitudes toward Modernization* (1965).*

status as the "symbol of the State and of the unity of the people," the emperor, whose popularity was attested by crowds greeting his public appearances, continued to be a powerful focus of political loyalties, but no longer did he receive homage as an awesome symbol of authority. Rather he became popular as the human, democratized figure whose personal life was detailed in the press and whose son, the crown prince, took a commoner for his wife.

These changed attitudes in national matters suggested to many Japanese that the nation had lost direction and that it had been cut loose from traditions which had offered guidance and direction. In an apparent effort to fill the void, Marxism, largely suppressed since its initial appearance in Japan in the 1920s, was seized upon by many intellectuals as an alternative to the discredited philosophy of military socialism. Communists and socialists in the press, on university faculties, and in the powerful teachers' union voiced a Marxian theme oddly at variance with Japan's actual political and economic experience. While profits and wages rose to unprecedented heights, Japanese in many walks of life spoke glibly of the collapse of capitalism. It became fashionable to ascribe war and international tension to "capitalist imperialism." Nevertheless, Japanese in general showed more enthusiasm for close relations with the United States and Western Europe than with the Soviet Union.

These tokens of intellectual unrest, along with sensational press reports on crime and violence, were often interpreted as signs of crisis. The press expressed concern over a high suicide rate among teenagers. Radical students, organized under a national federation, the *Zengakuren,* staged protest meetings, rallies, and demonstrations, which overflowed into the streets where demonstrators clashed with police. These protests stressed Marxist critiques of Japan's government, decried the continuing influence of the United States in Japanese life, and pictured the Japanese as victims of an oppressive social order. In 1970, the popular novelist and opponent of Marxism, Mishima Yukio, created a national sensation by his dramatically staged suicide. Through death, Mishima sought to call attention to the sterility of a society whose rich abundance was devoid of meaning.

Japan's returning self-confidence countered this discontent, reducing its popular base. In the 1960s, the suicide rate declined, and radical student groups lost much of their earlier appeal. Marxist orthodoxies were diluted as intellectuals showed a fresh receptivity to a variety of political and social ideas. Indeed, the Japanese mind, which had suffered from isolation during the era of militarism, was intent on joining the larger world. The works of European artists and writers proved especially influential among creative Japanese. American scholarship in the humanities and the social sciences became a model for young Japanese scholars. In turn, the Japanese derived deep satisfaction from the international recognition achieved by their own films, paintings, and sculpture. The writings of their contemporary authors reached a Western audience through translation; and Yasunari Kawabata, author of *The Sound of the Mountain*, received a Nobel Prize for literature in 1968.

The foregoing developments suggest that Japanese political and social thought was far less unified than before World War II. Not surprisingly, the younger generations accepted new attitudes more readily than their parents. Sharp differences among political parties and their followings accentuated ideological diversity. Even the newer attitudes were in constant flux. Increased contact with other nations not only contributed to the decline of Marxist dogma, but also lessened preoccupation with American influence. Thus attitudes that were strong during the first post-occupation decade were by no means constant in subsequent years.

But egalitarian tendencies made slow headway among rural inhabitants and the less educated city dwellers. Among some Japanese old attitudes on authority remained intact; and segments of the population retained the conviction that politics was a matter for leaders rather than a concern of the average citizen.

GOVERNMENT AND POLITICS

Although the Japanese political system underwent extensive reform during the occupation, politics retained a remarkable continuity from prewar days. If the military elite, uprooted and discredited, no longer was an important pressure group, government continued to be dominated by the bureaucracy and big business. The bureaucracy gained new power because of its near monopoly of expert opinion on the complex problems of modern government. The Diet and cabinet, ill-equipped to deal with these problems, were dependent on bureaucrats in making policy decisions and in formulating legislation. The same voice was also heard from bureaucrats who, upon retirement, filled elective offices. With few exceptions, Japanese cabinets after 1945 were headed by former bureaucrats; ex-bureaucrats also took many other cabinet posts and were heavily represented in the Diet. Also close, but less well defined, were the ties linking government and the highly integrated management of Japan's larger business firms, a revived *zaibatsu*. Big business became the principal source of funds for conservative parties, while party and business leaders maintained the closest cooperation.[6] Against these power combinations, other pressure groups, such as organized labor, were relatively ineffective.

Japan's postwar political parties were rooted in the past. The *Seiyukai* and *Minseito*, the two major prewar parties, reemerged after 1945 to dominate party politics as the Liberals (*Jiyuto*) and the Progressives (*Shimpoto*, reorganized in 1947 as the Democratic party or *Minshuto*). In resuming operations these parties retained much of their old leadership, cultivated their established constituencies in rural Japan, and were financed largely by business contributions. Left wing groups, Socialists and Communists, similarly could trace their origins to prewar parties having the support of intellectuals and urban workers.

Moreover, these postwar parties like their predecessors, were riddled by factionalism. The Liberal-Democratic party (*Jiyu-Minshuto*),

[6] See Chitoshi Yanaga, *Big Business in Japanese Politics* (1968),* Yamamura Kozo, "Zaibatsu, Prewar and *Zaibatsu,* Postwar," *Journal of Asian Studies,* 23 (1964), 539-54, rejects "*zaibatsu*" as an appropriate label for postwar industrial combinations.

Faces of Contemporary Japan

The industrial and urban Japan of today bears little outward resemblance to the traditional society. Customers shop in department stores that can scarcely be distinguished from those in the West; women increasingly have assumed responsibilities outside the home; agriculture has been supplanted by manufacturing; and standardized mass housing projects dot a landscape once renowned for its natural beauty.

which had been formed by a merger in 1955, was divided during the early months of Ikeda Hayato's leadership into no less than eight factions holding seats in the House of Representatives. On the left, repeated atttempts at a "united front" failed to effect a lasting union of Socialists and Communists. Meanwhile Socialist strength was dissipated by party feuds which led successively to the shearing off of splinter groups in 1948; a party split into right and left wing groups, 1950-1955; party reunification; and another split in 1960, resulting in establishment of the Japan Socialist party (*Nihon Shakaito*) and the Democratic Socialist party (*Nihon Minshu Shakaito*). The chief distinction between the various factions in parties of the left and right is not easily summarized. Between Socialists and Communists (the Communists organized under the *Nihon Kysanto*), party factions stemmed from ideological differences, whereas Liberal-Democratic factions arose almost entirely from more personal rivalries.

There was continuity, furthermore, in Japan's voting patterns. Politics was dominated by right wing parties, but opposition groups, particularly the Socialists, resumed the slow growth of popular support that had been noted before the war. In national elections the combined vote for all Socialist candidates rose from slightly better than twenty pervent of the total balloting in 1952 to a little less than forty percent ten years later. At this point, however, Socialist dreams of reaching majority status were dashed by their own quarrels and the appearance of strong rivals. Japanese Communists, who had enjoyed very little success in their doctrinaire role, emerged as pragmatic politicians ready to espouse a variety of causes. In 1969, the Communist party won fourteen Diet seats; three years later the party claimed thirty-nine seats and better than ten percent of the popular vote.

The *Komeito* or "Clean Government party," acting as the political arm of a newly-established religion, the *Soka Gakkai,* attracted a subsantial following as the proponent of humane and moral government, an end to corruption and rising prices, support for enlarged

social programs, and policies promoting peace.[7] In the elections of 1967 and 1969, the *Komeito's* seats in the House of Representatives rose from twenty-five to forty-seven. The combined efforts of the opposition destroyed the Liberal-Democratic majority but not its plurality. Since the opposition was unable to unite in a coalition, the Liberal-Democrats continued to form and control the governing cabinets, even though after the election of 1972 they held only 284 seats against an opposition total of 307. The legislative compromises which resulted from these emerging political balances indicated that Japan might be moving toward government under a multiparty system.

DECLINE OF THE "AMERICAN FIXATION"

Although American control of Japan was relaxed beginning in 1949 and was withdrawn altogether three years later, Japanese politics retained the flavor of defeat and foreign dominance for some years. To most Japanese, the United States appeared to enter and to meddle in every issue long after the end of the occupation. Japanese advocates of non-alignment, of neutrality, or of alignment with the Communist world attacked the Japanese-American security treaty and the presence of American military bases on Japanese soil. Conservative Japanese, welded to traditions, berated the United States for imposing democratic reforms which were held to be unsuited to Japanese circumstances and temperament. Still others criticized Japan's heavy economic dependence on the United States. These anxieties, whatever the degree of their substance or significance,

---

[7]Theologically the *Soka Gakkai* had its origins in Nichiren Buddhism. Its appeal, however, appeared to derive less from a religious than from a social orientation. The membership, which came largely from the urban lower class or lower middle class, was attracted by an emphasis on simple doctrines of absolute faith that gave direction in a confusing age. The *Soka Gakkai* first entered local elections in 1955. The organization's connections with the *Komeito* were severed shortly after the 1969 elections. For a study analyzing membership and ideology see James W. White, *The Sokagakkai and Mass Society* (1970).

made it quite evident that, many years after the end of the occupation, the United States was still regarded as unduly influential in Japan's national and international life.[8]

The Yoshida Years to 1954

The American presence was personified in the eyes of many Japanese by Prime Minister Yoshida Shigeru, whose Liberal party overwhelmingly carried the nation's first postoccupation election. A firm advocate of close Japanese-American relations, Yoshida had headed two ministries which had cooperated with SCAP in the implementation of fundamental reforms. His post-occupation policies directed Japan toward a firm alignment with the United States in a world torn by cold war rivalries. He envisioned an independent, revitalized Japan taking its place beside the United States as a full partner in the fight against world communism.

To this end Yoshida's government adopted anti-inflationary policies that in later years were said to have laid the foundations of Japan's economic boom of the 1960s. The prime minister also moved to check the power of the Japanese Communists, who had instigated a number of student strikes and whose strength at the polls had been growing steadily. Following pitched battles between radicals and police in Tokyo, May 1, 1952, Yoshida requested parliamentary approval of a new anti-subversive activity law and of a measure increasing the government's control over the police. The first of these was opposed unsuccessfully by organized labor on the grounds that a provision giving the cabinet power to ban activities leading to violence would endanger legitimate union operations. The proposed police law was even more controversial in that it provided for a return of some practices which had made the police, operating under the old home minister, a dreaded instrument of an authoritarian state. Protesting vehemently, opponents blocked the bill until 1954, when, following new general elections, additional votes were mustered for its passage. Meanwhile, some voters, reacting

[8] The phrase "American fixation" is E. O. Reischauer's. For a full discussion see his *Japan: Past and Present* (3rd rev. ed., 1964).

apparently to Communist violence at home and abroad, deserted the party. In the election of 1952, the Communists lost all thirty-five of their parliamentary seats, and their portion of the total vote declined to 2.6 percent.

Controversy also swirled about Yoshida as his government transformed the police reserve into a national security force and, in March, 1954, approved a mutual defense assistance agreement broadening the United States-Japanese security treaty into a defensive alliance. Under the agreement's terms the United States renewed its pledge to fight in Japan's defense, while Japan agreed to maintain prohibitions on trade with Communist China and to build its military forces against Communist aggression.

Both the agreement and the transformation of the police reserve violated deep Japanese convictions that war was reprehensible and that it might be avoided if Japan remained neutral and unarmed. Moreover, the changed status of the police reserve raised questions about the need to revise the constitution to eliminate the article on the renunciation of war. While Yoshida argued that constitutional revision was unnecessary since Japanese forces were purely defensive, he found many political, religious, and social groups arrayed against him. The Communists and left wing Socialists opposed rearmament and closer alliance with the United States; and they were not alone in this position. Many Japanese of other political persuasions feared the economic drain imposed by military reconstruction and resented being used by the United States as a buffer against Communism. Mixed with these feelings were fears that rearmament would lead to a new militarism. A few ultranationalists castigated the measures because they failed to provide the sufficiently rapid militarization.

Confrontations with the Socialists, 1955-1960

Yoshida prevailed against the opposition, carrying both controversial measures in the Diet, but the effort weakened his hold on power. The revelation that Japan suffered a trade deficit resulting from a drop in American procurement toppled the ministry, and in

December, 1954, control of the cabinet passed to Hatoyama Ichiro, who once had been president of the Liberal party but was then serving as leader of the Democrats (*Minshuto*). Subsequently, Hatoyama's cabinet was backed jointly by the Liberals and Democrats as those parties merged to meet the challenge of a united Socialist party.

Under Hatoyama, Japan tackled unsettled questions arising from the absence of a peace treaty with the Soviet Union. A fisheries agreement, May, 1956, and a joint statement, October 19, 1956, terminating the technical state of war and re-establishing diplomatic relations, served as initial steps toward the opening of limited trade under terms of a commercial treaty concluded at the end of the following year. Meanwhile, Japan joined the United Nations as a result of the Soviet Union's dropping its opposition. These accomplishments failed to produce entirely amicable relations. On the contrary, Japanese opinion was offended by the Russian failure to return several small islands off Hokkaido and by her procrastination in the repatriation of Japanese prisoners.[9] Dissatisfaction with the handling of Soviet affairs turned factions within the ruling party against the prime minister. These difficulties plus Hatoyama's failing health, forced the cabinet's collapse in December, 1956. Liberal-Democratic party leadership, however continued under governments headed first by Ishibashi Tanzan and later by Kishi Nobusuke.

While Kishi's parliamentary majority was soon confirmed by a Liberal-Democratic victory at the polls, his administration confronted dual hazards arising from factional rivalries and increased Socialist opposition. Furthermore, Kishi came to power as Japanese opinion demanded a new approach to questions relating to China and the United States as well as to the Soviet Union. With respect to China, Socialists and Communists led criticism of the nation's

isolation from its neighbor and urged reopening formal relations. The appeal of these arguments was not limited to left wing groups. Among Japanese in general, China was viewed with a peculiar mixture of admiration and condescension, an attitude encouraging support for the fullest contacts with a major source of Japanese civilization. Even right wing businessmen were attracted by the potentials of the China market. Such sentiments were scarcely satisfied by the informal contacts whereby the Kishi Ministry permitted limited Sino-Japanese trade under private agreement and allowed Japanese delegations to travel to China. Public opinion persisted in looking toward the expansion and formalization of these contacts, even though China's economic limitation promised to curtail trade volume and Peking's motives in promoting the relationship was clearly political.[10] For the Kishi ministry the problem was one of resolving these pressures while maintaining Japan's treaty commitments to the United States.

Related to but not identical with this problem was one of meeting the increasingly vehement attacks on Japan's close ties with the United States. The Socialist opposition charged that the Japanese-American alliance limited Japan's initiative in dealing with nations such as China, and threatened Japan with involvement in nuclear war. To a Japanese public aroused by American nuclear tests in the Pacific and irritated by the presence of American bases in Japan, these were telling arguments. By 1958, criticism was so widespread that the Kishi ministry and the Eisenhower administration opened negotiations which resulted in 1960 in the signing of a new treaty of mutual security and cooperation providing for (1) American consultations with

---

[9] Antipathy toward the Soviet Union was one of the few attitudes common to most Japanese. See James W. Morley, "Japan's Image of the Soviet Union, 1952-1961," *Pacific Affairs*, 35 (1962), 51-58.

[10] Popular enthusiasm for enlarged contacts with China was set back temporarily in May, 1958, when Peking, seizing upon the destruction of a Chinese Communist flag by a rightist youth in Nagasaki, cut off all trade. China's intent was to exert a favorable influence on the left wing vote in Japan's impending parliamentary elections. Not only did the effort fail, as Japanese were outraged by these crude tactics, but trade was slow in rebuilding to its earlier levels.

Japan before Japanese bases were employed for war in Asia or nuclear weapons were introduced to Japanese soil, and (2) the imposition of a ten-year limit on American claims to Japanese bases, after which either party might seek a cancellation. These concessions to Japanese sensibilities were intended to ease pressures on the Kishi ministry, but they failed to meet the basic charge that the alliance was unwise and should be terminated.

The Socialists did not have enough votes to block parliamentary approval of the treaty, but several incidents gained public support for their position and turned opinion against the Kishi ministry. Early in May, 1960, while a vote was pending, the downing of an American U-2 reconnaissance plane inside the Soviet Union, the cancellation of a scheduled summit conference between President Eisenhower and Premier Khrushchev, and the intensification of the cold war dramatized afresh for the Japanese the risks entailed by an alliance with the United States. Amid these events, Premier Kishi, desiring apparently to complete ratification of the new defense treaty before a scheduled visit by President Eisenhower to Japan, called a surprise vote on the treaty while opponents were not on the floor of the House of Representatives. These tactics won the treaty's approval, but the way was opened for a double-barrel attack on the substance of the alliance and on the ministry's "dictatorial" procedures. As the Eisenhower visit approached, demonstrations, which were spearheaded by left wing organizations but supported by a formidable number of persons with more moderate leanings, paralyzed Tokyo, humilating and intimidating the government. The Eisenhower visit was cancelled at Tokyo's request, and Kishi, badly shaken and confronted with the refusal of key factions within his own party to support his leadership, resigned in favor of the Liberal-Democrat Ikeda Hayato, another exbureaucrat and protégé of Yoshida.[11]

With Ikeda's appointment, Japanese politics entered a period of smoother sailing. Rioters disappeared and the aura of crisis no longer colored government operations. General elections in November, 1960, revealed no extensive damage to the Liberal-Democratic party. Its percentage (57.6) of the total popular vote was almost identical with that of 1958. Among its opponents, the Socialists made slight gains in voting but lost parliamentary seats through a party split, while the Communists managed to poll only 2.9 percent of all votes cast. These results confirmed the power of a political leadership whose largely rural constituency had remained calm throughout the turmoil. But even more important to the outcome were second thoughts entertained by many who had participated in the demonstrations. Except for the far left, most Japanese came to view riots threatening chaos as a dangerous corrective. After 1960 the press departed from its customary sharp criticism of government and adopted a more constructive tone.[12] Of importance, too, was the new look in government policies; on taking office Ikeda announced that he would assume a "low posture," meaning that his ministry would heed opposition views and avoid highly controversial issues.

Domestically, Ikeda focused attention on "income doubling" within ten years, a popular goal which, in view of Japan's overall economic growth, appeared attainable. In foreign affairs Ikeda emphasized the enhancement of Japan's international position and attainment of equality in dealings with the United States. Among the products of these latter efforts were: (1) the settlement on favorable terms of a debt owed the United States for costs of the occupation; (2) the establishment of the United States-Japan committee on trade and economic affairs, a body composed of cabinet-level officers who were periodically to

---

[11] The coalition opposing the mutual security treaty was unbelievably fragmented; yet it was not deadlocked because it was broadly based on a public mood that was concerned not with ideology but with Japan's involvement in nuclear war and with the threat to democracy inherent in the "tyranny of the major-

ity." See George R. Packard, *Protest in Tokyo: The Treaty Crisis of 1960* (1966); and J. A. A. Stockwin, *The Japanese Socialist Party and Neutralism* (1968).

[12] The role of the press in the rioting of 1960 is the basis of Edward P. Whittemore, *The Press in Japan Today: A Case Study* (1961).*

review problems upsetting commercial relationships; (3) the exchange of visits by high European and Japanese statesmen; and (4) the membership of Japan in the Organization for Economic Cooperation and Development (OECD), an international body admitting only the most economically advanced states. These steps were accompanied by the appearance of new Japanese attitudes toward their country's position in world affairs. Increasingly, Japan's relations with the United States were described as a "partnership," and, while in Europe in 1962, Ikeda spoke of Japan's serving with the United States and Western Europe as the "three pillars" of the free world. Thus, at the beginning of the 1960s Japan entered a new phase of postwar development characterized by a self-assurance that had been missing since the end of World War II.

EMERGENCE OF AN ASIAN GIANT

Japan's basic orientation in foreign matters during the 1960s and into the following decade was suggested by her firm commitment to the alliance with the United States. In June, 1970, the Japanese-American treaty of mutual security and cooperation was renewed. Yet within the framework of this alliance Japan exercised a new independence. As a preliminary to treaty negotiations, Japan took an exceedingly firm position, insisting on the return of islands which the United States had administered since World War II. In 1968, the United States returned the Ogasawara (Bonin) Islands, and the next year promised that Okinawa, on which the United States maintained a key military base, would revert to Japanese control in 1972.

Japan's new-found confidence also was manifest in the assumption of enlarged international responsibilities in financial and technical assistance. Some of this aid was a product of the nation's booming private enterprise. African and Latin American nations, for example, were assisted through technological advice, capital investment, and export credits provided by corporations. Government assistance was more prominent in Southeast Asia. Japan became a major contributor to the capital funds of the newly established Asian Development Bank, and the sponsor of the Ministerial Conference for Economic Development of Southeast Asia. Total governmental expenditures for these agencies—$538 million in 1966—averaged substantially less than the aid budgets of the United States or leading European industrial powers; nevertheless, these expenditures symbolized Japan's growing capacity and determination to make her own way in the world.[13]

Neither these new departures in foreign affairs nor the daily conduct of domestic politics excited the controversy of earlier years. Sato Eisaku, who became prime minister late in 1964 in the place of the ailing Ikeda, was to hold office until 1972, far longer than any other cabinet leader. He was replaced by still another Liberal-Democrat, Tanaka Kakuei, whose power was confirmed by general parliamentary election. The monotonous regularity with which the conservatives were returned to power was attributable only in part to the fragmentation of the opposition. More than any other party, the Liberal-Democrats were able to take credit for the nation's prosperity and its new prestige in foreign affairs, which voters found so satisfying. Indeed, it was a political era seemingly characterized by good feeling.

In concluding this brief survey on aspects of recent and contemporary Japan, it is evident that by the mid-1970s the nation had performed an economic miracle. From total defeat, poverty, and hunger in 1945, Japan had become the strongest economic power in Asia and the third-ranking industrial power in the world. This triumph in what the world calls success had been achieved, however, at

[13] For contemporary appraisals see Edwin O. Reischauer, "Japan Is One of the Biggest Countries in the World," *New York Times Magazine*, Oct. 16, 1966; and Robert A. Scalapino, "In Search of a Role: Japan and the Uncertainties of Power," *Encounter*, 27 (1966), 21-27. These essays sketch the bases of Japan's initiatives.

no bargain price. The nation's physical environment, once one of the most beautiful in the world, was threatened with extreme pollution, if not ruin. In addition, the entire massive economic structure was tied to foreign trade—to the importation of raw materials that were to be processed and exported at a profit. Japan had thereby made herself peculiarly sensitive and vulnerable to any change in the international climate, whether this change took the form of outright war or of economic sanctions, such as an oil embargo.

Less obvious but no less significant as indicators of the price Japan had paid for "success" were continuing and prevading intellectual and philosophical questions intruding into the Japanese mind. Was Japan's economic miracle an end in itself? Could Japan match her expanding economic power with a new and higher quality in her political and social life and structure? In a word, would this new Japan stand for anything other than unlimited economic growth?[14]

[14] Note the discussion by Hugh T. Patrick, "The Phoenix Risen from the Ashes: Postwar Japan," in *Modern East Asia: Essays in Interpretation,* James B. Crowley, ed. (1970),* 298-335. While the problems ahead presented great difficulties, the Sato and Tanaka governments devised various plans which suggested that the future was to be mastered in much the way Japan had met the consequences of military defeat and economic collapse. Tanaka indicated that his administration would depart from policies that would have "growth induce further growth," so that he might engage in "remodeling of the Japanese Archipelago" by shifting industrial development away from the highly congested Tokyo-Osaka-Nagoya area into less developed regions. The plan envisioned Japan's population distributed around cities of 250,000 inhabitants. This was seen as a way of providing a "lively" environment without the problems of overcrowding. All of Japan would be served with high speed railways, superhighways, and instantaneous communications. Intensive land-use studies would insure a protected environment. Meanwhile, as a remedy to "spiritual emptiness," Tanaka hoped that "new 'frontiers' other than private consumption, private equipment investment, and exports will be opened up for Japanese industry"; and that ". . . when both rural areas and big cities are remade . . . so that the people living there can live a truly human life. . . . the Japanese people [will] be able to have real pride in their towns and villages. . . ." Japan's national satisfaction would come, it was said, not from "excessive economic growth" or from the "path to becoming a military power," but from "the role of trail blazer in the service of the progress of welfare and civilization of the world." See Japan Information Service (Consulate General of Japan, New York), *Japan Report,* 18 (Dec. 1, 1972). Other issues of *Japan Report,* 1970-1974 summarize a variety of plans for dealing with social and economic problems.

Social Order. Donald Keene, *Living Japan* (1959) offers a delightful introduction to old and new aspects of contemporary Japanese life. Donald Richie, *The Inland Sea* (1972), an uncommonly thoughtful portrayal of changing social patterns. Other studies of the new social order are contained in R. P. Dore's two books: *City Life in Japan: A Study of a Tokyo Ward* (1958)*; and *Land Reform in Japan* (1959). Excellent descriptive material is found in Richard K. Beardsley, et al., *Village Japan* (1959)*; and Edward Norbeck, *Changing Japan* (1965).* David W. Plath, *The After Hours: Modern Japan and the Search for Enjoyment* (1964). Jean Stoetzel, *Without the Chrysanthemum and the Sword: A Study of the Attitudes of Postwar Japan* (1955); and Chie Nakane, *Japanese Society* (1970) give perspective to Ruth Benedict's famous study. Kazuko Tsurumi, *Social Change and the Individual: Japan Before and After Defeat in World War II* (1970). For specialized aspects of social life, see James C. Abegglen, *The Japanese Factory: Aspects of its Social Organization* (1958); Robert E. Cole, *Japanese Blue Collar: The Changing Tradition* (1971),* the most successful attempt to provide a first-hand account of conditions and attitudes to be found among factory workers. Solomon B. Levine, *Industrial Relations in Postwar Japan* (1958); Arthur M. Whitehall, Jr. and Shin-Ichi Takezama, *The Other Worker* (1968); and Fernando M. Basabe, *Religious Attitudes of Japanese Men, A Sociological Survey* (1968). Lawrence Olson, *Dimensions of Japan* (1963), perceptive essays. Edward Norbeck, *Religion and Society in Modern Japan: Continuity and Change* (1970),* the recent and new religious cults and what has happened to Shinto, Buddhism and Christianity in recent years. Agency for Cultural Affairs, Kodansha, Intl., *Japanese Religions* (1972), translations of essays by

Japanese specialists. Masataka Kosaka, *100 Million Japanese: The Postwar Experience* (1972), the most comprehensive single volume.

Japan's Economy. Jerome B. Cohen, *Japan's Postwar Economy* (1958). G.C. Allen, *Japan's Economic Expansion* (1965). William W. Lockwood, ed., *The State and Economic Enterprise in Japan* (1965).* Warren S. Hunsberger, *Japan and the United States in World Trade* (1964). Prue Dempster, *Japan Advances: A Geographical Study* (1967). Two articles by John D. Eyre, "Japan's Electric-Power Supply," *Geographic Review,* 55 (1965), 546-62; and "Development Trends in the Japanese Electric Power Industry, 1963-68," *The Professional Geographer,* 22 (1970), 26-30, examine the transformation of a basic industry. Eleanor Hadley, *Antitrust in Japan* (1970) deals with *zaibatsu* dissolution and its aftermath.

Contemporary Political Institutions and Practices. Theodore McNelly, *Politics and Government in Japan* (2nd rev. ed., 1972),* an excellent short portrayal. Frank Langdon, *Politics in Japan* (1967).* E. Wight Bakke, *Revolutionary Democracy: Challenge and Testing in Japan* (1968). John M. Maki, *Government and Politics in Japan: The Road to Democracy* (1962),* analysis of performance under the new constitution. Nathaniel B. Thayer, *How the Conservatives Rule Japan* (1969) is a detailed analysis of the Liberal-Democratic party's operations. Haruhiro Fukui, *Party in Power: The Japanese Liberal Democrats and Policy-Making* (1970), for the

sophisticated reader. Hiroshi Itoh, ed., and trans., *Japanese Politics—An Inside View: Readings from Japan* (1973),* reveals the highly critical view that Japanese scholars take of their political system. Gerald L. Curtis, *Election Campaigning Japanese Style* (1971), follows a Liberal Democratic candidate on his daily rounds. Allan B. Cole provides pioneering studies of political behavior in *Japanese Society and Politics: The Impact of Social Stratification and Mobility on Politics* (1956); and *Political Tendencies of Japanese in Small Enterprises, with Special Reference to the Social Democratic Party* (1959). Aspects of extremist activities are treated in: I. I. Morris, *Nationalism and the Right Wing in Japan: A Study of Post-war Trends* (1960); Paul F. Langer, *Communism in Japan* (1972), an excellent treatment. Lawrence H. Battistini, *The Postwar Student Struggles in Japan* (1956). Yoshida Shigeru, *The Yoshida Memoirs: The Story of Japan in Crisis* (1962); and Dan Kurzman, *Kishi and Japan: The Search for the Sun* (1960) provide details on two crucial administrations. Arthur T. von Mehren, ed., *Law in Japan: The Legal Order in a Changing Society* (1963).

Translations of Contemporary Literature. Tanizaki Junichiro, *Some Prefer Nettles,* Edward Seidensticker, trans. (1957).* Mishima Yukio, *The Sound of Waves,* Meredith Weatherby, trans. (1956).* Donald Keene, trans., *The Old Woman, The Wife, and The Archer: Three Modern Japanese Short Novels* (1961). Jiro Osaragi, *Homecoming,* Brewster Horwitz, trans. (1954).

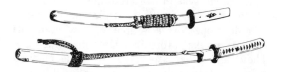

Wars
Cold and Hot:
Korea
and Taiwan
Since 1945

34

For Korea and Taiwan the year 1945 marked the end of Japanese colonialism and the beginning of a new and uncertain political future. As hostilities ended, the United Nations began implementation of the decisions of the Cairo conference of 1943, whereby Korea "in due course" was to be independent, and Japan was to be deprived of all territory seized since 1894. Korea was divided at the 38th parallel into two zones, the Japanese surrendering in the north to the Russians and in the south to the Americans. Taiwan was occupied by *Kuomintang*-Nationalist armies under authorization of General MacArthur. Thus the ties that had bound Korea and Taiwan to Japan for a half century were severed, but the end of Japanese colonialism did not mean that either Korea or Taiwan was to become its own master. Located on the border separating the Communist and non-Communist worlds, each was caught in the pressures of the cold war, which meant that Japanese influence was replaced by that of other great powers now contending for control of East Asia.

KOREA

One of the less obvious but vital results of the outbreak of World War II was a revival of Korean nationalism. Under Japanese rule Korea had suffered a prolonged and systematic attack on her cultural identity and had seen the progressive integration of her economy with Japan's. Operating through a strong central government and an oppressive police system, Japan had held Koreans in subjection, permitting them only limited educational and occupational opportunities.[1] The

[1] Authoritative decisions were made for Korea by the Japanese imperial government and the governor-general of Korea. The conduct of Korean foreign relations was controlled entirely by the Japanese foreign ministry. Korean participation in decision-making, limited to a small part of the society's elite, was largely consultative and advisory. A council of notables to advise the Japanese governor-general was established in 1910 and, subsequently, advisory councils were permitted to function in conjunction with lower levels of government. Koreans generally did not serve in the colonial bureaucracy.

educational system fostered the Japanization of the Korean populace, while the economy was developed as a source of raw materials and a market for Japanese manufactures. These and other aspects of her rule enabled Japan to suppress an infant national movement. In all the years of colonial rule, the only major outburst occurred in March, 1919, when the death of the last royal monarch sent a million or more people into the streets.

Firm government, however, did not eliminate widespread resentment of the Japanese or put an end to nationalist movements among Korean exiles. One exile group attempted unsuccessfully in 1919 to plead Korea's case for self-determination before the Paris peace conference. A Korean provisional government, unrecognized but nevertheless aided by China, existed first in the International Settlement at Shanghai and later at Nanking and Chungking. In the United States another group, headed by Syngman Rhee, vainly sought American recognition. Thus Korean nationalism survived Japanese repression, but there was no consensus among the nationalists as to Korea's future. At the end of World War II, two years after the Cairo declaration, neither Korean nationalists in exile nor the great powers themselves were agreed on the country's future beyond a commitment to independence. Moreover, the Korean people, who had lived under Japanese rule, were not consulted. The only positive step was the understanding reached at Yalta between Roosevelt and Stalin that for a time Korea might be made a trusteeship.

The collapse of Japanese power in Korea was accompanied not only by Russian and American military occupation but also by efforts on the part of Korean factions to seize political power. In the north these groups, heavily weighed with Korean Communists returned from exile, were encouraged and given authority by the Russians. In the south, on the other hand, revolutionary groups that had formed a people's republic at Seoul were not accepted by the American occupation forces as a de facto government. Indeed, for a time the Americans retained Japanese in administrative

posts and then set up an American military government employing Koreans. The net result was that in the south the government was American in appearance and power, while in the north the government seemed to be Korean, though the actual control was Russian.

THE MAKING OF THE TWO KOREAS

Against this background the American and Soviet commands in Korea were unable to reach any agreement on relations between the two zones. The respective commands also failed to agree on how to form a provisional government for all Korea or on what Korean parties were to be consulted and allowed to participate toward this end. In consequence the United States took the Korean problem to the United Nations in August, 1947, while Russia proposed that both powers withdraw their military forces. The United States and the United Nations General Assembly rejected this proposal for reasons that were quite clear: Russia was suspected of looking toward communist control of the south once American troops had left.

In the southern zone progress toward the appearance of some kind of Korean leadership was much slower than in the north. The United States wanted Korea to build a democratic system of government, but it did not wish to turn over authority to a Korean democracy that might be hostile to American policy. Here the dilemma was real and the ultimate solution not satisfactory. While the American military government tolerated agitation by all factions, it tended to support the moderate and conservative elements, and as American-Russian relations became more bitter, the American tendency to bolster the extreme Korean "conservatives" grew. The result was that the American-supervised election for an interim legislative assembly was regarded as fraudulent even by middle-of-the-road Korean leaders. At the same time, the continuing efforts of many North Koreans to escape to the south suggested that there were many who preferred to rely on ultimate

American purposes rather than on the imposed regime of the Communists.

THE DIVISION HARDENS

Aggravating these questions of internal politics operating under the pressure of external power was the country's economic plight. Korea, formerly a kingdom of self-sufficient farmers, had experienced an economic transformation under Japanese rule. Industry and mining were established chiefly in the north, while commercialized agriculture was developed in the south. In the postwar era, this modernized system, cut off from Japanese markets, deprived of Japanese capital and technical guidance, and disrupted by division at the 38th parallel, floundered badly. North Korea met the crisis with land reforms, Soviet economic and technical assistance, and the opening of trade with Russia. The American military government in the south had to save a larger population from starvation through the importation of food and fertilizer. Eventually the problem was further relieved by land reform which allotted Japanese-held land to Korean tenants. No fundamental solution to economic problems, however, was attempted while the political situation was deadlocked.

The deadlock continued. A United Nations temporary commission, sent late in 1947 to see that freely-elected representatives of the Korean people were permitted to determine the form of government for all Korea, was refused admittance to the Russian zone. Elections held in the south in 1948 under the commission's supervision (with seats reserved for the north) brought into being the first assembly of the Republic of Korea. Under a constitution adopted in July, 1948, the assembly elected Syngman Rhee the first president. The authority of the American military government was transferred to the new regime, which was approved by the United Nations General Assembly as a lawful government and was soon recognized by most countries except those in the Soviet bloc. The Soviet Union's answer to these steps was an election in the north for a supreme people's assembly. The assembly set up a rival constitu-

tion and government under Prime Minister Kim Il-song. Once established, this government was recognized by the Communist bloc and received further economic aid from the Soviet Union.

Withdrawal of American troops from South Korea was completed in June, 1949, while the Russians announced that their withdrawal would be complete by 1950. The resulting balance of power in the peninsula was uneven. In the north what amounted to a single-party Communist regime, backed by Russia, was intent on extending its power. In the south the government of Rhee, purportedly a free administration, was attacked from many quarters on the grounds that it had gained power by unscrupulous methods, that the cabinet was chosen unwisely, that no North Koreans were included, and that the president and the ministry were concerned primarily with achieving personal power.

Thus matters stood in 1949. As American and Russian troops left Korea, there seemed to be some prospect that the way was opening for the Koreans to settle their own affairs, but this was not to be the case. In 1949, China fell to Mao Tse-tung. It was also at this time that the United States, against strong Russian opposition, was preparing to conclude a peace treaty with Japan. In this atmosphere of worldwide rivalry, the Russians suspected an American plot to rearm Japan. Moscow's first countermove was the Sino-Soviet alliance of February, 1950. Its second appears to have been notice to North Korea that the time for an invasion of South Korea had arrived.[2]

WAR IN KOREA

Well-equipped North Korean armies struck across the 38th parallel in a surprise attack on June 25, 1950. Two assumptions underlay the attack: (1) that the United States, having already excluded Korea from the American security zone, would not intervene with military force, and (2) that the United Nations could not act in the absence of one of the

[2] Harold C. Hinton, *China's Turbulent Quest* (1970), 40ff.

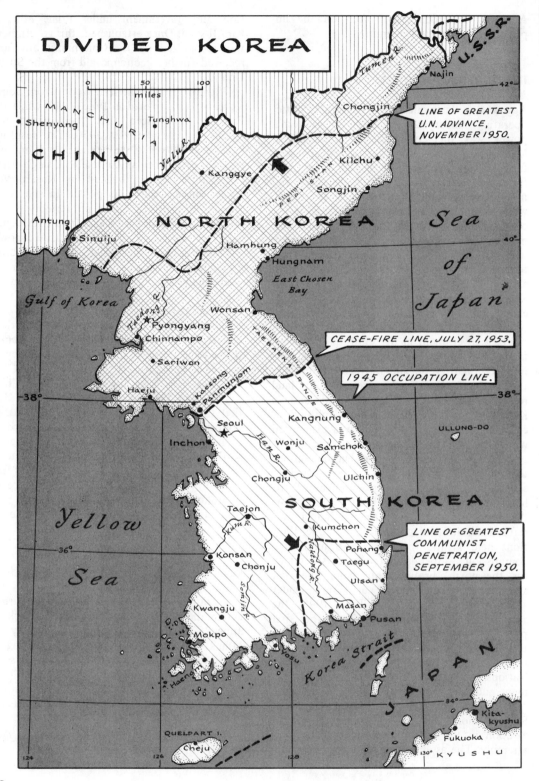

DIVIDED KOREA

miles
0   50   100

U.S.S.R.

MANCHURIA

Shenyang

Tunghwa

CHINA

Najin

Chongjin

LINE OF GREATEST U.N. ADVANCE, NOVEMBER 1950.

Kanggye

Kilchu

Songjin

Antung

NORTH KOREA

Sea

Sinuiju

Hamhung

of

Hungnam

East Chosen Bay

Japan

Gulf of Korea

Wonsan

Pyongyang

Chinnampo

Sariwon

Haeju

Kaesong

Panmunjom

CEASE-FIRE LINE, JULY 27, 1953.

1945 OCCUPATION LINE.

38°

Kangnung

ULLUNG-DO

Seoul

Inchon

Wonju

Samchok

Chongju

Ulchin

SOUTH KOREA

Taejon

Kumchon

LINE OF GREATEST COMMUNIST PENETRATION, SEPTEMBER 1950.

Pohang

Yellow

Konsan

Chonju

Taegu

Ulsan

36°

Sea

Masan

Kwangju

Pusan

Mokpo

Korea Strait

JAPAN

Kita-kyushu

QUELPART I.

Fukuoka

Cheju

KYUSHU

great powers, since Russia at the time was absenting herself from the Security Council. The Security Council, however, passed a resolution calling on the North Koreans to withdraw, and the United States authorized military supplies to the defenders. On June 27, American air and sea forces were ordered to cover and support South Korean troops, and when, on June 30, it was clear that South Korean forces were facing complete defeat, American ground forces were ordered to Korea. These American actions were in support of the resolution of the Security Council and, as aspects of American policy, were designed to halt Communism in its attack upon a free nation.[3]

On July 8, President Truman named General of the Army Douglas MacArthur as commander of United Nations forces in Korea. In addition, as precautionary measures, he proclaimed the

[3] The decisive and rapid military response of the United States was due to Washington's conviction: (1) that the North Korean attack was massive aggression; (2) that if not resisted it would lead to other attacks on the non-communist world elsewhere; (3) that resistance in Korea would demonstrate the need for America and Western Europe to rearm; (4) that the U.S. and the U.N. had a special responsibility because they had established the Republic of Korea; and (5) that the U.S. and the U.N. were in a favorable position to react because of the concentration of American troops in Japan, and Russia's absence from the Security Council. See H. Bradford Westerfield, *The Instruments of America's Foreign Policy* (1963), 136-37. In addition, President Truman's action gave notice that the United States would resist further Communist expansion wherever it might be attempted. Note Glenn D. Paige, *The Korean Decision: June 24-30, 1950* (1968). Differing interpretations on the wisdom of the American intervention are in Robert Osgood, *Limited War: The Challenge to American Strategy* (1957), and Alexander L. George, "American Policy-Making and the North Korean Aggression," *World Politics,* 7 (1955), 209-32. On the underlying causes of the war, there is a voluminous literature on the rivalries of the great powers in Korea and particularly on Russian aims. Less attention has been given to the rivalries among Koreans themselves as a cause of the war. See Gregory Henderson, *Korea: The Politics of the Vortex* (1968). On bibliography and further interpretations, see Robert Dalleck, "The Truman Years," in *American-East Asian Relations: A Survey,* Ernest R. May and James C. Thomson, Jr., eds., (1972), 356-76; also, William Stueck, and Joyce and Gabriel Kolko, "An Exchange of Opinion," *Pacific Historical Review,* 42 (1973), 537-75.

the neutralization of Taiwan by presidential mandate, and placed the U.S. Seventh Fleet in the Taiwan Straits to prevent hostilities between the Nationalist and the Communist Chinese. On August 1, Russia resumed her seat on the Security Council, taking the position that the conflict in Korea had been precipitated by a South Korean attack and that the resolutions of the Security Council were illegal. By October, with a reversal in the tide of battle, South Korean troops were invading the north. MacArthur had called upon the north to surrender, and had been authorized by the United Nations General Assembly to exercise civil authority on its behalf in territory north of the 38th parallel.

CHINA ENTERS THE WAR

An entirely new situation was created by the end of October when, as United Nations forces moved across the 38th parallel and as Republic of Korea troops in advance of them neared the Yalu river boundary with Manchuria, Communist Chinese armies, termed "volunteers," joined the North Korean forces.[4]

[4] Allen S. Whiting, *China Crosses the Yalu: The Decision to Enter the Korean War* (1960)* suggests the following reasons for Chinese intervention: (1) fear of American influence in the nearby anti-communist regimes of South Korea and Japan; (2) resentment occasioned by Peking's inability to occupy Taiwan and by the threatened destruction of North Korea; (3) anxiety lest anti-communist neighbors become bases for the overthrow of the People's Republic; and (4) the need to show a united front with Moscow.

The United Nation's military offensive north of the 38th parallel created a new situation not contemplated in the initial aim of repelling the North Korean attack. Dean Acheson, *Present at the Creation* (1969), 445-55, emphasizes the importance of this thrust as a tactical move. John Spanier, *The Truman-MacArthur Controversy and the Korean War* (1959)* suggests that a decision had been made to reunite Korea through military conquest. Walter Millis describes the crossing of the 38th parallel as a product of "blurred and fuzzy processes." See his *Arms and the State: Civil-Military Elements in National Policy* (1958), 272-79. Remarkable, too, was the American failure to anticipate Chinese intervention. MacArthur and his superiors at Washington were seemingly aware of the presence of some 300,000 Chinese troops in Manchuria. MacArthur,

By January, 1951, the Chinese Communists had entered the war in overwhelming force, had driven United Nations forces back to the 38th parallel, and had demonstrated their power to drive into South Korea far beyond the demarcation line. This offensive was contained by April, 1951, when U.N. forces were again north of the parallel. Meanwhile, negotiations for a political settlement were unsuccessful. The United States was prepared to discuss proposals once a cease-fire had been achieved. Russia and Communist China would discuss nothing until there was a prior acceptance on their terms of a general East Asian settlement. Their terms included: (1) evacuation of all foreign troops from Korea; (2) admission of Communist China to the U.N.; (3) termination of American "intervention" supporting the Chinese Nationalists on Taiwan; (4) a general East Asian conference to seek a comprehensive settlement; and (5) a peace treaty with Japan meeting the wishes of Moscow and Peking. In the face of these demands the United States appealed to the U.N. General Assembly, which on February 1, 1951, found Mao's government guilty of aggression.

Agreeing upon a unified policy was relatively simple for Russia and China, but not for the United States and other powers— European and Asian—supporting South Korea through the United Nations. In Western Europe it was feared that a major American involvement in East Asia would weaken the defense of Europe against Russia. The "neutralism" of the newly-created Asian states also posed problems. Led by India, these "neutrals," intent upon retaining their independ-

---

however, believed China would be deterred merely by the show of American power. MacArthur's successor, General Matthew B. Ridgway, linked the incautious approach to the Machurian border with MacArthur's desire to carry the war to China. See Ridgway, *The Korean War* (1967).* David S. McLellan, "Dean Acheson and the Korean War," *Political Science Quarterly*, 83 (1968), 16-39, indicates that the Truman administration was so clear in its determination not to provoke a wider war that it failed to note that the Chinese might feel menaced by American actions.

ence of judgment, refused to commit themselves to the dictates of American leadership and policy.

Nevertheless, in the spring of 1951, General MacArthur advocated broadening the United Nations role to include: (1) a blockade of China; (2) air reconnaisance over Manchuria and the China coast; and (3) authority for Chinese Nationalists on Taiwan to operate against the mainland. These measures, it was said, would terminate Chinese intervention, thus opening the way for reunification of Korea on American terms.

To these proposals the Truman administration reacted most unfavorably. The blockade was not regarded as a weapon that could be immediately effective against the Chinese economy, and air reconnaissance was seen as a first step toward the bombing of Manchurian bases, which might well bring Russia into the war. General Omar Bradley expressed the view of the U.S. Joint Chiefs of Staff when he said that participation in a general Asian conflict would involve the United States "in the wrong war, at the wrong place, at the wrong time, and with the wrong enemy." In consequence, Truman decided upon renewed efforts to obtain a cease-fire and an armistice, a decision that further inflamed bitterly partisan groups in their attack on American East Asian policy (see Chapter 31). Wide publicity was given to MacArthur's position through publication of a letter which the general had written to Congressman Joseph Martin. The president's subsequent action removing MacArthur from his command led to emotion-packed charges that an administration which had "lost China" was failing again in Korea. One effect of this unreasoning uproar was to limit the range of acceptable terms in the search for a Korean settlement. As a result, inconclusive negotiations and limited hostilities continued in Korea for the next two years.

Progress toward an armistice was made only after Dwight Eisenhower succeeded President Truman, and Georgi Malenkov became Soviet premier following the death of Stalin. These events cleared the way for a compromise settlement, July 27, 1953, calling for a cease-fire, the establishment of a neutral zone, and an exchange of prisoners.[5] A subsequent agreement provided for international supervision of these terms and a high-level political conference to discuss the peaceful settlement of the Korean question on the basis of reunification. While these understandings terminated hostilities, they failed to usher in a new era in Korea's political position. The Korean phase of an international conference meeting in Geneva in 1954 ended in stalemate. Meanwhile, the prospects for Korean reunification were complicated further by the continuing existence of two antagonistic Korean governments, one for the north and another for the south.[6]

TWO KOREAS

North Korean politics after 1953 was dominated by Kim Il-song. Although Kim had been initially little more than a figurehead operating

[5] With the election of Eisenhower, Congressional critics of the Truman administration became supporters of an attempt to find a compromise Korean settlement. The influence of Senator Joseph McCarthy, the administration's most publicized critic, declined, and McCarthy ultimately was censured in the Senate on a motion initiated and supported by Republican colleagues. The impact of "McCarthyism" on the American government and on American dealings with Asia, however, did not end with the man. Former Secretary of State Dean Acheson observed: "McCarthy's name has been given . . . to a phenomenon broader than his own participation in it, the hysteria growing out of fear of Communist subversion. . . . The result was deplorable. The Government's foreign and civil services, universities, and China-studies programs in them took a decade to recover from this sadistic program. . . ." *Present at the Creation*, 369. See also Ronald J. Caridi, *The Korean War and American Politics: The Republican Party as a Case Study* (1968).

[6] The costs of the Korean war for the United States included more than 23,000 Americans killed, some 105,000 wounded, and about $18 billion in direct military expenditures. On the credit side there was some reason to conclude that the war strengthened the military preparedness of the non-communist Western states and increased the general will to resist Communist expansion. For the Koreans, the war meant that their country would remain divided for the indefinite future and that it would continue to be a victim of great power rivalry, just as it had been in the late nineteenth and the early twentieth centuries. Note the discussion in Westerfield, *Instruments*, Chs. 7 and 8.

under Soviet direction, the close of the Korean war permitted him to eliminate rivals and convert his Communist Workers' party into an instrument for controlling the state.[7] Under his leadership, party enrollment, which stood at 360,000 in 1946, swelled by 1961 to 1,311,563, or about 12 percent of a total population estimated at 10.7 million. The army was guided by party members, and the party directed drastic reforms involving: (1) collectivization of the agricultural system; (2) nationalization of existing industry and construction of new plants under a series of long-range plans; and (3) development of a new educational system providing for the socialist reorientation of the populace, revival of Korean nationalism, and instruction in vital technical skills. The Soviet Union supported these programs with aid in the amount of some two billion rubles, the services of 1,500 technicians, and equipment for a variety of industrial enterprises. China and the Communist nations of Eastern Europe supplied help in roughly an equal amount. In consequence, North Korea's postwar decades were characterized by such expansion and diversification of the industrial system that the country could boast of the production of machine tools, automobiles, tractors, mining equipment, and chemicals. Slender agricultural resources were augmented, though self-sufficiency in producing food and fiber was not attained. Social transformations included a decline in farm population, growth of an industrial and clerical labor force, urbanization, and a steady rise in educational attainment. These gains, which were achieved through the well-known methods of the completely authori-

[7] Kim was one of several Communists to return to Korea with the occupying Soviet forces, and among these his credentials were not the most impressive. Kim Tu-bong was notable for leadership among Korean revolutionaries in Shanghai and Yenan; and Pak Honyang, a Communist since 1919 and founder of the Korean Communist party, was the most generally acknowledged leader. Kim Il-song, however, as a former exile in Siberia, received Soviet support because he was the Korean Communist whom the Russian military knew best. Once in power Kim posed as the only revolutionary leader of significance before 1945 and as the one who almost single-handedly defeated Japanese imperialism. Chong-sik Lee, "Kim Il-song of North Korea," *Asian Survey*, 7 (1967), 374-82.

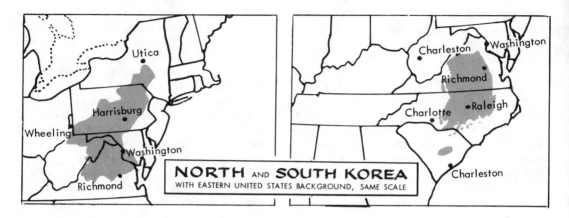

NORTH AND SOUTH KOREA
WITH EASTERN UNITED STATES BACKGROUND, SAME SCALE

tarian state, advanced North Korea toward its goal of "self-reliance" (*chuch'e*), but they contributed little to improving the material standards of living. Kim Il-song, noting these material deficiencies, defended his record, saying that his regime had provided the essentials of food, clothing, and shelter while building the nation's strength.[8]

Kim was committed to the reunification of all Korea under Communism. To this end, fol-

lowing the withdrawal of Chinese troops in 1958, he indicated a readiness to open trade with South Korea and to discuss establishment of a united Korean government on the basis of free elections, provided United Nations forces were first withdrawn from South Korea. These terms reflected his confidence that the Workers' party could capture any government developed through negotiations with South Korea. The founding of a military-controlled regime in Seoul, May 16, 1961, and the south's subsequent attack on elements which had been agitating for negotiations with the north, however, destroyed immediate prospects for the successful conclusion of these plans. In consequence, Kim signed mutual security treaties with the Chinese People's Republic and the Soviet Union and undertook to expand his military forces. This latter effort resulted in a well-trained, Soviet-equipped army of over 350,000, an air force boasting some 500 jet aircraft, modern air-defense missile complexes, and a militia of more than one million men and women. These forces backed the escalation of periodic violence against the south. North Korean troops clashed with United Nations forces along the demarcation line; the south's fishing boats were harassed and captured; and North Korean commandos staged raids aimed at the destruction of key facilities and the assassination of South Korean officials (one such squad penetrated to within 800 meters of President Park Chunghee's residence before being captured).

[8] Kim's leadership emphasized a view that popular satisfaction was not to be found primarily in a richer material life. Note his statement: "Our party has made the peasants masters of the land through democratic reform and is leading them along the road to a new, blissful life and continues to awaken them ideologically and enlighten them culturally." For the full text see Kim Il-song, *Selected Works* (1971), V, 1. It should be noted further that economic development in North Korea encountered grave difficulties. The goals of the seven-year plan, 1961-1967, for example, were not met, and the plan was extended for three years. Soviet aid proved uncertain since it was linked with North Korea's readiness (not always forthcoming) to submit to Moscow's leadership. Economic growth was hampered also by the country's heavy commitment to military spending. The result was a loss of momentum in economic development during the late 1960s. Yet the inauguration of a six-year economic development plan, 1971-1976, which was to raise productivity through mechanization and automation, demonstrated that North Korea had established an embryonic industrial complex in a war-ravaged country that, by Asian standards, was impressive.

North Korea's dependence upon its allies was paralleled in South Korea's relations with the United States. South Korea was the recipient of initially more than $3.5 million in American economic aid.[9] Moreover, in January, 1954, a treaty was concluded whereby the United States was pledged to "act to meet the common danger" in the event of an "armed attack" on South Korean territory. Support of this pledge was demonstrated by American military aid amounting to two billion dollars and the stationing of several thousand American troops near the 38th parallel. Yet, while these measures were essential to South Korea's survival, relations between Seoul and Washington were often strained. President Rhee reacted violently to the American decision to agree on a cease-fire short of Korean reunification. He all but ended the armistice negotiations in 1953 by releasing North Korean prisoners in violation of a key understanding, and his constant threats to use South Korean troops in "Marches North," led the United States in the treaty of 1954 to insist on a prohibition of unilateral South Korean military action. During an official visit to the United States in 1954, Rhee attacked American policy, calling upon Congress and the American people to launch a military crusade against communism on all fronts.

South Korea was also troubled by domestic turmoil. The functioning of democratic political institutions, installed under American guidance, was subverted by personalities and by authoritarian traditions. The political record became one of constant intrigue and shifting coalitions among rival factions grouped in two loosely organized parties known as the Liberals (headed by Rhee) and the Democrats—two labels that had very little, if any, meaning in Korea.[10] Rhee dominated the government by

fair means and foul. When it appeared in 1952 that the National Assembly, acting in its capacity of presidential elector, would not re-elect him, he forced amendment of the constitution to provide for election through a popular vote. He filled administrative posts with appointees whose chief qualification was loyalty to him; and the National Assembly, dominated by the Liberal party, was bribed or coerced to do the president's bidding. Notwithstanding his authoritarian tendencies, however, Rhee did not have full dictatorial powers. He was never without vocal opposition, and in the elections of May, 1956, his hand-picked candidate for the vice-presidency was defeated by the Democratic leader, John M. Chang (Chang Myun). Moreover, Rhee's rule was weakened by confusion and, at times, indecision. Lacking capable advisers, he refused to delegate authority, trying unsuccessfully to make all major decisions himself. During the latter years of his administration, bribe-taking and the diversion of foreign aid funds to the private enrichment of favorites became a public scandal.

In spite of this record, Rhee remained in power until April, 1960, a month after his election to a fourth term in balloting marked by police interference and gross corruption. His fall was preceded by mass rioting which the army refused to suppress. The United States at this point also exerted pressure for reform; Rhee in response resigned his office and fled to Hawaii. Following his departure, a new constitution was adopted making the presidency an honorary office and placing authority in the hands of a prime minister responsible to the National Assembly. In July, 1960, a new administration was installed under the control of the Democratic party led by John M. Chang.

While Chang took office pledging widespread reform in government, his task was complicated by the disintegration of his party into feuding factions. The new premier failed to eliminate political malpractice, to arrest growing eco-

---

[9] In addition to American financial assistance, South Korea received some $125 million through a special United Nations rehabilitation agency before that agency closed its operations in 1960.

[10] Political factionalism was a persistent barrier to the development of a consensus on important national questions. In South Korea more than 500 political parties were identified after 1945. Their sheer number and fluidity indicate the personalized

nature of politics and the absence of strong ideological or pragmatic orientations. Even the Communists did not escape the divisive effects of factionalism. In North Korea, however, since 1945, Kim's systematic elimination of his rivals was basic to the creation of a seemingly monolithic political system. See David I. Steinberg, *Korea: Nexus of East Asia* (1968), 9-17.

nomic instability, and to prevent Communist infiltration from the north. In the confusion, army leaders entered politics with a bloodless coup, May 16, 1961, that forced Chang from office and dissolved the National Assembly. An interim government functioning through a supreme council for national reconstruction was set up by the military junta. During a period of tutelage that was to end in the summer of 1963, the militarists proposed to punish those guilty of crimes against the state, to institute reforms, and to instruct the populace in the responsibilities of self-government. Former Premier Chang and some of his colleagues were charged with graft, while business leaders confessed to evasion of millions of dollars in income taxes. As a corrective to economic woes, the junta announced both an emergency economic program and a five-year economic reconstruction plan.

The attack thus launched on basic problems achieved its greatest success in the economic field. Unlike in the north, where expansion of productive capacity was pressed as early as 1945, economic programs in South Korea before 1960 had emphasized relief and rehabilitation. Under the new regime, the south's development was boosted by the conclusion of a treaty with Japan, June, 1965, restoring relations and providing access to Japanese capital. The United States also figured prominently as a source of economic aid.

As economic development continued under the third five-year plan, 1972-1976, South Korea exulted in its material achievements. The goals of the previous five-year plan had been more than met; the gross national product during the latter half of the 1960s grew at an annual average of more than 11 percent; and average annual per capita income, which had been $88 at the beginning of the 1960s, had reached $223 in 1970.

For a time this new prosperity contributed to internal political peace. To be sure, economic development aggravated serious social conditions: urban unemployment as high as 20 percent, wage levels scarcely above subsistence

and increasing contrasts between rich and poor. But the lack of political protest appears to have been related to the nature of the new regime. General Park Chung-hee, head of the junta and later president, had laid firm foundations for one-man rule with the loyalty of South Korea's 600,000 man army and an efficient secret police. The National Assembly, which should have provided a forum for opposition, had been reduced to virtual impotence; the press was controlled; and, in 1972, through elections conducted in an atmosphere of martial law, the constitution was revised to permit President Park to succeed himself indefinitely. The result was a governmental machine which functioned under a presidential dictatorship.[11]

In 1974, in an apparent effort to make this dictatorship even more complete, Park's government agents abducted a prominent opposition leader, Kim Dae-jung, from a hotel room in Tokyo and returned him to Korea, where he was placed under house arrest. The abduction, conducted in secret, was discovered and publicized in the international press. To avoid trouble, South Korea apologized to Japan for the incident, but Park's government found it less easy to deal with its own people, many of whom interpreted the bungled kidnapping and subsequent apology as evidence that Park was not infallible or invincible. A new political opposition, led by the Korean Christian Student Federation, protested against the president's high-handed revision of the constitution, the activities of the secret police, and a foreign policy that courted Japan, whose colonial rule continued to evoke bitter memories.[12] The

[11] See Chae-jin Lee, "South Korea: The Politics of Domestic-Foreign Linkage," *Asian Survey*, 13 (1973) 94-101.
[12] Not all of the students opposing the regime were Christian. Korean Christians constituted only about four million people in a population totaling more than 31 million. Christian students emerged prominently, however, partly because their pastors (most were Protestant) preached social action and partly because churches were one of the few places in a repressive society where public meetings were allowed.

president responded by closing the schools and engaging in other acts of political repression.

A DIVIDED PEOPLE

Despite their problems, the two Koreas, North and South, manifested a new self-confidence by the late 1960s. North Korea's behavior was marked by increasingly noisy assertions of her independence of all foreign powers. Sino-Soviet wrangling had been especially embarrassing to Kim Il-song, who was linked ideologically to Mao Tse-tung but tied to Moscow for foreign aid. Thus it became important to demonstrate that North Korea was not wholly dependent on either of these Communist neighbors. In a further demonstration of independence in January, 1968, North Korea defied American power, seizing a United States intelligence vessel, the *Pueblo,* and holding its eighty-two crew members for a year. Meanwhile South Korea's President Park embarked on a series of foreign visits, not only in the United States but also in Southeast Asia and Europe. His government sought to break its appearance of almost total dependence on America by diversifying its sources of foreign assistance. Moreover, South Korea's dispatch of some 50,000 men to fight in Vietnam contributed to the picture of a government which saw itself as an influence in Asian affairs.

The emergence of self-confident regimes also heightened old demands for Korean unification. Both Korean governments had long been pledged to national unity—each on its own terms. The south had looked toward elections throughout the country under the sponsorship and supervision of the United Nations. These would be held at a time when a politically united and economically powerful south might stand successfully against the north. The north, on the other hand, had looked toward reunification through methods unemcumbered by United Nations or American intervention. Actually the ideal of reunification had no substance even in principle until 1972. In that year, because of improved American relations with China and Russia, high North and South

Korean officials issued a joint communique pledging to seek a peaceful settlement uniting Korea "without . . . external imposition and interference" and transcending "differences in ideas, ideologies, and systems." Both sides agreed to avoid armed provocations. A "hot line" linking the two Korean capitals was to be installed and recriminatory propaganda campaigns were to be stopped. These pledges were hailed by Korean nationalists of all political shadings, but the hard fact was that actual reunification remained only an ideal. By 1974, there was no practical plan on how a unified government transcending "ideas, ideologies, and systems" might be put into operation. Moreover, while the cause of reunification was aided by some relaxation in international tensions, achievement of Korean unity was beyond the power of the Koreans alone. Korea was still a concern of great powers as it had been for a century.

TAIWAN

The history of Taiwan (Formosa) since 1945 is a dramatic chapter in the cold war.[13] During the immediate postwar years, and in the absence of a Japanese peace treaty, *Kuomintang-*Nationalist forces administered the island as an army of occupation. This early administration, adept in misgovernment, did not recommend itself to the native population. By January, 1949, however, the Chinese Nationalist government, foreseeing the need for a refuge, appointed one of its ablest officials, Ch'en Ch'eng, as governor. Ch'en eliminated some of the worst abuses. Later, when Chiang Kai-shek fled

[13] "Taiwan" is the mainland Chinese name for the island. "Formosa" is the name given by Portuguese explorers. The names assumed contemporary importance because Formosans, seeking an autonomous status for their homeland, have used the Portuguese name. Note the usage in the quarterly publication *The Independent Formosa,* published by the "United Formosans in America for Independence." See Douglas Mendel, *The Politics of Formosan Nationalism* (1970), based on extensive interviews both in Formosa and among Formosans living in the United States.

to the island with two million refugees from the mainland, Taiwan assumed a dual status as a Chinese province and as the temporary seat of government for the Republic of China. An additional defense against Communist "liberation" of Taiwan was provided shortly thereafter when the United States, having reexamined its strategic position in East Asia in the light of rising Communist power and the outbreak of the Korean War, set up a naval patrol of the Taiwan Straits and provided fresh military and economic aid to the Nationalists. Thus the march of events dictated that Taiwan was separated from the mainland and dependent on American aid. Taiwan's legal position, however, was not so clear. The decision of the Cairo conference to restore the island to China seemed clear enough, but after 1949 there was the question of restoration to which China— *Kuomintang* or Communist? Neither Chinese government abandoned its claim to Taiwan in any measure. Moreover, the San Francisco treaty of 1951, which divested Japan of its rights in Taiwan, did not otherwise dispose of the island or contribute to a settlement.[14]

Government on Taiwan

Government on Taiwan after 1949 consisted of a double system wherein a provincial regime governed the island, while Chiang Kai-shek's administration concerned itself in theory with the broader affairs of the lost mainland and its relations with the powers. Under this division of responsibility, Taiwanese participated in government to the extent of selecting local officials, voting for members of a provincial assembly, and having representation on the governor's council. The governor, however, was invariably a mainlander appointed by the Re-

public. Mainlanders also monopolized positions in the Republic, the governmental structure of which had been transferred almost intact to the island. Remnants of the national assembly met periodically to discharge such functions as re-electing Chiang Kai-shek. Many administrative officials from mainland days continued to hold titles as provincial governors, customs inspectors, or district magistrates even though the duties of their offices had disappeared.[15] The net result was to exclude Taiwanese from a major role in government and to perpetuate a huge bureaucracy that had too little to do. The rationale for this voiced by the *Kuomingtang*-Nationalist government was the necessity of holding political machinery in readiness for a return to the mainland. Pending that time, the bureacracy and the army served Chiang on Taiwan as a basis of power.

While local government on the island took on some surface characteristics of a democracy, Taiwan was a police state, though not a fully totalitarian one. The *Kuomintang's* domination of political life was scarcely challenged by the existence of a few opposition parties. *Kuomintang* party cells were organized throughout the island; ambitious local politicians were absorbed into its ranks; and party members holding official posts were safeguarded by laws proscribing discussion of such topics as Chiang's leadership, and making candidates criminally liable for their speeches. Other laws providing harsh treatment for Communist sympathizers

[14] Hungdah Chiu, *China and the Question of Taiwan: Documents and Analysis* (1973) explores the origins of the Taiwan question through the shifts in America's postwar policy, the legal issues involved, and the positions taken by Taipei and Peking. See also note 25 below. For still other perspectives see J. P. Jain, "Legal Status of Formosa: A Study of British, Chinese, and Indian Views," *American Journal of International Law*, 57 (1963), 25-45.

[15] Under the constitution of 1947 the national assembly was to function as a popularly elected body which would meet every six years to elect a president. The constitution's provisions, however, did not clearly distinguish between the functions of this body and the legislative *yuan*. Thus in its meetings on the mainland and in Taiwan, the national assembly sometimes insisted on hearing administrative reports, questioning officials, and passing resolutions. In assuming these additional functions, the national assembly embarrassed *Kuomintang*-Nationalist officialdom, but such independence never threatened Chiang's re-election. In practice the periodic meetings of the national assembly reflected more of a commitment to the appearance than to the spirit of constitutional government. See Mark A. Plummer, "Chiang Kai-shek and the National Assembly," in *Studies on Asia, 1967*, Sidney Brown, ed. (1967), 119-38.

and limiting civil rights were said to be justified by constant threats of invasion, infiltration, and subversion. Furthermore, as the *Kuomintang* tightened its grip on Taiwan, it became increasingly intolerant of any dissent from Chiang's leadership within its own ranks. In 1955, for example, Sun Li-jen, an able soldier, who objected to the activities of Chiang Ching-kuo (the generalissimo's son) in the political departments of his army, who had criticized the generalissimo, and who had expressed doubts about the return to the mainland, was retired in disgrace.[16]

Economic Progress

Taiwan's economic progress was substantial. Postwar development was founded on the work of the Japanese colonial regime, which had organized the island under a stable government, had raised the technological proficiency of the populace, and had built farming operations that exported substantial quantities of rice, sugar, and pineapples.[17] In addition, the United States after 1950 supplied military and economic assistance amounting to more than three billion dollars. These factors combined with favorable governmental programs to produce rapid development. By 1974 Taiwan's productive capacity not only sustained a population of some sixteen million at one of the highest levels in all Asia—$467 annual per capita income, a figure exceeded only by Japan—but it also converted the island into a trade center exporting the more traditional agricultural commodities and a variety of manufactured products.[18] Moreover, the *Kuomintang*-Nationalist government's support of such creative experiments as the industrial processing zone at Kaohsiung (an effort which capitalized on abundant labor by importing raw materials, manufacturing them at the water's edge, and re-exporting them to world markets) demonstrated its commitment to continued growth. In these circumstances of a thriving economy, American economic aid was terminated and Taiwan even extended technical assistance to developing nations in Africa, the Middle East, and Latin America.[19]

While these accomplishments gave Taiwan a new importance in East Asia, economic problems did not vanish. Population increased at a rate of better than 3 percent annually, creating the long-range task of finding thousands of new jobs each year.[20] Furthermore, in addition to the burdens imposed by a large bureaucracy, the economy was taxed to support an army of 600,000 men. Yet for understandable political reasons the government delayed official support of intensive birth control programs until 1968 and did not begin reductions in the army's manpower until the following year. The belated decisions in these matters were explained by the official view that rapid population increase and military power were essential to the reconquest of the mainland.[21]

---

[16] The persecution of Sun Li-jen was not an isolated case. For a brief description of government on Taiwan and its operation see Harold C. Hinton, "China," in *Major Governments of Asia,* George Kahin, ed. (2nd ed., 1963), 134-38.

[17] For a review and analysis of the Japanese era, see the essay by Hyman Kublin in *Taiwan in Modern Times,* Paul K. T. Shih, ed. (1973). See also the important contributions to Taiwanese history presented in this volume by Kuo Ting-yee. Specialized aspects of Japan's colonial rule are treated in E. Patricia Tsurumi, "Taiwan under Kodama Gentaro and Goto Shimpei," and Ching-chih Chen, "The Police and Hoko Systems in Taiwan under Japanese Administration," *Papers on Japan,* 4, published by the East Asia Research Center, Harvard University (1967), 95-146, and 147-76, respectively. See also Chang Han-yu and Ramon H. Myers, "Japanese Colonial Development Policy in Taiwan, 1895-1906: A Case of Bureaucratic Entrepreneurship," *Journal of Asian Studies,* 22 (1963), 433-49.

[18] Exports from Taiwan in 1952 were valued at $120 million. In 1973, they were valued at $8.2 billion. Exports of such agricultural commodities as sugar, tea, rice, and bananas, while reaching new records, declined in importance. Industrial goods constituted only fifty-two percent of all exports in 1963; ten years later they accounted for eighty-five percent of all foreign sales. Textile goods were the chief export, followed by electric and electronic products, plywood, and metal and plastic products. The United States, Japan, Western Europe, Southeast Asia, and Africa (in descending order of importance) comprised Taiwan's foreign markets.

[19] Karl Brandt, "Economic Development: Lessons in Statecraft in Taiwan," *Orbis,* 11 (1968), 1067-80.

[20] Irene B. Taeuber, "Population Growth in a Chinese Microcosm," *Population Index,* 27 (1961), 101-26.

[21] American military advisers had long advocated reduction in the *Kuomintang*-Nationalist army on grounds that it was too large for the defense of Taiwan and too small to take the mainland. Ameri-

Under Chiang's rule, military and political decisions were directed initially toward a return to the mainland. The *Kuomintang*-Nationalist government held that Communist rule had been imposed upon the Chinese people against their will; that the Peking regime was becoming more unpopular as crop failures, coercion, bureaucratic mistakes, and recurrent turmoil compounded human misery; and that throughout China millions were awaiting the moment to revolt. These views were linked to plans for a military invasion, predicated on the assumption that troop landings would trigger popular uprisings.[22] In the course of time, however, as the Chinese People's Republic persisted, *Kuomintang*-Nationalist plans underwent profound changes. During the mainland's Great Proletarian Cultural Revolution, Chiang responded to demands from within his party for an immediate invasion by saying that his plans for the return were 70 percent political (the nature of the politics was unspecified) and 30 percent military. In advancing this new formula, Chiang did not alter the contention that his was the only legitimate Chinese government. As such, the *Kuomintang*-Nationalist insisted upon retention of China's permanent seat in the Security Council of the United Nations and upon recognition by other nations as the legal government of China.

Taiwan Whither?

By 1974, the prospects for the *Kuomintang*-Nationalist government, well into its third decade of exile, had not been resolved. While the measure of economic achievement was notable, the island's development—like Japan's—was dependent on world conditions. Embargoes in the world petroleum trade, sharp rises in raw commodity prices, and general inflationary pressures combined in 1974 to frustrate optimistic predictions. In politics, the regime's boast of having given Taiwan (at least since 1950) a stable and efficient government was strengthened by some basic political reform. Native Taiwanese men, women, and young people were brought into government. New regulations, if strictly enforced, promised to root out corruption. Yet Chiang Kai-shek was in his eighties, and while the actual conduct of government had devolved upon his son, Chiang Ching-kuo, the generalissimo as titular head of state continued in control. Questions inevitably arose as to the ability of this leadership to attract popular loyalty, and as to whether it would continue to regard the return to the mainland as a practical and compelling goal.[23]

Taiwan's international status remained obscure. For twenty years, 1950-1970, the majority of the world's nations had recognized the *Kuomintang*-Nationalist regime as the legitimate government of all China. International support for this position, however, was eroded as cold war tensions eased. In October, 1971, the United Nations voted to oust Nationalist China and to seat representatives of the Chinese People's Republic. Meanwhile a number of individual governments moved to shift their representation to Peking. These steps did not result in the complete isolation of Taiwan. The *Kuomintang*-Nationalists displayed remarkable resilience in the face of adversity, collaborating with foreign groups in the establishment of unofficial liaison offices which permitted the continuation of economic and cultural contacts.

---

can pledges of new weapons and of facilities enabling the Chinese to manufacture their own helicopters, M-14 rifles, and F-4 fighters also encouraged the shift toward a smaller but more elite force. The *Kuomintang*-Nationalist regime was also concerned by the spectre of disloyalty among a force composed almost entirely of Taiwanese enlisted men and commanded by a diminishing supply of mainlanders. See Mark A. Plummer, "Taiwan: Toward a Second Generation of Mainlander Rule," *Asian Survey,* 10 (1970), 18-24.

[22] This thesis is developed more fully in two articles, Duncan Norton-Taylor, "The Sword at the Belly of China," *Fortune,* 67 (1963), 151-53; and Stanley Karnow, "How Communist Economics Failed in China," *ibid.,* 154-57.

[23] Chiang Ching-kuo was appointed minister of defense in 1965; vice-prime minister in 1969; and premier in 1972. His power, initially, however, stemmed less from any particular office than from his parentage and his control of the army and secret police. Chiang Kai-shek died in 1975.

These uncertainties were compounded further by limitations attached to American support. As defined in 1950, at the outset of the Korean war, American policy included: (1) nonrecognition of the Chinese People's Republic; (2) opposition to a shift in China's representation in the United Nations; (3) economic nonintercourse with mainland China; and (4) material military aid to the *Kuomintang*-Nationalist establishment. While this policy appeared to support Chiang's determination to return to the mainland, American practice, if not pronouncement, placed restrictions on aid to the Nationalists. American power was employed in defense of Taiwan and the neighboring Pescadores Islands, but the United States opposed Nationalist adventures which threatened war with Communist China.[24] Thus, despite outward appearances, American policy had come to view Chiang less as an alternative and successor to Mao Tse-tung than as head of a government maintaining Taiwan's freedom from Communist control.

After 1972, as the United States and the People's Republic entered an era of improved relations, even this limited measure of American support was called into question. Peking, which had characterized American support of the Nationalists as a "invasion" of Taiwan, insisted that a settlement with Washington was dependent on United States' withdrawal from the island. The Nixon administration responded by reaffirming its determination to uphold all commitments to preserve Taiwan's security, but these pledges apparently did not preclude changes in the island's status if these were effected by peaceful means. The American view, it seemed, was that the ultimate resolution of the Taiwan question was to be settled peacefully by the Chinese themselves. In 1974, the United States continued to recognize the

government at Taipei as the Republic of China. Yet, by then, it had also opened a "liaison office" in Peking and had removed most barriers to economic and cultural exchange with the Chinese mainland. Moreover, the United States was carrying forward a gradual withdrawal of American troops from Taiwan.[25]

[24] American military assistance was extended under a mutual defense treaty (1954). The limitations on American aid under this treaty were illustrated by the reaction of the Eisenhower administration in 1958 to a Nationalist proposal to bomb the Chinese mainland in defense of Quemoy Island. The United States insisted upon a pledge by Chiang that force would not be "the principal means" of overturning Communist rule. Tang Tsou, "The Quemoy Imbroglio: Chiang Kai-shek and the United States," *Western Political Quarterly,* 12 (1959), 1075-91.

[25] American relations with Taiwan and the place of Taiwan in American domestic politics form a very complex story. Here it is sufficient to note that, beginning in 1949 when Chiang K'ai-shek and what was left of the *Kuomintang*-Nationalists fled to Taiwan, the island became a troublesome subject in American policy. America's pronounced interest in Taiwan did not reflect a concern for the native Taiwanese since they and Americans were complete strangers. The official and the popular American concern stemmed from the fact that Taiwan had become the home of the fugitive *Kuomintang*-Nationalist government which the United States recognized as the government of all China when, in fact, all of mainland China was under the unmistakable control of the Chinese Communists. As events moved into 1950 there was no disposition in Washington or in Peking toward rapprochement. From then on during the 1950s and 1960s, Taiwan came to stand for the intricate mixture of two distinct American foreign policy questions: (1) the nature and extent of American ties with Chiang's government, and (2) American recognition policy toward Peking.

Prior to June, 1950, the Truman administration had made no important moves to prevent the possible takeover of Taiwan by Peking. At that time Washington was taking the position that Taiwan was a part of China and that the U.S. should avoid further involvement in a Chinese civil war.

It was the outbreak of the Korean war (June, 1950) that altered this U.S. policy. Truman promptly "neutralized" the Taiwan Straits with American naval power. The purpose was to prevent Peking from attacking Taiwan, though it was announced as an impartial neutralizing action designed to control the Nationalists as well as the Communists. This "neutralizing" brought a further change in U.S. policy (June 27) when the administration shifted from the previous position that Taiwan was a part of China to the position that the status of the island was undetermined. Until the outbreak of the Korean war even leading Republican senators appeared to agree that Chiang had lost the mainland and that the American purpose should simply be to keep Taiwan out of the hands of the Communists. After the Korean outbreak conservative American sentiment swung strongly to a policy of support for Chiang. By 1951, the administration was facing extreme pressure from Congress for an inflexible stand against Peking.

During the Eisenhower administration, nonrecognition of Peking and support for Chiang's government as the government of all China (both begun

FOR FURTHER READING

Korean War. Harold Vinacke, *Far Eastern Politics in the Post-War Period* (1956). Leon Gordenker, *The United Nations and the Peaceful Unification of Korea: The Politics of Field Operations, 1947-1950* (1959). Carl Berger, *The Korea Knot: A Military-Political History* (1957). L. M. Goodrich, *Korea: A Study of United States Policy in the United Nations* (1956). J. W. Spanier, *The Truman-MacArthur Controversy and the Korean War* (1959).* David Rees, *Korea: The Limited War* (1964).* William H. Vatcher, Jr., *Panmunjon: The Story of the Korean Military Armistic Negotiations* (1958). Kenneth T. Young, *Negotiating with the Chinese Communists: The United States Experience, 1953-1967* (1968).*

Korea. Three complementary studies emphasizing the years before 1945: William E. Henthorn, *A History of Korea* (1971); Sohn Powkey, *et al., The History of Korea* (1970); and Han Woo-keun, *The History of Korea,* trans. Lee Kyong-shik and Grafton K. Mintz, ed. (1972). Shannon McCune, *Korea's Heritage: A Regional and Social Geography* (1956); Kim Ik-tal, *Korea: Its Land, People, and Culture of All Ages* (1960); and Patricia M. Bartz, *South Korea: A Descriptive Geography*

(1972), are highly readable cultural geographies. Vincent S. R. Brandt, *A Korean Village: Between Farm and Sea* (1972), an example of the growing body of research by behavioral scientists. South Korea's political problems are examined in David C. Cole and Princeton N. Lyman, *Korean Development: the Interplay of Politics and Economics* (1971); Kim Kwon-bong, *The Korea-Japan Treaty Crisis and the Instability of Korean Political System* (1971); and Kim Se-jin, *The Politics of Military Revolution in Korea* (1971). Lee Chong-sik, *The Politics of Korean Nationalism* (1963), the standard study. Robert A. Scalapino, and Chong-sik Lee, *Communism in Korea* (2 vols., 1973), the most exhaustive study. On North Korea, see Philip Rudolph, *North Korea's Political and Economic Structure* (1959); Robert Scalapino, ed., *North Korea Today* (1963); and Joseph S. Chung, *Patterns of Economic Development: Korea* (1966). Lim Youngli, "Foreign Influence on the Economic Change in Korea: A Survey," *Journal of Asian Studies* 28 (1968), 77-99. W. D. Reeve, *The Republic of Korea: A Political and Economic Study* (1963), useful for the Rhee period. John K. Oh, *Korea: Democracy on Trial* (1968) is critical of achievements to 1967.

Taiwan. P. M. A. Linebarger, *et al., Far Eastern Governments and Politics* (2nd ed., 1956). On the earlier stages of *Kuomintang*-Nationalist rule, see Norton S. Ginsburg, *Economic Resources and Development of Formosa* (1953); Fred W. Riggs, *Formosa under Chinese Nationalist Rule* (1952); and George H. Kerr, *Formosa Betrayed* (1965). Hsieh Chiao-min, *Taiwan-Ilha Formosa: A Geography in Perspective* (1965). Aspects of agricultural development are treated in Teng-hui Lee, *Intersectoral Capital Flows in the Economic Development of Taiwan, 1895-1960* (1971); Anthony Y. C. Koo, *The Role of Land Reform in Economic Development: A Case Study* (1968); T. S. Shen, *Agricultural Development on Taiwan since World War II* (1964); and Charles Kao, "An Analysis of Agricultural Output Increase on Taiwan, 1953-1964," *Journal of Asian Studies* 26 (1967), 611-26. Norma Diamond, *K'un*

---

by Truman as temporary measures) became established American policy. This policy enjoyed an almost unanimous support in government and in American public opinion simply because it was based on fear and intense emotionalism rather than on reasoned analysis of actual American interests. Somewhat paradoxically, supporters of the policy sometimes described Mao's government as a passing phase.

The Kennedy administration did not accept the view that Mao's government was merely a transient phenomenon. This change was important for long-range purposes, but had no effect upon immediate policy. Kennedy was under the same domestic pressures as Eisenhower to support Chiang and to ignore or rebuff Peking. The Johnson administration made no significant change in the Kennedy policy toward Taiwan and Peking. See the detailed discussion in William M. Bueler, *U.S. China Policy and the Problem of Taiwan* (1971). For the impact of improved mainland Chinese relations with the United States and Japan, see J. Bruce Jacobs, "Taiwan, 1972: Political Season," *Asian Survey,* 13 (1973), 102-12.

Shen: A Taiwan Village (1969),* emphasizes relationships between the economy and social organization. Mark Mancall, ed., *Formosa Today* (1964), a collection of essays generally critical of *Kuomintang*-Nationalist rule.

American Relations with Korea and Taiwan. Essays by Shannon McCune, Robert Scalapino, and Allen S. Whiting in *The United States and the Far East,* Willard Thorp, ed. (2nd. ed., 1962).* An official statement of American policy is in the United States Department of State, *U.S. Policy on Nonrecognition of Communist China,* Public Services Division, Pub. No. 6705, Far Eastern Series (1958). Conlon Associates, Ltd., *United States Foreign Policy: Asia,* Study No. 5, United States Senate, 86th Cong. 1st Sess. (1959), a critical review made at the request of the Senate Foreign Relations Committee. Sheldon Appleton, *The Eternal Triangle? Communist China, the United States, and the United Nations* (1961) includes American and United Nations documents. Robert P. Newman, *Recognition of Communist China? A Study in Argument* (1961),* a convenient summary of this debate in the United States. Li Thianhok, "The China Impasse: A Formosan View," *Foreign Affairs* 36 (1958), 437-48.

Robert Scalapino, "The Question of 'Two Chinas'" in *China in Crisis: China's Heritage and the Communist Political System,* Ho Ping-ti and Tsou Tang, eds. (1968),* 109-20, argues for a two-China policy. Two studies debating the Taiwan question in the light of improved American relations with the People's Republic are: Jerome A. Cohen, *et al., Taiwan and American Policy: The Dilemma in U.S.-China Relations* (1971)*; and Richard Moorsteen and Morton Abramowitz, *Remaking China Policy: U.S. China Relations and Governmental Decision Making* (1971).

The Transactions of the Korea Branch of the Royal Asiatic Society is an important source for the cultural history of Korea. The *Korean Quarterly* is useful for political events. For current developments in Korea and Taiwan see *Pacific Affairs* and *Asian Survey.*

Nationalism and Conflict in Southeast Asia After 1945

35

World War II bequeathed to Southeast Asia a perplexing, frustrating legacy. The war had so crippled the old colonial orders that the way appeared to be open for the states of this vast region to move toward independence. After 1945, Southeast Asia did enjoy limited opportunities to nurture concepts of freedom, nationalism, and economic and social modernization. Yet even in this new era of "independence," the area was subjected to renewed and devastating international and domestic pressures. Local rivalries which had been suppressed under colonialism reappeared, along with embittered relations among native leaders attempting to present a united front against Western and Japanese imperialism. At the same time, the retreat of the colonial empires created a vacuum of political power—an invitation to new contestants seeking to control the region as it became involved in the cold war rivalries of the United States, the Soviet Union, and Communist China.

The revolutionary changes which engulfed Southeast Asia in the wake of World War II should not have come as a surprise to any informed observer: they were a logical product of history reaching back many years. The

Western impacts of the nineteenth and twentieth centuries, which contributed so profoundly to new and modern outlooks in Japan and China, inevitably influenced the history of Southeast Asia as well. But colonialism, whether Spanish or American in the Philippines, British in Burma and Malaya, Dutch in the East Indies, or French in Indochina, was in varying degrees a principal agent of its own eventual destruction. In Japan and China, as we have seen, Western infringements on those traditional states and the ultimate imposition of semi-colonial status upon them prepared the way for protest and modern nationalism. Southeast Asia after 1945 was responding to similar aspirations. What made Southeast Asia a special and tragic case was its lack of a single, overall cultural heritage. The new Southeast Asia was a conglomerate of many "states" and cultures, a region occupied by groups of people holding little in common, who just happened to live next door to each other.[1]

[1] Note Bernard K. Gordon, *The Dimensions of Conflict in Southeast Asia* (1966).* The student of contemporary history may find it useful to compare recent years in Southeast Asia with the plight of the Balkans following the collapse of the Ottoman empire.

THE MARCH TOWARD INDEPENDENCE

A goodly part of colonial Southeast Asia had achieved its independence within a decade after the Japanese surrender of 1945. The Philippine Commonwealth in 1946 became the Republic of the Philippines; in 1948, Burma, granted a very limited self-government in 1937, became a fully independent nation outside the Commonwealth; the Netherlands East Indies, following four years of sporadic warfare between the Dutch and native forces, became (except for the area known as Netherlands West New Guinea or West Irian) the Republic of Indonesia in 1950; in 1957 the former British colonies and protected states in Malaya became the Federation of Malaya, independent but a member of the British Commonwealth. (The Federation was expanded into the States of Malaysia in 1963 by the addition of Singapore, together with Sabad and Sarawak, two British colonies in Borneo; Singapore itself became an independent state in 1965.) And Thailand (Siam), the only state in Southeast Asia not taken over by a colonial power until the Japanese occupation of World War II, resumed its independence following the Japanese withdrawal.

In Indochina, however, where the French had created a great empire comprising Vietnam, Cambodia, and Laos, there was no easy transition to independence. Here native nationalisms were subverted by domestic turmoil, civil wars, and the vain efforts of the French to repossess their empire—and, when this failed, by efforts of the great powers (the United States, Russia, and China) to force a settlement according to their respective and irreconcilable ideas on who was to control what. The eventual result was a prolonged military struggle which brought frightful destruction throughout Indochina.

The effects of this ghastly conflict reached far beyond Indochina. Defeat at the hands of the North Vietnamese and the eventual loss of Indochina combined with other troubles to produce in France a prolonged political crisis. For the United States, the Vietnam war became the longest in its history, a costly involvement in money and lives, and one which,

as in the case of France, contributed in a major degree to a far-reaching domestic crisis. Furthermore, the Vietnam war may be regarded as part of a struggle to define a new international order in greater East Asia involving a resurgent China and Japan.

THE LURE OF REGIONAL UNITY

During the immediate postwar years, there were efforts throughout Southeast Asia to destroy the vestiges of imperialism and to foster regional unity. Conferences were convened by India in 1947 to strengthen Asian independence, to foster interstate relations, and, in 1949, to demand the departure of the Dutch from Indonesia. In 1953, Asian socialists led representatives from Indonesia, Burma, India, Pakistan, and Ceylon in condemning French policy in Vietnam, the arms race, the development of nuclear weapons, and other activities of the great powers. The most ambitious of these meetings, the Bandung conference, called by Indonesia in 1955, attempted to promote unity among the new states. Delegates to this meeting supported such matters as Indonesia's claims to West Irian and demands for an end to the production and testing of nuclear weapons, United Nations membership for states such as Laos and Cambodia, and the unification of Vietnam. Like the earlier meetings, Bandung was notable not only for its basic goals but also for its inability to translate its resolutions to action. In Southeast Asia, cooperation was an ideal, not a reality: Thailand pressed Burma and Cambodia for territorial adjustments; Cambodia protested alleged Vietnamese expansion at Cambodian expense; and the creation of Malaysia brought protests and threats from the Philippines and Indonesia. Furthermore, in a world dominated by great powers, the new states of Southeast Asia, unable to reconcile their own differences, had little influence on the world beyond their own region.[2]

[2] Territorial disputes, a frequent source of trouble in Southeast Asia, were rooted in border lines inherited from the colonial period. Modern Southeast Asian nationalists, however, tended to advance claims based on the domains of ancient kingdoms. The actual

FRANCE VERSUS THE *VIETMINH*

It was against this background of rival Southeast Asian nationalisms that the French attempted after 1945 to reestablish their Indochinese empire. Initially, the French return seemed simply a matter of taking over administrative authority from the Japanese. At the Potsdam conference (1945), however, victorious Allies commissioned the Chinese Nationalists to occupy northern Vietnam, while the British were to occupy the south. The Free French entered the south behind the British and, by early 1946 when the British withdrew, French control had been reestablished in most of Cochin China. But a very different situation prevailed in the north. There, during the interval between the Japanese surrender and the French reoccupation, Chinese Nationalist forces not only disarmed and evacuated the Japanese, but also tolerated a government, the Democratic Republic of Vietnam, established by Ho Chi Minh and the *Vietminh* at Hanoi in August, 1945. As a result, returning French forces met organized resistance.

By stressing such themes as "democracy" and "independence," Ho had fashioned a united popular front against French authority. His administration included non-Communists as well as Communists. These tactics alone, however, were not enough to sustain Vietnamese independence. Since neither the Chinese Nationalists nor the United States was disposed to offer Ho any aid, the Vietnamese leader had to come to terms with superior French power. Under an agreement reached on March 6, 1946, France recognized Ho's Democratic Republic as a free state having its own army, but this understanding was limited by the further stipulation that the Democratic Republic was to become part of an Indochinese Federation within a French "Union." The political realities of this deal were re-

extent of these kingdoms was not easy to determine as the old dynastic states, concerned with the protection of the throne, gave more attention to sources of income (the commodity trade, trading routes, cities, and such) than to the mere control of territory.

vealed when French troops marched back to Hanoi.

It was soon clear that this make-believe understanding had solved nothing. Ho quickly lost interest in the principle of a united front. Even before his relations with the French broke down, Vietnamese Communist forces had all but destroyed native non-Communist organizations in the north. The French set up a rival "independent" puppet regime in Cochin China and in November, 1946, unleashed a naval and air bombardment on Haiphong. A month later the forces of the Vietnamese Republic were attacking the French at Hanoi. Such, in brief outline, was the beginning of a seven-year Franco-Vietnamese war.

THE COLD WAR REACHES VIETNAM

From 1947 to 1954, France sought desperately to retain the substance of her colonial overlordship by working through native nationalist and anti-communist regimes. By 1949, the French had put together a government at Saigon headed by the ex-emperor Bao-Dai. The following year the French National Assembly declared Bao-Dai's Vietnam along with Cambodia and Laos to be "associated" states in the French Federation. Meanwhile, as French aims became all too clear, Ho's regime was ousted from Hanoi. All this was taking place at a time when the Chinese Communists were coming to power at Peking, when separate Communist-led outbreaks were occurring in Burma, Indonesia, Malaya, and the Philippines, and when there were dramatic intensifications of rivalries between Communist and anti-communist powers throughout the world. The result was that Communist China and the Soviet Union recognized Ho Chi Minh's Democratic Republic, and the United States and Great Britain recognized Bao-Dai's government. American aid and arms flowed promptly to the French in Vietnam, and Chinese aid crossed the border of Tonkin to the *Vietminh*. The cold war had reached Indochina.[3]

[3] American involvement in Vietnam, first as the supplier of aid to the French and, later, as a direct

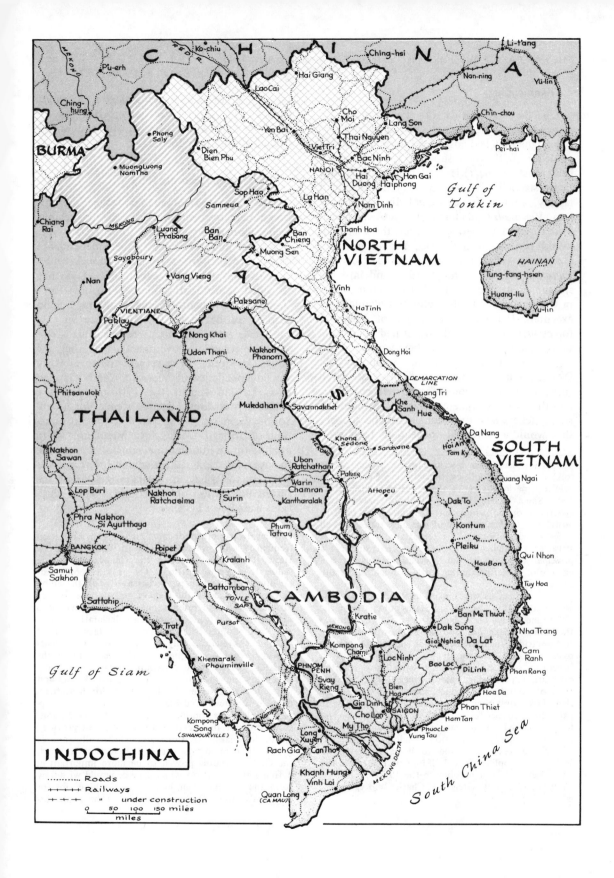

INDOCHINA

.... Roads
++++ Railways
+ + + " under construction

0 50 100 150 miles
miles

Dienbienphu

On the battlefields of the Franco-Vietnamese war, the French sustained military campaigns that had cost $1.5 billion by the end of 1949. With their superior firepower they held most of the cities and major towns, but their strength in the countryside declined rapidly. French forces repeatedly cut deeply into *Vietminh*-held territory; yet as French forces moved to new offensives, the *Vietminh* would return. In mid-1953, France gambled everything on a final effort to destroy the *Vietminh* armies. Through 1953 and into the spring, 1954, a series of offensives culminating in the battle of Dienbienphu was planned and executed. Heavy concentrations of *Vietminh* forces were to be lured into armed confrontations where, it was said, they would be destroyed by France's superior weaponry. At Dienbienphu the French correctly calculated that the *Vietminh* would accept their challenge, but they totally underestimated the fervor of the attackers and the quantity of the artillery that would be brought to bear on their posi-

tion. The French surrendered to *Vietminh* forces under General Vo Nguyen Giap, May, 7, 1954, a date which forecast the end of the French empire in Indochina.

The Geneva Accords, 1954

The fall of Dienbienphu brought a new government to power in Paris. The new regime, facing hard reality, decided to withdraw from Indochina and to recognize the independence of the former colonies. An international conference of the powers in session at Geneva then struggled to find some kind of formula for a Vietnam settlement. In the resultant Geneva accords, produced by the conference on July 21, 1954, with the United States and Bao-Dai's South Vietnamese government abstaining, the powers pledged: (1) to respect the sovereignty and independence of Vietnam, Cambodia, and Laos; (2) to accept the 17th parallel as a temporary dividing line between North and South Vietnam; (3) to prohibit the introduction of foreign troops into Vietnam; (4) to provide for an international control commission to supervise the agreements; and (5) to call for elections to be held in Vietnam in 1956 on the future unification of the country. These elections were never held.[4]

---

participant, has been described as an aspect of the folklore of power politics—that cluster of convictions held by nation-states in their dealings with other states. Since the late 1940s, this body of convictions in American opinion included a number of primary postulates; (1) the security of the state transcends all other considerations; (2) international politics is a struggle in which all states are involved; and (3) a principal safeguard of the international system is a balance of power preventing world domination by any single power.

These principles were linked in the American view with a conviction that United States policy during the 1920s and 1930s (as embodied in such documents as the Kellogg-Briand pact and the Stimson non-recognition doctrine) was naive because it ignored the decisive role of power. The result was a decided shift in American opinion and policy to a power-politics orientation, producing, among other things, the doctrine of containment, which, though garbed in the rhetoric of opposing communism, was in reality an expanded concern for national security. Security was to be assured by military strength, alliances, and threats of massive retaliation. Under this doctrine, security interests were said to be world-wide. See William D. Coplin, "The Folklore of Power Politics and American Foreign Policy in the 1970's," in *After Vietnam,* Robert W. Gregg and Charles W. Kegley, Jr., eds. (1971), 14-31.

[4] In later American debates on Vietnam, a question frequently asked was whether South Vietnam and the United States had violated the Geneva accords in failing to agree to elections. The answer is one that, pending a time when research may dispel the ambiguities produced by the Geneva negotiations, is very difficult to give in brief, simple fashion. It has been said of the final Geneva conference declaration that it was "non-adopted." Of the several pledges produced by the conference, only the cease-fire agreements appear to have been signed, and these bound only the signatories. The final declaration (containing the only statement on elections) was not signed. Russia and China appear to have "assented" to it; South Vietnam rejected it. The United States statement made its support of elections contingent upon: (1) United Nations supervision of the elections (which was not provided for in the final declaration), and (2) the willingness of South Vietnam to take part in the election. In short, the Geneva accords proved to be more important in defining the terms on which France would withdraw from the fighting than in providing a blueprint for Vietnam's future. On these points see John T. McAlis-

Within Vietnam the so-called regrouping zones provided by the Geneva accords (zones which were not be construed as setting up a political boundary) were not welcomed by nationalists of any political complexion. In the north, Ho Chi Minh's *Vietminh* regarded the 1954 settlement as better suited to the needs of its communist allies than to itself. Similarly, South Vietnam in later years commemorated the anniversary of the Geneva accords as "National Shame Day." Actual political conditions on both sides of the 17th parallel after 1954 made unification a very remote possibility, except through the conquest of one side by the other.

ter, Jr., *Vietnam: The Origins of Revolution* (1969), 351-52; George McTurnan Kahin and John W. Lewis, *The United States in Vietnam* (rev. ed., 1969),* 43-63; and Milton Sacks, "Background to the Vietnam War: An Introduction." in *Studies on the Soviet Union*, 6 (1966), 1-7. For further details see Robert F. Randle, *Geneva, 1954: The Settlement of the Indochinese War* (1969), 569-72.

The Geneva agreements were regarded by most of the major powers (France, Great Britain, the Soviet Union, and Communist China) as an acceptable and peaceful settlement of the Indochina problem. The United States took an opposing position, its National Security Council concluding (August, 1954) that the Geneva agreement was a "disaster," a major forward stride for communism that could lead "to the loss of Southeast Asia," a phrase reminiscent of the previous "loss of China." See *The Pentagon Papers, As Published by the New York Times* (1971), 14ff.

In the north, Ho Chi Minh and the Communist party, the *Lao Dong* (Worker's party), applied themselves to tasks of consolidation and development. Efforts were made to replace traditionally-oriented village leaders with trusted personnel; to foster the loyalty of intellectuals and skilled workers; to implement land reform as a preliminary to raising agricultural productivity; to establish state ownership of all levels of business; and to introduce economic planning, with an emphasis on heavy industry. These changes were so fundamental and their implementation so harsh that the government at first faced widespread uprisings. They were controlled, however, without causing injury to the regime's commanding position.[5] Considerable success was also achieved in expanding the nation's economic base. With help from Communist China and the Soviet Union, North Vietnam reopened railway connections with Southern China, repaired harbor facilities, and

[5] The *Lao Dong's* aim in carrying forward these transformations was to win the political commitment of the masses to its social programs and leadership. To achieve this commitment, the *Lao Dong* placed less stress on material incentives than on forging a new political community—a community that commanded loyalty by rewarding performance with upward mobility and by offering individuals access to the attributes of modernity (literally, technical skills, etc.) and to political power.

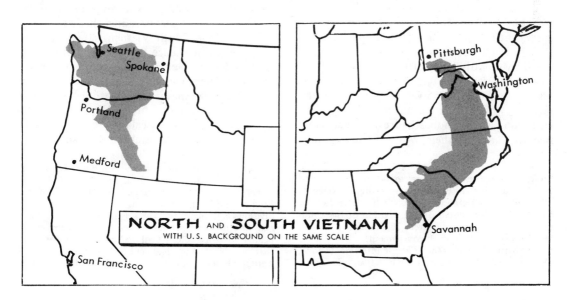

NORTH AND **SOUTH VIETNAM**
WITH U.S. BACKGROUND ON THE SAME SCALE

built factories, so that by the early 1960s, prior to the onset of American bombing raids, she could boast of industrial leadership in Southeast Asia. These accomplishments were the more notable because they were carried out in a land that had been stripped of facilities built by the French.[6] North Vietnam's economic development, however, contributed more to national power than to individual well-being. In spite of agricultural expansion, foodstuffs were chronically inadequate; and shortages in clothing and virtually all other consumer goods forced severe rationing.

The disciplined development of the North reflected a notable political stability. Operating initially through a provisional government, the *Lao Dong,* on January 1, 1960, provided for permanent leadership under a constitution that defined the institutions of a single-party dictatorship.[7] The elections which followed sanctioned *Lao Dong* control and confirmed Ho Chi Minh as president. Other key leaders were Pham Van Dong as premier and foreign minister; Vo Nguyen Giap, army commander-in-chief, as minister of defense; and Truong Chinh as leader of the National Assembly. Following Ho's death in 1969, these close associates continued the leadership on a cooperative basis.

DIEM AND SOUTH VIETNAM

In South Vietnam there was neither the equivalent of the personal leadership offered by Ho Chi Minh nor a party having the organizational basis or discipline of the *Lao Dong.* While France had regarded Bao Dai as chief of state, his government by 1955 was only one of several factions which exercised authority. Caodaists, Hoa Hao, and Catholics had established paramilitary forces of their own and had begun to

operate from separate territorial bases. Within Saigon, the seat of Bao Dai's government, a gangster organization known as *Binh Xuyen,* controlled the police. The army chief of staff, Nguyen Van Hinh, wanted the premiership for himself. And finally, among and between all these contending forces, dozens of splinter parties maneuvered for position. It was from this situation of growing and almost indescribable political chaos that Ngo Dinh Diem, a member of a prominent Roman Catholic family, and his brother, Ngo Dinh Nhu, emerged at the head of such government as South Vietnam was to have in the years 1955-1963. Serving first as Bao Dai's premier and then as president of the Republic of Vietnam (established in October, 1955), Diem's political fortunes were supported by aid from the United States throughout the Eisenhower administration. But it was an extraordinary capacity for political survival, as well as foreign aid, that explained Diem's tenure. Attacked on all sides, Diem and his brother played army faction against faction, made and broke alliances with the parties, and used their police and military authority to maintain themselves in power.

Complicating Diem's tasks was the fact that the government over which he presided was at war not only with itself but also with native Communists. While the Communist military in 1954 had followed Ho Chi Minh north of the 17th parallel, party cadres had remained behind in the South Vietnam countryside to organize the populace for the elections scheduled under the Geneva conference agreements. Although Diem jailed local leaders suspected of Communist sympathies, he was unable to root out the opposition entirely. His own officials were subjected to an escalating series of attacks as they attempted to establish their authority.[8]

---

[6] Under the Geneva agreement of 1954, all public institutions and services were to be handed over to Hanoi, but South Vietnam, operating through a "Committee for Defense of the North," carried off or destroyed what it could during division of the country. Hanoi ultimately received 265 million francs in restitution from the French government.

[7] Bernard B. Fall, *The Two Viet-Nams* (1963), 399-416, gives the full text of the constitution.

[8] The semantic aspects of the conflict in Indochina, especially since the Geneva accords of 1954, have been rather notable. For example, after the fall of the French empire in Indochina and the "temporary" division of the country, the hostilities between North and South Vietnam and within South Vietnam appeared to constitute a civil war in the obvious sense that peoples of the same general nationality and area were fighting each other for control of political power.

Moreover, by March, 1960, the *Vietcong,* as Diem had dubbed the Communists of the south, had established a political administration of their own through their political agency, the National Liberation Front. By this means the *Vietcong* collected taxes, conscripted troops, collected food and supplies, and provided rudimentary public services in territory supposed to be ruled by Diem.

Under Diem, some headway was made in consolidating political leadership in Saigon, but little was done to build a popular base for rule in the countryside. The quality of local leadership declined as established village chiefs were jailed in Diem's anti-Communist campaigns. A land reform program which was intended to win peasant loyalty through rent reductions and other benefits became, under faulty administration, a source of more political disaffection. Furthermore, the introduction of "strategic hamlets," a system of fortified villages which had served in Malaya to isolate guerrillas and thereby to rob them of their major supply base, failed to check the *Vietcong.* In fact, Diem's major accomplishment was the resettlement from the north of some 745,000 Catholic refugees. It was from members of this group and the army that Diem found his major support.

THE AMERICAN INVOLVEMENT

Diem's failure to rally his own people increased the pressures on the United States to assume a larger role in South Vietnamese politics. This

---

As the ally of the Saigon government, however, the United States took the position that only the conflict between Saigon and the National Liberation Front, a Communist-led coalition of insurgents opposing Diem, could be considered a civil war and that the infiltration of North Vietnamese forces was an international event in violation of the 1954 accord and, therefore, not a civil war but an aggression. Note United States, Department of States, News Release, December 6, 1973, and *A Threat to the Peace: North Viet-Nam's Effort to Conquer South Viet-Nam,* Publication #7308, Far Eastern Series 110 (1961), Part I, 12-13. Kahin and Lewis, *United States in Vietnam,* 384-87, is critical of this official thesis. A Communist view is developed in Wilfred G. Burchett: *The Fugitive War: The United States in Vietnam and Laos* (1963); and *Vietnam: The Inside Story of the Guerilla War* (1965).

growing American involvement had been forecast in principle as early as 1949 when Secretary of State Dean Acheson said it was as essential to contain communist aggression in Asia as in Europe. For the ensuing two decades this statement embodied the essence of American policy. It was a policy which, in the view of its critics, was based on predetermined assumptions, acceptable to the popular American mood, rather than on continuing analysis of on-going and changing conditions. Secretary Acheson's statement, it should be remembered, was made in the year that China fell to the Communists. Thus the secretary spoke against the background of a popular American theory to the effect that Russia (now joined by Communist China) was successfully promoting a world-wide Communist conspiracy. Americans were therefore receptive to notions of "containing" further Communist expansion. The strength of the American position lay in its simplicity and its implications of virtue; its weakness lay in its ignoring the fact that the Communist victory in China was a part of nationalistic and revolutionary movements which had been maturing in East Asia for a century. This weakness revealed a very imperfect reading by Americans of the modern history of East Asia.[9]

---

[9] Since the American involvement in Southeast Asia, particularly in Vietnam, Laos, Cambodia, and Thailand, became one of the most controversial subjects in the history of American foreign relations, it is well to be reminded that the history of this entire undertaking (beginning in 1945 and not yet ended) will continue, for some years to come, to be an aspect of current history—incomplete, fragmented, lacking the more definitive qualities which only the perspective of time can give. These qualifications persist even though the primary and secondary sources now available on the American involvement are already massive. These sources include: (1) memoirs and "histories" by participating statesmen and other officials; (2) books and articles by journalists and other observers; (3) early interpretative accounts by scholar-specialists; (4) non-classified government documents, records of press conferences, and the hearings of Congressional committees; and (5) secret government documents, leaked and published in various incomplete editions, such as the so-called "Pentagon Papers," a top secret history of the role of the United States in Indochina authorized in June, 1967, by Secretary of Defense Robert S. McNamara. Its official title is *History of U.S. Decision-Making Process on Vietnam Policy.* Various published

The Truman Years

Implementing the Acheson policy in 1950, the United States sent economic and military aid to the French as they attempted to re-establish their Indochinese empire. Since the French, however, were only interested in recovering their colonies, the United States was in the uncomfortable position of giving support to colonialism. Later that year, on the outbreak of the Korean war and at a time when Communist-led uprisings were breaking out in the Philippines, Malaya, Burma, and Indonesia, this American aid was increased, on the theory that what was happening in Indochina was indeed a part of a world-wide Communist conspiracy. The new aid included the sending of an American military mission to Saigon. During 1951, American aid to France in Indochina was in excess of $500 million.

The Eisenhower Years

The armistice of July, 1953, which brought an uneasy peace in the Korean war did not diminish official American fears concerning Indochina. The new American secretary of state, John Foster Dulles, was more devoted to the simplistic Acheson policy than was Acheson himself. Dulles saw in Communist China a supreme threat to American interests and was deeply disturbed by reports of Chinese Communist troop concentrations on the North Vietnamese border. By this time, on the credit side, the French were training and using additional native troops, a kind of "Vietnamization" program which, they said, would produce an early victory. In these

editions of parts of this study include: *The Pentagon Papers, As Published by the New York Times* (1971); *The Pentagon Papers: The Defense Department History of U.S. Decision-Making on Vietnam: The Senator Gravel Edition* (1971); and *United States-Vietnam Relations, 1945-1967: Study Prepared by the Department of Defense,* printed for the use of the House Committee on Armed Services (1971).

For a description and evaluation of sources on the Indochina involvement see James C. Thomson, Jr., "The Nineteen Sixties as History," in *American-East Asian Relations: A Survey,* Ernest R. May and James C. Thomson, Jr., eds. (1972), 390-409.

circumstances, the Eisenhower administration sought to increase popular American support for the French and their war in Vietnam by dwelling on the transcendent importance of Southeast Asia for the free world and by invoking the "falling domino" theory. On the other hand, the president, early in 1954, exercised a restraining influence on some top members of his own administration when he turned down the French request for American air strikes in Indochina to save Dienbienphu and its crumbling military fortunes.

Geneva and SEATO

In holding aloof from the Geneva accords (see p. 496), the United States had announced that it would refrain from any threat or use of force that might disturb the agreements so long as there was no renewal of Communist aggression in Indochina. Actually, the French withdrawal spurred Washington to seek a collective defense treaty covering Communist movements in Southeast Asia. A conference called at Manila on the initiative of Secretary Dulles, September, 1954, resulted in the formation of the Southeast Asia Treaty Organization (SEATO). Members of this organization—the United States, Great Britain, Australia, New Zealand, France, the Philippines, and Pakistan—pledged that, in the event of aggression or subversion, they would "consult immediately" on measures to be taken within the limits of their "constitutional processes." Under a special protocol, the terms of the SEATO agreement were extended to cover Laos, Cambodia, and "the free territory under the jurisdiction of the State of Vietnam." SEATO has sometimes been described as a pale reflection of the North Atlantic Treaty Organization. But unlike the latter, SEATO had no military forces of its own and no explicit pledges of support for its purposes. Moreover, four "neutral" states—India, Burma, Indonesia, and Ceylon—pointedly refused to join.

However great its deficiencies as a defense organization, SEATO was in fact an affirmation of American intent to assume enlarged responsibilities in a region evacuated by a European colonial powers. Along with the establishment of SEATO, the Eisenhower administration committed the United States in October, 1954, to military assistance to Ngo Dinh Diem, who had replaced Bao-Dai as head of South Vietnam. In this case, aid was coupled with American intervention in South Vietnam's political processes: Diem was told that he was expected to undertake needed reforms as a means for building popular support and curbing opposition.

Meanwhile, SEATO became still another source of friction in American relations with Communist China. While signing the SEATO pact in Manila, Secretary Dulles had singled out China as the great danger to Southeast Asia. These remarks were only the preliminary round in a battle of words and slogans that brought Sino-American hostility to new heights, thereby burying whatever chance there may have been for a peaceful settlement in Indochina.[10]

THE LAOTIAN CRISIS

A second arena of civil war and international rivalry in Indochina was the unhappy kingdom of Laos, a small and weak country (some 91,000 square miles with a population of about three million). The Geneva accords of 1954 had provided for the neutrality of Laos and Cambodia, but this status was quite beyond the capacity of Laos to maintain. During World War II a strong resistance movement in Laos, the *Lao Issara*, fought the Japanese and later the returning French. Its successor was the Pathet Lao organized in 1951, with most of its support coming from Communist North Vietnam. Indeed, the French stand at Dienbienphu was designed in part to stop *Vietminh* incursions into Laos and to prevent the development of supply routes through Laos to South Vietnam. The existence of the Pathet Lao meant Laos had two *de facto* governments and intermittent

[10] Dulles declared that "open military aggression by the Chinese Communist regime" and "disturbances fomented from Communist China" were the twofold danger the United States faced in Southeast Asia. Quoted in Foster Rhea Dulles, *American Policy toward Communist China: The Historical Record, 1949-1969* (1972), 146.

civil war.[11] Laos, therefore, presented a very troublesome problem for American policy makers, who were already becoming more deeply involved in the affairs of Vietnam. During the later 1950s, the United States, after supporting a neutralist central government, gave aid to right-wing regimes which, it was hoped, would create an anti-Communist bastion in Laos. These developments prompted dissident elements to appeal to the Soviet Union for assistance. Russia responded by air-lifting military supplies to the Pathet Lao and the North Vietnamese, who were infiltrating eastern Laos to aid the Pathet Lao and to open a supply route to support growing insurgency in South Vietnam. In these circumstances, the Kennedy administration, supported by Khrushchev at Vienna (June, 1961), decided to "neutralize" Laos in the general pattern of the earlier Geneva accords. Since the powers apparently desired to avoid a major conflict, and since no single Laotian faction had achieved a decisive advantage, the United States and the Soviet Union joined in a fourteen-nation declaration at Geneva (1962) providing a formula for Laotian independence, neutrality, and peace. Under this formula, foreign military missions were to be withdrawn, an international control commission would be provided, and a new coalition, the Royal Laotian government, would be formed representing the irreconcilables: the right, the center, and the left. For a time, tensions were eased as the contestants took stock of their new

[11] Some idea of the interminable rivalries within Laos may be gathered from the following record of events:

1957. Formation of a coalition government headed by Prince Souvanna Phouma and including his half-brother the "Red Prince" Souphanouvong, the head of the Pathet Lao.

1958. Collapse of the coalition.

1959. Seizure of power by the rightists under General Phoumi Nosavan.

1960. Defection of troops under Kong Le and the setting up of rival regimes under Souvanna Phouma and Phoumi Nosavan. Seizure of Vientiane by Phouma Nosavan, and the arrival of Russian aid to the Souvanna Phouma-Kong Le group.

1962. Formation of a new coalition headed by Souvanna Phouma and including Phoumi Nosavan and Souphanouvong, the leader of the Pathet Lao.

1963. The Pathet Lao leaves the coalition.

1965. Phoumi Nosavan ousted from the government.

positions. The calm did not last long. In 1963, the coalition collapsed, and by 1965, the Pathet Lao was at war with Royal Laotian government.[12]

AMERICANIZING THE WAR

As it first assumed office, the Kennedy administration seemed to move toward a re-examination of policies in East and Southeast Asia, particularly the Vietnam conflict. Avoiding much of the more emotional language sometimes employed by spokesmen of the Eisenhower administration, Kennedy spoke of America's need to maintain a balance of power in Asia as in Europe. Nevertheless, the president and his secretary of state, Dean Rusk, soon shared with their predecessors a conviction that "containment" was essential. Although the United States had accepted a compromise settlement in Laos, American policy in 1961-1962 was still predicated on a belief that China was intent on expanding her influence, if not her control, in border areas. When new tensions arose in the Taiwan Straits, Kennedy renewed the Eisenhower-Dulles formula in support of the Chinese Nationalists (see p. 512).

In October, 1962, as fighting broke out along the Indian-Chinese frontiers, the United States promised India large-scale military assistance to meet China's "violent and aggressive action." These steps, it should be noted, were taken at a time when Washington was aware of severe tensions in Sino-Russian relations, which should have called into question Secretary Dulles's contention that the United States was facing a disguised form of Russian imperialism in Asia. Moreover, the American government had reason to know that Chinese objectives in India were probably much more limited than was indicated by their diplomatic rhetoric proclaiming world revolution. Chinese troops, for example, had been pulled back along the Indian frontier, though an invasion of India was still quite possible. None of these facts, however, was sufficient to shake American faith in the need for "containment." Indeed, a revised American thesis saw an aggressive, determined China, freed from Soviet leadership, offering greater dangers in Asia than the combined efforts of Peking and Moscow had done previously.[13]

THE FALL OF DIEM

It was thus in an atmosphere of heightened tensions that Vietnam became the focus of "containment" in Southeast Asia. The problem there, however, was that Diem, like his predecessor Bao-Dai, was in as great danger from his own people as from the Communist North. In an effort to curb continuing political disintegration, American advice and aid had been increased and extended to non-military areas; yet, by 1962-1963, the political shambles of the Diem government had become all too apparent. The *Vietcong* was expanding the areas of South Vietnam under its control, Diem's own planes bombed his presidential palace, and protesting Buddhist monks burned themselves to death in the streets of Saigon. To these and similar

---

[12] Note Harold C. Hinton, *China's Turbulent Quest* (1970), *passim.*

[13] In June, 1962, Peng Chen, mayor of Peking and a prominent government spokesman, outlined what the United States must do if peace were to be assured: "The U.S. imperialists," he said, "must get out of Korea, get out of Taiwan, get out of South Vietnam, get out of Laos," and then he added for good measure, "get out of the whole area of Asia, Africa, and Latin America." Statements of this kind were referred to in justifying the need for "containment." Among some American officials, however, there was a belief that these Chinese views should not be taken literally. They were intended, it was said, to heighten Chinese nationalism and to identify it with the Peking government. Revision of American policy toward conciliation with China, it was held, was quite possible. According to Kennedy's closest advisers, the president was testing this theory in his last news conference when he denied that the United States was "wedded to a policy of hostility to Red China," and suggested the possible need for a reappraisal of American policy. Apparently, however, the president did not see his signal to the Chinese as a step leading to any immediate change; he remarked to an adviser that improved Sino-American relations were "a subject for the second term." See Dulles, *American Policy,* 188-210.

events, Diem replied by narrowing his political base. He arrested real or suspected political opponents and bestowed increasing power on relatives and a small circle of family friends. Finally, in November, 1963, Diem felt it necessary to bring troops into Saigon to protect government offices. At this point, the Kennedy administration, apparently despairing of Diem's capacity to govern, announced suspension of some American aid. Shortly thereafter a military coup engineered by officers of the South Vietnamese army drove Diem from office and assassinated him. In the months that followed, South Vietnam survived only because of the American presence. Even with this presence, nine administrations came to power and fell before a more permanent leadership emerged. In June, 1965, a new government took office that included General Nguyen Cao Ky, a Buddhist, as premier. Ky was ousted later, but Nguyen Van Thieu, his successor, ruled until faced with imminent defeat in 1975.

These unhappy events offered fresh illustrations of both the weaknesses and the strengths of American policy. By stressing ideological objectives above all others, the United States found that in Vietnam its efforts were directed against the forces which had seized the initiative in a national revolution. This fact alone presented a major obstacle to the implementation of American policy. But lack of success in Vietnam did not mean that American policy lost immediate favor at home. "Containment" throughout the early and mid-1960s drew unflagging support from political leaders of both major parties. This meant that there was ample support within the United States for ever larger commitments. In 1961, as the Eisenhower administration left office, the United States had less than 1,000 officers and men in South Vietnam; at the time of President Kennedy's death (a few days after Diem's ouster), American forces numbered more than 15,000. Although these forces had been assigned as advisers to South Vietnam, they were shortly to be involved in combat.

THE JOHNSON YEARS

The growing importance of Vietnam in American affairs was suggested, August 4, 1964, when President Lyndon B. Johnson announced that in retaliation for reported attacks on two American destroyers patrolling in the Gulf of Tonkin, the United States had carried out air strikes on four PT boat bases and an oil storage depot, thus for the first time carrying the war outside the south. Shortly thereafter, Congress approved the "Gulf of Tonkin resolution," whereby the administration was authorized to "take all necessary measures to repel any armed attack against the forces of the United States and to prevent further aggression." The United States, the resolution affirmed, was prepared "as the President determines to take all necessary steps, including the use of armed forces, to assist any member or protocol state of the Southeast Asia Collective Defense Treaty requesting assistance in defense of its freedom."[14] Taking note that this resolution had been passed in the midst of a presidential campaign, President Johnson asserted that, "Hostile nations must understand that in such a period the United States will continue to protect its national interests and that in these matters there is no division among us."[15]

By February, 1965, American air strikes were authorized against *Vietcong* military installations and troop concentrations in the south and against supply lines and logistical and industrial centers in the north. At the height of these raids, American planes were dropping a weekly bomb tonnage that exceeded the totals at the peak of attacks on Germany in World War II. Meanwhile, American ground forces swelled from 16,500 in 1964 to 267,000 in 1966, and to more than 500,000 in 1968.[16] In

[14] The text of the resolution is in the *United States Department of State, Bulletin*, 5 (August 24, 1964), 268. The resolution passed unanimously in the House of Representatives; the Senate vote was 88-2. For a critical appraisal of the Gulf of Tonkin incident and the American response, see Kahin and Lewis, *United States in Vietnam*, 157-59.

[15] President Johnson's order to strike North Vietnamese military installations improved his political fortunes. The Gallup poll, August 26, 1964, showed that public approval of the president's handling of the Vietnam situation rose from 38 percent to 71 percent; 16 percent were unfavorable; and 13 percent had no opinion.

[16] A chronology of events in 1965 suggests the rapidity of the shift of American ground forces from military assistance to actual combat: (1) March—Marines landed to guard air bases at Danang: (2)

addition, 44,000 South Koreans, 4,000 Australians, and small New Zealand, Philippine, and Thai contingents joined the conflict. American policy presumed that these determined efforts would speed the making of peace on terms favorable to non-Communist South Vietnam. The immediate results, however, were intensification of the north's determination to fight and the multiplication of American casualties. When United States forces eventually withdrew from Vietnam, January, 1973, some 56,000 Americans had died in battle, many thousands more had been wounded, and about $150 billion had been expended in direct war costs. For the Vietnamese, north and south, there was an even more dreadful price in casualties, both military and civilian, in villages destroyed, in lands laid waste, and in social and moral disintegration.

VIETNAM IN AMERICAN POLITICS

As the war in Vietnam brought unspeakable devastation to the land and death to uncounted thousands of its peoples, the American mood shifted dramatically. For the third time since World War II (the fall of China to the Communists and the Korean war were the other occasions), American domestic politics were stirred profoundly by Asian issues. Criticism of the American role was expressed by "teach-ins" in the colleges, by the public burning of draft cards, and by mass demonstrations, including one at the Pentagon in Washington. As in the case of the Korean involvement, the critics were at first out-voiced by strong public support of official policy; but as casualties mounted, as the heavy drain on national resources continued, and as the war took on a seemingly interminable character, public patience was eroded. There were increasing demands even in high places for the United States to get out of Vietnam.

April—President Johnson authorized Marines to take the offensive; (3) June—the American commander in Vietnam authorized to commit American forces to battle when South Vietnam required aid; and (4) July —the American commander's request for forty-four additional battalions was approved.

In this emotional, divisive debate, American critics of the war linked it to fundamental problems in American society. Some charged the government with flagrant wasting of resources that were needed at home. Many regarded the war as a serious affront to American democratic institutions and traditions. There was also pointed questioning of the leadership offered by the federal administration and its powerful bureaucracies. A so-called "credibility gap" was said to have resulted from a war which persisted in spite of repeated governmental assurances by civilian and military spokesmen that victory was just around the corner.[17] Furthermore, criticism of Washington's policies even by reputable, responsible, and patriotic Americans was sometimes equated with disloyalty, thus giving support to the thesis that democracies attempting to mold other states run the danger of destroying their own institutions in the process.[18]

[17] Some American newsmen charged deliberate distortion. Samuel G. Blackman, general news editor of the Associated Press, noted of the administration that "its misinformation on the progress of the war in Vietnam has been monumental." "The Gospel According to Blackman," *Saturday Review,* 52 (August 9, 1969), 45. The war between the press and American officialdom is described from the newsman's point of view in David Halberstam, *The Making of a Quagmire* (1965). With respect to charges of lack of frankness, John Mecklin, onetime chief of United States Information Services in Saigon, commented: ". . . the case against us was more complex than the sin of falsehood. The root of the problem was the fact that much of what the newsmen took to be lies was exactly what the Mission genuinely believed, and was reporting to Washington. Events were to prove that the Mission itself was unaware of how badly the war was going, operating in a world of illusion." *Mission in Torment: An Intimate Account of the U.S. Role in Vietnam* (1965), 100.

[18] For more extended analysis see Gregg and Kegley, eds., *After Vietnam,* 1-13; on the background of broad institutional effects, George F. Kennan, *American Diplomacy, 1900-1950* (1951),* passim;* on the military problems of strategy and tactics, Russell F. Weigley, *The American Way of War: A History of United States Military Strategy and Policy* (1973), 398, 465-70. The frustrations of the American military experience in Vietnam should be considered in the context of a significant change in the American concept of military strategy. As Weigley points out, U.S. military strategy prior to 1945 was defined narrowly as a means to the destruction of the enemy's

By the early 1970s American policy makers and their critics had set forth four principal interpretations of Vietnam's frustrating experience. The first, often entertained by military professionals and the right wing of American politics, saw the Vietnam intervention as a qualified success and as a justifiable use of American military power. The frustrations arose, they said, because American presidents had refused to draw upon the full resources of the nation's power—that is, the United States unwisely had sought limited ends through limited means. A second interpretation, often ascribed to the so-called liberals, regarded the American involvement as a failure to balance ends and means. This view accepted the initial objective to defend Saigon as proper, if it could be done in "reasonable" time and at "reasonable" cost. Where Washington had erred was in failing to modify its objectives in light of escalating costs in dollars, lives, and declining American morale. A third interpretation, credited to the Nixon administration, held that America's involvement in Vietnam, though sound in principle, suffered from a limited failure of tactics. In the so-called "Nixon doctrine" of 1969, the United States announced that the basic purposes of American policy would not change, but the application of the principles of "containment" would henceforth be governed by the requirement that the threatened country provide the ground forces essential for its own defense.[19]

armed forces. But the cold war and particularly the Korean war suggested that this ingrained tradition of regarding military victory as the sole objective of war was no longer wholly adequate in all types of war and in an atomic age. Accordingly, an effort was made to widen the American concept of strategy to comprehend political ends, a revolutionary change in American thought. It meant that American military strategy was no longer confined to the use of force in a conflict, but rather came to include efforts to deter potential enemies from either starting a conflict or pursuing it once it had begun. Vietnam demonstrated, however, that deeply rooted habits have a capacity to persist. Though the new theory of strategy was applicable to American problems in Vietnam, it was often forgotten; victory was still defined in terms of decisive ground and air attacks, as though the enemy were another Germany and the goal were her surrender rather than her cessation of hostilities. See also Thomas H. Etzold and Bruce W. Menning, "Riding the Tiger: Force and Diplomacy in a Nuclear Age," *Army* (January, 1974), 10-15.

[19] In President Nixon's statement, the United

A fourth interpretation challenged the fundamental basis of American involvement in Vietnam. It questioned the validity, the relevance, and the moral propriety of what were said to be the overall American objectives in East Asia: (1) to prevent the expansion of Chinese influence; and (2) to prevent any anti-Communist government from being overthrown by internal revolutionary forces. According to this point of view, the South Vietnamese regime, dominated by a native elite allied with defeated French colonialism, had remained in power only through American support and what was termed the "oppression" of its own people. But in the general debate on Vietnam, which gave primary emphasis to the effects of the war on the United States and to the wisdom of American tactics, relatively little attention was paid to these arguments about the political or moral grounds on which support for an independent South Vietnam might or might not be justified.[20]

THE SEARCH FOR PEACE

Since an escalating Vietnam war carried the threat of a wider conflict, the Johnson and Nixon administrations were under heavy

States appeared as a "Pacific" rather than an "Asian" power; America's future policy was to be keyed to Asian initiatives ("Peace and progress," President Nixon said in Manila, "must be shaped and protected primarily by Asian hands."), but the United States fully intended to honor existing treaties. These principles were said to mean that, "In some cases, assistance in economic and political development may be enough. In other cases aid in the form of training and equipment may be necessary. But the job of countering insurgency in the field is one which must be conducted by the government concerned, making use of its popular support, its resources, and its men. Large-scale intervention from abroad is, of course, something else again and must be considered against the backdrop of the total obligations and interests of the American people." Undersecretary of State Elliott L. Richardson, speaking at a meeting of the International Studies Association. Quoted in *The National Observer*, September 15, 1969.

[20] For a more detailed analysis of the Vietnam controversy, see Richard A. Falk, "What Shall We Learn from Vietnam?" in *After Vietnam*, Gregg and Kegley, eds., 324-39. Among the contributors to this notable contemporary study are George W. Ball, Richard J. Barnet, Kenneth E. Boudling, Morton A. Kaplan, Ernest R. May, Richard L. Park, and Adam Yarmolinsky.

foreign as well as domestic pressure to end the fighting. Thus the course of the war was paced by a peace diplomacy involving the United Nations and, at one time or another, all the major powers. In 1968, after President Johnson offered to restrict the American bombing of North Vietnam in return for negotiations, delegates representing the United States, North Vietnam, South Vietnam, and the National Liberation Front (the *Vietcong's* political arm) began talks that were to last through 1973. From the beginning these meetings were devoted to propaganda rather than to negotiation. The respective delegations repeatedly presented proposals doomed in advance to rejection. In effect, the negotiators were asked to resolve what had not been resolved on the battlefield—at best, a difficult task.

By June, 1969, however, a movement to terminate direct American involvement in hostilities was well under way. President Nixon, who had entered office pledging that he would end the Vietnam war, began applying a formula for withdrawing American combat ground forces. On the theory that Saigon under American tutelage and with American assistance was rapidly becoming politically self-reliant, and that her forces, freshly trained and supplied, could deal with the *Vietcong* and their North Vietnamese allies, the United States announced a policy of "Vietnamizing" the war. Stated simply, "Vietnamization" called for replacement of American forces with South Vietnamese troops. In practice, this transfer of responsibility proved to be a remarkably delicate business because: (1) it assumed that the *Vietcong,* having in recent months scaled down their military operations, would not soon resume major offensives; (2) it depended upon a relatively quick revitalization of a South Vietnamese army that since 1965 had played a secondary role in the fighting; (3) it required stable, effective leadership by the Saigon government; and (4) it assumed that an increasingly impatient American public would tolerate the uncertainties of a gradual withdrawal, to be undertaken with no announced deadlines. Failure in any one of these four areas could endanger the entire "Vietnamization" program.

Cambodia

Some of the perils besetting "Vietnamization" were dramatized when, beginning in May, 1970, American and South Vietnamese forces invaded Cambodia to destroy enemy command bases and supply depots long maintained in the jungle borders of this allegedly neutral state. This turn of events provoked a fury of American protests. At Kent State University, four students were killed by National Guardsmen who had been called to the campus to control the demonstration. Critics argued that President Nixon, far from "winding down" the war as he had promised to do, had in fact extended the area of hostilities by the invasion of Cambodia—to the point that it was no longer a "Vietnam war but an Indochina war." The conflict he had inherited from President Johnson became "Mr. Nixon's war." In Congress, Republicans and Democrats joined in an effort to restrain the president's war-making powers, and the Senate (but not the House) repealed the Gulf of Tonkin resolution. The President in turn emphasized the importance of the Cambodian invasion to his "Vietnamization" program: by destroying supplies, by driving the Communists from their sheltered sanctuaries, the invasion would provide additional time for strengthening South Vietnamese forces; furthermore, the action would serve as a warning that the United States would take whatever steps were required to safeguard American troops during their withdrawal from Vietnam.[21]

---

[21] As background to the invasion of the border sanctuaries, it should be noted that the very existence of Cambodia, a country of rice culture and a Khmer population of some 7 million in an area about the size of Missouri, rested during the past century in large part on the former French protectorate, which was credited with saving the country from partition by its neighbors, Vietnam and Thailand. Occupied by Japan during World War II, Cambodia became an associated state in the French Union in 1949. Prince Norodom Sihanouk, king of Cambodia after 1941, became a leader in the movement for independence from France, and took the title of chief of state in 1955. Earlier he had rejected the proferred protection of SEATO and declared Cambodia's neutrality, a status the country was unable to maintain. While abroad in 1970, Sihanouk was ousted from office by General

It was against this background that the United States began actual troop withdrawals. By mid-1971, American forces in Vietnam numbered 275,000, about half the number involved two years earlier. Meanwhile the outlook for American withdrawal of all forces was improved by an easing of tensions between the United States and North Vietnam's principal supporters, Communist China and the Soviet Union. A major step toward extracating the United States from the fighting came on January 23, 1973, when President Nixon and the North Vietnamese announced that their special representatives, Henry Kissinger and Le Duc Tho, had initialed an agreement providing for a ceasefire, an exchange of prisoners, and a withdrawal of all American forces. As these agreements were implemented, other steps were to be taken, under the supervision of an international control commission, which ultimately were supposed to lead to the peaceful reunification of Vietnam and to peace in the entire Indochina area.[22]

These new accords were acclaimed throughout the world; Henry Kissinger and Le Duc Tho were jointly awarded the Nobel Peace Prize. The hard reality, however, was that the new agreement, like the Geneva accords of 1954, was more successful in providing for the withdrawal of a foreign power than in defining the basis of peace. Warfare continued throughout Indochina after the ceasefire had been signed, though the United States was no longer directly involved in the fighting. The intensity of the hostilities was suggested by Saigon's admission in December, 1973, that more than 11,000 of its troops had been lost since the ceasefire was announced. Although Kissinger and Le Duc Tho reopened discussions on the ceasefire in

January, 1974, neither North nor South Vietnam, both of which continued to receive substantial military assistance from their Russian, Chinese, and American allies, appeared willing to compromise.

INTERNATIONAL PERSPECTIVES ON THE NEW SOUTHEAST ASIA

The American military withdrawal from Vietnam and the limits imposed by the Nixon doctrine on American intervention assumed that Southeast Asia during the 1970s would move toward constructive solutions. There is some evidence to support this view. In Vietnam, while both the north and the south have drawn heavily on foreign assistance, all of the great powers—the United States, the Soviet Union, and China—seem to sense a futility in dictating what the Vietnamese should do. Elsewhere in the region, Southeast Asia's leadership, once preoccupied with parochial nationalism and anti-Western sloganeering, at last began to support projects encouraging national development. The Asian Development Bank, backed with Asian capital and directed by a Japanese president, sponsored such diverse projects as irrigation programs in Indonesia, industrial expansion in Thailand, and the development of air transport in Nepal. Despite the Vietnam war, a start was made on development of the Mekong River basin. Moreover, a new sense of regional interdependence was evident in talks looking toward construction of transportation and communication systems to overcome the insularity of the Southeast Asian states. Yet the area still has neither the unity nor the strength to stand against big power pressures. Conflicting territorial ambitions within Southeast Asia remain strong, a further invitation to foreign intervention. In matters of trade, the area has not yet broken the patterns of an earlier colonial era. The new states continue to be linked through their exports of raw materials and imports of manufactured goods more closely with the industrial powers than with one another. Altogether, these conditions suggest a region which neither the United States nor any other power could rationally view in the simplistic terms of "containment" or "liberation." During

Lon Nol, the premier who approved the invasion of Cambodia's neutrality by American and South Vietnamese forces. After clearing the sanctuaries, the American troops withdrew but the Vietnamese stayed on, and the war thus moved into Cambodia. See Hal Kosut, ed., *Cambodia and the Vietnam War* (1971) for further details.

[22] The text of Nixon's announcement, Henry Kissinger's news conference on the American-North Vietnamese understanding, and the text of the "Agreement on Ending the War and Restoring Peace in Vietnam" are printed in the United States Department of State, *Bulletin* (February 12, 1973).

nearly thirty years of independence, the new states have proven remarkably resistant to the return of foreign rule. On the other hand, while the great powers finally agreed to limit the scale of their intervention in the case of Vietnam, there were no pledges to forswear intervention entirely. In this sense, Southeast Asia's role in the shaping of East Asia's new international order had not as yet been determined.

FOR FURTHER READING

Southeast Asia After 1945.   Rupert Emerson, *From Empire to Nation* (1960),* a classic examination of Southeast Asian nationalism. For problems of governing the new nations, see Richard Butwell, *Southeast Asia Today—And Tomorrow* (1960)*; and Michael Leifer, *Dilemmas of Statehood in Southeast Asia* (1972). Wayne Wilcox, *et al.*, eds., *Asia and the International Systems* (1972),* suggestive of Southeast Asia's growing capacity to resist foreign intrusions. Robert O. Tilman, ed., *Man, State and Society in Contemporary Southeast Asia* (1969),* forty essays by specialists, well-organized for introductory reading. Insights into the social and economic bases of Southeast Asian life are offered in Robbins Burling, *Hill Farms and Padi Fields: Life in Mainland Southeast Asia* (1965)*; Frank M. LaBar, *Ethnic Groups of Mainland Southeast Asia* (1964); and C. A. Fisher, *Southeast Asia: A Social, Economic, and Political Geography* (1964). Robert Shaplen, *Time Out of Hand* (1969),* essays by a capable journalist.

Indochina.   Ellen Hammer, *Vietnam: Yesterday and Today* (1966), a brief introduction. For description of life and customs, see Gerald Hickey, *Village in Vietnam* (1964).* On the impact of war and revolution on Vietnamese life are Jeffrey Race, *War Comes to Long An; Revolutionary Conflict in a Vietnamese Province* (1971)*; Jon M. Van Dyke, *North Vietnam's Strategy for Survival* (1972); and Ly Qui Chung, *Between Two Fires: The Unheard Voices of Vietnam* (1970).* Dennis J. Duncanson, *Government and Revolution in Vietnam*

(1968), insights into the Diem regime. On North Vietnam see P. J. Honey, ed., *North Vietnam Today* (1962); and Hoang Van Chi, *From Colonialism to Communism* (1964). Douglas Pike, *War, Peace, and the Viet Cong* (1969)* is a condensation and updating of an earlier study. On Vietnam's dealings with its neighbors see Paul E. Langer and Joseph J. Zasloff, *North Vietnam and the Pathet Lao* (1970). For other titles relating to Southeast Asia generally and the Indochina area particularly, see the listings at the end of Chapter 28.

The Vietnam War.   Allan B. Cole, ed., *Conflict in Indochina and International Repercussions: A Documentary History, 1945-1955* (1956), indispensable for France's struggle to retain her empire. Philippe Devillers and Jean LaCouture, *End of a War: Indo-China 1954* (rev. ed., 1969), a study of the Geneva Conference which argues that the meeting merely marked the transfer of the French role to the United States. Russell Fifield, *Southeast Asia in United States Policy* (1963),* a detailed accounting of the American economic and military posture through the Eisenhower years that pictures American involvement as a response to Communist aggression.

The escalation of the American effort in Vietnam and the college teach-ins produced a flood of literature, much, though not all, of which is polemical. Suggestive of the output of scholars, some of whom were not Asian specialists or social scientists, is the following list: Frank N. Trager, *Why Vietnam?* (1967); Wesley R. Fishel, ed., *Vietnam: Anatomy of a Conflict* (1968)*; and Chester A. Bain, *Vietnam: The Roots of Conflict* (1967).* All of the foregoing portray the war as necessary, if costly. For the thesis that Vietnam was a "tragic error," a war into which the United States stumbled inadvertantly, see the study by Kahin and Lewis cited in the footnotes of this chapter; A. M. Schlesinger, Jr., *The Bitter Heritage: Vietnam and American Diplomacy, 1941-1966* (1967)*; John K. Galbraith, *How to Get Out of Vietnam* (1967); and Hans Morgenthau, *Vietnam and the United States* (1965). Noam Chomsky, *Ameri-*

can *Power and the New Mandarins* (1969)*; Howard Zinn, *Vietnam: The Logic of Withdrawal* (1967)*; Gabriel Kolko, *The Roots of American Foreign Policy* (1969)*; David Horowitz, ed., *Containment and Revolution* (1967)*; and the Committee of Concerned Asian Scholars, *The Indochina Story* (1970),* treat the American involvement in imperialistic terms.

Among the most reliable of the journalistic treatments are: Theodore Draper, *Abuse of Power* (1967),* which deals with the escalation of the American effort; Robert Shaplen, *The Lost Revolution* (1965),* and *The Road from War, Vietnam, 1965-1970* (1970); Jonathan Schell, *The Village of Ben Suc* (1967); Don Oberdorfer, *Tet: The Story of a Battle and Its Historic Aftermath* (1971)*; and Frances Fitzgerald, *Fire in the Lake: The Vietnamese and the Americans in Vietnam* (1972).* David Halberstam, *The Best and the Brightest* (1972),* a compelling but undocumented portrayal of the personalities in the Kennedy and Johnson administrations who made the decisions on Vietnam.

New Powers in Asia: China, Japan, and the West Since 1953

America's withdrawal from the fighting in Vietnam was one indication of an altered international atmosphere in East Asia. The United States and the Soviet Union were less inclined than in earlier years to present themselves as unrelenting rivals. Their leaders spoke of "negotiation," while both sides explored openings through what once had been known as the "Iron Curtain." This recent attitude was to some extent a product of Asia's growing power and self-confidence. Neither the United States nor the Soviet Union enjoyed in Asia the prestige or the authority of previous years. The change in America's position was symbolized in Japan's insistence on treatment as a full and equal partner within the framework of the American-Japanese alliance. China, on the other hand, broke openly with the Soviet Union, confronting Russian forces along Inner Asian frontiers and charging Moscow with a variety of ideological sins. By 1974, cold war alignments no longer described the East Asian scene accurately. The region had not escaped, however, from its plague of international rivalries and war.[1]

[1] Akira Iriye has interpreted recent developments in Russian-American East Asian relations as a return to

CHINA: THE FOREIGN RELATIONS OF A REVOLUTIONARY SOCIETY

China's role in this picture reflected the on-going revolution reshaping her society. After 1949, China assumed a variety of faces before the world, ranging from militant advocacy of worldwide revolution and warfare to the softer language of "peaceful coexistence"; but whatever the line, the constant purpose was to restore China as a power in Asia and as a world ideological leader. Long at the mercy of the West, China proposed to meet the West at

the ideals that were expressed most frequently during World War II, particularly at the big power meeting at Yalta: "By the early 1970s, then, the Cold War . . . could no longer serve as a framework of Asian-Pacific international relations. . . . The United States and the Soviet Union now had to reckon with the resurgence of Japanese power and the achievement of near super-power status of China. Both of them were multilateralizing their foreign relations, departing from the earlier dependence on one of the Big Two. They were competitors with the United States and the Soviet Union for worldwide influence, economic expansion, or regional power. Whether these four could somehow cooperate, as another foursome had tried to do in the 1940s, and build a stable regional order was a key question of the 1970s." *The Cold War in Asia* (1974),* 189-90.

least as an equal, thereby ending Western political dominance in Asia. Peking assumed a loud, vocal role as the chief opponent of what it called "imperialism." The rhetoric of its foreign policy dwelt ceaselessly on ideological conflict, but its substance was based solidly in Chinese nationalism.[2]

Chinese Communist foreign policy in its first phase, 1949-1952, was guided by militant idealism. According to Peking's analysis, nations fell into one of three categories—the Communist bloc, the "imperialist" powers, and the "unliberated" ex-colonial countries of Asia and the third world. With respect to the Communist bloc, China would "lean to one side," uniting its forces in revolutionary endeavors with those of its ideological comrades. Against the "imperialist camp," China would wage continuous war. The "unliberated" countries were to be the target of revolutionary efforts to bring them into the Communist world. Basic to this policy was the assumption of continuing revolution until all countries were "free."

Expressed in more concrete terms, Chinese policy in this period involved aid to "People's Liberation Armies" seeking to overthrow existing governments (in Southeast Asia, for example), the buildup of armed forces along the China coast for an assault on Taiwan, and intensive propaganda attacks on Western activities in Japan and Southeast Asia.[3] Consistent with this posture, China first supported North Korea verbally following the outbreak of the Korean war in June, 1950, and later intervened directly as fighting tipped in favor of United Nations forces. At the same time, China's deference to the Soviet Union's position as an "elder brother" in matters pertaining to world affairs was formalized in a treaty of friendship and alliance.[4]

CHINA IN THE "COMMUNIST BLOC"

After 1952, however, this early militancy was mixed with the tactics of "peaceful coexistence." While this new diversity may have been encouraged by the Soviet Union's adoption of a similar line, "peaceful coexistence" certainly reflected China's own changing world view. Peking, having consolidated its position in some measure on the Chinese mainland, and having readied its first five-year plan, anticipated sufficient resources for spreading its influence through trade and aid. Furthermore, "peaceful coexistence" seemed ideal for circumventing

---

[2] In considering the intricate subject of Communist China's foreign policy, it will be helpful to keep China's objectives in mind: (1) deterring or avoiding external attack on China; (2) unifying the country and terminating the civil war through the "liberation" of Taiwan; (3) gaining acceptance by the powers of Communist China's status as a world influence through revolutionary as well as conventional means; and (4) increasing Chinese influence everywhere by posing as the most effective leader of an alleged world-wide struggle against American imperialism and, since 1960, against Soviet revisionism. These objectives are discussed ably by Harold C. Hinton, "Evolution of Foreign Policy," in *China: A Handbook*, Yuan-li Wu, ed. (1973), 281-99.

[3] A continuing important factor in Peking's foreign policy was some 19 million so-called "overseas Chinese," (people of Chinese extraction living in another country) of whom about 17 million were in Southeast Asia as late as 1966. The greatest concentrations of these people were in Thailand, Vietnam, Malaya, Singapore, Indonesia, and Hong Kong. They were regarded by Peking as potential agents in spreading the teachings of Mao Tse-tung. In a cultural sense, the overseas Chinese had long shown strong loyalties to mainland China. Ideologically, they often appeared to have no bonds with Peking. Their potential role was made all the more complex because in the new nationalistic states of Southeast Asia they were often subject to discriminatory legislation and outright violence. See Chen-hsi Wu, "Overseas Chinese," in *China: A Handbook*, Wu, ed., 413-42.

[4] The position of Communist China as a new and revolutionary power in East Asia has been inseparable from the history of its army, known since 1946 as the People's Liberation Army (PLA). Its functions have been varied, changing, and complex. It was the force which brought the new regime to power in 1949. At times it has been a principal arm in local administration and in economic and social affairs. As the "liberator" of the Chinese people, the PLA provided a model for what were described as "wars of liberation" and "People's Liberation Armies" in countries still under colonial or imperialistic control. Since 1949 when it was a semi-guerrilla force, it has become in many respects a modernized army. (Nuclear research dating from 1955 led to the first test of a nuclear weapon in 1964.) Its irregular and so-called "volunteer" system of recruitment was replaced by conscription in 1955. On the PLA and the doctrine of revolutionary war, note Ellis Joffe, "The People's Liberation Army," in *China: A Handbook*, Wu, ed., 261-80.

the countermeasures developed by the United States against China's militant policies. Thus, between 1952 and 1955, China in her contacts with the third world countries of Asia and Africa abandoned her insistence that "bourgeois nationalist" governments must be overthrown, agreed to a Korean truce, and participated in drawing up the Geneva accords of 1954, which brought a cease-fire to Indochina. In April, 1955, China joined twenty-eight Asian and African states at Bandung, Indonesia, in pledging increased economic and cultural cooperation, respect for human rights and self-determination, and peace through universal disarmament. She made gestures toward implementing these principles through increased trade with nonaligned countries and the extension of economic and technical aid to nations whose peoples were certainly in no greater plight than the Chinese themselves.[5]

[5] Among the nations receiving aid were North Korea, North Vietnam, the Mongolian People's Republic, Cambodia, Nepal, Hungary, and Egypt.

CRISES IN THE FORMOSAN STRAITS

But the politics of accommodation were not applied to China's relations with the United States. In 1954, while Secretary of State Dulles was in Manila shaping the SEATO pact, Chou En-lai reiterated Peking's determination to "liberate" Taiwan. In an apparent prelude to invasion, China threatened a string of small islands, including the Tachen, Matsu, and Quemoy groups, which stretched some 350 miles along the China coast and were held tenaciously by *Kuomintang* forces. A few days before the Manila conference began, Chinese Communist forces started a heavy bombardment of the two Quemoys, located about five miles outside the port of Amoy. The American response was to open talks with Chiang Kai-shek leading to the signing in December, 1954, of a mutual defense treaty similar to the SEATO pact. This treaty was adopted, it should be recalled, against the background of a furious debate within the United States over the "loss" of China, and at a time when the Eisenhower

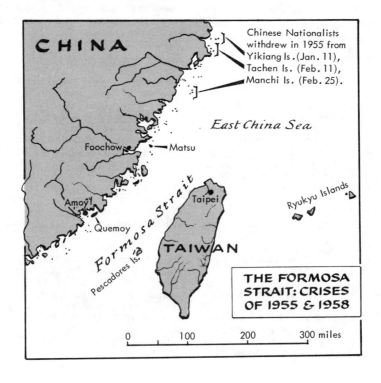

THE FORMOSA STRAIT: CRISES OF 1955 & 1958

administration identified Peking as Moscow's "puppet." The American view, therefore, held that the understanding with the Chinese Nationalists was essential to the "containment" of world communism. Peking saw the Washington-Taipei agreement as America's most serious intervention yet in China's internal affairs.[6]

Since American pledges to the Chinese Nationalists did not define precisely what territory was to be defended, it was impossible to know what action might touch off a general Sino-American war. On January 18, 1955, the Communists invaded the island of Yikiang, eight miles north of the Tachens. Washington promptly indicated that this island and the Tachens were not essential to the defense of Taiwan, some 200 miles away. Within weeks the Nationalists, acting under American pressure, removed their troops from the Tachens and neighboring islands. This step, however, was followed by Congressional action (January 25, 1955) on a "Formosan resolution" authorizing President Eisenhower to use American forces to protect Taiwan, the Pescadores, and "such related positions and territories of that area now in friendly hands. ..." America's course was further obscured by Washington's failure to disassociate itself from Chiang's announced intention of reconquering the mainland. Secretary Dulles testified later that the confrontation in the Taiwan Straits brought China and the United States to the "brink of war."[7]

[6] Shortly before his appointment as secretary of state, John Foster Dulles expressed his fundamental assumptions concerning the Sino-Soviet alliance: "By the test of conception, birth, nurture, and obedience, the Mao Tse-tung regime is a creature of the Moscow Politburo, and it is on behalf of Moscow, not of China, that it is betraying the friendship of the Chinese people toward the United States. ..." Foreshadowing his own later policy, he went on to declare that "we should treat the Mao Tse-tung regime for what it is—a puppet regime." It followed, therefore, that no American act should contribute to Mao's fastening "the yoke of Moscow on the Chinese people." Quoted in Foster Rhea Dulles, *American Policy toward Communist China: The Historical Record, 1949-1969* (1972), 121.

[7] An article praising Secretary Dulles's "brinkmanship" and giving his version of the Formosan Straits crisis appeared while the secretary was still in office. See James Shepley, "How Dulles Averted War," *Life*, 40 (January 16, 1956), 70-72. Another top presidential adviser, Sherman Adams, later expressed

Yet the immediate crisis passed in the spring of 1955 after Communist China and the United States began talks at Geneva and continued them on the ambassadorial level at Warsaw. The two sides exchanged assurances that circumvented a showdown, but they made absolutely no progress in reconciling their conflicting views on Taiwan and the offshore islands. Thus matters stood until August, 1958, when Communist forces began heavy artillery bombardment of Quemoy. This time, acting on the theory that the island was vital to the defense of Taiwan (Chiang had moved about a third of his total forces to Quemoy), Eisenhower informed both Peking and Moscow that the United States would protect Quemoy and the Matsu Islands further to the north. Again there were threats of war, renewed ambassadorial talks, and an inconclusive resolution of the contest. The United States, however, was accused by American critics and by its European allies of risking nuclear war in defense of a discredited Chinese government. Accordingly, the Eisenhower administration finally disavowed for the first time any commitment to aid a Nationalist return to the mainland, and it further pledged efforts to force a reduction of Nationalist forces on Quemoy. It thereby sought to assure the Communists that no invasion was contemplated, but in taking this step the United States renewed its pledges to sustain the Nationalists on Taiwan. The Communists in turn eased pressure on Quemoy without modifying their claims to Taiwan and all the offshore islands.[8]

MILITARY ACTION IN TIBET AND ON THE INDIAN BORDER

Peking's advocacy of "peaceful coexistence" was also qualified by military campaigning in central Asia, first against Tibetan insurgents and later against Indian border forces. Peking's

doubts that Eisenhower was as close to a decision on war as Dulles had claimed. Sherman Adams, *Firsthand Report: The Story of the Eisenhower Administration* (1961), 410.

[8] The assurances on Quemoy were announced by Secretary Dulles, September 30, 1958. See the *United States Department of State Bulletin*, 39 (October, 20, 1958), 599.

problems here grew out of her determination to carry the Communist revolution into Tibet and to incorporate that mountainous region into the areas under her administrative control. Under a Sino-Tibetan treaty, 1951, Tibet had recognized China's suzerainty in return for assurances of autonomy in internal matters.[9] This understanding, however, was soon followed by large-scale Chinese activities in Tibet. Several thousand Chinese were sent into northern areas to develop the rich mineral deposits; a highway was constructed linking Lhasa with China Proper; a Chinese garrison was stationed in the Tibetan capital; and preparations were made for the inauguration of a profound social revolution. These activities, which Lhasa charged were in violation of the earlier understanding, met sporadic resistance, particularly as the Chinese imposed heavy taxes, interfered with religious life, and initiated land reforms. A general uprising was precipitated in March, 1959, when the Chinese commander tried to force Tibet's key spiritual leader, the Dalai Lama, to support Peking's directives. During the fighting that ensued, the Dalai Lama fled to India, where he denounced the "cultural and physical genocide" being committed in Tibet. Meanwhile, the Chinese, having gained the support of another Tibetan luminary, the

---

[9] Following the revolution of 1911, a succession of Chinese governments had affirmed their title to Tibet. The political reality, however, was that Tibet had cut her ties with China in 1911—these ties had become progressively weaker in the later years of the Ch'ing dynasty—and, prior to 1951, no Chinese government was strong enough to implement its claims fully. The Nationalists under Chiang Kai-shek succeeded in converting eastern (or "Inner") Tibet into provinces under its administrative authority, but western ("Outer") Tibet continued to claim its independence and developed economic and cultural ties with India. A concise treatment of the difficult subject of minorities under Chinese Communist rule is William Liu, "Chinese Society: Stratification, Minorities, and the Family", in *China: A Handbook*, Wu, ed., 680ff. Here it may be noted that the *Kuomintang* did not have a systematic policy for drawing the minorities (Manchus, Mongols, Tibetans, etc.) into national life. In contrast, the Communists have insisted in theory and in law on the equal civil and political status of the minorities. But in practice they have sometimes returned to the methods used by the Manchu emperors in dealing with the border peoples: divide and rule.

Panchen Lama, proceeded with the suppression of resistance movements and the introduction of revolutionary and reform measures.

Peking's Tibetan policy emphasized the goal of national unification. India, however, did not regard the matter as being wholly a Chinese domestic concern. As an "independent" state having some economic and cultural ties with India, Tibet had served as a friendly buffer along India's northern frontiers. With China's advance, however, India met for the first time since its own independence a revolutionary power directly to the north. New Delhi expressed concern with this development, especially when the Chinese press, reporting India's welcome to the Dalai Lama and several thousand Tibetan refugees, accused India of continuing British imperialist meddling in Chinese politics. It was thus against a background of growing tension that China and India prepared in 1959-1962 to do battle along an ill-defined, mountainous border.

On the eastern end of the Sino-Indian frontier, India claimed as its boundary the so-called "McMahon line," which had been drawn by a British colonial officer and accepted by Tibet but not by China. On the western end of the border in a remote corner of Ladakh, a territory claimed by the Indian state of Kashmir, the Chinese had crossed the border defined by India to build a strategic highway linking Tibet with Sinkiang. Since a compromise was not in sight and both sides sent troops into the contested territory, China's advance into Tibet had become a prelude to new international troubles.

The first of a series of armed skirmishes occurred in Ladakh, October, 1959, but neither side was as yet prepared to push immediately toward a decisive resolution. China's tactic was to apply diplomatic pressure on India while building its forces in Tibet. In August, 1960, Peking signed border treaties with Nepal and Burma.[10] India was offered a settlement

---

[10] In 1962, two years after the Sino-Burmese boundary settlement, the Union of Burma, which began its independent political life in 1948 as a constitutional democracy, became a military dictatorship under a self-chosen revolutionary council. Opposition to continuing military rule came from former

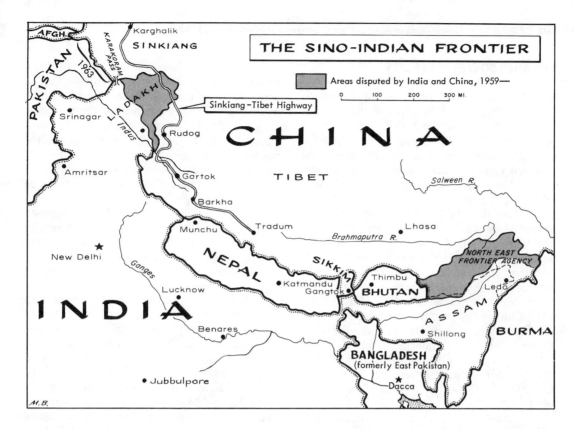

whereby she would concede 12,000 square miles in Ladakh (thus securing the Sinkiang-Tibet highway) and would be guaranteed in return 40,000 square miles claimed by China south of the McMahon line. Prime Minister Nehru, however, having vowed that India would never "bow down to the threats of forces," insisted on all of his country's claims. The Chinese responded to this refusal with offensives in Kashmir and along the eastern Himalayan border. Within a month Chinese forces commanded all of the territory claimed by Peking in the Ladakh area; in the east, Chinese forces drove well beyond the McMahon line to

the edge of the Assam plain. This latter offensive was so successful that northern India seemed open to a massive Chinese invasion, but the Chinese suddenly stopped their drive, withdrew their forces from their more advanced positions, repatriated Indian prisoners, returned captured military supplies, and offered to negotiate a settlement. Even at this point, however, a basis for agreement could not be found. Although the fighting stopped, the border remained legally undefined. The Sino-Indian border had been realigned only to the extent that Chinese forces remained in control of whatever Peking wanted at that time.[11]

---

constitutional leaders who were in exile and from the Burmese Communist party. Adding to the civil disorders were anti-Maoist riots in Rangoon in 1967 as a result of which Peking severed relations. In 1970, however, diplomatic relations were restored and the boundary treaty of 1960 was reinstated. These events of the 1960s were a constant reminder of Burma's strategic position between China and India. See *The Far East and Australia* (3rd ed., 1971). 395-98.

[11] As border tensions developed, India and China advanced conflicting claims grounded in history and law. It was the strategic stakes, however, that led the two countries to expose themselves to the risks of war. India, for example, adopted a "forward policy" along the eastern frontier as a counter to Chinese pressures in the west. Indian forces were ordered to advance close to Chinese lines, along their flanks, and, ultimately, even to the rear of Chinese forces (the "lines" in reality being little more than scattered outposts that

THE SINO-SOVIET CONFLICT

Some of the wider implications of this short-lived mountain war were noted in the previous chapter. Set against the background of bitter cold war rivalries—the fighting in the Himalayas coincided with the Cuban missile crisis and followed closely a Soviet-American confrontation in Laos—China's resort to military action in Tibet and against India reinforced American convictions that the Chinese Communists were embarked on a policy of expansion. The result was a strengthening of the American position along all of China's southern and eastern frontiers. India's pleas for military assistance were answered promptly, and American aid to South Vietnam was enlarged. In June, 1962, when Chinese Communist forces again started a military buildup opposite Taiwan, President Kennedy reiterated American pledges to the Chinese Nationalist government. The United States' position with respect to Taiwan and the offshore islands, he said, had not changed since 1955.

Yet even with apparent hardening of cold war attitudes, the roles of various nations in the Sino-Indian war revealed significant shifts in alignments. Pakistan, an American ally, protested United States arms shipments to India on the ground that the Indians would use the equipment against her. Indian-Pakistani quarrels were in fact revived, and, in June, 1963, Pakistan moved closer to China with the signing of a treaty defining their frontiers and of a non-aggression pact. There also was evidence that the Sino-Indian war was affecting the Russo-Chinese alliance. Moscow publicized its displeasure over China's assaults on India, pledging aid to India.

could be penetrated). For sharply conflicting views as to which side was responsible for the war, see Dorothy Woodman, *Himalayan Frontiers: A Political Review of British, Chinese, Indian, and Russian Rivalries* (1970), which labels Chinese claims of Indian aggression as "obvious nonsense"; and Neville Maxwell, *India's China War* (1972),* which claims that domestic pressures operating on the Nehru government led India into provocative actions. Stephen P. Cohen, "India's China War and After: A Review Article," *Journal of Asian Studies*, 30 (1971), 847-57, offers guidance to reading in often highly polemical literature.

Prior to 1962, American architects of "containment" had given scant heed to signs that all was not well between Peking and Moscow. Attention was focused instead on the seemingly insoluble bonds between the two Communist allies. China, it was said, had shouldered the burdens of advancing Communist revolutions in Asia and other developing areas. Meanwhile, she was pictured as loyally supporting Soviet policy in all matters pertaining to the West. This American fixation concentrated on a supposed ideological affinity between the Communist giants. It also assumed that the Chinese were heavily dependent on Russian aid for their own development.

Neither China nor Russia had initially discouraged this view of "monolithic international Communism." The facade of unity was regarded as an obvious asset in the general Communist cause. Yet there was little in the record to suggest a fundamental harmony of national interests between Russia and China. Tsarist Russia had encroached on Sinkiang, Mongolia, and Manchuria, and in the twentieth century there had been few signs of mutual admiration or cooperation before 1950. Even the aid proffered by the Soviet Union under the alliance was eventually to be repaid. In reality, China and the Soviet Union were adversaries on a broad range of issues.

The immediate grounds for Sino-Soviet conflict were fashioned in the years following the death of Joseph Stalin in 1953. While the new Russian leadership made concessions to Peking's requests for increased aid and to the Chinese resentment of Russian encroachment (Moscow was slow in relinquishing its authority in Port Arthur and in a number of "mixed companies" operating in China), Peking felt that the Soviets were determined to keep China in a subservient position. Mao was embarrassed by Premier Nikita Khrushchev's anti-Stalinist campaigns, since the Soviets' denunciation of "personality cults" and the "Stalinist line" reflected unfavorably on Chinese styles in leadership.[12] Moreover, the Chinese were dis-

[12] There is said to be no place in the Communist movement for a cult of personality. Curiously, however, the flowering of Communism in Russia and China is intimately associated with such names as

turbed when Moscow, which was beset by serious unrest among its East European satellites, summarily reduced its aid to China and moved toward negotiation with the West. In the face of this treatment, Peking declared that, while "Communist parties of all countries must be united." the common front must be based on recognition of equality and on "real, and not formal, consultation." This warning was not effective. The Soviet Union did not concede to an increasingly self-confident China an equal share in the leadership which it had exercised in the Communist movement since 1917.[13]

Furthermore, ideology proved to be less a unifying bond than a divisive force, converting differences in national policy into a source of heightened rivalry. In 1958, for example, Peking proclaimed the Great Leap Forward and the establishment of communes as significant advances in the application of Communist theory. Since the effect was to highlight China, rather than Russia, as the model for revolutions, Moscow ridiculed Chinese pretension and warned that Mao's fanaticism endangered the whole Communist movement. Subsequent efforts to repair these damaged relations led to a meeting of world Communist leaders in Moscow, November, 1960, but the reconciliation achieved there failed to survive the tensions engendered by the Sino-Indian war. The one-time fraternal Communist rhetoric of Moscow and Peking was supplanted by vituperative recrimination.

The Rivalry Full-Blown

As the Communist split widened, the Chinese sought to capture the leadership of the world's revolutionary forces. Peking no longer directed her appeals primarily to the developing nations of Asia, Africa, and Latin America. Her new line held that there were "third worlds" of underprivileged and exploited people everywhere (in the United States, poor whites, blacks, and the radical left were said to constitute a "third world" within a more generally developed society). According to Lin Piao, then Mao's heir-apparent, China would do all that she could to shape these oppressed elements into revolutionary vanguards. This was not to say that China's revolution was held in any direct sense to be exportable. Lin's thesis was that Chinese Communism could point the way for societies where conditions were right. In this sense, Peking presented herself as the ideological leader of a coming era of "national liberation." These claims, moreover, were advanced at a time when China was taking other steps that called attention to her importance in world politics. The successful testing of an atomic device in October, 1964, announced that China had entered the select company of nuclear powers.

These developments evoked world-wide speculation about China's ultimate goals. The official American view held that Lin Piao's remarks, delivered in an address, "Long Live the Victory of the People's War," September 3, 1965, were nothing less than a fresh blueprint for expansion that challenged United States policy.[14] At this point, however, China in fact

Lenin, Stalin, and Mao. In Communist doctrine, there is none but a subordinate place for the individual, yet Communist history tells its story by portraying heroes and villains, saints and heretics. See Adam B. Ulam, *Stalin: The Man and His Era* (1973), 6-11.

[13] Students of Sino-Soviet affairs have not identified exactly all sources of the rivalry. One problem has been to assess the role of ideological differences in a quarrel that assumed so many forms. Some suggestion of the spectrum of interpretations may be found in the following: Robert A. Scalapino, "Moscow, Peking, and the Communist Parties of Asia," *Foreign Affairs*, 41 (1963), 323-43, emphasizes ideology as a source of Sino-Soviet troubles in dealing as allies with fledging parties in Asia; John Gittings, *Survey of the Sino-Soviet Dispute* (1968) views the struggle as one involving the "dual challenge" of ideology and national power; and An Tai-sung, *The Sino-Soviet Territorial Dispute* (1973) focuses mainly on border issues. Edmund O. Clubb, *China and Russia: The "Great Game"* (1971) holds that China's stubborn persistence in a "bankrupt course in international Communist affairs" has been the prime source of trouble. Maury Lisann, "Moscow and the Chinese Power Struggle," *Problems of Communism*, 18 (1969), 32-41, surveys China's reactions to Russian threats. The argument that the Sino-Soviet split is likely to persist is given in Stefan T. Possony, "Peking and Moscow: The Permanence of Conflict," *Modern Age*, 16 (1972), 130-45.

[14] Dulles, *American Policy*, 224-25. By the mid-1960s, those American specialists who subscribed to the view of China as "expansionist" did not portray her as seeking additional territory. According to Franz Michael, "the Chinese Communist regime has demonstrated no territorial ambitions beyond its present

was moving away from any new international ventures. Between 1966 and 1969, as her energies were absorbed at home by the fantastic upheavals of the Cultural Revolution, China virtually isolated herself from the world. With the exception of her ambassador in Cairo, all top-ranking diplomats were recalled for political re-education. Thus the most immediate effect of the publicity focusing on China's independent posture was to dramatize for the

world the depth of Chinese and Russian differences. In these years, the two Communist nations appeared close to war.

The Cultural Revolution's intense campaigns frequently assumed an antiforeign character. Virtually all Western diplomats stationed in China were harassed at one time or another, but the Russians were in for special abuse. The Soviet embassy in Peking was surrounded and isolated for days at a time by demonstrating Red Guards; Soviet citizens making their way to the airport were reviled and threatened. Meanwhile in Moscow, Soviet police battled Chinese students who attempted to recite Mao's thoughts in front of Lenin's tomb. Most serious of all, however, was Premier Leonid Brezhnev's warning in 1968 that the Soviet Union might invade any Communist country when, in Moscow's judgment, the revolution there was threatened. While this "Brezhnev doctrine" had specific reference to the Soviet invasion of Czechoslovakia and destruction of a Czech government headed by Alexander Dubcek, Peking claimed that the Soviets intended to apply the principle in China.[15] Fighting broke out at several points on the Sino-Soviet border as both sides advanced conflicting territorial claims, but these were controlled incidents which resolved nothing. As the Cultural Revolution passed from the Chinese scene, tensions were lowered

---

borders—though within the latter it does, of course, lay claim to the lands of certain non-Chinese people who were part of the former Chinese empire. . . . Peking's disinterest in old-style empire-building has deflected Western attention from the far more important form of 'expansion' that it practices—the spread of Communist world revolution." "Is China Expansionist?" *Problems of Communism* 20 (1971), 62-74. To this argument Peter VanNess responded, saying that efforts to gain an enlarged world influence did not constitute expansion under any usual definition of the word. In a full-scale study of China's theory and practice with respect to "national liberation," VanNess concluded that Chinese support of insurrectionary groups was less than universal. China offered support to groups working to overthrow governments that had close ties with the United States or the Soviet Union, but an insurrectionary group in French Somiland, which theoretically qualified for support under Lin Piao's doctrines, received no aid, presumably because Peking did not wish to offend the DeGaulle government, a source of dissension within the Western world. Moreover, the Chinese gave support to a Nepalese monarchy which was asserting its independence from India. *Revolution and China's Foreign Policy: Peking's Support for Wars of National Liberation* (1970).

[15] See Harrison E. Salisbury, *War between Russia and China* (1969), a seasoned journalist's report on the tensions in Russia.

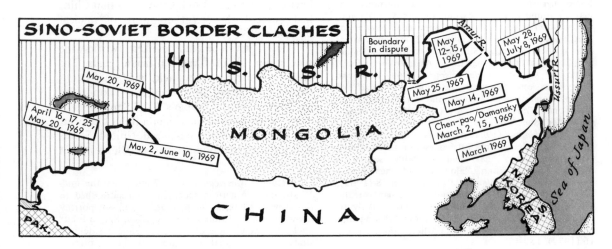

SINO-SOVIET BORDER CLASHES

U. S. S. R.

May 20, 1969

April 16, 17, 25, May 20, 1969

May 2, June 10, 1969

MONGOLIA

Boundary in dispute

May 12-15, 1969

Amur R.

May 28, July 8, 1969

May 25, 1969

May 14, 1969

Chen-pao/Damansky March 2, 15, 1969

March 1969

Ussuri R.

N. KOREA

Sea of Japan

CHINA

PAK.

somewhat along the Sino-Soviet frontier. The Soviet Union, however, kept a large part of its best military forces in the area. The Chinese, having constructed elaborate networks of air raid shelters, professed a continued readiness to meet any Soviet attack, whether staged with conventional or nuclear weapons.[16]

TOWARD IMPROVED SINO-AMERICAN RELATIONS

American policy for a time seemed to be unaffected by the Sino-Soviet conflict. As Peking's estrangement from the Russians became public, American official spokesmen abandoned the theory of coordinated Communist offensives, but the United States clung to its contention that Communist China must be "contained." Thus the escalation of the American military effort in Vietnam was accompanied by the prospect of a larger Chinese-American conflict. On April 23, 1965, American planes downed two North Vietnamese jets seventy miles north of Hanoi, near the China border. This incident prompted Secretary of State Dean Rusk to say that in this war, as opposed to Korea, there would be no privileged sanctuaries inside China. China's rejoinder, which was offered the day after China had conducted her third successful nuclear test, disclaimed any intention of provoking war with the United States but went on to warn: "The Chinese mean what they say. . . . China is prepared. . . . Once war breaks out, it will have no boundaries."[17]

Employing words that echoed those of John Foster Dulles, Rusk, in January, 1965, expounded the basic theme in American policy with reference to the Chinese Communists. "We think," he said, "that anything in terms of trade expansion, or recognition, or admission to the United Nations that tends to encourage them that their policy is paying dividends is not in the interest of getting peace established in the Pacific."[18] This view, designed to appear inflexible, was soon followed by signs that some high American officials were willing at least to reconsider the nation's stand on China. In March, 1964, the chairman of the Senate's foreign relations committee, J. William Fulbright, amplified an idea that had first been voiced during the Kennedy administration (see note, p. 502). The American people, Senator Fulbright said, should re-examine "old myths" concerning China, should be on guard lest American policies be "guided by emotionalism" and "thought processes by clichés," and should accept the fact that Red China was likely to remain where it was for some time to come.[19] Two years later, the senator, believing that the subject which had been "taboo for so long" was at last "respectable" enough to discuss, arranged for his foreign relations committee to

[16] Throughout the 1960s there were repeated incidents on the long Sino-Russian frontier. China accused the Soviets of fomenting subversion among minorities, particularly in Sinkiang. In 1964 the Soviets held large military maneuvers in the Soviet Far East and Mao, in an interview with Japanese visitors, criticized Russia for taking territory from its neighbors, including Outer Mongolia from China. See Hinton, "Evolution of Foreign Policy." The role of Mongolia as a buffer between China and Russia is of particular interest. The division of Mongolia into Inner and Outer Mongolia dated from the seventeenth century when the area was taken over by the Manchus in their conquest of China. They administered Outer Mongolia and Inner Mongolia separately. After the abdication of the Manchus in China, Outer Mongolia by a Russo-Chinese-Mongol agreement, 1915, acquired a nominal status of autonomy as a theocratic monarchy under Chinese suzerainty. Its actual status was that of a Russian protectorate. Inner Mongolia remained under direct Chinese rule. In the early 1920s Outer Mongolia, which was overrun by Chinese armies, became the seat of a Mongol People's Party supported by Russia, and an arena for White Russian counter-revolution. Out of this turmoil emerged a People's Republic with a Soviet-style constitution in 1924. From then on, Mongolia was increasingly under Russian control. Meanwhile China bowed to the inevitable and recognized Outer Mongolia's independence in 1946. It was admitted to the United Nations in 1961.

[17] Quoted in Roderick MacFarquhar, *Sino-American Relations, 1949-1971* (1972),* 214.
[18] Quoted in Dulles, *American Policy,* 219.
[19] The senator noted that he was not then advocating American recognition of the People's Republic, because Peking manifested an attitude of "implacable hostility", but the Chinese attitude, he added, was not "necessarily permanent." It would, therefore, be "extremely useful if we could introduce an element of flexibility, or, more precisely, of a capacity to be flexible, into our relations with Communist China." *Congressional Record,* 88th Congress, Second Session, 110 No. 56 (March 25, 1964), 6028-34.

hold nationally televised hearings on America's relations with China. The result was a great deal of publicity for expert testimony which held overwhelmingly that the United States was out of touch with the "new realities" in Asia. On May 21, 1968, Undersecretary of State Nicholas Katzenbach stressed the desirability of broader American contacts with China and assured China that the United States had no wish to imperil her security. Later that year, President Johnson invited Chinese correspondents to cover the upcoming presidential election; the invitation was not accepted.[20]

Despite these indications of a possibly softer line, Sino-American relations remained tense into the early 1970's. Against the background of American involvement in Vietnam, Peking continued to characterize American policy in pejorative terms. United States "imperialism" was held to be the "most ferocious enemy of the people of the whole world," while the newly elected President, Richard M. Nixon, was said to preside over a "hopeless mess and an insoluble economic crisis." When American and South Vietnamese troops struck at Communist forces inside Cambodia in May, 1970, Mao Tse-tung issued a rare personal statement denouncing the United States. On the American side, Nixon's election seemed to preclude basic changes in the nation's China policy. While the president spoke in his inaugural address of a coming "new era of negotiation," his own political record in Congress and as vice-

president did not suggest an accommodation with Communists. Meeting the press for the first time as president, Nixon indicated that he would continue to oppose Communist China's admission to the United Nations. Any shift from this position, he indicated, must be the result of improved Chinese behavior.[21]

Nixon's Visit to Peking

It was thus an astonished world that heard Nixon's brief, televised announcement, July 15, 1971, of his plans to visit Peking early the following year. In fact, however, neither Peking's invitation nor the president's acceptance was spontaneous. Each was the product of profound realignments that had been underway for a decade or more. The Nixon administration had sustained and expanded efforts that were begun during the Kennedy and Johnson years to negotiate the settlement of some basic issues with the Soviet Union. At a time when Moscow and Peking were insulting one another, American and Soviet diplomats were reaching agreements on such formerly explosive problems as the status of Berlin, (resolved in the four-power agreement of September 3, 1971) and the nuclear arms race, (the so-called SALT agreement of May, 1972, providing for partial control). Meanwhile, through such presidential pronouncements as the "Nixon doctrine" (see p. 505)., the United States gave notice of its intention to reduce the level of its involvement in Asian affairs. The "Vietnamization" of the Indochina war and reduction of American troop strength in South Vietnam, it was said, were aspects of the new American posture. By mid-1971, American troop levels in Vietnam were 250,000—about half the peak level of the previous year. Smaller numbers of American forces were withdrawn from other Asian areas: South Korea, Thailand, Japan, and the Philippines.

All of these steps came at a time when China, emerging from the turmoil of the Cul-

---

[20] For the full text see *U.S. Policy with Respect to Mainland China, Hearings before the Committee on Foreign Relations.* United States Senate, 89th Congress, Second Session. An edited version of this text with additional material from related hearings may be found in Akira Iriye, ed., *U.S. Policy toward China: Testimony taken from the Senate Foreign Relations Committee Hearings—1966* (1968).* The text of the remarks containing the President's invitation (quoted in MacFarquhar, *Sino-American Relations,* 246-47) is an example of the delicate signaling taking place between the Americans and Chinese. In referring to the Chinese capital city, the American official for the first time made use of the name "Peking," the designation meaning "northern capital." Prior to this, the United States had consistently followed the Chinese Nationalist usage by calling the city "Peiping."

[21] Partial texts of the president's inaugural address and his first press conference are in MacFarquhar, *Sino-American Relations,* 246-47.

tural Revolution, was attempting to re-establish contacts throughout the world. For the first time since the Korean war, China appeared to feel that American intentions might be less than wholly hostile. In any event, Peking regarded some general reordering of East Asian relations as vital. This attitude was related to fears that improved American-Russian relations would isolate China and reduce her influence. Japan's growing power and her increasing world role were also involved in these considerations. By 1969, Peking, which had enjoyed little success in its attempts to influence Japan through unofficial contacts with business and cultural groups, was condemning the massive return of Japanese investment to South Korea and Taiwan as evidence of revived imperialism.

In April, 1971, China gave its most positive response to American signals when it unexpectedly invited the United States table tennis team to visit China after the championship matches then underway in Japan were completed. Earlier, during a trip to Rumania, the president had planted the idea of his visiting China, and this was the first indication that it had taken root. American trade restrictions, first enforced twenty-one years earlier, were lifted on June 10, a move which cleared the way for preparatory meetings between presidential adviser Henry Kissinger and Chinese officials in Peking. Before 1971 ended, all was in readiness for summit meetings that were to symbolize the end of the Sino-American cold war.

The Substance of First Contacts

President Nixon told Congress in 1972 that the central purpose of his China policy was to encourage the People's Republic to "play its appropriate role in shaping international arrangements that affect its concerns. Only then will that great nation have a stake in such arrangements; only then will they endure." To advance this purpose, the administration indicated that it would modify its stand on the question of Chinese representation in the United Nations. Even before the president arrived in Peking, Secretary of State William Rogers said in October, 1971, that the United States would no longer oppose the seating of

the People's Republic in the Security Council. The American government, Rogers explained, had discovered overwhelming sentiment in other capitals favoring a change in China's representation. The United States, therefore, would work to insure a seat in the General Assembly for the Chinese government in Taiwan.[22] A second change in the American position came during the presidential visit in China. The final communiqué of the meetings noted that "the United States acknowledges that all Chinese on either side of the Taiwan Straits maintain there is but one China and that Taiwan is a part of China." The American view, the communiqué continued, held that jurisdiction over the island was a matter for the Chinese to settle without foreign interference.[23] Pending the resolution of this issue, Washington and Peking resorted to an ambiguous formula for circumventing the question of which government—Nationalist or Com-

[22] Documents pertaining to the proposed presidential visit are printed in MacFarquhar, *Sino-American Relations*, 250-56. The Nationalist government rejected the American suggestion of a seat in the General Assembly. When the United Nations voted to change the Chinese representation, the Nationalists walked out.

[23] The shift in the American position on Taiwan is indicated by comparison of two statements coming from the White House. In a press conference, April 29, 1971, President Nixon described speculation about negotiations between Peking and Taipei looking to a change in the status of Taiwan as "completely unrealistic." *New York Times*, April 30, 1971. A few months later, however, on November 30, 1971, presidential adviser Henry Kissinger was quoted at a press conference as follows: "The question which I was asked was: Will we settle the future of Taiwan in Peking? My answer to that was: It is our judgment that the future relationship between the People's Republic and Taiwan should be worked out between Taiwan and the People's Republic." Quoted in "Official Press Release from the Office of the White House Press Secretary, November 30, 1971," p. 7. During these months in which the United States was reconsidering its China policy, Richard Moorsteen, an American foreign service officer on temporary leave, and Morton Abramowitz, an employee of the Rand Corporation (a research organization often retained by the United States government for specialized consultation) published a study advocating a graded shift away from American support for an independent Chinese government on Taiwan. The recommendation was summed up in the phrase "one China but not now." See their *Remaking China Policy: U.S.–China Relations and Governmental Decision-Making* (1971).

munist—was truly legitimate. The United States retained its embassy in Taipei and reaffirmed the applicability of its mutual defense treaty with the Republic of China, which provided guarantees against an invasion from the mainland. Then, in 1973, the People's Republic and the United States opened "liaison offices" in the other's capital, but neither party held that opening such offices implied formal recognition. It was widely noted, however, that the "liaison offices" were headed by officials holding ambassadorial rank and that in the conduct of their business these offices functioned much like embassies.

While the Nixon visit failed to destroy entirely the barriers associated with the "Bamboo Curtain," the United States and China after 1972 enjoyed an enlarged trade and an expanded cultural exchange. Between 1971 and 1974, the value of commodities exchanged rose from zero to some $900,000,000. Both countries admitted, albeit under strict regulation, several thousand academicians, journalists, physicians, a variety of skilled professionals, athletes, and entertainers. Moreover, there was evidence that the Nixon administration believed that its closer relations with Peking nullified the importance of lingering support in some segments of American opinion for Chiang Kai-shek's claims to the leadership of China. The president's visit to China was a strong plank in his campaign for re-election in 1972.

JAPAN: RESURGENCE OF AN ASIAN POWER

World War II and the subsequent Allied (American) occupation brought radical change in Japan's life at home and in her relations with the outside world both near and far. The empire which had been built since 1895 was gone. The ultranationalism which had captured both domestic and foreign policy was merely a bitter memory. In the destruction and the resulting poverty of defeat most Japanese were repelled by their own recent history. They accepted, since there was no alternative, the political, economic, and social reforms imposed

by the victor, who in time seemed rather benevolent. Militaristic Japan accepted a constitution abolishing war as an instrument of its policy. Her role in international politics became that of a spectator—a strange status for a country which had sought and almost won the overlordship of East Asia.

As the occupation came to an end, Japan became the compliant ally of her erstwhile enemy, the United States. In the global cold war of the 1950s, she was an American military and economic base for the conflict in Korea and for American efforts to contain and isolate Communist China. Not surprisingly, therefore, her energies in the foreign field centered on rebuilding foreign trade with the "free world" under the protection of the American alliance.

In the 1960s with the renewal of the American-Japanese mutual security treaty, Japan's isolation from world politics continued, but her economic relations with the non-Communist states enjoyed an amazing growth (see Chapter 33), and there were marked increases in her trade with China and Russia. By the end of the decade, Japan had achieved a world position in industry and trade unprecedented in her history. The new prosperity rested in part on her technological and industrial skills, but to an even greater degree on an international environment favorable to Japanese economic and commercial growth: the economic needs of the new states of Southeast Asia, the escalation of the Vietnam war, and advantageous markets in American and Europe. Japan had become the world's third-ranking industrial power. All this came about at a time when she had no military establishment, when the remnants of her discredited nationalism were exclusively cultural, and when there was no meaningful pressure from her people to resume the game of world politics.[24]

Nevertheless, by the early 1970s there were unmistakable signs that Japan was under increasing pressure at home to modify its 25-year-old posture of isolation in foreign policy.

---

[24] See Donald C. Hellmann, *Japan and East Asia: The New International Order* (1972), 3-17.

By 1974, East Asian international relations seemed to be governed less by old Cold War rivalries than by forces creating new international alignments. President Richard Nixon, once a stern critic of Communist governments, flew to Peking where he met Mao Tse-tung and engaged in talks looking toward the relaxation of tensions between the United States and the People's Republic. Meanwhile, Japan was demonstrating through such steps as the provision of technological assistance (the picture above is of a Japanese agricultural technician working in the Middle East) that she had recovered from defeat and was entitled to a voice in the affairs of the great powers.

The Japanese could not but be concerned by what they regarded as a decreasing American military role in East Asia, by the boisterous rhetoric of China's foreign policy and its growing nuclear capability, and by the political implications of Japan's far-flung industrial and commercial relations. For increasing numbers of Japanese there was some question as to whether the policy of isolation within the American alliance would continue to serve Japan's vital interests in the new and turbulent East Asia. Attitudes which had been shaped by defeat and the occupation were disappearing. After 1970, Japanese public opinion, which now took pride in the nation's "miracle of production," was more and more sensitive to any suggestion that it was regarded by its American ally as a second-class power.

JAPAN AND THE "NIXON SHOCKS"

Such was the climate of Japanese opinion when in the summer of 1971 it was subjected to what the Japanese called the "Nixon shocks." The president's revelation that he would go to Peking was as electrifying to the Japanese as to the Americans. In general, it was a step which the Japanese approved, since improved Sino-American relations promised to give Japan increased latitude for dealing with China. The Japanese populace, however, learned that Nixon's action had caught their government by surprise. The United States had not only failed to consult with Japan on the new initiatives, but had also neglected the courtesy of informing an ally of its intentions. The Japanese ambassador in Washington had been told of the president's intentions only a few minutes before his nationally televised address. Thus it was the manner in which the United States conducted itself, not the substance of American action, which produced the "shock." Japanese press reactions suggested bluntly that this was not the way to treat an Asian partner.

This unpleasantness was compounded by still another unexpected American move. A few weeks after the president spoke on China, the United States announced that it was imposing a ten percent surcharge on all imports and was taking steps to revalue the dollar in international markets. In the closely linked worlds of Japanese government and business, these American moves were interpreted as being directed at Japan. The Americans, it was held, were attempting to force revaluation of the yen, thereby reducing the competitive advantages of Japanese goods in American markets, and were pressuring Japan to drop some of her barriers to American investment in Japan. The contention that the United States by these measures was trying to unload the costs of its own economic shortcomings on others only heightened resentment. Japanese businessmen grumbled that, while they were certain to suffer losses, the Nixon measures would not solve basic American problems—production costs that were pricing goods beyond the reach of world markets, inept marketing practices, and an inflationary spiral that had been accelerated by prolonged American involvement in the Vietnam war.

Tokyo's immediate and most apparent response was to fall in line with American policy. Prime Minister Sato flew to the President's San Clemente White House to accept assurances that none of the agreements which might be reached in Peking would be prejudicial to Japanese interests. On the economic front Tokyo moved quickly to revalue its own currency and steps were taken to admit larger amounts of American investment in Japan. The United States attempted to make all of these concessions somewhat easier for the prime minister by agreeing to a firm date (May 15, 1972) for the retrocession of Okinawa, thus terminating a long-standing territorial dispute in Japan's favor. None of these maneuvers, however, could allay popular resentment of American behavior or a growing uneasiness with respect to ultimate American intentions. Did American troop reductions in Vietnam and elsewhere in Asia, together with these dramatic approaches to China, foreshadow a total withdrawal from Asia, leaving Japan as the only major non-Communist state on Asia's eastern perimeter? Was the failure to consult frankly with Tokyo an indication of declining American interest in Japan? In this newly charged atmosphere it became somewhat more fashionable in Japan to advocate enlargement of the nation's self-defense forces, and there was a new seriousness to speculation that a "security shock," meaning an American refusal to renew the alliance, might eventually be in the offing. Indeed, a fundamental questioning of the premises on which the Japanese-American alliance

rested was one of the deeper effects of the "Nixon shocks."[25]

JAPANESE POLICY INITIATIVES

These tensions encouraged Japan toward a more independent role in foreign policy. In international economic affairs, for example, Tokyo took pains to show that she was not utterly dependent on the United States. Government policy encouraged foreign investments that would sustain national prosperity and foster favorable and broader political relationships. Investment capital, which had been permitted to flow abroad into such ventures as the construction of luxury vacation hotels in Hawaii, was turned toward enlarging supplies of basic commodities and providing Japan with a stake in the manufacturing enterprises of other countries. Japanese capital was exported to support the development of farm land, to operate mining enterprises, to build steel mills,

[25] In assessing these contemporary Japanese-American tensions, it should be noted that the adjustments required to bring the two nations into a working relationship based on approximate equality may be more difficult to effect than would first appear. The problems included (1) Japan's legacy of seven years of occupation and two decades of "low posture" diplomacy, both of which have left the nation with slim foundations for a more active role in world affairs; and (2) her development as an economic giant lacking most of the attributes of a major military power. This latter characteristic has made Japan something of an anomaly in a world where military power and the will to use it have been prime determinants of a nation's role and influence. The American tasks, according to John Maki, may be even more difficult, because they require the United States "to escape the psychology of the victor created by the physical mastery demonstrated by stark military superiority; to make the difficult adjustment from a position of easy dominance in its economic relations with Japan to a position as 'victim' of Japan's economic miracle to which . . . it contributed not a little; to take seriously, as a fellow major actor in world politics, a government which has played an almost completely subservient role to American policy since 1945; and to avoid even the . . . suggestion of racism." See Maki's "Japan and World Politics in the 1970s," *Pacific Affairs*, 46 (1973), 289-97.

and to gain control of companies manufacturing light aircraft. The fact that much of this investment was made in American enterprises was testimony to the continuing importance of the United States to Japan. Yet in the aftermath of the great oil crisis of 1973-1974, Japanese corporations sought to secure their supplies of energy by offering to underwrite a variety of large-scale projects in Arab countries.

Japan's efforts to diversify her foreign economic relations were welcomed by Communist China and the Soviet Union. In an era of cold war detente, both these Communist nations had a stake in encouraging a Japanese drift away from the United States. Moreover, their own bitter rivalry encouraged them to compete for favorable economic arrangements with Japan.

RELATIONS WITH COMMUNIST CHINA

The new postures in Sino-Japanese relations, an aftermath of Nixon's trip to Peking, were particularly notable. Japan had never been comfortable in applying the American line of isolating Communist China. In the early 1950s, Japanese intellectuals had denounced their government's role in the cold war. They advocated close relations with China and the solution of Japan's own problems through the application of Chinese revolutionary theories. Later, as China's own troubles became more readily apparent, Japanese enthusiasm for China as a model for Japanese society declined, but a high level of popular interest was maintained in China as a source of traditional culture, as a potential market and supplier of vital raw materials, and as a nearby power reaching toward nuclear capability. Thus the press spoke approvingly of the "Tanaka shock" (Tanaka Kakuei succeeded Sato as prime minister in July, 1972) when Tokyo moved, well in advance of the United States, to establish formal diplomatic ties with Peking in September, 1972. The reopening of formal ties seemed all the more welcome as evidence accumulated revealing a reduction of Sino-Japanese tensions and the opening of fresh economic channels. As Japan joined the United States in efforts to

improve relations with China, Peking ended her complaints against the presence of American military bases on Japanese soil, presumably because these bases could serve as a restraint on Russian action. Japanese businessmen entered negotiations which promised Chinese purchases of whole industrial plants and related technologies, and, during the oil crisis of 1973-1974, China, who was not a major petroleum exporter, rushed the conclusion of contracts that guaranteed Japanese importers significant annual deliveries of this vital energy source.

While these early contacts stressed the broadening of economic relations, the Japanese continually faced the political implications of dealing with China. With respect to Taiwan, for example, Japan found that she was no longer subject to Communist condemnation of her investments in her former island colony. Since Tokyo and Taipei had broken diplomatic relations, Communist China did not object to the invention of various "unofficial" devices to safeguard Japanese investments in trade with Taiwan. Yet on the one economic issue most imbued with political meaning—Japan's proposal to extend air service by its nationally owned line into Peking while continuing flights to Taipei—China's stand was firm. Japan Air Lines would not be permitted to schedule cities on the mainland until the national carrier had terminated all service to Taiwan.

JAPAN AND RUSSIA

A similar political atmosphere colored improving Japanese-Russian relations. Like the Chinese, the Russians could play to Japan's economic interests. Siberia's vast and still underdeveloped forest and mineral resources provided the incentive for closer ties. Moscow saw Japanese capital and technological expertise as speeding the development of her eastern regions, while Japan was attracted by opportunities to tap useful stores of industrial raw materials. In consequence, the two parties reached agreements by which the Japanese traded economic and technical assistance for access to coal, natural gas, and petroleum.

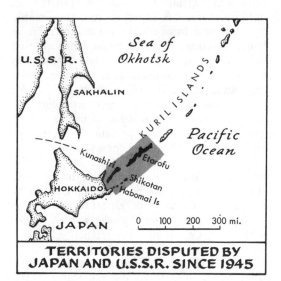

TERRITORIES DISPUTED BY JAPAN AND U.S.S.R. SINCE 1945

Despite the advantages offered by the Russians, Japan moved cautiously in the Siberian venture. Tokyo was sensitive to potential dangers in linking herself too closely to one side or the other in the Sino-Soviet dispute. Even more fundamental was Japan's mistrust of the Russians. The two nations were historic rivals, and they were still disputing issues arising from World War II. While a semblance of normal relations had been restored in 1956 through a "peace declaration," a formal peace treaty awaited the settlement of such matters as the ownership of the southern Kurile islands. The Soviets claimed them under a number of big power agreements of the World War II era and the San Francisco treaty, all of which were questioned by the Japanese. In one sense this quarrel, which involved only a few tiny islands, seemed rather odd when there were manifestly such larger stakes to be derived from improved relations, but neither side seemed anxious to retreat. The Russians viewed concessions on the Kuriles as an invitation to a host of other territorial claims. For the Japanese, the whole matter was a constant reminder of how difficult the Russians could be when they held the advantage. Tokyo's mood suggested that Japan was unwilling to sacrifice what she regarded as just territorial claims if all she received in return were economic concessions.

PERSPECTIVES ON CONTEMPORARY EAST ASIA

Major world capitals in 1974 tended to place positive interpretations on these emerging patterns of Asian politics.[26] They were seen as an end to confrontation and as the opening of a new era of negotiation and economic cooperation. Certainly there were encouraging signs. Nevertheless, in East Asia as in Southeast Asia, the new atmosphere had not been translated into a broadly accepted international order. Some of the foundations of the cold war alignments had been eroded, but in a region where massive revolutions were still under way, international stability remained an elusive blessing. The potentially explosive Sino-Soviet disagreements, the unresolved status of Taiwan, new Japanese relations with the United States and her Asian neighbors, and a continuing war in Southeast Asia were only some of the on-going problems.

Yet there were signs that the nations of East Asia in the 1970s were moving from one great historic era into a new domestic and international order. A century and a half ago, China and Japan faced the outside barbarian world with some confidence. The years prior to 1830, the point at which this history begins, recall a China able not only to limit trade with the West to the single port of Canton, but also to dictate the terms on which the Western barbarians might visit the great Middle Kingdom. It was

[26] The Soviet leader Leonid Brezhnev, speaking to American businessmen, in June 1973, stressed the importance of "economic cooperation" as a basis for mutually "advantageous relations between our two countries." The cold war, he said, "put the brake on the development of normal human relations between nations, and it slowed down the progress and advance of economic and scientific times. And I ask you gentlemen, as I ask myself, was that a good period? Did it serve the interests of the peoples? And my answer to that is no, no, no, and no again." President Nixon's foreign policy adviser, Henry Kissinger, had spoken in a similarly optimistic view a few weeks earlier: "We [the great powers] must identify interests and positive values beyond security in order to engage once again the commitment of peoples and parliaments. We need a shared view of the world we seek." Both are quoted in Iriye, *Cold War*, 190-91.

also an era when Japan could indulge her fancies in policies of exclusion and seclusion. Then came the Western impact with its gathering momentum. What followed was the era of East Asia's humiliation, its subjection to colonial and semi-colonial status, and its long revolutionary struggles, not yet ended, to regain self-confidence and power. Now, in the 1970s. this era of humiliation appears to be passing into history. During little more than a century, Japan has moved from isolation and feudal-military dictatorship to semi-colonial status, to modernization, to empire, to war and total defeat, to occupation and rule by the victor, and then to a new economic though not a political empire. During these same years, China, for centuries the cultural center of East Asia, accepted defeat at the hands of British forces numbering less than 10,000 men and witnessed the slow but inexorable collapse of her venerable Confucian order and its dynasty, the chaos of the warlord era, the beginnings of national unification under the *Kuomintang* "republicans," and, finally, full-scale civil war and the triumph of peasant-based, Communist, semi-guerilla armies.

How the states and the peoples of East Asia will use their new found confidence, their revolutionary nationalism, and their growing power belongs to a history that is yet to be written.

FOR FURTHER READING

China. J. D. Simmonds, *China's World: The Foreign Policy of a Developing State* (1971) argues that Chinese policy is primarily a response to domestic problems. For details on Communist China during her first decade, A. Doak Barnett, *Communist China and Asia* (1960).* Harold C. Hinton, *China's Turbulent Quest* (1970), a survey of foreign relations. Studies of China's dealings with particular regions: George V. H. Moseley, *The Consolidation of the South China Frontier* (1973), stresses historical continuity in China's approach to minorities along her southern borders; Bruce D. Larkin, *China and Africa, 1949-1970: The Foreign Policy of the People's Republic of China* (1971); and Cecil Johnson, *Communist China and Latin America, 1959-1967* (1970). Communist China's defense policy is treated in Arthur Huck, *The Security*

of China: Chinese Approaches to Problems of War and Strategy (1970).* China's nuclear capability and foreign policy is treated in Alice Hsieh, *Communist China's Strategy in the Nuclear Era* (1962); and Morton H. Halperin, *China and the Bomb* (1965).* More recent nuclear developments can be found in Harry G. Gelber, "Nuclear Weapons in Chinese Strategy," *Problems of Communism* 20 (1971). 33-44.

Sino-Soviet Split. H. L. Boorman, *et al., Moscow-Peking Axis: Strengths and Strains* (1957), an appraisal that preceded the rupture. Studies focusing on the break are: Donald S. Zagoria, *The Sino-Soviet Conflict, 1956-1961* (1962)*; Donald W. Treadgold, ed., *Soviet and Chinese Communism: Similarities and Differences* (1967)*; and Walter C. Clemens, Jr., *The Arms Race and Sino-Soviet Relations* (1968). Harry Schwartz, *Tsars, Mandarins, and Commissars: A History of Chinese-Russian Relations* (rev. ed., 1973),* and Klaus Menhart, *Peking and Moscow (1963).*

The Cultural Revolution and China's Foreign Relations. Tang Tsou, ed., *China in Crisis. Volume 2; China's Policies in Asia and America's Alternatives* (1968),* a comprehensive series of essays. Klaus Menhert, *Peking and the New Left at Home and Abroad* (1969),* treats relationships between the Cultural Revolution and revolutionary movements in the Third World and the West. Albert Feuerwerker, "Modern China?" *Michigan Quarterly Review* 11 (1972), 1-5, questions the theory that Maoist revolutionary models offer directions for industrialized nations.

Sino-American Relations. O.E. Clubb, "Formosa and the Offshore Islands in American Policy," *Political Science Quarterly* 74 (1959), 517-31; and Tang Tsou, *Embroilment over Quemoy* (1959). Fred Greene, *U.S. Policy and the Security of Asia* (1968),* an exposition of America's "containment" policy. Robert Blum, *The United States and China in World Affairs* (1966)*; and the latter portions of Warren I. Cohen, *America's Response to China* (1971)* are complementary studies. A. T. Steele, *The American People and China* (1966),* an examination of America's shifting popular attitudes.

Alexander Eckstein, ed., *China Trade Prospects and U.S. Policy* (1971). U.S. Department of State, *Issues in United States Foreign Policy, No. 4: The People's Republic of China.* Publication #8666 (rev. ed., 1972). Other notable studies are: Albert Feuerwerker, "Chinese History and the Foreign Relations of Contemporary China," *Annals of the American Academy of Political and Social Science*, 402 (1972), 1-14; and John K. Fairbank, *The People's Middle Kingdom and the U.S.A.* (1967).

Japan.   Herman Kahn, *The Emerging Japanese Superstate: Challenge and Response* (1970)*; and Zbigniew Brzezinski, *The Fragile Blossom: Crisis and Change in Japan* (1972)* offer conflicting views of Japan's future. A seasoned diplomat's appraisal of Japan's economic diplomacy is in John K. Emmerson's *Arms, Yen and Power: The Japanese Dilemma* (1971). F. C. Langdon, *Japan's Foreign Policy* (1973), an important recent study. Martin E. Weinstein, *Japan's Postwar Defense Policy, 1947-1968* (1971).

John S. Stephan, *Sakhalin: A History* (1971) suggests some of the legacies coloring current territorial disputes between Russia and Japan. Savitri Vishwanathan, *Normalization of Japanese-Soviet Relations, 1945-1970* (1973), based largely on Japanese records. Donald C. Hellman, *Japanese Domestic Politics and Foreign Policy: The Peace Agreement with the Soviet Union* (1969).

Aspects of changing American-Japanese relations can be seen in: Robert Scalpino, "The Foreign Policy of Modern Japan," in *Foreign Policy in World Politics*, Roy C. Macridis, ed. (2nd. ed., 1962)*; Herbert Passin, ed., *The United States and Japan* (1966); James Morley, *Japan and Korea: American Allies in the Pacific* (1965); Lawrence Olson, *Japan in Postwar Asia* (1970); Gerald L. Curtis, ed., *Japanese-American Relations in the 1970's* (1970)*; and Robert Scalpino, *American-Japanese Relations in a Changing Era* (1972).)

Epilogue: A Matter of Interpretation

As noted at the beginning of this survey, the task of the historian, and indeed of the concerned student of history, is to construct a record of the past, a record of what was thought, said, and done, to refine the record through critical analysis, and to suggest meanings that are derived from the evidence. It is these meanings that give point to man's experiences, enabling him to use them for good or for ill. In Old China, for example, the Confucian literati were much concerned with the writing of history and expounding the "lessons" that were supposed to be taught by that history. Moreover, they became expert in applying what they had learned to practical politics, a fact that had something to do with the richness and the longevity of Old China's great civilization.

The story of modern Asia which has been outlined in the foregoing pages suggests that the functions of history are no less urgent now than in the days of Old China. The meeting of East and West, together with the unfolding of Asia's revolutions, is producing an historical record without precedent in its complexity—a remarkable mixture of the noble and the ignoble, of the constructive and the destructive, of wisdom and unbelievable stupidity. In the overall view, one conclusion is that the peoples of East Asia have been moving in their own special ways into a world of modernization. But what further evaluations may the historian make of this record? One easy and popular view has held that Asia's trend toward modernity is to be equated with "progress." Such a view, however, gives way when it is recalled that the daily fare of the peoples of East Asia in the twentieth century has been war and revolutionary upheaval. As in the West, these in turn have nurtured extreme forms of nationalism and international confrontation. The great powers, it has been said, have twisted "progress" into a dedication to perpetual war, thereby reducing peace to an aberration, simply a memory from the nineteenth century.[1]

For the American student who seeks to develop his own historical interpretations on modern East Asia, these difficulties in sifting and weighing the evidence constitute only part of the problem. Even a limited acquaintance with Asia is something that Americans do not easily acquire. The area remains far removed from the educational tradition of the United

[1] Richard J. Barnet, *Roots of War* (1973).

529

States, and, in consequence, the American way of measuring Asia often has been emotional rather than intellectual. For example, Americans having only a sketchy knowledge of Asia's past became accustomed to viewing their country's role in the East as unfailingly benevolent. This was a pleasing theory, but one that left Americans ill-prepared to deal with perplexing questions posed by the events of recent years. How could it come about that America's good intentions and benevolence led to war in Vietnam, a war that has been described as the longest and, in some respects, the most calamitous in the nation's history?

This civil war in Vietnam had come to an end by April 1975. The Saigon government surrendered to the *Vietcong* and to Hanoi. A Thirty Years War (1945-1975) dating from the first futile efforts of France to repossess her colonial empire in Indochina had passed into history. After the defeat of France in 1954 a continuing and a growing American involvement eventually was to cost the United States alone more than 56,000 American lives and some 150 billion American dollars, hardly to be counted trivial expenditures. From whence came this American involvement which constantly promised so much, which cost so much, and which achieved so little? What were the origins of those American attitudes and beliefs with their resulting policies which led America into Vietnam? Could it be that they were attitudes and beliefs dating far back into the nineteenth century? Could they be related to what has been called an amazing American capacity to believe in an imaginary East Asia thirsting for Americanization—the picture Anson Burlingame first brought to Americans more than a century ago?

The student who is willing to struggle with such vexing problems of interpretation will find it helpful to review the thinking of scholars and statesmen whose findings have been tested by time and experience. Archibald Cary Collidge, at the turn of the century, was, in Carl Becker's phrase, anticipating the future when he wrote that all nations divide mankind into two categories—themselves and everybody else. He noted that Americans would be as eager as other peoples to nurture the happy belief that they had achieved greatness and power through their own virtues and the blessings of a kindly Providence, whereas the progress of other peoples was due to their unscrupulous rapacity. Some years later in 1922 Elihu Root enriched these conclusions when he said that in autocracies and oligarchies the danger of war lay in sinister purpose, whereas in democracies the danger of war lay in mistaken beliefs.[2]

These observations of Coolidge and Root have an intimate relevance to the narrative given in these pages, and to the problem of interpretation that faces each student. They are an uncomfortable reminder that Americans, like other peoples, have often preferred what Carl Becker called the history of the specious present. Elihu Root called it the history of mistaken beliefs.

---

[2] See the observations of Hamilton Fish Armstrong, "Isolated America," in *Fifty Years of Foreign Affairs,* Hamilton Fish Armstrong, ed., *et al.,* (1972). Burton F. Beers, "Americans in China? Some Historical Perspectives on a Contemporary Enthusiasm," *South Atlantic Quarterly* (Winter 1975), 1-11, emphasizes the sharply differing interpretations which Americans and Chinese have placed on the history of their relations. For contemporary background data on Vietnam, Cambodia, Laos, and other states recently divided in Asia, see Gregory Henderson et al., *Divided Nations in a Divided World* (1974).

Index

Index

Shao Yung, 11-15
Shaw, Major Samuel, 80
Shensi, 404
  Border Government, 376
  rebellion, 192
Sherman, John, 228
Shidehara Kijuro, 316, 322, 325-27, 360, 410-11, 425
Shih Huang-ti, 12-13
Shikoku, 418
Shimabara Revolt, 65
Shimoda, trade port, 125-26
Shimonoseki, treaty of (1895), 200-203, 205-7
Shingon Buddhism, 49. *See also* Buddhism; Zen Buddhism
Shintoism, 45
  in Meiji Japan, 153-55, 282-83
Shogun, Japanese, role of, 51
Shogunate, under Tokugawa, 111-13
Short, General Walter C., 385
Shotoku Taishi, 46
Shufeldt, Robert W., 197
Siam, 193
  in 19th century, 188
Siberia:
  Allied intervention (1918), 305-6
  and Bolshevik Revolution, 307
  Eastern, 3
  Far Eastern Republic, 339
  Four-Power Consortium, 307-8
  Sino-Russian relations, 103
  20th century, 325
Silk:
  Chinese industry, 58
  Japanese industry, 130; Meiji period, 283-84
Singapore:
  independence (1965), 493
  Japanese occupation (1942), 387
  Malaysia, States of, 493
Sinitic (Sino-Tibetan) languages, 3-4
Sinkiang, 34, 190. *See also* Turkestan, Chinese
Sino-Japanese Manchurian treaty (1915), 358
Sino-Japanese treaty (1905), 255-56
Sino-Japanese war (1894), 200-203, 205, 211, 278
Sino-Korean trade regulations, 197
Sino-Soviet Friendship Association, 445
Sino-Tibetan treaty (1951), 514
Sittang river, 194
Smith, Arthur, 72
Social Interpretation of History, The (Williams), 335
Socialism, Japan (1955-60), 468-70
Society, concept of in ancient China, 17. *See also* Clans
Solomon Islands, Japanese occupation, 387
Sone, Viscount, 261
Soong, T. V., 389
Sound of the Mountain, The (Kawataba), 466
Southeast Asia. *See also* East Asia; Indochina

Southeast Asia (*cont.*)
  contemporary perspectives, 526-27
  international perspectives after 1970, 507-8
  Japanese colonialism, 392
  Kennedy "containment" policy, 502-3
  nationalism after 1945, 395-96, 492
Southeast Asia Collective Defense Treaty, 503
Southeast Asia Treaty Organization (SEATO), 500-501
South Manchurian Railway Company, 255-56, 308, 358-59, 368
Soviet Union. *See also* Russia
  China, and revolution of 1927, 338-39
  Chinese Communist Party, 348. *See also* China, People's Republic of
  India, aid to, 516
  Japan, war with (1945). 391
  and Manchuria, 357
  Non-aggression treaty, Japan (1941), 381
  North Korea, security treaty of 1961, 482
  People's Republic of China: conflict with, 516-19; economic alliance (1950). 451-52
  Republic of China, Karakhan manifesto (1920), 298
  Siberian-Japanese negotiations, 525-26
  Vietnam, Democratic Republic of, 494
  World War II, alliances, 389
Spain:
  China, ancient, trade with, 61-62
  Japan, trade with, 63-64
  Korea, discovery of, 195
  Spanish-American war (1898), 218-20
Spice Islands, 62
Spratley Islands, Japanese occupation, 375
Spring and Autumn Annals, The (Confucius), 19
Stalin, Josef, 349, 389, 481, 516
Steel production, in People's Republic of China, 452. *See also* Industry
Sterling, Sir James, 125
Stilwell, General Joseph, 405, 407
Stimson, Henry L., 357, 360-62
Stimson nonaggression doctrine, 379
Straight, Willard, 254, 258-60
Strategic Arms Limitation Talks (SALT), (1972), 520
Suematsu Kencho, 285
Sugimura Yotaro, 327
Sui dynasty, China, 13
Sukarno, 414
Sumitomo, 319
Sun Chia-ku, 167
Sung Chiao-jen, 269
Sung dynasty (960-1279), 13-15
Sungari river, 192-93

Sun Wen, *see* Sun Yat-sen
Sun Yat-sen, 267-69, 272-73, 292, 320, 333-39, 343-44, 346, 348, 376, 402
  biography, 243-44
  Kuomintang, founding of, 269
  San min chu-i, 334-35
  socialism, principles of, 244-45
Suzuki Kantaro, 391, 410
Swift, John F., 178
Szechuan, 175, 347, 377

Tachen, 512
Taft, William Howard, 254, 258-59, 270
Taika Reform, ancient Japan, 46-47
T'ai-p'ing Rebellion, 16, 92-93, 106, 159-62
T'ai-p'ing rebels, 106, 164
T'ai-p'ing T'ien-kuo, 93
Tai language, 195
Taira Kiyomori, 50-51
Taisei Yokusan Kai (IRAA), 409
Taisho Tenno, emperor, 277
Taiwan (Formosa), 3
  Dutch trade, 62
  economic progress, postwar, 487-88
  government since 1949, 486-87
  international status (1950-70), 488-89
  Japanese colonialism, terminated 1945, 475
  Kuomintang occupation, 475
  language of, 4
  neutralization, Korean war, 479
  postwar development (1945), 485-89
  San Francisco treaty (1951), 486
  Straits of, 502; crisis (1954), 512-13
Takahashi Korekiyo, 367
Takahira, Ambassador, 259
Taku, forts, 101
Tale of the Taira Family, The (Heike Monogatari), 53
Tanaka, General Giichi, 320, 322-23
Tanaka Kakuei, 472
Tanaka "positive policy," towards China, 326-27
Tanegashima, 63
T'ang dynasty (618-906), 13
T'ang Shao-yi, 267
Tanuma Okitsugu, 119
Taoism, 18, 21-22, 31, 186
  in ancient China, 61
  versus Confucianism, 23
Tao Te Ching (Lao Tzu), 22
Tea, Japanese trade, 130
Technology, Chinese appeal to (19th century), 182
Tenasserim Peninsula, 194
Tendai Buddhism, 49. *See also* Buddhism; Zen Buddhism
Teng Hsiao-p'ing, 448
Terauchi, Masatake, 261, 280, 308, 318
Terauchi Juichi, 367
Terranova affair, 70-71
Thailand (Siam):